Java™

HOW TO PROGRAM

EARLY OBJECTS

ELEVENTH EDITION

Deitel® Series Page

How To Program Series

Android™ How to Program, 3/E
C++ How to Program, 10/E
C How to Program, 8/E
Java™ How to Program, Early Objects Version, 11/E
Java™ How to Program, Late Objects Version, 11/E
Internet & World Wide Web How to Program, 5/E
Visual Basic® 2012 How to Program, 6/E
Visual C#® How to Program, 6/E

Deitel® Developer Series

Android™ 6 for Programmers: An App-Driven Approach, 3/E
C for Programmers with an Introduction to C11
C++11 for Programmers
C# 6 for Programmers
Java™ for Programmers, 4/E
JavaScript for Programmers
Swift™ for Programmers

Simply Series

Simply Visual Basic® 2010: An App-Driven Approach, 4/E
Simply C++: An App-Driven Tutorial Approach

VitalSource Web Books

`http://bit.ly/DeitelOnVitalSource`

Android™ How to Program, 2/E and 3/E
C++ How to Program, 9/E and 10/E
Java™ How to Program, 10/E and 11/E
Simply C++: An App-Driven Tutorial Approach
Simply Visual Basic® 2010: An App-Driven Approach, 4/E
Visual Basic® 2012 How to Program, 6/E
Visual C#® How to Program, 6/E
Visual C#® 2012 How to Program, 5/E

LiveLessons Video Learning Products

`http://deitel.com/books/LiveLessons/`

Android™ 6 App Development Fundamentals, 3/E
C++ Fundamentals
Java SE 8™ Fundamentals, 2/E
Java SE 9™ Fundamentals, 3/E
C# 6 Fundamentals
C# 2012 Fundamentals
JavaScript Fundamentals
Swift™ Fundamentals

REVEL™ Interactive Multimedia

REVEL™ for Deitel Java™

To receive updates on Deitel publications, Resource Centers, training courses, partner offers and more, please join the Deitel communities on

- Facebook®—`http://facebook.com/DeitelFan`
- Twitter®—`http://twitter.com/deitel`
- LinkedIn®—`http://linkedin.com/company/deitel-&-associates`
- YouTube™—`http://youtube.com/DeitelTV`
- Google+™—`http://google.com/+DeitelFan`
- Instagram®—`http://instagram.com/DeitelFan`

and register for the free *Deitel® Buzz Online* e-mail newsletter at:

`http://www.deitel.com/newsletter/subscribe.html`

To communicate with the authors, send e-mail to:

`deitel@deitel.com`

For information on programming-languages corporate training seminars offered by Deitel & Associates, Inc. worldwide, write to `deitel@deitel.com` or visit:

`http://www.deitel.com/training/`

For continuing updates on Pearson/Deitel publications visit:

`http://www.deitel.com`
`http://www.pearsonhighered.com/deitel/`

Visit the Deitel Resource Centers, which will help you master programming languages, software development, Android™ and iOS® app development, and Internet- and web-related topics:

`http://www.deitel.com/ResourceCenters.html`

Java™

HOW TO PROGRAM

EARLY OBJECTS

ELEVENTH EDITION

Paul Deitel
Deitel & Associates, Inc.

Harvey Deitel
Deitel & Associates, Inc.

330 Hudson Street, NY, NY, 10013

Senior Vice President Courseware Portfolio Management: *Marcia J. Horton*
Director, Portfolio Management: Engineering, Computer Science & Global Editions: *Julian Partridge*
Higher Ed Portfolio Management: *Tracy Johnson (Dunkelberger)*
Portfolio Management Assistant: *Kristy Alaura*
Managing Content Producer: *Scott Disanno*
Content Producer: *Robert Engelhardt*
Web Developer: *Steve Wright*
Rights and Permissions Manager: *Ben Ferrini*
Manufacturing Buyer, Higher Ed, LSC Communications Inc : *Maura Zaldivar-Garcia*
Inventory Manager: *Ann Lam*
Product Marketing Manager: *Yvonne Vannatta*
Field Marketing Manager: *Demetrius Hall*
Marketing Assistant: *Jon Bryant*
Cover Designer: *Paul Deitel, Harvey Deitel, Chuti Prasertsith*
Cover Art: *©Joingate/ShutterStock*

Credits and acknowledgments borrowed from other sources and reproduced, with permission, in this textbook appear on page vi.

Library of Congress Cataloging-in-Publication Data
On file

50 2023

ISBN-10: 0-13-474335-0
ISBN-13: 978-0-13-474335-6

In memory of Dr. Henry Heimlich:

Barbara Deitel used your Heimlich maneuver to save Abbey Deitel's life. Our family is forever grateful to you.

Harvey, Barbara, Paul and Abbey Deitel

Trademarks

DEITEL and the double-thumbs-up bug are registered trademarks of Deitel and Associates, Inc.

Oracle and Java are registered trademarks of Oracle and/or its affiliates. Other names may be trademarks of their respective owners.

Microsoft and/or its respective suppliers make no representations about the suitability of the information contained in the documents and related graphics published as part of the services for any purpose. All such documents and related graphics are provided "as is" without warranty of any kind. Microsoft and/or its respective suppliers hereby disclaim all warranties and conditions with regard to this information, including all warranties and conditions of merchantability, whether express, implied or statutory, fitness for a particular purpose, title and non-infringement. In no event shall Microsoft and/or its respective suppliers be liable for any special, indirect or consequential damages or any damages whatsoever resulting from loss of use, data or profits, whether in an action of contract, negligence or other tortious action, arising out of or in connection with the use or performance of information available from the services.

The documents and related graphics contained herein could include technical inaccuracies or typographical errors. Changes are periodically added to the information herein. Microsoft and/or its respective suppliers may make improvements and/or changes in the product(s) and/or the program(s) described herein at any time. Partial screen shots may be viewed in full within the software version specified.

Microsoft® and Windows® are registered trademarks of the Microsoft Corporation in the U.S.A. and other countries. Screen shots and icons reprinted with permission from the Microsoft Corporation. This book is not sponsored or endorsed by or affiliated with the Microsoft Corporation.

UNIX is a registered trademark of The Open Group.

Apache is a trademark of The Apache Software Foundation.

CSS and XML are registered trademarks of the World Wide Web Consortium.

Firefox is a registered trademark of the Mozilla Foundation.

Google is a trademark of Google, Inc.

Mac and macOS are trademarks of Apple Inc., registered in the U.S. and other countries.

Linux is a registered trademark of Linus Torvalds. All trademarks are property of their respective owners.

Throughout this book, trademarks are used. Rather than put a trademark symbol in every occurrence of a trademarked name, we state that we are using the names in an editorial fashion only and to the benefit of the trademark owner, with no intention of infringement of the trademark.

Contents

The online chapters and appendices listed at the end of this Table of Contents are located on the book's Companion Website (`http://www.pearsonhighered.com/deitel/`)—see the inside front cover of your book for details.

5 Control Statements: Part 2; Logical Operators 164

6 Methods: A Deeper Look 212

17 Lambdas and Streams 694

Online Chapters and Appendices

The online chapters and appendices are located on the book's Companion Website. See the book's inside front cover for details.

Foreword

Throughout my career I've met and interviewed many expert Java developers who've learned from Paul and Harvey, through one or more of their college textbooks, professional books, videos and corporate training. Many Java User Groups have joined together around the Deitels' publications, which are used internationally in university courses and professional training programs. You are joining an elite group.

How do I become an expert Java developer?

This is one of the most common questions I receive at talks for university students and at events with Java professionals. Students want to become expert developers—and this is a great time to be one.

The market is wide open, full of opportunities and fascinating projects, especially for those who take the time to learn, practice and master software development. The world needs good, focused expert developers.

So, how do you do it? First, let's be clear: Software development is hard. But do not be discouraged. Mastering it opens the door to great opportunities. Accept that it's hard, embrace the complexity, enjoy the ride. There are no limits to how much you can expand your skills.

Software development is an amazing skill. It can take you anywhere. You can work in any field. From nonprofits making the world a better place, to bleeding-edge biological technologies. From the frenetic daily run of the financial world to the deep mysteries of religion. From sports to music to acting. Everything has software. The success or failure of initiatives everywhere will depend on developers' knowledge and skills.

The push for you to get the relevant skills is what makes *Java How to Program, 11/e* so compelling. Written for students and new developers, it's easy to follow. It's written by authors who are educators and developers, with input over the years from some of the world's leading academics and professional Java experts—Java Champions, open-source Java developers, even creators of Java itself. Their collective knowledge and experience will guide you. Even seasoned Java professionals will learn and grow their expertise with the wisdom in these pages.

How can this book help you become an expert?

Java was released in 1995—Paul and Harvey had the first edition of *Java How to Program* ready for Fall 1996 classes. Since that groundbreaking book, they've produced ten more editions, keeping current with the latest developments and idioms in the Java software-engineering community. You hold in your hands the map that will enable you to rapidly develop your Java skills.

The Deitels have broken down the humongous Java world into well-defined, specific goals. Put in your full attention, and consciously "beat" each chapter. You'll soon find yourself moving nicely along your road to excellence. And with both Java 8 and Java 9 in the same book, you'll have up-to-date skills on the latest Java technologies.

Most importantly, this book is not just meant for you to read—it's meant for you to practice. Be it in the classroom or at home after work, experiment with the abundant sample code and practice with the book's extraordinarily rich and diverse collection of exercises. Take the time to do all that is in here and you'll be well on your way to achieving a level of expertise that will challenge professional developers out there. After working with Java for more than 20 years, I can tell you that this is not an exaggeration.

For example, one of my favorite chapters is Lambdas and Streams. The chapter covers the topic in detail and the exercises shine—many real-world challenges that developers will encounter every day and that will help you sharpen your skills. After solving these exercises, novices and experienced developers alike will deeply understand these important Java features. And if you have a question, don't be shy—the Deitels publish their email address in every book they write to encourage interaction.

That's also why I love the chapter about JShell—the new Java 9 tool that enables interactive Java. JShell allows you to explore, discover and experiment with new concepts, language features and APIs, make mistakes—accidentally and intentionally—and correct them, and rapidly prototype new code. It may prove to be the most important tool for leveraging your learning and productivity. Paul and Harvey give a full treatment of JShell that both students and experienced developers will be able to put to use immediately.

I'm impressed with the care that the Deitels always take care to accommodate readers at all levels. They ease you into difficult concepts and deal with the challenges that professionals will encounter in industry projects.

There's lots of information about Java 9, the important new Java release. You can jump right in and learn the latest Java features. If you're still working with Java 8, you can ease into Java 9 at your own pace—be sure to begin with the extraordinary JShell coverage.

Another example is the amazing coverage of JavaFX—Java's latest GUI, graphics and multimedia capabilities. JavaFX is the recommended toolkit for new projects. But if you'll be working on legacy projects that use the older Swing API, those chapters are still available to you.

Make sure to dig in on Paul and Harvey's treatment of concurrency. They explain the basic concepts so clearly that the intermediate and advanced examples and discussions will be easy to master. You will be ready to maximize your applications' performance in an increasingly multi-core world.

I encourage you to participate in the worldwide Java community. There are many helpful folks out there who stand ready to help you. Ask questions, get answers and answer your peers' questions. Along with this book, the Internet and the academic and professional communities will help speed you on your way to becoming an expert Java developer. I wish you success!

Bruno Sousa
`bruno@javaman.com.br`
Java Champion
Java Specialist at ToolsCloud
President of SouJava (the Brazilian Java Society)
SouJava representative at the Java Community Process

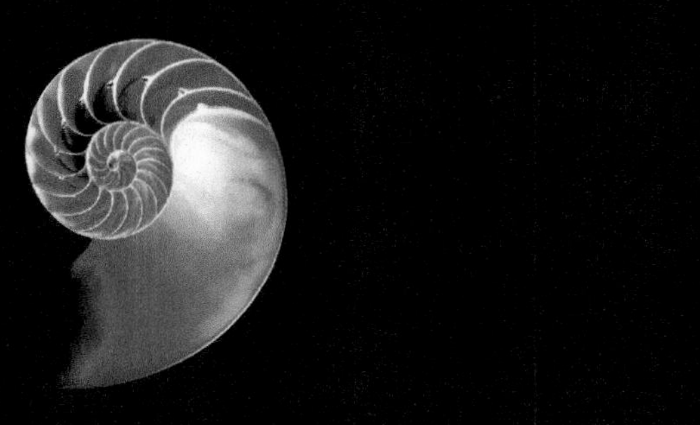

Preface

Welcome to the Java programming language and ***Java How to Program, Early Objects, Eleventh Edition***! This book presents leading-edge computing technologies for students, instructors and software developers. It's appropriate for introductory academic and professional course sequences based on the curriculum recommendations of the **ACM** and the **IEEE** professional societies,[1] and for *Advanced Placement (AP) Computer Science* exam preparation.[2] It also will help you prepare for most topics covered by the following Oracle Java Standard Edition 8 (Java SE 8) Certifications:[3]

- Oracle Certified Associate, Java SE 8 Programmer
- Oracle Certified Professional, Java SE 8 Programmer

If you haven't already done so, please read the bullet points and reviewer comments on the back cover and inside back cover—these concisely capture the essence of the book. In this Preface we provide more detail for students, instructors and professionals.

Our primary goal is to prepare college students to meet the Java programming challenges they'll encounter in upper-level courses and in industry. We focus on software engineering best practices. At the heart of the book is the Deitel signature **live-code approach**—we present most concepts in the context of hundreds of complete working programs that have been tested on **Windows®**, **macOS®** and **Linux®**. The complete code examples are accompanied by live sample executions.

New and Updated Features

In the following sections, we discuss the key features and updates we've made for *Java How to Program, 11/e*, including:

- Flexibility Using Java SE 8 or the New Java SE 9 (which includes Java SE 8)
- *Java How to Program, 11/e*'s Modular Organization
- Introduction and Programming Fundamentals
- Flexible Coverage of Java SE 9: JShell, the Module System and Other Java SE 9 Topics
- Object-Oriented Programming

---

1. *Computer Science Curricula 2013 Curriculum Guidelines for Undergraduate Degree Programs in Computer Science*, December 20, 2013, The Joint Task Force on Computing Curricula, Association for Computing Machinery (ACM), IEEE Computer Society.
2. `https://apstudent.collegeboard.org/apcourse/ap-computer-science-a/exam-practice`
3. `http://bit.ly/OracleJavaSE8Certification` (At the time of this writing, the Java SE 9 certification exams were not yet available.)

- Flexible JavaFX/Swing GUI, Graphics and Multimedia Coverage
- Data Structures and Generic Collections
- Flexible Lambdas and Streams Coverage
- Concurrency and Multi-Core Performance
- Database: JDBC and JPA
- Web-Application Development and Web Services
- Optional Online Object-Oriented Design Case Study

Flexibility Using Java SE 8 or the New Java SE 9

To meet the needs of our diverse audiences, we designed the book for college and professional courses based on Java SE 8 or Java SE 9, which from this point forward we'll refer
8 to as Java 8 and Java 9, respectively. Each feature first introduced in Java 8 or Java 9 is
accompanied by an 8 or 9 icon in the margin, like those to the left of this paragraph. The
9 new Java 9 capabilities are covered in clearly marked, *easy-to-include-or-omit* chapters and
sections—some in the print book and some online. Figures 1 and 2 list some key Java 8
and Java 9 features that we cover, respectively.

Java 8 features	
Lambdas and streams	Date & Time API (`java.time`)
Type-inference improvements	Parallel array sorting
`@FunctionalInterface` annotation	Java concurrency API improvements
Bulk data operations for Java Collections—`filter`, `map` and `reduce`	`static` and `default` methods in interfaces
Library enhancements to support lambdas (e.g., `java.util.stream`, `java.util.function`)	Functional interfaces that define only one `abstract` method and can include `static` and `default` methods

Fig. 1 | Some key features we cover that were introduced in Java 8.

Java 9 features	
In the Print Book	***On the Companion Website***
New JShell chapter	Module system
_ is no longer allowed as an identifier	HTML5 Javadoc enhancements
`private` interface methods	`Matcher` class's new method overloads
Effectively `final` variables can be used in `try`-with-resources statements	`CompletableFuture` enhancements
Mention of the Stack Walking API	JavaFX 9 skin APIs and other enhancements
Mention of JEP 254, Compact Strings	Mentions of:
Collection factory methods	Overview of Java 9 security enhancements
	G1 garbage collector
	Object serialization security enhancements
	Enhanced deprecation

Fig. 2 | Some key new features we cover that were introduced in Java 9.

Java How to Program, 11/e's Modular Organization[1]

The book's modular organization helps instructors plan their syllabi.

Java How to Program, 11/e, is appropriate for programming courses at various levels. Chapters 1–25 are popular in core CS 1 and CS 2 courses and introductory course sequences in related disciplines—these chapters appear in the **print book.** Chapters 26–36 are intended for advanced courses and are located on the book's **Companion Website.**

Part 1: Introduction
Chapter 1, Introduction to Computers, the Internet and Java
Chapter 2, Introduction to Java Applications; Input/Output and Operators
Chapter 3, Introduction to Classes, Objects, Methods and Strings

---

Chapter 25, Introduction to JShell: Java 9's REPL for Interactive Java

Part 2: Additional Programming Fundamentals
Chapter 4, Control Statements: Part 1; Assignment, `++` and `--` Operators
Chapter 5, Control Statements: Part 2; Logical Operators
Chapter 6, Methods: A Deeper Look
Chapter 7, Arrays and `ArrayList`s

Chapter 14, Strings, Characters and Regular Expressions
Chapter 15, Files, Input/Output Streams, NIO and XML Serialization

Part 3: Object-Oriented Programming
Chapter 8, Classes and Objects: A Deeper Look
Chapter 9, Object-Oriented Programming: Inheritance
Chapter 10, Object-Oriented Programming: Polymorphism and Interfaces
Chapter 11, Exception Handling: A Deeper Look

Part 4: JavaFX Graphical User Interfaces, Graphics and Multimedia
Chapter 12, JavaFX Graphical User Interfaces: Part 1
Chapter 13, JavaFX GUI: Part 2

Chapter 22, JavaFX Graphics and Multimedia

Part 5: Data Structures, Generic Collections, Lambdas and Streams
Chapter 16, Generic Collections
Chapter 17, Lambdas and Streams
Chapter 18, Recursion
Chapter 19, Searching, Sorting and Big O
Chapter 20, Generic Classes and Methods: A Deeper Look
Chapter 21, Custom Generic Data Structures

---

1. The online chapters and VideoNotes will be available on the book's Companion Website before Fall 2017 classes and will be updated as Java 9 evolves. Please write to `deitel@deitel.com` if you need them sooner.

Part 6: Concurrency; Networking
Chapter 23, Concurrency

Chapter 28, Networking

Part 7: Database-Driven Desktop Development
Chapter 24, Accessing Databases with JDBC

Chapter 29, Java Persistence API (JPA)

Part 8: Web App Development and Web Services
Chapter 30, JavaServer™ Faces Web Apps: Part 1
Chapter 31, JavaServer™ Faces Web Apps: Part 2
Chapter 32, REST Web Services

Part 9: Other Java 9 Topics
Chapter 36, Java Module System and Other Java 9 Features

Part 10: (Optional) Object-Oriented Design
Chapter 33, ATM Case Study, Part 1: Object-Oriented Design with the UML
Chapter 34, ATM Case Study Part 2: Implementing an Object-Oriented Design

Part 11: (Optional) Swing Graphical User Interfaces and Java 2D Graphics
Chapter 26, Swing GUI Components: Part 1
Chapter 27, Graphics and Java 2D

Chapter 35, Swing GUI Components: Part 2

Introduction and Programming Fundamentals (Parts 1 and 2)

Chapters 1 through 7 provide a friendly, example-driven treatment of traditional introductory programming topics. This book differs from most other Java textbooks in that it features an **early objects approach**—see the section "Object-Oriented Programming" later in this Preface. Note in the preceding outline that Part 1 includes the (optional) Chapter 25 on Java 9's new JShell. It's optional because not all courses will want to cover JShell. For those that do, instructors and students will appreciate how JShell's interactivity makes Java "come alive," leveraging the learning process—see the next section on JShell.

9 Flexible Coverage of Java 9: JShell, the Module System and Other Java 9 Topics (JShell Begins in Part 1; the Rest is in Part 9)

JShell: Java 9's REPL (Read-Eval-Print-Loop) for Interactive Java
JShell provides a friendly environment that enables you to quickly explore, discover and experiment with Java's language features and its extensive libraries. JShell replaces the tedious cycle of editing, compiling and executing with its **read-evaluate-print-loop**. Rather than complete programs, you write JShell commands and Java code snippets. When you enter a snippet, JShell *immediately*

- **reads** it,
- **evaluates** it and
- **prints** messages that help you see the effects of your code, then it
- **loops** to perform this process again for the next snippet.

As you work through Chapter 25's scores of examples and exercises, you'll see how JShell and its **instant feedback** keep your attention, enhance your performance and speed the learning and software development processes.

As a student you'll find JShell easy and fun to use. It will help you learn Java features faster and more deeply and will help you verify that these features work the way they're supposed to. As an instructor, you'll appreciate how JShell encourages your students to dig in, and that it **leverages the learning process.** As a professional you'll appreciate how JShell helps you rapidly prototype key code segments and how it helps you discover and experiment with new APIs.

We chose a modular approach with the JShell content packaged in Chapter 25. The chapter:

1. is **easy to include or omit.**
2. is organized as a series of 16 sections, many of which are designed to be covered after a specific earlier chapter of the book (Fig. 3).
3. offers rich coverage of JShell's capabilities. It's **example-intensive**—you should do each of the examples. Get JShell into your fingertips. You'll appreciate how quickly and conveniently you can do things.
4. includes **dozens of Self-Review Exercises, each with an answer.** These exercises can be done after you read Chapter 2 and Section 25.3. As you do each of them, flip the page and check your answer. This will help you master the basics of JShell quickly. Then as you do each of the examples in the remainder of the chapter you'll master the vast majority of JShell's capabilities.

JShell discussions	Can be covered after
Section 25.3 introduces **JShell**, including starting a session, executing statements, declaring variables, evaluating expressions, JShell's **type-inference** capabilities and more. Section 25.4 discusses command-line input with **Scanner** in JShell.	Chapter 2, Introduction to Java Applications; Input/Output and Operators
Section 25.5 discusses how to declare and use **classes** in JShell, including how to load a Java source-code file containing an existing class declaration. Section 25.6 shows how to use JShell's **auto-completion** capabilities to discover a class's capabilities and JShell commands.	Chapter 3, Introduction to Classes, Objects, Methods and Strings

Fig. 3 | Chapter 25 JShell discussions that are designed to be covered after specific earlier chapters. (Part 1 of 2.)

JShell discussions	Can be covered after
Section 25.7 presents additional JShell auto-completion capabilities for **experimentation and discovery**, including viewing method parameters, documentation and method overloads. Section 25.8 shows how to declare and use methods in JShell, including **forward referencing** a method that does not yet exist in the JShell session.	Chapter 6, Methods: A Deeper Look
Section 25.9 shows how **exceptions** are handled in JShell.	Chapter 7, Arrays and `ArrayLists`
Section 25.10 shows how to add existing **packages** to the classpath and import them for use in JShell.	Chapter 21, Custom Generic Data Structures
The remaining JShell sections are reference material that can be covered after Section 25.10. Topics include using an external editor, a summary of JShell commands, getting help in JShell, additional features of `/edit` command, `/reload` command, `/drop` command, feedback modes, other JShell features configurable with `/set`, keyboard shortcuts for snippet editing, how JShell reinterprets Java for interactive use and IDE JShell support.	

Fig. 3 | Chapter 25 JShell discussions that are designed to be covered after specific earlier chapters. (Part 2 of 2.)

9 *New Chapter—The Java Module System and Other Java 9 Topics*
Because Java 9 was still under development when this book was published, we included an online chapter on the book's Companion Website that discusses Java 9's module system and various other Java 9 topics. This **online content will be available before Fall 2017 courses.**

Object-Oriented Programming (Part 3)

Object-oriented programming. We use an **early objects approach**, introducing the basic concepts and terminology of object technology in Chapter 1. Students develop their first customized classes and objects in Chapter 3. Presenting objects and classes early gets students "thinking about objects" immediately and mastering these concepts more thoroughly. [For courses that require a **late-objects approach**, you may want to consider our sister book ***Java How to Program, Late Objects Version, 11/e.***]

Early objects real-world case studies. The early classes and objects presentation in Chapters 3–7 features `Account`, `Student`, `AutoPolicy`, `Time`, `Employee`, `GradeBook` and `Card` shuffling-and-dealing case studies, gradually introducing deeper OO concepts.

Inheritance, Interfaces, Polymorphism and Composition. The deeper treatment of object-oriented programming in Chapters 8–10 features additional real-world case studies, including class `Time`, an `Employee` class hierarchy, and a `Payable` interface implemented in disparate `Employee` and `Invoice` classes. We explain the use of current idioms, such as **"programming to an interface not an implementation"** and **"preferring composition to inheritance"** in building industrial-strength applications.

Exception handling. We integrate basic exception handling beginning in Chapter 7 then present a deeper treatment in Chapter 11. Exception handling is important for building **mission-critical** and **business-critical** applications. To use a Java component, you need to know not only how that component behaves when "things go well," but also what exceptions that component "throws" when "things go poorly" and how your code should handle those exceptions.

Class `Arrays` *and* `ArrayList`. Chapter 7 covers class `Arrays`—which contains methods for performing common array manipulations—and class `ArrayList`—which implements a dynamically resizable array-like data structure. This follows our philosophy of getting lots of practice using existing classes while learning how to define your own. The chapter's rich selection of exercises includes a substantial project on **building your own computer** through the technique of software simulation. Chapter 21 includes a follow-on project on **building your own compiler** that can compile high-level language programs into machine language code that will actually execute on your computer simulator. Students in first and second programming courses enjoy these challenges.

Flexible JavaFX GUI, Graphics and Multimedia Coverage (Part 4) and Optional Swing Coverage (Part II)

For instructors teaching introductory courses, we provide a **scalable JavaFX GUI, graphics and multimedia treatment** enabling instructors to choose the amount of JavaFX they want to cover:

- from none at all,
- to some or all of the *optional* **introductory** sections at the ends of the early chapters,
- to a **deep treatment** of JavaFX GUI, graphics and multimedia in Chapters 12, 13 and 22.

We also use JavaFX in several GUI-based examples in Chapter 23, Concurrency and Chapter 24, Accessing Databases with JDBC.

Flexible Early Treatment of JavaFX

Students enjoy building applications with GUI, graphics, animations and videos. For courses that gently introduce GUI and graphics early, we've integrated an ***optional*** **GUI and Graphics Case Study** that introduces JavaFX-based graphical user interfaces (GUIs) and **`Canvas`-based graphics.**[1] The goal of this case study is to create a simple polymorphic drawing application in which the user can select a shape to draw and the shape's characteristics (such as its color, stroke thickness and whether it's hollow or filled) then drag the mouse to position and size the shape. The case study builds gradually toward that goal, with the reader implementing a polymorphic drawing app in Chapter 10, and a more robust user interface in Exercise 13.9 (Fig. 4). For courses that include these optional early case study sections, instructors can opt to cover none, some or all of the deeper treatment in Chapters 12, 13 and 22 discussed in the next section.

---

1. The deeper graphics treatment in Chapter 22 uses JavaFX shape types that can be added directly to the GUI using **Scene Builder**.

Section or Exercise	What you'll do
Section 3.6: A Simple GUI	Display text and an image.
Section 4.15: Event Handling and Drawing Lines	In response to a `Button` click, draw lines using JavaFX graphics capabilities.
Section 5.11: Drawing Rectangles and Ovals	Draw rectangles and ovals.
Section 6.13: Colors and Filled Shapes	Draw filled shapes in multiple colors.
Section 7.17: Drawing Arcs	Draw a rainbow of colored arcs.
Section 8.16: Using Objects with Graphics	Store shapes as objects then have those objects to draw themselves on the screen.
Section 10.14: Drawing with Polymorphism	Identify the similarities between shape classes and create and use a shape class hierarchy.
Exercise 13.9: Interactive Polymorphic Drawing Application	A capstone exercise in which you'll enable users to select each shape to draw, configure its properties (such as color and fill), and drag the mouse to position and size the shape.

Fig. 4 | GUI and Graphics Case Study sections and exercise.

Deeper Treatment of JavaFX GUI, Graphics and Multimedia in Chapters 12, 13 and 22
For this 11th edition, we've significantly updated our JavaFX presentation and moved all three chapters into the print book, replacing our Swing GUI and graphics coverage (which is now online for instructors who want to continue with Swing). In the case study and in Chapters 12–13, we use JavaFX and **Scene Builder**—a drag-and-drop tool for creating JavaFX GUIs quickly and conveniently—to build several apps demonstrating various JavaFX layouts, controls and event-handling capabilities. In Swing, drag-and-drop tools and their generated code are *IDE dependent.* Scene Builder is a standalone tool that you can use separately or with any of the Java IDEs to do **portable drag-and-drop GUI design**. In Chapter 22, we present many JavaFX 2D and 3D graphics, animation and video capabilities. We also provide **36 programming exercises and projects** that students will find challenging and entertaining, including many **game-programming exercises.** Despite the fact that the JavaFX chapters are spread out in the book, **Chapter 22 can be covered immediately after Chapter 13.**

Swing GUI and Java 2D Graphics
Swing is still widely used, but Oracle will provide only minor updates going forward. For instructors and readers who wish to continue using Swing, we've moved to the book's **Companion Website** the 10th edition's

- optional Swing GUI and Graphics Case Study from Chapters 3–8, 10 and 13
- Chapter 26, Swing GUI Components: Part 1
- Chapter 27, Graphics and Java 2D
- Chapter 35, Swing GUI Components: Part 2.

See the "Companion Website" section later in this Preface.

Integrating Swing GUI Components in JavaFX GUIs
Even if you move to JavaFX, you still can use your favorite Swing capabilities. For example, in Chapter 24, we demonstrate how to display database data in a Swing `JTable` component that's embedded in a JavaFX GUI via a JavaFX 8 `SwingNode`. As you explore Java further, you'll see that you also can incorporate JavaFX capabilities into your Swing GUIs.

Data Structures and Generic Collections (Part 5)

Data structures presentation. Chapter 7 and the chapters of Part 5 form the core of a data structures course. We begin with generic class `ArrayList` in Chapter 7. Our later data structures discussions (Chapters 16–21) provide a deeper treatment of **generic collections**—showing how to use the built-in collections of the Java API.

We discuss **recursion**, which is important for many reasons including implementing tree-like, data-structure classes. For computer-science majors and students in related disciplines, we discuss popular **searching and sorting algorithms** for manipulating the contents of collections, and provide a friendly introduction to **Big O**—a means of describing mathematically how hard an algorithm might have to work to solve a problem. Most programmers should use the built-in searching and sorting capabilities of the collections classes.

We then show how to implement **generic methods and classes**, and **custom generic data structures** (this, too, is intended for computer-science majors—most programmers should use the pre-built generic collections). **Lambdas and streams** (introduced in Chapter 17) are especially useful for working with generic collections.

Flexible Lambdas and Streams Coverage (Chapter 17)

The most significant new features in Java 8 were lambdas and streams. This book has several 8
audiences, including

- those who'd like a significant treatment of lambdas and streams
- those who want a basic introduction with a few simple examples
- those who do not want to use lambdas and streams yet.

For this reason, we've placed most of the lambdas and streams treatment in Chapter 17, which is architected as a series of *easy-to-include-or-omit* sections that are keyed to the book's earlier sections and chapters. We do integrate lambdas and streams into a few examples after Chapter 17, because their capabilities are so compelling.

In Chapter 17, you'll see that lambdas and streams can help you write programs faster, more concisely, more simply, with fewer bugs and that are easier to **parallelize** (to realize performance improvements on **multi-core systems**) than programs written with previous techniques. You'll see that "functional programming" with lambdas and streams complements object-oriented programming.

Many of Chapter 17's sections are written so they can be covered earlier in the book (Fig. 5)—we suggest that students begin by covering Sections 17.2–17.7 after Chapter 7 and that professionals begin by covering Sections 17.2–17.5 after Chapter 5. After reading Chapter 17, you'll be able to cleverly reimplement many examples throughout the book.

Lambdas and streams discussions	Can be covered after
Sections 17.2–17.5 introduce basic lambda and streams capabilities that you can use to **replace counting loops**, and discuss the mechanics of how streams are processed.	Chapter 5, Control Statements: Part 2; Logical Operators
Section 17.6 introduces **method references** and additional streams capabilities.	Chapter 6, Methods: A Deeper Look
Section 17.7 introduces streams capabilities that process **one-dimensional arrays.**	Chapter 7, Arrays and `ArrayList`s
Sections 17.8–17.10 demonstrate additional streams capabilities and present various **functional interfaces used in streams processing.**	Chapter 10, Object-Oriented Programming: Polymorphism and Interfaces—Section 10.10 introduces Java 8 interface features (**`default` methods, `static` methods** and the concept of **functional interfaces**) for the functional interfaces that support lambdas and streams.
Section 17.11 shows how to use lambdas and streams to **process collections of `String` objects.**	Chapter 14, Strings, Characters and Regular Expressions
Section 17.12 shows how to use lambdas and streams to **process a `List<Employee>`.**	Chapter 16, Generic Collections
Section 17.13 shows how to use lambdas and streams to **process lines of text from a file.**	Chapter 15, Files, Input/Output Streams, NIO and XML Serialization
Section 17.14 introduces streams of random values	All earlier Chapter 17 sections.
Section 17.15 introduces infinite streams	All earlier Chapter 17 sections.
Section 17.16 shows how to use lambdas to implement **JavaFX event-listener interfaces.**	Chapter 12, JavaFX Graphical User Interfaces: Part 1
Chapter 23, Concurrency, shows that programs using lambdas and streams are often easier to **parallelize** so they can take advantage of **multi-core architectures** to enhance performance. The chapter demonstrates **parallel stream processing** and shows that **`Arrays` method `parallelSort`** improves performance on **multi-core architectures** when sorting large arrays.	

Fig. 5 | Java 8 lambdas and streams discussions and examples.

Concurrency and Multi-Core Performance (Part 6)

We were privileged to have as a reviewer of *Java How to Program, 10/e* Brian Goetz, co-author of *Java Concurrency in Practice* (Addison-Wesley). We updated Chapter 23, Concurrency, with Java 8 technology and idiom. We added a **`parallelSort`** vs. `sort` example
8 that uses the **Java 8 Date/Time API** to time each operation and demonstrate `parallelSort`'s better performance on a **multi-core** system. We included a **Java 8 parallel vs. sequential stream processing** example, again using the Date/Time API to show performance improvements. We added a Java 8 **`CompletableFuture`** example that demonstrates se-

quential and parallel execution of long-running calculations and we discuss **`Completable-Future` enhancements** in the online Java 9 chapter. Finally, we added several new 9 exercises, including one that demonstrates the problems with parallelizing Java 8 streams that apply non-associative operations and several that have the reader investigate and use the **Fork/Join framework** to **parallelize recursive algorithms.**

JavaFX concurrency. In this edition, we converted Chapter 23's Swing-based GUI examples to JavaFX. We now use **JavaFX concurrency** features, including class `Task` to execute long-running tasks in separate threads and display their results in the JavaFX application thread, and the `Platform` class's `runLater` method to schedule a `Runnable` for execution in the JavaFX application thread.

Database: JDBC and JPA (Part 7)

JDBC. Chapter 24 covers the widely used **JDBC** and uses the **Java DB database management system.** The chapter introduces **Structured Query Language** (SQL) and features a case study on developing a JavaFX database-driven address book that demonstrates **prepared statements.** In JDK 9, Oracle no longer bundles Java DB, which is simply an Ora- 9 cle-branded version of Apache Derby. JDK 9 users can download and use Apache Derby instead (`https://db.apache.org/derby/`).

Java Persistence API. Chapter 29 covers the newer **Java Persistence API** (JPA)—a standard for **object relational mapping (ORM)** that uses JDBC "under the hood." ORM tools can look at a database's **schema** and generate a set of classes that enabled you to interact with a database without having to use JDBC and SQL directly. This speeds database-application development, reduces errors and produces more portable code.

Web Application Development and Web Services (Part 8)

Java Server Faces (JSF). Chapters 30–31 introduce the **JavaServer™ Faces** (JSF) technology for building JSF web-based applications. Chapter 30 includes examples on building web application GUIs, validating forms and session tracking. Chapter 31 discusses data-driven JSF applications—including a **multi-tier web address book application** that allows users to add and search for contacts.

Web services. Chapter 32 now concentrates on creating and consuming **REST-based web services.** Most of today's web services use REST, which is simpler and more flexible than older web-services technologies that often required manipulating data in XML format. REST can use a variety of formats, such as JSON, HTML, plain text, media files and XML.

Optional Online Object-Oriented Design Case Study (Part 10)

Developing an Object-Oriented Design and Java Implementation of an ATM. Chapters 33–34 include an *optional* case study on object-oriented design using the UML (Unified Modeling Language™)—the industry-standard graphical language for modeling object-oriented systems. We design and implement the software for a simple automated teller machine (ATM). We analyze a typical **requirements document** that specifies the system to be built. We determine the **classes** needed to implement that system, the **attributes** the classes need to have, the **behaviors** the classes need to exhibit and specify how the classes must **interact** with one another to meet the system requirements. From the design we produce a **complete**

Java implementation. Students often report having a "light-bulb moment"—the case study helps them "tie it all together" and understand object orientation more deeply.

Teaching Approach

Java How to Program, 11/e, contains hundreds of complete working code examples. We stress program clarity and concentrate on building well-engineered software.

Syntax Coloring. For readability, we syntax color all the Java code, similar to the way most Java integrated-development environments and code editors syntax color code. Our syntax-coloring conventions are as follows:

```
comments appear in green
keywords appear in dark blue
errors appear in red
constants and literal values appear in light blue
all other code appears in black
```

Code Highlighting. We place transparent yellow rectangles around key code segments.

Using Fonts for Emphasis. We place the key terms and the index's page reference for each defining occurrence in **bold maroon** text for easier reference. We emphasize on-screen components in the **bold Helvetica** font (e.g., the **File** menu) and emphasize Java program text in the `Lucida` font (for example, `int x = 5;`).

Objectives. The list of chapter objectives provides a high-level overview of the chapter's contents.

Illustrations/Figures. Abundant tables, line drawings, UML diagrams, programs and program outputs are included.

Summary Bullets. We present a section-by-section bullet-list summary of the chapter. For ease of reference, we generally include the page number of each key term's defining occurrence in the text.

Self-Review Exercises and Answers. Extensive self-review exercises *and* answers are included for self study. All of the exercises in the optional ATM case study are fully solved.

Exercises. The chapter exercises include:

- simple recall of important terminology and concepts
- What's wrong with this code?
- What does this code do?
- writing individual statements and small portions of methods and classes
- writing complete methods, classes and programs
- major projects
- in many chapters, **Making a Difference exercises** that encourage you to use computers and the Internet to research and address significant social problems.
- In this edition, we added new exercises to our **game-programming** set (**SpotOn, Horse Race, Cannon, 15 Puzzle, Hangman, Block Breaker, Snake** and **Word Search**), as well as others on the **JavaMoney API**, `final` instance variables, com-

bining composition and inheritance, working with interfaces, drawing fractals, recursively searching directories, visualizing sorting algorithms and implementing parallel recursive algorithms with the Fork/Join framework. Many of these require students to research additional Java features online and use them.

Exercises that focus on either Java 8 or Java 9 are marked as such. Check out our **Programming Projects Resource Center** for lots of additional exercise and project possibilities (`www.deitel.com/ProgrammingProjects/`).

Index. We've included an extensive index. Defining occurrences of key terms are highlighted with a **bold maroon** page number. The print book index mentions only those terms used in the print book. **The online chapters index on the Companion Website includes all the print book terms and the online chapter terms.**

Programming Wisdom

We include hundreds of programming tips to help you focus on important aspects of program development. These represent the best we've gleaned from a combined nine decades of programming and teaching experience.

Good Programming Practices

The Good Programming Practices *call attention to techniques that will help you produce programs that are clearer, more understandable and more maintainable.*

Common Programming Errors

Pointing out these Common Programming Errors *reduces the likelihood that you'll make them.*

Error-Prevention Tips

These tips contain suggestions for exposing bugs and removing them from your programs; many describe aspects of Java that prevent bugs from getting into programs in the first place.

Performance Tips

These tips highlight opportunities for making your programs run faster or minimizing the amount of memory that they occupy.

Portability Tips

The Portability Tips *help you write code that will run on a variety of platforms.*

Software Engineering Observations

The Software Engineering Observations *highlight architectural and design issues that affect the construction of software systems, especially large-scale systems.*

Look-and-Feel Observations

The Look-and-Feel Observations *highlight graphical-user-interface conventions. These observations help you design attractive, user-friendly graphical user interfaces that conform to industry norms.*

What are JEPs, JSRs and the JCP?

Throughout the book we encourage you to research various aspects of Java online. Some acronyms you're likely to see are JEP, JSR and JCP.

JEPs (JDK Enhancement Proposals) are used by Oracle to gather proposals from the Java community for changes to the Java language, APIs and tools, and to help create the roadmaps for future Java Standard Edition (Java SE), Java Enterprise Edition (Java EE) and Java Micro Edition (Java ME) platform versions and the JSRs (Java Specification Requests) that define them. The complete list of JEPs can be found at

```
http://openjdk.java.net/jeps/0
```

JSRs (Java Specification Requests) are the formal descriptions of Java platform features' technical specifications. Each new feature that gets added to Java (Standard Edition, Enterprise Edition or Micro Edition) has a JSR that goes through a review and approval
8 process before the feature is added to Java. Sometimes JSRs are grouped together into an
umbrella JSR. For example JSR 337 is the umbrella for Java 8 features, and JSR 379 is the
9 umbrella for Java 9 features. The complete list of JSRs can be found at

```
https://www.jcp.org/en/jsr/all
```

The JCP (**Java Community Process**) is responsible for developing JSRs. JCP expert groups create the JSRs, which are publicly available for review and feedback. You can learn more about the JCP at:

```
https://www.jcp.org
```

Secure Java Programming

It's difficult to build industrial-strength systems that stand up to attacks from viruses, worms, and other forms of "malware." Today, via the Internet, such attacks can be instantaneous and global in scope. Building security into software from the beginning of the development cycle can greatly reduce vulnerabilities. We audited our book against the CERT Oracle Secure Coding Standard for Java

```
http://bit.ly/CERTOracleSecureJava
```

and adhered to various secure coding practices as appropriate for a textbook at this level.

The CERT® Coordination Center (`www.cert.org`) was created to analyze and respond promptly to attacks. CERT—the Computer Emergency Response Team—is a government-funded organization within the Carnegie Mellon University Software Engineering Institute™. CERT publishes and promotes secure coding standards for various popular programming languages to help software developers implement industrial-strength systems by employing programming practices that prevent system attacks from succeeding.

We'd like to thank Robert C. Seacord. A few years back, when Mr. Seacord was the Secure Coding Manager at CERT and an adjunct professor in the Carnegie Mellon University School of Computer Science, he was a technical reviewer for our book, *C How to Program, 7/e*, where he scrutinized our C programs from a security standpoint, recommending that we adhere to the *CERT C Secure Coding Standard*. This experience also influenced our coding practices in *C++ How to Program, 10/e* and *Java How to Program, 11/e*.

Companion Website: Source Code, VideoNotes, Online Chapters and Online Appendices

All the source code for the book's code examples is available at:

```
http://www.deitel.com/books/jhtp11
```

and at the book's **Companion Website**, which also contains extensive **VideoNotes** and the online chapters and appendices:

```
http://www.pearsonhighered.com/deitel
```

See the book's inside front cover for information on accessing the Companion Website.

In the extensive **VideoNotes**, co-author Paul Deitel patiently explains most of the programs in the book's core chapters. Students like viewing the VideoNotes for reinforcement of core concepts and for additional insights.

Software Used in *Java How to Program, 11/e*

All the software you'll need for this book is available free for download from the Internet.
See the **Before You Begin** section that follows this Preface for links to each download. We
wrote most of the examples in *Java How to Program, 11/e*, using the free Java Standard Edition Development Kit (JDK) 8. For the optional Java 9 content, we used the OpenJDK's 8
early access version of JDK 9. All of the Java 9 programs run on the early access versions
of JDK 9. All of the remaining programs run on both JDK 8 and early access versions of 9
JDK 9, and were tested on Windows, macOS and Linux. Several online chapters also use
the Netbeans IDE.

Java Documentation Links

Throughout the book, we provide links to Java documentation where you can learn more
about various topics that we present. For Java 8 documentation, the links begin with 8

```
http://docs.oracle.com/javase/8/
```

and for Java 9 documentation, the links currently begin with 9

```
http://download.java.net/java/jdk9/
```

The Java 9 documentation links will change when Oracle releases Java 9—*possibly* to links beginning with

```
http://docs.oracle.com/javase/9/
```

For any links that change after publication, we'll post updates at

```
http://www.deitel.com/books/jhtp11
```

Java How to Program, Late Objects Version, 11/e

There are several approaches to teaching first courses in Java programming. The two most popular are the **early objects approach** and the **late objects approach**. To meet these diverse needs, we've published two versions of this book:

- *Java How to Program, Early Objects Version, 11/e* (this book), and
- *Java How to Program, Late Objects Version, 11/e*

The key difference between them is the order in which we present Chapters 1–7. The books have identical content in Chapter 8 and higher. Instructors can request an examination copy of either of these books from their Pearson representative:

```
http://www.pearsonhighered.com/educator/replocator/
```

Instructor Supplements

The following supplements are available to qualified instructors only through Pearson Education's Instructor Resource Center (`www.pearsonhighered.com/irc`):

- *PowerPoint® slides* containing all the code and figures in the text, plus bulleted items that summarize key points.
- *Test Item File* of multiple-choice questions and answers (approximately two per book section).
- *Solutions Manual* with solutions to most of the end-of-chapter exercises. **Before assigning an exercise for homework, instructors should check the IRC to be sure it includes the solution. Solutions are *not* provided for "project" exercises.**

Please do not write to us requesting access to the Pearson Instructor's Resource Center which contains the book's instructor supplements, including the exercise solutions. Access is limited strictly to college instructors teaching from the book. Instructors may obtain access only through their Pearson representatives. Solutions are *not* provided for "project" exercises. If you're not a registered faculty member, contact your Pearson representative or visit

```
http://www.pearsonhighered.com/educator/replocator/
```

Online Practice and Assessment with MyProgrammingLab™

MyProgrammingLab™ helps students fully grasp the logic, semantics, and syntax of programming. Through practice exercises and immediate, personalized feedback, MyProgrammingLab improves the programming competence of beginning students who often struggle with the basic concepts and paradigms of popular high-level programming languages.

An optional self-study and homework tool, a MyProgrammingLab course consists of hundreds of small practice problems organized around the structure of this textbook. For students, the system automatically detects errors in the logic and syntax of their code submissions and offers targeted hints that enable students to figure out what went wrong—and why. For instructors, a comprehensive gradebook tracks correct and incorrect answers and stores the code inputted by students for review.

For a full demonstration, to see feedback from instructors and students or to get started using MyProgrammingLab in your course, instructors should visit

```
http://www.myprogramminglab.com
```

Keeping in Touch with the Authors

As you read the book, if you have **questions**, send an e-mail to us at

```
deitel@deitel.com
```

and we'll respond promptly. For **book updates**, visit

```
http://www.deitel.com/books/jhtp11
```

subscribe to the ***Deitel*® *Buzz Online*** **newsletter** at

```
http://www.deitel.com/newsletter/subscribe.html
```

and join the **Deitel social networking communities** on

- **Facebook®** (`http://www.deitel.com/deitelfan`)
- **Twitter®** (`@deitel`)
- **LinkedIn®** (`http://linkedin.com/company/deitel-&-associates`)
- **YouTube®** (`http://youtube.com/DeitelTV`)
- **Google+™** (`http://google.com/+DeitelFan`)
- **Instagram®** (`http://instagram.com/DeitelFan`)

Acknowledgments

We'd like to thank Barbara Deitel for long hours devoted to technical research on this project. We're fortunate to have worked with the dedicated team of publishing professionals at Pearson. We appreciate the guidance, wisdom and energy of Tracy Johnson, Executive Editor, Computer Science. Tracy and her team handle all of our academic textbooks. Kristy Alaura recruited the book's reviewers and managed the review process. Bob Engelhardt managed the book's publication. We selected the cover art and Chuti Prasertsith designed the cover.

Reviewers

We wish to acknowledge the efforts of our recent editions reviewers—a distinguished group of academics, Oracle Java team members, Oracle Java Champions and other industry professionals. They scrutinized the text and the programs and provided countless suggestions for improving the presentation. Any remaining faults in the book are our own.

We appreciate the guidance of JavaFX experts Jim Weaver and Johan Vos (co-authors of *Pro JavaFX 8*), Jonathan Giles and Simon Ritter on the three JavaFX chapters.

Eleventh Edition reviewers: Marty Allen (University of Wisconsin-La Crosse), Robert Field (JShell chapter only; JShell Architect, Oracle), Trisha Gee (JetBrains, Java Champion), Jonathan Giles (Consulting Member of Technical Staff, Oracle), Brian Goetz (JShell chapter only; Oracle's Java Language Architect), Edwin Harris (M.S. Instructor at The University of North Florida's School of Computing), Maurice Naftalin (Java Champion), José Antonio González Seco (Consultant), Bruno Souza (President of SouJava—the Brazilian Java Society, Java Specialist at ToolsCloud, Java Champion and SouJava representative at the Java Community Process), Dr. Venkat Subramaniam (President, Agile Developer, Inc. and Instructional Professor, University of Houston), Johan Vos (CTO, Cloud Products at Gluon, Java Champion).

Tenth Edition reviewers: Lance Andersen (Oracle Corporation), Dr. Danny Coward (Oracle Corporation), Brian Goetz (Oracle Corporation), Evan Golub (University of Maryland), Dr. Huiwei Guan (Professor, Department of Computer & Information Science, North Shore Community College), Manfred Riem (Java Champion), Simon Ritter (Oracle Corporation), Robert C. Seacord (CERT, Software Engineering Institute, Carnegie Mellon University), Khallai Taylor (Assistant Professor, Triton College and Adjunct Professor, Lonestar College—Kingwood), Jorge Vargas (Yumbling and a Java Champion), Johan Vos (LodgON and Oracle Java Champion) and James L. Weaver (Oracle Corporation and author of *Pro JavaFX 2*).

Earlier editions reviewers: Soundararajan Angusamy (Sun Microsystems), Joseph Bowbeer (Consultant), William E. Duncan (Louisiana State University), Diana Franklin (University of California, Santa Barbara), Edward F. Gehringer (North Carolina State University), Ric Heishman (George Mason University), Dr. Heinz Kabutz (JavaSpecialists.eu), Patty Kraft (San Diego State University), Lawrence Premkumar (Sun Microsystems), Tim Margush (University of Akron), Sue McFarland Metzger (Villanova University), Shyamal Mitra (The University of Texas at Austin), Peter Pilgrim (Consultant), Manjeet Rege, Ph.D. (Rochester Institute of Technology), Susan Rodger (Duke University), Amr Sabry (Indiana University), José Antonio González Seco (Parliament of Andalusia), Sang Shin (Sun Microsystems), S. Sivakumar (Astra Infotech Private Limited), Raghavan "Rags" Srinivas (Intuit), Monica Sweat (Georgia Tech), Vinod Varma (Astra Infotech Private Limited) and Alexander Zuev (Sun Microsystems).

A Special Thank You to Robert Field

Robert Field, Oracle's JShell Architect reviewed the new JShell chapter, responding to our numerous emails in which we asked JShell questions, reported bugs we encountered as JShell evolved and suggested improvements. It was a privilege having our content scrutinized by the person responsible for JShell.

A Special Thank You to Brian Goetz

Brian Goetz, Oracle's Java Language Architect and Specification Lead for Java 8's Project Lambda, and co-author of *Java Concurrency in Practice*, did a full-book review of the 10th edition. He provided us with an extraordinary collection of insights and constructive comments. For the 11th edition, he did a detailed review of our new JShell chapter and answered our Java questions throughout the project.

Well, there you have it! As you read the book, we'd appreciate your comments, criticisms, corrections and suggestions for improvement. Please send your questions and all other correspondence to:

```
deitel@deitel.com
```

We'll respond promptly. We hope you enjoy working with *Java How to Program, 11/e*, as much as we enjoyed researching and writing it!

Paul and Harvey Deitel

About the Authors

Paul J. Deitel, CEO and Chief Technical Officer of Deitel & Associates, Inc., is a graduate of MIT and has over 35 years of experience in computing. He holds the Java Certified Programmer and Java Certified Developer designations, and is an Oracle Java Champion. Through Deitel & Associates, Inc., he has delivered hundreds of programming courses worldwide to clients, including Cisco, IBM, Siemens, Sun Microsystems (now Oracle), Dell, Fidelity, NASA at the Kennedy Space Center, the National Severe Storm Laboratory, White Sands Missile Range, Rogue Wave Software, Boeing, SunGard Higher Education, Nortel Networks, Puma, iRobot, Invensys and many more. He and his co-author, Dr. Harvey M. Deitel, are the world's best-selling programming-language textbook/professional book/video authors.

Dr. Harvey M. Deitel, Chairman and Chief Strategy Officer of Deitel & Associates, Inc., has over 55 years of experience in computing. Dr. Deitel earned B.S. and M.S. degrees in Electrical Engineering from MIT and a Ph.D. in Mathematics from Boston University—he studied computing in each of these programs before they spun off Computer Science programs. He has extensive college teaching experience, including earning tenure and serving as the Chairman of the Computer Science Department at Boston College before founding Deitel & Associates, Inc., in 1991 with his son, Paul. The Deitels' publications have earned international recognition, with more than 100 translations published in Japanese, German, Russian, Spanish, French, Polish, Italian, Simplified Chinese, Traditional Chinese, Korean, Portuguese, Greek, Urdu and Turkish. Dr. Deitel has delivered hundreds of programming courses to academic, corporate, government and military clients.

About Deitel® & Associates, Inc.

Deitel & Associates, Inc., founded by Paul Deitel and Harvey Deitel, is an internationally recognized authoring and corporate training organization, specializing in computer programming languages, object technology, mobile app development and Internet and web software technology. The company's training clients include many of the world's largest companies, government agencies, branches of the military, and academic institutions. The company offers instructor-led training courses delivered at client sites worldwide on major programming languages and platforms, including Java™, Android app development, Swift and iOS app development, C++, C, Visual C#®, Visual Basic®, object technology, Internet and web programming and a growing list of additional programming and software development courses.

Through its 42-year publishing partnership with Pearson/Prentice Hall, Deitel & Associates, Inc., publishes leading-edge programming textbooks and professional books in print and e-book formats, **LiveLessons** video courses and **REVEL™** online interactive multimedia courses with integrated **MyProgrammingLab**. Deitel & Associates, Inc. and the authors can be reached at:

```
deitel@deitel.com
```

To learn more about Deitel's *Dive-Into® Series* Corporate Training curriculum, visit:

```
http://www.deitel.com/training
```

To request a proposal for worldwide on-site, instructor-led training, write to

```
deitel@deitel.com
```

Individuals wishing to purchase Deitel books and *LiveLessons* video training can do so through `www.deitel.com`. Bulk orders by corporations, the government, the military and academic institutions should be placed directly with Pearson. For more information, visit

```
http://www.informit.com/store/sales.aspx
```

About the Cover Art

The computer-generated art we selected picks up some key themes of *Java How to Program 11/e*:

©Joingate/ShutterStock

The art is in the shape of a "9" and this book covers key new features of **Java 9**.

The art represents a shell. One of the most important features in Java 9 is **JShell—Java 9's REPL** (read-eval-print-loop) for interactive Java. Many educators feel that JShell is the most important pedagogic enhancement to Java since it was announced in 1995. We discuss JShell in detail in Chapter 25 and show how you can use it for **experimentation** and **discovery** to learn Java faster beginning as early as Chapter 2.

The shell is composed of many compartments. There are analogous to Java 9 modules—the module system is Java 9's most important new software engineering capability.

The shell is computer-generated art, namely a recursively defined mathematical fractal. We discuss **generating fractal computer graphics** in Chapter 18, Recursion.

The shell's spiral shape is derived from the mathematical **Fibonacci series**, which we discuss in Chapter 18, Recursion.

Any sequence like the Fibonacci series can be treated as a stream. We discuss **Java streams** in Chapter 17, Lambdas and Streams.

The shell has lighting effects. JavaFX can apply lighting effects to 3D objects. We use the default **JavaFX lighting effects** in Chapter 22, JavaFX Graphics and Multimedia.

Before You Begin

This section contains information you should review before using this book. Any updates to the information presented here will be posted at:

```
http://www.deitel.com/books/jhtp11
```

In addition, we provide getting-started videos that demonstrate the instructions in this Before You Begin section.

Font and Naming Conventions

We use fonts to distinguish between on-screen components (such as menu names and menu items) and Java code or commands. Our convention is to emphasize on-screen components in a sans-serif bold **Helvetica** font (for example, **File** menu) and to emphasize Java code and commands in a sans-serif `Lucida` font (for example, `System.out.println()`).

Java SE Development Kit (JDK)

The software you'll need for this book is available free for download from the web. Most of the examples were tested with the Java SE Development Kit 8 (also known as JDK 8). The most recent JDK version is available from:

```
http://www.oracle.com/technetwork/java/javase/downloads/index.html
```

The current version of the JDK at the time of this writing is JDK 8 update 121.

Java SE 9

The Java SE 9-specific features that we discuss in optional sections and chapters require JDK 9. At the time of this writing, JDK 9 was available as an early access verion. If you're using this book before the final JDK 9 is released, see the section "Installing and Configuring JDK 9 Early Access Version" later in this Before You Begin. We also discuss in that section how you can manage multiple JDK versions on Windows, macOS and Linux.

JDK Installation Instructions

After downloading the JDK installer, be sure to carefully follow the installation instructions for your platform at:

```
https://docs.oracle.com/javase/8/docs/technotes/guides/install/
   install_overview.html
```

You'll need to update the JDK version number in any version-specific instructions. For example, the instructions refer to `jdk1.8.0`, but the current version at the time of this writing is `jdk1.8.0_121`. If you're a Linux user, your distribution's software package manager might provide an easier way to install the JDK. For example, you can learn how to install the JDK on Ubuntu here:

```
http://askubuntu.com/questions/464755/how-to-install-openjdk-8-on-
   14-04-lts
```

Setting the PATH Environment Variable

The PATH environment variable on your computer designates which directories the computer searches when looking for applications, such as the applications that enable you to compile and run your Java applications (called javac and java, respectively). *Carefully follow the installation instructions for Java on your platform to ensure that you set the* PATH *environment variable correctly.* The steps for setting environment variables differ by operating system. Instructions for various platforms are listed at:

```
http://www.java.com/en/download/help/path.xml
```

If you do not set the PATH variable correctly on Windows and some Linux installations, when you use the JDK's tools, you'll receive a message like:

```
'java' is not recognized as an internal or external command,
operable program or batch file.
```

In this case, go back to the installation instructions for setting the PATH and recheck your steps. If you've downloaded a newer version of the JDK, you may need to change the name of the JDK's installation directory in the PATH variable.

JDK Installation Directory and the bin *Subdirectory*

The JDK's installation directory varies by platform. The directories listed below are for Oracle's JDK 8 update 121:

- JDK on Windows:
  C:\Program Files\Java\jdk1.8.0_121
- macOS (formerly called OS X):
  /Library/Java/JavaVirtualMachines/jdk1.8.0_121.jdk/Contents/Home
- Ubuntu Linux:
  /usr/lib/jvm/java-8-oracle

Depending on your platform, the JDK installation folder's name might differ if you're using a different JDK 8 update. For Linux, the install location depends on the installer you use and possibly the Linux version as well. We used Ubuntu Linux. The PATH environment variable must point to the JDK installation directory's bin subdirectory.

When setting the PATH, be sure to use the proper JDK-installation-directory name for the specific version of the JDK you installed—as newer JDK releases become available, the JDK-installation-directory name changes with a new *update version number*. For example, at the time of this writing, the most recent JDK 8 release was update 121. For this version, the JDK-installation-directory name typically ends with _121.

CLASSPATH Environment Variable

If you attempt to run a Java program and receive a message like

```
Exception in thread "main" java.lang.NoClassDefFoundError: YourClass
```

then your system has a CLASSPATH environment variable that must be modified. To fix the preceding error, follow the steps in setting the PATH environment variable, to locate the CLASSPATH variable, then edit the variable's value to include the local directory—typically represented as a dot (.). On Windows add

```
.;
```

at the beginning of the CLASSPATH's value (with no spaces before or after these characters). On macOS and Linux, add

```
.:
```

Setting the JAVA_HOME Environment Variable

The Java DB database software that you'll use in Chapter 24 and several online chapters requires you to set the JAVA_HOME environment variable to your JDK's installation directory. The same steps you used to set the PATH may also be used to set other environment variables, such as JAVA_HOME.

Java Integrated Development Environments (IDEs)

There are many Java integrated development environments that you can use for Java programming. Because the steps for using them differ, we used only the JDK command-line tools for most of the book's examples. We provide getting-started videos that show how to download, install and use three popular IDEs—NetBeans, Eclipse and IntelliJ IDEA. We use NetBeans in several of the book's online chapters.

NetBeans Downloads
You can download the JDK/NetBeans bundle from:

```
http://www.oracle.com/technetwork/java/javase/downloads/index.html
```

The NetBeans version that's bundled with the JDK is for Java SE development. The online JavaServer Faces (JSF) chapters and web services chapter use the Java Enterprise Edition (Java EE) version of NetBeans, which you can download from:

```
https://netbeans.org/downloads/
```

This version supports both Java SE and Java EE development.

Eclipse Downloads
You can download the Eclipse IDE from:

```
https://eclipse.org/downloads/eclipse-packages/
```

For Java SE development choose the Eclipse IDE for Java Developers. For Java Enterprise Edition (Java EE) development (such as JSF and web services), choose the Eclipse IDE for Java EE Developers—this version supports both Java SE and Java EE development.

IntelliJ IDEA Community Edition Downloads
You can download the free IntelliJ IDEA Community from:

```
https://www.jetbrains.com/idea/download/index.html
```

The free version supports only Java SE development.

Scene Builder

Our JavaFX GUI, graphics and multimedia examples (starting in Chapter 12) use the free Scene Builder tool, which enables you to create graphical user interfaces (GUIs) with drag-and-drop techniques. You can download Scene Builder from:

```
http://gluonhq.com/labs/scene-builder/
```

Obtaining the Code Examples

Java How to Program, 11/e's examples are available for download at

```
http://www.deitel.com/books/jhtp11/
```

Click the **Download Code Examples** link to download a ZIP archive file containing the examples—typically, the file will be saved in you user account's `Downloads` folder.

Extract the contents of `examples.zip` using a ZIP extraction tool such as 7-Zip (`www.7-zip.org`), WinZip (`www.winzip.com`) or the built-in capabilities of your operating system. Instructions throughout the book assume that the examples are located at:

- `C:\examples` on Windows
- your user account's `Documents/examples` subfolder on macOS and Linux

Installing and Configuring JDK 9 Early Access Version

Throughout the book, we introduce various new Java 9 features in optional sections and chapters. The Java 9 features require JDK 9, which at the time of this writing was still early access software available from

```
https://jdk9.java.net/download/
```

This page provides installers for Windows and macOS (formerly Mac OS X). On these platforms, download the appropriate installer, double click it and follow the on-screen instructions. For Linux, the download page provides only a `tar.gz` archive file. You can download that file, then extract its contents to a folder on your system. *If you have both JDK 8 and JDK 9 installed*, we provide instructions below showing how to specify which JDK to use on Windows, macOS or Linux.

JDK Version Numbers

Prior to Java 9, JDK versions were numbered `1.X.0_`*updateNumber* where `X` was the major Java version. For example,

- Java 8's current JDK version number is `jdk1.8.0_121` and
- Java 7's final JDK version number was `jdk1.7.0_80`.

As of Java 9, Oracle has changed the numbering scheme. JDK 9 initially will be known as `jdk-9`. Once Java 9 is officially released, there will be future minor version updates that add new features, and security updates that fix security holes in the Java platform. These updates will be reflected in the JDK version numbers. For example, in `9.1.3`:

- `9`—is the major Java version number
- `1`—is the minor version update number and
- `3`—is the security update number.

So 9.2.5 would indicate the version of Java 9 for which there have been two minor version updates and five total security updates (across major and minor versions). For the new version-numbering scheme's details, see JEP (Java Enhancement Proposal) 223 at

```
http://openjdk.java.net/jeps/223
```

Managing Multiple JDKs on Windows

On Windows, you use the PATH environment variable to tell the operating system where to find a JDK's tools. The instructions at

```
https://docs.oracle.com/javase/8/docs/technotes/guides/install/
   windows_jdk_install.html#BABGDJFH
```

specify how to update the PATH. Replace the JDK version number in the instructions with the JDK version number you wish to use—currently jdk-9. You should check your JDK 9's installation folder name for an updated version number. This setting will automatically be applied to each new **Command Prompt** you open.

If you prefer not to modify your system's PATH—perhaps because you're also using JDK 8—you can open a **Command Prompt** window then set the PATH only for that window. To do so, use the command

```
set PATH=location;%PATH%
```

where *location* is the full path to JDK 9's bin folder and ;%PATH% appends the **Command Prompt** window's original PATH contents to the new PATH. Typically, the command would be

```
set PATH="C:\Program Files\Java\jdk-9\bin";%PATH%
```

Each time you open a new **Command Prompt** window to use JDK 9, you'll have to reissue this command.

Managing Multiple JDKs on macOS

On a Mac, you can determine which JDKs you have installed by opening a **Terminal** window and entering the command

```
/usr/libexec/java_home -V
```

which shows the version numbers, names and locations of your JDKs. In our case

```
Matching Java Virtual Machines (2):
    9, x86_64:  "Java SE 9-ea  "/Library/Java/JavaVirtualMachines/
       jdk-9.jdk/Contents/Home
    1.8.0_121, x86_64:  "Java SE 8  "/Library/Java/
       JavaVirtualMachines/jdk1.8.0_121.jdk/Contents/Home
```

the version numbers are 9 and 1.8.0_121. In "Java SE 9-ea" above, "ea" means "early access."

To set the default JDK version, enter

```
/usr/libexec/java_home -v # --exec javac -version
```

where # is the version number of the specific JDK that should be the default. At the time of this writing, for JDK 8, # should be 1.8.0_121 and, for JDK 9, # should be 9.

Next, enter the command:

```
export JAVA_HOME=`/usr/libexec/java_home -v #`
```

where # is the version number of the current default JDK. This sets the **Terminal** window's `JAVA_HOME` environment variable to that JDK's location. This environment variable will be used when launching JShell.

Managing Multiple JDKs on Linux

The way you manage multiple JDK versions on Linux depends on how you install your JDKs. If you use your Linux distribution's tools for installing software (we used `apt-get` on Ubuntu Linux), then on many Linux distributions you can use the following command to list the installed JDKs:

```
sudo update-alternatives --config java
```

If more than one is installed, the preceding command shows you a numbered list of JDKs—you then enter the number for the JDK you wish to use as the default. For a tutorial showing how to use `apt-get` to install JDKs on Ubuntu Linux, see

```
https://www.digitalocean.com/community/tutorials/how-to-install-
java-with-apt-get-on-ubuntu-16-04
```

If you installed JDK 9 by downloading the `tar.gz` file and extracting it to your system, you'll need to specify in a shell window the path to the JDK's `bin` folder. To do so, enter the following command in your shell window:

```
export PATH="location:$PATH"
```

where *location* is the path to JDK 9's `bin` folder. This updates the `PATH` environment variable with the location of JDK 9's commands, like `javac` and `java`, so that you can execute the JDK's commands in the shell window.

You're now ready to begin your Java studies with *Java How to Program, 11/e*. We hope you enjoy the book!

Introduction to Computers, the Internet and Java

1

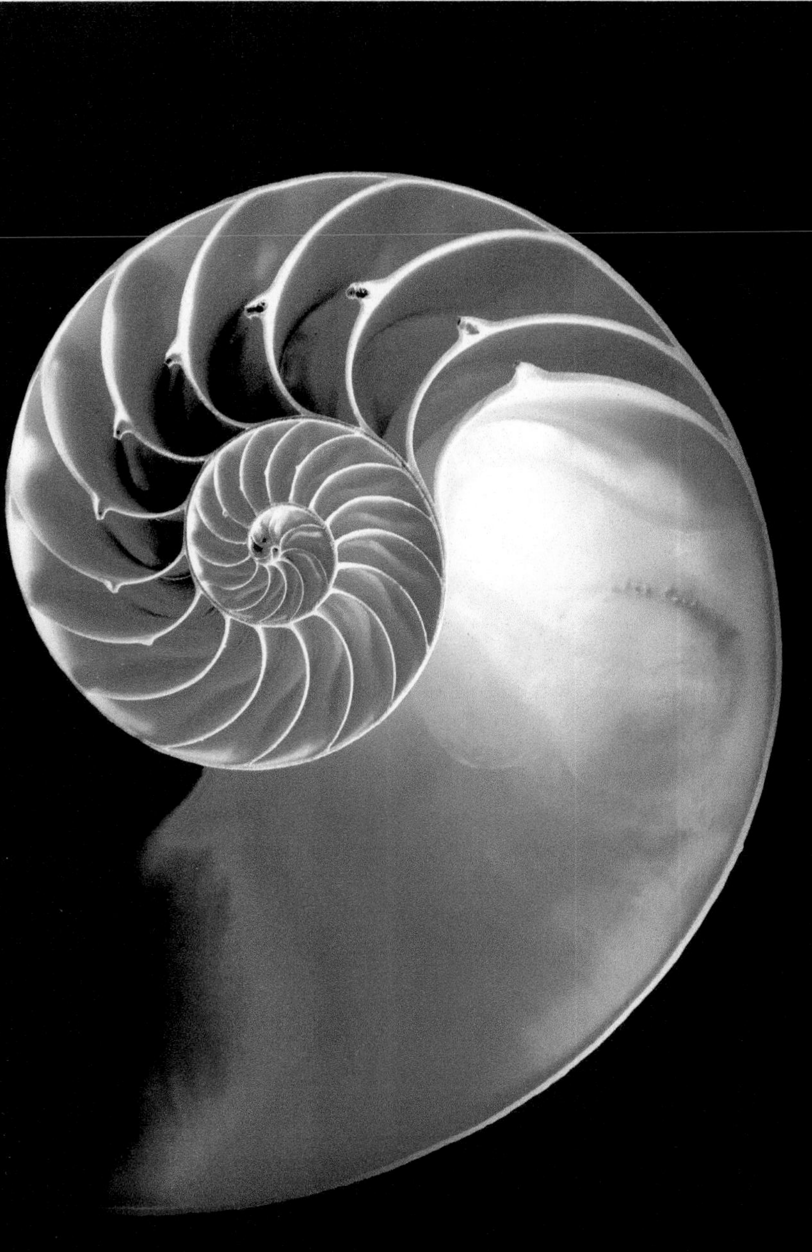

Objectives

In this chapter you'll:

- Learn about exciting recent developments in the computer field.
- Learn computer hardware, software and networking basics.
- Understand the data hierarchy.
- Understand the different types of programming languages.
- Understand the importance of Java and other leading programming languages.
- Understand object-oriented programming basics.
- Learn Internet and web basics.
- Learn a typical Java program-development environment.
- Test-drive a Java application.
- Learn some key recent software technologies.
- See how to keep up-to-date with information technologies.

Outline

1.1 Introduction

Welcome to Java—one of the world's most widely used computer programming languages and, according to the TIOBE Index, the world's most popular.[1] You're probably familiar with the powerful tasks computers perform. Using this textbook, you'll write instructions in the Java programming language commanding computers to perform those tasks. **Software** (i.e., the instructions you write) controls **hardware** (i.e., computers).

You'll learn *object-oriented programming*—today's key programming methodology. You'll create and work with many *software objects.*

For many organizations, the preferred language for meeting their enterprise programming needs is Java. Java is also widely used for implementing Internet-based applications and software for devices that communicate over a network.

There are billions of personal computers in use and an even larger number of mobile devices with computers at their core. According to Oracle's 2016 JavaOne conference keynote presentation,[2] there are now 10 million Java developers worldwide and Java runs on 15 billion devices (Fig. 1.1), including two billion vehicles and 350 million medical devices. In addition, the explosive growth of mobile phones, tablets and other devices is creating significant opportunities for programming mobile apps.

1. `http://www.tiobe.com/tiobe-index/`
2. `http://bit.ly/JavaOne2016Keynote`

Devices		
Access control systems	Airplane systems	ATMs
Automobiles	Blu-ray Disc™ players	Building controls
Cable boxes	Copiers	Credit cards
CT scanners	Desktop computers	e-Readers
Game consoles	GPS navigation systems	Home appliances
Home security systems	Internet-of-Things gateways	Light switches
Logic controllers	Lottery systems	Medical devices
Mobile phones	MRIs	Network switches
Optical sensors	Parking meters	Personal computers
Point-of-sale terminals	Printers	Robots
Routers	Servers	Smart cards
Smart meters	Smartpens	Smartphones
Tablets	Televisions	Thermostats
Transportation passes	TV set-top boxes	Vehicle diagnostic systems

Fig. 1.1 | Some devices that use Java.

Java Standard Edition

Java has evolved so rapidly that this eleventh edition of *Java How to Program*—based on **Java Standard Edition 8 (Java SE 8)** and the new **Java Standard Edition 9 (Java SE 9)**—was published just 21 years after the first edition. Java Standard Edition contains the capabilities needed to develop desktop and server applications. The book can be used conveniently with *either* Java SE 8 *or* Java SE 9 (released just after this book was published). For instructors and professionals who want to stay with Java 8 for a while, the Java SE 9 features are discussed in modular, easy-to-include-or-omit sections throughout this book and its Companion Website.

Prior to Java SE 8, Java supported three programming paradigms:

- *procedural programming,*
- *object-oriented programming* and
- *generic programming.*

Java SE 8 added the beginnings of *functional programming with lambdas and streams.* In Chapter 17, we'll show how to use lambdas and streams to write programs faster, more concisely, with fewer bugs and that are easier to *parallelize* (i.e., perform multiple calculations simultaneously) to take advantage of today's *multi-core* hardware architectures to enhance application performance.

Java Enterprise Edition

Java is used in such a broad spectrum of applications that it has two other editions. The **Java Enterprise Edition (Java EE)** is geared toward developing large-scale, distributed networking applications and web-based applications. In the past, most computer applications ran on "standalone" computers (that is, not networked together). Today's applications can be written with the aim of communicating among the world's computers via the Internet and the web. Later in this book we discuss how to build such web-based applications with Java.

Java Micro Edition
The **Java Micro Edition (Java ME)**—a subset of Java SE—is geared toward developing applications for resource-constrained embedded devices, such as smartwatches, television set-top boxes, smart meters (for monitoring electric energy usage) and more. Many of the devices in Fig. 1.1 use Java ME.

1.2 Hardware and Software

Computers can perform calculations and make logical decisions phenomenally faster than human beings can. Many of today's personal computers can perform billions of calculations in one second—more than a human can perform in a lifetime. *Supercomputers* are already performing *thousands of trillions (quadrillions)* of instructions per second! China's National Research Center of Parallel Computer Engineering & Technology (NRCPC) has developed the Sunway TaihuLight supercomputer can perform over 93 quadrillion calculations per second (93 *petaflops*)![3] To put that in perspective, *the Sunway TaihuLight supercomputer can perform in one second over 12 million calculations for every person on the planet!* And supercomputing upper limits are growing quickly.

Computers process data under the control of sequences of instructions called **computer programs**. These software programs guide the computer through ordered actions specified by people called computer **programmers**. In this book, you'll learn key programming methodologies that are enhancing programmer productivity, thereby reducing software development costs.

A computer consists of various devices referred to as hardware (e.g., the keyboard, screen, mouse, hard disks, memory, DVD drives and processing units). Computing costs are *dropping dramatically*, owing to rapid developments in hardware and software technologies. Computers that might have filled large rooms and cost millions of dollars decades ago are now inscribed on silicon chips smaller than a fingernail, costing perhaps a few dollars each. Ironically, silicon is one of the most abundant materials on Earth—it's an ingredient in common sand. Silicon-chip technology has made computing so economical that computers have become a commodity.

1.2.1 Moore's Law

Every year, you probably expect to pay at least a little more for most products and services. The opposite has been the case in the computer and communications fields, especially with regard to the hardware supporting these technologies. For many decades, hardware costs have fallen rapidly.

Every year or two, the capacities of computers have approximately *doubled* inexpensively. This remarkable trend often is called **Moore's Law**, named for the person who identified it in the 1960s, Gordon Moore, co-founder of Intel—the leading manufacturer of the processors in today's computers and embedded systems. Moore's Law *and related observations* apply especially to the amount of memory that computers have for programs,

3. `https://www.top500.org/lists/2016/06/`

the amount of secondary storage (such as solid-state drive storage) they have to hold programs and data over longer periods of time, and their processor speeds—the speeds at which they *execute* their programs (i.e., do their work).

Similar growth has occurred in the communications field—costs have plummeted as enormous demand for communications *bandwidth* (i.e., information-carrying capacity) has attracted intense competition. We know of no other fields in which technology improves so quickly and costs fall so rapidly. Such phenomenal improvement is truly fostering the *Information Revolution.*

1.2.2 Computer Organization

Regardless of differences in *physical* appearance, computers can be envisioned as divided into various **logical units** or sections (Fig. 1.2).

Logical unit	Description
Input unit	This "receiving" section obtains information (data and computer programs) from **input devices** and places it at the disposal of the other units for processing. Most user input is entered into computers through keyboards, touch screens and mouse devices. Other forms of input include receiving voice commands, scanning images and bar codes, reading from secondary storage devices (such as hard drives, DVD drives, Blu-ray Disc™ drives and USB flash drives—also called "thumb drives" or "memory sticks"), receiving video from a webcam and having your computer receive information from the Internet (such as when you stream videos from YouTube® or download e-books from Amazon). Newer forms of input include position data from a GPS device, motion and orientation information from an *accelerometer* (a device that responds to up/down, left/right and forward/backward acceleration) in a smartphone or game controller (such as Microsoft® Kinect® for Xbox®, Wii™ Remote and Sony® PlayStation® Move) and voice input from intelligent assistants like Amazon Echo and Google Home.
Output unit	This "shipping" section takes information the computer has processed and places it on various **output devices** to make it available for use outside the computer. Most information that's output from computers today is displayed on screens (including touch screens), printed on paper ("going green" discourages this), played as audio or video on PCs and media players (such as Apple's iPods) and giant screens in sports stadiums, transmitted over the Internet or used to control other devices, such as robots and "intelligent" appliances. Information is also commonly output to secondary storage devices, such as solid-state drives (SSDs), hard drives, DVD drives and USB flash drives. Popular recent forms of output are smartphone and game-controller vibration, virtual reality devices like Oculus Rift® and Google Cardboard™ and mixed reality devices like Microsoft's HoloLens™.

Fig. 1.2 | Logical units of a computer. (Part 1 of 2.)

Logical unit	Description
Memory unit	This rapid-access, relatively low-capacity "warehouse" section retains information that has been entered through the input unit, making it immediately available for processing when needed. The memory unit also retains processed information until it can be placed on output devices by the output unit. Information in the memory unit is *volatile*—it's typically lost when the computer's power is turned off. The memory unit is often called either **memory**, **primary memory** or RAM (Random Access Memory). Main memories on desktop and notebook computers contain as much as 128 GB of RAM, though 2 to 16 GB is most common. GB stands for gigabytes; a gigabyte is approximately one billion bytes. A **byte** is eight bits. A bit is either a `0` or a `1`.
Arithmetic and logic unit (ALU)	This "manufacturing" section performs *calculations*, such as addition, subtraction, multiplication and division. It also contains the *decision* mechanisms that allow the computer, for example, to compare two items from the memory unit to determine whether they're equal. In today's systems, the ALU is implemented as part of the next logical unit, the CPU.
Central processing unit (CPU)	This "administrative" section coordinates and supervises the operation of the other sections. The CPU tells the input unit when information should be read into the memory unit, tells the ALU when information from the memory unit should be used in calculations and tells the output unit when to send information from the memory unit to certain output devices. Many of today's computers have multiple CPUs and, hence, can perform many operations simultaneously. A **multicore processor** implements multiple processors on a single integrated-circuit chip—a *dual-core processor* has two CPUs, a *quad-core processor* has four and an *octa-core processor* has eight. Intel has some processors with up to 72 cores. Today's desktop computers have processors that can execute billions of instructions per second. Chapter 23 explores how to write apps that can take full advantage of multicore architecture.
Secondary storage unit	This is the long-term, high-capacity "warehousing" section. Programs or data not actively being used by the other units normally are placed on secondary storage devices (e.g., your *hard drive*) until they're again needed, possibly hours, days, months or even years later. Information on secondary storage devices is *persistent*—it's preserved even when the computer's power is turned off. Secondary storage information takes much longer to access than information in primary memory, but its cost per unit is much less. Examples of secondary storage devices include solid-state drives (SSDs), hard drives, DVD drives and USB flash drives, some of which can hold over 2 TB (TB stands for terabytes; a terabyte is approximately one trillion bytes). Typical hard drives on desktop and notebook computers hold up to 2 TB, and some desktop hard drives can hold up to 10 TB.

Fig. 1.2 | Logical units of a computer. (Part 2 of 2.)

1.3 Data Hierarchy

Data items processed by computers form a **data hierarchy** that becomes larger and more complex in structure as we progress from the simplest data items (called "bits") to richer ones, such as characters and fields. Figure 1.3 illustrates a portion of the data hierarchy.

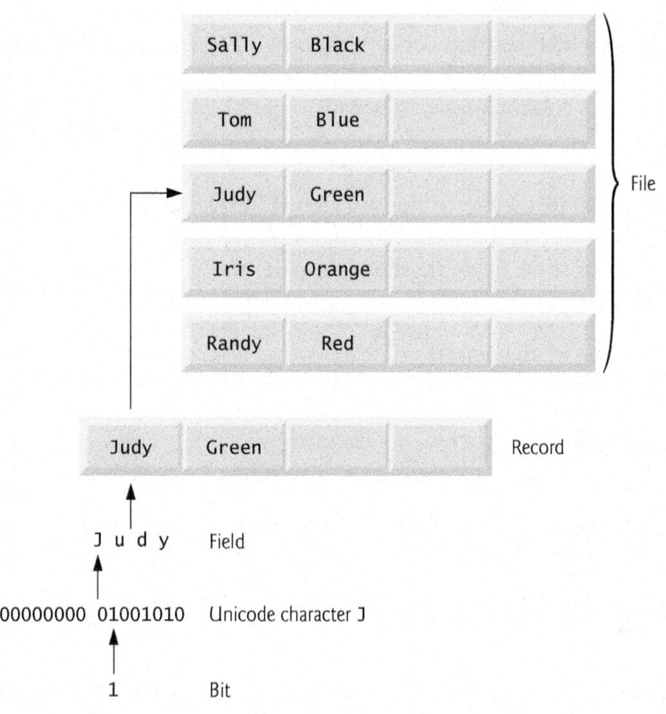

Fig. 1.3 | Data hierarchy.

Bits

The smallest data item in a computer can assume the value 0 or the value 1. It's called a **bit** (short for "binary digit"—a digit that can assume one of *two* values). Remarkably, the impressive functions performed by computers involve only the simplest manipulations of 0s and 1s—*examining a bit's value, setting a bit's value* and *reversing a bit's value* (from 1 to 0 or from 0 to 1).

Characters

It's tedious for people to work with data in the low-level form of bits. Instead, they prefer to work with *decimal digits* (0–9), *letters* (A–Z and a–z), and *special symbols* (e.g., $, @, %, &, *, (,), –, +, ", :, ? and /). Digits, letters and special symbols are known as **characters**. The computer's **character set** is the set of all the characters used to write programs and represent data items. Computers process only 1s and 0s, so a computer's character set represents every character as a pattern of 1s and 0s. Java uses **Unicode®** characters that are composed of one, two or four bytes (8, 16 or 32 bits). Unicode contains characters for many of the world's languages. See Appendix H for more information on Unicode. See Appendix B for more information on the **ASCII (American Standard Code for Information Interchange)** character set—the popular subset of Unicode that represents uppercase and lowercase letters, digits and some common special characters.

Fields

Just as characters are composed of bits, **fields** are composed of characters or bytes. A field is a group of characters or bytes that conveys meaning. For example, a field consisting of uppercase and lowercase letters can be used to represent a person's name, and a field consisting of decimal digits could represent a person's age.

Records

Several related fields can be used to compose a **record** (implemented as a `class` in Java). In a payroll system, for example, the record for an employee might consist of the following fields (possible types for these fields are shown in parentheses):

- Employee identification number (a whole number)
- Name (a string of characters)
- Address (a string of characters)
- Hourly pay rate (a number with a decimal point)
- Year-to-date earnings (a number with a decimal point)
- Amount of taxes withheld (a number with a decimal point)

Thus, a record is a group of related fields. In the preceding example, all the fields belong to the *same* employee. A company might have many employees and a payroll record for each.

Files

A **file** is a group of related records. [*Note:* More generally, a file contains arbitrary data in arbitrary formats. In some operating systems, a file is viewed simply as a *sequence of bytes*—any organization of the bytes in a file, such as organizing the data into records, is a view created by the application programmer. You'll see how to do that in Chapter 15.] It's not unusual for an organization to have many files, some containing billions, or even trillions, of characters of information.

Database

A **database** is a collection of data organized for easy access and manipulation. The most popular model is the *relational database*, in which data is stored in simple *tables*. A table includes *records* and *fields*. For example, a table of students might include first name, last name, major, year, student ID number and grade point average fields. The data for each student is a record, and the individual pieces of information in each record are the fields. You can *search*, *sort* and otherwise manipulate the data based on its relationship to multiple tables or databases. For example, a university might use data from the student database in combination with data from databases of courses, on-campus housing, meal plans, etc. We discuss databases in Chapter 24, Accessing Databases with JDBC and online Chapter 29, Java Persistence API (JPA).

Big Data

The amount of data being produced worldwide is enormous and growing quickly. According to IBM, approximately 2.5 quintillion bytes (2.5 *exabytes*) of data are created daily,[4] and according to Salesforce.com, as of October 2015 90% of the world's data was created in just the prior 12 months![5] According to an IDC study, the global data supply will reach 40 *zettabytes* (equal to 40 trillion gigabytes) annually by 2020.[6] Figure 1.4 shows some common byte measurements. **Big data** applications deal with massive amounts of data and this field is growing quickly, creating lots of opportunity for software developers. Millions of IT jobs globally already are supporting big data applications.

Unit	Bytes	Which is approximately
1 kilobyte (KB)	1024 bytes	10^3 (1024) bytes exactly
1 megabyte (MB)	1024 kilobytes	10^6 (1,000,000) bytes
1 gigabyte (GB)	1024 megabytes	10^9 (1,000,000,000) bytes
1 terabyte (TB)	1024 gigabytes	10^{12} (1,000,000,000,000) bytes
1 petabyte (PB)	1024 terabytes	10^{15} (1,000,000,000,000,000) bytes
1 exabyte (EB)	1024 petabytes	10^{18} (1,000,000,000,000,000,000) bytes
1 zettabyte (ZB)	1024 exabytes	10^{21} (1,000,000,000,000,000,000,000) bytes

Fig. 1.4 | Byte measurements.

1.4 Machine Languages, Assembly Languages and High-Level Languages

Programmers write instructions in various programming languages, some directly understandable by computers and others requiring intermediate *translation* steps. Hundreds of such languages are in use today. These may be divided into three general types:

1. Machine languages
2. Assembly languages
3. High-level languages

Machine Languages

Any computer can directly understand only its own **machine language**, defined by its hardware design. Machine languages generally consist of strings of numbers (ultimately reduced to 1s and 0s) that instruct computers to perform their most elementary operations one at a time. Machine languages are *machine dependent* (a particular machine language can be used on only one type of computer). Such languages are cumbersome for humans.

---

4. `http://www-01.ibm.com/software/data/bigdata/what-is-big-data.html`
5. `https://www.salesforce.com/blog/2015/10/salesforce-channel-ifttt.html`
6. `http://recode.net/2014/01/10/stuffed-why-data-storage-is-hot-again-really/`

For example, here's a section of an early machine-language payroll program that adds overtime pay to base pay and stores the result in gross pay:

```
+1300042774
+1400593419
+1200274027
```

Assembly Languages and Assemblers

Programming in machine language was simply too slow and tedious for most programmers. Instead of using the strings of numbers that computers could directly understand, programmers began using English-like abbreviations to represent elementary operations. These abbreviations formed the basis of **assembly languages.** *Translator programs* called **assemblers** were developed to convert early assembly-language programs to machine language at computer speeds. The following section of an assembly-language payroll program also adds overtime pay to base pay and stores the result in gross pay:

```
load    basepay
add     overpay
store   grosspay
```

Although such code is clearer to humans, it's incomprehensible to computers until translated to machine language.

High-Level Languages and Compilers

With the advent of assembly languages, computer usage increased rapidly, but programmers still had to use numerous instructions to accomplish even the simplest tasks. To speed the programming process, **high-level languages** were developed in which single statements could be written to accomplish substantial tasks. Translator programs called **compilers** convert high-level language programs into machine language. High-level languages allow you to write instructions that look almost like everyday English and contain commonly used mathematical notations. A payroll program written in a high-level language might contain a *single* statement such as

```
grossPay = basePay + overTimePay
```

From the programmer's standpoint, high-level languages are preferable to machine and assembly languages. Java is the world's most widely used high-level programming language.

Interpreters

Compiling a large high-level language program into machine language can take considerable computer time. *Interpreter* programs, developed to execute high-level language programs directly, avoid the delay of compilation, although they run slower than compiled programs. We'll say more about interpreters in Section 1.9, where you'll learn that Java uses a clever performance-tuned mixture of compilation and interpretation to run programs.

1.5 Introduction to Object Technology

Today, as demands for new and more powerful software are soaring, building software quickly, correctly and economically remains an elusive goal. *Objects,* or more precisely, the *classes* objects come from, are essentially *reusable* software components. There are date objects, time objects, audio objects, video objects, automobile objects, people objects, etc. Almost any *noun* can be reasonably represented as a software object in terms of *attributes* (e.g., name, color and size) and *behaviors* (e.g., calculating, moving and communicating). Software-development groups can use a modular, object-oriented design-and-implementation approach to be much more productive than with earlier popular techniques like "structured programming"—object-oriented programs are often easier to understand, correct and modify.

1.5.1 Automobile as an Object

To help you understand objects and their contents, let's begin with a simple analogy. Suppose you want to *drive a car and make it go faster by pressing its accelerator pedal.* What must happen before you can do this? Well, before you can drive a car, someone has to *design* it. A car typically begins as engineering drawings, similar to the *blueprints* that describe the design of a house. These drawings include the design for an accelerator pedal. The pedal *hides* from the driver the complex mechanisms that actually make the car go faster, just as the brake pedal "hides" the mechanisms that slow the car, and the steering wheel "hides" the mechanisms that turn the car. This enables people with little or no knowledge of how engines, braking and steering mechanisms work to drive a car easily.

Just as you cannot cook meals in the kitchen of a blueprint, you cannot drive a car's engineering drawings. Before you can drive a car, it must be *built* from the engineering drawings that describe it. A completed car has an *actual* accelerator pedal to make it go faster, but even that's not enough—the car won't accelerate on its own (hopefully!), so the driver must *press* the pedal to accelerate the car.

1.5.2 Methods and Classes

Let's use our car example to introduce some key object-oriented programming concepts. Performing a task in a program requires a **method**. The method houses the program statements that actually perform its tasks. The method hides these statements from its user, just as the accelerator pedal of a car hides from the driver the mechanisms of making the car go faster. In Java, we create a program unit called a **class** to house the set of methods that perform the class's tasks. For example, a class that represents a bank account might contain one method to *deposit* money to an account, another to *withdraw* money from an account and a third to *inquire* what the account's current balance is. A class is similar in concept to a car's engineering drawings, which house the design of an accelerator pedal, steering wheel, and so on.

1.5.3 Instantiation

Just as someone has to *build a car* from its engineering drawings before you can actually drive a car, you must *build an object* of a class before a program can perform the tasks that the class's methods define. The process of doing this is called *instantiation.* An object is then referred to as an **instance** of its class.

1.5.4 Reuse

Just as a car's engineering drawings can be *reused* many times to build many cars, you can *reuse* a class many times to build many objects. Reuse of existing classes when building new classes and programs saves time and effort. Reuse also helps you build more reliable and effective systems, because existing classes and components often have undergone extensive *testing*, *debugging* and *performance* tuning. Just as the notion of *interchangeable parts* was crucial to the Industrial Revolution, reusable classes are crucial to the software revolution that has been spurred by object technology.

Software Engineering Observation 1.1

Use a building-block approach to creating your programs. Avoid reinventing the wheel—use existing high-quality pieces wherever possible. This software reuse *is a key benefit of object-oriented programming.*

1.5.5 Messages and Method Calls

When you drive a car, pressing its gas pedal sends a *message* to the car to perform a task—that is, to go faster. Similarly, you *send messages to an object.* Each message is implemented as a **method call** that tells a method of the object to perform its task. For example, a program might call a bank-account object's *deposit* method to increase the account's balance.

1.5.6 Attributes and Instance Variables

A car, besides having capabilities to accomplish tasks, also has *attributes*, such as its color, its number of doors, the amount of gas in its tank, its current speed and its record of total miles driven (i.e., its odometer reading). Like its capabilities, the car's attributes are represented as part of its design in its engineering diagrams (which, for example, include an odometer and a fuel gauge). As you drive an actual car, these attributes are carried along with the car. Every car maintains its *own* attributes. For example, each car knows how much gas is in its own gas tank, but *not* how much is in the tanks of *other* cars.

An object, similarly, has attributes that it carries along as it's used in a program. These attributes are specified as part of the object's class. For example, a bank-account object has a *balance attribute* that represents the amount of money in the account. Each bank-account object knows the balance in the account it represents, but *not* the balances of the *other* accounts in the bank. Attributes are specified by the class's **instance variables.**

1.5.7 Encapsulation and Information Hiding

Classes (and their objects) **encapsulate**, i.e., encase, their attributes and methods. A class's (and its object's) attributes and methods are intimately related. Objects may communicate with one another, but they're normally not allowed to know how other objects are implemented—implementation details can be *hidden* within the objects themselves. This **information hiding**, as we'll see, is crucial to good software engineering.

1.5.8 Inheritance

A new class of objects can be created conveniently by **Inheritance**—the new class (called the **subclass**) starts with the characteristics of an existing class (called the **superclass**), possibly customizing them and adding unique characteristics of its own. In our car analogy, an object of class "convertible" certainly *is an* object of the more *general* class "automobile," but more *specifically*, the roof can be raised or lowered.

1.5.9 Interfaces

Java also supports **interfaces**—collections of related methods that typically enable you to 8
tell objects *what* to do, but not *how* to do it (we'll see exceptions to this in Java SE 8 and
Java SE 9 when we discuss interfaces in Chapter 10). In the car analogy, a "basic-driving- 9
capabilities" interface consisting of a steering wheel, an accelerator pedal and a brake pedal would enable a driver to tell the car *what* to do. Once you know how to use this interface for turning, accelerating and braking, you can drive many types of cars, even though manufacturers may *implement* these systems *differently*.

A class **implements** zero or more interfaces, each of which can have one or more methods, just as a car implements separate interfaces for basic driving functions, controlling the radio, controlling the heating and air conditioning systems, and the like. Just as car manufacturers implement capabilities *differently*, classes may implement an interface's methods *differently*. For example a software system may include a "backup" interface that offers the methods *save* and *restore*. Classes may implement those methods differently, depending on the types of things being backed up, such as programs, text, audios, videos, etc., and the types of devices where these items will be stored.

1.5.10 Object-Oriented Analysis and Design (OOAD)

Soon you'll be writing programs in Java. How will you create the **code** (i.e., the program instructions) for your programs? Perhaps, like many programmers, you'll simply turn on your computer and start typing. This approach may work for small programs (like the ones we present in the early chapters of the book), but what if you were asked to create a software system to control thousands of automated teller machines for a major bank? Or suppose you were asked to work on a team of 1,000 software developers building the next generation of the U.S. air traffic control system? For projects so large and complex, you should not simply sit down and start writing programs.

To create the best solutions, you should follow a detailed **analysis** process for determining your project's **requirements** (i.e., defining *what* the system is supposed to do) and developing a **design** that satisfies them (i.e., specifying *how* the system should do it). Ideally, you'd go through this process and carefully review the design (and have your design reviewed by other software professionals) before writing any code. If this process involves analyzing and designing your system from an object-oriented point of view, it's called an **object-oriented analysis-and-design (OOAD) process**. Languages like Java are object oriented. Programming in such a language, called **object-oriented programming** (OOP), allows you to implement an object-oriented design as a working system.

1.5.11 The UML (Unified Modeling Language)

Although many different OOAD processes exist, a single graphical language for communicating the results of *any* OOAD process has come into wide use. The Unified Modeling Language (UML) is now the most widely used graphical scheme for modeling object-oriented systems. We present our first UML diagrams in Chapters 3 and 4, then use them in our deeper treatment of object-oriented programming through Chapter 11. In our *optional* online ATM Software Engineering Case Study in Chapters 33–34 we present a simple subset of the UML's features as we guide you through an object-oriented design experience.

1.6 Operating Systems

Operating systems are software systems that make using computers more convenient for users, application developers and system administrators. They provide services that allow each application to execute safely, efficiently and *concurrently* (i.e., in parallel) with other applications. The software that contains the core components of the operating system is called the **kernel**. Popular desktop operating systems include Linux, Windows and macOS (formerly called OS X)—we used all three in developing this book. The most popular mobile operating systems used in smartphones and tablets are Google's Android and Apple's iOS (for iPhone, iPad and iPod Touch devices).

1.6.1 Windows—A Proprietary Operating System

In the mid-1980s, Microsoft developed the **Windows operating system**, consisting of a graphical user interface built on top of DOS (Disk Operating System)—an enormously popular personal-computer operating system that users interacted with by typing commands. Windows borrowed from many concepts (such as icons, menus and windows) developed by Xerox PARC and popularized by early Apple Macintosh operating systems. Windows 10 is Microsoft's latest operating system—its features include enhancements to the **Start** menu and user interface, Cortana personal assistant for voice interactions, Action Center for receiving notifications, Microsoft's new Edge web browser, and more. Windows is a *proprietary* operating system—it's controlled by Microsoft exclusively. Windows is by far the world's most widely used desktop operating system.

1.6.2 Linux—An Open-Source Operating System

The **Linux operating system** is perhaps the greatest success of the *open-source* movement. **Open-source software** departs from the *proprietary* software development style that dominated software's early years. With open-source development, individuals and companies *contribute* their efforts in developing, maintaining and evolving software in exchange for the right to use that software for their own purposes, typically at *no charge*. Open-source code is often scrutinized by a much larger audience than proprietary software, so errors often get removed faster. Open source also encourages innovation. Enterprise systems companies, such as IBM, Oracle and many others, have made significant investments in Linux open-source development.

Some key organizations in the open-source community are

- the Eclipse Foundation (the Eclipse Integrated Development Environment helps programmers conveniently develop software)
- the Mozilla Foundation (creators of the Firefox web browser)
- the Apache Software Foundation (creators of the Apache web server used to develop web-based applications)
- GitHub (which provides tools for managing open-source projects—it has millions of them under development).

Rapid improvements to computing and communications, decreasing costs and open-source software have made it much easier and more economical to create a software-based business now than just a decade ago. A great example is Facebook, which was launched from a college dorm room and built with open-source software.

The **Linux kernel** is the core of the most popular open-source, freely distributed, full-featured operating system. It's developed by a loosely organized team of volunteers and is popular in servers, personal computers and embedded systems (such as the computer systems at the heart of smartphones, smart TVs and automobile systems). Unlike that of proprietary operating systems like Microsoft's Windows and Apple's macOS, Linux source code (the program code) is available to the public for examination and modification and is free to download and install. As a result, Linux users benefit from a huge community of developers actively debugging and improving the kernel, and the ability to customize the operating system to meet specific needs.

A variety of issues—such as Microsoft's market power, the small number of user-friendly Linux applications and the diversity of Linux distributions, such as Red Hat Linux, Ubuntu Linux and many others—have prevented widespread Linux use on desktop computers. Linux has become extremely popular on servers and in embedded systems, such as Google's Android-based smartphones.

1.6.3 Apple's macOS and Apple's iOS for iPhone®, iPad® and iPod Touch® Devices

Apple, founded in 1976 by Steve Jobs and Steve Wozniak, quickly became a leader in personal computing. In 1979, Jobs and several Apple employees visited Xerox PARC (Palo Alto Research Center) to learn about Xerox's desktop computer that featured a graphical user interface (GUI). That GUI served as the inspiration for the Apple Macintosh, launched with much fanfare in a memorable Super Bowl ad in 1984.

The Objective-C programming language, created by Brad Cox and Tom Love at Stepstone in the early 1980s, added capabilities for object-oriented programming (OOP) to the C programming language. Steve Jobs left Apple in 1985 and founded NeXT Inc. In 1988, NeXT licensed Objective-C from StepStone and developed an Objective-C compiler and libraries which were used as the platform for the NeXTSTEP operating system's user interface, and Interface Builder—used to construct graphical user interfaces.

Jobs returned to Apple in 1996 when Apple bought NeXT. Apple's macOS operating system is a descendant of NeXTSTEP. Apple's proprietary operating system, **iOS**, is derived from Apple's macOS and is used in the iPhone, iPad, iPod Touch, Apple Watch and Apple TV devices. In 2014, Apple introduced its new Swift programming language, which became open source in 2015. The iOS app-development community is shifting from Objective-C to Swift.

1.6.4 Google's Android

Android—the fastest growing mobile and smartphone operating system—is based on the Linux kernel and Java. Android apps can also be developed in C++ and C. One benefit of developing Android apps is the openness of the platform. The operating system is open source and free.

The Android operating system was developed by Android, Inc., which was acquired by Google in 2005. In 2007, the Open Handset Alliance™

```
http://www.openhandsetalliance.com/oha_members.html
```

was formed to develop, maintain and evolve Android, driving innovation in mobile technology and improving the user experience while reducing costs. According to Statista.com, as of Q3 2016, Android had 87.8% of the global smartphone market share, compared to 11.5% for Apple.[7] The Android operating system is used in numerous smartphones, e-reader devices, tablets, in-store touch-screen kiosks, cars, robots, multimedia players and more.

We present an introduction to Android app development in our textbook, *Android How to Program, Third Edition,* and in our professional book, *Android 6 for Programmers: An App-Driven Approach, Third Edition*. After you learn Java, you'll find it straightforward to begin developing and running Android apps. You can place your apps on Google Play (`play.google.com`), and if they're successful, you may even be able to launch a business. Just remember—Facebook, Microsoft and Dell were all launched from college dorm rooms.

1.7 Programming Languages

Figure 1.6 provides brief comments on several popular programming languages. In the next section, we introduce Java.

Programming language	Description
Ada	Ada, based on Pascal, was developed under the sponsorship of the U.S. Department of Defense (DOD) during the 1970s and early 1980s. The DOD wanted a single language that would fill most of its needs. The Pascal-based language was named after Lady Ada Lovelace, daughter of the poet Lord Byron. She's credited with writing the world's first computer program in the early 1800s (for the Analytical Engine mechanical computing device designed by Charles Babbage). Ada also supports object-oriented programming.
Basic	Basic was developed in the 1960s at Dartmouth College to familiarize novices with programming techniques. Many of its latest versions are object oriented.
C	C was developed in the early 1970s by Dennis Ritchie at Bell Laboratories. It initially became widely known as the UNIX operating system's development language. Today, most code for general-purpose operating systems is written in C or C++.
C++	C++, which is based on C, was developed by Bjarne Stroustrup in the early 1980s at Bell Laboratories. C++ provides several features that "spruce up" the C language, but more important, it provides capabilities for object-oriented programming.
C#	Microsoft's three primary object-oriented programming languages are C# (based on C++ and Java), Visual C++ (based on C++) and Visual Basic (based on the original Basic). C# was developed to integrate the web into computer applications, and is now widely used to develop enterprise applications and for mobile application development.

Fig. 1.5 | Some other programming languages. (Part 1 of 3.)

7. `https://www.statista.com/statistics/266136/global-market-share-held-by-smartphone-operating-systems`

Programming language	Description
COBOL	COBOL (COmmon Business Oriented Language) was developed in the late 1950s by computer manufacturers, the U.S. government and industrial computer users, based on a language developed by Grace Hopper, a career U.S. Navy officer and computer scientist. (She was posthumously awarded the Presidential Medal of Freedom in November of 2016.) COBOL is still widely used for commercial applications that require precise and efficient manipulation of large amounts of data. Its latest version supports object-oriented programming.
Fortran	Fortran (FORmula TRANslator) was developed by IBM Corporation in the mid-1950s to be used for scientific and engineering applications that require complex mathematical computations. It's still widely used, and its latest versions support object-oriented programming.
JavaScript	JavaScript is the most widely used scripting language. It's primarily used to add programmability to web pages—for example, animations and interactivity with the user. All major web browsers support it.
Objective-C	Objective-C is an object-oriented language based on C. It was developed in the early 1980s and later acquired by NeXT, which in turn was acquired by Apple. It became the key programming language for the OS X operating system and all iOS-powered devices (such as iPods, iPhones and iPads).
Pascal	Research in the 1960s resulted in *structured programming*—a disciplined approach to writing programs that are clearer, easier to test and debug and easier to modify than programs produced with previous techniques. The Pascal language, developed by Professor Niklaus Wirth in 1971, grew out of this research. It was popular for teaching structured programming for several decades.
PHP	PHP is an object-oriented, *open-source* "scripting" language supported by a community of developers and used by numerous websites. PHP is platform independent—implementations exist for all major UNIX, Linux, Mac and Windows operating systems.
Python	Python, another object-oriented scripting language, was released publicly in 1991. Developed by Guido van Rossum of the National Research Institute for Mathematics and Computer Science in Amsterdam, Python draws heavily from Modula-3—a systems programming language. Python is "extensible"—it can be extended through classes and programming interfaces.
Ruby on Rails	Ruby—created in the mid-1990s by Yukihiro Matsumoto—is an open-source, object-oriented programming language with a simple syntax that's similar to Python. Ruby on Rails combines the scripting language Ruby with the Rails web-application framework developed by the company 37Signals. Their book, *Getting Real* (free at `http://gettingreal.37signals.com/toc.php`), is a must-read for web developers. Many Ruby on Rails developers have reported productivity gains over other languages when developing database-intensive web applications.

Fig. 1.5 | Some other programming languages. (Part 2 of 3.)

Programming language	Description
Scala	Scala (`http://www.scala-lang.org/what-is-scala.html`)—short for "scalable language"—was designed by Martin Odersky, a professor at École Polytechnique Fédérale de Lausanne (EPFL) in Switzerland. Released in 2003, Scala uses both the object-oriented programming and functional programming paradigms and is designed to integrate with Java. Programming in Scala can reduce the amount of code in your applications significantly.
Swift	Swift, which was introduced in 2014, is Apple's programming language of the future for developing iOS and OS X applications (apps). Swift is a contemporary language that includes popular programming-language features from languages such as Objective-C, Java, C#, Ruby, Python and others. According to the Tiobe Index, Swift has already become one of the most popular programming languages. Swift is now *open source*, so it can be used on non-Apple platforms as well.
Visual Basic	Microsoft's Visual Basic language was introduced in the early 1990s to simplify the development of Microsoft Windows applications. Its features are comparable to those of C#.

Fig. 1.5 | Some other programming languages. (Part 3 of 3.)

1.8 Java

The microprocessor revolution's most important contribution to date is that it enabled the development of personal computers. Microprocessors also have had a profound impact in intelligent consumer-electronic devices, including the recent explosion in the "Internet of Things." Recognizing this early on, Sun Microsystems in 1991 funded an internal corporate research project led by James Gosling, which resulted in a C++-based object-oriented programming language that Sun called Java. Using Java, you can write programs that will run on a great variety of computer systems and computer-controlled devices. This is sometimes called "write once, run anywhere."

Java drew the attention of the business community because of the phenomenal interest in the Internet. It's now used to develop large-scale enterprise applications, to enhance the functionality of web servers (the computers that provide the content we see in our web browsers), to provide applications for consumer devices (cell phones, smartphones, television set-top boxes and more), to develop robotics software and for many other purposes. It's also the key language for developing Android smartphone and tablet apps. Sun Microsystems was acquired by Oracle in 2010.

Java has become the most widely used general-purpose programming language with more than 10 million developers. In this textbook, you'll learn the two most recent versions of Java—Java Standard Edition 8 (Java SE 8) and Java Standard Edition 9 (Java SE 9).

Java Class Libraries

You can create each class and method you need to form your programs. However, most Java programmers take advantage of the rich collections of existing classes and methods in the **Java class libraries**, also known as the **Java APIs (Application Programming Interfaces)**.

Performance Tip 1.1

Using Java API classes and methods instead of writing your own versions can improve program performance, because they're carefully written to perform efficiently. This also shortens program development time.

1.9 A Typical Java Development Environment

We now explain the steps to create and execute a Java application. Normally there are five phases—edit, compile, load, verify and execute. We discuss them in the context of the Java SE 8 Development Kit (JDK). See the *Before You Begin* section *for information on downloading and installing the JDK on Windows, Linux and macOS.*

Phase 1: Creating a Program

Phase 1 consists of editing a file with an *editor program*, normally known simply as an *editor* (Fig. 1.6). Using the editor, you type a Java program (typically referred to as **source code**), make any necessary corrections and save it on a secondary storage device, such as your hard drive. Java source code files are given a name ending with the **`.java` extension**, indicating that the file contains Java source code.

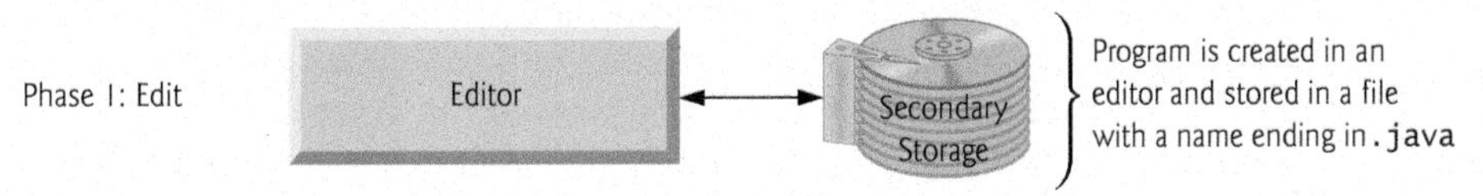

Fig. 1.6 | Typical Java development environment—editing phase.

Two editors widely used on Linux systems are `vi` and `emacs` (). Windows provides **Notepad**. macOS provides **TextEdit**. Many freeware and shareware editors are also available online, including Notepad++ (`http://notepad-plus-plus.org`), EditPlus (`http://www.editplus.com`), TextPad (`http://www.textpad.com`), jEdit (`http://www.jedit.org`) and more.

Integrated development environments (**IDEs**) provide tools that support the software development process, such as editors, debuggers for locating **logic errors** that cause programs to execute incorrectly and more. The most popular Java IDEs are:

- Eclipse (`http://www.eclipse.org`)
- IntelliJ IDEA (`http://www.jetbrains.com`)
- NetBeans (`http://www.netbeans.org`)

On the book's website at

```
http://www.deitel.com/books/jhtp11
```

we provide videos that show you how to execute this book's Java applications and how to develop new Java applications with Eclipse, NetBeans and IntelliJ IDEA.

Phase 2: Compiling a Java Program into Bytecodes

In Phase 2, you use the command **`javac`** (the **Java compiler**) to **compile** a program (Fig. 1.7). For example, to compile a program called `Welcome.java`, you'd type

```
javac Welcome.java
```

in your system's command window (i.e., the **Command Prompt** in Windows, the **Terminal** application in macOS) or a Linux shell (also called **Terminal** in some Linux versions). If the program compiles, the compiler produces a **`.class`** file called `Welcome.class`. IDEs typically provide a menu item, such as **Build** or **Make**, that invokes the `javac` command for you. If the compiler detects errors, you'll need to go back to Phase 1 and correct them. In Chapter 2, we'll say more about the kinds of errors the compiler can detect.

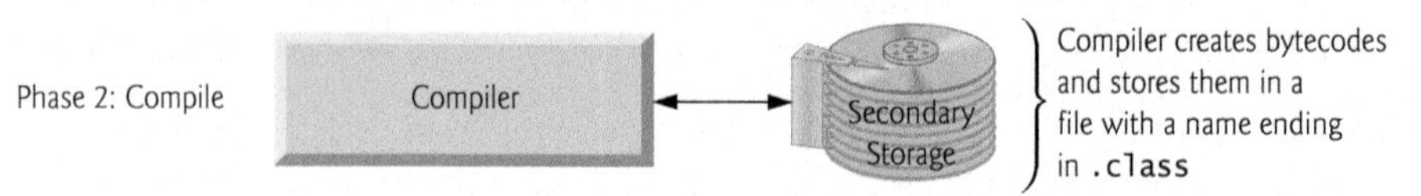
Phase 2: Compile
Compiler
Secondary Storage
Compiler creates bytecodes and stores them in a file with a name ending in .class

Fig. 1.7 | Typical Java development environment—compilation phase.

Common Programming Error 1.1

When using `javac`*, if you receive a message such as "*`bad command or filename`*," "*`javac: command not found`*" or "*`'javac' is not recognized as an internal or external command, operable program or batch file`*," then your Java software installation was not completed properly. This indicates that the system's* `PATH` *environment variable was not set properly. Carefully review the installation instructions in the Before You Begin section of this book. On some systems, after correcting the* `PATH`*, you may need to reboot your computer or open a new command window for these settings to take effect.*

The Java compiler translates Java source code into **bytecodes** that represent the tasks to execute in the execution phase (Phase 5). The **Java Virtual Machine** (**JVM**)—a part of the JDK and the foundation of the Java platform—executes bytecodes. A **virtual machine** (VM) is a software application that simulates a computer but hides the underlying operating system and hardware from the programs that interact with it. If the same VM is implemented on many computer platforms, applications written for that type of VM can be used on all those platforms. The JVM is one of the most widely used virtual machines. Microsoft's .NET uses a similar virtual-machine architecture.

Unlike machine-language instructions, which are *platform dependent* (that is, dependent on specific computer hardware), bytecode instructions are *platform independent*. So, Java's bytecodes are **portable**—without recompiling the source code, the same bytecode instructions can execute on any platform containing a JVM that understands the version of Java in which the bytecodes were compiled. The JVM is invoked by the **`java`** command. For example, to execute a Java application called `Welcome`, you'd type the command

```
java Welcome
```

in a command window to invoke the JVM, which would then initiate the steps necessary to execute the application. This begins Phase 3. IDEs typically provide a menu item, such as **Run**, that invokes the `java` command for you.

Phase 3: Loading a Program into Memory

In Phase 3, the JVM places the program in memory to execute it—this is known as **loading** (Fig. 1.8).The JVM's **class loader** takes the `.class` files containing the program's bytecodes and transfers them to primary memory. It also loads any of the `.class` files provided by Java that your program uses. The `.class` files can be loaded from a disk on your system or over a network (e.g., your local college or company network, or the Internet).

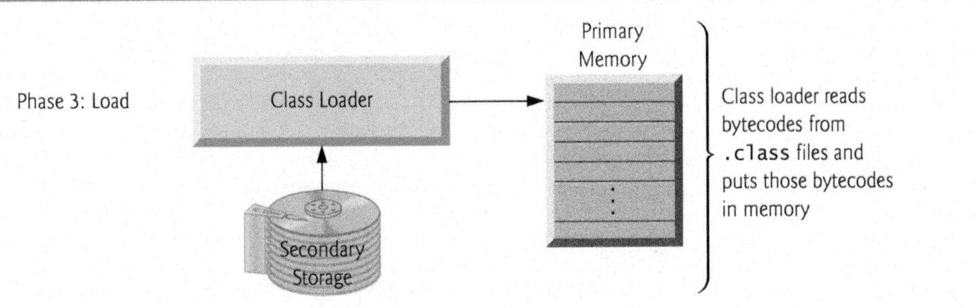
Phase 3: Load
Class Loader
Primary Memory
Secondary Storage
Class loader reads bytecodes from .class files and puts those bytecodes in memory

Fig. 1.8 | Typical Java development environment—loading phase.

Phase 4: Bytecode Verification

In Phase 4, as the classes are loaded, the **bytecode verifier** examines their bytecodes to ensure that they're valid and do not violate Java's security restrictions (Fig. 1.9). Java enforces strong security to make sure that Java programs arriving over the network do not damage your files or your system (as computer viruses and worms might).

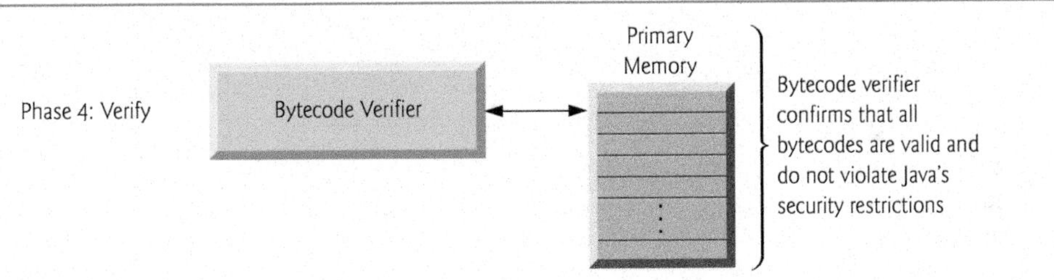
Phase 4: Verify
Bytecode Verifier
Primary Memory
Bytecode verifier confirms that all bytecodes are valid and do not violate Java's security restrictions

Fig. 1.9 | Typical Java development environment—verification phase.

Phase 5: Execution

In Phase 5, the JVM **executes** the bytecodes to perform the program's specified actions (Fig. 1.10). In early Java versions, the JVM was simply a Java-bytecode *interpreter*. Most programs would execute slowly, because the JVM would interpret and execute one bytecode at a time. Some modern computer architectures can execute several instructions in parallel. Today's JVMs typically execute bytecodes using a combination of interpretation and **just-in-time (JIT) compilation**. In this process, the JVM analyzes the bytecodes as they're interpreted, searching for *hot spots*—bytecodes that execute frequently. For these parts, a **just-in-time (JIT) compiler**, such as Oracle's **Java HotSpot™ compiler**, translates the bytecodes into the computer's machine language. When the JVM encounters these compiled parts again, the faster machine-language code executes. Thus programs actually go through *two* compilation phases—one in which Java code is translated into bytecodes (for portability across JVMs on different computer platforms) and a second in which, during execution, the bytecodes are translated into *machine language* for the computer on which the program executes.

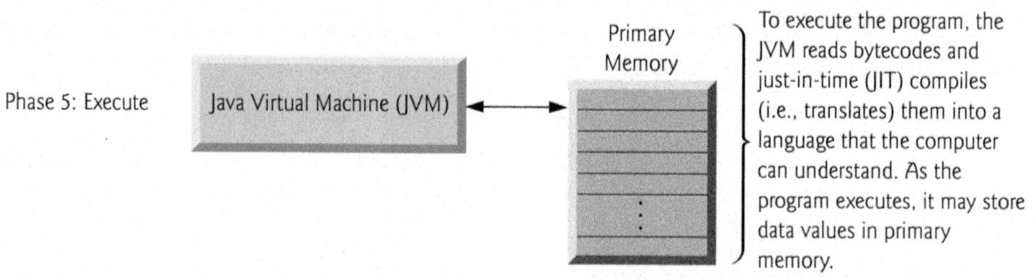
Phase 5: Execute
Java Virtual Machine (JVM)
Primary Memory
To execute the program, the JVM reads bytecodes and just-in-time (JIT) compiles (i.e., translates) them into a language that the computer can understand. As the program executes, it may store data values in primary memory.

Fig. 1.10 | Typical Java development environment—execution phase.

Problems That May Occur at Execution Time

Programs might not work on the first try. Each of the preceding phases can fail because of various errors that we'll discuss throughout this book. For example, an executing program might try to divide by zero (an illegal operation for whole-number arithmetic in Java). This would cause the Java program to display an error message. If this occurred, you'd return to the edit phase, make the necessary corrections and proceed through the remaining phases again to determine whether the corrections fixed the problem(s). [*Note:* Most programs in Java input or output data. When we say that a program displays a message, we normally mean that it displays that message on your computer's screen.]

Common Programming Error 1.2

Errors such as division by zero occur as a program runs, so they're called runtime errors or execution-time errors. Fatal runtime errors cause programs to terminate immediately without having successfully performed their jobs. Nonfatal runtime errors allow programs to run to completion, often producing incorrect results.

1.10 Test-Driving a Java Application

In this section, you'll run and interact with an existing Java **Painter** app, which you'll build in a later chapter. The elements and functionality you'll see are typical of what you'll learn to program in this book. Using the **Painter**'s graphical user interface (GUI), you choose a drawing color and pen size, then drag the mouse to draw circles in the specified color and size. You also can undo each drawing operation or clear the entire drawing. [*Note:* We emphasize screen features like window titles and menus (e.g., the **File** menu) in a **sans-serif font** and emphasize nonscreen elements, such as file names and program code (e.g., `ProgramName.java`), in a `fixed-width sans-serif font`.]

The steps in this section show you how to execute the **Painter** app from a **Command Prompt** (Windows), shell (Linux) or **Terminal** (macOS) window on your system. Throughout the book, we'll refer to these windows simply as *command windows*. We assume that the book's examples are located in `C:\examples` on Windows or in your user account's `Documents/examples` folder on Linux or macOS.

Checking Your Setup

Read the Before You Begin section that follows the Preface to set up Java on your computer and ensure that you've downloaded the book's examples to your hard drive.

Changing to the Completed Application's Directory

Open a command window and use the `cd` command to change to the directory (also called a *folder*) for the **Painter** application:

- On Windows type `cd C:\examples\ch01\Painter`, then press *Enter*.
- On Linux/macOS, type `cd ~/Documents/examples/ch01/Painter`, then press *Enter*.

Compiling the Application

In the command window, type the following command then press *Enter* to compile all the files for the **Painter** example:

```
javac *.java
```

The * indicates that all files with names that end in `.java` should be compiled.

Running the Painter Application

Recall from Section 1.9 that the `java` command, followed by the name of an app's `.class` file (in this case, `Painter`), executes the application. Type the command `java Painter` then press *Enter* to execute the app. Figure 1.11 shows the **Painter** app running on Windows, Linux and macOS, respectively. The app's capabilities are identical across operating systems, so the remaining steps in this section show only Windows screen captures. Java commands are *case sensitive*—that is, uppercase letters are different from lowercase letters. It's important to type `Painter` with a capital `P`. Otherwise, the application will *not* execute. Also, if you receive the error message, "`Exception in thread "main" java.lang.NoClassDefFoundError: Painter`," your system has a `CLASSPATH` problem. Please refer to the Before You Begin section for instructions to help you fix this problem.

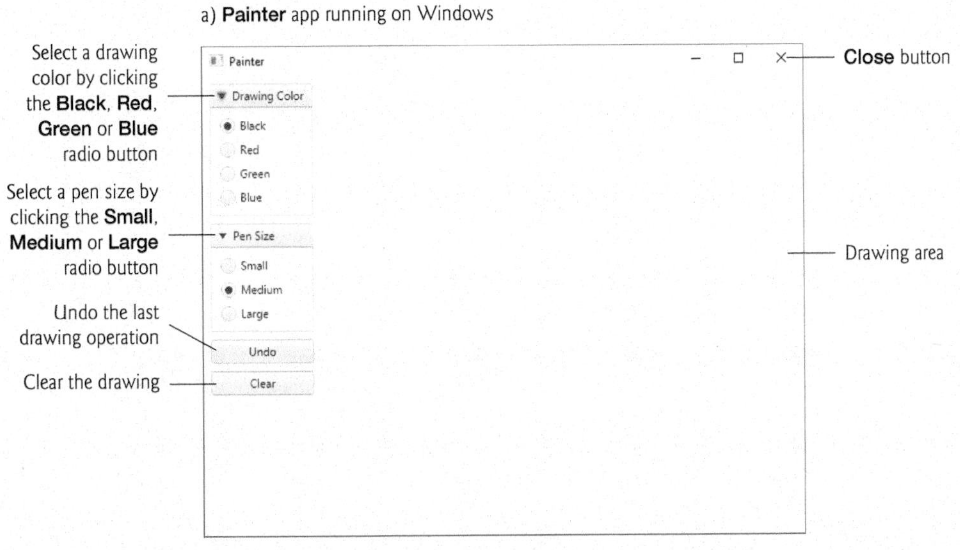
a) Painter app running on Windows
Painter
Close button
Select a drawing color by clicking the Black, Red, Green or Blue radio button
Drawing Color
Black
Red
Green
Blue
Select a pen size by clicking the Small, Medium or Large radio button
Pen Size
Small
Medium
Large
Drawing area
Undo the last drawing operation
Undo
Clear the drawing
Clear

Fig. 1.11 | **Painter** app executing in Windows, Linux and macOS. (Part 1 of 2.)

b) **Painter** app running on Linux.

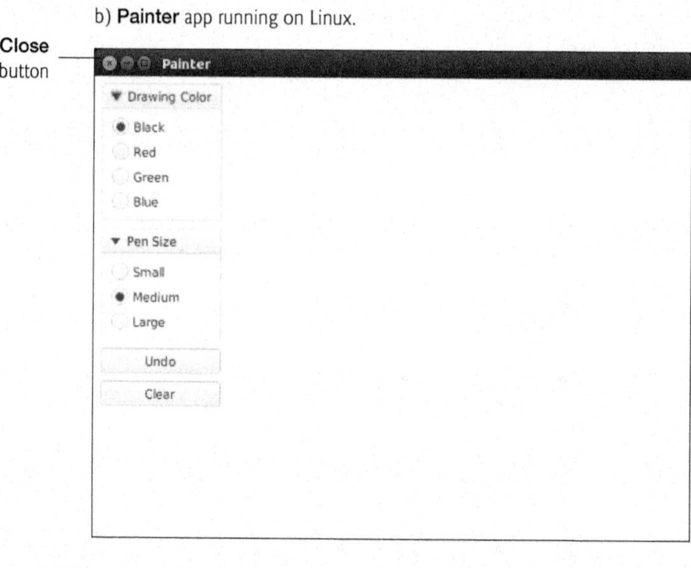

c) **Painter** app running on macOS.

Fig. 1.11 | **Painter** app executing in Windows, Linux and macOS. (Part 2 of 2.)

Drawing the Flower Petals

In this section's remaining steps, you'll draw a red flower with a green stem, green grass and blue rain. We'll begin with the flower petals in a red, medium-sized pen. Change the drawing color to red by clicking the **Red** radio button. Next, drag your mouse on the drawing area to draw flower petals (Fig. 1.12). If you don't like a portion of what you've drawn, you can click the **Undo** button repeatedly to remove the most recent circles that were drawn, or you can begin again by clicking the **Clear** button.

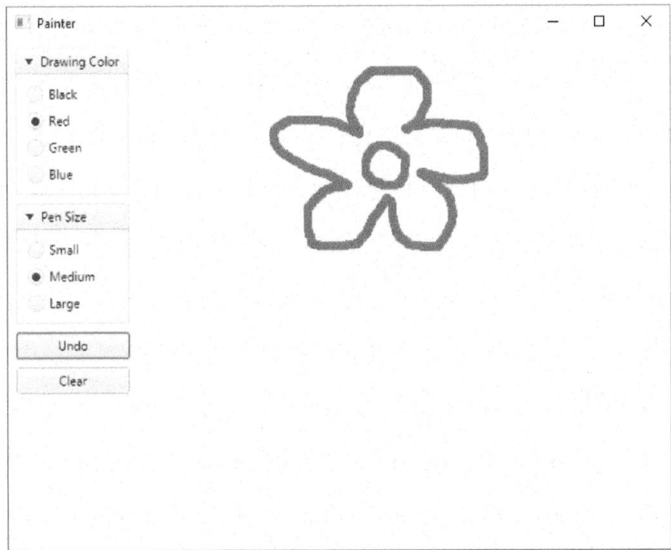

Fig. 1.12 | Drawing the flower petals.

Drawing the Stem, Leaves and Grass

Change the drawing color to green and the pen size to large by clicking the **Green** and **Large** radio buttons. Then, draw the stem and the leaves as shown in Fig. 1.13. Next, change the pen size to medium by clicking the **Medium** radio button, then draw the grass as shown in Fig. 1.13.

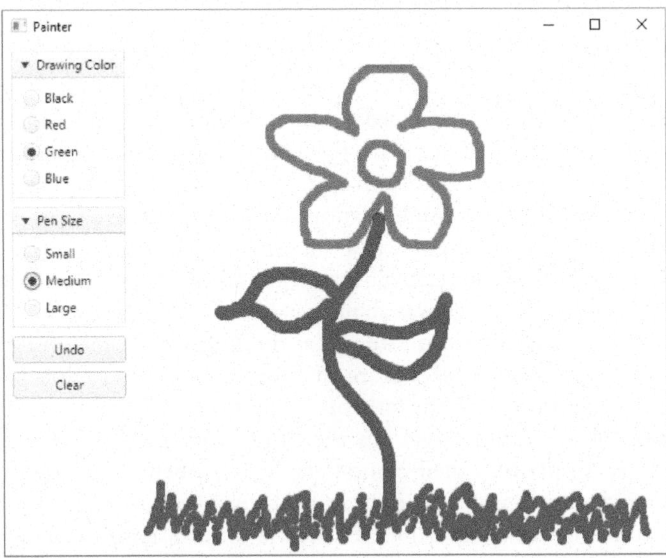

Fig. 1.13 | Drawing the stem and grass.

Drawing the Rain

Change the drawing color to blue and the pen size to small by clicking the **Blue** and **Small** radio buttons. Then, draw some rain as shown in Fig. 1.14.

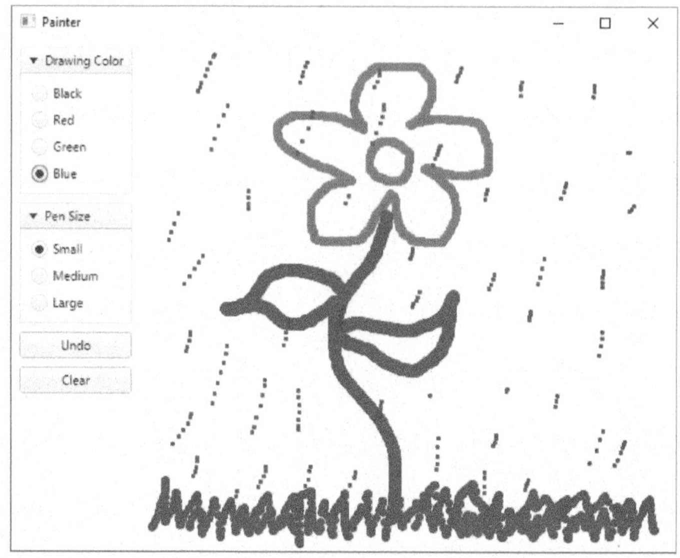

Fig. 1.14 | Drawing the rain.

Exiting the Painter App

At this point, you can close the **Painter** app. To do so, simply click the app's close box (shown for Windows, Linux and macOS in Fig. 1.11).

1.11 Internet and World Wide Web

In the late 1960s, ARPA—the Advanced Research Projects Agency of the United States Department of Defense—rolled out plans for networking the main computer systems of approximately a dozen ARPA-funded universities and research institutions. The computers were to be connected with communications lines operating at speeds on the order of 50,000 bits per second, a stunning rate at a time when most people (of the few who even had networking access) were connecting over telephone lines to computers at a rate of 110 bits per second. Academic research was about to take a giant leap forward. ARPA proceeded to implement what quickly became known as the ARPANET, the precursor to today's **Internet**. Today's fastest Internet speeds are on the order of billions of bits per second with trillion-bits-per-second speeds on the horizon!

Things worked out differently from the original plan. Although the ARPANET enabled researchers to network their computers, its main benefit proved to be the capability for quick and easy communication via what came to be known as electronic mail (e-mail). This is true even on today's Internet, with e-mail, instant messaging, file transfer and social media such as Facebook and Twitter enabling billions of people worldwide to communicate quickly and easily.

The protocol (set of rules) for communicating over the ARPANET became known as the **Transmission Control Protocol** (TCP). TCP ensured that messages, consisting of sequentially numbered pieces called *packets*, were properly routed from sender to receiver, arrived intact and were assembled in the correct order.

1.11.1 Internet: A Network of Networks

In parallel with the early evolution of the Internet, organizations worldwide were implementing their own networks for both intraorganization (that is, within an organization) and interorganization (that is, between organizations) communication. A huge variety of networking hardware and software appeared. One challenge was to enable these different networks to communicate with each other. ARPA accomplished this by developing the **Internet Protocol** (IP), which created a true "network of networks," the current architecture of the Internet. The combined set of protocols is now called TCP/IP. Each Internet-connected device has an **IP address**—a unique numerical identifier used by devices communicating via TCP/IP to locate one another on the Internet.

Businesses rapidly realized that by using the Internet, they could improve their operations and offer new and better services to their clients. Companies started spending large amounts of money to develop and enhance their Internet presence. This generated fierce competition among communications carriers and hardware and software suppliers to meet the increased infrastructure demand. As a result, **bandwidth**—the information-carrying capacity of communications lines—on the Internet has increased tremendously, while hardware costs have plummeted.

1.11.2 World Wide Web: Making the Internet User-Friendly

The **World Wide Web** (simply called "the web") is a collection of hardware and software associated with the Internet that allows computer users to locate and view documents (with various combinations of text, graphics, animations, audios and videos) on almost any subject. In 1989, Tim Berners-Lee of CERN (the European Organization for Nuclear Research) began developing **HyperText Markup Language** (HTML)—the technology for sharing information via "hyperlinked" text documents. He also wrote communication protocols such as **HyperText Transfer Protocol** (HTTP) to form the backbone of his new hypertext information system, which he referred to as the World Wide Web.

In 1994, Berners-Lee founded the **World Wide Web Consortium** (W3C, `http://www.w3.org`), devoted to developing web technologies. One of the W3C's primary goals is to make the web universally accessible to everyone regardless of disabilities, language or culture.

1.11.3 Web Services and Mashups

In online Chapter 32, we implement web services (Fig. 1.15). The applications-development methodology of *mashups* enables you to rapidly develop powerful software applications by combining (often free) complementary web services and other forms of information feeds. One of the first mashups combined the real-estate listings provided by `http://www.craigslist.org` with the mapping capabilities of *Google Maps* to offer maps that showed the locations of homes for sale or rent in a given area. ProgrammableWeb (`http://www.programmableweb.com/`) provides a directory of over 16,500 APIs and 6,300 mashups. Their API University (`https://www.programmableweb.com/api-university`) includes how-to guides and sample code for working with APIs and creating your own mashups. According to their website, some of the most widely used APIs are Facebook, Google Maps, Twitter and YouTube.

Web services source	How it's used
Google Maps	Mapping services
Twitter	Microblogging
YouTube	Video search
Facebook	Social networking
Instagram	Photo sharing
Foursquare	Mobile check-in
LinkedIn	Social networking for business
Groupon	Social commerce
Netflix	Movie rentals
eBay	Internet auctions
Wikipedia	Collaborative encyclopedia
PayPal	Payments
Last.fm	Internet radio
Amazon eCommerce	Shopping for books and many other products
Salesforce.com	Customer Relationship Management (CRM)
Skype	Internet telephony
Microsoft Bing	Search
Flickr	Photo sharing
Zillow	Real-estate pricing
Yahoo Search	Search
WeatherBug	Weather

Fig. 1.15 | Some popular web services (`https://www.programmableweb.com/category/all/apis`).

1.11.4 Internet of Things

The Internet is no longer just a network of computers—it's an **Internet of Things (IoT)**. A *thing* is any object with an IP address and the ability to send data automatically over the Internet. Such things include:

- a car with a transponder for paying tolls,
- monitors for parking-space availability in a garage,

- a heart monitor implanted in a human,
- monitors for drinkable water quality,
- a smart meter that reports energy usage,
- radiation detectors,
- item trackers in a warehouse,
- mobile apps that can track your movement and location,
- smart thermostats that adjust room temperatures based on weather forecasts and activity in the home
- intelligent home appliances
- and many more.

According to `statista.com`, there are already over 22 billion IoT devices in use today and there are expected to be over 50 billion IoT devices in 2020.[8]

1.12 Software Technologies

Figure 1.16 lists a number of buzzwords that you'll hear in the software development community. We've created Resource Centers on most of these topics, with more on the way.

Technology	Description
Agile software development	**Agile software development** is a set of methodologies that try to get software implemented faster and using fewer resources. Check out the Agile Alliance (`www.agilealliance.org`) and the Agile Manifesto (`www.agilemanifesto.org`).
Refactoring	**Refactoring** involves reworking programs to make them clearer and easier to maintain while preserving their correctness and functionality. It's widely employed with agile development methodologies. Many IDEs contain built-in *refactoring tools* to do major portions of the reworking automatically.
Design patterns	**Design patterns** are proven architectures for constructing flexible and maintainable object-oriented software. The field of design patterns tries to enumerate those recurring patterns, encouraging software designers to *reuse* them to develop better-quality software using less time, money and effort (see online Appendix N, Design Patterns).

Fig. 1.16 | Software technologies. (Part 1 of 2.)

8. `https://www.statista.com/statistics/471264/iot-number-of-connected-devices-worldwide/`

Technology	Description
LAMP	LAMP is an acronym for the open-source technologies that many developers use to build web applications inexpensively—it stands for *Linux*, *Apache*, *MySQL* and *PHP* (or *Perl* or *Python*—two other popular scripting languages). MySQL is an open-source database-management system. PHP is a popular open-source server-side "scripting" language for developing web applications. Apache is the most popular web server software. The equivalent for Windows development is WAMP—*Windows*, *Apache*, *MySQL* and *PHP*.
Software as a Service (SaaS)	Software has generally been viewed as a product; most software still is offered this way. If you want to run an application, you buy a software package from a software vendor—often a CD, DVD or web download. You then install that software on your computer and run it as needed. As new versions appear, you upgrade your software, often at considerable cost in time and money. This process can become cumbersome for organizations that must maintain tens of thousands of systems on a diverse array of computer equipment. With **Software as a Service (SaaS)**, the software runs on servers elsewhere on the Internet. When that server is updated, all clients worldwide see the new capabilities—no local installation is needed. You access the service through a browser. Browsers are quite portable, so you can run the same applications on a wide variety of computers from anywhere in the world. Salesforce.com, Google, Microsoft and many other companies offer SaaS.
Platform as a Service (PaaS)	**Platform as a Service (PaaS)** provides a computing platform for developing and running applications as a service over the web, rather than installing the tools on your computer. Some PaaS providers are Google App Engine, Amazon EC2 and Windows Azure™.
Cloud computing	SaaS and PaaS are examples of cloud computing. You can use software and data stored in the "cloud"—i.e., accessed on remote computers (or servers) via the Internet and available on demand—rather than having it stored locally on your desktop, notebook computer or mobile device. This allows you to increase or decrease computing resources to meet your needs at any given time, which is more cost effective than purchasing hardware to provide enough storage and processing power to meet occasional peak demands. Cloud computing also saves money by shifting to the service provider the burden of managing these apps (such as installing and upgrading the software, security, backups and disaster recovery).
Software Development Kit (SDK)	**Software Development Kits (SDKs)** include the tools and documentation developers use to program applications.

Fig. 1.16 | Software technologies. (Part 2 of 2.)

Software is complex. Large, real-world software applications can take many months or even years to design and implement. When large software products are under development, they typically are made available to the user communities as a series of releases, each more complete and polished than the last (Fig. 1.17).

Version	Description
Alpha	*Alpha* software is the earliest release of a software product that's still under active development. Alpha versions are often buggy, incomplete and unstable and are released to a relatively small number of developers for testing new features, getting early feedback, etc. Alpha software also is commonly called *early access* software.
Beta	*Beta* versions are released to a larger number of developers later in the development process after most major bugs have been fixed and new features are nearly complete. Beta software is more stable, but still subject to change.
Release candidates	*Release candidates* are generally *feature complete*, (mostly) bug free and ready for use by the community, which provides a diverse testing environment—the software is used on different systems, with varying constraints and for a variety of purposes.
Final release	Any bugs that appear in the release candidate are corrected, and eventually the final product is released to the general public. Software companies often distribute incremental updates over the Internet.
Continuous beta	Software that's developed using this approach (for example, Google search or Gmail) generally does not have version numbers. It's hosted in the *cloud* (not installed on your computer) and is constantly evolving so that users always have the latest version.

Fig. 1.17 | Software product-release terminology.

1.13 Getting Your Questions Answered

There are many online forums in which you can get your Java questions answered and interact with other Java programmers. Some popular Java and general programming forums include:

- `StackOverflow.com`
- `Coderanch.com`
- The Oracle Java Forum—`https://community.oracle.com/community/java`
- `</dream.in.code>`—`http://www.dreamincode.net/forums/forum/32-java/`

Self-Review Exercises

1.1 Fill in the blanks in each of the following statements:

a) Computers process data under the control of sets of instructions called ________.
b) The key logical units of the computer are the ________, ________, ________, ________, ________ and ________.
c) The three types of languages discussed in the chapter are ________, ________ and ________.
d) The programs that translate high-level language programs into machine language are called ________.

e) ________ is an operating system for mobile devices based on the Linux kernel and Java.
f) ________ software is generally feature complete, (supposedly) bug free and ready for use by the community.
g) The Wii Remote, as well as many smartphones, use a(n) ________ which allows the device to respond to motion.

1.2 Fill in the blanks in each of the following sentences about the Java environment:
a) The ________ command from the JDK executes a Java application.
b) The ________ command from the JDK compiles a Java program.
c) A Java source code file must end with the ________ file extension.
d) When a Java program is compiled, the file produced by the compiler ends with the ________ file extension.
e) The file produced by the Java compiler contains ________ that are executed by the Java Virtual Machine.

1.3 Fill in the blanks in each of the following statements (based on Section 1.5):
a) Objects enable the design practice of ________—although they may know how to communicate with one another across well-defined interfaces, they normally are not allowed to know how other objects are implemented.
b) Java programmers concentrate on creating ________, which contain fields and the set of methods that manipulate those fields and provide services to clients.
c) The process of analyzing and designing a system from an object-oriented point of view is called ________.
d) A new class of objects can be created conveniently by ________—the new class (called the subclass) starts with the characteristics of an existing class (called the superclass), possibly customizing them and adding unique characteristics of its own.
e) ________ is a graphical language that allows people who design software systems to use an industry-standard notation to represent them.
f) The size, shape, color and weight of an object are considered ________ of the object's class.

Answers to Self-Review Exercises

1.1 a) programs. b) input unit, output unit, memory unit, central processing unit, arithmetic and logic unit, secondary storage unit. c) machine languages, assembly languages, high-level languages. d) compilers. e) Android. f) Release candidate. g) accelerometer.

1.2 a) `java`. b) `javac`. c) `.java`. d) `.class`. e) bytecodes.

1.3 a) information hiding. b) classes. c) object-oriented analysis and design (OOAD). d) Inheritance. e) The Unified Modeling Language (UML). f) attributes.

Exercises

1.4 Fill in the blanks in each of the following statements:
a) The logical unit that receives information from outside the computer for use by the computer is the ________.
b) The process of instructing the computer to solve a problem is called ________.
c) ________ is a type of computer language that uses Englishlike abbreviations for machine-language instructions.
d) ________ is a logical unit that sends information which has already been processed by the computer to various devices so that it may be used outside the computer.
e) ________ and ________ are logical units of the computer that retain information.

f) _______ is a logical unit of the computer that performs calculations.
g) _______ is a logical unit of the computer that makes logical decisions.
h) _______ languages are most convenient to the programmer for writing programs quickly and easily.
i) The only language a computer can directly understand is that computer's _______.
j) _______ is a logical unit of the computer that coordinates the activities of all the other logical units.

1.5 Fill in the blanks in each of the following statements:

a) The _______ programming language is now used to develop large-scale enterprise applications, to enhance the functionality of web servers, to provide applications for consumer devices and for many other purposes.
b) _______ initially became widely known as the development language of the UNIX operating system.
c) The _______ ensures that messages, consisting of sequentially numbered pieces called bytes, were properly routed from sender to receiver, arrived intact and were assembled in the correct order.
d) The _______ programming language was developed by Bjarne Stroustrup in the early 1980s at Bell Laboratories.

1.6 Fill in the blanks in each of the following statements:

a) Java programs normally go through five phases—_______, _______, _______, _______ and _______.
b) A(n) _______ provides many tools that support the software development process, such as editors for writing and editing programs, debuggers for locating logic errors in programs, and many other features.
c) The command `java` invokes the _______, which executes Java programs.
d) A(n) _______ is a software application that simulates a computer, but hides the underlying operating system and hardware from the programs that interact with it.
e) The _______ takes the `.class` files containing the program's bytecodes and transfers them to primary memory.
f) The _______ examines bytecodes to ensure that they're valid.

1.7 Explain the two compilation phases of Java programs.

1.8 One of the world's most common objects is a wrist watch. Discuss how each of the following terms and concepts applies to the notion of a watch: object, attributes, behaviors, class, inheritance (consider, for example, an alarm clock), modeling, messages, encapsulation, interface and information hiding.

Making a Difference

The Making-a-Difference exercises will ask you to work on problems that really matter to individuals, communities, countries and the world.

1.9 *(Test Drive: Carbon Footprint Calculator)* Some scientists believe that carbon emissions, especially from the burning of fossil fuels, contribute significantly to global warming and that this can be combated if individuals take steps to limit their use of carbon-based fuels. Various organizations and individuals are increasingly concerned about their "carbon footprints." Websites such as TerraPass

```
http://www.terrapass.com/carbon-footprint-calculator-2/
```

and Carbon Footprint

```
http://www.carbonfootprint.com/calculator.aspx
```

provide carbon-footprint calculators. Test drive these calculators to determine your carbon footprint. Exercises in later chapters will ask you to program your own carbon-footprint calculator. To prepare for this, research the formulas for calculating carbon footprints.

1.10 *(Test Drive: Body-Mass-Index Calculator)* By recent estimates, two-thirds of the people in the United States are overweight and about half of those are obese. This causes significant increases in illnesses such as diabetes and heart disease. To determine whether a person is overweight or obese, you can use a measure called the body mass index (BMI). The United States Department of Health and Human Services provides a BMI calculator at `http://www.nhlbi.nih.gov/guidelines/obesity/BMI/bmicalc.htm`. Use it to calculate your own BMI. An exercise in Chapter 3 will ask you to program your own BMI calculator. To prepare for this, research the formulas for calculating BMI.

1.11 *(Attributes of Hybrid Vehicles)* In this chapter you learned the basics of classes. Now you'll begin "fleshing out" aspects of a class called "Hybrid Vehicle." Hybrid vehicles are becoming increasingly popular, because they often get much better mileage than purely gasoline-powered vehicles. Browse the web and study the features of four or five of today's popular hybrid cars, then list as many of their hybrid-related attributes as you can. For example, common attributes include city-miles-per-gallon and highway-miles-per-gallon. Also list the attributes of the batteries (type, weight, etc.).

1.12 *(Gender Neutrality)* Some people want to eliminate sexism in all forms of communication. You've been asked to create a program that can process a paragraph of text and replace gender-specific words with gender-neutral ones. Assuming that you've been given a list of gender-specific words and their gender-neutral replacements (e.g., replace "wife" with "spouse," "man" with "person," "daughter" with "child" and so on), explain the procedure you'd use to read through a paragraph of text and manually perform these replacements. How might your procedure generate a strange term like "woperchild?" In Chapter 4, you'll learn that a more formal term for "procedure" is "algorithm," and that an algorithm specifies the steps to be performed and the order in which to perform them.

1.13 *(Intelligent Assistants)* Developments in the field of artificial intelligence have been accelerating in recent years. Many companies now offer computerized intelligent assistants, such as IBM's Watson, Amazon's Alexa, Apple's Siri, Google's Google Now and Microsoft's Cortana. Research these and others and list uses that can improve people's lives.

1.14 *(Big Data)* Research the rapidly growing field of big data. List applications that hold great promise in fields such as healthcare and scientific research.

1.15 *(Internet of Things)* It's now possible to have a microprocessor at the heart of just about any device and to connect those devices to the Internet. This has led to the notion of the Internet of Things (IoT), which already interconnects tens of billions of devices. Research the IoT and indicate the many ways it's improving people's lives.

Introduction to Java Applications; Input/Output and Operators

2

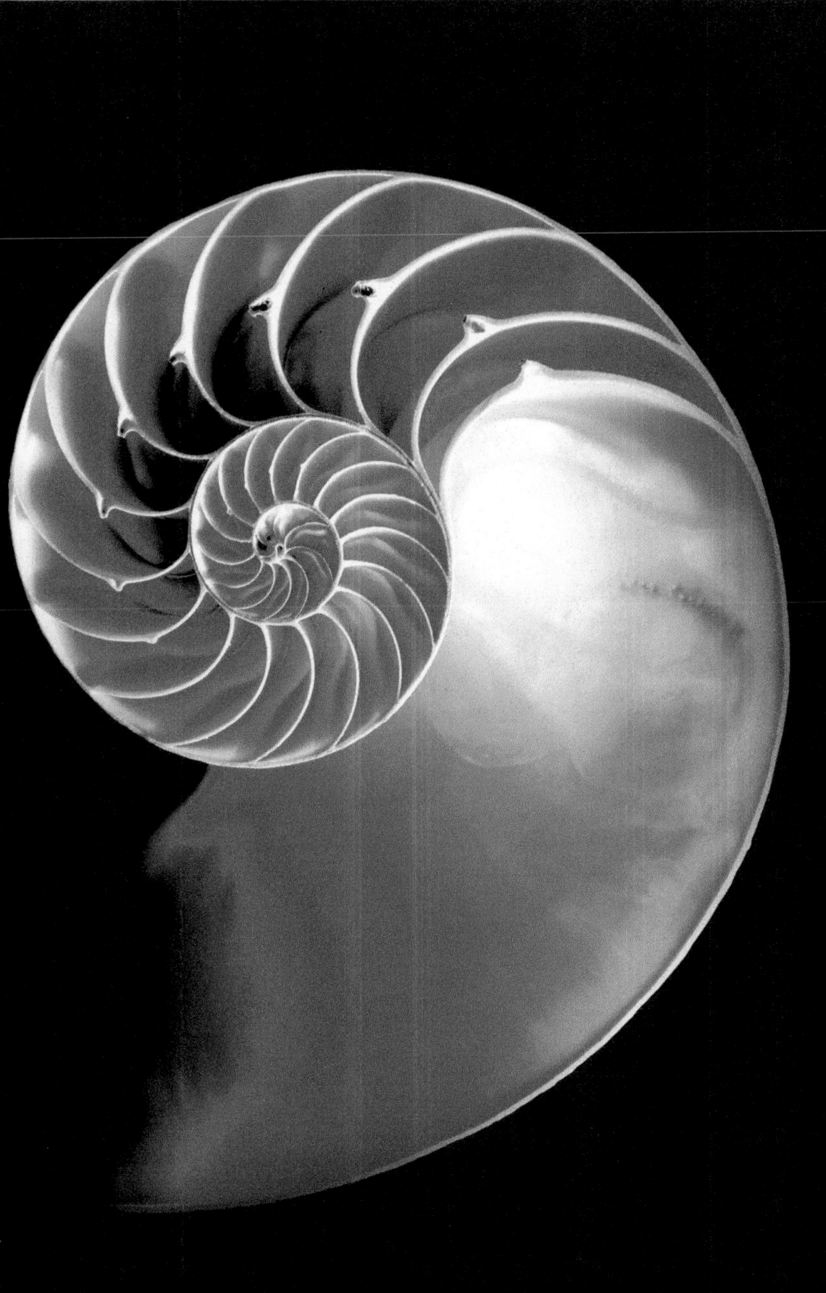

Objectives

In this chapter you'll:

- Write simple Java applications.
- Use input and output statements.
- Learn about Java's primitive types.
- Understand basic memory concepts.
- Use arithmetic operators.
- Learn the precedence of arithmetic operators.
- Write decision-making statements.
- Use relational and equality operators.

Outline

2.1 Introduction

This chapter introduces Java programming. We begin with examples of programs that display (output) messages on the screen. We then present a program that obtains (inputs) two numbers from a user, calculates their sum and displays the result. You'll learn how to instruct the computer to perform arithmetic calculations and save their results for later use. The last example demonstrates how to make decisions. The application compares two numbers, then displays messages that show the comparison results. You'll use the JDK command-line tools to compile and run this chapter's programs. If you prefer to use an integrated development environment (IDE), we've also posted getting-started videos at

```
http://www.deitel.com/books/jhtp11
```

for the three most popular Java IDEs—Eclipse, NetBeans and IntelliJ IDEA.

2.2 Your First Program in Java: Printing a Line of Text

A Java **application** is a computer program that executes when you use the **`java` command** to launch the Java Virtual Machine (JVM). Sections 2.2.1–2.2.2 discuss how to compile and run a Java application. First we consider a simple application that displays a line of text. Figure 2.1 shows the program followed by a box that displays its output.

```
// Fig. 2.1: Welcome1.java
// Text-printing program.

public class Welcome1 {
   // main method begins execution of Java application
   public static void main(String[] args) {
      System.out.println("Welcome to Java Programming!");
   } // end method main
} // end class Welcome1
```

Fig. 2.1 | Text-printing program. (Part 1 of 2.)

```
Welcome to Java Programming!
```

Fig. 2.1 | Text-printing program. (Part 2 of 2.)

We use line numbers for instructional purposes—they're *not* part of a Java program. This example illustrates several important Java features. We'll see that line 7 does the work—displaying the phrase `"Welcome to Java Programming!"` on the screen.

Commenting Your Programs

We insert **comments** to document programs and improve their readability. The Java compiler *ignores* comments, so they do *not* cause the computer to perform any action when the program is run.

By convention, we begin every program with a comment indicating the figure number and the program's filename. The comment in line 1

```
// Fig. 2.1: Welcome1.java
```

begins with `//`, indicating that it's an **end-of-line comment**—it terminates at the end of the line on which the `//` appears. An end-of-line comment need not begin a line; it also can begin in the middle of a line and continue until the end (as in lines 5, 8 and 9). Line 2,

```
// Text-printing program.
```

by our convention, is a comment that describes the purpose of the program.

Java also has **traditional comments**, which can be spread over several lines as in

```
/* This is a traditional comment. It
   can be split over multiple lines */
```

These begin with the delimiter `/*` and end with `*/`. The compiler ignores all text between the delimiters. Java incorporated traditional comments and end-of-line comments from the C and C++ programming languages, respectively.

Java provides comments of a third type—**Javadoc comments**. These are delimited by `/**` and `*/`. The compiler ignores all text between the delimiters. Javadoc comments enable you to embed program documentation directly in your programs. Such comments are the preferred Java documenting format in industry. The **`javadoc` utility program** (part of the JDK) reads Javadoc comments and uses them to prepare program documentation in HTML5 web-page format. We use `//` comments throughout our code, rather than traditional or Javadoc comments, to save space. We demonstrate Javadoc comments and the `javadoc` utility in online Appendix G, Creating Documentation with `javadoc`.

Common Programming Error 2.1

Forgetting one of the delimiters of a traditional or Javadoc comment is a syntax error. A ***syntax error*** *occurs when the compiler encounters code that violates Java's language rules (i.e., its syntax). These rules are similar to natural-language grammar rules specifying sentence structure, such as those in English, French, Spanish, etc. Syntax errors are also called* ***compiler errors, compile-time errors*** *or* ***compilation errors****, because the compiler detects them when compiling the program. When a syntax error is encountered, the compiler issues an error message. You must eliminate all compilation errors before your program will compile properly.*

Good Programming Practice 2.1

Some organizations require that every program begin with a comment that states the purpose of the program and the author, date and time when the program was last modified.

Using Blank Lines

Blank lines (like line 3), space characters and tabs can make programs easier to read. Together, they're known as **white space**. The compiler ignores white space.

Good Programming Practice 2.2

Use white space to enhance program readability.

Declaring a Class

Line 4

```
public class Welcome1 {
```

begins a **class declaration** for class `Welcome1`. Every Java program consists of at least one class that you define. The **`class` keyword** introduces a class declaration and is immediately followed by the **class name** (`Welcome1`). **Keywords** are reserved for use by Java and are spelled with all lowercase letters. The complete list of keywords is shown in Appendix C.

In Chapters 2–7, every class we define begins with the **`public`** keyword. For now, we simply require it. You'll learn more about `public` and non-`public` classes in Chapter 8.

Filename for a `public` Class

A `public` class *must* be placed in a file that has a filename of the form *ClassName*`.java`, so class `Welcome1` is stored in the file `Welcome1.java`.

Common Programming Error 2.2

A compilation error occurs if a `public` class's filename is not exactly the same name as the class (in terms of both spelling and capitalization) followed by the `.java` extension.

Class Names and Identifiers

By convention, class names begin with a capital letter and capitalize the first letter of each word they include (e.g., `SampleClassName`). A class name is an **identifier**—a series of characters consisting of letters, digits, underscores (_) and dollar signs ($) that does *not* begin with a digit and does *not* contain spaces. Some valid identifiers are `Welcome1`, `$value`, `_value`, `m_inputField1` and `button7`. The name `7button` is *not* a valid identifier because it begins with a digit, and the name `input field` is *not* a valid identifier because it contains a space. Normally, an identifier that does not begin with a capital letter is not a class name. Java is **case sensitive**—uppercase and lowercase letters are distinct—so `value` and `Value` are different (but both valid) identifiers.

Good Programming Practice 2.3

By convention, every word in a class-name identifier begins with an uppercase letter. For example, the class-name identifier `DollarAmount` starts its first word, `Dollar`, with an uppercase `D` and its second word, `Amount`, with an uppercase `A`. This naming convention is known as camel case, because the uppercase letters stand out like a camel's humps.

Underscore (_) in Java 9

9

As of Java 9, you can no longer use an underscore (_) by itself as an identifier.

Class Body

A **left brace** (at the end of line 4), `{`, begins the **body** of every class declaration. A corresponding **right brace** (at line 9), `}`, must end each class declaration. Lines 5–8 are indented.

Good Programming Practice 2.4

Indent the entire body of each class declaration one "level" between the braces that delimit the class's. This format emphasizes the class declaration's structure and makes it easier to read. We use three spaces to form a level of indent—many programmers prefer two or four spaces. Whatever you choose, use it consistently.

Good Programming Practice 2.5

IDEs typically indent code for you. The Tab *key may also be used to indent code. You can configure each IDE to specify the number of spaces inserted when you press* Tab.

Common Programming Error 2.3

It's a syntax error if braces do not occur in matching pairs.

Error-Prevention Tip 2.1

When you type an opening left brace, `{`, immediately type the closing right brace, `}`, then reposition the cursor between the braces and indent to begin typing the body. This practice helps prevent errors due to missing braces. Many IDEs do this for you.

Declaring a Method

Line 5

```
   // main method begins execution of Java application
```

is a comment indicating the purpose of lines 6–8 of the program. Line 6

```
   public static void main(String[] args) {
```

is the starting point of every Java application. The **parentheses** after the identifier `main` indicate that it's a program building block called a **method**. Java class declarations normally contain one or more methods. For a Java application, one of the methods *must* be called `main` and must be defined as in line 6; otherwise, the program will not execute.

Methods perform tasks and can return information when they complete their tasks. We'll explain the purpose of keyword `static` in Section 3.2.5. Keyword **`void`** indicates that this method will *not* return any information. Later, we'll see how a method can return information. For now, simply mimic `main`'s first line in your programs. The `String[] args` in parentheses is a required part of `main`'s declaration—we discuss this in Chapter 7.

The left brace at the end of line 6 begins the **body of the method declaration**. A corresponding right brace ends it (line 8). Line 7 is indented between the braces.

Good Programming Practice 2.6

Indent the entire body of each method declaration one "level" between the braces that define the method's body. This emphasizes the method's structure and makes it easier to read.

Performing Output with `System.out.println`

Line 7

```
System.out.println("Welcome to Java Programming!");
```

instructs the computer to perform an action—namely, to display the characters between the double quotation marks. The quotation marks themselves are *not* displayed. Together, the quotation marks and the characters between them are a **string**—also known as a **character string** or a **string literal**. White-space characters in strings are *not* ignored by the compiler. Strings *cannot* span multiple lines of code—later we'll show how to conveniently deal with long strings.

The **`System.out`** object—which is predefined for you—is known as the **standard output object**. It allows a program to display information in the **command window** from which the program executes. In Microsoft Windows, the command window is the **Command Prompt**. In UNIX/Linux/macOS, the command window is called a **terminal** or a **shell**. Many programmers call it simply the **command line**.

Method **`System.out.println`** displays (or prints) a *line* of text in the command window. The string in the parentheses in line 7 is the method's **argument**. When `System.out.println` completes its task, it positions the output cursor (the location where the next character will be displayed) at the beginning of the next line in the command window. This is similar to what happens when you press the *Enter* key while typing in a text editor—the cursor appears at the beginning of the next line in the document.

The entire line 7, including `System.out.println`, the argument `"Welcome to Java Programming!"` in the parentheses and the **semicolon** (`;`), is called a **statement**. A method typically contains statements that perform its task. Most statements end with a semicolon.

Using End-of-Line Comments on Right Braces for Readability

As an aid to programming novices, we include an end-of-line comment after a closing brace that ends a method declaration and after a closing brace that ends a class declaration. For example, line 8

```
   } // end method main
```

indicates the closing brace of method `main`, and line 9

```
} // end class Welcome1
```

indicates the closing brace of class `Welcome1`. Each comment indicates the method or class that the right brace terminates. We'll omit such ending comments after this chapter.

2.2.1 Compiling the Application

We're now ready to compile and execute the program. We assume you're using the Java Development Kit's command-line tools, not an IDE. The following instructions assume that the book's examples are located in `c:\examples` on Windows or in your user account's `Documents/examples` folder on Linux/macOS.

To prepare to compile the program, open a command window and change to the directory where the program is stored. Many operating systems use the command `cd` to change directories (or folders). On Windows, for example,

```
cd c:\examples\ch02\fig02_01
```

changes to the `fig02_01` directory. On UNIX/Linux/macOS, the command

```
cd ~/Documents/examples/ch02/fig02_01
```

changes to the `fig02_01` directory. To compile the program, type

```
javac Welcome1.java
```

If the program does not contain compilation errors, this command creates the file called `Welcome1.class` (known as `Welcome1`'s **class file**) containing the platform-independent Java bytecodes that represent our application. When we use the `java` command to execute the application on a given platform, the JVM will translate these bytecodes into instructions that are understood by the underlying operating system and hardware.

Common Programming Error 2.4

The compiler error message "`class Welcome1 is public, should be declared in a file named Welcome1.java`" indicates that the filename does not match the name of the `public` class in the file or that you typed the class name incorrectly when compiling the class.

When learning how to program, sometimes it's helpful to "break" a working program to get familiar with the compiler's error messages. These messages do not always state the exact problem in the code. When you encounter an error, it will give you an idea of what caused it. Try removing a semicolon or brace from the program of Fig. 2.1, then recompiling to see the error messages generated by the omission.

Error-Prevention Tip 2.2

When the compiler reports a syntax error, it may not be on the line that the error message indicates. First, check the line for which the error was reported. If you don't find an error on that line, check several preceding lines.

Each compilation-error message contains the filename and line number where the error occurred. For example, `Welcome1.java:6` indicates that an error occurred at line 6 in `Welcome1.java`. The rest of the message provides information about the syntax error.

2.2.2 Executing the Application

Now that you've compiled the program, type the following command and press *Enter*:

```
java Welcome1
```

to launch the JVM and load the `Welcome1.class` file. The command *omits* the `.class` filename extension; otherwise, the JVM will *not* execute the program. The JVM calls `Welcome1`'s `main` method. Next, line 7 of `main` displays `"Welcome to Java Programming!"`. Figure 2.2 shows the program executing in a Microsoft Windows **Command Prompt** window. [*Note:* Many environments show command windows with black backgrounds and white text. We adjusted these settings to make our screen captures more readable.]

Error-Prevention Tip 2.3

When attempting to run a Java program, if you receive a message such as "`Exception in thread "main" java.lang.NoClassDefFoundError: Welcome1`," your CLASSPATH environment variable has not been set properly. Please carefully review the installation instructions in the Before You Begin section of this book. On some systems, you may need to reboot your computer or open a new command window after configuring the CLASSPATH.

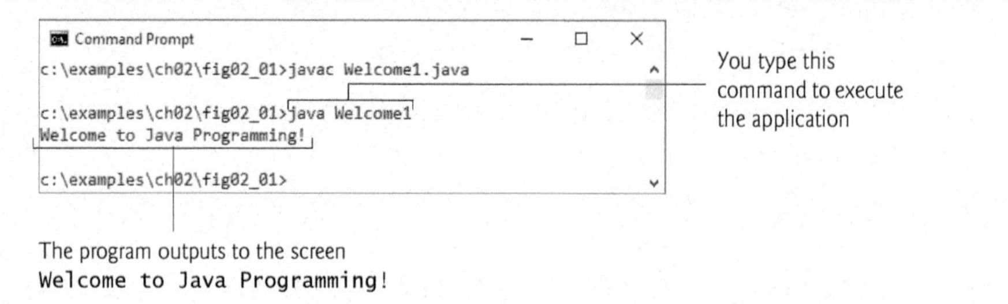

Fig. 2.2 | Executing `Welcome1` from the **Command Prompt**.

2.3 Modifying Your First Java Program

In this section, we modify the example in Fig. 2.1 to print text on one line by using multiple statements and to print text on several lines by using a single statement.

Displaying a Single Line of Text with Multiple Statements

`Welcome to Java Programming!` can be displayed several ways. Class `Welcome2`, shown in Fig. 2.3, uses two statements (lines 7–8) to produce the output shown in Fig. 2.1. [*Note:* From this point forward, we highlight with a yellow background the new and key features in each code listing, as we've done for lines 7–8.]

```
1  // Fig. 2.3: Welcome2.java
2  // Printing a line of text with multiple statements.
3
4  public class Welcome2 {
5     // main method begins execution of Java application
6     public static void main(String[] args) {
7        System.out.print("Welcome to ");
8        System.out.println("Java Programming!");
9     } // end method main
10 } // end class Welcome2
```

```
Welcome to Java Programming!
```

Fig. 2.3 | Printing a line of text with multiple statements.

The program is similar to Fig. 2.1, so we discuss only the changes here. Line 2

```
// Printing a line of text with multiple statements.
```

is an end-of-line comment stating the purpose of the program. Line 4 begins the `Welcome2` class declaration. Lines 7–8 in method `main`

```
System.out.print("Welcome to ");
System.out.println("Java Programming!");
```

display *one* line of text. The first statement uses `System.out`'s method `print` to display a string. Each `print` or `println` statement resumes displaying characters from where the last `print` or `println` statement stopped displaying characters. Unlike `println`, after displaying its argument, `print` does *not* position the output cursor at the beginning of the next line—the next character the program displays will appear *immediately after* the last character that `print` displays. So, line 8 positions the first character in its argument (the letter "`J`") immediately after the last character that line 7 displays (the *space character* before the string's closing double-quote character).

Displaying Multiple Lines of Text with a Single Statement

A single statement can display multiple lines by using **newline characters** (`\n`), which indicate to `System.out`'s `print` and `println` methods when to position the output cursor at the beginning of the next line in the command window. Like blank lines, space characters and tab characters, newline characters are white space characters. The program in Fig. 2.4 outputs four lines of text, using newline characters to determine when to begin each new line. Most of the program is identical to those in Figs. 2.1 and 2.3.

```
1  // Fig. 2.4: Welcome3.java
2  // Printing multiple lines of text with a single statement.
3
4  public class Welcome3 {
5     // main method begins execution of Java application
6     public static void main(String[] args) {
7        System.out.println("Welcome\nto\nJava\nProgramming!");
8     } // end method main
9  } // end class Welcome3
```

```
Welcome
to
Java
Programming!
```

Fig. 2.4 | Printing multiple lines of text with a single statement.

Line 7

```
System.out.println("Welcome\nto\nJava\nProgramming!");
```

displays four lines of text in the command window. Normally, the characters in a string are displayed *exactly* as they appear in the double quotes. However, the paired characters `\` and `n` (repeated three times in the statement) do *not* appear on the screen. The **backslash** (`\`) is an **escape character**, which has special meaning to `System.out`'s `print` and `println` methods. When a backslash appears in a string, Java combines it with the next character to form an **escape sequence**—`\n` represents the newline character. When a newline character appears in a string being output with `System.out`, the newline character causes the screen's output cursor to move to the beginning of the next line in the command window.

Figure 2.5 lists several escape sequences and describes how they affect the display of characters in the command window. For the complete list of escape sequences, visit

```
http://docs.oracle.com/javase/specs/jls/se8/html/jls-
   3.10.6
```

Escape sequence	Description
`\n`	Newline. Position the screen cursor at the beginning of the *next* line.
`\t`	Horizontal tab. Move the screen cursor to the next tab stop.
`\r`	Carriage return. Position the screen cursor at the beginning of the *current* line—do *not* advance to the next line. Any characters output after the carriage return *overwrite* the characters previously output on that line.
`\\`	Backslash. Used to print a backslash character.
`\"`	Double quote. Used to print a double-quote character. For example, `System.out.println("\"in quotes\"");` displays `"in quotes"`.

Fig. 2.5 | Some common escape sequences.

2.4 Displaying Text with `printf`

Method **`System.out.printf`** (`f` means "formatted") displays *formatted* data. Figure 2.6 uses this to output on two lines the strings `"Welcome to"` and `"Java Programming!"`.

```
1  // Fig. 2.6: Welcome4.java
2  // Displaying multiple lines with method System.out.printf.
3
4  public class Welcome4 {
5     // main method begins execution of Java application
6     public static void main(String[] args) {
7        System.out.printf("%s%n%s%n", "Welcome to", "Java Programming!");
8     } // end method main
9  } // end class Welcome4
```

```
Welcome to
Java Programming!
```

Fig. 2.6 | Displaying multiple lines with method `System.out.printf`.

Line 7

```
System.out.printf("%s%n%s%n", "Welcome to", "Java Programming!");
```

calls method `System.out.printf` to display the program's output. The method call specifies three arguments. When a method requires multiple arguments, they're placed in a **comma-separated list**. Calling a method is also referred to as **invoking** a method.

Good Programming Practice 2.7

Place a space after each comma (`,`) in an argument list to make programs more readable.

Method `printf`'s first argument is a **format string** that may consist of **fixed text** and **format specifiers**. Fixed text is output by `printf` just as it would be by `print` or `println`.

Each format specifier is a *placeholder* for a value and specifies the *type of data* to output. Format specifiers also may include optional formatting information.

Format specifiers begin with a percent sign (%) followed by a character that represents the *data type*. For example, the format specifier **%s** is a placeholder for a string. The format string specifies that `printf` should output two strings, each followed by a newline character. At the first format specifier's position, `printf` substitutes the value of the first argument after the format string. At each subsequent format specifier's position, `printf` substitutes the value of the next argument. So this example substitutes `"Welcome to"` for the first `%s` and `"Java Programming!"` for the second `%s`. The output shows that two lines of text are displayed on two lines.

Notice that instead of using the escape sequence `\n`, we used the **%n** format specifier, which is a line separator that's *portable* across operating systems. You cannot use `%n` in the argument to `System.out.print` or `System.out.println`; however, the line separator output by `System.out.println` *after* it displays its argument *is* portable across operating systems. Online Appendix I presents more details of formatting output with `printf`.

2.5 Another Application: Adding Integers

Our next application reads (or inputs) two **integers** (whole numbers, such as –22, 7, 0 and 1024) typed by a user at the keyboard, computes their sum and displays it. This program must keep track of the numbers supplied by the user for the calculation later in the program. Programs remember numbers and other data in the computer's memory and access that data through program elements called variables. The program of Fig. 2.7 demonstrates these concepts. In the sample output, we use bold text to identify the user's input (i.e., **45** and **72**). As per our convention in prior programs, lines 1–2 state the figure number, filename and purpose of the program.

```
 1  // Fig. 2.7: Addition.java
 2  // Addition program that inputs two numbers then displays their sum.
 3  import java.util.Scanner; // program uses class Scanner
 4
 5  public class Addition {
 6     // main method begins execution of Java application
 7     public static void main(String[] args) {
 8        // create a Scanner to obtain input from the command window
 9        Scanner input = new Scanner(System.in);
10
11        System.out.print("Enter first integer: "); // prompt
12        int number1 = input.nextInt(); // read first number from user
13
14        System.out.print("Enter second integer: "); // prompt
15        int number2 = input.nextInt(); // read second number from user
16
17        int sum = number1 + number2; // add numbers, then store total in sum
18
19        System.out.printf("Sum is %d%n", sum); // display sum
20     } // end method main
21  } // end class Addition
```

Fig. 2.7 | Addition program that inputs two numbers then, displays their sum. (Part 1 of 2.)

```
Enter first integer: 45
Enter second integer: 72
Sum is 117
```

Fig. 2.7 | Addition program that inputs two numbers then, displays their sum. (Part 2 of 2.)

2.5.1 `import` Declarations

A great strength of Java is its rich set of predefined classes that you can *reuse* rather than "reinventing the wheel." These classes are grouped into **packages**—*named groups of related classes*—and are collectively referred to as the **Java class library**, or the **Java Application Programming Interface (Java API)**. Line 3

```
import java.util.Scanner; // program uses class Scanner
```

is an **`import` declaration** that helps the compiler locate a class that's used in this program. It indicates that the program uses the predefined `Scanner` class (discussed shortly) from the package named **`java.util`**. The compiler then ensures that you use the class correctly.

Common Programming Error 2.5

All `import` declarations must appear before the first class declaration in the file. Placing an `import` declaration inside or after a class declaration is a syntax error.

Common Programming Error 2.6

Forgetting to include an `import` declaration for a class that must be imported results in a compilation error containing a message such as "`cannot find symbol`." When this occurs, check that you provided the proper `import` declarations and that the names in them are correct, including proper capitalization.

2.5.2 Declaring and Creating a `Scanner` to Obtain User Input from the Keyboard

A **variable** is a location in the computer's memory where a value can be stored for use later in a program. All Java variables *must* be declared with a **name** and a **type** *before* they can be used. A variable's *name* enables the program to access the variable's *value* in memory. A variable name can be any valid identifier—again, a series of characters consisting of letters, digits, underscores (_) and dollar signs ($) that does *not* begin with a digit and does *not* contain spaces. A variable's *type* specifies what kind of information is stored at that location in memory. Like other statements, declaration statements end with a semicolon (`;`).

Line 9 of `main`

```
Scanner input = new Scanner(System.in);
```

is a **variable declaration statement** that specifies the *name* (`input`) and *type* (`Scanner`) of a variable that's used in this program. A **`Scanner`** (package `java.util`) enables a program to read data (e.g., numbers and strings) for use in a program. The data can come from many sources, such as the user at the keyboard or a file on disk. Before using a `Scanner`, you must create it and specify the *source* of the data.

The `=` in line 9 indicates that `Scanner` variable `input` should be **initialized** (i.e., prepared for use in the program) in its declaration with the result of the expression to the right of the equals sign—`new Scanner(System.in)`. This expression uses the **new** keyword to create a `Scanner` object that reads characters typed by the user at the keyboard. The **standard input object, `System.in`**, enables applications to read *bytes* of data typed by the user. The `Scanner` translates these bytes into types (like `int`s) that can be used in a program.

Good Programming Practice 2.8

Choosing meaningful variable names helps a program to be self-documenting (i.e., one can understand the program simply by reading it rather than by reading associated documentation or creating and viewing an excessive number of comments).

Good Programming Practice 2.9

By convention, variable-name identifiers use the camel-case naming convention with a lowercase first letter—for example, `firstNumber`.

2.5.3 Prompting the User for Input

Line 11

```
System.out.print("Enter first integer: "); // prompt
```

uses `System.out.print` to display the message `"Enter first integer: "`. This message is called a **prompt** because it directs the user to take a specific action. We use method `print` here rather than `println` so that the user's input appears on the same line as the prompt. Recall from Section 2.2 that identifiers starting with capital letters typically represent class names. Class `System` is part of package **`java.lang`**.

Software Engineering Observation 2.1

By default, package `java.lang` is imported in every Java program; thus, classes in `java.lang` are the only ones in the Java API that do not require an `import` declaration.

2.5.4 Declaring a Variable to Store an Integer and Obtaining an Integer from the Keyboard

The variable declaration statement in line 12

```
int number1 = input.nextInt(); // read first number from user
```

declares that variable `number1` holds data of type **`int`**—that is, *integer* values, which are whole numbers such as `72`, `-1127` and `0`. The range of values for an `int` is –2,147,483,648 to +2,147,483,647. The `int` values you use in a program may not contain commas; however, for readability, you can place underscores in numbers. So `60_000_000` represents the `int` value 60,000,000.

Some other types of data are **`float`** and **`double`**, for holding real numbers, and **`char`**, for holding character data. Real numbers contain decimal points, such as in `3.4`, `0.0` and `-11.19`. Variables of type `char` represent individual characters, such as an uppercase letter (e.g., `A`), a digit (e.g., `7`), a special character (e.g., `*` or `%`) or an escape sequence (e.g., the tab character, `\t`). The types `int`, `float`, `double` and `char` are called **primitive types**. Primitive-type names are keywords and must appear in all lowercase letters. Appendix D summarizes the characteristics of the eight primitive types (`boolean`, `byte`, `char`, `short`, `int`, `long`, `float` and `double`).

The = in line 12 indicates that `int` variable `number1` should be initialized in its declaration with the result of `input.nextInt()`. This uses the `Scanner` object `input`'s `nextInt` method to obtain an integer from the user at the keyboard. At this point the program *waits* for the user to type the number and press the *Enter* key to submit the number to the program.

Our program assumes that the user enters a valid integer value. If not, a logic error will occur and the program will terminate. Chapter 11, Exception Handling: A Deeper Look, discusses how to make your programs more robust by enabling them to handle such errors. This is also known as making your program *fault tolerant*.

2.5.5 Obtaining a Second Integer

Line 14

```
System.out.print("Enter second integer: "); // prompt
```

prompts the user to enter the second integer. Line 15

```
int number2 = input.nextInt(); // read second number from user
```

declares the `int` variable `number2` and initializes it with a second integer read from the user at the keyboard.

2.5.6 Using Variables in a Calculation

Line 17

```
int sum = number1 + number2; // add numbers then store total in sum
```

declares the `int` variable `sum` and initializes it with the result of `number1 + number2`. When the program encounters the addition operation, it performs the calculation using the values stored in the variables `number1` and `number2`.

In the preceding statement, the addition operator is a **binary operator**, because it has *two* **operands**—`number1` and `number2`. Portions of statements that contain calculations are called **expressions**. In fact, an expression is any portion of a statement that has a *value*. The value of the expression `number1 + number2` is the *sum* of the numbers. Similarly, the value of the expression `input.nextInt()` (lines 12 and 15) is the integer typed by the user.

Good Programming Practice 2.10

Place spaces on either side of a binary operator for readability.

2.5.7 Displaying the Calculation Result

After the calculation has been performed, line 19

```
System.out.printf("Sum is %d%n", sum); // display sum
```

uses method `System.out.printf` to display the `sum`. The format specifier **%d** is a *placeholder* for an `int` value (in this case the value of `sum`)—the letter `d` stands for "decimal integer." The remaining characters in the format string are all fixed text. So, method `printf` displays `"Sum is "`, followed by the value of `sum` (in the position of the `%d` format specifier) and a newline.

Calculations also can be performed *inside* `printf` statements. We could have combined the statements at lines 17 and 19 into the statement

```
System.out.printf("Sum is %d%n", (number1 + number2));
```

The parentheses around the expression `number1 + number2` are optional—they're included to emphasize that the value of the *entire* expression is output in the position of the `%d` format specifier. Such parentheses are said to be **redundant**.

2.5.8 Java API Documentation

For each new Java API class we use, we indicate the package in which it's located. This information helps you locate descriptions of each package and class in the Java API documentation. A web-based version of this documentation can be found at

```
http://docs.oracle.com/javase/8/docs/api/index.html
```

You can download it from the Additional Resources section at

```
http://www.oracle.com/technetwork/java/javase/downloads
```

Appendix F shows how to use this documentation.

2.5.9 Declaring and Initializing Variables in Separate Statements

Each variable must have a value *before* you can use the variable in a calculation (or other expression). The variable declaration statement in line 12 both declared `number1` *and* initialized it with a value entered by the user.

Sometimes you declare a variable in one statement, then initialize in another. For example, line 12 could have been written in two statements as

```
int number1; // declare the int variable number1
number1 = input.nextInt(); // assign the user's input to number1
```

The first statement declares `number1`, but does *not* initialize it. The second statement uses the **assignment operator**, `=`, to *assign* (that is, give) `number1` the value entered by the user. You can read this statement as "`number1` *gets* the value of `input.nextInt()`." Everything to the *right* of the assignment operator, `=`, is always evaluated *before* the assignment is performed.

2.6 Memory Concepts

Variable names such as `number1`, `number2` and `sum` actually correspond to *locations* in the computer's memory. Every variable has a **name**, a **type**, a **size** (in bytes) and a **value**.

In the addition program of Fig. 2.7, when the following statement (line 12) executes:

```
int number1 = input.nextInt(); // read first number from user
```

the number typed by the user is placed into a memory location corresponding to the name `number1`. Suppose that the user enters `45`. The computer places that integer value into location `number1` (Fig. 2.8), replacing the previous value (if any) in that location. The previous value is lost, so this process is said to be *destructive*.

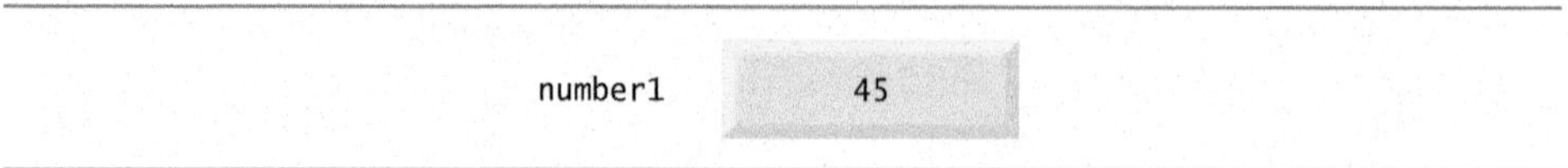

Fig. 2.8 | Memory location showing the name and value of variable `number1`.

When the statement (line 15)

```
int number2 = input.nextInt(); // read second number from user
```

executes, suppose that the user enters `72`. The computer places that integer value into location `number2`. The memory now appears as shown in Fig. 2.9.

number1	45
number2	72

Fig. 2.9 | Memory locations after storing values for `number1` and `number2`.

After the program of Fig. 2.7 obtains values for `number1` and `number2`, it adds the values and places the total into variable `sum`. The statement (line 17)

```
int sum = number1 + number2; // add numbers, then store total in sum
```

performs the addition, then replaces any previous value in `sum`. After `sum` has been calculated, memory appears as shown in Fig. 2.10. The values of `number1` and `number2` appear exactly as they did before they were used in the calculation of `sum`. These values were used, but *not* destroyed, as the computer performed the calculation. When a value is read from a memory location, the process is *nondestructive*.

number1	45
number2	72
sum	117

Fig. 2.10 | Memory locations after storing the sum of `number1` and `number2`.

2.7 Arithmetic

Most programs perform arithmetic calculations. The **arithmetic operators** are summarized in Fig. 2.11. Note the use of various special symbols not used in algebra. The **asterisk** (`*`) indicates multiplication, and the percent sign (`%`) is the **remainder operator**, which we'll discuss shortly. The arithmetic operators in Fig. 2.11 are *binary* operators, because each operates on *two* operands. For example, the expression `f + 7` contains the binary operator `+` and the two operands `f` and `7`.

Java operation	Operator	Algebraic expression	Java expression
Addition	+	$f + 7$	`f + 7`
Subtraction	–	$p - c$	`p - c`
Multiplication	*	bm	`b * m`
Division	/	x / y or $\frac{x}{y}$ or $x \div y$	`x / y`
Remainder	%	$r \bmod s$	`r % s`

Fig. 2.11 | Arithmetic operators.

Integer division yields an integer quotient. For example, the expression `7 / 4` evaluates to `1`, and the expression `17 / 5` evaluates to `3`. Any fractional part in integer division is simply *truncated* (i.e., *discarded*)—no *rounding* occurs. Java provides the remainder operator, `%`, which yields the remainder after division. The expression `x % y` yields the remainder after `x` is divided by `y`. Thus, `7 % 4` yields `3`, and `17 % 5` yields `2`. This operator is most commonly used with integer operands but it can also be used with other arithmetic types. In this chapter's exercises and in later chapters, we consider several interesting applications of the remainder operator, such as determining whether one number is a multiple of another.

Arithmetic Expressions in Straight-Line Form

Arithmetic expressions in Java must be written in **straight-line form** to facilitate entering programs into computers. Thus, expressions such as "a divided by `b`" must be written as `a / b`, so that all constants, variables and operators appear in a straight line. The following algebraic notation is generally not acceptable to compilers:

$$\frac{a}{b}$$

Parentheses for Grouping Subexpressions

Parentheses are used to group terms in Java expressions in the same manner as in algebraic expressions. For example, to multiply `a` times the quantity `b + c`, we write

```
a * (b + c)
```

If an expression contains **nested parentheses**, such as

```
((a + b) * c)
```

the expression in the *innermost* set of parentheses (`a + b` in this case) is evaluated *first*.

Rules of Operator Precedence

Java applies the arithmetic operators in a precise sequence determined by the **rules of operator precedence**, which are generally the same as those followed in algebra:

1. Multiplication, division and remainder operations are applied first. If an expression contains several such operations, they're applied from left to right. Multiplication, division and remainder operators have the same level of precedence.
2. Addition and subtraction operations are applied next. If an expression contains several such operations, the operators are applied from left to right. Addition and subtraction operators have the same level of precedence.

These rules enable Java to apply operators in the correct *order*.[1] When we say that operators are applied from left to right, we're referring to their **associativity**. Some associate from right to left. Figure 2.12 summarizes these rules of operator precedence. A complete precedence chart is included in Appendix A.

Operator(s)	Operation(s)	Order of evaluation (precedence)

`*`
`/`
`%`
	Multiplication
	Division
	Remainder
		Evaluated first. If there are several operators of this type, they're evaluated from *left to right*.

`+` `-`	Addition Subtraction	Evaluated next. If there are several operators of this type, they're evaluated from *left to right*.
`=`	Assignment	Evaluated last.

Fig. 2.12 | Precedence of arithmetic operators.

Sample Algebraic and Java Expressions

Let's consider several sample expressions. Each example shows an algebraic expression and its Java equivalent. The following is an example of an average of five terms:

Algebra: $m = \frac{a + b + c + d + e}{5}$

Java: `m = (a + b + c + d + e) / 5;`

The parentheses are required because division has higher precedence than addition. The entire quantity `(a + b + c + d + e)` is to be divided by `5`. If the parentheses are erroneously omitted, we obtain `a + b + c + d + e / 5`, which evaluates to the different expression

$$a + b + c + d + \frac{e}{5}$$

Here's an example of the equation of a straight line:

Algebra: $y = mx + b$

Java: `y = m * x + b;`

No parentheses are required. The multiplication operator is applied first because multiplication has a higher precedence than addition. The assignment occurs last because it has a lower precedence than multiplication or addition.

The following example contains remainder (`%`), multiplication, division, addition and subtraction operations:

Algebra: $z = pr\%q + w/x - y$

Java:

```
z  =  p  *  r  %  q  +  w  /  x  -  y;
   6     1     2     4     3     5
```

1. We use simple examples to explain the *order of evaluation*. Subtle order-of-evaluation issues occur in the more complex expressions. For more information, see Chapter 15 of *The Java™ Language Specification* (`https://docs.oracle.com/javase/specs/jls/se8/html/jls-15.html`).

The circled numbers under the statement indicate the *order* in which Java applies the operators. The *, % and / operations are evaluated first in *left-to-right* order (i.e., they associate from left to right), because they have higher precedence than + and -. The + and - operations are evaluated next. These operations are also applied from *left to right*. The assignment (=) operation is evaluated last.

Evaluation of a Second-Degree Polynomial

To develop a better understanding of the rules of operator precedence, consider the evaluation of an assignment expression that includes a second-degree polynomial $ax^2 + bx + c$:

```
y = a * x * x + b * x + c;
  6   1   2   4   3   5
```

The multiplication operations are evaluated first in left-to-right order (i.e., they associate from left to right), because they have higher precedence than addition. (Java has no arithmetic operator for exponentiation, so x^2 is represented as x * x. Section 5.4 shows an alternative for performing exponentiation.) The addition operations are evaluated next from *left to right*. Suppose that a, b, c and x are initialized (given values) as follows: a = 2, b = 3, c = 7 and x = 5. Figure 2.13 illustrates the order in which the operators are applied.

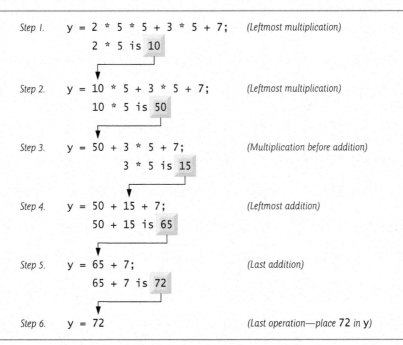

Step 1.	`y = 2 * 5 * 5 + 3 * 5 + 7;` `2 * 5 is 10`	*(Leftmost multiplication)*
Step 2.	`y = 10 * 5 + 3 * 5 + 7;` `10 * 5 is 50`	*(Leftmost multiplication)*
Step 3.	`y = 50 + 3 * 5 + 7;` `3 * 5 is 15`	*(Multiplication before addition)*
Step 4.	`y = 50 + 15 + 7;` `50 + 15 is 65`	*(Leftmost addition)*
Step 5.	`y = 65 + 7;` `65 + 7 is 72`	*(Last addition)*
Step 6.	`y = 72`	*(Last operation—place 72 in y)*

Fig. 2.13 | Order in which a second-degree polynomial is evaluated.

You can use redundant parentheses to make an expression clearer. For example, the preceding statement might be parenthesized as follows:

```
y = (a * x * x) + (b * x) + c;
```

2.8 Decision Making: Equality and Relational Operators

A **condition** is an expression that can be **true** or **false**. This section introduces Java's **if selection statement**, which allows a program to make a **decision** based on a condition's value. For example, the condition "grade is greater than or equal to 60" determines whether a student passed a test. If an `if` statement's condition is *true*, its body executes. If the condition is *false*, its body does not execute.

Conditions in `if` statements can be formed by using the **equality operators** (== and !=) and **relational operators** (>, <, >= and <=) summarized in Fig. 2.14. Both equality operators have the same level of precedence, which is *lower* than that of the relational operators. The equality operators associate from *left to right*. The relational operators all have the same level of precedence and also associate from *left to right*.

Algebraic operator	Java equality or relational operator	Sample Java condition	Meaning of Java condition
Equality operators			
=	==	`x == y`	x is equal to y
≠	!=	`x != y`	x is not equal to y
Relational operators			
>	>	`x > y`	x is greater than y
<	<	`x < y`	x is less than y
≥	>=	`x >= y`	x is greater than or equal to y
≤	<=	`x <= y`	x is less than or equal to y

Fig. 2.14 | Equality and relational operators.

Figure 2.15 uses six `if` statements to compare two integers input by the user. If the condition in any of these `if` statements is *true*, the statement associated with that `if` statement executes; otherwise, the statement is skipped. We use a `Scanner` to input the integers from the user and store them in variables `number1` and `number2`. The program *compares* the numbers and displays the results of the comparisons that are true. We show three sample outputs for different values entered by the user.

```java
// Fig. 2.15: Comparison.java
// Compare integers using if statements, relational operators
// and equality operators.
import java.util.Scanner; // program uses class Scanner

public class Comparison {
   // main method begins execution of Java application
   public static void main(String[] args) {
      // create Scanner to obtain input from command line
      Scanner input = new Scanner(System.in);
```

Fig. 2.15 | Compare integers using `if` statements, relational operators and equality operators. (Part 1 of 2.)

```

      System.out.print("Enter first integer: "); // prompt
      int number1 = input.nextInt(); // read first number from user

      System.out.print("Enter second integer: "); // prompt
      int number2 = input.nextInt(); // read second number from user

      if (number1 == number2)
         System.out.printf("%d == %d%n", number1, number2);
      }

      if (number1 != number2) {
         System.out.printf("%d != %d%n", number1, number2);
      }

      if (number1 < number2) {
         System.out.printf("%d < %d%n", number1, number2);
      }

      if (number1 > number2) {
         System.out.printf("%d > %d%n", number1, number2);
      }

      if (number1 <= number2) {
         System.out.printf("%d <= %d%n", number1, number2);
      }

      if (number1 >= number2) {
         System.out.printf("%d >= %d%n", number1, number2);
      }
   } // end method main
} // end class Comparison
```

```
Enter first integer: 777
Enter second integer: 777
777 == 777
777 <= 777
777 >= 777
```

```
Enter first integer: 1000
Enter second integer: 2000
1000 != 2000
1000 < 2000
1000 <= 2000
```

```
Enter first integer: 2000
Enter second integer: 1000
2000 != 1000
2000 > 1000
2000 >= 1000
```

Fig. 2.15 | Compare integers using `if` statements, relational operators and equality operators. (Part 2 of 2.)

Class `Comparison`'s `main` method (lines 8–41) begins the execution of the program. Line 10

```
Scanner input = new Scanner(System.in);
```

declares `Scanner` variable `input` and assigns it a `Scanner` that inputs data from the standard input (i.e., the keyboard).

Lines 12–13

```
System.out.print("Enter first integer: "); // prompt
int number1 = input.nextInt(); // read first number from user
```

prompt the user to enter the first integer and input the value, respectively. The value is stored in the `int` variable `number1`.

Lines 15–16

```
System.out.print("Enter second integer: "); // prompt
int number2 = input.nextInt(); // read second number from user
```

prompt the user to enter the second integer and input the value, respectively. The value is stored in the `int` variable `number2`.

Lines 18–20

```
if (number1 == number2) {
   System.out.printf("%d == %d%n", number1, number2);
}
```

compare the values of variables `number1` and `number2` to test for equality. If the values are equal, the statement in line 19 displays a line of text indicating that the numbers are equal. The `if` statements starting in lines 22, 26, 30, 34 and 38 compare `number1` and `number2` using the operators `!=`, `<`, `>`, `<=` and `>=`, respectively. If the conditions are `true` in one or more of those `if` statements, the corresponding body statement displays an appropriate line of text.

Each `if` statement in Fig. 2.15 contains a single body statement that's indented. Also notice that we've enclosed each body statement in a pair of braces, `{ }`, creating what's called a **compound statement** or a **block**.

Good Programming Practice 2.11

Indent the statement(s) in the body of an `if` *statement to enhance readability. IDEs typically do this for you, allowing you to specify the indent size.*

Error-Prevention Tip 2.4

You don't need to use braces, `{ }`*, around single-statement bodies, but you* must *include the braces around multiple-statement bodies. You'll see later that forgetting to enclose multiple-statement bodies in braces leads to errors. To avoid errors, as a rule, always enclose an* `if` *statement's body statement(s) in braces.*

Common Programming Error 2.7

Placing a semicolon immediately after the right parenthesis after the condition in an `if` *statement is often a logic error (although not a syntax error). The semicolon causes the body of the* `if` *statement to be empty, so the* `if` *statement performs no action, regardless of whether or not its condition is true. Worse yet, the original body statement of the* `if` *statement* always *executes, often causing the program to produce incorrect results.*

White Space

Note the use of white space in Fig. 2.15. Recall that the compiler normally ignores white space. So, statements may be split over several lines and may be spaced according to your preferences without affecting a program's meaning. It's incorrect to split identifiers and strings. Ideally, statements should be kept small, but this is not always possible.

Error-Prevention Tip 2.5

A lengthy statement can be spread over several lines. If a single statement must be split across lines, choose natural breaking points, such as after a comma in a comma-separated list, or after an operator in a lengthy expression. If a statement is split across two or more lines, indent all subsequent lines until the end of the statement.

Operators Discussed So Far

Figure 2.16 shows the operators discussed so far in decreasing order of precedence. All but the assignment operator, =, associate from *left to right*. The assignment operator, =, associates from *right to left*. An assignment expression's value is whatever was assigned to the variable on the = operator's left side—for example, the value of the expression `x = 7` is 7. So an expression like `x = y = 0` is evaluated as if it had been written as `x = (y = 0)`, which first assigns the value 0 to variable y, then assigns the result of that assignment, 0, to x.

Operators				Associativity	Type
*	/	%		left to right	multiplicative
+	-			left to right	additive
<	<=	>	>=	left to right	relational
==	!=			left to right	equality
=				right to left	assignment

Fig. 2.16 | Precedence and associativity of operators discussed.

Good Programming Practice 2.12

When writing expressions containing many operators, refer to the operator precedence chart (Appendix A). Confirm that the operations in the expression are performed in the order you expect. If, in a complex expression, you're uncertain about the order of evaluation, use parentheses to force the order, exactly as you'd do in algebraic expressions.

2.9 Wrap-Up

In this chapter, you learned many important features of Java, including displaying data on the screen in a command window, inputting data from the keyboard, performing calculations and making decisions. The applications presented here introduced you to many basic programming concepts. As you'll see in Chapter 3, Java applications typically contain just a few lines of code in method `main`—these statements normally create the objects that perform the work of the application. In Chapter 3, you'll learn how to implement your own classes and use objects of those classes in applications.

Summary

Section 2.2 Your First Program in Java: Printing a Line of Text

- A Java application (p. 36) executes when you use the `java` command to launch the JVM.
- Comments (p. 37) document programs and improve their readability. The compiler ignores them.
- An end-of-line comment begins with `//` and terminates at the end of the line on which it appears.
- Traditional comments (p. 37) can be spread over several lines and are delimited by `/*` and `*/`.
- Javadoc comments (p. 37), delimited by `/**` and `*/`, enable you to embed program documentation in your code. The `javadoc` program generates web pages based on these comments.
- A syntax error (p. 37) occurs when the compiler encounters code that violates Java's language rules. It's similar to a grammar error in a natural language.
- Blank lines, space characters and tab characters are known as white space (p. 38). White space makes programs easier to read and is normally ignored by the compiler.
- Keywords (p. 38) are reserved for use by Java and are always spelled with all lowercase letters.
- Keyword `class` (p. 38) introduces a class declaration.
- By convention, all class names in Java begin with a capital letter and capitalize the first letter of each word they include (e.g., `SampleClassName`).
- A Java class name is an identifier—a series of characters consisting of letters, digits, underscores (`_`) and dollar signs (`$`) that does not begin with a digit and does not contain spaces.
- A `public` (p. 38) class declaration must be saved in a file with the same name as the class followed by the "`.java`" filename extension.
- Java is case sensitive (p. 38)—that is, uppercase and lowercase letters are distinct.
- The body of every class declaration (p. 39) is delimited by braces, `{` and `}`.
- Method `main` (p. 39) is the starting point of every Java application and must begin with

```
public static void main(String[] args)
```

  otherwise, the JVM will not execute the application.
- Methods perform tasks and return information when they complete them. Keyword `void` (p. 39) indicates that a method will perform a task but return no information.
- Statements instruct the computer to perform actions.
- A string (p. 40) in double quotes is sometimes called a character string or a string literal.
- The standard output object (`System.out`; p. 40) displays characters in the command window.
- Method `System.out.println` (p. 40) displays its argument (p. 40) in the command window followed by a newline character to position the output cursor to the beginning of the next line.

Section 2.2.1 Compiling the Application

- You compile a program with the command `javac`. If the program contains no syntax errors, a class file (p. 41) containing the Java bytecodes that represent the application is created. These bytecodes are interpreted by the JVM when you execute the program.

Section 2.2.2 Executing the Application

- To run an application, type `java` followed by the name of the class that contains method `main`.

Section 2.3 Modifying Your First Java Program

- `System.out.print` (p. 42) displays its argument and positions the output cursor immediately after the last character displayed.

- A backslash (\) in a string is an escape character (p. 43). Java combines it with the next character to form an escape sequence (p. 43)—`\n` (p. 43) represents the newline character.

Section 2.4 Displaying Text with `printf`

- `System.out.printf` method (p. 44; `f` means "formatted") displays formatted data.
- Method `printf`'s first argument is a format string (p. 44) containing fixed text and/or format specifiers. Each format specifier (p. 44) indicates the type of data to output and is a placeholder for a corresponding argument that appears after the format string.
- Format specifiers begin with a percent sign (`%`) and are followed by a character that represents the data type. The format specifier `%s` (p. 45) is a placeholder for a string.
- The `%n` format specifier (p. 45) is a portable line separator. You cannot use `%n` in the argument to `System.out.print` or `System.out.println`; however, the line separator output by `System.out.println` after it displays its argument is portable across operating systems.

Section 2.5.1 `import` *Declarations*

- An `import` declaration (p. 46) helps the compiler locate a class that's used in a program.
- Java's rich set of predefined classes are grouped into packages (p. 46)—named groups of classes. These are referred to as the Java class library, or the Java Application Programming Interface (Java API; p. 46).

Section 2.5.2 Declaring and Creating a `Scanner` *to Obtain User Input from the Keyboard*

- A variable (p. 46) is a location in the computer's memory where a value can be stored for use later in a program. All variables must be declared with a name and a type before they can be used.
- A variable's name enables the program to access the variable's value in memory.
- A `Scanner` (package `java.util`; p. 46) enables a program to read data that the program will use. Before a `Scanner` can be used, the program must create it and specify the source of the data.
- Variables should be initialized (p. 46) to prepare them for use in a program.
- The expression `new Scanner(System.in)` creates a `Scanner` that reads from the standard input object (`System.in`; p. 47)—normally the keyboard.

Section 2.5.3 Prompting the User for Input

- A prompt (p. 47) directs the user to take a specific action.

Section 2.5.4 Declaring a Variable to Store an Integer and Obtaining an Integer from the Keyboard

- Data type `int` (p. 47) is used to declare variables that will hold integer values. The range of values for an `int` is –2,147,483,648 to +2,147,483,647.
- The `int` values you use in a program may not contain commas; however, for readability, you can place underscores in numbers (e.g., `60_000_000`).
- Types `float` and `double` (p. 47) specify real numbers with decimal points, such as `-11.19` and `3.4`.
- Variables of type `char` (p. 47) represent individual characters, such as an uppercase letter (e.g., `A`), a digit (e.g., `7`), a special character (e.g., `*` or `%`) or an escape sequence (e.g., tab, `\t`).
- Types such as `int`, `float`, `double` and `char` are primitive types (p. 47). Primitive-type names are keywords; thus, they must appear in all lowercase letters.
- `Scanner` method `nextInt` obtains an integer for use in a program.

Section 2.5.6 Using Variables in a Calculation

- Portions of statements that have values are called expressions (p. 48).

Section 2.5.7 Displaying the Calculation Result

- The format specifier `%d` (p. 48) is a placeholder for an `int` value.

Section 2.5.9 Declaring and Initializing Variables in Separate Statements

- A variable must be assigned a value before it's used in a program.
- The assignment operator, `=` (p. 49), enables the program to give a value to a variable.

Section 2.6 Memory Concepts

- Variable names (p. 49) correspond to locations in the computer's memory. Every variable has a name, a type, a size and a value.
- A value that's placed in a memory location replaces the location's previous value, which is lost.

Section 2.7 Arithmetic

- The arithmetic operators (p. 50) are `+` (addition), `-` (subtraction), `*` (multiplication), `/` (division) and `%` (remainder).
- Integer division (p. 51) yields an integer quotient.
- The remainder operator, `%` (p. 51), yields the remainder after division.
- Arithmetic expressions must be written in straight-line form (p. 51).
- If an expression contains nested parentheses (p. 51), the innermost set is evaluated first.
- Java applies the operators in arithmetic expressions in a precise sequence determined by the rules of operator precedence (p. 51).
- When we say that operators are applied from left to right, we're referring to their associativity (p. 52). Some operators associate from right to left.
- Redundant parentheses (p. 53) can make an expression clearer.

Section 2.8 Decision Making: Equality and Relational Operators

- The `if` statement (p. 54) makes a decision based on a condition's value (true or false).
- Conditions in `if` statements can be formed by using the equality (`==` and `!=`) and relational (`>`, `<`, `>=` and `<=`) operators (p. 54).
- An `if` statement begins with keyword `if` followed by a condition in parentheses and expects one statement in its body. You must include braces around multiple-statement bodies.

Self-Review Exercises

2.1 Fill in the blanks in each of the following statements:

a) A(n) ________ and a(n) ________ begin and end the body of every method.
b) You can use the ________ statement to make decisions.
c) ________ begins an end-of-line comment.
d) ________, ________ and ________ are called white space.
e) ________ are reserved for use by Java.
f) Java applications begin execution at method ________.
g) Methods ________, ________ and ________ display information in a command window.

2.2 State whether each of the following is *true* or *false*. If *false*, explain why.

a) Comments cause the computer to display the text after the `//` on the screen when the program executes.

b) All variables must be given a type when they're declared.
c) Java considers the variables `number` and `NuMbEr` to be identical.
d) The remainder operator (`%`) can be used only with integer operands.
e) The arithmetic operators `*`, `/`, `%`, `+` and `-` all have the same level of precedence.
f) The identifier `_` (underscore) is valid in Java 9.

2.3 Write statements to accomplish each of the following tasks:
a) Declare variables `c`, `thisIsAVariable`, `q76354` and `number` to be of type `int` and initialize each to `0`.
b) Prompt the user to enter an integer.
c) Input an integer and assign the result to `int` variable `value`. Assume `Scanner` variable `input` can be used to read a value from the keyboard.
d) Print `"This is a Java program"` on one line in the command window. Use method `System.out.println`.
e) Print `"This is a Java program"` on two lines in the command window. The first line should end with `Java`. Use method `System.out.printf` and two `%s` format specifiers.
f) If the variable `number` is not equal to `7`, display `"The variable number is not equal to 7"`.

2.4 Identify and correct the errors in each of the following statements:
a)
```
if (c < 7); {
    System.out.println("c is less than 7");
}
```
b)
```
if (c => 7) {
    System.out.println("c is equal to or greater than 7");
}
```

2.5 Write declarations, statements or comments that accomplish each of the following tasks:
a) State that a program will calculate the product of three integers.
b) Create a `Scanner` called `input` that reads values from the standard input.
c) Prompt the user to enter the first integer.
d) Read the first integer from the user and store it in the `int` variable `x`.
e) Prompt the user to enter the second integer.
f) Read the second integer from the user and store it in the `int` variable `y`.
g) Prompt the user to enter the third integer.
h) Read the third integer from the user and store it in the `int` variable `z`.
i) Compute the product of the three integers contained in variables `x`, `y` and `z`, and store the result in the `int` variable `result`.
j) Use `System.out.printf` to display the message `"Product is"` followed by the value of the variable `result`.

2.6 Using the statements you wrote in Exercise 2.5, write a complete program that calculates and prints the product of three integers.

Answers to Self-Review Exercises

2.1 a) left brace (`{`), right brace (`}`). b) `if`. c) `//`. d) Space characters, newlines and tabs. e) Keywords. f) `main`. g) `System.out.print`, `System.out.println` and `System.out.printf`.

2.2 The answers to Self-Review Exercise 2.2 are:
a) False. Comments do not cause any action to be performed when the program executes. They're used to document programs and improve their readability.
b) True.
c) False. Java is case sensitive, so these variables are distinct.
d) False. The remainder operator can also be used with noninteger operands in Java.

e) False. The operators `*`, `/` and `%` have higher precedence than operators `+` and `-`.
f) False. As of Java 9, `_` (underscore) by itself is no longer a valid identifier.

2.3 The answers to Self-Review Exercise 2.3 are:

a)
```
int c = 0;
int thisIsAVariable = 0;
int q76354 = 0;
int number = 0;
```
b) `System.out.print("Enter an integer: ");`
c) `int value = input.nextInt();`
d) `System.out.println("This is a Java program");`
e) `System.out.printf("%s%n%s%n", "This is a Java", "program");`
f)
```
if (number != 7) {
   System.out.println("The variable number is not equal to 7");
}
```

2.4 The answers to Self-Review Exercise 2.4 are:

a) Error: Semicolon after the right parenthesis of the condition `(c < 7)` in the `if`. As a result, the output statement executes regardless of whether the condition in the `if` is true.
Correction: Remove the semicolon after the right parenthesis.
b) Error: The relational operator `=>` is incorrect.
Correction: Change `=>` to `>=`.

2.5 The answers to Self-Review Exercise 2.5 are:

a) `// Calculate the product of three integers`
b) `Scanner input = new Scanner(System.in);`
c) `System.out.print("Enter first integer: ");`
d) `int x = input.nextInt();`
e) `System.out.print("Enter second integer: ");`
f) `int y = input.nextInt();`
g) `System.out.print("Enter third integer: ");`
h) `int z = input.nextInt();`
i) `int result = x * y * z;`
j) `System.out.printf("Product is %d%n", result);`

2.6 The answer to Self-Review Exercise 2.6 is:

```
// Ex. 2.6: Product.java
// Calculate the product of three integers.
import java.util.Scanner; // program uses Scanner

public class Product {
   public static void main(String[] args) {
      // create Scanner to obtain input from command window
      Scanner input = new Scanner(System.in);

      System.out.print("Enter first integer: "); // prompt for input
      int x = input.nextInt(); // read first integer

      System.out.print("Enter second integer: "); // prompt for input
      int y = input.nextInt(); // read second integer

      System.out.print("Enter third integer: "); // prompt for input
      int z = input.nextInt(); // read third integer

```

```
        int result = x * y * z; // calculate product of numbers

        System.out.printf("Product is %d%n", result);
    } // end method main
} // end class Product
```

```
Enter first integer: 10
Enter second integer: 20
Enter third integer: 30
Product is 6000
```

Exercises

2.7 Fill in the blanks in each of the following statements:

a) ________ are used to document a program and improve its readability.

b) A decision can be made in a Java program with a(n) ________.

c) The arithmetic operators with the same precedence as multiplication are ________ and ________.

d) When parentheses in an arithmetic expression are nested, the ________ set of parentheses is evaluated first.

e) A location in the computer's memory that may contain different values at various times throughout the execution of a program is called a(n) ________.

2.8 Write Java statements that accomplish each of the following tasks:

a) Display the message `"Enter an integer: "`, leaving the cursor on the same line.

b) Assign the product of variables `b` and `c` to the `int` variable `a`.

c) Use a comment to state that a program performs a sample payroll calculation.

2.9 State whether each of the following is *true* or *false*. If *false*, explain why.

a) Java operators are evaluated from left to right.

b) The following are all valid variable names: `_under_bar_`, `m928134`, `t5`, `j7`, `her_sales$`, `his_$account_total`, `a`, `b$`, `c`, `z` and `z2`.

c) A valid Java arithmetic expression with no parentheses is evaluated from left to right.

d) The following are all invalid variable names: `3g`, `87`, `67h2`, `h22` and `2h`.

2.10 Assuming that `x = 2` and `y = 3`, what does each of the following statements display?

a) `System.out.printf("x = %d%n", x);`

b) `System.out.printf("Value of %d + %d is %d%n", x, x, (x + x));`

c) `System.out.printf("x =");`

d) `System.out.printf("%d = %d%n", (x + y), (y + x));`

2.11 Which of the following Java statements contain variables whose values are modified?

a) `int p = i + j + k + 7;`

b) `System.out.println("variables whose values are modified");`

c) `System.out.println("a = 5");`

d) `int value = input.nextInt();`

2.12 Given that $y = ax^3 + 7$, which of the following are correct Java statements for this equation?

a) `int y = a * x * x * x + 7;`

b) `int y = a * x * x * (x + 7);`

c) `int y = (a * x) * x * (x + 7);`

d) `int y = (a * x) * x * x + 7;`

e) `int y = a * (x * x * x) + 7;`

f) `int y = a * x * (x * x + 7);`

2.13 State the order of evaluation of the operators in each of the following Java statements, and show the value of x after each statement is performed:

a) `int x = 7 + 3 * 6 / 2 - 1;`
b) `int x = 2 % 2 + 2 * 2 - 2 / 2;`
c) `int x = (3 * 9 * (3 + (9 * 3 / (3))));`

2.14 Write an application that displays the numbers 1 to 4 on the same line, with each pair of adjacent numbers separated by one space. Use the following techniques:

a) Use one `System.out.println` statement.
b) Use four `System.out.print` statements.
c) Use one `System.out.printf` statement.

2.15 *(Arithmetic)* Write an application that asks the user to enter two integers, obtains them from the user and prints their sum, product, difference and quotient (division). Use the techniques shown in Fig. 2.7.

2.16 *(Comparing Integers)* Write an application that asks the user to enter two integers, obtains them from the user and displays the larger number followed by the words `"is larger"`. If the numbers are equal, print the message `"These numbers are equal"`. Use the techniques shown in Fig. 2.15.

2.17 *(Arithmetic, Smallest and Largest)* Write an application that inputs three integers from the user and displays the sum, average, product, smallest and largest of the numbers. Use the techniques shown in Fig. 2.15. [*Note:* The calculation of the average in this exercise should result in an integer representation of the average. So, if the sum of the values is 7, the average should be 2, not 2.3333….]

2.18 *(Displaying Shapes with Asterisks)* Write an application that displays a box, an oval, an arrow and a diamond using asterisks (*), as follows:

```
*********     ***       *        *
*       *   *     *    ***      * *
*       *  *       *  *****    *   *
*       *  *       *    *     *     *
*       *  *       *    *    *       *
*       *  *       *    *     *     *
*       *  *       *    *      *   *
*       *   *     *     *       * *
*********     ***       *        *
```

2.19 What does the following code print?

```
System.out.printf("*%n**%n***%n****%n*****%n");
```

2.20 What does the following code print?

```
System.out.println("*");
System.out.println("***");
System.out.println("*****");
System.out.println("****");
System.out.println("**");
```

2.21 What does the following code print?

```
System.out.print("*");
System.out.print("***");
System.out.print("*****");
System.out.print("****");
System.out.println("**");
```

2.22 What does the following code print?

```
System.out.print("*");
System.out.println("***");
System.out.println("*****");
System.out.print("****");
System.out.println("**");
```

2.23 What does the following code print?

```
System.out.printf("%s%n%s%n%s%n", "*", "***", "*****");
```

2.24 *(Largest and Smallest Integers)* Write an application that reads five integers and determines and prints the largest and smallest integers in the group. Use only the programming techniques you learned in this chapter.

2.25 *(Odd or Even)* Write an application that reads an integer and determines and prints whether it's odd or even. [*Hint:* Use the remainder operator. An even number is a multiple of 2. Any multiple of 2 leaves a remainder of 0 when divided by 2.]

2.26 *(Multiples)* Write an application that reads two integers, determines whether the first is a multiple of the second and prints the result. [*Hint:* Use the remainder operator.]

2.27 *(Checkerboard Pattern of Asterisks)* Write an application that displays a checkerboard pattern, as follows:

```
* * * * * * * *
 * * * * * * * *
* * * * * * * *
 * * * * * * * *
* * * * * * * *
 * * * * * * * *
* * * * * * * *
 * * * * * * * *
```

2.28 *(Diameter, Circumference and Area of a Circle)* Here's a peek ahead. In this chapter, you learned about integers and the type `int`. Java can also represent floating-point numbers that contain decimal points, such as 3.14159. Write an application that inputs from the user the radius of a circle as an integer and prints the circle's diameter, circumference and area using the floating-point value 3.14159 for π. Use the techniques shown in Fig. 2.7. [*Note:* You may also use the predefined constant `Math.PI` for the value of π. This constant is more precise than the value 3.14159. Class `Math` is defined in package `java.lang`. Classes in that package are imported automatically, so you do not need to `import` class `Math` to use it.] Use the following formulas (r is the radius):

$$diameter = 2r$$
$$circumference = 2\pi r$$
$$area = \pi r^2$$

Do not store the results of each calculation in a variable. Rather, specify each calculation as the value that will be output in a `System.out.printf` statement. The values produced by the circumference and area calculations are floating-point numbers. Such values can be output with the format specifier `%f` in a `System.out.printf` statement. You'll learn more about floating-point numbers in Chapter 3.

2.29 *(Integer Value of a Character)* Here's another peek ahead. In this chapter, you learned about integers and the type `int`. Java can also represent uppercase letters, lowercase letters and a considerable variety of special symbols. Every character has a corresponding integer representation. The set of characters a computer uses together with the corresponding integer representations for those characters is called that computer's character set. You can indicate a character value in a program simply by enclosing that character in single quotes, as in 'A'.

You can determine a character's integer equivalent by preceding that character with (int), as in

```
(int) 'A'
```

An operator of this form is called a cast operator. (You'll learn about cast operators in Chapter 4.) The following statement outputs a character and its integer equivalent:

```
System.out.printf("The character %c has the value %d%n", 'A', ((int) 'A'));
```

When the preceding statement executes, it displays the character A and the value 65 (from the Unicode® character set) as part of the string. The format specifier %c is a placeholder for a character (in this case, the character 'A').

Using statements similar to the one shown earlier in this exercise, write an application that displays the integer equivalents of some uppercase letters, lowercase letters, digits and special symbols. Display the integer equivalents of the following: A B C a b c 0 1 2 $ * + / and the blank character.

2.30 *(Separating the Digits in an Integer)* Write an application that inputs one number consisting of five digits from the user, separates the number into its individual digits and prints the digits separated from one another by three spaces each. For example, if the user types in the number 42339, the program should print

```
4   2   3   3   9
```

Assume that the user enters the correct number of digits. What happens when you enter a number with more than five digits? What happens when you enter a number with fewer than five digits? [*Hint:* It's possible to do this exercise with the techniques you learned in this chapter. You'll need to use both division and remainder operations to "pick off" each digit.]

2.31 *(Table of Squares and Cubes)* Using only the programming techniques you learned in this chapter, write an application that calculates the squares and cubes of the numbers from 0 to 10 and prints the resulting values in table format, as shown below.

```
number  square  cube
0       0       0
1       1       1
2       4       8
3       9       27
4       16      64
5       25      125
6       36      216
7       49      343
8       64      512
9       81      729
10      100     1000
```

2.32 *(Negative, Positive and Zero Values)* Write a program that inputs five numbers and determines and prints the number of negative numbers input, the number of positive numbers input and the number of zeros input.

Making a Difference

2.33 *(Body Mass Index Calculator)* We introduced the body mass index (BMI) calculator in Exercise 1.10. The formulas for calculating BMI are

$$BMI = \frac{weightInPounds \times 703}{heightInInches \times heightInInches}$$

or

$$BMI = \frac{weightInKilograms}{heightInMeters \times heightInMeters}$$

Create a BMI calculator that reads the user's weight in pounds and height in inches (or, if you prefer, the user's weight in kilograms and height in meters), then calculates and displays the user's body mass index. Also, display the BMI categories and their values from the National Heart Lung and Blood Institute

`http://www.nhlbi.nih.gov/health/educational/lose_wt/BMI/bmicalc.htm`

so the user can evaluate his/her BMI.

[*Note:* In this chapter, you learned to use the `int` type to represent whole numbers. The BMI calculations when done with `int` values will both produce whole-number results. In Chapter 3 you'll learn to use the `double` type to represent numbers with decimal points. When the BMI calculations are performed with `double`s, they'll both produce numbers with decimal points—these are called "floating-point" numbers.]

2.34 *(World Population Growth Calculator)* Search the Internet to determine the current world population and the annual world population growth rate. Write an application that inputs these values, then displays the estimated world population after one, two, three, four and five years.

2.35 *(Car-Pool Savings Calculator)* Research several car-pooling websites. Create an application that calculates your daily driving cost, so that you can estimate how much money could be saved by car pooling, which also has other advantages such as reducing carbon emissions and reducing traffic congestion. The application should input the following information and display the user's cost per day of driving to work:

a) Total miles driven per day.
b) Cost per gallon of gasoline.
c) Average miles per gallon.
d) Parking fees per day.
e) Tolls per day.

3 Introduction to Classes, Objects, Methods and Strings

Objectives

In this chapter you'll:

- Declare a class and use it to create an object.
- Implement a class's behaviors as methods.
- Implement a class's attributes as instance variables.
- Call an object's methods to make them perform their tasks.
- Learn what local variables of a method are and how they differ from instance variables.
- Learn what primitive types and reference types are.
- Use a constructor to initialize an object's data.
- Represent and use numbers containing decimal points.
- Learn why classes are a natural way to model real-world things and abstract entities.

Outline

3.1 Introduction[1]

In Chapter 2, you worked with *existing* classes, objects and methods. You used the *predefined* standard output object `System.out`, *invoking* its methods `print`, `println` and `printf` to display information on the screen. You used the *existing* `Scanner` class to create an object that reads into memory integer data typed by the user at the keyboard. Throughout the book, you'll use many more *preexisting* classes and objects—this is one of the great strengths of Java as an object-oriented programming language.

In this chapter, you'll create your own classes and methods. Each new class you create becomes a new *type* that can be used to declare variables and create objects. You can declare new classes as needed; this is one reason why Java is known as an *extensible* language.

We present a case study on creating and using a simple, real-world bank-account class—`Account`. Such a class should maintain as *instance variables* attributes, such as its `name` and `balance`, and provide *methods* for tasks such as querying the balance (`getBalance`), making deposits that increase the balance (`deposit`) and making withdrawals that decrease the balance (`withdraw`). We'll build the `getBalance` and `deposit` methods into the class in the chapter's examples and you'll add the `withdraw` method in the exercises.

In Chapter 2, we used the data type `int` to represent integers. In this chapter, we introduce data type `double` to represent an account balance as a number that can contain a *decimal point*—such numbers are called *floating-point numbers*. In Chapter 8, when we

1. This chapter depends on the terminology and concepts of object-oriented programming introduced in Section 1.5, Introduction to Object Technology.

get a bit deeper into object technology, we'll begin representing monetary amounts precisely with class `BigDecimal` (package `java.math`), as you should do when writing industrial-strength monetary applications. [Alternatively, you could treat monetary amounts as whole numbers of pennies, then break the result into dollars and cents by using division and remainder operations, respectively, and insert a period between the dollars and the cents.]

Typically, the apps you develop in this book will consist of two or more classes. If you become part of a development team in industry, you might work on apps that contain hundreds, or even thousands, of classes.

3.2 Instance Variables, *set* Methods and *get* Methods

In this section, you'll create two classes—`Account` (Fig. 3.1) and `AccountTest` (Fig. 3.2). Class `AccountTest` is an *application class* in which the `main` method will create and use an `Account` object to demonstrate class `Account`'s capabilities.

3.2.1 Account Class with an Instance Variable, and *set* and *get* Methods

Different accounts typically have different names. For this reason, class `Account` (Fig. 3.1) contains a `name` *instance variable.* A class's instance variables maintain data for each object (that is, each instance) of the class. Later in the chapter we'll add an instance variable named `balance` so we can keep track of how much money is in the account. Class `Account` contains two methods—method `setName` stores a name in an `Account` object and method `getName` obtains a name from an `Account` object.

```
1  // Fig. 3.1: Account.java
2  // Account class that contains a name instance variable
3  // and methods to set and get its value.
4
5  public class Account {
6     private String name; // instance variable
7
8     // method to set the name in the object
9     public void setName(String name) {
10       this.name = name; // store the name
11    }
12
13    // method to retrieve the name from the object
14    public String getName() {
15       return name; // return value of name to caller
16    }
17 }
```

Fig. 3.1 | `Account` class that contains a `name` instance variable and methods to *set* and *get* its value.

Class Declaration

The *class declaration* begins in line 5:

```
public class Account {
```

The keyword `public` (which Chapter 8 explains in detail) is an **access modifier.** For now, we'll simply declare every class `public`. Each `public` class declaration must be stored in a file having the *same* name as the class and ending with the `.java` filename extension; otherwise, a compilation error will occur. Thus, `public` classes `Account` and `AccountTest` (Fig. 3.2) *must* be declared in the *separate* files `Account.java` and `AccountTest.java`, respectively.

Every class declaration contains the keyword `class` followed immediately by the class's name—in this case, `Account`. Every class's body is enclosed in a pair of left and right braces as in lines 5 and 17 of Fig. 3.1.

Identifiers and Camel-Case Naming

Recall from Chapter 2 that class names, method names and variable names are all *identifiers* and by convention all use the *camel-case* naming scheme. Also by convention, class names begin with an initial *uppercase* letter, and method names and variable names begin with an initial *lowercase* letter.

Instance Variable `name`

Recall from Section 1.5 that an object has attributes, implemented as instance variables and carried with it throughout its lifetime. Instance variables exist before methods are called on an object, while the methods are executing and after the methods complete execution. Each object (instance) of the class has its *own* copy of the class's instance variables. A class normally contains one or more methods that manipulate the instance variables belonging to particular objects of the class.

Instance variables are declared *inside* a class declaration but *outside* the bodies of the class's methods. Line 6

```
private String name; // instance variable
```

declares instance variable `name` of type `String` *outside* the bodies of methods `setName` (lines 9–11) and `getName` (lines 14–16). `String` variables can hold character string values such as `"Jane Green"`. If there are many `Account` objects, each has its own `name`. Because `name` is an instance variable, it can be manipulated by each of the class's methods.

Good Programming Practice 3.1

We prefer to list a class's instance variables first in the class's body, so that you see the names and types of the variables before they're used in the class's methods. You can list the class's instance variables anywhere in the class outside its method declarations, but scattering the instance variables can lead to hard-to-read code.

Access Modifiers `public` *and* `private`

Most instance-variable declarations are preceded with the keyword `private` (as in line 6). Like `public`, `private` is an *access modifier*. Variables or methods declared with `private` are accessible only to methods of the class in which they're declared. So, the variable `name` can be used only in each `Account` object's methods (`setName` and `getName` in this case). You'll soon see that this presents powerful software engineering opportunities.

`setName` *Method of Class* `Account`

Let's walk through the code of `setName`'s method declaration (lines 9–11):

```
public void setName(String name) {
   this.name = name; // store the name
}
```

We refer to the first line of each method declaration (line 9 in this case) as the *method header*. The method's **return type** (which appears before the method name) specifies the type of data the method returns to its *caller* after performing its task. As you'll soon see, the statement in line 19 of `main` (Fig. 3.2) *calls* method `setName`, so `main` is `setName`'s *caller* in this example. The return type `void` (line 9 in Fig. 3.1) indicates that `setName` will perform a task but will *not* return (i.e., give back) any information to its caller. In Chapter 2, you used methods that return information—for example, you used `Scanner` method `nextInt` to input an integer typed by the user at the keyboard. When `nextInt` reads a value from the user, it *returns* that value for use in the program. As you'll see shortly, `Account` method `getName` returns a value.

Method `setName` receives *parameter* `name` of type `String`—which represents the name that will be passed to the method as an *argument*. You'll see how parameters and arguments work together when we discuss the method call in line 19 of Fig. 3.2.

Parameters are declared in a **parameter list**, which is located inside the parentheses that follow the method name in the method header. When there are multiple parameters, each is separated from the next by a comma. Each parameter *must* specify a type (in this case, `String`) followed by a variable name (in this case, `name`).

Parameters Are Local Variables

In Chapter 2, we declared all of an app's variables in the `main` method. Variables declared in a particular method's body (such as `main`) are **local variables** which can be used *only* in that method. Each method can access its own local variables, not those of other methods. When a method terminates, the values of its local variables are *lost*. A method's parameters also are local variables of the method.

`setName` *Method Body*

Every *method body* is delimited by a pair of *braces* (as in lines 9 and 11 of Fig. 3.1) containing one or more statements that perform the method's task(s). In this case, the method body contains a single statement (line 10) that assigns the value of the `name` *parameter* (a `String`) to the class's `name` *instance variable*, thus storing the account name in the object.

If a method contains a local variable with the *same* name as an instance variable (as in lines 9 and 6, respectively), that method's body will refer to the local variable rather than the instance variable. In this case, the local variable is said to *shadow* the instance variable in the method's body. The method's body can use the keyword **`this`** to refer to the shadowed instance variable explicitly, as shown on the left side of the assignment in line 10. After line 10 executes, the method has completed its task, so it returns to its *caller*.

Good Programming Practice 3.2

We could have avoided the need for keyword `this` here by choosing a different name for the parameter in line 9, but using the `this` keyword as shown in line 10 is a widely accepted practice to minimize the proliferation of identifier names.

`getName` *Method of Class* **`Account`**

Method `getName` (lines 14–16)

```
public String getName() {
   return name; // return value of name to caller
}
```

returns a particular `Account` object's `name` to the caller. The method has an *empty* parameter list, so it does *not* require additional information to perform its task. The method returns a `String`. When a method that specifies a return type *other* than `void` is called and completes its task, it *must* return a result to its caller. A statement that calls method `getName` on an `Account` object (such as the ones in lines 14 and 24 of Fig. 3.2) expects to receive the `Account`'s name—a `String`, as specified in the method declaration's *return type*.

The **`return`** statement in line 15 of Fig. 3.1 passes the `String` value of instance variable `name` back to the caller. For example, when the value is returned to the statement in lines 23–24 of Fig. 3.2, the statement uses that value to output the name.

3.2.2 `AccountTest` Class That Creates and Uses an Object of Class `Account`

Next, we'd like to use class `Account` in an app and *call* each of its methods. A class that contains a `main` method begins the execution of a Java app. Class `Account` *cannot* execute by itself because it does *not* contain a `main` method—if you type `java Account` in the command window, you'll get an error indicating "`Main method not found in class Account.`" To fix this problem, you must either declare a *separate* class that contains a `main` method or place a `main` method in class `Account`.

Driver Class `AccountTest`

A person drives a car by telling it what to do (go faster, go slower, turn left, turn right, etc.)—without having to know how the car's internal mechanisms work. Similarly, a method (such as `main`) "drives" an `Account` object by calling its methods—without having to know how the class's internal mechanisms work. In this sense, the class containing method `main` is referred to as a **driver class**.

To help you prepare for the larger programs you'll encounter later in this book and in industry, we define class `AccountTest` and its `main` method in the file `AccountTest.java` (Fig. 3.2). Once `main` begins executing, it may call other methods in this and other classes; those may, in turn, call other methods, and so on. Class `AccountTest`'s `main` method creates one `Account` object and calls its `getName` and `setName` methods.

```
1  // Fig. 3.2: AccountTest.java
2  // Creating and manipulating an Account object.
3  import java.util.Scanner;
4
5  public class AccountTest {
6     public static void main(String[] args) {
7        // create a Scanner object to obtain input from the command window
8        Scanner input = new Scanner(System.in);
9
10       // create an Account object and assign it to myAccount
11       Account myAccount = new Account();
12
13       // display initial value of name (null)
14       System.out.printf("Initial name is: %s%n%n", myAccount.getName());
15
```

Fig. 3.2 | Creating and manipulating an `Account` object. (Part 1 of 2.)

```
16          // prompt for and read name
17          System.out.println("Please enter the name:");
18          String theName = input.nextLine(); // read a line of text
19          myAccount.setName(theName); // put theName in myAccount
20          System.out.println(); // outputs a blank line
21
22          // display the name stored in object myAccount
23          System.out.printf("Name in object myAccount is:%n%s%n",
24             myAccount.getName());
25       }
26    }
```

```
Initial name is: null

Please enter the name:
Jane Green

Name in object myAccount is:
Jane Green
```

Fig. 3.2 | Creating and manipulating an `Account` object. (Part 2 of 2.)

`Scanner` Object for Receiving Input from the User

Line 8 creates a `Scanner` object named `input` for inputting a name from the user. Line 17 prompts the user to enter a name. Line 18 uses the `Scanner` object's **`nextLine`** method to read the name from the user and assign it to the *local* variable `theName`. You type the name and press *Enter* to submit it to the program. Pressing *Enter* inserts a newline character after the characters you typed. Method `nextLine` reads characters (*including white-space characters,* such as the blank in `"Jane Green"`) until it encounters the newline, then returns a `String` containing the characters up to, but *not* including, the newline, which is *discarded.*

Class `Scanner` provides various other input methods, as you'll see throughout the book. A method similar to `nextLine`—named **`next`**—reads the *next word.* When you press *Enter* after typing some text, method `next` reads characters until it encounters a *white-space character* (such as a space, tab or newline), then returns a `String` containing the characters up to, but *not* including, the white-space character, which is *discarded.* All information after the first white-space character is *not lost*—it can be read by subsequent statements that call the `Scanner`'s methods later in the program.

Instantiating an Object—Keyword `new` and Constructors

Line 11 creates an `Account` object and assigns it to variable `myAccount` of type `Account`. The variable is initialized with the result of `new Account()`—a **class instance creation expression.** Keyword **`new`** creates a new object of the specified class—in this case, `Account`. The parentheses are *required.* As you'll learn in Section 3.3, those parentheses in combination with a class name represent a call to a **constructor**, which is *similar* to a method but is called implicitly by the `new` operator to *initialize* an object's instance variables when the object is *created.* In Section 3.3, you'll see how to place an *argument* in the parentheses to specify an *initial value* for an `Account` object's `name` instance variable—you'll enhance class `Account` to enable this. For now, we simply leave the parentheses *empty.* Line 8 contains a class instance creation expression for a `Scanner` object—the expression initializes the `Scanner` with `System.in`, which tells the `Scanner` where to read the input from (i.e., the keyboard).

Calling Class `Account`*'s* `getName` *Method*

Line 14 displays the *initial* name, which is obtained by calling the object's `getName` method. Just as we can use object `System.out` to call its methods `print`, `printf` and `println`, we can use object `myAccount` to call its methods `getName` and `setName`. Line 14 calls `getName` using the `myAccount` object created in line 11, followed by a **dot separator** (`.`), then the method name `getName` and an *empty* set of parentheses because no arguments are being passed. When `getName` is called:

1. The app transfers program execution from the call (line 14 in `main`) to method `getName`'s declaration (lines 14–16 of Fig. 3.1). Because `getName` was called via the `myAccount` object, `getName` "knows" which object's instance variable to manipulate.
2. Next, method `getName` performs its task—that is, it *returns* the `name` (line 15 of Fig. 3.1). When the `return` statement executes, program execution continues where `getName` was called (line 14 in Fig. 3.2).
3. `System.out.printf` displays the `String` returned by method `getName`, then the program continues executing at line 17 in `main`.

Error-Prevention Tip 3.1

Never use as a format-control a string that was input from the user. When method `System.out.printf` *evaluates the format-control string in its first argument, the method performs tasks based on the conversion specifier(s) in that string. If the format-control string were obtained from the user, a malicious user could supply conversion specifiers that would be executed by* `System.out.printf`*, possibly causing a security breach.*

`null`*—the Default Initial Value for* `String` *Variables*

The first line of the output shows the name "`null`." Unlike local variables, which are *not* automatically initialized, *every instance variable has a* **default initial value**—a value provided by Java when you do *not* specify the instance variable's initial value. Thus, *instance variables* are *not* required to be explicitly initialized before they're used in a program—unless they must be initialized to values *other than* their default values. The default value for an instance variable of type `String` (like `name` in this example) is `null`, which we discuss further in Section 3.5 when we consider *reference types*.

Calling Class `Account`*'s* `setName` *Method*

Line 19 calls `myAccounts`'s `setName` method. A method call can supply *arguments* whose *values* are assigned to the corresponding method parameters. In this case, the value of `main`'s local variable `theName` in parentheses is the *argument* that's passed to `setName` so that the method can perform its task. When `setName` is called:

1. The app transfers program execution from line 19 in `main` to `setName` method's declaration (lines 9–11 of Fig. 3.1), and the *argument value* in the call's parentheses (`theName`) is assigned to the corresponding *parameter* (`name`) in the method header (line 9 of Fig. 3.1). Because `setName` was called via the `myAccount` object, `setName` "knows" which object's instance variable to manipulate.
2. Next, method `setName` performs its task—that is, it assigns the `name` parameter's value to instance variable `name` (line 10 of Fig. 3.1).

3. When program execution reaches setName's closing right brace, it returns to where setName was called (line 19 of Fig. 3.2), then continues at line 20 of Fig. 3.2.

The number of *arguments* in a method call *must match* the number of *parameters* in the method declaration's parameter list. Also, the argument types in the method call must be *consistent* with the types of the corresponding parameters in the method's declaration. (As you'll learn in Chapter 6, an argument's type and its corresponding parameter's type are *not* required to be *identical.*) In our example, the method call passes one argument of type String (theName)—and the method declaration specifies one parameter of type String (name, declared in line 9 of Fig. 3.1). So in this example the type of the argument in the method call *exactly* matches the type of the parameter in the method header.

Displaying the Name That Was Entered by the User
Line 20 of Fig. 3.2 outputs a blank line. When the second call to method getName (line 24) executes, the name entered by the user in line 18 is displayed. After the statement at lines 23–24 completes execution, the end of method main is reached, so the program terminates.

Note that lines 23–24 represent only *one* statement. Java allows long statements to be split over multiple lines. We indent line 24 to indicate that it's a *continuation* of line 23.

Common Programming Error 3.1

Splitting a statement in the middle of an identifier or a string is a syntax error.

3.2.3 Compiling and Executing an App with Multiple Classes

You must compile the classes in Figs. 3.1 and 3.2 before you can *execute* the app. This is the first time you've created an app with *multiple* classes. Class AccountTest has a main method; class Account does not. To compile this app, first change to the directory that contains the app's source-code files. Next, type the command

```
javac Account.java AccountTest.java
```

to compile *both* classes at once. If the directory containing the app includes *only* this app's files, you can compile both classes with the command

```
javac *.java
```

The asterisk (*) in *.java is a wildcard that indicates *all* files in the *current* directory ending with the filename extension ".java" should be compiled. If both classes compile correctly—that is, no compilation errors are displayed—you can then run the app with the command

```
java AccountTest
```

3.2.4 Account UML Class Diagram

We'll often use UML class diagrams to help you visualize a class's *attributes* and *operations.* In industry, UML diagrams help systems designers specify a system in a concise, graphical, programming-language-independent manner, before programmers implement the system in a specific programming language. Figure 3.3 presents a UML **class diagram** for class `Account` of Fig. 3.1.

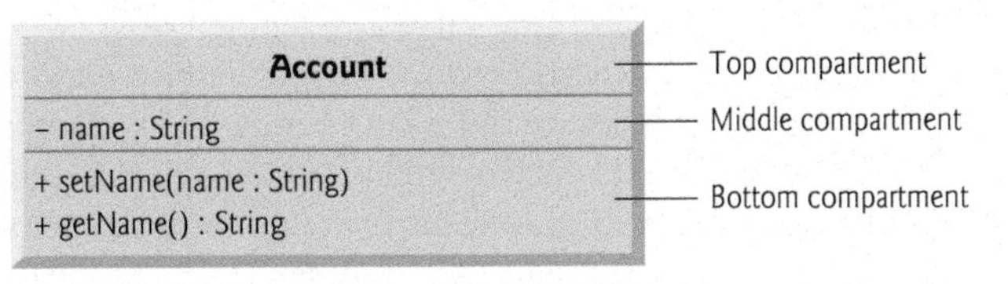

Fig. 3.3 | UML class diagram for class `Account` of Fig. 3.1.

Top Compartment

In the UML, each class is modeled in a class diagram as a rectangle with three compartments. In this diagram the *top* compartment contains the *class name* `Account` centered horizontally in boldface type.

Middle Compartment

The *middle* compartment contains the *class's attribute* `name`, which corresponds to the instance variable of the same name in Java. Instance variable `name` is `private` in Java, so the UML class diagram lists a *minus sign (-) access modifier* before the attribute name. Following the attribute name are a *colon* and the *attribute type*, in this case `String`.

Bottom Compartment

The *bottom* compartment contains the class's **operations**, `setName` and `getName`, which correspond to the methods of the same names in Java. The UML models operations by listing the operation name preceded by an *access modifier*, in this case `+ getName`. This plus sign (+) indicates that `getName` is a *public* operation in the UML (because it's a `public` method in Java). Operation `getName` does *not* have any parameters, so the parentheses following the operation name in the class diagram are *empty*, just as they are in the method's declaration in line 14 of Fig. 3.1. Operation `setName`, also a public operation, has a `String` parameter called `name`.

Return Types

The UML indicates the *return type* of an operation by placing a colon and the return type *after* the parentheses following the operation name. `Account` method `getName` (Fig. 3.1) has a `String` return type. Method `setName` *does not* return a value (because it returns `void` in Java), so the UML class diagram *does not* specify a return type after the parentheses of this operation.

Parameters

The UML models a parameter a bit differently from Java (recall that the UML is programming-language independent) by listing the parameter name, followed by a colon and the parameter type in the parentheses after the operation name. The UML has its own data types similar to those of Java, but for simplicity, we'll use the Java data types. `Account` method `setName` (Fig. 3.1) has a `String` parameter named `name`, so Fig. 3.3 lists `name : String` between the parentheses following the method name.

3.2.5 Additional Notes on Class AccountTest

static Method main

In Chapter 2, each class we declared had one main method. Recall that main is *always* called automatically by the Java Virtual Machine (JVM) when you execute an app. You must call most other methods *explicitly* to tell them to perform their tasks. In Chapter 6, you'll learn that method toString is commonly invoked *implicitly*.

Lines 6–25 of Fig. 3.2 declare method main. A key part of enabling the JVM to locate and call method main to begin the app's execution is the static keyword (line 6), which indicates that main is a static method. A static method is special, because you can call it *without first creating an object of the class in which the method is declared*—in this case class AccountTest. We discuss static methods in detail in Chapter 6.

Notes on import Declarations

Notice the import declaration in Fig. 3.2 (line 3), which indicates to the compiler that the program uses class Scanner. As you learned in Chapter 2, classes System and String are in package java.lang, which is *implicitly* imported into *every* Java program, so all programs can use that package's classes without explicitly importing them. Most other classes you'll use in Java programs must be imported *explicitly*.

There's a special relationship between classes that are compiled in the *same* directory, like classes Account and AccountTest. By default, such classes are considered to be in the *same* package—known as the **default package**. Classes in the same package are *implicitly imported* into the source-code files of other classes in that package. Thus, an import declaration is *not* required when one class in a package uses another in the same package—such as when class AccountTest uses class Account.

The import declaration in line 3 is *not* required if we refer to class Scanner throughout this file as java.util.Scanner, which includes the *full package name and class name*. This is known as the class's **fully qualified class name**. For example, line 8 of Fig. 3.2 also could be written as

```
java.util.Scanner input = new java.util.Scanner(System.in);
```

Software Engineering Observation 3.1

The Java compiler does not require import declarations in a Java source-code file if the fully qualified class name is specified every time a class name is used. Most Java programmers prefer the more concise programming style enabled by import declarations.

3.2.6 Software Engineering with private Instance Variables and public *set* and *get* Methods

As you'll see, through the use of *set* and *get* methods, you can *validate* attempted modifications to private data and control how that data is presented to the caller—these are compelling software engineering benefits. We'll discuss this in more detail in Section 3.4.

If the instance variable were public, any **client** of the class—that is, any other class that calls the class's methods—could see the data and do whatever it wanted with it, including setting it to an *invalid* value.

You might think that even though a client of the class cannot directly access a private instance variable, the client can do whatever it wants with the variable through public *set* and *get* methods. You would think that you could peek at the private data any time with the public *get* method and that you could modify the private data at will through the public *set* method. But *set* methods can be programmed to *validate* their arguments and reject any attempts to *set* the data to bad values, such as a negative body temperature, a day in March out of the range 1 through 31, a product code not in the company's product catalog, etc. And a *get* method can present the data in a different form. For example, a Grade class might store a grade as an int between 0 and 100, but a getGrade method might return a letter grade as a String, such as "A" for grades between 90 and 100, "B" for grades between 80 and 89, etc. Tightly controlling the access to and presentation of private data can greatly reduce errors, while increasing the robustness and security of your programs.

Declaring instance variables with access modifier private is known as *information hiding*. When a program creates (instantiates) an object of class Account, variable name is *encapsulated* (hidden) in the object and can be accessed only by methods of the object's class.

Software Engineering Observation 3.2

Precede each instance variable and method declaration with an access modifier. Generally, instance variables should be declared private *and methods* public*. Later in the book, we'll discuss why you might want to declare a method* private.

Conceptual View of an Account *Object with Encapsulated Data*

You can think of an Account object as shown in Fig. 3.4. The private instance variable name is *hidden inside* the object (represented by the inner circle containing name) and *protected by an outer layer* of public methods (represented by the outer circle containing getName and setName). Any client code that needs to interact with the Account object can do so *only* by calling the public methods of the protective outer layer.

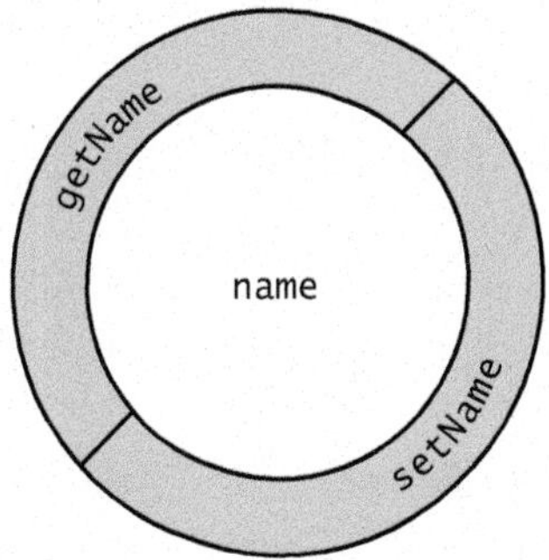

Fig. 3.4 | Conceptual view of an Account object with its encapsulated private instance variable name and protective layer of public methods.

3.3 Account Class: Initializing Objects with Constructors

As mentioned in Section 3.2, when an object of class Account (Fig. 3.1) is created, its String instance variable name is initialized to null by *default*. But what if you want to provide a name when you *create* an Account object?

Each class you declare can optionally provide a *constructor* with parameters that can be used to initialize an object of a class when the object is created. Java *requires* a constructor call for *every* object that's created, so this is the ideal point to initialize an object's instance variables. The next example enhances class `Account` (Fig. 3.5) with a constructor that can receive a name and use it to initialize instance variable `name` when an `Account` object is created (Fig. 3.6).

```
1  // Fig. 3.5: Account.java
2  // Account class with a constructor that initializes the name.
3
4  public class Account {
5     private String name; // instance variable
6
7     // constructor initializes name with parameter name
8     public Account(String name) { // constructor name is class name
9        this.name = name;
10    }
11
12    // method to set the name
13    public void setName(String name) {
14       this.name = name;
15    }
16
17    // method to retrieve the name
18    public String getName() {
19       return name;
20    }
21 }
```

Fig. 3.5 | `Account` class with a constructor that initializes the `name`.

3.3.1 Declaring an `Account` Constructor for Custom Object Initialization

When you declare a class, you can provide your own constructor to specify *custom initialization* for objects of your class. For example, you might want to specify a name for an `Account` object when the object is created, as you'll see in line 8 of Fig. 3.6:

```
Account account1 = new Account("Jane Green");
```

In this case, the `String` argument `"Jane Green"` is passed to the `Account` object's constructor and used to initialize the `name` instance variable. The preceding statement requires that the class provide a constructor that takes only a `String` parameter. Figure 3.5 contains a modified `Account` class with such a constructor.

`Account` *Constructor Declaration*

Lines 8–10 of Fig. 3.5 declare `Account`'s constructor, which *must* have the *same name* as the class. A constructor's *parameter list* specifies that the constructor requires zero or more pieces of data to perform its task. Line 8 indicates that the constructor has exactly one parameter—a `String` called `name`. When you create a new `Account` object, you'll pass a person's name to the constructor's name parameter. The constructor will then assign the name parameter's value to the *instance variable* name (line 9).

Error-Prevention Tip 3.2

Even though it's possible to do so, do not call methods from constructors. We'll explain this in Chapter 10, Object-Oriented Programming: Polymorphism and Interfaces.

***Parameter* `name` *of Class* `Account`*'s Constructor and Method* `setName`**

Recall from Section 3.2.1 that method parameters are local variables. In Fig. 3.5, the constructor and method setName both have a parameter called name. Although these parameters have the same identifier (name), the parameter in line 8 is a local variable of the constructor that's *not* visible to method setName, and the one in line 13 is a local variable of setName that's *not* visible to the constructor.

3.3.2 Class AccountTest: Initializing Account Objects When They're Created

The AccountTest program (Fig. 3.6) initializes two Account objects using the constructor. Line 8 creates and initializes the Account object account1. Keyword new requests memory from the system to store the Account object, then implicitly calls the class's constructor to *initialize* the object. The call is indicated by the parentheses after the class name, which contain the *argument* "Jane Green" that's used to initialize the new object's name. Line 8 assigns the new object to the variable account1. Line 9 repeats this process, passing the argument "John Blue" to initialize the name for account2. Lines 12–13 use each object's getName method to obtain the names and show that they were indeed initialized when the objects were *created*. The output shows *different* names, confirming that each Account maintains its *own copy* of the instance variable name.

```
1   // Fig. 3.6: AccountTest.java
2   // Using the Account constructor to initialize the name instance
3   // variable at the time each Account object is created.
4
5   public class AccountTest {
6      public static void main(String[] args) {
7         // create two Account objects
8         Account account1 = new Account("Jane Green");
9         Account account2 = new Account("John Blue");
10
11        // display initial value of name for each Account
12        System.out.printf("account1 name is: %s%n", account1.getName());
13        System.out.printf("account2 name is: %s%n", account2.getName());
14     }
15  }
```

```
account1 name is: Jane Green
account2 name is: John Blue
```

Fig. 3.6 | Using the Account constructor to initialize the name instance variable at the time each Account object is created.

Constructors Cannot Return Values
An important difference between constructors and methods is that *constructors cannot return values*, so they *cannot* specify a return type (not even `void`). Normally, constructors are declared `public`—later in the book we'll explain when to use `private` constructors.

Default Constructor
Recall that line 11 of Fig. 3.2

```
Account myAccount = new Account();
```

used `new` to create an `Account` object. The *empty* parentheses after "`new Account`" indicate a call to the class's **default constructor**—in any class that does *not* explicitly declare a constructor, the compiler provides a default constructor (which always has no parameters). When a class has only the default constructor, the class's instance variables are initialized to their *default values*. In Section 8.5, you'll learn that classes can have multiple constructors.

There's No Default Constructor in a Class That Declares a Constructor
If you declare a constructor for a class, the compiler will *not* create a *default constructor* for that class. In that case, you will not be able to create an `Account` object with the class instance creation expression `new Account()` as we did in Fig. 3.2—unless the custom constructor you declare takes *no* parameters.

Software Engineering Observation 3.3
Unless default initialization of your class's instance variables is acceptable, provide a custom constructor to ensure that your instance variables are properly initialized with meaningful values when each new object of your class is created.

Adding the Constructor to Class **`Account`***'s UML Class Diagram*
The UML class diagram of Fig. 3.7 models class `Account` of Fig. 3.5, which has a constructor with a `String name` parameter. As with operations, the UML models constructors in the *third* compartment of a class diagram. To distinguish a constructor from the class's operations, the UML requires that the word "constructor" be enclosed in **guillemets (« and »)** and placed before the constructor's name. It's customary to list constructors *before* other operations in the third compartment.

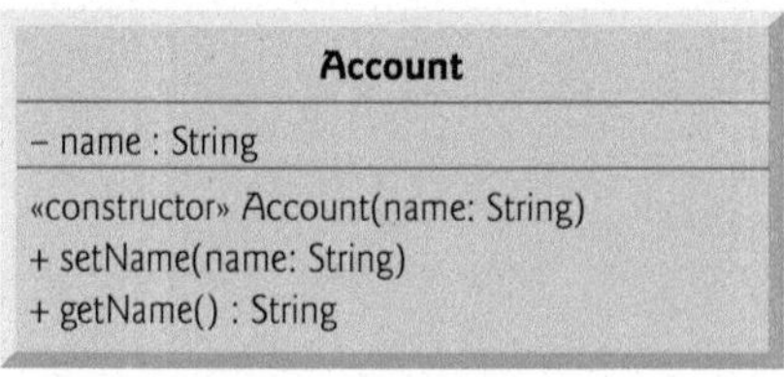

Fig. 3.7 | UML class diagram for `Account` class of Fig. 3.5.

3.4 `Account` Class with a Balance; Floating-Point Numbers

We now declare an `Account` class that maintains the *balance* of a bank account in addition to the name. Most account balances are not integers. So, class `Account` represents the account balance as a **floating-point number**—a number with a *decimal point*, such as 43.95, 0.0, –129.8873. [In Chapter 8, we'll begin representing monetary amounts precisely with class `BigDecimal` as you should do when writing industrial-strength monetary applications.]

Java provides two primitive types for storing floating-point numbers in memory—`float` and `double`. Variables of type **`float`** represent **single-precision floating-point numbers** and can hold up to *seven significant digits*. Variables of type **`double`** represent **double-precision floating-point numbers.** These require *twice* as much memory as `float` variables and can hold up to *15 significant digits*—about *double* the precision of `float` variables.

Most programmers represent floating-point numbers with type `double`. In fact, Java treats all floating-point numbers you type in a program's source code (such as 7.33 and 0.0975) as `double` values by default. Such values in the source code are known as **floating-point literals.** See Appendix D, Primitive Types, for the precise ranges of values for `floats` and `doubles`.

3.4.1 Account Class with a `balance` Instance Variable of Type `double`

Our next app contains a version of class `Account` (Fig. 3.8) that maintains as instance variables the `name` *and* the `balance` of a bank account. A typical bank services *many* accounts, each with its *own* balance, so line 7 declares an instance variable `balance` of type `double`. Every instance (i.e., object) of class `Account` contains its *own* copies of *both* the `name` and the `balance`.

```
1  // Fig. 3.8: Account.java
2  // Account class with a double instance variable balance and a constructor
3  // and deposit method that perform validation.
4
5  public class Account {
6     private String name; // instance variable
7     private double balance; // instance variable
8
9     // Account constructor that receives two parameters
10    public Account(String name, double balance) {
11       this.name = name; // assign name to instance variable name
12
13       // validate that the balance is greater than 0.0; if it's not,
14       // instance variable balance keeps its default initial value of 0.0
15       if (balance > 0.0) { // if the balance is valid
16          this.balance = balance; // assign it to instance variable balance
17       }
18    }
19
20    // method that deposits (adds) only a valid amount to the balance
21    public void deposit(double depositAmount) {
22       if (depositAmount > 0.0) { // if the depositAmount is valid
23          balance = balance + depositAmount; // add it to the balance
24       }
25    }
```

Fig. 3.8 | `Account` class with a `double` instance variable `balance` and a constructor and `deposit` method that perform validation. (Part 1 of 2.)

```
26
27      // method returns the account balance
28      public double getBalance() {
29         return balance;
30      }
31
32      // method that sets the name
33      public void setName(String name) {
34         this.name = name;
35      }
36
37      // method that returns the name
38      public String getName() {
39         return name;
40      }
41   }
```

Fig. 3.8 | `Account` class with a `double` instance variable `balance` and a constructor and `deposit` method that perform validation. (Part 2 of 2.)

`Account` *Class Two-Parameter Constructor*

The class has a *constructor* and four *methods*. It's common for someone opening an account to deposit money immediately, so the constructor (lines 10–18) now receives a second parameter—`balance` of type `double` that represents the *starting balance*. Lines 15–17 ensure that `initialBalance` is greater than `0.0`. If so, the `balance` parameter's value is assigned to the instance variable `balance`. Otherwise, the instance variable `balance` remains at `0.0`—its *default initial value*.

`Account` *Class* `deposit` *Method*

Method `deposit` (lines 21–25) does *not* return any data when it completes its task, so its return type is `void`. The method receives one parameter named `depositAmount`—a `double` value that's *added* to the instance variable `balance` *only* if the parameter value is *valid* (i.e., greater than zero). Line 23 first adds the current `balance` and `depositAmount`, forming a *temporary* sum which is *then* assigned to `balance`, *replacing* its prior value (recall that addition has a *higher* precedence than assignment). It's important to understand that the calculation on the right side of the assignment operator in line 23 does *not* modify the `balance`—that's why the assignment is necessary.

`Account` *Class* `getBalance` *Method*

Method `getBalance` (lines 28–30) allows *clients* of the class (i.e., other classes whose methods call the methods of this class) to obtain the value of a particular `Account` object's `balance`. The method specifies return type `double` and an *empty* parameter list.

`Account`*'s Methods Can All Use* `balance`

Once again, lines 15, 16, 23 and 29 use the variable `balance` even though it was *not* declared in *any* of the methods. We can use `balance` in these methods because it's an *instance variable* of the class.

3.4.2 AccountTest Class to Use Class Account

Class AccountTest (Fig. 3.9) creates two Account objects (lines 7–8) and initializes them with a *valid* balance of 50.00 and an *invalid* balance of -7.53, respectively—for the purpose of our examples, we assume that balances must be greater than or equal to zero. The calls to method System.out.printf in lines 11–14 output the account names and balances, which are obtained by calling each Account's getName and getBalance methods.

```
1  // Fig. 3.9: AccountTest.java
2  // Inputting and outputting floating-point numbers with Account objects.
3  import java.util.Scanner;
4
5  public class AccountTest {
6     public static void main(String[] args) {
7        Account account1 = new Account("Jane Green", 50.00);
8        Account account2 = new Account("John Blue", -7.53);
9
10       // display initial balance of each object
11       System.out.printf("%s balance: $%.2f%n",
12          account1.getName(), account1.getBalance());
13       System.out.printf("%s balance: $%.2f%n%n",
14          account2.getName(), account2.getBalance());
15
16       // create a Scanner to obtain input from the command window
17       Scanner input = new Scanner(System.in);
18
19       System.out.print("Enter deposit amount for account1: "); // prompt
20       double depositAmount = input.nextDouble(); // obtain user input
21       System.out.printf("%nadding %.2f to account1 balance%n%n",
22          depositAmount);
23       account1.deposit(depositAmount); // add to account1's balance
24
25       // display balances
26       System.out.printf("%s balance: $%.2f%n",
27          account1.getName(), account1.getBalance());
28       System.out.printf("%s balance: $%.2f%n%n",
29          account2.getName(), account2.getBalance());
30
31       System.out.print("Enter deposit amount for account2: "); // prompt
32       depositAmount = input.nextDouble(); // obtain user input
33       System.out.printf("%nadding %.2f to account2 balance%n%n",
34          depositAmount);
35       account2.deposit(depositAmount); // add to account2 balance
36
37       // display balances
38       System.out.printf("%s balance: $%.2f%n",
39          account1.getName(), account1.getBalance());
40       System.out.printf("%s balance: $%.2f%n%n",
41          account2.getName(), account2.getBalance());
42    }
43 }
```

Fig. 3.9 | Inputting and outputting floating-point numbers with Account objects. (Part 1 of 2.)

```
Jane Green balance: $50.00
John Blue balance: $0.00

Enter deposit amount for account1: 25.53

adding 25.53 to account1 balance

Jane Green balance: $75.53
John Blue balance: $0.00

Enter deposit amount for account2: 123.45

adding 123.45 to account2 balance

Jane Green balance: $75.53
John Blue balance: $123.45
```

Fig. 3.9 | Inputting and outputting floating-point numbers with Account objects. (Part 2 of 2.)

Displaying the Account *Objects' Initial Balances*

When method getBalance is called for account1 from line 12, the value of account1's balance is returned from line 29 of Fig. 3.8 and displayed by the System.out.printf statement (Fig. 3.9, lines 11–12). Similarly, when method getBalance is called for account2 from line 14, the value of the account2's balance is returned from line 29 of Fig. 3.8 and displayed by the System.out.printf statement (Fig. 3.9, lines 13–14). The balance of account2 is initially 0.00, because the constructor rejected the attempt to start account2 with a *negative* balance, so the balance retains its default initial value.

Formatting Floating-Point Numbers for Display

Each of the balances is output by printf with the format specifier %.2f. The **%f format specifier** is used to output values of type float or double. The .2 between % and f represents the number of *decimal places* (2) that should be output to the *right* of the decimal point in the floating-point number—also known as the number's **precision**. Any floating-point value output with %.2f will be *rounded* to the *hundredths position*—for example, 123.457 would be rounded to 123.46 and 27.33379 would be rounded to 27.33.

Reading a Floating-Point Value from the User and Making a Deposit

Line 19 (Fig. 3.9) prompts the user to enter a deposit amount for account1. Line 20 declares *local* variable depositAmount to store each deposit amount entered by the user. Unlike *instance* variables (such as name and balance in class Account), *local* variables (like depositAmount in main) are *not* initialized by default, so they normally must be initialized explicitly. As you'll learn momentarily, variable depositAmount's initial value will be determined by the user's input.

Common Programming Error 3.2

The Java compiler will issue a compilation error if you attempt to use the value of an uninitialized local variable. This helps you avoid dangerous execution-time logic errors. It's always better to get the errors out of your programs at compilation time rather than execution time.

Line 20 obtains the input from the user by calling `Scanner` object `input`'s **`nextDouble`** method, which returns a `double` value entered by the user. Lines 21–22 display the `depositAmount`. Line 23 calls object `account1`'s `deposit` method with the `depositAmount` as the method's *argument*. When the method is called, the argument's value is assigned to the parameter `depositAmount` of method `deposit` (line 21 of Fig. 3.8); then method `deposit` adds that value to the `balance`. Lines 26–29 (Fig. 3.9) output the `name`s and `balance`s of both `Accounts` *again* to show that *only* `account1`'s `balance` has changed.

Line 31 prompts the user to enter a deposit amount for `account2`. Line 32 obtains the input from the user by calling `Scanner` object `input`'s `nextDouble` method. Lines 33–34 display the `depositAmount`. Line 35 calls object `account2`'s `deposit` method with `depositAmount` as the method's *argument*; then method `deposit` adds that value to the `balance`. Finally, lines 38–41 output the `name`s and `balance`s of both `Accounts` *again* to show that *only* `account2`'s `balance` has changed.

Duplicated Code in Method `main`

The six statements at lines 11–12, 13–14, 26–27, 28–29, 38–39 and 40–41 are almost *identical*—they each output an `Account`'s `name` and `balance`. They differ only in the name of the `Account` object—`account1` or `account2`. Duplicate code like this can create *code maintenance problems* when that code needs to be updated—if *six* copies of the same code all have the same error or update to be made, you must make that change *six* times, *without making errors*. Exercise 3.15 asks you to modify Fig. 3.9 to include a `displayAccount` method that takes as a parameter an `Account` object and outputs the object's `name` and `balance`. You'll then replace `main`'s duplicated statements with six calls to `displayAccount`, thus reducing the size of your program and improving its maintainability by having *one* copy of the code that displays an `Account`'s `name` and `balance`.

Software Engineering Observation 3.4

Replacing duplicated code with calls to a method that contains one copy of that code can reduce the size of your program and improve its maintainability.

UML Class Diagram for Class `Account`

The UML class diagram in Fig. 3.10 concisely models class `Account` of Fig. 3.8. The diagram models in its *second* compartment the `private` attributes `name` of type `String` and `balance` of type `double`.

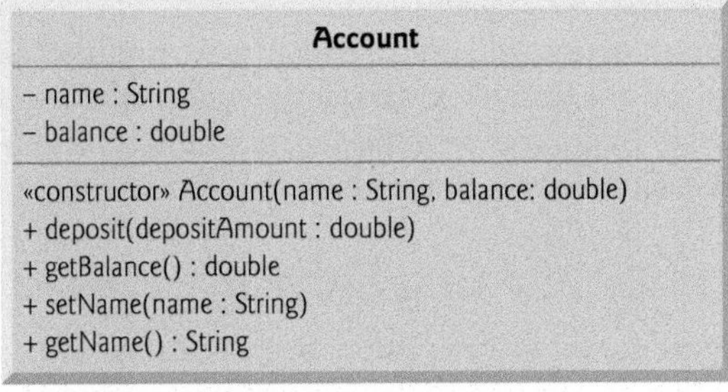

Fig. 3.10 | UML class diagram for `Account` class of Fig. 3.8.

Class Account's *constructor* is modeled in the *third* compartment with parameters name of type String and initialBalance of type double. The class's four public methods also are modeled in the *third* compartment—operation deposit with a depositAmount parameter of type double, operation getBalance with a return type of double, operation setName with a name parameter of type String and operation getName with a return type of String.

3.5 Primitive Types vs. Reference Types

Java's types are divided into primitive types and **reference types**. In Chapter 2, you worked with variables of type int—one of the primitive types. The other primitive types are boolean, byte, char, short, long, float and double, each of which we discuss in this book—these are summarized in Appendix D. All nonprimitive types are *reference types*, so classes, which specify the types of objects, are reference types.

A primitive-type variable can hold exactly *one* value of its declared type at a time. For example, an int variable can store one integer at a time. When another value is assigned to that variable, the new value replaces the previous one—which is *lost*.

Recall that local variables are *not* initialized by default. Primitive-type instance variables *are* initialized by default—instance variables of types byte, char, short, int, long, float and double are initialized to 0, and variables of type boolean are initialized to false. You can specify your own initial value for a primitive-type variable by assigning the variable a value in its declaration, as in

```
private int numberOfStudents = 10;
```

Programs use variables of reference types (normally called **references**) to store the *locations* of objects. Such a variable is said to **refer to an object** in the program. *Objects* that are referenced may each contain *many* instance variables. Line 8 of Fig. 3.2:

```
Scanner input = new Scanner(System.in);
```

creates an object of class Scanner, then assigns to the variable input a *reference* to that Scanner object. Line 11 of Fig. 3.2:

```
Account myAccount = new Account();
```

creates an object of class Account, then assigns to the variable myAccount a *reference* to that Account object. *Reference-type instance variables, if not explicitly initialized, are initialized by default to the value* null—which represents a "reference to nothing." That's why the first call to getName in line 14 of Fig. 3.2 returns null—the value of name has *not* yet been set, so the *default initial value* null is returned.

To call methods on an object, you need a reference to the object. In Fig. 3.2, the statements in method main use the variable myAccount to call methods getName (lines 14 and 24) and setName (line 19) to interact with the Account object. Primitive-type variables do *not* refer to objects, so such variables *cannot* be used to call methods.

3.6 (Optional) GUI and Graphics Case Study: A Simple GUI

This case study is designed for those who want to begin learning Java's powerful capabilities for creating graphical user interfaces (GUIs) and graphics early in the book, before our deeper discussions of these topics in Chapters 12, 13 and 22. We feature JavaFX—Java's GUI, graphics and multimedia technology of the future. The Swing version of this case study is still available on the book's Companion Website. The GUI and Graphics Case Study sections are summarized in Fig. 3.11. Each section introduces new concepts, provides examples with screen captures that show sample interactions and is followed immediately by one or more exercises in which you'll use the techniques you learned in that section.

Section or Exercise	What you'll do
Section 3.6: A Simple GUI	Display text and an image.
Section 4.15: Event Handling; Drawing Lines	In response to a `Button` click, draw lines using JavaFX graphics capabilities.
Section 5.11: Drawing Rectangles and Ovals	Draw rectangles and ovals.
Section 6.13: Colors and Filled Shapes	Draw filled shapes in multiple colors.
Section 7.17: Drawing Arcs	Draw a rainbow with arcs.
Section 8.16: Using Objects with Graphics	Store shapes as objects.
Section 10.14: Drawing with Polymorphism	Identify the similarities between shape classes and create a shape class hierarchy.
Exercise 13.9: Interactive Polymorphic Drawing Application	A capstone exercise in which you'll enable users to select each shape to draw, configure its properties (such as color and fill) and drag the mouse to size the shape.

Fig. 3.11 | Summary of the GUI and Graphics Case Study in each chapter.

In the early GUI and Graphics Case Study sections, you'll create your first graphical apps. In subsequent sections, you'll use object-oriented programming concepts to create an app that draws a variety of shapes. The case study's capstone is Exercise 13.9 in which you'll create a GUI-based drawing application that enables the user to choose each shape to draw and its color, then specify its size and location by dragging the mouse. We hope you find this case study informative and entertaining.

Chapter 22, JavaFX Graphics and Multimedia

If you enjoy working with GUI and graphics, be sure to read Chapter 22, which discusses JavaFX graphics and multimedia in detail, including JavaFX's powerful animation capabilities. The chapter features dozens of challenging and entertaining graphics and multimedia project exercises, including several game-programming exercises:

- **SpotOn** challenges the user to click moving spots before they disappear from the screen.
- **Horse Race** enhances the **SpotOn** game with a variation of the amusement-park horse-race game in which your horse moves in response to you rolling balls into a hole, hitting a target with a water gun, etc. In this app, the horse moves each time the user successfully clicks a spot.
- **Cannon** challenges the user to destroy a series of targets before time expires.

3.6.1 What Is a Graphical User Interface?

A **graphical user interface** (GUI) presents a user-friendly mechanism for interacting with an app. A GUI (pronounced "GOO-ee") gives an app a distinctive "look-and-feel." GUIs are built from **GUI components**—JavaFX refers to these as controls. **Controls** are GUI components, such as `Label` objects that display text, `TextField` objects that enable a program to receive text typed by the user and `Button` objects that users can click to initiate actions. When the user interacts with a control, such as clicking a `Button`, the control generates an **event**. Programs can respond to these events—known as **event handling**—to specify what should happen when each user interaction occurs. This first GUI and Graphics Case Study section in which you'll build a simple non-interactive GUI is a bit longer than the others, because we walk you through every step of building your first GUI.

3.6.2 JavaFX Scene Builder and FXML

In the GUI and Graphics Case Study sections, you'll use **Scene Builder**—a tool that enables you to create GUIs simply by dragging and dropping pre-built GUI components from Scene Builder's library onto a design area, then modifying and styling the GUI *without writing any code*. JavaFX Scene Builder's live editing and preview features allow you to view your GUI as you create and modify it, without compiling and running the app. You can download Scene Builder for Windows, macOS and Linux from:

```
http://gluonhq.com/labs/scene-builder/
```

FXML (FX Markup Language)

As you create and modify a GUI, JavaFX Scene Builder generates FXML (FX **Markup Language**)—a language for defining and arranging JavaFX GUI controls without writing any Java code. JavaFX uses FXML to concisely describe GUI, graphics and multimedia elements. *You do not need to know FXML to use this case study*—Scene Builder hides the FXML details from you.

3.6.3 Welcome App—Displaying Text and an Image

In this section, *without writing any code*, you'll build a GUI that displays text in a **`Label`** control and an image in an **`ImageView`** (Fig. 3.12) control. You'll use visual-programming techniques to *drag-and-drop* JavaFX components onto Scene Builder's content panel—the design area. Next, you'll use Scene Builder's **Inspector** to configure options, such as the `Label`s's text and font size, and the `ImageView`'s image. Finally, you'll view the completed GUI using Scene Builder's **Show Preview in Window** option.

3.6.4 Opening Scene Builder and Creating the File `Welcome.fxml`

Open Scene Builder so that you can create the file into which Scene Builder will place the FXML that defines the GUI. The window initially appears as shown in Fig. 3.13. **Untitled** at the top of the window indicates that Scene Builder has created a new FXML file that you have not yet saved.[2] Select **File > Save** to display the **Save As** dialog, then select a location in which to store the file, name the file `Welcome.fxml` and click the **Save** button.

2. We show the Scene Builder screen captures on Microsoft Windows 10, but Scene Builder is nearly identical on Windows, macOS and Linux. The key difference is that the menu bar on macOS is at the top of the screen, whereas the menu bar is part of the window on Windows and Linux.

Fig. 3.12 | Final **Welcome** GUI in a preview window on Microsoft Windows 10.

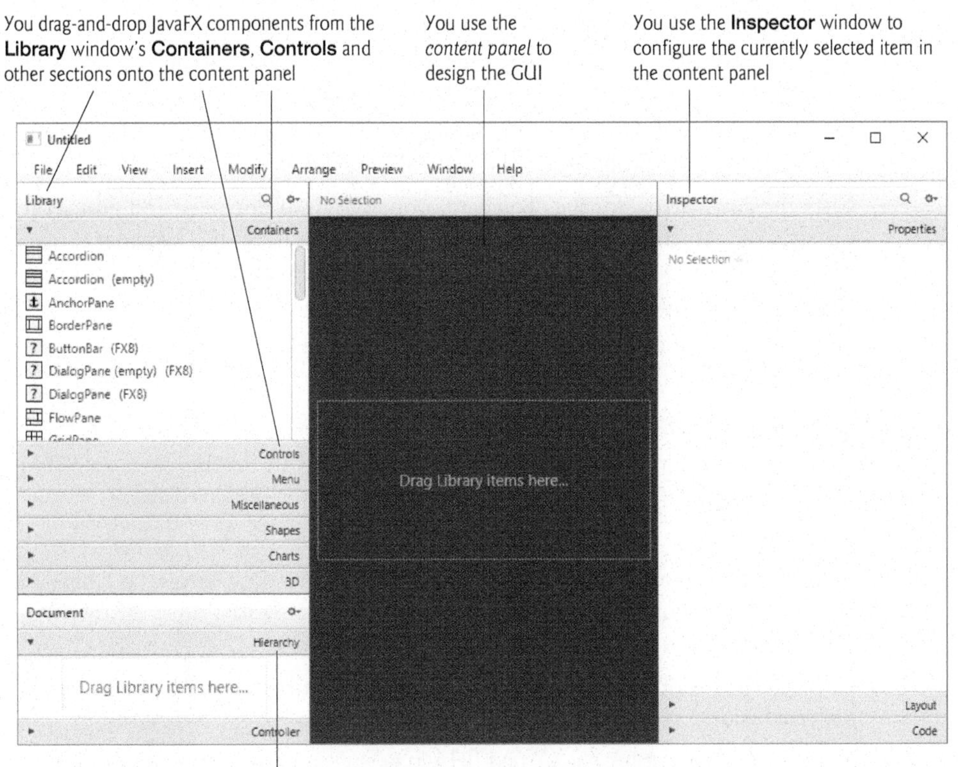

Fig. 3.13 | JavaFX Scene Builder when you first open it.

3.6.5 Adding an Image to the Folder Containing `Welcome.fxml`

The image you'll use for this app (`bug.png`) is located in the `images` subfolder of this chapter's `ch03` examples folder. To make it easy to find the image when you're ready to add it to the app, locate the `images` folder on your file system, then copy `bug.png` into the folder where you saved `Welcome.fxml`.

3.6.6 Creating a VBox Layout Container

JavaFX **Layout containers** help you arrange and size controls. For this app, you'll place a `Label` and an `ImageView` in a **`VBox` layout container**, which arranges its nodes *vertically* from top to bottom. To add a `VBox` to Scene Builder's content panel so you can begin designing the GUI, double-click **VBox** in the **Library** window's **Containers** section. (You also can drag-and-drop a **VBox** from the **Containers** section onto the content panel.)

3.6.7 Configuring the VBox

In this section, you'll specify the `VBox`'s alignment, initial size and padding.

*Specifying the **VBox**'s Alignment*

A `VBox`'s **alignment** determines the positioning of the controls in the `VBox`. In this app, we'd like the `Label` and the `ImageView` to be centered horizontally in the `VBox`, and we'd like both to be centered vertically, so that there is an equal amount of space above the `Label` and below the `ImageView` in the final design. To accomplish this:

1. Select the `VBox` in Scene Builder's content panel by clicking it once. Scene Builder displays many `VBox` properties in the Scene Builder **Inspector**'s **Properties** section.
2. Click the down arrow for the **Alignment** property's drop-down list and notice the variety of alignment values you can use. Click `CENTER` to set the **Alignment**—this indicates that the `VBox`'s contents should be centered within the `VBox` *both horizontally and vertically*.

Each property value you specify for a JavaFX object is used to set one of that object's instance variables when JavaFX creates the object at runtime.

*Specifying the **VBox**'s Preferred Size*

The **preferred size** (width and height) of a GUI's primary layout (in this case, the `VBox`) determines the default size of a JavaFX app's window. To set the preferred size:

1. Select the `VBox`.
2. Expand the **Inspector**'s **Layout** section by clicking the right arrow (▶) next to **Layout**—this expands the section and changes the arrow to a down arrow (▼). Clicking the down arrow would collapse the section.
3. Click the **Pref Width** property's text field, type `450` and press *Enter* to change the preferred width.
4. Click the **Pref Height** property's text field, type `300` and press *Enter* to change the preferred height.

3.6.8 Adding and Configuring a `Label`

Next, you'll create the `Label` that displays `Welcome to JavaFX!` on the screen.

Adding a **Label** *to the* **VBox**

Expand the Scene Builder **Library** window's **Controls** section by clicking the right arrow (▶) next to **Controls**, then drag-and-drop a **Label** from the **Controls** section onto the VBox in Scene Builder's content panel. (You also can double-click **Label** in the **Containers** section to add the Label.) Scene Builder automatically centers the Label object horizontally and vertically in the VBox, based on the VBox's **Alignment** property (Fig. 3.14).

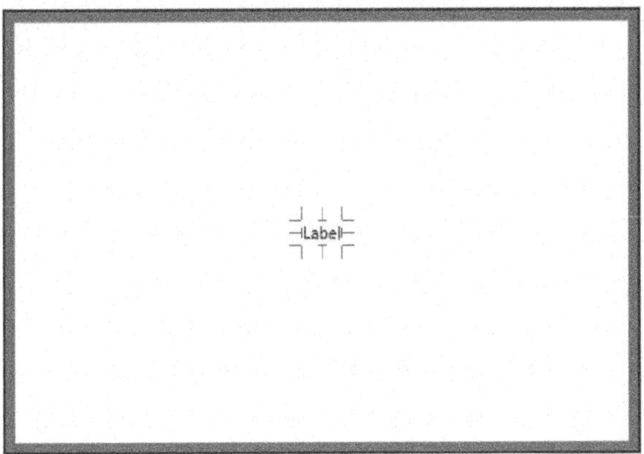

Fig. 3.14 | Label centered in a VBox.

Changing the **Label***'s Text*

You can set a Label's text either by double clicking it and typing the new text, or by selecting the Label and setting its **Text** property in the **Inspector**'s **Properties** section. Set the Label's text to "Welcome to JavaFX!".

Changing the **Label***'s Font*

For this app, we set the Label to display in a large bold font. To do so, select the Label, then in the **Inspector**'s **Properties** section, click the value to the right of the **Font** property (Fig. 3.15). In the window that appears, set the **Style** property to Bold and the **Size** property to 30. The design should now appear as shown in Fig. 3.16.

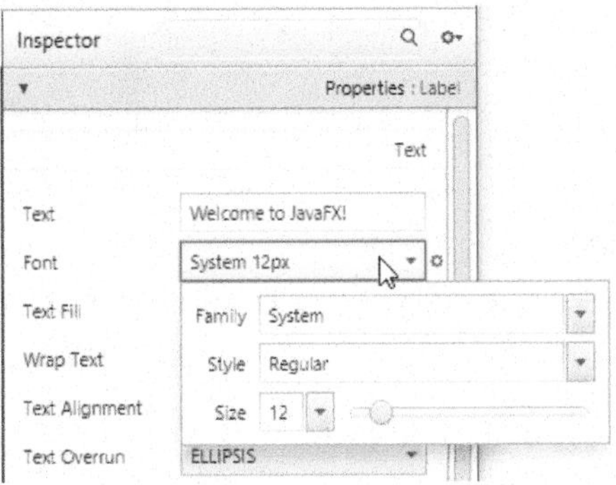

Fig. 3.15 | Setting the Label's **Font** property.

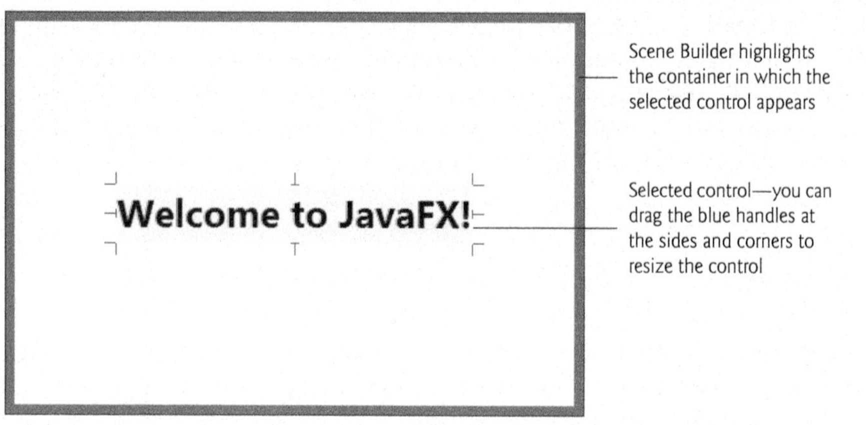
Welcome to JavaFX!
Scene Builder highlights the container in which the selected control appears
Selected control—you can drag the blue handles at the sides and corners to resize the control

Fig. 3.16 | **Welcome** GUI's design after adding and configuring a `Label`.

3.6.9 Adding and Configuring an `ImageView`

Finally, you'll add the `ImageView` that displays `bug.png`.

Adding an `ImageView` to the VBox

Drag and drop an **ImageView** from the **Library** window's **Controls** section to just below the `Label`, as shown in Fig. 3.17. You can also double-click **ImageView** in the **Library** window, in which case Scene Builder automatically places the new `ImageView` object below the `VBox`'s current contents.

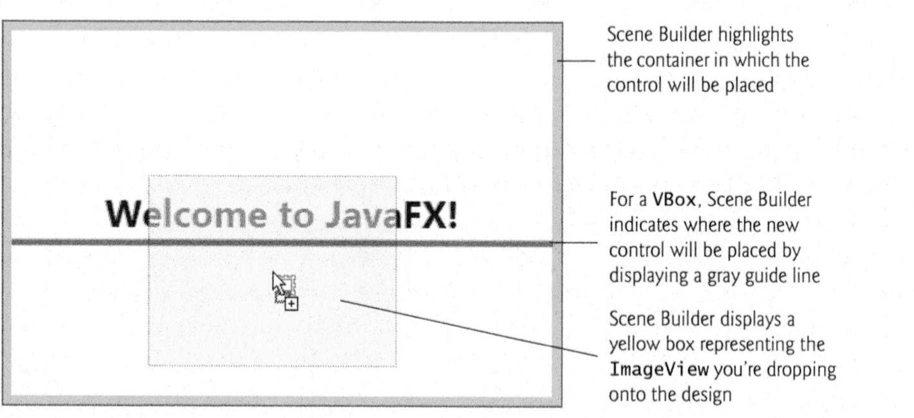
Welcome to JavaFX!
Scene Builder highlights the container in which the control will be placed
For a VBox, Scene Builder indicates where the new control will be placed by displaying a gray guide line
Scene Builder displays a yellow box representing the ImageView you're dropping onto the design

Fig. 3.17 | Dragging and dropping the `ImageView` below the `Label`.

Setting the `ImageView`'s Image

Next you'll set the image you'd like to display:

1. Select the `ImageView`, then in the **Inspector**'s **Properties** section click the ellipsis (...) button to the right of the **Image** property. By default, Scene Builder opens a

dialog showing the folder in which the FXML file is saved. This is where you placed the image file `bug.png` in Section 3.6.5.

2. Select the image file, then click **Open**. Scene Builder displays the image and resizes the `ImageView` to match the image's aspect ratio—the ratio of the image's width to its height.

Changing the `ImageView`'s Size

We'd like to display the image at its original size. If you reset the `ImageView`'s default **Fit Width** and **Fit Height** property values—which Scene Builder set for you when you dragged the `ImageView` onto the design—Scene Builder will resize the `ImageView` to the image's exact dimensions. To reset these properties:

1. Expand the **Inspector**'s **Layout** section.
2. Hover the mouse over the **Fit Width** property's value. This displays the button to the right of the property's value. Click the button and select **Reset to Default** to reset the value. This technique can be used with any property value to reset its default.
3. Repeat *Step 2* to reset the **Fit Height** property's value.

You've now completed the GUI. Scene Builder's content panel should now appear as shown in Fig. 3.18. Save the FXML file by selecting **File > Save.**

Fig. 3.18 | Completed **Welcome** GUI in Scene Builder's content panel.

3.6.10 Previewing the Welcome GUI

You can preview what the design will look like in a running application's window. To do so, select **Preview > Show Preview in Window**, which displays the window in Fig. 3.19.

Fig. 3.19 | Previewing the **Welcome** GUI on Microsoft Windows 10—only the window borders will differ on Linux, macOS and earlier Windows versions.

GUI and Graphics Case Study Exercise

3.1 Find four images of famous landmarks using websites such as Flickr. Create an app similar to the **Welcome** app in which you arrange the images in a collage. Add text that identifies each landmark. You can use images that are part of your project or you can specify the URL of an online image.

3.7 Wrap-Up

In this chapter, you learned how to create your own classes and methods, create objects of those classes and call methods of those objects to perform useful actions. You declared instance variables of a class to maintain data for each object of the class, and you declared your own methods to operate on that data. You learned how to call a method to tell it to perform its task, how to pass information to a method as arguments whose values are assigned to the method's parameters and how to receive the value returned by a method. You learned the difference between a local variable of a method and an instance variable of a class, and that only instance variables are initialized automatically. You also learned how to use a class's constructor to specify the initial values for an object's instance variables. You saw how to create UML class diagrams that model visually the methods, attributes and constructors of classes. Finally, you learned about floating-point numbers (numbers with decimal points)—how to store them with variables of primitive type `double`, how to input them with a `Scanner` object and how to format them with `printf` and format specifier `%f` for display purposes. [In Chapter 8, we'll begin representing monetary amounts precisely with class `BigDecimal`.] You may have also begun the optional GUI and Graphics case study, learning how to write your first GUI applications. In the next chapter we begin our introduction to control statements, which specify the order in which a program's actions are performed. You'll use these in your methods to specify how they should order their tasks.

Summary

Section 3.2 Instance Variables, set *Methods and* get *Methods*

- Each class you create becomes a new type that can be used to declare variables and create objects.
- You can declare new classes as needed; this is one reason Java is known as an extensible language.

Section 3.2.1 `Account` *Class with an Instance Variable, a* set *Method and a* get *Method*

- Each class declaration that begins with the access modifier (p. 70) `public` must be stored in a file that has the same name as the class and ends with the `.java` filename extension.
- Every class declaration contains keyword `class` followed immediately by the class's name.
- Class, method and variable names are identifiers. By convention all use camel-case names. Class names begin with an uppercase letter, and method and variable names begin with a lowercase letter.
- An object has attributes that are implemented as instance variables (p. 71) and carried with it throughout its lifetime.
- Instance variables exist before methods are called on an object, while the methods are executing and after the methods complete execution.
- A class normally contains one or more methods that manipulate the instance variables that belong to particular objects of the class.
- Instance variables are declared inside a class declaration but outside the bodies of the class's method declarations.
- Each object (instance) of the class has its own copy of each of the class's instance variables.
- Most instance-variable declarations are preceded with the keyword `private` (p. 71), which is an access modifier. Variables or methods declared with access modifier `private` are accessible only to methods of the class in which they're declared.
- Parameters are declared in a comma-separated parameter list (p. 72), which is located inside the parentheses that follow the method name in the method declaration. Multiple parameters are separated by commas. Each parameter must specify a type followed by a variable name.
- Variables declared in the body of a particular method are local variables and can be used only in that method. When a method terminates, the values of its local variables are lost. A method's parameters are local variables of the method.
- Every method's body is delimited by left and right braces (`{` and `}`).
- Each method's body contains one or more statements that perform the method's task(s).
- The method's return type specifies the type of data returned to a method's caller. Keyword `void` indicates that a method will perform a task but will not return any information.
- Empty parentheses following a method name indicate that the method does not require any parameters to perform its task.
- When a method that specifies a return type (p. 72) other than `void` is called and completes its task, the method must return a result to its calling method.
- The `return` statement (p. 73) passes a value from a called method back to its caller.
- Classes often provide `public` methods to allow the class's clients to *set* or *get* `private` instance variables.

Section 3.2.2 `AccountTest` *Class That Creates and Uses an Object of Class* `Account`

- A class that creates an object of another class, then calls the object's methods, is a driver class.
- `Scanner` method `nextLine` (p. 74) reads characters until a newline character is encountered, then returns the characters as a `String`.

- `Scanner` method `next` (p. 74) reads characters until any white-space character is encountered, then returns the characters as a `String`.
- A class instance creation expression (p. 74) begins with keyword `new` and creates a new object.
- A constructor is similar to a method but is called implicitly by the `new` operator to initialize an object's instance variables at the time the object is created.
- To call a method of an object, follow the object name with a dot separator (p. 75), the method name and a set of parentheses containing the method's arguments.
- Local variables are not automatically initialized. Every instance variable has a default initial value—a value provided by Java when you do not specify the instance variable's initial value.
- The default value for an instance variable of type `String` is `null`.
- A method call supplies values—known as arguments—for each of the method's parameters. Each argument's value is assigned to the corresponding parameter in the method header.
- The number of arguments in a method call must match the number of parameters in the method declaration's parameter list.
- The argument types in the method call must be consistent with the types of the corresponding parameters in the method's declaration.

Section 3.2.3 Compiling and Executing an App with Multiple Classes

- The `javac` command can compile multiple classes at once. Simply list the source-code filenames after the command with each filename separated by a space from the next. If the directory containing the app includes only one app's files, you can compile all of its classes with the command `javac *.java`. The asterisk (*) in `*.java` indicates that all files in the current directory ending with the filename extension "`.java`" should be compiled.

Section 3.2.4 **`Account`** *UML Class Diagram with an Instance Variable and* set *and* get *Methods*

- In the UML, each class is modeled in a class diagram (p. 77) as a rectangle with three compartments. The top one contains the class's name centered horizontally in boldface. The middle one contains the class's attributes, which correspond to instance variables in Java. The bottom one contains the class's operations (p. 77), which correspond to methods and constructors in Java.
- The UML represents instance variables as an attribute name, followed by a colon and the type.
- Private attributes are preceded by a minus sign (-) in the UML.
- The UML models operations by listing the operation name followed by a set of parentheses. A plus sign (+) in front of the operation name indicates that the operation is a public one in the UML (i.e., a `public` method in Java).
- The UML models a parameter of an operation by listing the parameter name, followed by a colon and the parameter type between the parentheses after the operation name.
- The UML indicates an operation's return type by placing a colon and the return type after the parentheses following the operation name.
- UML class diagrams do not specify return types for operations that do not return values.
- Declaring instance variables `private` is known as information hiding.

Section 3.2.5 Additional Notes on Class **`AccountTest`**

- You must call most methods other than `main` explicitly to tell them to perform their tasks.
- A key part of enabling the JVM to locate and call method `main` to begin the app's execution is the `static` keyword, which indicates that `main` is a `static` method that can be called without first creating an object of the class in which the method is declared.

- Most classes you'll use in Java programs must be imported explicitly. There's a special relationship between classes that are compiled in the same directory. By default, such classes are considered to be in the same package—known as the default package. Classes in the same package are implicitly imported into the source-code files of other classes in that package. An `import` declaration is not required when one class in a package uses another in the same package.
- An `import` declaration is not required if you always refer to a class with its fully qualified class name, which includes its package name and class name.

Section 3.2.6 Software Engineering with `private` *Instance Variables and* `public` set *and* get *Methods*

- Declaring instance variables `private` is known as information hiding.

Section 3.3 `Account` *Class: Initializing Objects with Constructors*

- Each class you declare can optionally provide a constructor with parameters that can be used to initialize an object of a class when the object is created.
- Java requires a constructor call for every object that's created.
- Constructors can specify parameters but not return types.
- If a class does not define constructors, the compiler provides a default constructor (p. 82) with no parameters, and the class's instance variables are initialized to their default values.
- If you declare a constructor for a class, the compiler will *not* create a *default constructor* for that class.
- The UML models constructors in the third compartment of a class diagram. To distinguish a constructor from a class's operations, the UML places the word "constructor" between guillemets (« and »; p. 82) before the constructor's name.

Section 3.4 `Account` *Class with a Balance; Floating-Point Numbers*

- A floating-point number (p. 83) is a number with a decimal point. Java provides two primitive types for storing floating-point numbers in memory—`float` and `double`.
- Variables of type `float` represent single-precision floating-point numbers and have seven significant digits. Variables of type `double` represent double-precision floating-point numbers. These require twice as much memory as `float` variables and provide 15 significant digits—approximately double the precision of `float` variables.
- Floating-point literals (p. 83) are of type `double` by default.
- The format specifier `%f` (p. 86) is used to output values of type `float` or `double`. The format specifier `%.2f` specifies that two digits of precision (p. 86) should be output to the right of the decimal point in the floating-point number.
- `Scanner` method `nextDouble` (p. 87) returns a `double` value.
- The default value for an instance variable of type `double` is `0.0` (or simply `0`), and the default value for an instance variable of type `int` is `0`.

Section 3.5 Primitive Types vs. Reference Types

- Types in Java are divided into two categories—primitive types and reference types. The primitive types are `boolean`, `byte`, `char`, `short`, `int`, `long`, `float` and `double`. All other types are reference types, so classes, which specify the types of objects, are reference types.
- A primitive-type variable can store exactly one value of its declared type at a time.
- Primitive-type instance variables are initialized by default. Variables of types `byte`, `char`, `short`, `int`, `long`, `float` and `double` are initialized to `0`. Variables of type `boolean` are initialized to `false`.

- Reference-type variables (called references; p. 88) store the location of an object in the computer's memory. Such variables refer to objects in the program. The object that's referenced may contain many instance variables and methods.
- Reference-type instance variables are initialized by default to the value `null`.
- A reference to an object (p. 88) is required to invoke an object's methods. A primitive-type variable does not refer to an object and therefore cannot be used to invoke a method.

Self-Review Exercises

3.1 Fill in the blanks in each of the following:

a) Each class declaration that begins with keyword ________ must be stored in a file that has exactly the same name as the class and ends with the `.java` filename extension.
b) Keyword ________ in a class declaration is followed immediately by the class's name.
c) Keyword ________ requests memory from the system to store an object, then calls the corresponding class's constructor to initialize the object.
d) Each parameter must specify both a(n) ________ and a(n) ________.
e) By default, classes that are compiled in the same directory are considered to be in the same package, known as the ________.
f) Java provides two primitive types for storing floating-point numbers in memory: ________ and ________.
g) Variables of type `double` represent ________ floating-point numbers.
h) `Scanner` method ________ returns a `double` value.
i) Keyword `public` is an access ________.
j) Return type ________ indicates that a method will not return a value.
k) `Scanner` method ________ reads characters until it encounters a newline character, then returns those characters as a `String`.
l) Class `String` is in package ________.
m) A(n) ________ is not required if you always refer to a class with its fully qualified class name.
n) A(n) ________ is a number with a decimal point, such as 7.33, 0.0975 or 1000.12345.
o) Variables of type `float` represent ________-precision floating-point numbers.
p) The format specifier ________ is used to output values of type `float` or `double`.
q) Types in Java are divided into two categories—________ types and ________ types.

3.2 State whether each of the following is *true* or *false*. If *false*, explain why.

a) By convention, method names begin with an uppercase first letter, and all subsequent words in the name begin with a capital first letter.
b) An `import` declaration is not required when one class in a package uses another in the same package.
c) Empty parentheses following a method name in a method declaration indicate that the method does not require any parameters to perform its task.
d) A primitive-type variable can be used to invoke a method.
e) Variables declared in the body of a particular method are known as instance variables and can be used in all methods of the class.
f) Every method's body is delimited by left and right braces (`{` and `}`).
g) Primitive-type local variables are initialized by default.
h) Reference-type instance variables are initialized by default to the value `null`.
i) Any class that contains `public static void main(String[] args)` can be used to execute an app.
j) The number of arguments in the method call must match the number of parameters in the method declaration's parameter list.

k) Floating-point values that appear in source code are known as floating-point literals and are type `float` by default.

3.3 What is the difference between a local variable and an instance variable?

3.4 Explain the purpose of a method parameter. What is the difference between a parameter and an argument?

Answers to Self-Review Exercises

3.1 a) `public`. b) `class`. c) `new`. d) type, name. e) default package. f) `float`, `double`. g) double-precision. h) `nextDouble`. i) modifier. j) `void`. k) `nextLine`. l) `java.lang`. m) `import` declaration. n) floating-point number. o) single. p) `%f`. q) primitive, reference.

3.2 a) False. By convention, method names begin with a lowercase first letter and all subsequent words in the name begin with a capital first letter. b) True. c) True. d) False. A primitive-type variable cannot be used to invoke a method—a reference to an object is required to invoke the object's methods. e) False. Such variables are called local variables and can be used only in the method in which they're declared. f) True. g) False. Primitive-type instance variables are initialized by default. Each local variable must explicitly be assigned a value. h) True. i) True. j) True. k) False. Such literals are of type `double` by default.

3.3 A local variable is declared in the body of a method and can be used only from the point at which it's declared through the end of the method declaration. An instance variable is declared in a class, but not in the body of any of the class's methods. Also, instance variables are accessible to all methods of the class. (We'll see an exception to this in Chapter 8.)

3.4 A parameter represents additional information that a method requires to perform its task. Each parameter required by a method is specified in the method's declaration. An argument is the actual value for a method parameter. When a method is called, the argument values are passed to the corresponding parameters of the method so that it can perform its task.

Exercises

3.5 *(Keyword **new**)* What's the purpose of keyword `new`? Explain what happens when you use it.

3.6 *(Default Constructors)* What is a default constructor? How are an object's instance variables initialized if a class has only a default constructor?

3.7 *(Instance Variables)* Explain the purpose of an instance variable.

3.8 *(Using Classes without Importing Them)* Most classes need to be imported before they can be used in an app. Why is every app allowed to use classes `System` and `String` without first importing them?

3.9 *(Using a Class without Importing It)* Explain how a program could use class `Scanner` without importing it.

3.10 *(set and get Methods)* Explain why a class might provide a *set* method and a *get* method for an instance variable.

3.11 *(Modified **Account** Class)* Modify class `Account` (Fig. 3.8) to provide a method called `withdraw` that withdraws money from an `Account`. Ensure that the withdrawal amount does not exceed the `Account`'s balance. If it does, the balance should be left unchanged and the method should print a message indicating `"Withdrawal amount exceeded account balance."` Modify class `AccountTest` (Fig. 3.9) to test method `withdraw`.

3.12 *(**Invoice** Class)* Create a class called `Invoice` that a hardware store might use to represent an invoice for an item sold at the store. An `Invoice` should include four pieces of information as instance variables—a part number (type `String`), a part description (type `String`), a quantity of the item being purchased (type `int`) and a price per item (`double`). Your class should have a constructor that initializes the four instance variables. Provide a *set* and a *get* method for each instance variable. In addition, provide a method named `getInvoiceAmount` that calculates the invoice amount (i.e., multiplies the quantity by the price per item), then returns the amount as a `double` value. If the quantity is not positive, it should be set to `0`. If the price per item is not positive, it should be set to `0.0`. Write a test app named `InvoiceTest` that demonstrates class `Invoice`'s capabilities.

3.13 *(`Employee` Class)* Create a class called `Employee` that includes three instance variables—a first name (type `String`), a last name (type `String`) and a monthly salary (`double`). Provide a constructor that initializes the three instance variables. Provide a *set* and a *get* method for each instance variable. If the monthly salary is not positive, do not set its value. Write a test app named `EmployeeTest` that demonstrates class `Employee`'s capabilities. Create two `Employee` objects and display each object's *yearly* salary. Then give each `Employee` a 10% raise and display each `Employee`'s yearly salary again.

3.14 *(`Date` Class)* Create a class called `Date` that includes three instance variables—a month (type `int`), a day (type `int`) and a year (type `int`). Provide a constructor that initializes the three instance variables and assumes that the values provided are correct. Provide a *set* and a *get* method for each instance variable. Provide a method `displayDate` that displays the month, day and year separated by forward slashes (/). Write a test app named `DateTest` that demonstrates class `Date`'s capabilities.

3.15 *(Removing Duplicated Code in Method `main`)* In the `AccountTest` class of Fig. 3.9, method `main` contains six statements (lines 11–12, 13–14, 26–27, 28–29, 38–39 and 40–41) that each display an `Account` object's `name` and `balance`. Study these statements and you'll notice that they differ only in the `Account` object being manipulated—`account1` or `account2`. In this exercise, you'll define a new `displayAccount` method that contains *one* copy of that output statement. The method's parameter will be an `Account` object and the method will output the object's `name` and `balance`. You'll then replace the six duplicated statements in `main` with calls to `displayAccount`, passing as an argument the specific `Account` object to output.

Modify class `AccountTest` of Fig. 3.9 to declare method `displayAccount` (Fig. 3.20) *after* the closing right brace of `main` and *before* the closing right brace of class `AccountTest`. Replace the comment in the method's body with a statement that displays `accountToDisplay`'s `name` and `balance`.

```
public static void displayAccount(Account accountToDisplay) {
   // place the statement that displays
   // accountToDisplay's name and balance here
}
```

Fig. 3.20 | Method `displayAccount` to add to class `Account`.

Recall that `main` is a `static` method, so it can be called without first creating an object of the class in which `main` is declared. We also declared method `displayAccount` as a `static` method. When `main` needs to call another method in the same class without first creating an object of that class, the other method *also* must be declared `static`.

Once you've completed `displayAccount`'s declaration, modify `main` to replace the statements that display each `Account`'s `name` and `balance` with calls to `displayAccount`—each receiving as its argument the `account1` or `account2` object, as appropriate. Then, test the updated `AccountTest` class to ensure that it produces the same output as shown in Fig. 3.9.

Making a Difference

3.16 *(Target-Heart-Rate Calculator)* While exercising, you can use a heart-rate monitor to see that your heart rate stays within a safe range suggested by your trainers and doctors. According to the American Heart Association (AHA) (`http://bit.ly/TargetHeartRates`), the formula for calculating your *maximum heart rate* in beats per minute is 220 minus your age in years. Your *target heart rate* is a range that's 50–85% of your maximum heart rate. [*Note:* These formulas are estimates provided by the AHA. Maximum and target heart rates may vary based on the health, fitness and gender of the individual. **Always consult a physician or qualified health-care professional before beginning or modifying an exercise program.**] Create a class called `HeartRates`. The class attributes should include the person's first name, last name and date of birth (consisting of separate attributes for the month, day and year of birth). Your class should have a constructor that receives this data as parameters. For each attribute provide *set* and *get* methods. The class also should include a method that calculates and returns the person's age (in years), a method that calculates and returns the person's maximum heart rate and a method that calculates and returns the person's target heart rate. Write a Java app that prompts for the person's information, instantiates an object of class `HeartRates` and prints the information from that object—including the person's first name, last name and date of birth—then calculates and prints the person's age in (years), maximum heart rate and target-heart-rate range.

3.17 *(Computerization of Health Records)* A health-care issue that has been in the news lately is the computerization of health records. This possibility is being approached cautiously because of sensitive privacy and security concerns, among others. [We address such concerns in later exercises.] Computerizing health records could make it easier for patients to share their health profiles and histories among their various health-care professionals. This could improve the quality of health care, help avoid drug conflicts and erroneous drug prescriptions, reduce costs and, in emergencies, could save lives. In this exercise, you'll design a "starter" `HealthProfile` class for a person. The class attributes should include the person's first name, last name, gender, date of birth (consisting of separate attributes for the month, day and year of birth), height (in inches) and weight (in pounds). Your class should have a constructor that receives this data. For each attribute, provide *set* and *get* methods. The class also should include methods that calculate and return the user's age in years, maximum heart rate and target-heart-rate range (see Exercise 3.16), and body mass index (BMI; see Exercise 2.33). Write a Java app that prompts for the person's information, instantiates an object of class `HealthProfile` for that person and prints the information from that object—including the person's first name, last name, gender, date of birth, height and weight—then calculates and prints the person's age in years, BMI, maximum heart rate and target-heart-rate range. It should also display the BMI values chart from Exercise 2.33.

4 Control Statements: Part I; Assignment, ++ and -- Operators

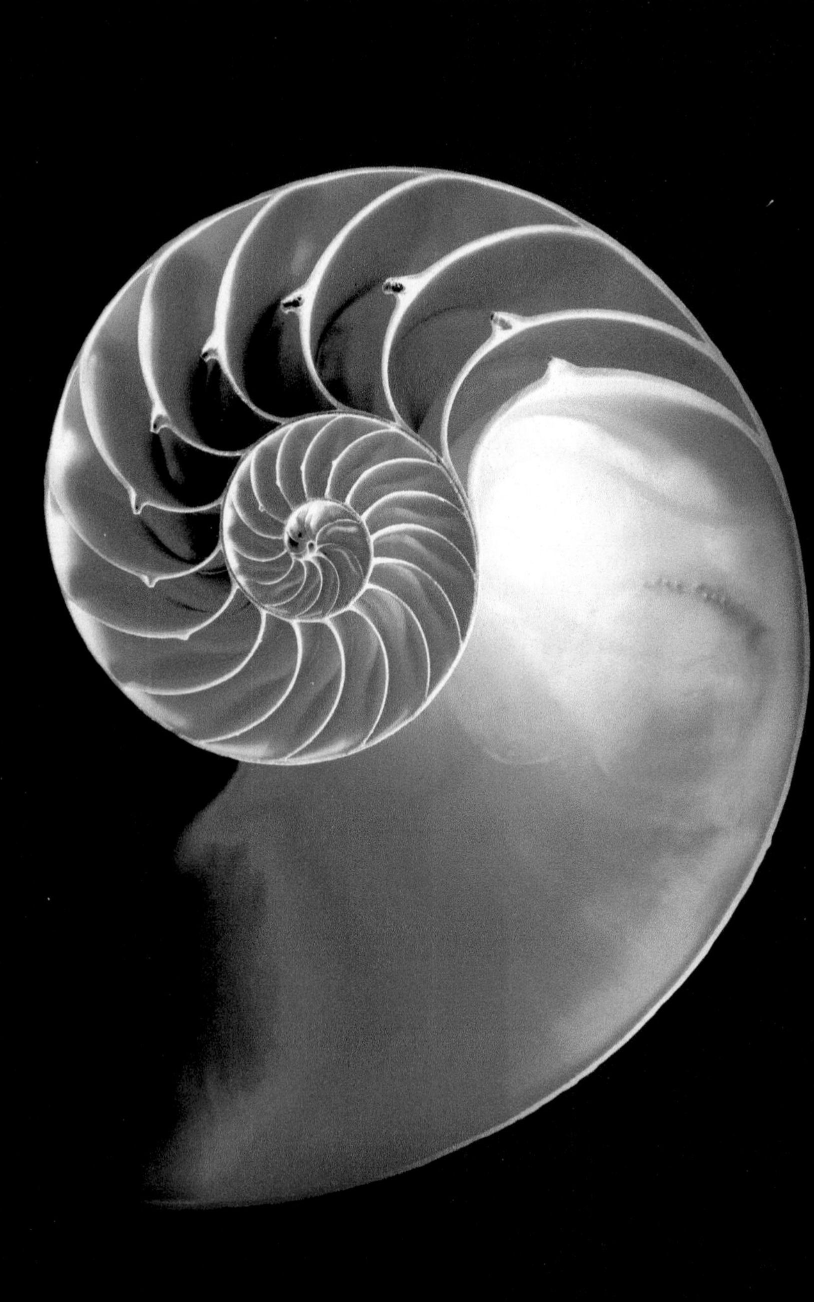

Objectives

In this chapter you'll:

- Learn basic problem-solving techniques.
- Develop algorithms through the process of top-down, stepwise refinement.
- Use the `if` and `if...else` selection statements to choose between alternative actions.
- Use the `while` iteration statement to execute statements in a program repeatedly.
- Use counter-controlled iteration and sentinel-controlled iteration.
- Use the compound assignment operator and the increment and decrement operators.
- Learn about the portability of primitive data types.

Outline

4.1 Introduction

Before writing a program to solve a problem, you should have a thorough understanding of the problem and a carefully planned approach to solving it. When writing a program, you also should understand the available building blocks and employ proven program-construction techniques. In this chapter and the next, we discuss these issues in presenting the theory and principles of structured programming. The concepts presented here are crucial in building classes and manipulating objects. We discuss Java's `if` statement in additional detail and introduce the `if...else` and `while` statements—all of these building blocks allow you to specify the logic required for methods to perform their tasks. We also introduce the compound assignment operator and the increment and decrement operators. Finally, we consider the portability of Java's primitive types.

4.2 Algorithms

Any computing problem can be solved by executing a series of actions in a specific order. A *procedure* for solving a problem in terms of

1. the **actions** to execute and
2. the **order** in which these actions execute

is called an **algorithm**. The following example demonstrates that correctly specifying the order in which the actions execute is important.

Consider the "rise-and-shine algorithm" followed by one executive for getting out of bed and going to work: (1) Get out of bed; (2) take off pajamas; (3) take a shower; (4) get dressed; (5) eat breakfast; (6) carpool to work. This routine gets the executive to work well prepared to make critical decisions. Suppose that the same steps are performed in a slightly different order: (1) Get out of bed; (2) take off pajamas; (3) get dressed; (4) take a shower; (5) eat breakfast; (6) carpool to work. In this case, our executive shows up for work soaking wet. Specifying the order in which statements (actions) execute in a program is called **program control**. This chapter investigates program control using Java's **control statements**.

4.3 Pseudocode

Pseudocode is an informal language that helps you develop algorithms without having to worry about the strict details of Java language syntax. The pseudocode we present is particularly useful for developing algorithms that will be converted to structured portions of Java programs. The pseudocode we use in this book is similar to everyday English—it's convenient and user friendly, but it's not an actual computer programming language. You'll see an algorithm written in pseudocode in Fig. 4.7. You may, of course, use your own native language(s) to develop your own pseudocode.

Pseudocode does not execute on computers. Rather, it helps you "think out" a program before attempting to write it in a programming language, such as Java. This chapter provides several examples of using pseudocode to develop Java programs.

The style of pseudocode we present consists purely of characters, so you can type pseudocode conveniently, using any text-editor program. A carefully prepared pseudocode program can easily be converted to a corresponding Java program.

Pseudocode normally describes only statements representing the *actions* that occur after you convert a program from pseudocode to Java and the program is run on a computer. Such actions might include *input*, *output* or *calculations*. In our pseudocode, we typically do *not* include variable declarations, but some programmers choose to list variables and mention their purposes.

4.4 Control Structures

Normally, statements in a program are executed one after the other in the order in which they're written. This process is called **sequential execution**. Various Java statements, which we'll soon discuss, enable you to specify that the next statement to execute is *not* necessarily the *next* one in sequence. This is called **transfer of control**.

During the 1960s, it became clear that the indiscriminate use of transfers of control was the root of much difficulty experienced by software development groups. The blame was pointed at the **goto statement** (used in most programming languages of the time), which allows you to specify a transfer of control to one of a wide range of destinations in a program. [*Note:* Java does *not* have a goto statement; however, the word goto is *reserved* by Java and should *not* be used as an identifier in programs.]

The research of Bohm and Jacopini[1] demonstrated that programs could be written *without* any goto statements. The challenge of the era for programmers was to shift their styles to "goto-less programming." The term **structured programming** became almost synonymous with "goto elimination." Not until the 1970s did most programmers start taking structured programming seriously. The results were impressive. Software develop-

1. C. Bohm and G. Jacopini, "Flow Diagrams, Turing Machines, and Languages with Only Two Formation Rules," *Communications of the ACM*, Vol. 9, No. 5, May 1966, pp. 336–371.

ment groups reported shorter development times, more frequent on-time delivery of systems and more frequent within-budget completion of software projects. The key to these successes was that structured programs were clearer, easier to debug and modify, and more likely to be bug free in the first place.

Bohm and Jacopini's work demonstrated that all programs could be written in terms of only three control structures—the **sequence structure**, the **selection structure** and the **iteration structure**. When we introduce Java's control-structure implementations, we'll refer to them in the terminology of the *Java Language Specification* as "control statements."

4.4.1 Sequence Structure in Java

The sequence structure is built into Java. Unless directed otherwise, the computer executes Java statements one after the other in the order in which they're written—that is, in sequence. The UML **activity diagram** in Fig. 4.1 illustrates a typical sequence structure in which two calculations are performed in order. Java lets you have as many actions as you want in sequence. As we'll soon see, anywhere a single action may be placed, we may place several actions in sequence.

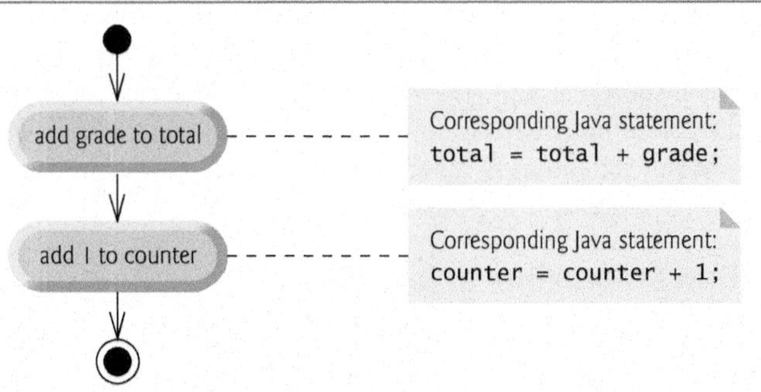

Fig. 4.1 | Sequence-structure activity diagram.

A UML activity diagram models the **workflow** (also called the **activity**) of a portion of a software system. Such workflows may include a portion of an algorithm, like the sequence structure in Fig. 4.1. Activity diagrams are composed of symbols, such as **action-state symbols** (rectangles with their left and right sides replaced with outward arcs), **diamonds** and **small circles**. These symbols are connected by **transition arrows**, which represent the *flow of the activity*—that is, the *order* in which the actions should occur.

Like pseudocode, activity diagrams help you develop and represent algorithms. Activity diagrams clearly show how control structures operate. We use the UML in this chapter and Chapter 5 to show control flow in control statements. Online Chapters 33–34 use the UML in a real-world automated-teller-machine case study.

Consider the activity diagram in Fig. 4.1. It contains two **action states**, each containing an **action expression**—"add grade to total" or "add 1 to counter"—that specifies a particular action to perform. Other actions might include calculations or input/output operations. The arrows represent **transitions**, which indicate the order in which the actions represented by the action states occur. The program that implements the activities illustrated by the diagram in Fig. 4.1 first adds `grade` to `total`, then adds `1` to `counter`.

The **solid circle** at the top of the activity diagram represents the **initial state**—the *beginning* of the workflow *before* the program performs the modeled actions. The **solid circle surrounded by a hollow circle** at the bottom of the diagram represents the **final state**—the *end* of the workflow *after* the program performs its actions.

Figure 4.1 also includes rectangles with the upper-right corners folded over. These are UML **notes** (like comments in Java)—explanatory remarks that describe the purpose of symbols in the diagram. Figure 4.1 uses notes to show the Java code associated with each action state. A **dotted line** connects each note with the element it describes. Activity diagrams normally do *not* show the corresponding Java code. We do this here to illustrate how the diagram relates to Java code. For more information on the UML, see our optional online object-oriented design case study (Chapters 33–34) or visit `http://www.uml.org`.

4.4.2 Selection Statements in Java

Java has three types of **selection statements** (discussed in this chapter and Chapter 5). The `if` *statement* either performs (selects) an action, if a condition is *true*, or skips it, if the condition is *false*. The `if...else` *statement* performs an action if a condition is *true* and performs a different action if the condition is *false*. The `switch` *statement* (Chapter 5) performs one of *many* different actions, depending on the value of an expression.

The `if` statement is a **single-selection statement** because it selects or ignores a *single* action (or, as we'll soon see, a *single group of actions*). The `if...else` statement is called a **double-selection statement** because it selects between *two different actions* (or *groups of actions*). The `switch` statement is called a **multiple-selection statement** because it selects among *many different actions* (or *groups of actions*).

4.4.3 Iteration Statements in Java

Java provides four **iteration statements** (also called **repetition statements** or **looping statements**) that enable programs to perform statements repeatedly as long as a condition (called the **loop-continuation condition**) remains *true*. The iteration statements are `while`, `do...while`, `for` and enhanced `for`. (Chapter 5 presents the `do...while` and `for` statements and Chapter 7 presents the enhanced `for` statement.) The `while` and `for` statements perform the action (or group of actions) in their bodies zero or more times—if the loop-continuation condition is initially *false*, the action (or group of actions) will *not* execute. The `do...while` statement performs the action (or group of actions) in its body *one or more* times. The words `if`, `else`, `switch`, `while`, `do` and `for` are Java keywords. A complete list of Java keywords appears in Appendix C.

4.4.4 Summary of Control Statements in Java

Java has only three kinds of control structures, which from this point forward we refer to as *control statements*: the *sequence statement*, *selection statements* (three types) and *iteration statements* (four types). Every program is formed by combining as many of these statements as is appropriate for the algorithm the program implements. We can model each control statement as an activity diagram. Like Fig. 4.1, each diagram contains an initial state and a final state that represent a control statement's entry point and exit point, respectively. **Single-entry/single-exit control statements** make it easy to build programs—we simply connect the exit point of one to the entry point of the next. We call this **control-statement stacking**. We'll learn that there's only one other way in which control statements may be connected—**control-statement nesting**—in which one control statement appears *inside* another. Thus, algorithms in Java programs are constructed from only three kinds of control statements, combined in only two ways. This is the essence of simplicity.

4.5 if Single-Selection Statement

Programs use selection statements to choose among alternative courses of action. For example, suppose that the passing grade on an exam is 60. The *pseudocode* statement

> *If student's grade is greater than or equal to 60*
> *Print "Passed"*

determines whether the *condition* "student's grade is greater than or equal to 60" is *true*. If so, "Passed" is printed, and the next pseudocode statement in order is "performed." If the condition is *false*, the *Print* statement is ignored, and the next pseudocode statement in order is performed. The indentation of the second line of this selection statement is optional, but recommended, because it emphasizes the inherent structure of structured programs.

The preceding pseudocode *If* statement may be written in Java as

```
if (studentGrade >= 60) {
   System.out.println("Passed");
}
```

The Java code corresponds closely to the pseudocode. This is one of the properties of pseudocode that makes it such a useful program development tool.

UML Activity Diagram for an `if` *Statement*

Figure 4.2 illustrates the single-selection `if` statement. This figure contains the most important symbol in an activity diagram—the *diamond*, or **decision symbol**, which indicates that a *decision* is to be made. The workflow continues along a path determined by the symbol's associated **guard conditions**, which can be *true* or *false*. Each transition arrow emerging from a decision symbol has a guard condition (specified in *square brackets* next to the arrow). If a guard condition is *true*, the workflow enters the action state to which the transition arrow points. In Fig. 4.2, if the grade is greater than or equal to 60, the program prints "Passed," then transitions to the activity's final state. If the grade is less than 60, the program immediately transitions to the final state without displaying a message.

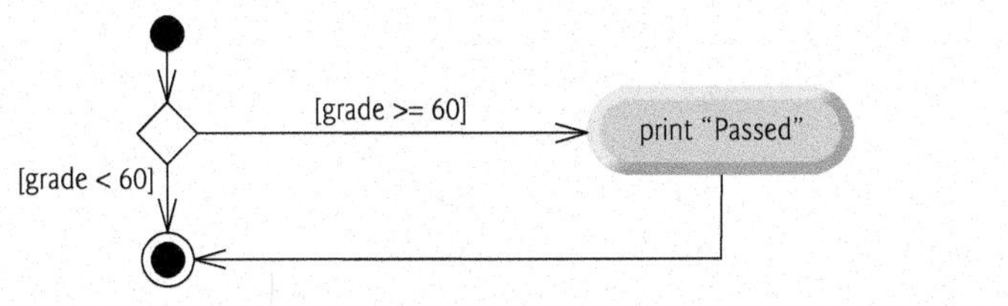

Fig. 4.2 | `if` single-selection statement UML activity diagram.

The `if` statement is a single-entry/single-exit control statement. We'll see that the activity diagrams for the remaining control statements also contain initial states, transition arrows, action states that indicate actions to perform, decision symbols (with associated guard conditions) that indicate decisions to be made, and final states.

4.6 `if...else` Double-Selection Statement

The `if` single-selection statement performs an indicated action only when the condition is `true`; otherwise, the action is skipped. The **`if...else` double-selection statement** allows you to specify an action to perform when the condition is *true* and another action when the condition is *false*. For example, the pseudocode statement

```
If student's grade is greater than or equal to 60
    Print "Passed"
Else
    Print "Failed"
```

prints "Passed" if the student's grade is greater than or equal to 60, but prints "Failed" if it's less than 60. In either case, after printing occurs, the next pseudocode statement in sequence is "performed."

The preceding *If...Else* pseudocode statement can be written in Java as

```
if (grade >= 60) {
   System.out.println("Passed");
}
else {
   System.out.println("Failed");
}
```

The body of the `else` is also indented. Whatever indentation convention you choose should be applied consistently throughout your programs.

Good Programming Practice 4.1

Indent both body statements of an `if...else` statement. Most IDEs do this for you.

Good Programming Practice 4.2

If there are several levels of indentation, each level should be indented the same additional amount of space.

UML Activity Diagram for an `if...else` Statement

Figure 4.3 illustrates the flow of control in the `if...else` statement. Once again, the symbols in the UML activity diagram (besides the initial state, transition arrows and final state) represent action states and decisions.

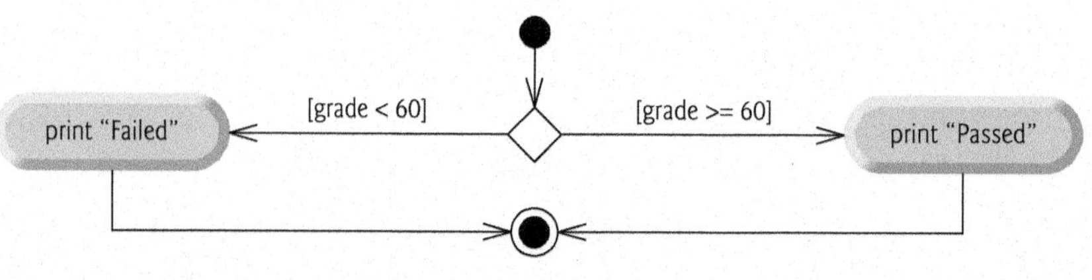

Fig. 4.3 | `if...else` double-selection statement UML activity diagram.

4.6.1 Nested if...else Statements

A program can test multiple cases by placing `if...else` statements inside other `if...else` statements to create **nested `if...else` statements**. For example, the following pseudocode represents a nested `if...else` that prints `A` for exam grades greater than or equal to 90, `B` for grades 80 to 89, `C` for grades 70 to 79, `D` for grades 60 to 69 and `F` for all other grades:

```
If student's grade is greater than or equal to 90
    Print "A"
else
    If student's grade is greater than or equal to 80
        Print "B"
    else
        If student's grade is greater than or equal to 70
            Print "C"
        else
            If student's grade is greater than or equal to 60
                Print "D"
            else
                Print "F"
```

This pseudocode may be written in Java as

```
if (studentGrade >= 90) {
   System.out.println("A");
}
else {
   if (studentGrade >= 80) {
      System.out.println("B");
   }
   else {
      if (studentGrade >= 70) {
         System.out.println("C");
      }
      else {
         if (studentGrade >= 60) {
            System.out.println("D");
         }
         else {
            System.out.println("F");
         }
      }
   }
}
```

Error-Prevention Tip 4.1

In a nested `if...else` statement, ensure that you test for all possible cases.

If variable `studentGrade` is greater than or equal to 90, the first four conditions in the nested `if...else` statement will be true, but only the statement in the `if` part of the first `if...else` statement will execute. After that statement executes, the `else` part of the "outermost" if...else statement is skipped. Many programmers prefer to write the preceding nested if...else statement as

```
if (studentGrade >= 90) {
   System.out.println("A");
}
else if (studentGrade >= 80) {
   System.out.println("B");
}
else if (studentGrade >= 70) {
   System.out.println("C");
}
else if (studentGrade >= 60) {
   System.out.println("D");
}
else {
   System.out.println("F");
}
```

The two forms are identical except for the spacing and indentation, which the compiler ignores. The latter form avoids deep indentation of the code to the right. Such indentation often leaves little room on a line of source code, forcing lines to be split.

4.6.2 Dangling-else Problem

Throughout the text, we always enclose control statement bodies in braces ({ and }). This avoids a logic error called the "dangling-else" problem. We investigate this problem in Exercises 4.27–4.29.

4.6.3 Blocks

The if statement normally expects only *one* statement in its body. To include *several* statements in the body of an if (or the body of an else for an if...else statement), enclose the statements in braces. Statements contained in braces (such as a method's body) form a **block**. A block can be placed anywhere in a method that a single statement can be placed.

The following example includes a block of multiple statements in the else part of an if...else statement:

```
if (grade >= 60) {
   System.out.println("Passed");
}
else {
   System.out.println("Failed");
   System.out.println("You must take this course again.");
}
```

In this case, if grade is less than 60, the program executes *both* statements in the body of the else and prints

```
Failed
You must take this course again.
```

Note the braces surrounding the two statements in the else clause. These braces are important. Without the braces, the statement

```
System.out.println("You must take this course again.");
```

would be outside the body of the else part of the if...else statement and would execute *regardless* of whether the grade was less than 60.

Syntax errors (such as a missing brace) are caught by the compiler. A **logic error** (e.g., when both braces in a block are left out of the program) has its effect at execution time. A **fatal logic error** causes a program to fail and terminate prematurely. A **nonfatal logic error** allows a program to continue executing but causes it to produce incorrect results.

Just as a block can be placed anywhere a single statement can be placed, it's also possible to have an empty statement. Recall from Section 2.8 that the empty statement is represented by placing a semicolon (;) where a statement would normally be.

Common Programming Error 4.1

Placing a semicolon after the condition in an if *or* if...else *statement leads to a logic error in single-selection* if *statements and a syntax error in double-selection* if...else *statements (when the* if*-part contains an actual body statement).*

4.6.4 Conditional Operator (?:)

Java provides the **conditional operator** (?:) that can be used in place of simple if...else statements. This can make your code shorter and clearer. The conditional operator is the only **ternary operator** (i.e., it takes *three* operands). Together, the operands and the ?: symbol form a **conditional expression.** The first operand (to the left of the ?) is a **boolean expression** (i.e., a *condition* that evaluates to a boolean value—**true** or **false**), the second operand (between the ? and :) is the value of the conditional expression if the condition is true and the third operand (to the right of the :) is the value of the conditional expression if the condition is false. For example, the following statement prints the value of println's conditional-expression argument:

```
System.out.println(studentGrade >= 60 ? "Passed" : "Failed");
```

The conditional expression in this statement evaluates to "Passed" if the boolean expression studentGrade >= 60 is true and to "Failed" if it's false. Thus, this statement with the conditional operator performs essentially the same function as the if...else statement shown earlier in this section. The precedence of the conditional operator is low, so the entire conditional expression is normally placed in parentheses. Conditional expressions can be used as parts of larger expressions where if...else statements cannot.

Error-Prevention Tip 4.2

Use expressions of the same type for the second and third operands of the ?: *operator to avoid subtle errors.*

4.7 Student Class: Nested if...else Statements

The example of Figs. 4.4–4.5 demonstrates a nested if...else statement that determines a student's letter grade based on the student's average in a course.

Class Student

Class Student (Fig. 4.4) has features similar to those of class Account (discussed in Chapter 3). Class Student stores a student's name and average and provides methods for manipulating these values.

```java
// Fig. 4.4: Student.java
// Student class that stores a student name and average.
public class Student {
   private String name;
   private double average;

   // constructor initializes instance variables
   public Student(String name, double average) {
      this.name = name;

      // validate that average is > 0.0 and <= 100.0; otherwise,
      // keep instance variable average's default value (0.0)
      if (average > 0.0) {
         if (average <= 100.0) {
            this.average = average; // assign to instance variable
         }
      }
   }

   // sets the Student's name
   public void setName(String name) {
      this.name = name;
   }

   // retrieves the Student's name
   public String getName() {
      return name;
   }

   // sets the Student's average
   public void setAverage(double studentAverage) {
      // validate that average is > 0.0 and <= 100.0; otherwise,
      // keep instance variable average's current value
      if (average > 0.0) {
         if (average <= 100.0) {
            this.average = average; // assign to instance variable
         }
      }
   }

   // retrieves the Student's average
   public double getAverage() {
      return average;
   }

   // determines and returns the Student's letter grade
   public String getLetterGrade() {
      String letterGrade = ""; // initialized to empty String

      if (average >= 90.0) {
         letterGrade = "A";
      }
```

Fig. 4.4 | Student class that stores a student name and average. (Part 1 of 2.)

```
53         else if (average >= 80.0) {
54            letterGrade = "B";
55         }
56         else if (average >= 70.0) {
57            letterGrade = "C";
58         }
59         else if (average >= 60.0) {
60            letterGrade = "D";
61         }
62         else {
63            letterGrade = "F";
64         }
65
66         return letterGrade;
67      }
68   }
```

Fig. 4.4 | `Student` class that stores a student name and average. (Part 2 of 2.)

The class contains:

- instance variable `name` of type `String` (line 4) to store a `Student`'s name
- instance variable `average` of type `double` (line 5) to store a `Student`'s average in a course
- a constructor (lines 8–18) that initializes the `name` and `average`—in Section 5.9, you'll learn how to express lines 13–14 and 34–35 more concisely with logical operators that can test multiple conditions
- methods `setName` and `getName` (lines 21–28) to *set* and *get* the `Student`'s `name`
- methods `setAverage` and `getAverage` (lines 31–44) to *set* and *get* the `Student`'s `average`
- method `getLetterGrade` (lines 47–67), which uses *nested* `if...else` *statements* to determine the `Student`'s *letter grade* based on the `Student`'s `average`

The constructor and method `setAverage` each use *nested* `if` *statements* (lines 13–17 and 34–38) to *validate* the value used to set the `average`—these statements ensure that the value is greater than `0.0` *and* less than or equal to `100.0`; otherwise, `average`'s value is left *unchanged*. Each `if` statement contains a *simple* condition. If the condition in line 13 is *true*, only then will the condition in line 14 be tested, and *only* if the conditions in both line 13 *and* line 14 are *true* will the statement in line 15 execute.

Software Engineering Observation 4.1

Recall from Chapter 3 that you should not call methods from constructors (we'll explain why in Chapter 10, Object-Oriented Programming: Polymorphism and Interfaces). For this reason, there is duplicated validation code in lines 13–17 and 34–38 of Fig. 4.4 and in subsequent examples.

Class `StudentTest`

To demonstrate the nested `if...else` statements in class `Student`'s `getLetterGrade` method, class `StudentTest`'s `main` method (Fig. 4.5) creates two `Student` objects (lines 5–

6). Next, lines 8–11 display each Student's name and letter grade by calling the objects' getName and getLetterGrade methods, respectively.

```
1  // Fig. 4.5: StudentTest.java
2  // Create and test Student objects.
3  public class StudentTest {
4     public static void main(String[] args) {
5        Student account1 = new Student("Jane Green", 93.5);
6        Student account2 = new Student("John Blue", 72.75);
7
8        System.out.printf("%s's letter grade is: %s%n",
9           account1.getName(), account1.getLetterGrade());
10       System.out.printf("%s's letter grade is: %s%n",
11          account2.getName(), account2.getLetterGrade());
12    }
13 }
```

```
Jane Green's letter grade is: A
John Blue's letter grade is: C
```

Fig. 4.5 | Create and test Student objects.

4.8 while Iteration Statement

An iteration statement allows you to specify that a program should repeat an action while some condition remains *true*. The pseudocode statement

While there are more items on my shopping list
Purchase next item and cross it off my list

describes the iteration during a shopping trip. The condition "there are more items on my shopping list" may be *true* or *false*. If it's *true*, then the action "Purchase next item and cross it off my list" is performed. This action will be performed *repeatedly* while the condition remains *true*. The statement(s) contained in the *While* iteration statement constitute its body, which may be a single statement or a block. Eventually, the condition will become *false* (when the shopping list's last item has been purchased and crossed off). At this point, the iteration terminates, and the first statement after the iteration statement executes.

As an example of Java's **while iteration statement**, consider a program segment that finds the first power of 3 larger than 100. After the following while statement executes, product contains the result:

```
int product = 3;

while (product <= 100) {
   product = 3 * product;
}
```

Each iteration of the while statement multiplies product by 3, so product takes on the values 9, 27, 81 and 243 successively. When product becomes 243, product <= 100 becomes false. This terminates the iteration, so the final value of product is 243. At this point, program execution continues with the next statement after the while statement.

Common Programming Error 4.2

Not providing in the body of a `while` *statement an action that eventually causes the condition in the* `while` *to become false normally results in a logic error called an infinite loop (the loop never terminates).*

UML Activity Diagram for a `while` *Statement*

The UML activity diagram in Fig. 4.6 illustrates the flow of control in the preceding `while` statement. Once again, the symbols in the diagram (besides the initial state, transition arrows, a final state and three notes) represent an action state and a decision. This diagram introduces the UML's **merge symbol**. The UML represents both the merge symbol and the decision symbol as diamonds. The merge symbol joins two flows of activity into one. In this diagram, the merge symbol joins the transitions from the initial state and from the action state, so they both flow into the decision that determines whether the loop should begin (or continue) executing.

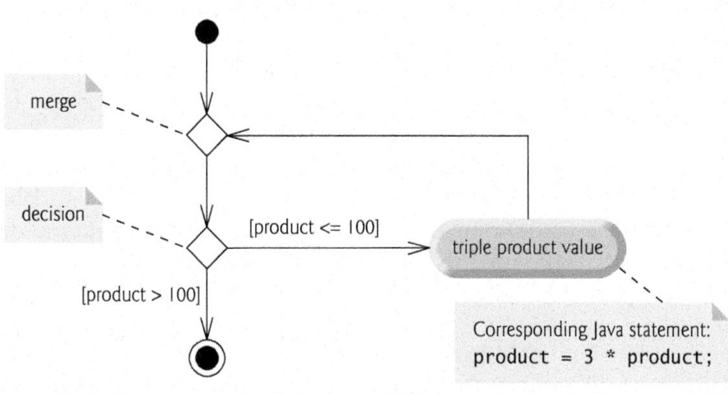

Fig. 4.6 | `while` iteration statement UML activity diagram.

The decision and merge symbols can be distinguished by the number of "incoming" and "outgoing" transition arrows. A decision symbol has one transition arrow pointing to the diamond and two or more pointing out from it to indicate possible transitions from that point. In addition, each transition arrow pointing out of a decision symbol has a guard condition next to it. A merge symbol has two or more transition arrows pointing to the diamond and only one pointing from the diamond, to indicate multiple activity flows merging to continue the activity. *None* of the transition arrows associated with a merge symbol has a guard condition.

Figure 4.6 clearly shows the iteration of the `while` statement discussed earlier in this section. The transition arrow emerging from the action state points back to the merge, from which program flow transitions back to the decision that's tested at the beginning of each iteration of the loop. The loop continues to execute until the guard condition `product > 100` becomes true. Then the `while` statement exits (reaches its final state), and control passes to the next statement in sequence in the program.

4.9 Formulating Algorithms: Counter-Controlled Iteration

To illustrate how algorithms are developed, we solve two variations of a problem that averages student grades. Consider the following problem statement:

> *A class of ten students took a quiz. The grades (integers in the range 0–100) for this quiz are available to you. Determine the class average on the quiz.*

The class average is equal to the sum of the grades divided by the number of students. The algorithm for solving this problem on a computer must input each grade, keep track of the total of all grades input, perform the averaging calculation and print the result.

Pseudocode Algorithm with Counter-Controlled Iteration

Let's use pseudocode to list the actions to execute and specify the order in which they should execute. We use **counter-controlled iteration** to input the grades one at a time. This technique uses a variable called a **counter** (or **control variable**) to control the number of times a set of statements will execute. Counter-controlled iteration is often called **definite iteration**, because the number of iterations is known *before* the loop begins executing. In this example, iteration terminates when the counter exceeds 10. This section presents a fully developed pseudocode algorithm (Fig. 4.7) and a corresponding Java program (Fig. 4.8) that implements the algorithm. In Section 4.10, we demonstrate how to use pseudocode to develop such an algorithm from scratch.

Note the references in the algorithm of Fig. 4.7 to a total and a counter. A **total** is a variable used to accumulate the sum of several values. A counter is a variable used to count—in this case, the grade counter indicates which of the 10 grades is about to be entered by the user. Variables used to store totals are normally initialized to zero before being used in a program.

Software Engineering Observation 4.2

Experience has shown that the most difficult part of solving a problem on a computer is developing the algorithm for the solution. Once a correct algorithm has been specified, producing a working Java program from it is usually straightforward.

```
Set total to zero
Set grade counter to one

While grade counter is less than or equal to ten
    Prompt the user to enter the next grade
    Input the next grade
    Add the grade into the total
    Add one to the grade counter

Set the class average to the total divided by ten
Print the class average
```

Fig. 4.7 | Pseudocode algorithm that uses counter-controlled iteration to solve the class-average problem.

Implementing Counter-Controlled Iteration

In Fig. 4.8, class `ClassAverage`'s `main` method implements the class-averaging algorithm described by the pseudocode in Fig. 4.7—it allows the user to enter 10 grades, then calculates and displays the average.

```
// Fig. 4.8: ClassAverage.java
// Solving the class-average problem using counter-controlled iteration.
import java.util.Scanner; // program uses class Scanner

public class ClassAverage {
   public static void main(String[] args) {
      // create Scanner to obtain input from command window
      Scanner input = new Scanner(System.in);

      // initialization phase
      int total = 0;  // initialize sum of grades entered by the user
      int gradeCounter = 1; // initialize # of grade to be entered next

      // processing phase uses counter-controlled iteration
      while (gradeCounter <= 10) { // loop 10 times
         System.out.print("Enter grade: "); // prompt
         int grade = input.nextInt(); // input next grade
         total = total + grade; // add grade to total
         gradeCounter = gradeCounter + 1; // increment counter by 1
      }

      // termination phase
      int average = total / 10; // integer division yields integer result

      // display total and average of grades
      System.out.printf("%nTotal of all 10 grades is %d%n", total);
      System.out.printf("Class average is %d%n", average);
   }
}
```

```
Enter grade: 67
Enter grade: 78
Enter grade: 89
Enter grade: 67
Enter grade: 87
Enter grade: 98
Enter grade: 93
Enter grade: 85
Enter grade: 82
Enter grade: 100

Total of all 10 grades is 846
Class average is 84
```

Fig. 4.8 | Solving the class-average problem using counter-controlled iteration.

Local Variables in Method `main`

Line 8 declares and initializes `Scanner` variable `input`, which is used to read values entered by the user. Lines 11, 12, 17 and 23 declare local variables `total`, `gradeCounter`, `grade` and `average`, respectively, to be of type `int`. Variable `grade` stores the user input.

These declarations appear in the body of method `main`. Recall that variables declared in a method body are local variables and can be used only from the line of their declaration to the closing right brace of the method declaration. A local variable's declaration must appear *before* the variable is used in that method. A local variable cannot be accessed outside the method in which it's declared. Variable `grade`, declared in the body of the `while` loop, can be used only in that block.

Initialization Phase: Initializing Variables `total` *and* `gradeCounter`

The assignments (in lines 11–12) initialize `total` to `0` and `gradeCounter` to `1`. These initializations occur *before* the variables are used in calculations.

Common Programming Error 4.3

Using the value of a local variable before it's initialized results in a compilation error. All local variables must be initialized before their values are used in expressions.

Error-Prevention Tip 4.3

Initialize each total and counter, either in its declaration or in an assignment statement. Totals are normally initialized to 0. Counters are normally initialized to 0 or 1, depending on how they're used (we'll show examples of when to use 0 and when to use 1).

Processing Phase: Reading 10 Grades from the User

Line 15 indicates that the `while` statement should continue looping (also called **iterating**) as long as `gradeCounter`'s value is less than or equal to 10. While this condition remains *true*, the `while` statement repeatedly executes the statements between the braces that delimit its body (lines 15–20).

Line 16 displays the prompt `"Enter grade: "`. Line 17 reads the grade entered by the user and assigns it to variable `grade`. Then line 18 adds the new `grade` entered by the user to the `total` and assigns the result to `total`, which replaces its previous value.

Line 19 adds `1` to `gradeCounter` to indicate that the program processed a grade and is ready to input the next grade from the user. Incrementing `gradeCounter` eventually causes it to exceed 10. Then the loop terminates, because its condition (line 15) becomes *false*.

Termination Phase: Calculating and Displaying the Class Average

When the loop terminates, line 23 performs the averaging calculation and assigns its result to the variable `average`. Line 26 uses `System.out`'s `printf` method to display the text `"Total of all 10 grades is "` followed by variable `total`'s value. Line 27 then uses `printf` to display the text `"Class average is "` followed by variable `average`'s value. When execution reaches line 28, the program terminates.

Notice that this example contains only one class, with method `main` performing all the work. In this chapter and in Chapter 3, you've seen examples consisting of two classes—one containing instance variables and methods that perform tasks using those variables and one containing method `main`, which creates an object of the other class and calls its methods. Occasionally, when it does not make sense to try to create a reusable class to demonstrate a concept, we'll place the program's statements entirely within a single class's `main` method.

Notes on Integer Division and Truncation

The averaging calculation performed by method `main` produces an integer result. The program's output indicates that the sum of the grade values in the sample execution is 846, which, when divided by 10, should yield the floating-point number 84.6. However, the result of the calculation `total / 10` (line 23 of Fig. 4.8) is the integer 84, because `total` and `10` are both integers. Dividing two integers results in **integer division**—any fractional part of the calculation is **truncated** (i.e., *lost*). In the next section we'll see how to obtain a floating-point result from the averaging calculation.

Common Programming Error 4.4

Assuming that integer division rounds (rather than truncates) can lead to incorrect results. For example, 7 ÷ 4, which yields 1.75 in conventional arithmetic, truncates to 1 in integer arithmetic, rather than rounding to 2.

A Note about Arithmetic Overflow

In Fig. 4.8, line 18

```
total = total + grade; // add grade to total
```

added each `grade` entered by the user to the `total`. Even this simple statement has a *potential* problem—adding the integers could result in a value that's *too large* to store in an `int` variable. This is known as **arithmetic overflow** and causes *undefined behavior*, which can lead to unintended results, as discussed at

```
http://en.wikipedia.org/wiki/
   Integer_overflow#Security_ramifications
```

Figure 2.7's `Addition` program had the same issue in line 17, which calculated the sum of two `int` values entered by the user:

```
int sum = number1 + number2; // add numbers, then store total in sum
```

The maximum and minimum values that can be stored in an `int` variable are represented by the constants `Integer.MIN_VALUE` and `Integer.MAX_VALUE`, respectively. There are similar constants for the other integral types and for floating-point types. Each primitive type has a corresponding class type in package `java.lang`. You can see the values of these constants in each class's online documentation. The online documentation for class `Integer` is located at:

```
http://docs.oracle.com/javase/8/docs/api/java/lang/Integer.html
```

It's considered a good practice to ensure, *before* you perform arithmetic calculations like those in line 18 of Fig. 4.8 and line 17 of Fig. 2.7, that they will *not* overflow. The code for doing this is shown on the CERT website:

```
http://www.securecoding.cert.org
```

Just search for guideline "NUM00-J." The code uses the `&&` (logical AND) and `||` (logical OR) operators, which are introduced in Chapter 5. In industrial-strength code, you should perform checks like these for *all* calculations.

A Deeper Look at Receiving User Input

Whenever a program receives input from the user, various problems might occur. For example, in line 17 of Fig. 4.8

```
int grade = input.nextInt(); // input next grade
```

we assume the user will enter an integer grade in the range 0 to 100. However, the person entering a grade could enter an integer less than 0, an integer greater than 100, an integer outside the range of values that can be stored in an `int` variable, a number containing a decimal point or a value containing letters or special symbols that's not even an integer.

To ensure that inputs are valid, industrial-strength programs must test for all possible erroneous cases. A program that inputs grades should **validate** the grades by using **range checking** to ensure that they are values from 0 to 100. You can then ask the user to reenter any value that's out of range. If a program requires inputs from a specific set of values (e.g., nonsequential product codes), you can ensure that each input matches a value in the set.

4.10 Formulating Algorithms: Sentinel-Controlled Iteration

Let's generalize Section 4.9's class-average problem. Consider the following problem:

> *Develop a class-averaging program that processes grades for an arbitrary number of students each time it's run.*

In the previous class-average example, the problem statement specified the number of students, so the number of grades (10) was known in advance. In this example, no indication is given of how many grades the user will enter during the program's execution. The program must process an arbitrary number of grades. How can it determine when to stop the input of grades? How will it know when to calculate and print the class average?

One way to solve this problem is to use a special value called a **sentinel value** (also called a **signal value**, a **dummy value** or a **flag value**) to indicate "end of data entry." The user enters grades until all legitimate grades have been entered. The user then types the sentinel value to indicate that no more grades will be entered. **Sentinel-controlled iteration** is often called **indefinite iteration** because the number of iterations is *not* known before the loop begins executing.

Clearly, a sentinel value must be chosen that cannot be confused with an acceptable input value. Grades on a quiz are nonnegative integers, so –1 is an acceptable sentinel value for this problem. Thus, a run of the class-average program might process a stream of inputs such as 95, 96, 75, 74, 89 and –1. The program would then compute and print the class average for the grades 95, 96, 75, 74 and 89; since –1 is the sentinel value, it should *not* enter into the averaging calculation.

Developing the Pseudocode Algorithm with Top-Down, Stepwise Refinement: The Top and First Refinement

We approach this class-average program with a technique called **top-down, stepwise refinement**, which is essential to the development of well-structured programs. We begin with a pseudocode representation of the **top**—a single statement that conveys the overall function of the program:

> *Determine the class average for the quiz*

The top is, in effect, a *complete* representation of a program. Unfortunately, the top rarely conveys sufficient detail from which to write a Java program. So we now begin the refinement process. We divide the top into a series of smaller tasks and list these in the order in which they'll be performed. This results in the following **first refinement**:

Initialize variables
Input, sum and count the quiz grades
Calculate and print the class average

This refinement uses only the *sequence structure*—the steps listed should execute in order, one after the other.

Software Engineering Observation 4.3

Each refinement, as well as the top itself, is a complete specification of the algorithm—only the level of detail varies.

Software Engineering Observation 4.4

Many programs can be divided logically into three phases: an initialization phase *that initializes the variables; a* processing phase *that inputs data values and adjusts program variables accordingly; and a* termination phase *that calculates and outputs the final results.*

Proceeding to the Second Refinement

The preceding Software Engineering Observation is often all you need for the first refinement in the top-down process. To proceed to the next level of refinement—that is, the **second refinement**—we commit to specific variables. In this example, we need a running total of the numbers, a count of how many numbers have been processed, a variable to receive the value of each grade as it's input by the user and a variable to hold the calculated average. The pseudocode statement

Initialize variables

can be refined as follows:

Initialize total to zero
Initialize counter to zero

Only the variables *total* and *counter* need to be initialized before they're used. The variables *average* and *grade* (for the calculated average and the user input, respectively) need not be initialized, because their values will be replaced as they're calculated or input.

The pseudocode statement

Input, sum and count the quiz grades

requires *iteration* to successively input each grade. We do not know in advance how many grades will be entered, so we'll use sentinel-controlled iteration. The user enters grades one at a time. After entering the last grade, the user enters the sentinel value. The program tests for the sentinel value after each grade is input and terminates the loop when the user enters the sentinel value. The second refinement of the preceding pseudocode statement is then

```
Prompt the user to enter the first grade
Input the first grade (possibly the sentinel)

While the user has not yet entered the sentinel
    Add this grade into the running total
    Add one to the grade counter
    Prompt the user to enter the next grade
    Input the next grade (possibly the sentinel)
```

In pseudocode, we do *not* use braces around the statements that form the body of the *While* structure. We simply indent the statements under the *While* to show that they belong to the *While*. Again, pseudocode is only an informal program development aid.

The pseudocode statement

```
Calculate and print the class average
```

can be refined as follows:

```
If the counter is not equal to zero
    Set the average to the total divided by the counter
    Print the average
Else
    Print "No grades were entered"
```

We're careful here to test for the possibility of *division by zero*—a *logic error* that, if undetected, would cause the program to fail or produce invalid output. The complete second refinement of the pseudocode for the class-average problem is shown in Fig. 4.9.

```
Initialize total to zero
Initialize counter to zero

Prompt the user to enter the first grade
Input the first grade (possibly the sentinel)

While the user has not yet entered the sentinel
    Add this grade into the running total
    Add one to the grade counter
    Prompt the user to enter the next grade
    Input the next grade (possibly the sentinel)

If the counter is not equal to zero
    Set the average to the total divided by the counter
    Print the average
Else
    Print "No grades were entered"
```

Fig. 4.9 | Class-average pseudocode algorithm with sentinel-controlled iteration.

Error-Prevention Tip 4.4

When performing division (/) or remainder (%) calculations in which the right operand could be zero, test for this and handle it (e.g., display an error message) rather than allowing the error to occur.

In Fig. 4.7 and Fig. 4.9, we included blank lines and indentation in the pseudocode to make it more readable. The blank lines separate the algorithms into their phases and set off control statements; the indentation emphasizes the bodies of the control statements.

The pseudocode algorithm in Fig. 4.9 solves the more general class-average problem. This algorithm was developed after two refinements. Sometimes more are needed.

Software Engineering Observation 4.5

Terminate the top-down, stepwise refinement process when you've specified the pseudocode algorithm in sufficient detail for you to convert the pseudocode to Java. Normally, implementing the Java program is then straightforward.

Software Engineering Observation 4.6

Some programmers do not use program development tools like pseudocode. They feel that their ultimate goal is to solve the problem on a computer and that writing pseudocode merely delays the production of final outputs. Although this may work for simple and familiar problems, it can lead to serious errors and delays in large, complex projects.

Implementing Sentinel-Controlled Iteration

In Fig. 4.10, method `main` implements the pseudocode algorithm of Fig. 4.9. Although each grade is an integer, the averaging calculation is likely to produce a number with a *decimal point*—in other words, a real (floating-point) number. The type `int` cannot represent such a number, so this class uses type `double` to do so. You'll also see that control statements may be *stacked* on top of one another (in sequence). The `while` statement (lines 20–27) is followed in sequence by an `if...else` statement (lines 31–42). Much of the code in this program is identical to that in Fig. 4.8, so we concentrate on the new concepts.

```
1  // Fig. 4.10: ClassAverage.java
2  // Solving the class-average problem using sentinel-controlled iteration.
3  import java.util.Scanner; // program uses class Scanner
4
5  public class ClassAverage {
6     public static void main(String[] args) {
7        // create Scanner to obtain input from command window
8        Scanner input = new Scanner(System.in);
9
10       // initialization phase
11       int total = 0; // initialize sum of grades
12       int gradeCounter = 0; // initialize # of grades entered so far
13
```

Fig. 4.10 | Solving the class-average problem using sentinel-controlled iteration. (Part 1 of 2.)

```
14        // processing phase
15        // prompt for input and read grade from user
16        System.out.print("Enter grade or -1 to quit: ");
17        int grade = input.nextInt();
18
19        // loop until sentinel value read from user
20        while (grade != -1) {
21           total = total + grade; // add grade to total
22           gradeCounter = gradeCounter + 1; // increment counter
23
24           // prompt for input and read next grade from user
25           System.out.print("Enter grade or -1 to quit: ");
26           grade = input.nextInt();
27        }
28
29        // termination phase
30        // if user entered at least one grade...
31        if (gradeCounter != 0) {
32           // use number with decimal point to calculate average of grades
33           double average = (double) total / gradeCounter;
34
35           // display total and average (with two digits of precision)
36           System.out.printf("%nTotal of the %d grades entered is %d%n",
37              gradeCounter, total);
38           System.out.printf("Class average is %.2f%n", average);
39        }
40        else { // no grades were entered, so output appropriate message
41           System.out.println("No grades were entered");
42        }
43     }
44  }
```

```
Enter grade or -1 to quit: 97
Enter grade or -1 to quit: 88
Enter grade or -1 to quit: 72
Enter grade or -1 to quit: -1

Total of the 3 grades entered is 257
Class average is 85.67
```

Fig. 4.10 | Solving the class-average problem using sentinel-controlled iteration. (Part 2 of 2.)

Program Logic for Sentinel-Controlled Iteration vs. Counter-Controlled Iteration

Line 12 initializes `gradeCounter` to `0`, because no grades have been entered yet. Remember that this program uses *sentinel-controlled iteration* to input the grades. To keep an accurate record of the number of grades entered, the program increments `gradeCounter` only when the user enters a valid grade.

Compare the logic for sentinel-controlled iteration used here with that for counter-controlled iteration in Fig. 4.8. In counter-controlled iteration, the `while` statement (lines 15–20 of Fig. 4.8) reads a value from the user for the specified number of iterations. In sentinel-controlled iteration, the program reads the first value (lines 16–17 of Fig. 4.10) *before* reaching the `while`. This value determines whether the program's flow of control should enter the `while`'s body. If the condition is `false`, the user entered the sentinel value, so the while's body does not execute (i.e., no grades were entered). If, on the other hand, the condition is true, the body executes, and the loop adds the grade value to the total and increments the gradeCounter (lines 21–22). Next, lines 25–26 *in the loop body* input another value from the user. Then, program control reaches the while's closing right brace (line 27), so execution continues by testing the while's condition (line 20), using the most recent grade input by the user. The value of grade is always input from the user immediately before the program tests the while condition, so the program can determine whether the value just input is the sentinel value *before* processing that value (i.e., adds it to the total). If the sentinel value is input, the loop terminates, and the program does not add –1 to the total.

Good Programming Practice 4.3

In a sentinel-controlled loop, prompts should remind the user of the sentinel.

After the loop terminates, the if...else statement at lines 31–42 executes. The condition at line 31 determines whether any grades were input. If none were input, the else part (lines 40–42) of the if...else statement executes and displays the message "No grades were entered" and the program terminates.

Braces in a while *statement*

Notice the while statement's *block* in Fig. 4.10 (lines 20–27). Without the braces, the loop would consider its body to be only the first statement, which adds the grade to the total. The last three statements in the block would fall outside the loop body, causing the computer to interpret the code incorrectly as follows:

```
while (grade != -1)
   total = total + grade; // add grade to total
gradeCounter = gradeCounter + 1; // increment counter

// prompt for input and read next grade from user
System.out.print("Enter grade or -1 to quit: ");
grade = input.nextInt();
```

The preceding code would cause an *infinite loop* in the program if the user did not input the sentinel -1 at line 17 (before the while statement).

Common Programming Error 4.5

Omitting the braces that delimit a block can lead to logic errors, such as infinite loops. To prevent this problem, some programmers enclose the body of every control statement in braces, even if the body contains only a single statement.

Explicitly and Implicitly Converting Between Primitive Types

If at least one grade was entered, line 33 of Fig. 4.10 calculates the average of the grades. Recall from Fig. 4.8 that integer division yields an integer result. Even though variable average is declared as a double, if we had written the averaging calculation as

```
double average = total / gradeCounter;
```

it would lose the fractional part of the quotient *before* the result of the division is assigned to average. This occurs because total and gradeCounter are *both* integers, and integer division yields an integer result.

Most averages are not whole numbers (e.g., 0, –22 and 1024). So, we calculate the class average in this example as a floating-point number. To perform a floating-point calculation with integer values, we must *temporarily* treat these values as floating-point numbers in the calculation. Java provides the **unary cast operator** to accomplish this task. Line 33 of Fig. 4.10 uses the **(double)** cast operator to create a *temporary* floating-point copy of its operand `total` (which appears to the operator's right). Using a cast operator in this manner is called **explicit conversion** or **type casting**. The value stored in `total` is still an integer.

The calculation now consists of a floating-point value (the temporary `double` copy of `total`) divided by the integer `gradeCounter`. Java can evaluate only arithmetic expressions in which the operands' types are *identical.* To ensure this, Java performs an operation called **promotion** (or **implicit conversion**) on selected operands. For example, in an expression containing `int` and `double` values, the `int` values are promoted to `double` values for use in the expression. In this example, the value of `gradeCounter` is promoted to type `double`, then floating-point division is performed and the result of the calculation is assigned to `average`. As long as the `(double)` cast operator is applied to *any* variable in the calculation, the calculation will yield a `double` result. Later in this chapter, we discuss all the primitive types. You'll learn more about the promotion rules in Section 6.7.

Common Programming Error 4.6

A cast operator can be used to convert between primitive numeric types, such as `int` *and* `double`*, and between related reference types (as we discuss in Chapter 10, Object-Oriented Programming: Polymorphism and Interfaces). Casting to the wrong type may cause compilation errors or runtime errors.*

You form a cast operator by placing parentheses around any type's name. The operator is a **unary operator**—it takes only one operand. Java also has unary plus (+) and minus (-) operators, so you can write expressions like `-7` or `+5`. Cast operators associate from *right to left* and have the same precedence as other unary operators. This precedence is one level higher than that of the **multiplicative operators** `*`, `/` and `%`. (See the operator precedence chart in Appendix A.) We indicate the cast operator with the notation `(`*type*`)` in our precedence charts, to indicate that any type name can be used to form a cast operator.

Line 38 of Fig. 4.10 displays the class average. In this example, we display the class average *rounded* to the nearest hundredth. The format specifier `%.2f` in `printf`'s format control string indicates that variable `average`'s value should be displayed with two digits of precision to the right of the decimal point—indicated by `.2` in the format specifier. The three grades entered during the sample execution total 257, which yields the average 85.666666…. Method `printf` uses the precision in the format specifier to round the value to the specified number of digits. In this program, the average is rounded to the hundredths position and is displayed as `85.67`.

Floating-Point Number Precision

Floating-point numbers are not always 100% precise, but they have numerous applications. For example, when we speak of a "normal" body temperature of 98.6, we do not need to be precise to a large number of digits. When we read the temperature on a thermometer as 98.6, it may actually be 98.5999473210643. Calling this number simply 98.6 is fine for most applications involving body temperatures.

Floating-point numbers often arise as a result of division, such as in this example's class-average calculation. In conventional arithmetic, when we divide 10 by 3, the result is

3.3333333..., with the sequence of 3s repeating infinitely. The computer allocates only a fixed amount of space to hold such a value, so clearly the stored floating-point value can be only an approximation.

Owing to the imprecise nature of floating-point numbers, type `double` is preferred over type `float`, because `double` variables can represent floating-point numbers more accurately. For this reason, we primarily use type `double` throughout the book. In some applications, the precision of `float` and `double` variables will be inadequate. For precise floating-point numbers (such as those required by monetary calculations), Java provides class `BigDecimal` (package `java.math`), which we'll discuss in Chapter 8.

Common Programming Error 4.7

Using floating-point numbers in a manner that assumes they're represented precisely can lead to incorrect results.

4.11 Formulating Algorithms: Nested Control Statements

For the next example, we once again formulate an algorithm by using pseudocode and top-down, stepwise refinement, and write a corresponding Java program. We've seen that control statements can be stacked on top of one another (in sequence). In this case study, we examine the only other structured way control statements can be connected—namely, by **nesting** one control statement within another.

Consider the following problem statement:

> *A college offers a course that prepares students for the state licensing exam for real-estate brokers. Last year, ten of the students who completed this course took the exam. The college wants to know how well its students did on the exam. You've been asked to write a program to summarize the results. You've been given a list of these 10 students. Next to each name is written a 1 if the student passed the exam or a 2 if the student failed.*
>
> *Your program should analyze the results of the exam as follows:*
>
> 1. *Input each test result (i.e., a 1 or a 2). Display the message "Enter result" on the screen each time the program requests another test result.*
> 2. *Count the number of test results of each type.*
> 3. *Display a summary of the test results, indicating the number of students who passed and the number who failed.*
> 4. *If more than eight students passed the exam, print "Bonus to instructor!"*

After reading the problem statement carefully, we make the following observations:

1. The program must process test results for 10 students. A counter-controlled loop can be used, because the number of test results is known in advance.
2. Each test result has a numeric value—either a 1 or a 2. Each time it reads a test result, the program must determine whether it's a 1 or a 2. We test for a 1 in our algorithm. If the number is not a 1, we assume that it's a 2. (Exercise 4.24 considers the consequences of this assumption.)
3. Two counters are used to keep track of the exam results—one to count the number of students who passed the exam and one to count the number who failed.
4. After the program has processed all the results, it must decide whether more than eight students passed the exam.

Let's begin the top-down, stepwise refinement with a representation of the top:

Analyze exam results and decide whether a bonus should be paid

Once again, the top is a *complete* representation of the program, but several refinements are likely to be needed before the pseudocode can evolve naturally into a Java program.

Our first refinement is

Initialize variables
Input the 10 exam results, and count passes and failures
Print a summary of the exam results and decide whether a bonus should be paid

Here, too, even though we have a *complete* representation of the program, further refinement is necessary. We now commit to specific variables. Counters are needed to record the passes and failures, a counter will be used to control the looping process and a variable is needed to store the user input. The variable in which the user input will be stored is *not* initialized at the start of the algorithm, because its value is input during each iteration of the loop.

The pseudocode statement

Initialize variables

can be refined as follows:

Initialize passes to zero
Initialize failures to zero
Initialize student counter to one

Notice that only the counters are initialized at the start of the algorithm.

The pseudocode statement

Input the 10 exam results, and count passes and failures

requires a loop that successively inputs the result of each exam. We know in advance that there are precisely 10 exam results, so counter-controlled looping is appropriate. Inside the loop (i.e., *nested* within the loop), a double-selection structure will determine whether each exam result is a pass or a failure and will increment the appropriate counter. The refinement of the preceding pseudocode statement is then

```
While student counter is less than or equal to 10
    Prompt the user to enter the next exam result
    Input the next exam result

    If the student passed
        Add one to passes
    Else
        Add one to failures

    Add one to student counter
```

We use blank lines to isolate the *If…Else* control structure, which improves readability.

The pseudocode statement

Print a summary of the exam results and decide whether a bonus should be paid

can be refined as follows:

```
Print the number of passes
Print the number of failures
If more than eight students passed
    Print "Bonus to instructor!"
```

Complete Second Refinement of Pseudocode and Conversion to Class `Analysis`

The complete second refinement appears in Fig. 4.11. Blank lines are also used to set off the *While* structure for program readability. This pseudocode is now sufficiently refined for conversion to Java.

```
Initialize passes to zero
Initialize failures to zero
Initialize student counter to one

While student counter is less than or equal to 10
    Prompt the user to enter the next exam result
    Input the next exam result

    If the student passed
        Add one to passes
    Else
        Add one to failures

    Add one to student counter

Print the number of passes
Print the number of failures

If more than eight students passed
    Print "Bonus to instructor!"
```

Fig. 4.11 | Pseudocode for examination-results problem.

The Java class that implements the pseudocode algorithm and two sample executions are shown in Fig. 4.12. Lines 11–13 and 19 of `main` declare the variables that are used to process the examination results.

Error-Prevention Tip 4.5

Initializing local variables when they're declared helps you avoid any compilation errors that might arise from attempts to use uninitialized variables. While Java does not require that local-variable initializations be incorporated into declarations, it does require that local variables be initialized before their values are used in an expression.

The `while` statement (lines 16–31) loops 10 times. During each iteration, the loop inputs and processes one exam result. Notice that the `if...else` statement (lines 22–27) for processing each result is *nested* in the `while` statement. If the `result` is `1`, the `if...else` statement increments `passes`; otherwise, it assumes the `result` is 2 and increments `failures`. Line 30 increments `studentCounter` before the loop condition is tested again at line 16. After 10 values have been input, the loop terminates and line 34 displays the number of `passes` and `failures`. The `if` statement at lines 37–39 determines whether more than eight students passed the exam and, if so, outputs the message `"Bonus to instructor!"`.

Figure 4.12 shows the input and output from two sample executions of the program. During the first, the condition at line 37 of method `main` is `true`—more than eight students passed the exam, so the program outputs a message to bonus the instructor.

```
1  // Fig. 4.12: Analysis.java
2  // Analysis of examination results using nested control statements.
3  import java.util.Scanner; // class uses class Scanner
4
5  public class Analysis {
6     public static void main(String[] args) {
7        // create Scanner to obtain input from command window
8        Scanner input = new Scanner(System.in);
9
10       // initializing variables in declarations
11       int passes = 0;
12       int failures = 0;
13       int studentCounter = 1;
14
15       // process 10 students using counter-controlled loop
16       while (studentCounter <= 10) {
17          // prompt user for input and obtain value from user
18          System.out.print("Enter result (1 = pass, 2 = fail): ");
19          int result = input.nextInt();
20
21          // if...else is nested in the while statement
22          if (result == 1) {
23             passes = passes + 1;
24          }
25          else {
26             failures = failures + 1;
27          }
28
29          // increment studentCounter so loop eventually terminates
30          studentCounter = studentCounter + 1;
31       }
32
33       // termination phase; prepare and display results
34       System.out.printf("Passed: %d%nFailed: %d%n", passes, failures);
35
36       // determine whether more than 8 students passed
37       if (passes > 8) {
38          System.out.println("Bonus to instructor!");
39       }
40    }
41 }
```

Fig. 4.12 | Analysis of examination results using nested control statements. (Part 1 of 2.)

```
Enter result (1 = pass, 2 = fail): 1
Enter result (1 = pass, 2 = fail): 2
Enter result (1 = pass, 2 = fail): 1
Enter result (1 = pass, 2 = fail): 1
Enter result (1 = pass, 2 = fail): 1
Enter result (1 = pass, 2 = fail): 1
Enter result (1 = pass, 2 = fail): 1
Enter result (1 = pass, 2 = fail): 1
Enter result (1 = pass, 2 = fail): 1
Enter result (1 = pass, 2 = fail): 1
Passed: 9
Failed: 1
Bonus to instructor!
```

```
Enter result (1 = pass, 2 = fail): 1
Enter result (1 = pass, 2 = fail): 2
Enter result (1 = pass, 2 = fail): 1
Enter result (1 = pass, 2 = fail): 2
Enter result (1 = pass, 2 = fail): 1
Enter result (1 = pass, 2 = fail): 2
Enter result (1 = pass, 2 = fail): 2
Enter result (1 = pass, 2 = fail): 1
Enter result (1 = pass, 2 = fail): 1
Enter result (1 = pass, 2 = fail): 1
Passed: 6
Failed: 4
```

Fig. 4.12 | Analysis of examination results using nested control statements. (Part 2 of 2.)

4.12 Compound Assignment Operators

The **compound assignment operators** enable you to abbreviate assignment expressions. For example, you can abbreviate the statement

```
c = c + 3; // adds 3 to c
```

with the **addition compound assignment operator, +=**, as

```
c += 3; // adds 3 to c more concisely
```

The += operator adds the value of the expression on its right to the value of the variable on its left and stores the result in the variable on the left. Thus, the assignment expression c += 3 adds 3 to c. In general, statements like

variable = *variable* *operator* *expression*;

where *operator* is one of the binary operators +, -, *, / or % (or others we discuss later in the text) and the same variable name is used can be written in the form

variable *operator*= *expression*;

Figure 4.13 shows the arithmetic compound assignment operators, sample expressions using the operators and explanations of what the operators do. Be sure to do Self-Review Exercise 4.1(h) to learn about a subtle feature of compound assignment operators.

Assignment operator	Sample expression	Explanation	Assigns
Assume: `int c = 3, d = 5, e = 4, f = 6, g = 12;`			
+=	`c += 7`	`c = c + 7`	10 to c
-=	`d -= 4`	`d = d - 4`	1 to d
*=	`e *= 5`	`e = e * 5`	20 to e
/=	`f /= 3`	`f = f / 3`	2 to f
%=	`g %= 9`	`g = g % 9`	3 to g

Fig. 4.13 | Arithmetic compound assignment operators.

4.13 Increment and Decrement Operators

Java provides two unary operators (summarized in Fig. 4.14) for adding 1 to or subtracting 1 from the value of a numeric variable. These are the unary **increment operator, ++**, and the unary **decrement operator, --**. A program can increment by 1 the value of a variable called `c` using the increment operator, `++`, rather than the expression `c = c + 1` or `c += 1`. An increment or decrement operator that's prefixed to (placed before) a variable is referred to as the **prefix increment** or **prefix decrement operator**, respectively. An increment or decrement operator that's postfixed to (placed after) a variable is referred to as the **postfix increment** or **postfix decrement operator**, respectively.

Operator	Sample expression	Explanation
++ (prefix increment)	`++a`	Increment `a` by 1, then use the new value of `a` in the expression in which `a` resides.
++ (postfix increment)	`a++`	Use the current value of `a` in the expression in which `a` resides, then increment `a` by 1.
-- (prefix decrement)	`--b`	Decrement `b` by 1, then use the new value of `b` in the expression in which `b` resides.
-- (postfix decrement)	`b--`	Use the current value of `b` in the expression in which `b` resides, then decrement `b` by 1.

Fig. 4.14 | Increment and decrement operators.

Using the prefix increment (or decrement) operator to add 1 to (or subtract 1 from) a variable is known as **preincrementing** (or **predecrementing**). This causes the variable to be incremented (decremented) by 1; then the new value of the variable is used in the expression in which it appears. Using the postfix increment (or decrement) operator to add 1 to (or subtract 1 from) a variable is known as **postincrementing** (or **postdecrementing**). This causes the current value of the variable to be used in the expression in which it appears; then the variable's value is incremented (decremented) by 1.

Good Programming Practice 4.4

Unlike binary operators, the unary increment and decrement operators should be placed next to their operands, with no intervening spaces.

Difference Between Prefix Increment and Postfix Increment Operators

Figure 4.15 demonstrates the difference between the prefix increment and postfix increment versions of the ++ increment operator. The decrement operator (--) works similarly.

```
1  // Fig. 4.15: Increment.java
2  // Prefix increment and postfix increment operators.
3
4  public class Increment {
5     public static void main(String[] args) {
6        // demonstrate postfix increment operator
7        int c = 5;
8        System.out.printf("c before postincrement: %d%n", c); // prints 5
9        System.out.printf("    postincrementing c: %d%n", c++); // prints 5
10       System.out.printf(" c after postincrement: %d%n", c); // prints 6
11
12       System.out.println(); // skip a line
13
14       // demonstrate prefix increment operator
15       c = 5;
16       System.out.printf(" c before preincrement: %d%n", c); // prints 5
17       System.out.printf("     preincrementing c: %d%n", ++c); // prints 6
18       System.out.printf("  c after preincrement: %d%n", c); // prints 6
19    }
20 }
```

```
c before postincrement: 5
    postincrementing c: 5
 c after postincrement: 6

 c before preincrement: 5
     preincrementing c: 6
  c after preincrement: 6
```

Fig. 4.15 | Prefix increment and postfix increment operators.

Line 7 initializes the variable c to 5, and line 8 outputs c's initial value. Line 9 outputs the value of the expression c++. This expression postincrements the variable c, so c's *original* value (5) is output, then c's value is incremented (to 6). Thus, line 9 outputs c's initial value (5) again. Line 10 outputs c's new value (6) to prove that the variable's value was indeed incremented in line 9.

Line 15 resets c's value to 5, and line 16 outputs c's value. Line 17 outputs the value of the expression ++c. This expression preincrements c, so its value is incremented; then the *new* value (6) is output. Line 18 outputs c's value again to show that the value of c is still 6 after line 17 executes.

Simplifying Statements with the Arithmetic Compound Assignment, Increment and Decrement Operators

The arithmetic compound assignment operators and the increment and decrement operators can be used to simplify program statements. For example, the three assignment statements in Fig. 4.12 (lines 23, 26 and 30)

```
passes = passes + 1;
failures = failures + 1;
studentCounter = studentCounter + 1;
```

can be written more concisely with compound assignment operators as

```
passes += 1;
failures += 1;
studentCounter += 1;
```

with prefix increment operators as

```
++passes;
++failures;
++studentCounter;
```

or with postfix increment operators as

```
passes++;
failures++;
studentCounter++;
```

When incrementing or decrementing a variable in a statement by itself, the prefix increment and postfix increment forms have the *same* effect, and the prefix decrement and postfix decrement forms have the *same* effect. It's only when a variable appears in the context of a larger expression that preincrementing and postincrementing the variable have different effects (and similarly for predecrementing and postdecrementing).

Common Programming Error 4.8

Attempting to use the increment or decrement operator on an expression other than one to which a value can be assigned is a syntax error. For example, writing `++(x + 1)` *is a syntax error, because* `(x + 1)` *is not a variable.*

Operator Precedence and Associativity

Figure 4.16 shows the precedence and associativity of the operators we've introduced. They're shown from top to bottom in decreasing order of precedence. The second column describes the operators' associativity. The conditional operator (`?:`); the unary operators increment (`++`), decrement (`--`), plus (`+`) and minus (`-`); the cast operators and the assignment operators `=`, `+=`, `-=`, `*=`, `/=` and `%=` associate from *right to left*. The other operators associate from left to right. The third column lists the type of each group of operators.

Error-Prevention Tip 4.6

Refer to the operator precedence and associativity chart (Appendix A) when writing expressions containing many operators. Confirm that the operators in the expression are performed in the order you expect. If you're uncertain about the order of evaluation in a complex expression, break the expression into smaller statements or use parentheses to force the order of evaluation, exactly as you'd do in an algebraic expression. Be sure to observe that some operators such as assignment (=) associate right to left rather than left to right.

Operators						Associativity	Type
++	--					right to left	unary postfix
++	--	+	-	(*type*)		right to left	unary prefix
*	/	%				left to right	multiplicative
+	-					left to right	additive
<	<=	>	>=			left to right	relational
==	!=					left to right	equality
?:						right to left	conditional
=	+=	-=	*=	/=	%=	right to left	assignment

Fig. 4.16 | Precedence and associativity of the operators discussed so far.

4.14 Primitive Types

The table in Appendix D lists the eight primitive types in Java. Like C and C++, Java requires all variables to have a type.[2]

In C and C++, programmers frequently have to write separate versions of programs to support different computer platforms, because the primitive types are not guaranteed to be identical from computer to computer. For example, an `int` on one machine might be represented by 16 bits (2 bytes) of memory, on a second machine by 32 bits (4 bytes), and on another machine by 64 bits (8 bytes). In Java, `int` values are always 32 bits (4 bytes).

Portability Tip 4.1

The primitive types in Java are portable across all computer platforms that support Java.

Each type in Appendix D is listed with its size in bits (there are eight bits to a byte) and its range of values. Because the designers of Java want to ensure portability, they use internationally recognized standards for character formats (Unicode; for more information, visit `http://www.unicode.org`) and floating-point numbers (IEEE 754; for more information, visit `http://grouper.ieee.org/groups/754/`).

Recall from Section 3.2 that variables of primitive types declared outside of a method as instance variables of a class are *automatically assigned default values unless explicitly initialized.* Instance variables of types `char`, `byte`, `short`, `int`, `long`, `float` and `double` are all given the value `0` by default. Instance variables of type `boolean` are given the value `false` by default. Reference-type instance variables are initialized by default to the value `null`.

2. We'll see an exception to this with lambdas in Chapter 17, Lambdas and Streams.

4.15 (Optional) GUI and Graphics Case Study: Event Handling; Drawing Lines

An appealing feature of Java is its graphics and multimedia support, which enables you to visually enhance your applications. Chapter 22, JavaFX Graphics and Multimedia, discusses these capabilities in detail.

In this and the next several GUI and Graphics Case Study sections, we introduce a few of JavaFX's graphics capabilities. In this section, you'll build the `DrawLines` app that draws lines on a **Canvas** control—a rectangular area in which you can draw. This app also introduces event handling—when the user clicks a **`Button`**, a method that we'll designate in Scene Builder will be called by JavaFX to draw the lines on the `Canvas`. Like Section 3.6, this GUI and Graphics Case Study section is a bit longer than the subsequent ones as we walk you through the steps to configure the GUI.

4.15.1 Test-Driving the Completed Draw Lines App

First, let's test-drive the completed app, so you can see it in action:

1. In a command window, change directories to the `GUIGraphicsCaseStudy04` directory in this chapter's `ch04` examples folder.
2. Compile the app with the following command, which compiles both of this app's Java source-code files:

```
javac *.java
```

3. Run the app with the following command:

```
java DrawLines
```

When the app's window appears on the screen (Fig. 4.17(a)), click the **Draw Lines** `Button`. Figure 4.17(b) shows the app's GUI after the user clicks the **Draw Lines** `Button`.

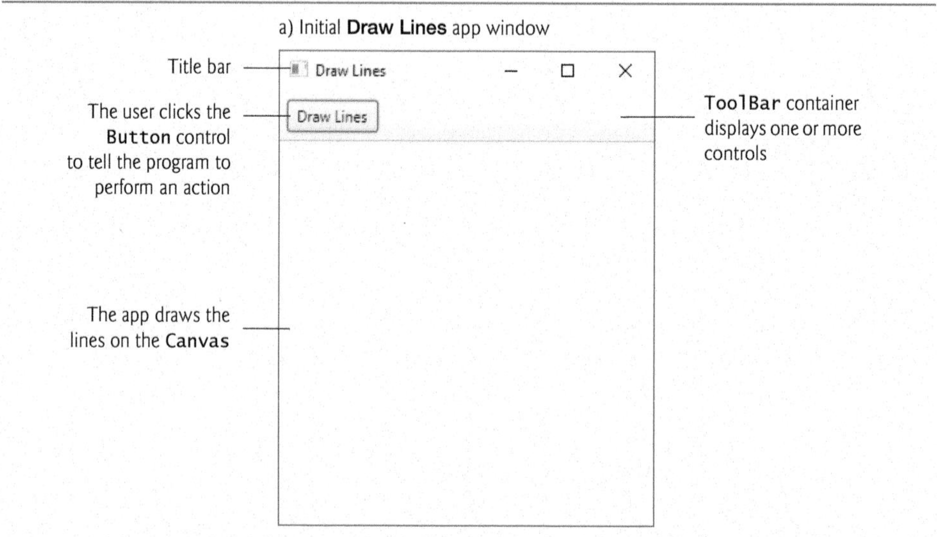
a) Initial Draw Lines app window
Title bar
Draw Lines
The user clicks the Button control to tell the program to perform an action
Draw Lines
ToolBar container displays one or more controls
The app draws the lines on the Canvas

Fig. 4.17 | **Draw Lines** app in action. (Part 1 of 2.)

b) **Draw Lines** app window after the user clicks the **Draw Lines** Button

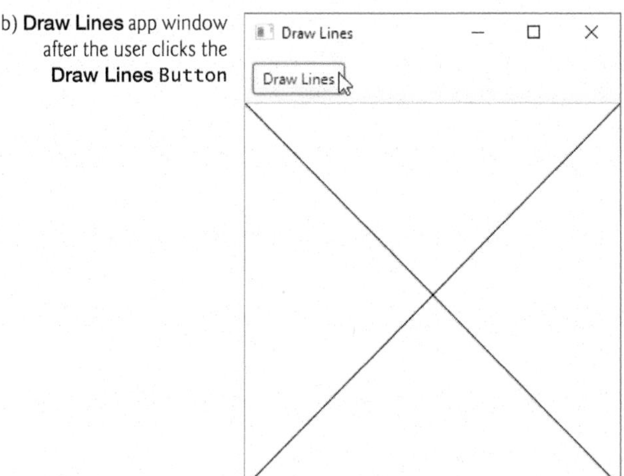

Fig. 4.17 | **Draw Lines** app in action. (Part 2 of 2.)

4.15.2 Building the App's GUI

You'll build the app's GUI in `DrawLines.fxml`, using the same techniques you learned in Section 3.6. The GUI contains the following controls:

- a `Button` that you press to draw the lines
- a `Canvas` that displays an image

You'll also use `BorderPane` and `ToolBar` layouts (discussed shortly), to help you arrange the `Button` and `Canvas` in the user interface.

Opening Scene Builder and Creating the File `DrawLines.fxml`

As you did in Section 3.6.4, open Scene Builder, then select **File > Save** to display the **Save As** dialog. Select a location in which to store the FXML file, name the file `DrawLines.fxml` and click the **Save** button to create the file.

Creating a **BorderPane** *Layout Container*

In Section 3.6, you arranged controls in a `VBox` layout container. For the remaining GUI and Graphics Case Study apps, you'll use a **BorderPane layout container**, which arranges controls into one or more of the five regions shown in Fig. 4.18.

Look-and-Feel Observation 4.1

All the areas in a `BorderPane` *are optional: If the top or bottom area is empty, the left, center and right areas expand vertically to fill that area. If the left or right area is empty, the center expands horizontally to fill that area.*

The top and bottom areas have the same width as the `BorderPane`. The left, center and right areas fill the vertical space between the top and bottom areas. Each area may contain only one control or one layout container that, in turn, may contain other controls. To begin designing the GUI, drag-and-drop a **BorderPane** from the **Library** window's **Containers** section onto Scene Builder's content panel. (You also can double-click **BorderPane** to add one to the content panel.)

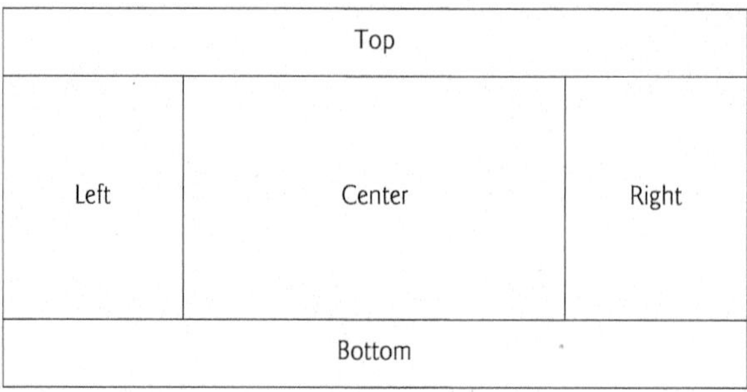
Top
Left
Center
Right
Bottom

Fig. 4.18 | BorderPane's five areas.

Adding a ToolBar and Configuring Its Button

Next, you'll add a **ToolBar layout container** to the BorderPane's top region. A ToolBar arranges controls horizontally by default. In this app, the ToolBar will contain only the app's **Draw Lines** Button—you'll see a ToolBar with two Buttons in Section 5.11, and later apps in the book will place other controls in a ToolBar.

Look-and-Feel Observation 4.2

ToolBars typically organize multiple controls at a layout's edges, such as in a BorderPane's top, right, bottom or left areas.

Drag a **ToolBar** from the Scene Builder **Library**'s **Containers** section onto the BorderPane's top area as shown in Fig. 4.19. As you drag over the BorderPane, Scene Builder shows you the five regions so you can determine where the ToolBar will appear when you drop it. By default, the ToolBar you drag onto your layout has one Button (Fig. 4.20).

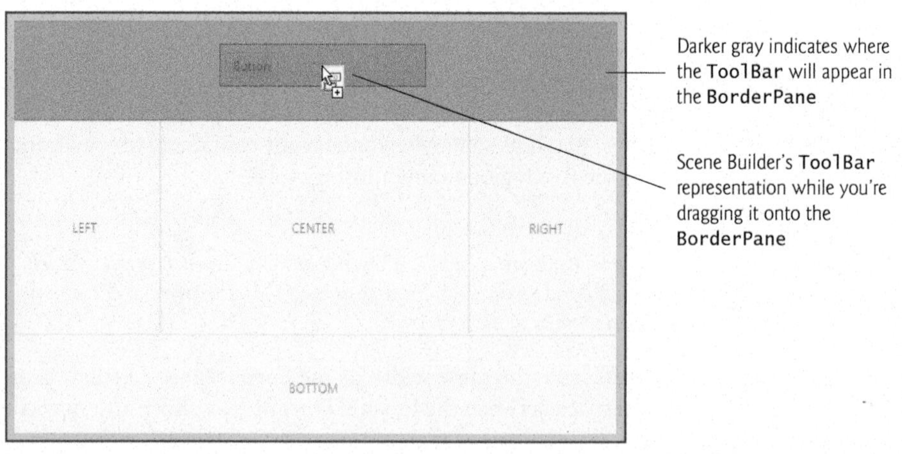
LEFT
CENTER
RIGHT
BOTTOM
Darker gray indicates where the ToolBar will appear in the BorderPane
Scene Builder's ToolBar representation while you're dragging it onto the BorderPane

Fig. 4.19 | Dragging a ToolBar onto a BorderPane.

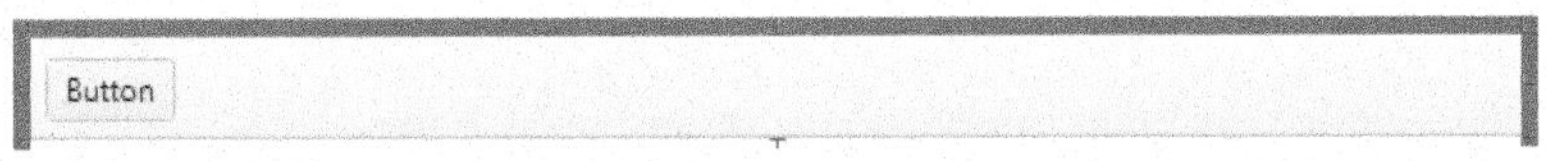

Fig. 4.20 | Initial `ToolBar` containing a `Button`—by default the `ToolBar` is the full width of the `BorderPane`'s top area.

Configuring the **`Button`***'s Text*

Next, double-click the `Button` to edit its text. Type `Draw Lines` and press *Enter*. The updated `Button` is shown in Fig. 4.21.

Fig. 4.21 | `ToolBar` containing the `Button` with its updated text.

Adding and Configuring a **`Canvas`**

Next, you'll create the `Canvas` in which the app draws lines. Drag-and-drop a **Canvas** from the Scene Builder **Library**'s **Miscellaneous** section to the `BorderPane`'s center area, as shown in Fig. 4.22. Scene Builder automatically creates a 200-by-200 pixel `Canvas` and centers it horizontally and vertically in the `BorderPane`'s center area.

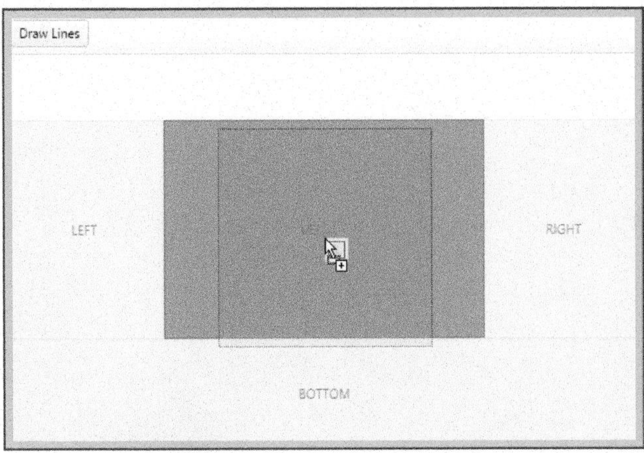

Fig. 4.22 | Dragging and dropping the `Canvas` onto the `BorderPane`'s center area.

Setting the **`Canvas`***'s Width and Height*

For this app, we increased the size of the `Canvas` to 300-by-300, which is the size we'll use in many of the subsequent GUI and Graphics Case Study apps. To do so:

1. Click the `Canvas` once to select it.

2. Expand the **Inspector**'s **Layout** section by clicking the right arrow (▶) next to **Layout**.
3. Type 300 for the **Width** property's value and press *Enter*.
4. Repeat *Step 3* for the **Height** property's value.

Configuring the **BorderPane** *Layout Container's Size*

Finally, you'll specify that the BorderPane should size itself, based on its contents. Recall from Section 3.6.7 that the preferred width and height of a GUI's primary layout (in this case, the BorderPane) determines the default size of the JavaFX app's window. To set the BorderPane's preferred size:

1. Select the BorderPane by clicking it in the content panel or by clicking it in the Scene Builder **Document** window's **Hierarchy** section (located in Scene Builder's bottom-left corner).
2. In the **Inspector**'s **Layout** section, click the **Pref Width** property's down arrow and select USE_COMPUTED_SIZE (Fig. 4.23). This tells the BorderPane to calculate its preferred width, based on the width of its contents. In this app, the widest item is the Canvas, so the BorderPane initially will be 300 pixels wide.
3. Repeat *Step 2* for the **Pref Height** property. This tells the BorderPane to calculate its preferred height, based on the height of its contents. In this case, the BorderPane's height will be the sum of the ToolBar's and Canvas's heights.

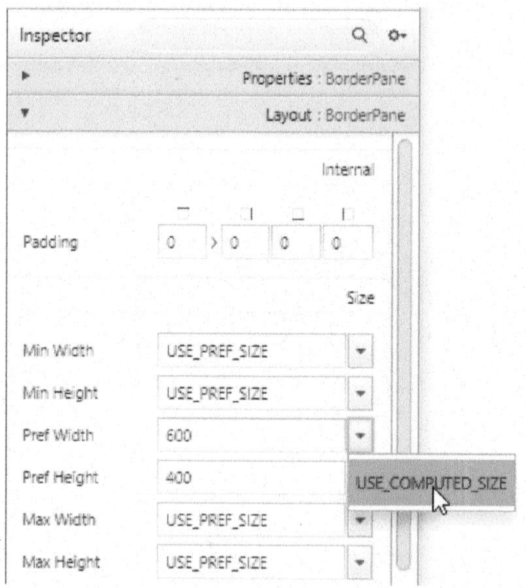

Fig. 4.23 | Selecting USE_COMPUTED_SIZE for the BorderPane's **Pref Width** property.

Saving the Design

You've now completed the GUI. The design should appear as shown in Fig. 4.24. Save the FXML file by selecting **File > Save**.

Fig. 4.24 | Completed GUI in Scene Builder's content panel.

4.15.3 Preparing to Interact with the GUI Programmatically

You've created objects (like `Scanner`, `Account` and `Student`), assigned them to variables and interacted with the objects programmatically through those variables. JavaFX GUI controls also are objects that you can interact with programmatically. For GUIs created in Scene Builder, *JavaFX creates the controls for you* when the app begins executing.

As you saw in Section 4.15.1, when you press the app's **Draw Lines** `Button`, the app responds to that event by drawing lines on the `Canvas`. In this section, you'll learn how to use Scene Builder to specify the names of variables and methods that will enable you to interact with the GUI's controls. We'll then show that Scene Builder can generate a class containing those variables and methods.

Specifying the App's Controller Class

Of course, instance variables and methods must be declared in a class. For an FXML GUI, these are declared in a class known as the **controller class**, because it controls what the app does in response to the user's GUI interactions. You'll see this app's controller class in Section 4.15.4. When you launch a JavaFX app with an FXML GUI, the JavaFX runtime:

- creates the GUI,
- creates an object of the controller class that you specified in Scene Builder,
- initializes any of the controller object's instance variables that you specified in Scene Builder, so they refer to the corresponding control objects, and
- configures any of the controller object's event handlers that you specified in Scene Builder, so that they'll be called when the user interacts with the corresponding control(s).

To specify the controller class's name:

1. Expand the Scene Builder **Document** window's **Controller** section (located in Scene Builder's bottom-left corner).
2. For the **Controller Class**, type `DrawLinesController` and press *Enter*. By convention, the controller class has the same base name as the FXML file (`DrawLines` in `DrawLines.fxml`) followed by `Controller`.

Specifying the **Canvas***'s Instance Variable Name*

To draw on the Canvas object, the program needs a variable that refers to it—this will be an instance variable in the controller class. A control's **fx:id property** specifies the instance variable's name—when the app begins executing, JavaFX initializes the instance variable with the corresponding control object. To specify the Canvas's **fx:id**:

1. Select the Canvas, then expand the Scene Builder **Inspector**'s **Code** section by clicking the right arrow (▶) next to **Code**.
2. For the **fx:id** property, type canvas and press *Enter*.

Specifying the **Button***'s Event-Handler Method*

An **event handler** is a method that's called in response to a user interaction, such as when the user clicks this app's **Draw Lines** Button. The method is called by the JavaFX runtime on an object of the controller class. To specify the Button event handler's name:

1. Click the Button to select it.
2. For the **On Action** property in the **Inspector**'s **Code** section, type the method name drawLinesButtonPressed and press *Enter*.
3. Save the FXML file by selecting **File > Save**.

Generating the Initial Controller Class

Scene Builder can generate a DrawLinesController class—which it calls the *controller skeleton*—containing the instance variables and event handlers you specified. Select **View > Show Sample Controller Skeleton** to display the class (Fig. 4.25), which has the controller-class name you specified, an instance variable with the Canvas's **fx:id** and the empty event-handler method drawLinesButtonPressed. We'll discuss the @FXML annotations shortly. To use this code in your controller class, click the **Copy** button, then create a Java source-code file named DrawLinesController.java in the same folder as DrawLines.fxml, paste the code into that file and save the file. You can add the program's logic into the file.

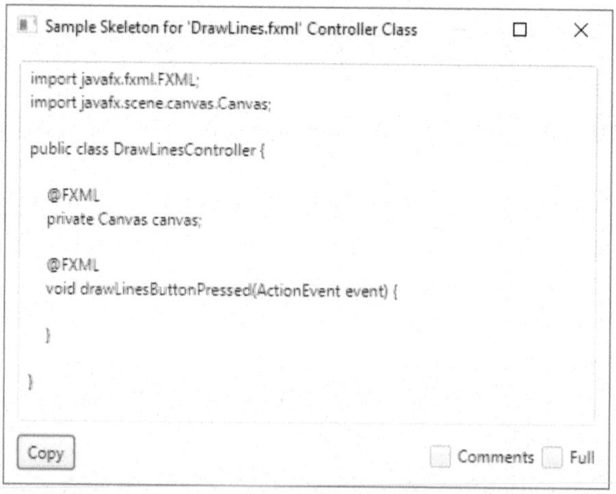

Sample Skeleton for 'DrawLines.fxml' Controller Class

```
import javafx.fxml.FXML;
import javafx.scene.canvas.Canvas;

public class DrawLinesController {

    @FXML
    private Canvas canvas;

    @FXML
    void drawLinesButtonPressed(ActionEvent event) {

    }
}
```

Copy   Comments   Full

Fig. 4.25 | Skeleton controller-class code generated by Scene Builder.

4.15.4 Class DrawLinesController

Each JavaFX app you'll see in this book has at least two Java source-code files:

- A controller class that defines the GUI's event handlers and logic. In this app, `DrawLinesController.java` (Fig. 4.26) contains the controller class.
- A main-application class that loads the app's FXML file, creates the GUI then creates and configures the corresponding controller-class object. In this app, `DrawLines.java` (Fig. 4.28) contains the main-application class. By convention, this class has the same base name as the FXML file (`DrawLines` in `DrawLines.fxml`).

Class `DrawLinesController` (Fig. 4.26) performs the drawing. The `import` statements in lines 5–6 allow us to use two classes from the package `javafx.scene.canvas`:

- `Canvas` provides the drawing area.
- **`GraphicsContext`** provides various methods for drawing onto a `Canvas`—every `Canvas` has a `GraphicsContext` object.

```
1  // Fig. 4.26: DrawLinesController.java
2  // Using strokeLine to connect the corners of a canvas.
3  import javafx.event.ActionEvent;
4  import javafx.fxml.FXML;
5  import javafx.scene.canvas.Canvas;
6  import javafx.scene.canvas.GraphicsContext;
7
8  public class DrawLinesController {
9     @FXML private Canvas canvas; // used to get the GraphicsContext
10
11    // when user presses Draw Lines button, draw two Lines in the Canvas
12    @FXML
13    void drawLinesButtonPressed(ActionEvent event) {
14       // get the GraphicsContext, which is used to draw on the Canvas
15       GraphicsContext gc = canvas.getGraphicsContext2D();
16
17       // draw line from upper-left to lower-right corner
18       gc.strokeLine(0, 0, canvas.getWidth(), canvas.getHeight());
19
20       // draw line from upper-right to lower-left corner
21       gc.strokeLine(canvas.getWidth(), 0, 0, canvas.getHeight());
22    }
23 }
```

Fig. 4.26 | Using `strokeLine` to connect the corners of a canvas.

@FXML Annotation

Recall from Section 4.15.3 that each control we manipulate programmatically needs an **fx:id**. Line 9 in Fig. 4.26 declares the controller class's corresponding instance variable canvas. The **@FXML annotation** preceding the declaration indicates that the variable name can be used in the GUI's FXML file. The variable name you specify in the controller class must precisely match the **fx:id** you specified when building the GUI. Note that we did *not* initialize this variable. When the `DrawLines` app executes, it initializes the canvas variable with the `Canvas` object from `DrawLines.fxml`.

The `@FXML` annotation preceding the method (line 12) indicates that this method can be used in the FXML file to specify a control's event handler. When the **Draw Lines** app executes, it configures `drawLinesButtonPressed` (lines 12–22) to execute when the user presses the **Draw Lines** `Button`. A `Button` press generates an `ActionEvent` object that contains information about the event that occurred. The corresponding event-handling method must return `void` and receive one `ActionEvent` parameter (line 13). (We don't use the information in `ActionEvent` parameter in this example.)

Getting a `GraphicsContext` *to Draw on a* `Canvas`

Every `Canvas` has a `GraphicsContext` object for drawing on the `Canvas`. You obtain the `GraphicsContext` by calling the `Canvas`'s **`getGraphicsContext2D`** method (line 15):

```
GraphicsContext gc = canvas.getGraphicsContext2D();
```

By convention, the variable name `gc` is used for this object.

`Canvas`*'s Coordinate System*

A **coordinate system** (Fig. 4.27) is a scheme for identifying points. In `Canvas`'s coordinate system, the upper-left corner has the coordinates (0, 0). An *x–y* coordinate pair is composed of an ***x*-coordinate** (the **horizontal coordinate**) and a ***y*-coordinate** (the **vertical coordinate**). The *x*-coordinate is the horizontal location moving from *left to right*. The *y*-coordinate is the vertical location moving from *top to bottom*. The ***x*-axis** describes every horizontal coordinate, and the ***y*-axis** describes every vertical coordinate. Coordinates indicate where graphics should be displayed. Coordinate units are measured in **pixels**. The term pixel stands for "picture element." A pixel is a display monitor's smallest addressable element.

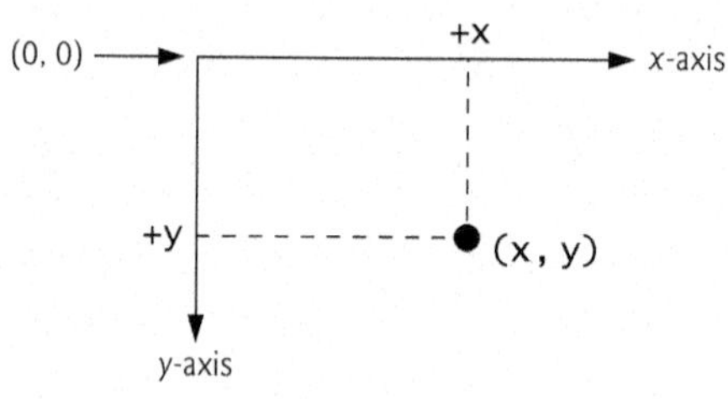

Fig. 4.27 | Java coordinate system. Units are measured in pixels.

Drawing Lines

Lines 18 and 21 in Fig. 4.26 use `GraphicsContext` variable `gc` to draw lines that diagonally connect the `Canvas`'s corners. Class `GraphicsContext`'s **`strokeLine`** method requires four arguments to draw a line—the first two are the start point's *x-y* coordinates and the last two are the end point's *x-y* coordinates. In line 18, the first two arguments represent the `Canvas`'s upper-left corner and the last two represent the `Canvas`'s bottom-right corner. `Canvas` methods **`getWidth`** and **`getHeight`** return the `Canvas`'s width and height in pixels, respectively. In line 21, the first two arguments represent the `Canvas`'s upper-right corner and the last two represent the `Canvas`'s bottom-left corner.

4.15.5 Class DrawLines—The Main Application Class

Figure 4.28 shows class `DrawLines`—the app's main-application class that begins the program's execution, creates the GUI from the FXML file, creates and configures the controller-class object and displays the GUI in a window. Every JavaFX app we present in this book uses a similar main-application class in which we make only three code changes (separate from the comments)—the class name (line 9), the FXML filename (line 14) and the text that's displayed in the application window's title bar (line 17). This class uses various concepts that we discuss in later chapters. For now, use class `DrawLines` as a template for the main-application class in each GUI and Graphics Case Study example and exercise. Simply copy it, rename it, then edit lines 9, 14 and 17. We discuss the details of a JavaFX app's main-application class in Section 12.5.4.

```
1  // Fig. 4.28: DrawLines.java
2  // Main application class that loads and displays the DrawLines GUI.
3  import javafx.application.Application;
4  import javafx.fxml.FXMLLoader;
5  import javafx.scene.Parent;
6  import javafx.scene.Scene;
7  import javafx.stage.Stage;
8
9  public class DrawLines extends Application {
10    @Override
11    public void start(Stage stage) throws Exception {
12       // loads DrawLines.fxml and configures the DrawLinesController
13       Parent root =
14          FXMLLoader.load(getClass().getResource("DrawLines.fxml"));
15
16       Scene scene = new Scene(root); // attach scene graph to scene
17       stage.setTitle("Draw Lines"); // displayed in window's title bar
18       stage.setScene(scene); // attach scene to stage
19       stage.show(); // display the stage
20    }
21
22    // application execution starts here
23    public static void main(String[] args) {
24       launch(args); // create a DrawLines object and call its start method
25    }
26 }
```

Fig. 4.28 | Main application class that loads and displays the **Draw Lines** GUI.

GUI and Graphics Case Study Exercises

4.1 Using loops and control statements to draw lines can lead to many interesting designs.

a) Create the design in Fig. 4.29. This design draws lines from the top-left corner, fanning them out until they cover the upper-left half of the `Canvas`. One approach is to divide the width and height into an equal number of steps (we found 20 steps works well). The first endpoint of each line will be the top-left corner (0, 0). The second endpoint can be found by starting at the bottom-left corner and moving up one vertical step and right one horizontal step. Draw a line between the two endpoints. Continue moving up and to the right one step to find each successive endpoint.

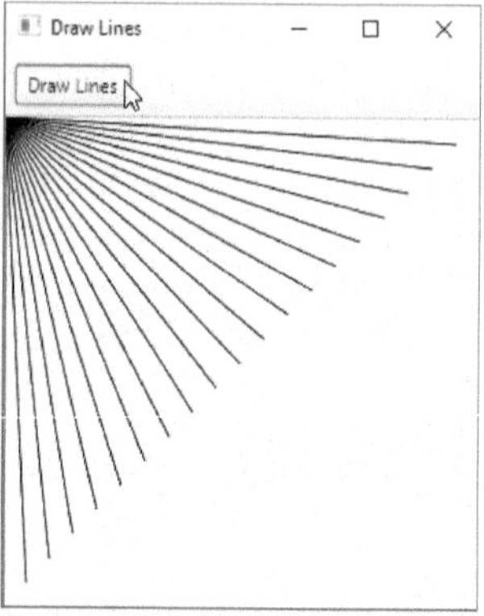

Fig. 4.29 | Lines fanning from a corner.

b) Modify part (a) to have lines fan out from all four corners, as shown in Fig. 4.30. Lines from opposite corners should intersect along the middle.

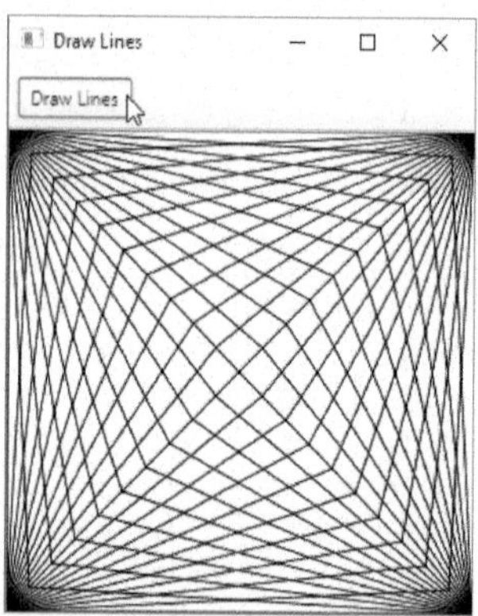

Fig. 4.30 | Lines fanning from all four corners.

4.2 Figures 4.31–4.32 display two additional designs created using loops and `strokeLine`.

a) Create the design in Fig. 4.31. Begin by dividing each edge into an equal number of increments (we chose 20 again). The first line starts in the top-left corner and ends one step right on the bottom edge. For each successive line, move down one increment on the left edge and right one increment on the bottom edge. Continue drawing lines until you reach the bottom-right corner.

b) Modify part (a) to mirror the design in all four corners, as shown in Fig. 4.32.

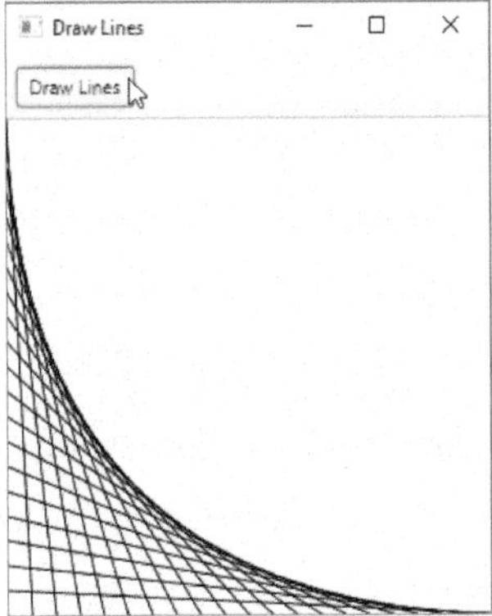

Fig. 4.31 | Line art with loops and `strokeLine`.

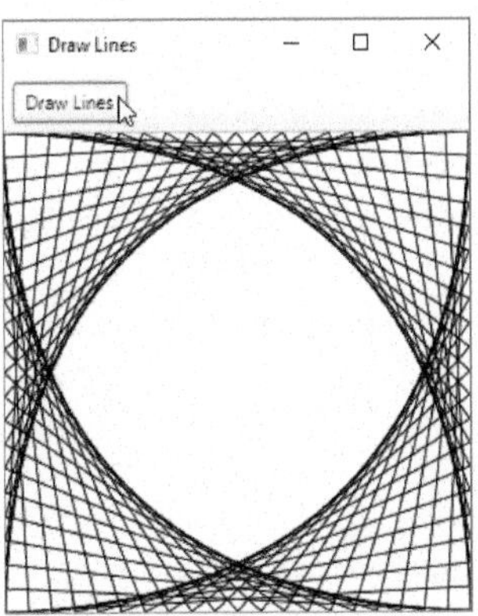

Fig. 4.32 | Line art with loops and `strokeLine`—repeating from all four corners.

4.16 Wrap-Up

This chapter presented basic problem solving for building classes and developing methods for these classes. We demonstrated how to construct an algorithm (i.e., an approach to solving a problem), then how to refine the algorithm through several phases of pseudocode development, resulting in Java code that can be executed as part of a method. The chapter showed how to use top-down, stepwise refinement to plan out the specific actions that a method must perform and the order in which the method must perform these actions.

Only three types of control structures—sequence, selection and iteration—are needed to develop any problem-solving algorithm. Specifically, this chapter demonstrated the `if` single-selection statement, the `if...else` double-selection statement and the `while` iteration statement. These are some of the building blocks used to construct solutions to many problems. We used control-statement stacking to total and compute the average of a set of student grades with counter- and sentinel-controlled iteration, and we used control-statement nesting to analyze and make decisions based on a set of exam results. We introduced Java's compound assignment operators and its increment and decrement operators.

Finally, we discussed Java's primitive types. In Chapter 5, we continue our discussion of control statements, introducing the `for`, `do...while` and `switch` statements.

Summary

Section 4.1 Introduction

- Before writing a program to solve a problem, you must have a thorough understanding of the problem and a carefully planned approach to solving it. You must also understand the building blocks that are available and employ proven program-construction techniques.

Section 4.2 Algorithms

- Any computing problem can be solved by executing a series of actions (p. 105) in a specific order.
- A procedure for solving a problem in terms of the actions to execute and the order in which they execute is called an algorithm (p. 105).
- Specifying the order in which statements execute in a program is called program control (p. 106).

Section 4.3 Pseudocode

- Pseudocode (p. 106) is an informal language that helps you develop algorithms without having to worry about the strict details of Java language syntax.
- Pseudocode is not an actual computer programming language. You may, of course, use your own native language(s) to develop your own pseudocode.
- Pseudocode helps you "think out" a program before attempting to write it in a programming language, such as Java.
- Carefully prepared pseudocode can easily be converted to a corresponding Java program.

Section 4.4 Control Structures

- Normally, statements in a program are executed one after the other in the order in which they're written. This process is called sequential execution (p. 106).
- Various Java statements enable you to specify that the next statement to execute is not necessarily the next one in sequence. This is called transfer of control (p. 106).
- Bohm and Jacopini demonstrated that all programs could be written in terms of only three control structures (p. 107)—the sequence structure, the selection structure and the iteration structure.
- The term "control structures" comes from the field of computer science. The *Java Language Specification* refers to "control structures" as "control statements."

Section 4.4.1 Sequence Structure in Java

- The sequence structure is built into Java. Unless directed otherwise, the computer executes Java statements one after the other in the order in which they're written—that is, in sequence.
- Anywhere a single action may be placed, several actions may be placed in sequence.
- Activity diagrams (p. 107) are part of the UML. An activity diagram models the workflow (p. 107; also called the activity) of a portion of a software system.
- Activity diagrams are composed of symbols (p. 107)—such as action-state symbols, diamonds and small circles—that are connected by transition arrows, which represent the flow of the activity.
- Action states (p. 107) contain action expressions that specify particular actions to perform.
- The arrows in an activity diagram represent transitions, which indicate the order in which the actions represented by the action states occur.

- The solid circle located at the top of an activity diagram represents the activity's initial state (p. 108)—the beginning of the workflow before the program performs the modeled actions.
- The solid circle surrounded by a hollow circle that appears at the bottom of the diagram represents the final state (p. 108)—the end of the workflow after the program performs its actions.
- Rectangles with their upper-right corners folded over are UML notes (p. 108)—explanatory remarks that describe the purpose of symbols in the diagram.

Section 4.4.2 Selection Statements in Java
- Java has three types of selection statements (p. 108).
- The `if` single-selection statement (p. 108) selects or ignores one or more actions.
- The `if...else` double-selection statement selects between two actions or groups of actions.
- The `switch` statement is called a multiple-selection statement (p. 108) because it selects among many different actions or groups of actions.

Section 4.4.3 Iteration Statements in Java
- Java provides the `while`, `do...while`, `for` and enhanced `for` iteration statements that enable programs to perform statements repeatedly as long as a loop-continuation condition remains true.
- The `while` and `for` statements perform the action(s) in their bodies zero or more times, based on their loop-continuation conditions (p. 108). The `do...while` statement its body one or more times.
- The words `if`, `else`, `switch`, `while`, `do` and `for` are Java keywords. Keywords cannot be used as identifiers, such as variable names.

Section 4.4.4 Summary of Control Statements in Java
- Every program is formed by combining as many sequence, selection and iteration statements (p. 108) as is appropriate for the algorithm the program implements.
- Single-entry/single-exit control statements (p. 108) are attached to one another by connecting the exit point of one to the entry point of the next. This is known as control-statement stacking.
- A control statement may also be nested (p. 109) inside another control statement.

Section 4.5 `if` Single-Selection Statement
- Programs use selection statements to choose among alternative courses of action.
- The single-selection `if` statement's activity diagram contains the diamond symbol, which indicates that a decision is to be made. The workflow follows a path determined by the symbol's associated guard conditions (p. 109). If a guard condition is true, the workflow enters the action state to which the corresponding transition arrow points.
- The `if` statement is a single-entry/single-exit control statement.

Section 4.6 `if...else` Double-Selection Statement
- The `if` single-selection statement executes its body only when the condition is `true`.
- The `if...else` double-selection statement performs one action (or group of actions) when the condition is true and another action (or group of actions) when the condition is false.

Section 4.6.1 Nested `if...else` Statements
- A program can test multiple cases with nested `if...else` statements (p. 111).

Section 4.6.2 Dangling-`else` Problem
- The Java compiler associates an `else` with the immediately preceding `if` unless told to do otherwise by the placement of braces.

Section 4.6.3 Blocks

- A block (p. 112) of statements can be placed anywhere that a single statement can be placed.
- A logic error (p. 113) has its effect at execution time. A fatal logic error (p. 113) causes a program to fail and terminate prematurely. A nonfatal logic error (p. 113) allows a program to continue executing, but causes it to produce incorrect results.
- Just as a block can be placed anywhere a single statement can be placed, you can also use an empty statement, represented by placing a semicolon (`;`) where a statement would normally be.

Section 4.6.4 Conditional Operator (`?:`)

- The conditional operator `?:` (p. 113) takes three operands. Together, the operands and the `?:` symbol form a conditional expression (p. 113). The first operand (to the left of the `?`) is a boolean expression, the second is the value of the conditional expression if the condition is `true` and the third is the value of the conditional expression if the condition is `false`.

Section 4.8 `while` Iteration Statement

- The `while` iteration statement (p. 116) allows you to specify that a program should repeat an action while some condition remains true.
- The UML's merge (p. 117) symbol joins two flows of activity into one.
- The decision and merge symbols can be distinguished by the number of incoming and outgoing transition arrows. A decision symbol has one transition arrow pointing to the diamond and two or more transition arrows pointing out from the diamond to indicate possible transitions from that point. Each transition arrow pointing out of a decision symbol has a guard condition. A merge symbol has two or more transition arrows pointing to the diamond and only one transition arrow pointing from the diamond, to indicate multiple activity flows merging to continue the activity. None of the transition arrows associated with a merge symbol has a guard condition.

Section 4.9 Formulating Algorithms: Counter-Controlled Iteration

- Counter-controlled iteration (p. 118) uses a variable called a counter (or control variable) to control the number of times a set of statements execute.
- Counter-controlled iteration is often called definite iteration (p. 118), because the number of iterations is known before the loop begins executing.
- A total (p. 118) is a variable used to accumulate the sum of several values. Variables used to store totals are normally initialized to zero before being used in a program.
- A local variable's declaration must appear before the variable is used in that method. A local variable cannot be accessed outside the method in which it's declared.
- Dividing two integers results in integer division—the calculation's fractional part is truncated.

Section 4.10 Formulating Algorithms: Sentinel-Controlled Iteration

- In sentinel-controlled iteration (p. 122), a special value called a sentinel value (also called a signal value, a dummy value or a flag value) is used to indicate "end of data entry."
- A sentinel value must be chosen that cannot be confused with an acceptable input value.
- Top-down, stepwise refinement (p. 122) is essential to the development of well-structured programs.
- Division by zero is a logic error.
- To perform a floating-point calculation with integer values, cast one of the integers to type `double`.
- Java knows how to evaluate only arithmetic expressions in which the operands' types are identical. To ensure this, Java performs an operation called promotion on selected operands.
- The unary cast operator is formed by placing parentheses around the name of a type.

Section 4.12 Compound Assignment Operators

- The compound assignment operators (p. 133) abbreviate assignments. Statements of the form

  variable = *variable operator expression*;

  where *operator* is one of the binary operators +, -, *, / or %, can be written in the form

  variable operator= *expression*;

- The += operator adds the value of the expression on the right of the operator to the value of the variable on the left of the operator and stores the result in the variable on the left of the operator.

Section 4.13 Increment and Decrement Operators

- The unary increment operator, ++, and the unary decrement operator, --, add 1 to or subtract 1 from the value of a numeric variable (p. 134).
- An increment or decrement operator that's prefixed (p. 134) to a variable is the prefix increment or prefix decrement operator, respectively. An increment or decrement operator that's postfixed (p. 134) to a variable is the postfix increment or postfix decrement operator, respectively.
- Using the prefix increment or decrement operator to add or subtract 1 is known as preincrementing or predecrementing, respectively.
- Preincrementing or predecrementing a variable causes the variable to be incremented or decremented by 1; then the new value of the variable is used in the expression in which it appears.
- Using the postfix increment or decrement operator to add or subtract 1 is known as postincrementing or postdecrementing, respectively.
- Postincrementing or postdecrementing the variable causes its value to be used in the expression in which it appears; then the variable's value is incremented or decremented by 1.
- When incrementing or decrementing a variable in a statement by itself, the prefix and postfix increment have the same effect, and the prefix and postfix decrement have the same effect.

Section 4.14 Primitive Types

- Java requires all variables to have a type.
- Java uses Unicode characters and IEEE 754 floating-point numbers.

Self-Review Exercises

4.1 Fill in the blanks in each of the following statements:

a) All programs can be written in terms of three types of control structures: ________, ________ and ________.

b) The ________ statement is used to execute one action when a condition is true and another when that condition is false.

c) Repeating a set of instructions a specific number of times is called ________ iteration.

d) When it's not known in advance how many times a set of statements will be repeated, a(n) ________ value can be used to terminate the iteration.

e) The ________ structure is built into Java; by default, statements execute in the order they appear.

f) Instance variables of types `char`, `byte`, `short`, `int`, `long`, `float` and `double` are all given the value ________ by default.

g) If the increment operator is ________ to a variable, first the variable is incremented by 1, then its new value is used in the expression.

h) When the declaration `int y = 5;` is followed by the assignment `y += 3.3;` the value of `y` is ________.

4.2 State whether each of the following is *true* or *false*. If *false*, explain why.

a) An algorithm is a procedure for solving a problem in terms of the actions to execute and the order in which they execute.
b) A set of statements contained within a pair of parentheses is called a block.
c) A selection statement repeats an action while a condition remains true.
d) A nested control statement appears in the body of another control statement.
e) Java provides the arithmetic compound assignment operators `+=`, `-=`, `*=`, `/=` and `%=` for abbreviating assignment expressions.
f) The primitive types (`boolean`, `char`, `byte`, `short`, `int`, `long`, `float` and `double`) are portable across only Windows platforms.
g) Specifying the order in which statements execute in a program is called program control.
h) The unary cast operator `(double)` creates a temporary integer copy of its operand.
i) Instance variables of type `boolean` are given the value `true` by default.
j) Pseudocode helps you think out a program before attempting to write it in a programming language.

4.3 Write four different Java statements that each add 1 to integer variable `x`.

4.4 Write Java statements to accomplish each of the following tasks:

a) Use one statement to assign the sum of `x` and `y` to `z`, then increment `x` by 1.
b) Test whether variable `count` is greater than 10. If it is, print `"Count is greater than 10"`.
c) Use one statement to decrement the variable `x` by 1, then subtract it from variable `total` and store the result in variable `total`.
d) Calculate the remainder after `q` is divided by `divisor`, and assign the result to `q`. Write this statement in two different ways.

4.5 Write a Java statement to accomplish each of the following tasks:

a) Declare variable `sum` of type `int` and initialize it to `0`.
b) Declare variable `x` of type `int` and initialize it to `1`.
c) Add variable `x` to variable `sum`, and assign the result to variable `sum`.
d) Print `"The sum is: "`, followed by the value of variable `sum`.

4.6 Combine the statements that you wrote in Exercise 4.5 into a Java application that calculates and prints the sum of the integers from 1 to 10. Use a `while` statement to loop through the calculation and increment statements. The loop should terminate when the value of `x` becomes 11.

4.7 Determine the value of the variables in the statement `product *= x++;` after the calculation is performed. Assume that all variables are type `int` and initially have the value 5.

4.8 Identify and correct the errors in each of the following code segments—assume that all variables have been properly declared and initialized:

a)

```
while (c <= 5) {
   product *= c;
   ++c;
```

b)

```
if (gender == 1) {
   System.out.println("Woman");
}
else; {
   System.out.println("Man");
}
```

4.9 What is wrong with the following `while` statement?

```
while (z >= 0) {
   sum += z;
}
```

Answers to Self-Review Exercises

4.1 a) sequence, selection, iteration. b) `if...else`. c) counter-controlled (or definite). d) sentinel, signal, flag or dummy. e) sequence. f) `0` (zero). g) prefixed. h) 8 [*Note:* You might expect a compilation error on the assignment statement. The Java Language Specification says that compound assignment operators perform an implicit cast on the right-hand expression's value to match the type of the variable on the operator's left side. So the calculated value `5 + 3.3 = 8.3` is actually cast to the `int` value `8`.].

4.2 a) True. b) False. A set of statements contained within a pair of braces (`{` and `}`) is called a block. c) False. An iteration statement specifies that an action is to be repeated while some condition remains true. d) True. e) True. f) False. The primitive types (`boolean`, `char`, `byte`, `short`, `int`, `long`, `float` and `double`) are portable across all computer platforms that support Java. g) True. h) False. The unary cast operator `(double)` creates a temporary floating-point copy of its operand. i) False. Instance variables of type `boolean` are given the value `false` by default. j) True.

4.3 The four ways to add `1` to `x` are:

```
x = x + 1;
x += 1;
++x;
x++;
```

4.4 Answers:

a) `z = x++ + y;`

b)

```
if (count > 10) {
   System.out.println("Count is greater than 10");
}
```

c) `total -= --x;`

d)

```
q %= divisor;
q = q % divisor;
```

4.5 Answers:

a) `int sum = 0;`

b) `int x = 1;`

c) `sum += x;` or `sum = sum + x;`

d) `System.out.printf("The sum is: %d%n", sum);`

4.6 The answer to Exercise 4.6 is as follows:

```
// Exercise 4.6: Calculate.java
// Calculate the sum of the integers from 1 to 10
public class Calculate {
   public static void main(String[] args) {
      int sum = 0;
      int x = 1;

      while (x <= 10) { // while x is less than or equal to 10
         sum += x; // add x to sum
         ++x; // increment x
      }

      System.out.printf("The sum is: %d%n", sum);
   }
}
```

```
The sum is: 55
```

4.7 `product = 25, x = 6`

4.8 Answers:

a) Error: The closing right brace of the `while` statement's body is missing.
Correction: Add a closing right brace after the statement `++c;`.

b) Error: The semicolon after `else` results in a logic error. The second output statement will always be executed.
Correction: Remove the semicolon after `else`.

4.9 The value of the variable `z` is never changed in the `while` statement. Therefore, if the loop-continuation condition `(z >= 0)` is true, an infinite loop is created. To prevent an infinite loop from occurring, `z` must be decremented so that it eventually becomes less than 0.

Exercises

4.10 Compare and contrast the `if` single-selection statement and the `while` iteration statement. How are these two statements similar? How are they different?

4.11 Explain what happens when a Java program attempts to divide one integer by another. What happens to the fractional part of the calculation? How can you avoid that outcome?

4.12 Describe the two ways in which control statements can be combined.

4.13 What type of iteration would be appropriate for calculating the sum of the first 100 positive integers? What type would be appropriate for calculating the sum of an arbitrary number of positive integers? Briefly describe how each of these tasks could be performed.

4.14 What is the difference between preincrementing and postincrementing a variable?

4.15 Identify and correct the errors in each of the following pieces of code. [*Note:* There may be more than one error in each piece of code.]

a)

```
int x = 1, total;
while (x <= 10) {
   total += x;
   ++x;
}
```

b)

```
while (x <= 100)
   total += x;
   ++x;
```

c)

```
while (y > 0) {a
   System.out.println(y);
   ++y;
```

4.16 What does the following program print?

```
// Exercise 4.16: Mystery.java
public class Mystery {
   public static void main(String[] args) {
      int x = 1;
      int total = 0;

      while (x <= 10) {
         int y = x * x;
         System.out.println(y);
         total += y;
         ++x;
      }

      System.out.printf("Total is %d%n", total);
   }
}
```

For Exercise 4.17 through Exercise 4.20, perform each of the following steps:

a) Read the problem statement.
b) Formulate the algorithm using pseudocode and top-down, stepwise refinement.
c) Write a Java program.
d) Test, debug and execute the Java program.
e) Process three complete sets of data.

4.17 *(Gas Mileage)* Drivers are concerned with the mileage their automobiles get. One driver has kept track of several trips by recording the miles driven and gallons used for each tankful. Develop a Java application that will input the miles driven and gallons used (both as integers) for each trip. The program should calculate and display the miles per gallon obtained for each trip and print the combined miles per gallon obtained for all trips up to this point. All averaging calculations should produce floating-point results. Use class `Scanner` and sentinel-controlled iteration to obtain the data from the user.

4.18 *(Credit Limit Calculator)* Develop a Java application that determines whether any of several department-store customers has exceeded the credit limit on a charge account. For each customer, the following facts are available:

a) account number
b) balance at the beginning of the month
c) total of all items charged by the customer this month
d) total of all credits applied to the customer's account this month
e) allowed credit limit.

The program should input all these facts as integers, calculate the new balance (= *beginning balance + charges – credits*), display the new balance and determine whether the new balance exceeds the customer's credit limit. For those customers whose credit limit is exceeded, the program should display the message `"Credit limit exceeded"`.

4.19 *(Sales Commission Calculator)* A large company pays its salespeople on a commission basis. The salespeople receive $200 per week plus 9% of their gross sales for that week. For example, a salesperson who sells $5,000 worth of merchandise in a week receives $200 plus 9% of $5,000, or a total of $650. You've been supplied with a list of the items sold by each salesperson. The values of these items are shown in Fig. 4.33. Develop a Java application that inputs one salesperson's items sold for last week and calculates and displays that salesperson's earnings. There's no limit to the number of items that can be sold.

Item	Value
1	239.99
2	129.75
3	99.95
4	350.89

Fig. 4.33 | Item values for Exercise 4.19.

4.20 *(Salary Calculator)* Develop a Java application that determines the gross pay for each of three employees. The company pays straight time for the first 40 hours worked by each employee and time and a half for all hours worked in excess of 40. You're given a list of the employees, their number of hours worked last week and their hourly rates. Your program should input this information for each employee, then determine and display the employee's gross pay. Use class `Scanner` to input the data.

4.21 *(Find the Largest Number)* The process of finding the largest value is used frequently in computer applications. For example, a program that determines the winner of a sales contest would input the number of units sold by each salesperson. The salesperson who sells the most units wins the contest. Write a pseudocode program, then a Java application that inputs a series of 10 integers and determines and prints the largest integer. Your program should use at least the following three variables:

a) `counter`: A counter to count to 10 (i.e., to keep track of how many numbers have been input and to determine when all 10 numbers have been processed).
b) `number`: The integer most recently input by the user.
c) `largest`: The largest number found so far.

4.22 *(Tabular Output)* Write a Java application that uses looping to print the following table of values:

```
N     10*N    100*N    1000*N

1     10      100      1000
2     20      200      2000
3     30      300      3000
4     40      400      4000
5     50      500      5000
```

4.23 *(Find the Two Largest Numbers)* Using an approach similar to that for Exercise 4.21, find the *two* largest values of the 10 values entered. [*Note:* You may input each number only once.]

4.24 *(Validating User Input)* Modify the program in Fig. 4.12 to validate its inputs. For any input, if the value entered is other than 1 or 2, keep looping until the user enters a correct value.

4.25 What does the following program print?

```java
// Exercise 4.25: Mystery2.java
public class Mystery2 {
   public static void main(String[] args) {
      int count = 1;

      while (count <= 10) {
         System.out.println(count % 2 == 1 ? "****" : "++++++++");
         ++count;
      }
   }
}
```

4.26 What does the following program print?

```java
// Exercise 4.26: Mystery3.java
public class Mystery3 {
   public static void main(String[] args) {
      int row = 10;

      while (row >= 1) {
         int column = 1;

         while (column <= 10) {
            System.out.print(row % 2 == 1 ? "<" : ">");
            ++column;
         }

         --row;
         System.out.println();
      }
   }
}
```

4.27 *(Dangling-`else` Problem)* The Java compiler always associates an `else` with the immediately preceding `if` unless told to do otherwise by the placement of braces (`{` and `}`). This behavior can lead to what is referred to as the **dangling-`else` problem.** The indentation of the nested statement

```java
if (x > 5)
   if (y > 5)
      System.out.println("x and y are > 5");
else
   System.out.println("x is <= 5");
```

appears to indicate that if `x` is greater than `5`, the nested `if` statement determines whether `y` is also greater than `5`. If so, the statement outputs the string `"x and y are > 5"`. Otherwise, it appears that if `x` is not greater than `5`, the `else` part of the `if...else` outputs the string `"x is <= 5"`. Beware! This nested `if...else` statement does *not* execute as it appears. The compiler actually interprets the statement as

```
if (x > 5)
   if (y > 5)
      System.out.println("x and y are > 5");
   else
      System.out.println("x is <= 5");
```

in which the body of the first `if` is a *nested* `if...else`. The outer `if` statement tests whether `x` is greater than `5`. If so, execution continues by testing whether `y` is also greater than `5`. If the second condition is *true*, the proper string—`"x and y are > 5"`—is displayed. However, if the second condition is *false*, the string `"x is <= 5"` is displayed, even though we know that `x` is greater than `5`. Equally bad, if the outer `if` statement's condition is *false*, the inner `if...else` is skipped and nothing is displayed. For this exercise, add braces to the preceding code snippet to force the nested `if...else` statement to execute as it was originally intended.

4.28 *(Another Dangling-`else` Problem)* Based on the dangling-`else` discussion in Exercise 4.27, state the output for each of the following code segments when `x` is `9` and `y` is `11` and when `x` is `11` and `y` is `9`. We eliminated the indentation from the following code to make the problem more challenging. [*Hint:* Apply the indentation conventions you've learned.]

a)

```
if (x < 10)
if (y > 10)
System.out.println("*****");
else
System.out.println("#####");
System.out.println("$$$$$");
```

b)

```
if (x < 10) {
if (y > 10)
System.out.println("*****");
}
else {
System.out.println("#####");
System.out.println("$$$$$");
}
```

4.29 *(Another Dangling-`else` Problem)* Based on the dangling-`else` discussion in Exercise 4.27, modify the following code to produce the output shown. Use proper indentation techniques. You must not make any additional changes other than inserting braces and changing the code's indentation. We've eliminated the indentation from the following code to make the problem more challenging. [*Note:* It's possible that no modification is necessary.]

```
if (y == 8)
if (x == 5)
System.out.println("@@@@@");
else
System.out.println("#####");
System.out.println("$$$$$");
System.out.println("&&&&&");
```

a) Assuming that `x = 5` and `y = 8`, the following output is produced:

```
@@@@@
$$$$$
&&&&&
```

b) Assuming that `x = 5` and `y = 8`, the following output is produced:

```
@@@@@
```

c) Assuming that `x = 5` and `y = 8`, the following output is produced:

```
@@@@@
&&&&&
```

d) Assuming that `x = 5` and `y = 7`, the following output is produced. [*Note:* The last three output statements after the `else` are all part of a block.]

```
#####
$$$$$
&&&&&
```

4.30 *(Square of Asterisks)* Write an application that prompts the user to enter the size of the side of a square, then displays a hollow square of that size made of asterisks. Your program should work for squares of all side lengths between 1 and 20.

4.31 *(Palindromes)* A palindrome is a sequence of characters that reads the same backward as forward. For example, each of the following five-digit integers is a palindrome: 12321, 55555, 45554 and 11611. Write an application that reads in a five-digit integer and determines whether it's a palindrome. If the number is not five digits long, display an error message and allow the user to enter a new value.

4.32 *(Printing the Decimal Equivalent of a Binary Number)* Write an application that inputs an integer containing only 0s and 1s (i.e., a binary integer) and prints its decimal equivalent. [*Hint:* Use the remainder and division operators to pick off the binary number's digits one at a time, from right to left. In the decimal number system, the rightmost digit has a positional value of 1 and the next digit to the left a positional value of 10, then 100, then 1000, and so on. The decimal number 234 can be interpreted as 4 * 1 + 3 * 10 + 2 * 100. In the binary number system, the rightmost digit has a positional value of 1, the next digit to the left a positional value of 2, then 4, then 8, and so on. The decimal equivalent of binary 1101 is 1 * 1 + 0 * 2 + 1 * 4 + 1 * 8, or 1 + 0 + 4 + 8 or, 13.]

4.33 *(Checkerboard Pattern of Asterisks)* Write an application that uses only the output statements

```
System.out.print("* ");
System.out.print(" ");
System.out.println();
```

to display the checkerboard pattern that follows. A `System.out.println` method call with no arguments causes the program to output a single newline character. [*Hint:* Iteration statements are required.]

```
* * * * * * * *
 * * * * * * * *
* * * * * * * *
 * * * * * * * *
* * * * * * * *
 * * * * * * * *
* * * * * * * *
 * * * * * * * *
```

4.34 *(Multiples of 2 with an Infinite Loop)* Write an application that keeps displaying in the command window the multiples of the integer 2—namely, 2, 4, 8, 16, 32, 64, and so on. Your loop should not terminate (i.e., it should create an infinite loop). What happens when you run this program?

4.35 *(What's Wrong with This Code?)* What is wrong with the following statement? Provide the correct statement to add one to the sum of x and y.

```
System.out.println(++(x + y));
```

4.36 *(Sides of a Triangle)* Write an application that reads three nonzero values entered by the user and determines and prints whether they could represent the sides of a triangle.

4.37 *(Sides of a Right Triangle)* Write an application that reads three nonzero integers and determines and prints whether they could represent the sides of a right triangle.

4.38 *(Factorial)* The factorial of a nonnegative integer n is written as $n!$ (pronounced "n factorial") and is defined for values of n greater than or equal to 1 as:

$$n! = n \cdot (n-1) \cdot (n-2) \cdot \ldots \cdot 1$$

and for the n value 0 as:

$$n! = 1$$

For example, $5! = 5 \cdot 4 \cdot 3 \cdot 2 \cdot 1$, which is 120.

a) Write an application that reads a nonnegative integer and computes and prints its factorial.

b) Write an application that estimates the value of the mathematical constant e by using the following formula. Allow the user to enter the number of terms to calculate.

$$e = 1 + \frac{1}{1!} + \frac{1}{2!} + \frac{1}{3!} + \ldots$$

c) Write an application that computes the value of e^x by using the following formula. Allow the user to enter the number of terms to calculate.

$$e^x = 1 + \frac{x}{1!} + \frac{x^2}{2!} + \frac{x^3}{3!} + \ldots$$

Making a Difference

4.39 *(Enforcing Privacy with Cryptography)* The explosive growth of Internet communications and data storage on Internet-connected computers has greatly increased privacy concerns. The field of cryptography is concerned with coding data to make it difficult (and hopefully—with the most advanced schemes—impossible) for unauthorized users to read. In this exercise you'll investigate a simple scheme for encrypting and decrypting data. A company that wants to send data over the Internet has asked you to write a program that will encrypt it so that it may be transmitted more securely. All the data is transmitted as four-digit integers. Your application should read a four-digit integer entered by the user and encrypt it as follows: Replace each digit with the result of adding 7 to the digit and getting the remainder after dividing the new value by 10. Then swap the first digit with the third, and swap the second digit with the fourth. Then print the encrypted integer. Write a separate application that inputs an encrypted four-digit integer and decrypts it (by reversing the encryption scheme) to form the original number. [*Optional reading project:* Research "public key cryptography" in general and the PGP (Pretty Good Privacy) specific public key scheme. You may also want to investigate the RSA scheme, which is widely used in industrial-strength applications.]

4.40 *(World Population Growth)* World population has grown considerably over the centuries. Continued growth could eventually challenge the limits of breathable air, drinkable water, arable cropland and other limited resources. There's evidence that growth has been slowing in recent years and that world population could peak some time this century, then start to decline.

For this exercise, research world population growth issues online. *Be sure to investigate various viewpoints.* Get estimates for the current world population and its growth rate (the percentage by which it's likely to increase this year). Write a program that calculates world population growth each year for the next 75 years, *using the simplifying assumption that the current growth rate will stay constant.* Print the results in a table. The first column should display the year from year 1 to year 75. The second column should display the anticipated world population at the end of that year. The third column should display the numerical increase in the world population that would occur that year. Using your results, determine the year in which the population would be double what it is today, if this year's growth rate were to persist.

5 Control Statements: Part 2; Logical Operators

Objectives

In this chapter you'll:

- Learn the essentials of counter-controlled iteration.
- Use the `for` and `do...while` iteration statements to execute statements in a program repeatedly.
- Understand multiple selection using the `switch` selection statement.
- Implement an object-oriented `AutoPolicy` case study using `Strings` in `switch` statements.
- Alter the flow of control with the `break` and `continue` program-control statements.
- Use the logical operators to form complex conditional expressions in control statements.

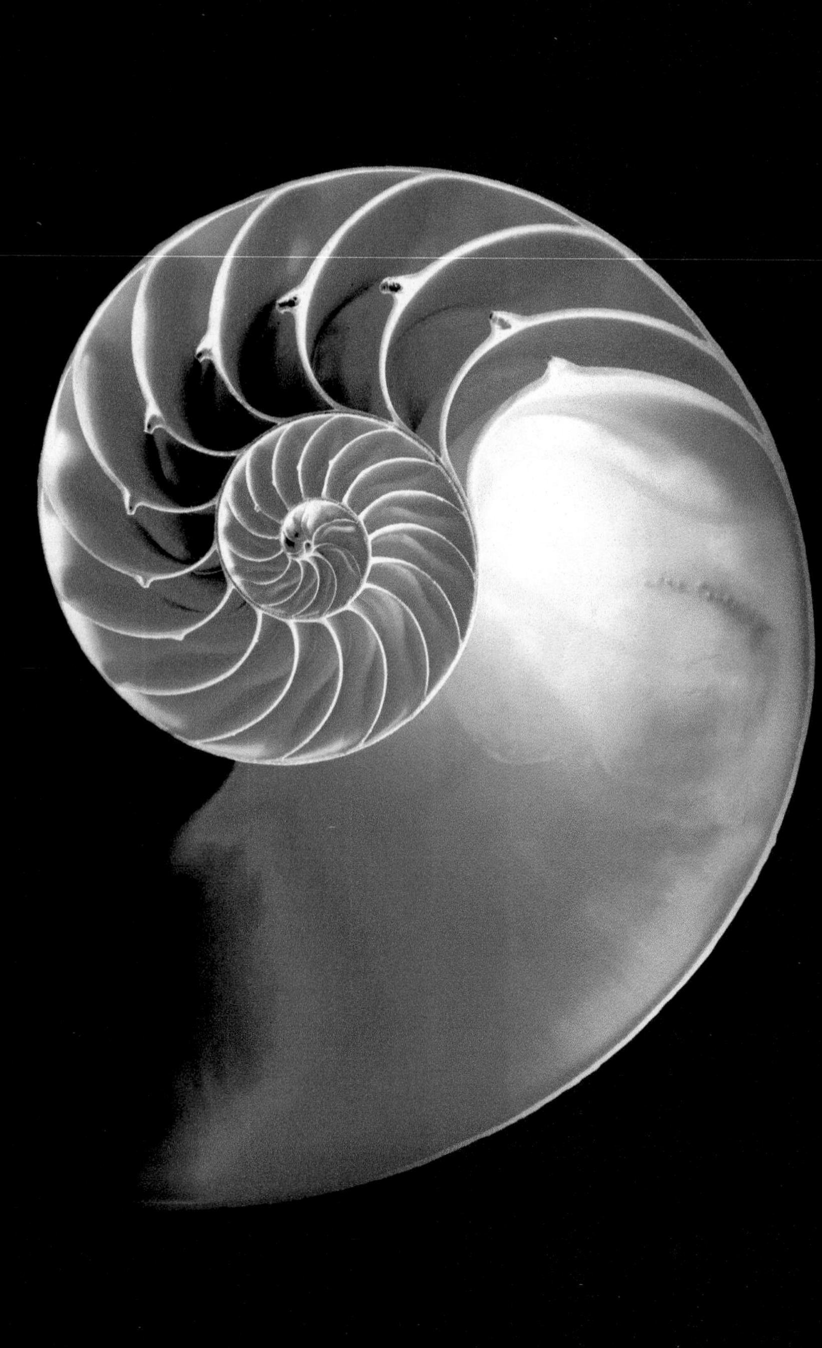

Outline

5.1 Introduction

This chapter continues our presentation of structured-programming theory and principles by introducing all but one of Java's remaining control statements. We demonstrate Java's `for`, `do...while` and `switch` statements. Through a series of short examples using `while` and `for`, we explore the essentials of counter-controlled iteration. We use a `switch` statement to count the number of A, B, C, D and F grade equivalents in a set of numeric grades entered by the user. We introduce the `break` and `continue` program-control statements. We discuss Java's logical operators, which enable you to use more complex conditional expressions in control statements. Finally, we summarize Java's control statements and the proven problem-solving techniques presented in this chapter and Chapter 4.

5.2 Essentials of Counter-Controlled Iteration

This section uses the `while` iteration statement introduced in Chapter 4 to formalize the elements required to perform counter-controlled iteration, which requires

1. a **control variable** (or loop counter)
2. the **initial value** of the control variable
3. the **increment** by which the control variable is modified each time through the loop (also known as **each iteration of the loop**)
4. the **loop-continuation condition** that determines if looping should continue.

To see these elements of counter-controlled iteration, consider the application of Fig. 5.1, which uses a loop to display the numbers from 1 through 10.

In Fig. 5.1, the elements of counter-controlled iteration are defined in lines 6, 8 and 10. Line 6 *declares* the control variable (`counter`) as an `int`, *reserves space* for it in memory

```
1  // Fig. 5.1: WhileCounter.java
2  // Counter-controlled iteration with the while iteration statement.
3
4  public class WhileCounter {
5     public static void main(String[] args) {
6        int counter = 1; // declare and initialize control variable
7
8        while (counter <= 10) { // loop-continuation condition
9           System.out.printf("%d  ", counter);
10          ++counter; // increment control variable
11       }
12
13       System.out.println();
14    }
15 }
```

```
1  2  3  4  5  6  7  8  9  10
```

Fig. 5.1 | Counter-controlled iteration with the `while` iteration statement.

and sets its *initial value* to `1`. Variable `counter` also could have been declared and initialized with the following local-variable declaration and assignment statements:

```
int counter; // declare counter
counter = 1; // initialize counter to 1
```

Line 9 displays control variable `counter`'s value during each iteration of the loop. Line 10 *increments* the control variable by 1 for each iteration of the loop. The loop-continuation condition in the `while` (line 8) tests whether the value of the control variable is less than or equal to `10` (the final value for which the condition is `true`). The program performs the body of this `while` even when the control variable is `10`. The loop terminates when the control variable exceeds `10` (i.e., `counter` becomes `11`).

Common Programming Error 5.1

Because floating-point values may be approximate, controlling loops with floating-point variables may result in imprecise counter values and inaccurate termination tests.

Error-Prevention Tip 5.1

Use integers to control counting loops.

5.3 for Iteration Statement

Section 5.2 presented the essentials of counter-controlled iteration. The `while` statement can be used to implement any counter-controlled loop. Java also provides the **`for` iteration statement**, which specifies the counter-controlled-iteration details in a single line of code. Figure 5.2 reimplements the application of Fig. 5.1 using `for`.

When the `for` statement (lines 8–10) begins executing, the control variable `counter` is *declared* and *initialized* to `1`. (Recall from Section 5.2 that the first two elements of counter-controlled iteration are the *control variable* and its *initial value*.) Next, the program checks the *loop-continuation condition*, `counter <= 10`, which is between the two

```
1  // Fig. 5.2: ForCounter.java
2  // Counter-controlled iteration with the for iteration statement.
3
4  public class ForCounter {
5     public static void main(String[] args) {
6        // for statement header includes initialization,
7        // loop-continuation condition and increment
8        for (int counter = 1; counter <= 10; counter++) {
9           System.out.printf("%d  ", counter);
10       }
11
12       System.out.println();
13    }
14 }
```

```
1  2  3  4  5  6  7  8  9  10
```

Fig. 5.2 | Counter-controlled iteration with the `for` iteration statement.

required semicolons. Because the initial value of `counter` is `1`, the condition initially is `true`. Therefore, the body statement (line 9) displays control variable `counter`'s value, namely `1`. After executing the loop's body, the program increments `counter` in the expression `counter++`, which appears to the right of the second semicolon. Then the loop-continuation test is performed again to determine whether the program should continue with the next iteration of the loop. At this point, the control variable's value is `2`, so the condition is still `true` (the *final value* is not exceeded)—thus, the program performs the body statement again (i.e., the next iteration of the loop). This process continues until the numbers 1 through 10 have been displayed and the `counter`'s value becomes `11`, causing the loop-continuation test to fail and iteration to terminate (after 10 iterations of the loop body). Then the program performs the first statement after the `for`—in this case, line 12.

Figure 5.2 uses (in line 8) the loop-continuation condition `counter <= 10`. If you incorrectly specified `counter < 10` as the condition, the loop would iterate only nine times. This is a common *logic error* called an **off-by-one error**.

Common Programming Error 5.2

Using an incorrect relational operator or an incorrect final value of a loop counter in the loop-continuation condition of an iteration statement can cause an off-by-one error.

Error-Prevention Tip 5.2

Using the final value and operator `<=` in a loop's condition helps avoid off-by-one errors. For a loop that outputs 1 to 10, the loop-continuation condition should be `counter <= 10` rather than `counter < 10` (which causes an off-by-one error) or `counter < 11` (which is correct). Many programmers prefer so-called zero-based counting, in which to count 10 times, `counter` would be initialized to zero and the loop-continuation test would be `counter < 10`.

Error-Prevention Tip 5.3

As Chapter 4 mentioned, integers can overflow, causing logic errors. A loop's control variable also could overflow. Write your loop conditions carefully to prevent this.

A Closer Look at the `for` *Statement's Header*

Figure 5.3 takes a closer look at the `for` statement in Fig. 5.2. The first line—including the keyword `for` and everything in parentheses after `for` (line 8 in Fig. 5.2)—is sometimes called the **`for` statement header**. The `for` header "does it all"—it specifies each item needed for counter-controlled iteration with a control variable. If there's more than one statement in the body of the `for`, braces are required to define the body of the loop.

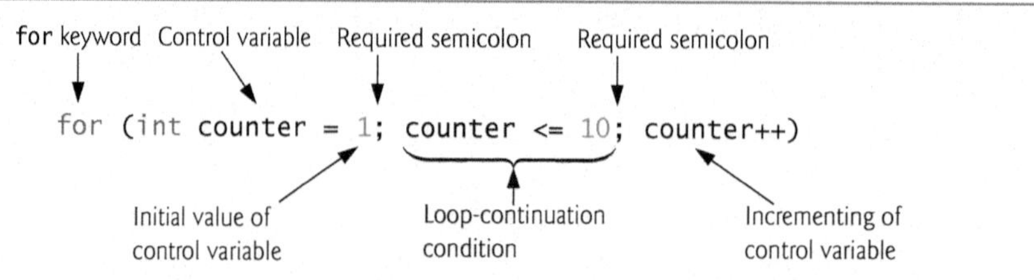

Fig. 5.3 | `for` statement header components.

General Format of a `for` *Statement*

The general format of the `for` statement is

```
for (initialization; loopContinuationCondition; increment) {
   statements
}
```

where the *initialization* expression names the loop's control variable and *optionally* provides its initial value, *loopContinuationCondition* determines whether the loop should continue executing and *increment* modifies the control variable's value, so that the loop-continuation condition eventually becomes `false`. The two semicolons in the `for` header are required. If the loop-continuation condition is initially `false`, the program does *not* execute the body. Instead, execution proceeds with the statement following the `for`.

Representing a `for` *Statement with an Equivalent* `while` *Statement*

The `for` statement often can be represented with an equivalent `while` statement as follows:

```
initialization;

while (loopContinuationCondition) {
   statements
   increment;
}
```

In Section 5.8, we show a case in which a `for` statement cannot be represented with an equivalent `while` statement. Typically, `for` statements are used for counter-controlled iteration and `while` statements for sentinel-controlled iteration. However, `while` and `for` can each be used for either iteration type.

Scope of a `for` *Statement's Control Variable*

If the *initialization* expression in the `for` header declares the control variable (i.e., the control variable's type is specified before the variable name, as in Fig. 5.2), the control variable can be used *only* in that `for` statement—it will not exist outside it. This restricted use is known as the variable's **scope**. The scope of a variable defines where it can be used in a program. For example, a *local variable* can be used *only* in the method that declares it and *only* from the point of declaration through the next right brace (}), which is often the brace that closes the method body. Scope is discussed in detail in Chapter 6, Methods: A Deeper Look.

Common Programming Error 5.3

When a `for` statement's control variable is declared in the initialization section of the `for`'s header, using the control variable after the `for`'s body is a compilation error.

Expressions in a `for` Statement's Header Are Optional

The three expressions in a `for` header are optional. If the *loopContinuationCondition* is omitted, Java assumes that it's *always* `true`, thus creating an *infinite loop*. You might omit the *initialization* expression if the program initializes the control variable *before* the loop. You might omit the *increment* expression if the program calculates the increment with statements in the loop's body or if no increment is needed. The increment expression in a `for` acts as if it were a standalone statement at the end of the `for`'s body. So, the expressions

```
counter = counter + 1
counter += 1
++counter
counter++
```

are equivalent increment expressions in a `for` statement. Many programmers prefer `counter++` because it's concise and because a `for` loop evaluates its increment expression *after* its body executes, so the postfix increment form seems more natural. In this case, the variable being incremented does not appear in a larger expression, so preincrementing and postincrementing actually have the *same* effect.

Common Programming Error 5.4

Placing a semicolon immediately to the right of the right parenthesis of a `for` header makes that `for`'s body an empty statement. This is normally a logic error.

Error-Prevention Tip 5.4

Infinite loops occur when the loop-continuation condition in an iteration statement never becomes `false`. To prevent this situation in a counter-controlled loop, ensure that the control variable is modified during each iteration of the loop so that the loop-continuation condition will eventually become `false`. In a sentinel-controlled loop, ensure that the sentinel value is able to be input.

Placing Arithmetic Expressions in a `for` Statement's Header

The initialization, loop-continuation condition and increment portions of a `for` statement can contain arithmetic expressions. For example, assume that `x = 2` and `y = 10`. If `x` and `y` are not modified in the body of the loop, the statement

```
for (int j = x; j <= 4 * x * y; j += y / x)
```

is equivalent to the statement

```
for (int j = 2; j <= 80; j += 5)
```

The increment of a `for` statement may also be *negative*, in which case it's a **decrement**, and the loop counts *downward*.

Using a **for** *Statement's Control Variable in the Statement's Body*

Programs frequently display the control-variable value or use it in calculations in the loop body, but this use is *not* required. The control variable is commonly used to control iteration *without* being mentioned in the body of the for.

> **Error-Prevention Tip 5.5**
> *Although the value of the control variable can be changed in the body of a* for *loop, avoid doing so, because this practice can lead to subtle errors.*

UML Activity Diagram for the **for** *Statement*

The for statement's UML activity diagram is similar to that of the while statement (Fig. 4.6). Figure 5.4 shows the activity diagram of the for statement in Fig. 5.2. The diagram makes it clear that initialization occurs *once before* the loop-continuation test is evaluated the first time, and that incrementing occurs *each* time through the loop *after* the body statement executes.

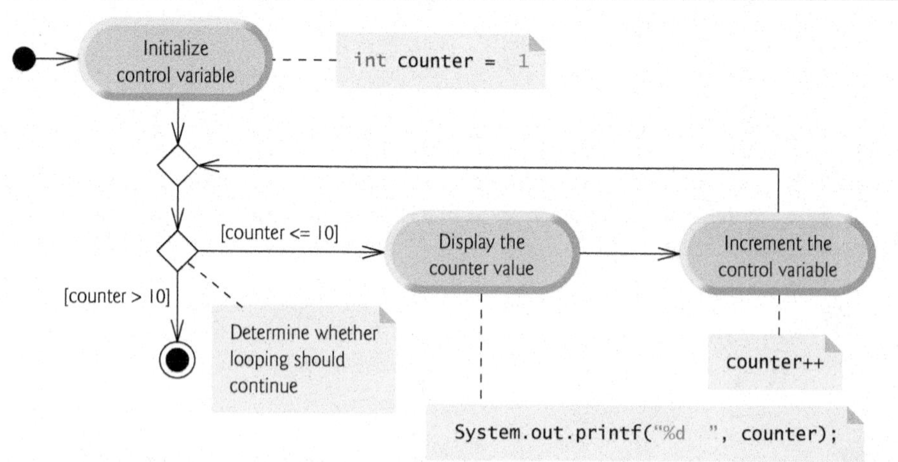

Fig. 5.4 | UML activity diagram for the for statement in Fig. 5.2.

5.4 Examples Using the for Statement

The following examples show techniques for varying the control variable in a for statement. In each case, we write *only* the appropriate for header. Note the change in the relational operator for the loops that *decrement* the control variable.

a) Vary the control variable from 1 to 100 in increments of 1.

```
for (int i = 1; i <= 100; i++)
```

b) Vary the control variable from 100 to 1 in *decrements* of 1.

```
for (int i = 100; i >= 1; i--)
```

c) Vary the control variable from 7 to 77 in increments of 7.

```
for (int i = 7; i <= 77; i += 7)
```

d) Vary the control variable from 20 to 2 in *decrements* of 2.

```
for (int i = 20; i >= 2; i -= 2)
```

e) Vary the control variable over the values 2, 5, 8, 11, 14, 17, 20.

```
for (int i = 2; i <= 20; i += 3)
```

f) Vary the control variable over the values 99, 88, 77, 66, 55, 44, 33, 22, 11, 0.

```
for (int i = 99; i >= 0; i -= 11)
```

Common Programming Error 5.5

Using an incorrect relational operator in the loop-continuation condition of a loop that counts downward (e.g., using `i <= 1` instead of `i >= 1` in a loop counting down to 1) is usually a logic error.

Common Programming Error 5.6

Do not use equality operators (`!=` or `==`) in a loop-continuation condition if the loop's control variable increments or decrements by more than 1. For example, consider the `for` statement header `for (int counter = 1; counter != 10; counter += 2)`. The loop-continuation test `counter != 10` never becomes `false` (resulting in an infinite loop*) because `counter` increments by 2 after each iteration.*

Error-Prevention Tip 5.6

Counting loops are error prone. In subsequent chapters, we'll introduce lambdas and streams—technologies that you can use to eliminate such errors.

5.4.1 Application: Summing the Even Integers from 2 to 20

We now consider two sample applications that demonstrate simple uses of `for`. The application in Fig. 5.5 uses a `for` statement to sum the even integers from 2 to 20 and store the result in an `int` variable called `total`.

```
// Fig. 5.5: Sum.java
// Summing integers with the for statement.

public class Sum {
   public static void main(String[] args) {
      int total = 0;

      // total even integers from 2 through 20
      for (int number = 2; number <= 20; number += 2) {
         total += number;
      }

      System.out.printf("Sum is %d%n", total);
   }
}
```

```
Sum is 110
```

Fig. 5.5 | Summing integers with the `for` statement.

The *initialization* and *increment* expressions can be comma-separated lists that enable you to use multiple initialization expressions or multiple increment expressions. For example, *although this is discouraged*, you could merge the for statement's body in lines 9–11 of Fig. 5.5 into the increment portion of the for header by using a comma as follows:

```
for (int number = 2; number <= 20; total += number, number += 2) {
   ; // empty statement
}
```

Good Programming Practice 5.1

For readability limit the size of control-statement headers to a single line if possible.

5.4.2 Application: Compound-Interest Calculations

Next, let's use the for statement to compute compound interest. Consider the following problem:

> *A person invests $1,000 in a savings account yielding 5% interest. Assuming that all the interest is left on deposit, calculate and print the amount of money in the account at the end of each year for 10 years. Use the following formula to determine the amounts:*
>
> $$a = p\,(1 + r)^n$$
>
> *where*
>
> *p is the original amount invested (i.e., the principal)*
> *r is the annual interest rate (e.g., use 0.05 for 5%)*
> *n is the number of years*
> *a is the amount on deposit at the end of the nth year.*

The solution to this problem (Fig. 5.6) involves a loop that performs the indicated calculation for each of the 10 years the money remains on deposit. Lines 6, 7 and 15 in main declare double variables principal, rate and amount. Lines 6–7 initialize principal to 1000.0 and rate to 0.05. Line 15 initializes amount to the result of the compound-interest calculation. Java treats floating-point constants like 1000.0 and 0.05 as type double. Similarly, Java treats whole-number constants like 7 and -22 as type int.

```
1  // Fig. 5.6: Interest.java
2  // Compound-interest calculations with for.
3
4  public class Interest {
5     public static void main(String[] args) {
6        double principal = 1000.0; // initial amount before interest
7        double rate = 0.05; // interest rate
8
9        // display headers
10       System.out.printf("%s%20s%n", "Year", "Amount on deposit");
11
```

Fig. 5.6 | Compound-interest calculations with for. (Part 1 of 2.)

```
12         // calculate amount on deposit for each of ten years
13         for (int year = 1; year <= 10; ++year) {
14            // calculate new amount on deposit for specified year
15            double amount = principal * Math.pow(1.0 + rate, year);
16
17            // display the year and the amount
18            System.out.printf("%4d%,20.2f%n", year, amount);
19         }
20      }
21   }
```

```
Year   Amount on deposit
   1            1,050.00
   2            1,102.50
   3            1,157.63
   4            1,215.51
   5            1,276.28
   6            1,340.10
   7            1,407.10
   8            1,477.46
   9            1,551.33
  10            1,628.89
```

Fig. 5.6 | Compound-interest calculations with `for`. (Part 2 of 2.)

Formatting Strings with Field Widths and Justification

Line 10 outputs the headers for two columns of output. The first column displays the year and the second column the amount on deposit at the end of that year. We use the format specifier `%20s` to output the `String` `"Amount on Deposit"`. The integer `20` between the `%` and the conversion character `s` indicates that the value should be displayed with a **field width** of 20—that is, `printf` displays the value with at least 20 character positions. If the value to be output is less than 20 character positions wide (17 characters in this example), the value is **right justified** in the field by default. If the `year` value to be output were more than four character positions wide, the field width would be extended to the right to accommodate the entire value—this would push the `amount` field to the right, upsetting the neat columns of our tabular output. To output values **left justified**, simply precede the field width with the **minus sign (-) formatting flag** (e.g., `%-20s`).

Performing the Interest Calculations with `static` *Method* `pow` *of Class* `Math`

The `for` statement (lines 13–19) executes its body 10 times, varying control variable `year` from 1 to 10 in increments of 1. This loop terminates when `year` becomes 11. (Variable `year` represents *n* in the problem statement.)

Classes provide methods that perform common tasks on objects. In fact, most methods must be called on a specific object. For example, to output text in Fig. 5.6, line 10 calls method `printf` on the `System.out` object. Some classes also provide methods that perform common tasks and do *not* require you to first create objects of those classes. These are called `static` methods. For example, Java does not include an exponentiation operator, so the designers of Java's `Math` class defined `static` method `pow` for raising a value to a power. You can call a `static` method by specifying the *class name* followed by a dot (`.`) and the method name, as in

```
ClassName.methodName(arguments)
```

In Chapter 6, you'll learn how to implement `static` methods in your own classes.

We use `static` method **`pow`** of class **`Math`** to perform the compound-interest calculation in Fig. 5.6. `Math.pow(x, y)` calculates the value of x raised to the yth power. The method receives two `double` arguments and returns a `double` value. Line 15 performs the calculation $a = p(1 + r)^n$, where a is `amount`, p is `principal`, r is `rate` and n is `year`. Class `Math` is defined in package `java.lang`, so you do *not* need to import class `Math` to use it.

The body of the `for` statement contains the calculation `1.0 + rate`, which appears as an argument to the `Math.pow` method. In fact, this calculation produces the *same* result each time through the loop, so repeating it in every iteration of the loop is wasteful.

Performance Tip 5.1

In loops, avoid calculations for which the result never changes—such calculations should typically be placed before the loop. Many of today's sophisticated optimizing compilers will place such calculations outside loops in the compiled code.

Formatting Floating-Point Numbers

After each calculation, line 18 outputs the year and the amount on deposit at the end of that year. The year is output in a field width of four characters (as specified by `%4d`). The amount is output as a floating-point number with the format specifier `%,20.2f`.

The **comma (`,`) formatting flag** indicates that the floating-point value should be output with a **grouping separator**. The actual separator used is specific to the user's locale (i.e., country). For example, in the United States, the number will be output using commas to separate every three digits and a decimal point to separate the fractional part of the number, as in 1,234.45. The number `20` in the format specification indicates that the value should be output right justified in a *field width* of 20 characters. The `.2` specifies the formatted number's *precision*—in this case, the number is *rounded* to the nearest hundredth and output with two digits to the right of the decimal point.

A Warning about Displaying Rounded Values

We declared variables `amount`, `principal` and `rate` to be of type `double` in this example. We're dealing with fractional parts of dollars and thus need a type that allows decimal points in its values. Unfortunately, floating-point numbers can cause trouble. Here's a simple explanation of what can go wrong when using `double` (or `float`) to represent dollar amounts (assuming that dollar amounts are displayed with two digits to the right of the decimal point): Two `double` dollar amounts stored in the machine could be 14.234 (which would normally be rounded to 14.23 for display purposes) and 18.673 (which would normally be rounded to 18.67 for display purposes). When these amounts are added, they produce the internal sum 32.907, which would normally be rounded to 32.91 for display purposes. Thus, your output could appear as

```
  14.23
+ 18.67
  32.91
```

but a person adding the individual numbers as displayed would expect the sum to be 32.90. You've been warned!

Error-Prevention Tip 5.7

Do not use variables of type `double` *(or* `float`*) to perform precise monetary calculations. The imprecision of floating-point numbers can lead to errors. In the exercises, you'll learn how to use integers to perform precise monetary calculations—Java also provides class* `java.math.BigDecimal` *for this purpose, which we demonstrate in Fig. 8.16.*

Error-Prevention Tip 5.8

In a global economy, dealing with currencies, monetary amounts, conversions, rounding and formatting is complex. The new JavaMoney API (`http://javamoney.github.io`*) was developed to meet these challenges. At the time of this writing, it was not yet incorporated into the JDK. Chapter 8 suggests a JavaMoney project exercise.*

5.5 do...while Iteration Statement

The **`do...while` iteration statement** is similar to the `while` statement. A `while` tests its loop-continuation condition at the *beginning* of the loop, *before* executing the loop's body; if the condition is `false`, the body *never* executes. A `do...while` tests its loop-continuation condition *after* executing the loop's body; therefore, *the body always executes at least once.* When a `do...while` statement terminates, execution continues with the next statement in sequence. Figure 5.7 uses a `do...while` to output the numbers 1–10.

```
1  // Fig. 5.7: DoWhileTest.java
2  // do...while iteration statement.
3
4  public class DoWhileTest {
5     public static void main(String[] args) {
6        int counter = 1;
7
8        do {
9           System.out.printf("%d  ", counter);
10          ++counter;
11       } while (counter <= 10);
12
13       System.out.println();
14    }
15 }
```

```
1  2  3  4  5  6  7  8  9  10
```

Fig. 5.7 | do...while iteration statement.

Line 6 declares and initializes control variable `counter`. Upon entering the `do...while` statement, line 9 outputs `counter`'s value and line 10 increments `counter`. Then the program evaluates the loop-continuation test at the *bottom* of the loop (line 11). If the condition is `true`, the loop continues at the first body statement (line 9). If the condition is `false`, the loop terminates and the program continues at the next statement after the loop.

UML Activity Diagram for the **`do...while`** *Iteration Statement*

Figure 5.8 contains the UML activity diagram for the `do...while` statement. This diagram makes it clear that the loop-continuation condition is not evaluated until *after* the loop performs the action state *at least once*. Compare this activity diagram with that of the `while` statement (Fig. 4.6).

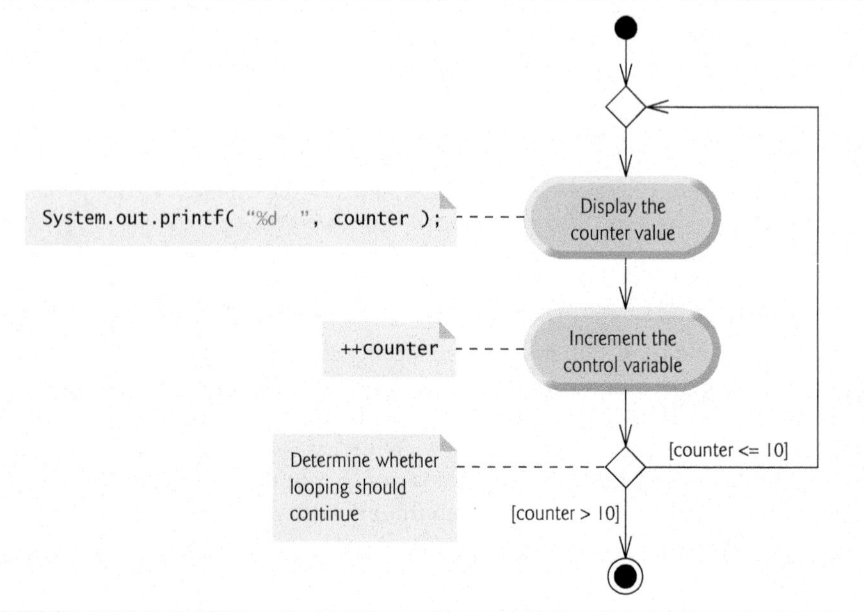

Fig. 5.8 | `do...while` iteration statement UML activity diagram.

5.6 `switch` Multiple-Selection Statement

Chapter 4 discussed the `if` single-selection statement and the `if...else` double-selection statement. The **`switch` multiple-selection statement** performs different actions based on the possible values of a **constant integral expression** of type `byte`, `short`, `int` or `char` (but not `long`). The expression may also be a `String`, which we demonstrate in Section 5.7.

Using a **`switch`** *Statement to Count A, B, C, D and F Grades*

Figure 5.9 calculates the class average of a set of user-entered numeric grades. The program's `switch` statement determines whether each grade is the equivalent of an A, B, C, D or F and increments the appropriate grade counter. The program also displays a summary of the number of students who received each grade.

```
// Fig. 5.9: LetterGrades.java
// LetterGrades class uses the switch statement to count letter grades.
import java.util.Scanner;

public class LetterGrades {
```

Fig. 5.9 | `LetterGrades` class uses the `switch` statement to count letter grades. (Part 1 of 3.)

```
   public static void main(String[] args) {
      int total = 0; // sum of grades
      int gradeCounter = 0; // number of grades entered
      int aCount = 0; // count of A grades
      int bCount = 0; // count of B grades
      int cCount = 0; // count of C grades
      int dCount = 0; // count of D grades
      int fCount = 0; // count of F grades

      Scanner input = new Scanner(System.in);

      System.out.printf("%s%n%s%n   %s%n   %s%n",
         "Enter the integer grades in the range 0-100.",
         "Type the end-of-file indicator to terminate input:",
         "On UNIX/Linux/macOS type <Ctrl> d then press Enter",
         "On Windows type <Ctrl> z then press Enter");

      // loop until user enters the end-of-file indicator
      while (input.hasNext()) {
         int grade = input.nextInt(); // read grade
         total += grade; // add grade to total
         ++gradeCounter; // increment number of grades

         //  increment appropriate letter-grade counter
         switch (grade / 10) {
            case 9:  // grade was between 90
            case 10: // and 100, inclusive
               ++aCount;
               break; // exits switch
            case 8: // grade was between 80 and 89
               ++bCount;
               break; // exits switch
            case 7: // grade was between 70 and 79
               ++cCount;
               break; // exits switch
            case 6: // grade was between 60 and 69
               ++dCount;
               break; // exits switch
            default: // grade was less than 60
               ++fCount;
               break; // optional; exits switch anyway
         }
      }

      // display grade report
      System.out.printf("%nGrade Report:%n");

      // if user entered at least one grade...
      if (gradeCounter != 0) {
         // calculate average of all grades entered
         double average = (double) total / gradeCounter;

```

Fig. 5.9 | LetterGrades class uses the switch statement to count letter grades. (Part 2 of 3.)

```
58          // output summary of results
59          System.out.printf("Total of the %d grades entered is %d%n",
60             gradeCounter, total);
61          System.out.printf("Class average is %.2f%n", average);
62          System.out.printf("%n%s%n%s%d%n%s%d%n%s%d%n%s%d%n%s%d%n",
63             "Number of students who received each grade:",
64             "A: ", aCount,  // display number of A grades
65             "B: ", bCount,  // display number of B grades
66             "C: ", cCount,  // display number of C grades
67             "D: ", dCount,  // display number of D grades
68             "F: ", fCount); // display number of F grades
69       }
70       else { // no grades were entered, so output appropriate message
71          System.out.println("No grades were entered");
72       }
73    }
74 }
```

```
Enter the integer grades in the range 0-100.
Type the end-of-file indicator to terminate input:
   On UNIX/Linux/macOS type <Ctrl> d then press Enter
   On Windows type <Ctrl> z then press Enter
99
92
45
57
63
71
76
85
90
100
^Z

Grade Report:
Total of the 10 grades entered is 778
Class average is 77.80

Number of students who received each grade:
A: 4
B: 1
C: 2
D: 1
F: 2
```

Fig. 5.9 | `LetterGrades` class uses the `switch` statement to count letter grades. (Part 3 of 3.)

Like earlier versions of the class-average program, the `main` method of class `LetterGrades` (Fig. 5.9) declares local variables `total` (line 7) and `gradeCounter` (line 8) to keep track of the sum of the grades entered by the user and the number of grades entered, respectively. Lines 9–13 declare counter variables for each grade category. Note that the variables in lines 7–13 are explicitly initialized to `0`.

Method `main` has two key parts. Lines 24–48 read an arbitrary number of integer grades from the user using sentinel-controlled iteration, update instance variables `total` and gradeCounter, and increment an appropriate letter-grade counter for each grade entered. Lines 51–72 output a report containing the total of all grades entered, the average of the grades and the number of students who received each letter grade. Let's examine these parts in more detail.

Reading Grades from the User

Lines 17–21 prompt the user to enter integer grades and to type the end-of-file indicator to terminate the input. The **end-of-file indicator** is a system-dependent keystroke combination which the user enters to indicate that there's *no more data to input.* In Chapter 15, Files, Input/Output Streams, NIO and XML Serialization, you'll see how the end-of-file indicator is used when a program reads its input from a file.

On UNIX/Linux/macOS systems, end-of-file is entered by typing the sequence

<Ctrl> d

on a line by itself. This notation means to simultaneously press both the *Ctrl* key and the *d* key. On Windows systems, end-of-file can be entered by typing

<Ctrl> z

[*Note:* On some systems, you must press *Enter* after typing the end-of-file key sequence. Also, Windows typically displays the characters ^Z on the screen when the end-of-file indicator is typed, as shown in the output of Fig. 5.9.]

Portability Tip 5.1

The keystroke combinations for entering end-of-file are system dependent.

The while statement (lines 24–48) obtains the user input. The condition at line 24 calls Scanner method **hasNext** to determine whether there's more data to input. This method returns the boolean value true if there's more data; otherwise, it returns false. The returned value is then used as the value of the condition in the while statement. Method hasNext returns false once the user types the end-of-file indicator.

Line 25 inputs a grade value from the user. Line 26 adds grade to total. Line 27 increments gradeCounter. These variables are used to compute the average of the grades. Lines 30–47 use a switch statement to increment the appropriate letter-grade counter based on the numeric grade entered.

Processing the Grades

The switch statement (lines 30–47) determines which counter to increment. We assume that the user enters a valid grade in the range 0–100. A grade in the range 90–100 represents A, 80–89 represents B, 70–79 represents C, 60–69 represents D and 0–59 represents F. The switch statement consists of a block that contains a sequence of **case labels** and an optional **default case.** These are used in this example to determine which counter to increment based on the grade.

When the flow of control reaches the switch, the program evaluates the expression in the parentheses (grade / 10) following keyword switch. This is the switch's **controlling expression.** The program compares this expression's value (which must evaluate to an integral value of type byte, char, short or int, or to a String) with each case label. The controlling expression in line 30 performs integer division, which *truncates the fractional part* of the result. Thus, when we divide a value from 0 to 100 by 10, the result is always a value from 0 to 10. We use several of these values in our `case` labels. For example, if the user enters the integer `85`, the controlling expression evaluates to 8. The `switch` compares `8` with each `case` label. If a match occurs (`case 8:` at line 35), the program executes that `case`'s statements. For the integer `8`, line 36 increments `bCount`, because a grade in the 80s is a B. The **`break` statement** (line 37) causes program control to proceed with the first statement after the `switch`—in this program, we reach the end of the `while` loop, so control returns to the loop-continuation condition in line 24 to determine whether the loop should continue executing.

The `case`s explicitly test for the values `10`, `9`, `8`, `7` and `6`. Note the cases at lines 31–32 that test for the values `9` and `10` (both of which represent the grade A). Listing cases consecutively in this manner with no statements between them enables the cases to perform the same set of statements—when the controlling expression evaluates to `9` or `10`, the statements in lines 33–34 will execute. The `switch` statement does *not* provide a mechanism for testing *ranges* of values, so *every* value you need to test must be listed in a separate `case` label. Each `case` can have multiple statements. The `switch` statement differs from other control statements in that it does *not* require braces around multiple statements in a `case`.

`case` *without a* `break` *Statement*

Without `break` statements, each time a match occurs in the `switch`, the statements for that case and subsequent cases execute until a `break` statement or the end of the `switch` is encountered. This is often referred to as "falling through" to the statements in subsequent `case`s. (This feature is perfect for writing a concise program that displays the iterative song "The Twelve Days of Christmas" in Exercise 5.29.)

Common Programming Error 5.7

Forgetting a `break` statement when one is needed in a `switch` is a logic error.

The `default` *Case*

If no match occurs between the controlling expression's value and a `case` label, the `default` case (lines 44–46) executes. We use the `default` case in this example to process all controlling-expression values that are less than `6`—that is, all failing grades. If no match occurs and the `switch` does not contain a `default` case, program control simply continues with the first statement after the `switch`.

Error-Prevention Tip 5.9

In a `switch` statement, ensure that you test all possible values of the controlling expression.

Displaying the Grade Report

Lines 51–72 output a report based on the grades entered (as shown in the input/output window in Fig. 5.9). Line 54 determines whether the user entered at least one grade—this helps us avoid dividing by zero. If so, line 56 calculates the average of the grades. Lines 59–68 then output the total of all the grades, the class average and the number of students who received each letter grade. If no grades were entered, line 71 outputs an appropriate message. The output in Fig. 5.9 shows a sample grade report based on 10 grades.

switch Statement UML Activity Diagram

Figure 5.10 shows the UML activity diagram for the general switch statement. Most switch statements use a break in each case to terminate the switch statement after processing the case. Figure 5.10 emphasizes this by including break statements in the activity diagram. The diagram makes it clear that the break statement at the end of a case causes control to exit the switch statement immediately.

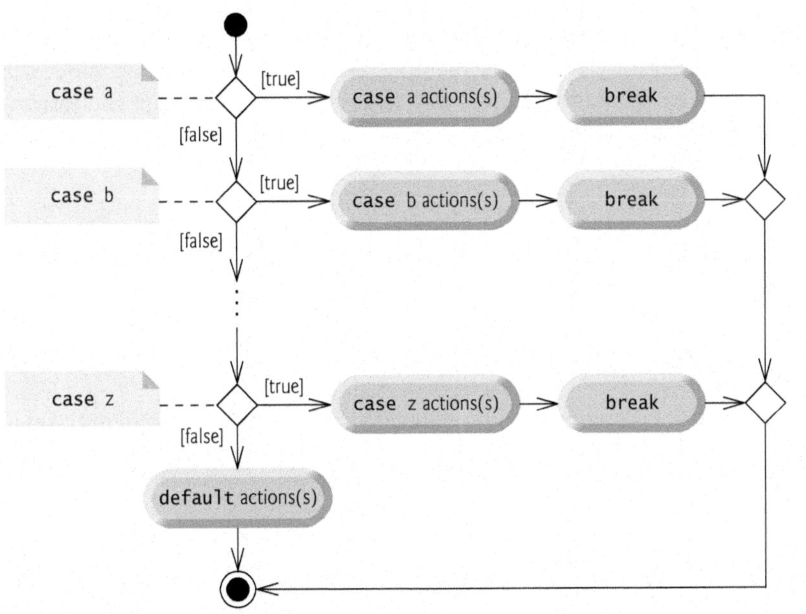

Fig. 5.10 | switch multiple-selection statement UML activity diagram with break statements.

The break statement is *not* required for the switch's last case (or the optional default case, when it appears last), because execution continues with the next statement after the switch.

Error-Prevention Tip 5.10

Provide a default *case in* switch *statements. This focuses you on the need to process exceptional conditions.*

Good Programming Practice 5.2

Although each case *and the* default *case in a* switch *can occur in any order, place the* default *case last. When the* default *case is last, the* break *for that case is not required.*

Notes on the Expression in Each case *of a* switch

When using a switch, remember that each case must contain a String or a constant integral expression—that is, any combination of integer constants that evaluates to a constant integer value (e.g., –7, 0 or 221). An integer constant is simply an integer value. In addition, you can use **character constants**—specific characters in single quotes, such as 'A', '7' or '$'—which represent the integer values of characters. (Appendix B shows the integer values of the characters in the ASCII character set, which is a subset of the Unicode® character set used by Java.)

The expression in each case can also be a **constant variable**—a variable containing a value which does not change for the entire program. Such a variable is declared with keyword `final` (discussed in Chapter 6). Java has a feature called `enum` types, which we also present in Chapter 6—`enum` type constants can also be used in `case` labels.

In Chapter 10, Object-Oriented Programming: Polymorphism and Interfaces, we present a more elegant way to implement `switch` logic—we use a technique called *polymorphism* to create programs that are often clearer, easier to maintain and easier to extend than programs using `switch` logic.

5.7 Class AutoPolicy Case Study: Strings in switch Statements

`String`s can be used as controlling expressions in `switch` statements, and `String` literals can be used in `case` labels. To demonstrate this, we'll implement an app that meets the following requirements:

> *You've been hired by an auto insurance company that serves these northeast states—Connecticut, Maine, Massachusetts, New Hampshire, New Jersey, New York, Pennsylvania, Rhode Island and Vermont. The company would like you to create a program that produces a report indicating for each of their auto insurance policies whether the policy is held in a state with "no-fault" auto insurance—Massachusetts, New Jersey, New York and Pennsylvania.*

The Java app that meets these requirements contains two classes—`AutoPolicy` (Fig. 5.11) and `AutoPolicyTest` (Fig. 5.12).

Class AutoPolicy

Class `AutoPolicy` (Fig. 5.11) represents an auto insurance policy. The class contains:

- `int` instance variable `accountNumber` (line 4) to store the policy's account number
- `String` instance variable `makeAndModel` (line 5) to store the car's make and model (such as a "`Toyota Camry`")
- `String` instance variable `state` (line 6) to store a two-character state abbreviation representing the state in which the policy is held (e.g., "`MA`" for Massachusetts)
- a constructor (lines 9–14) that initializes the class's instance variables
- methods `setAccountNumber` and `getAccountNumber` (lines 17–24) to *set* and *get* an `AutoPolicy`'s `accountNumber` instance variable
- methods `setMakeAndModel` and `getMakeAndModel` (lines 27–34) to *set* and *get* an `AutoPolicy`'s `makeAndModel` instance variable
- methods `setState` and `getState` (lines 37–44) to *set* and *get* an `AutoPolicy`'s `state` instance variable

- method `isNoFaultState` (lines 47–61) to return a `boolean` value indicating whether the policy is held in a no-fault auto insurance state; note the method name—the naming convention for a *get* method that returns a `boolean` value is to begin the name with `"is"` rather than `"get"` (such a method is commonly called a *predicate method*).

```
1  // Fig. 5.11: AutoPolicy.java
2  // Class that represents an auto insurance policy.
3  public class AutoPolicy {
4     private int accountNumber; // policy account number
5     private String makeAndModel; // car that the policy applies to
6     private String state; // two-letter state abbreviation
7
8     // constructor
9     public AutoPolicy(int accountNumber, String makeAndModel,
10       String state) {
11       this.accountNumber = accountNumber;
12       this.makeAndModel = makeAndModel;
13       this.state = state;
14    }
15
16    // sets the accountNumber
17    public void setAccountNumber(int accountNumber) {
18       this.accountNumber = accountNumber;
19    }
20
21    // returns the accountNumber
22    public int getAccountNumber() {
23       return accountNumber;
24    }
25
26    // sets the makeAndModel
27    public void setMakeAndModel(String makeAndModel) {
28       this.makeAndModel = makeAndModel;
29    }
30
31    // returns the makeAndModel
32    public String getMakeAndModel() {
33       return makeAndModel;
34    }
35
36    // sets the state
37    public void setState(String state) {
38       this.state = state;
39    }
40
41    // returns the state
42    public String getState() {
43       return state;
44    }
45
```

Fig. 5.11 | Class that represents an auto insurance policy. (Part 1 of 2.)

```
46      // predicate method returns whether the state has no-fault insurance
47      public boolean isNoFaultState() {
48         boolean noFaultState;
49
50         // determine whether state has no-fault auto insurance
51         switch (getState()) { // get AutoPolicy object's state abbreviation
52            case "MA": case "NJ": case "NY": case "PA":
53               noFaultState = true;
54               break;
55            default:
56               noFaultState = false;
57               break;
58         }
59
60         return noFaultState;
61      }
62   }
```

Fig. 5.11 | Class that represents an auto insurance policy. (Part 2 of 2.)

In method `isNoFaultState`, the `switch` statement's controlling expression (line 51) is the `String` returned by `AutoPolicy` method `getState`. The `switch` statement compares the controlling expression's value with the `case` labels (line 52) to determine whether the policy is held in Massachusetts, New Jersey, New York or Pennsylvania (the no-fault states). If there's a match, then line 53 sets local variable `noFaultState` to `true` and the `switch` statement terminates; otherwise, the `default` case sets `noFaultState` to `false` (line 56). Then method `isNoFaultState` returns local variable `noFaultState`'s value.

For simplicity, we did not validate an `AutoPolicy`'s data in the constructor or *set* methods, and we assume that state abbreviations are always two uppercase letters. In addition, a real `AutoPolicy` class would likely contain many other instance variables and methods for data such as the account holder's name, address, etc. In Exercise 5.30, you'll be asked to enhance class `AutoPolicy` by validating its state abbreviation using techniques that you'll learn in Section 5.9.

Class `AutoPolicyTest`

Class `AutoPolicyTest` (Fig. 5.12) creates two `AutoPolicy` objects (lines 6–9 in `main`). Lines 12–13 pass each object to `static` method `policyInNoFaultState` (lines 18–25), which uses `AutoPolicy` methods to determine and display whether the object it receives represents a policy in a no-fault auto insurance state.

```
1   // Fig. 5.12: AutoPolicyTest.java
2   // Demonstrating Strings in switch.
3   public class AutoPolicyTest {
4      public static void main(String[] args) {
5         // create two AutoPolicy objects
6         AutoPolicy policy1 =
7            new AutoPolicy(11111111, "Toyota Camry", "NJ");
```

Fig. 5.12 | Demonstrating `String`s in `switch`. (Part 1 of 2.)

```
        AutoPolicy policy2 =
           new AutoPolicy(22222222, "Ford Fusion", "ME");

        // display whether each policy is in a no-fault state
        policyInNoFaultState(policy1);
        policyInNoFaultState(policy2);
     }

     // method that displays whether an AutoPolicy
     // is in a state with no-fault auto insurance
     public static void policyInNoFaultState(AutoPolicy policy) {
        System.out.println("The auto policy:");
        System.out.printf(
           "Account #: %d; Car: %s;%nState %s %s a no-fault state%n%n",
           policy.getAccountNumber(), policy.getMakeAndModel(),
           policy.getState(),
           (policy.isNoFaultState() ? "is": "is not"));
     }
  }
```

```
The auto policy:
Account #: 11111111; Car: Toyota Camry;
State NJ is a no-fault state

The auto policy:
Account #: 22222222; Car: Ford Fusion;
State ME is not a no-fault state
```

Fig. 5.12 | Demonstrating `Strings` in `switch`. (Part 2 of 2.)

5.8 break and continue Statements

In addition to selection and iteration statements, Java provides statements `break` (which we discussed in the context of the `switch` statement) and **`continue`** (presented in this section and online Appendix L) to alter the flow of control. The preceding section showed how `break` can be used to terminate a `switch` statement's execution. This section discusses how to use `break` in iteration statements.

5.8.1 break Statement

The `break` statement, when executed in a `while`, `for`, `do…while` or `switch`, causes *immediate* exit from that statement. Execution continues with the first statement after the control statement. Common uses of `break` are to escape early from a loop or to skip the remainder of a `switch` (as in Fig. 5.9).

Figure 5.13 demonstrates a `break` statement exiting a `for`. When the `if` statement nested at lines 8–10 in the `for` statement detects that `count` is `5`, the `break` statement at line 9 executes. This terminates the `for` statement, and the program proceeds to line 15 (immediately after the `for` statement), which displays a message indicating the value of the control variable when the loop terminated. The loop fully executes its body only four times instead of 10.

```
// Fig. 5.13: BreakTest.java
// break statement exiting a for statement.
public class BreakTest {
   public static void main(String[] args) {
      int count; // control variable also used after loop terminates

      for (count = 1; count <= 10; count++) { // loop 10 times
         if (count == 5) {
            break; // terminates loop if count is 5
         }

         System.out.printf("%d ", count);
      }

      System.out.printf("%nBroke out of loop at count = %d%n", count);
   }
}
```

```
1 2 3 4
Broke out of loop at count = 5
```

Fig. 5.13 | break statement exiting a for statement.

5.8.2 continue Statement

The `continue` statement, when executed in a `while`, `for` or `do…while`, skips the remaining statements in the loop body and proceeds with the *next iteration* of the loop. In `while` and `do…while` statements, the program evaluates the loop-continuation test immediately after the `continue` statement executes. In a `for` statement, the increment expression executes, then the program evaluates the loop-continuation test.

Figure 5.14 uses `continue` (line 7) to skip the statement at line 10 when the nested `if` determines that `count`'s value is `5`. When the `continue` statement executes, program control continues with the increment of the control variable in the `for` statement (line 5).

```
1  // Fig. 5.14: ContinueTest.java
2  // continue statement terminating an iteration of a for statement.
3  public class ContinueTest {
4     public static void main(String[] args) {
5        for (int count = 1; count <= 10; count++) { // loop 10 times
6           if (count == 5) {
7              continue; // skip remaining code in loop body if count is 5
8           }
9
10          System.out.printf("%d ", count);
11       }
12
13       System.out.printf("%nUsed continue to skip printing 5%n");
14    }
15 }
```

Fig. 5.14 | continue statement terminating an iteration of a for statement. (Part 1 of 2.)

```
1 2 3 4 6 7 8 9 10
Used continue to skip printing 5
```

Fig. 5.14 | `continue` statement terminating an iteration of a `for` statement. (Part 2 of 2.)

In Section 5.3, we stated that `while` could be used in most cases in place of `for`. This is *not* true when the increment expression in the `while` follows a `continue` statement. In this case, the increment does *not* execute before the program evaluates the iteration-continuation condition, so the `while` does not execute in the same manner as the `for`.

Software Engineering Observation 5.1

Some programmers feel that `break` and `continue` violate structured programming. The same effects are achievable with structured-programming techniques, so these programmers do not use `break` or `continue`.

Software Engineering Observation 5.2

There's a tension between achieving quality software engineering and achieving the best-performing software. Sometimes one of these goals is achieved at the expense of the other. For all but the most performance-intensive situations, apply the following guideline: First, make your code simple and correct; then make it fast and small, but only if necessary.

5.9 Logical Operators

The `if`, `if...else`, `while`, `do...while` and `for` statements each require a *condition* to determine how to continue a program's flow of control. So far, we've studied only simple conditions, such as `count <= 10`, `number != sentinelValue` and `total > 1000`. Simple conditions are expressed in terms of the relational operators `>`, `<`, `>=` and `<=` and the equality operators `==` and `!=`, and each expression tests only one condition. To test *multiple* conditions in the process of making a decision, we performed these tests in separate statements or in nested `if` or `if...else` statements. Sometimes control statements require more complex conditions to determine a program's flow of control.

Java's **logical operators** enable you to *combine* simple conditions into more complex ones. The logical operators are `&&` (conditional AND), `||` (conditional OR), `&` (boolean logical AND), `|` (boolean logical inclusive OR), `^` (boolean logical exclusive OR) and `!` (logical NOT). [*Note:* The `&`, `|` and `^` operators are also bitwise operators when they're applied to integral operands. We discuss the bitwise operators in online Appendix K.]

5.9.1 Conditional AND (&&) Operator

Suppose we wish to ensure at some point in a program that two conditions are *both* `true` before we choose a certain path of execution. In this case, we can use the **&& (conditional AND)** operator, as follows:

```
if (gender == FEMALE && age >= 65) {
   ++seniorFemales;
}
```

This `if` statement contains two simple conditions. The condition `gender == FEMALE` compares variable `gender` to the constant `FEMALE` to determine whether a person is female. The condition age >= 65 might be evaluated to determine whether a person is a senior citizen. The if statement considers the combined condition

```
gender == FEMALE && age >= 65
```

which is true if and only if *both* simple conditions are true. In this case, the if statement's body increments seniorFemales by 1. If either or both of the simple conditions are false, the program skips the increment.

Similarly, the following condition ensures that a grade is in the range 1–100:

```
grade >= 1 && grade <= 100
```

This condition is true if and only if grade is greater than or equal to 1 *and* grade is less than or equal to 100. Some programmers find that the preceding combined condition is more readable when *redundant* parentheses are added, as in:

```
(grade >= 1) && (grade <= 100)
```

The table in Fig. 5.15 summarizes the && operator, showing all four possible combinations of false and true values for *expression1* and *expression2*. Such tables are called **truth tables**. Java evaluates to false or true all expressions that include relational operators, equality operators or logical operators.

expression1	expression2	expression1 && expression2
false	false	false
false	true	false
true	false	false
true	true	true

Fig. 5.15 | && (conditional AND) operator truth table.

5.9.2 Conditional OR (||) Operator

Now suppose we wish to ensure that *either or both* of two conditions are true before we choose a certain path of execution. In this case, we use the || (**conditional OR**) operator, as in the following program segment:

```
if ((semesterAverage >= 90) || (finalExam >= 90)) {
   System.out.println ("Student grade is A");
}
```

This statement also contains two simple conditions. The condition semesterAverage >= 90 evaluates to determine whether the student deserves an A in the course because of a solid performance throughout the semester. The condition finalExam >= 90 evaluates to determine whether the student deserves an A in the course because of an outstanding performance on the final exam. The if statement then considers the combined condition

```
(semesterAverage >= 90) || (finalExam >= 90)
```

and awards the student an A if *either or both* of the simple conditions are true. The only time the message "Student grade is A" is *not* printed is when *both* of the simple conditions are `false`. Figure 5.16 is a truth table for operator conditional OR (`||`). Operator `&&` has a higher precedence than operator `||`. Both operators associate from left to right.

expression1	expression2	expression1 || expression2
false	false	false
false	true	true
true	false	true
true	true	true

Fig. 5.16 | `||` (conditional OR) operator truth table.

5.9.3 Short-Circuit Evaluation of Complex Conditions

The parts of an expression containing `&&` or `||` operators are evaluated *only* until it's known whether the condition is `true` or `false`. Thus, evaluation of the expression

```
(gender == FEMALE) && (age >= 65)
```

stops immediately if `gender` *is not* equal to `FEMALE` (that is, the entire expression is `false`) and continues if `gender` *is* equal to `FEMALE` (that is, the entire expression could still be `true` if the condition `age >= 65` is `true`). This feature of conditional AND and conditional OR expressions is called **short-circuit evaluation.**

Common Programming Error 5.8

In expressions using `&&`, a condition—we'll call this the dependent condition*—may require another condition to be `true` for the dependent condition's evaluation to be meaningful. In this case, the dependent condition should be placed* after *the `&&` operator to prevent errors. Consider the expression `(i != 0) && (10 / i == 2)`. The dependent condition `(10 / i == 2)`* must *appear after the `&&` to prevent the possibility of division by zero.*

5.9.4 Boolean Logical AND (&) and Boolean Logical Inclusive OR (|) Operators

The **boolean logical AND** (`&`) and **boolean logical inclusive OR** (`|`) operators are identical to the `&&` and `||` operators, except that the `&` and `|` operators *always* evaluate *both* of their operands (i.e., they do *not* perform short-circuit evaluation). So, the expression

```
(gender == 1) & (age >= 65)
```

evaluates `age >= 65` *regardless* of whether `gender` is equal to `1`. This is useful if the right operand has a required **side effect**—a modification of a variable's value. For example,

```
(birthday == true) | (++age >= 65)
```

guarantees that the condition `++age >= 65` will be evaluated. Thus, the variable `age` is incremented, regardless of whether the overall expression is `true` or `false`.

Error-Prevention Tip 5.11

For clarity, avoid expressions with side effects (such as assignments) in conditions. They can make code harder to understand and can lead to subtle logic errors.

Error-Prevention Tip 5.12

Assignment (=) expressions generally should not *be used in conditions. Every condition* must *result in a* `boolean` *value; otherwise, a compilation error occurs. In a condition, an assignment will compile* only *if a* `boolean` *expression is assigned to a* `boolean` *variable.*

5.9.5 Boolean Logical Exclusive OR (^)

A simple condition containing the **boolean logical exclusive OR** (^) operator is `true` *if and only if one of its operands is* `true` *and the other is* `false`. If both are `true` or both are `false`, the entire condition is `false`. Figure 5.17 is a truth table for the boolean logical exclusive OR operator (^). This operator is guaranteed to evaluate *both* of its operands.

expression1	expression2	expression1 ^ expression2
false	false	false
false	true	true
true	false	true
true	true	false

Fig. 5.17 | ^ (boolean logical exclusive OR) operator truth table.

5.9.6 Logical Negation (!) Operator

The ! (**logical NOT**, also called **logical negation** or **logical complement**) operator "reverses" the meaning of a condition. Unlike the logical operators &&, ||, &, | and ^, which are ***binary*** operators that combine two conditions, the logical negation operator is a *unary* operator that has only one condition as an operand. The operator is placed *before* a condition to choose a path of execution if the original condition (without the logical negation operator) is `false`, as in the program segment

```
if (! (grade == sentinelValue)) {
   System.out.printf("The next grade is %d%n", grade);
}
```

which executes the `printf` call only if `grade` is *not* equal to `sentinelValue`. The parentheses around the condition `grade == sentinelValue` are needed because the logical negation operator has a *higher* precedence than the equality operator.

In most cases, you can avoid using logical negation by expressing the condition differently with an appropriate relational or equality operator. For example, the previous statement may also be written as follows:

```
if (grade != sentinelValue) {
   System.out.printf("The next grade is %d%n", grade);
}
```

This flexibility can help you express a condition in a more convenient manner. Figure 5.18 is a truth table for the logical negation operator.

expression	!expression
`false`	`true`
`true`	`false`

Fig. 5.18 | `!` (logical NOT) operator truth table.

5.9.7 Logical Operators Example

Figure 5.19 uses logical operators to produce the truth tables discussed in this section. The output shows the `boolean` expression that was evaluated and its result. We used the **`%b` format specifier** to display the word "true" or the word "false" based on a `boolean` expression's value. Lines 7–11 produce the truth table for `&&`. Lines 14–18 produce the truth table for `||`. Lines 21–25 produce the truth table for `&`. Lines 28–33 produce the truth table for `|`. Lines 36–41 produce the truth table for `^`. Lines 44–45 produce the truth table for `!`.

```
1  // Fig. 5.19: LogicalOperators.java
2  // Logical operators.
3
4  public class LogicalOperators {
5     public static void main(String[] args) {
6        // create truth table for && (conditional AND) operator
7        System.out.printf("%s%n%s: %b%n%s: %b%n%s: %b%n%s: %b%n%n",
8           "Conditional AND (&&)", "false && false", (false && false),
9           "false && true", (false && true),
10          "true && false", (true && false),
11          "true && true", (true && true));
12
13       // create truth table for || (conditional OR) operator
14       System.out.printf("%s%n%s: %b%n%s: %b%n%s: %b%n%s: %b%n%n",
15          "Conditional OR (||)", "false || false", (false || false),
16          "false || true", (false || true),
17          "true || false", (true || false),
18          "true || true", (true || true));
19
20       // create truth table for & (boolean logical AND) operator
21       System.out.printf("%s%n%s: %b%n%s: %b%n%s: %b%n%s: %b%n%n",
22          "Boolean logical AND (&)", "false & false", (false & false),
23          "false & true", (false & true),
24          "true & false", (true & false),
25          "true & true", (true & true));
26
27       // create truth table for | (boolean logical inclusive OR) operator
28       System.out.printf("%s%n%s: %b%n%s: %b%n%s: %b%n%s: %b%n%n",
29          "Boolean logical inclusive OR (|)",
30          "false | false", (false | false),
31          "false | true", (false | true),
32          "true | false", (true | false),
33          "true | true", (true | true));
```

Fig. 5.19 | Logical operators. (Part 1 of 2.)

```

      // create truth table for ^ (boolean logical exclusive OR) operator
      System.out.printf("%s%n%s: %b%n%s: %b%n%s: %b%n%s: %b%n%n",
         "Boolean logical exclusive OR (^)",
         "false ^ false", (false ^ false),
         "false ^ true", (false ^ true),
         "true ^ false", (true ^ false),
         "true ^ true", (true ^ true));

      // create truth table for ! (logical negation) operator
      System.out.printf("%s%n%s: %b%n%s: %b%n", "Logical NOT (!)",
         "!false", (!false), "!true", (!true));
   }
}
```

```
Conditional AND (&&)
false && false: false
false && true: false
true && false: false
true && true: true

Conditional OR (||)
false || false: false
false || true: true
true || false: true
true || true: true

Boolean logical AND (&)
false & false: false
false & true: false
true & false: false
true & true: true

Boolean logical inclusive OR (|)
false | false: false
false | true: true
true | false: true
true | true: true

Boolean logical exclusive OR (^)
false ^ false: false
false ^ true: true
true ^ false: true
true ^ true: false

Logical NOT (!)
!false: true
!true: false
```

Fig. 5.19 | Logical operators. (Part 2 of 2.)

Precedence and Associativity of the Operators Presented So Far

Figure 5.20 shows the precedence and associativity of the Java operators introduced so far. The operators are shown from top to bottom in decreasing order of precedence.

Operators	Associativity	Type
++ --	right to left	unary postfix
++ -- + - ! (*type*)	right to left	unary prefix
* / %	left to right	multiplicative
+ -	left to right	additive
< <= > >=	left to right	relational
== !=	left to right	equality
&	left to right	boolean logical AND
^	left to right	boolean logical exclusive OR
|	left to right	boolean logical inclusive OR
&&	left to right	conditional AND
||	left to right	conditional OR
?:	right to left	conditional
= += -= *= /= %=	right to left	assignment

Fig. 5.20 | Precedence/associativity of the operators discussed so far.

5.10 Structured-Programming Summary

Just as architects design buildings by employing the collective wisdom of their profession, so should programmers design programs. Our field is much younger than architecture, and our collective wisdom is considerably sparser. We've learned that structured programming produces programs that are easier than unstructured programs to understand, test, debug, modify and even prove correct in a mathematical sense.

Java Control Statements Are Single-Entry/Single-Exit

Figure 5.21 uses UML activity diagrams to summarize Java's control statements. The initial and final states indicate the *single entry point* and the *single exit point* of each control statement. Arbitrarily connecting individual symbols in an activity diagram can lead to unstructured programs. Therefore, the programming profession has chosen a limited set of control statements that can be combined in only two simple ways to build structured programs.

For simplicity, Java includes only *single-entry/single-exit* control statements—there's only one way to enter and only one way to exit each control statement. Connecting control statements in sequence to form structured programs is simple. The final state of one control statement is connected to the initial state of the next—that is, the control statements are placed one after another in a program in sequence. We call this *control-statement stacking*. The rules for forming structured programs also allow for control statements to be *nested*.

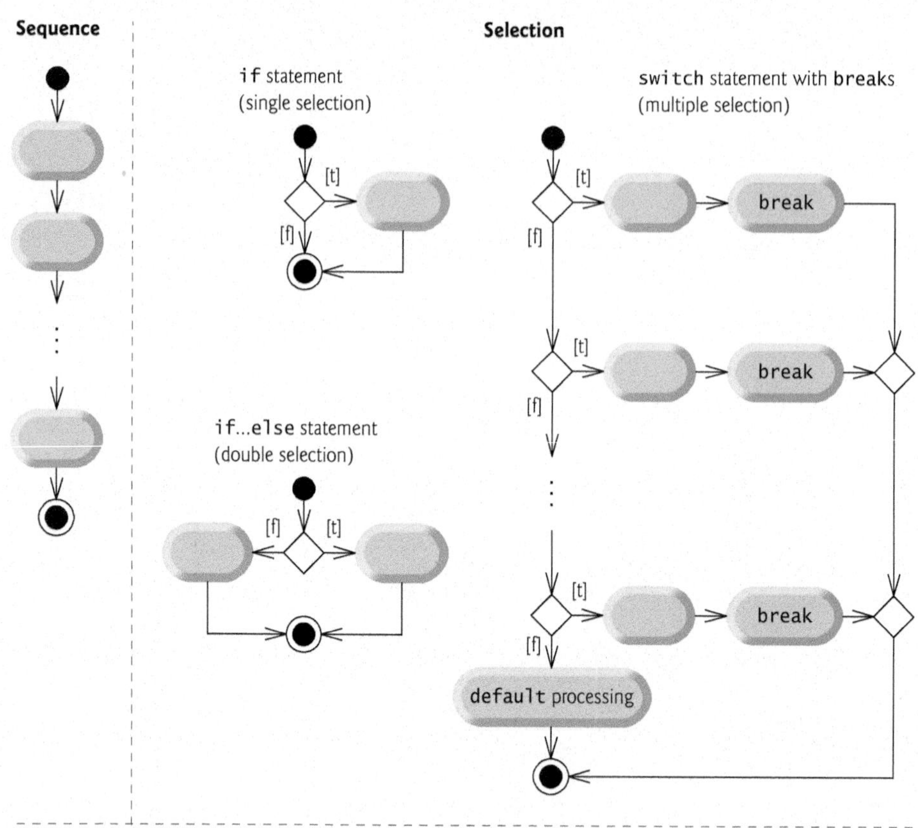

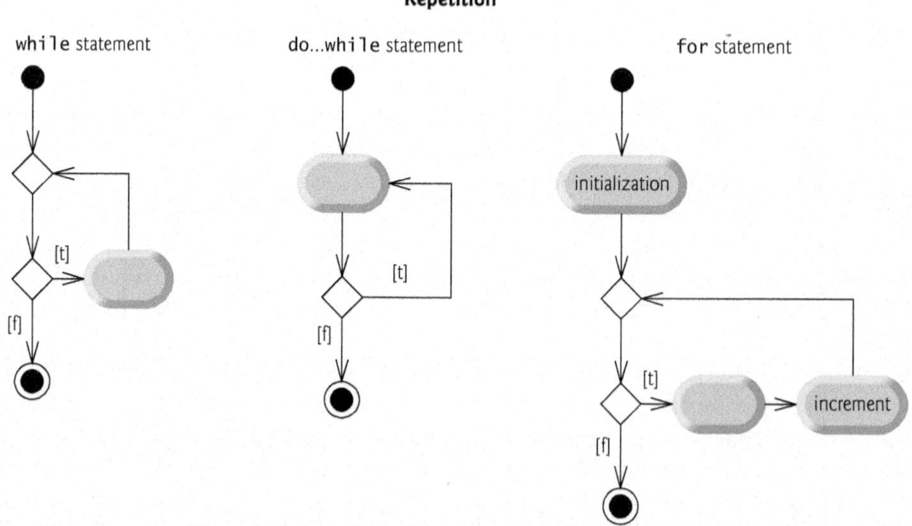

Fig. 5.21 | Java's single-entry/single-exit sequence, selection and iteration statements.

Rules for Forming Structured Programs

Figure 5.22 shows the rules for forming structured programs. The rules assume that action states may be used to indicate *any* action. The rules also assume that we begin with the simplest activity diagram (Fig. 5.23) consisting of only an initial state, an action state, a final state and transition arrows.

Rules for forming structured programs	
1.	Begin with the simplest activity diagram (Fig. 5.23).
2.	Any action state can be replaced by two action states in sequence.
3.	Any action state can be replaced by any control statement (`if`, `if...else`, `switch`, `while`, `do...while` or `for`).
4.	Rules 2 and 3 can be applied as often as you like and in any order.

Fig. 5.22 | Rules for forming structured programs.

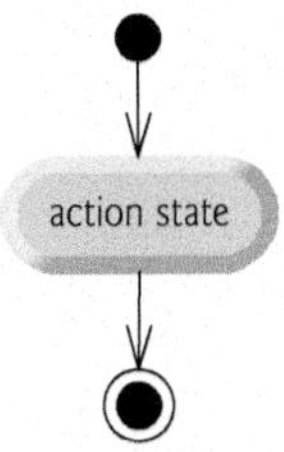

Fig. 5.23 | Simplest activity diagram.

Applying the rules in Fig. 5.22 always results in a properly structured activity diagram with a neat, building-block appearance. For example, repeatedly applying rule 2 to the simplest activity diagram results in an activity diagram containing many action states in sequence (Fig. 5.24). Rule 2 generates a *stack* of control statements, so let's call rule 2 the **stacking rule**. The vertical dashed lines in Fig. 5.24 are not part of the UML—we use them to separate the four activity diagrams that demonstrate rule 2 of Fig. 5.22 being applied.

Rule 3 is called the **nesting rule**. Repeatedly applying rule 3 to the simplest activity diagram results in one with neatly *nested* control statements. For example, in Fig. 5.25, the action state in the simplest activity diagram is replaced with a double-selection (`if...else`) statement. Then rule 3 is applied again to the action states in the double-selection statement, replacing each with a double-selection statement. The dashed action-state symbol around each double-selection statement represents the action state that was replaced. [*Note:* The dashed arrows and dashed action-state symbols shown in Fig. 5.25 are not part of the UML. They're used here to illustrate that *any* action state can be replaced with a control statement.]

Rule 4 generates larger, more involved and more deeply nested statements. The diagrams that emerge from applying the rules in Fig. 5.22 constitute the set of all possible structured activity diagrams and hence the set of all possible structured programs. The

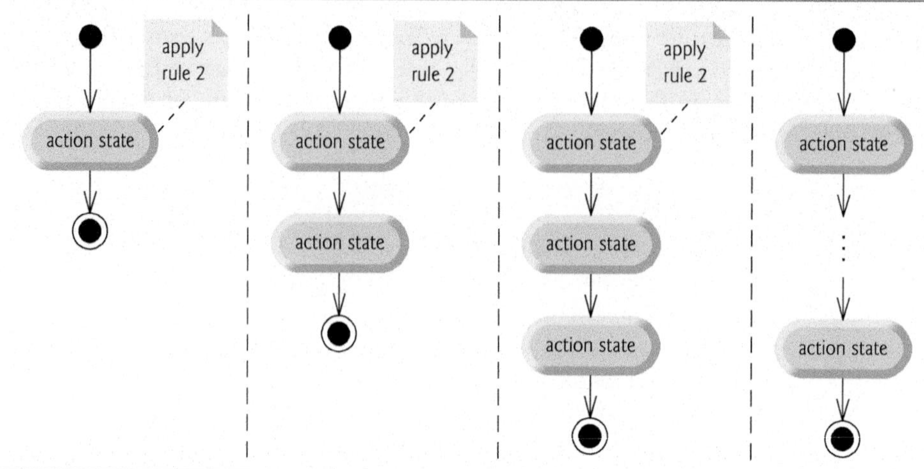

Fig. 5.24 | Repeatedly applying rule 2 of Fig. 5.22 to the simplest activity diagram.

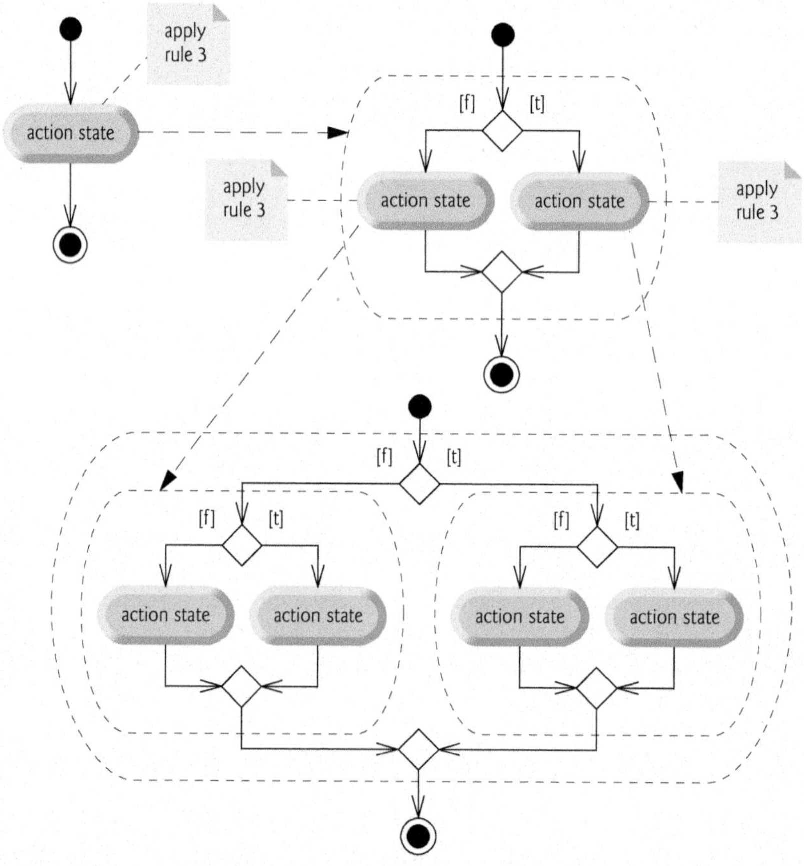

Fig. 5.25 | Repeatedly applying rule 3 of Fig. 5.22 to the simplest activity diagram.

beauty of the structured approach is that we use *only seven* simple single-entry/single-exit control statements and assemble them in *only two* simple ways.

If the rules in Fig. 5.22 are followed, an "unstructured' activity diagram (like the one in Fig. 5.26) cannot be created. If you're uncertain about whether a particular diagram is structured, apply the rules of Fig. 5.22 in reverse to reduce it to the simplest activity diagram. If you can reduce it, the original diagram is structured; otherwise, it's not.

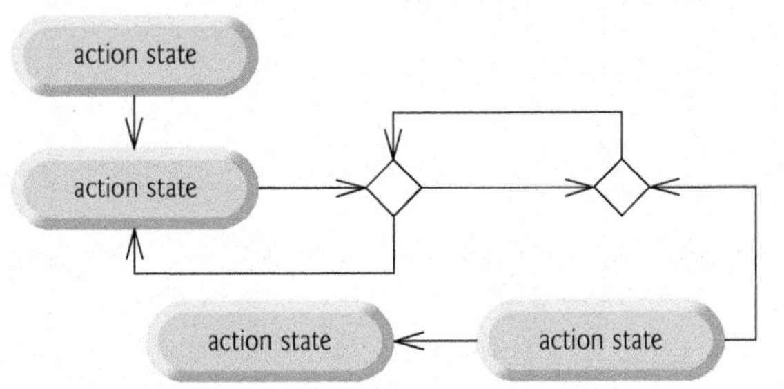

Fig. 5.26 | "Unstructured" activity diagram.

Three Forms of Control

Structured programming promotes simplicity. Only three forms of control are needed to implement an algorithm:

- sequence
- selection
- iteration

The sequence structure is trivial. Simply list the statements to execute in the order in which they should execute. Selection is implemented in one of three ways:

- `if` statement (single selection)
- `if...else` statement (double selection)
- `switch` statement (multiple selection)

In fact, it's straightforward to prove that the simple `if` statement is sufficient to provide *any* form of selection—everything that can be done with the `if...else` statement and the `switch` statement can be implemented by combining `if` statements (although perhaps not as clearly and efficiently).

Iteration is implemented in one of three ways:

- `while` statement
- `do...while` statement
- `for` statement

[*Note:* There's a fourth iteration statement—the *enhanced* `for` *statement*—that we discuss in Section 7.7.] It's straightforward to prove that the `while` statement is sufficient to provide *any* form of iteration. Everything that can be done with `do...while` and `for` can be done with the `while` statement (although perhaps not as conveniently).

Combining these results illustrates that *any* form of control ever needed in a Java program can be expressed in terms of

- sequence
- `if` statement (selection)
- `while` statement (iteration)

and that these can be combined in only two ways—*stacking* and *nesting*. Indeed, structured programming is the essence of simplicity.

5.11 (Optional) GUI and Graphics Case Study: Drawing Rectangles and Ovals

In this section, we'll discuss the **Draw Shapes** app, which demonstrates drawing rectangles and ovals using the `GraphicsContext` methods `strokeRect` and `strokeOval`, respectively.

Creating the **Draw Shapes** *App's GUI*

The app's GUI is defined in `DrawShapes.fxml` using the techniques you learned in Sections 3.6 and 4.15, and is nearly identical to the GUI in Fig. 4.17. To build the GUI, we copied `DrawLines.fxml` into a new directory and renamed it `DrawShapes.fxml`, then opened `DrawShapes.fxml` in Scene Builder and made the following changes:

- We specified `DrawShapesController` as the app's **Controller class** in the Scene Builder **Document** window's **Controller** section.
- We set the `Button`'s **Text** property to `Draw Rectangles` (in the **Inspector**'s **Properties** section) and set the `Button`'s **On Action** event handler to `drawRectangles-ButtonPressed` (**Inspector**'s **Code** section).
- We dragged another `Button` from the Scene Builder **Library**'s **Controls** section onto the `ToolBar`, then set that `Button`'s **Text** property to `Draw Ovals` and set its **On Action** event handler to `drawOvalsButtonPressed`.

If necessary, review the steps presented in Sections 4.15.2–4.15.3 to make these changes.

Class **`DrawLinesController`**

As in the prior Java FX example, this app has two Java source-code files:

- `DrawShapes.java` contains the JavaFX app's `main` application class that loads `DrawShapes.fxml` and configures the `DrawShapesController`.
- `DrawShapesController.java` contains the controller class that draws either rectangles or ovals, based on which `Button` the user presses.

To create `DrawShapes.java`, we copied `DrawLines.java`, renamed it and made the code edits described in Section 4.15.5. We do not show `DrawShapes.java`, because the only changes are the class name (`DrawShapes`), the name of the FXML file to load (`Draw-Shapes.fxml`) and the text displayed in the stage's title bar (`Draw Shapes`).

Class `DrawLinesController` (Fig. 5.27) performs the drawing when the user clicks either of the app's `Buttons`. When the `DrawShapes` app executes, it will

- configure the `DrawShapesController`'s `canvas` variable (line 9) to refer to the `Canvas` from `DrawShapes.fxml`,

- configure the method `drawRectanglesButtonPressed` (lines 12–15) to execute when the user presses the **Draw Rectangles** `Button`, and
- configure the method `drawOvalsButtonPressed` (lines 18–21) to execute when the user presses the **Draw Ovals** `Button`.

Methods `drawRectanglesButtonPressed` and `drawOvalsButtonPressed` each call method `draw` (lines 24–47)—passing the arguments `"rectangles"` or `"ovals"`, respectively, to indicate which shapes `draw` should display.

```
1  // Fig. 5.27: DrawShapesController.java
2  // Using strokeRect and strokeOval to draw rectangles and ovals.
3  import javafx.event.ActionEvent;
4  import javafx.fxml.FXML;
5  import javafx.scene.canvas.Canvas;
6  import javafx.scene.canvas.GraphicsContext;
7
8  public class DrawShapesController {
9     @FXML private Canvas canvas;
10
11    // when user presses Draw Rectangles button, call draw for rectangles
12    @FXML
13    void strokeRectanglesButtonPressed(ActionEvent event) {
14       draw("rectangles");
15    }
16
17    // when user presses Draw Ovals button, call draw for ovals
18    @FXML
19    void strokeOvalsButtonPressed(ActionEvent event) {
20       draw("ovals");
21    }
22
23    // draws rectangles or ovals based on which Button the user pressed
24    public void draw(String choice) {
25       // get the GraphicsContext, which is used to draw on the Canvas
26       GraphicsContext gc = canvas.getGraphicsContext2D();
27
28       // clear the canvas for next set of shapes
29       gc.clearRect(0, 0, canvas.getWidth(), canvas.getHeight());
30
31       int step = 10;
32
33       // draw 10 overlapping shapes
34       for (int i = 0; i < 10; i++) {
35          // pick the shape based on the user's choice
36          switch (choice) {
37             case "rectangles": // draw rectangles
38                gc.strokeRect(10 + i * step, 10 + i * step,
39                   90 + i * step, 90 + i * step);
40                break;
41             case "ovals": // draw ovals
```

Fig. 5.27 | Using `strokeRect` and `strokeOval` to draw rectangles and ovals. (Part 1 of 2.)

```
42                          gc.strokeOval(10 + i * step, 10 + i * step,
43                             90 + i * step, 90 + i * step);
44                          break;
45                    }
46                }
47          }
48    }
```

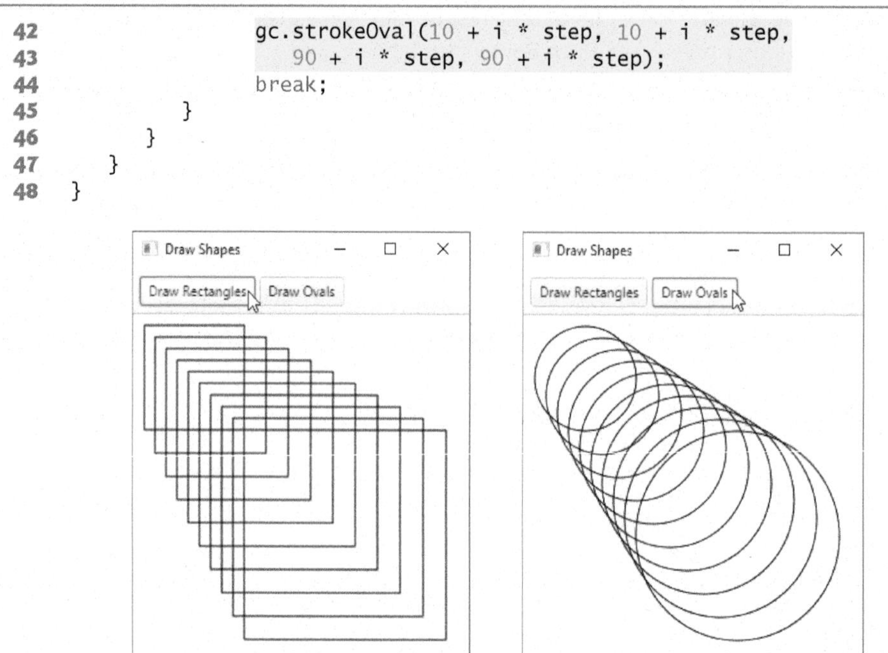

Fig. 5.27 | Using `strokeRect` and `strokeOval` to draw rectangles and ovals. (Part 2 of 2.)

Method `draw` performs the actual drawing. Each time the method is called, it uses `GraphicsContext` method **`clearRect`** to clear any prior drawing (line 29). This method clears a rectangular area by setting it to the `Canvas`'s background color. The method's four arguments are the *x*- and *y*-coordinates of the rectangle's upper-left corner and the rectangle's width and height. In this case, we clear the entire `Canvas` by starting from its upper-left corner (0, 0) and using its `getWidth` and `getHeight` methods to get the `Canvas`'s width and height, respectively.

Lines 34–46 loop 10 times to draw 10 shapes. The *nested* `switch` statement (lines 36–45) chooses between drawing rectangles and drawing ovals. If method `draw`'s `choice` parameter contains `"rectangles"`, then the method draws rectangles. Lines 38–39 call `GraphicsContext` method **`strokeRect`**, which requires four arguments. The first two represent the *x*- and *y*-coordinates of the upper-left corner of the rectangle; the next two represent the rectangle's width and height. In this example, we start at a position 10 pixels down and 10 pixels right of the top-left corner, and every iteration of the loop moves the upper-left corner another 10 pixels down and to the right. The width and the height of the rectangle start at 90 pixels and increase by 10 pixels in each iteration.

If method `draw`'s `choice` parameter contains `"ovals"`, the program draws ovals. It creates an imaginary rectangle called a **bounding rectangle** and places inside it an oval that touches the midpoints of all four sides. Method **`strokeOval`** (lines 42–43) requires the same four arguments as method `strokeRect`. The arguments specify the position and size of the *bounding rectangle* for the oval. The values passed to `strokeOval` in this example are the same as those passed to `strokeRect` in lines 38–39. Since the width and height of the bounding rectangle are identical in this example, lines 42–43 draw a *circle*.

GUI and Graphics Case Study Exercises

5.1 Draw 12 concentric circles in the center of a `Canvas` (Fig. 5.28). The innermost circle should have a radius of 10 pixels, and each successive circle should have a radius 10 pixels larger than the previous one. Begin by finding the `Canvas`'s center. To determine the upper-left corner location of a given circle's bounding rectangle, move up one radius (that is, `-10` pixels) and to the left one radius (that is, `-10` pixels) from the center. The bounding rectangle's width and height are both the same as the circle's diameter (that is, twice the radius).

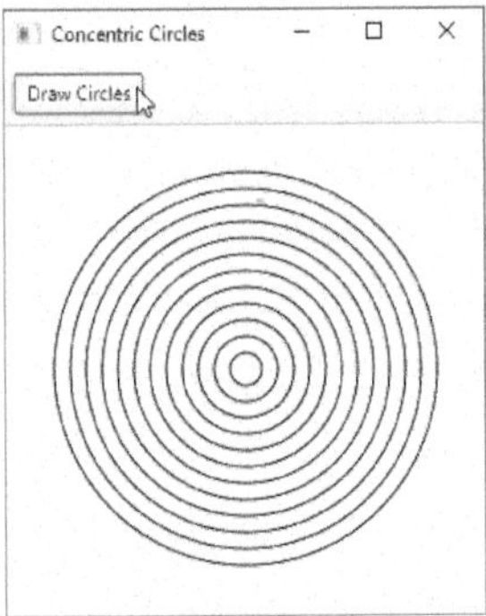

Fig. 5.28 | Drawing concentric circles.

5.2 Modify Exercise 5.1 so that it also displays each circle's bounding square (Fig. 5.29).

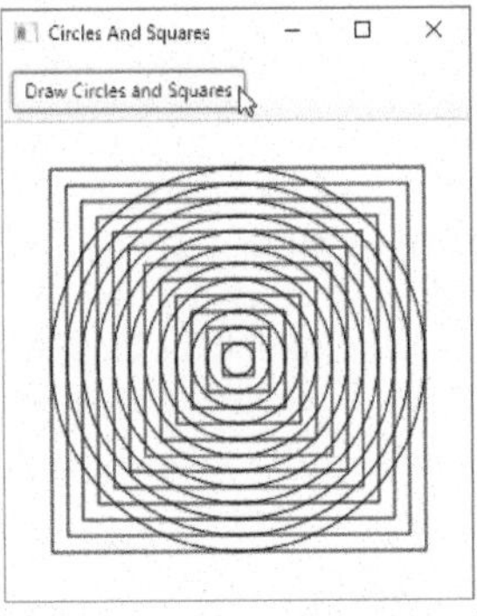

Fig. 5.29 | Drawing concentric circles and their bounding squares.

5.12 Wrap-Up

In this chapter, we completed our introduction to control statements, which enable you to control the flow of execution in methods. Chapter 4 discussed `if`, `if...else` and `while`. This chapter demonstrated `for`, `do...while` and `switch`. We showed that any algorithm can be developed using combinations of the sequence structure, the three types of selection statements—`if`, `if...else` and `switch`—and the three types of iteration statements—`while`, `do...while` and `for`. In this chapter and Chapter 4, we discussed how you can combine these building blocks to utilize proven program-construction and problem-solving techniques. You used the `break` statement to exit a `switch` statement and to immediately terminate a loop, and used a `continue` statement to terminate a loop's current iteration and proceed with the loop's next iteration. This chapter also introduced Java's logical operators, which enable you to use more complex conditional expressions in control statements. In Chapter 6, we examine methods in greater depth.

Summary

Section 5.2 Essentials of Counter-Controlled Iteration

- Counter-controlled iteration (p. 165) requires a control variable, the initial value of the control variable, the increment by which the control variable is modified each time through the loop (also known as each iteration of the loop) and the loop-continuation condition that determines whether looping should continue.
- You can declare a variable and initialize it in the same statement.

Section 5.3 `for` Iteration Statement

- The `while` statement can be used to implement any counter-controlled loop.
- The `for` statement (p. 166) specifies all the details of counter-controlled iteration in its header.
- When the `for` statement begins executing, its control variable is declared and initialized. If the loop-continuation condition is initially `true`, the body executes. After executing the loop's body, the increment expression executes. Then the loop-continuation test is performed again to determine whether the program should continue with the next iteration of the loop.
- The general format of the `for` statement is

```
for (initialization; loopContinuationCondition; increment) {
   statements
}
```

  where the *initialization* expression names the loop's control variable and provides its initial value, *loopContinuationCondition* determines whether the loop should continue executing and *increment* modifies the control variable's value, so that the loop-continuation condition eventually becomes `false`. The two semicolons in the `for` header are required.
- Most `for` statements can be represented with equivalent `while` statements as follows:

```
initialization;
while (loopContinuationCondition) {
   statements
   increment;
}
```

- Typically, `for` statements are used for counter-controlled iteration and `while` statements for sentinel-controlled iteration.
- If the *initialization* expression in the `for` header declares the control variable, the control variable can be used only in that `for` statement—it will not exist outside the `for` statement.
- The expressions in a `for` header are optional. If the *loopContinuationCondition* is omitted, Java assumes that it's always `true`, thus creating an infinite loop. You might omit the *initialization* expression if the control variable is initialized before the loop. You might omit the *increment* expression if the increment is calculated with statements in the loop's body or if no increment is needed.

- A `for`'s increment expression acts as if it's a standalone statement at the end of the `for`'s body.
- A `for` statement can count downward by using a negative increment—i.e., a decrement (p. 169).
- If the loop-continuation condition is initially `false`, the `for` statement's body does not execute.

Section 5.4.2 Application: Compound-Interest Calculations

- Java treats floating-point constants like `1000.0` and `0.05` as type `double`. Similarly, Java treats whole-number constants like `7` and `-22` as type `int`.
- The format specifier `%4s` outputs a `String` in a field width (p. 173) of 4—that is, 4 character positions. If the value to be output has fewer characters, it's right justified (p. 173) by default. If the value has more characters, the field width expands to accommodate the appropriate number of characters. To left justify (p. 173) the value, use a negative integer to specify the field width.
- `Math.pow(`*x*`,` *y*`)` (p. 174) calculates the value of *x* raised to the *y*th power. The method receives two `double` arguments and returns a `double` value.
- The comma (`,`) formatting flag (p. 174) in a format specifier indicates that a floating-point value should be output with a grouping separator (p. 174). The actual separator used is specific to the user's locale (i.e., country). In the United States, the number will have commas separating every three digits and a decimal point separating the fractional part of the number, as in 1,234.45.
- The `.` in a format specifier indicates that the integer to its right is the number's precision.

Section 5.5 `do…while` Iteration Statement

- The `do…while` statement (p. 175) is similar to the `while`. In the `while`, the program tests the loop-continuation condition at the beginning of the loop, before executing its body; if the condition is `false`, the body never executes. The `do…while` statement tests the loop-continuation condition *after* executing the loop's body; therefore, the body always executes at least once.

Section 5.6 `switch` Multiple-Selection Statement

- A `switch` statement (p. 176) performs different actions based on the possible values of a constant integral expression (a constant value of type `byte`, `short`, `int` or `char`, but not `long`), or a `String`.
- The end-of-file indicator is a system-dependent keystroke combination that terminates user input. On UNIX/Linux/macOS systems, end-of-file is entered by typing the sequence <*Ctrl*> *d* on a line by itself. This notation means to simultaneously press both the *Ctrl* key and the *d* key. On Windows systems, enter end-of-file by typing <*Ctrl*> *z*.
- `Scanner` method `hasNext` (p. 179) determines whether there's more data to input. This method returns the `boolean` value `true` if there's more data; otherwise, it returns `false`. As long as the end-of-file indicator has not been typed, method `hasNext` will return `true`.
- The `switch` statement consists of a block that contains a sequence of `case` labels (p. 179) and an optional `default` case (p. 179).
- In a `switch`, the program evaluates the controlling expression and compares its value with each `case` label. If a match occurs, the program executes the statements for that `case`.
- Listing `case`s consecutively with no statements between them enables the `case`s to perform the same set of statements.
- Every value you wish to test in a `switch` must be listed in a separate `case` label.
- Each `case` can have multiple statements, and these need not be placed in braces.
- A `case`'s statements typically end with a `break` (p. 180) that terminates the `switch`'s execution.
- Without `break` statements, each time a match occurs in the `switch`, the statements for that `case` and subsequent `case`s execute until a `break` statement or the end of the `switch` is encountered.

- If no match occurs between the controlling expression's value and a case label, the optional default case executes. If no match occurs and the switch does not contain a default case, program control simply continues with the first statement after the switch.

Section 5.7 Class **AutoPolicy** *Case Study:* **Strings** *in* **switch** *Statements*

- Strings can be used in a switch statement's controlling expression and case labels.

Section 5.8.1 **break** *Statement*

- The break statement, when executed in a while, for, do...while or switch, causes immediate exit from that statement.

Section 5.8.2 **continue** *Statement*

- The continue statement (p. 185), when executed in a while, for or do...while, skips the loop's remaining body statements and proceeds with its next iteration. In while and do...while statements, the program evaluates the loop-continuation test immediately. In a for statement, the increment expression executes, then the program evaluates the loop-continuation test.

Section 5.9 Logical Operators

- Simple conditions are expressed in terms of the relational operators >, <, >= and <= and the equality operators == and !=, and each expression tests only one condition.
- Logical operators (p. 187) enable you to form more complex conditions by combining simple conditions. The logical operators are && (conditional AND), || (conditional OR), & (boolean logical AND), | (boolean logical inclusive OR), ^ (boolean logical exclusive OR) and ! (logical NOT).

Section 5.9.1 Conditional AND (&&) Operator

- To ensure that two conditions are *both* true, use the && (conditional AND) operator. If either or both of the simple conditions are false, the entire expression is false.

Section 5.9.2 Conditional OR (||) Operator

- To ensure that either *or* both of two conditions are true, use the || (conditional OR) operator, which evaluates to true if either or both of its simple conditions are true.

Section 5.9.3 Short-Circuit Evaluation of Complex Conditions

- A condition using && or || operators (p. 189) uses short-circuit evaluation (p. 189)—they're evaluated only until it's known whether the condition is true or false.

Section 5.9.4 Boolean Logical AND (&) and Boolean Logical Inclusive OR (|) Operators

- The & and | operators (p. 189) work identically to the && and || operators but always evaluate both operands.

Section 5.9.5 Boolean Logical Exclusive OR (^)

- A simple condition containing the boolean logical exclusive OR (^; p. 190) operator is true *if and only if one of its operands is* true *and the other is* false. If both operands are true or both are false, the entire condition is false. This operator is also guaranteed to evaluate both of its operands.

Section 5.9.6 Logical Negation (!) Operator

- The unary ! (logical NOT; p. 190) operator "reverses" the value of a condition.

Self-Review Exercises

5.1 Fill in the blanks in each of the following statements:

a) Typically, ________ statements are used for counter-controlled iteration and ________ statements for sentinel-controlled iteration.

b) The `do...while` statement tests the loop-continuation condition ________ executing the loop's body; therefore, the body always executes at least once.

c) The ________ statement selects among multiple actions based on the possible values of an integer variable or expression, or a `String`.

d) The ________ statement, when executed in an iteration statement, skips the remaining statements in the loop body and proceeds with the next iteration of the loop.

e) The ________ operator (with short-circuit evaluation) can be used to ensure that two conditions are *both* true before choosing a certain path of execution.

f) If the loop-continuation condition in a `for` header is initially ________, the program does not execute the `for` statement's body.

g) Methods that perform common tasks and do not require objects are ________ methods.

5.2 State whether each of the following is *true* or *false*. If *false*, explain why.

a) The `default` case is required in the `switch` selection statement.

b) The `break` statement is required in the last case of a `switch` selection statement.

c) The expression `((x > y) && (a < b))` is `true` if either `x > y` is `true` or `a < b` is `true`.

d) An expression containing the `||` operator is `true` if either or both of its operands are `true`.

e) The comma (`,`) formatting flag in a format specifier (e.g., `%,20.2f`) indicates that a value should be output with a grouping separator.

f) To test for a range of values in a `switch` statement, use a hyphen (-) between the start and end values of the range in a `case` label.

g) Listing `case`s consecutively with no statements between them enables the `case`s to perform the same set of statements.

5.3 Write a Java statement or a set of Java statements to accomplish each of the following tasks:

a) Sum the odd integers between 1 and 99, using a `for` statement. Assume that the integer variables `sum` and `count` have been declared.

b) Calculate the value of `2.5` raised to the power of `3`, using the `pow` method.

c) Print the integers from 1 to 20, using a `while` loop and the counter variable `i`. Assume that the variable `i` has been declared, but not initialized. Print only five integers per line. [*Hint:* Use the calculation `i % 5`. When the value of this expression is 0, print a newline character; otherwise, print a tab character. Assume that this code is an application. Use the `System.out.println()` method to output the newline character, and use the `System.out.print('\t')` method to output the tab character.]

d) Repeat part (c), using a `for` statement.

5.4 Find the error in each of the following code segments, and explain how to correct it:

a)

```
i = 1;
while (i <= 10);
   ++i;
}
```

b)

```
for (k = 0.1; k != 1.0; k += 0.1) {
   System.out.println(k);
}
```

c)

```
switch (n) {
   case 1:
      System.out.println("The number is 1");
   case 2:
      System.out.println("The number is 2");
      break;
   default:
      System.out.println("The number is not 1 or 2");
      break;
}
```

d) The following code should print the values 1 to 10:

```
n = 1;
while (n < 10) {
   System.out.println(n++);
}
```

Answers to Self-Review Exercises

5.1 a) `for`, `while`. b) after. c) `switch`. d) `continue`. e) `&&` (conditional AND). f) `false`. g) `static`.

5.2 a) False. The `default` case is optional. If no default action is needed, then there's no need for a `default` case. b) False. The `break` statement is used to exit the `switch` statement. The `break` statement is not required for the last case in a `switch` statement. c) False. *Both* of the relational expressions must be `true` for the entire expression to be `true` when using the `&&` operator. d) True. e) True. f) False. The `switch` statement does not provide a mechanism for testing ranges of values, so every value that must be tested should be listed in a separate `case` label. g) True.

5.3 Answers:

a)

```
sum = 0;
for (count = 1; count <= 99; count += 2) {
   sum += count;
}
```

b) `double result = Math.pow(2.5, 3);`

c)

```
i = 1;

while (i <= 20) {
   System.out.print(i);

   if (i % 5 == 0) {
      System.out.println();
   }
   else {
      System.out.print('\t');
   }

   ++i;
}
```

d)

```
for (i = 1; i <= 20; i++) {
   System.out.print(i);

   if (i % 5 == 0) {
      System.out.println();
   }
   else {
      System.out.print('\t');
   }
}
```

5.4 Answers:

a) Error: The semicolon after the `while` header causes an infinite loop, and there's a missing left brace.
Correction: Replace the semicolon by a `{`, or remove both the `;` and the `}`.

b) Error: Using a floating-point number to control a `for` statement may not work, because floating-point numbers are represented only approximately by most computers.
Correction: Use an integer, and perform the proper calculation to get the values you desire, as in:

```
for (k = 1; k != 10; k++) {
   System.out.println((double) k / 10);
}
```

c) Error: The missing code is the `break` statement in the statements for the first `case`.
Correction: Add a `break` statement at the end of the statements for the first `case`. This omission is not necessarily an error if you want the statement of `case 2:` to execute every time the `case 1:` statement executes.

d) Error: An improper relational operator is used in the `while`'s continuation condition.
Correction: Use `<=` rather than `<`, or change `10` to `11`.

Exercises

5.5 Describe the four basic elements of counter-controlled iteration.

5.6 Compare and contrast the `while` and `for` iteration statements.

5.7 Discuss a situation in which it would be more appropriate to use a `do...while` statement than a `while` statement. Explain why.

5.8 Compare and contrast the `break` and `continue` statements.

5.9 Find and correct the error(s) in each of the following segments of code:

a)

```
For (i = 100, i >= 1, i++) {
   System.out.println(i);
}
```

b) The following code should print whether integer `value` is odd or even:

```
switch (value % 2) {
   case 0:
      System.out.println("Even integer");
   case 1:
      System.out.println("Odd integer");
}
```

c) The following code should output the odd integers from 19 to 1:

```
for (i = 19; i >= 1; i += 2) {
   System.out.println(i);
}
```

d) The following code should output the even integers from 2 to 100:

```
int counter = 2;

do {
   System.out.println(counter);
   counter += 2;
} While (counter < 100);
```

5.10 What does the following program do?

```
// Exercise 5.10: Printing.java
public class Printing {
   public static void main(String[] args) {
      for (int i = 1; i <= 10; i++) {
         for (int j = 1; j <= 5; j++) {
            System.out.print('@');
         }

         System.out.println();
      }
   }
}
```

5.11 *(Find the Smallest Value)* Write an application that finds the smallest of several integers. Assume that the first value read specifies the number of values to input from the user.

5.12 *(Calculating the Product of Odd Integers)* Write an application that calculates the product of the odd integers from 1 to 15.

5.13 *(Factorials) Factorials* are used frequently in probability problems. The factorial of a positive integer *n* (written *n*! and pronounced "*n* factorial") is equal to the product of the positive integers from 1 to *n*. Write an application that calculates the factorials of 1 through 20. Use type `long`. Display the results in tabular format. What difficulty might prevent you from calculating the factorial of 100?

5.14 *(Modified Compound-Interest Program)* Modify the compound-interest application of Fig. 5.6 to repeat its steps for interest rates of 5%, 6%, 7%, 8%, 9% and 10%. Use a `for` loop to vary the interest rate.

5.15 *(Triangle Printing Program)* Write an application that displays the following patterns separately, one below the other. Use `for` loops to generate the patterns. All asterisks (*) should be printed by a single statement of the form `System.out.print('*');` which causes the asterisks to print side by side. A statement of the form `System.out.println();` can be used to move to the next line. A statement of the form `System.out.print(' ');` can be used to display a space for the last two patterns. There should be no other output statements in the program. [*Hint:* The last two patterns require that each line begin with an appropriate number of blank spaces.]

```
(a)            (b)            (c)            (d)
*              **********     **********              *
**             *********       *********             **
***            ********         ********            ***
****           *******           *******           ****
*****          ******             ******          *****
******         *****               *****         ******
*******        ****                 ****        *******
********       ***                   ***       ********
*********      **                     **      *********
**********     *                       *     **********
```

5.16 *(Bar-Chart Printing Program)* One interesting application of computers is to display graphs and bar charts. Write an application that reads five numbers between 1 and 30. For each number that's read, your program should display the same number of adjacent asterisks. For example, if your program reads the number 7, it should display *******. Display the bars of asterisks *after* you read all five numbers.

5.17 *(Calculating Sales)* An online retailer sells five products whose retail prices are as follows: Product 1, $2.98; product 2, $4.50; product 3, $9.98; product 4, $4.49 and product 5, $6.87. Write an application that reads a series of pairs of numbers as follows:

a) product number
b) quantity sold

Your program should use a `switch` statement to determine the retail price for each product. It should calculate and display the total retail value of all products sold. Use a sentinel-controlled loop to determine when the program should stop looping and display the final results.

5.18 *(Modified Compound-Interest Program)* Modify the application in Fig. 5.6 to use only integers to calculate the compound interest. [*Hint:* Treat all monetary amounts as integral numbers of pennies. Then break the result into its dollars and cents portions by using the division and remainder operations, respectively. Insert a period between the dollars and the cents portions.]

5.19 Assume that `i = 1`, `j = 2`, `k = 3` and `m = 2`. What does each of the following statements print?

a) `System.out.println(i == 1);`
b) `System.out.println(j == 3);`
c) `System.out.println((i >= 1) && (j < 4));`
d) `System.out.println((m <= 99) & (k < m));`
e) `System.out.println((j >= i) || (k == m));`
f) `System.out.println((k + m < j) | (3 - j >= k));`
g) `System.out.println(!(k > m));`

5.20 *(Calculating the Value of π)* Calculate the value of π from the infinite series

$$\pi = 4 - \frac{4}{3} + \frac{4}{5} - \frac{4}{7} + \frac{4}{9} - \frac{4}{11} + \cdots$$

Print a table that shows the value of π approximated by computing the first 200,000 terms of this series. How many terms do you have to use before you first get a value that begins with 3.14159?

5.21 *(Pythagorean Triples)* A right triangle can have sides whose lengths are all integers. The set of three integer values for the lengths of the sides of a right triangle is called a Pythagorean triple. The lengths of the three sides must satisfy the relationship that the sum of the squares of two of the sides is equal to the square of the hypotenuse. Write an application that displays a table of the Pythagorean triples for `side1`, `side2` and the `hypotenuse`, all no larger than 500. Use a triple-nested `for` loop that tries all possibilities. This method is an example of "brute-force" computing. You'll learn in more advanced computer-science courses that for many interesting problems there's no known algorithmic approach other than using sheer brute force.

5.22 *(Modified Triangle-Printing Program)* Modify Exercise 5.15 to combine your code from the four separate triangles of asterisks such that all four patterns print side by side. [*Hint:* Make clever use of nested `for` loops.]

5.23 *(De Morgan's Laws)* In this chapter, we discussed the logical operators `&&`, `&`, `||`, `|`, `^` and `!`. De Morgan's laws can sometimes make it more convenient for us to express a logical expression. These laws state that the expression `!(`*condition1* `&&` *condition2*`)` is logically equivalent to the expression `(!`*condition1* `||` `!`*condition2*`)`. Also, the expression `!(`*condition1* `||` *condition2*`)` is logically equivalent to the expression `(!`*condition1* `&&` `!`*condition2*`)`. Use De Morgan's laws to write equivalent expressions for each of the following, then write an application to show that both the original expression and the new expression in each case produce the same value:

a) `!(x < 5) && !(y >= 7)`
b) `!(a == b) || !(g != 5)`
c) `!((x <= 8) && (y > 4))`
d) `!((i > 4) || (j <= 6))`

5.24 *(Diamond-Printing Program)* Write an application that prints the following diamond shape. You may use output statements that print a single asterisk (*), a single space or a single newline character. Maximize your use of iteration (with nested `for` statements), and minimize the number of output statements.

```
    *
   ***
  *****
 *******
*********
 *******
  *****
   ***
    *
```

5.25 *(Modified Diamond Printing Program)* Modify the application you wrote in Exercise 5.24 to read an odd number in the range 1 to 19 to specify the number of rows in the diamond. Your program should then display a diamond of the appropriate size.

5.26 A criticism of the `break` statement and the `continue` statement is that each is unstructured. Actually, these statements can always be replaced by structured statements, although doing so can be awkward. Describe in general how you'd remove any `break` statement from a loop in a program and replace it with some structured equivalent. [*Hint:* The `break` statement exits a loop from the body of the loop. The other way to exit is by failing the loop-continuation test. Consider using in the loop-continuation test a second test that indicates "early exit because of a 'break' condition."] Use the technique you develop here to remove the `break` statement from the application in Fig. 5.13.

5.27 What does the following program segment do?

```
for (i = 1; i <= 5; i++) {
   for (j = 1; j <= 3; j++) {
      for (k = 1; k <= 4; k++) {
         System.out.print('*');
      }

      System.out.println();
   }

   System.out.println();
}
```

5.28 Describe in general how you'd remove any `continue` statement from a loop in a program and replace it with some structured equivalent. Use the technique you develop here to remove the `continue` statement from the program in Fig. 5.14.

5.29 *("The Twelve Days of Christmas" Song)* Write an application that uses iteration and `switch` statements to print the song "The Twelve Days of Christmas." One `switch` statement should be used to print the day ("first," "second," and so on). A separate `switch` statement should be used to print the remainder of each verse. Visit the website `en.wikipedia.org/wiki/The_Twelve_Days_of_Christmas_(song)` for the lyrics of the song.

5.30 *(Modified `AutoPolicy` Class)* Modify class `AutoPolicy` in Fig. 5.11 to validate the two-letter state codes for the northeast states. The codes are: CT for Connecticut, MA for Massachusetts, ME for Maine, NH for New Hampshire, NJ for New Jersey, NY for New York, PA for Pennsylvania and VT for Vermont. In `AutoPolicy` method `setState`, use the logical OR (`||`) operator (Section 5.9) to create a compound condition in an `if...else` statement that compares the method's argument with each two-letter code. If the code is incorrect, the `else` part of the `if...else` statement should display an error message. In later chapters, you'll learn how to use exception handling to indicate that a method received an invalid argument.

Making a Difference

5.31 *(Global Warming Facts Quiz)* The controversial issue of global warming has been widely publicized by the film "An Inconvenient Truth," featuring former Vice President Al Gore. Mr. Gore and a U.N. network of scientists, the Intergovernmental Panel on Climate Change, shared the 2007 Nobel Peace Prize in recognition of "their efforts to build up and disseminate greater knowledge about man-made climate change." Research *both* sides of the issue online. Create a five-question multiple-choice quiz on global warming, each question having four possible answers (numbered 1–4). Be objective and try to fairly represent both sides of the issue. Next, write an application that administers the quiz, calculates the number of correct answers (zero through five) and returns a message to the user. If the user correctly answers five questions, print "Excellent"; if four, print "Very good"; if three or fewer, print "Time to brush up on your knowledge of global warming," and include a list of some of the websites where you found your facts.

5.32 *(Tax Plan Alternatives; The "FairTax")* There are many proposals to make taxation fairer. Check out the FairTax initiative in the United States at `http://www.fairtax.org`. Research how the proposed FairTax works. One suggestion is to eliminate income taxes and most other taxes in favor of a 23% consumption tax on all products and services that you buy. Some FairTax opponents question the 23% figure and say that because of the way the tax is calculated, it would be more accurate to say the rate is 30%—check this carefully. Write a program that prompts the user to enter expenses in various expense categories they have (e.g., housing, food, clothing, transportation, education, health care, vacations), then prints the estimated FairTax that person would pay.

6 Methods: A Deeper Look

Objectives

In this chapter you'll learn:

- How `static` methods and fields are associated with classes rather than objects.
- How the method-call/return mechanism is supported by the method-call stack.
- About argument promotion and casting.
- How packages group related classes.
- How to use secure random-number generation to implement game-playing applications.
- How the visibility of declarations is limited to specific regions of programs.
- What method overloading is and how to create overloaded methods.

Outline

6.1 Introduction

Experience has shown that the best way to develop and maintain a large program is to construct it from small, simple pieces. This technique is called **divide and conquer**. Methods, which we introduced in Chapter 3, help you modularize programs. In this chapter, we study methods in more depth.

You'll learn more about `static` methods, which can be called without the need for an object of the class to exist. You'll also learn how Java is able to keep track of which method is currently executing, how local variables of methods are maintained in memory and how a method knows where to return after it completes execution.

We'll take a brief diversion into simulation techniques with random-number generation and develop a version of the dice game called craps that uses most of the programming techniques you've used to this point in the book. In addition, you'll learn how to declare constants in your programs.

Many of the classes you'll use or create while developing applications will have more than one method of the same name. This technique, called *overloading*, is used to implement methods that perform similar tasks for arguments of different types or for different numbers of arguments. We continue our discussion of methods in Chapter 18, Recursion. Recursion provides an intriguing way of thinking about methods and algorithms.

6.2 Program Units in Java

You've already been working with various program units in Java. You write programs by combining new methods and classes with predefined ones available in the **Java Application Programming Interface** (also referred to as the **Java API** or **Java class library**) and in various other class libraries. Related classes are typically grouped into *packages* so that they can be *imported* into programs and *reused*. You'll learn how to group your own classes into *packages* in Section 21.4.10. Java 9 introduces another program unit called *modules*, which we discuss in Chapter 36, Java Module System and Other Java 9 Features. 9

The Java API provides a rich collection of predefined classes that contain methods for performing common mathematical calculations, string manipulations, character manipulations, input/output operations, database operations, networking operations, file processing, error checking and more.

Software Engineering Observation 6.1

Familiarize yourself with the rich collection of classes and methods provided by the Java API (`http://docs.oracle.com/javase/8/docs/api`). Section 6.8 overviews several common packages. Online Appendix F explains how to navigate the API documentation. Don't reinvent the wheel. When possible, reuse Java API classes and methods. This reduces program development time and avoids introducing programming errors.

Divide and Conquer with Classes and Methods

Classes and methods help you modularize a program by separating its tasks into self-contained units. The statements in the method bodies are written only once, are hidden from other methods and can be reused from several locations in a program.

One motivation for modularizing a program into classes and methods is the *divide-and-conquer* approach, which makes program development more manageable by constructing programs from small, simple pieces. Another is **software reusability**—using existing classes and methods as building blocks to create new programs. Often, you can create programs mostly from existing classes and methods rather than by building customized code. For example, in earlier programs, we did not define how to read data from the keyboard—Java provides these capabilities in the methods of class `Scanner`. A third motivation is to *avoid repeating code*. Dividing a program into meaningful classes and methods makes the program easier to debug and maintain.

Software Engineering Observation 6.2

To promote software reusability, every method should be limited to performing a single, well-defined task, and the name of the method should express that task effectively.

Error-Prevention Tip 6.1

A method that performs one task is easier to test and debug than one that performs many tasks.

Software Engineering Observation 6.3

If you cannot choose a concise name that expresses a method's task, your method might be attempting to perform too many tasks. Break such a method into several smaller ones.

Hierarchical Relationship Between Method Calls

As you know, a method is invoked by a method call, and when the called method completes its task, it returns control and possibly a result to the caller. An analogy to this program structure is the hierarchical form of management (Fig. 6.1). A boss (the caller) asks a worker (the called method) to perform a task and report back (return) the results after completing the task. The boss method does not know how the worker method performs its designated tasks. The worker may also call other worker methods, unbeknown to the boss. This "hiding" of implementation details promotes good software engineering. Figure 6.1 shows the `boss` method communicating with several worker methods in a hierarchical manner. The boss method divides its responsibilities among the various worker methods. Here, worker1 acts as a "boss method" to worker4 and worker5.

Error-Prevention Tip 6.2

Some methods return a value indicating whether the method performed its task successfully. When you call such a method, be sure to check the return value of that method and, if that method was unsuccessful, deal with the issue appropriately.

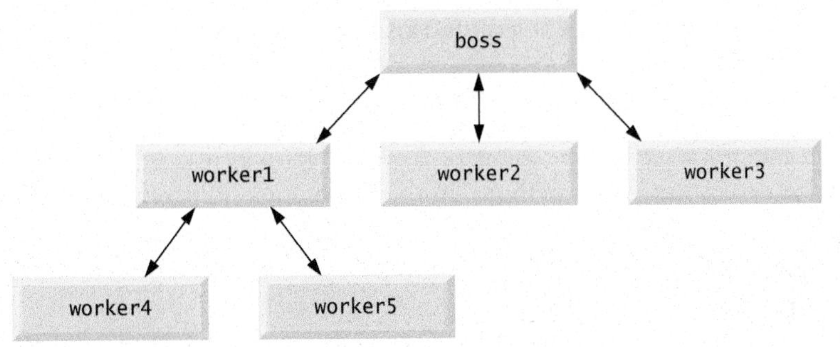

Fig. 6.1 | Hierarchical boss-method/worker-method relationship.

6.3 static Methods, static Fields and Class Math

Most methods execute in response to method calls *on specific objects*. However, sometimes a method performs a task that does not depend on an object. Such a method applies to the class in which it's declared as a whole and is known as a static method or a **class method**. (In Section 10.10, you'll see that interfaces also may contain static methods.)

Classes often contain convenient static methods to perform common tasks. For example, recall that we used class Math's static method pow to raise a value to a power in Fig. 5.6. To declare a method as static, place the keyword static before the return type in the method's declaration. For any class imported into your program, you can call the class's static methods by specifying the class's name, followed by a dot (.) and the method name, as in

```
ClassName.methodName(arguments)
```

Math *Class Methods*

We use various Math class methods here to present the concept of static methods. Class Math provides a collection of methods that enable you to perform common mathematical calculations. For example, you can calculate the square root of 900.0 with the static method call

```
Math.sqrt(900.0)
```

This expression evaluates to 30.0. Method sqrt takes an argument of type double and returns a result of type double. To output the value of the preceding method call in the command window, you might write the statement

```
System.out.println(Math.sqrt(900.0));
```

In this statement, the value that `sqrt` returns becomes the argument to method `println`. There was no need to create a `Math` object before calling method `sqrt`. Also *all* `Math` class methods are `static`—therefore, each is called by preceding its name with the class name `Math` and the dot (`.`) separator.

Software Engineering Observation 6.4

Class `Math` is part of the `java.lang` package, which is implicitly imported by the compiler, so it's not necessary to import class `Math` to use its methods.

Method arguments may be constants, variables or expressions. If `c = 13.0`, `d = 3.0` and `f = 4.0`, then the statement

```
System.out.println(Math.sqrt(c + d * f));
```

calculates and prints the square root of `13.0 + 3.0 * 4.0 = 25.0`—namely, `5.0`. Figure 6.2 summarizes several `Math` class methods. In the figure, *x* and *y* are of type `double`.

Method	Description	Example

`abs(`*x*`)`	absolute value of *x*	`abs(23.7)` is `23.7`
		`abs(0.0)` is `0.0`
		`abs(-23.7)` is `23.7`

`ceil(`*x*`)`	rounds *x* to the smallest integer not less than *x*	`ceil(9.2)` is `10.0` `ceil(-9.8)` is `-9.0`
`cos(`*x*`)`	trigonometric cosine of *x* (*x* in radians)	`cos(0.0)` is `1.0`
`exp(`*x*`)`	exponential method e^x	`exp(1.0)` is `2.71828` `exp(2.0)` is `7.38906`
`floor(`*x*`)`	rounds *x* to the largest integer not greater than *x*	`floor(9.2)` is `9.0` `floor(-9.8)` is `-10.0`
`log(`*x*`)`	natural logarithm of *x* (base *e*)	`log(Math.E)` is `1.0` `log(Math.E * Math.E)` is `2.0`
`max(`*x*`, `*y*`)`	larger value of *x* and *y*	`max(2.3, 12.7)` is `12.7` `max(-2.3, -12.7)` is `-2.3`
`min(`*x*`, `*y*`)`	smaller value of *x* and *y*	`min(2.3, 12.7)` is `2.3` `min(-2.3, -12.7)` is `-12.7`
`pow(`*x*`, `*y*`)`	*x* raised to the power *y* (i.e., x^y)	`pow(2.0, 7.0)` is `128.0` `pow(9.0, 0.5)` is `3.0`
`sin(`*x*`)`	trigonometric sine of *x* (*x* in radians)	`sin(0.0)` is `0.0`
`sqrt(`*x*`)`	square root of *x*	`sqrt(900.0)` is `30.0`
`tan(`*x*`)`	trigonometric tangent of *x* (*x* in radians)	`tan(0.0)` is `0.0`

Fig. 6.2 | `Math` class methods.

`static` *Variables*

Recall from Section 3.2 that each object of a class maintains its *own* copy of every instance variable of the class. There are variables for which each object of a class does *not* need its own separate copy (as you'll see momentarily). Such variables are declared `static` and are also known as **class variables**. When objects of a class containing `static` variables are created, all the objects of that class share *one* copy of the `static` variables. Together a class's `static` variables and instance variables are known as its **fields**. You'll learn more about `static` fields in Section 8.11.

`Math` *Class* `static` *Constants* `PI` *and* `E`

Class `Math` declares two constants, `Math.PI` and `Math.E`, that represent *high-precision approximations* to commonly used mathematical constants:

- `Math.PI` (3.141592653589793) is the ratio of a circle's circumference to its diameter.
- `Math.E` (2.718281828459045) is the base value for natural logarithms (calculated with class `Math`'s `static` method `log`).

These constants are declared in class `Math` with the modifiers `public`, `final` and `static`. Making them `public` allows you to use them in your own classes. Any field declared with keyword **`final`** is *constant*—its value cannot change after the field is initialized. Making these fields `static` allows them to be accessed via the class name `Math` and a dot (`.`) separator, just as class `Math`'s methods are.

Why Is Method `main` *Declared* `static`*?*

When you execute the Java Virtual Machine (JVM) with the `java` command, the JVM attempts to invoke the `main` method of the class you specify—at this point no objects of the class have been created. Declaring `main` as `static` allows the JVM to invoke `main` without creating an instance of the class. When you execute your application, you specify its class name as an argument to the `java` command, as in

```
java ClassName argument1 argument2 ...
```

The JVM loads the class specified by *ClassName* and uses that class name to invoke method `main`. In the preceding command, *ClassName* is a **command-line argument** to the JVM that tells it which class to execute. Following the *ClassName*, you can also specify a list of `String`s (separated by spaces) as command-line arguments that the JVM will pass to your application. Such arguments might be used to specify options (e.g., a filename) to run the application. Every class may contain `main`—only the `main` of the class used to execute the application is called. As you'll learn in Chapter 7, Arrays and `ArrayList`s, your application can access those command-line arguments and use them to customize the application.

6.4 Methods with Multiple Parameters

Methods often require more than one piece of information to perform their tasks. We now consider how to write your own methods with *multiple* parameters.

Figure 6.3 uses a method called `maximum` to determine and return the largest of three `double` values. In `main`, lines 11–15 prompt the user to enter three `double` values, then read them from the user. Line 18 calls method `maximum` (declared in lines 25–39) to determine the largest of the three values it receives as arguments. When method `maximum` returns the result to line 18, the program assigns `maximum`'s return value to local variable `result`. Then line 21 outputs the maximum value. At the end of this section, we'll discuss the use of operator + in line 21.

```
// Fig. 6.3: MaximumFinder.java
// Programmer-declared method maximum with three double parameters.
import java.util.Scanner;

public class MaximumFinder {
   public static void main(String[] args) {
      // create Scanner for input from command window
      Scanner input = new Scanner(System.in);

      // prompt for and input three floating-point values
      System.out.print(
         "Enter three floating-point values separated by spaces: ");
      double number1 = input.nextDouble(); // read first double
      double number2 = input.nextDouble(); // read second double
      double number3 = input.nextDouble(); // read third double

      // determine the maximum value
      double result = maximum(number1, number2, number3);

      // display maximum value
      System.out.println("Maximum is: " + result);
   }

   // returns the maximum of its three double parameters
   public static double maximum(double x, double y, double z) {
      double maximumValue = x; // assume x is the largest to start

      // determine whether y is greater than maximumValue
      if (y > maximumValue) {
         maximumValue = y;
      }

      // determine whether z is greater than maximumValue
      if (z > maximumValue) {
         maximumValue = z;
      }

      return maximumValue;
   }
}
```

```
Enter three floating-point values separated by spaces: 9.35 2.74 5.1
Maximum is: 9.35
```

```
Enter three floating-point values separated by spaces: 5.8 12.45 8.32
Maximum is: 12.45
```

```
Enter three floating-point values separated by spaces: 6.46 4.12 10.54
Maximum is: 10.54
```

Fig. 6.3 | Programmer-declared method `maximum` with three `double` parameters.

The `public` *and* `static` *Keywords*

Method `maximum`'s declaration begins with keyword `public` to indicate that the method is "available to the public"—it can be called from methods of other classes. The keyword `static` enables the `main` method (another `static` method) to call `maximum` as shown in line 18 without qualifying the method name with the class name `MaximumFinder`—`static` methods in the same class can call each other directly. Any other class that uses `maximum` must fully qualify the method name, as in `MaximumFinder.maximum(10, 30, 20)`.

Method `maximum`

Consider `maximum`'s declaration (lines 25–39). Line 25 indicates that it returns a `double` value, that the method's name is `maximum` and that the method requires three `double` parameters (`x`, `y` and `z`) to accomplish its task. Multiple parameters are specified as a comma-separated list. When `maximum` is called from line 18, the parameters `x`, `y` and `z` are initialized with copies of the values of arguments `number1`, `number2` and `number3`, respectively. There must be one argument in the method call for each parameter in the method declaration. Each argument also must be *consistent* with the corresponding parameter's type. For example, a parameter of type `double` can receive values like 7.35, 22 or –0.03456, but not `String`s like `"hello"` nor the `boolean` values `true` or `false`. Section 6.7 discusses the argument types that you can provide in a method call for each primitive-type parameter.

To determine the maximum value, we initially assume that parameter `x` contains the largest value, so line 26 declares local variable `maximumValue` and initializes it with the value of parameter `x`. Of course, it's possible that parameter `y` or `z` contains the actual largest value, so we must compare each of these with `maximumValue`. Lines 29–31 determine whether `y` is greater than `maximumValue`. If so, line 30 assigns `y` to `maximumValue`. Lines 34–36 determine whether `z` is greater than `maximumValue`. If so, line 35 assigns `z` to `maximumValue`. At this point the largest value resides in `maximumValue`, so line 38 returns that value to line 18. When program control returns to where `maximum` was called, `maximum`'s parameters `x`, `y` and `z` no longer exist in memory.

Software Engineering Observation 6.5

Methods can return at most one value, but the returned value could be a reference to an object that contains many values in its instance variables.

Software Engineering Observation 6.6

Variables should be declared as fields only if they're required for use in more than one method of the class or if the program should save their values between calls to the class's methods.

Common Programming Error 6.1

Declaring method parameters of the same type as `float x, y` *instead of* `float x, float y` *is a syntax error—a type is required for each parameter in the parameter list.*

Implementing Method `maximum` *by Reusing Method* `Math.max`

The entire body of our maximum method could also be implemented with two calls to `Math.max`, as follows:

```
return Math.max(x, Math.max(y, z));
```

The first call to `Math.max` specifies arguments `x` and `Math.max(y, z)`. *Before* any method can be called, its arguments must be evaluated to determine their values. If an argument is a method call, the method call must be performed to determine its return value. So, in the preceding statement, `Math.max(y, z)` is evaluated to determine the maximum of `y` and `z`. Then the result is passed as the second argument to the other call to `Math.max`, which returns the larger of its two arguments. This is a good example of *software reuse*—we find the largest of three values by reusing `Math.max`, which finds the larger of two values. Note how concise this code is compared to lines 26–38 of Fig. 6.3.

Assembling Strings with String Concatenation

Java allows you to assemble `String` objects into larger strings by using operators + or +=. This is known as **string concatenation**. When both operands of operator + are `String` objects, operator + creates a new `String` object containing the characters of the left operand followed by those of the right operand—so the expression `"hello " + "there"` creates the `String "hello there"`.

In line 21 of Fig. 6.3, the expression

```
"Maximum is: " + result
```

uses operator + with operands of types `String` and `double`. *Every primitive value and object in Java can be represented as a* `String`. When one of the + operator's operands is a `String`, the other is converted to a `String`, then the two are *concatenated*. In line 21, the `double` value is converted to its `String` representation and placed at the end of `"Maximum is: "`. If there are any *trailing zeros* in a `double` value, these will be *discarded* when the number is converted to a `String`—for example, 9.3500 would be represented as 9.35.

Primitive values used in `String` concatenation are converted to `String`s. A `boolean` concatenated with a `String` is converted to the `String "true"` or `"false"`. *All objects have a* `toString` *method that returns a* `String` *representation of the object.* (We discuss `toString` in more detail in subsequent chapters.) When an object is concatenated with a `String`, the object's `toString` method is called implicitly and returns the object's `String` representation. Method `toString` also can be called explicitly.

You can break large `String` literals into several smaller `String`s and place them on multiple lines of code for readability. In this case, the `String`s can be reassembled using concatenation. We discuss the details of `String`s in Chapter 14.

Common Programming Error 6.2

It's a syntax error to break a `String` *literal across lines. If necessary, you can split a* `String` *into several smaller* `String`*s and use concatenation to form the desired* `String`*.*

Common Programming Error 6.3

Confusing the + operator used for string concatenation with the + operator used for addition can lead to strange results. Java evaluates the operands of an operator from left to right. For example, if integer variable `y` *has the value* 5*, the expression* `"y + 2 = " + y + 2` *results in the string* `"y + 2 = 52"`*, not* `"y + 2 = 7"`*, because first the value of* `y` *(5) is concatenated to the string* `"y + 2 = "`*, then the value* 2 *is concatenated to the new larger string* `"y + 2 = 5"`*. The expression* `"y + 2 = " + (y + 2)` *produces the desired result* `"y + 2 = 7"`*.*

6.5 Notes on Declaring and Using Methods

Calling Methods
There are three ways to call a method:

1. Using a method name by itself to call another method of the *same* class—such as `maximum(number1, number2, number3)` in line 18 of Fig. 6.3.
2. Using a variable that contains a reference to an object, followed by a dot (`.`) and the method name to call a non-`static` method of the referenced object—such as the method call in line 14 of Fig. 3.2, `myAccount.getName()`, which calls a method of class `Account` from the `main` method of `AccountTest`. Non-`static` methods are typically called **instance methods**.
3. Using the class name and a dot (`.`) to call a `static` method of a class—such as `Math.sqrt(900.0)` in Section 6.3.

Returning from Methods
There are three ways to return control to the statement that calls a method:

- When the method-ending right brace is reached in a method with return type `void`.
- When the following statement executes in a method with return type `void`

```
return;
```

- When a method returns a result with a statement of the following form in which the *expression* is evaluated and its result (and control) are returned to the caller:

```
return expression;
```

Common Programming Error 6.4
Declaring a method outside the body of a class declaration or inside the body of another method is a syntax error.

Common Programming Error 6.5
Declaring a local variable in a method with the same name as one of the method's parameters is a compilation error.

Common Programming Error 6.6
Forgetting to return a value from a method that should return a value is a compilation error. If a return type other than `void` *is specified, the method* must *contain a* `return` *statement that returns a value consistent with the method's return type. Returning a value from a method whose return type has been declared* `void` *is a compilation error.*

`static` Members Can Access Only the Class's Other `static` Members Directly
A `static` method can call directly (that is, using the method name by itself) *only* other `static` methods of the same class and can manipulate directly *only* `static` variables in the same class. To access a class's instance variables and instance methods (that is, its non-`static` members), a `static` method must use a reference to an object of that class. Instance methods can access all fields (`static` variables and instance variables) and methods of the class.

Many objects of a class, each with its own copies of the instance variables, may exist at the same time. Suppose a `static` method were to invoke a non-`static` method directly. How would the method know which object's instance variables to manipulate? What would happen if no objects of the class existed at the time the non-`static` method was invoked?

6.6 Method-Call Stack and Activation Records

To understand how Java performs method calls, we first need to consider a data structure (i.e., collection of related data items) known as a **stack**. Think of a stack as analogous to a pile of dishes. When a dish is placed on the pile, it's placed at the *top*—referred to as **pushing** the dish onto the stack. Similarly, when a dish is removed from the pile, it's removed from the top—referred to as **popping** the dish off the stack. Stacks are known as **last-in, first-out (LIFO) data structures**—the last item pushed (inserted) on the stack is the first item popped (removed) from the stack.

6.6.1 Method-Call Stack

One of the most important mechanisms for computer science students to understand is the **method-call stack** (sometimes referred to as the **program-execution stack**). This data structure—working "behind the scenes"—supports the method-call/return mechanism. It also supports the creation, maintenance and destruction of each called method's local variables. Last-in, first-out (LIFO) behavior is *exactly* what a method needs in order to return to the method that called it.

6.6.2 Stack Frames

As each method is called, it may, in turn, call other methods, which may, in turn, call other methods—all *before* any of the methods return. Each method eventually must return control to the method that called it. So, somehow, the system must keep track of the *return addresses* that each method needs in order to return control to the method that called it. The method-call stack is the perfect data structure for handling this information. Each time a method calls another method, an entry is *pushed* onto the stack. This entry, called a **stack frame** or an **activation record**, contains the *return address* that the called method needs in order to return to the calling method. It also contains some additional information we'll soon discuss. If the called method simply returns instead of calling another method before returning, the stack frame for the method call is *popped*, and control transfers to the return address in the popped stack frame.

The beauty of the call stack is that each called method *always* finds the information it needs to return to its caller at the *top* of the call stack. And, if a method makes a call to another method, a stack frame for the new method call is simply *pushed* onto the call stack. Thus, the return address required by the newly called method to return to its caller is now located at the *top* of the stack.

6.6.3 Local Variables and Stack Frames

The stack frames have another important responsibility. Most methods have local variables—parameters and any local variables the method declares. Local variables need to exist while a method is executing. They need to remain active if the method makes calls to other methods. But when a called method returns to its caller, the called method's local variables need to "go away." The called method's stack frame is a perfect place to reserve the memory for the called method's local variables. That stack frame exists as long as the called method is active. When that method returns—and no longer needs its local variables—its stack frame is *popped* from the stack, and those local variables no longer exist.

6.6.4 Stack Overflow

Of course, the amount of memory in a computer is finite, so only a certain amount of memory can be used to store activation records on the method-call stack. If more method calls occur than can have their activation records stored on the method-call stack, a fatal error known as **stack overflow** occurs[1]—this typically is caused by infinite recursion (Chapter 18).

6.7 Argument Promotion and Casting

Another important feature of method calls is **argument promotion**—converting an *argument's value*, if possible, to the type that the method expects to receive in its corresponding *parameter*. For example, a program can call `Math` method `sqrt` with an `int` argument even though a `double` argument is expected. The statement

```
System.out.println(Math.sqrt(4));
```

correctly evaluates `Math.sqrt(4)` and prints the value `2.0`. The method declaration's parameter list causes Java to convert the `int` value `4` to the `double` value `4.0` *before* passing the value to method `sqrt`. Such conversions may lead to compilation errors if Java's **promotion rules** are not satisfied. These rules specify which conversions are allowed—that is, which ones can be performed *without losing data*. In the `sqrt` example above, an `int` is converted to a `double` without changing its value. However, converting a `double` to an `int` *truncates* the fractional part of the `double` value—thus, part of the value is lost. Converting large integer types to small integer types (for example, `long` to `int`, or `int` to `short`) may also result in changed values.

The promotion rules apply to expressions containing values of two or more primitive types and to primitive-type values passed as arguments to methods. Each value is promoted to the "highest" type in the expression. Actually, the expression uses a *temporary copy* of each value—the types of the original values remain unchanged. Figure 6.4 lists the primitive types and the types to which each can be promoted. The valid promotions for a given type are always to a type higher in the table. For example, an `int` can be promoted to the higher types `long`, `float` and `double`.

Converting values to types lower in the table of Fig. 6.4 will result in different values if the lower type cannot represent the value of the higher type (for example, the `int` value 2000000 cannot be represented as a `short`, and any floating-point number with digits after its decimal point cannot be represented in an integer type such as `long`, `int` or `short`). Therefore, in cases where information may be lost due to conversion, the Java compiler requires you to use a *cast operator* (introduced in Section 4.10) to explicitly force

---

1. This is how the website `stackoverflow.com` got its name. This is a great website for getting answers to your programming questions.

Type	Valid promotions
double	None
float	double
long	float or double
int	long, float or double
char	int, long, float or double
short	int, long, float or double (but not char)
byte	short, int, long, float or double (but not char)
boolean	None (boolean values are not considered to be numbers in Java)

Fig. 6.4 | Promotions allowed for primitive types.

the conversion to occur—otherwise a compilation error occurs. This enables you to "take control" from the compiler. You essentially say, "I know this conversion might cause loss of information, but for my purposes here, that's fine." Suppose method square calculates the square of an integer and thus requires an int argument. To call square with a double argument named doubleValue, we would be required to write the method call as

```
square((int) doubleValue)
```

This method call explicitly casts (converts) doubleValue's value to a a temporary integer for use in method square. Thus, if doubleValue's value is 4.5, the method receives the value 4 and returns 16, not 20.25.

Common Programming Error 6.7

Casting a primitive-type value to another primitive type may change the value if the new type is not a valid promotion. For example, casting a floating-point value to an integer value may introduce truncation errors (loss of the fractional part) into the result.

6.8 Java API Packages

As you've seen, Java contains many *predefined* classes that are grouped into categories of related classes called *packages*. Together, these are known as the Java Application Programming Interface (Java API), or the Java class library. A great strength of Java is the Java API's thousands of classes. Some key Java API packages that we use in this book are described in Fig. 6.5, which represents only a small portion of the *reusable components* in the Java API.

Package	Description
java.awt.event	The **Java Abstract Window Toolkit Event Package** contains classes and interfaces that enable event handling for GUI components in both the java.awt and javax.swing packages. (See Chapter 26, Swing GUI Components: Part 1, and Chapter 35, Swing GUI Components: Part 2.)

Fig. 6.5 | Java API packages (a subset). (Part 1 of 2.)

Package	Description
`java.awt.geom`	The **Java 2D Shapes Package** contains classes and interfaces for working with Java's advanced two-dimensional graphics capabilities. (See Chapter 27, Graphics and Java 2D.)
`java.io`	The **Java Input/Output Package** contains classes and interfaces that enable programs to input and output data. (See Chapter 15, Files, Input/Output Streams, NIO and XML Serialization.)
`java.lang`	The **Java Language Package** contains classes and interfaces (discussed throughout the book) that are required by many Java programs. This package is imported by the compiler into all programs.
`java.net`	The **Java Networking Package** contains classes and interfaces that enable programs to communicate via computer networks like the Internet. (See online Chapter 28, Networking.)
`java.security`	The **Java Security Package** contains classes and interfaces for enhancing application security.
`java.sql`	The **JDBC Package** contains classes and interfaces for working with databases. (See Chapter 24, Accessing Databases with JDBC.)
`java.util`	The **Java Utilities Package** contains utility classes and interfaces that enable storing and processing of large amounts of data. Many of these classes and interfaces have been updated to support Java SE 8's lambda capabilities. (See Chapter 16, Generic Collections.)
`java.util.concurrent`	The **Java Concurrency Package** contains utility classes and interfaces for implementing programs that can perform multiple tasks in parallel. (See Chapter 23, Concurrency.)
`javax.swing`	The **Java Swing GUI Components Package** contains classes and interfaces for Java's Swing GUI components. This package still uses some elements of the older `java.awt` package. (See Chapter 26, Swing GUI Components: Part 1, and Chapter 35, Swing GUI Components: Part 2.)
`javax.swing.event`	The **Java Swing Event Package** contains classes and interfaces that enable event handling (for example, responding to button clicks) for GUI components in package `javax.swing`. (See Chapter 26, Swing GUI Components: Part 1, and Chapter 35, Swing GUI Components: Part 2.)
`javax.xml.ws`	The **JAX-WS Package** contains classes and interfaces for working with web services in Java. (See online Chapter 32, Web Services.)
`javafx` packages	JavaFX is Java's preferred GUI, graphics and multimedia technology for the future. We cover JavaFX extensively throughout the book.
Some Java SE 8 Packages Used in This Book	
`java.time`	The Java SE 8 **Date/Time API Package** contains classes and interfaces for working with dates and times. (See Chapter 23, Concurrency.)
`java.util.function` and `java.util.stream`	These packages contain classes and interfaces for working with Java SE 8's functional programming capabilities. (See Chapter 17, Lambdas and Streams.)

Fig. 6.5 | Java API packages (a subset). (Part 2 of 2.)

The set of packages available in Java is quite large. In addition to those summarized in Fig. 6.5, Java includes packages for complex graphics, advanced graphical user interfaces, printing, advanced networking, security, database processing, multimedia, accessibility (for people with disabilities), concurrent programming, cryptography, XML processing and many other capabilities. For an overview of the packages in Java, visit

```
http://docs.oracle.com/javase/8/docs/api/overview-summary.html
```

You can locate additional information about a predefined Java class's methods in the Java API documentation at

```
http://docs.oracle.com/javase/8/docs/api
```

When you visit this site, click the **Index** link to see an alphabetical listing of all the classes and methods in the Java API. Locate the class name and click its link to see the online description of the class. Click the **METHOD** link to see a table of the class's methods. Each `static` method will be listed with the word "`static`" preceding its return type.

6.9 Case Study: Secure Random-Number Generation

We now take a brief diversion into a popular type of programming application—simulation and game playing. In this and the next section, we develop a game-playing program with multiple methods. The program uses most of the control statements presented thus far in the book and introduces several new programming concepts.

The **element of chance** can be introduced in a program via an object of class **`SecureRandom`** (package `java.security`). Such objects can produce random `boolean`, `byte`, `float`, `double`, `int`, `long` and Gaussian values. In the next several examples, we use objects of class `SecureRandom` to produce random values.

Moving to Secure Random Numbers

Recent editions of this book used Java's `Random` class to obtain "random" values. This class produced *deterministic* values that could be *predicted* by malicious programmers. `SecureRandom` objects produce **nondeterministic random numbers** that *cannot* be predicted.

Deterministic random numbers have been the source of many software security breaches. Most programming languages now have library features similar to `SecureRandom` for producing nondeterministic random numbers to help prevent such problems. From this point forward in the text, when we refer to "random numbers" we mean "secure random numbers."

Software Engineering Observation 6.7

9 *For developers concerned with building increasingly secure applications, Java 9 enhances `SecureRandom`'s capabilities as defined by JEP 273.*

Creating a `SecureRandom` Object

A new secure random-number generator object can be created as follows:

```
SecureRandom randomNumbers = new SecureRandom();
```

It can then be used to generate random values—we discuss only random `int` values here. For more information on the `SecureRandom` class, see

```
http://docs.oracle.com/javase/8/docs/api/java/security/
    SecureRandom.html
```

Obtaining a Random `int` *Value*

Consider the following statement:

```
int randomValue = randomNumbers.nextInt();
```

`SecureRandom` method **`nextInt`** generates a random `int` value. If it truly produces values *at random*, then every value in the range should have an *equal chance* (or probability) of being chosen each time `nextInt` is called.

Changing the Range of Values Produced By `nextInt`

The range of values produced by method `nextInt` generally differs from the range of values required in a particular Java application. For example, a program that simulates coin tossing might require only 0 for "heads" and 1 for "tails." A program that simulates the rolling of a six-sided die might require random integers in the range 1–6. A program that randomly predicts the next type of spaceship (out of four possibilities) that will fly across the horizon in a video game might require random integers in the range 1–4. For cases like these, class `SecureRandom` provides another version of method `nextInt` that receives an `int` argument and returns a value from 0 up to, but not including, the argument's value. For example, for coin tossing, the following statement returns 0 or 1.

```
int randomValue = randomNumbers.nextInt(2);
```

Rolling a Six-Sided Die

To demonstrate random numbers, let's develop a program that simulates 20 rolls of a six-sided die and displays the value of each roll. We begin by using `nextInt` to produce random values in the range 0–5, as follows:

```
int face = randomNumbers.nextInt(6);
```

The argument `6`—called the **scaling factor**—represents the number of unique values that `nextInt` should produce (in this case six—0, 1, 2, 3, 4 and 5). This manipulation is called **scaling** the range of values produced by `SecureRandom` method `nextInt`.

A six-sided die has the numbers 1–6 on its faces, not 0–5. So we **shift** the range of numbers produced by adding a **shifting value**—in this case 1—to our previous result, as in

```
int face = 1 + randomNumbers.nextInt(6);
```

The shifting value (`1`) specifies the *first* value in the desired range of random integers. The preceding statement assigns `face` a random integer in the range 1–6.

Rolling a Six-Sided Die 20 Times

Figure 6.6 shows two sample outputs which confirm that the results of the preceding calculation are integers in the range 1–6, and that each run of the program can produce a *different* sequence of random numbers. Line 3 imports class `SecureRandom` from the `java.security` package. Line 8 creates the `SecureRandom` object `randomNumbers` to produce random values. Line 13 executes 20 times in a loop to roll the die. The `if` statement (lines 18–20) in the loop starts a new line of output after every five numbers to create a neat, five-column format.

```
1  // Fig. 6.6: RandomIntegers.java
2  // Shifted and scaled random integers.
3  import java.security.SecureRandom; // program uses class SecureRandom
4
5  public class RandomIntegers {
6     public static void main(String[] args) {
7        // randomNumbers object will produce secure random numbers
8        SecureRandom randomNumbers = new SecureRandom();
9
10       // loop 20 times
11       for (int counter = 1; counter <= 20; counter++) {
12          // pick random integer from 1 to 6
13          int face = 1 + randomNumbers.nextInt(6);
14
15          System.out.printf("%d  ", face); // display generated value
16
17          // if counter is divisible by 5, start a new line of output
18          if (counter % 5 == 0) {
19             System.out.println();
20          }
21       }
22    }
23 }
```

```
1  5  3  6  2
5  2  6  5  2
4  4  4  2  6
3  1  6  2  2
```

```
6  5  4  2  6
1  2  5  1  3
6  3  2  2  1
6  4  2  6  4
```

Fig. 6.6 | Shifted and scaled random integers.

Rolling a Six-Sided Die 60,000,000 Times

To show that the numbers produced by `nextInt` occur with approximately equal likelihood, let's simulate 60,000,000 rolls of a die with the application in Fig. 6.7. Each integer from 1 to 6 should appear approximately 10,000,000 times. Note in line 18 that we used the _ digit separator to make the `int` value `60_000_000` more readable. Recall that you cannot separate digits with commas. For example, if you replace the `int` value `60_000_000` with `60,000,000`, the JDK 8 compiler generates several compilation errors throughout the `for` statement's header (line 18). Note that this example might take several seconds to execute—see our note about `SecureRandom` performance following the example.

```
// Fig. 6.7: RollDie.java
// Roll a six-sided die 60,000,000 times.
import java.security.SecureRandom;

public class RollDie {
   public static void main(String[] args) {
      // randomNumbers object will produce secure random numbers
      SecureRandom randomNumbers = new SecureRandom();

      int frequency1 = 0; // count of 1s rolled
      int frequency2 = 0; // count of 2s rolled
      int frequency3 = 0; // count of 3s rolled
      int frequency4 = 0; // count of 4s rolled
      int frequency5 = 0; // count of 5s rolled
      int frequency6 = 0; // count of 6s rolled

      // tally counts for 60,000,000 rolls of a die
      for (int roll = 1; roll <= 60_000_000; roll++) {
         int face = 1 + randomNumbers.nextInt(6); // number from 1 to 6

         // use face value 1-6 to determine which counter to increment
         switch (face) {
            case 1:
               ++frequency1; // increment the 1s counter
               break;
            case 2:
               ++frequency2; // increment the 2s counter
               break;
            case 3:
               ++frequency3; // increment the 3s counter
               break;
            case 4:
               ++frequency4; // increment the 4s counter
               break;
            case 5:
               ++frequency5; // increment the 5s counter
               break;
            case 6:
               ++frequency6; // increment the 6s counter
               break;
         }
      }

      System.out.println("Face\tFrequency"); // output headers
      System.out.printf("1\t%d%n2\t%d%n3\t%d%n4\t%d%n5\t%d%n6\t%d%n",
         frequency1, frequency2, frequency3, frequency4,
         frequency5, frequency6);
   }
}
```

Fig. 6.7 | Roll a six-sided die 60,000,000 times. (Part 1 of 2.)

```
Face    Frequency
1       10001086
2       10000185
3       9999542
4       9996541
5       9998787
6       10003859
```

```
Face    Frequency
1       10003530
2       9999925
3       9994766
4       10000707
5       9998150
6       10002922
```

Fig. 6.7 | Roll a six-sided die 60,000,000 times. (Part 2 of 2.)

As the sample outputs show, scaling and shifting the values produced by `nextInt` enables the program to simulate rolling a six-sided die. The application uses nested control statements (the `switch` is nested inside the `for`) to determine the number of times each side of the die appears. The `for` statement (lines 18–42) iterates 60,000,000 times. During each iteration, line 19 produces a random value from 1 to 6. That value is then used as the controlling expression (line 22) of the `switch` statement (lines 22–41). Based on the `face` value, the `switch` statement increments one of the six counter variables during each iteration of the loop. This `switch` statement has no `default` case, because we have a `case` for every possible die value that the expression in line 19 could produce. Run the program, and observe the results. As you'll see, every time you run this program, it produces *different* results.

When we study arrays in Chapter 7, we'll show an elegant way to replace the entire `switch` statement in this program with a *single* statement. Then, when we study Java SE 8's functional programming capabilities in Chapter 17, we'll show how to replace the loop that rolls the dice, the `switch` statement *and* the statement that displays the results with a *single* statement!

A Note about **SecureRandom** *Performance*

Using `SecureRandom` instead of `Random` to achieve higher levels of security incurs a significant performance penalty. For "casual" applications, you might want to use class `Random` from package `java.util`—simply replace `SecureRandom` with `Random`.

Generalized Scaling and Shifting of Random Numbers

Previously, we simulated the rolling of a six-sided die with the statement

```
int face = 1 + randomNumbers.nextInt(6);
```

This statement always assigns to variable `face` an integer in the range `1 ≤ face ≤ 6`. The *width* of this range (i.e., the number of consecutive integers in the range) is `6`, and the *starting number* in the range is `1`. In the preceding statement, the width of the range is determined by the number 6 that's passed as an argument to `SecureRandom` method `nextInt`, and the starting number of the range is the number 1 that's added to `randomNumbers.nextInt(6)`. We can generalize this result as

```
int number = shiftingValue + randomNumbers.nextInt(scalingFactor);
```

where *shiftingValue* specifies the *first number* in the desired range of consecutive integers and *scalingFactor* specifies *how many numbers* are in the range.

It's also possible to choose integers at random from sets of values other than ranges of consecutive integers. For example, to obtain a random value from the sequence 2, 5, 8, 11 and 14, you could use the statement

```
int number = 2 + 3 * randomNumbers.nextInt(5);
```

In this case, `randomNumbers.nextInt(5)` produces values in the range 0–4. Each value produced is multiplied by 3 to produce a number in the sequence 0, 3, 6, 9 and 12. We add 2 to that value to *shift* the range of values and obtain a value from the sequence 2, 5, 8, 11 and 14. We can generalize this result as

```
int number = shiftingValue +
   differenceBetweenValues * randomNumbers.nextInt(scalingFactor);
```

where *shiftingValue* specifies the first number in the desired range of values, *differenceBetweenValues* represents the *constant difference* between consecutive numbers in the sequence and *scalingFactor* specifies how many numbers are in the range.

6.10 Case Study: A Game of Chance; Introducing enum Types

A popular game of chance is a dice game known as craps, which is played in casinos and back alleys throughout the world. The rules of the game are straightforward:

> *You roll two dice. Each die has six faces, which contain one, two, three, four, five and six spots, respectively. After the dice have come to rest, the sum of the spots on the two upward faces is calculated. If the sum is 7 or 11 on the first throw, you win. If the sum is 2, 3 or 12 on the first throw (called "craps"), you lose (i.e., the "house" wins). If the sum is 4, 5, 6, 8, 9 or 10 on the first throw, that sum becomes your "point." To win, you must continue rolling the dice until you "make your point" (i.e., roll that same point value). You lose by rolling a 7 before making your point.*

Figure 6.8 simulates the game of craps, using methods to implement the game's logic. The `main` method (lines 20–66) calls the `rollDice` method (lines 69–80) as necessary to roll the dice and compute their sum. The sample outputs show winning and losing on the first roll, and winning and losing on a subsequent roll.

```
1  // Fig. 6.8: Craps.java
2  // Craps class simulates the dice game craps.
3  import java.security.SecureRandom;
4
5  public class Craps {
```

Fig. 6.8 | `Craps` class simulates the dice game craps. (Part 1 of 3.)

```java
   // create secure random number generator for use in method rollDice
   private static final SecureRandom randomNumbers = new SecureRandom();

   // enum type with constants that represent the game status
   private enum Status {CONTINUE, WON, LOST};

   // constants that represent common rolls of the dice
   private static final int SNAKE_EYES = 2;
   private static final int TREY = 3;
   private static final int SEVEN = 7;
   private static final int YO_LEVEN = 11;
   private static final int BOX_CARS = 12;

   // plays one game of craps
   public static void main(String[] args) {
      int myPoint = 0; // point if no win or loss on first roll
      Status gameStatus; // can contain CONTINUE, WON or LOST

      int sumOfDice = rollDice(); // first roll of the dice

      // determine game status and point based on first roll
      switch (sumOfDice) {
         case SEVEN: // win with 7 on first roll
         case YO_LEVEN: // win with 11 on first roll
            gameStatus = Status.WON;
            break;
         case SNAKE_EYES: // lose with 2 on first roll
         case TREY: // lose with 3 on first roll
         case BOX_CARS: // lose with 12 on first roll
            gameStatus = Status.LOST;
            break;
         default: // did not win or lose, so remember point
            gameStatus = Status.CONTINUE; // game is not over
            myPoint = sumOfDice; // remember the point
            System.out.printf("Point is %d%n", myPoint);
            break;
      }

      // while game is not complete
      while (gameStatus == Status.CONTINUE) { // not WON or LOST
         sumOfDice = rollDice(); // roll dice again

         // determine game status
         if (sumOfDice == myPoint) { // win by making point
            gameStatus = Status.WON;
         }
         else {
            if (sumOfDice == SEVEN) { // lose by rolling 7 before point
               gameStatus = Status.LOST;
            }
         }
      }

```

Fig. 6.8 | Craps class simulates the dice game craps. (Part 2 of 3.)

```
59          // display won or lost message
60          if (gameStatus == Status.WON) {
61             System.out.println("Player wins");
62          }
63          else {
64             System.out.println("Player loses");
65          }
66       }
67
68       // roll dice, calculate sum and display results
69       public static int rollDice() {
70          // pick random die values
71          int die1 = 1 + randomNumbers.nextInt(6); // first die roll
72          int die2 = 1 + randomNumbers.nextInt(6); // second die roll
73
74          int sum = die1 + die2; // sum of die values
75
76          // display results of this roll
77          System.out.printf("Player rolled %d + %d = %d%n", die1, die2, sum);
78
79          return sum;
80       }
81    }
```

```
Player rolled 5 + 6 = 11
Player wins
```

```
Player rolled 5 + 4 = 9
Point is 9
Player rolled 4 + 2 = 6
Player rolled 3 + 6 = 9
Player wins
```

```
Player rolled 1 + 2 = 3
Player loses
```

```
Player rolled 2 + 6 = 8
Point is 8
Player rolled 5 + 1 = 6
Player rolled 2 + 1 = 3
Player rolled 1 + 6 = 7
Player loses
```

Fig. 6.8 | Craps class simulates the dice game craps. (Part 3 of 3.)

Method `rollDice`

In the rules of the game, the player must roll *two* dice on each roll. We declare method `rollDice` (lines 69–80) to roll the dice and compute and print their sum. Method `roll-`

Dice is declared once, but it's called from two places (lines 24 and 46) in main, which contains the logic for one complete game of craps. Method rollDice takes no arguments, so it has an empty parameter list. Each time it's called, rollDice returns the sum of the dice, so the return type int is indicated in the method header (line 69). Although lines 71 and 72 look the same (except for the die names), they do not necessarily produce the same result. Each statement produces a *random* value in the range 1–6. Variable randomNumbers (used in lines 71–72) is *not* declared in the method. Instead it's declared as a private static final variable of the class and initialized in line 7. This enables us to create one SecureRandom object that's reused in each call to rollDice. If there were a program that contained multiple instances of class Craps, they'd all share this one SecureRandom object.

Method main*'s Local Variables*

The game is reasonably involved. The player may win or lose on the first roll, or may win or lose on any subsequent roll. Method main (lines 20–66) uses

- local variable myPoint (line 21) to store the "point" if the player doesn't win or lose on the first roll,
- local variable gameStatus (line 22) to keep track of the overall game status and
- local variable sumOfDice (line 24) to hold the sum of the dice for the most recent roll.

Variable myPoint is initialized to 0 to ensure that the application will compile. If you do not initialize myPoint, the compiler issues an error, because myPoint is not assigned a value in *every* case of the switch statement, and thus the program could try to use myPoint before it's assigned a value. By contrast, gameStatus *is* assigned a value in *every* case of the switch statement (including the default case)—thus, it's guaranteed to be initialized before it's used, so we do not need to initialize it in line 22.

enum *Type* Status

Local variable gameStatus (line 22) is declared to be of a new type called Status (declared at line 10). Type Status is a private member of class Craps, because Status will be used only in that class. Status is a type called an **enum type**, which, in its simplest form, declares a set of constants represented by identifiers. An enum type is a special kind of class that's introduced by the keyword enum and a type name (in this case, Status). As with classes, braces delimit an enum declaration's body. Inside the braces is a comma-separated list of **enum constants**, each representing a unique value. The identifiers in an enum must be *unique*. You'll learn more about enum types in Chapter 8.

Good Programming Practice 6.1

Use only uppercase letters in the names of enum *constants to make them stand out and remind you that they're not variables.*

Variables of type Status can be assigned only the three constants declared in the enum (line 10) or a compilation error will occur. When the game is won, the program sets local variable gameStatus to Status.WON (lines 30 and 50). When the game is lost, the program sets local variable gameStatus to Status.LOST (lines 35 and 54). Otherwise, the program sets local variable gameStatus to Status.CONTINUE (line 38) to indicate that the game is not over and the dice must be rolled again.

Good Programming Practice 6.2

Using enum *constants (like* Status.WON, Status.LOST *and* Status.CONTINUE) *rather than literal values (such as 0, 1 and 2) makes programs easier to read and maintain.*

Logic of the main *Method*

Line 24 in main calls rollDice, which picks two random values from 1 to 6, displays the values of the first die, the second die and their sum, and returns the sum. Method main next enters the switch statement (lines 27–42), which uses the sumOfDice value from line 24 to determine whether the game has been won or lost, or should continue with another roll. The values that result in a win or loss on the first roll are declared as private static final int constants in lines 13–17. The identifier names use casino parlance for these sums. These constants, like enum constants, are declared by convention with all capital letters, to make them stand out in the program. Lines 28–31 determine whether the player won on the first roll with SEVEN (7) or YO_LEVEN (11). Lines 32–36 determine whether the player lost on the first roll with SNAKE_EYES (2), TREY (3), or BOX_CARS (12). After the first roll, if the game is not over, the default case (lines 37–41) sets gameStatus to Status.CONTINUE, saves sumOfDice in myPoint and displays the point.

If we're still trying to "make our point" (i.e., the game is continuing from a prior roll), lines 45–57 execute. Line 46 rolls the dice again. If sumOfDice matches myPoint (line 49), line 50 sets gameStatus to Status.WON, then the loop terminates because the game is complete. If sumOfDice is SEVEN (line 53), line 54 sets gameStatus to Status.LOST, and the loop terminates because the game is complete. When the game completes, lines 60–65 display a message indicating whether the player won or lost, and the program terminates.

The program uses the various program-control mechanisms we've discussed. The Craps class uses two methods—main and rollDice (called twice from main)—and the switch, while, if...else and nested if control statements. Note also the use of multiple case labels in the switch statement to execute the same statements for sums of SEVEN and YO_LEVEN (lines 28–29) and for sums of SNAKE_EYES, TREY and BOX_CARS (lines 32–34).

Why Some Constants Are Not Defined as enum *Constants*

You might be wondering why we declared the sums of the dice as private static final int constants rather than as enum constants. The reason is that the program must compare the int variable sumOfDice (line 24) to these constants to determine the outcome of each roll. Suppose we declared enum Sum containing constants representing the five sums used in the game, then used these constants in the switch statement (lines 27–42). Doing so would prevent us from using sumOfDice as the switch statement's controlling expression, because Java does *not* allow you to compare an int to an enum constant. To achieve the same functionality as the current program, we'd have to use a variable currentSum of type Sum as the switch's controlling expression. Unfortunately, Java does not provide an easy way to convert an int value to a particular enum constant. This could be done with a separate switch statement. This would be cumbersome and would not improve the program's readability (thus defeating the purpose of using an enum).

6.11 Scope of Declarations

You've seen declarations of various Java entities, such as classes, methods, variables and parameters. Declarations introduce names that can be used to refer to such Java entities. The **scope** of a declaration is the portion of the program that can refer to the declared entity by its name. Such an entity is said to be "in scope" for that portion of the program. This section introduces several important scope issues.

The basic scope rules are as follows:

1. The scope of a parameter declaration is the body of the method in which the declaration appears.
2. The scope of a local-variable declaration is from the point at which the declaration appears to the end of that block.
3. The scope of a local-variable declaration that appears in the initialization section of a `for` statement's header is the body of the `for` statement and the other expressions in the header.
4. A method or field's scope is the entire body of the class. This enables a class's instance methods to use the fields and other methods of the class.

Any block may contain variable declarations. If a local variable or parameter in a method has the same name as a field of the class, the field is *hidden* until the block terminates execution—this is called **shadowing**. To access a shadowed field in a block:

- If the field is an instance variable, precede its name with the `this` keyword and a dot (`.`), as in `this.x`.
- If the field is a `static` class variable, precede its name with the class's name and a dot (`.`), as in *ClassName*`.x`.

It's a compilation error if multiple *local* variables have the same name in the same method.

Figure 6.9 demonstrates field and local-variable scopes. Line 6 declares and initializes the field `x` to `1`. This field is *shadowed* in any block (or method) that declares a local variable named `x`. Method `main` declares a local variable `x` (line 11) and initializes it to `5`. This local variable's value is output to show that the field `x` (whose value is `1`) is *shadowed* in `main`.

```
1  // Fig. 6.9: Scope.java
2  // Scope class demonstrates field and local-variable scopes.
3
4  public class Scope {
5     // field that is accessible to all methods of this class
6     private static int x = 1;
7
8     // method main creates and initializes local variable x
9     // and calls methods useLocalVariable and useField
10    public static void main(String[] args) {
11       int x = 5; // method's local variable x shadows field x
12
13       System.out.printf("local x in main is %d%n", x);
14
```

Fig. 6.9 | Scope class demonstrates field and local-variable scopes. (Part 1 of 2.)

```
15         useLocalVariable(); // useLocalVariable has local x
16         useField(); // useField uses class Scope's field x
17         useLocalVariable(); // useLocalVariable reinitializes local x
18         useField(); // class Scope's field x retains its value
19
20         System.out.printf("%nlocal x in main is %d%n", x);
21      }
22
23      // create and initialize local variable x during each call
24      public static void useLocalVariable() {
25         int x = 25; // initialized each time useLocalVariable is called
26
27         System.out.printf(
28            "%nlocal x on entering method useLocalVariable is %d%n", x);
29         ++x; // modifies this method's local variable x
30         System.out.printf(
31            "local x before exiting method useLocalVariable is %d%n", x);
32      }
33
34      // modify class Scope's field x during each call
35      public static void useField() {
36         System.out.printf(
37            "%nfield x on entering method useField is %d%n", x);
38         x *= 10; // modifies class Scope's field x
39         System.out.printf(
40            "field x before exiting method useField is %d%n", x);
41      }
42   }
```

```
local x in main is 5

local x on entering method useLocalVariable is 25
local x before exiting method useLocalVariable is 26

field x on entering method useField is 1
field x before exiting method useField is 10

local x on entering method useLocalVariable is 25
local x before exiting method useLocalVariable is 26

field x on entering method useField is 10
field x before exiting method useField is 100

local x in main is 5
```

Fig. 6.9 | Scope class demonstrates field and local-variable scopes. (Part 2 of 2.)

The program declares two other methods—`useLocalVariable` (lines 24–32) and `useField` (lines 35–41)—that take no arguments and return no results. Method `main` calls each method twice (lines 15–18). Method `useLocalVariable` declares local variable `x` (line 25). When `useLocalVariable` is first called (line 15), it creates local variable `x` and initializes it to `25`, outputs the value of `x` (lines 27–28), increments `x` (line 29) and outputs the value of `x` again (lines 30–31). When `uselLocalVariable` is called a second time (line 17), it *recreates* local variable `x` and *reinitializes* it to `25`, so the output of each `useLocalVariable` call is identical.

Method useField does not declare any local variables. Therefore, when it refers to x, the field x (line 6) of the class is used. When method useField is first called (line 16), it outputs the value (1) of field x (lines 36–37), multiplies the field x by 10 (line 38) and outputs the value (10) of field x again (lines 39–40) before returning. The next time method useField is called (line 18), the field has its modified value (10), so the method outputs 10, then 100. Finally, in method main, the program outputs the value of local variable x again (line 20) to show that none of the method calls modified main's local variable x, because the methods all referred to variables named x in other scopes.

Principle of Least Privilege

In a general sense, "things" should have the capabilities they need to get their job done, but no more. An example is the scope of a variable. A variable should not be visible when it's not needed.

Good Programming Practice 6.3

Declare variables as close to where they're first used as possible.

6.12 Method Overloading

Methods of the *same* name can be declared in the same class, as long as they have *different* sets of parameters (determined by the number, types and order of the parameters)—this is called **method overloading**. When an overloaded method is called, the compiler selects the appropriate method by examining the number, types and order of the arguments in the call. Method overloading is commonly used to create several methods with the *same* name that perform the *same* or *similar* tasks, but on *different* types or *different* numbers of arguments. For example, Math methods abs, min and max (summarized in Section 6.3) are overloaded with four versions each:

1. One with two double parameters.
2. One with two float parameters.
3. One with two int parameters.
4. One with two long parameters.

Our next example demonstrates declaring and invoking overloaded methods. We demonstrate overloaded constructors in Chapter 8.

6.12.1 Declaring Overloaded Methods

Class MethodOverload (Fig. 6.10) declares two overloaded square methods—one calculates the square of an int (and returns an int) and one calculates the square of a double (and returns a double). Although these methods have the same name and similar parameter lists and bodies, think of them simply as *different* methods. It may help to think of the method names as "square of int" and "square of double," respectively.

Line 7 invokes method square with the argument 7. Literal integer values are treated as type int, so the method call in line 7 invokes the version of square at lines 12–16 that specifies an int parameter. Similarly, line 8 invokes method square with the argument 7.5. Literal floating-point values are treated as type double, so the method call in line 8

```
1  // Fig. 6.10: MethodOverload.java
2  // Overloaded method declarations.
3
4  public class MethodOverload {
5     // test overloaded square methods
6     public static void main(String[] args) {
7        System.out.printf("Square of integer 7 is %d%n", square(7));
8        System.out.printf("Square of double 7.5 is %f%n", square(7.5));
9     }
10
11    // square method with int argument
12    public static int square(int intValue) {
13       System.out.printf("%nCalled square with int argument: %d%n",
14          intValue);
15       return intValue * intValue;
16    }
17
18    // square method with double argument
19    public static double square(double doubleValue) {
20       System.out.printf("%nCalled square with double argument: %f%n",
21          doubleValue);
22       return doubleValue * doubleValue;
23    }
24 }
```

```
Called square with int argument: 7
Square of integer 7 is 49

Called square with double argument: 7.500000
Square of double 7.5 is 56.250000
```

Fig. 6.10 | Overloaded method declarations.

invokes the version of `square` at lines 19–23 that specifies a `double` parameter. Each method first outputs a line of text to prove that the proper method was called in each case. The values in lines 8 and 20 are displayed with the format specifier `%f`. We did not specify a precision in either case. By default, floating-point values are displayed with six digits of precision if the precision is *not* specified in the format specifier.

6.12.2 Distinguishing Between Overloaded Methods

The compiler distinguishes overloaded methods by their **signatures**—a combination of the method's *name* and the *number*, *types* and *order* of its parameters, but *not* its return type. If the compiler looked only at method names during compilation, the code in Fig. 6.10 would be ambiguous—the compiler would not know how to distinguish between the two `square` methods (lines 12–16 and 19–23). Internally, the compiler uses longer method names that include the original method name, the types of each parameter and the exact order of the parameters to determine whether the methods in a class are *unique* in that class.

For example, in Fig. 6.10, the compiler might (internally) use the logical name "`square` of `int`" for the `square` method that specifies an `int` parameter and "`square` of double" for the square method that specifies a double parameter (the actual names the compiler uses are messier). If method1's declaration begins as

```
void method1(int a, float b)
```

then the compiler might use the logical name "method1 of int and float." If the parameters are specified as

```
void method1(float a, int b)
```

then the compiler might use the logical name "method1 of float and int." The *order* of the parameter types is important—the compiler considers the preceding two method1 headers to be *distinct*.

6.12.3 Return Types of Overloaded Methods

In discussing the logical names of methods used by the compiler, we did not mention the return types of the methods. *Method calls cannot be distinguished only by return type.* When two methods have the *same* signature and *different* return types, the compiler issues an error message indicating that the method is already defined in the class. Overloaded methods *can* have *different* return types if the methods have *different* parameter lists. Also, overloaded methods need *not* have the same number of parameters.

Common Programming Error 6.8

Declaring overloaded methods with identical parameter lists is a compilation error regardless of whether the return types are different.

6.13 (Optional) GUI and Graphics Case Study: Colors and Filled Shapes

Class GraphicsContext provides many more capabilities than drawing lines, rectangles and ovals. The next two features we introduce are colors and filled shapes. Adding color enriches the drawings a user sees on the computer screen. For example, IDEs generally "syntax color" Java code to help you distinguish different code elements, like keywords and comments. Shapes can be filled with solid colors. As we show in Chapter 22, shapes also can be filled with images or with so-called gradients that transition gradually between colors. In this section, we'll create the DrawSmiley app that uses solid colors and filled shapes to draw a smiley face.

Solid colors displayed on computer screens are defined by their *red*, *green*, and *blue* components (called **RGB values**) that each have an integer value from 0 to 255, inclusive. The higher the value of a component color, the richer that color's shade will be. Class **Color** (package javafx.scene.paint) represents colors using their RGB values. For convenience, class Color contains dozens of predefined static Color objects that each can be accessed via the class name and a dot (.), as in Color.RED. For a complete list of the predefined colors see class Color's documentation at

```
https://docs.oracle.com/javase/8/javafx/api/javafx/scene/paint/
   Color.html
```

Class Color also provides methods that enable you to create custom Colors, though we do not use them in this example.

Creating the Draw Smiley *App's GUI*

The app's GUI is defined in `DrawSmiley.fxml`. We reused the `DrawLines.fxml` GUI shown in Fig. 4.17, but made the following changes to `DrawSmiley.fxml`:

- We specified `DrawSmileyController` as the app's **Controller class** in the Scene Builder **Document** window's **Controller** section.
- We set the `Button`'s **Text** property to `Draw Smiley` (in the **Inspector**'s **Properties** section) and set the `Button`'s **On Action** event handler to `drawSmileyButtonPressed` (in the **Inspector**'s **Code** section).

Class `DrawSmileyController`

Again, we do not show the code for `DrawSmiley.java`, because the only changes from earlier examples are the name of the FXML file to load (`DrawSmiley.fxml`) and the text displayed in the stage's title bar (`Draw Smiley`). Class `DrawSmileyController` (Fig. 6.11) performs the drawing. `GraphicsContext` methods **`fillRect`** and **`fillOval`** draw filled rectangles and ovals, respectively. These have the same parameters as `strokeRect` and `strokeOval` (Section 5.11); the first two are the coordinates for the shape's *upper-left corner*, while the next two determine the *width* and *height*—recall that for an oval these specify the bounding rectangle in which the oval is displayed.

```
// Fig. 6.11: DrawSmileyController.java
// Drawing a smiley face using colors and filled shapes.
import javafx.event.ActionEvent;
import javafx.fxml.FXML;
import javafx.scene.canvas.Canvas;
import javafx.scene.canvas.GraphicsContext;
import javafx.scene.paint.Color;

public class DrawSmileyController {
   @FXML private Canvas canvas;

   // draws a smiley face
   @FXML
   void drawSmileyButtonPressed(ActionEvent event) {
      // get the GraphicsContext, which is used to draw on the Canvas
      GraphicsContext gc = canvas.getGraphicsContext2D();

      // draw the face
      gc.setFill(Color.YELLOW);
      gc.fillOval(10, 10, 280, 280);
      gc.strokeOval(10, 10, 280, 280);

      // draw the eyes
      gc.setFill(Color.BLACK);
      gc.fillOval(75, 85, 40, 40);
      gc.fillOval(185, 85, 40, 40);

      // draw the mouth
      gc.fillOval(50, 130, 200, 120);

```

Fig. 6.11 | Drawing a smiley face using colors and filled shapes. (Part 1 of 2.)

```
31         // "touch up" the mouth into a smile
32         gc.setFill(Color.YELLOW);
33         gc.fillRect(50, 130, 200, 60);
34         gc.fillOval(50, 140, 200, 90);
35     }
36 }
```

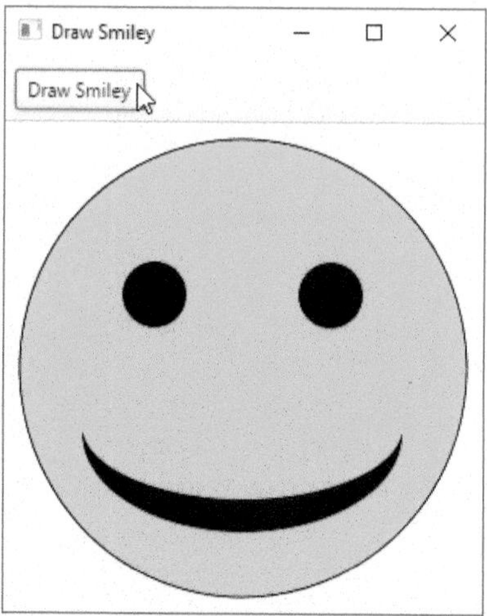

Fig. 6.11 | Drawing a smiley face using colors and filled shapes. (Part 2 of 2.)

Method `drawSmileyButtonPressed` draws the smiley face when the user presses the **Draw Smiley** `Button`. Line 19 uses `GraphicsContext` method **`setFill`** to set the current fill color to the predefined `Color.YELLOW`—all filled shapes will use this fill until you change it with a subsequent call to `setFill`.

Line 20 draws a filled circle with diameter 280 to represent the face—when the width and height arguments are identical, method `fillOval` draws a circle. Line 21 uses `strokeOval` with the same arguments as `fillOval` to outline the face with a black line for better contrast with the window's background. Note that the `GraphicsContext` separately maintains the fill color and stroke color—as you've seen, the default stroke color is black. You can change the stroke color with `GraphicsContext` method **`setStroke`**. Next, line 24 sets the fill color to `Color.BLACK`, and lines 25–26 draw two filled circles for the eyes.

Line 29 draws the mouth as an oval, but this is not quite what we want. To create a happy face, we'll touch up the mouth. Line 32 sets the fill color to `Color.YELLOW`, so any shapes we draw will blend in with the face. Line 33 draws a rectangle that's half the mouth's height. This erases the top half of the mouth, leaving just the bottom half. To create a better smile, line 34 draws another oval to slightly cover the upper portion of the mouth.

GUI and Graphics Case Study Exercises

6.1 Using method `fillOval`, draw a bull's-eye that alternates between two random colors, as in Fig. 6.12. To generate a random color, use the following method call in which `red`, `green` and `blue` are random values in the range 0–255

```
Color.rgb(red, green, blue)
```

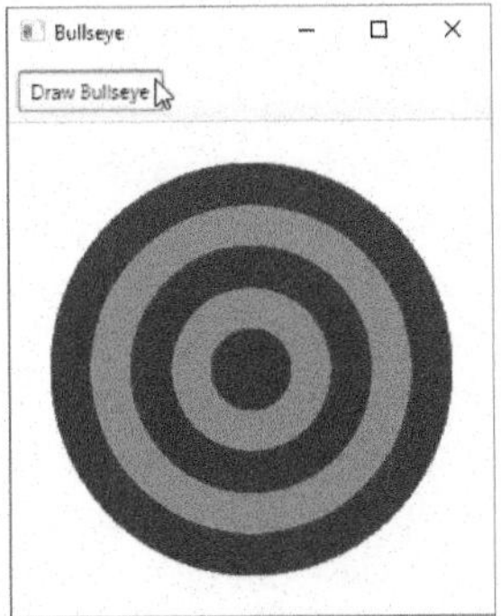

Fig. 6.12 | A bulls-eye with two alternating, random colors.

6.2 Create a program that draws 10 random filled shapes in random colors, positions and sizes (Fig. 6.13). The event handler for the **Draw Shapes** `Button` should contain a loop that iterates 10 times. In each iteration, the loop should use a random number to determine whether to draw a filled rectangle or an oval, create a random color and choose the shape's coordinates and dimensions at random. The coordinates should be chosen based on the `Canvas`'s width and height. Lengths of sides should be limited to half the width or height of the window.

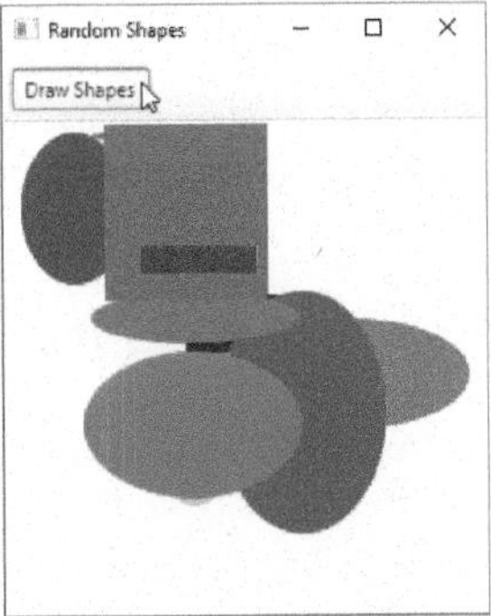

Fig. 6.13 | Randomly generated shapes.

6.3 Enhance Exercise 6.2 to randomly choose bordered or filled shapes.

6.4 Enhance the **Draw Smiley** app by using white rectangles to draw teeth and a pink oval to make a tongue. Use the `Color` objects `Color.WHITE` and `Color.PINK`.

6.5 Enhance the **Draw Smiley** app by drawing the eyes as white circles containing pupils drawn as brown circles (`Color.BROWN`).

6.6 Enhance the **Draw Smiley** app to make the eyes blink each time the user clicks a `Button`.

6.14 Wrap-Up

In this chapter, you learned more about method declarations. You also learned the difference between instance methods and `static` methods and how to call `static` methods by preceding the method name with the name of the class in which it appears and the dot (.) separator. You learned how to use operators + and += to perform string concatenations. We discussed how the method-call stack and stack frames keep track of the methods that have been called and where each method must return to when it completes its task. We also discussed Java's promotion rules for converting implicitly between primitive types and ways to perform explicit conversions with cast operators. Next, you learned about some of the commonly used packages in the Java API.

You saw how to declare named constants using both `enum` types and `private static final` variables. You used class `SecureRandom` to generate random numbers for simulations. You also learned about the scope of fields and local variables in a class. Finally, you learned that multiple methods in one class can be overloaded by providing methods with the same name and different signatures. Such methods can be used to perform the same or similar tasks using different types or different numbers of parameters.

In Chapter 7, you'll learn how to maintain lists and tables of data in arrays. You'll see a more elegant implementation of the application that rolls a die 60,000,000 times. We'll present two versions of a `GradeBook` case study that stores sets of student grades in a `GradeBook` object. You'll also learn how to access an application's command-line arguments that are passed to method `main` when an application begins execution.

Summary

Section 6.1 Introduction

- Experience has shown that the best way to develop and maintain a large program is to construct it from small, simple pieces. This technique is called divide and conquer (p. 213).

Section 6.2 Program Units in Java

- Methods are declared within classes. Classes are typically grouped into packages so they can be imported and reused.
- Methods allow you to modularize a program by separating its tasks into self-contained units. The statements in a method are written only once and hidden from other methods.
- Using existing methods as building blocks to create new programs is a form of software reusability (p. 214) that allows you to avoid repeating code within a program.

Section 6.3 `static` Methods, `static` Fields and Class `Math`

- A method call specifies the name of the method to call and provides the arguments that the called method requires to perform its task. When the method call completes, the method returns either a result, or simply control, to its caller.
- A class may contain `static` methods to perform common tasks that do not require an object of the class. Any data a `static` method might require to perform its tasks can be sent to the method as arguments in a method call. A `static` method is called by specifying the name of the class in which the method is declared followed by a dot (.) and the method name, as in

  ClassName.*methodName*(*arguments*)

- Class `Math` provides `static` methods for performing common mathematical calculations.
- The constant `Math.PI` (3.141592653589793; p. 217) is the ratio of a circle's circumference to its diameter. The constant `Math.E` (2.718281828459045; p. 217) is the base value for natural logarithms (calculated with `static Math` method `log`).

- `Math.PI` and `Math.E` are declared with the modifiers `public`, `final` and `static`. Making them `public` allows you to use these fields in your own classes. A field declared with keyword `final` (p. 217) is constant—its value cannot be changed after it's initialized. Both `PI` and `E` are declared `final` because their values never change. Making these fields `static` allows them to be accessed via the class name `Math` and a dot (`.`) separator, just like class `Math`'s methods.
- All the objects of a class share one copy of the class's `static` fields. Together the class variables (p. 217) and instance variables represent the fields of a class.
- When you execute the Java Virtual Machine (JVM) with the `java` command, the JVM loads the class you specify and uses that class name to invoke method `main`. You can specify additional command-line arguments (p. 217) that the JVM will pass to your application.
- You can place a `main` method in every class you declare—only the `main` method in the class you use to execute the application will be called by the `java` command.

Section 6.4 Methods with Multiple Parameters

- When a method is called, the program makes a copy of the method's argument values and assigns them to the method's corresponding parameters. When program control returns to the point in the program where the method was called, the method's parameters are removed from memory.
- A method can return at most one value, but the returned value could be a reference to an object that contains many values.
- Variables should be declared as fields of a class only if they're required for use in more than one method of the class or if the program should save their values between calls to the class's methods.
- A method specifies parameters in a comma-separated list. There must be one argument for each parameter. Also, each argument must be consistent with the type of the corresponding parameter. If a method does not accept arguments, the parameter list is empty.
- `String`s can be concatenated (p. 220) using operator `+`, which creates a new `String` containfing the characters of the left operand followed by those of the right operand.
- Every primitive value and object in Java can be represented as a `String`. When an object is concatenated with a `String`, the object is converted to a `String`, then the two `String`s are concatenated.
- If a `boolean` is concatenated with a `String`, the word `"true"` or the word `"false"` is used to represent the `boolean` value.
- All objects in Java have a special method named `toString` that returns a `String` representation of the object's contents. When an object is concatenated with a `String`, the JVM implicitly calls the object's `toString` method to obtain the string representation of the object.
- You can break large `String` literals into several smaller `String`s and place them on multiple lines of code for readability, then reassemble the `String`s using concatenation.

Section 6.5 Notes on Declaring and Using Methods

- You've seen three ways to call a method—using a method name by itself to call another method of the same class; using a variable that contains a reference to an object, followed by a dot (`.`) and the method name to call a non-`static` method of the referenced object; and using the class name and a dot (`.`) to call a `static` method of a class.
- A `static` method can call directly only other `static` methods of the same class and can manipulate directly only `static` variables in the same class.
- There are three ways to return control to the statement that calls a method—when the method-ending right brace is reached in a method with return type `void`, when the following statement executes in a method with return type `void`:

```
return;
```

and when a method returns a result with a statement of the following form in which the *expression* is evaluated and its result (and control) are returned to the caller:

```
return expression;
```

Section 6.6 Method-Call Stack and Activation Records

- Stacks are known as last-in, first-out (LIFO) data structures—the last item pushed (inserted) onto the stack is the first item popped (removed) from the stack.
- A called method must know how to return to its caller, so the return address of the calling method is pushed onto the method-call stack when the method is called. If a series of method calls occurs, the successive return addresses are pushed onto the stack in last-in, first-out order so that the last method to execute will be the first to return to its caller.
- The method-call stack contains the memory for the local variables used in each invocation of a method during a program's execution. This data is known as the method call's stack frame or activation record. When a method call is made, the stack frame for that method call is pushed onto the method-call stack. When the method returns to its caller, its stack frame is popped off the stack and the local variables are no longer known to the program.
- If there are more method calls than can have their stack frames stored on the method-call stack, an error known as a stack overflow occurs. The application will compile correctly, but its execution causes a stack overflow.

Section 6.7 Argument Promotion and Casting

- Argument promotion (p. 223) converts an argument's value to the type that the method expects to receive in its corresponding parameter.
- Promotion rules (p. 223) apply to expressions containing values of two or more primitive types and to primitive-type values passed as arguments to methods. Each value is promoted to the "highest" type in the expression. In cases where information may be lost due to conversion, the Java compiler requires you to use a cast operator to explicitly force the conversion to occur.

Section 6.9 Case Study: Secure Random-Number Generation

- Objects of class `SecureRandom` (package `java.security`; p. 226) can produce nondeterministic random values.
- `SecureRandom` method `nextInt` (p. 227) generates a random `int` value.
- Class `SecureRandom` provides another version of method `nextInt` that receives an `int` argument and returns a value from 0 up to, but not including, the argument's value.
- Random numbers in a range (p. 227) can be generated with

```
int number = shift + randomNumbers.nextInt(scale);
```

where *shift* specifies the first number in the desired range of consecutive integers, and *scale* specifies how many numbers are in the range.

- Random numbers can be chosen from nonconsecutive integer ranges, as in

```
int number = shift + difference * randomNumbers.nextInt(scale);
```

where *shift* specifies the first number in the sequence, *difference* represents the difference between consecutive numbers in the sequence and *scale* specifies how many numbers are in the sequence.

Section 6.10 Case Study: A Game of Chance; Introducing **`enum`** *Types*

- An `enum` type (p. 234) is introduced by the keyword `enum` and a type name. As with any class, braces (`{` and `}`) delimit the body of an `enum` declaration. Inside the braces is a comma-separated list of `enum` constants, each representing a unique value. The identifiers in an `enum` must be unique. Variables of an `enum` type can be assigned only constants of that `enum` type.

- Constants can also be declared as `private static final` variables. Such constants are declared by convention with all capital letters to make them stand out in the program.

Section 6.11 Scope of Declarations

- Scope (p. 236) is the portion of the program in which an entity, such as a variable or a method, can be referred to by its name. Such an entity is said to be "in scope" for that portion of the program.
- The scope of a parameter declaration is the body of the method in which the declaration appears.
- The scope of a local-variable declaration is from the point at which the declaration appears to the end of that block.
- The scope of a local-variable declaration that appears in the initialization section of a `for` statement's header is the body of the `for` statement and the other expressions in the header.
- The scope of a method or field of a class is the entire body of the class. This enables a class's methods to use simple names to call the class's other methods and to access the class's fields.
- Any block may contain variable declarations. If a local variable or parameter in a method has the same name as a field, the field is shadowed (p. 236) until the block terminates execution.

Section 6.12 Method Overloading

- Java allows overloaded methods (p. 238) in a class, as long as the methods have different sets of parameters (determined by the number, order and types of the parameters).
- Overloaded methods are distinguished by their signatures (p. 239)—combinations of the methods' names and the number, types and order of their parameters, but not their return types.

Self-Review Exercises

6.1 Fill in the blanks in each of the following statements:

a) A method is invoked with a(n) ________.

b) A variable known only within the method in which it's declared is called a(n) ________.

c) The ________ statement in a called method can be used to pass the value of an expression back to the calling method.

d) The keyword ________ indicates that a method does not return a value.

e) Data can be added or removed only from the ________ of a stack.

f) Stacks are known as ________ data structures; the last item pushed (inserted) onto the stack is the first item popped (removed) from the stack.

g) The three ways to return control from a called method to a caller are ________, ________ and ________.

h) An object of class ________ produces truly random numbers.

i) The method-call stack contains the memory for local variables on each invocation of a method during a program's execution. This data, stored as a portion of the method-call stack, is known as the ________ or ________ of the method call.

j) If there are more method calls than can be stored on the method-call stack, an error known as a(n) ________ occurs.

k) The ________ of a declaration is the portion of a program that can refer to the entity in the declaration by name.

l) It's possible to have several methods with the same name, each operating on different types or numbers of arguments. This feature is called method ________.

6.2 For the class `Craps` in Fig. 6.8, state the scope of each of the following entities:

a) the variable `randomNumbers`.

b) the variable `die1`.
c) the method `rollDice`.
d) the method `main`.
e) the variable `sumOfDice`.

6.3 Write an application that tests whether the examples of the `Math` class method calls shown in Fig. 6.2 actually produce the indicated results.

6.4 Give the method header for each of the following methods:

a) Method `hypotenuse`, which takes two double-precision, floating-point arguments `side1` and `side2` and returns a double-precision, floating-point result.
b) Method `smallest`, which takes three integers `x`, `y` and `z` and returns an integer.
c) Method `instructions`, which does not take any arguments and does not return a value. [*Note:* Such methods are commonly used to display instructions to a user.]
d) Method `intToFloat`, which takes integer argument `number` and returns a `float`.

6.5 Find the error in each of the following program segments. Explain how to correct the error.

a)

```
void g() {
   System.out.println("Inside method g");

   void h() {
      System.out.println("Inside method h");
   }
}
```

b)

```
int sum(int x, int y) {
   int result;
   result = x + y;
}
```

c)

```
void f(float a); {
   float a;
   System.out.println(a);
}
```

d)

```
void product() {
   int a = 6;
   int b = 5;
   int c = 4;
   int result = a * b * c;
   System.out.printf("Result is %d%n", result);
   return result;
}
```

6.6 Declare method `sphereVolume` to calculate and return the volume of the sphere. Use the following statement to calculate the volume:

```
double volume = (4.0 / 3.0) * Math.PI * Math.pow(radius, 3)
```

Write a Java application that prompts the user for the `double` radius of a sphere, calls `sphereVolume` to calculate the volume and displays the result.

Answers to Self-Review Exercises

6.1 a) method call. b) local variable. c) `return`. d) `void`. e) top. f) last-in, first-out (LIFO). g) `return;` or `return` *expression*; or encountering the closing right brace of a method. h) `SecureRandom`. i) stack frame, activation record. j) stack overflow. k) scope. l) overloading.

6.2 a) class body. b) block that defines method `rollDice`'s body. c) class body. d) class body. e) block that defines method `main`'s body.

6.3 The following solution demonstrates the `Math` class methods in Fig. 6.2:

```
// Exercise 6.3: MathTest.java
// Testing the Math class methods.
public class MathTest {
   public static void main(String[] args) {
      System.out.printf("Math.abs(23.7) = %f%n", Math.abs(23.7));
      System.out.printf("Math.abs(0.0) = %f%n", Math.abs(0.0));
      System.out.printf("Math.abs(-23.7) = %f%n", Math.abs(-23.7));
      System.out.printf("Math.ceil(9.2) = %f%n", Math.ceil(9.2));
      System.out.printf("Math.ceil(-9.8) = %f%n", Math.ceil(-9.8));
      System.out.printf("Math.cos(0.0) = %f%n", Math.cos(0.0));
      System.out.printf("Math.exp(1.0) = %f%n", Math.exp(1.0));
      System.out.printf("Math.exp(2.0) = %f%n", Math.exp(2.0));
      System.out.printf("Math.floor(9.2) = %f%n", Math.floor(9.2));
      System.out.printf("Math.floor(-9.8) = %f%n", Math.floor(-9.8));
      System.out.printf("Math.log(Math.E) = %f%n", Math.log(Math.E));
      System.out.printf("Math.log(Math.E * Math.E) = %f%n",
         Math.log(Math.E * Math.E));
      System.out.printf("Math.max(2.3, 12.7) = %f%n", Math.max(2.3, 12.7));
      System.out.printf("Math.max(-2.3, -12.7) = %f%n", Math.max(-2.3, -12.7));
      System.out.printf("Math.min(2.3, 12.7) = %f%n", Math.min(2.3, 12.7));
      System.out.printf("Math.min(-2.3, -12.7) = %f%n", Math.min(-2.3, -12.7));
      System.out.printf("Math.pow(2.0, 7.0) = %f%n", Math.pow(2.0, 7.0));
      System.out.printf("Math.pow(9.0, 0.5) = %f%n", Math.pow(9.0, 0.5));
      System.out.printf("Math.sin(0.0) = %f%n", Math.sin(0.0));
      System.out.printf("Math.sqrt(900.0) = %f%n", Math.sqrt(900.0));
      System.out.printf("Math.tan(0.0) = %f%n", Math.tan(0.0));
   }
}
```

```
Math.abs(23.7) = 23.700000
Math.abs(0.0) = 0.000000
Math.abs(-23.7) = 23.700000
Math.ceil(9.2) = 10.000000
Math.ceil(-9.8) = -9.000000
Math.cos(0.0) = 1.000000
Math.exp(1.0) = 2.718282
Math.exp(2.0) = 7.389056
Math.floor(9.2) = 9.000000
Math.floor(-9.8) = -10.000000
Math.log(Math.E) = 1.000000
Math.log(Math.E * Math.E) = 2.000000
Math.max(2.3, 12.7) = 12.700000
Math.max(-2.3, -12.7) = -2.300000
Math.min(2.3, 12.7) = 2.300000
Math.min(-2.3, -12.7) = -12.700000
Math.pow(2.0, 7.0) = 128.000000
Math.pow(9.0, 0.5) = 3.000000
```

```
Math.sin(0.0) = 0.000000
Math.sqrt(900.0) = 30.000000
Math.tan(0.0) = 0.000000
```

6.4 Answers:

a) `double hypotenuse(double side1, double side2)`
b) `int smallest(int x, int y, int z)`
c) `void instructions()`
d) `float intToFloat(int number)`

6.5 Answers:

a) Error: Method `h` is declared within method `g`.
Correction: Move the declaration of `h` outside the declaration of `g`.
b) Error: The method is supposed to return an integer, but does not.
Correction: Delete the variable `result`, and place the statement
`return x + y;`
in the method, or add the following statement at the end of the method body:
`return result;`
c) Error: The semicolon after the right parenthesis of the parameter list is incorrect, and the parameter a should not be redeclared in the method.
Correction: Delete the semicolon after the right parenthesis of the parameter list, and delete the declaration `float a;`.
d) Error: The method returns a value when it's not supposed to.
Correction: Change the return type from `void` to `int`.

6.6 The following solution calculates the volume of a sphere, using the radius entered by the user:

```java
// Exercise 6.6: Sphere.java
// Calculate the volume of a sphere.
import java.util.Scanner;

public class Sphere {
   // obtain radius from user and display volume of sphere
   public static void main(String[] args) {
      Scanner input = new Scanner(System.in);

      System.out.print("Enter radius of sphere: ");
      double radius = input.nextDouble();

      System.out.printf("Volume is %f%n", sphereVolume(radius));
   }

   // calculate and return sphere volume
   public static double sphereVolume(double radius) {
      double volume = (4.0 / 3.0) * Math.PI * Math.pow(radius, 3);
      return volume;
   }
}
```

```
Enter radius of sphere: 4
Volume is 268.082573
```

Exercises

6.7 What is the value of x after each of the following statements is executed?

a) `double x = Math.abs(7.5);`

b) `double x = Math.floor(7.5);`
c) `double x = Math.abs(0.0);`
d) `double x = Math.ceil(0.0);`
e) `double x = Math.abs(-6.4);`
f) `double x = Math.ceil(-6.4);`
g) `double x = Math.ceil(-Math.abs(-8 + Math.floor(-5.5)));`

6.8 *(Parking Charges)* A parking garage charges a $2.00 minimum fee to park for up to three hours. The garage charges an additional $0.50 per hour for each hour *or part thereof* in excess of three hours. The maximum charge for any given 24-hour period is $10.00. Assume that no car parks for longer than 24 hours at a time. Write an application that calculates and displays the parking charges for each customer who parked in the garage yesterday. You should enter the hours parked for each customer. The program should display the charge for the current customer and should calculate and display the running total of yesterday's receipts. It should use the method `calculateCharges` to determine the charge for each customer.

6.9 *(Rounding Numbers)* `Math.floor` can be used to round values to the nearest integer—e.g.,

```
double y = Math.floor(x + 0.5);
```

will round the number `x` to the nearest integer and assign the result to `y`. Write an application that reads `double` values and uses the preceding statement to round each of the numbers to the nearest integer. For each number processed, display both the original number and the rounded number.

6.10 *(Rounding Numbers)* To round numbers to specific decimal places, use a statement like

```
double y = Math.floor(x * 10 + 0.5) / 10;
```

which rounds `x` to the tenths position (i.e., the first position to the right of the decimal point), or

```
double y = Math.floor(x * 100 + 0.5) / 100;
```

which rounds `x` to the hundredths position (i.e., the second position to the right of the decimal point). Write an application that defines four methods for rounding a number `x` in various ways:

a) `roundToInteger(number)`
b) `roundToTenths(number)`
c) `roundToHundredths(number)`
d) `roundToThousandths(number)`

For each value read, your program should display the original value, the number rounded to the nearest integer, the number rounded to the nearest tenth, the number rounded to the nearest hundredth and the number rounded to the nearest thousandth.

6.11 Answer each of the following questions:

a) What does it mean to choose numbers "at random"?
b) Why is the `nextInt` method of class `SecureRandom` useful for simulating games of chance?
c) Why is it often necessary to scale or shift the values produced by a `SecureRandom` object?
d) Why is computerized simulation of real-world situations a useful technique?

6.12 Write statements that assign random integers to the variable n in the following ranges:

a) $1 \leq n \leq 2$.
b) $1 \leq n \leq 100$.
c) $0 \leq n \leq 9$.
d) $1000 \leq n \leq 1112$.
e) $-1 \leq n \leq 1$.
f) $-3 \leq n \leq 11$.

6.13 Write statements that will display a random number from each of the following sets:

a) 2, 4, 6, 8, 10.

b) 3, 5, 7, 9, 11.
c) 6, 10, 14, 18, 22.

6.14 *(Exponentiation)* Write a method `integerPower(base, exponent)` that returns the value of

$base^{exponent}$

For example, `integerPower(3, 4)` calculates 3^4 (or `3 * 3 * 3 * 3`). Assume that `exponent` is a positive, nonzero integer and that `base` is an integer. Use a `for` or `while` statement to control the calculation. Do not use any `Math` class methods. Incorporate this method into an application that reads integer values for `base` and `exponent` and performs the calculation with the `integerPower` method.

6.15 *(Hypotenuse Calculations)* Define a method `hypotenuse` that calculates the hypotenuse of a right triangle when the lengths of the other two sides are given. The method should take two arguments of type `double` and return the hypotenuse as a `double`. Incorporate this method into an application that reads values for `side1` and `side2` and performs the calculation with the `hypotenuse` method. Use `Math` methods `pow` and `sqrt` to determine the length of the hypotenuse for each of the triangles in Fig. 6.14. [*Note:* Class `Math` also provides method `hypot` to perform this calculation.]

Triangle	Side 1	Side 2
1	3.0	4.0
2	5.0	12.0
3	8.0	15.0

Fig. 6.14 | Values for the sides of triangles in Exercise 6.15.

6.16 *(Multiples)* Write a method `isMultiple` that determines, for a pair of integers, whether the second integer is a multiple of the first. The method should take two integer arguments and return `true` if the second is a multiple of the first and `false` otherwise. [*Hint:* Use the remainder operator.] Incorporate this method into an application that inputs a series of pairs of integers (one pair at a time) and determines whether the second value in each pair is a multiple of the first.

6.17 *(Even or Odd)* Write a method `isEven` that uses the remainder operator (%) to determine whether an integer is even. The method should take an integer argument and return `true` if the integer is even and `false` otherwise. Incorporate this method into an application that inputs a sequence of integers (one at a time) and determines whether each is even or odd.

6.18 *(Displaying a Square of Asterisks)* Write a method `squareOfAsterisks` that displays a solid square (the same number of rows and columns) of asterisks whose side is specified in integer parameter `side`. For example, if `side` is 4, the method should display

```
****
****
****
****
```

Incorporate this method into an application that reads an integer value for `side` from the user and outputs the asterisks with the `squareOfAsterisks` method.

6.19 *(Displaying a Square of Any Character)* Modify the method created in Exercise 6.18 to receive a second parameter of type `char` called `fillCharacter`. Form the square using the `char` provided as an argument. Thus, if `side` is 5 and `fillCharacter` is #, the method should display

```
#####
#####
#####
#####
#####
```

Use the following statement (in which `input` is a `Scanner` object) to read a character from the user at the keyboard:

```
// next() returns a String and charAt(0) gets the String's first character
char fill = input.next().charAt(0);
```

6.20 *(Circle Area)* Write an application that prompts the user for the radius of a circle and uses a method called `circleArea` to calculate the area of the circle.

6.21 *(Separating Digits)* Write methods that accomplish each of the following tasks:

a) Calculate the integer part of the quotient when integer `a` is divided by integer `b`.
b) Calculate the integer remainder when integer `a` is divided by integer `b`.
c) Use the methods developed in parts (a) and (b) to write a method `displayDigits` that receives an integer between `1` and `99999` and displays it as a sequence of digits, separating each pair of digits by two spaces. For example, the integer `4562` should appear as

```
4  5  6  2
```

Incorporate the methods into an application that inputs an integer and calls `displayDigits` by passing the method the integer entered. Display the results.

6.22 *(Temperature Conversions)* Implement the following integer methods:

a) Method `celsius` returns the Celsius equivalent of a Fahrenheit temperature, using the calculation

```
celsius = 5.0 / 9.0 * (fahrenheit - 32);
```

b) Method `fahrenheit` returns the Fahrenheit equivalent of a Celsius temperature, using the calculation

```
fahrenheit = 9.0 / 5.0 * celsius + 32;
```

c) Use the methods from parts (a) and (b) to write an application that enables the user either to enter a Fahrenheit temperature and display the Celsius equivalent or to enter a Celsius temperature and display the Fahrenheit equivalent.

6.23 *(Find the Minimum)* Write a method `minimum3` that returns the smallest of three floating-point numbers. Use the `Math.min` method to implement `minimum3`. Incorporate the method into an application that reads three values from the user, determines the smallest value and displays the result.

6.24 *(Perfect Numbers)* An integer number is said to be a *perfect number* if its factors, including 1 (but not the number itself), sum to the number. For example, 6 is a perfect number, because 6 = 1 + 2 + 3. Write a method `isPerfect` that determines whether parameter `number` is a perfect number. Use this method in an application that displays all the perfect numbers between 1 and 1000. Display the factors of each perfect number to confirm that the number is indeed perfect. Challenge the computing power of your computer by testing numbers much larger than 1000. Display the results.

6.25 *(Prime Numbers)* A positive integer is *prime* if it's divisible by only 1 and itself. For example, 2, 3, 5 and 7 are prime, but 4, 6, 8 and 9 are not. The number 1, by definition, is not prime.

a) Write a method that determines whether a number is prime.

b) Use this method in an application that determines and displays all the prime numbers less than 10,000. How many numbers up to 10,000 do you have to test to ensure that you've found all the primes?

c) Initially, you might think that $n/2$ is the upper limit for which you must test to see whether a number n is prime, but you need only go as high as the square root of n. Rewrite the program, and run it both ways.

6.26 *(Reversing Digits)* Write a method that takes an integer value and returns the number with its digits reversed. For example, given the number 7631, the method should return 1367. Incorporate the method into an application that reads a value from the user and displays the result.

6.27 *(Greatest Common Divisor)* The *greatest common divisor* (*GCD*) of two integers is the largest integer that evenly divides each of the two numbers. Write a method `gcd` that returns the greatest common divisor of two integers. [*Hint:* You might want to use Euclid's algorithm. You can find information about it at `en.wikipedia.org/wiki/Euclidean_algorithm`.] Incorporate the method into an application that reads two values from the user and displays the result.

6.28 Write a method `qualityPoints` that inputs a student's average and returns `4` if it's 90–100, `3` if 80–89, `2` if 70–79, `1` if 60–69 and `0` if lower than 60. Incorporate the method into an application that reads a value from the user and displays the result.

6.29 *(Coin Tossing)* Write an application that simulates coin tossing. Let the program toss a coin each time the user chooses the "`Toss Coin`" menu option. Count the number of times each side of the coin appears. Display the results. The program should call a separate method `flip` that takes no arguments and returns a value from a `Coin` `enum` (`HEADS` and `TAILS`). [*Note:* If the program realistically simulates coin tossing, each side of the coin should appear approximately half the time.]

6.30 *(Guess the Number)* Write an application that plays "guess the number" as follows: Your program chooses the number to be guessed by selecting a random integer in the range 1 to 1000. The application displays the prompt `Guess a number between 1 and 1000`. The player inputs a first guess. If the player's guess is incorrect, your program should display `Too high. Try again.` or `Too low. Try again.` to help the player "zero in" on the correct answer. The program should prompt the user for the next guess. When the user enters the correct answer, display `Congratulations. You guessed the number!`, and allow the user to choose whether to play again. [*Note:* The guessing technique employed in this problem is similar to a binary search, which is discussed in Chapter 19, Searching, Sorting and Big O.]

6.31 *(Guess-the-Number Modification)* Modify the program of Exercise 6.30 to count the number of guesses the player makes. If the number is 10 or fewer, display `Either you know the secret or you got lucky!` If the player guesses the number in 10 tries, display `Aha! You know the secret!` If the player makes more than 10 guesses, display `You should be able to do better!` Why should it take no more than 10 guesses? Well, with each "good guess," the player should be able to eliminate half of the numbers, then half of the remaining numbers, and so on.

6.32 *(Distance Between Points)* Write method `distance` to calculate the distance between two points ($x1$, $y1$) and ($x2$, $y2$). All numbers and return values should be of type `double`. Incorporate this method into an application that enables the user to enter the coordinates of the points.

6.33 *(Craps Game Modification)* Modify the craps program of Fig. 6.8 to allow wagering. Initialize variable `bankBalance` to 1000 dollars. Prompt the player to enter a `wager`. Check that `wager` is less than or equal to `bankBalance`, and if it's not, have the user reenter `wager` until a valid `wager` is entered. Then, run one game of craps. If the player wins, increase `bankBalance` by `wager` and display the new `bankBalance`. If the player loses, decrease `bankBalance` by `wager`, display the new `bankBalance`, check whether `bankBalance` has become zero and, if so, display the message `"Sorry. You busted!"` As the game progresses, display various messages to create some "chatter," such as `"Oh, you're going for broke, huh?"` or `"Aw c'mon, take a chance!"` or `"You're up big. Now's the time` `to cash in your chips!"`. Implement the "chatter" as a separate method that randomly chooses the string to display.

6.34 *(Table of Binary, Octal and Hexadecimal Numbers)* Write an application that displays a table of the binary, octal and hexadecimal equivalents of the decimal numbers in the range 1 through 256. If you aren't familiar with these number systems, read online Appendix J first.

Making a Difference

As computer costs decline, it becomes feasible for every student, regardless of economic circumstance, to have a computer and use it in school. This creates exciting possibilities for improving the educational experience of all students worldwide, as suggested by the following exercises. [*Note:* Check out initiatives such as the One Laptop Per Child Project (`http://www.laptop.org`). Also, research "green" laptops—what are some key "going green" characteristics of these devices? Look into the Electronic Product Environmental Assessment Tool (`http://www.epeat.net`), which can help you assess the "greenness" of desktops, notebooks and monitors to help you decide which products to purchase.]

6.35 *(Computer-Assisted Instruction)* The use of computers in education is referred to as *computer-assisted instruction (CAI)*. Write a program that will help an elementary school student learn multiplication. Use a `SecureRandom` object to produce two positive one-digit integers. The program should then prompt the user with a question, such as

```
How much is 6 times 7?
```

The student then inputs the answer. Next, the program checks the student's answer. If it's correct, display the message `"Very good!"` and ask another multiplication question. If the answer is wrong, display the message `"No. Please try again."` and let the student try the same question repeatedly until the student finally gets it right. A separate method should be used to generate each new question. This method should be called once when the application begins execution and each time the user answers the question correctly.

6.36 *(Computer-Assisted Instruction: Reducing Student Fatigue)* One problem in CAI environments is student fatigue. This can be reduced by varying the computer's responses to hold the student's attention. Modify the program of Exercise 6.35 so that various comments are displayed for each answer as follows:

Possible responses to a correct answer:

```
Very good!
Excellent!
Nice work!
Keep up the good work!
```

Possible responses to an incorrect answer:

```
No. Please try again.
Wrong. Try once more.
Don't give up!
No. Keep trying.
```

Use random-number generation to choose a number from 1 to 4 that will be used to select one of the four appropriate responses to each correct or incorrect answer. Use a `switch` statement to issue the responses.

6.37 *(Computer-Assisted Instruction: Monitoring Student Performance)* More sophisticated computer-assisted instruction systems monitor the student's performance over a period of time. The decision to begin a new topic is often based on the student's success with previous topics. Modify the program of Exercise 6.36 to count the number of correct and incorrect responses typed by the student. After the student types 10 answers, your program should calculate the percentage that are correct. If the percentage is lower than 75%, display `"Please ask your teacher for extra help."`, then reset the program so another student can try it. If the percentage is 75% or higher, display `"Congratulations, you are ready to go to the next level!"`, then reset the program so another student can try it.

6.38 *(Computer-Assisted Instruction: Difficulty Levels)* Exercises 6.35–6.37 developed a computer-assisted instruction program to help teach an elementary school student multiplication. Modify the program to allow the user to enter a difficulty level. At a difficulty level of 1, the program should use only single-digit numbers in the problems; at a difficulty level of 2, numbers as large as two digits, and so on.

6.39 *(Computer-Assisted Instruction: Varying the Types of Problems)* Modify the program of Exercise 6.38 to allow the user to pick a type of arithmetic problem to study. An option of `1` means addition problems only, `2` means subtraction problems only, `3` means multiplication problems only, `4` means division problems only and `5` means a random mixture of all these types.

Arrays and ArrayLists

7

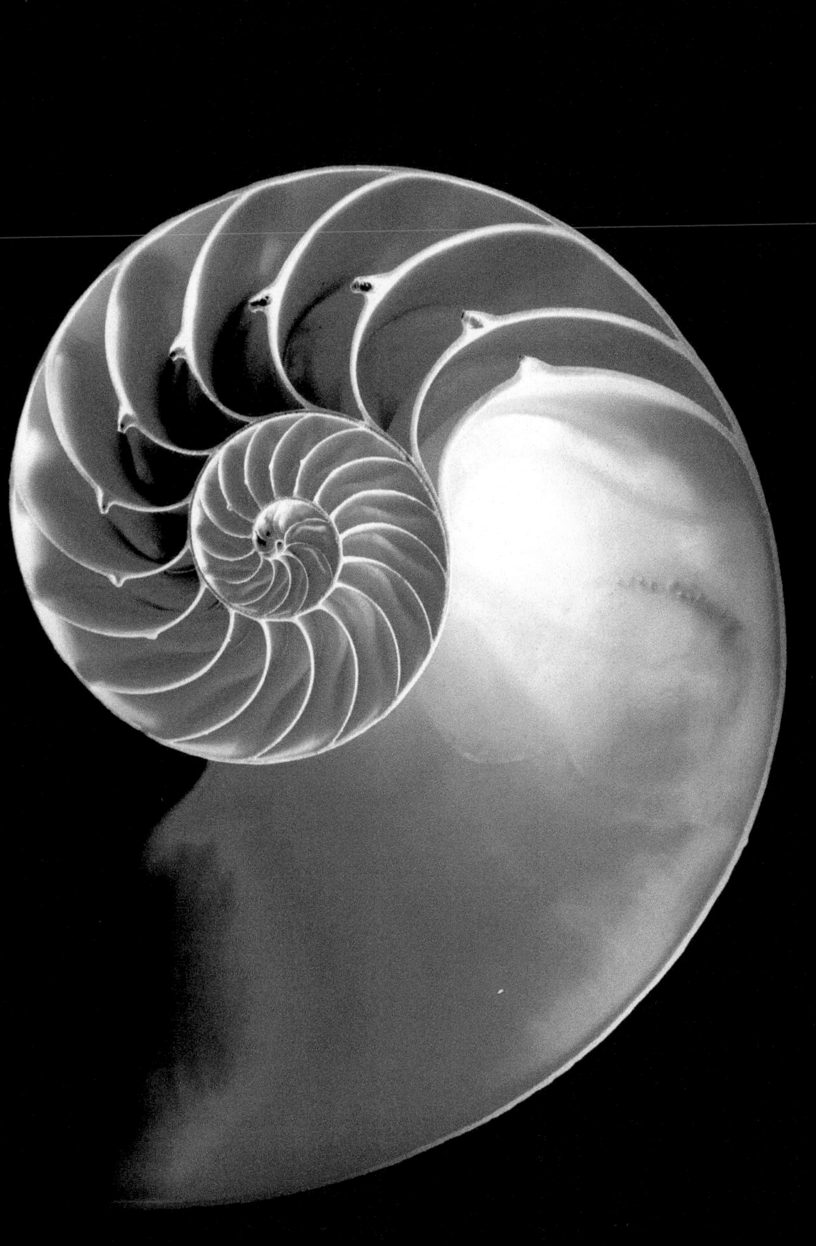

Objectives

In this chapter you'll:

- Learn what arrays are.
- Use arrays to store data in and retrieve data from lists and tables of values.
- Declare arrays, initialize arrays and refer to individual elements of arrays.
- Iterate through arrays with the enhanced `for` statement.
- Pass arrays to methods.
- Declare and manipulate multidimensional arrays.
- Use variable-length argument lists.
- Read command-line arguments into a program.
- Build an object-oriented instructor gradebook class.
- Perform common array manipulations with the methods of class `Arrays`.
- Use class `ArrayList` to manipulate a dynamically resizable array-like data structure.

Outline

7.1 Introduction

This chapter introduces **data structures**—collections of related data items. **Array** objects are data structures consisting of related data items of the same type. Arrays make it convenient to process related groups of values. Arrays remain the same length once they're created. We study data structures in depth in Chapters 16–21.

After discussing how arrays are declared, created and initialized, we present practical examples that demonstrate common array manipulations. We introduce Java's *exception-handling* mechanism and use it to allow a program to continue executing when it attempts to access an array element that does not exist. We also present a case study that examines how arrays can help simulate the shuffling and dealing of playing cards in a card-game application. We introduce Java's *enhanced `for` statement*, which allows a program to access the data in an array more easily than does the counter-controlled `for` statement presented in Section 5.3. We build two versions of an instructor `GradeBook` case study that use arrays to maintain sets of student grades *in memory* and analyze student grades. We show how to use *variable-length argument lists* to create methods that can be called with varying numbers of arguments, and we demonstrate how to process *command-line arguments* in method `main`. Next, we present some common array manipulations with `static` methods of class `Arrays` from the `java.util` package.

Although commonly used, arrays have limited capabilities. For example, you must specify an array's size, and if at execution time you wish to modify it, you must do so by creating a new array. At the end of this chapter, we introduce one of Java's prebuilt data structures from the Java API's *collection classes*. These offer greater capabilities than traditional arrays. They're reusable, reliable, powerful and efficient. We focus on the `ArrayList` collection. `ArrayList`s are similar to arrays but provide additional functionality, such as **dynamic resizing** as necessary to accommodate more or fewer elements.

Java SE 8

After reading Chapter 17, Lambdas and Streams, you'll be able to reimplement many of Chapter 7's examples in a more concise and elegant manner, and in a way that makes them easier to parallelize to improve performance on today's multi-core systems.

Recall from the Preface that Chapter 17 is keyed to many earlier sections of the book so that you can conveniently cover lambdas and streams if you'd like. If so, we recommend that after you complete Chapter 7, you read Sections 17.1–17.7, which introduce the lambdas and streams concepts and use them to rework examples from Chapters 4–7.

7.2 Arrays

An array is a group of variables (called **elements** or **components**) containing values that all have the *same* type. Arrays are *objects*, so they're considered *reference types*. As you'll soon see, what we typically think of as an array is actually a *reference* to an array object in memory. The *elements* of an array can be either *primitive types* or *reference types* (including arrays, as we'll see in Section 7.11). To refer to a particular element in an array, we specify the *name* of the reference to the array and the *position number* of the element in the array. The position number of the element is called the element's **index** or **subscript**.

Logical Array Representation

Figure 7.1 shows a logical representation of an integer array called `c`. This array contains 12 *elements*. A program refers to any one of these elements with an **array-access expression** that includes the *name* of the array followed by the *index* of the particular element in **square brackets** (`[]`). The first element in every array has **index zero** and is sometimes called the **zeroth element**. Thus, the elements of array `c` are `c[0]`, `c[1]`, `c[2]` and so on. The highest index in array `c` is 11, which is 1 less than 12—the number of elements in the array. Array names follow the same conventions as other variable names.

An index must be a *nonnegative integer* that's less than the array's size. A program can use an expression as an index. For example, if we assume that variable `a` is `5` and variable `b` is `6`, then the statement

```
c[a + b] += 2;
```

adds `2` to array element `c[11]`. An indexed array name is an *array-access expression*, which can be used on the left side of an assignment to place a new value into an array element.

Common Programming Error 7.1

An index must be an `int` value or a value of a type that can be promoted to `int`—namely, `byte`, `short` or `char`, but not `long`; otherwise, a compilation error occurs.

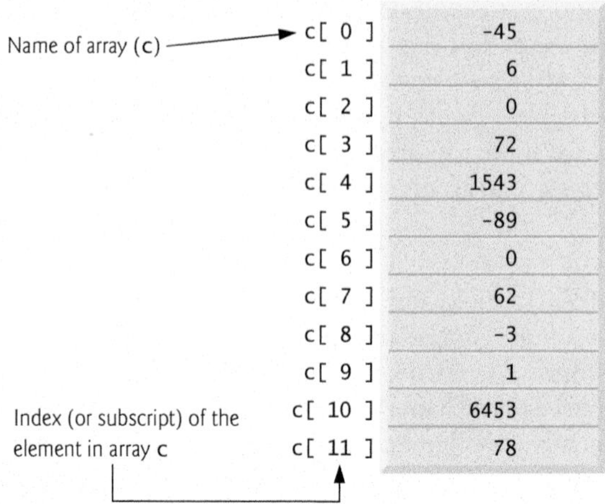

Fig. 7.1 | A 12-element array.

Let's examine array c in Fig. 7.1 more closely. The **name** of the array is c. Every array object knows its own length and stores it in a **length instance variable**. The expression c.length returns array c's length. Even though the length instance variable of an array is public, it cannot be changed because it's a final variable. This array's 12 elements are referred to as c[0], c[1], c[2], ..., c[11]. The value of c[0] is -45, the value of c[1] is 6, the value of c[2] is 0, the value of c[7] is 62 and the value of c[11] is 78. To calculate the sum of the values contained in the first three elements of array c and store the result in variable sum, we would write

```
sum = c[0] + c[1] + c[2];
```

To divide the value of c[6] by 2 and assign the result to the variable x, we would write

```
x = c[6] / 2;
```

7.3 Declaring and Creating Arrays

Array objects occupy space in memory. Like other objects, arrays are created with keyword new. To create an array object, you specify the type of the array elements and the number of elements as part of an **array-creation expression** that uses keyword new. Such an expression returns a *reference* that can be stored in an array variable. The following declaration and array-creation expression create an array object containing 12 int elements and store the array's reference in the array variable named c:

```
int[] c = new int[12];
```

This expression can be used to create the array in Fig. 7.1. When an array is created, each of its elements receives a default value—zero for the numeric primitive-type elements, false for boolean elements and null for references. As you'll soon see, you can provide nondefault element values when you create an array.

Creating the array in Fig. 7.1 can also be performed in two steps as follows:

```
int[] c; // declare the array variable
c = new int[12]; // create the array; assign to array variable
```

In the declaration, the *square brackets* following the type indicate that c is a variable that will refer to an array (i.e., the variable will store an array *reference*). In the assignment statement, the array variable c receives the reference to a new array of 12 int elements.

Common Programming Error 7.2

In an array declaration, specifying the number of elements in the square brackets of the declaration (e.g., `int[12] c;`*) is a syntax error.*

A program can create several arrays in a single declaration. The following declaration reserves 100 elements for b and 27 elements for x:

```
String[] b = new String[100], x = new String[27];
```

When the type of the array and the square brackets are combined at the beginning of the declaration, all the identifiers in the declaration are array variables. In this case, variables b and x refer to String arrays. For readability, we prefer to declare only *one* variable per declaration. The preceding declaration is equivalent to:

```
String[] b = new String[100]; // create array b
String[] x = new String[27]; // create array x
```

Good Programming Practice 7.1

For readability, declare only one variable per declaration. Keep each declaration on a separate line, and include a comment describing the variable being declared.

When only one variable is declared in each declaration, the square brackets can be placed either after the type or after the array variable name, as in:

```
String b[] = new String[100]; // create array b
String x[] = new String[27]; // create array x
```

but placing the square brackets after the type is preferred.

Common Programming Error 7.3

Declaring multiple array variables in a single declaration can lead to subtle errors. Consider the declaration `int[] a, b, c;`*. If* a*,* b *and* c *should be declared as array variables, then this declaration is correct—placing square brackets directly following the type indicates that* all *the identifiers in the declaration are array variables. However, if only* a *is intended to be an array variable, and* b *and* c *are intended to be individual* int *variables, then this declaration is incorrect—the declaration* `int a[], b, c;` *would achieve the desired result.*

A program can declare arrays of any type. Every element of a primitive-type array contains a value of the array's declared element type. Similarly, in an array of a reference type, every element is a reference to an object of the array's declared element type. For example, every element of an int array is an int value, and every element of a String array is a reference to a String object.

7.4 Examples Using Arrays

This section presents several examples that demonstrate declaring arrays, creating arrays, initializing arrays and manipulating array elements.

7.4.1 Creating and Initializing an Array

The application of Fig. 7.2 uses keyword new to create an array of 10 int elements, which are initially zero (the default initial value for int variables). Line 7 declares array—a reference capable of referring to an array of int elements—then initializes the variable with a reference to an array object containing 10 int elements. Line 9 outputs the column headings. The first column contains the index (0–9) of each array element, and the second column contains the default initial value (0) of each array element.

```
1  // Fig. 7.2: InitArray.java
2  // Initializing the elements of an array to default values of zero.
3
4  public class InitArray {
5     public static void main(String[] args) {
6        // declare variable array and initialize it with an array object
7        int[] array = new int[10]; // create the array object
8
9        System.out.printf("%s%8s%n", "Index", "Value"); // column headings
10
11       // output each array element's value
12       for (int counter = 0; counter < array.length; counter++) {
13          System.out.printf("%5d%8d%n", counter, array[counter]);
14       }
15    }
16 }
```

```
Index   Value
    0       0
    1       0
    2       0
    3       0
    4       0
    5       0
    6       0
    7       0
    8       0
    9       0
```

Fig. 7.2 | Initializing the elements of an array to default values of zero.

The for statement (lines 12–14) outputs the index (represented by counter) and value of each array element (represented by array[counter]). Control variable counter is initially 0—index values start at 0, so using **zero-based counting** allows the loop to access every element of the array. The for's loop-continuation condition uses the expression array.length (line 12) to determine the length of the array. In this example, the length of the array is 10, so the loop continues executing as long as the value of control variable `counter` is less than 10. The highest index value of a 10-element array is 9, so using the less-than operator in the loop-continuation condition guarantees that the loop does not attempt to access an element *beyond* the end of the array (i.e., during the final iteration of the loop, `counter` is `9`). We'll soon see what Java does when it encounters such an *out-of-range index* at execution time.

7.4.2 Using an Array Initializer

You can create an array and initialize its elements with an **array initializer**—a comma-separated list of expressions (called an **initializer list**) enclosed in braces. In this case, the array length is determined by the number of elements in the initializer list. For example,

```
int[] n = {10, 20, 30, 40, 50};
```

creates a *five*-element array with index values `0–4`. Element `n[0]` is initialized to `10`, `n[1]` is initialized to `20`, and so on. When the compiler encounters an array declaration that includes an initializer list, it *counts* the number of initializers in the list to determine the size of the array, then sets up the appropriate `new` operation "behind the scenes."

The application in Fig. 7.3 initializes an integer array with 10 values (line 7) and displays the array in tabular format. The code for displaying the array elements (lines 12–14) is identical to that in Fig. 7.2 (lines 12–14).

```
1  // Fig. 7.3: InitArray.java
2  // Initializing the elements of an array with an array initializer.
3
4  public class InitArray {
5     public static void main(String[] args) {
6        // initializer list specifies the initial value for each element
7        int[] array = {32, 27, 64, 18, 95, 14, 90, 70, 60, 37};
8
9        System.out.printf("%s%8s%n", "Index", "Value"); // column headings
10
11       // output each array element's value
12       for (int counter = 0; counter < array.length; counter++) {
13          System.out.printf("%5d%8d%n", counter, array[counter]);
14       }
15    }
16 }
```

```
Index   Value
    0      32
    1      27
    2      64
    3      18
    4      95
    5      14
    6      90
    7      70
    8      60
    9      37
```

Fig. 7.3 | Initializing the elements of an array with an array initializer.

7.4.3 Calculating the Values to Store in an Array

The application in Fig. 7.4 creates a 10-element array and assigns to each element one of the even integers from 2 to 20 (2, 4, 6, …, 20). Then the application displays the array in tabular format. The `for` statement at lines 10–12 calculates an array element's value by multiplying the current value of the control variable `counter` by `2`, then adding `2`.

```
1  // Fig. 7.4: InitArray.java
2  // Calculating the values to be placed into the elements of an array.
3
4  public class InitArray {
5     public static void main(String[] args) {
6        final int ARRAY_LENGTH = 10; // declare constant
7        int[] array = new int[ARRAY_LENGTH]; // create array
8
9        // calculate value for each array element
10       for (int counter = 0; counter < array.length; counter++) {
11          array[counter] = 2 + 2 * counter;
12       }
13
14       System.out.printf("%s%8s%n", "Index", "Value"); // column headings
15
16       // output each array element's value
17       for (int counter = 0; counter < array.length; counter++) {
18          System.out.printf("%5d%8d%n", counter, array[counter]);
19       }
20    }
21 }
```

```
Index   Value
    0       2
    1       4
    2       6
    3       8
    4      10
    5      12
    6      14
    7      16
    8      18
    9      20
```

Fig. 7.4 | Calculating the values to be placed into the elements of an array.

Line 6 uses the modifier `final` to declare the constant variable `ARRAY_LENGTH` with the value `10`. Constant variables must be initialized *before* they're used and *cannot* be modified thereafter. If you attempt to *modify* a `final` variable after it's initialized in its declaration, the compiler issues an error message like

```
cannot assign a value to final variable variableName
```

Good Programming Practice 7.2

*Constant variables also are called **named constants**. They often make programs more readable—a named constant such as* `ARRAY_LENGTH` *clearly indicates its purpose, whereas a literal value such as* `10` *could have different meanings based on its context.*

Good Programming Practice 7.3

Constants use all uppercase letters by convention and multiword named constants should have each word separated from the next with an underscore (_) as in ARRAY_LENGTH.

Common Programming Error 7.4

Assigning a value to a previously initialized `final` *variable is a compilation error. Similarly, attempting to access the value of a* `final` *variable before it's initialized results in a compilation error like, "*`variable` *variableName* `might not have been initialized.`*"*

7.4.4 Summing the Elements of an Array

Often, array elements represent values for use in a calculation. If, for example, they're exam grades, a professor may wish to total the array elements and use that sum to calculate the class average. The `GradeBook` examples in Figs. 7.14 and 7.18 use this technique.

Figure 7.5 sums the values contained in a 10-element array. The program declares, creates and initializes the array at line 6. Lines 10–12 perform the calculations.

```
1  // Fig. 7.5: SumArray.java
2  // Computing the sum of the elements of an array.
3
4  public class SumArray {
5     public static void main(String[] args) {
6        int[] array = {87, 68, 94, 100, 83, 78, 85, 91, 76, 87};
7        int total = 0;
8
9        // add each element's value to total
10       for (int counter = 0; counter < array.length; counter++) {
11          total += array[counter];
12       }
13
14       System.out.printf("Total of array elements: %d%n", total);
15    }
16 }
```

```
Total of array elements: 849
```

Fig. 7.5 | Computing the sum of the elements of an array.

Note that the values supplied as array initializers are often read into a program rather than specified in an initializer list. For example, you could input the values from a user or from a file on disk, as discussed in Chapter 15, Files, Input/Output Streams, NIO and XML Serialization. Reading the data into a program (rather than "hand coding" it into the program) makes the program more reusable, because it can be used with *different* sets of data.

7.4.5 Using Bar Charts to Display Array Data Graphically

Many programs present data to users in a graphical manner. For example, numeric values are often displayed as bars in a bar chart. In such a chart, longer bars represent proportionally larger numeric values. One simple way to display numeric data graphically is with a bar chart that shows each numeric value as a bar of asterisks (*).

Professors often like to examine the grade distribution on an exam. A professor might visualize this with a graph of the number of grades in each of several categories. Suppose the grades were 87, 68, 94, 100, 83, 78, 85, 91, 76 and 87. They include one grade of 100, two grades in the 90s, four grades in the 80s, two grades in the 70s, one grade in the 60s and no grades below 60. Figure 7.6 stores this grade distribution data in an array of 11 elements, each corresponding to a category of grades. For example, `array[0]` indicates the number of grades in the range 0–9, `array[7]` the number of grades in the range 70–79 and `array[10]` the number of 100 grades.

```java
// Fig. 7.6: BarChart.java
// Bar chart printing program.

public class BarChart {
   public static void main(String[] args) {
      int[] array = {0, 0, 0, 0, 0, 0, 1, 2, 4, 2, 1};

      System.out.println("Grade distribution:");

      // for each array element, output a bar of the chart
      for (int counter = 0; counter < array.length; counter++) {
         // output bar label ("00-09: ", ..., "90-99: ", "100: ")
         if (counter == 10) {
            System.out.printf("%5d: ", 100);
         }
         else {
            System.out.printf("%02d-%02d: ",
               counter * 10, counter * 10 + 9);
         }

         // print bar of asterisks
         for (int stars = 0; stars < array[counter]; stars++) {
            System.out.print("*");
         }

         System.out.println();
      }
   }
}
```

```
Grade distribution:
00-09:
10-19:
20-29:
30-39:
40-49:
50-59:
60-69: *
70-79: **
80-89: ****
90-99: **
  100: *
```

Fig. 7.6 | Bar chart printing program.

The GradeBook classes later in the chapter (Figs. 7.14 and 7.18) contain code that calculates these grade frequencies based on a set of grades. For now, we manually create the array with the given grade frequencies. The application reads the numbers from the array and graphs the information as a bar chart. It displays each grade range followed by a bar of asterisks indicating the number of grades in that range. To label each bar, lines 13–19 output a grade range (e.g., "70-79: ") based on the current counter value. When counter is 10, line 14 outputs 100 with a field width of 5, followed by a colon and a space, to align the label "100: " with the other bar labels. The nested for statement (lines 22–24) outputs the bars. Note the loop-continuation condition at line 22 (stars < array[counter]). Each time the program reaches the inner for, the loop counts from 0 up to array[counter], thus using a value in array to determine the number of asterisks to display. In this example, *no* students received a grade below 60, so array[0]–array[5] contain zeroes, and *no* asterisks are displayed next to the first six grade ranges. In line 17, the format specifier %02d indicates that an int value should be formatted as a field of two digits. The **0 flag** in the format specifier displays a leading 0 for values with fewer digits than the field width (2).

7.4.6 Using the Elements of an Array as Counters

Sometimes, programs use counter variables to summarize data, such as the results of a survey. In Fig. 6.7, we used separate counters in our die-rolling program to track the number of occurrences of each side of a six-sided die as the program rolled the die 60,000,000 times. An array version of this application is shown in Fig. 7.7.

```
// Fig. 7.7: RollDie.java
// Die-rolling program using arrays instead of switch.
import java.security.SecureRandom;

public class RollDie {
   public static void main(String[] args) {
      SecureRandom randomNumbers = new SecureRandom();
      int[] frequency = new int[7]; // array of frequency counters

      // roll die 60,000,000 times; use die value as frequency index
      for (int roll = 1; roll <= 60_000_000; roll++) {
         ++frequency[1 + randomNumbers.nextInt(6)];
      }

      System.out.printf("%s%10s%n", "Face", "Frequency");

      // output each array element's value
      for (int face = 1; face < frequency.length; face++) {
         System.out.printf("%4d%10d%n", face, frequency[face]);
      }
   }
}
```

Fig. 7.7 | Die-rolling program using arrays instead of switch. (Part 1 of 2.)

```
Face Frequency
   1    9995532
   2   10003079
   3   10000564
   4   10000726
   5    9998994
   6   10001105
```

Fig. 7.7 | Die-rolling program using arrays instead of `switch`. (Part 2 of 2.)

Figure 7.7 uses the array `frequency` (line 8) to count the occurrences of each side of the die. *The single statement in line 12 of this program replaces lines 19–41 of Fig. 6.7.* Line 12 uses the random value to determine which `frequency` element to increment . The calculation in line 12 produces random numbers from 1 to 6, so the array `frequency` must be large enough to store six counters. However, we use a seven-element array in which we ignore `frequency[0]`—it's more logical to have the face value 1 increment `frequency[1]` than `frequency[0]`. Thus, each face value is used as an index for array `frequency`. In line 12, the calculation inside the square brackets evaluates first to determine which element of the array to increment, then the `++` operator adds one to that element. We also replaced lines 45–47 from Fig. 6.7 by looping through array `frequency` to output the results (lines
8 18–20). When we study Java SE 8's functional programming capabilities in Chapter 17, we'll show how to replace lines 11–13 and 18–20 with a *single* statement!

7.4.7 Using Arrays to Analyze Survey Results

Our next example uses arrays to summarize data collected in a survey. Consider the following problem statement:

> *Twenty students were asked to rate on a scale of 1 to 5 the quality of the food in the student cafeteria, with 1 being "awful" and 5 being "excellent." Place the 20 responses in an integer array and determine the frequency of each rating.*

This is a typical array-processing application (Fig. 7.8). We wish to summarize the number of responses of each type (that is, 1–5). Array `responses` (lines 7–8) is a 20-element integer array containing the students' survey responses. The last value in the array *is intentionally* an incorrect response (`14`). When a Java program executes, array element indices are checked for validity—all indices must be greater than or equal to 0 and less than the length of the array. Any attempt to access an element outside that range of indices results in a runtime error that's known as an `ArrayIndexOutOfBoundsException`. At the end of this section, we'll discuss the invalid response value, demonstrate array **bounds checking** and introduce Java's *exception-handling* mechanism, which can be used to detect and handle an `ArrayIndexOutOfBoundsException`.

The `frequency` *Array*

We use the *six-element* array `frequency` (line 9) to count the number of occurrences of each response. Each element (except element 0) is used as a *counter* for one of the possible survey-response values—`frequency[1]` counts the number of students who rated the food as 1, `frequency[2]` counts the number of students who rated the food as 2, and so on.

```
1  // Fig. 7.8: StudentPoll.java
2  // Poll analysis program.
3
4  public class StudentPoll {
5     public static void main(String[] args) {
6        // student response array (more typically, input at runtime)
7        int[] responses =
8           {1, 2, 5, 4, 3, 5, 2, 1, 3, 3, 1, 4, 3, 3, 3, 2, 3, 3, 2, 14};
9        int[] frequency = new int[6]; // array of frequency counters
10
11       // for each answer, select responses element and use that value
12       // as frequency index to determine element to increment
13       for (int answer = 0; answer < responses.length; answer++) {
14          try {
15             ++frequency[responses[answer]];
16          }
17          catch (ArrayIndexOutOfBoundsException e) {
18             System.out.println(e); // invokes toString method
19             System.out.printf("   responses[%d] = %d%n%n",
20                answer, responses[answer]);
21          }
22       }
23
24       System.out.printf("%s%10s%n", "Rating", "Frequency");
25
26       // output each array element's value
27       for (int rating = 1; rating < frequency.length; rating++) {
28          System.out.printf("%6d%10d%n", rating, frequency[rating]);
29       }
30    }
31 }
```

```
java.lang.ArrayIndexOutOfBoundsException: 14
   responses[19] = 14

Rating Frequency
     1         3
     2         4
     3         8
     4         2
     5         2
```

Fig. 7.8 | Poll analysis program.

Summarizing the Results

The `for` statement (lines 13–22) reads the responses from the array `responses` one at a time and increments one of the counters `frequency[1]` to `frequency[5]`; we ignore `frequency[0]` because the survey responses are limited to the range 1–5. The key statement in the loop appears in line 15. This statement increments the appropriate `frequency` counter as determined by the value of `responses[answer]`.

Let's step through the first few iterations of the `for` statement:

- When `answer` is `0`, `responses[answer]` is the value of `responses[0]` (that is, 1—see line 8). So, `frequency[responses[answer]]` evaluates to `frequency[1]` and counter `frequency[1]` is incremented by one. To evaluate the expression, we begin with the value in the *innermost* set of brackets (`answer`, currently `0`). The value of `answer` is plugged into the expression, and the next set of brackets (`responses[answer]`) is evaluated. That value is used as the index for the `frequency` array to determine which counter to increment (in this case, `frequency[1]`).

- The next time through the loop `answer` is `1`, `responses[answer]` is the value of `responses[1]` (that is, `2`—see line 8), so `frequency[responses[answer]]` is interpreted as `frequency[2]`, causing `frequency[2]` to be incremented.
- When `answer` is `2`, `responses[answer]` is the value of `responses[2]` (that is, `5`—see line 8), so `frequency[responses[answer]]` is interpreted as `frequency[5]`, causing `frequency[5]` to be incremented, and so on.

Regardless of the number of responses processed, only a six-element array (in which we ignore element zero) is required to summarize the results, because all the correct responses are from 1 to 5, and the index values for a six-element array are 0–5. In the program's output, the `Frequency` column summarizes only 19 of the 20 values in the `responses` array—the last element of the array `responses` contains an (intentionally) incorrect response that was not counted. Section 7.5 discusses what happens when the program in Fig. 7.8 encounters the invalid response (`14`) in the last element of array `responses`.

7.5 Exception Handling: Processing the Incorrect Response

An **exception** indicates a problem that occurs while a program executes. **Exception handling** helps you create **fault-tolerant programs** that can resolve (or handle) exceptions. In some cases, this allows a program to continue executing as if no problems were encountered. For example, the `StudentPoll` application still displays results (Fig. 7.8), even though one of the responses was out of range. More severe problems might prevent a program from continuing normal execution, instead requiring it to notify the user of the problem, then terminate. When the JVM or a method detects a problem, such as an invalid array index or an invalid method argument, it **throws** an exception—that is, an exception occurs. Methods in your own classes can also throw exceptions, as you'll learn in Chapter 8.

7.5.1 The `try` Statement

To handle an exception, place any code that might throw an exception in a **`try` statement** (lines 14–21 of Fig. 7.8). The **`try` block** (lines 14–16) contains the code that might *throw* an exception, and the **`catch` block** (lines 17–21) contains the code that *handles* the exception if one occurs. You can have *many* `catch`es to handle different *types* of exceptions that might be thrown in the corresponding `try` block. When line 15 correctly increments a `frequency` array element, lines 17–21 are ignored. The braces that delimit the bodies of the `try` and `catch` blocks are required.

7.5.2 Executing the `catch` Block

When the program encounters the invalid value `14` in the `responses` array, it attempts to add `1` to `frequency[14]`, which is *outside* the bounds of the array—the `frequency` array has only six elements (with indexes 0–5). Because array bounds checking is performed at execution time, the JVM generates an *exception*—specifically line 15 throws an **`ArrayIndexOutOfBoundsException`** to notify the program of this problem. At this point the `try` block terminates and the `catch` block begins executing—if you declared any local variables in the `try` block, they're now *out of scope* (and no longer exist), so they're not accessible in the `catch` block.

The `catch` block declares an exception parameter (`e`) of type `ArrayIndexOutOfBoundsException`. The `catch` block can handle exceptions of the specified type. Inside the `catch` block, you can use the parameter's identifier to interact with a caught exception object.

Error-Prevention Tip 7.1

When writing code to access an array element, ensure that the array index remains greater than or equal to 0 and less than the length of the array. This will prevent `ArrayIndexOutOfBoundsException`s if your program is correct.

Software Engineering Observation 7.1

Systems in industry that have undergone extensive testing are still likely to contain bugs. Our preference for industrial-strength systems is to catch and deal with runtime exceptions, such as `ArrayIndexOutOfBoundsException`s, to ensure that a system either stays up and running or degrades gracefully, and to inform the system's developers of the problem.

7.5.3 `toString` Method of the Exception Parameter

When lines 17–21 *catch* the exception, the program displays a message indicating the problem that occurred. Line 18 *implicitly* calls the exception object's `toString` method to get the error message that's implicitly stored in the exception object and display it. Once the message is displayed in this example, the exception is considered *handled* and the program continues with the next statement after the `catch` block's closing brace. In this example, the end of the `for` statement is reached (line 22), so the program continues with the increment of the control variable in line 13. We discuss exception handling again in Chapter 8, and more deeply in Chapter 11.

7.6 Case Study: Card Shuffling and Dealing Simulation

The examples in the chapter thus far have used arrays containing elements of primitive types. Recall from Section 7.2 that the elements of an array can be either primitive types or reference types. This section uses random-number generation and an array of reference-type elements, namely objects representing playing cards, to develop a class that simulates card shuffling and dealing. This class can then be used to implement applications that play specific card games. The exercises at the end of the chapter use the classes developed here to build a simple poker application.

We first develop class `Card` (Fig. 7.9), which represents a playing card that has a face (e.g., `"Ace"`, `"Deuce"`, `"Three"`, …, `"Jack"`, `"Queen"`, `"King"`) and a suit (e.g., `"Hearts"`, `"Diamonds"`, `"Clubs"`, `"Spades"`). Next, we develop the `DeckOfCards` class (Fig. 7.10), which creates a deck of 52 playing cards in which each element is a `Card` object. We then build a test application (Fig. 7.11) that demonstrates class `DeckOfCards`'s card shuffling and dealing capabilities.

Class Card

Class Card (Fig. 7.9) contains two String instance variables—face and suit—that are used to store references to the face name and suit name for a specific Card. The constructor for the class (lines 9–12) receives two Strings that it uses to initialize face and suit. Method toString (lines 15–17) creates a String consisting of the face of the card, the String " of " and the suit of the card.[1] Card's toString method can be invoked *explicitly* to obtain a string representation of a Card object (e.g., "Ace of Spades"). The toString method of an object is called *implicitly* when the object is used where a String is expected (e.g., when printf outputs the object as a String using the %s format specifier or when the object is concatenated to a String using the + operator). For this behavior to occur, toString must be declared with the header shown in Fig. 7.9.

```
1  // Fig. 7.9: Card.java
2  // Card class represents a playing card.
3
4  public class Card {
5     private final String face; // face of card ("Ace", "Deuce", ...)
6     private final String suit; // suit of card ("Hearts", "Diamonds", ...)
7
8     // two-argument constructor initializes card's face and suit
9     public Card(String cardFace, String cardSuit) {
10       this.face = cardFace; // initialize face of card
11       this.suit = cardSuit; // initialize suit of card
12    }
13
14    // return String representation of Card
15    public String toString() {
16       return face + " of " + suit;
17    }
18 }
```

Fig. 7.9 | Card class represents a playing card.

Class DeckOfCards

Class DeckOfCards (Fig. 7.10) creates and manages an array of Card references. The named constant NUMBER_OF_CARDS (line 8) specifies the number of Cards in a deck (52). Line 10 declares and initializes an instance variable named deck that refers to a new array of Cards that has NUMBER_OF_CARDS (52) elements—the deck array's elements are null by default. Recall from Chapter 3 that null represents a "reference to nothing," so no Card objects exist yet. An array of a *reference* type is declared like any other array. Class DeckOfCards also declares int instance variable currentCard (line 11), representing the sequence number (0–51) of the next Card to be dealt from the deck array.

1. You'll learn in Chapter 9 that when we provide a custom toString method for a class, we are actually "overriding" a version of that method supplied by class Object from which all Java classes "inherit." As of Chapter 9, every method we explicitly override will be preceded by the "annotation" @Override, which prevents a common programming error.

```java
// Fig. 7.10: DeckOfCards.java
// DeckOfCards class represents a deck of playing cards.
import java.security.SecureRandom;

public class DeckOfCards {
   // random number generator
   private static final SecureRandom randomNumbers = new SecureRandom();
   private static final int NUMBER_OF_CARDS = 52; // constant # of Cards

   private Card[] deck = new Card[NUMBER_OF_CARDS]; // Card references
   private int currentCard = 0; // index of next Card to be dealt (0-51)

   // constructor fills deck of Cards
   public DeckOfCards() {
      String[] faces = {"Ace", "Deuce", "Three", "Four", "Five", "Six",
         "Seven", "Eight", "Nine", "Ten", "Jack", "Queen", "King"};
      String[] suits = {"Hearts", "Diamonds", "Clubs", "Spades"};

      // populate deck with Card objects
      for (int count = 0; count < deck.length; count++) {
         deck[count] =
            new Card(faces[count % 13], suits[count / 13]);
      }
   }

   // shuffle deck of Cards with one-pass algorithm
   public void shuffle() {
      // next call to method dealCard should start at deck[0] again
      currentCard = 0;

      // for each Card, pick another random Card (0-51) and swap them
      for (int first = 0; first < deck.length; first++) {
         // select a random number between 0 and 51
         int second = randomNumbers.nextInt(NUMBER_OF_CARDS);

         // swap current Card with randomly selected Card
         Card temp = deck[first];
         deck[first] = deck[second];
         deck[second] = temp;
      }
   }

   // deal one Card
   public Card dealCard() {
      // determine whether Cards remain to be dealt
      if (currentCard < deck.length) {
         return deck[currentCard++]; // return current Card in array
      }
      else {
         return null; // return null to indicate that all Cards were dealt
      }
   }
}
```

Fig. 7.10 | DeckOfCards class represents a deck of playing cards.

DeckOfCards Constructor

The class's constructor uses a for statement (lines 20–23) to fill the deck instance variable with Card objects. The loop initializes control variable count to 0 and loops while count is less than deck.length, causing count to take on each integer value from 0 through 51 (the deck array's indices). Each Card is instantiated and initialized with two Strings—one from the faces array (which contains the Strings "Ace" through "King") and one from the suits array (which contains the Strings "Hearts", "Diamonds", "Clubs" and "Spades"). The calculation count % 13 always results in a value from 0 to 12 (the 13 indices of the faces array in lines 15–16), and the calculation count / 13 always results in a value from 0 to 3 (the four indices of the suits array in line 17). When the loop completes, deck contains the Cards with faces "Ace" through "King" in order for each suit (13 "Hearts", then 13 "Diamonds", then 13 "Clubs", then 13 "Spades"). We use arrays of Strings to represent the faces and suits in this example. In Exercise 7.34, we ask you to modify this example to use arrays of enum constants to represent the faces and suits.

DeckOfCards Method shuffle

Method shuffle (lines 27–41) shuffles the Cards in the deck. The method loops through all 52 Cards (array indices 0 to 51). For each Card, line 34 selects a random index between 0 and 51 to select another Card. Next, lines 37–39 swap the current Card and the randomly selected Card in the array. The extra variable temp (line 37) temporarily stores one of the two Card objects being swapped. After the for loop terminates, the Card objects are randomly ordered. A total of only 52 swaps are made in a single pass of the entire array, and the array of Card objects is shuffled!

The swap in lines 37–39 cannot be performed with only the two statements

```
deck[first] = deck[second];
deck[second] = deck[first];
```

If deck[first] is the "Ace" of "Spades" and deck[second] is the "Queen" of "Hearts", after the first assignment, both array elements contain the "Queen" of "Hearts" and the "Ace" of "Spades" is lost—so, the extra variable temp is needed.

[*Note:* It's recommended that you use a so-called *unbiased* shuffling algorithm for real card games. Such an algorithm ensures that all possible shuffled card sequences are equally likely to occur. Exercise 7.35 asks you to research the popular unbiased Fisher-Yates shuffling algorithm and use it to reimplement the DeckOfCards method shuffle.]

DeckOfCards Method dealCard

Method dealCard (lines 44–52) deals one Card in the array. Recall that currentCard indicates the index of the next Card to be dealt (i.e., the Card at the *top* of the deck). Thus, line 46 compares currentCard to the length of the deck array. If the deck is not empty (i.e., currentCard is less than 52), line 47 returns the "top" Card and postincrements currentCard to prepare for the next call to dealCard—otherwise, line 50 returns null.

Shuffling and Dealing Cards

Figure 7.11 demonstrates class DeckOfCards. Line 7 creates a DeckOfCards object named myDeckOfCards. The DeckOfCards constructor creates the deck with the 52 Card objects in order by suit and face. Line 8 invokes `myDeckOfCards`'s `shuffle` method to rearrange the `Card` objects. Lines 11–18 deal all 52 `Card`s and print them in four columns of 13 `Card`s each. Line 13 deals one `Card` object by invoking `myDeckOfCards`'s `dealCard` method, then displays the `Card` left justified in a field of 19 characters. When a `Card` is output as a `String`, the `Card`'s `toString` method (Fig. 7.9) is implicitly invoked. Lines 15–17 in Fig. 7.11 start a new line after every four `Card`s.

```
1  // Fig. 7.11: DeckOfCardsTest.java
2  // Card shuffling and dealing.
3
4  public class DeckOfCardsTest {
5     // execute application
6     public static void main(String[] args) {
7        DeckOfCards myDeckOfCards = new DeckOfCards();
8        myDeckOfCards.shuffle(); // place Cards in random order
9
10       // print all 52 Cards in the order in which they are dealt
11       for (int i = 1; i <= 52; i++) {
12          // deal and display a Card
13          System.out.printf("%-19s", myDeckOfCards.dealCard());
14
15          if (i % 4 == 0) { // output a newline after every fourth card
16             System.out.println();
17          }
18       }
19    }
20 }
```

```
Six of Spades      Eight of Spades    Six of Clubs       Nine of Hearts
Queen of Hearts    Seven of Clubs     Nine of Spades     King of Hearts
Three of Diamonds  Deuce of Clubs     Ace of Hearts      Ten of Spades
Four of Spades     Ace of Clubs       Seven of Diamonds  Four of Hearts
Three of Clubs     Deuce of Hearts    Five of Spades     Jack of Diamonds
King of Clubs      Ten of Hearts      Three of Hearts    Six of Diamonds
Queen of Clubs     Eight of Diamonds  Deuce of Diamonds  Ten of Diamonds
Three of Spades    King of Diamonds   Nine of Clubs      Six of Hearts
Ace of Spades      Four of Diamonds   Seven of Hearts    Eight of Clubs
Deuce of Spades    Eight of Hearts    Five of Hearts     Queen of Spades
Jack of Hearts     Seven of Spades    Four of Clubs      Nine of Diamonds
Ace of Diamonds    Queen of Diamonds  Five of Clubs      King of Spades
Five of Diamonds   Ten of Clubs       Jack of Spades     Jack of Clubs
```

Fig. 7.11 | Card shuffling and dealing.

Preventing `NullPointerException`*s*

In Fig. 7.10, we created a `deck` array of 52 `Card` references—by default, each element of a reference-type array created with new is initialized to `null`. Similarly, reference-type fields of a class are also initialized to `null` by default. A `NullPointerException` occurs when you try to call a method on a `null` reference. In industrial-strength code, ensuring that references are not `null` before you use them to call methods prevents `NullPointerException`s.

7.7 Enhanced for Statement

The **enhanced `for` statement** iterates through the elements of an array *without* using a counter, thus avoiding the possibility of "stepping outside" the array. We show how to use the enhanced `for` statement with the Java API's prebuilt data structures (called collections) in Section 7.16. The syntax of an enhanced `for` statement is:

```
for (parameter : arrayName) {
   statement
}
```

where *parameter* has a *type* and an *identifier* (e.g., `int number`), and *arrayName* is the array through which to iterate. The type of the parameter must be *consistent* with the type of the elements in the array. As the next example illustrates, the identifier represents successive element values in the array on successive iterations of the loop.

Figure 7.12 uses the enhanced `for` statement (lines 10–12) to sum the integers in an array of student grades. The enhanced `for`'s parameter is of type `int`, because `array` contains `int` values—the loop selects one `int` value from the array during each iteration. The enhanced `for` statement iterates through successive values in the array one by one. The statement's header can be read as "for each iteration, assign the next element of `array` to `int` variable `number`, then execute the following statement." Thus, for each iteration, identifier `number` represents an `int` value in `array`. Lines 10–12 are equivalent to the following counter-controlled iteration used in lines 10–12 of Fig. 7.5 to total the integers in `array`, except that the counting details are hidden from you in the enhanced `for` statement:

```
for (int counter = 0; counter < array.length; counter++) {
   total += array[counter];
}
```

```
1  // Fig. 7.12: EnhancedForTest.java
2  // Using the enhanced for statement to total integers in an array.
3
4  public class EnhancedForTest {
5     public static void main(String[] args) {
6        int[] array = {87, 68, 94, 100, 83, 78, 85, 91, 76, 87};
7        int total = 0;
8
9        // add each element's value to total
10       for (int number : array) {
11          total += number;
12       }
13
14       System.out.printf("Total of array elements: %d%n", total);
15    }
16 }
```

```
Total of array elements: 849
```

Fig. 7.12 | Using the enhanced `for` statement to total integers in an array.

The enhanced `for` statement can be used *only* to obtain array elements—it *cannot* be used to *modify* elements. If your program needs to modify elements, use the traditional counter-controlled `for` statement.

The enhanced `for` statement can be used in place of the counter-controlled `for` statement whenever code looping through an array does *not* require access to the counter indicating the index of the current array element. For example, totaling the integers in an array requires access only to the element values—the index of each element is irrelevant. However, if a program must use a counter for some reason other than simply to loop through an array (e.g., to print an index number next to each array element value, as in the examples earlier in this chapter), use the counter-controlled `for` statement.

Error-Prevention Tip 7.2

The enhanced `for` *statement simplifies iterating through an array. This makes the code more readable and eliminates several error possibilities, such as improperly specifying the control variable's initial value, the loop-continuation test and the increment expression.*

Java SE 8 8

The `for` statement and the enhanced `for` statement each iterate sequentially from a starting value to an ending value. In Chapter 17, Lambdas and Streams, you'll learn about streams. As you'll see, streams provide an elegant, more concise and less error-prone means for iterating through collections in a manner that enables some iterations to occur in parallel with others to achieve better multi-core system performance.

7.8 Passing Arrays to Methods

This section demonstrates how to pass arrays and individual array elements as arguments to methods. To pass an array argument to a method, specify the name of the array *without any brackets*. For example, if array `hourlyTemperatures` is declared as

```
double[] hourlyTemperatures = new double[24];
```

then the method call

```
modifyArray(hourlyTemperatures);
```

passes the reference of array `hourlyTemperatures` to method `modifyArray`. Every array object "knows" its own length. Thus, when we pass an array object's reference into a method, we need not pass the array length as an additional argument.

For a method to receive an array reference through a method call, the method's parameter list must specify an *array parameter*. For example, the method header for method `modifyArray` might be written as

```
void modifyArray(double[] b)
```

indicating that `modifyArray` receives the reference of a `double` array in parameter `b`. The method call passes array `hourlyTemperature`'s reference, so when the called method uses the array variable `b`, it *refers to* the same array object as `hourlyTemperatures` in the caller.

When an argument to a method is an entire array or an individual array element of a reference type, the called method receives a *copy* of the reference. However, when an argument to a method is an individual array element of a primitive type, the called method receives a copy of the element's *value*. Such primitive values are called **scalars** or **scalar** quantities. To pass an individual array element to a method, use the indexed name of the array element as an argument in the method call.

Figure 7.13 demonstrates the difference between passing an entire array and passing a primitive-type array element to a method. Method `main` invokes `static` methods `modifyArray` (line 18) and `modifyElement` (line 30). Recall that a `static` method can invoke other `static` methods of the same class without using the class name and a dot (.).

```
1  // Fig. 7.13: PassArray.java
2  // Passing arrays and individual array elements to methods.
3
4  public class PassArray {
5     // main creates array and calls modifyArray and modifyElement
6     public static void main(String[] args) {
7        int[] array = {1, 2, 3, 4, 5};
8
9        System.out.printf(
10          "Effects of passing reference to entire array:%n" +
11          "The values of the original array are:%n");
12
13       // output original array elements
14       for (int value : array) {
15          System.out.printf("   %d", value);
16       }
17
18       modifyArray(array); // pass array reference
19       System.out.printf("%n%nThe values of the modified array are:%n");
20
21       // output modified array elements
22       for (int value : array) {
23          System.out.printf("   %d", value);
24       }
25
26       System.out.printf(
27          "%n%nEffects of passing array element value:%n" +
28          "array[3] before modifyElement: %d%n", array[3]);
29
30       modifyElement(array[3]); // attempt to modify array[3]
31       System.out.printf(
32          "array[3] after modifyElement: %d%n", array[3]);
33    }
34
35    // multiply each element of an array by 2
36    public static void modifyArray(int[] array2) {
37       for (int counter = 0; counter < array2.length; counter++) {
38          array2[counter] *= 2;
39       }
40    }
41
42    // multiply argument by 2
43    public static void modifyElement(int element) {
44       element *= 2;
```

Fig. 7.13 | Passing arrays and individual array elements to methods. (Part 1 of 2.)

```
45          System.out.printf(
46             "Value of element in modifyElement: %d%n", element);
47       }
48    }
```

```
Effects of passing reference to entire array:
The values of the original array are:
   1   2   3   4   5

The values of the modified array are:
   2   4   6   8   10

Effects of passing array element value:
array[3] before modifyElement: 8
Value of element in modifyElement: 16
array[3] after modifyElement: 8
```

Fig. 7.13 | Passing arrays and individual array elements to methods. (Part 2 of 2.)

The enhanced `for` statement in lines 14–16 outputs `array`'s elements. Line 18 invokes `modifyArray` (lines 36–40), passing `array` as an argument. The method receives a copy of `array`'s reference and uses it to multiply each of `array`'s elements by 2. To prove that `array`'s elements were modified, lines 22–24 output the elements again. As the output shows, method `modifyArray` doubled the value of each element. We could *not* use the enhanced `for` statement in lines 37–39 because we're modifying the array's elements.

Figure 7.13 next demonstrates that when a copy of an individual primitive-type array element is passed to a method, modifying the *copy* in the called method does *not* affect the original value of that element in the calling method's array. Lines 26–28 output the value of `array[3]` *before* invoking method `modifyElement`. Remember that the value of this element is now 8 after it was modified in the call to `modifyArray`. Line 30 calls method `modifyElement` and passes `array[3]` as an argument. Remember that `array[3]` is actually one `int` value (8) in `array`. Therefore, the program passes a copy of `array[3]`'s value. Method `modifyElement` (lines 43–47) multiplies the value received as an argument by 2, stores the result in its parameter `element`, then outputs the value of `element` (16). Since method parameters, like local variables, cease to exist when the method in which they're declared completes execution, the method parameter `element` is destroyed when `modifyElement` terminates. When the program returns control to `main`, lines 31–32 output the *unmodified* value of `array[3]` (i.e., 8).

7.9 Pass-By-Value vs. Pass-By-Reference

The preceding example demonstrated how arrays and primitive-type array elements are passed as arguments to methods. We now take a closer look at how arguments in general are passed to methods. Two ways to pass arguments in method calls in many programming languages are **pass-by-value** and **pass-by-reference** (sometimes called **call-by-value** and **call-by-reference**). When an argument is passed by value, a *copy* of the argument's *value* is passed to the called method. The called method works exclusively with the copy. Changes to the called method's copy do *not* affect the original variable's value in the caller.

When an argument is passed by reference, the called method can access the argument's value in the caller directly and modify that data, if necessary. Pass-by-reference improves performance by eliminating the need to copy possibly large amounts of data.

Unlike some other languages, Java does *not* allow you to choose pass-by-value or pass-by-reference—*all arguments are passed by value*. A method call can pass two types of values to a method—copies of primitive values (e.g., values of type `int` and `double`) and copies of references to objects. Objects themselves cannot be passed to methods. When a method modifies a primitive-type parameter, changes to the parameter have no effect on the original argument value in the calling method. For example, when line 30 in `main` of Fig. 7.13 passes `array[3]` to method `modifyElement`, the statement in line 44 that doubles the value of parameter `element` has *no* effect on the value of `array[3]` in `main`. This is also true for reference-type parameters. If you modify a reference-type parameter so that it refers to another object, only the parameter refers to the new object—the reference stored in the caller's variable still refers to the original object.

Although an object's reference is passed by value, a method can still interact with the referenced object by calling its `public` methods using the copy of the object's reference. Since the reference stored in the parameter is a copy of the reference that was passed as an argument, the parameter in the called method and the argument in the calling method refer to the *same* object in memory. For example, in Fig. 7.13, both parameter `array2` in method `modifyArray` and variable `array` in `main` refer to the *same* array object in memory. Any changes made using the parameter `array2` are carried out on the object that `array` references in the calling method. In Fig. 7.13, the changes made in `modifyArray` using `array2` affect the contents of the array object referenced by `array` in `main`. Thus, with a reference to an object, the called method *can* manipulate the caller's object directly.

Performance Tip 7.1

Passing references to arrays, instead of the array objects themselves, makes sense for performance reasons. Because Java arguments are passed by value, if array objects were passed, a copy of each element would be passed. For large arrays, this would waste time and consume considerable storage for the copies of the elements.

7.10 Case Study: Class GradeBook Using an Array to Store Grades

We now present the first part of our case study on developing a `GradeBook` class that instructors can use to maintain students' grades on an exam and display a grade report that includes the grades, class average, lowest grade, highest grade and a grade-distribution bar chart. The version of class `GradeBook` presented in this section stores the grades for one exam in a one-dimensional array. In Section 7.12, we present a version of class `GradeBook` that uses a two-dimensional array to store students' grades for *several* exams.

Storing Student Grades in an Array in Class GradeBook

Class `GradeBook` (Fig. 7.14) uses an array of `int`s to store several students' grades on a single exam. Array `grades` is declared as an instance variable (line 6), so each `GradeBook` object maintains its *own* set of grades. The constructor (lines 9–12) has two parameters—the name of the course and an array of grades. When an application (e.g., class `GradeBookTest` in Fig. 7.15) creates a `GradeBook` object, the application passes an existing `int` array to the constructor, which assigns the array's reference to instance variable `grades` (line 11). The `grades` array's *size* is determined by the `length` instance variable of the constructor's array parameter. Thus, a `GradeBook` object can process a *variable* number of grades. The grade values in the argument could have been input from a user, read from a file on disk (as discussed in Chapter 15) or come from a variety of other sources. In class `GradeBookTest`, we initialize an array with grade values (Fig. 7.15, line 7). Once the grades are stored in *instance variable* `grades` of class `GradeBook`, all the class's methods can access the elements of `grades`.

```
1  // Fig. 7.14: GradeBook.java
2  // GradeBook class using an array to store test grades.
3
4  public class GradeBook {
5     private String courseName; // name of course this GradeBook represents
6     private int[] grades; // array of student grades
7
8     // constructor
9     public GradeBook(String courseName, int[] grades) {
10       this.courseName = courseName;
11       this.grades = grades;
12    }
13
14    // method to set the course name
15    public void setCourseName(String courseName) {
16       this.courseName = courseName;
17    }
18
19    // method to retrieve the course name
20    public String getCourseName() {
21       return courseName;
22    }
23
24    // perform various operations on the data
25    public void processGrades() {
26       // output grades array
27       outputGrades();
28
29       // call method getAverage to calculate the average grade
30       System.out.printf("%nClass average is %.2f%n", getAverage());
31
32       // call methods getMinimum and getMaximum
33       System.out.printf("Lowest grade is %d%nHighest grade is %d%n%n",
34          getMinimum(), getMaximum());
35
36       // call outputBarChart to print grade distribution chart
37       outputBarChart();
38    }
39
40    // find minimum grade
41    public int getMinimum() {
42       int lowGrade = grades[0]; // assume grades[0] is smallest
```

Fig. 7.14 | GradeBook class using an array to store test grades. (Part 1 of 3.)

```

      // loop through grades array
      for (int grade : grades) {
         // if grade lower than lowGrade, assign it to lowGrade
         if (grade < lowGrade) {
            lowGrade = grade; // new lowest grade
         }
      }

      return lowGrade;
   }

   // find maximum grade
   public int getMaximum() {
      int highGrade = grades[0]; // assume grades[0] is largest

      // loop through grades array
      for (int grade : grades) {
         // if grade greater than highGrade, assign it to highGrade
         if (grade > highGrade) {
            highGrade = grade; // new highest grade
         }
      }

      return highGrade;
   }

   // determine average grade for test
   public double getAverage() {
      int total = 0;

      // sum grades for one student
      for (int grade : grades) {
         total += grade;
      }

      // return average of grades
      return (double) total / grades.length;
   }

   // output bar chart displaying grade distribution
   public void outputBarChart() {
      System.out.println("Grade distribution:");

      // stores frequency of grades in each range of 10 grades
      int[] frequency = new int[11];

      // for each grade, increment the appropriate frequency
      for (int grade : grades) {
         ++frequency[grade / 10];
      }

```

Fig. 7.14 | GradeBook class using an array to store test grades. (Part 2 of 3.)

```
95          // for each grade frequency, print bar in chart
96          for (int count = 0; count < frequency.length; count++) {
97             // output bar label ("00-09: ", ..., "90-99: ", "100: ")
98             if (count == 10) {
99                System.out.printf("%5d: ", 100);
100            }
101            else {
102               System.out.printf("%02d-%02d: ", count * 10, count * 10 + 9);
103            }
104
105            // print bar of asterisks
106            for (int stars = 0; stars < frequency[count]; stars++) {
107               System.out.print("*");
108            }
109
110            System.out.println();
111         }
112      }
113
114      // output the contents of the grades array
115      public void outputGrades() {
116         System.out.printf("The grades are:%n%n");
117
118         // output each student's grade
119         for (int student = 0; student < grades.length; student++) {
120            System.out.printf("Student %2d: %3d%n",
121               student + 1, grades[student]);
122         }
123      }
124   }
```

Fig. 7.14 | GradeBook class using an array to store test grades. (Part 3 of 3.)

Method processGrades (lines 25–38) contains a series of method calls that output a report summarizing the grades. Line 27 calls method outputGrades to print the contents of the array grades. Lines 119–122 in method outputGrades output the students' grades. A counter-controlled for statement *must* be used in this case, because lines 120–121 use counter variable student's value to output each grade next to a particular student number (see the output in Fig. 7.15). Although array indices start at 0, a professor might typically number students starting at 1. Thus, lines 120–121 output student + 1 as the student number to produce grade labels "Student 1: ", "Student 2: ", and so on.

Method processGrades next calls method getAverage (line 30) to obtain the average of the grades in the array. Method getAverage (lines 71–81) uses an enhanced for statement to total the values in array grades before calculating the average. The parameter in the enhanced for's header (e.g., int grade) indicates that for each iteration, the int variable grade takes on a value in the array grades. The averaging calculation in line 80 uses grades.length to determine the number of grades being averaged.

Lines 33–34 in method processGrades call methods getMinimum and getMaximum to determine the lowest and highest grades of any student on the exam, respectively. Each of these methods uses an enhanced for statement to loop through array grades. Lines 45–50 in method getMinimum loop through the array. Lines 47–49 compare each grade to lowGrade; if a grade is less than lowGrade, lowGrade is set to that grade. When line 52 executes, lowGrade contains the lowest grade in the array. Method getMaximum (lines 56–68) works similarly to method getMinimum.

Finally, line 37 in method processGrades calls outputBarChart to print a grade-distribution chart using a technique similar to that in Fig. 7.6. In that example, we manually calculated the number of grades in each category (i.e., 0–9, 10–19, …, 90–99 and 100) by simply looking at a set of grades. Here, lines 91–93 use a technique similar to that in Figs. 7.7–7.8 to calculate the frequency of grades in each category. Line 88 declares and creates array frequency of 11 ints to store the frequency of grades in each category. For each grade in array grades, lines 91–93 increment the appropriate frequency array element. To determine which one to increment, line 92 divides the current grade by 10 using *integer division*—e.g., if grade is 85, line 92 increments frequency[8] to update the count of grades in the range 80–89. Lines 96–111 print the bar chart (as shown in Fig. 7.15) based on the values in array frequency. Lines 106–108 of Fig. 7.14 use a value in array frequency to determine the number of asterisks to display in each bar.

Class GradeBookTest *That Demonstrates Class* GradeBook

The application of Fig. 7.15 creates an object of class GradeBook using the int array gradesArray (declared and initialized in line 7). Lines 9–10 pass a course name and gradesArray to the GradeBook constructor. Lines 11–12 display a welcome message that includes the course name stored in the GradeBook object. Line 13 invokes the GradeBook object's processGrades method. The output summarizes the 10 grades in myGradeBook.

Software Engineering Observation 7.2

A test harness (or test application) is responsible for creating an object of the class being tested and providing it with data. This data could come from any of several sources. Test data can be placed directly into an array with an array initializer, it can come from the user at the keyboard, from a file (as you'll see in Chapter 15), from a database (as you'll see in Chapter 24) or from a network (as you'll see in online Chapter 28). After passing this data to the class's constructor to instantiate the object, the test harness should call upon the object to test its methods and manipulate its data. Gathering data in the test harness like this allows the class to be more reusable, able to manipulate data from several sources.

```
1  // Fig. 7.15: GradeBookTest.java
2  // GradeBookTest creates a GradeBook object using an array of grades,
3  // then invokes method processGrades to analyze them.
4  public class GradeBookTest {
5     public static void main(String[] args) {
6        // array of student grades
7        int[] gradesArray = {87, 68, 94, 100, 83, 78, 85, 91, 76, 87};
8
9        GradeBook myGradeBook = new GradeBook(
10          "CS101 Introduction to Java Programming", gradesArray);
11       System.out.printf("Welcome to the grade book for%n%s%n%n",
12          myGradeBook.getCourseName());
```

Fig. 7.15 | GradeBookTest creates a GradeBook object using an array of grades, then invokes method processGrades to analyze them. (Part 1 of 2.)

```
        myGradeBook.processGrades();
    }
}
```

```
Welcome to the grade book for
CS101 Introduction to Java Programming

The grades are:

Student  1:  87
Student  2:  68
Student  3:  94
Student  4: 100
Student  5:  83
Student  6:  78
Student  7:  85
Student  8:  91
Student  9:  76
Student 10:  87

Class average is 84.90
Lowest grade is 68
Highest grade is 100

Grade distribution:
00-09:
10-19:
20-29:
30-39:
40-49:
50-59:
60-69: *
70-79: **
80-89: ****
90-99: **
  100: *
```

Fig. 7.15 | `GradeBookTest` creates a `GradeBook` object using an array of grades, then invokes method `processGrades` to analyze them. (Part 2 of 2.)

Java SE 8

In Chapter 17, Lambdas and Streams, the example of Fig. 17.9 uses stream methods `min`, `max`, `count` and `average` to process the elements of an `int` array elegantly and concisely without having to write iteration statements. In Chapter 23, Concurrency, the example of Fig. 23.30 uses stream method `summaryStatistics` to perform all of these operations in one method call.

7.11 Multidimensional Arrays

Multidimensional arrays with two dimensions often represent *tables* of values with data arranged in *rows* and *columns*. To identify a particular table element, you specify *two* indices. *By convention*, the first identifies the element's row and the second its column. Arrays that require two indices to identify each element are called **two-dimensional arrays**. (Multidimensional arrays can have more than two dimensions.) Java does not support multidimensional arrays directly, but it allows you to specify one-dimensional arrays whose elements are also one-dimensional arrays, thus achieving the same effect. Figure 7.16 illustrates a two-dimensional array named a with three rows and four columns (i.e., a three-by-four array). In general, an array with *m* rows and *n* columns is called an ***m*-by-*n* array**.

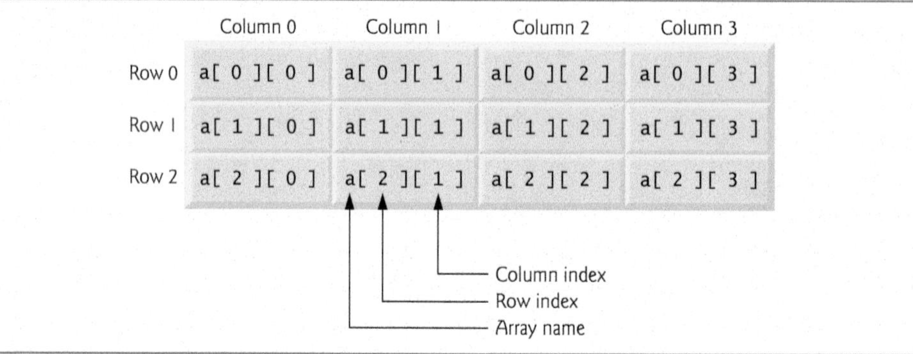

Fig. 7.16 | Two-dimensional array with three rows and four columns.

Every element in array a is identified in Fig. 7.16 by an *array-access expression* of the form `a[`*row*`][`*column*`]`; a is the name of the array, and *row* and *column* are the indices that uniquely identify each element by row and column index. The element names in *row* 0 all have a *first* index of `0`, and the element names in *column* 3 all have a *second* index of `3`.

7.11.1 Arrays of One-Dimensional Arrays

Like one-dimensional arrays, multidimensional arrays can be initialized with array initializers in declarations. A two-dimensional array b with two rows and two columns could be declared and initialized with **nested array initializers** as follows:

```
int[][] b = {{1, 2}, {3, 4}};
```

The initial values are *grouped by row* in braces. So `1` and `2` initialize `b[0][0]` and `b[0][1]`, respectively, and `3` and `4` initialize `b[1][0]` and `b[1][1]`, respectively. The compiler counts the number of nested array initializers (represented by sets of braces within the outer braces) to determine the number of *rows* in array `b`. The compiler counts the initializer values in the nested array initializer for a row to determine the number of *columns* in that row. As we'll see momentarily, this means that *rows can have different lengths*.

Multidimensional arrays are maintained as *arrays of one-dimensional arrays*. Therefore array `b` in the preceding declaration is actually composed of two separate one-dimensional arrays—one containing the values in the first nested initializer list `{1, 2}` and one containing the values in the second nested initializer list `{3, 4}`. Thus, array `b` itself is an array of two elements, each a one-dimensional array of `int` values.

7.11.2 Two-Dimensional Arrays with Rows of Different Lengths

The manner in which multidimensional arrays are represented makes them quite flexible. In fact, the lengths of the rows in array `b` are *not* required to be the same. For example,

```
int[][] b = {{1, 2}, {3, 4, 5}};
```

creates integer array b with two elements (determined by the number of nested array initializers) that represent the rows of the two-dimensional array. Each element of b is a *reference* to a one-dimensional array of int variables. The int array for row 0 is a one-dimensional array with *two* elements (1 and 2), and the int array for row 1 is a one-dimensional array with *three* elements (3, 4 and 5).

7.11.3 Creating Two-Dimensional Arrays with Array-Creation Expressions

A multidimensional array with the *same* number of columns in every row can be created with an array-creation expression. For example, the following line declares array b and assigns it a reference to a three-by-four array:

```
int[][] b = new int[3][4];
```

In this case, we use the literal values 3 and 4 to specify the number of rows and number of columns, respectively, but this is *not* required. Programs can also use variables to specify array dimensions, because *new creates arrays at execution time—not at compile time.* The elements of a multidimensional array are initialized when the array object is created.

A multidimensional array in which each row has a *different* number of columns can be created as follows:

```
int[][] b = new int[2][];    // create 2 rows
b[0] = new int[5]; // create 5 columns for row 0
b[1] = new int[3]; // create 3 columns for row 1
```

The preceding statements create a two-dimensional array with two rows. Row 0 has *five* columns, and row 1 has *three* columns.

7.11.4 Two-Dimensional Array Example: Displaying Element Values

Figure 7.17 demonstrates initializing two-dimensional arrays with array initializers and using nested for loops to **traverse** the arrays (i.e., manipulate *every* element of each array). Class InitArray's main declares two arrays. The declaration of array1 (line 7) uses nested array initializers of the *same* length to initialize the first row to the values 1, 2 and 3, and the second row to the values 4, 5 and 6. The declaration of array2 (line 8) uses nested initializers of *different* lengths. In this case, the first row is initialized to two elements with the values 1 and 2, respectively. The second row is initialized to one element with the value 3. The third row is initialized to three elements with the values 4, 5 and 6, respectively.

```
1  // Fig. 7.17: InitArray.java
2  // Initializing two-dimensional arrays.
3
4  public class InitArray {
5     // create and output two-dimensional arrays
6     public static void main(String[] args) {
7        int[][] array1 = {{1, 2, 3}, {4, 5, 6}};
8        int[][] array2 = {{1, 2}, {3}, {4, 5, 6}};
9
```

Fig. 7.17 | Initializing two-dimensional arrays. (Part 1 of 2.)

```
10        System.out.println("Values in array1 by row are");
11        outputArray(array1); // displays array1 by row
12
13        System.out.printf("%nValues in array2 by row are%n");
14        outputArray(array2); // displays array2 by row
15     }
16
17     // output rows and columns of a two-dimensional array
18     public static void outputArray(int[][] array) {
19        // loop through array's rows
20        for (int row = 0; row < array.length; row++) {
21           // loop through columns of current row
22           for (int column = 0; column < array[row].length; column++) {
23              System.out.printf("%d  ", array[row][column]);
24           }
25
26           System.out.println();
27        }
28     }
29  }
```

```
Values in array1 by row are
1  2  3
4  5  6

Values in array2 by row are
1  2
3
4  5  6
```

Fig. 7.17 | Initializing two-dimensional arrays. (Part 2 of 2.)

Lines 11 and 14 call method `outputArray` (lines 18–28) to output the elements of `array1` and `array2`, respectively. Method `outputArray`'s parameter—`int[][] array`—indicates that the method receives a two-dimensional array. The nested `for` statement (lines 20–27) outputs the rows of a two-dimensional array. In the loop-continuation condition of the outer `for` statement, the expression `array.length` determines the number of rows in the array. In the inner `for` statement, the expression `array[row].length` determines the number of columns in the current row of the array. The inner `for` statement's condition enables the loop to determine the exact number of columns in each row. We demonstrate nested enhanced `for` statements in Fig. 7.18.

7.11.5 Common Multidimensional-Array Manipulations Performed with for Statements

Many common array manipulations use `for` statements. As an example, the following `for` statement sets all the elements in row 2 of array a in Fig. 7.16 to zero:

```
for (int column = 0; column < a[2].length; column++) {
   a[2][column] = 0;
}
```

We specified row 2; therefore, we know that the *first* index is always 2 (0 is the first row, and 1 is the second row). This for loop varies only the *second* index (i.e., the column index). If row 2 of array a contains four elements, then the preceding for statement is equivalent to the assignment statements

```
a[2][0] = 0;
a[2][1] = 0;
a[2][2] = 0;
a[2][3] = 0;
```

The following nested for statement totals the values of all the elements in array a:

```
int total = 0;
for (int row = 0; row < a.length; row++) {
   for (int column = 0; column < a[row].length; column++) {
      total += a[row][column];
   }
}
```

These nested for statements total the array elements *one row at a time*. The outer for statement begins by setting the row index to 0 so that the first row's elements can be totaled by the inner for statement. The outer for then increments row to 1 so that the second row can be totaled. Then, the outer for increments row to 2 so that the third row can be totaled. The variable total can be displayed when the outer for statement terminates. In the next example, we show how to process a two-dimensional array in a similar manner using nested enhanced for statements.

7.12 Case Study: Class GradeBook Using a Two-Dimensional Array

In Section 7.10, we presented class GradeBook (Fig. 7.14), which used a one-dimensional array to store student grades on a single exam. In most semesters, students take several exams. Professors are likely to want to analyze grades across the entire semester, both for a single student and for the class as a whole.

Storing Student Grades in a Two-Dimensional Array in Class GradeBook

Figure 7.18 contains a GradeBook class that uses a two-dimensional array grades to store the grades of *several* students on *multiple* exams. Each *row* of the array represents a *single* student's grades for the entire course, and each *column* represents the grades of *all* the students who took a particular exam. Class GradeBookTest (Fig. 7.19) passes the array as an argument to the GradeBook constructor. In this example, we use a ten-by-three array for ten students' grades on three exams. Five methods perform array manipulations to process the grades. Each method is similar to its counterpart in the earlier one-dimensional array version of GradeBook (Fig. 7.14). Method getMinimum (lines 39–55 of Fig. 7.18) determines the lowest grade of any student for the semester. Method getMaximum (lines 58–74) determines the highest grade of any student for the semester. Method getAverage (lines 77–87) determines a particular student's semester average. Method outputBarChart (lines 90–121) outputs a grade bar chart for the entire semester's student grades. Method outputGrades (lines 124–148) outputs the array in a tabular format, along with each student's semester average.

```java
// Fig. 7.18: GradeBook.java
// GradeBook class using a two-dimensional array to store grades.

public class GradeBook {
   private String courseName; // name of course this grade book represents
   private int[][] grades; // two-dimensional array of student grades

   // two-argument constructor initializes courseName and grades array
   public GradeBook(String courseName, int[][] grades) {
      this.courseName = courseName;
      this.grades = grades;
   }

   // method to set the course name
   public void setCourseName(String courseName) {
      this.courseName = courseName;
   }

   // method to retrieve the course name
   public String getCourseName() {
      return courseName;
   }

   // perform various operations on the data
   public void processGrades() {
      // output grades array
      outputGrades();

      // call methods getMinimum and getMaximum
      System.out.printf("%n%s %d%n%s %d%n%n",
         "Lowest grade in the grade book is", getMinimum(),
         "Highest grade in the grade book is", getMaximum());

      // output grade distribution chart of all grades on all tests
      outputBarChart();
   }

   // find minimum grade
   public int getMinimum() {
      // assume first element of grades array is smallest
      int lowGrade = grades[0][0];

      // loop through rows of grades array
      for (int[] studentGrades : grades) {
         // loop through columns of current row
         for (int grade : studentGrades) {
            // if grade less than lowGrade, assign it to lowGrade
            if (grade < lowGrade) {
               lowGrade = grade;
            }
         }
      }
```

Fig. 7.18 | GradeBook class using a two-dimensional array to store grades. (Part 1 of 3.)

```

      return lowGrade;
   }

   // find maximum grade
   public int getMaximum() {
      // assume first element of grades array is largest
      int highGrade = grades[0][0];

      // loop through rows of grades array
      for (int[] studentGrades : grades) {
         // loop through columns of current row
         for (int grade : studentGrades) {
            // if grade greater than highGrade, assign it to highGrade
            if (grade > highGrade) {
               highGrade = grade;
            }
         }
      }

      return highGrade;
   }

   // determine average grade for particular set of grades
   public double getAverage(int[] setOfGrades) {
      int total = 0;

      // sum grades for one student
      for (int grade : setOfGrades) {
         total += grade;
      }

      // return average of grades
      return (double) total / setOfGrades.length;
   }

   // output bar chart displaying overall grade distribution
   public void outputBarChart() {
      System.out.println("Overall grade distribution:");

      // stores frequency of grades in each range of 10 grades
      int[] frequency = new int[11];

      // for each grade in GradeBook, increment the appropriate frequency
      for (int[] studentGrades : grades) {
         for (int grade : studentGrades) {
            ++frequency[grade / 10];
         }
      }

```

Fig. 7.18 | GradeBook class using a two-dimensional array to store grades. (Part 2 of 3.)

```
103         // for each grade frequency, print bar in chart
104         for (int count = 0; count < frequency.length; count++) {
105            // output bar label ("00-09: ", ..., "90-99: ", "100: ")
106            if (count == 10) {
107               System.out.printf("%5d: ", 100);
108            }
109            else {
110               System.out.printf("%02d-%02d: ",
111                  count * 10, count * 10 + 9);
112            }
113
114            // print bar of asterisks
115            for (int stars = 0; stars < frequency[count]; stars++) {
116               System.out.print("*");
117            }
118
119            System.out.println();
120         }
121      }
122
123      // output the contents of the grades array
124      public void outputGrades() {
125         System.out.printf("The grades are:%n%n");
126         System.out.print("            "); // align column heads
127
128         // create a column heading for each of the tests
129         for (int test = 0; test < grades[0].length; test++) {
130            System.out.printf("Test %d  ", test + 1);
131         }
132
133         System.out.println("Average"); // student average column heading
134
135         // create rows/columns of text representing array grades
136         for (int student = 0; student < grades.length; student++) {
137            System.out.printf("Student %2d", student + 1);
138
139            for (int test : grades[student]) { // output student's grades
140               System.out.printf("%8d", test);
141            }
142
143            // call method getAverage to calculate student's average grade;
144            // pass row of grades as the argument to getAverage
145            double average = getAverage(grades[student]);
146            System.out.printf("%9.2f%n", average);
147         }
148      }
149   }
```

Fig. 7.18 | GradeBook class using a two-dimensional array to store grades. (Part 3 of 3.)

Methods `getMinimum` *and* `getMaximum`

Methods `getMinimum`, `getMaximum`, `outputBarChart` and `outputGrades` each loop through array `grades` by using nested `for` statements—for example, the nested enhanced `for` statement (lines 44–52) from the declaration of method `getMinimum`. The outer enhanced for statement iterates through the two-dimensional array grades, assigning successive rows to parameter studentGrades on successive iterations. The square brackets following the parameter name indicate that studentGrades refers to a one-dimensional int array—namely, a row in array grades containing one student's grades. To find the lowest overall grade, the inner for statement compares the elements of the current one-dimensional array studentGrades to variable lowGrade. For example, on the first iteration of the outer for, row 0 of grades is assigned to parameter studentGrades. The inner enhanced for statement then loops through studentGrades and compares each grade value with lowGrade. If a grade is less than lowGrade, lowGrade is set to that grade. On the second iteration of the outer enhanced for statement, row 1 of grades is assigned to studentGrades, and the elements of this row are compared with variable lowGrade. This repeats until all rows of grades have been traversed. When execution of the nested statement is complete, lowGrade contains the lowest grade in the two-dimensional array. Method getMaximum works similarly to method getMinimum.

Method outputBarChart

Method outputBarChart in Fig. 7.18 is nearly identical to the one in Fig. 7.14. However, to output the overall grade distribution for a whole semester, the method here uses nested enhanced for statements (lines 97–101) to create the one-dimensional array frequency based on all the grades in the two-dimensional array. The rest of the code in each of the two outputBarChart methods that displays the chart is identical.

Method outputGrades

Method outputGrades (lines 124–148) uses nested for statements to output values of the array grades and each student's semester average. The output (Fig. 7.19) shows the result, which resembles the tabular format of a professor's physical grade book. Lines 129–131 of of Fig. 7.18 print the column headings for each test. We use a counter-controlled for statement here so that we can identify each test with a number. Similarly, the for statement in lines 136–147 first outputs a row label using a counter variable to identify each student (line 137). Although array indices start at 0, lines 130 and 137 output test + 1 and student + 1, respectively, to produce test and student numbers starting at 1 (see the output in Fig. 7.19). The inner for statement (lines 139–141 of Fig. 7.18) uses the outer for statement's counter variable student to loop through a specific row of array grades and output each student's test grade. An enhanced for statement can be nested in a counter-controlled for statement, and vice versa. Finally, line 145 obtains each student's semester average by passing the current row of grades (i.e., grades[student]) to method getAverage.

Method getAverage

Method getAverage (lines 77–87) takes one argument—a one-dimensional array of test results for a particular student. When line 145 calls getAverage, the argument is grades[student], which specifies that a particular row of the two-dimensional array grades should be passed to getAverage. For example, based on the array created in Fig. 7.19, the argument grades[1] represents the three values (a one-dimensional array of grades) stored in row 1 of the two-dimensional array grades. Recall that a two-dimensional array is one whose elements are one-dimensional arrays. Method getAverage calculates the sum of the array elements, divides the total by the number of test results and returns the floating-point result as a double value (line 86 of Fig. 7.18).

Class **GradeBookTest** *That Demonstrates Class* **GradeBook**

Figure 7.19 creates an object of class `GradeBook` using the two-dimensional array of `int`s named `gradesArray` (declared and initialized in lines 8–17). Lines 19–20 pass a course name and `gradesArray` to the `GradeBook` constructor. Lines 21–22 display a welcome message containing the course name, then line 23 invokes `myGradeBook`'s `processGrades` method to display a report summarizing the students' grades for the semester.

```
1  // Fig. 7.19: GradeBookTest.java
2  // GradeBookTest creates GradeBook object using a two-dimensional array
3  // of grades, then invokes method processGrades to analyze them.
4  public class GradeBookTest {
5     // main method begins program execution
6     public static void main(String[] args) {
7        // two-dimensional array of student grades
8        int[][] gradesArray = {{87, 96, 70},
9                               {68, 87, 90},
10                              {94, 100, 90},
11                              {100, 81, 82},
12                              {83, 65, 85},
13                              {78, 87, 65},
14                              {85, 75, 83},
15                              {91, 94, 100},
16                              {76, 72, 84},
17                              {87, 93, 73}};
18
19       GradeBook myGradeBook = new GradeBook(
20          "CS101 Introduction to Java Programming", gradesArray);
21       System.out.printf("Welcome to the grade book for%n%s%n%n",
22          myGradeBook.getCourseName());
23       myGradeBook.processGrades();
24    }
25 }
```

```
Welcome to the grade book for
CS101 Introduction to Java Programming

The grades are:

            Test 1  Test 2  Test 3  Average
Student  1      87      96      70    84.33
Student  2      68      87      90    81.67
Student  3      94     100      90    94.67
Student  4     100      81      82    87.67
Student  5      83      65      85    77.67
Student  6      78      87      65    76.67
Student  7      85      75      83    81.00
Student  8      91      94     100    95.00
Student  9      76      72      84    77.33
Student 10      87      93      73    84.33
```

Fig. 7.19 | `GradeBookTest` creates `GradeBook` object using a two-dimensional array of grades, then invokes method `processGrades` to analyze them. (Part 1 of 2.)

```
Lowest grade in the grade book is 65
Highest grade in the grade book is 100

Overall grade distribution:
00-09:
10-19:
20-29:
30-39:
40-49:
50-59:
60-69: ***
70-79: ******
80-89: ***********
90-99: *******
  100: ***
```

Fig. 7.19 | `GradeBookTest` creates `GradeBook` object using a two-dimensional array of grades, then invokes method `processGrades` to analyze them. (Part 2 of 2.)

7.13 Variable-Length Argument Lists

With **variable-length argument lists**, you can create methods that receive an unspecified number of arguments. A type followed by an **ellipsis** (`...`) in a method's parameter list indicates that the method receives a variable number of arguments of that particular type. This use of the ellipsis can occur only *once* in a parameter list, and the ellipsis, together with its type and the parameter name, must be placed at the *end* of the parameter list. While you can use method overloading and array passing to accomplish much of what is accomplished with variable-length argument lists, using an ellipsis in a method's parameter list is more concise.

Figure 7.20 demonstrates method `average` (lines 6–15), which receives a variable-length sequence of `double`s. Java treats the variable-length argument list as an array whose elements are all of the same type. So, the method body can manipulate the parameter `numbers` as an array of `double`s. Lines 10–12 use the enhanced `for` loop to walk through the array and calculate the total of the `double`s in the array. Line 14 accesses `numbers.length` to obtain the size of the `numbers` array for use in the averaging calculation. Lines 27, 29 and 31 in `main` call method `average` with two, three and four arguments, respectively. Method `average` has a variable-length argument list (line 6), so it can average as many `double` arguments as the caller passes. The output shows that each call to method `average` returns the correct value.

Common Programming Error 7.5

Placing an ellipsis indicating a variable-length argument list in the middle of a parameter list is a syntax error. An ellipsis may be placed only at the end of the parameter list.

```
1  // Fig. 7.20: VarargsTest.java
2  // Using variable-length argument lists.
3
```

Fig. 7.20 | Using variable-length argument lists. (Part 1 of 2.)

```java
public class VarargsTest {
   // calculate average
   public static double average(double... numbers) {
      double total = 0.0;

      // calculate total using the enhanced for statement
      for (double d : numbers) {
         total += d;
      }

      return total / numbers.length;
   }

   public static void main(String[] args) {
      double d1 = 10.0;
      double d2 = 20.0;
      double d3 = 30.0;
      double d4 = 40.0;

      System.out.printf("d1 = %.1f%nd2 = %.1f%nd3 = %.1f%nd4 = %.1f%n%n",
         d1, d2, d3, d4);

      System.out.printf("Average of d1 and d2 is %.1f%n",
         average(d1, d2));
      System.out.printf("Average of d1, d2 and d3 is %.1f%n",
         average(d1, d2, d3));
      System.out.printf("Average of d1, d2, d3 and d4 is %.1f%n",
         average(d1, d2, d3, d4));
   }
}
```

```
d1 = 10.0
d2 = 20.0
d3 = 30.0
d4 = 40.0

Average of d1 and d2 is 15.0
Average of d1, d2 and d3 is 20.0
Average of d1, d2, d3 and d4 is 25.0
```

Fig. 7.20 | Using variable-length argument lists. (Part 2 of 2.)

7.14 Using Command-Line Arguments

It's possible to pass arguments from the command line to an application via method `main`'s `String[]` parameter, which receives an array of `String`s. By convention, this parameter is named `args`. When an application is executed using the `java` command, Java passes the **command-line arguments** that appear after the class name in the `java` command to the application's `main` method as `String`s in the array `args`. The number of command-line arguments is obtained by accessing the array's `length` attribute. Common uses of command-line arguments include passing options and filenames to applications.

Our next example uses command-line arguments to determine the size of an array, the value of its first element and the increment used to calculate the values of the array's remaining elements. The command

```
java InitArray 5 0 4
```

passes three arguments, `5`, `0` and `4`, to the application `InitArray`. Command-line arguments are separated by white space, *not* commas. When this command executes, `InitArray`'s `main` method receives the three-element array `args` (i.e., `args.length` is `3`) in which `args[0]` contains the `String` `"5"`, `args[1]` contains the `String` `"0"` and `args[2]` contains the `String` `"4"`. The program determines how to use these arguments—in Fig. 7.21 we convert the three command-line arguments to `int` values and use them to initialize an array. When the program executes, if `args.length` is not `3`, the program prints an error message and terminates (lines 7–11). Otherwise, lines 12–32 initialize and display the array based on the values of the command-line arguments.

```
1  // Fig. 7.21: InitArray.java
2  // Initializing an array using command-line arguments.
3
4  public class InitArray {
5     public static void main(String[] args) {
6        // check number of command-line arguments
7        if (args.length != 3) {
8           System.out.printf(
9              "Error: Please re-enter the entire command, including%n" +
10             "an array size, initial value and increment.%n");
11       }
12       else {
13          // get array size from first command-line argument
14          int arrayLength = Integer.parseInt(args[0]);
15          int[] array = new int[arrayLength];
16
17          // get initial value and increment from command-line arguments
18          int initialValue = Integer.parseInt(args[1]);
19          int increment = Integer.parseInt(args[2]);
20
21          // calculate value for each array element
22          for (int counter = 0; counter < array.length; counter++) {
23             array[counter] = initialValue + increment * counter;
24          }
25
26          System.out.printf("%s%8s%n", "Index", "Value");
27
28          // display array index and value
29          for (int counter = 0; counter < array.length; counter++) {
30             System.out.printf("%5d%8d%n", counter, array[counter]);
31          }
32       }
33    }
34 }
```

Fig. 7.21 | Initializing an array using command-line arguments. (Part 1 of 2.)

```
java InitArray
Error: Please re-enter the entire command, including
an array size, initial value and increment.
```

```
java InitArray 5 0 4
Index   Value
    0       0
    1       4
    2       8
    3      12
    4      16
```

```
java InitArray 8 1 2
Index   Value
    0       1
    1       3
    2       5
    3       7
    4       9
    5      11
    6      13
    7      15
```

Fig. 7.21 | Initializing an array using command-line arguments. (Part 2 of 2.)

Line 14 gets `args[0]`—a `String` that specifies the array size—and converts it to an `int` value that the program uses to create the array in line 15. The `static` method `parseInt` of class `Integer` converts its `String` argument to an `int`.

Lines 18–19 convert the `args[1]` and `args[2]` command-line arguments to `int` values and store them in `initialValue` and `increment`, respectively. Lines 22–24 calculate the value for each array element.

The output of the first execution shows that the application received an insufficient number of command-line arguments. The second execution uses command-line arguments 5, 0 and 4 to specify the size of the array (5), the value of the first element (0) and the increment of each value in the array (4), respectively. The corresponding output shows that these values create an array containing the integers 0, 4, 8, 12 and 16. The output from the third execution shows that the command-line arguments 8, 1 and 2 produce an array whose 8 elements are the nonnegative odd integers from 1 to 15.

7.15 Class Arrays

Class **`Arrays`** helps you avoid reinventing the wheel by providing `static` methods for common array manipulations. These methods include **`sort`** for *sorting* an array (i.e., arranging elements into ascending order), **`binarySearch`** for *searching* a *sorted* array (i.e., determining whether an array contains a specific value and, if so, where the value is located), **`equals`** for *comparing* arrays and **`fill`** for *placing values into an array*. These methods are overloaded for primitive-type arrays and for arrays of objects. Our focus in this section is on using the built-in capabilities provided by the Java API. Chapter 19, Searching, Sorting and Big O, shows how to implement your own sorting and searching algorithms, a subject of great interest to computer-science researchers and students, and to developers of high-performance systems.

Figure 7.22 uses `Arrays` methods `sort`, `binarySearch`, `equals` and `fill`, and shows how to *copy* arrays with class `System`'s `static` **arraycopy method**. In `main`, line 9 sorts the elements of array `doubleArray`. The `static` method `sort` of class `Arrays` orders the array's elements in *ascending* order by default. We discuss how to sort in *descending* order later in the chapter. Overloaded versions of `sort` allow you to sort a specific range of elements within the array. Lines 10–14 output the sorted array.

```
1  // Fig. 7.22: ArrayManipulations.java
2  // Arrays class methods and System.arraycopy.
3  import java.util.Arrays;
4
5  public class ArrayManipulations {
6     public static void main(String[] args) {
7        // sort doubleArray into ascending order
8        double[] doubleArray = {8.4, 9.3, 0.2, 7.9, 3.4};
9        Arrays.sort(doubleArray);
10       System.out.printf("%ndoubleArray: ");
11
12       for (double value : doubleArray) {
13          System.out.printf("%.1f ", value);
14       }
15
16       // fill 10-element array with 7s
17       int[] filledIntArray = new int[10];
18       Arrays.fill(filledIntArray, 7);
19       displayArray(filledIntArray, "filledIntArray");
20
21       // copy array intArray into array intArrayCopy
22       int[] intArray = {1, 2, 3, 4, 5, 6};
23       int[] intArrayCopy = new int[intArray.length];
24       System.arraycopy(intArray, 0, intArrayCopy, 0, intArray.length);
25       displayArray(intArray, "intArray");
26       displayArray(intArrayCopy, "intArrayCopy");
27
28       // compare intArray and intArrayCopy for equality
29       boolean b = Arrays.equals(intArray, intArrayCopy);
30       System.out.printf("%n%nintArray %s intArrayCopy%n",
31          (b ? "==" : "!="));
32
33       // compare intArray and filledIntArray for equality
34       b = Arrays.equals(intArray, filledIntArray);
35       System.out.printf("intArray %s filledIntArray%n",
36          (b ? "==" : "!="));
37
38       // search intArray for the value 5
39       int location = Arrays.binarySearch(intArray, 5);
40
```

Fig. 7.22 | `Arrays` class methods and `System.arraycopy`. (Part 1 of 2.)

```
41          if (location >= 0) {
42             System.out.printf(
43                "Found 5 at element %d in intArray%n", location);
44          }
45          else {
46             System.out.println("5 not found in intArray");
47          }
48
49          // search intArray for the value 8763
50          location = Arrays.binarySearch(intArray, 8763);
51
52          if (location >= 0) {
53             System.out.printf(
54                "Found 8763 at element %d in intArray%n", location);
55          }
56          else {
57             System.out.println("8763 not found in intArray");
58          }
59       }
60
61       // output values in each array
62       public static void displayArray(int[] array, String description) {
63          System.out.printf("%n%s: ", description);
64
65          for (int value : array) {
66             System.out.printf("%d ", value);
67          }
68       }
69    }
```

```
doubleArray: 0.2 3.4 7.9 8.4 9.3
filledIntArray: 7 7 7 7 7 7 7 7 7 7
intArray: 1 2 3 4 5 6
intArrayCopy: 1 2 3 4 5 6

intArray == intArrayCopy
intArray != filledIntArray
Found 5 at element 4 in intArray
8763 not found in intArray
```

Fig. 7.22 | `Arrays` class methods and `System.arraycopy`. (Part 2 of 2.)

Line 18 calls `static` method `fill` of class `Arrays` to populate all 10 elements of `filledIntArray` with 7s. Overloaded versions of `fill` allow you to populate a specific range of elements with the same value. Line 19 calls our class's `displayArray` method (declared at lines 62–68) to output the contents of `filledIntArray`.

Line 24 copies the elements of `intArray` into `intArrayCopy`. The first argument (`intArray`) passed to `System` method `arraycopy` is the array from which elements are to be copied. The second argument (`0`) is the index that specifies the *starting point* in the range of elements to copy from the array. This value can be any valid array index. The third argument (`intArrayCopy`) specifies the *destination array* that will store the copy. The fourth argument (`0`) specifies the index in the destination array *where the first copied ele-*

ment should be stored. The last argument specifies the *number of elements to copy* from the array in the first argument. In this case, we copy all the elements in the array.

Lines 29 and 34 call `static` method `equals` of class `Arrays` to determine whether all the elements of two arrays are equivalent. If the arrays contain the same elements in the same order, the method returns `true`; otherwise, it returns `false`.

Error-Prevention Tip 7.3

When comparing array contents, always use `Arrays.equals(array1, array2)`*, which compares the two arrays' contents, rather than* `array1.equals(array2)`*, which compares whether* `array1` *and* `array2` *refer to the same array object.*

Lines 39 and 50 call `static` method `binarySearch` of class `Arrays` to perform a binary search on `intArray`, using the second argument (`5` and `8763`, respectively) as the key. If the value is found, `binarySearch` returns the index of the element; otherwise, `binarySearch` returns a negative value. The negative value returned is based on the search key's *insertion point*—the index where the key would be inserted in the array if we were performing an insert operation. After `binarySearch` determines the insertion point, it changes its sign to negative and subtracts `1` to obtain the return value. For example, in Fig. 7.22, the insertion point for the value `8763` is the element with index `6` in the array. Method `binarySearch` changes the insertion point to `-6`, subtracts `1` from it and returns the value `-7`. Subtracting `1` from the insertion point guarantees that method `binarySearch` returns positive values (>= 0) if and only if the key is found. This return value is useful for inserting elements in a sorted array. Chapter 19 discusses binary searching in detail.

Common Programming Error 7.6

Passing an unsorted array to `binarySearch` *is a logic error—the value returned is undefined.*

Java SE 8—Class `Arrays` *Method* `parallelSort`

The `Arrays` class now has several new "parallel" methods that take advantage of multi-core 8
hardware. `Arrays` method `parallelSort` can sort large arrays more efficiently on multi-core systems. In Section 23.12, we create a very large array and use features of the Date/Time API to compare how long it takes to sort the array with `sort` and `parallelSort`.

7.16 Introduction to Collections and Class ArrayList

The Java API provides several predefined data structures, called **collections**, used to store groups of related objects in memory. These classes provide efficient methods that organize, store and retrieve your data *without* requiring knowledge of how the data is being *stored.* This reduces application-development time.

You've used arrays to store sequences of objects. Arrays do not automatically change their size at execution time to accommodate additional elements. The collection class **`ArrayList<E>`** (package `java.util`) provides a convenient solution to this problem—it can *dynamically* change its size to accommodate more elements. The `E` (by convention) is a *placeholder*—when declaring a new `ArrayList`, replace it with the type of elements that you want the `ArrayList` to hold. For example,

```
ArrayList<String> list;
```

declares list as an ArrayList collection that can store only Strings. Classes with this kind of placeholder that can be used with any type are called **generic classes.** *Only reference types can be used to declare variables and create objects of generic classes.* However, Java provides a mechanism—known as *boxing*—that allows primitive values to be wrapped as objects for use with generic classes. So, for example,

```
ArrayList<Integer> integers;
```

declares integers as an ArrayList that can store only Integers. When you place an int value into an ArrayList<Integer>, the int value is *boxed* (wrapped) as an Integer object, and when you get an Integer object from an ArrayList<Integer>, then assign the object to an int variable, the int value inside the object is *unboxed* (unwrapped).

Additional generic collection classes and generics are discussed in Chapters 16 and 20, respectively. Figure 7.23 shows some common methods of class ArrayList<E>.

Method	Description
add	Overloaded to add an element to the *end* of the ArrayList or at a specific index in the ArrayList.
clear	Removes all the elements from the ArrayList.
contains	Returns true if the ArrayList contains the specified element; otherwise, returns false.
get	Returns the element at the specified index.
indexOf	Returns the index of the first occurrence of the specified element in the ArrayList.
remove	Overloaded. Removes the first occurrence of the specified value or the element at the specified index.
size	Returns the number of elements stored in the ArrayList.
trimToSize	Trims the capacity of the ArrayList to the current number of elements.

Fig. 7.23 | Some methods of class ArrayList<E>.

Demonstrating an ArrayList<String>

Figure 7.24 demonstrates some common ArrayList capabilities. Line 8 creates a new empty ArrayList of Strings with a default initial capacity of 10 elements. The capacity indicates how many items the ArrayList can hold *without growing*. ArrayList is implemented using a conventional array behind the scenes. When the ArrayList grows, it must create a larger internal array and *copy* each element to the new array. This is a time-consuming operation. It would be inefficient for the ArrayList to grow each time an element is added. Instead, it grows only when an element is added *and* the number of elements is equal to the capacity—i.e., there's no space for the new element.

```
1  // Fig. 7.24: ArrayListCollection.java
2  // Generic ArrayList<E> collection demonstration.
3  import java.util.ArrayList;
4
```

Fig. 7.24 | Generic ArrayList<E> collection demonstration. (Part 1 of 3.)

```
public class ArrayListCollection {
   public static void main(String[] args) {
      // create a new ArrayList of Strings with an initial capacity of 10
      ArrayList<String> items = new ArrayList<String>();

      items.add("red"); // append an item to the list
      items.add(0, "yellow"); // insert "yellow" at index 0

      // header
      System.out.print(
         "Display list contents with counter-controlled loop:");

      // display the colors in the list
      for (int i = 0; i < items.size(); i++) {
         System.out.printf(" %s", items.get(i));
      }

      // display colors using enhanced for in the display method
      display(items,
         "%nDisplay list contents with enhanced for statement:");

      items.add("green"); // add "green" to the end of the list
      items.add("yellow"); // add "yellow" to the end of the list
      display(items, "List with two new elements:");

      items.remove("yellow"); // remove the first "yellow"
      display(items, "Remove first instance of yellow:");

      items.remove(1); // remove item at index 1
      display(items, "Remove second list element (green):");

      // check if a value is in the List
      System.out.printf("\"red\" is %sin the list%n",
         items.contains("red") ? "": "not ");

      // display number of elements in the List
      System.out.printf("Size: %s%n", items.size());
   }

   // display the ArrayList's elements on the console
   public static void display(ArrayList<String> items, String header) {
      System.out.printf(header); // display header

      // display each element in items
      for (String item : items) {
         System.out.printf(" %s", item);
      }

      System.out.println();
   }
}
```

Fig. 7.24 | Generic ArrayList<E> collection demonstration. (Part 2 of 3.)

```
Display list contents with counter-controlled loop: yellow red
Display list contents with enhanced for statement: yellow red
List with two new elements: yellow red green yellow
Remove first instance of yellow: red green yellow
Remove second list element (green): red yellow
"red" is in the list
Size: 2
```

Fig. 7.24 | Generic ArrayList<E> collection demonstration. (Part 3 of 3.)

The **add** method adds elements to the ArrayList (lines 10–11). The add method with *one* argument *appends* its argument to the *end* of the ArrayList. The add method with *two* arguments *inserts* a new element at the specified *position*. The first argument is an index. As with arrays, collection indices start at zero. The second argument is the *value* to insert at that *index*. The indices of all subsequent elements are incremented by one. Inserting an element is usually slower than adding an element to the end of the ArrayList.

Lines 18–20 display the items in the ArrayList. Method **size** returns the number of elements currently in the ArrayList. Method **get** (line 19) obtains the element at a specified index. Lines 23–24 display the elements again by invoking method display (defined at lines 45–54). Lines 26–27 add two more elements to the ArrayList, then line 28 displays the elements again to confirm that the two elements were added to the *end* of the collection.

The **remove** method is used to remove an element with a specific value (line 30). It removes only the first such element. If no such element is in the ArrayList, remove does nothing. An overloaded version of the method removes the element at the specified index (line 33). When an element is removed, the indices of any elements after the removed element decrease by one.

Line 38 uses the **contains** method to check if an item is in the ArrayList. The contains method returns true if the element is found in the ArrayList, and false otherwise. The method compares its argument to each element of the ArrayList in order, so using contains on a large ArrayList can be *inefficient*. Line 41 displays the ArrayList's size.

Diamond (<>) Notation for Creating an Object of a Generic Class

Consider line 8 of Fig. 7.24:

```
ArrayList<String> items = new ArrayList<String>();
```

Notice that ArrayList<String> appears in the variable declaration *and* in the class instance creation expression. The **diamond (<>) notation** simplifies statements like this. Using <> in a class instance creation expression for an object of a *generic* class tells the compiler to determine what belongs in the angle brackets. The preceding statement can be written as:

```
ArrayList<String> items = new ArrayList<>();
```

When the compiler encounters the diamond (<>) in the class instance creation expression, it uses the declaration of variable items to determine the ArrayList's element type (String)—this is known as *inferring the element type*.

7.17 (Optional) GUI and Graphics Case Study: Drawing Arcs

In this section, we build a **Draw Rainbow** app that uses arrays and iteration statements to draw a rainbow with `GraphicsContext` method `fillArc`. Drawing arcs in JavaFX is similar to drawing ovals—an arc is simply a section of an oval.

Creating the Draw Rainbow *App's GUI*

The app's GUI is defined in `DrawRainbow.fxml`. We reused the `DrawLines.fxml` GUI shown in Fig. 4.17, but made the following changes to `DrawRainbow.fxml`:

- We specified `DrawRainbowController` as the app's **Controller class** in the Scene Builder **Document** window's **Controller** section.
- We set the `Button`'s **Text** property to `Draw Rainbow` (in the **Inspector**'s **Properties** section) and set the `Button`'s **On Action** event handler to `drawRainbowButtonPressed` (in the **Inspector**'s **Code** section).
- We changed the `Canvas`'s **Width** and **Height** properties (in the **Inspector**'s **Layout** section) to `400` and `200`, respectively.

Class `DrawSmileyController`

Again, we do not show the code for `DrawRainbow.java`, because the only changes from earlier examples are the name of the FXML file to load (`DrawRainbow.fxml`) and the text displayed in the stage's title bar (`Draw Rainbow`).

In Fig. 7.25, lines 16–17 use various predefined `Color`s to initialize an array with the colors of the rainbow, starting with the innermost arcs first. The array begins with two `Color.WHITE` elements, which, as you'll soon see, are for drawing the empty arcs at the center of the rainbow.

```
1  // Fig. 7.25: DrawRainbowController.java
2  // Drawing a rainbow using arcs.
3  import javafx.event.ActionEvent;
4  import javafx.fxml.FXML;
5  import javafx.scene.canvas.Canvas;
6  import javafx.scene.canvas.GraphicsContext;
7  import javafx.scene.paint.Color;
8  import javafx.scene.shape.ArcType;
9
10 public class DrawRainbowController {
11    @FXML private Canvas canvas;
12
13    // colors to use in the rainbow, starting from the innermost
14    // The two white entries result in an empty arc in the center
15    private final Color[] colors = {
16       Color.WHITE, Color.WHITE, Color.VIOLET, Color.INDIGO, Color.BLUE,
17       Color.GREEN, Color.YELLOW, Color.ORANGE, Color.RED};
18
19    // draws a rainbow using arcs
20    @FXML
21    void drawRainbowButtonPressed(ActionEvent event) {
```

Fig. 7.25 | Drawing a rainbow using arcs. (Part 1 of 2.)

```
22        // get the GraphicsContext, which is used to draw on the Canvas
23        GraphicsContext gc = canvas.getGraphicsContext2D();
24
25        final int radius = 20; // radius of an arc
26
27        // draw the rainbow near the bottom-center
28        final double centerX = canvas.getWidth() / 2;
29        final double maxY = canvas.getHeight() - 10;
30
31        // draws filled arcs starting with the outermost
32        for (int counter = colors.length; counter > 0; counter--) {
33           // set the color for the current arc
34           gc.setFill(colors[counter - 1]);
35
36           // fill the arc from 0 to 180 degrees
37           gc.fillArc(centerX - counter * radius,
38              maxY - counter * radius, counter * radius * 2,
39              counter * radius * 2, 0, 180, ArcType.OPEN);
40        }
41     }
42  }
```

Fig. 7.25 | Drawing a rainbow using arcs. (Part 2 of 2.)

Line 25 in method `drawRainbowButtonPressed` declares local variable `radius`, which determines each arc's radius. Local variables `centerX` and `maxY` (lines 28–29) determine the location of the midpoint on the rainbow's base. Lines 32–40 use control variable `counter` to count backwards from the array's elements, drawing the largest arcs first and placing each successive smaller arc on top of the previous one. Line 34 uses an element from the `colors` array to set the fill color for the current arc. The two `Color.WHITE` entries at the beginning of the array create the empty white arc in the center. You can change the individual colors and the number of entries in the array to create new designs.

The **`fillArc`** method call at lines 37–39 draws a filled semicircle. Method `fillArc` requires six parameters. The first four represent the bounding rectangle in which the arc will be drawn. The first two of these specify the coordinates for the bounding rectangle's upper-left corner, and the next two specify its width and height. The fifth parameter is the starting angle on the oval, and the sixth specifies the **sweep**, or the amount of arc to cover. The starting angle and sweep are measured in degrees, with zero degrees pointing right. A *positive* sweep draws the arc *counterclockwise*, while a *negative* sweep draws the arc *clockwise*. The last argument—`ArcType.OPEN`—specifies that the arc's endpoints should not be connected with a line. You can see the other `ArcType` options at

```
https://docs.oracle.com/javase/8/javafx/api/javafx/scene/shape/
   ArcType.html
```

Method **`strokeArc`** requires the same parameters as `fillArc`, but draws the edge of the arc rather than filling it.

GUI and Graphics Case Study Exercises

7.1 ***(Drawing a Spiral with Lines)*** Draw a square-shaped spiral (Fig. 7.26), centered on the `Canvas`, using method `strokeLine`. One technique is to use a loop that increases the line length after drawing every second line. The direction in which to draw the next line should follow a distinct pattern, such as down, left, up, right.

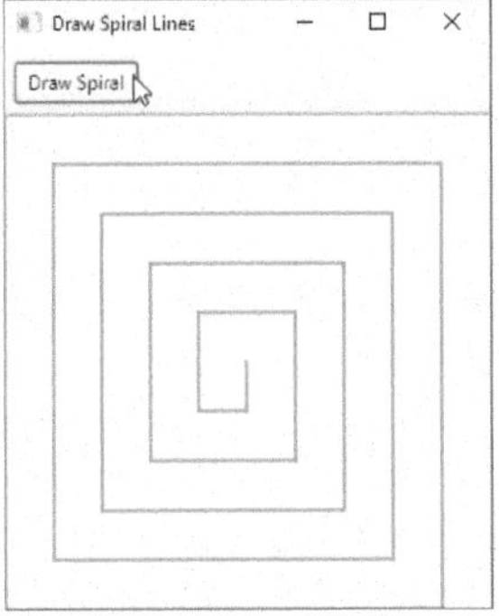

Fig. 7.26 | Drawing a spiral using `strokeLine`.

7.2 ***(Drawing a Spiral with Arcs)*** Draw a circular spiral (Fig. 7.27), using method `strokeArc` to draw one semicircle at a time. Each successive semicircle should have a larger radius (as specified by the bounding rectangle's width) and should continue drawing where the previous semicircle finished.

Fig. 7.27 | Drawing a spiral using `strokeArc`.

7.3 *(Rotating Spiral)* Enhance Exercise 7.2 so that the spiral rotates slightly on each `Button` click.

7.4 *(Color Changing Spiral)* Enhance Exercise 7.2 so that each arc segment in the spiral uses a slightly brighter version of the previous `Color`. Start with a dark `Color`, then use the `Color` method `brighter` to create the next segment's `Color`.

7.5 *(Enhanced Rainbow)* Enhance the **Draw Rainbow** app to use thinner arcs and to transition through additional color variations to create a more realistic looking rainbow.

7.18 Wrap-Up

This chapter began our introduction to data structures, exploring the use of arrays to store data in and retrieve data from lists and tables of values. The chapter examples demonstrated how to declare an array, initialize an array and refer to individual elements of an array. The chapter introduced the enhanced `for` statement to iterate through arrays. We used exception handling to test for `ArrayIndexOutOfBoundsException`s that occur when a program attempts to access an array element outside the bounds of an array. We also illustrated how to pass arrays to methods and how to declare and manipulate multidimensional arrays. Finally, the chapter showed how to write methods that use variable-length argument lists and how to read arguments passed to a program from the command line.

We introduced the `ArrayList<E>` generic collection, which provides all the functionality and performance of arrays, along with other useful capabilities such as dynamic resizing. We used the `add` methods to add new items to the end of an `ArrayList` and to insert items in an `ArrayList`. The `remove` method was used to remove the first occurrence of a specified item, and an overloaded version of `remove` was used to remove an item at a specified index. We used the `size` method to obtain number of items in the `ArrayList`.

We continue our coverage of data structures in Chapter 16, Generic Collections. Chapter 16 introduces the Java Collections Framework, which uses generics to allow you to specify the exact types of objects that a particular data structure will store. Chapter 16 also introduces Java's other predefined data structures. Chapter 16 covers additional methods of class `Arrays`. You'll be able to use some of the `Arrays` methods discussed in Chapter 16 after reading the current chapter, but some of the `Arrays` methods require knowledge of concepts presented later in the book. Chapter 20 discusses generics, which enable you to create general models of methods and classes that can be declared once, but used with many different data types. Chapter 21, Custom Generic Data Structures, shows how to build dynamic data structures, such as lists, queues, stacks and trees, that can grow and shrink as programs execute.

We've now introduced the basic concepts of classes, objects, control statements, methods, arrays and collections. In Chapter 8, we take a deeper look at classes and objects.

Summary

Section 7.1 Introduction

- Arrays (p. 258) are fixed-length data structures consisting of related data items of the same type.

Section 7.2 Arrays

- An array is a group of variables (called elements or components; p. 259) containing values that all have the same type. Arrays are objects, so they're considered reference types.

- A program refers to any one of an array's elements with an array-access expression (p. 259) that includes the name of the array followed by the index of the particular element in square brackets (`[]`; p. 259).
- The first element in every array has index zero (p. 259) and is sometimes called the zeroth element.
- An index must be a nonnegative integer. A program can use an expression as an index.
- An array object knows its own length and stores this information in a `length` instance variable (p. 260).

Section 7.3 Declaring and Creating Arrays

- To create an array object, specify the array's element type and the number of elements as part of an array-creation expression (p. 260) that uses keyword `new`.
- When an array is created, each element receives a default value—zero for numeric primitive-type elements, `false` for boolean elements and `null` for references.
- In an array declaration, the type and the square brackets can be combined at the beginning of the declaration to indicate that all the identifiers in the declaration are array variables.
- Every element of a primitive-type array contains a variable of the array's declared type. Every element of a reference-type array is a reference to an object of the array's declared type.

Section 7.4 Examples Using Arrays

- A program can create an array and initialize its elements with an array initializer (p. 263).
- Constant variables (p. 264) are declared with keyword `final`, must be initialized before they're used and cannot be modified thereafter.

Section 7.5 Exception Handling: Processing the Incorrect Response

- An exception indicates a problem that occurs while a program executes.
- Exception handling (p. 270) enables you to create fault-tolerant programs.
- When a Java program executes, the JVM checks array indices to ensure that they're greater than or equal to 0 and less than the array's length. If a program uses an invalid index, Java generates an exception (p. 270) to indicate that an error occurred in the program at execution time.
- To handle an exception, place any code that might throw an exception (p. 270) in a `try` statement.
- The `try` block (p. 270) contains the code that might throw an exception, and the `catch` block (p. 270) contains the code that handles the exception if one occurs.
- You can have many `catch` blocks to handle different types of exceptions that might be thrown in the corresponding `try` block.
- When a `try` block terminates, any variables declared in the `try` block go out of scope.
- A `catch` block declares a type and an exception parameter. Inside the `catch` block, you can use the parameter's identifier to interact with a caught exception object.
- When a program is executed, array element indices are checked for validity—all indices must be greater than or equal to 0 and less than the length of the array. If an attempt is made to use an invalid index to access an element, an `ArrayIndexOutOfBoundsException` (p. 271) exception occurs.
- An exception object's `toString` method returns the exception's error message.

Section 7.6 Case Study: Card Shuffling and Dealing Simulation

- The `toString` method of an object is called implicitly when the object is used where a `String` is expected (e.g., when `printf` outputs the object as a `String` using the `%s` format specifier or when the object is concatenated to a `String` using the `+` operator).

Section 7.7 Enhanced `for` Statement

- The enhanced `for` statement (p. 276) allows you to iterate through the elements of an array or a collection without using a counter. The syntax of an enhanced `for` statement is:

```
for (Type parameter : arrayName) {
   statement
}
```

- The enhanced `for` statement cannot be used to modify elements in an array. If a program needs to modify elements, use the traditional counter-controlled `for` statement.

Section 7.8 Passing Arrays to Methods

- When an argument is passed by value, a copy of the argument's value is made and passed to the called method. The called method works exclusively with the copy.

Section 7.9 Pass-By-Value vs. Pass-By-Reference

- When an argument is passed by reference (p. 279), the called method can access the argument's value in the caller directly and possibly modify it.
- All arguments in Java are passed by value. A method call can pass two types of values to a method—copies of primitive values and copies of references to objects. Although an object's reference is passed by value (p. 279), a method can still interact with the referenced object by calling its `public` methods using the copy of the object's reference.
- When you pass an array or an individual array element of a reference type to a method, the called method receives a copy of the array or element's reference. When you pass an individual element of a primitive type, the called method receives a copy of the element's value.
- To pass an individual array element to a method, use the indexed name of the array.

Section 7.11 Multidimensional Arrays

- Multidimensional arrays with two dimensions are often used to represent tables of values consisting of information arranged in rows and columns.
- A two-dimensional array (p. 285) with *m* rows and *n* columns is called an *m*-by-*n* array. Such an array can be initialized with an array initializer of the form

```
arrayType[][] arrayName = {{row1 initializer}, {row2 initializer}, ...};
```

- Multidimensional arrays are maintained as arrays of separate one-dimensional arrays. As a result, the lengths of the rows in a two-dimensional array are not required to be the same.
- A multidimensional array with the same number of columns in every row can be created with an array-creation expression of the form

```
arrayType[][] arrayName = new arrayType[numRows][numColumns];
```

Section 7.13 Variable-Length Argument Lists

- An argument type followed by an ellipsis (`...`; p. 295) in a method's parameter list indicates that the method receives a variable number of arguments of that particular type. The ellipsis can occur only once in a method's parameter list. It must be at the end of the parameter list.
- A variable-length argument list (p. 295) is treated as an array within the method body. The number of arguments in the array can be obtained using the array's `length` field.

Section 7.14 Using Command-Line Arguments

- Passing arguments to `main` (p. 296) from the command line is achieved by including a parameter of type `String[]` in the parameter list of `main`. By convention, `main`'s parameter is named `args`.

- Java passes command-line arguments that appear after the class name in the `java` command to the application's `main` method as `String`s in the array `args`.

Section 7.15 Class `Arrays`

- Class `Arrays` (p. 298) provides `static` methods that peform common array manipulations, including `sort` to sort an array, `binarySearch` to search a sorted array, `equals` to compare arrays and `fill` to place items in an array.
- Class `System`'s `arraycopy` method (p. 299) enables you to copy the elements of one array into another.

Section 7.16 Introduction to Collections and Class `ArrayList`

- The Java API's collection classes provide efficient methods that organize, store and retrieve data without requiring knowledge of how the data is being stored.
- An `ArrayList<E>` (p. 301) is similar to an array but can be dynamically resized.
- The `add` method (p. 304) with one argument appends an element to the end of an `ArrayList`.
- The `add` method with two arguments inserts a new element at a specified position in an `ArrayList`.
- The `size` method (p. 304) returns the number of elements currently in an `ArrayList`.
- The `remove` method with a reference to an object as an argument removes the first element that matches the argument's value, and all elements above the removed element's index are shifted down by one.
- The `remove` method with an integer argument removes the element at the specified index, and all elements above that index are shifted down by one.
- The `contains` method returns `true` if the element is found in the `ArrayList`, and `false` otherwise.

Self-Review Exercises

7.1 Fill in the blank(s) in each of the following statements:

a) Lists and tables of values can be stored in ________ and ________.
b) An array is a group of ________ (called elements or components) containing values that all have the same ________.
c) The ________ allows you to iterate through an array's elements without using a counter.
d) The number used to refer to a particular array element is called the element's ________.
e) An array that uses two indices is referred to as a(n) ________ array.
f) Use the enhanced `for` statement ________ to walk through `double` array `numbers`.
g) Command-line arguments are stored in ________.
h) Use the expression ________ to receive the total number of arguments in a command line. Assume that command-line arguments are stored in `String[] args`.
i) Given the command `java MyClass test`, the first command-line argument is ________.
j) A(n) ________ in the parameter list of a method indicates that the method can receive a variable number of arguments.

7.2 Determine whether each of the following is *true* or *false*. If *false*, explain why.

a) An array can store many different types of values.
b) An array index should normally be of type `float`.
c) An individual array element that's passed to a method and modified in that method will contain the modified value when the called method completes execution.
d) Command-line arguments are separated by commas.

7.3 Perform the following tasks for an array called `fractions`:

a) Declare a constant `ARRAY_SIZE` that's initialized to 10.

b) Declare an array with ARRAY_SIZE elements of type double, and initialize the elements to 0.
c) Refer to array element 4.
d) Assign the value 1.667 to array element 9.
e) Assign the value 3.333 to array element 6.
f) Sum all the elements of the array, using a for statement. Declare the integer variable x as a control variable for the loop.

7.4 Perform the following tasks for an array called table:
a) Declare and create the array as an integer array that has three rows and three columns. Assume that the constant ARRAY_SIZE has been declared to be 3.
b) How many elements does the array contain?
c) Use a for statement to initialize each element of the array to the sum of its indices. Assume that the integer variables x and y are declared as control variables.

7.5 Find and correct the error in each of the following program segments:
a)

```
final int ARRAY_SIZE = 5;
ARRAY_SIZE = 10;
```

b)

```
int[] b = new int[10];
for (int i = 0; i <= b.length; i++)
   b[i] = 1;
```

c)

```
int[][] a = {{1, 2}, {3, 4}};
a[1, 1] = 5;
```

Answers to Self-Review Exercises

7.1 a) arrays, collections. b) variables, type. c) enhanced for statement. d) index (or subscript or position number). e) two-dimensional. f) for (double d : numbers). g) an array of Strings, called args by convention. h) args.length. i) test. j) ellipsis (...).

7.2 Answers:
a) False. An array can store only values of the same type.
b) False. An array index must be an integer or an integer expression.
c) For individual primitive-type elements of an array: False. A called method receives and manipulates a copy of the value of such an element, so modifications do not affect the original value. If the reference of an array is passed to a method, however, modifications to the array elements made in the called method are indeed reflected in the original. For individual elements of a reference type: True. A called method receives a copy of the reference of such an element, and changes to the referenced object will be reflected in the original array element.
d) False. Command-line arguments are separated by white space.

7.3 Answers:
a) `final int ARRAY_SIZE = 10;`
b) `double[] fractions = new double[ARRAY_SIZE];`
c) `fractions[4]`

d) `fractions[9] = 1.667;`

e) `fractions[6] = 3.333;`

f)

```
double total = 0.0;
for (int x = 0; x < fractions.length; x++)
   total += fractions[x];
```

7.4 Answers:

a) `int[][] table = new int[ARRAY_SIZE][ARRAY_SIZE];`

b) Nine.

c)

```
for (int x = 0; x < table.length; x++)
   for (int y = 0; y < table[x].length; y++)
      table[x][y] = x + y;
```

7.5 Answers:

a) Error: Assigning a value to a constant after it has been initialized.
Correction: Assign the correct value to the constant in a `final int ARRAY_SIZE` declaration or declare another variable.

b) Error: Referencing an array element outside the bounds of the array (`b[10]`).
Correction: Change the `<=` operator to `<`.

c) Error: Array indexing is performed incorrectly.
Correction: Change the statement to `a[1][1] = 5;`.

Exercises

7.6 Fill in the blanks in each of the following statements:

a) One-dimensional array `p` contains four elements. The names of those elements are ________, ________, ________ and ________.

b) Naming an array, stating its type and specifying the number of dimensions in the array is called ________ the array.

c) In a two-dimensional array, the first index identifies the ________ of an element and the second index identifies the ________ of an element.

d) An *m*-by-*n* array contains ________ rows, ________ columns and ________ elements.

e) The name of the element in row 3 and column 5 of array `d` is ________.

7.7 Determine whether each of the following is *true* or *false*. If *false*, explain why.

a) To refer to a particular location or element within an array, we specify the name of the array and the value of the particular element.

b) An array declaration reserves space for the array.

c) To indicate that 100 locations should be reserved for integer array `p`, you write the declaration

```
p[100];
```

d) An application that initializes the elements of a 15-element array to zero must contain at least one `for` statement.

e) An application that totals the elements of a two-dimensional array must contain nested `for` statements.

7.8 Write Java statements to accomplish each of the following tasks:

a) Display the value of element 6 of array `f`.

b) Initialize each of the five elements of one-dimensional integer array `g` to `8`.
c) Total the 100 elements of floating-point array `c`.
d) Copy 11-element array a into the first portion of array `b`, which contains 34 elements.
e) Determine and display the smallest and largest values contained in 99-element floating-point array `w`.

7.9 Consider a two-by-three integer array `t`.
a) Write a statement that declares and creates `t`.
b) How many rows does `t` have?
c) How many columns does `t` have?
d) How many elements does `t` have?
e) Write access expressions for all the elements in row 1 of `t`.
f) Write access expressions for all the elements in column 2 of `t`.
g) Write a single statement that sets the element of `t` in row 0 and column 1 to zero.
h) Write individual statements to initialize each element of `t` to zero.
i) Write a nested `for` statement that initializes each element of `t` to zero.
j) Write a nested `for` statement that inputs the values for the elements of `t` from the user.
k) Write a series of statements that determines and displays the smallest value in `t`.
l) Write a single `printf` statement that displays the elements of the first row of `t`.
m) Write a statement that totals the elements of the third column of `t`. Do not use iteration.
n) Write a series of statements that displays the contents of `t` in tabular format. List the column indices as headings across the top, and list the row indices at the left of each row.

7.10 *(Sales Commissions)* Use a one-dimensional array to solve the following problem: A company pays its salespeople on a commission basis. The salespeople receive $200 per week plus 9% of their gross sales for that week. For example, a salesperson who grosses $5,000 in sales in a week receives $200 plus 9% of $5,000, or a total of $650. Write an application (using an array of counters) that determines how many of the salespeople earned salaries in each of the following ranges (assume that each salesperson's salary is truncated to an integer amount):
a) $200–299
b) $300–399
c) $400–499
d) $500–599
e) $600–699
f) $700–799
g) $800–899
h) $900–999
i) $1,000 and over

Summarize the results in tabular format.

7.11 Write statements that perform the following one-dimensional-array operations:
a) Set the 10 elements of integer array `counts` to zero.
b) Add one to each of the 15 elements of integer array `bonus`.
c) Display the five values of integer array `bestScores` in column format.

7.12 *(Duplicate Elimination)* Use a one-dimensional array to solve the following problem: Write an application that inputs five numbers, each between 10 and 100, inclusive. As each number is read, display it only if it's not a duplicate of a number already read. Provide for the "worst case," in which all five numbers are different. Use the smallest possible array to solve this problem. Display the complete set of unique values input after the user enters each new value.

7.13 Label the elements of three-by-five two-dimensional array `sales` to indicate the order in which they're set to zero by the following program segment:

```
for (int row = 0; row < sales.length; row++) {
   for (int col = 0; col < sales[row].length; col++) {
      sales[row][col] = 0;
   }
}
```

7.14 *(Variable-Length Argument List)* Write an application that calculates the product of a series of integers that are passed to method `product` using a variable-length argument list. Test your method with several calls, each with a different number of arguments.

7.15 *(Command-Line Arguments)* Rewrite Fig. 7.2 so that the size of the array is specified by the first command-line argument. If no command-line argument is supplied, use 10 as the default size of the array.

7.16 *(Using the Enhanced `for` Statement)* Write an application that uses an enhanced `for` statement to sum the `double` values passed by the command-line arguments. [*Hint:* Use the `static` method `parseDouble` of class `Double` to convert a `String` to a `double` value.]

7.17 *(Dice Rolling)* Write an application to simulate the rolling of two dice. The application should use an object of class `Random` once to roll the first die and again to roll the second die. The sum of the two values should then be calculated. Each die can show an integer value from 1 to 6, so the sum of the values will vary from 2 to 12, with 7 being the most frequent sum, and 2 and 12 the least frequent. Figure 7.28 shows the 36 possible combinations of the two dice. Your application should roll the dice 36,000,000 times. Use a one-dimensional array to tally the number of times each possible sum appears. Display the results in tabular format.

	1	2	3	4	5	6
1	2	3	4	5	6	7
2	3	4	5	6	7	8
3	4	5	6	7	8	9
4	5	6	7	8	9	10
5	6	7	8	9	10	11
6	7	8	9	10	11	12

Fig. 7.28 | The 36 possible sums of two dice.

7.18 *(Game of Craps)* Write an application that runs 1,000,000 games of craps (Fig. 6.8) and answers the following questions:

a) How many games are won on the first roll, second roll, …, twentieth roll and after the twentieth roll?
b) How many games are lost on the first roll, second roll, …, twentieth roll and after the twentieth roll?
c) What are the chances of winning at craps? [*Note:* You should discover that craps is one of the fairest casino games. What do you suppose this means?]
d) What is the average length of a game of craps?
e) Do the chances of winning improve with the length of the game?

7.19 *(Airline Reservations System)* A small airline has just purchased a computer for its new automated reservations system. You've been asked to develop the new system. You're to write an application to assign seats on each flight of the airline's only plane (capacity: 10 seats).

Your application should display the following alternatives: `Please type 1 for First Class` and `Please type 2 for Economy`. If the user types `1`, your application should assign a seat in the first-class section (seats 1–5). If the user types `2`, your application should assign a seat in the economy section (seats 6–10). Your application should then display a boarding pass indicating the person's seat number and whether it's in the first-class or economy section of the plane.

Use a one-dimensional array of primitive type `boolean` to represent the seating chart of the plane. Initialize all the elements of the array to `false` to indicate that all the seats are empty. As each seat is assigned, set the corresponding element of the array to `true` to indicate that the seat is no longer available.

Your application should never assign a seat that has already been assigned. When the economy section is full, your application should ask the person if it's acceptable to be placed in the first-class section (and vice versa). If yes, make the appropriate seat assignment. If no, display the message `"Next flight leaves in 3 hours."`

7.20 *(Total Sales)* Use a two-dimensional array to solve the following problem: A company has four salespeople (1 to 4) who sell five different products (1 to 5). Once a day, each salesperson passes in a slip for each type of product sold. Each slip contains the following:

a) The salesperson number
b) The product number
c) The total dollar value of that product sold that day

Thus, each salesperson passes in between 0 and 5 sales slips per day. Assume that the information from all the slips for last month is available. Write an application that will read all this information for last month's sales and summarize the total sales by salesperson and by product. All totals should be stored in the two-dimensional array `sales`. After processing all the information for last month, display the results in tabular format, with each column representing a salesperson and each row representing a particular product. Cross-total each row to get the total sales of each product for last month. Cross-total each column to get the total sales by salesperson for last month. Your output should include these cross-totals to the right of the totaled rows and to the bottom of the totaled columns.

7.21 *(Turtle Graphics)* The Logo language made the concept of *turtle graphics* famous. Imagine a mechanical turtle that walks around the room under the control of a Java application. The turtle holds a pen in one of two positions, up or down. While the pen is down, the turtle traces out shapes as it moves, and while the pen is up, the turtle moves about freely without writing anything. In this problem, you'll simulate the operation of the turtle and create a computerized sketchpad.

Use a 20-by-20 array `floor` that's initialized to zeros. Read commands from an array that contains them. Keep track of the current position of the turtle at all times and whether the pen is currently up or down. Assume that the turtle always starts at position (0, 0) of the floor with its pen up. The set of turtle commands your application must process are shown in Fig. 7.29.

Command	Meaning
`1`	Pen up
`2`	Pen down
`3`	Turn right
`4`	Turn left
`5,10`	Move forward 10 spaces (replace 10 for a different number of spaces)
`6`	Display the 20-by-20 array
`9`	End of data (sentinel)

Fig. 7.29 | Turtle graphics commands.

Suppose that the turtle is somewhere near the center of the floor. The following "program" would draw and display a 12-by-12 square, leaving the pen in the up position:

```
2
5,12
3
5,12
3
5,12
3
5,12
1
6
9
```

As the turtle moves with the pen down, set the appropriate elements of array `floor` to `1`s. When the `6` command (display the array) is given, wherever there's a `1` in the array, display an asterisk or any character you choose. Wherever there's a `0`, display a blank.

Write an application to implement the turtle graphics capabilities discussed here. Write several turtle graphics programs to draw interesting shapes. Add other commands to increase the power of your turtle graphics language.

7.22 *(Knight's Tour)* An interesting puzzler for chess buffs is the Knight's Tour problem, originally proposed by the mathematician Euler. Can the knight piece move around an empty chessboard and touch each of the 64 squares once and only once? We study this intriguing problem in depth here.

The knight makes only L-shaped moves (two spaces in one direction and one space in a perpendicular direction). Thus, as shown in Fig. 7.30, from a square near the middle of an empty chessboard, the knight (labeled K) can make eight different moves (numbered 0 through 7).

	0	1	2	3	4	5	6	7
0								
1				2		1		
2			3				0	
3					K			
4			4				7	
5				5		6		
6								
7								

Fig. 7.30 | The eight possible moves of the knight.

a) Draw an eight-by-eight chessboard on a sheet of paper, and attempt a Knight's Tour by hand. Put a `1` in the starting square, a `2` in the second square, a `3` in the third, and so on. Before starting the tour, estimate how far you think you'll get, remembering that a full tour consists of 64 moves. How far did you get? Was this close to your estimate?

b) Now let's develop an application that will move the knight around a chessboard. The board is represented by an eight-by-eight two-dimensional array `board`. Each square is initialized to zero. We describe each of the eight possible moves in terms of its horizontal and vertical components. For example, a move of type 0, as shown in Fig. 7.30, consists of moving two squares horizontally to the right and one square vertically upward.

A move of type 2 consists of moving one square horizontally to the left and two squares vertically upward. Horizontal moves to the left and vertical moves upward are indicated with negative numbers. The eight moves may be described by two one-dimensional arrays, `horizontal` and `vertical`, as follows:

```
horizontal[0] = 2          vertical[0] = -1
horizontal[1] = 1          vertical[1] = -2
horizontal[2] = -1         vertical[2] = -2
horizontal[3] = -2         vertical[3] = -1
horizontal[4] = -2         vertical[4] = 1
horizontal[5] = -1         vertical[5] = 2
horizontal[6] = 1          vertical[6] = 2
horizontal[7] = 2          vertical[7] = 1
```

Let the variables `currentRow` and `currentColumn` indicate the row and column, respectively, of the knight's current position. To make a move of type `moveNumber`, where `moveNumber` is between 0 and 7, your application should use the statements

```
currentRow += vertical[moveNumber];
currentColumn += horizontal[moveNumber];
```

Write an application to move the knight around the chessboard. Keep a counter that varies from `1` to `64`. Record the latest count in each square the knight moves to. Test each potential move to see if the knight has already visited that square. Test every potential move to ensure that the knight does not land off the chessboard. Run the application. How many moves did the knight make?

c) After attempting to write and run a Knight's Tour application, you've probably developed some valuable insights. We'll use these insights to develop a *heuristic* (i.e., a common-sense rule) for moving the knight. Heuristics do not guarantee success, but a carefully developed heuristic greatly improves the chance of success. You may have observed that the outer squares are more troublesome than the squares nearer the center of the board. In fact, the most troublesome or inaccessible squares are the four corners.

Intuition may suggest that you should attempt to move the knight to the most troublesome squares first and leave open those that are easiest to get to, so that when the board gets congested near the end of the tour, there will be a greater chance of success.

We could develop an "accessibility heuristic" by classifying each of the squares according to how accessible it is and always moving the knight (using the knight's L-shaped moves) to the most inaccessible square. We label a two-dimensional array `accessibility` with numbers indicating from how many squares each particular square is accessible. On a blank chessboard, each of the 16 squares nearest the center is rated as `8`, each corner square is rated as `2`, and the other squares have accessibility numbers of `3`, `4` or `6` as follows:

```
2 3 4 4 4 4 3 2
3 4 6 6 6 6 4 3
4 6 8 8 8 8 6 4
4 6 8 8 8 8 6 4
4 6 8 8 8 8 6 4
4 6 8 8 8 8 6 4
3 4 6 6 6 6 4 3
2 3 4 4 4 4 3 2
```

Write a new version of the Knight's Tour, using the accessibility heuristic. The knight should always move to the square with the lowest accessibility number. In case of a tie, the knight may move to any of the tied squares. Therefore, the tour may begin in any of the four corners. [*Note:* As the knight moves around the chessboard, your application should reduce the accessibility numbers as more squares become occupied. In this way, at any given time during the tour, each available square's accessibility number will remain equal to precisely the number of squares from which that square may be reached.] Run this version of your application. Did you get a full tour? Modify the application to run 64 tours, one starting from each square of the chessboard. How many full tours did you get?

d) Write a version of the Knight's Tour application that, when encountering a tie between two or more squares, decides what square to choose by looking ahead to those squares reachable from the "tied" squares. Your application should move to the tied square for which the next move would arrive at a square with the lowest accessibility number.

7.23 *(Knight's Tour: Brute-Force Approaches)* In part (c) of Exercise 7.22, we developed a solution to the Knight's Tour problem. The approach used, called the "accessibility heuristic," generates many solutions and executes efficiently.

As computers continue to increase in power, we'll be able to solve more problems with sheer computer power and relatively unsophisticated algorithms. Let's call this approach "brute-force" problem solving.

a) Use random-number generation to enable the knight to walk around the chessboard (in its legitimate L-shaped moves) at random. Your application should run one tour and display the final chessboard. How far did the knight get?

b) Most likely, the application in part (a) produced a relatively short tour. Now modify your application to attempt 1,000 tours. Use a one-dimensional array to keep track of the number of tours of each length. When your application finishes attempting the 1,000 tours, it should display this information in neat tabular format. What was the best result?

c) Most likely, the application in part (b) gave you some "respectable" tours, but no full tours. Now let your application run until it produces a full tour. [*Caution:* This version of the application could run for hours on a powerful computer.] Once again, keep a table of the number of tours of each length, and display this table when the first full tour is found. How many tours did your application attempt before producing a full tour? How much time did it take?

d) Compare the brute-force version of the Knight's Tour with the accessibility-heuristic version. Which required a more careful study of the problem? Which algorithm was more difficult to develop? Which required more computer power? Could we be certain (in advance) of obtaining a full tour with the accessibility-heuristic approach? Could we be certain (in advance) of obtaining a full tour with the brute-force approach? Argue the pros and cons of brute-force problem solving in general.

7.24 *(Eight Queens)* Another puzzler for chess buffs is the Eight Queens problem, which asks the following: Is it possible to place eight queens on an empty chessboard so that no queen is "attacking" any other (i.e., no two queens are in the same row, in the same column or along the same diagonal)? Use the thinking developed in Exercise 7.22 to formulate a heuristic for solving the Eight Queens problem. Run your application. [*Hint:* It's possible to assign a value to each square of the chessboard to indicate how many squares of an empty chessboard are "eliminated" if a queen is placed in that square. Each of the corners would be assigned the value 22, as demonstrated by Fig. 7.31. Once these "elimination numbers" are placed in all 64 squares, an appropriate heuristic might be as follows: Place the next queen in the square with the smallest elimination number. Why is this strategy intuitively appealing?]

7.25 *(Eight Queens: Brute-Force Approaches)* In this exercise, you'll develop several brute-force approaches to solving the Eight Queens problem introduced in Exercise 7.24.

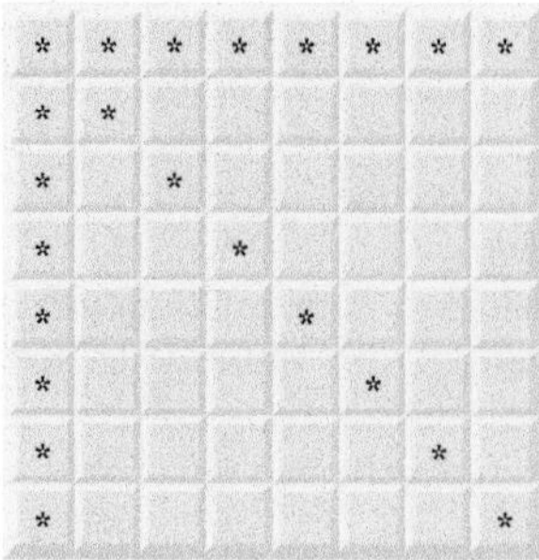

Fig. 7.31 | The 22 squares eliminated by placing a queen in the upper left corner.

a) Use the random brute-force technique developed in Exercise 7.23 to solve the Eight Queens problem.
b) Use an exhaustive technique (i.e., try all possible combinations of eight queens on the chessboard) to solve the Eight Queens problem.
c) Why might the exhaustive brute-force approach not be appropriate for solving the Knight's Tour problem?
d) Compare and contrast the random brute-force and exhaustive brute-force approaches.

7.26 *(Knight's Tour: Closed-Tour Test)* In the Knight's Tour (Exercise 7.22), a full tour occurs when the knight makes 64 moves, touching each square of the chessboard once and only once. A closed tour occurs when the 64th move is one move away from the square in which the knight started the tour. Modify the application you wrote in Exercise 7.22 to test for a closed tour if a full tour has occurred.

7.27 *(Sieve of Eratosthenes)* A prime number is any integer greater than 1 that's evenly divisible only by itself and 1. The Sieve of Eratosthenes is a method of finding prime numbers. It operates as follows:

a) Create a primitive-type `boolean` array with all elements initialized to `true`. Array elements with prime indices will remain `true`. All other array elements will eventually be set to `false`.
b) Starting with array index 2, determine whether a given element is `true`. If so, loop through the remainder of the array and set to `false` every element whose index is a multiple of the index for the element with value `true`. Then continue the process with the next element with value `true`. For array index 2, all elements beyond element 2 in the array that have indices which are multiples of 2 (indices 4, 6, 8, 10, etc.) will be set to `false`; for array index 3, all elements beyond element 3 in the array that have indices which are multiples of 3 (indices 6, 9, 12, 15, etc.) will be set to `false`; and so on.

When this process completes, the array elements that are still `true` indicate that the index is a prime number. These indices can be displayed. Write an application that uses an array of 1,000 elements to determine and display the prime numbers between 2 and 999. Ignore elements 0 and 1.

7.28 *(Simulation: The Tortoise and the Hare)* In this problem, you'll re-create the classic race of the tortoise and the hare. You'll use random-number generation to develop a simulation of this memorable event.

Our contenders begin the race at square 1 of 70 squares. Each square represents a possible position along the race course. The finish line is at square 70. The first contender to reach or pass square 70 is rewarded with a pail of fresh carrots and lettuce. The course weaves its way up the side of a slippery mountain, so occasionally the contenders lose ground.

A clock ticks once per second. With each tick of the clock, your application should adjust the position of the animals according to the rules in Fig. 7.32. Use variables to keep track of the positions of the animals (i.e., position numbers are 1–70). Start each animal at position 1 (the "starting gate"). If an animal slips left before square 1, move it back to square 1.

Animal	Move type	Percentage of the time	Actual move
Tortoise	Fast plod	50%	3 squares to the right
	Slip	20%	6 squares to the left
	Slow plod	30%	1 square to the right
Hare	Sleep	20%	No move at all
	Big hop	20%	9 squares to the right
	Big slip	10%	12 squares to the left
	Small hop	30%	1 square to the right
	Small slip	20%	2 squares to the left

Fig. 7.32 | Rules for adjusting the positions of the tortoise and the hare.

Generate the percentages in Fig. 7.32 by producing a random integer i in the range $1 \le i \le 10$. For the tortoise, perform a "fast plod" when $1 \le i \le 5$, a "slip" when $6 \le i \le 7$ or a "slow plod" when $8 \le i \le 10$. Use a similar technique to move the hare.

Begin the race by displaying

```
BANG !!!!!
AND THEY'RE OFF !!!!!
```

Then, for each tick of the clock (i.e., each iteration of a loop), display a 70-position line showing the letter `T` in the position of the tortoise and the letter `H` in the position of the hare. Occasionally, the contenders will land on the same square. In this case, the tortoise bites the hare, and your application should display `OUCH!!!` beginning at that position. All output positions other than the `T`, the `H` or the `OUCH!!!` (in case of a tie) should be blank.

After each line is displayed, test for whether either animal has reached or passed square 70. If so, display the winner and terminate the simulation. If the tortoise wins, display `TORTOISE WINS!!! YAY!!!` If the hare wins, display `Hare wins. Yuch.` If both animals win on the same tick of the clock, you may want to favor the tortoise (the "underdog"), or you may want to display `It's a tie.` If neither animal wins, perform the loop again to simulate the next tick of the clock. When you're ready to run your application, assemble a group of fans to watch the race. You'll be amazed at how involved your audience gets!

Later in the book, we introduce a number of Java capabilities, such as graphics, images, animation, sound and multithreading. As you study those features, you might enjoy enhancing your tortoise-and-hare contest simulation.

7.29 *(Fibonacci Series)* The Fibonacci series

0, 1, 1, 2, 3, 5, 8, 13, 21, …

begins with the terms 0 and 1 and has the property that each succeeding term is the sum of the two preceding terms.

a) Write a method `fibonacci(n)` that calculates the nth Fibonacci number. Incorporate this method into an application that enables the user to enter the value of `n`.

b) Determine the largest Fibonacci number that can be displayed on your system.
c) Modify the application you wrote in part (a) to use `double` instead of `int` to calculate and return Fibonacci numbers, and use this modified application to repeat part (b).

Exercises 7.30–7.34 are reasonably challenging. Once you've done them, you ought to be able to implement most popular card games easily.

7.30 *(Card Shuffling and Dealing)* Modify Fig. 7.11 to deal a five-card poker hand. Then modify class `DeckOfCards` of Fig. 7.10 to include methods that determine whether a hand contains

a) a pair
b) two pairs
c) three of a kind (e.g., three jacks)
d) four of a kind (e.g., four aces)
e) a flush (i.e., all five cards of the same suit)
f) a straight (i.e., five cards of consecutive face values)
g) a full house (i.e., two cards of one face value and three cards of another face value)

[*Hint:* Add methods `getFace` and `getSuit` to class `Card` of Fig. 7.9.]

7.31 *(Card Shuffling and Dealing)* Use the methods developed in Exercise 7.30 to write an application that deals two five-card poker hands, evaluates each hand and determines which is better.

7.32 *(Project: Card Shuffling and Dealing)* Modify the application developed in Exercise 7.31 so that it can simulate the dealer. The dealer's five-card hand is dealt "face down," so the player cannot see it. The application should then evaluate the dealer's hand, and, based on the quality of the hand, the dealer should draw one, two or three more cards to replace the corresponding number of unneeded cards in the original hand. The application should then reevaluate the dealer's hand. [*Caution:* This is a difficult problem!]

7.33 *(Project: Card Shuffling and Dealing)* Modify the application developed in Exercise 7.32 so that it can handle the dealer's hand automatically, but the player is allowed to decide which cards of the player's hand to replace. The application should then evaluate both hands and determine who wins. Now use this new application to play 20 games against the computer. Who wins more games, you or the computer? Have a friend play 20 games against the computer. Who wins more games? Based on the results of these games, refine your poker-playing application. (This, too, is a difficult problem.) Play 20 more games. Does your modified application play a better game?

7.34 *(Project: Card Shuffling and Dealing)* Modify the application of Figs. 7.9–7.11 to use `Face` and `Suit` `enum` types to represent the faces and suits of the cards. Declare each of these `enum` types as a `public` type in its own source-code file. Each `Card` should have a `Face` and a `Suit` instance variable. These should be initialized by the `Card` constructor. In class `DeckOfCards`, create an array of `Face`s that's initialized with the names of the constants in the `Face` `enum` type and an array of `Suit`s that's initialized with the names of the constants in the `Suit` `enum` type. [*Note:* When you output an `enum` constant as a `String`, the name of the constant is displayed.]

7.35 *(Fisher-Yates Shuffling Algorithm)* Research the Fisher-Yates shuffling algorithm online, then use it to reimplement the `shuffle` method in Fig. 7.10.

Special Section: Building Your Own Computer

In the next several problems, we take a temporary diversion from the world of high-level language programming to "peel open" a computer and look at its internal structure. We introduce machine-language programming and write several machine-language programs. To make this an especially valuable experience, we then build a computer (through the technique of software-based *simulation*) on which you can execute your machine-language programs.

7.36 *(Machine-Language Programming)* Let's create a computer called the Simpletron. As its name implies, it's a simple machine, but powerful. The Simpletron runs programs written in the only language it directly understands: Simpletron Machine Language (SML).

The Simpletron contains an *accumulator*—a special register in which information is put before the Simpletron uses that information in calculations or examines it in various ways. All the information in the Simpletron is handled in terms of *words*. A word is a signed four-digit decimal number, such as `+3364`, `-1293`, `+0007` and `-0001`. The Simpletron is equipped with a 100-word memory, and these words are referenced by their location numbers `00`, `01`, …, `99`.

Before running an SML program, we must *load*, or place, the program into memory. The first instruction (or statement) of every SML program is always placed in location `00`. The simulator will start executing at this location.

Each instruction written in SML occupies one word of the Simpletron's memory (so instructions are signed four-digit decimal numbers). We shall assume that the sign of an SML instruction is always plus, but the sign of a data word may be either plus or minus. Each location in the Simpletron's memory may contain an instruction, a data value used by a program or an unused (and so undefined) area of memory. The first two digits of each SML instruction are the *operation code* specifying the operation to be performed. SML operation codes are summarized in Fig. 7.33.

The last two digits of an SML instruction are the *operand*—the address of the memory location containing the word to which the operation applies. Let's consider several simple SML programs.

Operation code	Meaning
Input/output operations:	
`final int READ = 10;`	Read a word from the keyboard into a specific location in memory.
`final int WRITE = 11;`	Write a word from a specific location in memory to the screen.
Load/store operations:	
`final int LOAD = 20;`	Load a word from a specific location in memory into the accumulator.
`final int STORE = 21;`	Store a word from the accumulator into a specific location in memory.
Arithmetic operations:	
`final int ADD = 30;`	Add a word from a specific location in memory to the word in the accumulator (leave the result in the accumulator).
`final int SUBTRACT = 31;`	Subtract a word from a specific location in memory from the word in the accumulator (leave the result in the accumulator).
`final int DIVIDE = 32;`	Divide a word from a specific location in memory into the word in the accumulator (leave result in the accumulator).
`final int MULTIPLY = 33;`	Multiply a word from a specific location in memory by the word in the accumulator (leave the result in the accumulator).
Transfer-of-control operations:	
`final int BRANCH = 40;`	Branch to a specific location in memory.
`final int BRANCHNEG = 41;`	Branch to a specific location in memory if the accumulator is negative.
`final int BRANCHZERO = 42;`	Branch to a specific location in memory if the accumulator is zero.
`final int HALT = 43;`	Halt. The program has completed its task.

Fig. 7.33 | Simpletron Machine Language (SML) operation codes.

The first SML program (Fig. 7.34) reads two numbers from the keyboard and computes and displays their sum. The instruction +1007 reads the first number from the keyboard and places it into location 07 (which has been initialized to 0). Then instruction +1008 reads the next number into location 08. The *load* instruction, +2007, puts the first number into the accumulator, and the *add* instruction, +3008, adds the second number to the number in the accumulator. *All SML arithmetic instructions leave their results in the accumulator.* The *store* instruction, +2109, places the result back into memory location 09, from which the *write* instruction, +1109, takes the number and displays it (as a signed four-digit decimal number). The *halt* instruction, +4300, terminates execution.

Location	Number	Instruction
00	+1007	(Read A)
01	+1008	(Read B)
02	+2007	(Load A)
03	+3008	(Add B)
04	+2109	(Store C)
05	+1109	(Write C)
06	+4300	(Halt)
07	+0000	(Variable A)
08	+0000	(Variable B)
09	+0000	(Result C)

Fig. 7.34 | SML program that reads two integers and computes their sum.

The second SML program (Fig. 7.35) reads two numbers from the keyboard and determines and displays the larger value. Note the use of the instruction +4107 as a conditional transfer of control, much the same as Java's `if` statement.

Location	Number	Instruction
00	+1009	(Read A)
01	+1010	(Read B)
02	+2009	(Load A)
03	+3110	(Subtract B)
04	+4107	(Branch negative to 07)
05	+1109	(Write A)
06	+4300	(Halt)
07	+1110	(Write B)
08	+4300	(Halt)
09	+0000	(Variable A)
10	+0000	(Variable B)

Fig. 7.35 | SML program that reads two integers and determines the larger.

Now write SML programs to accomplish each of the following tasks:

a) Use a sentinel-controlled loop to read 10 positive numbers. Compute and display their sum.
b) Use a counter-controlled loop to read seven numbers, some positive and some negative, and compute and display their average.
c) Read a series of numbers, and determine and display the largest number. The first number read indicates how many numbers should be processed.

7.37 *(Computer Simulator)* In this problem, you're going to build your own computer. No, you'll not be soldering components together. Rather, you'll use the powerful technique of *software-based simulation* to create an object-oriented *software model* of the Simpletron of Exercise 7.36. Your Simpletron simulator will turn the computer you're using into a Simpletron, and you'll actually be able to run, test and debug the SML programs you wrote in Exercise 7.36.

When you run your Simpletron simulator, it should begin by displaying:

```
*** Welcome to Simpletron! ***
*** Please enter your program one instruction    ***
*** (or data word) at a time. I will display     ***
*** the location number and a question mark (?). ***
*** You then type the word for that location.    ***
*** Type -99999 to stop entering your program.   ***
```

Your application should simulate the memory of the Simpletron with a one-dimensional array `memory` that has 100 elements. Now assume that the simulator is running, and let's examine the dialog as we enter the program of Fig. 7.35 (Exercise 7.36):

```
00 ? +1009
01 ? +1010
02 ? +2009
03 ? +3110
04 ? +4107
05 ? +1109
06 ? +4300
07 ? +1110
08 ? +4300
09 ? +0000
10 ? +0000
11 ? -99999
```

Your program should display the memory location followed by a question mark. Each value to the right of a question mark is input by the user. When the sentinel value `-99999` is input, the program should display the following:

```
*** Program loading completed ***
*** Program execution begins  ***
```

The SML program has now been placed (or loaded) in array `memory`. Now the Simpletron executes the SML program. Execution begins with the instruction in location `00` and, as in Java, continues sequentially, unless directed to some other part of the program by a transfer of control.

Use the variable `accumulator` to represent the accumulator register. Use the variable `instructionCounter` to keep track of the location in memory that contains the instruction being performed. Use the variable `operationCode` to indicate the operation currently being performed (i.e., the left two digits of the instruction word). Use the variable `operand` to indicate the memory location on which the current instruction operates. Thus, `operand` is the rightmost two digits of the instruction currently being performed. Do not execute instructions directly from memory. Rather, transfer the next instruction to be performed from memory to a variable called `instructionRegister`. Then pick off the left two digits and place them in `operationCode`, and pick off the right two digits and place them in `operand`. When the Simpletron begins execution, the special registers are all initialized to zero.

Now, let's walk through execution of the first SML instruction, +1009 in memory location 00. This procedure is called an *instruction-execution cycle.*

The instructionCounter tells us the location of the next instruction to be performed. We *fetch* the contents of that location from memory by using the Java statement

```
instructionRegister = memory[instructionCounter];
```

The operation code and the operand are extracted from the instruction register by the statements

```
operationCode = instructionRegister / 100;
operand = instructionRegister % 100;
```

Now the Simpletron must determine that the operation code is actually a *read* (versus a *write,* a *load,* and so on). A switch differentiates among the 12 operations of SML. In the switch statement, the behavior of various SML instructions is simulated as shown in Fig. 7.36. We discuss branch instructions shortly and leave the others to you.

Instruction	Description
read:	Display the prompt "Enter an integer", then input the integer and store it in location memory[operand].
load:	accumulator = memory[operand];
add:	accumulator += memory[operand];
halt:	Terminate the SML program's execution and display the following message: *** Simpletron execution terminated ***

Fig. 7.36 | Behavior of several SML instructions in the Simpletron.

When the SML program completes execution, the name and contents of each register as well as the complete contents of memory should be displayed. Such a printout is often called a computer dump (no, a computer dump is not a place where old computers go). To help you program your dump method, a sample dump format is shown in Fig. 7.37. A dump after executing a Simpletron program would show the actual values of instructions and data values at the moment execution terminated.

```
REGISTERS:
accumulator          +0000
instructionCounter      00
instructionRegister  +0000
operationCode           00
operand                 00

MEMORY:
       0     1     2     3     4     5     6     7     8     9
 0 +0000 +0000 +0000 +0000 +0000 +0000 +0000 +0000 +0000 +0000
10 +0000 +0000 +0000 +0000 +0000 +0000 +0000 +0000 +0000 +0000
20 +0000 +0000 +0000 +0000 +0000 +0000 +0000 +0000 +0000 +0000
30 +0000 +0000 +0000 +0000 +0000 +0000 +0000 +0000 +0000 +0000
40 +0000 +0000 +0000 +0000 +0000 +0000 +0000 +0000 +0000 +0000
50 +0000 +0000 +0000 +0000 +0000 +0000 +0000 +0000 +0000 +0000
60 +0000 +0000 +0000 +0000 +0000 +0000 +0000 +0000 +0000 +0000
70 +0000 +0000 +0000 +0000 +0000 +0000 +0000 +0000 +0000 +0000
80 +0000 +0000 +0000 +0000 +0000 +0000 +0000 +0000 +0000 +0000
90 +0000 +0000 +0000 +0000 +0000 +0000 +0000 +0000 +0000 +0000
```

Fig. 7.37 | A sample dump.

Let's proceed with the execution of our program's first instruction—namely, the +1009 in location 00. As we've indicated, the switch statement simulates this task by prompting the user to enter a value, reading the value and storing it in memory location memory[operand]. The value is then read into location 09.

At this point, simulation of the first instruction is completed. All that remains is to prepare the Simpletron to execute the next instruction. Since the instruction just performed was not a transfer of control, we need merely increment the instruction-counter register as follows:

```
instructionCounter++;
```

This action completes the simulated execution of the first instruction. The entire process (i.e., the instruction-execution cycle) begins anew with the fetch of the next instruction to execute.

Now let's consider how the branching instructions—the transfers of control—are simulated. All we need to do is adjust the value in the instruction counter appropriately. Therefore, the unconditional branch instruction (40) is simulated within the switch as

```
instructionCounter = operand;
```

The conditional "branch if accumulator is zero" instruction is simulated as

```
if (accumulator == 0) {
   instructionCounter = operand;
}
```

At this point, you should implement your Simpletron simulator and run each of the SML programs you wrote in Exercise 7.36. If you desire, you may embellish SML with additional features and provide for these features in your simulator.

Your simulator should check for various types of errors. During the program-loading phase, for example, each number the user types into the Simpletron's memory must be in the range -9999 to +9999. Your simulator should test that each number entered is in this range and, if not, keep prompting the user to re-enter the number until the user enters a correct number.

During the execution phase, your simulator should check for various serious errors, such as attempts to divide by zero, attempts to execute invalid operation codes, and accumulator overflows (i.e., arithmetic operations resulting in values larger than +9999 or smaller than -9999). Such serious errors are called *fatal errors*. When a fatal error is detected, your simulator should display an error message, such as

```
*** Attempt to divide by zero ***
*** Simpletron execution abnormally terminated ***
```

and should display a full computer dump in the format we discussed previously. This treatment will help the user locate the error in the program.

7.38 *(Simpletron Simulator Modifications)* In Exercise 7.37, you wrote a software simulation of a computer that executes programs written in Simpletron Machine Language (SML). In this exercise, we propose several modifications and enhancements to the Simpletron Simulator. In the exercises of Chapter 21, we propose building a compiler that converts programs written in a high-level programming language (a variation of Basic) to Simpletron Machine Language. Some of the following modifications and enhancements may be required to execute the programs produced by the compiler:

a) Extend the Simpletron Simulator's memory to contain 1,000 memory locations to enable the Simpletron to handle larger programs.
b) Allow the simulator to perform remainder calculations. This modification requires an additional SML instruction.
c) Allow the simulator to perform exponentiation calculations. This modification requires an additional SML instruction.

d) Modify the simulator to use hexadecimal rather than integer values to represent SML instructions.
e) Modify the simulator to allow output of a newline. This modification requires an additional SML instruction.
f) Modify the simulator to process floating-point values in addition to integer values.
g) Modify the simulator to handle string input. [*Hint:* Each Simpletron word can be divided into two groups, each holding a two-digit integer. Each two-digit integer represents the ASCII (see Appendix B) decimal equivalent of a character. Add a machine-language instruction that will input a string and store the string, beginning at a specific Simpletron memory location. The first half of the word at that location will be a count of the number of characters in the string (i.e., the length of the string). Each succeeding half-word contains one ASCII character expressed as two decimal digits. The machine-language instruction converts each character into its ASCII equivalent and assigns it to a half-word.]
h) Modify the simulator to handle output of strings stored in the format of part (g). [*Hint:* Add a machine-language instruction that will display a string, beginning at a certain Simpletron memory location. The first half of the word at that location is a count of the number of characters in the string (i.e., the length of the string). Each succeeding half-word contains one ASCII character expressed as two decimal digits. The machine-language instruction checks the length and displays the string by translating each two-digit number into its equivalent character.]

7.39 *(Enhanced `GradeBook`)* Modify the `GradeBook` class of Fig. 7.18 so that the constructor accepts as parameters the number of students and the number of exams, then builds an appropriately sized two-dimensional array, rather than receiving a preinitialized two-dimensional array as it does now. Set each element of the new two-dimensional array to `-1` to indicate that no grade has been entered for that element. Add a `setGrade` method that sets one grade for a particular student on a particular exam. Modify class `GradeBookTest` of Fig. 7.19 to input the number of students and number of exams for the `GradeBook` and to allow the instructor to enter one grade at a time.

Making a Difference

7.40 *(Polling)* The Internet and the web are enabling more people to network, join a cause, voice opinions, and so on. Recent presidential candidates have used the Internet intensively to get out their messages and raise money for their campaigns. In this exercise, you'll write a simple polling program that allows users to rate five social-consciousness issues from 1 (least important) to 10 (most important). Pick five causes that are important to you (e.g., political issues, global environmental issues). Use a one-dimensional array `topics` (of type `String`) to store the five causes. To summarize the survey responses, use a 5-row, 10-column two-dimensional array `responses` (of type `int`), each row corresponding to an element in the `topics` array. When the program runs, it should ask the user to rate each issue. Have your friends and family respond to the survey. Then have the program display a summary of the results, including:
a) A tabular report with the five topics down the left side and the 10 ratings across the top, listing in each column the number of ratings received for each topic.
b) To the right of each row, show the average of the ratings for that issue.
c) Which issue received the highest point total? Display both the issue and the point total.
d) Which issue received the lowest point total? Display both the issue and the point total.

Classes and Objects: A Deeper Look

8

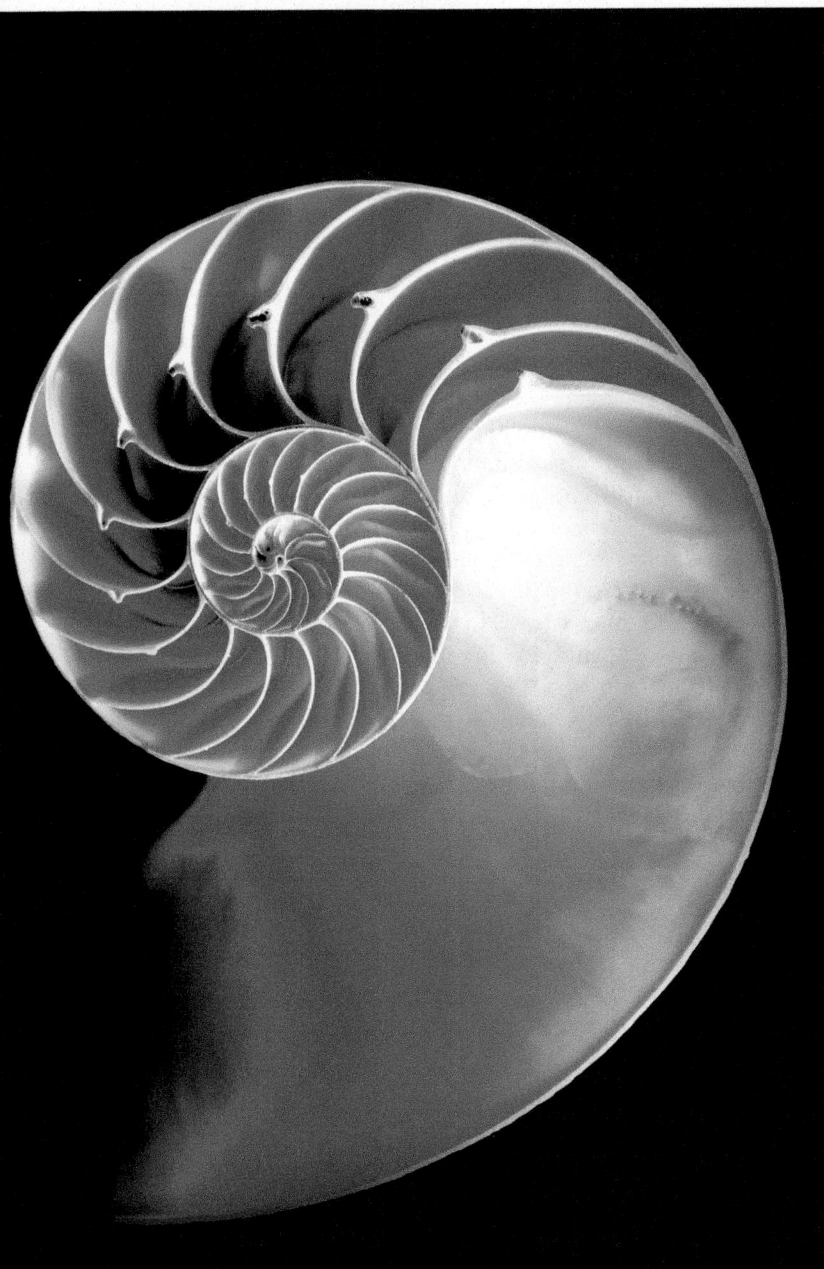

Objectives

In this chapter you'll:

- See additional details of creating class declarations.
- Use the `throw` statement to indicate that a problem has occurred.
- Use keyword `this` in a constructor to call another constructor in the same class.
- Use `static` variables and methods.
- Import `static` members of a class.
- Use the `enum` type to create sets of constants with unique identifiers.
- Declare `enum` constants with parameters.
- Use `BigDecimal` for precise monetary calculations.

Outline

8.1 Introduction

We now take a deeper look at building classes, controlling access to members of a class and creating constructors. We show how to throw an exception to indicate that a problem has occurred—Section 7.5 discussed catching exceptions. We use the this keyword to enable one constructor to conveniently call another constructor of the same class. We discuss *composition*—a capability that allows a class to have references to objects of other classes as members. We reexamine the use of *set* and *get* methods. Recall that Section 6.10 introduced the basic enum type to declare a set of constants. In this chapter, we discuss the relationship between enum types and classes, demonstrating that an enum type, like a class, can be declared in its own file with constructors, methods and fields. The chapter also discusses static class members and final instance variables in detail. We show a special relationship between classes in the same package. Finally, we demonstrate how to use class BigDecimal to perform precise monetary calculations. Two additional types of classes—nested classes and anonymous inner classes—are discussed in detail in our later chapters on GUI, graphics and multimedia.

8.2 Time Class Case Study

Our first example consists of two classes—Time1 (Fig. 8.1) and Time1Test (Fig. 8.2). Class Time1 represents the time of day. Class Time1Test's main method creates one object of class Time1 and invokes its methods. The output of this program appears in Fig. 8.2.

Time1 Class Declaration

Class Time1's private int instance variables hour, minute and second (Fig. 8.1, lines 5–7) represent the time in universal-time format (24-hour clock format in which hours are in the range 0–23, and minutes and seconds are each in the range 0–59). Time1 contains public methods setTime (lines 11–22), toUniversalString (lines 25–27) and toString (lines 30–34). These methods are also called the **public services** or the **public interface** that the class provides to its clients.

```
1  // Fig. 8.1: Time1.java
2  // Time1 class declaration maintains the time in 24-hour format.
3
4  public class Time1 {
5     private int hour; // 0 - 23
6     private int minute; // 0 - 59
7     private int second; // 0 - 59
8
9     // set a new time value using universal time; throw an
10    // exception if the hour, minute or second is invalid
11    public void setTime(int hour, int minute, int second) {
12       // validate hour, minute and second
13       if (hour < 0 || hour >= 24 || minute < 0 || minute >= 60 ||
14          second < 0 || second >= 60) {
15          throw new IllegalArgumentException(
16             "hour, minute and/or second was out of range");
17       }
18
19       this.hour = hour;
20       this.minute = minute;
21       this.second = second;
22    }
23
24    // convert to String in universal-time format (HH:MM:SS)
25    public String toUniversalString() {
26       return String.format("%02d:%02d:%02d", hour, minute, second);
27    }
28
29    // convert to String in standard-time format (H:MM:SS AM or PM)
30    public String toString() {
31       return String.format("%d:%02d:%02d %s",
32          ((hour == 0 || hour == 12) ? 12 : hour % 12),
33          minute, second, (hour < 12 ? "AM" : "PM"));
34    }
35 }
```

Fig. 8.1 | `Time1` class declaration maintains the time in 24-hour format.

Default Constructor

In this example, class `Time1` does *not* declare a constructor, so the compiler supplies a default constructor (as we discussed in Section 3.3.2). Each instance variable implicitly receives the default `int` value. Instance variables also can be initialized when they're declared in the class body, using the same initialization syntax as with a local variable.

Method `setTime` *and Throwing Exceptions*

Method `setTime` (lines 11–22) is a `public` method that declares three `int` parameters and uses them to set the time. Lines 13–14 test each argument to determine whether the value is outside the proper range. The `hour` value must be greater than or equal to `0` and less than `24`, because universal-time format represents hours as integers from 0 to 23 (e.g., 1 PM is hour 13 and 11 PM is hour 23; midnight is hour 0 and noon is hour 12). Similarly, both `minute` and `second` values must be greater than or equal to `0` and less than `60`. For values outside these ranges, `setTime` **throws an exception** of type **`IllegalArgumentException`** (lines 15–16), which notifies the client code that an invalid argument was passed to the method. As you learned in Section 7.5, you can use `try...catch` to catch exceptions and attempt to recover from them, which we'll do in Fig. 8.2. The class instance creation expression in the **throw statement** (Fig. 8.1; line 15) creates a new object of type `IllegalArgumentException`. The parentheses indicate a call to the `IllegalArgumentException` constructor. In this case, we call the constructor that allows us to specify a custom error message. After the exception object is created, the `throw` statement immediately terminates method `setTime` and the exception is returned to the calling method that attempted to set the time. If the argument values are all valid, lines 19–21 assign them to the `hour`, `minute` and `second` instance variables.

Software Engineering Observation 8.1

For a method like `setTime` in Fig. 8.1, validate all of the method's arguments before using them to set instance variable values to ensure that the object's data is modified only if all the arguments are valid.

Method `toUniversalString`

Method `toUniversalString` (lines 25–27) takes no arguments and returns a `String` in *universal-time format*, consisting of two digits each for the hour, minute and second—recall that you can use the `0` flag in a `printf` format specification (e.g., `"%02d"`) to display leading zeros for a value that doesn't use all the character positions in the specified field width. For example, if the time were 1:30:07 PM, the method would return `13:30:07`. Line 26 uses `static` method **`format`** of class `String` to return a `String` containing the formatted `hour`, `minute` and `second` values, each with two digits and possibly a leading `0` (specified with the `0` flag). Method `format` is similar to method `System.out.printf` except that `format` *returns* a formatted `String` rather than displaying it in a command window. The formatted `String` is returned by method `toUniversalString`.

Method `toString`

Method `toString` (lines 30–34) takes no arguments and returns a `String` in *standard-time format*, consisting of the `hour`, `minute` and `second` values separated by colons and followed by AM or PM (e.g., `11:30:17 AM` or `1:27:06 PM`). Like method `toUniversalString`, method `toString` uses `static String` method `format` to format the `minute` and `second` as two-digit values, with leading zeros if necessary. Line 32 uses a conditional operator (`?:`) to determine the value for `hour` in the `String`—if the `hour` is `0` or `12` (AM or PM), it appears as 12; otherwise, it appears as a value from 1 to 11. The conditional operator in line 33 determines whether AM or PM will be returned as part of the `String`.

Recall that all objects in Java have a `toString` method that returns a `String` representation of the object. We chose to return a `String` containing the time in standard-time format. Method `toString` is called *implicitly* whenever a `Time1` object appears in the code where a `String` is needed, such as the value to output with a `%s` format specifier in a call to `System.out.printf`. You may also call `toString` *explicitly* to obtain a `String` representation of a `Time` object.

Using Class `Time1`

Class `Time1Test` (Fig. 8.2) uses class `Time1`. Line 7 declares the `Time1` variable `time` and initializes it with a new `Time1` object. Operator `new` implicitly invokes class `Time1`'s default constructor, because `Time1` does not declare any constructors. To confirm that the `Time1` object was initialized properly, line 10 calls the `private` method `displayTime` (lines 31–34), which, in turn, calls the `Time1` object's `toUniversalString` and `toString` methods to output the time in universal-time format and standard-time format, respectively. Note that `toString` could have been called implicitly here rather than explicitly. Next, line 14 invokes method `setTime` of the `time` object to change the time. Then line 15 calls `displayTime` again to output the time in both formats to confirm that it was set correctly.

Software Engineering Observation 8.2

Recall from Chapter 3 that methods declared with access modifier `private` *can be called* only *by other methods of the class in which the* `private` *methods are declared. Such methods are commonly referred to as utility methods or helper methods because they're typically used to support the operation of the class's other methods.*

```
1  // Fig. 8.2: Time1Test.java
2  // Time1 object used in an app.
3
4  public class Time1Test {
5     public static void main(String[] args) {
6        // create and initialize a Time1 object
7        Time1 time = new Time1(); // invokes Time1 constructor
8
9        // output string representations of the time
10       displayTime("After time object is created", time);
11       System.out.println();
12
13       // change time and output updated time
14       time.setTime(13, 27, 6);
15       displayTime("After calling setTime", time);
16       System.out.println();
17
18       // attempt to set time with invalid values
19       try {
20          time.setTime(99, 99, 99); // all values out of range
21       }
22       catch (IllegalArgumentException e) {
23          System.out.printf("Exception: %s%n%n", e.getMessage());
24       }
25
26       // display time after attempt to set invalid values
27       displayTime("After calling setTime with invalid values", time);
28    }
29
30    // displays a Time1 object in 24-hour and 12-hour formats
31    private static void displayTime(String header, Time1 t) {
32       System.out.printf("%s%nUniversal time: %s%nStandard time: %s%n",
33          header, t.toUniversalString(), t.toString());
34    }
35 }
```

Fig. 8.2 | `Time1` object used in an app. (Part 1 of 2.)

```
After time object is created
Universal time: 00:00:00
Standard time: 12:00:00 AM

After calling setTime
Universal time: 13:27:06
Standard time: 1:27:06 PM

Exception: hour, minute and/or second was out of range

After calling setTime with invalid values
Universal time: 13:27:06
Standard time: 1:27:06 PM
```

Fig. 8.2 | `Time1` object used in an app. (Part 2 of 2.)

Calling `Time1` Method `setTime` with Invalid Values

To illustrate that method `setTime` *validates* its arguments, line 20 calls method `setTime` with *invalid* arguments of `99` for the `hour`, `minute` and `second`. This statement is placed in a `try` block (lines 19–21) in case `setTime` throws an `IllegalArgumentException`, which it will do since the arguments are all invalid. When this occurs, the exception is caught at lines 22–24, and line 23 displays the exception's error message by calling its `getMessage` method. Line 27 outputs the time again in both formats to confirm that `setTime` did *not* change the time when invalid arguments were supplied.

Software Engineering of the `Time1` Class Declaration

Consider several issues of class design with respect to class `Time1`. The instance variables `hour`, `minute` and `second` are each declared `private`. The actual data representation used within the class is of no concern to the class's clients. For example, it would be perfectly reasonable for `Time1` to represent the time internally as the number of seconds since midnight or the number of minutes and seconds since midnight. Clients could use the same `public` methods and get the same results without being aware of this. (Exercise 8.5 asks you to represent the time in class `Time2` of Fig. 8.5 as the number of seconds since midnight and show that indeed no change is visible to the clients of the class.)

Software Engineering Observation 8.3

Classes simplify programming, because the client can use only a class's `public` *methods. Such methods are usually client oriented rather than implementation oriented. Clients are neither aware of, nor involved in, a class's implementation. Clients generally care about* what *the class does but not* how *the class does it.*

Software Engineering Observation 8.4

Interfaces change less frequently than implementations. When an implementation changes, implementation-dependent code must change accordingly. Hiding the implementation reduces the possibility that other program parts will become dependent on a class's implementation details.

Java SE 8—Date/Time API

This section's example and several of this chapter's later examples demonstrate various class-implementation concepts in classes that represent dates and times. In professional

Java development, rather than building your own date and time classes, you'll typically reuse the ones provided by the Java API. Though Java has always had classes for manipulating dates and times, Java SE 8 introduced a new **Date/Time API**—defined by the classes in the package **`java.time`**. Applications built with Java SE 8 should use the Date/Time API's capabilities, rather than those in earlier Java versions. The new API fixes various issues with the older classes and provides more robust, easier-to-use capabilities for manipulating dates, times, time zones, calendars and more. We use some Date/Time API features in Chapter 23. You can learn more about the Date/Time API's classes at:

```
http://docs.oracle.com/javase/8/docs/api/java/time/package-
   summary.html
```

8.3 Controlling Access to Members

The access modifiers `public` and `private` control access to a class's variables and methods. In Chapter 9, we'll introduce the additional access modifier `protected`. The primary purpose of `public` methods is to present to the class's clients a view of the services the class provides (i.e., the class's `public` interface). Clients need not be concerned with how the class accomplishes its tasks. For this reason, the class's `private` variables and `private` methods (i.e., its *implementation details*) are *not* accessible to its clients.

Figure 8.3 demonstrates that `private` class members are *not* accessible outside the class. Lines 7–9 attempt to access the `private` instance variables `hour`, `minute` and `second` of the `Time1` object `time`. When this program is compiled, the compiler generates error messages that these `private` members are not accessible. This program assumes that the `Time1` class from Fig. 8.1 is used.

```
1  // Fig. 8.3: MemberAccessTest.java
2  // Private members of class Time1 are not accessible.
3  public class MemberAccessTest {
4     public static void main(String[] args) {
5        Time1 time = new Time1(); // create and initialize Time1 object
6
7        time.hour = 7; // error: hour has private access in Time1
8        time.minute = 15; // error: minute has private access in Time1
9        time.second = 30; // error: second has private access in Time1
10    }
11 }
```

```
MemberAccessTest.java:7: error: hour has private access in Time1
      time.hour = 7; // error: hour has private access in Time1
          ^
MemberAccessTest.java:8: error: minute has private access in Time1
      time.minute = 15; // error: minute has private access in Time1
          ^
MemberAccessTest.java:9: error: second has private access in Time1
      time.second = 30; // error: second has private access in Time1
          ^
3 errors
```

Fig. 8.3 | Private members of class `Time1` are not accessible.

Common Programming Error 8.1

An attempt by a method that's not a member of a class to access a `private` *member of that class generates a compilation error.*

8.4 Referring to the Current Object's Members with the `this` Reference

Every object can access a *reference to itself* with keyword **this** (sometimes called the **this reference**). When an instance method is called for a particular object, the method's body *implicitly* uses keyword `this` to refer to the object's instance variables and other methods. This enables the class's code to know which object should be manipulated. As you'll see in Fig. 8.4, you can also use keyword `this` *explicitly* in an instance method's body. Section 8.5 shows another interesting use of keyword `this`. Section 8.11 explains why keyword `this` cannot be used in a `static` method.

Figure 8.4 demonstrates implicit and explicit use of the `this` reference. This example is the first in which we declare *two* classes in one file—class `ThisTest` is declared in lines 4–9, and class `SimpleTime` in lines 12–41. When you compile a `.java` file containing more than one class, the compiler produces a separate `.class` file for every class. In this case, two separate files are produced—`SimpleTime.class` and `ThisTest.class`. When one source-code (`.java`) file contains multiple class declarations, the compiler places the `.class` files in the *same* directory. Note also in Fig. 8.4 that only class `ThisTest` is declared `public`. A source-code file can contain only *one* `public` class—otherwise, a compilation error occurs. *Non-*`public` *classes* can be used only by other classes in the *same package*—recall from Section 3.2.5 that classes compiled into the same directory are in the same package. So, in this example, class `SimpleTime` can be used only by class `ThisTest`.

```
1  // Fig. 8.4: ThisTest.java
2  // this used implicitly and explicitly to refer to members of an object.
3
4  public class ThisTest {
5     public static void main(String[] args) {
6        SimpleTime time = new SimpleTime(15, 30, 19);
7        System.out.println(time.buildString());
8     }
9  }
10
11 // class SimpleTime demonstrates the "this" reference
12 class SimpleTime {
13    private int hour; // 0-23
14    private int minute; // 0-59
15    private int second; // 0-59
16
17    // if the constructor uses parameter names identical to
18    // instance variable names the "this" reference is
19    // required to distinguish between the names
20    public SimpleTime(int hour, int minute, int second) {
21       this.hour = hour; // set "this" object's hour
```

Fig. 8.4 | `this` used implicitly and explicitly to refer to members of an object. (Part 1 of 2.)

```
22        this.minute = minute; // set "this" object's minute
23        this.second = second; // set "this" object's second
24     }
25
26     // use explicit and implicit "this" to call toUniversalString
27     public String buildString() {
28        return String.format("%24s: %s%n%24s: %s",
29           "this.toUniversalString()", this.toUniversalString(),
30           "toUniversalString()", toUniversalString());
31     }
32
33     // convert to String in universal-time format (HH:MM:SS)
34     public String toUniversalString() {
35        // "this" is not required here to access instance variables,
36        // because method does not have local variables with same
37        // names as instance variables
38        return String.format("%02d:%02d:%02d",
39           this.hour, this.minute, this.second);
40     }
41  }
```

```
this.toUniversalString(): 15:30:19
     toUniversalString(): 15:30:19
```

Fig. 8.4 | `this` used implicitly and explicitly to refer to members of an object. (Part 2 of 2.)

Class `SimpleTime` (lines 12–41) declares three `private` instance variables—`hour`, `minute` and `second` (lines 13–15). The class's constructor (lines 20–24) receives three `int` arguments to initialize a `SimpleTime` object. Once again, we used parameter names for the constructor that are *identical* to the class's instance-variable names (lines 13–15), so we use the `this` reference to refer to the instance variables in lines 21–23.

Error-Prevention Tip 8.1

Most IDEs will issue a warning if you say `x = x;` *instead of* `this.x = x;`. *The statement* `x = x;` *is often called a no-op (no operation).*

Method `buildString` (lines 27–31) returns a `String` created by a statement that uses the `this` reference explicitly and implicitly. Line 29 uses it *explicitly* to call method `toUniversalString`. Line 30 uses it *implicitly* to call the same method. Both lines perform the same task. You typically will not use `this` explicitly to reference other methods within the current object. Also, line 39 in method `toUniversalString` explicitly uses the `this` reference to access each instance variable. This is *not* necessary here, because the method does *not* have any local variables that shadow the instance variables of the class.

Performance Tip 8.1

There's only one copy of each method per class—every object of the class shares the method's code. Each object, on the other hand, has its own copy of the class's instance variables. The class's non-`static` *methods implicitly use* `this` *to determine the specific object of the class to manipulate.*

Class `ThisTest`'s `main` method (lines 5–8) demonstrates class `SimpleTime`. Line 6 creates an instance of class `SimpleTime` and invokes its constructor. Line 7 invokes the object's `buildString` method, then displays the results.

8.5 Time Class Case Study: Overloaded Constructors

As you know, you can declare your own constructor to specify how objects of a class should be initialized. Next, we demonstrate a class with several **overloaded constructors** that enable objects of that class to be initialized in different ways. To overload constructors, simply provide multiple constructor declarations with different signatures.

Class `Time2` with Overloaded Constructors

The `Time1` class's default constructor in Fig. 8.1 initialized `hour`, `minute` and `second` to their default `0` values (i.e., midnight in universal time). The default constructor does not enable the class's clients to initialize the time with nonzero values. Class `Time2` (Fig. 8.5) contains five overloaded constructors that provide convenient ways to initialize objects. In this program, four of the constructors invoke a fifth, which in turn ensures that the value supplied for `hour` is in the range 0 to 23, and the values for `minute` and `second` are each in the range 0 to 59. The compiler invokes the appropriate constructor by matching the number, types and order of the types of the arguments specified in the constructor call with the number, types and order of the types of the parameters specified in each constructor declaration. Class `Time2` also provides *set* and *get* methods for each instance variable.

```
// Fig. 8.5: Time2.java
// Time2 class declaration with overloaded constructors.

public class Time2 {
   private int hour; // 0 - 23
   private int minute; // 0 - 59
   private int second; // 0 - 59

   // Time2 no-argument constructor:
   // initializes each instance variable to zero
   public Time2() {
      this(0, 0, 0); // invoke constructor with three arguments
   }

   // Time2 constructor: hour supplied, minute and second defaulted to 0
   public Time2(int hour) {
      this(hour, 0, 0); // invoke constructor with three arguments
   }

   // Time2 constructor: hour and minute supplied, second defaulted to 0
   public Time2(int hour, int minute) {
      this(hour, minute, 0); // invoke constructor with three arguments
   }

```

Fig. 8.5 | `Time2` class declaration with overloaded constructors. (Part 1 of 3.)

```java
   // Time2 constructor: hour, minute and second supplied
   public Time2(int hour, int minute, int second) {
      if (hour < 0 || hour >= 24) {
         throw new IllegalArgumentException("hour must be 0-23");
      }

      if (minute < 0 || minute >= 60) {
         throw new IllegalArgumentException("minute must be 0-59");
      }

      if (second < 0 || second >= 60) {
         throw new IllegalArgumentException("second must be 0-59");
      }

      this.hour = hour;
      this.minute = minute;
      this.second = second;
   }

   // Time2 constructor: another Time2 object supplied
   public Time2(Time2 time) {
      // invoke constructor with three arguments
      this(time.hour, time.minute, time.second);
   }

   // Set Methods
   // set a new time value using universal time;
   // validate the data
   public void setTime(int hour, int minute, int second) {
      if (hour < 0 || hour >= 24) {
         throw new IllegalArgumentException("hour must be 0-23");
      }

      if (minute < 0 || minute >= 60) {
         throw new IllegalArgumentException("minute must be 0-59");
      }

      if (second < 0 || second >= 60) {
         throw new IllegalArgumentException("second must be 0-59");
      }

      this.hour = hour;
      this.minute = minute;
      this.second = second;
   }

   // validate and set hour
   public void setHour(int hour) {
      if (hour < 0 || hour >= 24) {
         throw new IllegalArgumentException("hour must be 0-23");
      }

```

Fig. 8.5 | Time2 class declaration with overloaded constructors. (Part 2 of 3.)

```
77          this.hour = hour;
78       }
79
80       // validate and set minute
81       public void setMinute(int minute) {
82          if (minute < 0 || minute >= 60) {
83             throw new IllegalArgumentException("minute must be 0-59");
84          }
85
86          this.minute = minute;
87       }
88
89       // validate and set second
90       public void setSecond(int second) {
91          if (second < 0 || second >= 60) {
92             throw new IllegalArgumentException("second must be 0-59");
93          }
94
95          this.second = second;
96       }
97
98       // Get Methods
99       // get hour value
100      public int getHour() {return hour;}
101
102      // get minute value
103      public int getMinute() {return minute;}
104
105      // get second value
106      public int getSecond() {return second;}
107
108      // convert to String in universal-time format (HH:MM:SS)
109      public String toUniversalString() {
110         return String.format(
111            "%02d:%02d:%02d", getHour(), getMinute(), getSecond());
112      }
113
114      // convert to String in standard-time format (H:MM:SS AM or PM)
115      public String toString() {
116         return String.format("%d:%02d:%02d %s",
117            ((getHour() == 0 || getHour() == 12) ? 12 : getHour() % 12),
118            getMinute(), getSecond(), (getHour() < 12 ? "AM" : "PM"));
119      }
120   }
```

Fig. 8.5 | `Time2` class declaration with overloaded constructors. (Part 3 of 3.)

Class `Time2`'s Constructors—Calling One Constructor from Another via `this`

Lines 11–13 declare a so-called **no-argument constructor** that's invoked without arguments. Once you declare any constructors in a class, the compiler will *not* provide a *default constructor*. This no-argument constructor ensures that class `Time2`'s clients can create `Time2` objects with default values. Such a constructor simply initializes the object as specified in the constructor's body. In the body, we introduce a use of `this` that's allowed only as the *first* statement in a constructor's body. Line 12 uses `this` in method-call syntax to invoke the `Time2` constructor that takes three parameters (lines 26–42) with values of 0 for the `hour`, `minute` and `second`. Using `this` as shown here is a popular way to *reuse* initialization code provided by another of the class's constructors rather than defining similar code in the no-argument constructor's body. A constructor that calls another constructor in this manner is known as a **delegating constructor**. We use this syntax in four of the five `Time2` constructors to make the class easier to maintain and modify. If we need to change how objects of class `Time2` are initialized, only the constructor that the class's other constructors call will need to be modified.

Common Programming Error 8.2

It's a compilation error when `this` is used in a constructor's body to call another of the class's constructors if that call is not the first statement in the constructor. It's also a compilation error when a method attempts to invoke a constructor directly via `this`.

Lines 16–18 declare a `Time2` constructor with a single `int` parameter representing the `hour`, which is passed with 0 for the `minute` and `second` to the constructor at lines 26–42. Lines 21–23 declare a `Time2` constructor that receives two `int` parameters representing the `hour` and `minute`, which are passed with 0 for the `second` to the constructor at lines 26–42. Like the no-argument constructor, each of these constructors invokes the three-argument constructor to minimize code duplication. Lines 26–42 declare the `Time2` constructor that receives three `int` parameters representing the `hour`, `minute` and `second`. This constructor validates and initializes the instance variables.

Lines 45–48 declare a `Time2` constructor that receives a reference to another `Time2` object. The argument object's values are passed to the three-argument constructor to initialize the `hour`, `minute` and `second`. Line 47 directly accesses the `hour`, `minute` and `second` values of the argument `time` with the expressions `time.hour`, `time.minute` and `time.second`—even though `hour`, `minute` and `second` are declared as `private` variables of class `Time2`. This is due to a special relationship between objects of the same class.

Software Engineering Observation 8.5

When one object of a class has a reference to another object of the same class, the first object can access all *the second object's data and methods (including those that are `private`).*

Class `Time2`*'s* `setTime` *Method*

Method `setTime` (lines 53–69) throws an `IllegalArgumentException` (lines 55, 59 and 63) if any of the method's arguments is out of range. Otherwise, it sets `Time2`'s instance variables to the argument values (lines 66–68).

Notes Regarding Class `Time2`*'s* Set *and* Get *Methods and Constructors*

`Time2`'s *get* methods are called from other methods of the class. In particular, methods `toUniversalString` and `toString` call `getHour`, `getMinute` and `getSecond` in line 111 and lines 117–118, respectively. In each case, these methods could have accessed the class's private data directly without calling the *get* methods. However, consider changing the representation of the time from three `int` values (requiring 12 bytes of memory) to a single `int` value representing the total number of seconds that have elapsed since midnight (requiring only four bytes of memory). If we made such a change, only the bodies of the methods that access the `private` data directly would need to change—in particular, the three-argument constructor, the `setTime` method and the individual *set* and *get* methods for the `hour`, `minute` and `second`. There would be no need to modify the bodies of methods `toUniversalString` or `toString` because they do *not* access the data directly. Designing the class in this manner reduces the likelihood of programming errors when altering the class's implementation.

Similarly, each `Time2` constructor could include a copy of the appropriate statements from the three-argument constructor. Doing so may be slightly more efficient, because the extra constructor calls are eliminated. But, *duplicating* statements makes changing the class's internal data representation more difficult. Having the `Time2` constructors call the constructor with three arguments requires that any changes to the implementation of the three-argument constructor be made only once. Also, the compiler can optimize programs by removing calls to simple methods and replacing them with the expanded code of their declarations—a technique known as **inlining the code**, which improves program performance.

Using Class `Time2`'s Overloaded Constructors

Class `Time2Test` (Fig. 8.6) invokes the overloaded `Time2` constructors (lines 6–10 and 21). Line 6 invokes the `Time2` no-argument constructor. Lines 7–10 demonstrate passing arguments to the other `Time2` constructors. Line 7 invokes the single-argument constructor that receives an `int` at lines 16–18 of Fig. 8.5. Line 8 of Fig. 8.6 invokes the two-argument constructor at lines 21–23 of Fig. 8.5. Line 9 of Fig. 8.6 invokes the three-argument constructor at lines 26–42 of Fig. 8.5. Line 10 of Fig. 8.6 invokes the single-argument constructor that takes a `Time2` at lines 45–48 of Fig. 8.5. Next, the app displays the `String` representations of each `Time2` object to confirm that it was initialized properly (lines 13–17 of Fig. 8.6). Line 21 attempts to initialize `t6` by creating a new `Time2` object and passing three *invalid* values to the constructor. When the constructor attempts to use the invalid `hour` value to initialize the object's `hour`, an `IllegalArgumentException` occurs. We catch this exception at line 23 and display its error message, which results in the last line of the output.

```
1   // Fig. 8.6: Time2Test.java
2   // Overloaded constructors used to initialize Time2 objects.
3
4   public class Time2Test {
5      public static void main(String[] args) {
6         Time2 t1 = new Time2(); // 00:00:00
7         Time2 t2 = new Time2(2); // 02:00:00
8         Time2 t3 = new Time2(21, 34); // 21:34:00
9         Time2 t4 = new Time2(12, 25, 42); // 12:25:42
10        Time2 t5 = new Time2(t4); // 12:25:42
11
12        System.out.println("Constructed with:");
13        displayTime("t1: all default arguments", t1);
14        displayTime("t2: hour specified; default minute and second", t2);
15        displayTime("t3: hour and minute specified; default second", t3);
16        displayTime("t4: hour, minute and second specified", t4);
17        displayTime("t5: Time2 object t4 specified", t5);
```

Fig. 8.6 | Overloaded constructors used to initialize `Time2` objects. (Part 1 of 2.)

```

      // attempt to initialize t6 with invalid values
      try {
         Time2 t6 = new Time2(27, 74, 99); // invalid values
      }
      catch (IllegalArgumentException e) {
         System.out.printf("%nException while initializing t6: %s%n",
            e.getMessage());
      }
   }

   // displays a Time2 object in 24-hour and 12-hour formats
   private static void displayTime(String header, Time2 t) {
      System.out.printf("%s%n   %s%n   %s%n",
         header, t.toUniversalString(), t.toString());
   }
}
```

```
Constructed with:
t1: all default arguments
   00:00:00
   12:00:00 AM
t2: hour specified; default minute and second
   02:00:00
   2:00:00 AM
t3: hour and minute specified; default second
   21:34:00
   9:34:00 PM
t4: hour, minute and second specified
   12:25:42
   12:25:42 PM
t5: Time2 object t4 specified
   12:25:42
   12:25:42 PM

Exception while initializing t6: hour must be 0-23
```

Fig. 8.6 | Overloaded constructors used to initialize `Time2` objects. (Part 2 of 2.)

8.6 Default and No-Argument Constructors

Every class *must* have at least *one* constructor. If you do not provide any in a class's declaration, the compiler creates a *default constructor* that takes *no* arguments when it's invoked. The default constructor initializes the instance variables to the initial values specified in their declarations or to their default values (zero for primitive numeric types, `false` for `boolean` values and `null` for references).

Recall that if your class declares constructors, the compiler will *not* create a default constructor. In this case, you must declare a no-argument constructor if default initialization is required. Like a default constructor, a no-argument constructor is invoked with empty parentheses. The `Time2` no-argument constructor (lines 11–13 of Fig. 8.5) explicitly initializes a `Time2` object by passing to the three-argument constructor 0 for each parameter. Since 0 is the default value for `int` instance variables, the no-argument constructor in this example could actually be declared with an empty body. In this case, each instance variable would receive its default value when the no-argument constructor is called. If we were to omit the no-argument constructor, clients of this class would not be able to create a `Time2` object with the expression `new Time2()`.

Error-Prevention Tip 8.2

Ensure that you do not *include a return type in a constructor definition. Java allows other methods of the class besides its constructors to have the same name as the class and to specify return types. Such methods are* not *constructors and will* not *be called when an object of the class is instantiated.*

Common Programming Error 8.3

A compilation error occurs if a program attempts to initialize an object of a class by passing the wrong number or types of arguments to the class's constructor.

8.7 Notes on *Set* and *Get* Methods

As you know, client code can manipulate a class's `private` fields *only* through the class's methods. A typical manipulation might be the adjustment of a customer's bank balance (e.g., a `private` instance variable of a class `BankAccount`) by a method `computeInterest`. *Set* methods are also commonly called **mutator methods**, because they typically *change* an object's state—i.e., *modify* the values of instance variables. *Get* methods are also commonly called **accessor methods** or **query methods**.

Set *and* Get *Methods vs.* `public` *Data*

It would seem that providing *set* and *get* capabilities is essentially the same as making a class's instance variables `public`. This is one of the subtleties that makes Java so desirable for software engineering. A `public` instance variable can be read or written by any method that has a reference to an object containing that variable. If an instance variable is declared `private`, a `public` *get* method certainly allows other methods to access it, but the *get* method can *control* how the client can access it. For example, a *get* method might control the format of the data it returns, shielding the client code from the actual data representation. A `public` *set* method can—and should—carefully scrutinize attempts to modify the variable's value and throw an exception if necessary. For example, attempts to *set* the day of the month to 37 or a person's weight to a negative value should be rejected. Thus, although *set* and *get* methods provide access to `private` data, the access is restricted by the implementation of the methods. This helps promote good software engineering.

Software Engineering Observation 8.6

Classes should never have `public` *nonconstant data, but declaring data* `public static final` *enables you to make constants available to clients of your class. For example, class* `Math` *offers* `public static final` *constants* `Math.E` *and* `Math.PI`*.*

Validity Checking in Set *Methods*

The benefits of data integrity do not follow automatically simply because instance variables are declared `private`—you must provide validity checking. A class's *set* methods could determine that attempts were made to assign invalid data to objects of the class. Typically *set* methods have `void` return type and use exception handling to indicate attempts to assign invalid data. We discuss exception handling in detail in Chapter 11.

Software Engineering Observation 8.7

When appropriate, provide `public` *methods to change and retrieve the values of* `private` *instance variables. This architecture helps hide the implementation of a class from its clients, which improves program modifiability.*

Error-Prevention Tip 8.3

Using set *and* get *methods helps you create classes that are easier to debug and maintain. If only one method performs a particular task, such as setting an instance variable in an object, it's easier to debug and maintain the class. If the instance variable is not being set properly, the code that actually modifies instance variable is localized to one* set *method. Your debugging efforts can be focused on that one method.*

Predicate Methods

Another common use for accessor methods is to test whether a condition is *true* or *false*—such methods are often called **predicate methods**. An example would be class `ArrayList`'s `isEmpty` method, which returns `true` if the `ArrayList` is empty and `false` otherwise. A program might test `isEmpty` before attempting to read another item from an `ArrayList`.

Good Programming Practice 8.1

By convention, predicate method names begin with `is` *rather than* `get`.

8.8 Composition

A class can have references to objects of other classes as members. This is called **composition** and is sometimes referred to as a ***has-a* relationship**. For example, an `AlarmClock` object needs to know the current time *and* the time when it's supposed to sound its alarm, so it's reasonable to include *two* references to `Time` objects in an `AlarmClock` object. A car *has-a* steering wheel, a break pedal, an accelerator pedal and more.

Class `Date`

This composition example contains classes `Date` (Fig. 8.7), `Employee` (Fig. 8.8) and `EmployeeTest` (Fig. 8.9). Class `Date` (Fig. 8.7) declares instance variables `month`, `day` and `year` (lines 5–7) to represent a date. The constructor receives three `int` parameters. Lines 15–18 validate the `month`—if it's out-of-range, lines 16–17 throw an exception. Lines 21–25 validate the `day`. If the day is incorrect based on the number of days in the particular `month` (except February 29th which requires special testing for leap years), lines 23–24 throw an exception. Lines 28–29 perform the leap year testing for February. If the month is February and the day is 29 and the `year` is not a leap year, lines 30–31 throw an exception. If no exceptions are thrown, then lines 34–36 initialize the `Date`'s instance variables and line 38 output the `this` reference as a `String`. Since `this` is a reference to the current `Date` object, the object's `toString` method (lines 42–44) is called *implicitly* to obtain the object's `String` representation. In this example, we assume that the value for `year` is correct—an industrial-strength `Date` class should also validate the year.

```
// Fig. 8.7: Date.java
// Date class declaration.

public class Date {
   private int month; // 1-12
   private int day; // 1-31 based on month
   private int year; // any year

   private static final int[] daysPerMonth =
      {0, 31, 28, 31, 30, 31, 30, 31, 31, 30, 31, 30, 31};

   // constructor: confirm proper value for month and day given the year
   public Date(int month, int day, int year) {
      // check if month in range
      if (month <= 0 || month > 12) {
         throw new IllegalArgumentException(
            "month (" + month + ") must be 1-12");
      }

      // check if day in range for month
      if (day <= 0 ||
         (day > daysPerMonth[month] && !(month == 2 && day == 29))) {
         throw new IllegalArgumentException("day (" + day +
            ") out-of-range for the specified month and year");
      }

      // check for leap year if month is 2 and day is 29
      if (month == 2 && day == 29 && !(year % 400 == 0 ||
           (year % 4 == 0 && year % 100 != 0))) {
         throw new IllegalArgumentException("day (" + day +
            ") out-of-range for the specified month and year");
      }

      this.month = month;
      this.day = day;
      this.year = year;

      System.out.printf("Date object constructor for date %s%n", this);
   }

   // return a String of the form month/day/year
   public String toString() {
      return String.format("%d/%d/%d", month, day, year);
   }
}
```

Fig. 8.7 | Date class declaration.

Class Employee

Class Employee (Fig. 8.8) has reference-type instance variables firstName (String), lastName (String), birthDate (Date) and hireDate (Date), showing that a class can have as instance variables references to objects of other classes. The Employee constructor (lines 11–17) takes four parameters representing the first name, last name, birth date and hire date. The objects referenced by the parameters are assigned to an `Employee` object's instance variables. When `Employee`'s `toString` method is called, it returns a `String` containing the employee's name and the `String` representations of the two `Date` objects. Each of these `Strings` is obtained with an *implicit* call to the `Date` class's `toString` method.

```
// Fig. 8.8: Employee.java
// Employee class with references to other objects.

public class Employee {
   private String firstName;
   private String lastName;
   private Date birthDate;
   private Date hireDate;

   // constructor to initialize name, birth date and hire date
   public Employee(String firstName, String lastName, Date birthDate,
      Date hireDate) {
      this.firstName = firstName;
      this.lastName = lastName;
      this.birthDate = birthDate;
      this.hireDate = hireDate;
   }

   // convert Employee to String format
   public String toString() {
      return String.format("%s, %s  Hired: %s  Birthday: %s",
         lastName, firstName, hireDate, birthDate);
   }
}
```

Fig. 8.8 | `Employee` class with references to other objects.

Class `EmployeeTest`

Class `EmployeeTest` (Fig. 8.9) creates two `Date` objects to represent an `Employee`'s birthday and hire date, respectively. Line 8 creates an `Employee` and initializes its instance variables by passing to the constructor two `Strings` (representing the `Employee`'s first and last names) and two `Date` objects (representing the birthday and hire date). Line 10 *implicitly* invokes the `Employee`'s `toString` method to display the values of its instance variables and demonstrate that the object was initialized properly.

```
1  // Fig. 8.9: EmployeeTest.java
2  // Composition demonstration.
3
4  public class EmployeeTest {
5     public static void main(String[] args) {
6        Date birth = new Date(7, 24, 1949);
7        Date hire = new Date(3, 12, 1988);
8        Employee employee = new Employee("Bob", "Blue", birth, hire);
9
```

Fig. 8.9 | Composition demonstration. (Part 1 of 2.)

```
        System.out.println(employee);
    }
}
```

```
Date object constructor for date 7/24/1949
Date object constructor for date 3/12/1988
Blue, Bob  Hired: 3/12/1988  Birthday: 7/24/1949
```

Fig. 8.9 | Composition demonstration. (Part 2 of 2.)

8.9 enum Types

In Fig. 6.8, we introduced the basic enum type, which defines a set of constants represented as unique identifiers. In that program the enum constants represented the game's status. In this section we discuss the relationship between enum types and classes. Like classes, all enum types are *reference* types. An enum type is declared with an **enum declaration**, which is a comma-separated list of *enum constants*—the declaration may optionally include other components of traditional classes, such as constructors, fields and methods (as you'll see momentarily). Each enum declaration declares an enum class with the following restrictions:

1. enum constants are *implicitly* `final`.
2. enum constants are *implicitly* `static`.
3. Any attempt to create an object of an enum type with operator new results in a compilation error.

The enum constants can be used anywhere constants can be used, such as in the `case` labels of `switch` statements and to control enhanced `for` statements.

Declaring Instance Variables, a Constructor and Methods in an enum *Type*

Figure 8.10 demonstrates instance variables, a constructor and methods in an enum type. The enum declaration contains two parts—the enum constants and the other members of the enum type.

```
// Fig. 8.10: Book.java
// Declaring an enum type with a constructor and explicit instance fields
// and accessors for these fields

public enum Book {
    // declare constants of enum type
    JHTP("Java How to Program", "2018"),
    CHTP("C How to Program", "2016"),
    IW3HTP("Internet & World Wide Web How to Program", "2012"),
    CPPHTP("C++ How to Program", "2017"),
    VBHTP("Visual Basic How to Program", "2014"),
    CSHARPHTP("Visual C# How to Program", "2017");

```

Fig. 8.10 | Declaring an enum type with a constructor and explicit instance fields and accessors for these fields. (Part 1 of 2.)

```
14      // instance fields
15      private final String title; // book title
16      private final String copyrightYear; // copyright year
17
18      // enum constructor
19      Book(String title, String copyrightYear) {
20         this.title = title;
21         this.copyrightYear = copyrightYear;
22      }
23
24      // accessor for field title
25      public String getTitle() {
26         return title;
27      }
28
29      // accessor for field copyrightYear
30      public String getCopyrightYear() {
31         return copyrightYear;
32      }
33   }
```

Fig. 8.10 | Declaring an `enum` type with a constructor and explicit instance fields and accessors for these fields. (Part 2 of 2.)

The first part (lines 7–12) declares six constants. Each is optionally followed by arguments that are passed to the **enum constructor** (lines 19–22). Like the constructors in classes, an `enum` constructor can specify any number of parameters and can be overloaded. In this example, the `enum` constructor requires two `String` parameters—one that specifies the book's title and one that specifies its copyright year. To properly initialize each `enum` constant, we follow it with parentheses containing two `String` arguments.

The second part (lines 15–32) declares the `enum` type's other members—instance variables `title` and `copyrightYear` (lines 15–16), a constructor (lines 19–22) and two methods (lines 25–27 and 30–32) that return the book title and copyright year, respectively. Each `enum` constant in `enum` type `Book` is an object of `enum` type `Book` that has its own copy of instance variables.

Using enum *type* Book

Figure 8.11 tests the `Book` `enum` and illustrates how to iterate through a range of its constants. For every `enum`, the compiler generates the `static` method **`values`** (called in line 10), which returns an array of the `enum`'s constants in the order they were declared. Lines 10–13 display the constants. Line 12 invokes the `enum` `Book`'s `getTitle` and `getCopyrightYear` methods to get the title and copyright year associated with the constant. When an `enum` constant is converted to a `String` (e.g., `book` in line 11), the constant's identifier is used as the `String` representation (e.g., `JHTP` for the first `enum` constant).

```
1   // Fig. 8.11: EnumTest.java
2   // Testing enum type Book.
3   import java.util.EnumSet;
```

Fig. 8.11 | Testing `enum` type `Book`. (Part 1 of 2.)

```
4
5  public class EnumTest {
6     public static void main(String[] args) {
7        System.out.println("All books:");
8
9        // print all books in enum Book
10       for (Book book : Book.values()) {
11          System.out.printf("%-10s%-45s%s%n", book,
12              book.getTitle(), book.getCopyrightYear());
13       }
14
15       System.out.printf("%nDisplay a range of enum constants:%n");
16
17       // print first four books
18       for (Book book : EnumSet.range(Book.JHTP, Book.CPPHTP)) {
19          System.out.printf("%-10s%-45s%s%n", book,
20              book.getTitle(), book.getCopyrightYear());
21       }
22    }
23 }
```

```
All books:
JHTP      Java How to Program                          2018
CHTP      C How to Program                             2016
IW3HTP    Internet & World Wide Web How to Program     2012
CPPHTP    C++ How to Program                           2017
VBHTP     Visual Basic How to Program                  2014
CSHARPHTP Visual C# How to Program                     2017

Display a range of enum constants:
JHTP      Java How to Program                          2018
CHTP      C How to Program                             2016
IW3HTP    Internet & World Wide Web How to Program     2012
CPPHTP    C++ How to Program                           2017
```

Fig. 8.11 | Testing enum type Book. (Part 2 of 2.)

Lines 18–21 use the static method **range** of class **EnumSet** (package java.util) to display a range of the enum Book's constants. Method range takes two parameters—the first and the last enum constants in the range—and returns an EnumSet that contains all the constants between these two constants, inclusive. For example, the expression EnumSet.range(Book.JHTP, Book.CPPHTP) returns an EnumSet containing Book.JHTP, Book.CHTP, Book.IW3HTP and Book.CPPHTP. The enhanced for statement can be used with an EnumSet just as it can with an array, so lines 18–21 use it to display the title and copyright year of every book in the EnumSet. Class EnumSet provides several other static methods for creating sets of enum constants from the same enum type.

Common Programming Error 8.4

In an enum declaration, it's a syntax error to declare enum constants after the enum type's constructors, fields and methods.

8.10 Garbage Collection

Every object uses system resources, such as memory. We need a disciplined way to give resources back to the system when they're no longer needed; otherwise, "resource leaks" might occur that would prevent resources from being reused by your program or possibly by other programs. The JVM performs automatic **garbage collection** to reclaim the *memory* occupied by objects that are no longer used. When there are *no more references* to an object, the object is *eligible* to be collected. Collection typically occurs when the JVM executes its **garbage collector**, which may not happen for a while, or even at all before a program terminates. So, memory leaks that are common in other languages like C and C++ (because memory is *not* automatically reclaimed in those languages) are *less* likely in Java, but some can still happen in subtle ways. Resource leaks other than memory leaks can also occur. For example, an app may open a file on disk to modify its contents—if the app does not close the file, it must terminate before any other app can use the file.

A Note about Class `Object`'s `finalize` Method

Every class in Java has the methods of class `Object` (package `java.lang`), one of which is method **`finalize`**. (You'll learn more about class `Object` in Chapter 9.) You should *never* use method `finalize`, because it can cause many problems and there's uncertainty as to whether it will *ever* get called before a program terminates.

The original intent of `finalize` was to allow the garbage collector to perform **termination housekeeping** on an object just before reclaiming the object's memory. Now, it's considered better practice for any class that uses system resources—such as files on disk—to provide a method that programmers can call to release resources when they're no longer needed in a program. `AutoClosable` objects reduce the likelihood of resource leaks when you use them with the `try`-with-resources statement. As its name implies, an `AutoClosable` object is closed automatically, once a `try`-with-resources statement finishes using the object. We discuss this in more detail in Section 11.12.

Software Engineering Observation 8.8

Many Java API classes (e.g., class `Scanner` and classes that read files from or write files to disk) provide `close` or `dispose` methods that programmers can call to release resources when they're no longer needed in a program.

8.11 `static` Class Members

Every object has its own copy of all the instance variables of the class. In certain cases, only one copy of a particular variable should be *shared* by all objects of a class. A **`static` field**—called a **class variable**—is used in such cases. A `static` variable represents **classwide information**—all objects of the class share the *same* piece of data. The declaration of a `static` variable begins with the keyword `static`.

Motivating `static`

Let's motivate `static` data with an example. Suppose that we have a video game with `Martian`s and other space creatures. Each `Martian` tends to be brave and willing to attack other space creatures when the `Martian` is aware that at least four other `Martian`s are present. If fewer than five `Martian`s are present, each of them becomes cowardly. Thus, each `Martian` needs to know the `martianCount`. We could endow class `Martian` with `martianCount` as an *instance variable*. If we do this, then every `Martian` will have *a separate copy* of the instance variable, and every time we create a new `Martian`, we'll have to update the instance variable `martianCount` in every `Martian` object. This wastes space with the redundant copies, wastes time in updating the separate copies and is error prone. Instead, we declare `martianCount` to be `static`, making `martianCount` classwide data. Every `Martian` can see the `martianCount` as if it were an instance variable of class `Martian`, but only *one* copy of the `static martianCount` is maintained. This saves space. We save time by having the `Martian` constructor increment the `static martianCount`—there's only one copy, so we do not have to increment separate copies for each `Martian` object.

Software Engineering Observation 8.9

Use a `static` variable when all objects of a class must use the same copy of the variable.

Class Scope

Static variables have *class scope*—they can be used in all of the class's methods. We can access a class's `public static` members through a reference to any object of the class, or by qualifying the member name with the class name and a dot (`.`), as in `Math.sqrt(2)`. A class's `private static` class members can be accessed by client code only through methods of the class. Actually, *`static` class members exist even when no objects of the class exist*—they're available as soon as the class is loaded into memory at execution time. To access a `public static` member when no objects of the class exist (and even when they do), prefix the class name and a dot (`.`) to the `static` member, as in `Math.PI`. To access a `private static` member when no objects of the class exist, provide a `public static` method and call it by qualifying its name with the class name and a dot.

Software Engineering Observation 8.10

Static class variables and methods exist, and can be used, even if no objects of that class have been instantiated.

`static` *Methods Cannot Directly Access Instance Variables and Instance Methods*

A `static` method *cannot* directly access a class's instance variables and instance methods, because a `static` method can be called even when no objects of the class have been instantiated. For the same reason, the `this` reference *cannot* be used in a `static` method. The `this` reference must refer to a specific object of the class, and when a `static` method is called, there might not be any objects of its class in memory.

Common Programming Error 8.5

A compilation error occurs if a `static` method calls an instance method in the same class by using only the method name. Similarly, a compilation error occurs if a `static` method attempts to access an instance variable in the same class by using only the variable name.

Common Programming Error 8.6

Referring to `this` in a `static` method is a compilation error.

Tracking the Number of Employee Objects That Have Been Created

Our next program declares two classes—Employee (Fig. 8.12) and EmployeeTest (Fig. 8.13). Class Employee declares private static variable count (Fig. 8.12, line 6) and public static method getCount (lines 32–34). The static variable count maintains a count of the number of objects of class Employee that have been created so far. This class variable is initialized to 0 in line 6. If a static variable is *not* initialized, the compiler assigns it a default value—in this case 0, the default value for type int.

```
1   // Fig. 8.12: Employee.java
2   // static variable used to maintain a count of the number of
3   // Employee objects in memory.
4
5   public class Employee {
6      private static int count = 0; // number of Employees created
7      private String firstName;
8      private String lastName;
9
10     // initialize Employee, add 1 to static count and
11     // output String indicating that constructor was called
12     public Employee(String firstName, String lastName) {
13        this.firstName = firstName;
14        this.lastName = lastName;
15
16        ++count;  // increment static count of employees
17        System.out.printf("Employee constructor: %s %s; count = %d%n",
18           firstName, lastName, count);
19     }
20
21     // get first name
22     public String getFirstName() {
23        return firstName;
24     }
25
26     // get last name
27     public String getLastName() {
28        return lastName;
29     }
30
31     // static method to get static count value
32     public static int getCount() {
33        return count;
34     }
35  }
```

Fig. 8.12 | static variable used to maintain a count of the number of Employee objects in memory.

When Employee objects exist, variable count can be used in any method of an Employee object—this example increments count in the constructor (line 16). The public static method getCount (lines 32–34) returns the number of Employee objects that have been created so far. When no objects of class Employee exist, client code can access variable count by calling method getCount via the class name, as in Employee.getCount().

Good Programming Practice 8.2

Invoke every `static` method by using the class name and a dot (`.`) to emphasize that the method being called is a `static` method.

When objects exist, `static` method `getCount` also can be called via any reference to an `Employee` object. This contradicts the preceding Good Programming Practice and, in fact, the Java SE 9 compiler issues warnings on lines 16–17 of Fig. 8.13. 9

Class `EmployeeTest`

`EmployeeTest` method `main` (Fig. 8.13) instantiates two `Employee` objects (lines 11–12). When each `Employee` object's constructor is invoked, lines 13–14 of Fig. 8.12 assign the `Employee`'s first name and last name to instance variables `firstName` and `lastName`. These statements do *not* copy the original `String` arguments. `String`s in Java are **immutable**—they cannot be modified after they're created. Therefore, it's safe to have *many* references to one `String` object. This is not normally the case for objects of most other classes in Java. If `String` objects are immutable, you might wonder why we're able to use operators + and += to concatenate `String` objects. String concatenation actually results in a *new* `String` object containing the concatenated values. The original `String` objects are *not* modified.

```
1  // Fig. 8.13: EmployeeTest.java
2  // static member demonstration.
3
4  public class EmployeeTest {
5     public static void main(String[] args) {
6        // show that count is 0 before creating Employees
7        System.out.printf("Employees before instantiation: %d%n",
8           Employee.getCount());
9
10       // create two Employees; count should be 2
11       Employee e1 = new Employee("Susan", "Baker");
12       Employee e2 = new Employee("Bob", "Blue");
13
14       // show that count is 2 after creating two Employees
15       System.out.printf("%nEmployees after instantiation:%n");
16       System.out.printf("via e1.getCount(): %d%n", e1.getCount());
17       System.out.printf("via e2.getCount(): %d%n", e2.getCount());
18       System.out.printf("via Employee.getCount(): %d%n",
19          Employee.getCount());
20
21       // get names of Employees
22       System.out.printf("%nEmployee 1: %s %s%nEmployee 2: %s %s%n",
23          e1.getFirstName(), e1.getLastName(),
24          e2.getFirstName(), e2.getLastName());
25    }
26 }
```

```
Employees before instantiation: 0
Employee constructor: Susan Baker; count = 1
Employee constructor: Bob Blue; count = 2
```

Fig. 8.13 | `static` member demonstration. (Part 1 of 2.)

```
Employees after instantiation:
via e1.getCount(): 2
via e2.getCount(): 2
via Employee.getCount(): 2

Employee 1: Susan Baker
Employee 2: Bob Blue
```

Fig. 8.13 | static member demonstration. (Part 2 of 2.)

When main terminates, local variables e1 and e2 are discarded—remember that a local variable exists *only* until the block in which it's declared completes execution. Because e1 and e2 were the only references to the Employee objects created in lines 11–12 (Fig. 8.13), these objects become "eligible for garbage collection" as main terminates.

In a typical app, the garbage collector *might* eventually reclaim the memory for any objects that are eligible for collection. If any objects are not reclaimed before the program terminates, the operating system will reclaim the memory used by the program. The JVM does *not* guarantee when, or even whether, the garbage collector will execute. When it does, it's possible that no objects or only a subset of the eligible objects will be collected.

8.12 static Import

In Section 6.3, you learned about the static fields and methods of class Math. We access class Math's static fields and *methods* by preceding each with the class name Math and a dot (.). A **static import** declaration enables you to import the static members of a class or interface so you can access them via their *unqualified names* in your class—that is, the class name and a dot (.) are *not* required when using an imported static member.

static *Import Forms*

A static import declaration has two forms—one that imports a particular static member (which is known as **single static import**) and one that imports *all* static members of a class (known as **static import on demand**). The following syntax imports a particular static member:

```
import static packageName.ClassName.staticMemberName;
```

where *packageName* is the package of the class (e.g., java.lang), *ClassName* is the name of the class (e.g., Math) and *staticMemberName* is the name of the static field or method (e.g., PI or abs). In the following syntax, the asterisk (*) indicates that *all* static members of a class should be available for use in the file:

```
import static packageName.ClassName.*;
```

static import declarations import *only* static class members. Regular import statements should be used to specify the classes used in a program.

Demonstrating static *Import*

Figure 8.14 demonstrates a static import. Line 3 is a static import declaration, which imports *all* static fields and methods of class Math from package java.lang. Lines 7–10 access the Math class's static methods sqrt (line 7) and ceil (line 8) and its static fields

E (line 9) and PI (line 10) *without* preceding the field names or method names with class name Math and a dot.

Common Programming Error 8.7

A compilation error occurs if a program attempts to import two or more classes' `static` *methods that have the same signature or* `static` *fields that have the same name.*

```
1  // Fig. 8.14: StaticImportTest.java
2  // Static import of Math class methods.
3  import static java.lang.Math.*;
4
5  public class StaticImportTest {
6     public static void main(String[] args) {
7        System.out.printf("sqrt(900.0) = %.1f%n", sqrt(900.0));
8        System.out.printf("ceil(-9.8) = %.1f%n", ceil(-9.8));
9        System.out.printf("E = %f%n", E);
10       System.out.printf("PI = %f%n", PI);
11    }
12 }
```

```
sqrt(900.0) = 30.0
ceil(-9.8) = -9.0
E = 2.718282
PI = 3.141593
```

Fig. 8.14 | `static` import of `Math` class methods.

8.13 `final` Instance Variables

The *principle of least privilege* is fundamental to good software engineering. In the context of an app's code, it states that code should be granted only the amount of privilege and access that it needs to accomplish its designated task, but no more. This makes your programs more robust by preventing code from accidentally (or maliciously) modifying variable values and calling methods that should *not* be accessible.

Let's see how this principle applies to instance variables. Some need to be *modifiable* and some do not. You can use the keyword `final` to specify that a variable is *not* modifiable (i.e., it's a *constant*) and that any attempt to modify it is an error. For example,

```
private final int INCREMENT;
```

declares a `final` (constant) instance variable `INCREMENT` of type `int`. Such variables can be initialized when they're declared. If they're not, they *must* be initialized in every constructor of the class. Initializing constants in constructors enables each object of the class to have a different value for the constant. If a `final` variable is *not* initialized in its declaration or in every constructor, a compilation error occurs.

Common Programming Error 8.8

Attempting to modify a `final` *instance variable after it's initialized is a compilation error.*

Error-Prevention Tip 8.4

Attempts to modify a `final` *instance variable are caught at compilation time rather than causing execution-time errors. It's always preferable to get bugs out at compilation time, if possible, rather than allow them to slip through to execution time (where experience has shown that repair is often many times more expensive).*

Software Engineering Observation 8.11

Declaring an instance variable as `final` *helps enforce the principle of least privilege. If an instance variable should not be modified, declare it to be* `final` *to prevent modification. For example, in Fig. 8.8, the instance variables* `firstName`, `lastName`, `birthDate` *and* `hireDate` *are never modified after they're initialized, so they should be declared* `final` *(Exercise 8.20). We'll enforce this practice in all programs going forward. Testing, debugging and maintaining programs is easier when every variable that can be* `final` *is, in fact,* `final`. *You'll see additional benefits of* `final` *in Chapter 23, Concurrency.*

Software Engineering Observation 8.12

A `final` *field should also be declared* `static` *if it's initialized in its declaration to a value that's the same for all objects of the class. After this initialization, its value can never change. Therefore, we don't need a separate copy of the field for every object of the class. Making the field* `static` *enables all objects of the class to share the* `final` *field.*

8.14 Package Access

If no access modifier (`public`, `protected` or `private`—we discuss `protected` in Chapter 9) is specified for a method or variable when it's declared in a class, the method or variable is considered to have **package access**. In a program that consists of one class declaration, this has no specific effect. However, if a program uses *multiple* classes from the *same* package (i.e., a group of related classes), these classes can access each other's package-access members directly through references to objects of the appropriate classes, or in the case of `static` members through the class name. Package access is rarely used.

Figure 8.15 demonstrates package access. The app contains two classes in one source-code file—the `PackageDataTest` class (lines 5–19) containing `main` and the `PackageData` class (lines 22–30). Classes in the same source file are part of the same package. Consequently, class `PackageDataTest` is allowed to modify the package-access data of `PackageData` objects. When you compile this program, the compiler produces two separate `.class` files—`PackageDataTest.class` and `PackageData.class`. The compiler places the two `.class` files in the same directory. You can also place class `PackageData` (lines 22–30) in a separate source-code file.

```
1  // Fig. 8.15: PackageDataTest.java
2  // Package-access members of a class are accessible by other classes
3  // in the same package.
4
5  public class PackageDataTest {
```

Fig. 8.15 | Package-access members of a class are accessible by other classes in the same package. (Part 1 of 2.)

```
 6      public static void main(String[] args) {
 7         PackageData packageData = new PackageData();
 8
 9         // output String representation of packageData
10         System.out.printf("After instantiation:%n%s%n", packageData);
11
12         // change package access data in packageData object
13         packageData.number = 77;
14         packageData.string = "Goodbye";
15
16         // output String representation of packageData
17         System.out.printf("%nAfter changing values:%n%s%n", packageData);
18      }
19   }
20
21   // class with package access instance variables
22   class PackageData {
23      int number = 0; // package-access instance variable
24      String string = "Hello"; // package-access instance variable
25
26      // return PackageData object String representation
27      public String toString() {
28         return String.format("number: %d; string: %s", number, string);
29      }
30   }
```

```
After instantiation:
number: 0; string: Hello

After changing values:
number: 77; string: Goodbye
```

Fig. 8.15 | Package-access members of a class are accessible by other classes in the same package. (Part 2 of 2.)

In the `PackageData` class declaration, lines 23–24 declare the instance variables `number` and `string` with no access modifiers—therefore, these are package-access instance variables. Class `PackageDataTest`'s `main` method creates an instance of the `PackageData` class (line 7) to demonstrate the ability to modify the `PackageData` instance variables directly (as shown in lines 13–14). The results of the modification can be seen in the output window.

8.15 Using BigDecimal for Precise Monetary Calculations

In earlier chapters, we demonstrated monetary calculations using values of type `double`. In Chapter 5, we discussed the fact that some `double` values are represented *approximately*. Any application that requires precise floating-point calculations—such as those in financial applications—should instead use class **`BigDecimal`** (from package **`java.math`**).[1]

Interest Calculations Using `BigDecimal`

Figure 8.16 reimplements the interest-calculation example of Fig. 5.6 using objects of class `BigDecimal` to perform the calculations. We also introduce class **`NumberFormat`** (package **`java.text`**) for formatting numeric values as *locale-specific* `String`s—for example, in the U.S. locale, the value 1234.56, would be formatted as `"1,234.56"`, whereas in many European locales it would be formatted as `"1.234,56"`.

```java
// Fig. 8.16: Interest.java
// Compound-interest calculations with BigDecimal.
import java.math.BigDecimal;
import java.text.NumberFormat;

public class Interest {
   public static void main(String args[]) {
      // initial principal amount before interest
      BigDecimal principal = BigDecimal.valueOf(1000.0);
      BigDecimal rate = BigDecimal.valueOf(0.05); // interest rate

      // display headers
      System.out.printf("%s%20s%n", "Year", "Amount on deposit");

      // calculate amount on deposit for each of ten years
      for (int year = 1; year <= 10; year++) {
         // calculate new amount for specified year
         BigDecimal amount =
            principal.multiply(rate.add(BigDecimal.ONE).pow(year));

         // display the year and the amount
         System.out.printf("%4d%20s%n", year,
            NumberFormat.getCurrencyInstance().format(amount));
      }
   }
}
```

```
Year   Amount on deposit
   1           $1,050.00
   2           $1,102.50
   3           $1,157.62
   4           $1,215.51
   5           $1,276.28
   6           $1,340.10
   7           $1,407.10
   8           $1,477.46
   9           $1,551.33
  10           $1,628.89
```

Fig. 8.16 | Compound-interest calculations with `BigDecimal`.

1. Dealing with currencies, monetary amounts, conversions, rounding and formatting is complex. The new JavaMoney API (`http://javamoney.github.io`) was developed to meet these challenges. At this time, JavaMoney is not part of Java SE or Java EE. Exercise 8.22 asks you to investigate JavaMoney and use it to build a currency converter app.

Creating `BigDecimal` Objects

Lines 9–10 declare and initialize `BigDecimal` variables `principal` and `rate` using the `BigDecimal` `static` method **`valueOf`** that receives a `double` argument and returns a `BigDecimal` object that represents the *exact* value specified.

Performing the Interest Calculations with `BigDecimal`

Lines 18–19 perform the interest calculation using `BigDecimal` methods **`multiply`**, **`add`** and **`pow`**. The expression in line 19 evaluates as follows:

1. First, the expression `rate.add(BigDecimal.ONE)` adds `1` to the `rate` to produce a `BigDecimal` containing `1.05`—this is equivalent to `1.0 + rate` in line 15 of Fig. 5.6. The `BigDecimal` constant **`ONE`** represents the value `1`. Class `BigDecimal` also provides the commonly used constants **`ZERO`** (`0`) and **`TEN`** (`10`).
2. Next, `BigDecimal` method `pow` is called on the preceding result to raise `1.05` to the power `year`—this is equivalent to passing `1.0 + rate` and `year` to method `Math.pow` in line 15 of Fig. 5.6.
3. Finally, we call `BigDecimal` method `multiply` on the `principal` object, passing the preceding result as the argument. This returns a `BigDecimal` representing the amount on deposit at the end of the specified `year`.

Since the expression `rate.add(BigDecimal.ONE)` produces the same value in each iteration of the loop, we could have simply initialized rate to `1.05` in line 10 of Fig. 8.16; however, we chose to mimic the precise calculations we used in line 15 of Fig. 5.6.

Formatting Currency Values with `NumberFormat`

During each iteration of the loop, line 23 of Fig. 8.16

```
NumberFormat.getCurrencyInstance().format(amount)
```

evaluates as follows:

1. First, the expression uses `NumberFormat`'s `static` method **`getCurrencyInstance`** to get a `NumberFormat` that's preconfigured to format numeric values as locale-specific currency `Strings`—for example, in the U.S. locale, the numeric value 1628.89 is formatted as $1,628.89. Locale-specific formatting is an important part of **internationalization**—the process of customizing your applications for users' various locales and spoken languages.
2. Next, the expression invokes method `NumberFormat` method **`format`** (on the object returned by `getCurrencyInstance`) to perform the formatting of the `amount` value. Method `format` then returns the locale-specific `String` representation. For the U.S. locale, the result is rounded to two digits to the right of the decimal point.

Rounding `BigDecimal` Values

In addition to precise calculations, `BigDecimal` gives you control over rounding—by default all calculations are exact and *no* rounding occurs. If you do not specify how to round `BigDecimal` values and a given value cannot be represented exactly—such as the result of 1 divided by 3, which is 0.3333333...—an `ArithmeticException` occurs.

Though we do not do so in this example, you can specify the *rounding mode* for `BigDecimal` by supplying a `MathContext` object (package `java.math`) to class `BigDecimal`'s constructor when you create a `BigDecimal`. You may also provide a `MathContext` to various `BigDecimal` methods that perform calculations. Class `MathContext` contains several preconfigured `MathContext` objects that you can learn about at

```
http://docs.oracle.com/javase/8/docs/api/java/math/MathContext.html
```

By default, each preconfigured `MathContext` uses so-called "banker's rounding" as explained for the `RoundingMode` constant `HALF_EVEN` at:

```
http://docs.oracle.com/javase/8/docs/api/java/math/
   RoundingMode.html#HALF_EVEN
```

Scaling `BigDecimal` *Values*

A `BigDecimal`'s scale is the number of digits to the right of its decimal point. If you need a `BigDecimal` rounded to a specific digit, you can call `BigDecimal` method `setScale`. For example, the following expression returns a `BigDecimal` with two digits to the right of the decimal point and using banker's rounding:

```
amount.setScale(2, RoundingMode.HALF_EVEN)
```

8.16 (Optional) GUI and Graphics Case Study: Using Objects with Graphics

Recall from Section 3.6 that one of our goals in this case study is to use object-oriented programming concepts to create an app that draws a variety of shapes. Eventually, we'll want to store the shapes the user draws in a collection. Each shape will know its own location, size and color. Then, the app will be able to recreate the drawing by iterating through the collection and displaying each shape. Also, by using a collection, you'll easily be able to add an *undo* capability to the drawing app—each time the user presses an **Undo** `Button`, you can simply remove the last shape in the collection and then iterate through the collection and redraw the shapes that remain. To do this, we'll create a set of shape classes that store information about each shape. We'll make these classes "smart" by allowing objects of these classes to *draw themselves* when provided with a JavaFX `GraphicsContext` object. In this section's `DrawRandomLines` example, we'll begin with a class named `MyLine` that encapsulates the information for drawing a line. For this section's example, we'll store the `MyLine` objects in an array, but you could also use an `ArrayList<MyLine>` (Section 7.16).

Class `MyLine`

Figure 8.17 declares class `MyLine`, which imports classes `GraphicsContext` and `Color` (lines 3–4). Lines 7–10 declare instance variables for the line's starting and ending coordinates, and line 11 declares the instance variable that stores the line's stroke color. The constructor at lines 14–22 takes five parameters, one for each instance variable that it initializes. Method `draw` at lines 25–28 receives a `GraphicsContext` object and uses it to draw a line in the proper color between the start and end points.

```
// Fig. 8.17: MyLine.java
// MyLine class represents a line.
import javafx.scene.canvas.GraphicsContext;
import javafx.scene.paint.Color;

public class MyLine {
   private double x1; // x-coordinate of first endpoint
   private double y1; // y-coordinate of first endpoint
   private double x2; // x-coordinate of second endpoint
   private double y2; // y-coordinate of second endpoint
   private Color strokeColor; // color of this line

   // constructor with input values
   public MyLine(
      double x1, double y1, double x2, double y2, Color strokeColor) {

      this.x1 = x1;
      this.y1 = y1;
      this.x2 = x2;
      this.y2 = y2;
      this.strokeColor = strokeColor;
   }

   // draw the line in the specified color
   public void draw(GraphicsContext gc) {
      gc.setStroke(strokeColor);
      gc.strokeLine(x1, y1, x2, y2);
   }
}
```

Fig. 8.17 | `MyLine` class represents a line.

Creating the **Draw Random Lines** *App's GUI*

The app's GUI is defined in `DrawRandomLines.fxml`. We reused the `DrawLines.fxml` GUI shown in Fig. 4.17, but made the following change to `DrawRandomLines.fxml`:

- We specified `DrawRandomLinesController` as the app's **Controller class** in the Scene Builder **Document** window's **Controller** section.

Class `DrawRandomLinesController`

Again, we do not show the code for `DrawRandomLines.java`, because the only changes from earlier examples are the name of the FXML file to load (`DrawRandomLines.fxml`) and the text displayed in the stage's title bar (`Draw Random Lines`).

In method `drawLinesButtonPressed` (Fig. 8.18), line 21 creates the `MyLine` array `lines` to store 100 lines to draw. Lines 23 and 24 store the `Canvas`'s `width` and `height`, which we use in lines 29–32 when choosing random coordinates. Lines 27–40 create a new `MyLine` for every array element. Lines 29–32 generate random coordinates for each line's endpoints, and lines 35–36 generate a random color. Line 39 creates a new `MyLine` object with the randomly generated values and stores it in the array. Finally, lines 43–47 clear the `Canvas` then iterate through the `MyLine` objects in array `lines` using an enhanced for statement. Each iteration calls the current MyLine's draw method and passes it the Canvas's GraphicsContext. The MyLine object actually draws itself.

```
// Fig. 8.18: DrawRandomLinesController.java
// Drawing random lines using MyLine objects.
import java.security.SecureRandom;
import javafx.event.ActionEvent;
import javafx.fxml.FXML;
import javafx.scene.canvas.Canvas;
import javafx.scene.canvas.GraphicsContext;
import javafx.scene.paint.Color;
import javafx.scene.shape.ArcType;

public class DrawRandomLinesController {
   private static final SecureRandom randomNumbers = new SecureRandom();
   @FXML private Canvas canvas;

   // draws random lines
   @FXML
   void drawLinesButtonPressed(ActionEvent event) {
      // get the GraphicsContext, which is used to draw on the Canvas
      GraphicsContext gc = canvas.getGraphicsContext2D();

      MyLine[] lines = new MyLine[100]; // stores the MyLine objects

      final nt width = (int) canvas.getWidth();
      final int height = (int) canvas.getHeight();

      // create lines
      for (int count = 0; count < lines.length; count++) {
         // generate random coordinates
         double x1 = randomNumbers.nextInt(width);
         double y1 = randomNumbers.nextInt(height);
         double x2 = randomNumbers.nextInt(width);
         double y2 = randomNumbers.nextInt(height);

         // generate a random color
         Color color = Color.rgb(randomNumbers.nextInt(256),
            randomNumbers.nextInt(256), randomNumbers.nextInt(256));

         // add a new MyLine to the array
         lines[count] = new MyLine(x1, y1, x2, y2, color);
      }

      // clear the Canvas then draw the lines
      gc.clearRect(0, 0, canvas.getWidth(), canvas.getHeight());

      for (MyLine line : lines) {
         line.draw(gc);
      }
   }
}
```

Fig. 8.18 | Drawing random lines using MyLine objects. (Part 1 of 2.)

Fig. 8.18 | Drawing random lines using `MyLine` objects. (Part 2 of 2.)

GUI and Graphics Case Study Exercise

8.1 Enhance the program in Figs. 8.17–8.18 to draw the lines in random thicknesses. You can set the line thickness with `GraphicsContext` method `setLineWidth`.

8.2 Enhance the program in Figs. 8.17–8.18 to randomly draw rectangles and ovals. Create classes `MyRectangle` and `MyOval`. Both classes should include *x1*, *y1*, *x2*, *y2* coordinates, a stroke color, a fill color and a `boolean` flag to determine whether the shape is filled. Declare a constructor in each class with arguments for initializing all the instance variables. To help draw rectangles and ovals, each class should provide methods `getUpperLeftX`, `getUpperLeftY`, `getWidth` and `getHeight` that calculate the upper-left *x*-coordinate, upper-left *y*-coordinate, width and height, respectively, based on the *x1*, *y1*, *x2*, *y2* coordinates. The upper-left *x*-coordinate is the smaller of the two *x*-coordinate values, the upper-left *y*-coordinate is the smaller of the two *y*-coordinate values, the width is the absolute value of the difference between the *x*-coordinate values, and the height is the absolute value of the difference between the *y*-coordinate values. (Declaring classes `MyRectangle` and `MyOval` as described here will make it easier for you to support drawing with the mouse in Exercise 13.9 after you learn about mouse event handling in Section 13.3.)

The app's GUI should provide separate `Button`s that draw 100 random `MyRectangle`s and 100 random `MyOval`s, respectively. Each `Button` should have a corresponding event handler in the app's controller.

In addition, modify classes `MyLine`, `MyRectangle` and `MyOval` to include the following capabilities that you'll use in Section 10.14:

a) A constructor with no arguments that sets the shape's coordinates to `0`, the stroke color and—for classes `MyRectangle` and `MyOval` only—the `filled` flag to `false` and the fill color to `Color.BLACK`.
b) *Set* methods for the instance variables in each class. The methods that *set* a coordinate value should verify that the argument is greater than or equal to zero before setting the coordinate—if it's not, they should set the coordinate to zero.
c) *Get* methods for the instance variables in each class. Method `draw` should reference the coordinates by the *get* methods rather than access them directly.

8.17 Wrap-Up

In this chapter, we presented additional class concepts. The `Time` class case study showed a complete class declaration consisting of `private` data, overloaded `public` constructors for initialization flexibility, *set* and *get* methods for manipulating the class's data, and methods that returned `String` representations of a `Time` object in two different formats. You also learned that every class can declare a `toString` method that returns a `String` representation of an object of the class and that method `toString` can be called implicitly whenever an object of a class appears in the code where a `String` is expected. We showed how to `throw` an exception to indicate that a problem has occurred.

You learned that the `this` reference is used implicitly in a class's instance methods to access the class's instance variables and other instance methods. You also saw explicit uses of the `this` reference to access the class's members (including shadowed fields) and how to use keyword `this` in a constructor to call another constructor of the class.

We discussed the differences between default constructors provided by the compiler and no-argument constructors provided by the programmer. You learned that a class can have references to objects of other classes as members—a concept known as composition. You learned more about `enum` types and how they can be used to create a set of constants for use in a program. You learned about Java's garbage-collection capability and how it (unpredictably) reclaims the memory of objects that are no longer used. The chapter explained the motivation for `static` fields in a class and demonstrated how to declare and use `static` fields and methods in your own classes. You also learned how to declare and initialize `final` variables.

You learned that fields declared without an access modifier are given package access by default. You saw the relationship between classes in the same package that allows each class in a package to access the package-access members of other classes in the package. Finally, we demonstrated how to use class `BigDecimal` to perform precise monetary calculations.

In the next chapter, you'll learn about an important aspect of object-oriented programming in Java—inheritance. You'll see that all classes in Java are related by inheritance, directly or indirectly, to the class called `Object`. You'll also begin to understand how the relationships between classes enable you to build more powerful apps.

Summary

Section 8.2 `Time` *Class Case Study*

- The `public` methods of a class are also known as the class's `public` services or `public` interface (p. 330). They present to the class's clients a view of the services the class provides.
- A class's `private` members are not accessible to its clients.
- `String` class `static` method `format` (p. 332) is similar to method `System.out.printf` except that `format` returns a formatted `String` rather than displaying it in a command window.
- All objects in Java have a `toString` method that returns a `String` representation of the object. Method `toString` is called implicitly when an object appears in code where a `String` is needed.

Section 8.3 Controlling Access to Members

- The access modifiers `public` and `private` control access to a class's variables and methods.

- The primary purpose of `public` methods is to present to the class's clients a view of the services the class provides. Clients need not be concerned with how the class accomplishes its tasks.
- A class's `private` variables and `private` methods (i.e., its implementation details) are not accessible to its clients.

Section 8.4 Referring to the Current Object's Members with the `this` *Reference*

- An instance method of an object implicitly uses keyword `this` (p. 336) to refer to the object's instance variables and other methods. Keyword `this` can also be used explicitly.
- The compiler produces a separate file with the `.class` extension for every compiled class.
- If a local variable has the same name as a class's field, the local variable shadows the field. You can use the `this` reference in a method to refer to the shadowed field explicitly.

Section 8.5 `Time` *Class Case Study: Overloaded Constructors*

- Overloaded constructors enable objects of a class to be initialized in different ways. The compiler differentiates overloaded constructors (p. 338) by their signatures.
- To call one constructor of a class from another of the same class, you can use the `this` keyword followed by parentheses containing the constructor arguments. If used, such a constructor call must appear as the first statement in the constructor's body.

Section 8.6 Default and No-Argument Constructors

- If no constructors are provided in a class, the compiler creates a default constructor.
- If a class declares constructors, the compiler will not create a default constructor. In this case, you must declare a no-argument constructor (p. 340) if default initialization is required.

Section 8.7 Notes on Set *and* Get *Methods*

- *Set* methods are commonly called mutator methods (p. 344) because they typically change a value. *Get* methods are commonly called accessor methods (p. 344) or query methods. A predicate method (p. 345) tests whether a condition is true or false.

Section 8.8 Composition

- A class can have references to objects of other classes as members. This is called composition (p. 345) and is sometimes referred to as a *has-a* relationship.

Section 8.9 `enum` *Types*

- All `enum` types (p. 348) are reference types. An `enum` type is declared with an `enum` declaration, which is a comma-separated list of `enum` constants. The declaration may optionally include other components of traditional classes, such as constructors, fields and methods.
- `enum` constants are implicitly `final`, because they declare constants that should not be modified.
- `enum` constants are implicitly `static`.
- Any attempt to create an object of an `enum` type with operator `new` results in a compilation error.
- `enum` constants can be used anywhere constants can be used, such as in the `case` labels of `switch` statements and to control enhanced `for` statements.
- Each `enum` constant in an `enum` declaration is optionally followed by arguments which are passed to the `enum` constructor.
- For every `enum`, the compiler generates a `static` method called `values` (p. 349) that returns an array of the `enum`'s constants in the order in which they were declared.
- `EnumSet` `static` method `range` (p. 350) receives the first and last `enum` constants in a range and returns an `EnumSet` that contains all the constants between these two constants, inclusive.

Section 8.10 Garbage Collection

- The Java Virtual Machine (JVM) performs garbage collection (p. 351) to reclaim the memory occupied by objects that are no longer in use. When there are no more references to an object, the object is eligible for garbage collection the next time the JVM executes its garbage collector.

Section 8.11 `static` *Class Members*

- A `static` variable (p. 351) represents classwide information that's shared among the class's objects.
- `static` variables have class scope. A class's `public static` members can be accessed through a reference to any object of the class, or they can be accessed by qualifying the member name with the class name and a dot (`.`). Client code can access a class's `private static` class members only through methods of the class.
- `static` class members exist as soon as the class is loaded into memory.
- A method declared `static` cannot directly access a class's instance variables and instance methods, because a `static` method can be called even when no objects of the class have been instantiated.
- The `this` reference cannot be used in a `static` method.

Section 8.12 `static` *Import*

- A `static` import declaration (p. 355) enables you to refer to imported `static` members without the class name and a dot (`.`). A single `static` import declaration imports one `static` member, and a `static` import on demand imports all `static` members of a class.

Section 8.13 `final` *Instance Variables*

- In the context of an app's code, the principle of least privilege states that code should be granted only the amount of privilege and access that it needs to accomplish its designated task.
- Keyword `final` specifies that a variable is not modifiable. Such variables must be initialized when they're declared or by each of a class's constructors.

Section 8.14 Package Access

- If no access modifier is specified for a method or variable when it's declared in a class, the method or variable is considered to have package access (p. 357).
- Classes from the same package can access each other's package-access members directly through references to objects of the appropriate classes, or for `static` members through the class name.

Section 8.15 Using `BigDecimal` *for Precise Monetary Calculations*

- Any application that requires precise floating-point calculations without rounding errors—such as those in financial applications—should use class `BigDecimal` (package `java.math`; p. 358).
- `BigDecimal static` method `valueOf` (p. 360) with a `double` argument returns a `BigDecimal` that represents the exact value specified.
- `BigDecimal` method `add` (p. 360) adds its argument `BigDecimal` to the `BigDecimal` on which the method is called and returns the result.
- `BigDecimal` provides the constants `ONE` (`1`), `ZERO` (`0`) and `TEN` (`10`).
- `BigDecimal` method `pow` (p. 360) raises its first argument to the power in its second argument.
- `BigDecimal` method `multiply` (p. 360) multiplies its argument `BigDecimal` with the `BigDecimal` on which the method is called and returns the result.
- Class `NumberFormat` (package `java.text;` p. 360) provides capabilities for formatting numeric values as locale-specific `Strings`. The class's `static` method `getCurrencyInstance` returns a preconfigured `NumberFormat` for local-specific currency values. `NumberFormat` method `format` performs the formatting.

- Locale-specific formatting is an important part of internationalization—the process of customizing your applications for users' various locales and spoken languages.
- `BigDecimal` gives you control over how values are rounded—by default all calculations are exact and no rounding occurs. If you do not specify how to round `BigDecimal` values and a given value cannot be represented exactly, an `ArithmeticException` occurs.
- You can specify the rounding mode for `BigDecimal` by supplying a `MathContext` object (package `java.math`) to class `BigDecimal`'s constructor when you create a `BigDecimal`. You may also provide a `MathContext` to various `BigDecimal` methods that perform calculations. By default, each preconfigured `MathContext` uses so called "banker's rounding."
- A `BigDecimal`'s scale is the number of digits to the right of its decimal point. If you need a `BigDecimal` rounded to a specific digit, you can call `BigDecimal` method `setScale`.

Self-Review Exercises

8.1 Fill in the blanks in each of the following statements:

a) A(n) ________ imports all `static` members of a class.
b) `String` class `static` method ________ is similar to method `System.out.printf`, but returns a formatted `String` rather than displaying a `String` in a command window.
c) If a method contains a local variable with the same name as one of its class's fields, the local variable ________ the field in that method's scope.
d) The `public` methods of a class are also known as the class's ________ or ________.
e) A(n) ________ declaration imports one `static` member.
f) If a class declares constructors, the compiler will not create a(n) ________.
g) An object's ________ method is called implicitly when an object appears in code where a `String` is needed.
h) *Get* methods are commonly called ________ or ________.
i) A(n) ________ method tests whether a condition is true or false.
j) For every `enum`, the compiler generates a `static` method called ________ that returns an array of the `enum`'s constants in the order in which they were declared.
k) Composition is sometimes referred to as a(n) ________ relationship.
l) A(n) ________ declaration contains a comma-separated list of constants.
m) A(n) ________ variable represents classwide information that's shared by all the objects of the class.
n) A(n) ________ declaration imports one `static` member.
o) The ________ states that code should be granted only the amount of privilege and access that it needs to accomplish its designated task.
p) Keyword ________ specifies that a variable is not modifiable after initialization in a declaration or constructor.
q) A(n) ________ imports all `static` members of a class.
r) *Set* methods are commonly called ________ because they typically change a value.
s) Use class ________ to perform precise monetary calculations.
t) Use the ________ statement to indicate that a problem has occurred.

Answers to Self-Review Exercises

8.1 a) `static` import on demand. b) `format`. c) shadows. d) `public` services, `public` interface. e) single `static` import. f) default constructor. g) `toString`. h) accessor methods, query methods. i) predicate. j) `values`. k) *has-a*. l) `enum`. m) `static`. n) single `static` import. o) principle of least privilege. p) `final`. q) `static` import on demand. r) mutator methods. s) `BigDecimal`. t) `throw`.

Exercises

8.2 *(Based on Section 8.14)* Explain the notion of package access in Java. Explain the negative aspects of package access.

8.3 What happens when a return type, even `void`, is specified for a constructor?

8.4 *(Rectangle Class)* Create a class `Rectangle` with attributes `length` and `width`, each of which defaults to 1. Provide methods that calculate the rectangle's perimeter and area. It has *set* and *get* methods for both `length` and `width`. The *set* methods should verify that `length` and `width` are each floating-point numbers larger than 0.0 and less than 20.0. Write a program to test class `Rectangle`.

8.5 *(Modifying the Internal Data Representation of a Class)* It would be perfectly reasonable for the `Time2` class of Fig. 8.5 to represent the time internally as the number of seconds since midnight rather than the three integer values `hour`, `minute` and `second`. Clients could use the same `public` methods and get the same results. Modify the `Time2` class of Fig. 8.5 to implement the time as the number of seconds since midnight and show that no change is visible to the clients of the class.

8.6 *(Savings Account Class)* Create class `SavingsAccount`. Use a `static` variable `annualInterestRate` to store the annual interest rate for all account holders. Each object of the class contains a `private` instance variable `savingsBalance` indicating the amount the saver currently has on deposit. Provide method `calculateMonthlyInterest` to calculate the monthly interest by multiplying the `savingsBalance` by `annualInterestRate` divided by 12—this interest should be added to `savingsBalance`. Provide a `static` method `modifyInterestRate` that sets the `annualInterestRate` to a new value. Write a program to test class `SavingsAccount`. Instantiate two `savingsAccount` objects, `saver1` and `saver2`, with balances of $2000.00 and $3000.00, respectively. Set `annualInterestRate` to 4%, then calculate the monthly interest for each of 12 months and print the new balances for both savers. Next, set the `annualInterestRate` to 5%, calculate the next month's interest and print the new balances for both savers.

8.7 *(Enhancing Class `Time2`)* Modify class `Time2` of Fig. 8.5 to include a `tick` method that increments the time stored in a `Time2` object by one second. Provide method `incrementMinute` to increment the minute by one and method `incrementHour` to increment the hour by one. Write a program that tests the `tick` method, the `incrementMinute` method and the `incrementHour` method to ensure that they work correctly. Be sure to test the following cases:

a) incrementing into the next minute,
b) incrementing into the next hour and
c) incrementing into the next day (i.e., 11:59:59 PM to 12:00:00 AM).

8.8 *(Enhancing Class `Date`)* Modify class `Date` of Fig. 8.7 to perform error checking on the initializer values for variables `month`, `day` and `year` (currently it validates only the month and day). Provide a method `nextDay` to increment the day by one. Write a program that tests method `nextDay` in a loop that prints the date during each iteration to illustrate that the method works correctly. Test the following cases:

a) incrementing into the next month and
b) incrementing into the next year.

8.9 Rewrite the code in Fig. 8.14 to use a separate `import` declaration for each `static` member of class `Math` that's used in the example.

8.10 Write an `enum` type `TrafficLight`, whose constants (`RED`, `GREEN`, `YELLOW`) take one parameter—the duration of the light. Write a program to test the `TrafficLight` `enum` so that it displays the `enum` constants and their durations.

8.11 *(Complex Numbers)* Create a class called `Complex` for performing arithmetic with complex numbers. Complex numbers have the form

realPart + *imaginaryPart* * *i*

where i is

$$\sqrt{-1}$$

Write a program to test your class. Use floating-point variables to represent the `private` data of the class. Provide a constructor that enables an object of this class to be initialized when it's declared. Provide a no-argument constructor with default values in case no initializers are provided. Provide `public` methods that perform the following operations:

a) Add two `Complex` numbers: The real parts are added together and the imaginary parts are added together.
b) Subtract two `Complex` numbers: The real part of the right operand is subtracted from the real part of the left operand, and the imaginary part of the right operand is subtracted from the imaginary part of the left operand.
c) Print `Complex` numbers in the form `(`*realPart*`,` *imaginaryPart*`)`.

8.12 *(Date and Time Class)* Create class `DateAndTime` that combines the modified `Time2` class of Exercise 8.7 and the modified `Date` class of Exercise 8.8. Modify method `incrementHour` to call method `nextDay` if the time is incremented into the next day. Modify methods `toString` and `toUniversalString` to output the date in addition to the time. Write a program to test the new class `DateAndTime`. Specifically, test incrementing the time to the next day.

8.13 *(Set of Integers)* Create class `IntegerSet`. Each `IntegerSet` object can hold integers in the range 0–100. The set is represented by an array of `boolean`s. Array element `a[i]` is `true` if integer i is in the set. Array element `a[j]` is `false` if integer j is not in the set. The no-argument constructor initializes the array to the "empty set" (i.e., all `false` values).

8.14 Provide the following methods: The `static` method `union` creates a set that's the set-theoretic union of two existing sets (i.e., an element of the new set's array is set to `true` if that element is `true` in either or both of the existing sets—otherwise, the new set's element is set to `false`). The `static` method `intersection` creates a set which is the set-theoretic intersection of two existing sets (i.e., an element of the new set's array is set to `false` if that element is `false` in either or both of the existing sets—otherwise, the new set's element is set to `true`). Method `insertElement` inserts a new integer k into a set (by setting `a[k]` to `true`). Method `deleteElement` deletes integer m (by setting `a[m]` to `false`). Method `toString` returns a `String` containing a set as a list of numbers separated by spaces. Include only those elements that are present in the set. Use `---` to represent an empty set. Method `isEqualTo` determines whether two sets are equal. Write a program to test class `IntegerSet`. Instantiate several `IntegerSet` objects. Test that all your methods work properly.

8.15 *(Date Class)* Create class `Date` with the following capabilities:

a) Output the date in multiple formats, such as

```
MM/DD/YYYY
June 14, 1992
DDD YYYY
```

b) Use overloaded constructors to create `Date` objects initialized with dates of the formats in part (a). In the first case the constructor should receive three integer values. In the second case it should receive a `String` and two integer values. In the third case it should receive two integer values, the first of which represents the day number in the year.

8.16 *(Rational Numbers)* Create a class called `Rational` for performing arithmetic with fractions. Write a program to test your class. Use integer variables to represent the `private` instance variables of the class—the `numerator` and the `denominator`. Provide a constructor that enables an object of this class to be initialized when it's declared. The constructor should store the fraction in reduced form. The fraction

```
2/4
```

is equivalent to `1/2` and would be stored in the object as 1 in the `numerator` and 2 in the `denominator`. Provide a no-argument constructor with default values in case no initializers are provided. Provide `public` methods that perform each of the following operations:

a) Add two `Rational` numbers: The result of the addition should be stored in reduced form. Implement this as a `static` method.
b) Subtract two `Rational` numbers: The result of the subtraction should be stored in reduced form. Implement this as a `static` method.
c) Multiply two `Rational` numbers: The result of the multiplication should be stored in reduced form. Implement this as a `static` method.
d) Divide two `Rational` numbers: The result of the division should be stored in reduced form. Implement this as a `static` method.
e) Return a `String` representation of a `Rational` number in the form `a/b`, where `a` is the `numerator` and `b` is the `denominator`.
f) Return a `String` representation of a `Rational` number in floating-point format. (Consider providing formatting capabilities that enable the user of the class to specify the number of digits of precision to the right of the decimal point.)

8.17 *(`HugeInteger` Class)* Create a class `HugeInteger` which uses a 40-element array of digits to store integers as large as 40 digits each. Provide methods `parse`, `toString`, `add` and `subtract`. Method `parse` should receive a `String`, extract each digit using method `charAt` and place the integer equivalent of each digit into the integer array. For comparing `HugeInteger` objects, provide the following methods: `isEqualTo`, `isNotEqualTo`, `isGreaterThan`, `isLessThan`, `isGreaterThanOrEqualTo` and `isLessThanOrEqualTo`. Each of these is a predicate method that returns `true` if the relationship holds between the two `HugeInteger` objects and returns `false` if the relationship does not hold. Provide a predicate method `isZero`. If you feel ambitious, also provide methods `multiply`, `divide` and `remainder`. [*Note:* Primitive `boolean` values can be output as the word "true" or the word "false" with format specifier `%b`.]

8.18 *(Tic-Tac-Toe)* Create a class `TicTacToe` that will enable you to write a program to play Tic-Tac-Toe. The class contains a private 3-by-3 two-dimensional array. Use an `enum` type to represent the value in each cell of the array. The `enum`'s constants should be named `X`, `O` and `EMPTY` (for a position that does not contain an `X` or an `O`). The constructor should initialize the board elements to `EMPTY`. Allow two human players. Wherever the first player moves, place an `X` in the specified square, and place an `O` wherever the second player moves. Each move must be to an empty square. After each move, determine whether the game has been won and whether it's a draw. If you feel ambitious, modify your program so that the computer makes the moves for one of the players. Also, allow the player to specify whether he or she wants to go first or second. If you feel exceptionally ambitious, develop a program that will play three-dimensional Tic-Tac-Toe on a 4-by-4-by-4 board [*Note:* This is an extremely challenging project!].

8.19 *(`Account` Class with `BigDecimal balance`)* Rewrite the `Account` class of Section 3.4 to store the `balance` as a `BigDecimal` object and to perform all calculations using `BigDecimals`.

8.20 *(`final` Instance Variables)* In Fig. 8.8, class `Employee`'s instance variables are never modified after they're initialized. Any such instance variable should be declared `final`. Modify class `Employee` accordingly, then compile and run the program again to demonstrate that it produces the same results.

Making a Difference

8.21 *(Project: Emergency Response Class)* The North American emergency response service, *9-1-1*, connects callers to a *local* Public Service Answering Point (PSAP). Traditionally, the PSAP would ask the caller for identification information—including the caller's address, phone number and the nature of the emergency, then dispatch the appropriate emergency responders (such as the police, an ambulance or the fire department). *Enhanced 9-1-1 (or E9-1-1)* uses computers and databases to determine the caller's physical address, directs the call to the nearest PSAP, and displays the caller's phone number and address to the call taker. *Wireless Enhanced 9-1-1* provides call takers with identification information for wireless calls. Rolled out in two phases, the first phase required carriers to provide the wireless phone number and the location of the cell site or base station transmitting the call. The second phase required carriers to provide the location of the caller (using technologies such as GPS). To learn more about 9-1-1, visit `https://www.fcc.gov/general/9-1-1-and-e9-1-1-services` and `http://people.howstuffworks.com/9-1-1.htm`.

An important part of creating a class is determining the class's attributes (instance variables). For this class design exercise, research 9-1-1 services on the Internet. Then, design a class called `Emergency` that might be used in an object-oriented 9-1-1 emergency response system. List the attributes that an object of this class might use to represent the emergency. For example, the class might include information on who reported the emergency (including their phone number), the location of the emergency, the time of the report, the nature of the emergency, the type of response and the status of the response. The class attributes should completely describe the nature of the problem and what's happening to resolve that problem.

8.22 ***(Project: Dealing with Currencies in a Global Economy—JavaMoney)*** In a global economy, dealing with currencies, monetary amounts, conversions, rounding and formatting is complex. The new JavaMoney API was developed to meet these challenges. At the time of this writing, it was not yet incorporated into either Java SE or Java EE. You can read about JavaMoney at

```
https://java.net/projects/javamoney/pages/Home
http://jsr354.blogspot.ch
```

and you can obtain the software and documentation at

```
http://javamoney.github.io
```

Use JavaMoney to develop an application that will convert between two currencies specified by the user.

Object-Oriented Programming: Inheritance

9

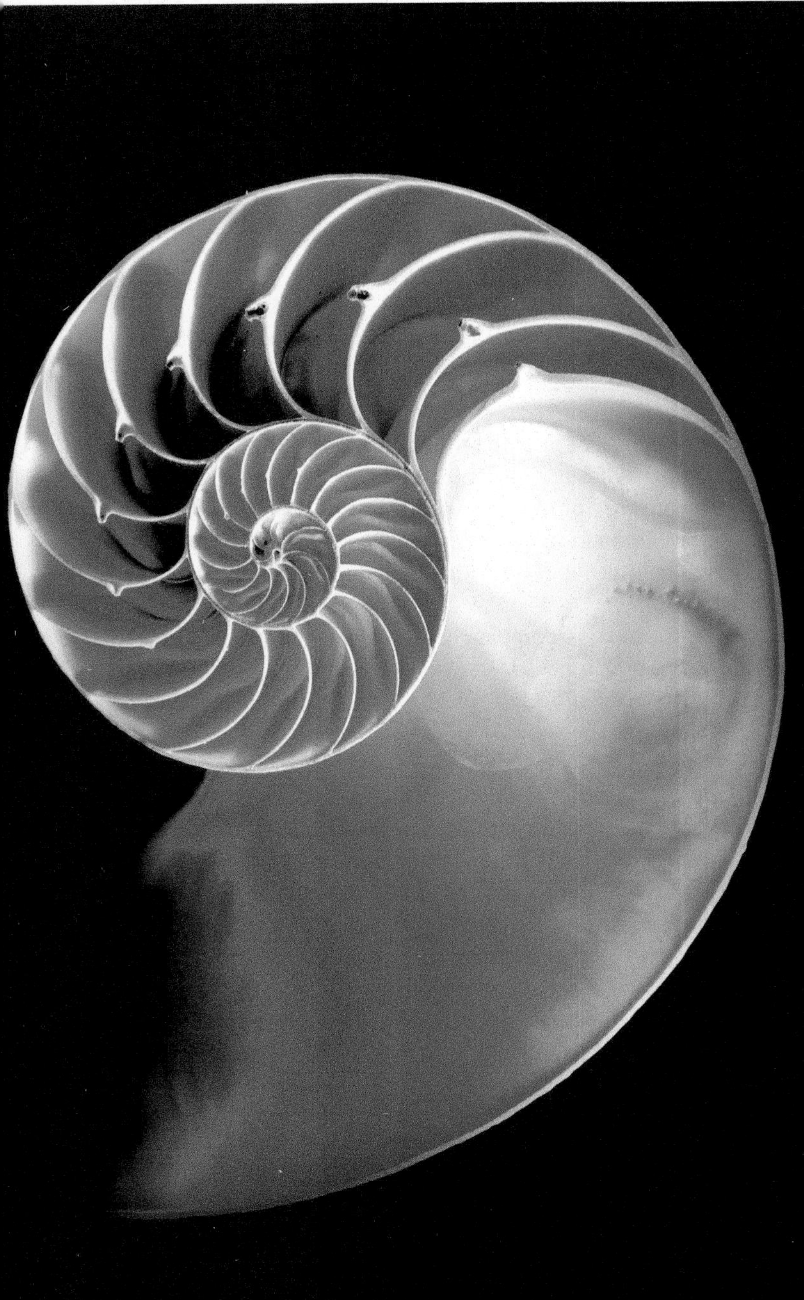

Objectives

In this chapter you'll:

- Understand inheritance and how to use it to develop new classes based on existing classes.
- Learn the notions of superclasses and subclasses and the relationship between them.
- Use keyword `extends` to create a class that inherits attributes and behaviors from another class.
- Use access modifier `protected` in a superclass to give subclass methods access to these superclass members.
- Access superclass members with `super` from a subclass.
- Learn how constructors are used in inheritance hierarchies.
- Learn about the methods of class `Object`, the direct or indirect superclass of all classes.

Outline

9.1 Introduction

This chapter continues our discussion of object-oriented programming (OOP) by introducing **inheritance**, in which a new class is created by acquiring an existing class's members and possibly embellishing them with new or modified capabilities. With inheritance, you can save time during program development by basing new classes on existing proven and debugged high-quality software. This also increases the likelihood that a system will be implemented and maintained effectively.

When creating a class, rather than declaring completely new members, you can designate that the new class should *inherit* the members of an existing class. The existing class is called the **superclass**, and the new class is the **subclass**. (The C++ programming language refers to the superclass as the **base class** and the subclass as the **derived class**.) A subclass can become a superclass for future subclasses.

A subclass can add its own fields and methods. Therefore, a subclass is *more specific* than its superclass and represents a more specialized group of objects. The subclass exhibits the behaviors of its superclass and can modify those behaviors so that they operate appropriately for the subclass. This is why inheritance is sometimes referred to as **specialization**.

The **direct superclass** is the superclass from which the subclass explicitly inherits. An **indirect superclass** is any class above the direct superclass in the **class hierarchy**, which defines the inheritance relationships among classes—as you'll see in Section 9.2, diagrams help you understand these relationships. In Java, the class hierarchy begins with class `Object` (in package `java.lang`), which *every* class in Java directly or indirectly **extends** (or "inherits from"). Section 9.6 lists the methods of class `Object` that are inherited by all other Java classes. Java supports only **single inheritance**, in which each class is derived from exactly *one* direct superclass. Unlike C++, Java does *not* support multiple inheritance (which occurs when a class is derived from more than one direct superclass). Chapter 10, Object-Oriented Programming: Polymorphism and Interfaces, explains how to use Java *interfaces* to realize many of the benefits of multiple inheritance while avoiding the associated problems.

We distinguish between the *is-a* **relationship** and the *has-a* **relationship**. *Is-a* represents inheritance. In an *is-a* relationship, *an object of a subclass can also be treated as an object of its superclass*—e.g., a car *is a* vehicle. By contrast, *has-a* represents composition (see Chapter 8). In a *has-a* relationship, *an object contains as members references to other objects*—e.g., a car *has a* steering wheel (and a car object has a reference to a steering-wheel object).

New classes can inherit from classes in **class libraries**. Organizations develop their own class libraries and can take advantage of others available worldwide. Some day, most new software likely will be constructed from **standardized reusable components**, just as automobiles and most computer hardware are constructed today. This will facilitate the rapid development of more powerful, abundant and economical software.

9.2 Superclasses and Subclasses

Often, an object of one class *is an* object of another class as well. For example, a `CarLoan` *is a* `Loan` as are `HomeImprovementLoans` and `MortgageLoans`. Thus, in Java, class `CarLoan` can be said to inherit from class `Loan`. In this context, class `Loan` is a superclass and class `CarLoan` is a subclass. A `CarLoan` *is a* specific type of `Loan`, but it's incorrect to claim that every `Loan` *is a* `CarLoan`—the `Loan` could be any type of loan. Figure 9.1 lists several simple examples of superclasses and subclasses—superclasses tend to be "more general" and subclasses "more specific."

Superclass	Subclasses
`Student`	`GraduateStudent`, `UndergraduateStudent`
`Shape`	`Circle`, `Triangle`, `Rectangle`, `Sphere`, `Cube`
`Loan`	`CarLoan`, `HomeImprovementLoan`, `MortgageLoan`
`Employee`	`Faculty`, `Staff`
`BankAccount`	`CheckingAccount`, `SavingsAccount`

Fig. 9.1 | Inheritance examples.

Because every subclass object *is an* object of its superclass, and one superclass can have many subclasses, the set of objects represented by a superclass is often larger than the set of objects represented by any of its subclasses. For example, the superclass `Vehicle` represents *all* vehicles, including cars, trucks, boats, bicycles and so on. By contrast, subclass `Car` represents a smaller, more specific subset of vehicles.

University Community Member Hierarchy

Inheritance relationships form treelike *hierarchical* structures. A superclass exists in a hierarchical relationship with its subclasses. Let's develop a sample class hierarchy (Fig. 9.2), also called an **inheritance hierarchy**. A university community has thousands of members, including employees, students and alumni. Employees are either faculty or staff members. Faculty members are either administrators (e.g., deans and department chairpersons) or teachers. The hierarchy could contain many other classes. For example, students can be graduate or undergraduate students. Undergraduate students can be freshmen, sophomores, juniors or seniors.

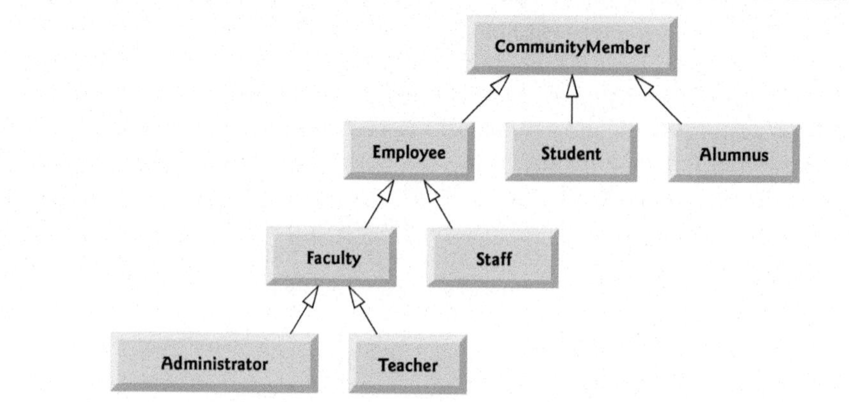

Fig. 9.2 | Inheritance hierarchy UML class diagram for university `CommunityMembers`.

Each arrow in the hierarchy represents an *is-a* relationship. As we follow the arrows upward in this class hierarchy, we can state, for example, that "an `Employee` *is a* `CommunityMember`" and "a `Teacher` *is a* `Faculty` member." `CommunityMember` is the direct superclass of `Employee`, `Student` and `Alumnus` and is an indirect superclass of all the other classes in the diagram. Starting from the bottom, you can follow the arrows and apply the *is-a* relationship up to the topmost superclass. For example, an `Administrator` *is a* `Faculty` member, *is an* `Employee`, *is a* `CommunityMember` and, of course, *is an* `Object`.

Shape Hierarchy

Now consider the `Shape` inheritance hierarchy in Fig. 9.3. This hierarchy begins with superclass `Shape`, which is extended by subclasses `TwoDimensionalShape` and `ThreeDimensionalShape`—`Shape`s are either `TwoDimensionalShape`s or `ThreeDimensionalShape`s. The third level of this hierarchy contains *specific* types of `TwoDimensionalShape`s and `ThreeDimensionalShape`s. As in Fig. 9.2, we can follow the arrows from the bottom of the diagram to the topmost superclass in this class hierarchy to identify several *is-a* relationships. For example, a `Triangle` *is a* `TwoDimensionalShape` and *is a* `Shape`, while a `Sphere` *is a* `ThreeDimensionalShape` and *is a* `Shape`. This hierarchy could contain many other classes. For example, ellipses and trapezoids also are `TwoDimensionalShape`s.

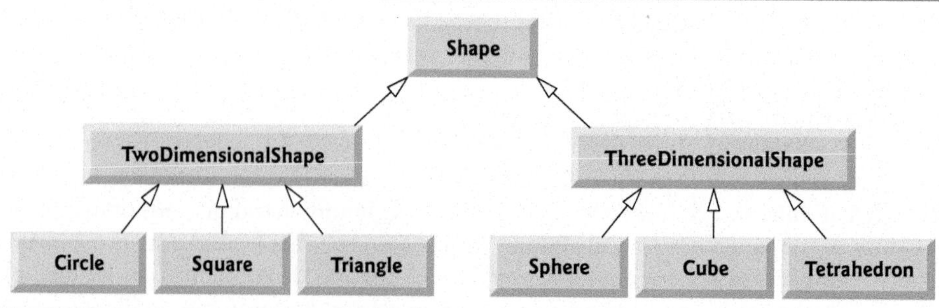

Fig. 9.3 | Inheritance hierarchy UML class diagram for `Shape`s.

Not every class relationship is an inheritance relationship. In Chapter 8, we discussed the *has-a* relationship, in which classes have members that are references to objects of other classes. Such relationships create classes by *composition* of existing classes. For example, given the classes `Employee`, `BirthDate` and `TelephoneNumber`, it's improper to say that an `Employee` *is a* `BirthDate` or that an `Employee` *is a* `TelephoneNumber`. However, an `Employee` *has a* `BirthDate`, and an `Employee` *has a* `TelephoneNumber`.

It's possible to treat superclass objects and subclass objects similarly—their commonalities are expressed in the superclass's members. Objects of all classes that extend a common superclass can be treated as objects of that superclass—such objects have an *is-a* relationship with the superclass. Later in this chapter and in Chapter 10, we consider many examples that take advantage of the *is-a* relationship.

A subclass can customize methods that it inherits from its superclass. To do this, the subclass **overrides** (*redefines*) the superclass method with an appropriate implementation, as we'll see in the chapter's code examples.

9.3 protected Members

Chapter 8 discussed access modifiers `public` and `private`. A class's `public` members are accessible wherever the program has a *reference* to an *object* of that class or one of its *subclasses*. A class's `private` members are accessible only within the class itself. In this section, we introduce the access modifier **`protected`**. Using `protected` access offers an intermediate level of access between `public` and `private`. A superclass's `protected` members can be accessed by members of that superclass, by members of its subclasses and by members of other classes in the *same package*—`protected` members also have *package access*.

All `public` and `protected` superclass members retain their original access modifier when they become members of the subclass—`public` members of the superclass become `public` members of the subclass, and `protected` members of the superclass become `protected` members of the subclass. A superclass's `private` members are *not* accessible outside the class itself. Rather, they're *hidden* from its subclasses and can be accessed only through the `public` or `protected` methods inherited from the superclass.

Subclass methods can refer to `public` and `protected` members inherited from the superclass simply by using the member names. When a subclass method *overrides* an inherited superclass method, the *superclass* version of the method can be accessed from the *subclass* by preceding the superclass method name with keyword **`super`** and a dot (.) separator. We discuss accessing overridden members of the superclass in Section 9.4.

Software Engineering Observation 9.1

Methods of a subclass cannot directly access `private` members of their superclass. A subclass can change the state of `private` superclass instance variables only through non-`private` methods provided in the superclass and inherited by the subclass.

Software Engineering Observation 9.2

Declaring `private` instance variables helps you test, debug and correctly modify systems. If a subclass could access its superclass's `private` instance variables, classes that inherit from that subclass could access the instance variables as well. This would propagate access to what should be `private` instance variables, and the benefits of information hiding would be lost.

9.4 Relationship Between Superclasses and Subclasses

We now use an inheritance hierarchy containing types of *employees* in a company's payroll application to discuss the relationship between a superclass and its subclass. In this company, *commission employees* (who will be represented as objects of a superclass) are paid a percentage of their sales, while *base-salaried commission employees* (who will be represented as objects of a subclass) receive a base salary *plus* a percentage of their sales.

We divide our discussion of the relationship between these classes into five examples. The first declares class `CommissionEmployee`, which directly inherits from class `Object` and declares as `private` instance variables a first name, last name, social security number, commission rate and gross (i.e., total) sales amount.

The second example declares class `BasePlusCommissionEmployee`, which also directly inherits from class `Object` and declares as `private` instance variables a first name, last name, social security number, commission rate, gross sales amount *and* base salary. We create this class by *writing every line of code* the class requires—we'll soon see that it's much more efficient to create it by inheriting from class `CommissionEmployee`.

The third example declares a new `BasePlusCommissionEmployee` class that *extends* class `CommissionEmployee` (i.e., a `BasePlusCommissionEmployee` *is a* `CommissionEmployee` who also has a base salary). This *software reuse lets us write much less code* when developing the new subclass. In this example, class `BasePlusCommissionEmployee` attempts to access class `CommissionEmployee`'s `private` members—this results in compilation errors, because the subclass *cannot* access the superclass's `private` instance variables.

The fourth example shows that if `CommissionEmployee`'s instance variables are declared as `protected`, the `BasePlusCommissionEmployee` subclass *can* access that data directly. Both `BasePlusCommissionEmployee` classes contain identical functionality, but we show how the inherited version is easier to create and manage.

After we discuss the convenience of using `protected` instance variables, we create the fifth example, which sets the `CommissionEmployee` instance variables back to `private` to enforce good software engineering. Then we show how the `BasePlusCommissionEmployee` subclass can use `CommissionEmployee`'s `public` methods to manipulate (in a controlled manner) the `private` instance variables inherited from `CommissionEmployee`.

9.4.1 Creating and Using a `CommissionEmployee` Class

We begin by declaring class `CommissionEmployee` (Fig. 9.4). Line 4 begins the class declaration and indicates that class `CommissionEmployee` **`extends`** (i.e., *inherits from*) class `Object` (from package `java.lang`). This causes class `CommissionEmployee` to inherit the class `Object`'s methods—class `Object` does not have any fields. If you don't explicitly specify which class a new class extends, the class extends `Object` implicitly. For this reason, you typically will not include "`extends Object`" in your code—we do so in this one example only for demonstration purposes.

```
1  // Fig. 9.4: CommissionEmployee.java
2  // CommissionEmployee class represents an employee paid a
3  // percentage of gross sales.
```

Fig. 9.4 | `CommissionEmployee` class represents an employee paid a percentage of gross sales. (Part 1 of 3.)

```
public class CommissionEmployee extends Object {
   private final String firstName;
   private final String lastName;
   private final String socialSecurityNumber;
   private double grossSales; // gross weekly sales
   private double commissionRate; // commission percentage

   // five-argument constructor
   public CommissionEmployee(String firstName, String lastName,
      String socialSecurityNumber, double grossSales,
      double commissionRate) {
      // implicit call to Object's default constructor occurs here

      // if grossSales is invalid throw exception
      if (grossSales < 0.0) {
         throw new IllegalArgumentException("Gross sales must be >= 0.0");
      }

      // if commissionRate is invalid throw exception
      if (commissionRate <= 0.0 || commissionRate >= 1.0) {
         throw new IllegalArgumentException(
            "Commission rate must be > 0.0 and < 1.0");
      }

      this.firstName = firstName;
      this.lastName = lastName;
      this.socialSecurityNumber = socialSecurityNumber;
      this.grossSales = grossSales;
      this.commissionRate = commissionRate;
   }

   // return first name
   public String getFirstName() {return firstName;}

   // return last name
   public String getLastName() {return lastName;}

   // return social security number
   public String getSocialSecurityNumber() {return socialSecurityNumber;}

   // set gross sales amount
   public void setGrossSales(double grossSales) {
      if (grossSales < 0.0) {
         throw new IllegalArgumentException("Gross sales must be >= 0.0");
      }

      this.grossSales = grossSales;
   }

   // return gross sales amount
   public double getGrossSales() {return grossSales;}
```

Fig. 9.4 | CommissionEmployee class represents an employee paid a percentage of gross sales. (Part 2 of 3.)

```
55
56       // set commission rate
57       public void setCommissionRate(double commissionRate) {
58          if (commissionRate <= 0.0 || commissionRate >= 1.0) {
59             throw new IllegalArgumentException(
60                "Commission rate must be > 0.0 and < 1.0");
61          }
62
63          this.commissionRate = commissionRate;
64       }
65
66       // return commission rate
67       public double getCommissionRate() {return commissionRate;}
68
69       // calculate earnings
70       public double earnings() {return commissionRate * grossSales;}
71
72       // return String representation of CommissionEmployee object
73       @Override // indicates that this method overrides a superclass method
74       public String toString() {
75          return String.format("%s: %s %s%n%s: %s%n%s: %.2f%n%s: %.2f",
76             "commission employee", firstName, lastName,
77             "social security number", socialSecurityNumber,
78             "gross sales", grossSales,
79             "commission rate", commissionRate);
80       }
81    }
```

Fig. 9.4 | `CommissionEmployee` class represents an employee paid a percentage of gross sales. (Part 3 of 3.)

Overview of Class `CommissionEmployee`*'s Methods and Instance Variables*

Class `CommissionEmployee`'s `public` services include a constructor (lines 12–33) and methods `earnings` (line 70) and `toString` (lines 73–80). Lines 36–42 declare `public` *get* methods for the class's `final` instance variables (declared in lines 5–7) `firstName`, `lastName` and `socialSecurityNumber`. These three instance variables are declared `final` because they do not need to be modified after they're initialized—this is also why we do not provide corresponding *set* methods. Lines 45–67 declare `public` *set* and *get* methods for the class's `grossSales` and `commissionRate` instance variables (declared in lines 8–9). The class declares its instance variables as `private`, so objects of other classes cannot directly access these variables.

Class `CommissionEmployee`*'s Constructor*

Constructors are *not* inherited, so class `CommissionEmployee` does not inherit class `Object`'s constructor. However, a superclass's constructors are still available to be called by subclasses. In fact, Java requires that *the first task of any subclass constructor is to call its direct superclass's constructor*, either explicitly or implicitly (if no constructor call is specified), to ensure that the instance variables inherited from the superclass are initialized properly. The syntax for calling a superclass constructor explicitly is discussed in Section 9.4.3. In this example, class `CommissionEmployee`'s constructor calls class `Object`'s constructor implicitly. If the code does not include an explicit call to the superclass constructor, Java *implic-*

itly calls the superclass's default or *no-argument* constructor. The comment in line 15 of Fig. 9.4 indicates where the implicit call to the superclass `Object`'s default constructor is made (you do *not* write the code for this call). `Object`'s default constructor does nothing. Even if a class does not have constructors, the default constructor that the compiler implicitly declares for the class will call the superclass's default or no-argument constructor.

After the implicit call to `Object`'s constructor, lines 18–20 and 23–26 validate the `grossSales` and `commissionRate` arguments. If these are valid (that is, the constructor does not throw an `IllegalArgumentException`), lines 28–32 assign the constructor's arguments to the class's instance variables.

We did not validate the values of arguments `firstName`, `lastName` and `socialSecurityNumber` before assigning them to the corresponding instance variables. We could validate the first and last names—perhaps to ensure that they're of a reasonable length. Similarly, a social security number could be validated using regular expressions (Section 14.7) to ensure that it contains nine digits, with or without dashes (e.g., `123-45-6789` or `123456789`).

Class `CommissionEmployee`*'s* `earnings` *Method*

Method `earnings` (line 70) calculates a `CommissionEmployee`'s earnings. The method multiplies the `commissionRate` by the `grossSales` and returns the result.

Class `CommissionEmployee`*'s* `toString` *Method*

Method `toString` (lines 73–80) is special—it's one of the methods that *every* class inherits directly or indirectly from class `Object` (summarized in Section 9.6). Method `toString` returns a `String` representing an object. It's called implicitly whenever an object must be converted to a `String` representation, such as when an object is output by `printf` or output by `String` method `format` via the `%s` format specifier. Class `Object`'s `toString` method returns a `String` that includes the name of the object's class and the object's so-called hashcode (see Section 9.6). It's primarily a placeholder that can be *overridden* by a subclass to specify an appropriate `String` representation of the data in a subclass object.

Method `toString` of class `CommissionEmployee` overrides (redefines) class `Object`'s `toString` method. When invoked, `CommissionEmployee`'s `toString` method uses `String` method `format` to return a `String` containing information about the `CommissionEmployee`. To override a superclass method, a subclass must declare a method with the *same signature* (method name, number of parameters, parameter types and order of parameter types) as the superclass method—`Object`'s `toString` method takes no parameters, so `CommissionEmployee` declares `toString` with no parameters.

`@Override` *Annotaton*

Line 73 uses the optional **`@Override` annotation** to indicate that the following method declaration (i.e., `toString`) should *override* an *existing* superclass method. This annotation helps the compiler catch a few common errors. For example, in this case, you intend to override superclass method `toString`, which is spelled with a lowercase "`t`" and an uppercase "`S`." If you inadvertently use a lowercase "`s`," the compiler will flag this as an error because the superclass does not contain a method named `tostring` with a lowercase "`s`." If you didn't use the `@Override` annotation, `tostring` would be an entirely different method that would *not* be called if a `CommissionEmployee` were used where a `String` was needed.

Another common overriding error is declaring the wrong number or types of parameters in the parameter list. This creates an *unintentional overload* of the superclass method, rather than overriding the existing method. If you then attempt to call the method (with the correct number and types of parameters) on a subclass object, the superclass's version is invoked—potentially leading to subtle logic errors. When the compiler encounters a method declared with `@Override`, it compares the method's signature with the superclass's method signatures. If there isn't an exact match, the compiler issues an error message, such as "method does not override or implement a method from a supertype." You can then correct your method's signature so that it matches one in the superclass.

Error-Prevention Tip 9.1

Though the `@Override` annotation is optional, declare overridden methods with it to ensure at compilation time that you defined their signatures correctly. It's always better to find errors at compile time rather than at runtime. For this reason, the `toString` methods in Fig. 7.9 and in Chapter 8's examples should have been declared with `@Override`.

Common Programming Error 9.1

It's a compilation error to override a method with a more restricted access modifier—a `public` superclass method cannot become a `protected` or `private` subclass method; a `protected` superclass method cannot become a `private` subclass method. Doing so would break the is-a *relationship, which requires that all subclass objects be able to respond to method calls made to `public` methods declared in the superclass. If a `public` method could be overridden as a `protected` or `private` method, the subclass objects would not be able to respond to the same method calls as superclass objects. Once a method is declared `public` in a superclass, the method remains `public` for all that class's direct and indirect subclasses.*

Class `CommissionEmployeeTest`

Figure 9.5 tests class `CommissionEmployee`. Lines 6–7 instantiate a `CommissionEmployee` object and invoke `CommissionEmployee`'s constructor (lines 12–33 of Fig. 9.4) to initialize it with `"Sue"` as the first name, `"Jones"` as the last name, `"222-22-2222"` as the social security number, `10000` as the gross sales amount ($10,000) and `.06` as the commission rate (i.e., 6%). Lines 11–20 use `CommissionEmployee`'s *get* methods to retrieve the object's instance-variable values for output. Lines 22–23 invoke the object's `setGrossSales` and `setCommissionRate` methods to change the values of instance variables `grossSales` and `commissionRate`. Lines 25–26 output the `String` representation of the updated `CommissionEmployee`. When an object is output using the `%s` format specifier, the object's `toString` method is invoked *implicitly* to obtain the object's `String` representation. [*Note:* In this chapter, we do not use the `earnings` method in each class, but it's used extensively in Chapter 10.]

```
1  // Fig. 9.5: CommissionEmployeeTest.java
2  // CommissionEmployee class test program.
3  public class CommissionEmployeeTest {
4     public static void main(String[] args) {
```

Fig. 9.5 | `CommissionEmployee` class test program. (Part 1 of 2.)

```
      // instantiate CommissionEmployee object
      CommissionEmployee employee = new CommissionEmployee(
         "Sue", "Jones", "222-22-2222", 10000, .06);

      // get commission employee data
      System.out.println("Employee information obtained by get methods:");
      System.out.printf("%n%s %s%n", "First name is",
         employee.getFirstName());
      System.out.printf("%s %s%n", "Last name is",
         employee.getLastName());
      System.out.printf("%s %s%n", "Social security number is",
         employee.getSocialSecurityNumber());
      System.out.printf("%s %.2f%n", "Gross sales is",
         employee.getGrossSales());
      System.out.printf("%s %.2f%n", "Commission rate is",
         employee.getCommissionRate());

      employee.setGrossSales(5000);
      employee.setCommissionRate(.1);

      System.out.printf("%n%s:%n%n%s%n",
         "Updated employee information obtained by toString", employee);
   }
}
```

```
Employee information obtained by get methods:

First name is Sue
Last name is Jones
Social security number is 222-22-2222
Gross sales is 10000.00
Commission rate is 0.06

Updated employee information obtained by toString:

commission employee: Sue Jones
social security number: 222-22-2222
gross sales: 5000.00
commission rate: 0.10
```

Fig. 9.5 | `CommissionEmployee` class test program. (Part 2 of 2.)

9.4.2 Creating and Using a `BasePlusCommissionEmployee` Class

We now discuss the second part of our introduction to inheritance by declaring and testing (a completely new and independent) class `BasePlusCommissionEmployee` (Fig. 9.6), which contains a first name, last name, social security number, gross sales amount, commission rate *and* base salary. Class `BasePlusCommissionEmployee`'s `public` services include a `BasePlusCommissionEmployee` constructor (lines 13–40) and methods `earnings` (lines 89–91) and `toString` (lines 94–102). Lines 43–86 declare `public` *get* and *set* methods for the class's `private` instance variables (declared in lines 5–10) `firstName`, `lastName`, `socialSecurityNumber`, `grossSales`, `commissionRate` and `baseSalary`. These variables and methods encapsulate all the necessary features of a base-salaried commission employee. Note the *similarity* between this class and class `CommissionEmployee` (Fig. 9.4)—in this example, we'll not yet exploit that similarity.

```java
// Fig. 9.6: BasePlusCommissionEmployee.java
// BasePlusCommissionEmployee class represents an employee who receives
// a base salary in addition to commission.
public class BasePlusCommissionEmployee {
   private final String firstName;
   private final String lastName;
   private final String socialSecurityNumber;
   private double grossSales; // gross weekly sales
   private double commissionRate; // commission percentage
   private double baseSalary; // base salary per week

   // six-argument constructor
   public BasePlusCommissionEmployee(String firstName, String lastName,
      String socialSecurityNumber, double grossSales,
      double commissionRate, double baseSalary) {
      // implicit call to Object's default constructor occurs here

      // if grossSales is invalid throw exception
      if (grossSales < 0.0) {
         throw new IllegalArgumentException("Gross sales must be >= 0.0");
      }

      // if commissionRate is invalid throw exception
      if (commissionRate <= 0.0 || commissionRate >= 1.0) {
         throw new IllegalArgumentException(
            "Commission rate must be > 0.0 and < 1.0");
      }

      // if baseSalary is invalid throw exception
      if (baseSalary < 0.0) {
         throw new IllegalArgumentException("Base salary must be >= 0.0");
      }

      this.firstName = firstName;
      this.lastName = lastName;
      this.socialSecurityNumber = socialSecurityNumber;
      this.grossSales = grossSales;
      this.commissionRate = commissionRate;
      this.baseSalary = baseSalary;
   }

   // return first name
   public String getFirstName() {return firstName;}

   // return last name
   public String getLastName() {return lastName;}

```

Fig. 9.6 | `BasePlusCommissionEmployee` class represents an employee who receives a base salary in addition to a commission. (Part 1 of 3.)

```
   // return social security number
   public String getSocialSecurityNumber() {return socialSecurityNumber;}

   // set gross sales amount
   public void setGrossSales(double grossSales) {
      if (grossSales < 0.0) {
         throw new IllegalArgumentException("Gross sales must be >= 0.0");
      }

      this.grossSales = grossSales;
   }

   // return gross sales amount
   public double getGrossSales() {return grossSales;}

   // set commission rate
   public void setCommissionRate(double commissionRate) {
      if (commissionRate <= 0.0 || commissionRate >= 1.0) {
         throw new IllegalArgumentException(
            "Commission rate must be > 0.0 and < 1.0");
      }

      this.commissionRate = commissionRate;
   }

   // return commission rate
   public double getCommissionRate() {return commissionRate;}

   // set base salary
   public void setBaseSalary(double baseSalary) {
      if (baseSalary < 0.0) {
         throw new IllegalArgumentException("Base salary must be >= 0.0");
      }

      this.baseSalary = baseSalary;
   }

   // return base salary
   public double getBaseSalary() {return baseSalary;}

   // calculate earnings
   public double earnings() {
      return baseSalary + (commissionRate * grossSales);
   }

   // return String representation of BasePlusCommissionEmployee
   @Override
   public String toString() {
      return String.format(
         "%s: %s %s%n%s: %s%n%s: %.2f%n%s: %.2f%n%s: %.2f",
         "base-salaried commission employee", firstName, lastName,
```

Fig. 9.6 | BasePlusCommissionEmployee class represents an employee who receives a base salary in addition to a commission. (Part 2 of 3.)

```
99            "social security number", socialSecurityNumber,
100           "gross sales", grossSales, "commission rate", commissionRate,
101           "base salary", baseSalary);
102    }
103 }
```

Fig. 9.6 | `BasePlusCommissionEmployee` class represents an employee who receives a base salary in addition to a commission. (Part 3 of 3.)

Class `BasePlusCommissionEmployee` does *not* specify "`extends Object`" in line 4, so the class *implicitly* extends `Object`. Also, like class `CommissionEmployee`'s constructor (lines 12–33 of Fig. 9.4), class `BasePlusCommissionEmployee`'s constructor invokes class `Object`'s default constructor *implicitly*, as noted in the comment in line 16 of Fig. 9.6.

Class `BasePlusCommissionEmployee`'s `earnings` method (lines 89–91) returns the result of adding the `BasePlusCommissionEmployee`'s base salary to the product of the commission rate and the employee's gross sales.

Class `BasePlusCommissionEmployee` overrides `Object` method `toString` to return a `String` containing the `BasePlusCommissionEmployee`'s information. Once again, we use format specifier `%.2f` to format the gross sales, commission rate and base salary with two digits of precision to the right of the decimal point (line 97).

Testing Class `BasePlusCommissionEmployee`

Figure 9.7 tests class `BasePlusCommissionEmployee`. Lines 7–9 create a `BasePlusCommissionEmployee` object and pass `"Bob"`, `"Lewis"`, `"333-33-3333"`, `5000`, `.04` and `300` to the constructor as the first name, last name, social security number, gross sales, commission rate and base salary, respectively. Lines 14–25 use `BasePlusCommissionEmployee`'s *get* methods to retrieve the values of the object's instance variables for output. Line 27 invokes the object's `setBaseSalary` method to change the base salary. Method `setBaseSalary` (Fig. 9.6, lines 77–83) ensures that instance variable `baseSalary` is not assigned a negative value. Line 31 of Fig. 9.7 invokes method `toString` *explicitly* to get the object's `String` representation.

```
1  // Fig. 9.7: BasePlusCommissionEmployeeTest.java
2  // BasePlusCommissionEmployee test program.
3
4  public class BasePlusCommissionEmployeeTest {
5     public static void main(String[] args) {
6        // instantiate BasePlusCommissionEmployee object
7        BasePlusCommissionEmployee employee =
8           new BasePlusCommissionEmployee(
9           "Bob", "Lewis", "333-33-3333", 5000, .04, 300);
10
11       // get base-salaried commission employee data
12       System.out.printf(
13          "Employee information obtained by get methods:%n");
14       System.out.printf("%s %s%n", "First name is",
15          employee.getFirstName());
```

Fig. 9.7 | `BasePlusCommissionEmployee` test program. (Part 1 of 2.)

```
      System.out.printf("%s %s%n", "Last name is",
         employee.getLastName());
      System.out.printf("%s %s%n", "Social security number is",
         employee.getSocialSecurityNumber());
      System.out.printf("%s %.2f%n", "Gross sales is",
         employee.getGrossSales());
      System.out.printf("%s %.2f%n", "Commission rate is",
         employee.getCommissionRate());
      System.out.printf("%s %.2f%n", "Base salary is",
         employee.getBaseSalary());

      employee.setBaseSalary(1000);

      System.out.printf("%n%s:%n%n%s%n",
         "Updated employee information obtained by toString",
          employee.toString());
   }
}
```

```
Employee information obtained by get methods:

First name is Bob
Last name is Lewis
Social security number is 333-33-3333
Gross sales is 5000.00
Commission rate is 0.04
Base salary is 300.00

Updated employee information obtained by toString:

base-salaried commission employee: Bob Lewis
social security number: 333-33-3333
gross sales: 5000.00
commission rate: 0.04
base salary: 1000.00
```

Fig. 9.7 | BasePlusCommissionEmployee test program. (Part 2 of 2.)

Notes on Class **BasePlusCommissionEmployee**

Much of class BasePlusCommissionEmployee's code (Fig. 9.6) is *similar*, or *identical*, to that of class CommissionEmployee (Fig. 9.4). For example, private instance variables firstName and lastName and methods getFirstName and getLastName are identical to those of class CommissionEmployee. The classes also both contain private instance variables socialSecurityNumber, commissionRate and grossSales, and corresponding *get* and *set* methods. In addition, the BasePlusCommissionEmployee constructor is *almost* identical to that of class CommissionEmployee, except that BasePlusCommissionEmployee's constructor also sets the baseSalary. The other additions to class BasePlusCommissionEmployee are private instance variable baseSalary and methods setBaseSalary and getBaseSalary. Class BasePlusCommissionEmployee's toString method is *almost* identical to that of class CommissionEmployee except that it also outputs instance variable baseSalary with two digits of precision to the right of the decimal point.

We literally *copied* code from class `CommissionEmployee` and *pasted* it into class `BasePlusCommissionEmployee`, then modified class `BasePlusCommissionEmployee` to include a base salary and methods that manipulate the base salary. This *"copy-and-paste" approach* is often error prone and time consuming. Worse yet, it spreads copies of the same code throughout a system, creating code-maintenance problems—changes to the code would need to be made in multiple classes. Is there a way to "acquire" the instance variables and methods of one class in a way that makes them part of other classes *without duplicating code*? Next we answer this question, using a more elegant approach to building classes that emphasizes the benefits of inheritance.

Software Engineering Observation 9.3

With inheritance, the instance variables and methods that are the same for all the classes in the hierarchy are declared in a superclass. Changes made to these common features in the superclass are inherited by the subclass. Without inheritance, changes would need to be made to all the source-code files that contain a copy *of the code in question.*

9.4.3 Creating a `CommissionEmployee`–`BasePlusCommissionEmployee` Inheritance Hierarchy

Now we declare class `BasePlusCommissionEmployee` (Fig. 9.8) to *extend* class `CommissionEmployee` (Fig. 9.4). A `BasePlusCommissionEmployee` object *is a* `CommissionEmployee`, because inheritance passes on class `CommissionEmployee`'s capabilities. Class `BasePlusCommissionEmployee` also has instance variable `baseSalary` (Fig. 9.8, line 4). Keyword `extends` (line 3) indicates inheritance. `BasePlusCommissionEmployee` *inherits* `CommissionEmployee`'s instance variables and methods.

Software Engineering Observation 9.4

At the design stage in an object-oriented system, you'll often find that certain classes are closely related. You should "factor out" common instance variables and methods and place them in a superclass. Then use inheritance to develop subclasses, specializing them with capabilities beyond those inherited from the superclass.

Software Engineering Observation 9.5

Declaring a subclass does not affect its superclass's source code. Inheritance preserves the integrity of the superclass.

```
1  // Fig. 9.8: BasePlusCommissionEmployee.java
2  // private superclass members cannot be accessed in a subclass.
3  public class BasePlusCommissionEmployee extends CommissionEmployee {
4     private double baseSalary; // base salary per week
5
6     // six-argument constructor
7     public BasePlusCommissionEmployee(String firstName, String lastName,
8        String socialSecurityNumber, double grossSales,
9        double commissionRate, double baseSalary) {
```

Fig. 9.8 | `private` superclass members cannot be accessed in a subclass. (Part 1 of 3.)

```
      // explicit call to superclass CommissionEmployee constructor
      super(firstName, lastName, socialSecurityNumber,
         grossSales, commissionRate);

      // if baseSalary is invalid throw exception
      if (baseSalary < 0.0) {
         throw new IllegalArgumentException("Base salary must be >= 0.0");
      }

      this.baseSalary = baseSalary;
   }

   // set base salary
   public void setBaseSalary(double baseSalary) {
      if (baseSalary < 0.0) {
         throw new IllegalArgumentException("Base salary must be >= 0.0");
      }

      this.baseSalary = baseSalary;
   }

   // return base salary
   public double getBaseSalary() {return baseSalary;}

   // calculate earnings
   @Override
   public double earnings() {
      // not allowed: commissionRate and grossSales private in superclass
      return baseSalary + (commissionRate * grossSales);
   }

   // return String representation of BasePlusCommissionEmployee
   @Override
   public String toString() {
      // not allowed: attempts to access private superclass members
      return String.format(
         "%s: %s %s%n%s: %s%n%s: %.2f%n%s: %.2f%n%s: %.2f",
         "base-salaried commission employee", firstName, lastName,
         "social security number", socialSecurityNumber,
         "gross sales", grossSales, "commission rate", commissionRate,
         "base salary", baseSalary);
   }
}
```

```
BasePlusCommissionEmployee.java:38: error: commissionRate has private access
in CommissionEmployee
      return baseSalary + (commissionRate * grossSales);
                           ^
BasePlusCommissionEmployee.java:38: error: grossSales has private access in
CommissionEmployee
      return baseSalary + (commissionRate * grossSales);
                                            ^
```

Fig. 9.8 | `private` superclass members cannot be accessed in a subclass. (Part 2 of 3.)

```
BasePlusCommissionEmployee.java:47: error: firstName has private access in
CommissionEmployee
        "base-salaried commission employee", firstName, lastName,
                                             ^
BasePlusCommissionEmployee.java:47: error: lastName has private access in
CommissionEmployee
        "base-salaried commission employee", firstName, lastName,
                                                        ^
BasePlusCommissionEmployee.java:48: error: socialSecurityNumber has private
access in CommissionEmployee
        "social security number", socialSecurityNumber,
                                  ^
BasePlusCommissionEmployee.java:49: error: grossSales has private access in
CommissionEmployee
        "gross sales", grossSales, "commission rate", commissionRate,
                       ^
BasePlusCommissionEmployee.java:49: error: commissionRate has private access
inCommissionEmployee
        "gross sales", grossSales, "commission rate", commissionRate,
                                                      ^
```

Fig. 9.8 | `private` superclass members cannot be accessed in a subclass. (Part 3 of 3.)

Only `CommissionEmployee`'s `public` and `protected` members are directly accessible in the subclass. The `CommissionEmployee` constructor is *not* inherited. So, the `public` `BasePlusCommissionEmployee` services include its constructor (lines 7–20), `public` methods inherited from `CommissionEmployee`, and methods `setBaseSalary` (lines 23–29), `getBaseSalary` (line 32), `earnings` (lines 35–39) and `toString` (lines 42–51). Methods `earnings` and `toString` *override* the corresponding methods in class `CommissionEmployee` because their superclass versions do not properly calculate a `BasePlusCommissionEmployee`'s earnings or return an appropriate `String` representation, respectively.

A Subclass's Constructor Must Call Its Superclass's Constructor

Each subclass constructor must implicitly or explicitly call one of its superclass's constructors to initialize the instance variables inherited from the superclass. Lines 11–12 in `BasePlusCommissionEmployee`'s six-argument constructor (lines 7–20) explicitly call class `CommissionEmployee`'s five-argument constructor (declared at lines 12–33 of Fig. 9.4) to initialize the superclass portion of a `BasePlusCommissionEmployee` object (i.e., variables `firstName`, `lastName`, `socialSecurityNumber`, `grossSales` and `commissionRate`). We do this by using the **superclass constructor call syntax**—keyword `super`, followed by a set of parentheses containing the superclass constructor arguments, which are used to initialize the superclass instance variables `firstName`, `lastName`, `socialSecurityNumber`, `grossSales` and `commissionRate`, respectively. The explicit superclass constructor call in lines 11–12 of Fig. 9.8 must be the *first* statement in the constructor's body.

If `BasePlusCommissionEmployee`'s constructor did not invoke the superclass's constructor explicitly, the compiler would attempt to insert a call to the superclass's default or no-argument constructor. Class `CommissionEmployee` does not have such a constructor, so the compiler would issue an error. When a superclass contains a no-argument constructor, you can use `super()` to call that constructor explicitly, but this is rarely done.

Software Engineering Observation 9.6

You learned previously that you should not call a class's instance methods from its constructors and that we'll say why in Chapter 10. Calling a superclass constructor from a subclass constructor does not contradict this advice.

BasePlusCommissionEmployee *Methods* Earnings *and* toString

The compiler generates errors for line 38 (Fig. 9.8) because CommissionEmployee's instance variables commissionRate and grossSales are private—subclass BasePlusCommissionEmployee's methods are *not* allowed to access superclass CommissionEmployee's private instance variables. The compiler issues additional errors at lines 47–49 of BasePlusCommissionEmployee's toString method for the same reason. The errors in BasePlusCommissionEmployee could have been prevented by using the *get* methods inherited from class CommissionEmployee. For example, line 38 could have called getCommissionRate and getGrossSales to access CommissionEmployee's private instance variables commissionRate and grossSales, respectively. Lines 47–49 also could have used appropriate *get* methods to retrieve the values of the superclass's instance variables.

9.4.4 CommissionEmployee-BasePlusCommissionEmployee Inheritance Hierarchy Using protected Instance Variables

To enable class BasePlusCommissionEmployee to directly access superclass instance variables firstName, lastName, socialSecurityNumber, grossSales and commissionRate, we can declare those members as protected in the superclass. As we discussed in Section 9.3, a superclass's protected members are accessible by all subclasses of that superclass. In the new CommissionEmployee class, we modified only lines 5–9 of Fig. 9.4 to declare the instance variables with the protected access modifier as follows:

```
protected final String firstName;
protected final String lastName;
protected final String socialSecurityNumber;
protected double grossSales; // gross weekly sales
protected double commissionRate; // commission percentage
```

The rest of the class declaration (which is not shown here) is identical to that of Fig. 9.4.

We could have declared CommissionEmployee's instance variables public to enable subclass BasePlusCommissionEmployee to access them. However, declaring public instance variables is poor software engineering because it allows unrestricted access to the these variables from any class, greatly increasing the chance of errors. With protected instance variables, the subclass gets access to the instance variables, but classes that are not subclasses and classes that are not in the same package cannot access these variables directly—recall that protected class members are also visible to other classes in the same package.

Class BasePlusCommissionEmployee

Class BasePlusCommissionEmployee (Fig. 9.9) extends the new version of class CommissionEmployee with protected instance variables. BasePlusCommissionEmployee objects inherit CommissionEmployee's protected instance variables firstName, lastName, socialSecurityNumber, grossSales and commissionRate—all these variables are now protected members of BasePlusCommissionEmployee. As a result, the compiler does not generate errors when compiling line 38 of method `earnings` and lines 46–48 of method `toString`. If another class extends this version of class `BasePlusCommissionEmployee`, the new subclass also can access the `protected` members.

```
1  // Fig. 9.9: BasePlusCommissionEmployee.java
2  // BasePlusCommissionEmployee inherits protected instance
3  // variables from CommissionEmployee.
4
5  public class BasePlusCommissionEmployee extends CommissionEmployee {
6     private double baseSalary; // base salary per week
7
8     // six-argument constructor
9     public BasePlusCommissionEmployee(String firstName, String lastName,
10       String socialSecurityNumber, double grossSales,
11       double commissionRate, double baseSalary) {
12       super(firstName, lastName, socialSecurityNumber,
13          grossSales, commissionRate);
14
15       // if baseSalary is invalid throw exception
16       if (baseSalary < 0.0) {
17          throw new IllegalArgumentException("Base salary must be >= 0.0");
18       }
19
20       this.baseSalary = baseSalary;
21    }
22
23    // set base salary
24    public void setBaseSalary(double baseSalary) {
25       if (baseSalary < 0.0) {
26          throw new IllegalArgumentException("Base salary must be >= 0.0");
27       }
28
29       this.baseSalary = baseSalary;
30    }
31
32    // return base salary
33    public double getBaseSalary() {return baseSalary;}
34
35    // calculate earnings
36    @Override // indicates that this method overrides a superclass method
37    public double earnings() {
38       return baseSalary + (commissionRate * grossSales);
39    }
40
41    // return String representation of BasePlusCommissionEmployee
42    @Override
43    public String toString() {
44       return String.format(
45          "%s: %s %s%n%s: %s%n%s: %.2f%n%s: %.2f%n%s: %.2f",
46          "base-salaried commission employee", firstName, lastName,
47          "social security number", socialSecurityNumber,
```

Fig. 9.9 | `BasePlusCommissionEmployee` inherits `protected` instance variables from `CommissionEmployee`. (Part 1 of 2.)

```
48          "gross sales", grossSales, "commission rate", commissionRate,
49          "base salary", baseSalary);
50     }
51  }
```

Fig. 9.9 | `BasePlusCommissionEmployee` inherits `protected` instance variables from `CommissionEmployee`. (Part 2 of 2.)

A Subclass Object Contains the Instance Variables of All of Its Superclasses

When you create a `BasePlusCommissionEmployee`, it contains all instance variables declared in the class hierarchy to that point—that is, those from classes `Object` (which does not have instance variables), `CommissionEmployee` and `BasePlusCommissionEmployee`. Class `BasePlusCommissionEmployee` does *not* inherit `CommissionEmployee`'s constructor, but *explicitly invokes* it (lines 12–13) to initialize the `BasePlusCommissionEmployee` instance variables inherited from `CommissionEmployee`. Similarly, `CommissionEmployee`'s constructor *implicitly* calls class `Object`'s constructor. `BasePlusCommissionEmployee`'s constructor must *explicitly* call `CommissionEmployee`'s constructor because `CommissionEmployee` does *not* have a no-argument constructor that could be invoked implicitly.

Testing Class `BasePlusCommissionEmployee`

Class `BasePlusCommissionEmployeeTest` for this example is identical to that of Fig. 9.7 and produces the same output, so we do not show it here. Although the version of class `BasePlusCommissionEmployee` in Fig. 9.6 does not use inheritance and the version in Fig. 9.9 does, both classes provide the *same* functionality. The source code in Fig. 9.9 (51 lines) is considerably shorter than that in Fig. 9.6 (103 lines), because most of the class's functionality is now inherited from `CommissionEmployee`—there's now only one copy of the `CommissionEmployee` functionality. This makes the code easier to maintain, modify and debug, because the code related to a `CommissionEmployee` exists only in that class.

Notes on Using `protected` *Instance Variables*

In this example, we declared superclass instance variables as `protected` so that subclasses could access them. Inheriting `protected` instance variables enables direct access to the variables by subclasses. In most cases, however, it's better to use `private` instance variables to encourage proper software engineering. Your code will be easier to maintain, modify and debug.

Using `protected` instance variables creates several potential problems. First, the subclass object can set an inherited variable's value directly without using a *set* method. Therefore, a subclass object can assign an invalid value to the variable, possibly leaving the object in an inconsistent state. For example, if we were to declare `CommissionEmployee`'s instance variable `grossSales` as `protected`, a subclass object (e.g., `BasePlusCommissionEmployee`) could then assign a negative value to `grossSales`.

Another problem with using `protected` instance variables is that subclass methods are more likely to be written so that they depend on the superclass's data implementation. In practice, subclasses should depend only on the superclass services (i.e., non-`private` methods) and not on the superclass data implementation. With `protected` instance variables in the superclass, we may need to modify all the subclasses of the superclass if the superclass implementation changes. For example, if for some reason we were to change the names of instance variables `firstName` and `lastName` to `first` and `last`, then we would have to do so for all occurrences in which a subclass directly references superclass instance variables `firstName` and `lastName`. Such a class is said to be **fragile** or **brittle**, because a small change in the superclass can "break" subclass implementation. You should be able to change the superclass implementation while still providing the same services to the subclasses. Of course, if the superclass services change, we must reimplement our subclasses.

A third problem is that a class's `protected` members are visible to all classes in the same package as the class containing the `protected` members. This is not always desirable.

Software Engineering Observation 9.7

Use the `protected` *access modifier when a superclass should provide a method only to its subclasses and other classes in the same package, but not to other clients.*

Software Engineering Observation 9.8

Declaring superclass instance variables `private` *(as opposed to* `protected`*) enables the superclass implementation of these instance variables to change without affecting subclass implementations.*

Error-Prevention Tip 9.2

Avoid `protected` *instance variables. Instead, include non-*`private` *methods that access* `private` *instance variables. This will help ensure that objects of the class maintain consistent states.*

9.4.5 `CommissionEmployee`–`BasePlusCommissionEmployee` Inheritance Hierarchy Using `private` Instance Variables

Let's reexamine our hierarchy once more, this time using good software engineering practices.

Class `CommissionEmployee`

Class `CommissionEmployee` (Fig. 9.10) declares instance variables `firstName`, `lastName`, `socialSecurityNumber`, `grossSales` and `commissionRate` as *`private`* (lines 5–9) and provides `public` methods `getFirstName`, `getLastName`, `getSocialSecurityNumber`, `setGrossSales`, `getGrossSales`, `setCommissionRate`, `getCommissionRate`, `earnings` and `toString` for manipulating these values. Methods `earnings` (lines 70–72) and `toString` (lines 75–82) use the class's *get* methods to obtain the values of its instance variables. If we decide to change the names of the instance variables, the `earnings` and `toString` declarations will *not* require modification—only the bodies of the *get* and *set* methods that directly manipulate the instance variables will need to change. These changes occur solely within the superclass—no changes to the subclass are needed. *Localizing the effects of changes* like this is a good software engineering practice.

```
1  // Fig. 9.10: CommissionEmployee.java
2  // CommissionEmployee class uses methods to manipulate its
3  // private instance variables.
```

Fig. 9.10 | `CommissionEmployee` class uses methods to manipulate its `private` instance variables. (Part 1 of 3.)

```java
public class CommissionEmployee {
   private final String firstName;
   private final String lastName;
   private final String socialSecurityNumber;
   private double grossSales; // gross weekly sales
   private double commissionRate; // commission percentage

   // five-argument constructor
   public CommissionEmployee(String firstName, String lastName,
      String socialSecurityNumber, double grossSales,
      double commissionRate) {
      // implicit call to Object constructor occurs here

      // if grossSales is invalid throw exception
      if (grossSales < 0.0) {
         throw new IllegalArgumentException("Gross sales must be >= 0.0");
      }

      // if commissionRate is invalid throw exception
      if (commissionRate <= 0.0 || commissionRate >= 1.0) {
         throw new IllegalArgumentException(
            "Commission rate must be > 0.0 and < 1.0");
      }

      this.firstName = firstName;
      this.lastName = lastName;
      this.socialSecurityNumber = socialSecurityNumber;
      this.grossSales = grossSales;
      this.commissionRate = commissionRate;
   }

   // return first name
   public String getFirstName() {return firstName;}

   // return last name
   public String getLastName() {return lastName;}

   // return social security number
   public String getSocialSecurityNumber() {return socialSecurityNumber;}

   // set gross sales amount
   public void setGrossSales(double grossSales) {
      if (grossSales < 0.0) {
         throw new IllegalArgumentException("Gross sales must be >= 0.0");
      }

      this.grossSales = grossSales;
   }

   // return gross sales amount
   public double getGrossSales() {return grossSales;}
```

Fig. 9.10 | CommissionEmployee class uses methods to manipulate its private instance variables. (Part 2 of 3.)

```java

   // set commission rate
   public void setCommissionRate(double commissionRate) {
      if (commissionRate <= 0.0 || commissionRate >= 1.0) {
         throw new IllegalArgumentException(
            "Commission rate must be > 0.0 and < 1.0");
      }

      this.commissionRate = commissionRate;
   }

   // return commission rate
   public double getCommissionRate() {return commissionRate;}

   // calculate earnings
   public double earnings() {
      return getCommissionRate() * getGrossSales();
   }

   // return String representation of CommissionEmployee object
   @Override
   public String toString() {
      return String.format("%s: %s %s%n%s: %s%n%s: %.2f%n%s: %.2f",
         "commission employee", getFirstName(), getLastName(),
         "social security number", getSocialSecurityNumber(),
         "gross sales", getGrossSales(),
         "commission rate", getCommissionRate());
   }
}
```

Fig. 9.10 | CommissionEmployee class uses methods to manipulate its private instance variables. (Part 3 of 3.)

Class BasePlusCommissionEmployee

Subclass BasePlusCommissionEmployee (Fig. 9.11) inherits CommissionEmployee's non-private methods and can access (in a controlled way) the private superclass members via those methods. Class BasePlusCommissionEmployee has several changes that distinguish it from Fig. 9.9. Methods earnings (lines 36–37 of Fig. 9.11) and toString (lines 40–44) each invoke method getBaseSalary to obtain the base salary value, rather than accessing baseSalary directly. If we decide to rename instance variable baseSalary, only the bodies of method setBaseSalary and getBaseSalary will need to change.

```java
1  // Fig. 9.11: BasePlusCommissionEmployee.java
2  // BasePlusCommissionEmployee class inherits from CommissionEmployee
3  // and accesses the superclass's private data via inherited
4  // public methods.
5  public class BasePlusCommissionEmployee extends CommissionEmployee {
6     private double baseSalary; // base salary per week
7
```

Fig. 9.11 | BasePlusCommissionEmployee class inherits from CommissionEmployee and accesses the superclass's private data via inherited public methods. (Part 1 of 2.)

```
8      // six-argument constructor
9      public BasePlusCommissionEmployee(String firstName, String lastName,
10        String socialSecurityNumber, double grossSales,
11        double commissionRate, double baseSalary) {
12        super(firstName, lastName, socialSecurityNumber,
13           grossSales, commissionRate);
14
15        // if baseSalary is invalid throw exception
16        if (baseSalary < 0.0) {
17           throw new IllegalArgumentException("Base salary must be >= 0.0");
18        }
19
20        this.baseSalary = baseSalary;
21     }
22
23     // set base salary
24     public void setBaseSalary(double baseSalary) {
25        if (baseSalary < 0.0) {
26           throw new IllegalArgumentException("Base salary must be >= 0.0");
27        }
28
29        this.baseSalary = baseSalary;
30     }
31
32     // return base salary
33     public double getBaseSalary() {return baseSalary;}
34
35     // calculate earnings
36     @Override
37     public double earnings() {return getBaseSalary() + super.earnings();}
38
39     // return String representation of BasePlusCommissionEmployee
40     @Override
41     public String toString() {
42        return String.format("%s %s%n%s: %.2f", "base-salaried",
43           super.toString(), "base salary", getBaseSalary());
44     }
45  }
```

Fig. 9.11 | `BasePlusCommissionEmployee` class inherits from `CommissionEmployee` and accesses the superclass's `private` data via inherited `public` methods. (Part 2 of 2.)

Class `BasePlusCommissionEmployee`'s `earnings` Method

Method `earnings` (lines 36–37) overrides class `CommissionEmployee`'s `earnings` method (Fig. 9.10, lines 70–72) to calculate a base-salaried commission employee's earnings. The new version obtains the portion of the earnings based on commission alone by calling `CommissionEmployee`'s `earnings` method with `super.earnings()` (line 37 of Fig. 9.11), then adds the base salary to this value to calculate the total earnings. Note the syntax used to invoke an *overridden* superclass method from a subclass—place the keyword `super` and a dot (`.`) separator before the superclass method name. This method invocation is a good software engineering practice—if a method performs all or some of the actions needed by another method, call that method rather than duplicate its code. By having `BasePlusCom-`

missionEmployee's earnings method invoke CommissionEmployee's earnings method to calculate part of a BasePlusCommissionEmployee object's earnings, we *avoid duplicating the code* and *reduce code-maintenance problems.*

Common Programming Error 9.2

When a superclass method is overridden in a subclass, the subclass version often calls the superclass version to do a portion of the work. Failure to prefix the superclass method name with the keyword super *and the dot* (.) *separator when calling the superclass's method causes the subclass method to call itself, potentially creating an error called infinite recursion, which would eventually cause the method-call stack to overflow—a fatal runtime error. Recursion, used correctly, is a powerful capability discussed in Chapter 18.*

Class BasePlusCommissionEmployee*'s* toString *Method*

Similarly, BasePlusCommissionEmployee's toString method (Fig. 9.11, lines 40–44) overrides CommissionEmployee's toString method (Fig. 9.10, lines 75–82) to return a String representation that's appropriate for a base-salaried commission employee. The new version creates part of a BasePlusCommissionEmployee object's String representation (i.e., the String "commission employee" and the values of class CommissionEmployee's private instance variables) by calling CommissionEmployee's toString method with the expression super.toString() (Fig. 9.11, line 43). BasePlusCommissionEmployee's toString method then completes the remainder of a BasePlusCommissionEmployee object's String representation (i.e., the value of class BasePlusCommissionEmployee's base salary).

Testing Class BasePlusCommissionEmployee

Class BasePlusCommissionEmployeeTest performs the same manipulations on a BasePlusCommissionEmployee object as in Fig. 9.7 and produces the same output, so we do not show it here. Although each BasePlusCommissionEmployee class you've seen behaves identically, the version in Fig. 9.11 is the best engineered. By using inheritance and by calling methods that hide the data and ensure consistency, we've efficiently and effectively constructed a well-engineered class.

9.5 Constructors in Subclasses

As we explained, instantiating a subclass object begins a chain of constructor calls in which the subclass constructor, before performing its own tasks, explicitly uses super to call one of the constructors in its direct superclass or implicitly calls the superclass's default or no-argument constructor. Similarly, if the superclass is derived from another class—true of every class except Object—the superclass constructor invokes the constructor of the next class up the hierarchy, and so on. The last constructor called in the chain is *always* Object's constructor. The original subclass constructor's body finishes executing *last.* Each superclass's constructor manipulates the superclass instance variables that the subclass object inherits. For example, consider again the CommissionEmployee–BasePlusCommissionEmployee hierarchy from Figs. 9.10–9.11. When an app creates a BasePlusCommissionEmployee object, its constructor is called. That constructor calls CommissionEmployee's constructor, which in turn calls Object's constructor. Class Object's constructor has an *empty body,* so it immediately returns control to CommissionEmployee's constructor, which then initializes the CommissionEmployee instance variables that are part of the

BasePlusCommissionEmployee object. When CommissionEmployee's constructor completes execution, it returns control to BasePlusCommissionEmployee's constructor, which initializes the baseSalary.

Software Engineering Observation 9.9

Java ensures that even if a constructor does not assign a value to an instance variable, the variable is still initialized to its default value (e.g., `0` *for primitive numeric types,* `false` *for* `boolean`*s,* `null` *for references).*

9.6 Class Object

As we discussed earlier in this chapter, all classes in Java inherit directly or indirectly from class Object (package java.lang), so its 11 methods (some are overloaded) are inherited by all other classes. Figure 9.12 summarizes Object's methods. We discuss several Object methods throughout this book (as indicated in Fig. 9.12).

Method	Description
equals	This method compares two objects for equality and returns true if they're equal and false otherwise. The method takes any Object as an argument. When objects of a particular class must be compared for equality, the class should override method equals to compare the *contents* of the two objects. For the requirements of implementing this method (which include also overriding method hashCode), refer to the method's documentation at http://docs.oracle.com/javase/8/docs/api/java/lang/Object.html. The default equals implementation uses operator == to determine whether two references *refer to the same object* in memory. Section 14.3.3 demonstrates class String's equals method and differentiates between comparing String objects with == and with equals.
hashCode	Hashcodes are int values used for high-speed storage and retrieval of information stored in a hashtable data structure (see Section 16.10). This method is also called as part of Object's default toString method implementation.
toString	This method (introduced in Section 9.4.1) returns a String representation of an object. The default implementation of this method returns the package name and class name of the object's class typically followed by a hexadecimal representation of the value returned by the object's hashCode method.
wait, notify, notifyAll	Methods notify, notifyAll and the three overloaded versions of wait are related to multithreading, which is discussed in Chapter 23.
getClass	Every object in Java knows its own type at execution time. Method getClass (used in Sections 10.5 and 12.5) returns an object of class Class (package java.lang) that contains information about the object's type, such as its class name (returned by Class method getName).
finalize	This protected method is called by the garbage collector to perform termination housekeeping on an object just before the garbage collector reclaims the object's memory. Recall from Section 8.10 that it's unclear whether, or when, finalize will be called. For this reason, most programmers should avoid method finalize.

Fig. 9.12 | Object methods. (Part 1 of 2.)

Method	Description
`clone`	This `protected` method, which takes no arguments and returns an `Object` reference, makes a copy of the object on which it's called. The default implementation performs a so-called **shallow copy**—instance-variable values in one object are copied into another object of the same type. For reference types, only the references are copied. A typical overridden `clone` method's implementation would perform a **deep copy** that creates a new object for each reference-type instance variable. *Implementing `clone` correctly is difficult. For this reason, its use is discouraged.* Some industry experts suggest that object serialization should be used instead. We discuss object serialization in Chapter 15. Recall from Chapter 7 that arrays are objects. As a result, like all other objects, arrays inherit the members of class `Object`. Every array has an overridden `clone` method that copies the array. However, if the array stores references to objects, the objects are not copied—a shallow copy is performed.

Fig. 9.12 | `Object` methods. (Part 2 of 2.)

9.7 Designing with Composition vs. Inheritance

There's much discussion in the software engineering community about the relative merits of composition and inheritance. Each has its own place, but inheritance is often overused and composition is more appropriate in many cases. A mix of composition and inheritance often is a reasonable design approach, as you'll see in Exercise 9.16.[1]

Software Engineering Observation 9.10

As a college student, you learn tools for creating solutions. In industry, problems are larger and more complex than you see in college courses. Often the demands of the problem you're solving will be unique and may require you to rethink the proper way to use the tools at your disposal. As a college student, you tend to work on problems yourself. In industry, problem solving often requires interaction among many colleagues. Rarely will you be able to get everyone on a project to agree on the "right" approach to a solution. Also, rarely will any particular approach be "perfect." You'll often compare the relative merits of different approaches, as we do in this section.

Inheritance-Based Designs

Inheritance creates *tight coupling* among the classes in a hierarchy—each subclass typically depends on its direct or indirect superclasses' implementations. Changes in superclass implementation can affect the behavior of subclasses, often in subtle ways. Tightly coupled designs are more difficult to modify than those in loosely coupled, composition-based designs (discussed momentarily). Change is the rule rather than the exception—this encourages composition.

1. The concepts we present in this section are widely discussed in the software engineering community and derived from many sources, most notably the books: Gamma, Erich et al. *Design Patterns: Elements of Reusable Object-Oriented Software.* Reading, MA: Addison-Wesley, 1995, and Bloch, Joshua. *Effective Java.* Upper Saddle River, NJ: Addison-Wesley, 2008.

In general, you should use inheritance only for true *is-a* relationships in which you can assign a subclass object to a superclass reference. When you invoke a method via a superclass reference to a subclass object, the subclass's corresponding method executes. This is called polymorphic behavior, which we explore in Chapter 10.

Software Engineering Observation 9.11

Some of the difficulties with inheritance occur on large projects where different classes in the hierarchy are controlled by different people. An inheritance hierarchy is less problematic when it's entirely under one person's control.

Composition-Based Designs

Composition is loosely coupled. When you compose a reference as an instance variable of a class, it's part of the class's implementation details that are hidden from the class's client code. If the reference's class type changes, you may need to make changes to the composing class's internal details, but those changes do not affect the client code.

In addition, inheritance is done at compile time. Composition is more flexible—it, too, can be done at compile time, but it also can be done at execution time because non-`final` references to composed objects can be modified. We call this dynamic composition. This is another aspect of loose coupling—if the reference is of a superclass type, you can replace the referenced object with an object of *any* type that has an *is-a* relationship with the reference's class type.

When you use a composition approach instead of inheritance, you'll typically create a larger number of smaller classes, each focused on one responsibility. Smaller classes generally are easier to test, debug and modify.

Java does not offer multiple inheritance—each class in Java may extend only one class. However, a new class may reuse the capabilities of one or more other classes by composition. As you'll see in Chapter 10, Object-Oriented Programming: Polymorphism and Interfaces, we also can get many of the benefits of multiple inheritance by implementing multiple interfaces.

Performance Tip 9.1

A potential disadvantage of composition is that it typically requires more objects at runtime, which might negatively impact garbage-collection and virtual-memory performance. Virtual-memory architectures and performance issues are typically discussed in operating systems courses.

Software Engineering Observation 9.12

A `public` *method of a composing class can call a method of a composed object to perform a task for the benefit of the composing class's clients. This is known as forwarding the method call and is a common way to reuse a class's capabilities via composition rather than inheritance.*

Software Engineering Observation 9.13

When implementing a new class and choosing whether you should reuse an existing class via inheritance or composition, use composition if the existing class's `public` *methods should not be part of the new class's* `public` *interface.*

Recommended Exercises

Exercise 9.3 asks you to reimplement this chapter's `CommissionEmployee–BasePlusCommissionEmployee` hierarchy using composition, rather than inheritance. Exercise 9.16 asks you to reimplement the hierarchy using a combination of composition and inheritance in which you'll see the benefits of composition's loose coupling.

9.8 Wrap-Up

This chapter introduced inheritance—the ability to create classes by acquiring an existing class's members (without copying and pasting the code) and having the ability to embellish them with new capabilities. You learned the notions of superclasses and subclasses and used keyword `extends` to create a subclass that inherits members from a superclass. We showed how to use the `@Override` annotation to prevent unintended overloading by indicating that a method overrides a superclass method. We introduced the access modifier `protected`; subclass methods can directly access `protected` superclass members. You learned how to use `super` to access overridden superclass members. You also saw how constructors are used in inheritance hierarchies. you learned about the methods of class `Object`, the direct or indirect superclass of all Java classes. Finally, we discussed designing classes with composition vs. inheritance.

In Chapter 10, Object-Oriented Programming: Polymorphism and Interfaces, we build on our discussion of inheritance by introducing *polymorphism*—an object-oriented concept that enables us to write programs that conveniently handle, in a more general and convenient manner, objects of a wide variety of classes related by inheritance, by interfaces or both. After studying Chapter 10, you'll be familiar with classes, objects, encapsulation, inheritance and polymorphism—the key technologies of object-oriented programming.

Summary

Section 9.1 Introduction

- Inheritance (p. 374) reduces program-development time.
- The direct superclass (p. 374) of a subclass is the one from which the subclass inherits. An indirect superclass (p. 374) of a subclass is two or more levels up the class hierarchy from that subclass.
- In single inheritance (p. 374), a class is derived from one superclass. In multiple inheritance, a class is derived from more than one direct superclass. Java does not support multiple inheritance.
- A subclass is more specific than its superclass and represents a smaller group of objects (p. 374).
- Every object of a subclass is also an object of that class's superclass. However, a superclass object is not an object of its class's subclasses.
- An *is-a* relationship (p. 375) represents inheritance. In an *is-a* relationship, an object of a subclass also can be treated as an object of its superclass.
- A *has-a* relationship (p. 375) represents composition. In a *has-a* relationship, a class object contains references to objects of other classes.

Section 9.2 Superclasses and Subclasses

- Single-inheritance relationships form treelike hierarchical structures—a superclass exists in a hierarchical relationship with its subclasses.

Section 9.3 **`protected`** *Members*

- A superclass's `public` members are accessible wherever the program has a reference to an object of that superclass or one of its subclasses.
- A superclass's `private` members can be accessed directly only within the superclass's declaration.
- A superclass's `protected` members (p. 377) have an intermediate level of protection between `public` and `private` access. They can be accessed by members of the superclass, by members of its subclasses and by members of other classes in the same package.
- A superclass's `private` members are hidden in its subclasses and can be accessed only through the `public` or `protected` methods inherited from the superclass.
- An overridden superclass method can be accessed from a subclass if the superclass method name is preceded by `super` (p. 377) and a dot (`.`) separator.

Section 9.4 Relationship Between Superclasses and Subclasses

- A subclass cannot access the `private` members of its superclass, but it can access the non-`private` members.
- A subclass can invoke a constructor of its superclass by using the keyword `super`, followed by a set of parentheses containing the superclass constructor arguments. This must appear as the first statement in the subclass constructor's body.
- A superclass method can be overridden in a subclass to declare an appropriate implementation for the subclass.
- The `@Override` annotation (p. 381) indicates that a method should override a superclass method. When the compiler encounters a method declared with `@Override`, it compares the method's signature with the superclass's method signatures. If there isn't an exact match, the compiler issues an error message, such as "method does not override or implement a method from a supertype."
- Method `toString` takes no arguments and returns a `String`. The `Object` class's `toString` method is normally overridden by a subclass.
- When an object is output using the `%s` format specifier, the object's `toString` method is called implicitly to obtain its `String` representation.

Section 9.5 Constructors in Subclasses

- The first task of a subclass constructor is to call its direct superclass's constructor to ensure that the instance variables inherited from the superclass are initialized.

Section 9.6 Class **`Object`**

- See the table of class `Object`'s methods in Fig. 9.12.

Self-Review Exercises

9.1 Fill in the blanks in each of the following statements:

a) ________ is a form of software reusability in which new classes acquire the members of existing classes and embellish those classes with new capabilities.

b) A superclass's ________ members can be accessed in the superclass declaration *and in* subclass declarations.

c) In a(n) ________ relationship, an object of a subclass can also be treated as an object of its superclass.

d) In a(n) ________ relationship, a class object has references to objects of other classes as members.

e) In single inheritance, a class exists in a(n) ________ relationship with its subclasses.

f) A superclass's ________ members are accessible anywhere that the program has a reference to an object of that superclass or to an object of one of its subclasses.
g) When an object of a subclass is instantiated, a superclass ________ is called implicitly or explicitly.
h) Subclass constructors can call superclass constructors via the ________ keyword.

9.2 State whether each of the following is *true* or *false*. If a statement is *false*, explain why.
a) Superclass constructors are not inherited by subclasses.
b) A *has-a* relationship is implemented via inheritance.
c) A `Car` class has an *is-a* relationship with the `SteeringWheel` and `Brakes` classes.
d) When a subclass redefines a superclass method by using the same signature, the subclass is said to overload that superclass method.

Answers to Self-Review Exercises

9.1 a) Inheritance. b) `public` and `protected`. c) *is-a* or inheritance. d) *has-a* or composition. e) hierarchical. f) `public`. g) constructor. h) `super`.

9.2 a) True. b) False. A *has-a* relationship is implemented via composition. An *is-a* relationship is implemented via inheritance. c) False. This is an example of a *has-a* relationship. Class `Car` has an *is-a* relationship with class `Vehicle`. d) False. This is known as overriding, not overloading—an overloaded method has the same name, but a different signature.

Exercises

9.3 *(Recommended: Using Composition Rather Than Inheritance)* Many programs written with inheritance could be written with composition instead, and vice versa. Rewrite class `BasePlusCommissionEmployee` (Fig. 9.11) of the `CommissionEmployee`–`BasePlusCommissionEmployee` hierarchy so that it contains a reference to a `CommissionEmployee` object, rather than inheriting from class `CommissionEmployee`. Retest `BasePlusCommissionEmployee` to demonstrate that it still provides the same functionality.

9.4 *(Software Reuse)* Discuss the ways in which inheritance promotes software reuse, saves time during program development and helps prevent errors.

9.5 *(`Student` Inheritance Hierarchy)* Draw an inheritance hierarchy for students at a university similar to the hierarchy shown in Fig. 9.2. Use `Student` as the superclass of the hierarchy, then extend `Student` with classes `UndergraduateStudent` and `GraduateStudent`. Continue to extend the hierarchy as deep (i.e., as many levels) as possible. For example, `Freshman`, `Sophomore`, `Junior` and `Senior` might extend `UndergraduateStudent`, and `DoctoralStudent` and `MastersStudent` might be subclasses of `GraduateStudent`. After drawing the hierarchy, discuss the relationships that exist between the classes. [*Note:* You do not need to write any code for this exercise.]

9.6 *(`Shape` Inheritance Hierarchy)* The world of shapes is much richer than the shapes included in the inheritance hierarchy of Fig. 9.3. Write down all the shapes you can think of—both two-dimensional and three-dimensional—and form them into a more complete `Shape` hierarchy with as many levels as possible. Your hierarchy should have class `Shape` at the top. Classes `TwoDimensionalShape` and `ThreeDimensionalShape` should extend `Shape`. Add additional subclasses, such as `Quadrilateral` and `Sphere`, at their correct locations in the hierarchy as necessary.

9.7 *(`protected` vs. `private`)* Some programmers prefer not to use `protected` access, because they believe it breaks the encapsulation of the superclass. Discuss the relative merits of using `protected` access vs. using `private` access in superclasses.

9.8 *(`Quadrilateral` Inheritance Hierarchy)* Write an inheritance hierarchy for classes `Quadrilateral`, `Trapezoid`, `Parallelogram`, `Rectangle` and `Square`. Use `Quadrilateral` as the superclass of the hierarchy. Create and use a `Point` class to represent the points in each shape. Make the hierarchy as deep (i.e., as many levels) as possible. Specify the instance variables and methods for each class. The `private` instance variables of `Quadrilateral` should be the *x-y* coordinate pairs for the four endpoints of the `Quadrilateral`. Write a program that instantiates objects of your classes and outputs each object's area (except `Quadrilateral`).

9.9 *(What Does Each Code Snippet Do?)*

a) Assume the following method call is in an overridden `earnings` method in a subclass:

```
super.earnings()
```

b) Assume that the following line of code appears before a method declaration:

```
@Override
```

c) Assume the following line of code appears as the first statement in a constructor's body:

```
super(firstArgument, secondArgument);
```

9.10 *(Write a Line of Code)* Write a line of code that performs each of the following tasks:

a) Specify that class `PieceWorker` inherits from class `Employee`.
b) Call superclass `Employee`'s `toString` method from subclass `PieceWorker`'s `toString` method.
c) Call superclass `Employee`'s constructor from subclass `PieceWorker`'s constructor—assume that the superclass constructor receives three `String`s representing the first name, last name and social security number.

9.11 *(Using `super` in a Constructor's Body)* Explain why you would use `super` in the first statement of a subclass constructor's body.

9.12 *(Using `super` in an Instance Method's Body)* Explain why you would use `super` in the body of a subclass's instance method.

9.13 *(Calling* get *Methods in a Class's Body)* In Figs. 9.10–9.11 methods `earnings` and `toString` each call various *get* methods within the same class. Explain the benefits of calling these *get* methods within the classes.

9.14 *(`Employee` Hierarchy)* In this chapter, you studied an inheritance hierarchy in which class `BasePlusCommissionEmployee` inherited from class `CommissionEmployee`. However, not all types of employees are `CommissionEmployee`s. In this exercise, you'll create a more general `Employee` superclass that *factors out* the attributes and behaviors in class `CommissionEmployee` that are common to all `Employee`s. The common attributes and behaviors for all `Employee`s are `firstName`, `lastName`, `socialSecurityNumber`, `getFirstName`, `getLastName`, `getSocialSecurityNumber` and a portion of method `toString`. Create a new superclass `Employee` that contains these instance variables and methods and a constructor. Next, rewrite class `CommissionEmployee` from Section 9.4.5 as a subclass of `Employee`. Class `CommissionEmployee` should contain only the instance variables and methods that are not declared in superclass `Employee`. Class `CommissionEmployee`'s constructor should invoke class `Employee`'s constructor, and `CommissionEmployee`'s `toString` method should invoke `Employee`'s `toString` method. Once you've completed these modifications, run the `CommissionEmployeeTest` and `BasePlusCommissionEmployeeTest` apps using these new classes to ensure that the apps still display the same results for a `CommissionEmployee` object and `BasePlusCommissionEmployee` object, respectively.

9.15 *(Creating a New Subclass of `Employee`)* Other types of `Employee`s might include `SalariedEmployee`s who get paid a fixed weekly salary, `PieceWorker`s who get paid by the number of pieces they produce or `HourlyEmployee`s who get paid an hourly wage with time-and-a-half—1.5 times the hourly wage—for hours worked over 40 hours.

Create class `HourlyEmployee` that inherits from class `Employee` (Exercise 9.14) and has instance variable `hours` (a `double`) that represents the hours worked, instance variable `wage` (a `dou-`

ble) that represents the wages per hour, a constructor that takes as arguments a first name, a last name, a social security number, an hourly wage and the number of hours worked, *set* and *get* methods for manipulating the hours and wage, an earnings method to calculate an HourlyEmployee's earnings based on the hours worked and a toString method that returns the HourlyEmployee's String representation. Method setWage should ensure that wage is nonnegative, and setHours should ensure that the value of hours is between 0 and 168 (the total number of hours in a week). Use class HourlyEmployee in a test program that's similar to the one in Fig. 9.5.

9.16 *(Recommended Project: Combining Composition and Inheritance[2])* In this chapter, we created the CommissionEmployee–BasePlusCommissionEmployee inheritance hierarchy to model the relationship between two types of employees and how to calculate the earnings for each. Another way to look at the problem is that CommissionEmployees and BasePlusCommissionEmployees are each Employees and that each *has a* different CompensationModel object.

A CompensationModel would provide an earnings method. Subclasses of CompensationModel would contain the details of a particular Employee's compensation:

a) CommissionCompensationModel—For Employees who are paid by commission, this CompensationModel subclass would contain grossSales and commissionRate instance variables, and would define earnings to return grossSales * commissionRate.
b) BasePlusCommissionCompensationModel—For Employees who are paid a base salary and commission, this CompensationModel subclass would contain instance variables grossSales, commissionRate and baseSalary and would define earnings to return baseSalary + grossSales * commissionRate.

Class Employee's earnings method would simply call the composed CompensationModel's earnings method and return its result.

This approach is more flexible than our original hierarchy. For example, consider an Employee who gets promoted. With the approach described here, you can simply change that Employee's CompensationModel by assigning the composed CompensationModel reference an appropriate subclass object. With the CommissionEmployee–BasePlusCommissionEmployee hierarchy, you'd need to change the employee's type by creating a new object of the appropriate class and moving data from the old object into the new one.

Implement the Employee class and CompensationModel hierarchy discussed in this exercise. In addition to the firstName, lastName, socialSecurityNumber and CompensationModel instance variables, class Employee should provide:

a) A constructor that receives three Strings and a CompensationModel to initialize the instance variables.
b) A set method that allows the client code to change an Employee's CompensationModel.
c) An earnings method that calls the CompensationModel's earnings method and returns its result.

When you invoke method earnings via the superclass CompensationModel reference to a subclass object (of type CommissionCompensationModel or BasePlusCommissionCompensationModel), you might expect superclass CompensationModel's earnings method to execute. What actually happens? The subclass object's earnings method executes. This is called polymorphic behavior, which we explore in Chapter 10.

In your test application, create two Employee objects—one with a CommissionCompensationModel and one with a BasePlusCommissionCompensationModel—then display each Employee's earnings. Next, change each Employee's CompensationModel dynamically and redisplay each Employee's earnings. In Chapter 10's exercises, we'll examine how to implement CompensationModel as an interface rather than a class.

---

2. Our thanks to Brian Goetz, Oracle's Java Language Architect, for suggesting the class architecture we use in this exercise.

Object-Oriented Programming: Polymorphism and Interfaces

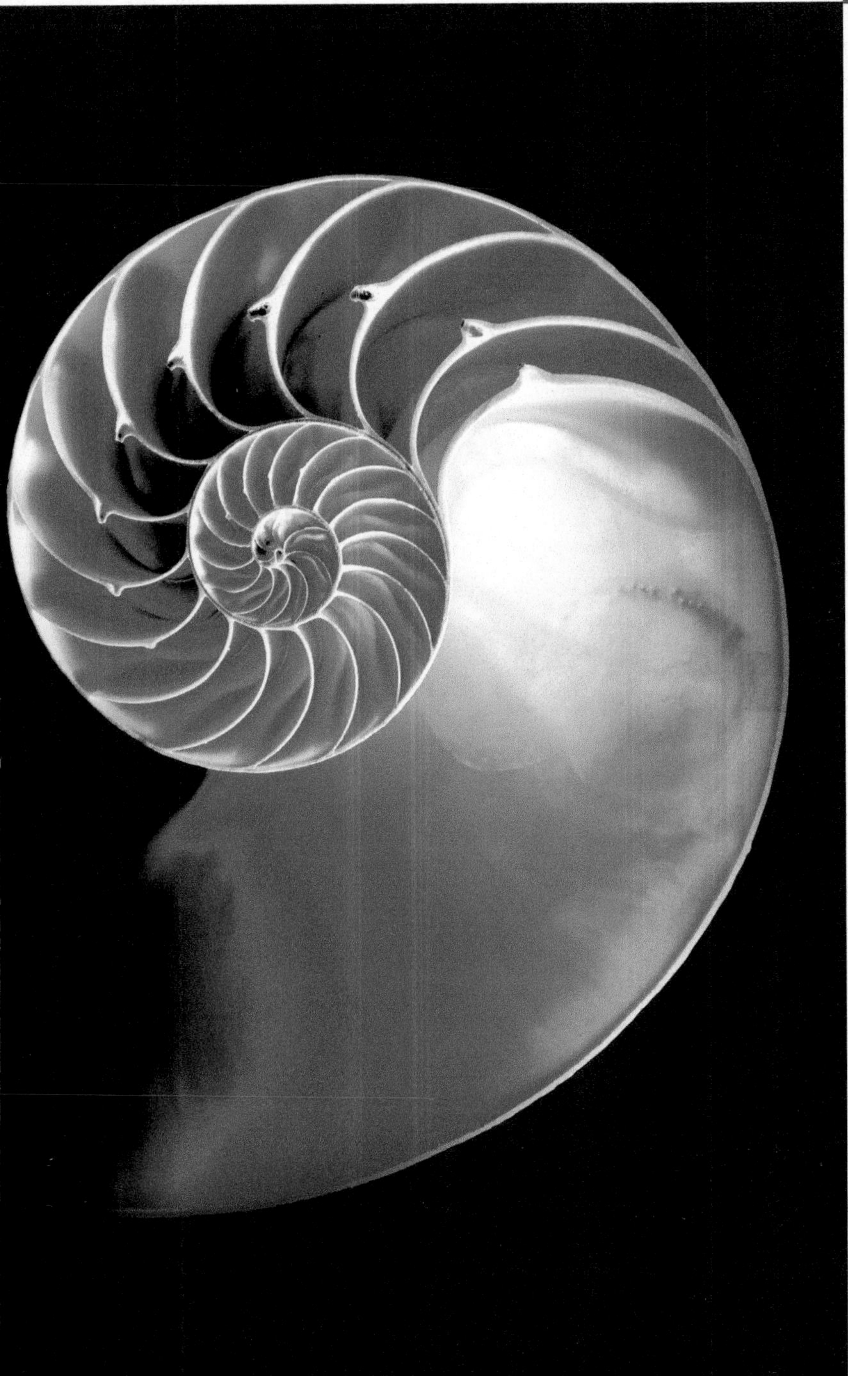

Objectives

In this chapter you'll:

- Learn the concept of polymorphism and how it enables "programming in the general."
- Use overridden methods to effect polymorphism.
- Distinguish between abstract and concrete classes.
- Declare abstract methods to create abstract classes.
- Learn how polymorphism makes systems extensible and maintainable.
- Determine an object's type at execution time.
- Declare and implement interfaces, and become familiar with the Java SE 8 interface enhancements.

Outline

10.1 Introduction

We continue our study of object-oriented programming by explaining and demonstrating **polymorphism** with inheritance hierarchies. Polymorphism enables you to "program in the *general*" rather than "program in the *specific*." In particular, polymorphism enables you to write programs that process objects that share the same superclass, either directly or indirectly, as if they were all objects of the superclass; this can simplify programming.

Consider the following example of polymorphism. Suppose we create a program that simulates the movement of several types of animals for a biological study. Classes `Fish`, `Frog` and `Bird` represent the types of animals under investigation. Imagine that each class extends superclass `Animal`, which contains a method `move` and maintains an animal's current location as *x-y* coordinates. Each subclass implements method `move`. Our program maintains an `Animal` array containing references to objects of the various `Animal` subclasses. To simulate the animals' movements, the program sends each object the *same* message once per second—namely, `move`. Each specific type of `Animal` responds to a `move` message in its own way—a `Fish` might swim three feet, a `Frog` might jump five feet and a `Bird` might fly ten feet. Each object knows how to modify its *x-y* coordinates appropriately for its *specific* type of movement. Relying on each object to know how to "do the right thing" (i.e., do what's appropriate for that type of object) in response to the *same* method call is the key concept of polymorphism. The *same* message (in this case, `move`) sent to a *variety* of objects has *many forms* of results—hence the term polymorphism.

Implementing for Extensibility

With polymorphism, we can design and implement systems that are easily *extensible*—new classes can be added with little or no modification to the general portions of the program, as long as the new classes are part of the inheritance hierarchy that the program processes generically. The new classes simply "plug right in." The only parts of a program that must be altered are those that require direct knowledge of the new classes that we add to the hierarchy. For example, if we extend class `Animal` to create class `Tortoise` (which might respond to a `move` message by crawling one inch), we need to write only the `Tortoise` class and the part of the simulation that instantiates a `Tortoise` object. The portions of the simulation that tell each `Animal` to move generically can remain the same.

Chapter Overview

First, we discuss common examples of polymorphism. We then provide a simple example demonstrating polymorphic behavior. We use superclass references to manipulate *both* superclass objects and subclass objects polymorphically.

We then present a case study that revisits the employee hierarchy of Section 9.4.5. We develop a simple payroll application that polymorphically calculates the weekly pay of several different types of employees using each employee's `earnings` method. Though the earnings of each type of employee are calculated in a *specific* way, polymorphism allows us to process the employees "in the *general*." In the case study, we enlarge the hierarchy to include two new classes—`SalariedEmployee` (for people paid a fixed weekly salary) and `HourlyEmployee` (for people paid an hourly salary and "time-and-a-half" for overtime). We declare the common functionality for all the classes in the updated hierarchy in an "abstract" `Employee` class from which "concrete" classes `SalariedEmployee`, `HourlyEmployee` and `CommissionEmployee` inherit directly and "concrete" class `BasePlusCommissionEmployee` inherits indirectly. As you'll see, *when we invoke each employee's* `earnings` *method off a superclass* `Employee` *reference (regardless of the employee's type), the correct earnings subclass calculation is performed,* due to Java's built-in polymorphic capabilities.

Programming in the Specific

Occasionally, when performing polymorphic processing, we need to program "in the *specific*." Our `Employee` case study demonstrates that a program can determine the *type* of an object at *execution time* and act on that object accordingly. In the case study, we've decided that `BasePlusCommissionEmployees` should receive 10% raises on their base salaries. So, we use these capabilities to determine whether a particular employee object *is a* `BasePlusCommissionEmployee`. If so, we increase that employee's base salary by 10%.

Interfaces

The chapter continues with an introduction to Java *interfaces*, which are particularly useful for assigning *common* functionality to possibly *unrelated* classes. This allows objects of these classes to be processed polymorphically—objects of classes that **implement** the *same* interface can respond to all of the interface method calls. To demonstrate creating and using interfaces, we modify our payroll application to create a generalized accounts payable application that can calculate payments due for company employees *and* invoice amounts to be billed for purchased goods.

10.2 Polymorphism Examples

Let's consider several additional examples of polymorphism.

Quadrilaterals

If class `Rectangle` is derived from class `Quadrilateral`, then a `Rectangle` object *is a* more *specific* version of a `Quadrilateral`. Any operation (e.g., calculating the perimeter or the area) that can be performed on a `Quadrilateral` can also be performed on a `Rectangle`. These operations can also be performed on other `Quadrilateral`s, such as `Square`s, `Parallelogram`s and `Trapezoid`s. The polymorphism occurs when a program invokes a method through a superclass `Quadrilateral` variable—at execution time, the correct subclass version of the method is called, based on the type of the reference stored in the superclass variable. You'll see a simple code example that illustrates this process in Section 10.3.

Space Objects in a Video Game

Suppose we design a video game that manipulates objects of classes `Martian`, `Venusian`, `Plutonian`, `SpaceShip` and `LaserBeam`. Imagine that each class inherits from the superclass `SpaceObject`, which contains method `draw`. Each subclass implements this method. A screen manager maintains a collection (e.g., a `SpaceObject` array) of references to objects of the various classes. To refresh the screen, the screen manager periodically sends each object the *same* message—namely, `draw`. However, each object responds its *own* way, based on its class. For example, a `Martian` object might draw itself in red with green eyes and the appropriate number of antennae. A `SpaceShip` object might draw itself as a bright silver flying saucer. A `LaserBeam` object might draw itself as a bright red beam across the screen. Again, the *same* message (in this case, `draw`) sent to a *variety* of objects has "many forms" of results.

A screen manager might use polymorphism to facilitate adding new classes to a system with minimal modifications to the system's code. Suppose that we want to add `Mercurian` objects to our video game. To do so, we'd build a class `Mercurian` that extends `SpaceObject` and provides its own `draw` method implementation. When `Mercurian` objects appear in the `SpaceObject` collection, the screen-manager code *invokes method* `draw`*, exactly as it does for every other object in the collection, regardless of its type.* So the new `Mercurian` objects simply "plug right in" without any modification of the screen-manager code by the programmer. Thus, without modifying the system (other than to build new classes and modify the code that creates new objects), you can use polymorphism to conveniently include additional types that were not even considered when the system was created.

Software Engineering Observation 10.1

Polymorphism enables you to deal in generalities and let the execution-time environment handle the specifics. You can tell objects to behave in manners appropriate to those objects, without knowing their specific types, as long as they belong to the same inheritance hierarchy.

Software Engineering Observation 10.2

Polymorphism promotes extensibility: Software that invokes polymorphic behavior is independent of the object types to which messages are sent. New object types that can respond to existing method calls can be incorporated into a system without modifying the base system. Only client code that instantiates new objects must be modified to accommodate new types.

10.3 Demonstrating Polymorphic Behavior

Section 9.4 created a class hierarchy, in which class `BasePlusCommissionEmployee` inherited from `CommissionEmployee`. The examples in that section manipulated `CommissionEmployee` and `BasePlusCommissionEmployee` objects by using references to them to invoke their methods—we aimed superclass variables at superclass objects and subclass variables at subclass objects. These assignments are natural and straightforward—superclass variables are *intended* to refer to superclass objects, and subclass variables are *intended* to refer to subclass objects. However, as you'll soon see, other assignments are possible.

In the next example, we aim a *superclass* reference at a *subclass* object. We then show how invoking a method on a subclass object via a superclass reference invokes the *subclass* functionality—the type of the *referenced object*, *not* the type of the *variable*, determines which method is called. This example demonstrates that *an object of a subclass can be treated as an object of its superclass*, enabling various interesting manipulations. A program can create an array of superclass variables that refer to objects of many subclass types. This is allowed because each subclass object *is an* object of its superclass. For example, we can assign the reference of a `BasePlusCommissionEmployee` object to a superclass `CommissionEmployee` variable, because a `BasePlusCommissionEmployee` *is a* `CommissionEmployee`—so we can treat a `BasePlusCommissionEmployee` as a `CommissionEmployee`.

As you'll learn later in the chapter, you *cannot treat a superclass object as a subclass object*, because a superclass object is *not* an object of any of its subclasses. For example, we cannot assign the reference of a `CommissionEmployee` object to a subclass `BasePlusCommissionEmployee` variable, because a `CommissionEmployee` is *not* a `BasePlusCommissionEmployee`—a `CommissionEmployee` does *not* have a `baseSalary` instance variable and does *not* have methods `setBaseSalary` and `getBaseSalary`. The *is-a* relationship applies only *up the hierarchy* from a subclass to its direct (and indirect) superclasses, and *not* vice versa (i.e., not down the hierarchy from a superclass to its subclasses or indirect subclasses).

The Java compiler *does* allow the assignment of a superclass reference to a subclass variable if we explicitly *cast* the superclass reference to the subclass type. Why would we ever want to perform such an assignment? A superclass reference can be used to invoke *only* the methods declared in the superclass—attempting to invoke *subclass-only* methods through a superclass reference results in compilation errors. If a program needs to perform a subclass-specific operation on a subclass object referenced by a superclass variable, the program must first cast the superclass reference to a subclass reference through a technique known as **downcasting**. This enables the program to invoke subclass methods that are *not* in the superclass. We demonstrate the mechanics of downcasting in Section 10.5.

Software Engineering Observation 10.3

Although it's allowed, you should generally avoid downcasting.

The example in Fig. 10.1 demonstrates three ways to use superclass and subclass variables to store references to superclass and subclass objects. The first two are straightforward—as in Section 9.4, we assign a superclass reference to a superclass variable, and a subclass reference to a subclass variable. Then we demonstrate the relationship between subclasses and superclasses (i.e., the *is-a* relationship) by assigning a subclass reference to a superclass variable. This program uses classes `CommissionEmployee` and `BasePlusCommissionEmployee` from Fig. 9.10 and Fig. 9.11, respectively.

```
// Fig. 10.1: PolymorphismTest.java
// Assigning superclass and subclass references to superclass and
// subclass variables.

public class PolymorphismTest {
   public static void main(String[] args) {
      // assign superclass reference to superclass variable
      CommissionEmployee commissionEmployee = new CommissionEmployee(
         "Sue", "Jones", "222-22-2222", 10000, .06);

      // assign subclass reference to subclass variable
      BasePlusCommissionEmployee basePlusCommissionEmployee =
         new BasePlusCommissionEmployee(
         "Bob", "Lewis", "333-33-3333", 5000, .04, 300);

      // invoke toString on superclass object using superclass variable
      System.out.printf("%s %s:%n%n%s%n%n",
         "Call CommissionEmployee's toString with superclass reference ",
         "to superclass object", commissionEmployee.toString());

      // invoke toString on subclass object using subclass variable
      System.out.printf("%s %s:%n%n%s%n%n",
         "Call BasePlusCommissionEmployee's toString with subclass",
         "reference to subclass object",
         basePlusCommissionEmployee.toString());

      // invoke toString on subclass object using superclass variable
      CommissionEmployee commissionEmployee2 =
         basePlusCommissionEmployee;
      System.out.printf("%s %s:%n%n%s%n",
         "Call BasePlusCommissionEmployee's toString with superclass",
         "reference to subclass object", commissionEmployee2.toString());
   }
}
```

```
Call CommissionEmployee's toString with superclass reference to superclass
object:

commission employee: Sue Jones
social security number: 222-22-2222
gross sales: 10000.00
commission rate: 0.06
```

Fig. 10.1 | Assigning superclass and subclass references to superclass and subclass variables. (Part 1 of 2.)

```
Call BasePlusCommissionEmployee's toString with subclass reference to
subclass object:

base-salaried commission employee: Bob Lewis
social security number: 333-33-3333
gross sales: 5000.00
commission rate: 0.04
base salary: 300.00

Call BasePlusCommissionEmployee's toString with superclass reference to
subclass object:

base-salaried commission employee: Bob Lewis
social security number: 333-33-3333
gross sales: 5000.00
commission rate: 0.04
base salary: 300.00
```

Fig. 10.1 | Assigning superclass and subclass references to superclass and subclass variables. (Part 2 of 2.)

In Fig. 10.1, lines 8–9 create a `CommissionEmployee` object and assign its reference to a `CommissionEmployee` variable. Lines 12–14 create a `BasePlusCommissionEmployee` object and assign its reference to a `BasePlusCommissionEmployee` variable. These assignments are natural—for example, a `CommissionEmployee` variable's primary purpose is to hold a reference to a `CommissionEmployee` object. Lines 17–19 use `commissionEmployee` to invoke `toString` *explicitly*. Because `commissionEmployee` refers to a `CommissionEmployee` object, superclass `CommissionEmployee`'s version of `toString` is called. Similarly, lines 22–25 use `basePlusCommissionEmployee` to invoke `toString` *explicitly* on the `BasePlusCommissionEmployee` object. This invokes subclass `BasePlusCommissionEmployee`'s version of `toString`.

Lines 28–29 then assign the reference of subclass object `basePlusCommissionEmployee` to a superclass `CommissionEmployee` variable, which lines 30–32 use to invoke method `toString`. *When a superclass variable contains a reference to a subclass object, and that reference is used to call a method, the subclass version of the method is called.* Hence, `commissionEmployee2.toString()` in line 32 actually calls class `BasePlusCommissionEmployee`'s `toString` method. The Java compiler allows this "crossover" because an object of a subclass *is an* object of its superclass (but *not* vice versa). When the compiler encounters a method call made through a variable, the compiler determines if the method can be called by checking the variable's class type. If that class contains the proper method declaration (or inherits one), the call is compiled. At execution time, the type of the object to which the variable refers determines the actual method to use. This process, called *dynamic binding*, is discussed in detail in Section 10.5.

10.4 Abstract Classes and Methods

When we think of a class, we assume that programs will create objects of that type. Sometimes it's useful to declare classes—called **abstract classes**—for which you *never* intend to create objects. Because they're used only as superclasses in inheritance hierarchies, we refer to them as **abstract superclasses**. These classes cannot be used to instantiate objects, because, as we'll soon see, abstract classes are *incomplete*. Subclasses must declare the "missing pieces" to become "concrete" classes, from which you can instantiate objects. Otherwise, these subclasses, too, will be abstract. We demonstrate abstract classes in Section 10.5.

Purpose of Abstract Classes

An abstract class's purpose is to provide an appropriate superclass from which other classes can inherit and thus share a common design. In the `Shape` hierarchy of Fig. 9.3, for example, subclasses inherit the notion of what it means to be a `Shape`—perhaps common attributes such as `location`, `color` and `borderThickness`, and behaviors such as `draw`, `move`, `resize` and `changeColor`. Classes that can be used to instantiate objects are called **concrete classes**. Such classes provide implementations of *every* method they declare (some of the implementations can be inherited). For example, we could derive concrete classes `Circle`, `Square` and `Triangle` from abstract superclass `TwoDimensionalShape`. Similarly, we could derive concrete classes `Sphere`, `Cube` and `Tetrahedron` from abstract superclass `ThreeDimensionalShape`. Abstract superclasses are *too general* to create real objects—they specify only what is common among subclasses. We need to be more *specific* before we can create objects. For example, if you send the `draw` message to abstract class `TwoDimensionalShape`, the class knows that two-dimensional shapes should be *drawable*, but it does not know what *specific* shape to draw, so it cannot implement a real `draw` method. Concrete classes provide the specifics that make it reasonable to instantiate objects.

Not all hierarchies contain abstract classes. However, you'll often write client code that uses only abstract superclass types to reduce the client code's dependencies on a range of subclass types. For example, you can write a method with a parameter of an abstract superclass type. When called, such a method can receive an object of *any* concrete class that directly or indirectly extends the superclass specified as the parameter's type.

Abstract classes sometimes constitute several levels of a hierarchy. For example, the `Shape` hierarchy of Fig. 9.3 begins with abstract class `Shape`. On the next level of the hierarchy are *abstract* classes `TwoDimensionalShape` and `ThreeDimensionalShape`. The next level of the hierarchy declares *concrete* classes for `TwoDimensionalShapes` (`Circle`, `Square` and `Triangle`) and for `ThreeDimensionalShapes` (`Sphere`, `Cube` and `Tetrahedron`).

Declaring an Abstract Class and Abstract Methods

You make a class abstract by declaring it with keyword **`abstract`**. An abstract class normally contains one or more **abstract methods**. An abstract method is an *instance method* with keyword `abstract` in its declaration, as in

```
public abstract void draw(); // abstract method
```

Abstract methods do *not* provide implementations. A class that contains *any* abstract methods must be explicitly declared `abstract` even if that class contains some concrete (nonabstract) methods. Each concrete subclass of an abstract superclass also must provide concrete implementations of each of the superclass's abstract methods. Constructors and `static` methods cannot be declared `abstract`. Constructors are *not* inherited, so an `abstract` constructor could never be implemented. Though non-`private static` methods are inherited, they cannot be overridden. Since `abstract` methods are meant to be overridden so that they can process objects based on their types, it would not make sense to declare a `static` method as `abstract`.

Software Engineering Observation 10.4

An `abstract` *class declares common attributes and behaviors (both* `abstract` *and concrete) of the classes in a class hierarchy. An* `abstract` *class typically contains one or more* `abstract` *methods that subclasses must override if they are to be concrete. The instance variables and concrete methods of an* `abstract` *class are subject to the normal rules of inheritance.*

Common Programming Error 10.1

Attempting to instantiate an object of an abstract class is a compilation error.

Common Programming Error 10.2

Classes must be declared `abstract` *if they declare* `abstract` *methods or if they inherit* `abstract` *methods and do not provide concrete implementations of them; otherwise, compilation errors occur.*

Using Abstract Classes to Declare Variables

Although we cannot instantiate objects of abstract superclasses, you'll soon see that we *can* use abstract superclasses to declare variables that can hold references to objects of *any* concrete class *derived from* those abstract superclasses. We'll use such variables to manipulate subclass objects *polymorphically*. You also can use abstract superclass names to invoke `static` methods declared in those abstract superclasses.

Consider another application of polymorphism. A drawing program needs to display many shapes, including types of new shapes that you'll *add* to the system *after* writing the drawing program. The drawing program might need to display shapes, such as `Circle`s, `Triangle`s, `Rectangle`s or others, that derive from abstract class `Shape`. The drawing program uses `Shape` variables to manage the objects that are displayed. To draw any object in this inheritance hierarchy, the drawing program uses a superclass `Shape` variable containing a reference to the subclass object to invoke the object's `draw` method. This method is declared `abstract` in superclass `Shape`, so each concrete subclass *must* implement method `draw` in a manner specific to that shape—each object in the `Shape` inheritance hierarchy *knows how to draw itself.* The drawing program does not have to worry about the type of each object or whether the program has ever encountered objects of that type.

Layered Software Systems

Polymorphism is particularly effective for implementing so-called *layered software systems.* In operating systems, for example, each type of physical device could operate quite differently from the others. Even so, commands to read or write data from and to devices may have a certain uniformity. For each device, the operating system uses a piece of software called a *device driver* to control all communication between the system and the device. The write message sent to a device-driver object needs to be interpreted specifically in the context of that driver and how it manipulates devices of a specific type. However, the write call itself really is no different from the write to any other device in the system—place some number of bytes from memory onto that device. An object-oriented operating system might use an abstract superclass to provide an "interface" appropriate for all device drivers. Then, through inheritance from that abstract superclass, subclasses are formed that all behave similarly. The device-driver methods are declared as abstract methods in the abstract superclass. The implementations of these abstract methods are provided in the concrete subclasses that correspond to the specific types of device drivers. New devices are always being developed, often long after the operating system has been released. When you buy a new device, it comes with a device driver provided by the device vendor. The device is immediately operational after you connect it to your computer and install the driver. This is another elegant example of how polymorphism makes systems *extensible*.

10.5 Case Study: Payroll System Using Polymorphism

This section reexamines the `CommissionEmployee-BasePlusCommissionEmployee` hierarchy that we explored throughout Section 9.4. Now we use an abstract method and polymorphism to perform payroll calculations based on an enhanced employee inheritance hierarchy that meets the following requirements:

> *A company pays its employees on a weekly basis. The employees are of four types: Salaried employees are paid a fixed weekly salary regardless of the number of hours worked, hourly employees are paid by the hour and receive overtime pay (i.e., 1.5 times their hourly salary rate) for all hours worked in excess of 40 hours, commission employees are paid a percentage of their sales and base-salaried commission employees receive a base salary plus a percentage of their sales. For the current pay period, the company has decided to reward base-salaried commission employees by adding 10% to their base salaries. The company wants you to write an application that performs its payroll calculations polymorphically.*

We use `abstract` class `Employee` to represent the general concept of an employee. The classes that extend `Employee` are `SalariedEmployee`, `CommissionEmployee` and `HourlyEmployee`. Class `BasePlusCommissionEmployee`—which extends `CommissionEmployee`—represents the last employee type. The UML class diagram in Fig. 10.2 shows the inheritance hierarchy for our polymorphic employee-payroll application. Abstract class name `Employee` is *italicized*—a convention of the UML.

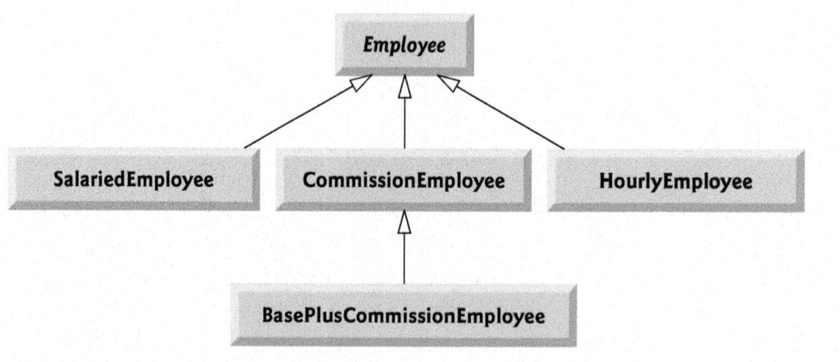

Fig. 10.2 | `Employee` hierarchy UML class diagram.

Abstract superclass `Employee` declares the "interface" to the hierarchy—that is, the set of methods that a program can invoke on all `Employee` objects. We use the term "interface" here in a *general* sense to refer to the various ways programs can communicate with objects of *any* `Employee` subclass. Be careful not to confuse the general notion of an "interface" with the formal notion of a Java interface, the subject of Section 10.9. Each employee, regardless of the way his or her earnings are calculated, has a first name, a last name and a social security number, so `private` instance variables `firstName`, `lastName` and `socialSecurityNumber` appear in abstract superclass `Employee`.

The diagram in Fig. 10.3 shows each of the five classes in the hierarchy down the left side and methods `earnings` and `toString` across the top. For each class, the diagram shows the desired results of each method. We do not list superclass `Employee`'s *get* methods because they're *not* overridden in any of the subclasses—each of these methods is inherited and used "as is" by each subclass.

	earnings	toString
Employee	abstract	*firstName lastName* social security number: *SSN*
Salaried- Employee	weeklySalary	salaried employee: *firstName lastName* social security number: *SSN* weekly salary: *weeklySalary*

Hourly-
Employee
	if (hours <= 40) {
	  wage * hours
	}
	else if (hours > 40) {
	  40 * wage +
	  (hours - 40) *
	  wage * 1.5
	}
		hourly employee: *firstName lastName*
		social security number: *SSN*
		hourly wage: *wage*; hours worked: *hours*

Commission- Employee	commissionRate * grossSales	commission employee: *firstName lastName* social security number: *SSN* gross sales: *grossSales*; commission rate: *commissionRate*
BasePlus- Commission- Employee	(commissionRate * grossSales) + baseSalary	base salaried commission employee: *firstName lastName* social security number: *SSN* gross sales: *grossSales*; commission rate: *commissionRate*; base salary: *baseSalary*

Fig. 10.3 | Polymorphic interface for the `Employee` hierarchy classes.

The following sections implement the `Employee` class hierarchy of Fig. 10.2. The first section implements *abstract superclass* `Employee`. The next four sections each implement one of the *concrete* classes. The last section implements a test program that builds objects of all these classes and processes those objects polymorphically.

10.5.1 Abstract Superclass `Employee`

Class `Employee` (Fig. 10.4) provides methods `earnings` and `toString`, in addition to the *get* methods that return the values of `Employee`'s instance variables. An `earnings` method certainly applies *generically* to all employees. But each earnings calculation depends on the employee's particular class. So we declare `earnings` as `abstract` in superclass `Employee` because a *specific* default implementation does not make sense for that method—there isn't enough information to determine what amount `earnings` should return.

Each subclass overrides `earnings` with an appropriate implementation. To calculate an employee's earnings, the program assigns to a superclass `Employee` variable a reference to the employee's object, then invokes the `earnings` method on that variable. We maintain an array of `Employee` variables, each holding a reference to an `Employee` object. You *cannot* use class `Employee` directly to create `Employee` *objects*, because `Employee` is an *abstract* class. Due to inheritance, however, all objects of all `Employee` subclasses may be thought of as `Employee` objects. The program will iterate through the array and call method `earnings` for each `Employee` object. Java processes these method calls *polymorphically*. Declaring `earnings` as an `abstract` method in `Employee` enables the calls to `earnings` through `Employee` variables to compile and forces every direct *concrete* subclass of `Employee` to *override* `earnings`.

Method `toString` in class `Employee` returns a `String` containing the first name, last name and social security number of the employee. As we'll see, each subclass of `Employee` *overrides* method `toString` to create a `String` representation of an object of that class that contains the employee's type (e.g., `"salaried employee:"`) followed by the rest of the employee's information.

Let's consider class `Employee`'s declaration (Fig. 10.4). The class includes a constructor that receives the first name, last name and social security number (lines 10–15); *get* methods that return the first name, last name and social security number (lines 18, 21 and 24, respectively); method `toString` (lines 27–31), which returns the `String` representation of an `Employee`; and `abstract` method `earnings` (line 34), which will be implemented by each of the *concrete* subclasses. The `Employee` constructor does *not* validate its parameters in this example; normally, such validation should be provided.

```
1  // Fig. 10.4: Employee.java
2  // Employee abstract superclass.
3
4  public abstract class Employee {
5     private final String firstName;
6     private final String lastName;
7     private final String socialSecurityNumber;
8
9     // constructor
10    public Employee(String firstName, String lastName,
11       String socialSecurityNumber) {
12       this.firstName = firstName;
13       this.lastName = lastName;
14       this.socialSecurityNumber = socialSecurityNumber;
15    }
16
17    // return first name
18    public String getFirstName() {return firstName;}
19
20    // return last name
21    public String getLastName() {return lastName;}
```

Fig. 10.4 | `Employee` abstract superclass. (Part 1 of 2.)

```

   // return social security number
   public String getSocialSecurityNumber() {return socialSecurityNumber;}

   // return String representation of Employee object
   @Override
   public String toString() {
      return String.format("%s %s%nsocial security number: %s",
         getFirstName(), getLastName(), getSocialSecurityNumber());
   }

   // abstract method must be overridden by concrete subclasses
   public abstract double earnings(); // no implementation here
}
```

Fig. 10.4 | `Employee` abstract superclass. (Part 2 of 2.)

Why did we decide to declare `earnings` as an `abstract` method? It simply does not make sense to provide a *specific* implementation of this method in class `Employee`. We cannot calculate the earnings for a *general* `Employee`—we first must know the *specific* type of `Employee` to determine the appropriate earnings calculation. By declaring this method `abstract`, we indicate that each concrete subclass *must* provide an appropriate `earnings` implementation and that a program will be able to use superclass `Employee` variables to invoke method `earnings` *polymorphically* for any type of `Employee`.

10.5.2 Concrete Subclass `SalariedEmployee`

Class `SalariedEmployee` (Fig. 10.5) extends class `Employee` (line 4) and overrides *abstract* method `earnings` (lines 34–35), which makes `SalariedEmployee` a *concrete* class. The class includes a constructor (lines 8–18) that receives a first name, a last name, a social security number and a weekly salary; a *set* method to assign a new *nonnegative* value to instance variable `weeklySalary` (lines 21–28); a *get* method to return `weeklySalary`'s value (line 31); a method `earnings` (lines 34–35) to calculate a `SalariedEmployee`'s earnings; and a method `toString` (lines 38–42), which returns a `String` including `"salaried employee: "` followed by employee-specific information produced by superclass `Employee`'s `toString` method and `SalariedEmployee`'s `getWeeklySalary` method. Class `SalariedEmployee`'s constructor passes the first name, last name and social security number to the `Employee` constructor (line 10) to initialize the `private` instance variables of the superclass. Once again, we've duplicated the `weeklySalary` validation code in the constructor and the `setWeeklySalary` method. Recall that more complex validation could be placed in a `static` class method that's called from the constructor and the *set* method.

Error-Prevention Tip 10.1

We've said that you should not call a class's instance methods from its constructors—you can call `static` *class methods and make the required call to one of the superclass's constructors. If you follow this advice, you'll avoid the problem of calling the class's overridable methods either directly or indirectly, which can lead to runtime errors. See Section 10.8 for additional details.*

```java
1  // Fig. 10.5: SalariedEmployee.java
2  // SalariedEmployee concrete class extends abstract class Employee.
3
4  public class SalariedEmployee extends Employee {
5     private double weeklySalary;
6
7     // constructor
8     public SalariedEmployee(String firstName, String lastName,
9        String socialSecurityNumber, double weeklySalary) {
10       super(firstName, lastName, socialSecurityNumber);
11
12       if (weeklySalary < 0.0) {
13          throw new IllegalArgumentException(
14             "Weekly salary must be >= 0.0");
15       }
16
17       this.weeklySalary = weeklySalary;
18    }
19
20    // set salary
21    public void setWeeklySalary(double weeklySalary) {
22       if (weeklySalary < 0.0) {
23          throw new IllegalArgumentException(
24             "Weekly salary must be >= 0.0");
25       }
26
27       this.weeklySalary = weeklySalary;
28    }
29
30    // return salary
31    public double getWeeklySalary() {return weeklySalary;}
32
33    // calculate earnings; override abstract method earnings in Employee
34    @Override
35    public double earnings() {return getWeeklySalary();}
36
37    // return String representation of SalariedEmployee object
38    @Override
39    public String toString() {
40       return String.format("salaried employee: %s%n%s: $%,.2f",
41          super.toString(), "weekly salary", getWeeklySalary());
42    }
43 }
```

Fig. 10.5 | `SalariedEmployee` concrete class extends `abstract` class `Employee`.

Method `earnings` overrides `Employee`'s *abstract* method `earnings` to provide a *concrete* implementation that returns the `SalariedEmployee`'s weekly salary. If we do not implement `earnings`, class `SalariedEmployee` must be declared `abstract`—otherwise, class `SalariedEmployee` will not compile. Of course, we want `SalariedEmployee` to be a *concrete* class in this example.

Method `toString` (lines 38–42) overrides `Employee`'s `toString`. If class `SalariedEmployee` did *not* override `toString`, it would have inherited `Employee`'s version. In that case, `SalariedEmployee`'s `toString` method would simply return the employee's full name and social security number, which does *not* adequately represent a `SalariedEmployee`. To produce a complete `String` representation of a `SalariedEmployee`, the subclass's `toString` method returns `"salaried employee: "` followed by the superclass `Employee`-specific information (i.e., first name, last name and social security number) obtained by invoking the *superclass's* `toString` method (line 41)—this is a nice example of *code reuse*. The `String` representation of a `SalariedEmployee` also contains the employee's weekly salary obtained by invoking the class's `getWeeklySalary` method.

10.5.3 Concrete Subclass `HourlyEmployee`

Class `HourlyEmployee` (Fig. 10.6) also extends `Employee` (line 4). The class includes a constructor (lines 9–24) that receives a first name, a last name, a social security number, an hourly wage and the number of hours worked. Lines 27–33 and 39–46 declare *set* methods that assign new values to instance variables `wage` and `hours`, respectively. Method `setWage` ensures that `wage` is *nonnegative*, and method `setHours` ensures that the value of `hours` is between 0 and 168 (the total number of hours in a week) inclusive. Class `HourlyEmployee` also includes *get* methods (lines 36 and 49) to return the values of `wage` and `hours`, respectively; a method `earnings` (lines 52–60) to calculate an `HourlyEmployee`'s earnings; and a method `toString` (lines 63–68), which returns a `String` containing the employee's type (`"hourly employee: "`) and the employee-specific information. The `HourlyEmployee` constructor, like the `SalariedEmployee` constructor, passes the first name, last name and social security number to the superclass `Employee` constructor (line 11) to initialize the `private` instance variables. In addition, method `toString` calls *superclass* method `toString` (line 66) to obtain the `Employee`-specific information (i.e., first name, last name and social security number)—this is another nice example of *code reuse*.

```
1  // Fig. 10.6: HourlyEmployee.java
2  // HourlyEmployee class extends Employee.
3
4  public class HourlyEmployee extends Employee {
5     private double wage; // wage per hour
6     private double hours; // hours worked for week
7
8     // constructor
9     public HourlyEmployee(String firstName, String lastName,
10       String socialSecurityNumber, double wage, double hours) {
11       super(firstName, lastName, socialSecurityNumber);
12
13       if (wage < 0.0) { // validate wage
14          throw new IllegalArgumentException("Hourly wage must be >= 0.0");
15       }
16
17       if ((hours < 0.0) || (hours > 168.0)) { // validate hours
18          throw new IllegalArgumentException(
19             "Hours worked must be >= 0.0 and <= 168.0");
20       }
21
```

Fig. 10.6 | `HourlyEmployee` class extends `Employee`. (Part 1 of 2.)

```
      this.wage = wage;
      this.hours = hours;
   }

   // set wage
   public void setWage(double wage) {
      if (wage < 0.0) { // validate wage
         throw new IllegalArgumentException("Hourly wage must be >= 0.0");
      }

      this.wage = wage;
   }

   // return wage
   public double getWage() {return wage;}

   // set hours worked
   public void setHours(double hours) {
      if ((hours < 0.0) || (hours > 168.0)) { // validate hours
         throw new IllegalArgumentException(
            "Hours worked must be >= 0.0 and <= 168.0");
      }

      this.hours = hours;
   }

   // return hours worked
   public double getHours() {return hours;}

   // calculate earnings; override abstract method earnings in Employee
   @Override
   public double earnings() {
      if (getHours() <= 40) { // no overtime
         return getWage() * getHours();
      }
      else {
         return 40 * getWage() + (getHours() - 40) * getWage() * 1.5;
      }
   }

   // return String representation of HourlyEmployee object
   @Override
   public String toString() {
      return String.format("hourly employee: %s%n%s: $%,.2f; %s: %,.2f",
         super.toString(), "hourly wage", getWage(),
         "hours worked", getHours());
   }
}
```

Fig. 10.6 | `HourlyEmployee` class extends `Employee`. (Part 2 of 2.)

10.5.4 Concrete Subclass `CommissionEmployee`

Class `CommissionEmployee` (Fig. 10.7) extends class `Employee` (line 4). The class includes a constructor (lines 9–25) that takes a first name, a last name, a social security number, a sales amount and a commission rate; *set* methods (lines 28–34 and 40–47) to assign valid new values to instance variables `grossSales` and `commissionRate`, respectively; *get* methods (lines 37 and 50) that retrieve the values of these instance variables; method `earnings` (lines 53–56) to calculate a `CommissionEmployee`'s earnings; and method `toString` (lines 59–65), which returns `"commission employee: "` followed by the employee's specific information. The constructor also passes the first name, last name and social security number to *superclass* `Employee`'s constructor (line 12) to initialize `Employee`'s `private` instance variables. Method `toString` calls *superclass* method `toString` (line 62) to obtain the `Employee`-specific information (i.e., first name, last name and social security number).

```
1  // Fig. 10.7: CommissionEmployee.java
2  // CommissionEmployee class extends Employee.
3
4  public class CommissionEmployee extends Employee {
5     private double grossSales; // gross weekly sales
6     private double commissionRate; // commission percentage
7
8     // constructor
9     public CommissionEmployee(String firstName, String lastName,
10       String socialSecurityNumber, double grossSales,
11       double commissionRate) {
12       super(firstName, lastName, socialSecurityNumber);
13
14       if (commissionRate <= 0.0 || commissionRate >= 1.0) { // validate
15          throw new IllegalArgumentException(
16             "Commission rate must be > 0.0 and < 1.0");
17       }
18
19       if (grossSales < 0.0) { // validate
20          throw new IllegalArgumentException("Gross sales must be >= 0.0");
21       }
22
23       this.grossSales = grossSales;
24       this.commissionRate = commissionRate;
25    }
26
27    // set gross sales amount
28    public void setGrossSales(double grossSales) {
29       if (grossSales < 0.0) { // validate
30          throw new IllegalArgumentException("Gross sales must be >= 0.0");
31       }
32
33       this.grossSales = grossSales;
34    }
35
36    // return gross sales amount
37    public double getGrossSales() {return grossSales;}
38
39    // set commission rate
40    public void setCommissionRate(double commissionRate) {
41       if (commissionRate <= 0.0 || commissionRate >= 1.0) { // validate
```

Fig. 10.7 | `CommissionEmployee` class extends `Employee`. (Part 1 of 2.)

```
         throw new IllegalArgumentException(
            "Commission rate must be > 0.0 and < 1.0");
      }

      this.commissionRate = commissionRate;
   }

   // return commission rate
   public double getCommissionRate() {return commissionRate;}

   // calculate earnings; override abstract method earnings in Employee
   @Override
   public double earnings() {
      return getCommissionRate() * getGrossSales();
   }

   // return String representation of CommissionEmployee object
   @Override
   public String toString() {
      return String.format("%s: %s%n%s: $%,.2f; %s: %.2f",
         "commission employee", super.toString(),
         "gross sales", getGrossSales(),
         "commission rate", getCommissionRate());
   }
}
```

Fig. 10.7 | `CommissionEmployee` class extends `Employee`. (Part 2 of 2.)

10.5.5 Indirect Concrete Subclass BasePlusCommissionEmployee

Class `BasePlusCommissionEmployee` (Fig. 10.8) extends class `CommissionEmployee` (line 4) and therefore is an *indirect* subclass of class `Employee`. Class `BasePlusCommissionEmployee` has a constructor (lines 8–19) that receives a first name, a last name, a social security number, a sales amount, a commission rate and a base salary. It then passes all of these except the base salary to the `CommissionEmployee` constructor (lines 11–12) to initialize the superclass instance variables. `BasePlusCommissionEmployee` also contains a *set* method (lines 22–28) to assign a new value to instance variable `baseSalary` and a *get* method (line 31) to return `baseSalary`'s value. Method `earnings` (lines 34–35) calculates a `BasePlusCommissionEmployee`'s earnings. Line 35 in method `earnings` calls *superclass* `CommissionEmployee`'s `earnings` method to calculate the commission-based portion of the employee's earnings—this is another nice example of *code reuse*. `BasePlusCommissionEmployee`'s `toString` method (lines 38–43) creates a `String` representation of a `BasePlusCommissionEmployee` that contains `"base-salaried"`, followed by the `String` obtained by invoking *superclass* `CommissionEmployee`'s `toString` method (line 41), then the base salary. The result is a `String` beginning with `"base-salaried commission employee"` followed by the rest of the `BasePlusCommissionEmployee`'s information. Recall that `CommissionEmployee`'s `toString` obtains the employee's first name, last name and social security number by invoking the `toString` method of its *superclass* (i.e., `Employee`)—yet another example of *code reuse*. `BasePlusCommissionEmployee`'s `toString` method initiates a *chain of method calls* that span all three levels of the `Employee` hierarchy.

```java
// Fig. 10.8: BasePlusCommissionEmployee.java
// BasePlusCommissionEmployee class extends CommissionEmployee.

public class BasePlusCommissionEmployee extends CommissionEmployee {
   private double baseSalary; // base salary per week

   // constructor
   public BasePlusCommissionEmployee(String firstName, String lastName,
      String socialSecurityNumber, double grossSales,
      double commissionRate, double baseSalary) {
      super(firstName, lastName, socialSecurityNumber,
         grossSales, commissionRate);

      if (baseSalary < 0.0) { // validate baseSalary
         throw new IllegalArgumentException("Base salary must be >= 0.0");
      }

      this.baseSalary = baseSalary;
   }

   // set base salary
   public void setBaseSalary(double baseSalary) {
      if (baseSalary < 0.0) { // validate baseSalary
         throw new IllegalArgumentException("Base salary must be >= 0.0");
      }

      this.baseSalary = baseSalary;
   }

   // return base salary
   public double getBaseSalary() {return baseSalary;}

   // calculate earnings; override method earnings in CommissionEmployee
   @Override
   public double earnings() {return getBaseSalary() + super.earnings();}

   // return String representation of BasePlusCommissionEmployee object
   @Override
   public String toString() {
      return String.format("%s %s; %s: $%,.2f",
         "base-salaried", super.toString(),
         "base salary", getBaseSalary());
   }
}
```

Fig. 10.8 | `BasePlusCommissionEmployee` class extends `CommissionEmployee`.

10.5.6 Polymorphic Processing, Operator `instanceof` and Downcasting

To test our `Employee` hierarchy, the application in Fig. 10.9 creates an object of each of the four *concrete* classes `SalariedEmployee`, `HourlyEmployee`, `CommissionEmployee` and `BasePlusCommissionEmployee`. The program manipulates these objects *nonpolymorphically*, via variables of each object's own type, then *polymorphically*, using an array of `Employ-`

ee variables. While processing the objects polymorphically, the program increases the base salary of each `BasePlusCommissionEmployee` by 10%—this requires *determining the object's type at execution time*. Finally, the program polymorphically determines and outputs the *type* of each object in the `Employee` array. Lines 7–16 create objects of each of the four concrete `Employee` subclasses. Lines 20–28 output the `String` representation and earnings of each of these objects *nonpolymorphically*. Each object's `toString` method is called *implicitly* by `printf` when the object is output as a `String` with the `%s` format specifier.

```
1  // Fig. 10.9: PayrollSystemTest.java
2  // Employee hierarchy test program.
3
4  public class PayrollSystemTest {
5     public static void main(String[] args) {
6        // create subclass objects
7        SalariedEmployee salariedEmployee =
8           new SalariedEmployee("John", "Smith", "111-11-1111", 800.00);
9        HourlyEmployee hourlyEmployee =
10          new HourlyEmployee("Karen", "Price", "222-22-2222", 16.75, 40);
11       CommissionEmployee commissionEmployee =
12          new CommissionEmployee(
13          "Sue", "Jones", "333-33-3333", 10000, .06);
14       BasePlusCommissionEmployee basePlusCommissionEmployee =
15          new BasePlusCommissionEmployee(
16          "Bob", "Lewis", "444-44-4444", 5000, .04, 300);
17
18       System.out.println("Employees processed individually:");
19
20       System.out.printf("%n%s%n%s: $%,.2f%n%n",
21          salariedEmployee, "earned", salariedEmployee.earnings());
22       System.out.printf("%s%n%s: $%,.2f%n%n",
23          hourlyEmployee, "earned", hourlyEmployee.earnings());
24       System.out.printf("%s%n%s: $%,.2f%n%n",
25          commissionEmployee, "earned", commissionEmployee.earnings());
26       System.out.printf("%s%n%s: $%,.2f%n%n",
27          basePlusCommissionEmployee,
28          "earned", basePlusCommissionEmployee.earnings());
29
30       // create four-element Employee array
31       Employee[] employees = new Employee[4];
32
33       // initialize array with Employees
34       employees[0] = salariedEmployee;
35       employees[1] = hourlyEmployee;
36       employees[2] = commissionEmployee;
37       employees[3] = basePlusCommissionEmployee;
38
39       System.out.printf("Employees processed polymorphically:%n%n");
40
41       // generically process each element in array employees
42       for (Employee currentEmployee : employees) {
43          System.out.println(currentEmployee); // invokes toString
```

Fig. 10.9 | Employee hierarchy test program. (Part 1 of 3.)

```java

         // determine whether element is a BasePlusCommissionEmployee
         if (currentEmployee instanceof BasePlusCommissionEmployee) {
            // downcast Employee reference to
            // BasePlusCommissionEmployee reference
            BasePlusCommissionEmployee employee =
               (BasePlusCommissionEmployee) currentEmployee;

            employee.setBaseSalary(1.10 * employee.getBaseSalary());

            System.out.printf(
               "new base salary with 10%% increase is: $%,.2f%n",
               employee.getBaseSalary());
         }

         System.out.printf(
            "earned $%,.2f%n%n", currentEmployee.earnings());
      }

      // get type name of each object in employees array
      for (int j = 0; j < employees.length; j++) {
         System.out.printf("Employee %d is a %s%n", j,
            employees[j].getClass().getName());
      }
   }
}
```

```
Employees processed individually:

salaried employee: John Smith
social security number: 111-11-1111
weekly salary: $800.00
earned: $800.00

hourly employee: Karen Price
social security number: 222-22-2222
hourly wage: $16.75; hours worked: 40.00
earned: $670.00

commission employee: Sue Jones
social security number: 333-33-3333
gross sales: $10,000.00; commission rate: 0.06
earned: $600.00

base-salaried commission employee: Bob Lewis
social security number: 444-44-4444
gross sales: $5,000.00; commission rate: 0.04; base salary: $300.00
earned: $500.00

Employees processed polymorphically:

salaried employee: John Smith
social security number: 111-11-1111
weekly salary: $800.00
earned $800.00
```

Fig. 10.9 | Employee hierarchy test program. (Part 2 of 3.)

```
hourly employee: Karen Price
social security number: 222-22-2222
hourly wage: $16.75; hours worked: 40.00
earned $670.00

commission employee: Sue Jones
social security number: 333-33-3333
gross sales: $10,000.00; commission rate: 0.06
earned $600.00

base-salaried commission employee: Bob Lewis
social security number: 444-44-4444
gross sales: $5,000.00; commission rate: 0.04; base salary: $300.00
new base salary with 10% increase is: $330.00
earned $530.00

Employee 0 is a SalariedEmployee
Employee 1 is a HourlyEmployee
Employee 2 is a CommissionEmployee
Employee 3 is a BasePlusCommissionEmployee
```

Fig. 10.9 | `Employee` hierarchy test program. (Part 3 of 3.)

Creating the Array of `Employees`

Line 31 declares `employees` and assigns it an array of four `Employee` variables. Lines 34–37 assign to the elements a reference to a `SalariedEmployee`, an `HourlyEmployee`, a `CommissionEmployee` and a `BasePlusCommissionEmployee`, respectively. These assignments are allowed, because a `SalariedEmployee` *is an* `Employee`, an `HourlyEmployee` *is an* `Employee`, a `CommissionEmployee` *is an* `Employee` and a `BasePlusCommissionEmployee` *is an* `Employee`. Therefore, we can assign the references of `SalariedEmployee`, `HourlyEmployee`, `CommissionEmployee` and `BasePlusCommissionEmployee` objects to *superclass* `Employee` variables, *even though* `Employee` *is an abstract class.*

Polymorphically Processing `Employees`

Lines 42–61 iterate through array `employees` and invoke methods `toString` and `earnings` with `Employee` variable `currentEmployee`, which is assigned the reference to a different `Employee` in the array on each iteration. The output illustrates that the specific methods for each class are indeed invoked. All calls to method `toString` and `earnings` are resolved at *execution* time, based on the *type* of the object to which `currentEmployee` refers. This process is known as **dynamic binding** or **late binding**. For example, line 43 *implicitly* invokes method `toString` of the object to which `currentEmployee` refers. As a result of *dynamic binding*, Java decides which class's `toString` method to call *at execution time rather than at compile time.* Only the methods of class `Employee` can be called via an `Employee` variable (and `Employee`, of course, includes the methods of class `Object`). A superclass reference can be used to invoke only methods of the *superclass*—the *subclass* method implementations are invoked *polymorphically*.

Performing Type-Specific Operations on `BasePlusCommissionEmployees`

We perform special processing on `BasePlusCommissionEmployee` objects—as we encounter these objects at execution time, we increase their base salary by 10%. When processing objects *polymorphically*, we typically do not need to worry about the *specifics*, but to adjust the base salary, we *do* have to determine the *specific* type of `Employee` object at *execution time*. Line 46 uses the **`instanceof`** operator to determine whether a particular `Employee` object's type is `BasePlusCommissionEmployee`. The condition in line 46 is *true* if the object referenced by `currentEmployee` *is a* `BasePlusCommissionEmployee`. This would also be *true* for any object of a `BasePlusCommissionEmployee` subclass because of the *is-a* relationship a subclass has with its superclass. Lines 49–50 *downcast* `currentEmployee` from type `Employee` to type `BasePlusCommissionEmployee`—this cast is allowed only if the object has an *is-a* relationship with `BasePlusCommissionEmployee`. The condition at line 46 ensures that this is the case. This cast is required if we're to invoke subclass `BasePlusCommissionEmployee` methods `getBaseSalary` and `setBaseSalary` on the current `Employee` object—as you'll see momentarily, *attempting to invoke a subclass-only method directly on a superclass reference is a compilation error.*

Common Programming Error 10.3

Assigning a superclass variable to a subclass variable is a compilation error.

Common Programming Error 10.4

When downcasting a reference, a `ClassCastException` occurs if the referenced object at execution time does not have an is-a *relationship with the type specified in the cast operator.*

If the `instanceof` expression in line 46 is `true`, lines 49–56 perform the special processing required for the `BasePlusCommissionEmployee` object. Using `BasePlusCommissionEmployee` variable `employee`, line 52 invokes subclass-only methods `getBaseSalary` and `setBaseSalary` to retrieve and update the employee's base salary with the 10% raise.

Calling `earnings` *Polymorphically*

Lines 59–60 invoke method `earnings` on `currentEmployee`, which polymorphically calls the appropriate subclass object's `earnings` method. Obtaining the earnings of the `SalariedEmployee`, `HourlyEmployee` and `CommissionEmployee` polymorphically in lines 59–60 produces the same results as obtaining these employees' earnings individually in lines 20–25. The earnings amount obtained for the `BasePlusCommissionEmployee` in lines 59–60 is higher than that obtained in lines 26–28, due to the 10% increase in its base salary.

Getting Each `Employee`*'s Class Name*

Lines 64–67 display each employee's type as a `String`. Every object *knows its own class* and can access this information through the **`getClass`** method, which all classes inherit from class `Object`. Method `getClass` returns an object of type **`Class`** (from package `java.lang`), which contains information about the object's type, including its class name. Line 66 invokes `getClass` on the current object to get its class. The result of the `getClass` call is used to invoke **`getName`** to get the object's class name.

Avoiding Compilation Errors with Downcasting

In the previous example, we avoided several compilation errors by *downcasting* an `Employee` variable to a `BasePlusCommissionEmployee` variable in lines 49–50. If you remove the cast operator `(BasePlusCommissionEmployee)` from line 50 and attempt to assign `Em-`

`ployee` variable `currentEmployee` directly to `BasePlusCommissionEmployee` variable `employee`, you'll receive an "`incompatible types`" compilation error. This error indicates that the attempt to assign the reference of superclass object `currentEmployee` to subclass variable `employee` is *not* allowed. The compiler prevents this assignment because a `CommissionEmployee` is *not* a `BasePlusCommissionEmployee`—*the* is-a *relationship applies only between the subclass and its superclasses, not vice versa.*

Similarly, if lines 52 and 56 used superclass variable `currentEmployee` to invoke subclass-only methods `getBaseSalary` and `setBaseSalary`, we'd receive "`cannot find symbol`" compilation errors at these lines. Attempting to invoke subclass-only methods via a superclass variable is *not* allowed—even though lines 52 and 56 execute only if `instanceof` in line 46 returns `true` to indicate that `currentEmployee` holds a reference to a `BasePlusCommissionEmployee` object. Using a superclass `Employee` variable, we can invoke only methods found in class `Employee`—`earnings`, `toString` and `Employee`'s *get* and *set* methods.

Software Engineering Observation 10.5

Although the actual method that's called depends on the runtime type of the object to which a variable refers, a variable can be used to invoke only those methods that are members of that variable's type, which the compiler verifies.

10.6 Allowed Assignments Between Superclass and Subclass Variables

Now that you've seen a complete application that processes diverse subclass objects *polymorphically*, we summarize what you can and cannot do with superclass and subclass objects and variables. Although a subclass object also *is a* superclass object, the two classes are nevertheless different. As discussed previously, subclass objects can be treated as objects of their superclass. But because the subclass can have additional subclass-only members, assigning a superclass reference to a subclass variable is not allowed without an *explicit cast*—such an assignment would leave the subclass members undefined for the superclass object.

We've discussed three proper ways to assign superclass and subclass references to variables of superclass and subclass types:

1. Assigning a superclass reference to a superclass variable is straightforward.
2. Assigning a subclass reference to a subclass variable is straightforward.
3. Assigning a subclass reference to a superclass variable is safe, because the subclass object *is an* object of its superclass. However, the superclass variable can be used to refer *only* to superclass members. If this code refers to subclass-only members through the superclass variable, the compiler reports errors.

10.7 `final` Methods and Classes

We saw in Sections 6.3 and 6.10 that variables can be declared `final` to indicate that they cannot be modified *after* they're initialized—such variables represent constant values. You also declare method parameters `final` to prevent them from being modified in the method's body. It's also possible to declare methods and classes with the `final` modifier.

Final Methods Cannot Be Overridden

A **`final` method** in a superclass *cannot* be overridden in a subclass—this guarantees that the `final` method implementation will be used by all direct and indirect subclasses in the hierarchy. Methods that are declared `private` are implicitly `final`, because it's not possible to override them in a subclass. Methods that are declared `static` are also implicitly `final`. A `final` method's declaration can never change, so all subclasses use the same method implementation, and calls to `final` methods are resolved at compile time—this is known as **static binding.**

Final Classes Cannot Be Superclasses

A **`final` class** cannot be extended to create a subclass. All methods in a `final` class are implicitly `final`. Class `String` is an example of a `final` class. If you were allowed to create a subclass of `String`, objects of that subclass could be used wherever `String`s are expected. Since class `String` cannot be extended, programs that use `String`s can rely on the functionality of `String` objects as specified in the Java API. Making the class `final` also prevents programmers from creating subclasses that might bypass security restrictions.

We've now discussed declaring variables, methods and classes `final`, and we've emphasized that if something *can* be `final` it *should* be `final`—this is another example of the *principle of least privilege*. When we study concurrency in Chapter 23, you'll see that `final` variables make it much easier to parallelize your programs for use on today's multi-core processors. For more insights on the use of `final`, visit

```
http://docs.oracle.com/javase/tutorial/java/IandI/final.html
```

Common Programming Error 10.5

Attempting to declare a subclass of a `final` class is a compilation error.

Software Engineering Observation 10.6

In the Java API, the vast majority of classes are not declared `final`. This enables inheritance and polymorphism. However, in some cases, it's important to declare classes `final`—typically for security reasons. Also, unless you carefully design a class for extension, you should declare the class as `final` to avoid (often subtle) errors.

Software Engineering Observation 10.7

Though `final` classes cannot be extended, you can reuse them via composition.

10.8 A Deeper Explanation of Issues with Calling Methods from Constructors

We've stated that you should not call overridable methods from constructors. To understand why, recall that when you construct a subclass object, the *subclass* constructor first calls a constructor in its direct *superclass*. At this point, any subclass instance-variable initialization code in the subclass constructor's body has not yet executed. If the *superclass* constructor then calls a method that the subclass overrides, the *subclass's* version executes. This could lead to subtle, difficult-to-detect errors if the subclass method uses instance variables that have not yet been initialized properly, because the subclass constructor hasn't finished executing.

Let's assume that a constructor and a *set* method perform the same validation for a particular instance variable. How should you handle the common code?

- If the validation code is brief, you can duplicate it in the constructor and the *set* method. This is a simple way to eliminate the problem we're considering here.
- For lengthier validation, you can define a `static` validation method—typically a `private static` helper method—then call it from the constructor and from the *set* method. It's acceptable to call a `static` method from a constructor, because `static` methods are not overridable.

It's also acceptable for a constructor to call a `final` instance method, provided that the method does not directly or indirectly call any overridable instance methods.

10.9 Creating and Using Interfaces

8 *[Note: Java SE 8 interface enhancements are introduced in Section 10.10 and discussed in more detail in Chapter 17. Java SE 9 interface enhancements are introduced in Section 10.11.]*

Our next example (Figs. 10.11–10.14) reexamines the payroll system of Section 10.5. Suppose that the company involved wishes to perform several accounting operations in a single accounts payable application—in addition to calculating the earnings that must be paid to each employee, the company must also calculate the payment due on each of several invoices (i.e., bills for goods purchased). Though applied to *unrelated* things—employees and invoices—both operations have to do with obtaining a payment amount. For an employee, the payment is the employee's earnings. For an invoice, the payment is the total cost of the goods listed on the invoice. Can we calculate such *different* things as the payments due for employees and invoices in *a single* application *polymorphically*? Does Java offer a capability requiring that *unrelated* classes implement a set of *common* methods (e.g., a method that calculates a payment amount)? Java **interfaces** offer exactly this capability.

Standardizing Interactions

Interfaces define and standardize the ways in which things such as people and systems can interact with one another. For example, the controls on a radio serve as an interface between radio users and a radio's internal components. The controls allow users to perform only a limited set of operations (e.g., change the station, adjust the volume, choose between AM and FM), and different radios may implement the controls in different ways (e.g., using push buttons, dials, voice commands). The interface specifies *what* operations a radio must permit users to perform but does not specify *how* the operations are performed.

Similarly, in our car analogy from Section 1.5, a "basic-driving-capabilities" interface consisting of a steering wheel, an accelerator pedal and a brake pedal would enable a driver to tell the car *what* to do. Once you know how to use this interface for turning, accelerating and braking, you can drive many types of cars, even though manufacturers may *implement* these systems *differently*. For example, there are many types of braking systems—disc brakes, drum brakes, antilock brakes, hydraulic brakes, air brakes and more. When you press the brake pedal, your car's actual brake system is irrelevant—all that matters is that the car slows down when you press the brake.

Software Objects Communicate Via Interfaces

Software objects also communicate via interfaces. A Java interface describes a set of methods that can be called on an object to tell it, for example, to perform some task or return some piece of information. The next example introduces an interface named `Payable` to describe the functionality of any object that must be "capable of being paid" and thus must offer a method to determine the proper payment amount due. An **interface declaration** begins with the keyword **`interface`** and contains *only* constants and `abstract` methods. Unlike classes, all interface members *must* be `public`, and *interfaces may not specify any implementation details*, such as concrete method declarations and instance variables.[1] All methods declared in an interface are implicitly `public abstract` methods, and all fields are implicitly `public`, `static` and `final`.

Using an Interface

To use an interface, a concrete class must specify that it **`implements`** the interface and must declare each method in the interface with the signature specified in the interface declaration. To specify that a class implements an interface, add the `implements` keyword and the name of the interface to the end of your class declaration's first line, as in:

```
public class ClassName extends SuperclassName implements InterfaceName
```

or

```
public class ClassName implements InterfaceName
```

InterfaceName in the preceding snippets may be a comma-separated list of interface names.

Implementing an interface is like signing a *contract* with the compiler that states, "I will declare all the `abstract` methods specified by the interface or I will declare my class `abstract`."

Common Programming Error 10.6

In a concrete class that `implements` *an interface, failing to implement any of the interface's* `abstract` *methods results in a compilation error indicating that the class must be declared* `abstract`.

Relating Disparate Types

An interface is often used when *disparate* classes—i.e., classes that are not related by a class hierarchy—need to share common methods and constants. This allows objects of *unrelated* classes to be processed *polymorphically*—objects of classes that implement the *same* interface can respond to the *same* method calls (for methods of that interface). You can create an interface that describes the desired functionality, then implement this interface in any classes that require that functionality. For example, in the accounts payable application developed in this section, we implement interface `Payable` in any class that must be able to calculate a payment amount (e.g., `Employee` and `Invoice`).

Interfaces vs. Abstract Classes

An interface should be used in place of an `abstract` *class when there's no default implementation to inherit*—that is, no fields and no concrete method implementations. Like `public`

---

1. Sections 10.10–10.11 introduce the Java SE 8 and Java SE 9 interface enhancements that allow method implementations and `private` methods, respectively, in interfaces.

abstract classes, interfaces are typically public types. Like a public class, a public interface must be declared in a file with the same name as the interface and the .java filename extension.

Software Engineering Observation 10.8

Many developers feel that interfaces are an even more important modeling technology than classes, especially with the interface enhancements in Java SE 8 (see Section 10.10).

Tagging Interfaces

A *tagging interface* (also called a *marker interface*) is an empty interfaces that have *no* methods or constant values. They're used to add *is-a* relationships to classes. For example, Java has a mechanism called *object serialization*, which can convert objects to byte representations and can convert those byte representations back to objects, using classes ObjectOutputStream and ObjectInputStream. To enable this mechanism to work with your objects, you simply have to *tag* them as Serializable by adding implements Serializable to the end of your class declaration's first line. Then all the objects of your class have the *is-a* relationship with Serializable—that's all it takes to implement basic object serialization.

10.9.1 Developing a Payable Hierarchy

To build an application that can determine payments for employees and invoices alike, we first create interface Payable, which contains method getPaymentAmount that returns a double amount that must be paid for an object of any class that implements the interface. Method getPaymentAmount is a general-purpose version of method earnings of the Employee hierarchy—method earnings calculates a payment amount specifically for an Employee, while getPaymentAmount can be applied to a broad range of possibly unrelated objects. After declaring interface Payable, we introduce class Invoice, which implements interface Payable. We then modify class Employee such that it also implements interface Payable.

Classes Invoice and Employee both represent things for which the company must be able to calculate a payment amount. Both classes implement the Payable interface, so a program can invoke method getPaymentAmount on Invoice objects and Employee objects alike. As we'll soon see, this enables the *polymorphic* processing of Invoices and Employees required for the company's accounts payable application.

Good Programming Practice 10.1

When declaring a method in an interface, choose a method name that describes the method's purpose in a general *manner, because the method may be implemented by many* unrelated *classes.*

UML Diagram Containing an Interface

The UML class diagram in Fig. 10.10 shows the interface and class hierarchy used in our accounts payable application. The hierarchy begins with interface Payable. The UML distinguishes an interface from classes by placing the word "interface" in guillemets (« and ») above the interface name. The UML expresses the relationship between a class and an interface through a relationship known as **realization**. A class is said to *realize*, or *implement*, the methods of an interface. A class diagram models a realization as a dashed arrow with a hollow arrowhead pointing from the implementing class to the interface. The diagram in Fig. 10.10 indicates that classes `Invoice` and `Employee` each realize interface `Payable`. As in the class diagram of Fig. 10.2, class `Employee` appears in *italics*, indicating that it's an *abstract class*. *Concrete* class `SalariedEmployee` extends `Employee`, *inheriting its superclass's realization relationship* with interface `Payable`.

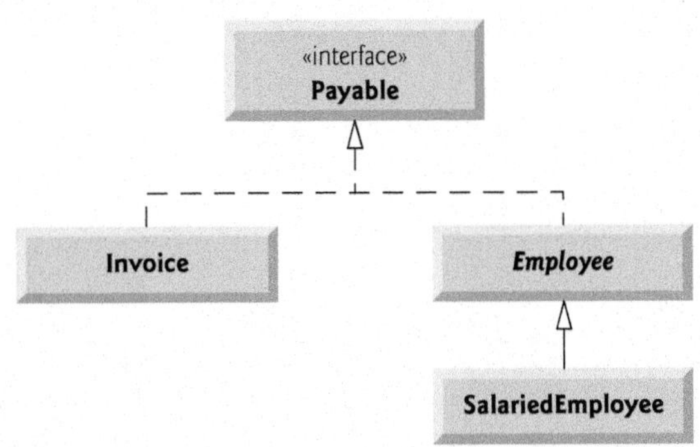

Fig. 10.10 | `Payable` hierarchy UML class diagram.

10.9.2 Interface `Payable`

Interface `Payable`'s declaration begins in Fig. 10.11 at line 4 with the `interface` keyword. The interface contains the `public abstract` method named `getPaymentAmount`. Interface methods are `public` and `abstract` by default, so they do not need to be declared as such. Interface `Payable` has only one method, but interfaces can have *any* number of methods. In addition, method `getPaymentAmount` has no parameters, but interface methods *can* have parameters. Interfaces may also contain `final static` constants.

Good Programming Practice 10.2

Use `public` *and* `abstract` *explicitly when declaring interface methods to make your intentions clear. As you'll see in Sections 10.10–10.11, Java SE 8 and Java SE 9 allow other kinds of methods in interfaces.*

```
1 // Fig. 10.11: Payable.java
2 // Payable interface declaration.
3
4 public interface Payable {
5    public abstract double getPaymentAmount(); // no implementation
6 }
```

Fig. 10.11 | `Payable` interface declaration.

10.9.3 Class `Invoice`

Class `Invoice` (Fig. 10.12) represents a simple invoice that contains billing information for only one kind of part. The class declares `private` instance variables `partNumber`, `part-`

Description, quantity and pricePerItem (in lines 5–8) that indicate the part number, a description of the part, the quantity of the part ordered and the price per item. Class Invoice also contains a constructor (lines 11–26), *get* methods (lines 29–38) and a toString method (lines 41–46) that returns a String representation of an Invoice object.

```
1  // Fig. 10.12: Invoice.java
2  // Invoice class that implements Payable.
3
4  public class Invoice implements Payable {
5     private final String partNumber;
6     private final String partDescription;
7     private final int quantity;
8     private final double pricePerItem;
9
10    // constructor
11    public Invoice(String partNumber, String partDescription, int quantity,
12       double pricePerItem) {
13       if (quantity < 0) { // validate quantity
14          throw new IllegalArgumentException("Quantity must be >= 0");
15       }
16
17       if (pricePerItem < 0.0) { // validate pricePerItem
18          throw new IllegalArgumentException(
19             "Price per item must be >= 0");
20       }
21
22       this.quantity = quantity;
23       this.partNumber = partNumber;
24       this.partDescription = partDescription;
25       this.pricePerItem = pricePerItem;
26    }
27
28    // get part number
29    public String getPartNumber() {return partNumber;}
30
31    // get description
32    public String getPartDescription() {return partDescription;}
33
34    // get quantity
35    public int getQuantity() {return quantity;}
36
37    // get price per item
38    public double getPricePerItem() {return pricePerItem;}
39
40    // return String representation of Invoice object
41    @Override
42    public String toString() {
43       return String.format("%s: %n%s: %s (%s) %n%s: %d %n%s: $%,.2f",
44          "invoice", "part number", getPartNumber(), getPartDescription(),
45          "quantity", getQuantity(), "price per item", getPricePerItem());
46    }
```

Fig. 10.12 | Invoice class that implements Payable. (Part 1 of 2.)

```
47
48     // method required to carry out contract with interface Payable
49     @Override
50     public double getPaymentAmount() {
51        return getQuantity() * getPricePerItem(); // calculate total cost
52     }
53  }
```

Fig. 10.12 | `Invoice` class that implements `Payable`. (Part 2 of 2.)

Line 4 indicates that class `Invoice` implements interface `Payable`. Like all classes, class `Invoice` also *implicitly* extends `Object`. Class `Invoice` implements the one `abstract` method in interface `Payable`—method `getPaymentAmount` is declared in lines 49–52. The method calculates the total payment required to pay the invoice. The method multiplies the values of `quantity` and `pricePerItem` (obtained through the appropriate *get* methods) and returns the result. This method satisfies the implementation requirement for this method in interface `Payable`—we've *fulfilled* the *interface contract* with the compiler.

A Class Can Extend Only One Other Class But Can Implement Many Interfaces

Java does not allow subclasses to inherit from more than one superclass, but it allows a class to *inherit* from one *superclass* and *implement* as many *interfaces* as it needs. To implement more than one interface, use a comma-separated list of interface names after keyword `implements` in the class declaration, as in:

```
public class ClassName extends SuperclassName implements FirstInterface,
   SecondInterface, …
```

Software Engineering Observation 10.9

All objects of a class that implements multiple interfaces have the is-a *relationship with each implemented interface type.*

Class `ArrayList` (Section 7.16) is one of many Java API classes that implement multiple interfaces. For example, `ArrayList` implements interface `Iterable`, which enables the enhanced `for` statement to iterate over an `ArrayList`'s elements. `ArrayList` also implements interface `List` (Section 16.6), which declares the common methods (such as `add`, `remove` and `contains`) that you can call on any object that represents a lists of items.

10.9.4 Modifying Class `Employee` to Implement Interface `Payable`

We now modify class `Employee` to implement interface `Payable` (Fig. 10.13). This class declaration is identical to that of Fig. 10.4 with two exceptions:

- Line 4 of Fig. 10.13 indicates that class `Employee` now implements `Payable`.
- Line 38 implements interface `Payable`'s `getPaymentAmount` method.

Notice that `getPaymentAmount` simply calls `Employee`'s `abstract` method `earnings`. At execution time, when `getPaymentAmount` is called on an object of an `Employee` subclass, `getPaymentAmount` calls that subclass's concrete `earnings` method, which knows how to calculate earnings for objects of that subclass type.

```java
// Fig. 10.13: Employee.java
// Employee abstract superclass that implements Payable.

public abstract class Employee implements Payable {
   private final String firstName;
   private final String lastName;
   private final String socialSecurityNumber;

   // constructor
   public Employee(String firstName, String lastName,
      String socialSecurityNumber) {
      this.firstName = firstName;
      this.lastName = lastName;
      this.socialSecurityNumber = socialSecurityNumber;
   }

   // return first name
   public String getFirstName() {return firstName;}

   // return last name
   public String getLastName() {return lastName;}

   // return social security number
   public String getSocialSecurityNumber() {return socialSecurityNumber;}

   // return String representation of Employee object
   @Override
   public String toString() {
      return String.format("%s %s%nsocial security number: %s",
         getFirstName(), getLastName(), getSocialSecurityNumber());
   }

   // abstract method must be overridden by concrete subclasses
   public abstract double earnings(); // no implementation here

   // implementing getPaymentAmount here enables the entire Employee
   // class hierarchy to be used in an app that processes Payables
   public double getPaymentAmount() {return earnings();}
}
```

Fig. 10.13 | `Employee` `abstract` superclass that implements `Payable`.

Subclasses of `Employee` *and Interface* `Payable`

When a class implements an interface, the same *is-a* relationship as inheritance applies. Class `Employee` implements `Payable`, so we can say that an `Employee` *is a* `Payable`, and thus any object of an `Employee` subclass also *is a* `Payable`. So, if we update the class hierarchy in Section 10.5 with the new `Employee` superclass in Fig. 10.13, then `SalariedEmployees`, `HourlyEmployees`, `CommissionEmployees` and `BasePlusCommissionEmployees` are all `Payable` objects. Just as we can assign the reference of a `SalariedEmployee` subclass object to a superclass `Employee` variable, we can assign the reference of a `SalariedEmployee` object (or any other `Employee` derived-class object) to a `Payable` variable. `Invoice` implements `Payable`, so an `Invoice` object also *is a* `Payable` object, and we can assign the reference of an `Invoice` object to a `Payable` variable.

Software Engineering Observation 10.10

Inheritance and interfaces are similar in their implementation of the is-a *relationship. An object of a class that implements an interface may be thought of as an object of that interface type. An object of any subclass of a class that implements an interface also can be thought of as an object of the interface type.*

Software Engineering Observation 10.11

The is-a *relationship that exists between superclasses and subclasses, and between interfaces and the classes that implement them, holds when passing an object to a method. When a method parameter receives an argument of a superclass or interface type, the method polymorphically processes the object received as an argument.*

Software Engineering Observation 10.12

Using a superclass reference, we can polymorphically invoke any method declared in the superclass and its superclasses (e.g., class `Object`). Using an interface reference, we can polymorphically invoke any method declared in the interface, its superinterfaces (one interface can extend another) and in class `Object`—a variable of an interface type must refer to an object to call methods, and all objects have the methods of class `Object`.

10.9.5 Using Interface `Payable` to Process `Invoices` and `Employees` Polymorphically

`PayableInterfaceTest` (Fig. 10.14) illustrates that interface `Payable` can be used to process a set of `Invoices` and `Employees` *polymorphically* in a single application. Lines 7–12 declare and initialize the four-element array `payableObjects`. Lines 8–9 place the references of `Invoice` objects in `payableObjects`' first two elements. Lines 10–11 then place the references of `SalariedEmployee` objects in `payableObjects`' last two elements. The elements are allowed to be initialized with `Invoices` and `SalariedEmployees`, because an `Invoice` *is a* `Payable`, a `SalariedEmployee` *is an* `Employee` and an `Employee` *is a* `Payable`.

```
1  // Fig. 10.14: PayableInterfaceTest.java
2  // Payable interface test program processing Invoices and
3  // Employees polymorphically.
4  public class PayableInterfaceTest {
5     public static void main(String[] args) {
6        // create four-element Payable array
7        Payable[] payableObjects = new Payable[] {
8           new Invoice("01234", "seat", 2, 375.00),
9           new Invoice("56789", "tire", 4, 79.95),
10          new SalariedEmployee("John", "Smith", "111-11-1111", 800.00),
11          new SalariedEmployee("Lisa", "Barnes", "888-88-8888", 1200.00)
12       };
13
```

Fig. 10.14 | `Payable` interface test program processing `Invoices` and `Employees` polymorphically. (Part 1 of 2.)

```
14          System.out.println(
15             "Invoices and Employees processed polymorphically:");
16
17          // generically process each element in array payableObjects
18          for (Payable currentPayable : payableObjects) {
19             // output currentPayable and its appropriate payment amount
20             System.out.printf("%n%s %npayment due: $%,.2f%n",
21                currentPayable.toString(), // could invoke implicitly
22                currentPayable.getPaymentAmount());
23          }
24       }
25    }
```

```
Invoices and Employees processed polymorphically:

invoice:
part number: 01234 (seat)
quantity: 2
price per item: $375.00
payment due: $750.00

invoice:
part number: 56789 (tire)
quantity: 4
price per item: $79.95
payment due: $319.80

salaried employee: John Smith
social security number: 111-11-1111
weekly salary: $800.00
payment due: $800.00

salaried employee: Lisa Barnes
social security number: 888-88-8888
weekly salary: $1,200.00
payment due: $1,200.00
```

Fig. 10.14 | Payable interface test program processing Invoices and Employees polymorphically. (Part 2 of 2.)

Lines 18–23 *polymorphically* process each Payable object in payableObjects, displaying each object's String representation and payment amount. Line 21 invokes method toString via a Payable interface reference, even though toString is not declared in interface Payable—*all references (including those of interface types) refer to objects that extend Object and therefore have a toString method.* (Method toString also can be invoked *implicitly* here.) Line 22 invokes Payable method getPaymentAmount to obtain the payment amount for each object in payableObjects, regardless of the actual type of the object. The output reveals that each of the method calls in lines 21–22 invokes the appropriate class's toString and getPaymentAmount methods.

10.9.6 Some Common Interfaces of the Java API

You'll use interfaces extensively when developing Java applications. The Java API contains numerous interfaces, and many of the Java API methods take interface arguments and return interface values. Figure 10.15 overviews a few of the more popular interfaces of the Java API that we use in later chapters.

Interface	Description
`Comparable`	Java contains several comparison operators (e.g., `<`, `<=`, `>`, `>=`, `==`, `!=`) that allow you to compare primitive values. However, these operators *cannot* be used to compare objects. Interface `Comparable` is used to allow objects of a class that `implements` the interface to be compared to one another. Interface `Comparable` is commonly used for ordering objects in a collection such as an `ArrayList`. We use `Comparable` in Chapter 16, Generic Collections, and Chapter 20, Generic Classes and Methods: A Deeper Look.
`Serializable`	An interface used to identify classes whose objects can be written to (i.e., serialized) or read from (i.e., deserialized) some type of storage (e.g., file on disk, database field) or transmitted across a network.
`Runnable`	Implemented by any class that represents a task to perform. Objects of such a class are often executed in parallel using a technique called *multithreading* (discussed in Chapter 23, Concurrency). The interface contains one method, `run`, which specifies the behavior of an object when executed.
GUI event-listener interfaces	You work with graphical user interfaces (GUIs) every day. In your web browser, you might type the address of a website to visit, or you might click a button to return to a previous site. The browser responds to your interaction and performs the desired task. Your interaction is known as an *event*, and the code that the browser uses to respond to an event is known as an *event handler*. In Chapter 12, JavaFX Graphical User Interfaces: Part 1, you'll begin learning how to build GUIs with event handlers that respond to user interactions. Event handlers are declared in classes that implement an appropriate *event-listener interface*. Each event-listener interface specifies one or more methods that must be implemented to respond to user interactions.
`AutoCloseable`	Implemented by classes that can be used with the `try`-with-resources statement (Chapter 11, Exception Handling: A Deeper Look) to help prevent resource leaks. We use this interface in Chapter 15, Files, Input/Output Streams, NIO and XML Serialization, and Chapter 24, Accessing Databases with JDBC.

Fig. 10.15 | Common interfaces of the Java API.

10.10 Java SE 8 Interface Enhancements 8

This section introduces interface features that were added in Java SE 8. We discuss these in more detail in later chapters.

10.10.1 `default` Interface Methods

Prior to Java SE 8, interface methods could be *only* `public abstract` methods. This meant that an interface specified *what* operations an implementing class must perform but not *how* the class should perform them.

As of Java SE 8, interfaces also may contain `public` **`default` methods** with *concrete* default implementations that specify *how* operations are performed when an implementing class does not override the methods. If a class implements such an interface, the class also receives the interface's `default` implementations (if any). To declare a `default` method, place the keyword `default` before the method's return type and provide a concrete method implementation.

Adding Methods to Existing Interfaces

Prior to Java SE 8, adding methods to an interface would break any implementing classes that did not implement the new methods. Recall that if you didn't implement each of an interface's methods, you had to declare your class `abstract`.

Any class that implements the original interface will *not* break when a `default` method is added—the class simply receives the new `default` method. When a class implements a Java SE 8 interface, the class "signs a contract" with the compiler that says, "I will declare all the *`abstract`* methods specified by the interface or I will declare my class `abstract`"—the implementing class is not required to override the interface's `default` methods, but it can if necessary.

Software Engineering Observation 10.13

Java SE 8 `default` methods enable you to evolve existing interfaces by adding new methods to those interfaces without breaking code that uses them.

Interfaces vs. **`abstract`** *Classes*

Prior to Java SE 8, an interface was typically used (rather than an `abstract` class) when there were no implementation details to inherit—no fields and no method implementations. With `default` methods, you can instead declare common method implementations in interfaces. This gives you more flexibility in designing your classes, because a class can implement many interfaces, but can extend only one superclass.

10.10.2 `static` Interface Methods

Prior to Java SE 8, it was common to associate with an interface a class containing `static` helper methods for working with objects that implemented the interface. In Chapter 16, you'll learn about class `Collections` which contains many `static` helper methods for working with objects that implement interfaces `Collection`, `List`, `Set` and more. For example, `Collections` method `sort` can sort objects of *any* class that implements interface `List`. With `static` interface methods, such helper methods can now be declared directly in interfaces rather than in separate classes.

10.10.3 Functional Interfaces

As of Java SE 8, any interface containing only one `abstract` method is known as a **functional interface**—these are also called SAM (single `abstract` method) interfaces. There are many such interfaces throughout the Java APIs. Some functional interfaces that you'll use in this book include:

- `ChangeListener` (Chapter 12)—You'll implement this interface to define a method that's called when the interacts with a slider graphical user interface control.
- `Comparator` (Chapter 16)—You'll implement this interface to define a method that can compare two objects of a given type to determine whether the first object is less than, equal to or greater than the second.

- Runnable (Chapter 23)—You'll implement this interface to define a task that may be run in parallel with other parts of your program.

Functional interfaces are used extensively with Java's lambda capabilities that we introduce in Chapter 17. Lambdas provide a shorthand notation for implementing functional interfaces.

10.11 Java SE 9 private Interface Methods

9

As you know, a class's private helper methods may be called only by the class's other methods. As of Java SE 9, you can declare helper methods in *interfaces* via **private interface methods**. An interface's private instance methods can be called directly (i.e., without an object reference) only by the interface's other instance methods. An interface's private static methods can be called by any of the interface's instance or static methods.

Common Programming Error 10.7

Including the default *keyword in a* private *interface method's declaration is a compilation error—*default *methods must be* public.

10.12 private Constructors

In Section 3.4, we mentioned that constructors are normally declared public. Sometimes it's useful to declare one or more of a class's constructors as private.

Preventing Object Instantiation

You can prevent client code from creating objects of a class by making the class's constructors private. For example, consider class Math, which contains only public static constants and public static methods. There's no need to create a Math object to use the class's constants and methods, so its constructor is private.

Sharing Initialization Code in Constructors

One common use of a private constructor is sharing initialization code among a class's other constructors. You can use delegating constructors (introduced in Fig. 8.5) to call the private constructor that contains the shared initialization code.

Factory Methods

Another common use of private constructors is to force client code to use so-called "factory methods" to create objects. A **factory method** is a public static method that creates and initializes an object of a specified type (possibly of the same class), then returns a reference to it. A key benefit of this architecture is that the method's return type can be an interface or a superclass (either abstract or concrete). We discuss factory methods in more detail in the online Design Patterns appendix.[2]

---

2. Gamma, Erich et al. *Design Patterns: Elements of Reusable Object-Oriented Software*. Reading, MA: Addison-Wesley, 1995.

10.13 Program to an Interface, Not an Implementation[3]

Implementation inheritance via `extends` has been explained in detail in Chapters 9 and 10. Recall that Java does not allow a class to inherit from more than one superclass.

With interface inheritance, a class `implements` an interface describing various `abstract` methods that the new class must provide. The new class also may inherit some
8 method implementations (allowed in interfaces as of Java SE 8), but no instance variables. Recall that Java allows a class to implement multiple interfaces in addition to extending one class. An interface also may extend one or more other interfaces.

10.13.1 Implementation Inheritance Is Best for Small Numbers of Tightly Coupled Classes

Implementation inheritance is primarily used to declare closely related classes that have many of the same instance variables and method implementations. Every subclass object has the *is-a* relationship with the superclass, so anywhere a superclass object is expected, a subclass object may be provided.

Classes declared with implementation inheritance are tightly coupled—you define the common instance variables and methods once in a superclass, then inherit them into subclasses. Changes to a superclass directly affect all corresponding subclasses. When you use a superclass variable, only a superclass object or one of its subclass objects may be assigned to the variable.

A key disadvantage of implementation inheritance is that the tight coupling among the classes can make it difficult to modify the hierarchy. For example, consider supporting retirement plans in Section 10.5's `Employee` hierarchy. There are many different types of retirement plans (such as 401Ks and IRAs). We might add a `makeRetirementDeposit` method to class `Employee`, then define various subclasses such as `SalariedEmployeeWith401K`, `SalariedEmployeeWithIRA`, `HourlyEmployeeWith401K`, `HourlyEmployeeWithIRA`, etc. Each subclass would override `makeRetirementDeposit` as appropriate for a given employee and retirement-plan type. As you can see, you quickly wind up with a proliferation of subclasses, making the hierarchy hard to maintain.

As we mentioned in Chapter 9, small inheritance hierarchies under the control of one person tend to be more manageable than large ones maintained by many people. This is true even with the tight coupling associated with implementation inheritance.

10.13.2 Interface Inheritance Is Best for Flexibility

Interface inheritance often requires more work than implementation inheritance, because you must provide implementations of the interface's `abstract` methods—even if those implementations are similar or identical among classes. However, this gives you additional flexibility by eliminating the tight coupling between classes. When you use a variable of an interface type, you can assign it an object of *any* type that implements the interface, either directly or indirectly. This allows you to add new types to your code easily and to replace existing objects with objects of new and improved implementation classes. The dis-

3. Defined in Gamma, Erich et al. *Design Patterns: Elements of Reusable Object-Oriented Software.* Reading, MA: Addison-Wesley, 1995, 17–18, and further emphasized and discussed in Bloch, Joshua. *Effective Java.* Upper Saddle River, NJ: Addison-Wesley, 2008.

cussion of device drivers in the context of abstract classes at the end of Section 10.4 is a good example of how interfaces enable systems to be modified easily.

Software Engineering Observation 10.14

Java SE 8's and Java SE 9's `interface` *enhancements (Sections 10.10–10.11)—which allow* `interfaces` *to contain* `public` *and* `private` *instance methods and* `static` *methods with implementations—make programming with* `interfaces` *appropriate for almost all cases in which you would have used* `abstract` *classes previously. With the exception of fields, you get all the benefits that classes provide, plus classes can implement any number of interfaces but can extend only one class (*`abstract` *or concrete).*

Software Engineering Observation 10.15

Just as superclasses can change, so can interfaces. If the signature of an interface method changes, all corresponding classes would require modification. Experience has shown that interfaces change much less frequently than implementations.

10.13.3 Rethinking the Employee Hierarchy

Let's reconsider Section 10.5's `Employee` hierarchy with composition and an interface. We can say that each type of employee in the hierarchy is an `Employee` that *has a* `CompensationModel`. We can declare `CompensationModel` as an interface with an `abstract` `earnings` method, then declare implementations of `CompensationModel` that specify the various ways in which an `Employee` gets paid:

- A `SalariedCompensationModel` would contain a `weeklySalary` instance variable and would implement method `earnings` to return the `weeklySalary`.
- An `HourlyCompensationModel` would contain `wage` and `hours` instance variables and would implement method `earnings` based on the number of `hours` worked, with `1.5 * wage` for any `hours` over `40`.
- A `CommissionCompensationModel` would contain `grossSales` and `commissionRate` instance variables and would implement method `earnings` to return `grossSales * commissionRate`.
- A `BasePlusCommissionCompensationModel` would contain instance variables `grossSales`, `commissionRate` and `baseSalary` and would implement `earnings` to return `baseSalary + grossSales * commissionRate`.

Each `Employee` object you create can then be initialized with an object of the appropriate `CompensationModel` implementation. Class `Employee`'s `earnings` method would simply use the class's composed `CompensationModel` instance variable to call the `earnings` method of the corresponding `CompensationModel` object.

Flexibility if Compensation Models Change

Declaring the `CompensationModel`s as separate classes that implement the same interface provides flexibility for future changes. Let's assume `Employee`s who are paid purely by commission based on gross sales should get an extra 10% commission, but those who have a base salary should not. In Section 10.5's `Employee` hierarchy, making this change to class `CommissionEmployee`'s `earnings` method (Fig. 10.7) directly affects how `BasePlusCommissionEmployee`s are paid, because `BasePlusCommissionEmployee`'s `earnings` method calls CommissionEmployee's earnings method. However, changing the CommissionCompensationModel's earnings implementation does not affect class BasePlusCommissionCompensationModel, because these classes are not tightly coupled by inheritance.

Flexibility if Employees *Are Promoted*

Interface-based composition is more flexible than Section 10.5's class hierarchy if an Employee gets promoted. Class Employee can provide a setCompensationModel method that receives a CompensationModel and assigns it to the Employee's composed CompensationModel variable. When an Employee gets promoted, you'd simply call setCompensationModel to replace the Employee's existing CompensationModel object with an appropriate new one. To promote an employee using Section 10.5's Employee hierarchy, you'd need to change the employee's type by creating a new object of the appropriate class and moving data from the old object into the new one. Exercise 10.17 asks you to reimplement Exercise 9.16 using interface CompensationModel as described in this section.

Flexibility if Employees *Acquire New Capabilities*

Using composition and interfaces also is more flexible than Section 10.5's class hierarchy for enhancing class Employee. Let's assume we decide to support retirement plans (such as 401Ks and IRAs). We could say that every Employee *has a* RetirementPlan and define interface RetirementPlan with a makeRetirementDeposit method. Then, we can provide appropriate implementations for various retirement-plan types.

10.14 (Optional) GUI and Graphics Case Study: Drawing with Polymorphism

You may have noticed in the drawing program created in GUI and Graphics Case Study Exercise 8.2 that shape classes have many similarities. Using inheritance, we can "factor out" the common features from classes MyLine, MyRectangle and MyOval and place them in a single shape *superclass*. Then, using variables of the superclass type, we can manipulate shape objects *polymorphically*. Removing the redundant code will result in a smaller, more flexible program that's easier to maintain.

GUI and Graphics Case Study Exercises

10.1 Modify the MyLine, MyOval and MyRectangle classes of GUI and Graphics Case Study Exercise 8.2 to create the class hierarchy in Fig. 10.16. Classes of the MyShape hierarchy should be "smart" shape classes that know how to draw themselves (if provided with a GraphicsContext object that tells them where to draw). Once the program creates an object from this hierarchy, it can manipulate it *polymorphically* for the rest of its lifetime as a MyShape.

In your solution, class MyShape in Fig. 10.16 *must* be abstract. Since MyShape represents any shape in general, you cannot implement a draw method without knowing *specifically* what shape it is. The data representing the coordinates and color of the shapes in the hierarchy should be declared as private instance variables of class MyShape. In addition to the common data, class MyShape should declare the following methods:

a) A *no-argument constructor* that sets all the coordinates of the shape to 0 and the stroke color to Color.BLACK.
b) A constructor that initializes the coordinates and stroke color to the values of the arguments supplied.

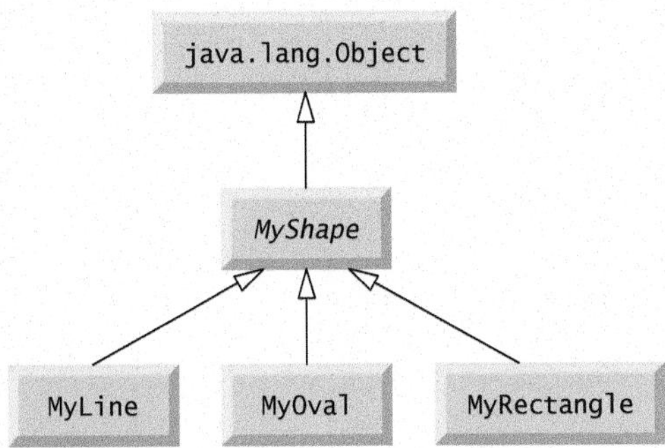

Fig. 10.16 | MyShape hierarchy.

c) *Set* methods for the individual coordinates and color that allow the programmer to set any piece of data independently for a shape in the hierarchy.
d) *Get* methods for the individual coordinates and color that allow the programmer to retrieve any piece of data independently for a shape in the hierarchy.
e) The abstract method

```
public abstract void draw(GraphicsContext gc);
```

which the program will call to tell a MyShape to draw itself on the screen.

To ensure proper encapsulation, all data in class MyShape must be private. This requires declaring proper *set* and *get* methods to manipulate the data. Class MyLine should provide a no-argument constructor and a constructor with arguments for the coordinates and stroke color. Classes MyOval and MyRectangle should provide a no-argument constructor and a constructor with arguments for the coordinates, stroke color, fill color and determining whether the shape is filled. The no-argument constructor should, in addition to setting the default values, set the shape's filled flag to false so that an unfilled shape is the default.

You can draw lines, rectangles and ovals if you know two points in space. Lines require *x1*, *y1*, *x2* and *y2* coordinates. GraphicsContext method strokeLine will connect the two points supplied with a line. If you have the same four coordinate values (*x1*, *y1*, *x2* and *y2*) for ovals and rectangles, you can calculate the four arguments needed to draw them. Each requires an upper-left *x*-coordinate value (the smaller of the two *x*-coordinate values), an upper-left *y*-coordinate value (the smaller of the two *y*-coordinate values), a *width* (the absolute value of the difference between the two *x*-coordinate values) and a *height* (the absolute value of the difference between the two *y*-coordinate values).

There should be no MyLine, MyOval or MyRectangle variables in the program—only MyShape variables that contain references to MyLine, MyOval and MyRectangle objects. The program should generate random shapes and store them in an ArrayList<MyShape>. When it's time to draw the MyShape objects, iterate through the ArrayList<MyShape> and polymorphically call every shape's draw method. Allow the user to specify the number of shapes to generate. The program will then generate and display the specified number of shapes. When creating the shapes, use random-number generation to select which shape to create and to specify the default values for that shape's coordinates, stroke color and, for rectangles and ovals, whether the shape is filled and its fill color.

10.2 ***(Drawing Application Modification)*** In the preceding exercise, you created a MyShape hierarchy in which classes MyLine, MyOval and MyRectangle extend MyShape directly. Notice the similarities between the MyOval and MyRectangle classes. Redesign and reimplement the code for the MyOval and MyRectangle classes to "factor out" the common features into the abstract class MyBoundedShape to produce the hierarchy in Fig. 10.17. Class MyBoundedShape should declare two constructors that mimic those of class MyShape, but with an added parameter specifying whether the shape is filled. Class `MyBoundedShape` should also declare *get* and *set* methods for manipulating the `filled` flag and fill color, and methods that calculate the upper-left *x*-coordinate, upper-left *y*-coordinate, width and height. Remember, the values needed to draw an oval or a rectangle can be calculated from two (*x*, *y*) coordinates. If designed properly, the new `MyOval` and `MyRectangle` classes should each have only two constructors and a `draw` method.

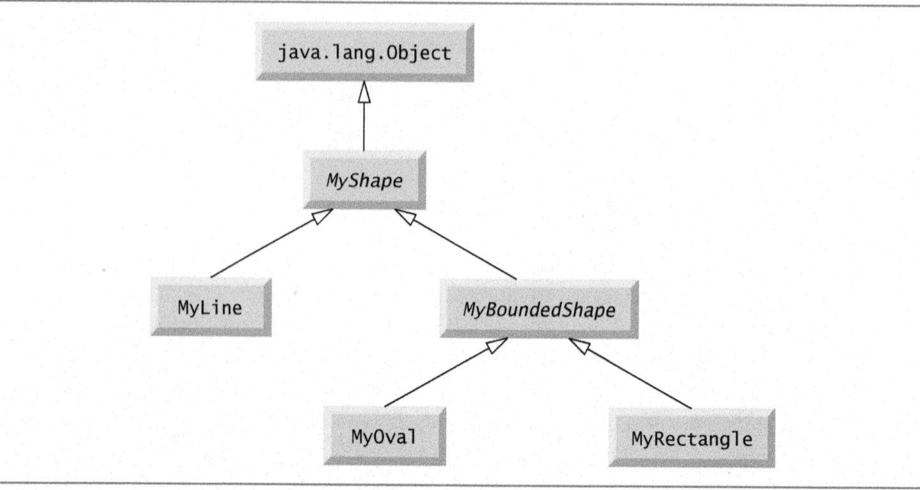

Fig. 10.17 | `MyShape` hierarchy with `MyBoundedShape`.

10.15 Wrap-Up

This chapter introduced polymorphism—the ability to process objects that share the same superclass in a class hierarchy as if they were all objects of the superclass. We discussed how polymorphism makes systems extensible and maintainable, then demonstrated how to use overridden methods to effect polymorphic behavior. We introduced abstract classes, which allow you to provide an appropriate superclass from which other classes can inherit. You learned that an abstract class can declare abstract methods that each subclass must implement to become a concrete class and that a program can use variables of an abstract class to invoke the subclasses' implementations of abstract methods polymorphically. You also learned how to determine an object's type at execution time. We explained the notions of `final` methods and classes. The chapter discussed declaring and implementing an interface as a way for possibly disparate classes to implement common functionality, enabling objects of those classes to be processed polymorphically.

We introduced the interface enhancements in Java SE 8—`default` methods and `static` methods—and in Java SE 9—`private` methods. Next, we discussed the purpose of `private` constructors. Finally, we discussed programming to an interface vs. programming to an implementation, and how the `Employee` hierarchy can be reimplemented using a `CompensationModel` interface.

You should now be familiar with classes, objects, encapsulation, inheritance, interfaces and polymorphism—the most essential aspects of object-oriented programming.

In the next chapter, you'll learn about exceptions, useful for handling errors during a program's execution. Exception handling provides for more robust programs.

Summary

Section 10.1 Introduction

- Polymorphism (p. 408) enables us to write programs that process objects that share the same superclass as if they were all objects of the superclass; this can simplify programming.
- With polymorphism, we can design and implement systems that are easily extensible. The only parts of a program that must be altered to accommodate new classes are those that require direct knowledge of the new classes that you add to the hierarchy.

Section 10.3 Demonstrating Polymorphic Behavior

- When the compiler encounters a method call made through a variable, it determines if the method can be called by checking the variable's class type. If that class contains the proper method declaration (or inherits one), the call is compiled. At execution time, the type of the object to which the variable refers determines the actual method to use.

Section 10.4 Abstract Classes and Methods

- Abstract classes (p. 413) cannot be used to instantiate objects, because they're incomplete.
- The primary purpose of an abstract class is to provide an appropriate superclass from which other classes can inherit and thus share a common design.
- Classes that can be used to instantiate objects are called concrete classes (p. 414). They provide implementations of every method they declare (some of the implementations can be inherited).
- Programmers often write client code that uses only abstract superclasses (p. 414) to reduce client code's dependencies on specific subclass types.
- Abstract classes sometimes constitute several levels of a hierarchy.
- An abstract class normally contains one or more abstract methods (p. 414).
- Abstract methods do not provide implementations.
- A class that contains any abstract methods must be declared as an `abstract` class (p. 414). Each concrete subclass must provide implementations of each of the superclass's abstract methods.
- Constructors and `static` methods cannot be declared `abstract`.
- Abstract superclass variables can hold references to objects of any concrete class derived from the superclass. Programs typically use such variables to manipulate subclass objects polymorphically.
- Polymorphism is particularly effective for implementing layered software systems.

Section 10.5 Case Study: Payroll System Using Polymorphism

- A hierarchy designer can demand that each concrete subclass provide an appropriate method implementation by including an `abstract` method in a superclass.
- Most method calls are resolved at execution time, based on the type of the object being manipulated. This process is known as dynamic binding (p. 428) or late binding.
- A superclass variable can be used to invoke only methods declared in the superclass.
- Operator `instanceof` (p. 429) determines if an object has the *is-a* relationship with a specific type.
- Every object in Java knows its own class and can access it through `Object` method `getClass` (p. 429), which returns an object of type `Class` (package `java.lang`).
- The *is-a* relationship applies only between the subclass and its superclasses, not vice versa.

Section 10.6 Allowed Assignments Between Superclass and Subclass Variables

- Assigning a superclass reference to a subclass variable is not allowed without an explicit cast.

Section 10.7 `final` Methods and Classes

- A method that's declared `final` (p. 431) in a superclass cannot be overridden in a subclass.
- Methods declared `private` are implicitly `final`, because you can't override them in a subclass.
- Methods that are declared `static` are implicitly `final`.
- A `final` method's declaration can never change, so all subclasses use the same implementation, and calls to `final` methods are resolved at compile time—this is known as static binding (p. 431).
- The compiler can optimize programs by removing calls to `final` methods and inlining their expanded code at each method-call location.
- A class that's declared `final` cannot be extended (p. 431).
- All methods in a `final` class are implicitly `final`.

Section 10.8 A Deeper Explanation of Issues with Calling Methods from Constructors

- If a constructor and a *set* method perform the same validation for a particular instance variable and the validation code is brief, you can duplicate it in the constructor and the *set* method.
- For lengthier validation, you can define a `static` validation method.

Section 10.9 Creating and Using Interfaces

- An interface (p. 432) specifies *what* operations are allowed but not *how* they're performed.
- A Java interface describes a set of methods that can be called on an object.
- An interface declaration begins with the keyword `interface` (p. 433).
- All methods declared in an interface are implicitly `public abstract` methods and all fields are implicitly `public`, `static` and `final`.
- To use an interface, a concrete class must specify that it `implements` (p. 433) the interface and must declare each interface `abstract` method with the signature specified in the interface declaration. A class that does not implement all the interface's `abstract` methods must be declared `abstract`.
- Implementing an interface is like signing a contract with the compiler that states, "I will declare all the `abstract` methods specified by the interface or I will declare my class `abstract`."
- An interface is typically used when disparate (i.e., unrelated) classes need to share common methods and constants. This allows objects of unrelated classes to be processed polymorphically—objects of classes that implement the same interface can respond to the same method calls.
- You can create an interface that describes the desired functionality, then implement the interface in any classes that require that functionality.
- An interface is often used in place of an `abstract` class when there's no default implementation to inherit—that is, no instance variables and no default method implementations.
- Like `public abstract` classes, interfaces are typically `public` types, so they're normally declared in files by themselves with the same name as the interface and the `.java` filename extension.
- Java does not allow subclasses to inherit from more than one superclass, but it does allow a class to inherit from a superclass and implement more than one interface.
- All objects of a class that implement multiple interfaces have the *is-a* relationship with each implemented interface type.
- An interface can declare constants. The constants are implicitly `public`, `static` and `final`.

Section 10.10 Java SE 8 Interface Enhancements

- In Java SE 8, an interface may declare `default` methods—that is, `public` methods with concrete implementations that specify how an operation should be performed.
- When a class implements an interface, the class receives the interface's `default` concrete implementations if it does not override them.
- To declare a `default` method in an interface, you simply place the keyword `default` before the method's return type and provide a complete method body.
- When you enhance an existing an interface with `default` methods—any classes that implemented the original interface will not break—it'll simply receive the `default` method implementations.
- With `default` methods, you can declare common method implementations in interfaces (rather than `abstract` classes), which gives you more flexibility in designing your classes.
- As of Java SE 8, interfaces may include `public static` methods.
- As of Java SE 8, any interface containing only one method is known as a functional interface. There are many such interfaces throughout the Java APIs.
- Functional interfaces are used extensively with Java SE 8's lambda capabilities. As you'll see, lambdas provide a shorthand notation for implementing functional interfaces.

Section 10.11 Java SE 9 `private` Interface Methods

- As of Java SE 9, you can declare helper methods in interfaces via `private` interface instance methods and `static` methods.

Section 10.12 `private` Constructors

- You can prevent client code from creating of objects of a class by making the class's constructors `private`.
- You can use delegating constructors to call a `private` constructor that contains shared initialization code.
- You can use `private` constructors is to force client code to use a factory method to create and initialize an object.

Section 10.13 Program to an Interface, Not an Implementation

- With interface inheritance, a class implements an interface describing various `abstract` methods that the new class must provide. The new class also may inherit some method implementations (allowed in interfaces as of Java SE 8), but no instance variables.
- An interface also may extend one or more other interfaces.
- Implementation inheritance is primarily used to declare closely related classes that have many of the same instance variables and method implementations.
- Classes declared with implementation inheritance are tightly coupled. Changes to a superclass directly affect all corresponding subclasses.
- A key disadvantage of implementation inheritance is that the tight coupling among the classes can make it difficult to modify the hierarchy.
- Interface inheritance often requires more work than implementation inheritance, because you must provide implementations of the interface's `abstract` methods—even if those implementations are similar or identical among classes.
- Interface inheritance gives you additional flexibility by eliminating the tight coupling between classes. When you use a variable of an interface type, you can assign it an object of any type that implements the interface, either directly or indirectly.

- Java SE 8's and Java SE 9's interface enhancements make programming with interfaces appropriate for almost all cases in which you would have used `abstract` classes previously.

Self-Review Exercises

10.1 Fill in the blanks in each of the following statements:

a) If a class contains at least one abstract method, it's a(n) ________ class.
b) Classes from which objects can be instantiated are called ________ classes.
c) ________ involves using a superclass variable to invoke methods on superclass and subclass objects, enabling you to "program in the general."
d) Methods that are not interface methods and that do not provide implementations must be declared using keyword ________.
e) Casting a reference stored in a superclass variable to a subclass type is called ________.

10.2 State whether each of the statements that follows is *true* or *false*. If *false*, explain why.

a) All methods in an `abstract` class must be declared as `abstract` methods.
b) Invoking a subclass-only method through a subclass variable is not allowed.
c) If a superclass declares an `abstract` method, a subclass must implement that method.
d) An object of a class that implements an interface may be thought of as an object of that interface type.

10.3 *(Java SE 8 and Java SE 9 interfaces)* Fill in the blanks in each of the following statements:

a) In Java SE 8, an interface may declare ________—that is, `public` methods with concrete implementations that specify how an operation should be performed.
b) As of Java SE 8, interfaces can include ________ helper methods.
c) As of Java SE 8, any interface containing only one method is known as a(n) ________.
d) As of Java SE 9, any interface may contain ________ instance and `static` methods.

Answers to Self-Review Exercises

10.1 a) abstract. b) concrete. c) Polymorphism. d) `abstract`. e) downcasting.

10.2 a) False. An abstract class can include methods with implementations and `abstract` methods. b) False. Trying to invoke a subclass-only method with a superclass variable is not allowed. c) False. Only a concrete subclass must implement the method. d) True.

10.3 a) `default` methods. b) `static`. c) functional interface. d) `private`.

Exercises

10.4 How does polymorphism enable you to program "in the general" rather than "in the specific"? Discuss the key advantages of programming "in the general."

10.5 What are abstract methods? Describe the circumstances in which an abstract method would be appropriate.

10.6 How does polymorphism promote extensibility?

10.7 Discuss three proper ways in which you can assign superclass and subclass references to variables of superclass and subclass types.

10.8 Compare and contrast abstract classes and interfaces. Why would you use an abstract class? Why would you use an interface?

10.9 *(Java SE 8 Interfaces)* Explain how `default` methods enable you to add new methods to an existing interface without breaking the classes that implemented the original interface.

10.10 *(Java SE 8 Interfaces)* What is a functional interface?

10.11 *(Java SE 8 Interfaces)* Why is it useful to be able to add `static` methods to interfaces?

10.12 *(Java SE 9 Interfaces)* Why is it useful to be able to add `private` methods to interfaces?

10.13 *(Payroll System Modification)* Modify the payroll system of Figs. 10.4–10.9 to include `private` instance variable `birthDate` in class `Employee`. Use class `Date` of Fig. 8.7 to represent an employee's birthday. Add *get* methods to class `Date`. Assume that payroll is processed once per month. Create an array of `Employee` variables to store references to the various employee objects. In a loop, calculate the payroll for each `Employee` (polymorphically), and add a $100.00 bonus to the person's payroll amount if the current month is the one in which the `Employee`'s birthday occurs.

10.14 *(Project: `Shape` Hierarchy)* Implement the `Shape` hierarchy shown in Fig. 9.3. Each `TwoDimensionalShape` should contain method `getArea` to calculate the area of the two-dimensional shape. Each `ThreeDimensionalShape` should have methods `getArea` and `getVolume` to calculate the surface area and volume, respectively, of the three-dimensional shape. Create a program that uses an array of `Shape` references to objects of each concrete class in the hierarchy. The program should print a text description of the object to which each array element refers. Also, in the loop that processes all the shapes in the array, determine whether each shape is a `TwoDimensionalShape` or a `ThreeDimensionalShape`. If it's a `TwoDimensionalShape`, display its area. If it's a `ThreeDimensionalShape`, display its area and volume.

10.15 *(Payroll System Modification)* Modify the payroll system of Figs. 10.4–10.9 to include an additional `Employee` subclass `PieceWorker` that represents an employee whose pay is based on the number of pieces of merchandise produced. Class `PieceWorker` should contain `private` instance variables `wage` (to store the employee's wage per piece) and `pieces` (to store the number of pieces produced). Provide a concrete implementation of method `earnings` in class `PieceWorker` that calculates the employee's earnings by multiplying the number of pieces produced by the wage per piece. Create an array of `Employee` variables to store references to objects of each concrete class in the new `Employee` hierarchy. For each `Employee`, display its `String` representation and earnings.

10.16 *(Accounts Payable System Modification)* In this exercise, we modify the accounts payable application of Figs. 10.11–10.14 to include the complete functionality of the payroll application of Figs. 10.4–10.9. The application should still process two `Invoice` objects, but now should process one object of each of the four `Employee` subclasses. If the object currently being processed is a `BasePlusCommissionEmployee`, the application should increase the `BasePlusCommissionEmployee`'s base salary by 10%. Finally, the application should output the payment amount for each object. Complete the following steps to create the new application:

a) Modify classes `HourlyEmployee` (Fig. 10.6) and `CommissionEmployee` (Fig. 10.7) to place them in the `Payable` hierarchy as subclasses of the version of `Employee` (Fig. 10.13) that implements `Payable`. [*Hint:* Change the name of method `earnings` to `getPaymentAmount` in each subclass so that the class satisfies its inherited contract with interface `Payable`.]

b) Modify class `BasePlusCommissionEmployee` (Fig. 10.8) such that it extends the version of class `CommissionEmployee` created in part (a).

c) Modify `PayableInterfaceTest` (Fig. 10.14) to polymorphically process two `Invoice`s, one `SalariedEmployee`, one `HourlyEmployee`, one `CommissionEmployee` and one `BasePlusCommissionEmployee`. First output a `String` representation of each `Payable` object. Next, if an object is a `BasePlusCommissionEmployee`, increase its base salary by 10%. Finally, output the payment amount for each `Payable` object.

10.17 *(Recommended Project: Combining Composition and Inheritance[4])* Exercise 9.16 asked you to remodel Chapter 9's `CommissionEmployee`–`BasePlusCommissionEmployee` inheritance hierar-

4. We'd like to thank Brian Goetz, Oracle's Java Language Architect, for suggesting the class architecture we use in this exercise.

chy as a class `Employee` in which each `Employee` *has a* different `CompensationModel` object. In this exercise, reimplement Exercise 9.16's `CompensationModel` class as an interface that provides a `public abstract` method `earnings` that receives no parameters and returns a `double`. Then create the following classes that implement interface `CompensationModel`:

a) `SalariedCompensationModel`—For `Employees` who are paid a fixed weekly salary, this class should contain a `weeklySalary` instance variable, and should implement method `earnings` to return the `weeklySalary`.
b) `HourlyCompensationModel`—For `Employees` who are paid by the hour and receive overtime pay for all hours worked in excess of 40 hours per week, this class should contain `wage` and `hours` instance variables, and should implement method `earnings` based on the number of hours worked (see class `HourlyEmployee`'s `earnings` method in Fig. 10.6).
c) `CommissionCompensationModel`—For `Employees` who are paid by commission, this class should contain `grossSales` and `commissionRate` instance variables, and should implement method `earnings` to return `grossSales * commissionRate`.
d) `BasePlusCommissionCompensationModel`—For `Employees` who are paid a base salary and commission, this class should contain instance variables `grossSales`, `commissionRate` and `baseSalary` and should implement `earnings` to return `baseSalary + grossSales * commissionRate`.

In your test application, create `Employee` objects with each of the CompensationModels described above, then display each `Employee`'s earnings. Next, change each `Employee`'s `CompensationModel` dynamically and redisplay each `Employee`'s earnings.

10.18 ***(Recommended Project: Implementing the `Payable` Interface)*** Modify class `Employee` from Exercise 10.17 so that it implements the `Payable` interface of Fig. 10.11. Replace the `SalariedEmployee` objects in the application of Fig. 10.14 with the `Employee` objects from Exercise 10.17 and demonstrate processing the `Employee` and `Invoice` objects polymorphically.

Making a Difference

10.19 ***(`CarbonFootprint` Interface: Polymorphism)*** Using interfaces, as you learned in this chapter, you can specify similar behaviors for possibly disparate classes. Governments and companies worldwide are becoming increasingly concerned with carbon footprints (annual releases of carbon dioxide into the atmosphere) from buildings burning various types of fuels for heat, vehicles burning fuels for power, and the like. Many scientists blame these greenhouse gases for the phenomenon called global warming. Create three small classes unrelated by inheritance—classes `Building`, `Car` and `Bicycle`. Give each class some unique appropriate attributes and behaviors that it does not have in common with other classes. Write an interface `CarbonFootprint` with a `getCarbonFootprint` method. Have each of your classes implement that interface, so that its `getCarbonFootprint` method calculates an appropriate carbon footprint for that class (check out a few websites that explain how to calculate carbon footprints). Write an application that creates objects of each of the three classes, places references to those objects in `ArrayList<CarbonFootprint>`, then iterates through the `ArrayList`, polymorphically invoking each object's `getCarbonFootprint` method. For each object, print some identifying information and the object's carbon footprint.

Exception Handling: A Deeper Look

11

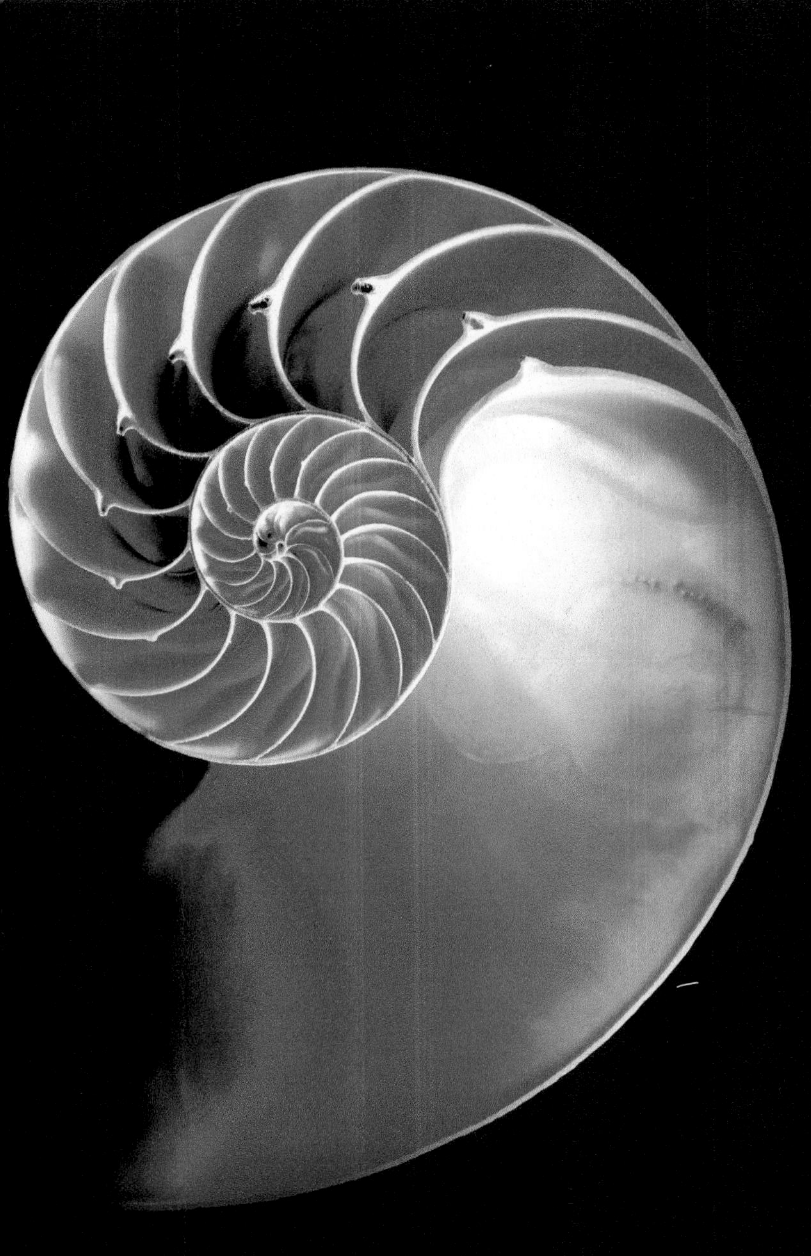

Objectives

In this chapter you'll:

- Learn why exception handling is an effective mechanism for responding to runtime problems.
- Use `try` blocks to delimit code in which exceptions might occur.
- Use `throw` to indicate a problem.
- Use `catch` blocks to specify exception handlers.
- Learn when to use exception handling.
- Understand the exception class hierarchy.
- Use the `finally` block to release resources.
- Chain exceptions by catching one exception and throwing another.
- Create user-defined exceptions.
- Use the debugging feature `assert` to state conditions that should be true at a particular point in a method.
- Learn how `try`-with-resources can automatically release a resource when the `try` block terminates.

Outline

11.1 Introduction

As you know from Chapters 7–8, an exception indicates a problem during a program's execution. Exception handling enables applications to resolve (or handle) exceptions. In some cases, a program can continue executing as if no problem had been encountered. The features presented in this chapter help you write *robust* and *fault-tolerant* programs that can deal with problems and continue executing or *terminate gracefully*.[1]

First, we handle an exception that occurs when a method attempts to divide an integer by zero. We discuss when to use exception handling and show a portion of the exception-handling class hierarchy. As you'll see, only subclasses of `Throwable` can be used with exception handling. We introduce the `try` statement's `finally` block, which executes whether or not an exception occurs. We then show how to use *chained exceptions* to add application-specific information to an exception and how to create your own exception types. Next, we introduce *preconditions* and *postconditions*, which must be true when your methods are called and when they return, respectively. We then present *assertions*, which you can use at development time to help debug your code. We also discuss catching multiple exceptions with one `catch` handler, and the `try`-with-resources statement that automatically releases a resource after it's used in the `try` block.

This chapter focuses on the exception-handling concepts and presents several mechanical examples that demonstrate various features. Many Java API methods throw exceptions that we handle in our code. Figure 11.1 shows some of the exception types you've already seen and others you'll learn about.

Software Engineering Observation 11.1

In industry, you're likely to find that companies have strict design, coding, testing, debugging and maintenance standards. These often vary among companies. Companies often have their own exception-handling standards that are sensitive to the type of application, such as real-time systems, high-performance mathematical calculations, big data, network-based distributed systems, etc. This chapter's tips provide observations consistent with these types of industry policies.

1. Java exception handling is based in part on the work of Andrew Koenig and Bjarne Stroustrup—A. Koenig and B. Stroustrup, "Exception Handling for C++ (revised)," *Proceedings of the Usenix C++ Conference*, pp. 149–176, San Francisco, April 1990.

Chapter	Sample of exceptions used
Chapter 7	`ArrayIndexOutOfBoundsException`
Chapters 8–10	`IllegalArgumentException`
Chapter 11	`ArithmeticException`, `InputMismatchException`
Chapter 15	`SecurityException`, `FileNotFoundException`, `IOException`, `ClassNotFoundException`, `IllegalStateException`, `FormatterClosedException`, `NoSuchElementException`
Chapter 16	`ClassCastException`, `UnsupportedOperationException`, `NullPointerException`, custom exception types
Chapter 20	`ClassCastException`, custom exception types
Chapter 21	`IllegalArgumentException`, custom exception types
Chapter 23	`InterruptedException`, `IllegalMonitorStateException`, `ExecutionException`, `CancellationException`
Chapter 24	`SQLException`, `IllegalStateException`, `PatternSyntaxException`
Chapter 28	`MalformedURLException`, `EOFException`, `SocketException`, `InterruptedException`, `UnknownHostException`
Chapter 31	`SQLException`

Fig. 11.1 | Various exception types that you'll see throughout this book

11.2 Example: Divide by Zero without Exception Handling

First we demonstrate what happens when errors arise in an application that does not use exception handling. Figure 11.2 prompts the user for two integers and passes them to method `quotient`, which calculates the integer quotient and returns an `int` result. In this example, you'll see that exceptions are **thrown** (i.e., the exception occurs) by a method when it detects a problem and is unable to handle it.

```
// Fig. 11.2: DivideByZeroNoExceptionHandling.java
// Integer division without exception handling.
import java.util.Scanner;

public class DivideByZeroNoExceptionHandling {
   // demonstrates throwing an exception when a divide-by-zero occurs
   public static int quotient(int numerator, int denominator) {
      return numerator / denominator; // possible division by zero
   }

   public static void main(String[] args) {
      Scanner scanner = new Scanner(System.in);

      System.out.print("Please enter an integer numerator: ");
      int numerator = scanner.nextInt();
```

Fig. 11.2 | Integer division without exception handling. (Part 1 of 2.)

```
        System.out.print("Please enter an integer denominator: ");
        int denominator = scanner.nextInt();

        int result = quotient(numerator, denominator);
        System.out.printf(
           "%nResult: %d / %d = %d%n", numerator, denominator, result);
    }
}
```

```
Please enter an integer numerator: 100
Please enter an integer denominator: 7

Result: 100 / 7 = 14
```

```
Please enter an integer numerator: 100
Please enter an integer denominator: 0
Exception in thread "main" java.lang.ArithmeticException: / by zero
        at DivideByZeroNoExceptionHandling.quotient(
           DivideByZeroNoExceptionHandling.java:8)
        at DivideByZeroNoExceptionHandling.main(
           DivideByZeroNoExceptionHandling.java:19)
```

```
Please enter an integer numerator: 100
Please enter an integer denominator: hello
Exception in thread "main" java.util.InputMismatchException
        at java.util.Scanner.throwFor(Unknown Source)
        at java.util.Scanner.next(Unknown Source)
        at java.util.Scanner.nextInt(Unknown Source)
        at java.util.Scanner.nextInt(Unknown Source)
        at DivideByZeroNoExceptionHandling.main(
            DivideByZeroNoExceptionHandling.java:17)
```

Fig. 11.2 | Integer division without exception handling. (Part 2 of 2.)

Stack Trace

The first sample execution in Fig. 11.2 shows a successful division. In the second execution, the user enters the value `0` as the denominator. Several lines of information are displayed in response to this invalid input. This information is known as a **stack trace**, which includes the name of the exception (`java.lang.ArithmeticException`) in a descriptive message that indicates the problem and the method-call stack (i.e., the call chain) at the time the problem occurred. The stack trace includes the path of execution that led to the exception method by method. This helps you debug the program. Even if a problem has not occurred, you can see the stack trace any time by calling `Thread.dumpStack()`.

Stack Trace for an `ArithmeticException`

The first line specifies that an `ArithmeticException` has occurred. The text after the name of the exception ("`/ by zero`") indicates that this exception occurred as a result of an attempt to divide by zero. Java does not allow division by zero in integer arithmetic. When this occurs, Java throws an **`ArithmeticException`**. `ArithmeticException`s can arise from a number of different problems, so the extra data ("`/ by zero`") provides more specific information.

Starting from the last line of the stack trace, we see that the exception was detected in line 19 of method `main`. Each line of the stack trace contains the class name and method (e.g., `DivideByZeroNoExceptionHandling.main`) followed by the filename and line number (e.g., `DivideByZeroNoExceptionHandling.java:19`). Moving up the stack trace, we see that the exception occurs in line 8, in method `quotient`. The top row of the call chain indicates the **throw point**—the initial point at which the exception occurred. The throw point of this exception is in line 8 of method `quotient`.

Side Note Regarding Floating-Point Arithmetic

Java *does* allow division by zero with floating-point values. Such a calculation results in positive or negative infinity, which is represented as a floating-point value that displays as `"Infinity"` or `"-Infinity"`. If you divide 0.0 by 0.0, the result is `NaN` (not a number), which is represented as a floating-point value that displays as `"NaN"`. If you need to compare a floating-point value to `NaN`, use the method `isNaN` of class `Float` (for `float` values) or of class `Double` (for `double` values). Classes `Float` and `Double` are in package `java.lang`.

Stack Trace for an `InputMismatchException`

In the third execution, the user enters the string `"hello"` as the denominator. Notice again that a stack trace is displayed. This informs us that an `InputMismatchException` has occurred (package `java.util`). Our prior examples that input numeric values assumed that the user would input a proper integer value. However, users sometimes make mistakes and input noninteger values. An **`InputMismatchException`** occurs when `Scanner` method `nextInt` receives a `string` that does not represent a valid integer. Starting from the end of the stack trace, we see that the exception was detected in line 17 of method `main`. Moving up the stack trace, we see that the exception occurred in method `nextInt`. Notice that in place of the filename and line number, we're provided with the text `Unknown Source`. This means that the so-called *debugging symbols* that provide the filename and line number information for that method's class were not available to the JVM—this is typically the case for the classes of the Java API. Many IDEs have access to the Java API source code and will display filenames and line numbers in stack traces.

Program Termination

In the sample executions of Fig. 11.2 when exceptions occur and stack traces are displayed, the program also *exits*. This does not always occur in Java. Sometimes a program may continue even though an exception has occurred and a stack trace has been printed. In such cases, the application may produce unexpected results. For example, a graphical user interface (GUI) application will often continue executing. In Fig. 11.2 both types of exceptions were detected in method `main`. In the next example, we'll see how to *handle* these exceptions so that you can enable the program to run to normal completion.

11.3 Example: Handling ArithmeticExceptions and InputMismatchExceptions

The application in Fig. 11.3, which is based on Fig. 11.2, uses *exception handling* to process any `ArithmeticExceptions` and `InputMistmatchExceptions` that arise. The application still prompts the user for two integers and passes them to method `quotient`, which calculates the quotient and returns an `int` result. This version of the application uses exception handling so that if the user makes a mistake, the program catches and handles (i.e., deals with) the exception—in this case, allowing the user to re-enter the input.

```
// Fig. 11.3: DivideByZeroWithExceptionHandling.java
// Handling ArithmeticExceptions and InputMismatchExceptions.
import java.util.InputMismatchException;
import java.util.Scanner;

public class DivideByZeroWithExceptionHandling
{
   // demonstrates throwing an exception when a divide-by-zero occurs
   public static int quotient(int numerator, int denominator)
      throws ArithmeticException {
      return numerator / denominator; // possible division by zero
   }

   public static void main(String[] args) {
      Scanner scanner = new Scanner(System.in);
      boolean continueLoop = true; // determines if more input is needed

      do {
         try { // read two numbers and calculate quotient
            System.out.print("Please enter an integer numerator: ");
            int numerator = scanner.nextInt();
            System.out.print("Please enter an integer denominator: ");
            int denominator = scanner.nextInt();

            int result = quotient(numerator, denominator);
            System.out.printf("%nResult: %d / %d = %d%n", numerator,
               denominator, result);
            continueLoop = false; // input successful; end looping
         }
         catch (InputMismatchException inputMismatchException) {
            System.err.printf("%nException: %s%n",
               inputMismatchException);
            scanner.nextLine(); // discard input so user can try again
            System.out.printf(
               "You must enter integers. Please try again.%n%n");
         }
         catch (ArithmeticException arithmeticException) {
            System.err.printf("%nException: %s%n", arithmeticException);
            System.out.printf(
               "Zero is an invalid denominator. Please try again.%n%n");
         }
      } while (continueLoop);
   }
}
```

Fig. 11.3 | Handling `ArithmeticExceptions` and `InputMismatchExceptions`. (Part 1 of 2.)

```
Please enter an integer numerator: 100
Please enter an integer denominator: 7

Result: 100 / 7 = 14
```

```
Please enter an integer numerator: 100
Please enter an integer denominator: 0

Exception: java.lang.ArithmeticException: / by zero
Zero is an invalid denominator. Please try again.

Please enter an integer numerator: 100
Please enter an integer denominator: 7

Result: 100 / 7 = 14
```

```
Please enter an integer numerator: 100
Please enter an integer denominator: hello

Exception: java.util.InputMismatchException
You must enter integers. Please try again.

Please enter an integer numerator: 100
Please enter an integer denominator: 7

Result: 100 / 7 = 14
```

Fig. 11.3 | Handling `ArithmeticException`s and `InputMismatchException`s. (Part 2 of 2.)

The first sample execution in Fig. 11.3 does *not* encounter any problems. In the second execution the user enters a *zero denominator*, and an `ArithmeticException` exception occurs. In the third execution the user enters the string `"hello"` as the denominator, and an `InputMismatchException` occurs. For each exception, the user is informed of the mistake and asked to try again, then is prompted for two new integers. In each sample execution, the program runs to completion successfully.

Class `InputMismatchException` is imported in line 3. Class `ArithmeticException` does not need to be imported because it's in package `java.lang`. Line 16 creates the `boolean` variable `continueLoop`, which is `true` if the user has *not* yet entered valid input. Lines 18–42 repeatedly ask users for input until a *valid* input is received.

Enclosing Code in a `try` *Block*

Lines 19–29 contain a **try block**, which encloses the code that *might* `throw` an exception and the code that should *not* execute if an exception occurs (i.e., if an exception occurs, the remaining code in the `try` block will be skipped). A `try` block consists of the keyword `try` followed by a block of code enclosed in curly braces. [*Note:* The term "`try` block" sometimes refers only to the block of code that follows the `try` keyword (not including the `try` keyword itself). For simplicity, we use the term "`try` block" to refer to the block of code that follows the try keyword, as well as the try keyword.] The statements that read the integers from the keyboard (lines 21 and 23) each use method nextInt to read an int value. Method nextInt throws an InputMismatchException if the value read in is *not* an integer.

The division that can cause an ArithmeticException is not performed in the try block. Rather, the call to method quotient (line 25) invokes the code that attempts the division (line 11); the JVM *throws* an ArithmeticException object when the denominator is zero.

Software Engineering Observation 11.2

Exceptions may surface through explicitly mentioned code in a try *block, through deeply nested method calls initiated by code in a* try *block or from the Java Virtual Machine as it executes Java bytecodes.*

Catching Exceptions

The try block in this example is followed by two catch blocks—one that handles an InputMismatchException (lines 30–36) and one that handles an ArithmeticException (lines 37–41). A **catch block** (also called a **catch clause** or **exception handler**) *catches* (i.e., receives) and *handles* an exception. A catch block begins with the keyword catch followed by a parameter in parentheses (called the *exception parameter*, discussed shortly) and a block of code enclosed in curly braces.

At least one catch block or a **finally block** (discussed in Section 11.6) *must* immediately follow the try block. Each catch block specifies in parentheses an **exception parameter** that identifies the exception type the handler can process. When an exception occurs in a try block, the catch block that executes is the *first* one whose type matches the type of the exception that occurred (i.e., the type in the catch block matches the thrown exception type exactly or is a direct or indirect superclass of it). The exception parameter's name enables the catch block to interact with a caught exception object—e.g., to implicitly invoke the caught exception's toString method (as in lines 31–32 and 38), which displays basic information about the exception. Notice that we use the **System.err (standard error stream) object** to output error messages. By default, System.err's print methods, like those of System.out, display data to the *command prompt*.

Line 33 in the first catch block calls Scanner method nextLine. Because an InputMismatchException occurred, the call to method nextInt never successfully read in the user's data—so we read that input with a call to method nextLine. We do not do anything with the input at this point, because we know that it's *invalid*. Each catch block displays an error message and asks the user to try again. After either catch block terminates, the user is prompted for input. We'll soon take a deeper look at how this flow of control works in exception handling.

Common Programming Error 11.1

It's a syntax error to place code between a try *block and its corresponding* catch *blocks.*

Multi-catch

It's relatively common for a try block to be followed by several catch blocks to handle various types of exceptions. If the bodies of several catch blocks are identical, you can use the **multi-catch** feature to catch those exception types in a *single* catch handler and perform the same task. The syntax for a *multi-catch* is:

```
catch (Type1 | Type2 | Type3 e)
```

Each exception type is separated from the next with a vertical bar (|). The preceding line of code indicates that *any* of the types (or their subclasses) can be caught in the exception handler. Any number of Throwable types can be specified in a multi-catch. In this case, the exception parameter's type is the common superclass of the specified types.

Uncaught Exceptions

An **uncaught exception** is one for which there are no matching catch blocks. You saw uncaught exceptions in the second and third outputs of Fig. 11.2. Recall that when exceptions occurred in that example, the application terminated early (after displaying the exception's *stack trace*). This does not always occur as a result of uncaught exceptions. Java uses a "multithreaded" model of program execution—each **thread** is a *concurrent activity*. One program can have many threads. If a program has only *one* thread, an uncaught exception will cause the program to terminate. If a program has *multiple* threads, an uncaught exception will terminate *only* the thread in which the exception occurred. In such programs, however, certain threads may rely on others, and if one thread terminates due to an uncaught exception, there may be adverse effects on the rest of the program. Chapter 23, Concurrency, discusses these issues in depth.

Termination Model of Exception Handling

If an exception occurs in a try block (such as an InputMismatchException being thrown as a result of the code at line 23 of Fig. 11.3), the try block *terminates* immediately and program control transfers to the *first* of the following catch blocks in which the exception parameter's type matches the thrown exception's type. In Fig. 11.3, the first catch block catches InputMismatchExceptions (which occur if invalid input is entered) and the second catch block catches ArithmeticExceptions (which occur if an attempt is made to divide by zero). After the exception is handled, program control does *not* return to the throw point, because the try block has *expired* (and its *local variables* have been *lost*). Rather, control resumes after the last catch block. This is known as the **termination model of exception handling.** Some languages use the **resumption model of exception handling,** in which, after an exception is handled, control resumes just after the *throw point*.

Notice that we name our exception parameters (inputMismatchException and arithmeticException) based on their type. Java programmers often simply use the letter e as the name of their exception parameters.

After executing a catch block, this program's flow of control proceeds to the first statement after the last catch block (line 42 in this case). The condition in the do…while statement is true (variable continueLoop contains its initial value of true), so control returns to the beginning of the loop and the user is again prompted for input. This control statement will loop until *valid* input is entered. At that point, program control reaches line 28, which assigns false to variable continueLoop. The try block then *terminates*. If no exceptions are thrown in the try block, the catch blocks are *skipped* and control continues with the first statement after the catch blocks (we'll learn about another possibility when we discuss the finally block in Section 11.6). Now the condition for the do…while loop is false, and method main ends.

The try block and its corresponding catch and/or finally blocks form a **try statement**. Do not confuse the terms "try block" and "try statement"—the latter includes the try block as well as the following catch blocks and/or finally block.

As with any other block of code, when a try block terminates, *local variables* declared in the block *go out of scope* and are no longer accessible; thus, the local variables of a try block are not accessible in the corresponding catch blocks. When a catch block *terminates, local variables* declared within the catch block (including the exception parameter of that catch block) also *go out of scope* and are *destroyed.* Any remaining catch blocks in the try statement are *ignored*, and execution resumes at the first line of code after the try...catch sequence—this will be a finally block, if one is present.

Using the throws *Clause*

In method quotient (Fig. 11.3, lines 9–12), line 10 is known as a **throws clause**. It specifies the exceptions the method *might* throw if problems occur. This clause, which must appear after the method's parameter list and before the body, contains a comma-separated list of the exception types. Such exceptions may be thrown by statements in the method's body or by methods called from there. We've added the throws clause to this application to indicate that this method might throw an ArithmeticException. Method quotient's callers are thus informed that the method might throw an ArithmeticException. Some exception types, such as ArithmeticException, are not required to be listed in the throws clause. For those that are, the method can throw exceptions that have the *is-a* relationship with the classes listed in the throws clause. You'll learn more about this in Section 11.5.

Error-Prevention Tip 11.1

Read a method's online API documentation before using it in a program. The documentation specifies exceptions thrown by the method (if any) and indicates reasons why such exceptions may occur. Next, read the online API documentation for the specified exception classes. The documentation for an exception class typically contains potential reasons that such exceptions occur. Finally, provide for handling those exceptions in your program.

When line 11 executes, if the denominator is zero, the JVM throws an ArithmeticException object. This object will be caught by the catch block at lines 37–41, which displays basic information about the exception by *implicitly* invoking the exception's toString method, then asks the user to try again.

If the denominator is not zero, method quotient performs the division and returns the result to the point of invocation of method quotient in the try block (line 25). Lines 26–27 display the result of the calculation and line 28 sets continueLoop to false. In this case, the try block completes successfully, so the program skips the catch blocks and fails the condition at line 42, and method main completes execution normally.

When quotient throws an ArithmeticException, quotient *terminates* and does *not* return a value, and quotient's *local variables go out of scope* (and are destroyed). If quotient contained local variables that were references to objects and there were no other references to those objects, the objects would be marked for *garbage collection*. Also, when an exception occurs, the try block from which quotient was called *terminates* before lines 26–28 can execute. Here, too, if local variables were created in the try block prior to the exception's being thrown, these variables would go out of scope.

If an `InputMismatchException` is generated by lines 21 or 23, the `try` block *terminates* and execution *continues* with the `catch` block at lines 30–36. In this case, method `quotient` is not called. Then method `main` continues after the last `catch` block.

11.4 When to Use Exception Handling

Exception handling is designed to process **synchronous errors**, which occur when a statement executes. Common examples we'll see throughout the book are *out-of-range array indices, arithmetic overflow* (i.e., a value outside the representable range of values), *division by zero, invalid method parameters* and *thread interruption* (as we'll see in Chapter 23). Exception handling is not designed to process problems associated with **asynchronous events** (e.g., disk I/O completions, network message arrivals, mouse clicks and keystrokes), which occur in parallel with, and *independent of*, the program's flow of control.

Software Engineering Observation 11.3

Incorporate your exception-handling and error-recovery strategy into your system from the inception of the design process—including these after a system has been implemented can be difficult.

Software Engineering Observation 11.4

Exception handling provides a single, uniform technique for documenting, detecting and recovering from errors. This helps programmers working on large projects understand each other's error-processing code.

Software Engineering Observation 11.5

A great variety of situations can generate exceptions—some exceptions are easier to recover from than others.

Software Engineering Observation 11.6

Sometimes you can prevent an exception by validating data first. For example, before you perform integer division, you can ensure that the denominator is not zero, which prevents the `ArithmeticException` that occurs when you divide by zero.

11.5 Java Exception Hierarchy

All Java exception classes inherit directly or indirectly from class **`Exception`**, forming an *inheritance hierarchy*. You can extend this hierarchy with your own exception classes.

Figure 11.4 shows a small portion of the inheritance hierarchy for class **`Throwable`** (a subclass of `Object`), which is the superclass of class `Exception`. Only `Throwable` objects can be used with the exception-handling mechanism. Class `Throwable` has two direct subclasses: `Exception` and `Error`. Class `Exception` and its subclasses—for example, `RuntimeException` (package `java.lang`) and `IOException` (package `java.io`)—represent exceptional situations that can occur in a Java program and that can be caught by the application. Class **`Error`** and its subclasses represent *abnormal situations* that happen in the JVM. Most `Error`*s happen infrequently and should not be caught by applications—it's usually not possible for applications to recover from* `Error`*s.*

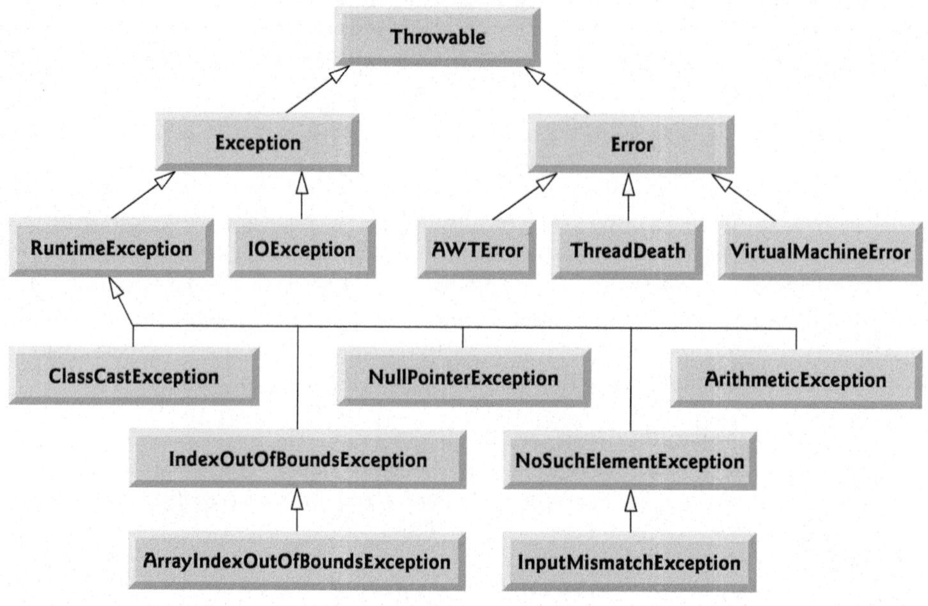

Fig. 11.4 | Portion of class `Throwable`'s inheritance hierarchy.

The Java exception hierarchy contains hundreds of classes. Information about Java's exception classes can be found throughout the Java API. You can view `Throwable`'s documentation at

```
http://docs.oracle.com/javase/8/docs/api/java/lang/Throwable.html
```

From there, you can look at this class's subclasses to get more information about Java's `Exception`s and `Error`s.

Checked vs. Unchecked Exceptions

Java distinguishes between **checked exceptions** and **unchecked exceptions**. This distinction is important, because the Java compiler enforces special requirements for *checked* exceptions (discussed momentarily). An exception's type determines whether it's checked or unchecked.

`RuntimeException`s Are Unchecked Exceptions

All exception types that are direct or indirect subclasses of **`RuntimeException`** (package `java.lang`) are *unchecked* exceptions. These are typically caused by defects in your program's code. Examples of unchecked exceptions include:

- `ArrayIndexOutOfBoundsException`s (discussed in Chapter 7)—You can avoid these by ensuring that your array indices are always greater than or equal to 0 and less than the array's `length`.
- `ArithmeticException`s (shown in Fig. 11.3)—You can avoid the `ArithmeticException` that occurs when you divide by zero by checking the denominator to determine whether it's 0 *before* performing the calculation.

Classes that inherit directly or indirectly from class `Error` (Fig. 11.4) are *unchecked*, because `Errors` typically are unrecoverable, so your program should not even attempt to deal with them. For example, the documentation for `VirtualMachineError` says that these are "thrown to indicate that the Java Virtual Machine is broken or has run out of resources necessary for it to continue operating." At this point, there's nothing your program can do.

Checked Exceptions

All classes that inherit from class `Exception` but *not* directly or indirectly from class `RuntimeException` are considered to be *checked* exceptions. Such exceptions are typically caused by conditions that are not under the control of the program—for example, in file processing, the program can't open a file if it does not exist.

The Compiler and Checked Exceptions

The compiler checks each method call and method declaration to determine whether the method throws a checked exception. If so, the compiler verifies that the checked exception is *caught* or is *declared* in a `throws` clause—this is known as the **catch-or-declare requirement**. We show how to catch or declare checked exceptions in the next several examples. Recall from Section 11.3 that the `throws` clause specifies the exceptions a method throws. Such exceptions are not caught in the method's body. To satisfy the *catch* part of the *catch-or-declare requirement*, the code that generates the exception must be wrapped in a `try` block and must provide a `catch` handler for the checked-exception type (or one of its superclasses). To satisfy the *declare* part of the catch-or-declare requirement, the method containing the code that generates the exception must provide a `throws` clause containing the checked-exception type after its parameter list and before its method body. If the catch-or-declare requirement is not satisfied, the compiler will issue an error message. This forces you to think about the problems that may occur when a method that throws checked exceptions is called.

Error-Prevention Tip 11.2

You must deal with checked exceptions. This results in more robust code than would be created if you were able to simply ignore them.

Common Programming Error 11.2

If a subclass method overrides a superclass method, it's an error for the subclass method to list more exceptions in its `throws` *clause than the superclass method does. However, a subclass's* `throws` *clause can contain a subset of a superclass's* `throws` *clause.*

Software Engineering Observation 11.7

If your method calls other methods that throw checked exceptions, those exceptions must be caught or declared. If an exception can be handled meaningfully in a method, the method should catch the exception rather than declare it.

Software Engineering Observation 11.8

Checked exceptions represent problems from which programs often can recover, so programmers are required to deal with them.

The Compiler and Unchecked Exceptions

Unlike checked exceptions, the Java compiler does *not* examine the code to determine whether an unchecked exception is caught or declared. Unchecked exceptions typically can be *prevented* by proper coding. For example, the unchecked `ArithmeticException` thrown by method `quotient` (lines 9–12) in Fig. 11.3 can be avoided if the method ensures that the denominator is not zero *before* performing the division. Unchecked exceptions are *not* required to be listed in a method's `throws` clause—even if they are, it's *not* required that such exceptions be caught by an application.

Software Engineering Observation 11.9

Although the compiler does not enforce the `catch-or-declare` *requirement for unchecked exceptions, provide appropriate exception-handling code when it's known that such exceptions might occur. For example, a program should process the* `NumberFormatException` *from* `Integer` *method* `parseInt`*, even though* `NumberFormatException` *is an indirect subclass of* `RuntimeException` *(and thus an unchecked exception). This makes your programs more robust.*

Catching Subclass Exceptions

If a `catch` handler is written to catch *superclass* exception objects, it can also catch all objects of that class's *subclasses.* This enables `catch` to handle related exceptions polymorphically. You can catch each subclass individually if they require different processing.

Only the First Matching `catch` *Executes*

If *multiple* `catch` blocks match a particular exception type, only the *first* matching `catch` block executes when an exception of that type occurs. It's a compilation error to catch the *exact same type* in two different `catch` blocks associated with a particular `try` block. However, there can be several `catch` blocks that match an exception—i.e., several `catch` blocks whose types are the same as the exception type or a superclass of that type. For example, we could follow a `catch` block for type `ArithmeticException` with a `catch` block for type `Exception`—both would match `ArithmeticException`s, but only the first matching `catch` block would execute.

Common Programming Error 11.3

Placing a `catch` *block for a superclass exception type before other* `catch` *blocks that catch subclass exception types would prevent those* `catch` *blocks from executing, so a compilation error occurs.*

Error-Prevention Tip 11.3

Catching subclass types individually is subject to error if you forget to test for one or more of the subclass types explicitly; catching the superclass guarantees that objects of all subclasses will be caught. Positioning a `catch` *block for the superclass type after all other subclass* `catch` *blocks ensures that all subclass exceptions are eventually caught.*

Software Engineering Observation 11.10

In industry, throwing or catching type `Exception` *is discouraged—we use it in this chapter simply to demonstrate exception-handling mechanics. In subsequent chapters, we generally throw and catch more specific exception types.*

11.6 `finally` Block

Programs that obtain certain resources must return them to the system to avoid so-called **resource leaks.** In programming languages such as C and C++, the most common resource leak is a *memory leak.* Java performs automatic *garbage collection* of memory no longer used by programs, thus avoiding most memory leaks. However, other types of resource leaks can occur. For example, files, database connections and network connections that are not closed properly after they're no longer needed might not be available for use in other programs.

Error-Prevention Tip 11.4

A subtle issue is that Java does not entirely eliminate memory leaks. Java will not garbage-collect an object until there are no remaining references to it. Thus, if you erroneously keep references to unwanted objects, memory leaks can occur.

The optional `finally` block (sometimes referred to as the **`finally` clause**) consists of the `finally` keyword, followed by code enclosed in curly braces. If it's present, it's placed after the last `catch` block. If there are no `catch` blocks, the `finally` block is required and immediately follows the `try` block.

When the `finally` Block Executes

The `finally` block will execute *whether or not* an exception is thrown in the corresponding `try` block. The `finally` block also will execute if a `try` block exits by using a `return`, `break` or `continue` statement or simply by reaching its closing right brace. The one case in which the `finally` block will *not* execute is if the application *exits early* from a `try` block by calling method **`System.exit`**. This method, which we demonstrate in Chapter 15, *immediately* terminates an application.

If an exception that occurs in a `try` block cannot be caught by one of that `try` block's `catch` handlers, the program skips the rest of the `try` block and control proceeds to the `finally` block. Then the program passes the exception to the next outer `try` block—normally in the calling method—where an associated `catch` block might catch it. This process can occur through many levels of `try` blocks. Also, the exception could go *uncaught* (as we discussed in Section 11.3).

If a `catch` block throws an exception, the `finally` block still executes. Then the exception is passed to the next outer `try` block—again, normally in the calling method.

Releasing Resources in a `finally` Block

Because a `finally` block always executes, it typically contains *resource-release code.* Suppose a resource is allocated in a `try` block. If no exception occurs, the `catch` blocks are *skipped* and control proceeds to the `finally` block, which frees the resource. Control then proceeds to the first statement after the `finally` block. If an exception occurs in the `try` block, the `try` block *terminates.* If the program catches the exception in one of the corresponding `catch` blocks, it processes the exception, then the `finally` block *releases the resource* and control proceeds to the first statement after the `finally` block. If the program doesn't catch the exception, the `finally` block *still* releases the resource and an attempt is made to catch the exception in a calling method.

Error-Prevention Tip 11.5

The `finally` block is an ideal place to release resources acquired in a `try` block (such as opened files), which helps eliminate resource leaks.

Performance Tip 11.1

Always release a resource explicitly and at the earliest possible moment at which it's no longer needed. This makes resources available for reuse as early as possible, thus improving resource utilization and program performance.

Demonstrating the `finally` Block

Figure 11.5 demonstrates that the `finally` block executes even if an exception is *not* thrown in the corresponding `try` block. The program contains `static` methods `main` (lines 5–14), `throwException` (lines 17–35) and `doesNotThrowException` (lines 38–50). Methods `throwException` and `doesNotThrowException` are declared `static`, so `main` can call them directly without instantiating a `UsingExceptions` object.

```
1  // Fig. 11.5: UsingExceptions.java
2  // try...catch...finally exception handling mechanism.
3
4  public class UsingExceptions {
5     public static void main(String[] args) {
6        try {
7           throwException();
8        }
9        catch (Exception exception) { // exception thrown by throwException
10          System.err.println("Exception handled in main");
11       }
12
13       doesNotThrowException();
14    }
15
16    // demonstrate try...catch...finally
17    public static void throwException() throws Exception {
18       try { // throw an exception and immediately catch it
19          System.out.println("Method throwException");
20          throw new Exception(); // generate exception
21       }
22       catch (Exception exception) { // catch exception thrown in try
23          System.err.println(
24             "Exception handled in method throwException");
25          throw exception; // rethrow for further processing
26
27          // code here would not be reached; would cause compilation errors
28
29       }
30       finally { // executes regardless of what occurs in try...catch
31          System.err.println("Finally executed in throwException");
32       }
33
```

Fig. 11.5 | `try`...`catch`...`finally` exception-handling mechanism. (Part 1 of 2.)

```
34          // code here would not be reached; would cause compilation errors
35       }
36
37       // demonstrate finally when no exception occurs
38       public static void doesNotThrowException() {
39          try { // try block does not throw an exception
40             System.out.println("Method doesNotThrowException");
41          }
42          catch (Exception exception) { // does not execute
43             System.err.println(exception);
44          }
45          finally { // executes regardless of what occurs in try...catch
46             System.err.println("Finally executed in doesNotThrowException");
47          }
48
49          System.out.println("End of method doesNotThrowException");
50       }
51    }
```

```
Method throwException
Exception handled in method throwException
Finally executed in throwException
Exception handled in main
Method doesNotThrowException
Finally executed in doesNotThrowException
End of method doesNotThrowException
```

Fig. 11.5 | `try`...`catch`...`finally` exception-handling mechanism. (Part 2 of 2.)

`System.out` and `System.err` are **streams**—sequences of bytes. While `System.out` (known as the **standard output stream**) displays a program's output, `System.err` (known as the **standard error stream**) displays a program's errors. Output from these streams can be *redirected* (i.e., sent to somewhere other than the *command prompt*, such as to a *file*). Using two different streams enables you to easily *separate* error messages from other output. For example, data output from `System.err` could be sent to a log file, while data output from `System.out` can be displayed on the screen. For simplicity, this chapter will *not* redirect output from `System.err` but will display such messages to the *command prompt*. You'll learn more about input/output streams in Chapter 15.

Throwing Exceptions Using the `throw` *Statement*

Method `main` (Fig. 11.5) begins executing, enters its `try` block and immediately calls method `throwException` (line 7). Method `throwException` throws an `Exception`. The statement at line 20 is known as a **`throw` statement**—it's executed to indicate that an exception has occurred. So far, you've caught only exceptions thrown by called methods. You can throw exceptions yourself by using the `throw` statement. Just as with exceptions thrown by the Java API's methods, this indicates to client applications that an error has occurred. A `throw` statement specifies an object to be thrown. The operand of a `throw` can be of any class derived from class `Throwable`.

Software Engineering Observation 11.11

When `toString` is invoked on any `Throwable` object, its resulting `String` includes the descriptive `string` that was supplied to the constructor, or simply the class name if no `string` was supplied.

Software Engineering Observation 11.12

An exception can be thrown without containing information about the problem that occurred. In this case, simply knowing that an exception of a particular type occurred may provide sufficient information for the handler to process the problem correctly.

Software Engineering Observation 11.13

Throw exceptions from constructors to indicate that the constructor parameters are not valid—this prevents an object from being created in an invalid state.

Rethrowing Exceptions

Line 25 of Fig. 11.5 **rethrows the exception**. Exceptions are rethrown when a `catch` block, upon receiving an exception, decides either that it cannot process that exception or that it can only partially process it. Rethrowing an exception defers the exception handling (or perhaps a portion of it) to another `catch` block associated with an outer `try` statement. An exception is rethrown by using the **`throw` keyword**, followed by a reference to the exception object that was just caught. Exceptions cannot be rethrown from a `finally` block, as the exception parameter (a local variable) from the `catch` block no longer exists.

When a rethrow occurs, the *next enclosing `try` block* detects the rethrown exception, and that `try` block's `catch` blocks attempt to handle it. In this case, the next enclosing `try` block is found at lines 6–8 in method `main`. Before the rethrown exception is handled, however, the `finally` block (lines 30–32) executes. Then method `main` detects the rethrown exception in the `try` block and handles it in the `catch` block (lines 9–11).

Next, `main` calls method `doesNotThrowException` (line 13). No exception is thrown in `doesNotThrowException`'s `try` block (lines 39–41), so the program skips the `catch` block (lines 42–44), but the `finally` block (lines 45–47) nevertheless executes. Control proceeds to the statement after the `finally` block (line 49). Then control returns to `main` and the program terminates.

Common Programming Error 11.4

If an exception has not been caught when control enters a `finally` block and the `finally` block throws an exception that's not caught in the `finally` block, the first exception will be lost *and the exception from the `finally` block will be returned to the calling method.*

Error-Prevention Tip 11.6

Avoid placing in a `finally` block code that can `throw` an exception. If such code is required, enclose the code in a `try...catch` within the `finally` block.

Common Programming Error 11.5

Assuming that an exception thrown from a `catch` block will be processed by that `catch` block or any other `catch` block associated with the same `try` statement can lead to logic errors.

Good Programming Practice 11.1

Exception handling removes error-processing code from the main line of a program's code to improve program clarity. Do not place `try...catch... finally` *around every statement that may throw an exception. This decreases readability. Rather, place one* `try` *block around a significant portion of your code, follow the* `try` *with* `catch` *blocks that handle each possible exception and follow the* `catch` *blocks with a single* `finally` *block (if one is required).*

11.7 Stack Unwinding and Obtaining Information from an Exception

When an exception is thrown but *not caught* in a particular method, the method-call stack is "unwound," and an attempt is made to `catch` the exception in the next outer `try` block. This process is called **stack unwinding**. Unwinding the method-call stack means that the method in which the exception was not caught *terminates*, all local variables in that method *go out of scope* and control returns to the statement that originally invoked that method. If a `try` block encloses that statement, an attempt is made to `catch` the exception. If a `try` block does not enclose that statement or if the exception is not caught, stack unwinding occurs again. Figure 11.6 demonstrates stack unwinding, and the exception handler in `main` shows how to access the data in an exception object.

```java
// Fig. 11.6: UsingExceptions.java
// Stack unwinding and obtaining data from an exception object.

public class UsingExceptions {
   public static void main(String[] args) {
      try {
         method1();
      }
      catch (Exception exception) { // catch exception thrown in method1
         System.err.printf("%s%n%n", exception.getMessage());
         exception.printStackTrace();

         // obtain the stack-trace information
         StackTraceElement[] traceElements = exception.getStackTrace();

         System.out.printf("%nStack trace from getStackTrace:%n");
         System.out.println("Class\t\tFile\t\t\tLine\tMethod");

         // loop through traceElements to get exception description
         for (StackTraceElement element : traceElements) {
            System.out.printf("%s\t", element.getClassName());
            System.out.printf("%s\t", element.getFileName());
            System.out.printf("%s\t", element.getLineNumber());
            System.out.printf("%s%n", element.getMethodName());
         }
      }
   }
```

Fig. 11.6 | Stack unwinding and obtaining data from an exception object. (Part 1 of 2.)

```
28
29    // call method2; throw exceptions back to main
30    public static void method1() throws Exception {
31       method2();
32    }
33
34    // call method3; throw exceptions back to method1
35    public static void method2() throws Exception {
36       method3();
37    }
38
39    // throw Exception back to method2
40    public static void method3() throws Exception {
41       throw new Exception("Exception thrown in method3");
42    }
43 }
```

```
Exception thrown in method3

java.lang.Exception: Exception thrown in method3
        at UsingExceptions.method3(UsingExceptions.java:41)
        at UsingExceptions.method2(UsingExceptions.java:36)
        at UsingExceptions.method1(UsingExceptions.java:31)
        at UsingExceptions.main(UsingExceptions.java:7)

Stack trace from getStackTrace:
Class           File                     Line    Method
UsingExceptions UsingExceptions.java     41      method3
UsingExceptions UsingExceptions.java     36      method2
UsingExceptions UsingExceptions.java     31      method1
UsingExceptions UsingExceptions.java     7       main
```

Fig. 11.6 | Stack unwinding and obtaining data from an exception object. (Part 2 of 2.)

Stack Unwinding

In main, the try block (lines 6–8) calls method1 (declared at lines 30–32), which in turn calls method2 (declared at lines 35–37), which in turn calls method3 (declared at lines 40–42). Line 41 in method3 throws an Exception object—this is the *throw point.* Because the throw statement is *not* enclosed in a try block, *stack unwinding* occurs—method3 terminates at line 41, then returns control to the statement in method2 that invoked method3 (i.e., line 36). Because *no* try block encloses line 36, *stack unwinding* occurs again—method2 terminates at line 36 and returns control to the statement in method1 that invoked method2 (i.e., line 31). Because *no* try block encloses line 31, *stack unwinding* occurs one more time—method1 terminates at line 31 and returns control to the statement in main that invoked method1 (i.e., line 7). The try block at lines 6–8 encloses this statement. The exception has not been handled, so the try block terminates and the first matching catch block (lines 9–26) catches and processes the exception. If there were no matching catch blocks, and the exception is *not declared* in each method that throws it, a compilation error would occur—main does not have a throws clause because main catches the exception. Remember that this is not always the case—for *unchecked* exceptions, the application will compile, but it will run with unexpected results.

Obtaining Data from an Exception Object

All exceptions derive from class `Throwable`, which has a **`printStackTrace`** method that outputs to the standard error stream the *stack trace* (discussed in Section 11.2). Often this is helpful in testing and debugging. Class `Throwable` also provides a **`getStackTrace`** method that retrieves the stack-trace information that might be printed by `printStackTrace`. Class `Throwable`'s **`getMessage`** method (inherited by all `Throwable` subclasses) returns the descriptive string stored in an exception. `Throwable` method `toString` (also inherited by all `Throwable` subclasses) returns a `String` containing the name of the exception's class and a descriptive message.

An exception that's not caught in an application causes Java's *default exception handler* to run. This displays the name of the exception, a descriptive message that indicates the problem that occurred and a complete execution stack trace. In an application with a single thread of execution, the application terminates. In an application with multiple threads, the thread that caused the exception terminates. We discuss multithreading in Chapter 23.

The `catch` handler in Fig. 11.6 (lines 9–26) demonstrates `getMessage`, `printStackTrace` and `getStackTrace`. If we wanted to output the stack-trace information to streams other than the standard error stream, we could use the information returned from `getStackTrace` and output it to another stream or use one of the overloaded versions of method `printStackTrace`. Sending data to other streams is discussed in Chapter 15.

Line 10 invokes the exception's `getMessage` method to get the *exception description*. Line 11 invokes the exception's `printStackTrace` method to output the *stack trace* that indicates where the exception occurred. Line 14 invokes the exception's `getStackTrace` method to obtain the stack-trace information as an array of **`StackTraceElement`** objects. Lines 20–25 get each `StackTraceElement` in the array and invoke its methods **`getClassName`**, **`getFileName`**, **`getLineNumber`** and **`getMethodName`** to get the class name, filename, line number and method name, respectively, for that `StackTraceElement`. Each `StackTraceElement` represents *one* method call on the *method-call stack*.

The program's output shows that the output of `printStackTrace` follows the pattern: *className.methodName(fileName:lineNumber)*, where *className*, *methodName* and *fileName* indicate the names of the class, method and file in which the exception occurred, respectively, and the *lineNumber* indicates where in the file the exception occurred. You saw this in the output for Fig. 11.2. Method `getStackTrace` enables custom processing of the exception information. Compare the output of `printStackTrace` with the output created from the `StackTraceElement`s to see that both contain the same stack-trace information.

Software Engineering Observation 11.14

Occasionally, you might want to ignore an exception by writing a `catch` handler with an empty body. Before doing so, ensure that the exception doesn't indicate a condition that code higher up the stack might want to know about or recover from.

Java SE 9: Stack-Walking API 9

`Throwable` methods `printStackTrace` and `getStackTrace` each process the entire method-call stack. When debugging, this can be inefficient—for example, you may be interested only in stack frames corresponding to methods of a specific class. Java SE 9 introduces the **Stack-Walking API** (class **`StackWalker`** in package `java.lang`), which uses lambdas and streams (introduced in Chapter 17) to access method-call-stack information in a more efficient manner. You can learn more about this API at:

```
http://openjdk.java.net/jeps/259
```

11.8 Chained Exceptions

Sometimes a method responds to an exception by throwing a different exception type that's specific to the current application. If a `catch` block throws a new exception, the original exception's information and stack trace are *lost*. Earlier Java versions provided no mechanism to wrap the original exception information with the new exception's information to provide a complete stack trace showing where the original problem occurred. This made debugging such problems particularly difficult. **Chained exceptions** enable an exception object to maintain the complete stack-trace information from the original exception. Figure 11.7 demonstrates chained exceptions.

```java
// Fig. 11.7: UsingChainedExceptions.java
// Chained exceptions.

public class UsingChainedExceptions {
   public static void main(String[] args) {
      try {
         method1();
      }
      catch (Exception exception) { // exceptions thrown from method1
         exception.printStackTrace();
      }
   }

   // call method2; throw exceptions back to main
   public static void method1() throws Exception {
      try {
         method2();
      }
      catch (Exception exception) { // exception thrown from method2
         throw new Exception("Exception thrown in method1", exception);
      }
   }

   // call method3; throw exceptions back to method1
   public static void method2() throws Exception {
      try {
         method3();
      }
      catch (Exception exception) { // exception thrown from method3
         throw new Exception("Exception thrown in method2", exception);
      }
   }

```

Fig. 11.7 | Chained exceptions. (Part 1 of 2.)

```
34     // throw Exception back to method2
35     public static void method3() throws Exception {
36        throw new Exception("Exception thrown in method3");
37     }
38  }
```

```
java.lang.Exception: Exception thrown in method1
        at UsingChainedExceptions.method1(UsingChainedExceptions.java:17)
        at UsingChainedExceptions.main(UsingChainedExceptions.java:7)
Caused by: java.lang.Exception: Exception thrown in method2
        at UsingChainedExceptions.method2(UsingChainedExceptions.java:27)
        at UsingChainedExceptions.method1(UsingChainedExceptions.java:17)
        ... 1 more
Caused by: java.lang.Exception: Exception thrown in method3
        at UsingChainedExceptions.method3(UsingChainedExceptions.java:36)
        at UsingChainedExceptions.method2(UsingChainedExceptions.java:27)
        ... 2 more
```

Fig. 11.7 | Chained exceptions. (Part 2 of 2.)

Program Flow of Control

The program has four methods—main (lines 5–12), method1 (lines 15–22), method2 (lines 25–32) and method3 (lines 35–37). Line 7 in main's try block calls method1. Line 17 in method1's try block calls method2. Line 27 in method2's try block calls method3. In method3, line 36 throws a new Exception. Because line 36 is not in a try block, method3 terminates, and the exception is returned to the calling method (method2) at line 27. This statement *is* in a try block; therefore, the try block terminates and the exception is caught at lines 29–31. Line 30 in the catch block throws a new exception. We call the Exception constructor with *two* arguments—the second represents the exception that was the original cause of the problem. In this program, that exception occurred at line 36. Because an exception is thrown from the catch block, method2 terminates and returns the new exception to method1 at line 17. Once again, this statement is in a try block, so the try block terminates and the exception is caught at lines 19–21. Line 20 in the catch block throws a new exception and uses the exception that was caught as the second argument to Exception's constructor. Because an exception is thrown from the catch block, method1 terminates and returns the new exception to main at line 7. The try block in main terminates, and the exception is caught at lines 9–11. Line 10 prints a stack trace.

Throwable *Method* **getCause**

For any chained exception, you can get the Throwable that initially caused that exception by calling Throwable method **getCause**.

Program Output

Notice in the program output that the first three lines show the most recent exception that was thrown (i.e., the one from method1 at line 20). The next four lines indicate the exception that was thrown from method2 at line 27. Finally, the last four lines represent the exception that was thrown from method3 at line 36. Also notice that, as you read the output in reverse, it shows how many more chained exceptions remain.

11.9 Declaring New Exception Types

Most Java programmers use *existing* classes from the Java API, third-party vendors and freely available class libraries (usually downloadable from the Internet) to build Java applications. The methods of those classes typically are declared to throw appropriate exceptions when problems occur. You write code that processes these existing exceptions to make your programs more robust.

If you build classes that other programmers will use, it's often appropriate to declare your own exception classes that are specific to the problems that can occur when another programmer uses your reusable classes.

A New Exception Type Must Extend an Existing One

A new exception class must extend an existing exception class to ensure that the class can be used with the exception-handling mechanism. An exception class is like any other class; however, a typical new exception class contains no members other than four constructors:

- one that takes no arguments and passes a default error message `String` to the superclass constructor
- one that receives a customized error message as a `String` and passes it to the superclass constructor
- one that receives a customized error message as a `String` and a `Throwable` (for chaining exceptions) and passes both to the superclass constructor
- one that receives a `Throwable` (for chaining exceptions) and passes it to the superclass constructor.

Good Programming Practice 11.2

Associating each type of serious execution-time malfunction with an appropriately named `Exception` *class improves program clarity.*

Software Engineering Observation 11.15

Most programmers will not need to declare their own exception classes. Before defining your own, study the existing ones in the Java API and try to choose one that already exists. If there is not an appropriate existing class, try to extend a related exception class. For example, if you're creating a new class to represent when a method attempts a division by zero, you might extend class `ArithmeticException` *because division by zero occurs during arithmetic. If the existing classes are not appropriate superclasses for your new exception class, decide whether your new class should be a checked or an unchecked exception class. If clients should be* required *to handle the exception, the new exception class should be a checked exception (i.e., extend* `Exception` *but not* `RuntimeException`*). The client application should be able to reasonably recover from such an exception. If the client code should be able to ignore the exception (i.e., the exception is an unchecked one), the new exception class should extend* `RuntimeException`.

Good Programming Practice 11.3

By convention, all exception-class names should end with the word `Exception`.

11.10 Preconditions and Postconditions

Programmers spend significant amounts of time maintaining and debugging code. To facilitate these tasks and to improve the overall design, you can specify the expected states before and after a method's execution. These states are called preconditions and postconditions, respectively.

Preconditions

A **precondition** must be true when a method is *invoked.* Preconditions describe constraints on method parameters and any other expectations the method has about the current state of a program *just before it begins executing.* If the preconditions are *not* met, then the method's behavior is *undefined*—it may *throw an exception, proceed with an illegal value* or *attempt to recover* from the error. You should not expect consistent behavior if the preconditions are not satisfied.

Postconditions

A **postcondition** is true *after the method successfully returns.* Postconditions describe *constraints on the return value* and any other *side effects* the method may have. When defining a method, you should document all postconditions so that others know what to expect when they call your method, and you should make certain that your method honors all its postconditions if its preconditions are indeed met.

Throwing Exceptions When Preconditions or Postconditions Are Not Met

When their preconditions or postconditions are not met, methods typically throw exceptions. As an example, examine `String` method `charAt`, which has one `int` parameter—an index in the `String`. For a precondition, method `charAt` assumes that `index` is greater than or equal to zero and less than the length of the `String`. If the precondition is met, the postcondition states that the method will return the character at the position in the `String` specified by the parameter `index`. Otherwise, the method throws an `IndexOutOfBoundsException`. We trust that method `charAt` satisfies its postcondition, provided that we meet the precondition. We need not be concerned with the details of how the method actually retrieves the character at the index.

Typically, a method's preconditions and postconditions are described as part of its specification. When designing your own methods, you typically state the preconditions and postconditions in a comment before the method declaration.

11.11 Assertions

When implementing and debugging a class, it's sometimes useful to state conditions that should be true at a particular point in a method. These conditions, called **assertions**, help ensure a program's validity by catching potential bugs and identifying possible logic errors during development. Preconditions and postconditions are two types of assertions. Preconditions are assertions about a program's state when a method is invoked, and postconditions are assertions about its state after a method finishes.

While assertions can be stated as comments to guide you during program development, Java includes two versions of the **assert** statement for validating assertions programatically. The assert statement evaluates a boolean expression and, if false, throws an **AssertionError** (a subclass of Error). The first form of the assert statement is

```
assert expression;
```

which throws an AssertionError if *expression* is false. The second form is

```
assert expression1 : expression2;
```

which evaluates *expression1* and throws an AssertionError with *expression2* as the error message if *expression1* is false.

You can use assertions to implement *preconditions* and *postconditions* programmatically or to verify any other *intermediate* states that help you ensure that your code is working correctly. Figure 11.8 demonstrates the assert statement. Line 9 prompts the user to enter a number between 0 and 10, then line 10 reads the number. Line 13 determines whether the user entered a number within the valid range. If the number is out of range, the assert statement reports an error; otherwise, the program proceeds normally.

```
1  // Fig. 11.8: AssertTest.java
2  // Checking with assert that a value is within range
3  import java.util.Scanner;
4
5  public class AssertTest {
6     public static void main(String[] args) {
7        Scanner input = new Scanner(System.in);
8
9        System.out.print("Enter a number between 0 and 10: ");
10       int number = input.nextInt();
11
12       // assert that the value is >= 0 and <= 10
13       assert (number >= 0 && number <= 10) : "bad number: " + number;
14
15       System.out.printf("You entered %d%n", number);
16    }
17 }
```

```
Enter a number between 0 and 10: 5
You entered 5
```

```
Enter a number between 0 and 10: 50
Exception in thread "main" java.lang.AssertionError: bad number: 50
        at AssertTest.main(AssertTest.java:13)
```

Fig. 11.8 | Checking with assert that a value is within range.

You use assertions primarily for debugging and identifying logic errors in an application. You must explicitly enable assertions when executing a program, because they reduce performance and are unnecessary for the program's user. To do so, use the `java` command's `-ea` command-line option, as in

```
java -ea AssertTest
```

Software Engineering Observation 11.16

Users shouldn't encounter `AssertionErrors`*—these should be used only during program development. For this reason, you shouldn't catch* `AssertionErrors`*. Instread, allow the program to terminate, so you can see the error message, then locate and fix the source of the problem. You should not use* `assert` *to indicate runtime problems in production code (as we did in Fig. 11.8 for demonstration purposes)—use the exception mechanism for this purpose.*

11.12 try-with-Resources: Automatic Resource Deallocation

Typically *resource-release code* should be placed in a `finally` block to ensure that a resource is released, regardless of whether there were exceptions when the resource was used in the corresponding `try` block. An alternative notation—the **try-with-resources** statement—simplifies writing code in which you obtain one or more resources, use them in a `try` block and release them in a corresponding `finally` block. For example, a file-processing application could process a file with a `try`-with-resources statement to ensure that the file is closed properly when it's no longer needed—we demonstrate this in Chapter 15. Each resource must be an object of a class that implements the **`AutoCloseable`** interface and thus provides a `close` method.

The general form of a `try`-with-resources statement is

```
try (ClassName theObject = new ClassName()) {
   // use theObject here, then release its resources at
   // the end of the try block
}
catch (Exception e) {
   // catch exceptions that occur while using the resource
}
```

where *ClassName* is a class that implements `AutoCloseable`. This code creates a *ClassName* object, uses it in the `try` block, then calls its `close` method *at the end of the* `try` *block—or, if an exception occurs, at the end of a* `catch` *block*—to release the object's resources. You can create multiple `AutoCloseable` objects in the parentheses following `try` by separating them with a semicolon (`;`). You'll see examples of the `try`-with-resources statement in Chapters 15 and 24.

Java SE 9: `try`*-with-Resources Can Use Effectively* `final` *Variables*

Java SE 8 introduced **effectively `final`** local variables. If the compiler can *infer* that the 8
variable could have been declared `final`, because its enclosing method never modifies the variable after it's declared and initialized, then the variable is effectively `final`. Such variables frequently are used with lambdas (Chapter 17, Lambdas and Streams).

As of Java SE 9, you can create an `AutoCloseable` object and assign it to a local variable 9
that's explicitly declared `final` or that's effectively `final`. Then, you can use it in a `try`-with-resources statement that releases the object's resources at the end of the `try` block.

```
ClassName theObject = new ClassName();

try (theObject) {
   // use theObject here, then release its resources at
   // the end of the try block
}
catch (Exception e) {
   // catch exceptions that occur while using the resource
}
```

As before, you can separate with a semicolon (;) multiple `AutoCloseable` objects in the parentheses following `try`. This simplifies the `try`-with-resources statement's code, especially for cases in which the statement uses and releases multiple `AutoCloseable` objects.

11.13 Wrap-Up

In this chapter, you learned how to use exception handling to deal with errors. You learned that exception handling enables you to remove error-handling code from the "main line" of the program's execution. We showed how to use `try` blocks to enclose code that may throw an exception, and how to use `catch` blocks to deal with exceptions that may arise.

You learned about the termination model of exception handling, which dictates that after an exception is handled, program control does not return to the throw point. We discussed checked vs. unchecked exceptions, and how to specify with the `throws` clause the exceptions that a method might throw.

You learned how to use the `finally` block to release resources whether or not an exception occurs. You also learned how to throw and rethrow exceptions. We showed how to obtain information about an exception using methods `printStackTrace`, `getStackTrace` and `getMessage`. Next, we presented chained exceptions, which allow you to wrap original exception information with new exception information. Then, we showed how to create your own exception classes.

We introduced preconditions and postconditions to help programmers using your methods understand conditions that must be true when the method is called and when it returns, respectively. When preconditions and postconditions are not met, methods typically throw exceptions. We discussed the `assert` statement and how it can be used to help you debug your programs. In particular, `assert` can be used to ensure that preconditions and postconditions are met.

We also introduced multi-`catch` for processing several types of exceptions in the same `catch` handler and the `try`-with-resources statement for automatically deallocating a resource after it's used in the `try` block. In the next chapter, we take a deeper look at graphical user interfaces (GUIs).

Summary

Section 11.1 Introduction

- An exception is an indication of a problem that occurs during a program's execution.
- Exception handling enables programmers to create applications that can resolve exceptions.

Section 11.2 Example: Divide by Zero without Exception Handling

- Exceptions are thrown (p. 457) when a method detects a problem and is unable to handle it.

- An exception's stack trace (p. 458) includes the exception's name in a message that indicates the problem that occurred and the complete method-call stack at the time the exception occurred.
- The point in the program at which an exception occurs is called the throw point (p. 459).

Section 11.3 Example: Handling `ArithmeticExceptions` *and* `InputMismatchExceptions`

- A `try` block (p. 461) encloses code that might `throw` an exception and code that should not execute if that exception occurs.
- Exceptions may surface through explicitly mentioned code in a `try` block, through calls to other methods or even through deeply nested method calls initiated by code in the `try` block.
- A `catch` block (p. 462) begins with keyword `catch` and an exception parameter followed by a block of code that handles the exception. This code executes when the `try` block detects the exception.
- At least one `catch` block or a `finally` block (p. 462) must immediately follow the `try` block.
- A `catch` block specifies in parentheses an exception parameter identifying the exception type to handle. The parameter's name enables the `catch` block to interact with a caught exception object.
- An uncaught exception (p. 463) is an exception that occurs for which there are no matching `catch` blocks. An uncaught exception will cause a program to terminate early if that program contains only one thread. Otherwise, only the thread in which the exception occurred will terminate. The rest of the program will run but possibly with adverse results.
- Multi-`catch` (p. 463) enables you to catch multiple exception types in a single `catch` handler and perform the same task for each type of exception. The syntax for a multi-`catch` uses a vertical bar (`|`) to separate the types, as in:

```
catch (Type1 | Type2 | Type3 e)
```

- If an exception occurs in a `try` block, the `try` block terminates immediately and program control transfers to the first `catch` block with a parameter type that matches the thrown exception's type.
- After an exception is handled, program control does not return to the throw point, because the `try` block has expired. This is known as the termination model of exception handling (p. 463).
- If there are multiple matching `catch` blocks when an exception occurs, only the first is executed.
- A `throws` clause (p. 464) specifies after the method's parameter list and before the method body a comma-separated list of exceptions that the method might throw.

Section 11.4 When to Use Exception Handling

- Exception handling processes synchronous errors (p. 465), which occur when a statement executes.
- Exception handling is not designed to process problems associated with asynchronous events (p. 465), which occur in parallel with, and independent of, the program's flow of control.

Section 11.5 Java Exception Hierarchy

- All Java exception classes inherit directly or indirectly from class `Exception`.
- Programmers can extend the Java exception hierarchy with their own exception classes.
- Class `Throwable` is the superclass of class `Exception` and is therefore also the superclass of all exceptions. Only `Throwable` objects can be used with the exception-handling mechanism.
- Class `Throwable` (p. 465) has two subclasses: `Exception` and `Error`.

- Class `Exception` and its subclasses represent problems that could occur in a Java program and be caught by the application.
- Class `Error` and its subclasses represent problems that could happen in the Java runtime system. `Error`s happen infrequently and typically should not be caught by an application.
- Java distinguishes between two categories of exceptions (p. 466): checked and unchecked.
- The Java compiler does not check to determine if an unchecked exception is caught or declared. Unchecked exceptions typically can be prevented by proper coding.
- Subclasses of `RuntimeException` represent unchecked exceptions. All exception types that inherit from class `Exception` but not from `RuntimeException` (p. 466) are checked.
- If a `catch` block is written to catch exception objects of a superclass type, it can also catch all objects of that class's subclasses. This allows for polymorphic processing of related exceptions.

Section 11.6 `finally` Block

- Programs that obtain certain types of resources must return them to the system to avoid so-called resource leaks (p. 469). Resource-release code typically is placed in a `finally` block (p. 469).
- The `finally` block is optional. If it's present, it's placed after the last `catch` block.
- The `finally` block will execute whether or not an exception is thrown in the corresponding `try` block or any of its corresponding `catch` blocks.
- If an exception cannot be caught by one of that `try` block's associated `catch` handlers, control proceeds to the `finally` block. Then the exception is passed to the next outer `try` block.
- If a `catch` block throws an exception, the `finally` block still executes. Then the exception is passed to the next outer `try` block.
- A `throw` statement (p. 471) can throw any `Throwable` object.
- Exceptions are rethrown (p. 472) when a `catch` block, upon receiving an exception, decides either that it cannot process that exception or that it can only partially process it. Rethrowing an exception defers the exception handling (or perhaps a portion of it) to another `catch` block.
- When a rethrow occurs, the next enclosing `try` block detects the rethrown exception, and that `try` block's `catch` blocks attempt to handle it.

Section 11.7 Stack Unwinding and Obtaining Information from an Exception

- When an exception is thrown but not caught in a particular method, the method-call stack is unwound, and an attempt is made to `catch` the exception in the next outer `try` statement.
- Class `Throwable` offers a `printStackTrace` method that prints the method-call stack. Often, this is helpful in testing and debugging.
- Class `Throwable` also provides a `getStackTrace` method that obtains the same stack-trace information that's printed by `printStackTrace` (p. 475).
- Class `Throwable`'s `getMessage` method (p. 475) returns the descriptive string stored in an exception.
- Method `getStackTrace` (p. 475) obtains the stack-trace information as an array of `StackTraceElement` objects. Each `StackTraceElement` represents one method call on the method-call stack.
- `StackTraceElement` methods (p. 475) `getClassName`, `getFileName`, `getLineNumber` and `getMethodName` get the class name, filename, line number and method name, respectively.

Section 11.8 Chained Exceptions

- Chained exceptions (p. 476) enable an exception object to maintain the complete stack-trace information, including information about previous exceptions that caused the current exception.

Section 11.9 Declaring New Exception Types

- A new exception class must extend an existing exception class to ensure that the class can be used with the exception-handling mechanism.

Section 11.10 Preconditions and Postconditions

- A method's precondition (p. 479) must be true when the method is invoked.
- A method's postcondition (p. 479) is true after the method successfully returns.
- When designing your own methods, you should state the preconditions and postconditions in a comment before the method declaration.

Section 11.11 Assertions

- Assertions (p. 479) help catch potential bugs and identify possible logic errors.
- The `assert` statement (p. 480) allows for validating assertions programmatically.
- To enable assertions at runtime, use the `-ea` switch when running the `java` command.

Section 11.12 `try`*-with-Resources: Automatic Resource Deallocation*

- The `try`-with-resources statement (p. 481) simplifies writing code in which you obtain a resource, use it in a `try` block and release the resource in a corresponding `finally` block. Instead, you allocate the resource in the parentheses following the `try` keyword and use the resource in the `try` block; then the statement implicitly calls the resource's `close` method at the end of the `try` block.
- Each resource specified in the parentheses following the `try` keyword must be an object of a class that implements the `AutoCloseable` interface (p. 481)—such a class has a `close` method.
- You can allocate multiple resources in the parentheses following `try` by separating them with a semicolon (`;`).

Self-Review Exercises

11.1 List five common examples of exceptions.

11.2 Why are exceptions particularly appropriate for dealing with errors produced by methods of classes in the Java API?

11.3 What is a "resource leak"?

11.4 If no exceptions are thrown in a `try` block, where does control proceed when the `try` block completes execution?

11.5 Give a key advantage of using `catch(Exception` *exceptionName*`)`.

11.6 Should a conventional application catch `Error` objects? Explain.

11.7 What happens if no `catch` handler matches the type of a thrown object?

11.8 What happens if several `catch` blocks match the type of the thrown object?

11.9 Why would a programmer specify a superclass type as the type in a `catch` block?

11.10 What is the key reason for using `finally` blocks?

11.11 What happens when a `catch` block throws an `Exception`?

11.12 What does the statement `throw` *exceptionReference* do in a `catch` block?

11.13 What happens to a local reference in a `try` block when that block throws an `Exception`?

Answers to Self-Review Exercises

11.1 Memory exhaustion, array index out of bounds, arithmetic overflow, division by zero, invalid method parameters.

11.2 It's unlikely that methods of classes in the Java API could perform error processing that would meet the unique needs of all users.

11.3 A "resource leak" occurs when an executing program does not properly release a resource when it's no longer needed.

11.4 The `catch` blocks for that `try` statement are skipped, and the program resumes execution after the last `catch` block. If there's a `finally` block, it's executed first; then the program resumes execution after the `finally` block.

11.5 The form `catch(Exception` *exceptionName*) catches any type of exception thrown in a `try` block. An advantage is that no thrown `Exception` can slip by without being caught. You can handle the exception or rethrow it.

11.6 `Errors` are usually serious problems with the underlying Java system; most programs will not want to catch `Errors` because they will not be able to recover from them.

11.7 This causes the search for a match to continue in the next enclosing `try` statement. If there's a `finally` block, it will be executed before the exception goes to the next enclosing `try` statement. If there are no enclosing `try` statements for which there are matching `catch` blocks and the exceptions are declared (or unchecked), a stack trace is printed and the current thread terminates early. If the exceptions are checked, but not caught or declared, compilation errors occur.

11.8 The first matching `catch` block after the `try` block is executed.

11.9 This enables a program to catch related types of exceptions and process them in a uniform manner. However, it's often useful to process the subclass types individually for more precise exception handling.

11.10 The `finally` block is the preferred means for releasing resources to prevent resource leaks.

11.11 First, control passes to the `finally` block if there is one. Then the exception will be processed by a `catch` block (if one exists) associated with an enclosing `try` block (if one exists).

11.12 It rethrows the exception for processing by an exception handler of an enclosing `try` statement, after the `finally` block of the current `try` statement executes.

11.13 The reference goes out of scope. If the referenced object becomes unreachable, the object can be garbage collected.

Exercises

11.14 *(Exceptional Conditions)* List the various exceptional conditions that have occurred in programs throughout this text so far. List as many additional exceptional conditions as you can. For each of these, describe briefly how a program typically would handle the exception by using the exception-handling techniques discussed in this chapter. Typical exceptions include division by zero and array index out of bounds.

11.15 *(Exceptions and Constructor Failure)* Until this chapter, we've found dealing with errors detected by constructors to be a bit awkward. Explain why exception handling is an effective means for dealing with constructor failure.

11.16 *(Catching Exceptions with Superclasses)* Use inheritance to create an exception superclass (called `ExceptionA`) and exception subclasses `ExceptionB` and `ExceptionC`, where `ExceptionB` inherits from `ExceptionA` and `ExceptionC` inherits from `ExceptionB`. Write a program to demonstrate that the `catch` block for type `ExceptionA` catches exceptions of types `ExceptionB` and `ExceptionC`.

11.17 *(Catching Exceptions Using Class* **`Exception`***)* Write a program that demonstrates how various exceptions are caught with

```
catch (Exception exception)
```

This time, define classes `ExceptionA` (which inherits from class `Exception`) and `ExceptionB` (which inherits from class `ExceptionA`). In your program, create `try` blocks that throw exceptions of types `ExceptionA`, `ExceptionB`, `NullPointerException` and `IOException`. All exceptions should be caught with `catch` blocks specifying type `Exception`.

11.18 *(Order of* **`catch`** *Blocks)* Write a program demonstrating that the order of `catch` blocks is important. If you try to catch a superclass exception type before a subclass type, the compiler should generate errors.

11.19 *(Constructor Failure)* Write a program that shows a constructor passing information about constructor failure to an exception handler. Define class `SomeClass`, which throws an `Exception` in the constructor. Your program should try to create an object of type `SomeClass` and catch the exception that's thrown from the constructor.

11.20 *(Rethrowing Exceptions)* Write a program that illustrates rethrowing an exception. Define methods `someMethod` and `someMethod2`. Method `someMethod2` should initially throw an exception. Method `someMethod` should call `someMethod2`, catch the exception and rethrow it. Call `someMethod` from method `main`, and catch the rethrown exception. Print the stack trace of this exception.

11.21 *(Catching Exceptions Using Outer Scopes)* Write a program showing that a method with its own `try` block does not have to catch every possible error generated within the `try`. Some exceptions can slip through to, and be handled in, other scopes.

12 JavaFX Graphical User Interfaces: Part 1

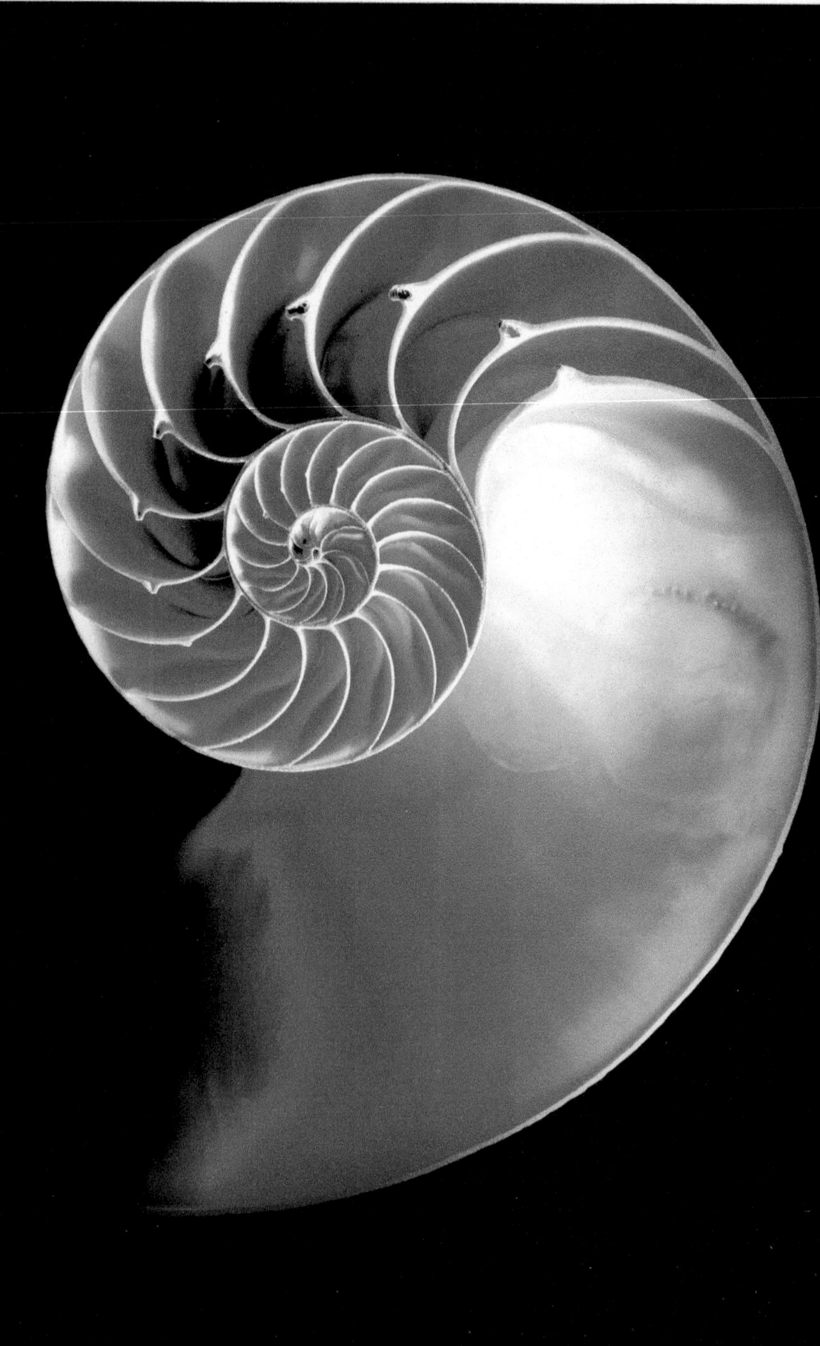

Objectives

In this chapter you'll:

- Build JavaFX GUIs and handle events generated by user interactions with them.
- Understand the structure of a JavaFX app window.
- Use JavaFX Scene Builder to create FXML files that describe JavaFX scenes containing `Labels`, `ImageViews`, `TextFields`, `Sliders` and `Buttons` without writing any code.
- Arrange GUI components using the `VBox` and `GridPane` layout containers.
- Use a controller class to define event handlers for JavaFX FXML GUI.
- Build two JavaFX apps.

Outline

12.1 Introduction

A **graphical user interface** (GUI) presents a user-friendly mechanism for interacting with an app. A GUI (pronounced "GOO-ee") gives an app a distinctive "look-and-feel." GUIs are built from **GUI components**—also called *controls* or *widgets* (short for window gadgets). A GUI component is an object with which the user interacts via the mouse, the keyboard or another form of input, such as voice recognition.

Look-and-Feel Observation 12.1

Providing different apps with consistent, intuitive user-interface components gives users a sense of familiarity with a new app, so that they can learn it more quickly and use it more productively.

History of GUI in Java

Java's original GUI library was the Abstract Window Toolkit (AWT). Swing was added to the platform in Java SE 1.2. Until recently, Swing was the primary Java GUI technology. Swing will remain part of Java and is still widely used. We discuss Swing in online Chapters 26 and 35.

JavaFX is Java's GUI, graphics and multimedia API of the future. Sun Microsystems (acquired by Oracle in 2010) announced JavaFX in 2007 as a competitor to Adobe Flash and Microsoft Silverlight. JavaFX 1.0 was released in 2008. Prior to version 2.0, developers wrote JavaFX apps in JavaFX Script, which compiled to Java bytecode, allowing JavaFX apps to run on the Java Virtual Machine. Starting with version 2.0 in 2011, JavaFX was reimplemented as Java libraries that could be used directly in Java apps. Some of the benefits of JavaFX over Swing include:

- JavaFX is easier to use—it provides one API for client functionality, including GUI, graphics and multimedia (images, animation, audio and video). Swing is only for GUIs, so you need to use other APIs for graphics and multimedia apps.
- With Swing, many IDEs provided GUI design tools for dragging and dropping components onto a layout; however, each IDE produced different code (such as different variable and method names). JavaFX Scene Builder (Section 12.2) can

be used standalone or integrated with many IDEs and it produces the same code regardless of the IDE.

- Though Swing components could be customized, JavaFX gives you complete control over a JavaFX GUI's look-and-feel (Chapter 13) via Cascading Style Sheets (CSS)—the same technology used to style web pages.
- JavaFX has better threading support, which is important for getting the best application performance on today's multi-core systems.
- JavaFX uses the GPU (graphics processing unit) for hardware-accelerated rendering.
- JavaFX supports transformations for repositioning and reorienting JavaFX components, and animations for changing the properties of JavaFX components over time. These can be used to make apps more intuitive and easier to use.
- JavaFX provides multiple upgrade paths for enhancing existing GUIs—Swing GUI capabilities may be embedded into JavaFX apps via class `SwingNode` and JavaFX capabilities may be embedded into Swing apps via class `JFXPanel`.

This chapter introduces JavaFX GUI basics—we present a more detailed treatment of Java FX GUI in the next chapter. Chapter 22 discusses graphics and multimedia. We placed the *Java How to Program, 10/e* Swing and Java 2D chapters on the book's Companion Website—see the inside front cover for Companion Website access instructions.

12.2 JavaFX Scene Builder

Most Java textbooks that introduce GUI programming provide hand-coded GUIs—that is, the authors build the GUIs from scratch in Java code, rather than using a visual GUI design tool. This is due to the fractured Java IDE market—there are many Java IDEs, so authors can't depend on any one IDE being used, and each generates different code.

JavaFX is organized differently. The **Scene Builder** tool is a standalone JavaFX GUI visual layout tool that can also be used with various IDEs, including the most popular ones—Eclipse, IntelliJ IDEA and NetBeans. You can download Scene Builder at:

```
http://gluonhq.com/labs/scene-builder/
```

JavaFX Scene Builder enables you to create GUIs by dragging and dropping GUI components from Scene Builder's library onto a design area, then modifying and styling the GUI—all without writing any code. JavaFX Scene Builder's live editing and preview features allow you to view your GUI as you create and modify it, without compiling and running the app. You can use **Cascading Style Sheets** (CSS) to change the entire look-and-feel of your GUI—a concept sometimes called **skinning**. In Chapter 22, we'll introduce styling with CSS.

FXML (FX Markup Language)

As you create and modify a GUI, JavaFX Scene Builder generates **FXML** (**FX Markup Language**)—an XML vocabulary for defining and arranging JavaFX GUI controls without writing any Java code. XML (eXtensible Markup Language) is a widely used language for describing things—it's readable both by computers and by humans. In JavaFX, FXML concisely describes GUI, graphics and multimedia elements. *You do not need to know FXML or XML to study this chapter.* As you'll see in Section 12.4, JavaFX Scene Builder hides the FXML details from you, so you can focus on defining *what* the GUI should contain without specifying *how* to generate it—this is an example of *declarative programming.*

Software Engineering Observation 12.1

The FXML code is separate from the program logic that's defined in Java source code—this separation of the interface (the GUI) from the implementation (the Java code) makes it easier to debug, modify and maintain JavaFX GUI apps.

12.3 JavaFX App Window Structure

A JavaFX app window consists of several parts (Fig. 12.1).

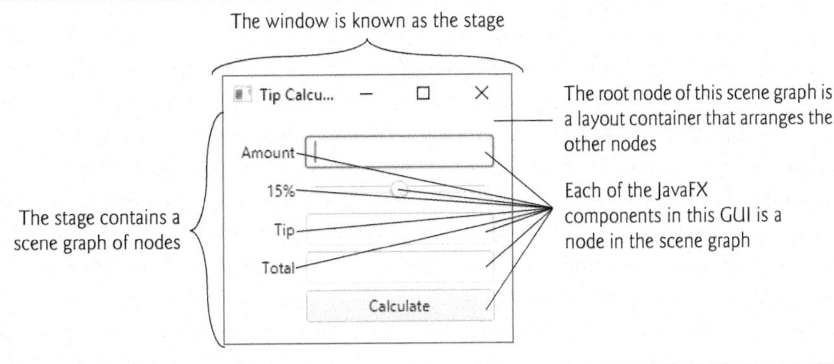

Fig. 12.1 | JavaFX app window parts.

Controls

Controls are GUI components, such as `Labels` that display text, `TextFields` that enable a program to receive user input, `Buttons` that users click to initiate actions, and more.

Stage

The window in which a JavaFX app's GUI is displayed is known as the **stage** and is an instance of class **`Stage`** (package `javafx.stage`).

Scene

The stage contains one active **scene** that defines the GUI as a **scene graph**—a tree data structure of an app's visual elements, such as GUI controls, shapes, images, video, text and more (trees are discussed in Section 21.7). The scene is an instance of class **`Scene`** (package `javafx.scene`).

Nodes

Each visual element in the scene graph is a **node**—an instance of a subclass of **`Node`** (package `javafx.scene`), which defines common attributes and behaviors for all nodes. With the exception of the first node in the scene graph—the **root node**—each node in the scene graph has one parent. Nodes can have transforms (e.g., moving, rotating and scaling), opacity (whether a node is transparent, partially transparent or opaque), effects (e.g., drop shadows, blurs, reflection and lighting) and more that we'll introduce in Chapter 22.

Layout Containers
Nodes that have children are typically **layout containers** that arrange their child nodes in the scene. You'll use two layout containers (`VBox` and `GridPane`) in this chapter and learn several more in Chapters 13–22. The nodes arranged in a layout container are a combination of controls and, in more complex GUIs, possibly other layout containers.

Event Handler and Controller Class
When the user interacts with a control, such as clicking a `Button` or typing text into a `TextField`, the control generates an event. Programs can respond to these events—known as event handling—to specify what should happen when each user interaction occurs. An **event handler** is a method that responds to a user interaction. An FXML GUI's event handlers are defined in a so-called **controller class** (as you'll see in Section 12.5.5).

12.4 Welcome App—Displaying Text and an Image

In this section, *without writing any code*, you'll build a GUI that displays text in a **`Label`** and an image in an **`ImageView`** (Fig. 12.2). You'll use visual-programming techniques to *drag-and-drop* JavaFX components onto Scene Builder's content panel—the design area. Next, you'll use Scene Builder's **Inspector** to configure options, such as the `Label`s's text and font size, and the `ImageView`'s image. Finally, you'll view the completed GUI using Scene Builder's **Show Preview in Window** option. In Section 12.5's **Tip Calculator** app, we'll discuss the Java code necessary to load and display an FXML GUI. Then, in Exercise 12.3, you'll create the Java application that displays the **Welcome** GUI you build in this section.

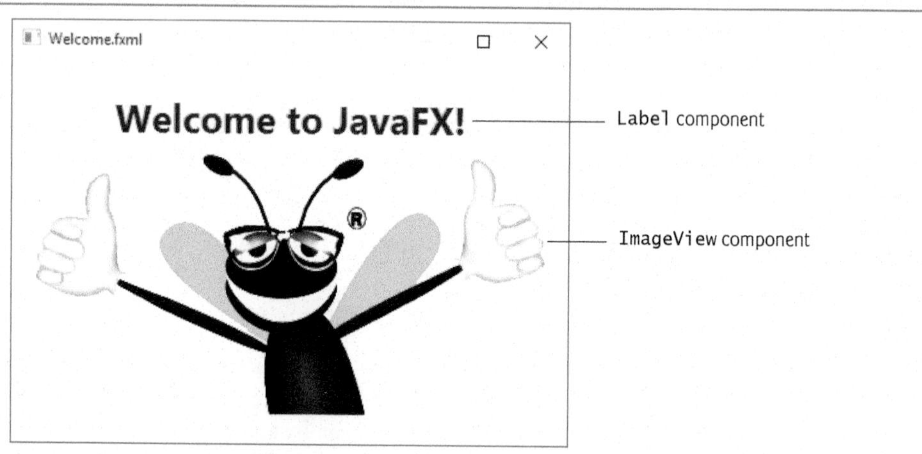

Fig. 12.2 | Final **Welcome** GUI in a preview window on Microsoft Windows 10.

12.4.1 Opening Scene Builder and Creating the File `Welcome.fxml`

Open Scene Builder so that you can create the FXML file that defines the GUI. The window initially appears as shown in Fig. 12.3. **Untitled** at the top of the window indicates that Scene Builder has created a new FXML file that you have not yet saved.[1] Select **File > Save** to display the **Save As** dialog, then select a location in which to store the file, name the file `Welcome.fxml` and click the **Save** button.

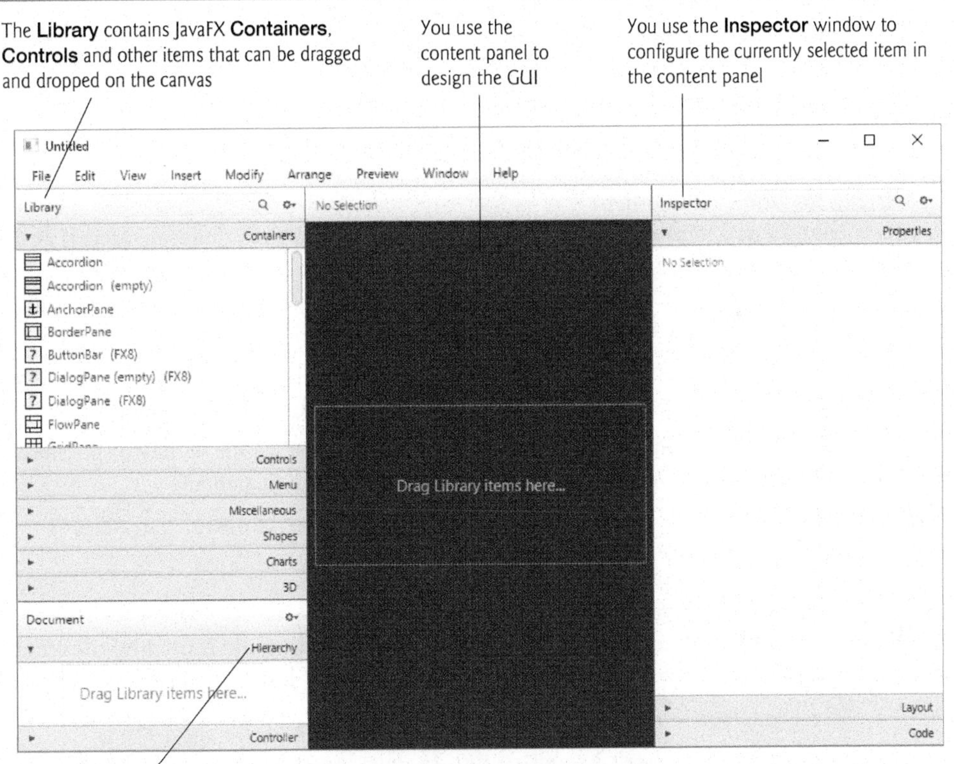
The **Library** contains JavaFX **Containers**, **Controls** and other items that can be dragged and dropped on the canvas
You use the content panel to design the GUI
You use the **Inspector** window to configure the currently selected item in the content panel
Untitled
File Edit View Insert Modify Arrange Preview Window Help
Library
Containers
Accordion
Accordion (empty)
AnchorPane
BorderPane
ButtonBar (FX8)
DialogPane (empty) (FX8)
DialogPane (FX8)
FlowPane
Controls
Menu
Miscellaneous
Shapes
Charts
3D
Document
Hierarchy
Drag Library items here...
Controller
No Selection
Drag Library items here...
Inspector
Properties
No Selection
Layout
Code
The **Document** window's **Hierarchy** section shows the structure of the GUI and allows you to select and reorganize controls

Fig. 12.3 | JavaFX Scene Builder when you first open it.

12.4.2 Adding an Image to the Folder Containing `Welcome.fxml`

The image you'll use for this app (`bug.png`) is located in the `images` subfolder of this chapter's examples folder. To make it easy to find the image when you're ready to add it to the app, locate the `images` folder on your file system, then copy `bug.png` into the folder where you saved `Welcome.fxml`.

12.4.3 Creating a VBox Layout Container

For this app, you'll place a `Label` and an `ImageView` in a **VBox layout container** (package `javafx.scene.layout`), which will be the scene graph's root node. Layout containers help you arrange and size GUI components. A `VBox` arranges its nodes *vertically* from top to bottom. We discuss the `GridPane` layout container in Section 12.5 and several others in Chapter 13. To add a `VBox` to Scene Builder's content panel so you can begin designing

1. We show the Scene Builder screen captures on Microsoft Windows 10, but Scene Builder is nearly identical on Windows, macOS and Linux. The key difference is that the menu bar on macOS is at the top of the screen, whereas the menu bar is part of the window on Windows and Linux.

the GUI, double-click **VBox** in the **Library** window's **Containers** section. (You also can drag-and-drop a VBox from the **Containers** section onto Scene Builder's content panel.)

12.4.4 Configuring the VBox Layout Container

You'll now specify the VBox's alignment, initial size and padding.

Specifying the **VBox***'s Alignment*

A VBox's **alignment** determines the layout positioning of the VBox's children. In this app, we'd like each child node (the Label and the ImageView) to be centered horizontally in the scene, and we'd like both children to be centered vertically, so that there is an equal amount of space above the Label and below the ImageView. To accomplish this:

1. Select the VBox in Scene Builder's content panel by clicking it. Scene Builder displays many VBox properties in the Scene Builder **Inspector**'s **Properties** section.
2. Click the **Alignment** property's drop-down list and notice the variety of potential alignment values you can use. Click CENTER to set the **Alignment**.

Each property value you specify for a JavaFX object is used to set one of that object's instance variables when JavaFX creates the object at runtime.

Specifying the **VBox***'s Preferred Size*

The **preferred size** (width and height) of the scene graph's root node is used by the scene to determine its window size when the app begins executing. To set the preferred size:

1. Select the VBox.
2. Expand the **Inspector**'s **Layout** section by clicking the right arrow (▶) next to **Layout**. The section expands and the right arrow changes to a down arrow. Clicking the arrow again would collapse the section.
3. Click the **Pref Width** property's text field, type 450 and press *Enter* to change the preferred width.
4. Click the **Pref Height** property's text field, type 300 and press *Enter* to change the preferred height.

12.4.5 Adding and Configuring a Label

Next, you'll create the Label that displays "Welcome to JavaFX!".

Adding a **Label** *to the* **VBox**

Expand the Scene Builder **Library** window's **Controls** section by clicking the right arrow (▶) next to **Controls**, then drag-and-drop a **Label** from the **Controls** section onto the VBox in Scene Builder's content panel. (You also can double-click **Label** in the **Containers** section to add the Label.) Scene Builder automatically centers the Label object horizontally and vertically in the VBox, based on the VBox's **Alignment** property.

Changing the **Label***'s Text*

You can set a Label's text either by double clicking it and typing the new text, or by selecting the Label and setting its **Text** property in the **Inspector**'s **Properties** section. Set the Label's text to "Welcome to JavaFX!".

Changing the `Label`'s Font

For this app, we set the `Label` to display in a large bold font. To do so, select the `Label`, then in the **Inspector**'s **Properties** section, click the value to the right of the **Font** property. In the window that appears, set the **Style** property to `Bold` and the **Size** property to `30`. The design should now appear as shown in Fig. 12.4.

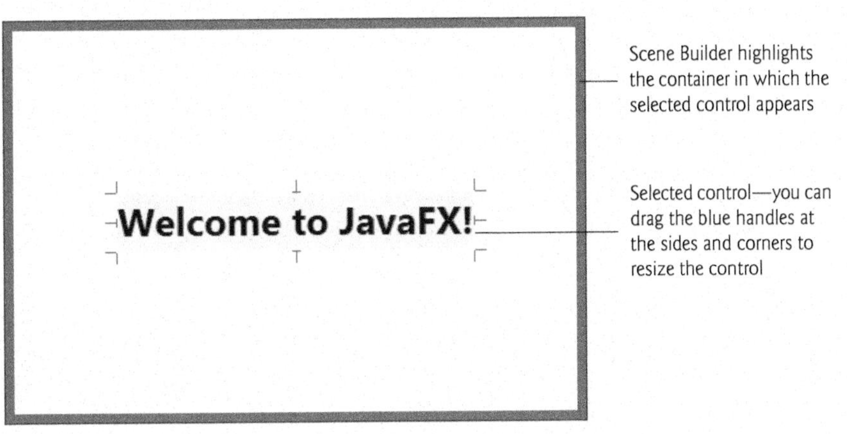
Welcome to JavaFX!
Scene Builder highlights the container in which the selected control appears
Selected control—you can drag the blue handles at the sides and corners to resize the control

Fig. 12.4 | Welcome GUI's design after adding and configuring a `Label`.

12.4.6 Adding and Configuring an `ImageView`

Finally, you'll add the `ImageView` that displays `bug.png`.

Adding an `ImageView` to the `VBox`

Drag and drop an **ImageView** from the **Library** window's **Controls** section to just below the `Label`, as shown in Fig. 12.5. You can also double-click **ImageView** in the **Library** window, in which case Scene Builder automatically places the new `ImageView` object below the `Label`. You can reorder a `VBox`'s controls by dragging them in the `VBox` or in the **Document** window's **Hierarchy** section (Fig. 12.3). Scene Builder automatically centers the `ImageView` horizontally in the `VBox`. Also notice that the `Label` and `ImageView` are centered vertically such that the same amount of space appears above the `Label` and below the `ImageView`.

Setting the `ImageView`'s Image

Next you'll set the image to display:

1. Select the `ImageView`, then in the **Inspector**'s **Properties** section click the ellipsis (...) button to the right of the **Image** property. By default, Scene Builder opens a dialog showing the folder in which the FXML file is saved. This is where you placed the image file `bug.png` in Section 12.4.2.
2. Select the image file, then click **Open**. Scene Builder displays the image and resizes the `ImageView` to match the image's aspect ratio—that is, the ratio of the image's width to its height.

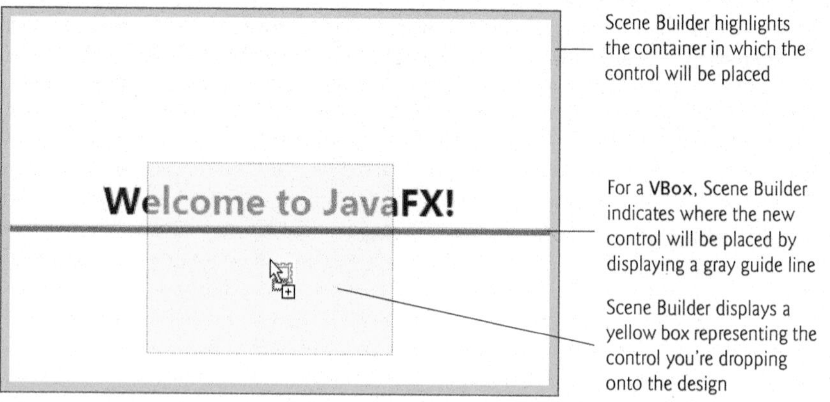
Welcome to JavaFX!
Scene Builder highlights the container in which the control will be placed
For a VBox, Scene Builder indicates where the new control will be placed by displaying a gray guide line
Scene Builder displays a yellow box representing the control you're dropping onto the design

Fig. 12.5 | Dragging and dropping the `ImageView` below the `Label`.

Changing the `ImageView`*'s Size*

We'd like to display the image at its original size. If you reset the `ImageView`'s default **Fit Width** and **Fit Height** property values—which Scene Builder set when you added the `ImageView` to the design—Scene Builder will resize the `ImageView` to the image's exact dimensions. To reset these properties:

1. Expand the **Inspector**'s **Layout** section.
2. Hover the mouse over the **Fit Width** property's value. This displays the button to the right property's value. Click the button and select **Reset to Default** to reset the value. This technique can be used with any property value to reset its default.
3. Repeat *Step 2* to reset the **Fit Height** property's value.

You've now completed the GUI. Scene Builder's content panel should now appear as shown in Fig. 12.6. Save the FXML file by selecting **File > Save**.

VBox
ImageView
Welcome to JavaFX!

Fig. 12.6 | Completed **Welcome** GUI in Scene Builder's content panel.

12.4.7 Previewing the `Welcome` GUI

You can preview what the design will look like in a running application's window. To do so, select **Preview > Show Preview in Window**, which displays the window in Fig. 12.7.

Fig. 12.7 | Previewing the **Welcome** GUI on Microsoft Windows 10—only the window borders will differ on Linux, macOS and earlier Windows versions.

12.5 Tip Calculator App—Introduction to Event Handling

The **Tip Calculator** app (Fig. 12.8(a)) calculates and displays a restaurant bill tip and total. By default, the app calculates the total with a 15% tip. You can specify a tip percentage from 0% to 30% by moving the `Slider` *thumb*—this updates the tip percentage (Fig. 12.8(b) and (c)). In this section, you'll build a **Tip Calculator** app using several JavaFX components and learn how to respond to user interactions with the GUI.

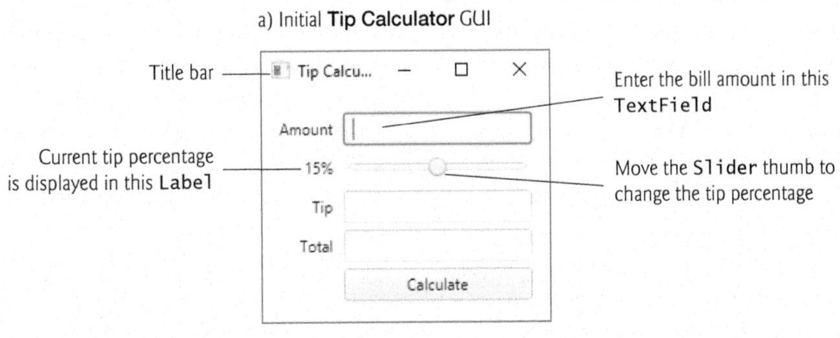

Fig. 12.8 | Entering the bill amount and calculating the tip. (Part 1 of 2.)

b) GUI after you enter the amount 34.56 and click the **Calculate** `Button`

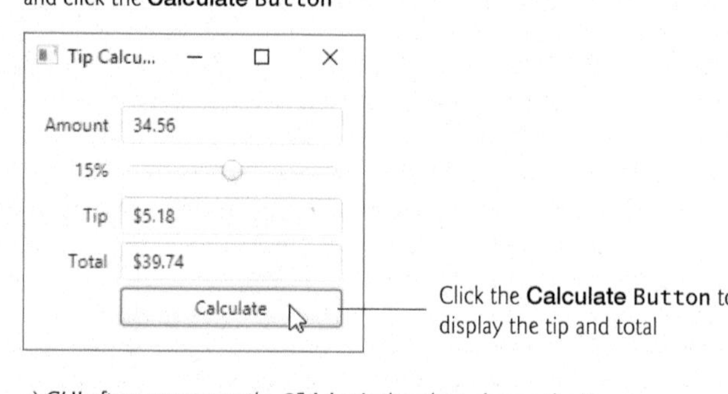

c) GUI after user moves the `Slider`'s thumb to change the tip percentage to 20%, then clicks the **Calculate** `Button`

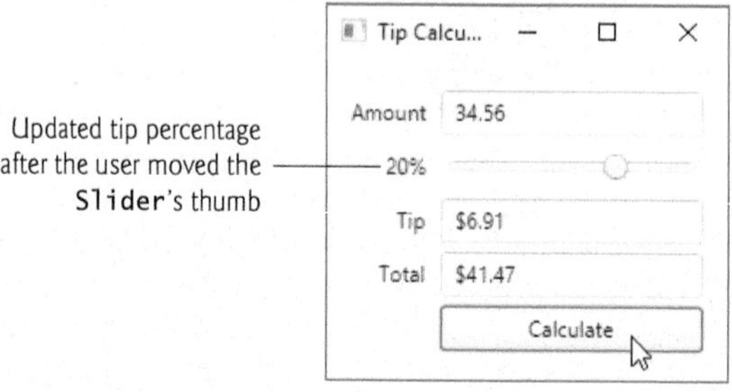

Fig. 12.8 | Entering the bill amount and calculating the tip. (Part 2 of 2.)

You'll begin by test-driving the app, using it to calculate 15% and 20% tips. Then we'll overview the technologies you'll use to create the app. You'll build the app's GUI using the Scene Builder. Finally, we'll present the complete Java code for the app and do a detailed code walkthrough.

12.5.1 Test-Driving the Tip Calculator App

Compile and run the app located in the `TipCalculator` folder with this chapter's examples. The class containing the `main` method is named `TipCalculator`.

Entering a Bill Total

Using your keyboard, enter `34.56`, then press the **Calculate** `Button`. The **Tip** and **Total** `TextField`s show the tip amount and the total bill for a 15% tip (Fig. 12.8(b)).

Selecting a Custom Tip Percentage

Use the `Slider` to specify a *custom* tip percentage. Drag the `Slider`'s *thumb* until the percentage reads **20%** (Fig. 12.8(c)), then press the **Calculate** `Button` to display the updated tip and total. As you drag the thumb, the tip percentage in the `Label` to the `Slider`'s left updates continuously. By default, the `Slider` allows you to select values from 0.0 to 100.0, but in this app we'll restrict the `Slider` to selecting whole numbers from 0 to 30.

12.5.2 Technologies Overview

This section introduces the technologies you'll use to build the **Tip Calculator** app.

Class `Application`

The class responsible for launching a JavaFX app is a subclass of **`Application`** (package **`javafx.application`**). When the subclass's `main` method is called:

1. Method `main` calls class `Application`'s `static` **`launch`** method to begin executing the app.
2. The `launch` method, in turn, causes the JavaFX runtime to create an object of the `Application` subclass and call its **`start`** method.
3. The `Application` subclass's `start` method creates the GUI, attaches it to a `Scene` and places it on the `Stage` that `start` receives as an argument.

Arranging JavaFX Components with a `GridPane`

Recall that layout containers arrange JavaFX components in a `Scene`. A **`GridPane`** (package **`javafx.scene.layout`**) arranges JavaFX components into *columns* and *rows* in a rectangular grid.

This app uses a `GridPane` (Fig. 12.9) to arrange views into two columns and five rows. Each cell in a `GridPane` can be empty or can hold one or more JavaFX components, including layout containers that arrange other controls. Each component in a `GridPane` can span *multiple* columns or rows, though we did not use that capability in this GUI. When you drag a `GridPane` onto Scene Builder's content panel, Scene Builder creates the `GridPane` with two columns and three rows by default. You can add and remove columns and rows as necessary. We'll discuss other `GridPane` features as we present the GUI-building steps. To learn more about class `GridPane`, visit:

```
https://docs.oracle.com/javase/8/javafx/api/javafx/scene/layout/
   GridPane.html
```

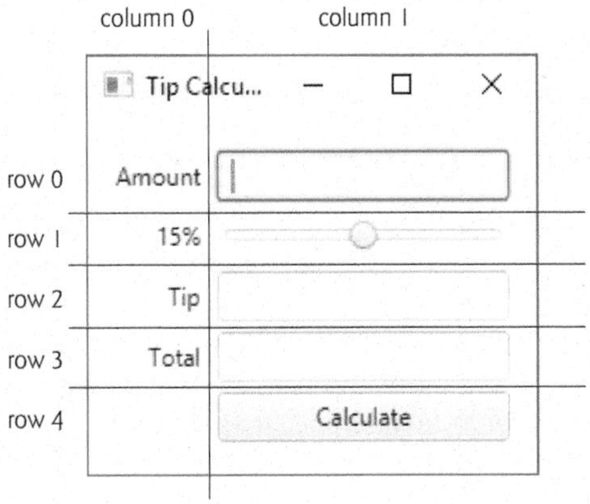

Fig. 12.9 | **Tip Calculator** GUI's `GridPane` labeled by its rows and columns.

Creating and Customizing the GUI with Scene Builder

You'll create `Label`s, `TextField`s, a `Slider` and a `Button` by dragging them onto Scene Builder's content panel, then customize them using the **Inspector** window.

- A **`TextField`** (package `javafx.scene.control`) can accept text input from the user or display text. You'll use one editable `TextField` to input the bill amount from the user and two *uneditable* `TextField`s to display the tip and total amounts.
- A **`Slider`** (package `javafx.scene.control`) represents a value in the range 0.0–100.0 by default and allows the user to select a number in that range by moving the `Slider`'s thumb. You'll customize the `Slider` so the user can choose a custom tip percentage *only* from the more limited integer range 0 to 30.
- A **`Button`** (package `javafx.scene.control`) allows the user to initiate an action—in this app, pressing the **Calculate** `Button` calculates and displays the tip and total amounts.

Formatting Numbers as Locale-Specific Currency and Percentage Strings

You'll use class **`NumberFormat`** (package **`java.text`**) to create *locale-specific* currency and percentage strings—an important part of *internationalization.*[2]

Event Handling

Normally, a user interacts with an app's GUI to indicate the tasks that the app should perform. For example, when you write an e-mail, clicking the e-mail app's **Send** button tells the app to send the e-mail to the specified e-mail addresses.

GUIs are **event driven.** When the user interacts with a GUI component, the interaction—known as an **event**—drives the program to perform a task. Some common user interactions that cause an app to perform a task include *clicking* a button, *typing* in a text field, *selecting* an item from a menu, *closing* a window and *moving* the mouse. The code that performs a task in response to an event is called an **event handler,** and the process of responding to events is known as **event handling.**

Before an app can respond to an event for a particular control, you must:

1. Define an event handler that implements an appropriate interface—known as an **event-listener interface.**
2. Indicate that an object of that class should be notified when the event occurs—known as **registering the event handler.**

In this app, you'll respond to two events—when the user moves the `Slider`'s thumb, the app will update the `Label` that displays the current tip percentage, and when the user clicks the **Calculate** `Button`, the app will calculate and display the tip and total bill amount.

You'll see that for certain events—such as when the user clicks a `Button`—you can link a control to its event-handling method by using the **Code** section of Scene Builder's **Inspector** window. In this case, the event-listener interface is implemented for you to call the method that you specify. For events that occur when the value of a control's property

2. Recall that the new JavaMoney API (`http://javamoney.github.io`) was developed to meet the challenges of handling currencies, monetary amounts, conversions, rounding and formatting. At the time of this writing, it was not yet incorporated into the JDK.

changes—such as when the user moves a `Slider`'s thumb to change the `Slider`'s value—you'll see that you must create the event handler entirely in code.

Implementing Interface **ChangeListener** *for Handling* **Slider** *Thumb Position Changes*

You'll implement interface **ChangeListener** (package `javafx.beans.value`) to respond when the user moves the `Slider`'s thumb. In particular, you'll use the interface's **changed** method to display the updated tip percentage as the user moves the `Slider`'s thumb.

Model-View-Controller (MVC) Architecture

JavaFX applications in which the GUI is implemented as FXML adhere to the **Model-View-Controller (MVC) design pattern**, which separates an app's data (contained in the **model**) from the app's GUI (the **view**) and the app's processing logic (the **controller**).

The controller implements logic for processing user inputs. The model contains application data, and the view presents the data stored in the model. When a user provides some input, the controller modifies the model with the given input. In the **Tip Calculator**, the model is the bill amount, the tip and the total. When the model changes, the controller updates the view to present the changed data.

In a JavaFX FXML app, a **controller class** defines instance variables for interacting with controls programmatically, as well as event-handling methods that respond to the user's interactions. The controller class may also declare additional instance variables, `static` variables and methods that support the app's operation. In a simple app like the **Tip Calculator**, the model and controller are often combined into a single class, as we'll do in this example.

FXMLLoader *Class*

When a JavaFX FXML app begins executing, class **FXMLLoader**'s `static` method **load** is used to load the FXML file that represents the app's GUI. This method:

- Creates the GUI's scene graph—containing the GUI's layouts and controls—and returns a **Parent** (package `javafx.scene`) reference to the scene graph's root node.
- Initializes the controller's instance variables for the components that are manipulated programmatically.
- Creates and registers the event handlers for any events specified in the FXML.

We'll discuss these steps in more detail in Sections 12.5.4–12.5.5.

12.5.3 Building the App's GUI

In this section, we'll show the precise steps for creating the **Tip Calculator**'s GUI. The GUI will not look like the one shown in Fig. 12.8 until you've completed the steps.

fx:id *Property Values for This App's Controls*

If the controller class will manipulate a control or layout programmatically (as we'll do with one `Label`, all the `TextField`s and the `Slider`), you must provide a name for that control or layout. In Section 12.5.4, you'll learn how to declare Java variables for each such component in the FXML, and we'll discuss how those variables are initialized for you. Each object's name is specified via its **fx:id property**. You can set this property's value by selecting a component in your scene, then expanding the **Inspector** window's **Code** section—the **fx:id** property appears at the top of the **Code** section. Figure 12.10 shows the **fx:id** properties of the **Tip Calculator**'s programmatically manipulated controls. For clarity, our naming convention is to use the control's class name in the **fx:id** property.

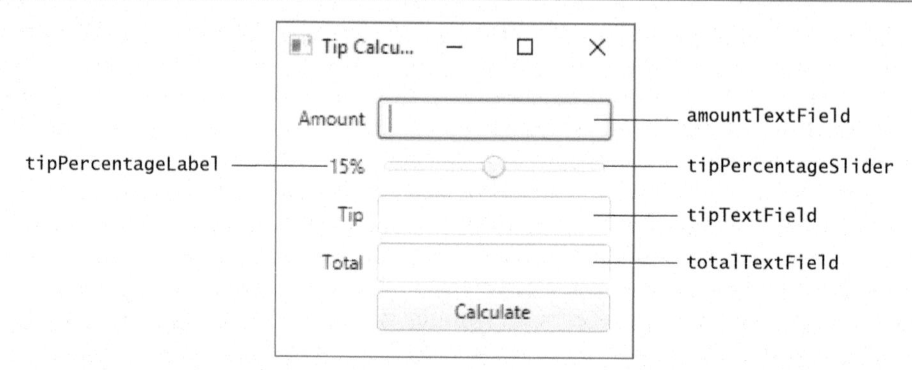

Fig. 12.10 | **Tip Calculator**'s programmatically manipulated controls labeled with their **fx:ids**.

Creating the `TipCalculator.fxml` File

As you did in Section 12.4.1, open Scene Builder to create a new FXML file. Then, select **File > Save** to display the **Save As** dialog, specify the location in which to store the file, name the file `TipCalculator.fxml` and click the **Save** button.

Step 1: Adding a `GridPane`

Drag a `GridPane` from the **Library** window's **Containers** section onto Scene Builder's content panel. By default, the `GridPane` contains two columns and three rows as shown in Fig. 12.11.

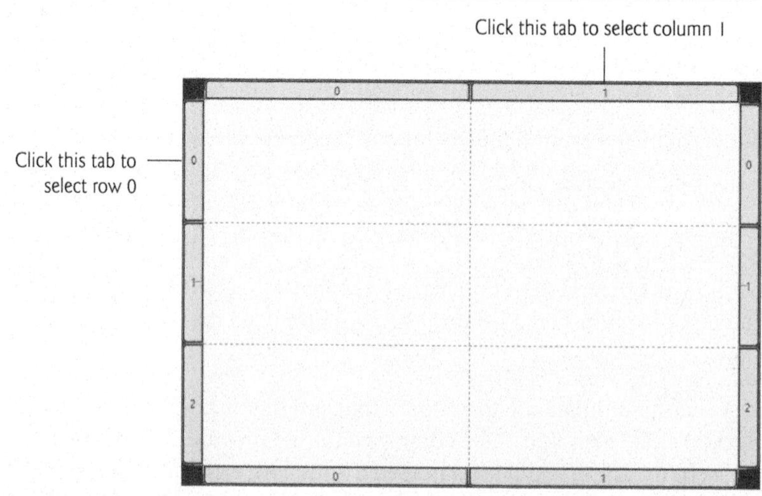

Fig. 12.11 | `GridPane` with two columns (0 and 1) and three rows (0, 1 and 2).

Step 2: Adding Rows to the `GridPane`

Recall that the GUI in Fig. 12.9 has two columns and five rows. Here you'll add two more rows. To add a row above or below an existing row:

1. Right click any row's row number tab and select either **Grid Pane > Add Row Above** or **Grid Pane > Add Row Below.**
2. Repeat this process to add another row.

After adding two rows, the `GridPane` should appear as shown in Fig. 12.12. You can use similar steps to add columns. You can delete a row or column by right clicking the tab containing its row or column number and selecting **Delete.**

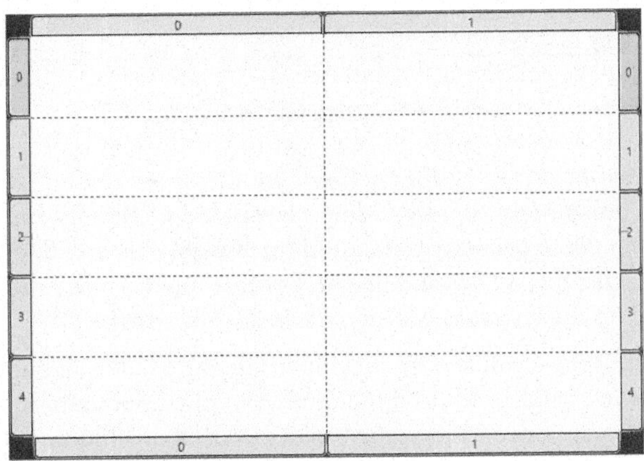

Fig. 12.12 | `GridPane` after adding two more rows.

Step 3: Adding the Controls to the `GridPane`

You'll now add the controls in Fig. 12.9 to the `GridPane`. For each control that has an **fx:id** in Fig. 12.10, when you drag the control onto the `GridPane`, set the control's **fx:id** property in the **Inspector** window's **Code** section. Perform the following steps:

1. ***Adding the*** `Labels`. Drag `Labels` from the **Library** window's **Controls** section into the first four rows of column 0 (the `GridPane`'s left column). As you add each `Label`, set its text as shown Fig. 12.9.
2. ***Adding the*** `TextFields`. Drag `TextFields` from the **Library** window's **Controls** section into rows 0, 2 and 3 of column 1 (the `GridPane`'s right column).
3. ***Adding a*** `Slider`. Drag a horizontal `Slider` from the **Library** window's **Controls** section into row 1 of column 1.
4. ***Adding a*** `Button`. Drag a `Button` from the **Library** window's **Controls** section into row 4 of column 1. Change the `Button`'s text to **Calculate.** You can set the `Button`'s text by double clicking it, or by selecting the `Button`, then setting its **Text** property in the **Inspector** window's **Properties** section.

The `GridPane` should appear as shown in Fig. 12.13.

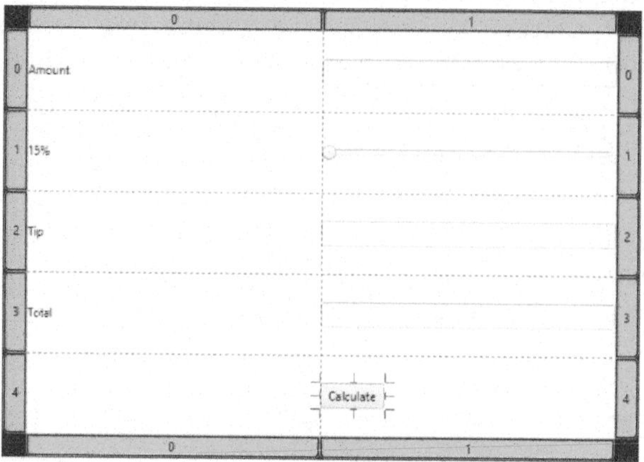

Fig. 12.13 | GridPane filled with the **Tip Calculator**'s controls.

Step 4: Sizing the GridPane *to Fit Its Contents*

When you begin designing a GUI by adding a layout, Scene Builder automatically sets the layout object's **Pref Width** property to 600 and **Pref Height** property to 400, which is much larger than this GUI's final width and height. For this app, we'd like the layout's size to be computed, based on the layout's contents. To make this change:

1. First, select the GridPane by clicking inside the GridPane, but not on any of the controls you've placed into its columns and rows. Sometimes, it's easier to select the GridPane node in the Scene Builder **Document** window's **Hierarchy** section.
2. In the **Inspector**'s **Layout** section, reset the **Pref Width** and **Pref Height** property values to their defaults (as you did in Section 12.4.4). This sets both properties' values to USE_COMPUTED_SIZE, so the layout calculates its own size.

The layout now appears as shown in Fig. 12.14.

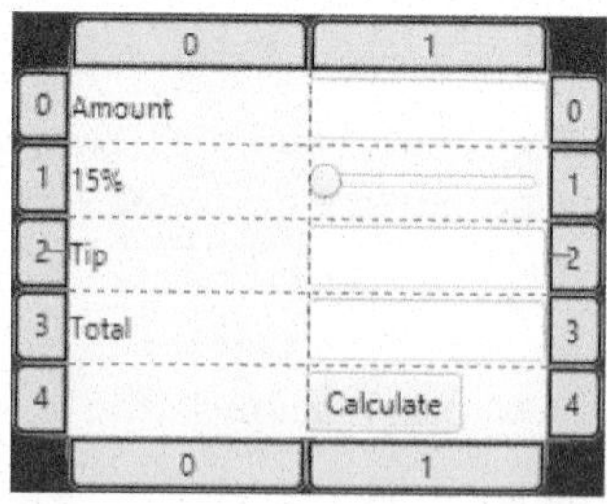

Fig. 12.14 | GridPane sized to fit its contents.

Step 5: Right-Aligning GridPane *Column 0's Contents*

A GridPane column's contents are left-aligned by default. To right-align the contents of column 0, select it by clicking the tab at the top or bottom of the column, then in the **Inspector**'s **Layout** section, set the **Halignment** (horizontal alignment) property to RIGHT.

Step 6: Sizing the **GridPane** *Columns to Fit Their Contents*

By default, Scene Builder sets each GridPane column's width to 100 pixels and each row's height to 30 pixels to ensure that you can easily drag controls into the GridPane's cells. In this app, we sized each column to fit its contents. To do so, select the column 0 by clicking the tab at the top or bottom of the column, then in the **Inspector**'s **Layout** section, reset the **Pref Width** property to its default size (that is, USE_COMPUTED_SIZE) to indicate that the column's width should be based on its widest child—the **Amount** Label in this case. Repeat this process for column 1. The GridPane should appear as shown in Fig. 12.15.

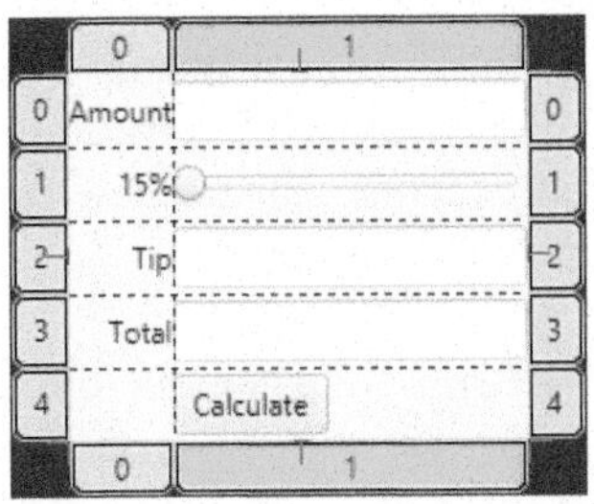

Fig. 12.15 | GridPane with columns sized to fit their contents.

Step 7: Sizing the **Button**

By default, Scene Builder sets a Button's width based on its text. For this app, we chose to make the Button the same width as the other controls in the GridPane's right column. To do so, select the Button, then in the **Inspector**'s **Layout** section, set the **Max Width** property to MAX_VALUE. This causes the Button's width to grow to fill the column's width.

Previewing the GUI

Preview the GUI by selecting **Preview > Show Preview in Window.** As you can see in Fig. 12.16, there's no space between the Labels in the left column and the controls in the right column. In addition, there's no space around the GridPane, because by default the Stage is sized to fit the Scene's contents. Thus, many of the controls touch the window's borders. You'll fix these issues in the next step.

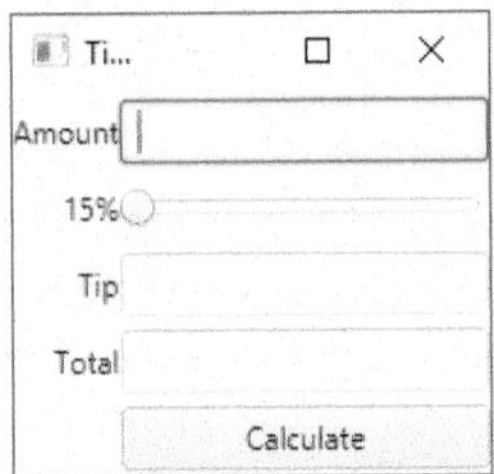

Fig. 12.16 | GridPane with the TextFields and Button resized.

Step 8: Configuring the **GridPane***'s Padding and Horizontal Gap Between Its Columns*

The space between a node's contents and its top, right, bottom and left edges is known as the **padding**, which separates the contents from the node's edges. Since the GridPane's size determines the Stage's window size, the GridPane's padding separates its children from the window's edges. To set the padding, select the GridPane, then in the **Inspector**'s **Layout** section, set the **Padding** property's four values (which represent the **TOP**, **RIGHT**, **BOTTOM** and **LEFT**) to 14—the JavaFX recommended distance between a control's edge and the Scene's edge.

You can specify the default amount of space between a GridPane's columns and rows with its **Hgap** (horizontal gap) and **Vgap** (vertical gap) properties, respectively. Because Scene Builder sets each GridPane row's height to 30 pixels—which is greater than the heights of this app's controls—there's already some vertical space between the components. To specify the horizontal gap between the columns, select the GridPane in the **Document** window's **Hierarchy** section, then in the **Inspector**'s **Layout** section, set the **Hgap** property to 8—the recommended distance between controls. If you'd like to precisely control the vertical space between components, you can reset each row's **Pref Height** to its default value, then set the GridPane's **Vgap** property.

Step 9: Making the `tipTextField` and `totalTextField` Uneditable and Not Focusable

The tipTextField and totalTextField are used in this app only to display results, not receive text input. For this reason, they should not be interactive. You can type in a TextField only if it's "in focus"—that is, it's the control that the user is interacting with. When you click an interactive control, it receives the focus. Similarly, when you press the *Tab* key, the focus transfers from the current focusable control to the next one—this occurs in the order the controls were added to the GUI. Interactive controls—such as TextFields, Sliders and Buttons—are focusable by default. Non-interactive controls—like Labels—are not focusable.

In this app, the tipTextField and totalTextField are neither editable nor focusable. To make these changes, select both TextFields, then in the **Inspector**'s **Properties** section uncheck the **Editable** and **Focus Traversable** properties. To select multiple controls at once, you can click the first (in the **Document** window's **Hierarchy** section or in the content panel), then hold the *Shift* key and click each of the others.

Step 10: Setting the `Slider`'s Properties

To complete the GUI, you'll now configure the **Tip Calculator**'s Slider. By default, a Slider's range is 0.0 to 100.0 and its initial value is 0.0. This app allows only integer tip percentages in the range 0 to 30 with a default of 15. To make these changes, select the Slider, then in the **Inspector**'s **Properties** section, set the Slider's **Max** property to 30 and the **Value** property to 15. We also set the **Block Increment** property to 5—this is the amount by which the **Value** property increases or decreases when the user clicks between an end of the Slider and the Slider's thumb. Save the FXML file by selecting **File > Save.**

Though we set the **Max**, **Value** and **Block Increment** properties to integer values, the Slider still produces floating-point values as the user moves its thumb. In the app's Java code, we'll restrict the Slider's values to integers when we respond to its events.

Previewing the Final Layout

You've now completed the **Tip Calculator**'s design. Select **Preview > Show Preview in Window** to view the final GUI (Fig. 12.17). When we discuss the TipCalculatorController class in Section 12.5.5, we'll show how to specify the **Calculate** Button's event handler in the FXML file.

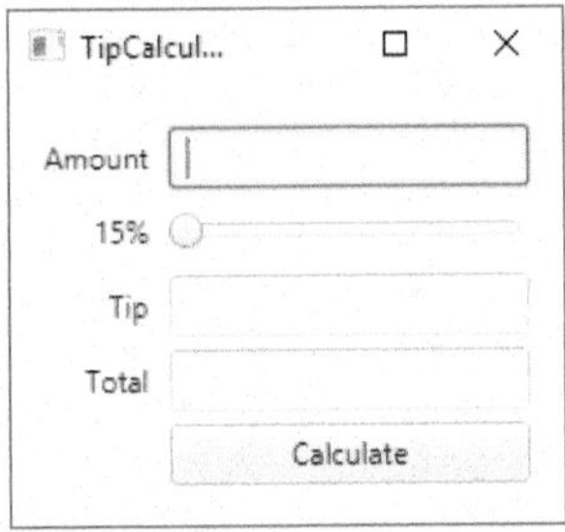

Fig. 12.17 | Final GUI design previewed in Scene Builder.

Specifying the Controller Class's Name

As we mentioned in Section 12.5.2, in a JavaFX FXML app, the app's controller class typically defines instance variables for interacting with controls programmatically, as well as event-handling methods. To ensure that an object of the controller class is created when the app loads the FXML file at runtime, you must specify the controller class's name in the FXML file:

1. Expand Scene Builder **Document** window's **Controller** section (located below the **Hierarchy** section in Fig. 12.3).
2. In the **Controller Class** field, type `TipCalculatorController`—by convention, the controller class's name starts with the same name as the FXML file (`TipCalculator`) and ends with `Controller`.

Specifying the **Calculate** *`Button`'s Event-Handler Method Name*

You can specify in the FXML file the names of the methods that will be called to handle specific control's events. When you select a control, the **Inspector** window's **Code** section shows all the events for which you can specify event handlers in the FXML file. When the user clicks a `Button`, the method specified in the **On Action** field is called—this method is defined in the controller class you specify in Scene Builder's **Controller** window. Enter `calculateButtonPressed` in the **On Action** field.

Generating a Sample Controller Class

You can have Scene Builder generate the initial controller class containing the variables you'll use to interact with controls programmatically and the empty **Calculate** `Button` event handler. Scene Builder calls this the "controller skeleton." Select **View > Show Sample Controller Skeleton** to generate the skeleton (Fig. 12.18). As you can see, the sample class has the class name you specified, a variable for each control that has an **fx:id** and an empty **Calculate** `Button` event handler. We'll discuss the `@FXML` annotation in Section 12.5.5 To use this skeleton to create your controller class, you can click the **Copy** button, then paste the contents into a file named `TipCalculatorController.java` in the same folder as the `TipCalculator.fxml` file you created in this section.

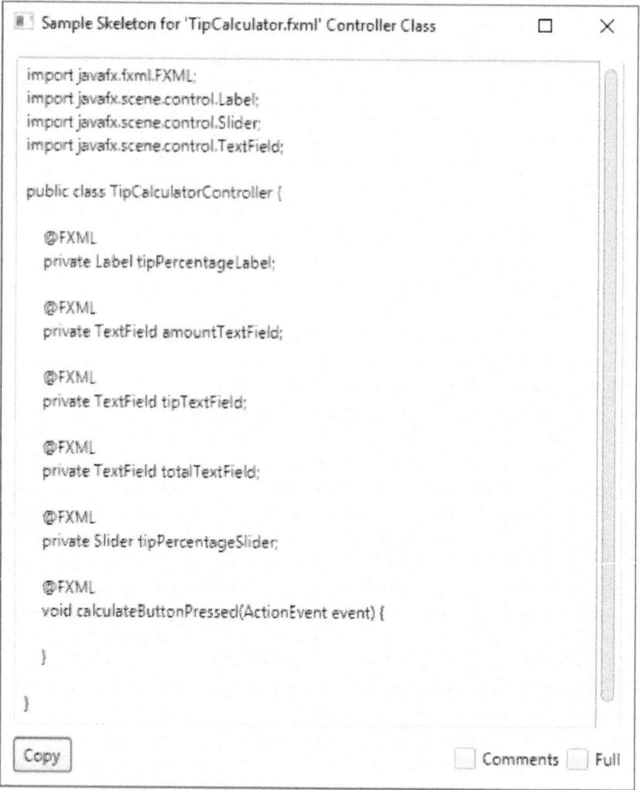

Fig. 12.18 | Skeleton code generated by Scene Builder.

12.5.4 `TipCalculator` Class

A simple JavaFX FXML-based app has two Java source-code files. For the **Tip Calculator** app these are:

- `TipCalculator.java`—This file contains the `TipCalculator` class (discussed in this section), which declares the `main` method that loads the FXML file to create the GUI and attaches the GUI to a `Scene` displayed on the app's `Stage`.
- `TipCalculatorController.java`—This file contains the `TipCalculatorController` class (discussed in Section 12.5.5), where you'll specify the `Slider` and `Button` controls' event handlers.

Figure 12.19 presents class `TipCalculator`. As we discussed in Section 12.5.2, the starting point for a JavaFX app is an `Application` subclass, so class `TipCalculator` extends `Application` (line 9). The `main` method calls class `Application`'s `static` `launch` method (line 23) to initialize the JavaFX runtime and to begin executing the app. This method causes the JavaFX runtime to create an object of the `TipCalculator` class and calls its `start` method (lines 10–19), passing the `Stage` object representing the window in which the app will be displayed. The JavaFX runtime creates the window.

```
1  // Fig. 12.19: TipCalculator.java
2  // Main app class that loads and displays the Tip Calculator's GUI
3  import javafx.application.Application;
4  import javafx.fxml.FXMLLoader;
5  import javafx.scene.Parent;
6  import javafx.scene.Scene;
7  import javafx.stage.Stage;
8
9  public class TipCalculator extends Application {
10    @Override
11    public void start(Stage stage) throws Exception {
12       Parent root =
13          FXMLLoader.load(getClass().getResource("TipCalculator.fxml"));
14
15       Scene scene = new Scene(root); // attach scene graph to scene
16       stage.setTitle("Tip Calculator"); // displayed in window's title bar
17       stage.setScene(scene); // attach scene to stage
18       stage.show(); // display the stage
19    }
20
21    public static void main(String[] args) {
22       // create a TipCalculator object and call its start method
23       launch(args);
24    }
25 }
```

Fig. 12.19 | Main app class that loads and displays the **Tip Calculator**'s GUI.

Overridden `Application` *Method* `start`

Method `start` (lines 11–19) creates the GUI, attaches it to a `Scene` and places it on the `Stage` that method `start` receives as an argument. Lines 12–13 use class `FXMLLoader`'s `static` method `load` to create the GUI's scene graph. This method:

- Returns a `Parent` (package `javafx.scene`) reference to the scene graph's root node—this is a reference to the GUI's `GridPane` in this app.
- Creates an object of the `TipCalculatorController` class that we specified in the FXML file.
- Initializes the controller's instance variables for the components that are manipulated programmatically.
- Attaches the event handlers specified in the FXML to the appropriate controls. This is known as registering the event handlers and enables the controls to call the corresponding methods when the user interacts with the app.

We discuss the initialization of the controller's instance variables and the registration of the event handlers in Section 12.5.5.

Creating the `Scene`

To display the GUI, you must attach it to a `Scene`, then attach the `Scene` to the `Stage` that method `start` receives as an argument. To attach the GUI to a `Scene`, line 15 creates a `Scene`, passing `root` (the scene graph's root node) as an argument to the constructor. By default, the `Scene`'s size is determined by the size of the scene graph's root node. Overloaded versions of the `Scene` constructor allow you to specify the `Scene`'s size and fill (a color, gradient or image), which appears in the `Scene`'s background. Line 16 uses `Stage` method `setTitle` to specify the text that appears in the `Stage` window's title bar. Line 17 calls `Stage` method `setScene` to place the `Scene` onto the `Stage`. Finally, line 18 calls `Stage` method `show` to display the `Stage` window.

12.5.5 `TipCalculatorController` Class

Figures 12.20–12.23 present the `TipCalculatorController` class that responds to user interactions with the app's `Button` and `Slider`.

Class `TipCalculatorController`'s `import` Statements

Figure 12.20 shows class `TipCalculatorController`'s `import` statements.

```
1  // TipCalculatorController.java
2  // Controller that handles calculateButton and tipPercentageSlider events
3  import java.math.BigDecimal;
4  import java.math.RoundingMode;
5  import java.text.NumberFormat;
6  import javafx.beans.value.ChangeListener;
7  import javafx.beans.value.ObservableValue;
8  import javafx.event.ActionEvent;
9  import javafx.fxml.FXML;
10 import javafx.scene.control.Label;
11 import javafx.scene.control.Slider;
12 import javafx.scene.control.TextField;
13
```

Fig. 12.20 | `TipCalculatorController`'s `import` declarations.

The classes and interfaces used by class `TipCalculatorController` include:

- Class `BigDecimal` of package `java.math` (line 3) is used to perform precise monetary calculations. The `RoundingMode` `enum` of package `java.math` (line 4) is used to specify how `BigDecimal` values are rounded during calculations or when formatting floating-point numbers as `String`s.
- Class `NumberFormat` of package `java.text` (line 5) provides numeric formatting capabilities, such as locale-specific currency and percentage formats. For example, in the U.S. locale, the monetary value 34.95 is formatted as $34.95 and the percentage 15 is formatted as 15%. Class `NumberFormat` determines the locale of the system on which your app runs, then formats currency amounts and percentages accordingly.
- You implement interface `ChangeListener` of package `javafx.beans.value` (line 6) to respond when the user moves the `Slider`'s thumb. This interface's `changed` method receives an object that implements interface `ObservableValue` (line 7)—that is, a value that generates an event when it changes.
- A `Button`'s event handler receives an `ActionEvent` object (line 8; package `javafx.event`) indicating which `Button` the user clicked. As you'll see in Chapter 13, many JavaFX controls support `ActionEvent`s.

- The annotation `FXML` (line 9; package `javafx.fxml`) is used in a JavaFX controller class's code to mark instance variables that should refer to JavaFX components in the GUI's FXML file and methods that can respond to the events of JavaFX components in the GUI's FXML file.
- Package `javafx.scene.control` (lines 10–12) contains many JavaFX control classes, including `Label`, `Slider` and `TextField`.

`TipCalculatorController`'s `static` Variables and Instance Variables

Lines 16—37 of Fig. 12.21 present class `TipCalculatorController`'s `static` and instance variables. The `NumberFormat` objects (lines 16–19) are used to format currency values and percentages, respectively. `NumberFormat` method `getCurrencyInstance` returns a `NumberFormat` object that formats values as currency using the default locale for the system on which the app is running. Similarly, `NumberFormat` method `getPercentInstance` returns a `NumberFormat` object that formats values as percentages using the system's default locale. The `BigDecimal` object `tipPercentage` (line 21) stores the current tip percentage and is used in the tip calculation (Fig. 12.22) when the user clicks the **Calculate** `Button`.

```
14 public class TipCalculatorController {
15    // formatters for currency and percentages
16    private static final NumberFormat currency =
17       NumberFormat.getCurrencyInstance();
18    private static final NumberFormat percent =
19       NumberFormat.getPercentInstance();
20
21    private BigDecimal tipPercentage = new BigDecimal(0.15); // 15% default
22
23    // GUI controls defined in FXML and used by the controller's code
24    @FXML
25    private TextField amountTextField;
26
27    @FXML
28    private Label tipPercentageLabel;
29
30    @FXML
31    private Slider tipPercentageSlider;
32
33    @FXML
34    private TextField tipTextField;
35
36    @FXML
37    private TextField totalTextField;
38
```

Fig. 12.21 | `TipCalculatorController`'s `static` and instance variables.

`@FXML` Annotation

Recall from Section 12.5.3 that each control that this app manipulates in its Java source code needs an **fx:id**. Lines 24–37 (Fig. 12.21) declare the controller class's corresponding instance variables. The **`@FXML` annotation** that precedes each declaration (lines 24, 27, 30, 33 and 36) indicates that the variable name can be used in the FXML file that describes the app's GUI. The variable names that you specify in the controller class must precisely match the **fx:id** values you specified when building the GUI. When the `FXMLLoader` loads `TipCalculator.fxml` to create the GUI, it also initializes each of the controller's instance variables that are declared with `@FXML` to ensure that they refer to the corresponding GUI components in the FXML file.

`TipCalculatorController`'s `calculateButtonPressed` Event Handler

Figure 12.22 presents class `TipCalculatorController`'s `calculateButtonPressed` method, which is called when the user clicks the **Calculate** `Button`. The `@FXML` annotation (line 40) preceding the method indicates that this method can be used to specify a control's event handler in the FXML file that describes the app's GUI. For a control that generates an `ActionEvent` (as is the case for many JavaFX controls), the event-handling method must return `void` and receive one `ActionEvent` parameter (line 41).

```
39     // calculates and displays the tip and total amounts
40     @FXML
41     private void calculateButtonPressed(ActionEvent event) {
42        try {
43           BigDecimal amount = new BigDecimal(amountTextField.getText());
44           BigDecimal tip = amount.multiply(tipPercentage);
45           BigDecimal total = amount.add(tip);
46
47           tipTextField.setText(currency.format(tip));
48           totalTextField.setText(currency.format(total));
49        }
50        catch (NumberFormatException ex) {
51           amountTextField.setText("Enter amount");
52           amountTextField.selectAll();
53           amountTextField.requestFocus();
54        }
55     }
56
```

Fig. 12.22 | `TipCalculatorController`'s `calculateButtonPressed` event handler.

Registering the Calculate Button's Event Handler

When the `FXMLLoader` loads `TipCalculator.fxml` to create the GUI, it creates and registers an event handler for the **Calculate** `Button`'s `ActionEvent`. The event handler for this event must implement interface **`EventHandler<ActionEvent>`**—`EventHandler` is a generic type, like `ArrayList` (introduced in Chapter 7). This interface contains a `handle` method that returns `void` and receives an `ActionEvent` parameter. This method's body, in turn, calls method `calculateButtonPressed` when the user clicks the **Calculate** `Button`. `FXMLLoader` performs similar tasks for every event listener you specify via the Scene Builder **Inspector** window's **Code** section.

Calculating and Displaying the Tip and Total Amounts

Lines 43–48 calculate and display the tip and total. Line 43 calls the `amountTextField`'s `getText` method to get the bill amount typed by the user. This `String` is passed to `BigDecimal`'s constructor, which throws a `NumberFormatException` if its argument is not a number. In that case, line 51 calls amountTextField's setText method to display the message "Enter amount" in the TextField. Line 52 then calls method selectAll to select the TextField's text and line 53 calls requestFocus to give the TextField the focus. Now the user can immediately type a value in the amountTextField without having to first select its text. Methods getText, setText and selectAll are inherited into class TextField from class TextInputControl (package javafx.scene.control), and method requestFocus is inherited into class TextField from class Node (package javafx.scene).

If line 43 does not throw an exception, line 44 calculates the tip by calling method multiply to multiply the amount by the tipPercentage, and line 45 calculates the total by adding the tip to the bill amount. Next lines 47 and 48 use the currency object's format method to create currency-formatted Strings representing the tip and total amounts, which we display in tipTextField and totalTextField, respectively.

TipCalculatorController's initalize Method

Figure 12.23 presents class TipCalculatorController's initialize method. This method can be used to configure the controller before the GUI is displayed. Line 60 calls the currency object's setRoundingMode method to specify how currency values should be rounded. The value RoundingMode.HALF_UP indicates that values greater than or equal to .5 should round up—for example, 34.567 would be formatted as 34.57 and 34.564 would be formatted as 34.56.

```
57       // called by FXMLLoader to initialize the controller
58       public void initialize() {
59          // 0-4 rounds down, 5-9 rounds up
60          currency.setRoundingMode(RoundingMode.HALF_UP);
61
62          // listener for changes to tipPercentageSlider's value
63          tipPercentageSlider.valueProperty().addListener(
64             new ChangeListener<Number>() {
65                @Override
66                public void changed(ObservableValue<? extends Number> ov,
67                   Number oldValue, Number newValue) {
68                   tipPercentage =
69                      BigDecimal.valueOf(newValue.intValue() / 100.0);
70                   tipPercentageLabel.setText(percent.format(tipPercentage));
71                }
72             }
73          );
74       }
75    }
```

Fig. 12.23 | TipCalculatorController's initalize method.

Using an Anonymous Inner Class for Event Handling

Each JavaFX control has properties. Some—such as a Slider's value—can generate events when they change. For such events, you must manually register as the event handler an object that implements the ChangeListener interface (package javafx.beans.value).

ChangeListener is a generic type that's specialized with the property's type. The call to valueProperty (line 63) returns a DoubleProperty (package javax.beans.property) that represents the Slider's value. A DoubleProperty is an ObservableValue<Number> that can notify listeners when a value changes. Each class that implements interface ObservableValue provides method addListener (called on line 63) to register an event-handler that implements interface ChangeListener. For a Slider's value, addListener's argument is an object that implements ChangeListener<Number>, because the Slider's value is a numeric value.

If an event handler is not reused, you often define it as an instance of an **anonymous inner class**—a class that's declared without a name and typically appears inside a method. The addListener method's argument is specified in lines 64–72 as one statement that

- declares the event listener's class,
- creates an object of that class and
- registers it as the listener for changes to the tipPercentageSlider's value.

Since an anonymous inner class has no name, you must create an object of the class at the point where it's declared (thus the keyword new in line 64). A reference to that object is then passed to addListener. After the new keyword, the syntax

```
ChangeListener<Number>()
```

in line 64 begins the declaration of an anonymous inner class that implements interface ChangeListener<Number>. This is similar to beginning a class declaration with

```
public class MyHandler implements ChangeListener<Number>
```

The opening left brace at 64 and the closing right brace at line 72 delimit the anonymous inner class's body. Lines 65–71 declare the interface's changed method, which receives a reference to the ObservableValue that changed, a Number containing the Slider's old value before the event occurred and a Number containing the Slider's new value. When the user moves the Slider's thumb, lines 68–69 store the new tip percentage and line 70 updates the tipPercentageLabel. (The notation ? extends Number in line 66 indicates that the ObservableValue's type argument is a Number or a subclass of Number. We explain this notation in more detail in Section 20.7.)

Anonymous Inner Class Notes

An anonymous inner class can access its top-level class's instance variables, static variables and methods—in this case, the anonymous inner class uses the instance variables tipPercentage and tipPercentageLabel, and the static variable percent. However, an anonymous inner class has limited access to the local variables of the method in which it's
8 declared—it can access only the final or effectively final (Java SE 8) local variables declared in the enclosing method's body.

Software Engineering Observation 12.2

The event listener for an event must implement the appropriate event-listener interface.

Common Programming Error 12.1

If you forget to register an event-handler object for a particular GUI component's event type, events of that type will be ignored.

Java SE 8: Using a Lambda to Implement the `ChangeListener` 8

Recall from Section 10.10 that in Java SE 8 an interface containing one method—such as `ChangeListener` in Fig. 12.23—is a functional interface. We'll show how to implement such interfaces with lambdas in Chapter 17.

12.6 Features Covered in the Other JavaFX Chapters

JavaFX is a robust GUI, graphics and multimedia technology. In Chapters 13 and 22, you'll:

- Learn additional JavaFX layouts and controls.
- Handle other event types (such as `MouseEvents`).
- Apply transformations (such as moving, rotating, scaling and skewing) and effects (such as drop shadows, blurs, reflection and lighting) to a scene graph's nodes.
- Use CSS to specify the look-and-feel of controls.
- Use JavaFX properties and data binding to enable automatic updating of controls as corresponding data changes.
- Use JavaFX graphics capabilities.
- Perform JavaFX animations.
- Use JavaFX multimedia capabilities to play audio and video.

In addition, our JavaFX Resource Center

```
http://www.deitel.com/JavaFX
```

contains links to online resources where you can learn more about JavaFX's capabilities.

12.7 Wrap-Up

In this chapter, we introduced JavaFX. We presented the structure of a JavaFX stage (the application window). You learned that the stage displays a scene graph, that the scene graph is composed of nodes and that nodes consist of layouts and controls.

You designed GUIs using visual programming techniques in JavaFX Scene Builder, which enabled you to create GUIs without writing any Java code. You arranged `Label`, `ImageView`, `TextField`, `Slider` and `Button` controls using the `VBox` and `GridPane` layout containers. You learned how class `FXMLLoader` uses the FXML created in Scene Builder to create the GUI.

You implemented a controller class to respond to user interactions with `Button` and `Slider` controls. We showed that certain event handlers can be specified directly in FXML from Scene Builder, but event handlers for changes to a control's property values must be implemented directly in the controllers code. You also learned that the `FXMLLoader` creates and initializes an instance of an application's controller class, initializes the controller's instance variables that are declared with the `@FXML` annotation, and creates and registers event handlers for any events specified in the FXML.

In the next chapter, you'll use additional JavaFX controls and layouts and use CSS to style your GUI. You'll also learn more about JavaFX properties and how to use a technique called data binding to automatically update elements in a GUI with new data.

Summary

Section 12.1 Introduction

- A graphical user interface (GUI) presents a user-friendly mechanism for interacting with an app. A GUI (pronounced "GOO-ee") gives an app a distinctive "look-and-feel."
- GUIs are built from GUI components—sometimes called controls or widgets.
- Providing different apps with consistent, intuitive user-interface components gives users a sense of familiarity with a new app, so that they can learn it more quickly and use it more productively.
- Java's GUI, graphics and multimedia API of the future is JavaFX.

Section 12.2 JavaFX Scene Builder

- The Scene Builder tool is a standalone JavaFX GUI visual layout tool that can also be used with various IDEs.
- JavaFX Scene Builder enables you to create GUIs by dragging and dropping GUI components from Scene Builder's library onto a design area, then modifying and styling the GUI—all without writing any code.
- JavaFX Scene Builder's live editing and preview features allow you to view your GUI as you create and modify it, without compiling and running the app.
- You can use Cascading Style Sheets (CSS) to change the entire look-and-feel of your GUI—a concept sometimes called skinning.
- As you create and modify a GUI, JavaFX Scene Builder generates FXML (FX Markup Language)—an XML vocabulary for defining and arranging JavaFX GUI controls without writing any Java code.
- XML (eXtensible Markup Language) is a widely used language for describing things—it's readable both by computers and by humans.
- FXML concisely describes GUI, graphics and multimedia elements.
- The FXML code is separate from the program logic that's defined in Java source code.
- Separation of the interface (the GUI) from the implementation (the Java code) makes it easier to debug, modify and maintain JavaFX GUI apps.

Section 12.3 JavaFX App Window Structure

- The window in which a JavaFX app's GUI is displayed is known as the stage and is an instance of class `Stage` (package `javafx.stage`).
- The stage contains one scene that defines the GUI as a scene graph—a tree structure of an app's visual elements, such as GUI controls, shapes, images, video, text and more. The scene is an instance of class `Scene` (package `javafx.scene`).
- Each visual element in the scene graph is a node—an instance of a subclass of `Node` (package `javafx.scene`), which defines common attributes and behaviors for all nodes in the scene graph.
- The first node in the scene graph is known as the root node.
- Nodes that have children are typically layout containers that arrange their child nodes in the scene.
- The nodes arranged in a layout container are a combination of controls and possibly other layout containers.
- When the user interacts with a control, it generates an event. Programs can use event handling to specify what should happen when each user interaction occurs.
- An event handler is a method that responds to a user interaction. An FXML GUI's event handlers are defined in a controller class.

Section 12.4 Welcome *App—Displaying Text and an Image*

- Visual-programming techniques enable you to drag-and-drop JavaFX components onto Scene Builder's design area (known as the content panel), then use Scene Builder's Inspector to configure options.
- Layout containers help you arrange and size GUI components.
- A `VBox` layout container (package `javafx.scene.layout`) arranges its nodes vertically from top to bottom.
- To add a layout to Scene Builder's content panel, double-click the layout in the **Library** window's **Containers** section or drag-and-drop the layout from the **Containers** section onto Scene Builder's content panel.
- A `VBox`'s **Alignment** property determines the layout positioning of the `VBox`'s children.
- Each property value you specify for a JavaFX object is used to set one of that object's instance variables when JavaFX creates the object at runtime.
- The preferred size (width and height) of the scene graph's root node is used by the scene to determine its window size when the app begins executing.
- To add a control to a layout, drag-and-drop the control from the **Library** onto a layout in Scene Builder's content panel. You also can double-click an item in the **Library** to add it.
- You can set a `Label`'s text either by double clicking it and typing the new text, or by selecting the `Label` and setting its **Text** property in the **Inspector**'s **Properties** section.
- To set a `Label`'s font, select the `Label`, then in the **Inspector**'s **Properties** section, click the value to the right of the **Font** property. In the window that appears, set the font's attributes.
- You can reorder a `VBox`'s controls by dragging them in the `VBox` or in Scene Builder **Document** window's **Hierarchy** section.
- To specify an `ImageView`'s image, select the `ImageView`, then in the **Inspector**'s **Properties** section click the ellipsis (...) button to the right of the **Image** property. Select the image from the dialog.
- To reset a property to its default value, hover the mouse over the property's value. This displays a button to the right of the property's value. Click the button and select **Reset to Default** to reset the value.
- You can preview what a design will look like in a running application's window by selecting **Preview > Show Preview in Window.**

Section 12.5.2 Technologies Overview

- A JavaFX app's main class inherits from `Application` (package `javafx.application`).
- The main class's `main` method calls class `Application`'s `static launch` method to begin executing a JavaFX app. This method, in turn, causes the JavaFX runtime to create an object of the `Application` subclass and call its `start` method, which creates the GUI, attaches it to a `Scene` and places it on the `Stage` that method start receives as an argument.
- A `GridPane` (package `javafx.scene.layout`) arranges JavaFX nodes into columns and rows in a rectangular grid.
- Each cell in a `GridPane` can be empty or can hold one or more JavaFX components, including layout containers that arrange other controls.
- Each component in a `GridPane` can span multiple columns or rows.
- A `TextField` (package `javafx.scene.control`) can accept text input or display text.
- A `Slider` (package `javafx.scene.control`) represents a value in the range 0.0–100.0 by default and allows the user to select a number in that range by moving the `Slider`'s thumb.

- A Button (package javafx.scene.control) allows the user to initiate an action.
- Class NumberFormat (package java.text) can format locale-specific currency and percentage strings.
- GUIs are event driven. When the user interacts with a GUI component, the interaction—known as an event—drives the program to perform a task.
- The code that performs a task in response to an event is called an event handler.
- For certain events you can link a control to its event-handling method by using the **Code** section of Scene Builder's **Inspector** window. In this case, the class that implements the event-listener interface will be created for you and will call the method you specify.
- For events that occur when the value of a control's property changes, you must create the event handler entirely in code.
- You implement the ChangeListener interface (package javafx.beans.value) to respond when the user moves the Slider's thumb.
- JavaFX applications in which the GUI is implemented as FXML adhere to the Model-View-Controller (MVC) design pattern, which separates an app's data (contained in the model) from the app's GUI (the view) and the app's processing logic (the controller). The controller implements logic for processing user inputs. The view presents the data stored in the model. When a user provides input, the controller modifies the model with the given input. When the model changes, the controller updates the view to present the changed data. In a simple app, the model and controller are often combined into a single class.
- In a JavaFX FXML app, you define the app's event handlers in a controller class. The controller class defines instance variables for interacting with controls programmatically, as well as event-handling methods.
- Class FXMLLoader's static method load uses the FXML file that represents the app's GUI to creates the GUI's scene graph and returns a Parent (package javafx.scene) reference to the scene graph's root node. It also initializes the controller's instance variables, and creates and registers the event handlers for any events specified in the FXML.

Section 12.5.3 Building the App's GUI

- If a control or layout will be manipulated programmatically in the controller class, you must provide a name for that control or layout. Each object's name is specified via its **fx:id** property. You can set this property's value by selecting a component in your scene, then expanding the **Inspector** window's **Code** section—the **fx:id** property appears at the top.
- By default, the GridPane contains two columns and three rows. To add a row above or below an existing row, right click the row's tab and select either **Grid Pane > Add Row Above** or **Grid Pane > Add Row Below.**
- You can delete a row or column by right clicking the tab containing its row or column number and selecting **Delete.**
- You can set a Button's text by double clicking it, or by selecting the Button, then setting its **Text** property in the **Inspector** window's **Properties** section.
- A GridPane column's contents are left-aligned by default. To change the alignment, select the column by clicking the tab at the top or bottom of the column, then in the **Inspector**'s **Layout** section, set the **Halignment** property.
- Setting a node's **Pref Width** property of a GridPane column to its default USE_COMPUTED_SIZE value indicates that the width should be based on the widest child.
- To size a Button the same width as the other controls in a GridPane's column, select the Button, then in the **Inspector**'s **Layout** section, set the **Max Width** property to MAX_VALUE.

- The space between a node's contents and its top, right, bottom and left edges is known as the padding, which separates the contents from the node's edges. To set the padding, select the node, then in the **Inspector**'s **Layout** section set the **Padding** property's values.
- You can specify the default amount of space between a `GridPane`'s columns and rows with its **Hgap** (horizontal gap) and **Vgap** (vertical gap) properties, respectively.
- You can type in a `TextField` only if it's "in focus"—that is, it's the control that the user is interacting with. When you click an interactive control, it receives the focus. Similarly, when you press the *Tab* key, the focus transfers from the current focusable control to the next one—this occurs in the order the controls were added to the GUI.

Section 12.5.4 `TipCalculator` Class

- To display a GUI, you must attach it to a `Scene`, then attach the `Scene` to the `Stage` that's passed into `Application` method `start`.
- By default, the `Scene`'s size is determined by the size of the scene graph's root node. Overloaded versions of the `Scene` constructor allow you to specify the Scene's size and fill (a color, gradient or image), which appears in the `Scene`'s background.
- `Stage` method `setTitle` specifies the text that appears in the `Stage` window's title bar.
- `Stage` method `setScene` places a `Scene` onto a `Stage`.
- `Stage` method `show` displays the `Stage` window.

Section 12.5.5 `TipCalculatorController` Class

- The `RoundingMode` `enum` of package `java.math` is used to specify how `BigDecimal` values are rounded during calculations or when formatting floating-point numbers as `Strings`.
- Class `NumberFormat` of package `java.text` provides numeric formatting capabilities, such as locale-specific currency and percentage formats.
- A `Button`'s event handler receives an `ActionEvent`, which indicates that the `Button` was clicked. Many JavaFX controls support `ActionEvents`.
- Package `javafx.scene.control` contains many JavaFX control classes.
- The `@FXML` annotation preceding an instance variable indicates that the variable's name can be used in the FXML file that describes the app's GUI. The variable names that you specify in the controller class must precisely match the **fx:id** values you specified when building the GUI.
- When the `FXMLLoader` loads an FXML file to create a GUI, it also initializes each of the controller's instance variables that are declared with `@FXML` to ensure that they refer to the corresponding GUI components in the FXML file.
- The `@FXML` annotation preceding a method indicates that the method can be used to specify a control's event handler in the FXML file that describes the app's GUI.
- When the `FXMLLoader` creates an object of a controller class, it determines whether the class contains an `initialize` method with no parameters and, if so, calls that method to initialize the controller. This method can be used to configure the controller before the GUI is displayed.
- An anonymous inner class is a class that's declared without a name and typically appears inside a method declaration.
- Since an anonymous inner class has no name, one object of the class must be created at the point where the class is declared.
- An anonymous inner class can access its top-level class's instance variables, `static` variables and methods but has limited access to the local variables of the method in which it's declared—it can

access only the `final` or effectively `final` (Java SE 8) local variables declared in the enclosing method's body.

Self-Review Exercises

12.1 Fill in the blanks in each of the following statements:

a) A(n) ________ can display text and accept text input from the user.
b) Use a(n) ________ to arrange GUI components into cells in a rectangular grid.
c) JavaFX Scene Builder **Document** window's ________ section shows the structure of the GUI and allows you to select and reorganize controls.
d) You implement interface ________ to respond to events when the user moves a `Slider`'s thumb.
e) A(n) ________ represents the app's window.
f) The method ________ is called by the `FXMLLoader` before the GUI is displayed.
g) The contents of a scene are placed in its ________.
h) The elements in the scene graph are called ________.
i) ________ allows you to build JavaFX GUIs using drag-and-drop techniques.
j) A(n) ________ file contains the description of a JavaFX GUI.

12.2 State whether each of the following is *true* or *false*. If *false*, explain why.

a) You must create JavaFX GUIs by hand coding them in Java.
b) The layout `VBox` arranges components vertically in a scene.
c) To right align controls in a `GridPane` column, set its **Alignment** property to `RIGHT`.
d) The `FXMLLoader` initializes the controller's `@FXML` instance variables.
e) You override class `Application`'s `launch` method to display a JavaFX app's stage.
f) The control that the user is interacting with "has the focus."
g) By default, a `Slider` allows you to select values from 0 to 255.
h) A node can span multiple columns in a `GridPane`.
i) Every concrete `Application` subclass must directly or indirectly override method `start`.

Answers to Self-Review Exercises

12.1 a) `TextField`. b) `GridPane`. c) **Hierarchy**. d) `ChangeListener<Number>`. e) `Stage`. f) `initialize`. g) scene graph. h) nodes. i) JavaFX Scene Builder. j) FXML.

12.2 a) False. You can use JavaFX Scene Builder to create JavaFX GUIs without writing any code. b) True. c) False. The name of the property is **Halignment**. d) True. e) False. You override class `Application`'s `start` method to display a JavaFX app's stage. f) True. g) False. By default a `Slider` allows you to select values from 0.0 to 100.0. h) True. i) True.

Exercises

12.3 *(Running the* **Welcome** *App)* In Section 12.4, you built the **Welcome** app's GUI and previewed it using Scene Builder's **Show Preview in Window** option. Create an `Application` subclass—like the one shown in Section 12.5.4—to load and display `Welcome.fxml` in a JavaFX window.

12.1 *(Addition App)* Create a JavaFX version of the addition program in Fig. 2.7. Use two `TextFields` to receive the user's input and a `Button` to initiate the calculation. Display the results in a `Label`. Since `TextField` method `getText` returns a `String`, you must convert the `String` the user enters to an `int` for use in calculations. Recall that the `static` method `parseInt` of class `Integer` takes a `String` argument representing an integer and returns the value as an `int`.

12.2 *(Scrapbooking App)* Find four images of famous landmarks using websites such as Flickr. Create an app similar to the **Welcome** app in which you arrange the images in a collage. Add text that identifies each landmark. You can use images that are part of your project or you can specify the URL of an image that's online.

12.3 *(Enhanced* ***Tip Calculator*** *App)* Modify the **Tip Calculator** app to allow the user to enter the number of people in the party. Calculate and display the amount owed by each person if the bill were to be split evenly among the party members.

12.4 *(****Mortgage Calculator*** *App)* Create a mortgage calculator app that allows the user to enter a purchase price, down-payment amount and an interest rate. Based on these values, the app should calculate the loan amount (purchase price minus down payment) and display the monthly payment for 10-, 20- and 30-year loans. Allow the user to select a custom loan duration (in years) by using a `Slider` and display the monthly payment for that custom loan duration.

12.5 *(****College Loan Payoff Calculator*** *App)* A bank offers college loans that can be repaid in 5, 10, 15, 20, 25 or 30 years. Write an app that allows the user to enter the amount of the loan and the annual interest rate. Based on these values, the app should display the loan lengths in years and their corresponding monthly payments.

12.6 *(****Car Payment Calculator*** *App)* Typically, banks offer car loans for periods ranging from two to five years (24 to 60 months). Borrowers repay the loans in monthly installments. The amount of each monthly payment is based on the length of the loan, the amount borrowed and the interest rate. Create an app that allows the customer to enter the price of a car, the down-payment amount and the loan's annual interest rate. The app should display the loan's duration in months and the monthly payments for two-, three-, four- and five-year loans. The variety of options allows the user to easily compare repayment plans and choose the most appropriate.

12.7 *(****Miles-Per-Gallon Calculator*** *App)* Drivers often want to know the miles per gallon their cars get so they can estimate gasoline costs. Develop an app that allows the user to input the number of miles driven and the number of gallons used and calculates and displays the corresponding miles per gallon.

Making a Difference

12.8 *(****Body Mass Index Calculator*** *App)* The formulas for calculating the BMI are

$$BMI = \frac{weightInPounds \times 703}{heightInInches \times heightInInches}$$

or

$$BMI = \frac{weightInKilograms}{heightInMeters \times heightInMeters}$$

Create a BMI calculator app that allows users to enter their weight and height and whether they are entering these values in English or metric units, then calculates and displays the user's body mass index. The app should also display the following information from the Department of Health and Human Services/National Institutes of Health so that users can evaluate their BMIs:

```
BMI VALUES
Underweight: less than 18.5
Normal:      between 18.5 and 24.9
Overweight:  between 25 and 29.9
Obese:       30 or greater
```

12.9 *(****Target-Heart-Rate Calculator*** *App)* While exercising, you can use a heart-rate monitor to see that your heart rate stays within a safe range suggested by your trainers and doctors. According to the American Heart Association (AHA), the formula for calculating your *maximum heart rate* in beats per minute is *220 minus your age in years* (`http://bit.ly/AHATargetHeartRates`). Your *target heart rate* is a range that is 50–85% of your maximum heart rate. [*Note:* These formulas are estimates provided by the AHA. Maximum and target heart rates may vary based on the health, fitness and gender of the individual. Always consult a physician or qualified health care professional before beginning or modifying an exercise program.] Write an app that inputs the person's age, then calculates and displays the person's maximum heart rate and target-heart-rate range.

JavaFX GUI: Part 2

13

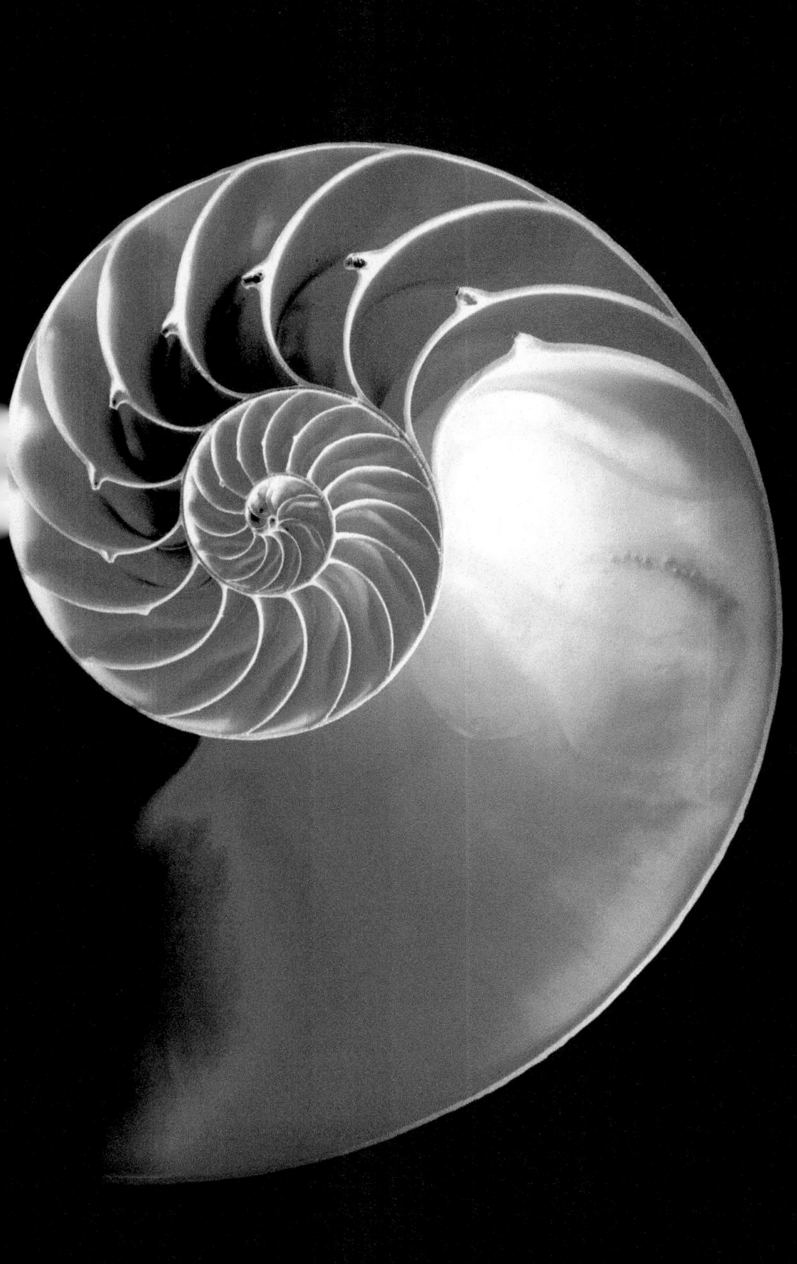

Objectives

In this chapter you'll:

- Learn more details of laying out nodes in a scene graph with JavaFX layout panels.
- Continue building JavaFX GUIs with Scene Builder.
- Create and manipulate `RadioButton`s and `ListView`s.
- Use `BorderPane`s and `TitledPane`s to layout controls.
- Handle mouse events.
- Use property binding and property listeners to perform tasks when a control's property value changes.
- Programmatically create layouts and controls.
- Customize a `ListView`'s cells with a custom cell factory.
- See an overview of other JavaFX capabilities.
- Be introduced to the JavaFX 9 updates in Java SE 9.

Outline

13.1 Introduction

This chapter continues our JavaFX presentation[1] that began in Chapter 12. In this chapter, you'll:

- Use additional layouts (`TitledPane`, `BorderPane` and `Pane`) and controls (`RadioButton` and `ListView`).
- Handle mouse and `RadioButton` events.
- Set up event handlers that respond to property changes on controls (such as the value of a `Slider`).
- Display `Rectangles` and `Circles` as nodes in the scene graph.
- Bind a collection of objects to a `ListView` that displays the collection's contents.
- Customize the appearance of a `ListView`'s cells.

Finally, we overview other JavaFX capabilities and mention Java SE 9's JavaFX changes that are discussed in our online Java SE 9 chapters.

13.2 Laying Out Nodes in a Scene Graph

A layout determines the size and positioning of nodes in the scene graph.

Node Size

In general, a node's size should *not* be defined *explicitly*. Doing so often creates a design that looks pleasing when it first loads, but deteriorates when the app is resized or the con-

1. The corresponding Swing GUI chapter is now online Chapter 35 and can be covered after online Chapter 26, which requires as prerequisites the only Chapters 1 through 11.

tent updates. In addition to the `width` and `height` properties, most JavaFX nodes have the properties **`prefWidth`**, **`prefHeight`**, **`minWidth`**, **`minHeight`**, **`maxWidth`** and **`maxHeight`** that specify a node's *range* of acceptable sizes as it's laid out within its parent node:

- The minimum size properties specify a node's smallest allowed size in points.
- The maximum size properties specify a node's largest allowed size in points.
- The preferred size properties specify a node's preferred width and height that should be used by the layout in most cases.

Node Position and Layout Panes

A node's position should be defined *relative* to its parent node and the other nodes in its parent. JavaFX **layout panes** are container nodes that arrange their child nodes in a scene graph relative to one another, based on their sizes and positions. Child nodes are controls, other layout panes, shapes and more.

Most JavaFX layout panes use *relative positioning*—if a layout-pane node is resized, it adjusts its children's sizes and positions accordingly, based on their preferred, minimum and maximum sizes. Figure 13.1 describes each of the JavaFX layout panes, including those presented in Chapter 12. In this chapter, we'll use `Pane`, `BorderPane`, `GridPane` and `VBox` from the `javafx.scene.layout` package.

Layout	Description
`AnchorPane`	Enables you to set the position of child nodes relative to the pane's edges. Resizing the pane does not alter the layout of the nodes.
`BorderPane`	Includes five areas—top, bottom, left, center and right—where you can place nodes. The top and bottom regions fill the `BorderPane`'s width and are vertically sized to their children's preferred heights. The left and right regions fill the `BorderPane`'s height and are horizontally sized to their children's preferred widths. The center area occupies all of the `BorderPane`'s remaining space. You might use the different areas for tool bars, navigation, a main content area, etc.
`FlowPane`	Lays out nodes consecutively—either horizontally or vertically. When the boundary for the pane is reached, the nodes wrap to a new line in a horizontal `FlowPane` or a new column in a vertical `FlowPane`.
`GridPane`	Creates a flexible grid for laying out nodes in rows and columns.
`Pane`	The base class for layout panes. This can be used to position nodes at fixed locations—known as absolute positioning.
`StackPane`	Places nodes in a stack. Each new node is stacked atop the previous node. You might use this to place text on top of images, for example.
`TilePane`	A horizontal or vertical grid of equally sized tiles. Nodes that are tiled horizontally wrap at the `TilePane`'s width. Nodes that are tiled vertically wrap at the `TilePane`'s height.
`HBox`	Arranges nodes horizontally in one row.
`VBox`	Arranges nodes vertically in one column.

Fig. 13.1 | JavaFX layout panes.

13.3 Painter App: RadioButtons, Mouse Events and Shapes

In this section, you'll create a simple **Painter** app (Fig. 13.2) that allows you to drag the mouse to draw. First, we'll overview the technologies you'll use, then we'll discuss creating the app's project and building its GUI. Finally, we'll present the source code for its `Painter` and `PainterController` classes.

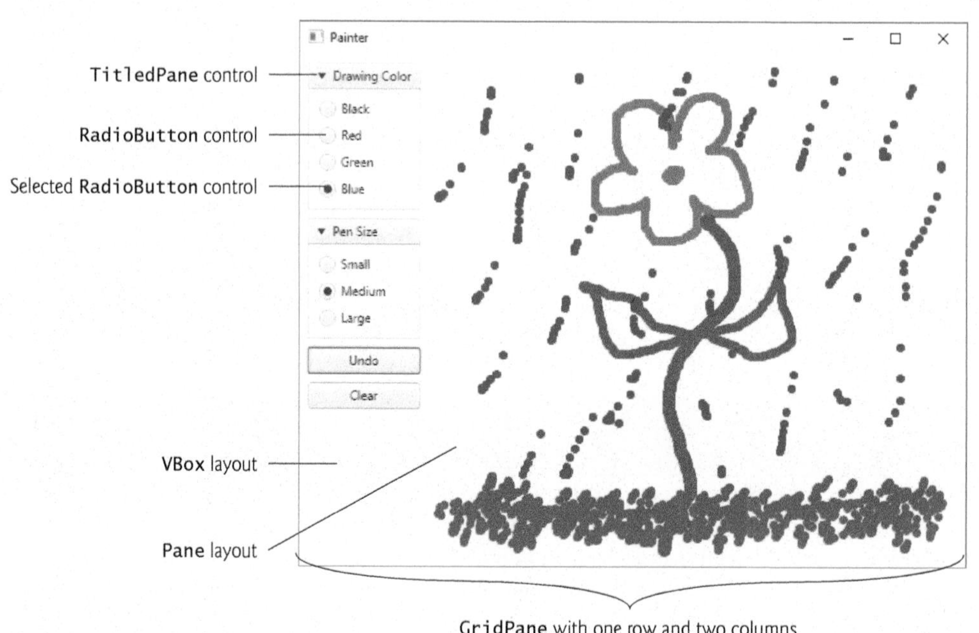

Fig. 13.2 | **Painter** app.

13.3.1 Technologies Overview

This section introduces the JavaFX features you'll use in the **Painter** app.

RadioButtons and ToggleGroups

`RadioButtons` function as *mutually exclusive* options. You add multiple `RadioButtons` to a **`ToggleGroup`** to ensure that only one `RadioButton` in a given group is selected at a time. For this app, you'll use JavaFX Scene Builder's capability for specifying each `RadioButton`'s `ToggleGroup` in FXML; however, you can also create a `ToggleGroup` in Java, then use a `RadioButton`'s **`setToggleGroup`** method to specify its `ToggleGroup`.

BorderPane Layout Container

A **`BorderPane` layout container** arranges controls into one or more of the five regions shown in Fig. 13.3. The top and bottom areas have the same width as the `BorderPane`. The left, center and right areas fill the vertical space between the top and bottom areas.

Each area may contain only one control or one layout container that, in turn, may contain other controls.

Look-and-Feel Observation 13.1

All the areas in a `BorderPane` *are optional: If the top or bottom area is empty, the left, center and right areas expand vertically to fill that area. If the left or right area is empty, the center expands horizontally to fill that area.*

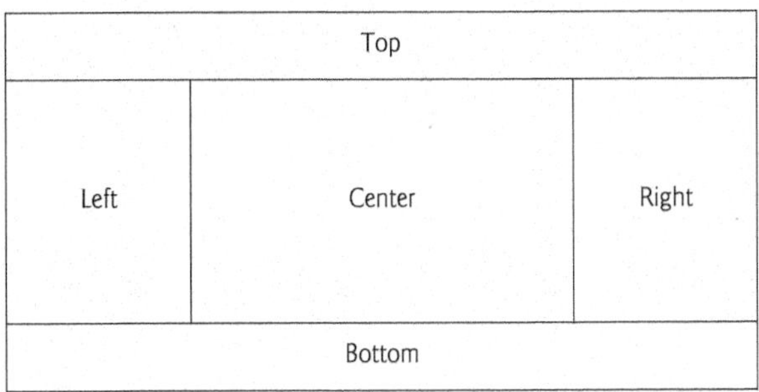

Fig. 13.3 | `BorderPane`'s five areas.

`TitledPane` Layout Container

A **`TitledPane` layout container** displays a title at its top and is a collapsible panel containing a layout node, which in turn contains other nodes. You'll use `TitledPane`s to organize the app's `RadioButton`s and to help the user understand the purpose of each `RadioButton` group.

JavaFX Shapes

The **`javafx.scene.shape`** package contains various classes for creating 2D and 3D shape nodes that can be displayed in a scene graph. In this app, you'll programmatically create **`Circle`** objects as the user drags the mouse, then attach them to the app's drawing area so that they're displayed in the scene graph.

`Pane` Layout Container

Each `Circle` you programmatically create is attached to an **`Pane`** layout (the drawing area) at a specified *x-y* coordinate measured from the `Pane`'s upper-left corner.

Mouse Event Handling

When you drag the mouse, the app's controller responds by displaying a `Circle` (in the currently selected color and pen size) at the current mouse position in the `Pane`. JavaFX nodes support various mouse events, which are summarized in Fig. 13.4. For this app, you'll configure an **`onMouseDragged`** event handler for the `Pane`. JavaFX also supports other types of input events. For example, for touchscreen devices there are various touch-oriented events and for keyboards there are various key events. For a complete list of JavaFX node events, see the `Node` class's properties that begin with the word "on" at:

```
http://docs.oracle.com/javase/8/javafx/api/javafx/scene/Node.html
```

Mouse events	When the event occurs for a given node
`onMouseClicked`	When the user clicks a mouse button—that is, presses and releases a mouse button without moving the mouse—with the mouse cursor within that node.
`onMouseDragEntered`	When the mouse cursor enters a node's bounds during a mouse drag—that is, the user is moving the mouse with a mouse button pressed.
`onMouseDragExited`	When the mouse cursor exits the node's bounds during a mouse drag.
`onMouseDragged`	When the user begins a mouse drag with the mouse cursor within that node and continues moving the mouse with a mouse button pressed.
`onMouseDragOver`	When a drag operation that started in a *different* node continues with the mouse cursor over the given node.
`onMouseDragReleased`	When the user completes a drag operation that began in that node.
`onMouseEntered`	When the mouse cursor enters that node's bounds.
`onMouseExited`	When the mouse cursor exits that node's bounds.
`onMouseMoved`	When the mouse cursor moves within that node's bounds.
`onMousePressed`	When user presses a mouse button with the mouse cursor within that node's bounds.
`onMouseReleased`	When user releases a mouse button with the mouse cursor within that node's bounds.

Fig. 13.4 | Mouse events.

Setting a Control's User Data

Each JavaFX control has a **`setUserData` method** that receives an `Object`. You can use this to store any object you'd like to associate with that control. With each drawing-color `RadioButton`, we store the specific `Color` that the `RadioButton` represents. With each pen size `RadioButton`, we store an `enum` constant for the corresponding pen size. We then use these objects when handling the `RadioButton` events.

13.3.2 Creating the `Painter.fxml` File

Create a folder on your system for this example's files, then open Scene Builder and save the new FXML file as `Painter.fxml`. If you already have an FXML file open, you also can choose **File > New** to create a new FXML file, then save it.

13.3.3 Building the GUI

In this section, we'll discuss the **Painter** app's GUI. Rather than providing the exact steps as we did in Chapter 12, we'll provide general instructions for building the GUI and focus on specific details for new concepts.

Software Engineering Observation 13.1

As you build a GUI, it's often easier to manipulate layouts and controls via Scene Builder's **Hierarchy** *window than directly in the stage design area.*

fx:id Property Values for This App's Controls

Figure 13.5 shows the **fx:id** properties of the **Painter** app's programmatically manipulated controls. As you build the GUI, you should set the corresponding **fx:id** properties in the FXML document, as we discussed in Chapter 12.

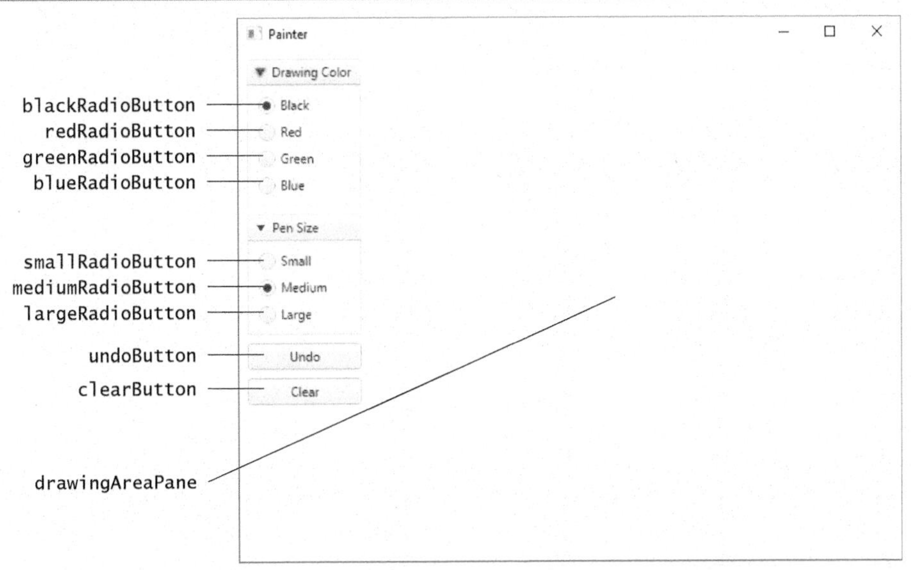

Fig. 13.5 | **Painter** GUI labeled with **fx:id**s for the programmatically manipulated controls.

Step 1: Adding a **BorderPane** *as the Root Layout Node*

Drag a `BorderPane` from the Scene Builder **Library** window's **Containers** section onto the content panel.

Step 2: Configuring the **BorderPane**

We set the `GridPane`'s **Pref Width** and **Pref Height** properties to `640` and `480` respectively. Recall that the stage's size is determined based on the size of the root node in the FXML document. Set the `BorderPane`'s **Padding** property to `8` to inset it from the stage's edges.

Step 3: Adding the **VBox** *and* **Pane**

Drag a `VBox` into the `BorderPane`'s left area and an `Pane` into the center area. As you drag over the `BorderPane`, Scene Builder shows the layout's five areas and highlights the area in which area the item you're dragging will be placed when you release the mouse. Set the `Pane`'s **fx:id** to `drawingAreaPane` as specified in Fig. 13.5.

For the `VBox`, set its **Spacing** property (in the **Inspector**'s **Layout** section) to `8` to add some vertical spacing between the controls that will be added to this container. Set its right **Margin** property to `8` to add some horizontal spacing between the `VBox` and the `Pane` be added to this container. Also reset its **Pref Width** and **Pref Height** properties to their default values (`USE_COMPUTED_SIZE`) and set its **Max Height** property to `MAX_VALUE`. This will enable the `VBox` to be as wide as it needs to be to accommodate its child nodes and occupy the full column height.

Reset the Pane's **Pref Width** and **Pref Height** to their default USE_COMPUTED_SIZE values, and set its **Max Width** and **Max Height** to MAX_VALUE so that it occupies the full width and height of the BorderPane's center area. In the **JavaFX CSS** category of the **Inspector** window's **Properties** section, click the field below **Style** (which is initially empty) and select -fx-background-color to indicate that you'd like to specify the Pane's background color. In the field to the right, specify white.

Step 4: Adding the ***TitledPanes*** *to the* ***VBox***
From the **Library** window's **Containers** section, drag two **TitledPane (empty)** objects onto the VBox. For the first TitledPane, set its **Text** property to Drawing Color. For the second, set its **Text** property to Pen Size.

Step 5: Customizing the ***TitledPanes***
Each TitledPane in the completed GUI contains multiple RadioButtons. We'll use a VBox within each TitledPane to help arrange those controls. Drag a VBox onto each TitledPane. For each VBox, set its **Spacing** property to 8 and its **Pref Width** and **Pref Height** to USE_COMPUTED_SIZE so the VBoxes will be sized based on their contents.

Step 6: Adding the ***RadioButtons*** *to the* ***VBox***
From the **Library** window's **Controls** section, drag four RadioButtons onto the VBox for the **Drawing Color** TitledPane, and three RadioButtons onto the VBox for the **Pen Size** TitledPane, then configure their **Text** properties and **fx:ids** as shown in Fig. 13.5. Select the blackRadioButton and ensure that its **Selected** property is checked, then do the same for the mediumRadioButton.

Step 7: Specifying the ***ToggleGroups*** *for the* ***RadioButtons***
Select all four RadioButtons in the first TitledPane's VBox, then set the **Toggle Group** property to colorToggleGroup. When the FXML file is loaded, a ToggleGroup object by that name will be created and these four RadioButtons will be associated with it to ensure that only one is selected at a time. Repeat this step for the three RadioButtons in the second TitledPane's VBox, but set the **Toggle Group** property to sizeToggleGroup.

Step 8: Changing the ***TitledPanes'*** *Preferred Width and Height*
For each TitledPane, set its **Pref Width** and **Pref Height** to USE_COMPUTED_SIZE so the TitledPanes will be sized based on their contents.

Step 9: Adding the ***Buttons***
Add two Buttons below the TitledPanes, then configure their **Text** properties and **fx:ids** as shown in Fig. 13.5. Set each Button's **Max Width** property to MAX_VALUE so that they fill the VBox's width.

Step 10: Setting the Width the ***VBox***
We'd like the VBox to be only as wide as it needs to be to display the controls in that column. To specify this, select the VBox in the **Document** window's **Hierarchy** section. Set the column's **Min Width** and **Pref Width** to USE_COMPUTED_SIZE, then set the **Max Width** to USE_PREF_SIZE (which indicates that the maximum width should be the preferred width). Also, reset the **Max Height** to its default USE_COMPUTED_SIZE value. The GUI is now complete and should appear as shown in Fig. 13.5.

Step 11: Specifying the Controller Class's Name

As we mentioned in Section 12.5.2, in a JavaFX FXML app, the app's controller class typically defines instance variables for interacting with controls programmatically, as well as event-handling methods. To ensure that an object of the controller class is created when the app loads the FXML file at runtime, you must specify the controller class's name in the FXML file:

1. Expand Scene Builder's **Controller** window (located below the **Hierarchy** window).
2. In the **Controller Class** field, type `PainterController`.

Step 12: Specifying the Event-Handler Method Names

Next, you'll specify in the **Inspector** window's **Code** section the names of the methods that will be called to handle specific control's events:

- For the `drawingAreaPane`, specify `drawingAreaMouseDragged` as the **On Mouse Dragged** event handler (located under the **Mouse** heading in the **Code** section). This method will draw a circle in the specified color and size for each mouse-dragged event.
- For the four **Drawing Color** `RadioButtons`, specify `colorRadioButtonSelected` as each `RadioButton`'s **On Action** event handler. This method will set the current drawing color, based on the user's selection.
- For the three **Pen Size** `RadioButtons`, specify `sizeRadioButtonSelected` as each `RadioButton`'s **On Action** event handler. This method will set the current pen size, based on the user's selection.
- For the **Undo** `Button`, specify `undoButtonPressed` as the **On Action** event handler. This method will remove the last circle the user drew on the screen.
- For the **Clear** `Button`, specify `clearButtonPressed` as the **On Action** event handler. This method will clear the entire drawing.

Step 13: Generating a Sample Controller Class

As you saw in Section 12.5, Scene Builder generates the initial controller-class skeleton for you when you select **View > Show Sample Controller Skeleton.** You can copy this code into a `PainterController.java` file and store the file in the same folder as `Painter.fxml`. We show the completed `PainterController` class in Section 13.3.5.

13.3.4 Painter Subclass of Application

Figure 13.6 shows class `Painter` subclass of `Application` that launches the app, which performs the same tasks to start the **Painter** app as described for the **Tip Calculator** app in Section 12.5.4.

```
// Fig. 13.5: Painter.java
// Main application class that loads and displays the Painter's GUI.
import javafx.application.Application;
import javafx.fxml.FXMLLoader;
```

Fig. 13.6 | Main application class that loads and displays the **Painter**'s GUI.

```
import javafx.scene.Parent;
import javafx.scene.Scene;
import javafx.stage.Stage;

public class Painter extends Application {
   @Override
   public void start(Stage stage) throws Exception {
      Parent root =
         FXMLLoader.load(getClass().getResource("Painter.fxml"));

      Scene scene = new Scene(root);
      stage.setTitle("Painter"); // displayed in window's title bar
      stage.setScene(scene);
      stage.show();
   }

   public static void main(String[] args) {
      launch(args);
   }
}
```

Fig. 13.6 | Main application class that loads and displays the **Painter**'s GUI.

13.3.5 PainterController Class

Figure 13.7 shows the final version of class `PainterController` with this app's new features highlighted. Recall from Chapter 12 that the controller class defines instance variables for interacting with controls programmatically, as well as event-handling methods. The controller class may also declare additional instance variables, `static` variables and methods that support the app's operation.

```
// Fig. 13.6: PainterController.java
// Controller for the Painter app
import javafx.event.ActionEvent;
import javafx.fxml.FXML;
import javafx.scene.control.RadioButton;
import javafx.scene.control.ToggleGroup;
import javafx.scene.input.MouseEvent;
import javafx.scene.layout.Pane;
import javafx.scene.paint.Color;
import javafx.scene.paint.Paint;
import javafx.scene.shape.Circle;

public class PainterController {
   // enum representing pen sizes
   private enum PenSize {
      SMALL(2),
      MEDIUM(4),
      LARGE(6);
```

Fig. 13.7 | Controller for the **Painter** app. (Part 1 of 3.)

```

   private final int radius;

   PenSize(int radius) {this.radius = radius;} // constructor

   public int getRadius() {return radius;}
};

// instance variables that refer to GUI components
@FXML private RadioButton blackRadioButton;
@FXML private RadioButton redRadioButton;
@FXML private RadioButton greenRadioButton;
@FXML private RadioButton blueRadioButton;
@FXML private RadioButton smallRadioButton;
@FXML private RadioButton mediumRadioButton;
@FXML private RadioButton largeRadioButton;
@FXML private Pane drawingAreaPane;
@FXML private ToggleGroup colorToggleGroup;
@FXML private ToggleGroup sizeToggleGroup;

// instance variables for managing Painter state
private PenSize radius = PenSize.MEDIUM; // radius of circle
private Paint brushColor = Color.BLACK; // drawing color

// set user data for the RadioButtons
public void initialize() {
   // user data on a control can be any Object
   blackRadioButton.setUserData(Color.BLACK);
   redRadioButton.setUserData(Color.RED);
   greenRadioButton.setUserData(Color.GREEN);
   blueRadioButton.setUserData(Color.BLUE);
   smallRadioButton.setUserData(PenSize.SMALL);
   mediumRadioButton.setUserData(PenSize.MEDIUM);
   largeRadioButton.setUserData(PenSize.LARGE);
}

// handles drawingArea's onMouseDragged MouseEvent
@FXML
private void drawingAreaMouseDragged(MouseEvent e) {
   Circle newCircle = new Circle(e.getX(), e.getY(),
      radius.getRadius(), brushColor);
   drawingAreaPane.getChildren().add(newCircle);
}

// handles color RadioButton's ActionEvents
@FXML
private void colorRadioButtonSelected(ActionEvent e) {
   // user data for each color RadioButton is the corresponding Color
   brushColor =
      (Color) colorToggleGroup.getSelectedToggle().getUserData();
}

```

Fig. 13.7 | Controller for the **Painter** app. (Part 2 of 3.)

```
71     // handles size RadioButton's ActionEvents
72     @FXML
73     private void sizeRadioButtonSelected(ActionEvent e) {
74        // user data for each size RadioButton is the corresponding PenSize
75        radius =
76           (PenSize) sizeToggleGroup.getSelectedToggle().getUserData();
77     }
78
79     // handles Undo Button's ActionEvents
80     @FXML
81     private void undoButtonPressed(ActionEvent event) {
82        int count = drawingAreaPane.getChildren().size();
83
84        // if there are any shapes remove the last one added
85        if (count > 0) {
86           drawingAreaPane.getChildren().remove(count - 1);
87        }
88     }
89
90     // handles Clear Button's ActionEvents
91     @FXML
92     private void clearButtonPressed(ActionEvent event) {
93        drawingAreaPane.getChildren().clear(); // clear the canvas
94     }
95  }
```

Fig. 13.7 | Controller for the **Painter** app. (Part 3 of 3.)

PenSize enum

Lines 15–25 define the nested `enum` type `PenSize`, which specifies three pen sizes—`SMALL`, `MEDIUM` and `LARGE`. Each has a corresponding radius that will be used when creating a `Circle` object to display in response to a mouse-drag event.

Java allows you to declare classes, interfaces and `enum`s as **nested types** inside other classes. Except for the anonymous inner class introduced in Section 12.5.5, all the classes, interfaces and `enum`s we've discussed were **top level**—that is, they *were* not declared *inside* another type. The `enum` type `PenSize` is declared here as a `private` nested type because it's used only by class `PainterController`. We'll say more about nested types later in the book.

Instance Variables

Lines 28–37 declare the `@FXML` instance variables that the controller uses to programmatically interact with the GUI. Recall that the names of these variables must match the corresponding **fx:id** values that you specified in `Painter.fxml`; otherwise, the `FXMLLoader` will not be able to connect the GUI components to the instance variables. Two of the `@FXML` instance variables are `ToggleGroups`—in the `RadioButton` event handlers, we'll use these to determine which `RadioButton` was selected. Lines 40–41 define two additional instance variables that store the current drawing `Color` and the current `PenSize`, respectively.

Method `initialize`

Recall that when the `FXMLLoader` creates a controller-class object, `FXMLLoader` determines whether the class contains an `initialize` method with no parameters and, if so, calls that method to initialize the controller. Lines 44–53 define method `initialize` to specify each `RadioButton`'s corresponding user data object—either a `Color` or a `PenSize`. You'll use these objects in the `RadioButton`s' event handlers.

`drawingAreaMouseDragged` Event Handler

Lines 56–61 define `drawingAreaMouseDragged`, which responds to drag events in the `drawingAreaPane`. Each mouse event handler you define must have one **`MouseEvent`** parameter (package **`javafx.scene.input`**). When the event occurs, this parameter contains information about the event, such as its location, whether any mouse buttons were pressed, which node the user interacted with and more. You specified `drawingAreaMouseDragged` in Scene Builder as the `drawingAreaPane`'s **On Mouse Dragged** event handler.

Lines 58–59 create a new `Circle` object using the constructor that takes as arguments the center point's *x*-coordinate, the center point's *y*-coordinate, the `Circle`'s radius and the `Circle`'s `Color`.

Next, line 60 attaches the new `Circle` to the `drawingAreaPane`. Each layout pane has a **`getChildren`** method that returns an **`ObservableList<Node>`** collection containing the layout's child nodes. An `ObservableList` provides methods for adding and removing elements. You'll learn more about `ObservableList` later in this chapter. Line 60 uses the `ObservableList`'s `add` method to add a new `Node` to the `drawingAreaPane`—all JavaFX shapes inherit indirectly from class `Node` in the `javafx.scene` package.

`colorRadioButtonSelected` Event Handler

Lines 64–69 define `colorRadioButtonSelected`, which responds to the `ActionEvent`s of the **Drawing Color** `RadioButton`s—these occur each time a new color `RadioButton` is selected. You specified this event handler in Scene Builder as the **On Action** event handler for all four **Drawing Color** `RadioButton`s.

Lines 67–68 set the current drawing `Color`. `ColorToggleGroup` method **`getSelectedToggle`** returns the `Toggle` that's currently selected. Class `RadioButton` is one of several controls (others are `RadioButtonMenuItem` and `ToggleButton`) that implement interface **`Toggle`**. We then use the `Toggle`'s **`getUserData`** method to get the user data `Object` that was associated with the corresponding `RadioButton` in method `initialize`. For the color `RadioButton`s, this `Object` is aways a `Color`, so we cast the `Object` to a `Color` and assign it to `brushColor`.

`sizeRadioButtonSelected` Event Handler

Lines 72–77 define `sizeRadioButtonSelected`, which responds to the pen size `RadioButton`s' `ActionEvent`s. You specified this event handler as the **On Action** event handler for all three **Pen Size** `RadioButton`s. Lines 75–76 set the current `PenSize`, using the same approach as setting the current color in method `colorRadioButtonSelected`.

`undoButtonPressed` Event Handler

Lines 80–88 define `undoButtonPressed`, which responds to an `ActionEvent` from the `undoButton` by removing the last `Circle` displayed. You specified this event handler in Scene Builder as the `undoButton`'s **On Action** event handler.

To undo the last `Circle`, we remove the last child from the `drawingAreaPane`'s collection of child nodes. First, line 82 gets the number of elements in that collection. Then, if that's greater than 0, line 86 removes the node at the last index in the collection.

`clearButtonPressed` *Event Handler*

Lines 91–94 define `clearButtonPressed`, which responds to the `ActionEvent` from the `clearButton` by clearing `drawingAreaPane`'s collection of child nodes. You specified this event handler in Scene Builder as the `clearButton`'s **On Action** event handler. Line 93 clears the collection of child nodes to erase the entire drawing.

13.4 Color Chooser App: Property Bindings and Property Listeners

In this section, we present a **Color Chooser** app (Fig. 13.8) that demonstrates property bindings and property listeners.

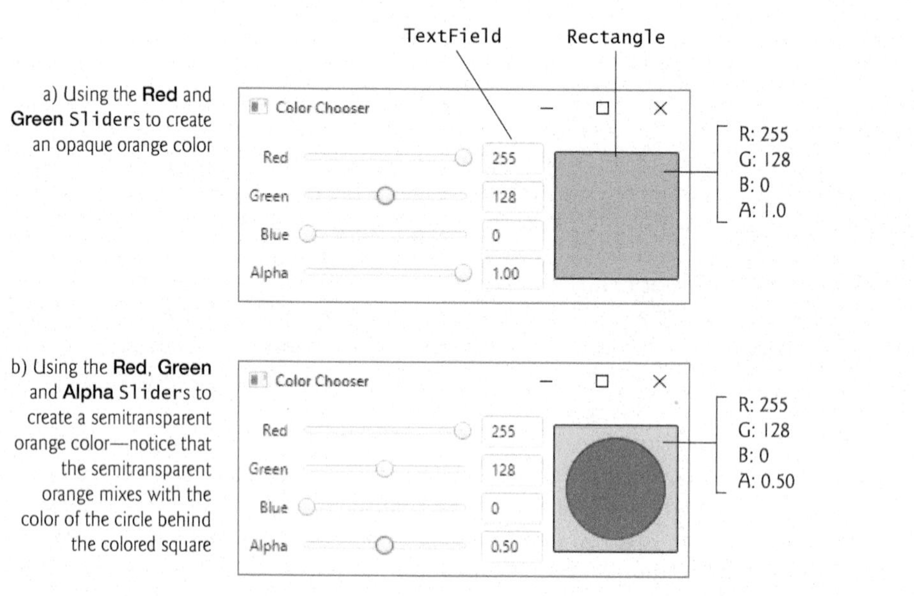

Fig. 13.8 | **Color Chooser** app with opaque and semitransparent orange colors.

13.4.1 Technologies Overview

In this section, we introduce the technologies you'll use to build the **Color Chooser**.

RGBA Colors

The app uses the **RGBA color system** to display a rectangle of color based on the values of four `Sliders`. In RGBA, every color is represented by its red, green and blue color values, each ranging from 0 to 255, where 0 denotes no color and 255 full color. For example, a color with a red value of 0 would contain no red component. The alpha value (A)—which ranges from 0.0 to 1.0—represents a color's *opacity*, with 0.0 being completely *transparent* and 1.0 completely *opaque*. The two colors in Fig. 13.8's sample outputs have the same RGB values, but the color displayed in Fig. 13.8(b) is *semitransparent*. You'll use a `Color` object that's created with RGBA values to fill a `Rectangle` that displays the `Color`.

Properties of a Class

JavaFX makes extensive use of properties. A **property** is defined by creating *set* and *get* methods with specific naming conventions. In general, the pair of methods that define a read/write property have the form:

```
public final void setPropertyName(Type propertyName)
public final Type getPropertyName()
```

Typically, such methods manipulate a corresponding *private* instance variable that has the same name as the property, but this is not required. For example, methods `setHour` and `getHour` together represent a property named `hour` and typically would manipulate a private `hour` instance variable. If the property represents a `boolean` value, its *get* method name typically begins with "`is`" rather than "`get`"—for example, `ArrayList` method `isEmpty`.

Software Engineering Observation 13.2

Methods that define properties should be declared `final` to prevent subclasses from overriding the methods, which could lead to unexpected results in client code.

Property Bindings

JavaFX properties are implemented in a manner that makes them *observable*—when a property's value changes, other objects can respond accordingly. This is similar to event handling. One way to respond to a property change is via a **property binding**, which enables a property of one object to be updated when a property of another object changes. For example, you'll use property bindings to enable a `TextField` to display the corresponding `Slider`'s current value when the user moves that `Slider`'s thumb. Property bindings are not limited to JavaFX controls. Package **`javafx.beans.property`** contains many classes that you can use to define bindable properties in your own classes.

Property Listeners

Property listeners are similar to property bindings. A **property listener** is an event handler that's invoked when a property's value changes. In the event handler, you can respond to the property change in a manner appropriate for your app. In this app, when a `Slider`'s value changes, a property listener will store the value in a corresponding instance variable, create a new `Color` based on the values of all four `Sliders` and set that `Color` as the fill color of a `Rectangle` object that displays the current color. For more information on properties, property bindings and property listeners, visit:

```
http://docs.oracle.com/javase/8/javafx/properties-binding-tutorial/
binding.htm
```

13.4.2 Building the GUI

In this section, we'll discuss the **Color Chooser** app's GUI. Rather than providing the exact steps as we did in Chapter 12, we'll provide general instructions for building the GUI and focus on specific details for new concepts. As you build the GUI, recall that it's often easier to manipulate layouts and controls via the Scene Builder **Document** window's **Hierarchy** section than directly in the stage design area. Before proceeding, open Scene Builder and create an FXML file named `ColorChooser.fxml`.

fx:id Property Values for This App's Controls

Figure 13.9 shows the **fx:id** properties of the **Color Chooser** app's programmatically manipulated controls. As you build the GUI, you should set the corresponding **fx:id** properties in the FXML document, as you learned in Chapter 12.

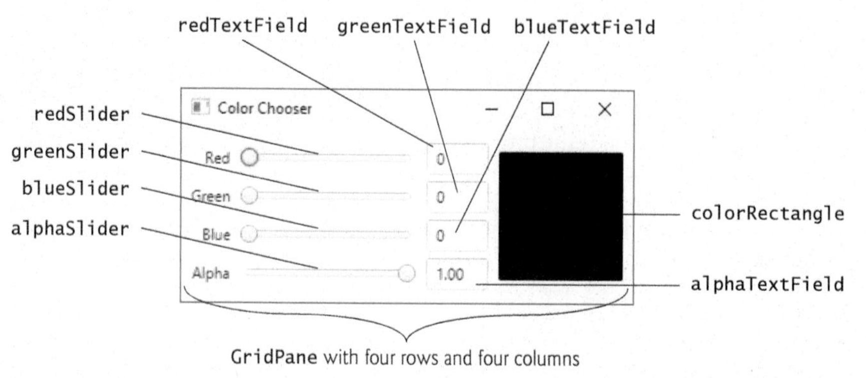

Fig. 13.9 | **Color Chooser** app's programmatically manipulated controls labeled with their **fx:id**s.

Step 1: Adding a `GridPane`

Drag a `GridPane` from the **Library** window's **Containers** section onto Scene Builder's content panel.

Step 2: Configuring the `GridPane`

This app's `GridPane` requires four rows and four columns. Use the techniques you've learned previously to add two columns and one row to the `GridPane`. Set the `GridPane`'s **Hgap** and **Padding** properties to `8` to inset the `GridPane` from the stage's edges and to provide space between its columns.

Step 3: Adding the Controls

Using Fig. 13.9 as a guide, add the `Label`s, `Slider`s, `TextField`s, a `Circle` and a `Rectangle` to the `GridPane`—`Circle` and `Rectangle` are located in the Scene Builder **Library**'s **Shapes** section. When adding the `Circle` and `Rectangle`, place both into the rightmost column's first row. Be sure to add the `Circle` *before* the `Rectangle` so that it will be located *behind* the rectangle in the layout. Set the text of the `Label`s and `TextField`s as shown and set all the appropriate **fx:id** properties as you add each control.

Step 4: Configuring the `Slider`*s*

For the red, green and blue `Slider`s, set the **Max** properties to `255` (the maximum amount of a given color in the RGBA color scheme). For the alpha `Slider`, set its **Max** property to `1.0` (the maximum opacity in the RGBA color scheme).

Step 5: Configuring the `TextField`*s*

Set all of the `TextField`'s **Pref Width** properties to `50`.

Step 6: Configuring the **Rectangle**
Set the Rectangle's **Width** and **Height** properties to 100, then set its **Row Span** property to Remainder so that it spans all four rows.

Step 7: Configuring the **Circle**
Set the Circle's **Radius** property to 40, then set its **Row Span** property to Remainder so that it spans all four rows.

Step 8: Configuring the Rows
Set all four columns' **Pref Height** properties to USE_COMPUTED_SIZE so that the rows are only as tall as their content.

Step 9: Configuring the Columns
Set all four columns' **Pref Width** properties to USE_COMPUTED_SIZE so that the columns are only as wide as their content. For the leftmost column, set the **Halignment** property to RIGHT. For the rightmost column, set the **Halignment** property to CENTER.

Step 10: Configuring the **GridPane**
Set the GridPane's **Pref Width** and **Pref Height** properties to USE_COMPUTED_SIZE so that it sizes itself, based on its contents. Your GUI should now appear as shown in Fig. 13.9.

Step 11: Specifying the Controller Class's Name
To ensure that an object of the controller class is created when the app loads the FXML file at runtime, specify ColorChooserController as the controller class's name in the FXML file as you've done previously.

Step 12: Generating a Sample Controller Class
Select **View > Show Sample Controller Skeleton**, then copy this code into a ColorChooser-Controller.java file and store the file in the same folder as ColorChooser.fxml. We show the completed ColorChooserController class in Section 13.4.4.

13.4.3 ColorChooser Subclass of Application

Figure 13.6 shows the ColorChooser subclass of Application that launches the app. This class loads the FXML and displays the app as in the prior JavaFX examples.

```
// Fig. 13.8: ColorChooser.java
// Main application class that loads and displays the ColorChooser's GUI.
import javafx.application.Application;
import javafx.fxml.FXMLLoader;
import javafx.scene.Parent;
import javafx.scene.Scene;
import javafx.stage.Stage;

public class ColorChooser extends Application {
   @Override
   public void start(Stage stage) throws Exception {
      Parent root =
         FXMLLoader.load(getClass().getResource("ColorChooser.fxml"));
```

Fig. 13.10 | Application class that loads and displays the **Color Chooser**'s GUI. (Part 1 of 2.)

```
      Scene scene = new Scene(root);
      stage.setTitle("Color Chooser");
      stage.setScene(scene);
      stage.show();
   }

   public static void main(String[] args) {
      launch(args);
   }
}
```

Fig. 13.10 | Application class that loads and displays the **Color Chooser**'s GUI. (Part 2 of 2.)

13.4.4 ColorChooserController Class

Figure 13.11 shows the final version of class ColorChooserController with this app's new features highlighted.

```
// Fig. 13.9: ColorChooserController.java
// Controller for the ColorChooser app
import javafx.beans.value.ChangeListener;
import javafx.beans.value.ObservableValue;
import javafx.fxml.FXML;
import javafx.scene.control.Slider;
import javafx.scene.control.TextField;
import javafx.scene.paint.Color;
import javafx.scene.shape.Rectangle;

public class ColorChooserController {
   // instance variables for interacting with GUI components
   @FXML private Slider redSlider;
   @FXML private Slider greenSlider;
   @FXML private Slider blueSlider;
   @FXML private Slider alphaSlider;
   @FXML private TextField redTextField;
   @FXML private TextField greenTextField;
   @FXML private TextField blueTextField;
   @FXML private TextField alphaTextField;
   @FXML private Rectangle colorRectangle;

   // instance variables for managing
   private int red = 0;
   private int green = 0;
   private int blue = 0;
   private double alpha = 1.0;

   public void initialize() {
      // bind TextField values to corresponding Slider values
      redTextField.textProperty().bind(
         redSlider.valueProperty().asString("%.0f"));
```

Fig. 13.11 | Controller for the ColorChooser app. (Part 1 of 2.)

```
      greenTextField.textProperty().bind(
         greenSlider.valueProperty().asString("%.0f"));
      blueTextField.textProperty().bind(
         blueSlider.valueProperty().asString("%.0f"));
      alphaTextField.textProperty().bind(
         alphaSlider.valueProperty().asString("%.2f"));

      // listeners that set Rectangle's fill based on Slider changes
      redSlider.valueProperty().addListener(
         new ChangeListener<Number>() {
            @Override
            public void changed(ObservableValue<? extends Number> ov,
               Number oldValue, Number newValue) {
               red = newValue.intValue();
               colorRectangle.setFill(Color.rgb(red, green, blue, alpha));
            }
         }
      );
      greenSlider.valueProperty().addListener(
         new ChangeListener<Number>() {
            @Override
            public void changed(ObservableValue<? extends Number> ov,
               Number oldValue, Number newValue) {
               green = newValue.intValue();
               colorRectangle.setFill(Color.rgb(red, green, blue, alpha));
            }
         }
      );
      blueSlider.valueProperty().addListener(
         new ChangeListener<Number>() {
            @Override
            public void changed(ObservableValue<? extends Number> ov,
               Number oldValue, Number newValue) {
               blue = newValue.intValue();
               colorRectangle.setFill(Color.rgb(red, green, blue, alpha));
            }
         }
      );
      alphaSlider.valueProperty().addListener(
         new ChangeListener<Number>() {
            @Override
            public void changed(ObservableValue<? extends Number> ov,
               Number oldValue, Number newValue) {
               alpha = newValue.doubleValue();
               colorRectangle.setFill(Color.rgb(red, green, blue, alpha));
            }
         }
      );
   }
}
```

Fig. 13.11 | Controller for the ColorChooser app. (Part 2 of 2.)

Instance Variables

Lines 13–27 declare the controller's instance variables. Variables `red`, `green`, `blue` and `alpha` store the current values of the `redSlider`, `greenSlider`, `blueSlider` and `alphaSlider`, respectively. These values are used to update the `colorRectangle`'s fill color each time the user moves a `Slider`'s thumb.

Method `initialize`

Lines 29–81 define method `initialize`, which initializes the controller after the GUI is created. In this app, `initialize` configures the property bindings and property listeners.

Property-to-Property Bindings

Lines 31–38 set up property bindings between a `Slider`'s value and the corresponding `TextField`'s text so that changing a `Slider` updates the corresponding `TextField`. Consider lines 31–32, which bind the `redSlider`'s `valueProperty` to the `redTextField's` `textProperty`:

```
redTextField.textProperty().bind(
   redSlider.valueProperty().asString("%.0f"));
```

Each `TextField` has a `text` property that's returned by its **`textProperty`** method as a **`StringProperty`** (package `javafx.beans.property`). `StringProperty` method **`bind`** receives an **`ObservableValue`** as an argument. When the `ObservableValue` changes, the bound property updates accordingly. In this case the `ObservableValue` is the result of the expression `redSlider.valueProperty().asString("%.0f")`. `Slider`'s `valueProperty` method returns the `Slider`'s `value` property as a **`DoubleProperty`**—an observable `double` value. Because the `TextField`'s `text` property must be bound to a `String`, we call `DoubleProperty` method **`asString`**, which returns a **`StringBinding`** object (an `ObservableValue`) that produces a `String` representation of the `DoubleProperty`. This version of `asString` receives a format-control `String` specifying the `DoubleProperty`'s format.

Property Listeners

To perform an arbitrary task when a property's value changes, register a property listener. Lines 41–80 register property listeners for the `Sliders`' `value` properties. Consider lines 41–50, which register the `ChangeListener` that executes when the user moves the `redSlider`'s thumb. As we did in Section 12.5 for the **Tip Calculator**'s `Slider`, we use an anonymous inner class to define the listener. Each `ChangeListener` stores the `int` value of the `newValue` parameter in a corresponding instance variable, then calls the `colorRectangle`'s `setFill` method to change its color, using `Color` method `rgb` to create the new `Color` object.

13.5 Cover Viewer App: Data-Driven GUIs with JavaFX Collections

Often an app needs to edit and display data. JavaFX provides a comprehensive model for allowing GUIs to interact with data. In this section, you'll build the **Cover Viewer** app (Fig. 13.12), which binds a list of `Book` objects to a `ListView`. When the user selects an item in the `ListView`, the corresponding `Book`'s cover image is displayed in an `ImageView`.

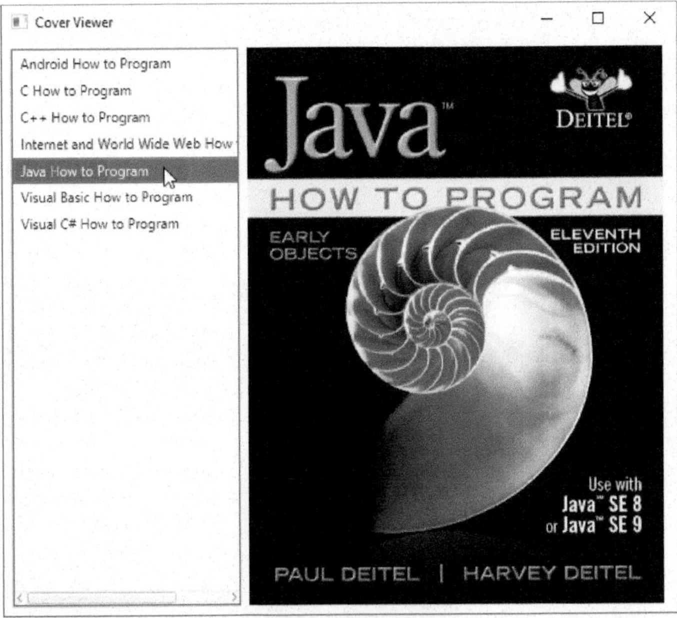

Fig. 13.12 | **Cover Viewer** with *Java How to Program* selected.

13.5.1 Technologies Overview

This app uses a `ListView` control to display a collection of book titles. Though you can individually add items to a `ListView`, in this app you'll bind an **`ObservableList`** object to the `ListView`. If you make changes to an `ObservableList`, its observer (the `ListView` in this app) will automatically be notified of those changes. Package **`javafx.collections`** defines `ObservableList` (similar to an `ArrayList`) and other observable collection interfaces. The package also contains class **`FXCollections`**, which provides `static` methods for creating and manipulating observable collections. You'll use a property listener to display the correct image when the user selects an item from the `ListView`—in this case, the property that changes is the selected item.

13.5.2 Adding Images to the App's Folder

From this chapter's examples folder, copy the `images` folder (which contains the `large` and `small` subfolders) into the folder where you'll save this app's FXML file, and the source-code files `CoverViewer.java` and `CoverViewerController.java`. Though you'll use only the `large` images in this example, you'll copy this app's folder to create the next example, which uses both sets of images.

13.5.3 Building the GUI

In this section, we'll discuss the **Cover Viewer** app's GUI. As you've done previously, create a new FXML file, then save it as `CoverViewer.fxml`.

fx:id Property Values for This App's Controls

Figure 13.13 shows the **fx:id** properties of the **Cover Viewer** app's programmatically manipulated controls. As you build the GUI, you should set the corresponding **fx:id** properties in the FXML document.

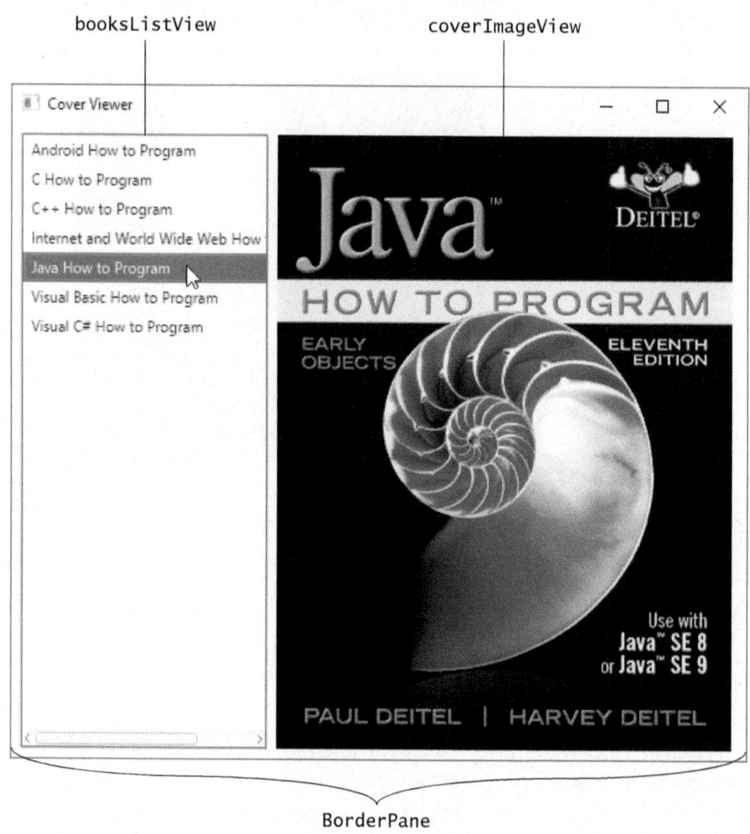

Fig. 13.13 | **Cover Viewer** app's programmatically manipulated controls labeled with their **fx:ids**.

Adding and Configuring the Controls

Using the techniques you learned previously, create a `BorderPane`. In the left area, place a `ListView` control, and in the center area, place an `ImageView` control.

For the `ListView`, set the following properties:

- **Margin**—`8` (for the right margin) to separate the `ListView` from the `ImageView`
- **Pref Width**—`200`
- **Max Height**—`MAX_VALUE`
- **Min Width**, **Min Height**, **Pref Height** and **Max Width**—`USE_COMPUTED_SIZE`

For the `ImageView`, set the **Fit Width** and **Fit Height** properties to `370` and `480`, respectively. To size the `BorderPane` based on its contents, set its **Pref Width** and **Pref Height** to `USE_COMPUTED_SIZE`. Also, set the **Padding** property to `8` to inset the `BorderPane` from the stage.

Specifying the Controller Class's Name

To ensure that an object of the controller class is created when the app loads the FXML file at runtime, specify `CoverViewerController` as the controller class's name in the FXML file as you've done previously.

Generating a Sample Controller Class

Select **View > Show Sample Controller Skeleton**, then copy this code into a `CoverViewer-Controller.java` file and store the file in the same folder as `CoverViewer.fxml`. We show the completed `CoverViewerController` class in Section 13.5.5.

13.5.4 CoverViewer Subclass of Application

Figure 13.14 shows class `CoverViewer` subclass of `Application`.

```
// Fig. 13.13: CoverViewer.java
// Main application class that loads and displays the CoverViewer's GUI.
import javafx.application.Application;
import javafx.fxml.FXMLLoader;
import javafx.scene.Parent;
import javafx.scene.Scene;
import javafx.stage.Stage;

public class CoverViewer extends Application {
   @Override
   public void start(Stage stage) throws Exception {
      Parent root =
         FXMLLoader.load(getClass().getResource("CoverViewer.fxml"));

      Scene scene = new Scene(root);
      stage.setTitle("Cover Viewer");
      stage.setScene(scene);
      stage.show();
   }

   public static void main(String[] args) {
      launch(args);
   }
}
```

Fig. 13.14 | Main application class that loads and displays the **Cover Viewer**'s GUI.

13.5.5 CoverViewerController Class

Figure 13.15 shows the final version of class `CoverViewerController` with the app's new features highlighted.

```
// Fig. 13.14: CoverViewerController.java
// Controller for Cover Viewer application
import javafx.beans.value.ChangeListener;
```

Fig. 13.15 | Controller for **Cover Viewer** application. (Part 1 of 2.)

```java
import javafx.beans.value.ObservableValue;
import javafx.collections.FXCollections;
import javafx.collections.ObservableList;
import javafx.fxml.FXML;
import javafx.scene.control.ListView;
import javafx.scene.image.Image;
import javafx.scene.image.ImageView;

public class CoverViewerController {
   // instance variables for interacting with GUI
   @FXML private ListView<Book> booksListView;
   @FXML private ImageView coverImageView;

   // stores the list of Book Objects
   private final ObservableList<Book> books =
      FXCollections.observableArrayList();

   // initialize controller
   public void initialize() {
      // populate the ObservableList<Book>
      books.add(new Book("Android How to Program",
         "/images/small/androidhtp.jpg", "/images/large/androidhtp.jpg"));
      books.add(new Book("C How to Program",
         "/images/small/chtp.jpg", "/images/large/chtp.jpg"));
      books.add(new Book("C++ How to Program",
         "/images/small/cpphtp.jpg", "/images/large/cpphtp.jpg"));
      books.add(new Book("Internet and World Wide Web How to Program",
         "/images/small/iw3htp.jpg", "/images/large/iw3htp.jpg"));
      books.add(new Book("Java How to Program",
         "/images/small/jhtp.jpg", "/images/large/jhtp.jpg"));
      books.add(new Book("Visual Basic How to Program",
         "/images/small/vbhtp.jpg", "/images/large/vbhtp.jpg"));
      books.add(new Book("Visual C# How to Program",
         "/images/small/vcshtp.jpg", "/images/large/vcshtp.jpg"));
      booksListView.setItems(books); // bind booksListView to books

      // when ListView selection changes, show large cover in ImageView
      booksListView.getSelectionModel().selectedItemProperty().
         addListener(
            new ChangeListener<Book>() {
               @Override
               public void changed(ObservableValue<? extends Book> ov,
                  Book oldValue, Book newValue) {
                  coverImageView.setImage(
                     new Image(newValue.getLargeImage()));
               }
            }
         );
   }
}
```

Fig. 13.15 | Controller for **Cover Viewer** application. (Part 2 of 2.)

`@FXML` *Instance Variables*

Lines 14–15 declare the controller's `@FXML` instance variables. Notice that `ListView` is a generic class. In this case, the `ListView` displays `Book` objects. Class `Book` contains three `String` instance variables with corresponding *set* and *get* methods:

- `title`—the book's title.
- `thumbImage`—the path to the book's thumbnail image (used in the next example).
- `largeImage`—the path to the book's large cover image.

The class also provides a `toString` method that returns the `Book`'s title and a constructor that initializes the three instance variables. You should copy class `Book` from this chapter's examples folder into the folder that contains `CoverViewer.fxml`, `CoverViewer.java` and `CoverViewerController.java`.

Instance Variable `books`

Lines 18–19 define the `books` instance variable as an `ObservableList<Book>` and initialize it by calling `FXCollections` `static` method **`observableArrayList`**. This method returns an empty collection object (similar to an `ArrayList`) that implements the `ObservableList` interface.

Initializing the `books` `ObservableList`

Lines 24–37 in method `initialize` create and add `Book` objects to the `books` collection. Line 38 passes this collection to `ListView` method **`setItems`**, which binds the `ListView` to the `ObservableList`. This *data binding* allows the `ListView` to display the `Book` objects automatically. By default, the `ListView` displays each `Book`'s `String` representation. (In the next example, you'll customize this.)

Listening for `ListView` *Selection Changes*

To synchronize the book cover that's being displayed with the currently selected book, we listen for changes to the `ListView`'s selected item. By default a `ListView` supports single selection—one item at a time may be selected. `ListView`s also support multiple selection. The type of selection is managed by the `ListView`'s **`MultipleSelectionModel`** (a subclass of **`SelectionModel`** from package `javafx.scene.control`), which contains observable properties and various methods for manipulating the corresponding `ListView`'s items.

To respond to selection changes, you register a listener for the `MultipleSelectionModel`'s `selectedItem` property (lines 41–51). `ListView` method **`getSelectionModel`** returns a `MultipleSelectionModel` object. In this example, `MultipleSelectionModel`'s **`selectedItemProperty`** method returns a **`ReadOnlyObjectProperty<Book>`**, and the corresponding `ChangeListener` receives as its `oldValue` and `newValue` parameters the previously selected and newly selected `Book` objects, respectively.

Lines 47–48 use `newValue`'s large image path to initialize a new **`Image`** (package `javafx.scene.image`)—this loads the image from that path. We then pass the new `Image` to the `coverImageView`'s **`setImage`** method to display the `Image`.

13.6 Cover Viewer App: Customizing `ListView` Cells

In the preceding example, the `ListView` displayed a `Book`'s `String` representation (i.e., its title). In this example, you'll create a custom `ListView` cell factory to create cells that display each book as its thumbnail image and title using a VBox, an ImageView and a Label (Fig. 13.16).

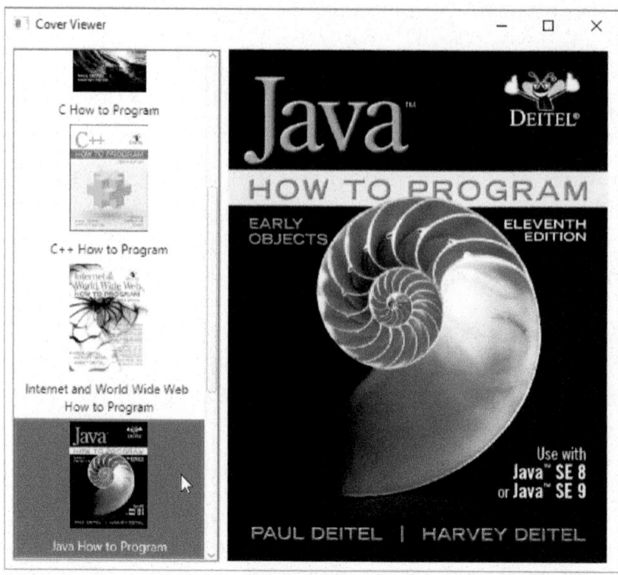

Fig. 13.16 | **Cover Viewer** app with *Java How to Program* selected.

13.6.1 Technologies Overview

`ListCell` Generic Class for Custom `ListView` Cell Formats

As you saw in Section 13.5, `ListView` cells display the `String` representations of a `ListView`'s items by default. To create a custom cell format, you must first define a subclass of the **`ListCell`** generic class (package `javafx.scene.control`) that specifies how to create a `ListView` cell. As the `ListView` displays items, it gets `ListCell`s from its cell factory. You'll use the `ListView`'s **`setCellFactory`** method to replace the default cell factory with one that returns objects of the `ListCell` subclass. You'll override this class's **`updateItem`** method to specify the cells' custom layout and contents.

Programmatically Creating Layouts and Controls

So far, you've created GUIs visually using JavaFX Scene Builder. In this app, you'll also create a portion of the GUI programmatically—in fact, everything we've shown you in Scene Builder also can be accomplished in Java code directly. In particular, you'll create and configure a `VBox` layout containing an `ImageView` and a `Label`. The `VBox` represents the custom `ListView` cell format.

13.6.2 Copying the `CoverViewer` App

This app's FXML layout and classes `Book` and `CoverViewer` are identical to those in Section 13.5, and the `CoverViewerController` class has only one new statement. For this example, we'll show a new class that implements the custom `ListView` cell factory and the one new statement in class `CoverViewerController`. Rather than creating a new app from scratch, copy the CoverViewer app from the previous example into a new folder named CoverViewerCustomListView.

13.6.3 ImageTextCell Custom Cell Factory Class

Class ImageTextCell (Fig. 13.17) defines the custom ListView cell layout for this version of the **Cover Viewer** app. The class extends ListCell<Book> because it defines a customized presentation of a Book in a ListView cell.

```
// Fig. 13.16: ImageTextCell.java
// Custom ListView cell factory that displays an Image and text
import javafx.geometry.Pos;
import javafx.scene.control.Label;
import javafx.scene.control.ListCell;
import javafx.scene.image.Image;
import javafx.scene.image.ImageView;
import javafx.scene.layout.VBox;
import javafx.scene.text.TextAlignment;

public class ImageTextCell extends ListCell<Book> {
   private VBox vbox = new VBox(8.0); // 8 points of gap between controls
   private ImageView thumbImageView = new ImageView(); // initially empty
   private Label label = new Label();

   // constructor configures VBox, ImageView and Label
   public ImageTextCell() {
      vbox.setAlignment(Pos.CENTER); // center VBox contents horizontally

      thumbImageView.setPreserveRatio(true);
      thumbImageView.setFitHeight(100.0); // thumbnail 100 points tall
      vbox.getChildren().add(thumbImageView); // attach to Vbox

      label.setWrapText(true); // wrap if text too wide to fit in label
      label.setTextAlignment(TextAlignment.CENTER); // center text
      vbox.getChildren().add(label); // attach to VBox

      setPrefWidth(USE_PREF_SIZE); // use preferred size for cell width
   }

   // called to configure each custom ListView cell
   @Override
   protected void updateItem(Book item, boolean empty) {
      // required to ensure that cell displays properly
      super.updateItem(item, empty)

      if (empty || item == null) {
         setGraphic(null); // don't display anything
      }
      else {
         // set ImageView's thumbnail image
         thumbImageView.setImage(new Image(item.getThumbImage()));
         label.setText(item.getTitle()); // configure Label's text
```

Fig. 13.17 | Custom ListView cell factory that displays an image and text.

```
44              setGraphic(vbox); // attach custom layout to ListView cell
45          }
46      }
47  }
```

Fig. 13.17 | Custom `ListView` cell factory that displays an image and text.

Constructor

The constructor (lines 17–29) configures the instance variables we use to build the custom presentation. Line 18 indicates that the `VBox`'s children should be centered. Lines 20–22 configure the `ImageView` and attach it to the `VBox`'s collection of children. Line 20 indicates that the `ImageView` should preserve the image's aspect ratio, and line 21 indicates that the `ImageView` should be 100 points tall. Line 22 attaches the `ImageView` to the `VBox`.

Lines 24–26 configure the `Label` and attach it to the `VBox`'s collection of children. Line 24 indicates that the `Label` should wrap its text if its too wide to fit in the `Label`'s width, and line 25 indicates that the text should be centered in the `Label`. Line 26 attaches the `Label` to the `VBox`. Finally, line 28 indicates that the cell should use its preferred width, which is determined from the width of its parent `ListView`.

Method `updateItem`

Method `updateItem` (lines 32–46) configures the `Label`'s text and the `ImageView`'s `Image` then displays the custom presentation in the `ListView`. This method is called by the `ListView`'s cell factory when a `ListView` cell is required—that is, when the `ListView` is first displayed and when `ListView` cells are about to scroll onto the screen. The method receives the `Book` to display and a `boolean` indicating whether the cell that's about to be created is empty. You must call the superclass's version of `updateItem` (line 35) to ensure that the custom cells display correctly.

If the cell is empty or the item parameter is `null`, then there is no `Book` to display and line 38 calls the `ImageTextCell`'s inherited **`setGraphic`** method with `null`. This method receives as its argument the `Node` that should be displayed in the cell. Any JavaFX `Node` can be provided, giving you tremendous flexibility for customizing a cell's appearance.

If there is a `Book` to display, lines 40–45 configure the `ImageTextCell`'s the `Label` and `ImageView`. Line 42 configures the `Book`'s `Image` and sets it to display in the `ImageView`. Line 43 sets the `Label`'s text to the `Book`'s title. Finally, line 38 uses method `setGraphic` to set the `ImageTextCell`'s `VBox` as the custom cell's presentation.

Performance Tip 13.1

For the best `ListView` performance, it's considered best practice to define the custom presentation's controls as instance variables in the `ListCell` subclass and configure them in the subclass's constructor. This minimizes the amount of work required in each call to method `updateItem`.

13.6.4 `CoverViewerController` Class

Once you've defined the custom cell layout, updating the `CoverViewerController` to use it requires that you set the `ListView`'s cell factory. Insert the following code as the last statement in the `CoverViewerController`'s `initialize` method:

```
booksListView.setCellFactory(
   new Callback<ListView<Book>, ListCell<Book>>() {
      @Override
      public ListCell<Book> call(ListView<Book> listView) {
         return new ImageTextCell();
      }
   }
);
```

and add an import for `javafx.util.Callback`.

The argument to `ListView` method `setCellFactory` is an implementation of the functional interface **`CallBack`** (package **`javafx.util`**). This generic interface provides a `call` method that receives one argument and returns a value. In this case, we implement interface `Callback` with an object of an anonymous inner class. In `Callback`'s angle brackets the first type (`ListView<Book>`) is the parameter type for the interface's `call` method and the second (`ListCell<Book>`) is the `call` method's return type. The parameter represents the `ListView` in which the custom cells will appear. The `call` method call simply creates and returns an object of the `ImageTextCell` class.

Each time the `ListView` requires a new cell, the anonymous inner class's `call` method will be invoked to get a new `ImageTextCell`. Then the `ImageTextCell`'s `update` method
will be called to create the custom cell presentation. Note that by using a Java SE 8 lambda 8
(Chapter 17) rather than an anonymous inner class, you can replace the entire statement that sets the cell factory with a single line of code.

13.7 Additional JavaFX Capabilities

This section overviews various additional JavaFX capabilities that are available in JavaFX 8 and JavaFX 9.

`TableView` Control

Section 13.5 demonstrated how to bind data to a `ListView` control. You often load such data from a database (Chapter 24, Accessing Databases with JDBC, and Chapter 29, Java Persistence API (JPA)). JavaFX's `TableView` control (package `javafx.scene.control`) displays tabular data in rows and columns, and supports user interactions with that data.

Accessibility

In a Java SE 8 update, JavaFX added *accessibility* features to help people with visual im- 8
pairments use their devices. For example, the screen readers in various operating systems can speak screen text or text that you provide to help users with visual impairments understand the purpose of a control. Visually impaired users must enable their operating systems' screen-reading capabilities. JavaFX controls also support:

- GUI navigation via the keyboard—for example, the user can press the *Tab* key to jump from one control to the next. If a screen reader also is enabled, as the user moves the focus from control to control, the screen reader will speak appropriate information about each control (discussed below).
- A high-contrast mode to make controls more readable—as with screen readers, visually impaired users must enable this feature in their operating systems.

See your operating system's documentation for information on enabling its screen reader and high-contrast mode.

Every JavaFX `Node` subclass also has the following accessibility-related properties:

- `accessibleTextProperty`—A `String` that a screen reader speaks for a control. For example, a screen reader normally speaks the text displayed on a `Button`, but setting this property for a `Button` causes the screen reader to speak this property's text instead. You also can set this property to provide accessibility text for controls that do not have text, such as `ImageViews`.
- `accessibleHelpProperty`—A more detailed control description `String` than that provided by the `accessibleTextProperty`. This property's text should help the user understand the purpose of the control in the context of your app.
- `accessibleRoleProperty`—A value from the `enum AccessibleRole` (package `javafx.scene`). A screen reader uses this property value to determine the attributes and actions supported for a given control.
- `accessibleRoleDescriptionProperty`—A `String` text description of a control that a screen reader typically speaks followed by the control's contents (such as the text on a `Button`) or the value of the `accessibleTextProperty`.

In addition, you can add `Labels` to a GUI that describe other controls. In such cases, you should set each `Label`'s `labelFor` property to the specific control the `Label` describes. For example, a `TextField` in which the user can enter a phone number might be preceded by a `Label` containing the text `"Phone Number"`. If the `Label`'s `labelFor` property references the `TextField`, then a screen reader will read the `Label`'s text as well when describing the `TextField` to the user.

Third-Party JavaFX Libraries

JavaFX continues to become more popular. There are various open-source, third-party libraries, which define additional JavaFX capabilities that you can incorporate into your own apps. Some popular JavaFX libraries include:

- ControlsFX (`http://www.controlsfx.org/`) provides common dialogs, additional controls, validation capabilities, `TextField` enhancements, a `SpreadSheetView`, `TableView` enhancements and more. You can find the API documentation at `http://docs.controlsfx.org/` and various code samples at `http://code.controlsfx.org`. We use one of the open-source ControlsFX dialogs in Chapter 22.
- JFXtras (`http://jfxtras.org/`) also provides many additional JavaFX controls, including date/time pickers, controls for maintaining an agenda, a calendar control, additional window features and more.
- Medusa provides many JavaFX gauges that look like clocks, speedometers and more. You can view samples at `https://github.com/HanSolo/Medusa/blob/master/README.md`.

Creating Custom JavaFX Controls

You can create custom controls by extending existing JavaFX control classes to customize them or by extending JavaFX's `Control` class directly.

JavaFXPorts: JavaFX for Mobile and Embedded Devices

A key Java benefit is writing apps that can run on any device with a Java Virtual Machine (JVM), including notebook computers, desktop computers, servers, mobile devices and embedded devices (such as those used in the Internet of Things). Oracle officially supports JavaFX only for desktop apps. Gluon's open-source JavaFXPorts project brings the desktip version of JavaFX to mobile devices (iOS and Android) and devices like the inexpensive Raspberry Pi (`https://www.raspberrypi.org/`), which can be used as a standalone computer or for embedded-device applications. For more information on JavaFXPorts, visit

```
http://javafxports.org/
```

In addition, Gluon Mobile provides a mobile-optimized JavaFX implementation for iOS and Android. For more information, see

```
http://gluonhq.com/products/mobile/
```

Scenic View *for Debugging JavaFX Scenes and Nodes*

Scenic View is a debugging tool for JavaFX scenes and nodes. You embed **Scenic View** directly into your apps or run it as a standalone app. You can inspect your JavaFX scenes and nodes, and modify them dynamically to see how changes affect their presentation on the screen—without having to edit your code, recompile it and re-run it for each change. For more information, visit

```
http://www.scenic-view.org
```

JavaFX Resources and JavaFX in the Real World

Visit

```
http://bit.ly/JavaFXResources
```

for a lengthy and growing list of JavaFX resources that includes links to:

- articles
- tutorials (free and for purchase)
- key blogs and websites
- YouTube® videos
- books (for purchase)
- many libraries, tools, projects and frameworks
- slide shows from JavaFX presentations and
- various real-world examples of JavaFX in use.

13.8 JavaFX 9: Java SE 9 JavaFX Updates

This section overviews several JavaFX 9 changes and enhancements.

Java SE 9 Modularization

Java SE 9's biggest new software-engineering feature is the module system. This applies to JavaFX 9 as well. The key JavaFX 9 modules are: 9

- `javafx.base`—Contains the packages required by all JavaFX 9 apps. All the other JavaFX 9 modules depend on this one.
- `javafx.controls`—Contains the packages for controls, layouts and charts, including the various controls we demonstrated in this chapter and Chapter 12.
- `javafx.fxml`—Contains the packages for working with FXML, including the FXML features we demonstrated in this chapter and Chapter 12.
- `javafx.graphics`—Contains the packages for working with graphics, animation, CSS (for styling nodes), text and more (Chapter 22, JavaFX Graphics and Multimedia).
- `javafx.media`—Contains the packages for incorporating audio and video (Chapter 22, JavaFX Graphics and Multimedia).
- `javafx.swing`—Contains the packages for integrating into JavaFX 9 apps Swing GUI components (Chapter 26, Swing GUI Components: Part 1, and Chapter 35, Swing GUI Components: Part 2).
- `javafx.web`—Contains the package for integrating web content.

In your apps, if you use modularization and JDK 9, only the modules required by your app will be loaded at runtime. Otherwise, your app will continue to work as it did previously, provided that you did not use so-called internal APIs—that is, undocumented Java APIs that are not meant for public use. In the modularized JDK 9, such APIs are automatically *private* and inaccessible to your apps—any code that depends on pre-Java-SE-9 internal APIs will not compile. We discuss modularization in more detail in our online Java SE 9 treatment. See the Preface for details.

9 *New Public Skinning APIs*

In Chapter 22, JavaFX Graphics and Multimedia, we demonstrate how to format JavaFX objects using a technology called *Cascading Style Sheets (CSS)* that was originally developed for styling the elements in web pages. As you'll see, CSS allows you to specify *presentation* (e.g., fonts, spacing, sizes, colors, positioning) separately from the GUI's *structure* and *content* (layout containers, shapes, text, GUI components, etc.). If a JavaFX GUI's presentation is determined entirely by a style sheet (which specifies the rules for styling the GUI), you can simply swap in a new style sheet—sometimes called a **skin**—to change the GUI's appearance. This is commonly called **skinning**.

Each JavaFX control also has a skin class that determines its default appearance. In JavaFX 8, skin classes are defined as internal APIs, but many developers create custom skins by extending these skin classes. In JavaFX 9, the skin classes are now public APIs in the package `javafx.scene.control.skin`. You can extend the appropriate skin class to customize the look-and-feel for a given type of control. You then create an object of your custom skin class and set it for a control via its `setSkin` method.

9 *GTK+ 3 Support on Linux*

GTK+ (GIMP Toolkit—`http://gtk.org`) is a GUI toolkit that JavaFX uses behind the scenes to render GUIs and graphics on Linux. In Java SE 9, JavaFX now supports GTK+ 3—the latest version of GTK+.

High-DPI Screen Support 9

In a Java SE 8 update, JavaFX added support for High DPI (dots-per-inch) screens on Windows and macOS. Java SE 9 adds Linux High-DPI support, as well as capabilities to programmatically manipulate the scale at which JavaFX apps are rendered on Windows, macOS and Linux.

Updated GStreamer 9

JavaFX implements its audio and video multimedia capabilities using the open-source GStreamer framework (`https://gstreamer.freedesktop.org`). JavaFX 9 incorporates a more recent version of GStreamer with various bug fixes and performance enhancements.

Updated WebKit 9

JavaFX's `WebView` control enables you to embed web content in your JavaFX apps. `WebView` is based on the open source WebKit framework (`http://www.webkit.org`)—a web browser engine that supports loading and rendering web pages. JavaFX 9 incorporates an updated version of WebKit.

13.9 Wrap-Up

In this chapter, we continued our presentation of JavaFX. We discussed JavaFX layout panes in more detail and used `BorderPane`, `TitledPane` and `Pane` to arrange controls.

You learned about the many mouse events supported by JavaFX nodes, and we used the `onMouseDragged` event in a simple **Painter** app that displayed `Circles` as the user dragged the mouse across an `Pane`. The **Painter** app allowed the user to choose the current color and pen size from groups of mutually exclusive `RadioButtons`. You used `ToggleGroups` to manage the relationship between the `RadioButtons` in each group. You also learned how to provide a so-called user data `Object` for a control. When a `RadioButton` was selected, you obtained it from the `ToggleGroup`, then accessed the `RadioButton`'s user data `Object` to determine the drawing color or pen size.

We discussed property binding and property listeners, then used them to implement a **Color Chooser** app. You bound a `TextField`'s text to a `Slider`'s value to automatically update the `TextField` when the user moved the `Slider`'s thumb. You also used a property listener to allow the app's controller to update the color of a `Rectangle` when a `Slider`'s value changed.

In our **Cover Viewer** app, we showed how to bind an `ObservableList` collection to a `ListView` control to populate it with the collection's elements. By default, each object in the collection was displayed as a `String` in the `ListView`. You configured a property listener to display an image in an `ImageView` when the user selected an item in the `ListView`. We modified the **Cover Viewer** app to use a custom `ListView` cell factory to specify the exact layout of a `ListView` cell's contents. Finally, we introduced several other JavaFX capabilities and the Java SE 9 changes to JavaFX.

In the next chapter, we discuss class `String` and its methods. We introduce regular expressions for pattern matching in strings and demonstrate how to validate user input with regular expressions.

Summary

Section 13.2 Laying Out Nodes in a Scene Graph

- A layout determines the size and positioning of nodes in the scene graph.
- In general, a node's size should not be defined explicitly.
- In addition to the `width` and `height` properties associated with every JavaFX node, most JavaFX nodes have the properties `prefWidth`, `prefHeight`, `minWidth`, `minHeight`, `maxWidth` and `maxHeight` that specify a node's *range* of acceptable sizes as it's laid out within its parent node.
- The minimum size properties specify a node's smallest allowed size in points.
- The maximum size properties specify a node's largest allowed size in points.
- The preferred size properties specify a node's preferred width and height that should be used by a layout in most cases.
- A node's position should be defined relative to its parent node and the other nodes in its parent.
- Layout panes are container nodes that arrange their child nodes in a scene graph relative to one another, based on their sizes and positions.
- Most JavaFX layout panes use relative positioning.

Section 13.3.1 Technologies Overview

- `RadioButtons` function as mutually exclusive options.
- You add multiple `RadioButtons` to a `ToggleGroup` to ensure that only one `RadioButton` in a given group is selected at a time.
- If you programmatically create a `ToggleGroup` (rather than declaring it in FXML), you can call `RadioButton`'s `setToggleGroup` method to specify its `ToggleGroup`.
- A `BorderPane` layout container arranges controls into one or more of five regions—top, right, bottom, left and center. The top and bottom areas have the same width as the `BorderPane`. The left, center and right areas fill the vertical space between the top and bottom areas. Each area may contain only one control or one layout container that, in turn, may contain other controls.
- All the areas in a `BorderPane` are optional: If the top or bottom area is empty, the left, center and right areas expand vertically to fill that area. If the left or right area is empty, the center expands horizontally to fill that area.
- A `TitledPane` displays a title at its top and is a collapsible panel containing a layout node, which in turn contains other nodes.
- The `javafx.scene.shape` package contains various classes for creating 2D and 3D shape nodes that can be displayed in a scene graph.
- Nodes are attached to an `Pane` layout at a specified *x-y* coordinate measured from the `Pane`'s upper-left corner.
- JavaFX nodes support various mouse events.
- JavaFX supports other types of input events, such as touch-oriented events and key events.
- Each JavaFX control has a `setUserData` method that receives an `Object`. You can use this to store any object you'd like to associate with that control—typically this `Object` is used when responding to the control's events.

Section 13.3.2 Creating the `Painter.fxml` File

- If you already have an FXML file open in Scene Builder, you can choose **File > New** to create a new FXML file, then save it.

Section 13.3.3 Building the GUI

- A `VBox`'s **Spacing** property specifies vertical spacing between its controls.
- Setting a node's **Max Height** property to `MAX_VALUE` enables the node to occupy the full height of its parent node.
- The **Style** `-fx-background-color` specifies a node's background color.
- A `TitledPane`'s **Text** property specifies the title at the top of the `TitledPane`.
- A `RadioButton`'s **Text** property specifies the text that appears next to the `RadioButton`.
- A `RadioButton`'s **Selected** property specifies whether the `RadioButton` is selected.
- Setting a `RadioButton`'s **Toggle Group** property in FXML adds the `RadioButton` to that `ToggleGroup`.
- Setting a control's **Max Width** property to `MAX_VALUE` enables the control to fill its parent node's width.
- A control's **On Mouse Dragged** event handler (located under the **Mouse** heading in the **Code** section) specifies what to do when the user drags the mouse on the control.
- To specify what to do when a user interacts with a `RadioButton`, set its **On Action** event handler.
- To specify what to do when a user interacts with a `Button`, set its **On Action** event handler.

Section 13.3.5 `PainterController` Class

- Top-level types are not declared inside another type.
- Java allows you to declare classes, interfaces and `enum`s inside other classes—these are called nested types.
- Each mouse event handler you define must provide one parameter of type `MouseEvent` (package `javafx.scene.input`). When the event occurs, this parameter contains information about the event, such as its location, whether any mouse buttons were pressed, which node the user interacted with and more.
- Each layout pane has a `getChildren` method that returns an `ObservableList<Node>` collection containing the layout's child nodes. An `ObservableList` provides methods for adding and removing elements.
- All JavaFX shapes inherit indirectly from class `Node` in the `javafx.scene` package.
- `ToggleGroup` method `getSelectedToggle` returns the `Toggle` that's currently selected. Class `RadioButton` is one of several controls (others are `RadioButtonMenuItem` and `ToggleButton`) that implements interface `Toggle`.
- `Toggle`'s `getUserData` method gets the user data `Object` that's associated with a control.

Section 13.4.1 Technologies Overview

- In the RGBA color system, every color is represented by its red, green and blue color values, each ranging from 0 to 255, where 0 denotes no color and 255 full color. The alpha value (A)—which ranges from 0.0 to 1.0—represents a color's opacity, with 0.0 being completely transparent and 1.0 completely opaque.
- A property is defined by creating *set* and *get* methods with specific naming conventions. Typically, such methods manipulate a corresponding `private` instance variable that has the same name as the property, but this is not required. If the property represents a `boolean` value, its *get* method name typically begins with "`is`" rather than "`get`."
- JavaFX properties are observable—when a property's value changes, other objects can respond accordingly.

- One way to respond to a property change is via a property binding, which enables a property of one object to be updated when a property of another object changes.
- Property bindings are not limited to JavaFX controls. Package `javafx.beans.property` contains many classes that you can use to define bindable properties in your own classes.
- A property listener is an event handler that's invoked when a property's value changes. In the event handler, you can respond to the property change in a manner appropriate for your app.

Section 13.4.2 Building the GUI

- `Circle` and `Rectangle` are located in the Scene Builder **Library**'s **Shapes** section.

Section 13.4.4 **`ColorChooserController`** *Class*

- A controller class's `initialize` method often configures property bindings and property listeners.
- Each `TextField` has a `text` property that's returned by its `textProperty` method as a `StringProperty` (package `javafx.beans.property`).
- `StringProperty` method `bind` receives an `ObservableValue` as an argument. When the `ObservableValue` changes, the bound property is updated accordingly.
- `Slider` method `valueProperty` returns a `Slider`'s `value` property as an object of class `DoubleProperty`—an observable `double` value.
- `DoubleProperty` method `asString` returns a `StringBinding` object (which is an `ObservableValue`) that produces a `String` representation of the `DoubleProperty`.
- To perform an arbitrary task when a property's value changes, you can register a property listener.

Section 13.5 **Cover Viewer** *App: Data-Driven GUIs with JavaFX Collections*

- JavaFX provides a comprehensive model for allowing GUIs to interact with data.

Section 13.5.1 Technologies Overview

- A `ListView` control displays a collection of objects.
- Though you can individually add items to a `ListView`, you'll often bind an `ObservableList` object to the `ListView`.
- If you make changes to an `ObservableList`, its observer (such as a `ListView`) will automatically be notified of those changes.
- Package `javafx.collections` defines `ObservableList` (similar to an `ArrayList`) and other observable collection interfaces.
- Class `FXCollections` provides `static` methods for creating and manipulating observable collections.

Section 13.5.5 **`CoverViewerController`** *Class*

- `FXCollections` `static` method `observableArrayList` returns an empty collection object (similar to an `ArrayList`) that implements the `ObservableList` interface.
- `ListView` method `setItems` receives an `ObservableList` and binds the `ListView` to it. This data binding allows the `ListView` to display the `ObservableList`'s objects automatically—as `Strings` by default.
- By default a `ListView` supports single selection—one item at a time may be selected. `ListViews` also support multiple selection. The type of selection is managed by the `ListView`'s `MultipleSelectionModel` (a subclass of `SelectionModel` from package `javafx.scene.control`), which contains observable properties and various methods for manipulating the corresponding `ListView`'s items.

- To respond to selection changes, register a listener for the `MultipleSelectionModel`'s `selectedItem` property.
- `ListView` method `getSelectionModel` returns a `MultipleSelectionModel` object.
- `MultipleSelectionModel`'s `selectedItemProperty` method returns a `ReadOnlyObjectProperty`, and the corresponding `ChangeListener` receives as its `oldValue` and `newValue` parameters the previously selected and newly selected objects, respectively.

Section 13.6.1 Technologies Overview

- To create a custom `ListView` cell format, you must first define a subclass of the `ListCell` generic class (package `javafx.scene.control`) that specifies how to create a `ListView` cell.
- As the `ListView` displays items, it gets `ListView` cells from its cell factory.
- You'll use the `ListView`'s `setCellFactory` method to replace the default cell factory with one that returns objects of the `ListCell` subclass. You override this class's `updateItem` method to specify the cells' custom layout and contents.
- Everything you can do in Scene Builder also can be accomplished in Java code.

Section 13.6.3 `ImageTextCell` Custom Cell Factory Class

- A custom `ListView` cell layout is defined as a subclass of `ListCell<`*Type*`>`, where *Type* is the type of the object displayed in a `ListView` cell.
- The `ListCell<`*Type*`>` subclass's `updateItem` method creates the custom presentation. This method is called by the `ListView`'s cell factory when a `ListView` cell is required—that is, when the `ListView` is first displayed and when `ListView` cells are about to scroll onto the screen.
- Method `updateItem` receives the object to display and a `boolean` indicating whether the cell that's about to be created is empty. You must call the superclass's version of `updateItem` to ensure that the custom cells display correctly.
- `ListCell<`*Type*`>`'s `setGraphic` method receives a JavaFX `Node` representing the customized cell's appearance.

Section 13.6.4 `CoverViewerController` Class

- Once you've defined the custom cell layout, you must set the `ListView`'s cell factory.
- The argument to `ListView` method `setCellFactory` is an implementation of interface `CallBack` (package `javafx.util`). This generic interface provides a `call` method that receives one argument and returns an object of the custom `ListCell<`*Type*`>` subclass.

Section 13.7 Additional JavaFX Capabilities

- JavaFX's `TableView` control (package `javafx.scene.control`) displays tabular data in rows and columns, and supports user interactions with that data.
- In a Java SE 8 update, JavaFX added accessibility features to help people with visual impairments use their devices. These features include screen-reader support, GUI navigation via the keyboard and a high-contrast mode to make controls more readable.
- See your operating system's documentation for information on enabling its screen reader and high-contrast mode.
- Every JavaFX `Node` subclass also has accessibility-related properties.
- The `accessibleTextProperty` is a `String` that a screen reader speaks for a control.
- The `accessibleHelpProperty` is a more detailed control description `String` than that provided by the `accessibleTextProperty`. This property's text should help the user understand the purpose of the control in the context of your app.

- The accessibleRoleProperty is a value from the enum AccessibleRole (package javafx.scene). A screen reader uses this property value to determine the attributes and actions supported for a given control.
- The accessibleRoleDescriptionProperty is a String text description of a control that a screen reader typically speaks followed by the control's contents or the value of the accessibleTextProperty.
- You can add Labels to a GUI that describe other controls. In such cases, you should set each Label's labelFor property to the specific control the Label describes. If a Label's labelFor property references another control, a screen reader will read the Label's text when describing the control to the user.
- You can create custom controls by extending existing JavaFX control classes to customize them or by extending JavaFX's Control class directly.
- **Scenic View** (http://www.scenic-view.org/) is a debugging tool for JavaFX scenes and nodes. You embed **Scenic View** directly into your apps or run it as a standalone app. You can inspect your JavaFX scenes and nodes, and modify them dynamically to see how changes affect their presentation on the screen—without having to edit your code, recompile it and re-run it for each change.

Section 13.8 JavaFX 9: Java SE 9 JavaFX Updates

- JavaFX 9's biggest new feature is modularization.
- In your apps, if you use modularization and JDK 9, only the modules required by your app will be loaded at runtime. Otherwise, your app will continue to work as it did previously, provided that you did not use so-called internal APIs—that is, undocumented Java APIs that are not meant for public use.
- If a JavaFX GUI's presentation is determined entirely by a style sheet (which specifies the rules for styling the GUI), you can simply swap in a new style sheet—sometimes called a skin—to change the GUI's appearance. This is commonly called skinning.
- Each JavaFX control also has a skin class that determines its default appearance.
- In JavaFX 8, skin classes are defined as internal APIs. In JavaFX 9, the skin classes are now public APIs in the package javafx.scene.control.skin.
- You can extend the appropriate skin class to customize the look-and-feel for a given type of control. You then create an object of your custom skin class and set it for a control via its setSkin method.
- JavaFX 9 supports GTK+ 3—the latest version of GTK+.
- In a Java SE 8 update, JavaFX added support for High-DPI (dots-per-inch) screens on Windows and macOS. Java SE 9 adds Linux High-DPI support.
- JavaFX 9 adds features to programmatically manipulate the scale at which JavaFX apps are rendered on Windows, macOS and Linux.
- JavaFX implements its audio and video multimedia capabilities using the open-source GStreamer framework (https://gstreamer.freedesktop.org). JavaFX 9 incorporates a more recent version of GStreamer with various bug fixes and performance enhancements.
- JavaFX's WebView control enables you to embed web content in your JavaFX apps. WebView is based on the open source WebKit framework (http://www.webkit.org)—a web browser engine that supports loading and rendering web pages. JavaFX 9 incorporates an updated version of WebKit.

Self-Review Exercises

13.1 Fill in the blanks in each of the following:

a) You add multiple `RadioButton`s to a(n) ________ to ensure that only one `RadioButton` in a given group is selected at a time.

b) A(n) ________ determines the size and positioning of nodes in the scene graph.

c) A(n) ________ displays a title at its top and is a collapsible panel containing a layout node, which in turn contains other nodes.

d) The ________ package contains various classes for creating 2D and 3D shape nodes that can be displayed in a scene graph.

e) A control's ________ event handler specifies what to do when the user drags the mouse on the control.

f) To specify what to do when a user interacts with a `RadioButton`, set its ________ event handler.

g) Each `TextField` has a `text` property that's returned by its `textProperty` method as a(n) ________ (package `javafx.beans.property`).

h) `DoubleProperty` method `asString` returns a(n) ________ object (which is an `ObservableValue`) that produces a `String` representation of the `DoubleProperty`.

i) Though you can individually add `ListView` items you'll often bind a(n) ________ object to the `ListView`.

j) Class ________ provides `static` methods for creating and manipulating observable collections.

k) As the `ListView` displays items, it gets `ListView` cells from its ________.

l) JavaFX's ________ control enables you to embed web content in your JavaFX apps.

m) In a Java SE 8 update, JavaFX added ________ to help people with visual impairments use their devices. These features include screen-reader support, GUI navigation via the keyboard and a high-contrast mode to make controls more readable.

13.2 State whether each of the following is *true* or *false*. If *false*, explain why:

a) In general, a node's size should be defined explicitly.

b) A node's position should be defined relative to its parent node and the other nodes in its parent.

c) Most JavaFX layout panes use fixed positioning.

d) `RadioButtons` function as mutually exclusive options.

e) Layout panes are container nodes that arrange their child nodes in a scene graph relative to one another, based on their sizes and positions.

f) `ToggleGroup` method `getToggle` returns the `Toggle` that's currently selected.

g) Each layout pane has a `getChildren` method that returns an `ObservableList<Node>` collection containing the layout's child nodes.

h) The only way to respond to a property change is via a property binding, which enables a property of one object to be updated when a property of another object changes.

i) JavaFX properties are observable—when a property's value changes, other objects can respond accordingly.

j) Property bindings are limited to JavaFX controls.

k) In the RGBA color system, every color is represented by its red, green and blue color values, each ranging from 0 to 255, where 0 denotes no color and 255 full color. The alpha value (A)—which ranges from 0.0 to 1.0—represents a color's opacity, with 0.0 being completely transparent and 1.0 completely opaque.

l) To respond to `ListView` selection changes, you register a listener for the `SingleSelectionModel`'s `selectedItem` property.

m) To create a custom `ListView` cell format, you must first define a subclass of the `CellFormat` generic class (package `javafx.scene.control`) that specifies how to create a `ListView` cell.
n) You can build JavaFX GUIs only by using Scene Builder.
o) JavaFX's `TableView` control (package `javafx.scene.control`) displays tabular data in rows and columns, and supports user interactions with that data.
p) You can add `Labels` to a GUI that describe other controls. In such cases, you should set each `Label`'s `describesControl` property to the specific control the `Label` describes.

Answers to Self-Review Exercises

13.1 a) `ToggleGroup`. b) layout. c) `TitledPane`. d) `javafx.scene.shape`. e) **On Mouse Dragged**. f) **On Action**. g) `StringProperty`. h) `StringBinding`. i) `ObservableList`. j) `FXCollections`. k) cell factory. l) `WebView`. m) accessibility features.

13.2 a) False. In general, a node's size shouldn't be defined explicitly. b) True. c) False. Most JavaFX layout panes use relative positioning. d) True. e) True. f) False. `ToggleGroup` method `getSelectedToggle` returns the `Toggle` that's currently selected. g) True. h) False. You can also respond to property changes with a property listener, which is an event handler that's invoked when a property's value changes. i) True. j) False. Property bindings are not limited to JavaFX controls. Package `javafx.beans.property` contains many classes that you can use to define bindable properties in your own classes. k) True. l) False. To respond to `ListView` selection changes, you register a listener for the `MultipleSelectionModel`'s `selectedItem` property. m) False. To create a custom `ListView` cell format, you must first define a subclass of the `ListCell` generic class (package `javafx.scene.control`) that specifies how to create a `ListView` cell. n) False. Everything you can do in Scene Builder also can be accomplished in Java code. o) True. p) You can add `Labels` to a GUI that describe other controls. In such cases, you should set each `Label`'s `labelFor` property to the specific control the `Label` describes.

Exercises

13.3 *(Painter App Modification)* Incorporate the RGBA color chooser you created in the **Color Chooser** app (Section 13.4) into the **Painter** app (Section 13.3) so that the user can choose any drawing color. Changing a `Slider`'s value should update the color swatch displayed to the user and set the `brushColor` instance variable to the current `Color`.

13.4 *(Contacts App)* Create a **Contacts** app modeled after the **Cover Viewer** app (Sections 13.5–13.6). Store the contact information in an `ObservableList` of `Contact` objects. A `Contact` should contain first name, last name, email and phone number properties (you can provide others). When the user selects a contact from the contacts list, its information should display in a `Grid` of `TextFields`. As the information is modified (a `Contact`'s data is updated, a new `Contact` is added or an existing `Contact` is deleted), the contacts `ListView` should display the updates. The `ListView` should display the `Contact`'s last names.

13.5 *(Contacts App Modification)* Modify the **Contacts** app from the preceding exercises to include an image for each `Contact`. Provide a custom `ListView` cell factory that displays the `Contact`'s full name and picture with the names in sorted order by last name.

13.6 *(Tip Calculator Modification)* The **Tip Calculator** app from Section 12.5 does not need a `Button` to perform its calculations. Reimplement this app to use property listeners to perform the calculations whenever the user modifies the bill amount or changes the custom tip percentage. Also use a property binding to update the `Label` that displays the tip percentage.

13.7 *(Advanced Project: Color Chooser App Modification)* The property bindings we created in the Color Chooser app (Section 13.4) allowed a `TextField`'s text to update when a `Slider`'s value changed, but not vice versa. JavaFX also supports bi-directional property bindings. Research bidirectional property bindings online, then create bidirectional bindings between the `Sliders` and the `TextFields` such that modifying a `TextField`'s value updates the corresponding slider.

13.8 *(Project: Mini Web Browser)* Investigate the capabilities of JavaFX's `WebView` control and `WebEngine` class, then create a JavaFX app that provides basic web browsing capabilities. For an introduction to these classes visit `https://docs.oracle.com/javase/8/javafx/embedded-browser-tutorial/overview.htm`.

(Optional) GUI and Graphics Case Study Exercise: Interactive Polymorphic Drawing App

13.9 *(Project: Interactive Polymorphic Drawing App)* Implement a JavaFX app that uses the `MyShape` hierarchy from GUI and Graphics Case Study Exercise 10.2 to create a fully interactive drawing application. The classes of the `MyShape` hierarchy require no additional changes. Your app should store the shapes in an `ArrayList<MyShape>`. The user should be able to specify drawing characteristics such as which shape to draw, the stroke color, the fill color and whether the shape should be hollow or filled. Provide mouse event handling to enable the user to position and size each shape by dragging the mouse. Also enable the user to undo the last shape drawn and to clear the entire drawing.

14 Strings, Characters and Regular Expressions

Objectives

In this chapter you'll:

- Create and manipulate immutable character-string objects of class `String`.
- Create and manipulate mutable character-string objects of class `StringBuilder`.
- Create and manipulate objects of class `Character`.
- Break a `String` object into tokens using `String` method `split`.
- Use regular expressions to validate `String` data entered into an application.

Outline

14.1 Introduction

This chapter introduces Java's string- and character-processing capabilities. The techniques discussed here are appropriate for validating program input, displaying information to users and performing other text-based manipulations. They're also appropriate for developing text editors, word processors, page-layout software and other kinds of text-processing software. We've presented several string-processing capabilities in earlier chapters. This chapter discusses in detail the capabilities of classes `String`, `StringBuilder` and `Character` from the `java.lang` package—these classes provide the foundation for string and character manipulation in Java.

The chapter also discusses regular expressions that provide applications with the capability to validate input. The functionality is located in the `String` class along with classes `Matcher` and `Pattern` located in the `java.util.regex` package.

14.2 Fundamentals of Characters and Strings

Characters are the fundamental building blocks of Java source programs. Every program is composed of a sequence of characters that—when grouped together meaningfully—are interpreted by the Java compiler as a series of instructions used to accomplish a task. A program may contain **character literals**. A character literal is an integer value represented as a character in single quotes. For example, `'z'` represents the integer value of `z`, and `'\t'` represents the integer value of a tab character. The value of a character literal is the integer value of the character in the **Unicode character set**. Appendix B presents the integer equivalents of the characters in the ASCII character set, which is a subset of Unicode (discussed in online Appendix H).

Recall from Section 2.2 that a string is a sequence of characters treated as a single unit. A string may include letters, digits and various **special characters**, such as +, -, *, / and $. A string is an object of class `String`. **String literals** (stored in memory as `String` objects) are written as a sequence of characters in double quotation marks, as in:

`"John Q. Doe"`	(a name)
`"9999 Main Street"`	(a street address)
`"Waltham, Massachusetts"`	(a city and state)
`"(201) 555-1212"`	(a telephone number)

A string literal may be assigned to a `String` reference. The declaration

```
String color = "blue";
```

initializes `String` variable `color` to refer to a `String` object that contains the string `"blue"`.

Performance Tip 14.1

To conserve memory, Java treats all string literals with the same contents as a single `String` *object that has many references to it.*

14.3 Class `String`

Class `String` is used to represent strings in Java. The next several subsections cover many of class `String`'s capabilities.

Performance Tip 14.2

9 *As of Java SE 9, Java uses a more compact* `String` *representation. This significantly reduces the amount of memory used to store* `String`*s containing only Latin-1 characters—that is, those with the character codes 0–255. For more information, see JEP 254's proposal at* `http://openjdk.java.net/jeps/254`.

14.3.1 `String` Constructors

Class `String` provides constructors for initializing `String` objects in a variety of ways. Four of the constructors are demonstrated in the `main` method of Fig. 14.1.

```
// Fig. 14.1: StringConstructors.java
// String class constructors.

public class StringConstructors {
   public static void main(String[] args) {
      char[] charArray = {'b', 'i', 'r', 't', 'h', ' ', 'd', 'a', 'y'};
      String s = new String("hello");

      // use String constructors
      String s1 = new String();
      String s2 = new String(s);
      String s3 = new String(charArray);
      String s4 = new String(charArray, 6, 3);

```

Fig. 14.1 | `String` class constructors. (Part 1 of 2.)

```
15        System.out.printf(
16           "s1 = %s%ns2 = %s%ns3 = %s%ns4 = %s%n", s1, s2, s3, s4);
17     }
18  }
```

```
s1 =
s2 = hello
s3 = birth day
s4 = day
```

Fig. 14.1 | `String` class constructors. (Part 2 of 2.)

Line 10 instantiates a new `String` using class `String`'s no-argument constructor and assigns its reference to `s1`. The new `String` object contains no characters (i.e., the **empty string**, which can also be represented as `""`) and has a length of 0. Line 11 instantiates a new `String` object using class `String`'s constructor that takes a `String` object as an argument and assigns its reference to `s2`. The new `String` object contains the same sequence of characters as the `String` object `s` that's passed as an argument to the constructor.

Performance Tip 14.3

It's not necessary to copy an existing `String` object. `String` objects are immutable, because class `String` does not provide methods that allow the contents of a `String` object to be modified after it is created. In fact, it's rarely necessary to call `String` constructors.

Line 12 instantiates a new `String` object and assigns its reference to `s3` using class `String`'s constructor that takes a `char` array as an argument. The new `String` object contains a copy of the characters in the array.

Line 13 instantiates a new `String` object and assigns its reference to `s4` using class `String`'s constructor that takes a `char` array and two integers as arguments. The second argument specifies the starting position (the *offset*) from which characters in the array are accessed. Remember that the first character is at position `0`. The third argument specifies the number of characters (the count) to access in the array. The new `String` object is formed from the accessed characters. If the offset or the count specified as an argument results in accessing an element outside the bounds of the character array, a `StringIndexOutOfBoundsException` is thrown.

14.3.2 `String` Methods `length`, `charAt` and `getChars`

`String` methods **`length`**, **`charAt`** and **`getChars`** return the length of a `String`, obtain the character at a specific location in a `String` and retrieve a set of characters from a `String` as a `char` array, respectively. Figure 14.2 demonstrates each of these methods.

```
// Fig. 14.2: StringMiscellaneous.java
// This application demonstrates the length, charAt and getChars
// methods of the String class.

```

Fig. 14.2 | `String` methods `length`, `charAt` and `getChars`. (Part 1 of 2.)

```
5   public class StringMiscellaneous {
6      public static void main(String[] args) {
7         String s1 = "hello there";
8         char[] charArray = new char[5];
9
10        System.out.printf("s1: %s", s1);
11
12        // test length method
13        System.out.printf("%nLength of s1: %d", s1.length());
14
15        // loop through characters in s1 with charAt and display reversed
16        System.out.printf("%nThe string reversed is: ");
17
18        for (int count = s1.length() - 1; count >= 0; count--) {
19           System.out.printf("%c ", s1.charAt(count));
20        }
21
22        // copy characters from string into charArray
23        s1.getChars(0, 5, charArray, 0);
24        System.out.printf("%nThe character array is: ");
25
26        for (char character : charArray) {
27           System.out.print(character);
28        }
29
30        System.out.println();
31     }
32  }
```

```
s1: hello there
Length of s1: 11
The string reversed is: e r e h t   o l l e h
The character array is: hello
```

Fig. 14.2 | `String` methods `length`, `charAt` and `getChars`. (Part 2 of 2.)

Line 13 uses `String` method `length` to determine the number of characters in `String` `s1`. Like arrays, strings know their own length. However, unlike arrays, you access a `String`'s length via class `String`'s `length` method.

Lines 18–20 print the characters of the `String` `s1` in reverse order (and separated by spaces). `String` method `charAt` (line 19) returns the character at a specific position in the `String`. Method `charAt` receives an integer argument that's used as the index and returns the character at that position. Like arrays, the first element of a `String` is at position 0.

Line 23 uses `String` method `getChars` to copy the characters of a `String` into a character array. The first argument is the starting index from which characters are to be copied. The second argument is the index that's one past the last character to be copied from the `String`. The third argument is the character array into which the characters are to be copied. The last argument is the starting index where the copied characters are placed in the target character array. Next, lines 26–28 print the `char` array contents one character at a time.

14.3.3 Comparing Strings

Chapter 19 discusses sorting and searching arrays. Frequently, the information being sorted or searched consists of Strings that must be compared to place them into order or to determine whether a string appears in an array (or other collection). Class String provides methods for *comparing* strings, as demonstrated in the next two examples.

To understand what it means for one string to be greater than or less than another, consider the process of alphabetizing a series of last names. No doubt, you'd place "Jones" before "Smith" because the first letter of "Jones" comes before the first letter of "Smith" in the alphabet. But the alphabet is more than just a list of 26 letters—it's an *ordered* list of characters. Each letter occurs in a specific position within the list. Z is more than just a letter of the alphabet—it's specifically the twenty-sixth letter of the alphabet.

How does the computer know that one letter "comes before" another? All characters are represented in the computer as numeric codes (see Appendix B). When the computer compares Strings, it actually compares the numeric codes of the characters in the Strings.

Figure 14.3 demonstrates String methods **equals**, **equalsIgnoreCase**, **compareTo** and **regionMatches** and using the equality operator == to compare String objects.

```java
// Fig. 14.3: StringCompare.java
// String methods equals, equalsIgnoreCase, compareTo and regionMatches.

public class StringCompare {
   public static void main(String[] args) {
      String s1 = new String("hello"); // s1 is a copy of "hello"
      String s2 = "goodbye";
      String s3 = "Happy Birthday";
      String s4 = "happy birthday";

      System.out.printf(
         "s1 = %s%ns2 = %s%ns3 = %s%ns4 = %s%n%n", s1, s2, s3, s4);

      // test for equality
      if (s1.equals("hello")) {  // true
         System.out.println("s1 equals \"hello\"");
      }
      else {
         System.out.println("s1 does not equal \"hello\"");
      }

      // test for equality with ==
      if (s1 == "hello") { // false; they are not the same object
         System.out.println("s1 is the same object as \"hello\"");
      }
      else {
         System.out.println("s1 is not the same object as \"hello\"");
      }

```

Fig. 14.3 | String methods equals, equalsIgnoreCase, compareTo and regionMatches. (Part 1 of 3.)

```
      // test for equality (ignore case)
      if (s3.equalsIgnoreCase(s4)) { // true
         System.out.printf("%s equals %s with case ignored%n", s3, s4);
      }
      else {
         System.out.println("s3 does not equal s4");
      }

      // test compareTo
      System.out.printf(
         "%ns1.compareTo(s2) is %d", s1.compareTo(s2));
      System.out.printf(
         "%ns2.compareTo(s1) is %d", s2.compareTo(s1));
      System.out.printf(
         "%ns1.compareTo(s1) is %d", s1.compareTo(s1));
      System.out.printf(
         "%ns3.compareTo(s4) is %d", s3.compareTo(s4));
      System.out.printf(
         "%ns4.compareTo(s3) is %d%n%n", s4.compareTo(s3));

      // test regionMatches (case sensitive)
      if (s3.regionMatches(0, s4, 0, 5)) {
         System.out.println("First 5 characters of s3 and s4 match");
      }
      else {
         System.out.println(
            "First 5 characters of s3 and s4 do not match");
      }

      // test regionMatches (ignore case)
      if (s3.regionMatches(true, 0, s4, 0, 5)) {
         System.out.println(
            "First 5 characters of s3 and s4 match with case ignored");
      }
      else {
         System.out.println(
            "First 5 characters of s3 and s4 do not match");
      }
   }
}
```

```
s1 = hello
s2 = goodbye
s3 = Happy Birthday
s4 = happy birthday

s1 equals "hello"
s1 is not the same object as "hello"
Happy Birthday equals happy birthday with case ignored
```

Fig. 14.3 | String methods equals, equalsIgnoreCase, compareTo and regionMatches. (Part 2 of 3.)

```
s1.compareTo(s2) is 1
s2.compareTo(s1) is -1
s1.compareTo(s1) is 0
s3.compareTo(s4) is -32
s4.compareTo(s3) is 32

First 5 characters of s3 and s4 do not match
First 5 characters of s3 and s4 match with case ignored
```

Fig. 14.3 | String methods equals, equalsIgnoreCase, compareTo and regionMatches. (Part 3 of 3.)

String Method equals

Line 15 uses method equals (an Object method overridden in String) to compare String s1 and the String literal "hello" for equality. For Strings, the method determines whether the contents of the two Strings are *identical*. If so, it returns true; otherwise, it returns false. The preceding condition is true because String s1 was initialized with the literal "hello". Method equals uses a **lexicographical comparison**—it compares the integer Unicode values (see online Appendix H for more information) that represent each character in each String. Thus, if the String "hello" is compared to the string "HELLO", the result is false, because the integer representation of a lowercase letter is *different* from that of the corresponding uppercase letter.

Comparing Strings with the == Operator

The condition at line 23 uses the equality operator == to compare String s1 for equality with the String literal "hello". When primitive-type values are compared with ==, the result is true if *both values are identical*. When references are compared with ==, the result is true if *both references refer to the same object in memory*. To compare the actual contents (or state information) of objects for equality, a method must be invoked. In the case of Strings, that method is equals. The condition evaluates to false at line 23 because the reference s1 was initialized with the statement

```
s1 = new String("hello");
```

which creates a new String object with a copy of string literal "hello" and assigns the new object to variable s1. If s1 had been initialized with the statement

```
s1 = "hello";
```

which directly assigns the string literal "hello" to variable s1, the condition would be true. Remember that Java treats all string literal objects with the same contents as one String object to which there can be many references. Thus, the "hello" literals in lines 6, 15 and 23 all refer to the same String object.

Common Programming Error 14.1

Comparing references with == can lead to logic errors, because == compares the references to determine whether they refer to the same object, *not whether two objects have the* same contents. *When two separate objects that contain the same values are compared with ==, the result will be* false. *When comparing objects to determine whether they have the same contents, use method* equals.

`String` *Method* `equalsIgnoreCase`

When sorting `String`s, you might compare them for equality with method `equalsIgnoreCase`, which performs a case-insensitive comparison. Thus, `"hello"` and `"HELLO"` compare as equal. Line 31 uses `String` method `equalsIgnoreCase` to compare `String s3`—`Happy Birthday`—for equality with `String s4`—`happy birthday`. The result of this comparison is `true` because the comparison ignores case.

`String` *Method* `compareTo`

Lines 39–48 use method `compareTo` to compare `String`s. Class `String` implements interface `Comparable` which declares method `compareTo`. Line 40 compares `String s1` to `String s2`. Method `compareTo` returns 0 if the `String`s are equal, a negative number if the `String` that invokes `compareTo` is less than the `String` that's passed as an argument and a positive number if the `String` that invokes `compareTo` is greater than the `String` that's passed as an argument. Method `compareTo` uses a *lexicographical* comparison—it compares the numeric values of corresponding characters in each `String`.

`String` *Method* `regionMatches`

The condition at line 51 uses a version of `String` method `regionMatches` to compare portions of two `String`s for equality. The first argument to this version of the method is the starting index in the `String` that invokes the method. The second argument is a comparison `String`. The third argument is the starting index in the comparison `String`. The last argument is the number of characters to compare between the two `String`s. The method returns `true` only if the specified number of characters are lexicographically equal.

Finally, the condition at line 60 uses a five-argument version of `String` method `regionMatches` to compare portions of two `String`s for equality. When the first argument is `true`, the method ignores the case of the characters being compared. The remaining arguments are identical to those described for the four-argument `regionMatches` method.

`String` *Methods* `startsWith` *and* `endsWith`

Figure 14.4 demonstrates `String` methods **`startsWith`** and **`endsWith`**. Method `main` creates array `strings` containing `"started"`, `"starting"`, `"ended"` and `"ending"`. The remainder of method `main` consists of three `for` statements that test the elements of the array to determine whether they start with or end with a particular set of characters.

```
// Fig. 14.4: StringStartEnd.java
// String methods startsWith and endsWith.

public class StringStartEnd {
   public static void main(String[] args) {
      String[] strings = {"started", "starting", "ended", "ending"};

      // test method startsWith
      for (String string : strings) {
         if (string.startsWith("st")) {
            System.out.printf("\"%s\" starts with \"st\"%n", string);
         }
      }
```

Fig. 14.4 | `String` methods `startsWith` and `endsWith`. (Part 1 of 2.)

```
14
15         System.out.println();
16
17         // test method startsWith starting from position 2 of string
18         for (String string : strings) {
19            if (string.startsWith("art", 2)) {
20               System.out.printf(
21                  "\"%s\" starts with \"art\" at position 2%n", string);
22            }
23         }
24
25         System.out.println();
26
27         // test method endsWith
28         for (String string : strings) {
29            if (string.endsWith("ed")) {
30               System.out.printf("\"%s\" ends with \"ed\"%n", string);
31            }
32         }
33      }
34   }
```

```
"started" starts with "st"
"starting" starts with "st"

"started" starts with "art" at position 2
"starting" starts with "art" at position 2

"started" ends with "ed"
"ended" ends with "ed"
```

Fig. 14.4 | `String` methods `startsWith` and `endsWith`. (Part 2 of 2.)

Lines 9–13 use the version of method `startsWith` that takes a `String` argument. The condition in the `if` statement (line 10) determines whether each `String` in the array starts with the characters `"st"`. If so, the method returns `true` and the application prints that `String`. Otherwise, the method returns `false` and nothing happens.

Lines 18–23 use the `startsWith` method that takes a `String` and an integer as arguments. The integer specifies the index at which the comparison should begin in the `String`. The condition in the `if` statement (line 19) determines whether each `String` in the array has the characters `"art"` beginning with the third character in each `String`. If so, the method returns `true` and the application prints the `String`.

The third `for` statement (lines 28–32) uses method `endsWith`, which takes a `String` argument. The condition at line 29 determines whether each `String` in the array ends with the characters `"ed"`. If so, the method returns `true` and the application prints the `String`.

14.3.4 Locating Characters and Substrings in Strings

Often it's useful to search a string for a character or set of characters. For example, if you're creating your own word processor, you might want to provide a capability for searching through documents. Figure 14.5 demonstrates the many versions of `String` methods **`indexOf`** and **`lastIndexOf`** that search for a specified character or substring in a `String`.

```
// Fig. 14.5: StringIndexMethods.java
// String searching methods indexOf and lastIndexOf.

public class StringIndexMethods {
   public static void main(String[] args) {
      String letters = "abcdefghijklmabcdefghijklm";

      // test indexOf to locate a character in a string
      System.out.printf(
         "'c' is located at index %d%n", letters.indexOf('c'));
      System.out.printf(
         "'a' is located at index %d%n", letters.indexOf('a', 1));
      System.out.printf(
         "'$' is located at index %d%n%n", letters.indexOf('$'));

      // test lastIndexOf to find a character in a string
      System.out.printf("Last 'c' is located at index %d%n",
         letters.lastIndexOf('c'));
      System.out.printf("Last 'a' is located at index %d%n",
         letters.lastIndexOf('a', 25));
      System.out.printf("Last '$' is located at index %d%n%n",
         letters.lastIndexOf('$'));

      // test indexOf to locate a substring in a string
      System.out.printf("\"def\" is located at index %d%n",
         letters.indexOf("def"));
      System.out.printf("\"def\" is located at index %d%n",
         letters.indexOf("def", 7));
      System.out.printf("\"hello\" is located at index %d%n%n",
         letters.indexOf("hello"));

      // test lastIndexOf to find a substring in a string
      System.out.printf("Last \"def\" is located at index %d%n",
         letters.lastIndexOf("def"));
      System.out.printf("Last \"def\" is located at index %d%n",
         letters.lastIndexOf("def", 25));
      System.out.printf("Last \"hello\" is located at index %d%n",
         letters.lastIndexOf("hello"));
   }
}
```

```
'c' is located at index 2
'a' is located at index 13
'$' is located at index -1

Last 'c' is located at index 15
Last 'a' is located at index 13
Last '$' is located at index -1

"def" is located at index 3
"def" is located at index 16
"hello" is located at index -1
```

Fig. 14.5 | String-searching methods `indexOf` and `lastIndexOf`. (Part 1 of 2.)

```
Last "def" is located at index 16
Last "def" is located at index 16
Last "hello" is located at index -1
```

Fig. 14.5 | String-searching methods `indexOf` and `lastIndexOf`. (Part 2 of 2.)

All the searches in this example are performed on the `String` `letters` (initialized with `"abcdefghijklmabcdefghijklm"`). Lines 9–14 use method `indexOf` to locate the first occurrence of a character in a `String`. If the method finds the character, it returns the character's index in the `String`—otherwise, it returns `-1`. There are two versions of `indexOf` that search for characters in a `String`. The expression in line 10 uses the version of method `indexOf` that takes an integer representation of the character to find. The expression at line 12 uses another version of method `indexOf`, which takes two integer arguments—the character and the starting index at which the search of the `String` should begin.

Lines 17–22 use method `lastIndexOf` to locate the last occurrence of a character in a `String`. The method searches from the end of the `String` toward the beginning. If it finds the character, it returns the character's index in the `String`—otherwise, it returns –1. There are two versions of `lastIndexOf` that search for characters in a `String`. The expression at line 18 uses the version that takes the integer representation of the character. The expression at line 20 uses the version that takes two integer arguments—the integer representation of the character and the index from which to begin searching *backward*.

Lines 25–38 demonstrate versions of methods `indexOf` and `lastIndexOf` that each take a `String` as the first argument. These versions perform identically to those described earlier except that they search for sequences of characters (or substrings) that are specified by their `String` arguments. If the substring is found, these methods return the index in the `String` of the first character in the substring.

14.3.5 Extracting Substrings from Strings

Class `String` provides two `substring` methods to enable a new `String` object to be created by copying part of an existing `String` object. Each method returns a new `String` object. Both methods are demonstrated in Fig. 14.6.

```java
// Fig. 14.6: SubString.java
// String class substring methods.

public class SubString {
   public static void main(String[] args) {
      String letters = "abcdefghijklmabcdefghijklm";

      // test substring methods
      System.out.printf("Substring from index 20 to end is \"%s\"%n",
         letters.substring(20));
      System.out.printf("%s \"%s\"%n",
         "Substring from index 3 up to, but not including, 6 is",
         letters.substring(3, 6));
   }
}
```

Fig. 14.6 | `String` class `substring` methods. (Part 1 of 2.)

```
Substring from index 20 to end is "hijklm"
Substring from index 3 up to, but not including, 6 is "def"
```

Fig. 14.6 | `String` class `substring` methods. (Part 2 of 2.)

The expression `letters.substring(20)` at line 10 uses the `substring` method that takes one integer argument. The argument specifies the starting index in the original `String letters` from which characters are to be copied. The substring returned contains a copy of the characters from the starting index to the end of the `String`. Specifying an index outside the bounds of the `String` causes a **`StringIndexOutOfBoundsException`**.

Line 13 uses the `substring` method that takes two integer arguments—the starting index from which to copy characters in the original `String` and the index one beyond the last character to copy (i.e., copy up to, but *not including*, that index in the `String`). The substring returned contains a copy of the specified characters from the original `String`. An index outside the bounds of the `String` causes a `StringIndexOutOfBoundsException`.

14.3.6 Concatenating Strings

`String` method **concat** (Fig. 14.7) concatenates two `String` objects (similar to using the + operator) and returns a new `String` object containing the characters from both original `Strings`. The expression `s1.concat(s2)` at line 11 forms a `String` by appending the characters in `s2` to the those in `s1`. The original `Strings` to which `s1` and `s2` refer are *not modified.*

```
1  // Fig. 14.7: StringConcatenation.java
2  // String method concat.
3
4  public class StringConcatenation {
5     public static void main(String[] args) {
6        String s1 = "Happy ";
7        String s2 = "Birthday";
8
9        System.out.printf("s1 = %s%ns2 = %s%n%n",s1, s2);
10       System.out.printf(
11          "Result of s1.concat(s2) = %s%n", s1.concat(s2));
12       System.out.printf("s1 after concatenation = %s%n", s1);
13    }
14 }
```

```
s1 = Happy
s2 = Birthday

Result of s1.concat(s2) = Happy Birthday
s1 after concatenation = Happy
```

Fig. 14.7 | `String` method `concat`.

14.3.7 Miscellaneous String Methods

Class `String` provides several methods that return `String`s or character arrays containing modified copies of an original `String`'s contents. These methods—none of which modify the `String` on which they're called—are demonstrated in Fig. 14.8.

```java
// Fig. 14.8: StringMiscellaneous2.java
// String methods replace, toLowerCase, toUpperCase, trim and toCharArray.

public class StringMiscellaneous2 {
   public static void main(String[] args) {
      String s1 = "hello";
      String s2 = "GOODBYE";
      String s3 = "   spaces   ";

      System.out.printf("s1 = %s%ns2 = %s%ns3 = %s%n%n", s1, s2, s3);

      // test method replace
      System.out.printf(
         "Replace 'l' with 'L' in s1: %s%n%n", s1.replace('l', 'L'));

      // test toLowerCase and toUpperCase
      System.out.printf("s1.toUpperCase() = %s%n", s1.toUpperCase());
      System.out.printf("s2.toLowerCase() = %s%n%n", s2.toLowerCase());

      // test trim method
      System.out.printf("s3 after trim = \"%s\"%n%n", s3.trim());

      // test toCharArray method
      char[] charArray = s1.toCharArray();
      System.out.print("s1 as a character array = ");

      for (char character : charArray) {
         System.out.print(character);
      }

      System.out.println();
   }
}
```

```
s1 = hello
s2 = GOODBYE
s3 =    spaces

Replace 'l' with 'L' in s1: heLLo

s1.toUpperCase() = HELLO
s2.toLowerCase() = goodbye

s3 after trim = "spaces"

s1 as a character array = hello
```

Fig. 14.8 | `String` methods `replace`, `toLowerCase`, `toUpperCase`, `trim` and `toCharArray`.

Line 14 uses `String` method `replace` to return a new `String` object in which every occurrence in `s1` of character `'l'` (lowercase el) is replaced with character `'L'`. Method `replace` leaves the original `String` unchanged. If there are no occurrences of the first argument in the `String`, method `replace` returns the original `String`. An overloaded version of method `replace` enables you to replace substrings rather than individual characters.

Line 17 uses `String` method **`toUpperCase`** to generate a new `String` with uppercase letters where corresponding lowercase letters exist in `s1`. The method returns a new `String` object containing the converted `String` and leaves the original `String` unchanged. If there are no characters to convert, method `toUpperCase` returns the original `String`.

Line 18 uses `String` method **`toLowerCase`** to return a new `String` object with lowercase letters where corresponding uppercase letters exist in `s2`. The original `String` remains unchanged. If there are no characters in the original `String` to convert, `toLowerCase` returns the original `String`.

Line 21 uses `String` method **`trim`** to generate a new `String` object that removes all white-space characters that appear at the beginning and/or end of the `String` on which `trim` operates. The method returns a new `String` object containing the `String` without leading or trailing white space. The original `String` remains unchanged. If there are no white-space characters at the beginning and end, `trim` returns the original `String`.

Line 24 uses `String` method **`toCharArray`** to create a new character array containing a copy of the characters in `s1`. Lines 27–29 output each `char` in the array.

14.3.8 `String` Method `valueOf`

As we've seen, every object in Java has a `toString` method that enables a program to obtain the object's *string representation*. Unfortunately, this technique cannot be used with primitive types because they do not have methods. Class `String` provides `static` methods that take an argument of any type and convert it to a `String` object. Figure 14.9 demonstrates the `String` class **`valueOf`** methods.

```java
// Fig. 14.9: StringValueOf.java
// String valueOf methods.

public class StringValueOf {
   public static void main(String[] args) {
      char[] charArray = {'a', 'b', 'c', 'd', 'e', 'f'};
      boolean booleanValue = true;
      char characterValue = 'Z';
      int integerValue = 7;
      long longValue = 10000000000L; // L suffix indicates long
      float floatValue = 2.5f; // f indicates that 2.5 is a float
      double doubleValue = 33.333; // no suffix, double is default
      Object objectRef = "hello"; // assign string to an Object reference

      System.out.printf(
         "char array = %s%n", String.valueOf(charArray));
      System.out.printf("part of char array = %s%n",
         String.valueOf(charArray, 3, 3));
```

Fig. 14.9 | `String` `valueOf` methods. (Part 1 of 2.)

```
19          System.out.printf(
20             "boolean = %s%n", String.valueOf(booleanValue));
21          System.out.printf(
22             "char = %s%n", String.valueOf(characterValue));
23          System.out.printf("int = %s%n", String.valueOf(integerValue));
24          System.out.printf("long = %s%n", String.valueOf(longValue));
25          System.out.printf("float = %s%n", String.valueOf(floatValue));
26          System.out.printf(
27             "double = %s%n", String.valueOf(doubleValue));
28          System.out.printf("Object = %s", String.valueOf(objectRef));
29       }
30    }
```

```
char array = abcdef
part of char array = def
boolean = true
char = Z
int = 7
long = 10000000000
float = 2.5
double = 33.333
Object = hello
```

Fig. 14.9 | `String` `valueOf` methods. (Part 2 of 2.)

The expression `String.valueOf(charArray)` at line 16 uses the character array `charArray` to create a new `String` object. The expression `String.valueOf(charArray, 3, 3)` at line 18 uses a portion of the character array `charArray` to create a new `String` object. The second argument specifies the starting index from which the characters are used. The third argument specifies the number of characters to be used.

There are seven other versions of method `valueOf`, which take arguments of type `boolean`, `char`, `int`, `long`, `float`, `double` and `Object`, respectively. These are demonstrated in lines 19–28. The version of `valueOf` that takes an `Object` as an argument can do so because all `Object`s can be converted to `String`s with method `toString`.

[*Note:* Lines 10–11 use literal values `10000000000L` and `2.5f` as the initial values of `long` variable `longValue` and `float` variable `floatValue`, respectively. By default, Java treats integer literals as type `int` and floating-point literals as type `double`. Appending the letter `L` to the literal `10000000000` and appending the letter `f` to the literal `2.5` indicates to the compiler that `10000000000` should be treated as a `long` and `2.5` as a `float`. An uppercase `L` or lowercase `l` can be used to denote a variable of type `long` and an uppercase `F` or lowercase `f` can be used to denote a variable of type `float`.]

14.4 Class StringBuilder

We now discuss the features of class **`StringBuilder`** for creating and manipulating *dynamic* string information—that is, *modifiable* strings. Every `StringBuilder` is capable of storing a number of characters specified by its *capacity*. If a `StringBuilder`'s capacity is exceeded, the capacity expands to accommodate the additional characters.

Performance Tip 14.4

Java can perform certain optimizations involving `String` objects (such as referring to one `String` object from multiple variables) because it knows these objects will not change. `Strings` (not `StringBuilders`) should be used if the data will not change.

Performance Tip 14.5

In programs that frequently perform string concatenation, or other string modifications, it's often more efficient to implement the modifications with class `StringBuilder`.

Software Engineering Observation 14.1

`StringBuilders` are not thread safe. If multiple threads require access to the same dynamic string information, use class `StringBuffer` in your code. Classes `StringBuilder` and `StringBuffer` provide identical capabilities, but class `StringBuffer` is thread safe. For more details on threading, see Chapter 23.

14.4.1 `StringBuilder` Constructors

Class `StringBuilder` provides four constructors. We demonstrate three of these in Fig. 14.10. Line 6 uses the no-argument `StringBuilder` constructor to create a `StringBuilder` with no characters in it and an initial capacity of 16 characters (the default for a `StringBuilder`). Line 7 uses the `StringBuilder` constructor that takes an integer argument to create a `StringBuilder` with no characters in it and the initial capacity specified by the integer argument (i.e., `10`). Line 8 uses the `StringBuilder` constructor that takes a `String` argument to create a `StringBuilder` containing the characters in the `String` argument. The initial capacity is the number of characters in the `String` argument plus 16. Lines 10–12 implicitly use the method `toString` of class `StringBuilder` to output the `StringBuilders` with the `printf` method. In Section 14.4.4, we discuss how Java uses `StringBuilder` objects to implement the + and += operators for string concatenation.

```
1  // Fig. 14.10: StringBuilderConstructors.java
2  // StringBuilder constructors.
3
4  public class StringBuilderConstructors {
5     public static void main(String[] args) {
6        StringBuilder buffer1 = new StringBuilder();
7        StringBuilder buffer2 = new StringBuilder(10);
8        StringBuilder buffer3 = new StringBuilder("hello");
9
10       System.out.printf("buffer1 = \"%s\"%n", buffer1);
11       System.out.printf("buffer2 = \"%s\"%n", buffer2);
12       System.out.printf("buffer3 = \"%s\"%n", buffer3);
13    }
14 }
```

```
buffer1 = ""
buffer2 = ""
buffer3 = "hello"
```

Fig. 14.10 | `StringBuilder` constructors.

14.4.2 StringBuilder Methods length, capacity, setLength and ensureCapacity

Class StringBuilder's **length** and **capacity** method return the number of characters currently in a StringBuilder and the number of characters that can be stored without allocating more memory, respectively. Method **ensureCapacity** guarantees that a StringBuilder has at least the specified capacity. Method **setLength** increases or decreases the length of a StringBuilder. Figure 14.11 demonstrates these methods.

```
1  // Fig. 14.11: StringBuilderCapLen.java
2  // StringBuilder length, setLength, capacity and ensureCapacity methods.
3
4  public class StringBuilderCapLen {
5     public static void main(String[] args) {
6        StringBuilder buffer = new StringBuilder("Hello, how are you?");
7
8        System.out.printf("buffer = %s%nlength = %d%ncapacity = %d%n%n",
9           buffer.toString(), buffer.length(), buffer.capacity());
10
11       buffer.ensureCapacity(75);
12       System.out.printf("New capacity = %d%n%n", buffer.capacity());
13
14       buffer.setLength(10));
15       System.out.printf("New length = %d%nbuffer = %s%n",
16          buffer.length(), buffer.toString());
17    }
18 }
```

```
buffer = Hello, how are you?
length = 19
capacity = 35

New capacity = 75

New length = 10
buffer = Hello, how
```

Fig. 14.11 | StringBuilder length, setLength, capacity and ensureCapacity methods.

The application contains one StringBuilder called buffer. Line 6 uses the StringBuilder constructor that takes a String argument to initialize the StringBuilder with "Hello, how are you?". Lines 8–9 print the contents, length and capacity of the StringBuilder. Note in the output window that the capacity of the StringBuilder is initially 35. Recall that the StringBuilder constructor that takes a String argument initializes the capacity to the length of the string passed as an argument plus 16.

Line 11 uses method ensureCapacity to expand the capacity of the StringBuilder to a minimum of 75 characters. Actually, if the original capacity is less than the argument, the method ensures a capacity that's the greater of the number specified as an argument and twice the original capacity plus 2. The StringBuilder's current capacity remains unchanged if it's more than the specified capacity.

Performance Tip 14.6

Dynamically increasing the capacity of a `StringBuilder` *can take a relatively long time. Executing a large number of these operations can degrade the performance of an application. If a* `StringBuilder` *is going to increase greatly in size, possibly multiple times, setting its capacity high at the beginning will increase performance.*

Line 14 uses method `setLength` to set the length of the `StringBuilder` to 10. If the specified length is less than the current number of characters in the `StringBuilder`, its contents are truncated to the specified length (i.e., the characters in the `StringBuilder` after the specified length are discarded). If the specified length is greater than the number of characters currently in the `StringBuilder`, `null` characters (characters with the numeric representation 0) are appended until the total number of characters in the `StringBuilder` is equal to the specified length.

14.4.3 `StringBuilder` Methods `charAt`, `setCharAt`, `getChars` and `reverse`

Class `StringBuilder` provides methods **`charAt`**, **`setCharAt`**, **`getChars`** and **`reverse`** to manipulate the characters in a `StringBuilder` (Fig. 14.12). Method `charAt` (line 10) takes an integer argument and returns the character in the `StringBuilder` at that index. Method `getChars` (line 13) copies characters from a `StringBuilder` into the character array passed as an argument. This method takes four arguments—the starting index from which characters should be copied in the `StringBuilder`, the index one past the last character to be copied from the `StringBuilder`, the character array into which the characters are to be copied and the starting location in the character array where the first character should be placed. Method `setCharAt` (lines 20 and 21) takes an integer and a character argument and sets the character at the specified position in the `StringBuilder` to the character argument. Method `reverse` (line 24) reverses the contents of the `StringBuilder`. Attempting to access a character that's outside the bounds of a `StringBuilder` results in a `StringIndexOutOfBoundsException`.

```
1  // Fig. 14.12: StringBuilderChars.java
2  // StringBuilder methods charAt, setCharAt, getChars and reverse.
3
4  public class StringBuilderChars {
5     public static void main(String[] args) {
6        StringBuilder buffer = new StringBuilder("hello there");
7
8        System.out.printf("buffer = %s%n", buffer.toString());
9        System.out.printf("Character at 0: %s%nCharacter at 4: %s%n%n",
10          buffer.charAt(0), buffer.charAt(4));
11
12       char[] charArray = new char[buffer.length()];
13       buffer.getChars(0, buffer.length(), charArray, 0);
14       System.out.print("The characters are: ");
15
```

Fig. 14.12 | `StringBuilder` methods `charAt`, `setCharAt`, `getChars` and `reverse`. (Part 1 of 2.)

```
      for (char character : charArray) {
         System.out.print(character);
      }

      buffer.setCharAt(0, 'H');
      buffer.setCharAt(6, 'T');
      System.out.printf("%n%nbuffer = %s", buffer.toString());

      buffer.reverse();
      System.out.printf("%n%nbuffer = %s%n", buffer.toString());
   }
}
```

```
buffer = hello there
Character at 0: h
Character at 4: o

The characters are: hello there

buffer = Hello There

buffer = erehT olleH
```

Fig. 14.12 | StringBuilder methods charAt, setCharAt, getChars and reverse. (Part 2 of 2.)

14.4.4 StringBuilder append Methods

Class StringBuilder provides *overloaded* **append** methods (Fig. 14.13) to allow values of various types to be appended to the end of a StringBuilder. Versions are provided for each of the primitive types and for character arrays, Strings, Objects, and more. (Remember that method toString produces a string representation of any Object.) Each method takes its argument, converts it to a string and appends it to the StringBuilder. The call System.getProperty("line.separator") returns a platform-independent newline.

```
// Fig. 14.13: StringBuilderAppend.java
// StringBuilder append methods.

public class StringBuilderAppend
{
   public static void main(String[] args)
   {
      Object objectRef = "hello";
      String string = "goodbye";
      char[] charArray = {'a', 'b', 'c', 'd', 'e', 'f'};
      boolean booleanValue = true;
      char characterValue = 'Z';
      int integerValue = 7;
      long longValue = 10000000000L;
      float floatValue = 2.5f;
      double doubleValue = 33.333;
```

Fig. 14.13 | StringBuilder append methods. (Part 1 of 2.)

```

      StringBuilder lastBuffer = new StringBuilder("last buffer");
      StringBuilder buffer = new StringBuilder();

      buffer.append(objectRef)
            .append(System.getProperty("line.separator"))
            .append(string)
            .append(System.getProperty("line.separator"))
            .append(charArray)
            .append(System.getProperty("line.separator"))
            .append(charArray, 0, 3)
            .append(System.getProperty("line.separator"))
            .append(booleanValue)
            .append(System.getProperty("line.separator"))
            .append(characterValue);
            .append(System.getProperty("line.separator"))
            .append(integerValue)
            .append(System.getProperty("line.separator"))
            .append(longValue)
            .append(System.getProperty("line.separator"))
            .append(floatValue)
            .append(System.getProperty("line.separator"))
            .append(doubleValue)
            .append(System.getProperty("line.separator"))
            .append(lastBuffer);

      System.out.printf("buffer contains%n%s%n", buffer.toString());
   }
}
```

```
buffer contains
hello
goodbye
abcdef
abc
true
Z
7
10000000000
2.5
33.333
last buffer
```

Fig. 14.13 | `StringBuilder` append methods. (Part 2 of 2.)

The compiler can use `StringBuilder` and the `append` methods to implement the + and += `String` concatenation operators. For example, assuming the declarations

```
String string1 = "hello";
String string2 = "BC";
int value = 22;
```

the statement

```
String s = string1 + string2 + value;
```

concatenates "hello", "BC" and 22. The concatenation can be performed as follows:

```
String s = new StringBuilder().append("hello").append("BC").
   append(22).toString();
```

First, the preceding statement creates an *empty* StringBuilder, then appends to it the strings "hello" and "BC" and the integer 22. Next, StringBuilder's toString method converts the StringBuilder to a String object to be assigned to String s. The statement

```
s += "!";
```

can be performed as follows (this may differ by compiler):

```
s = new StringBuilder().append(s).append("!").toString();
```

This creates an empty StringBuilder, then appends to it the current contents of s followed by "!". Next, StringBuilder's method toString (which must be called *explicitly* here) returns the StringBuilder's contents as a String, and the result is assigned to s.

14.4.5 StringBuilder Insertion and Deletion Methods

StringBuilder provides overloaded **insert** methods to insert values of various types at any position in a StringBuilder. Versions are provided for the primitive types and for character arrays, Strings, Objects and CharSequences. Each method takes its second argument and inserts it at the index specified by the first argument. If the first argument is less than 0 or greater than the StringBuilder's length, a StringIndexOutOfBoundsException occurs. Class StringBuilder also provides methods **delete** and **deleteCharAt** to delete characters at any position in a StringBuilder. Method delete takes two arguments—the starting index and the index one past the end of the characters to delete. All characters beginning at the starting index up to but *not* including the ending index are deleted. Method deleteCharAt takes one argument—the index of the character to delete. Invalid indices cause both methods to throw a StringIndexOutOfBoundsException. Figure 14.14 demonstrates methods insert, delete and deleteCharAt.

```
// Fig. 14.14: StringBuilderInsertDelete.java
// StringBuilder methods insert, delete and deleteCharAt.

public class StringBuilderInsertDelete {
   public static void main(String[] args) {
      Object objectRef = "hello";
      String string = "goodbye";
      char[] charArray = {'a', 'b', 'c', 'd', 'e', 'f'};
      boolean booleanValue = true;
      char characterValue = 'K';
      int integerValue = 7;
      long longValue = 10000000;
      float floatValue = 2.5f; // f suffix indicates that 2.5 is a float
      double doubleValue = 33.333;

      StringBuilder buffer = new StringBuilder();
```

Fig. 14.14 | StringBuilder methods insert, delete and deleteCharAt. (Part 1 of 2.)

```

      buffer.insert(0, objectRef);
      buffer.insert(0, "  "); // each of these contains two spaces
      buffer.insert(0, string);
      buffer.insert(0, "  ");
      buffer.insert(0, charArray);
      buffer.insert(0, "  ");
      buffer.insert(0, charArray, 3, 3);
      buffer.insert(0, "  ");
      buffer.insert(0, booleanValue);
      buffer.insert(0, "  ");
      buffer.insert(0, characterValue);
      buffer.insert(0, "  ");
      buffer.insert(0, integerValue);
      buffer.insert(0, "  ");
      buffer.insert(0, longValue);
      buffer.insert(0, "  ");
      buffer.insert(0, floatValue);
      buffer.insert(0, "  ");
      buffer.insert(0, doubleValue);

      System.out.printf(
         "buffer after inserts:%n%s%n%n", buffer.toString());

      buffer.deleteCharAt(10); // delete 5 in 2.5
      buffer.delete(2, 6); // delete .333 in 33.333

      System.out.printf(
         "buffer after deletes:%n%s%n", buffer.toString());
   }
}
```

```
buffer after inserts:
33.333  2.5  10000000  7  K  true  def  abcdef  goodbye  hello

buffer after deletes:
33  2.  10000000  7  K  true  def  abcdef  goodbye  hello
```

Fig. 14.14 | `StringBuilder` methods `insert`, `delete` and `deleteCharAt`. (Part 2 of 2.)

14.5 Class Character

Java provides eight **type-wrapper classes**—`Boolean`, `Character`, `Double`, `Float`, `Byte`, `Short`, `Integer` and `Long`—that enable primitive-type values to be treated as objects. In this section, we present class `Character`—the type-wrapper class for primitive type `char`.

Most `Character` methods are `static` methods designed for convenience in processing individual `char` values. These methods take at least a character argument and perform either a test or a manipulation of the character. Class `Character` also contains a constructor that receives a `char` argument to initialize a `Character` object. Most of the methods of class `Character` are presented in the next three examples. For more information on class Character (and all the type-wrapper classes), see the java.lang package in the Java API documentation.

Figure 14.15 demonstrates static methods that test characters to determine whether they're a specific character type and the static methods that perform case conversions on characters. You can enter any character and apply the methods to the character.

```
// Fig. 14.15: StaticCharMethods.java
// Character static methods for testing characters and converting case.
import java.util.Scanner;

public class StaticCharMethods {
   public static void main(String[] args) {
      Scanner scanner = new Scanner(System.in); // create scanner
      System.out.println("Enter a character and press Enter");
      String input = scanner.next();
      char c = input.charAt(0); // get input character

      // display character info
      System.out.printf("is defined: %b%n", Character.isDefined(c));
      System.out.printf("is digit: %b%n", Character.isDigit(c));
      System.out.printf("is first character in a Java identifier: %b%n",
         Character.isJavaIdentifierStart(c));
      System.out.printf("is part of a Java identifier: %b%n",
         Character.isJavaIdentifierPart(c));
      System.out.printf("is letter: %b%n", Character.isLetter(c));
      System.out.printf(
         "is letter or digit: %b%n", Character.isLetterOrDigit(c));
      System.out.printf(
         "is lower case: %b%n", Character.isLowerCase(c));
      System.out.printf(
         "is upper case: %b%n", Character.isUpperCase(c));
      System.out.printf(
         "to upper case: %s%n", Character.toUpperCase(c));
      System.out.printf(
         "to lower case: %s%n", Character.toLowerCase(c));
   }
}
```

```
Enter a character and press Enter
A
is defined: true
is digit: false
is first character in a Java identifier: true
is part of a Java identifier: true
is letter: true
is letter or digit: true
is lower case: false
is upper case: true
to upper case: A
to lower case: a
```

Fig. 14.15 | Character static methods for testing characters and converting case. (Part 1 of 2.)

```
Enter a character and press Enter
8
is defined: true
is digit: true
is first character in a Java identifier: false
is part of a Java identifier: true
is letter: false
is letter or digit: true
is lower case: false
is upper case: false
to upper case: 8
to lower case: 8
```

```
Enter a character and press Enter
$
is defined: true
is digit: false
is first character in a Java identifier: true
is part of a Java identifier: true
is letter: false
is letter or digit: false
is lower case: false
is upper case: false
to upper case: $
to lower case: $
```

Fig. 14.15 | Character static methods for testing characters and converting case. (Part 2 of 2.)

Line 13 uses `Character` method **`isDefined`** to determine whether character `c` is defined in the Unicode character set. If so, the method returns `true`; otherwise, it returns `false`. Line 14 uses `Character` method **`isDigit`** to determine whether character `c` is a defined Unicode digit. If so, the method returns `true`, and otherwise, `false`.

Line 16 uses `Character` method **`isJavaIdentifierStart`** to determine whether `c` is a character that can be the first character of an identifier in Java—that is, a letter, an underscore (_) or a dollar sign (`$`). If so, the method returns `true`, and otherwise, `false`. Line 18 uses `Character` method **`isJavaIdentifierPart`** to determine whether character `c` is a character that can be used in an identifier in Java—that is, a digit, a letter, an underscore (_) or a dollar sign (`$`). If so, the method returns `true`, and otherwise, `false`.

Line 19 uses `Character` method **`isLetter`** to determine whether character `c` is a letter. If so, the method returns `true`, and otherwise, `false`. Line 21 uses `Character` method **`isLetterOrDigit`** to determine whether character `c` is a letter or a digit. If so, the method returns `true`, and otherwise, `false`.

Line 23 uses `Character` method **`isLowerCase`** to determine whether `c` is a lowercase letter. If so, the method returns `true`, and otherwise, `false`. Line 25 uses **`isUpperCase`** to determine whether `c` is an uppercase letter. If so, the method returns `true`, and otherwise, `false`. Line 27 uses `Character` method **`toUpperCase`** to convert the character `c` to its uppercase equivalent. The method returns the converted character if the character has an uppercase equivalent, and otherwise, the method returns its original argument. Line 29 uses `Character` method **`toLowerCase`** to convert the character `c` to its lowercase equivalent. The method returns the converted character if the character has a lowercase equivalent, and otherwise, the method returns its original argument.

Figure 14.16 demonstrates static `Character` methods **`digit`** and **`forDigit`**, which convert characters to digits and digits to characters, respectively, in different number systems. Common number systems include decimal (base 10), octal (base 8), hexadecimal (base 16) and binary (base 2). The base of a number is also known as its **radix**. For more information on conversions between number systems, see online Appendix J.

```java
// Fig. 14.16: StaticCharMethods2.java
// Character class static conversion methods.
import java.util.Scanner;

public class StaticCharMethods2 {
   public static void main(String[] args) {
      Scanner scanner = new Scanner(System.in);

      // get radix
      System.out.println("Please enter a radix:");
      int radix = scanner.nextInt();

      // get user choice
      System.out.printf("Please choose one:%n1 -- %s%n2 -- %s%n",
         "Convert digit to character", "Convert character to digit");
      int choice = scanner.nextInt();

      // process request
      switch (choice) {
         case 1: // convert digit to character
            System.out.println("Enter a digit:");
            int digit = scanner.nextInt();
            System.out.printf("Convert digit to character: %s%n",
               Character.forDigit(digit, radix));
            break;
         case 2: // convert character to digit
            System.out.println("Enter a character:");
            char character = scanner.next().charAt(0);
            System.out.printf("Convert character to digit: %s%n",
               Character.digit(character, radix));
            break;
      }
   }
}
```

```
Please enter a radix:
16
Please choose one:
1 -- Convert digit to character
2 -- Convert character to digit
2
Enter a character:
A
Convert character to digit: 10
```

Fig. 14.16 | `Character` class `static` conversion methods. (Part 1 of 2.)

```
Please enter a radix:
16
Please choose one:
1 -- Convert digit to character
2 -- Convert character to digit
1
Enter a digit:
13
Convert digit to character: d
```

Fig. 14.16 | `Character` class `static` conversion methods. (Part 2 of 2.)

Line 24 uses method `forDigit` to convert the integer `digit` into a character in the number system specified by the integer `radix` (the base of the number). For example, the decimal integer `13` in base 16 (the `radix`) has the character value `'d'`. Lowercase and uppercase letters represent the *same* value in number systems. Line 30 uses method `digit` to convert variable `character` into an integer in the number system specified by the integer `radix` (the base of the number). For example, the character `'A'` is the base 16 (the `radix`) representation of the base 10 value 10. The radix must be between 2 and 36, inclusive.

Figure 14.17 demonstrates the constructor and several instance methods of class `Character`—**`charValue`**, `toString` and `equals`. Lines 5–6 instantiate two `Character` objects by assigning the character constants `'A'` and `'a'`, respectively, to the `Character` variables. Java automatically converts these `char` literals into `Character` objects—a process known as *autoboxing* that we discuss in more detail in Section 16.4. Line 9 uses `Character` method `charValue` to return the `char` value stored in `Character` object `c1`. Line 9 also gets a string representation of `Character` object `c2` using method `toString`. The condition in line 11 uses method `equals` to determine whether the object `c1` has the same contents as the object `c2` (i.e., the characters inside each object are equal).

```
1  // Fig. 14.17: OtherCharMethods.java
2  // Character class instance methods.
3  public class OtherCharMethods {
4     public static void main(String[] args) {
5        Character c1 = 'A';
6        Character c2 = 'a';
7
8        System.out.printf(
9           "c1 = %s%nc2 = %s%n%n", c1.charValue(), c2.toString());
10
11       if (c1.equals(c2)) {
12          System.out.println("c1 and c2 are equal%n");
13       }
14       else {
15          System.out.println("c1 and c2 are not equal%n");
16       }
17    }
18 }
```

Fig. 14.17 | `Character` class instance methods. (Part 1 of 2.)

```
c1 = A
c2 = a

c1 and c2 are not equal
```

Fig. 14.17 | `Character` class instance methods. (Part 2 of 2.)

14.6 Tokenizing Strings

When you read a sentence, your mind breaks it into **tokens**—individual words and punctuation marks that convey meaning to you. Compilers also perform tokenization. They break up statements into individual pieces like keywords, identifiers, operators and other programming-language elements. We now study class `String`'s **`split`** method, which breaks a `String` into its component tokens. Tokens are separated from one another by **delimiters**, typically white-space characters such as space, tab, newline and carriage return. Other characters can also be used as delimiters to separate tokens. The application in Fig. 14.18 demonstrates `String`'s `split` method.

When the user presses the *Enter* key, the input sentence is stored in variable `sentence`. Line 14 invokes `String` method `split` with the `String` argument `" "`, which returns an array of `String`s. The space character in the argument `String` is the delimiter that method `split` uses to locate the tokens in the `String`. As you'll learn in the next section, the argument to method split can be a regular expression for more complex tokenizing. Lines 15–16 display the length of the array `tokens`—i.e., the number of tokens in `sentence`. Lines 18–20 output each token on a separate line.

```
1  // Fig. 14.18: TokenTest.java
2  // Tokenizing with String method split
3  import java.util.Scanner;
4
5  public class TokenTest {
6     // execute application
7     public static void main(String[] args) {
8        // get sentence
9        Scanner scanner = new Scanner(System.in);
10       System.out.println("Enter a sentence and press Enter");
11       String sentence = scanner.nextLine();
12
13       // process user sentence
14       String[] tokens = sentence.split(" ");
15       System.out.printf("Number of elements: %d%nThe tokens are:%n",
16          tokens.length);
17
18       for (String token : tokens) {
19          System.out.println(token);
20       }
21    }
22 }
```

Fig. 14.18 | Tokenizing with `String` method `split`. (Part 1 of 2.)

```
Enter a sentence and press Enter
This is a sentence with seven tokens
Number of elements: 7
The tokens are:
This
is
a
sentence
with
seven
tokens
```

Fig. 14.18 | Tokenizing with `String` method `split`. (Part 2 of 2.)

14.7 Regular Expressions, Class `Pattern` and Class `Matcher`

A **regular expression** is a `String` that describes a *search pattern* for *matching* characters in other `String`s. Such expressions are useful for *validating input* and ensuring that data is in a particular format. For example, a ZIP code must consist of five digits, and a last name must contain only letters, spaces, apostrophes and hyphens. One application of regular expressions is to facilitate the construction of a compiler. Often, a large and complex regular expression is used to *validate the syntax of a program*. If the program code does *not* match the regular expression, the compiler knows that there's a syntax error in the code.

Class `String` provides several methods for performing regular-expression operations, the simplest of which is the matching operation. `String` method **`matches`** receives a `String` that specifies the regular expression and matches the contents of the `String` object on which it's called to the regular expression. The method returns a `boolean` indicating whether the match succeeded.

A regular expression consists of literal characters and special symbols. Figure 14.19 specifies some **predefined character classes** that can be used with regular expressions. A character class is an *escape sequence* that represents a group of characters. A digit is any numeric character. A **word character** is any letter (uppercase or lowercase), any digit or the underscore character. A white-space character is a space, a tab, a carriage return, a newline or a form feed. Each character class matches a single character in the `String` we're attempting to match with the regular expression.

Character	Matches	Character	Matches
`\d`	any digit	`\D`	any nondigit
`\w`	any word character	`\W`	any nonword character
`\s`	any white-space character	`\S`	any non-whitespace character

Fig. 14.19 | Predefined character classes.

Regular expressions are not limited to these predefined character classes. The expressions employ various operators and other forms of notation to match complex patterns.

We examine several of these techniques in the application in Figs. 14.20 and 14.21, which *validates user input* via regular expressions. [*Note:* This application is not designed to match all possible valid user input.]

```
// Fig. 14.20: ValidateInput.java
// Validating user information using regular expressions.

public class ValidateInput {
   // validate first name
   public static boolean validateFirstName(String firstName) {
      return firstName.matches("[A-Z][a-zA-Z]*");
   }

   // validate last name
   public static boolean validateLastName(String lastName) {
      return lastName.matches("[a-zA-z]+(['-][a-zA-Z]+)*");
   }

   // validate address
   public static boolean validateAddress(String address) {
      return address.matches(
         "\\d+\\s+([a-zA-Z]+|[a-zA-Z]+\\s[a-zA-Z]+)");
   }

   // validate city
   public static boolean validateCity(String city) {
      return city.matches("([a-zA-Z]+|[a-zA-Z]+\\s[a-zA-Z]+)");
   }

   // validate state
   public static boolean validateState(String state) {
      return state.matches("([a-zA-Z]+|[a-zA-Z]+\\s[a-zA-Z]+)");
   }

   // validate zip
   public static boolean validateZip(String zip) {
      return zip.matches("\\d{5}");
   }

   // validate phone
   public static boolean validatePhone(String phone) {
      return phone.matches("[1-9]\\d{2}-[1-9]\\d{2}-\\d{4}");
   }
}
```

Fig. 14.20 | Validating user information using regular expressions.

```
// Fig. 14.21: Validate.java
// Input and validate data from user using the ValidateInput class.
import java.util.Scanner;
```

Fig. 14.21 | Input and validate data from user using the ValidateInput class. (Part 1 of 3.)

```

public class Validate {
   public static void main(String[] args) {
      // get user input
      Scanner scanner = new Scanner(System.in);
      System.out.println("Please enter first name:");
      String firstName = scanner.nextLine();
      System.out.println("Please enter last name:");
      String lastName = scanner.nextLine();
      System.out.println("Please enter address:");
      String address = scanner.nextLine();
      System.out.println("Please enter city:");
      String city = scanner.nextLine();
      System.out.println("Please enter state:");
      String state = scanner.nextLine();
      System.out.println("Please enter zip:");
      String zip = scanner.nextLine();
      System.out.println("Please enter phone:");
      String phone = scanner.nextLine();

      // validate user input and display error message
      System.out.printf("%nValidate Result:");

      if (!ValidateInput.validateFirstName(firstName)) {
         System.out.println("Invalid first name");
      }
      else if (!ValidateInput.validateLastName(lastName)) {
         System.out.println("Invalid last name");
      }
      else if (!ValidateInput.validateAddress(address)) {
         System.out.println("Invalid address");
      }
      else if (!ValidateInput.validateCity(city)) {
         System.out.println("Invalid city");
      }
      else if (!ValidateInput.validateState(state)) {
         System.out.println("Invalid state");
      }
      else if (!ValidateInput.validateZip(zip)) {
         System.out.println("Invalid zip code");
      }
      else if (!ValidateInput.validatePhone(phone)) {
         System.out.println("Invalid phone number");
      }
      else {
         System.out.println("Valid input.  Thank you.");
      }
   }
}
```

Fig. 14.21 | Input and validate data from user using the `ValidateInput` class. (Part 2 of 3.)

```
Please enter first name:
Jane
Please enter last name:
Doe
Please enter address:
123 Some Street
Please enter city:
Some City
Please enter state:
SS
Please enter zip:
123
Please enter phone:
123-456-7890

Validate Result:
Invalid zip code
```

```
Please enter first name:
Jane
Please enter last name:
Doe
Please enter address:
123 Some Street
Please enter city:
Some City
Please enter state:
SS
Please enter zip:
12345
Please enter phone:
123-456-7890

Validate Result:
Valid input.  Thank you.
```

Fig. 14.21 | Input and validate data from user using the `ValidateInput` class. (Part 3 of 3.)

Figure 14.20 validates user input. Line 7 validates the first name. To match a set of characters that does not have a predefined character class, use square brackets, `[]`. For example, the pattern `"[aeiou]"` matches a single character that's a vowel. Character ranges are represented by placing a dash (-) between two characters. In the example, `"[A-Z]"` matches a single uppercase letter. If the first character in the brackets is `"^"`, the expression accepts any character other than those indicated. However, `"[^Z]"` is not the same as `"[A-Y]"`, which matches uppercase letters A–Y—`"[^Z]"` matches *any character other than* capital Z, including lowercase letters and nonletters such as the newline character. Ranges in character classes are determined by the letters' integer values. In this example, `"[A-Za-z]"` matches all uppercase and lowercase letters. The range `"[A-z]"` matches all letters and also matches those characters (such as `[` and `\`) with an integer value between uppercase `Z` and lowercase `a` (for more information on integer values of characters see Appendix B). Like predefined character classes, character classes delimited by square brackets match a single character in the search object.

In line 7, the asterisk after the second character class indicates that any number of letters can be matched. In general, when the regular-expression operator "*" appears in a regular expression, the application attempts to match zero or more occurrences of the subexpression immediately preceding the "*". Operator "+" attempts to match one or more occurrences of the subexpression immediately preceding "+". So both "A*" and "A+" will match "AAA" or "A", but only "A*" will match an empty string.

If method `validateFirstName` returns `true` (line 27 of Fig. 14.21), the application attempts to validate the last name (line 30) by calling `validateLastName` (lines 11–13 of Fig. 14.20). The regular expression to validate the last name matches any number of letters split by apostrophes or hyphens.

Line 33 of Fig. 14.21 calls method `validateAddress` (lines 16–19 of Fig. 14.20) to validate the address. The first character class matches any digit one or more times (`\\d+`). Two `\` characters are used, because `\` normally starts an escape sequence in a string. So `\\d` in a `String` represents the regular-expression pattern `\d`. Then we match one or more white-space characters (`\\s+`). The character "`|`" matches the expression to its left or to its right. For example, "`Hi (John|Jane)`" matches both "`Hi John`" and "`Hi Jane`". The parentheses are used to group parts of the regular expression. In this example, the left side of `|` matches a single word, and the right side matches two words separated by any amount of white space. So the address must contain a number followed by one or two words. Therefore, "`10 Broadway`" and "`10 Main Street`" are both valid addresses in this example. The city (lines 22–24 of Fig. 14.20) and state (lines 27–29 of Fig. 14.20) methods also match any word of at least one character or, alternatively, any two words of at least one character if the words are separated by a single space, so both `Waltham` and `West Newton` would match.

Quantifiers

The asterisk (*) and plus (+) are formally called **quantifiers**. Figure 14.22 lists all the quantifiers. We've already discussed how the asterisk (*) and plus (+) quantifiers work. All quantifiers affect only the subexpression immediately preceding the quantifier. Quantifier question mark (?) matches zero or one occurrences of the expression that it quantifies. A set of braces containing one number (`{n}`) matches exactly *n* occurrences of the expression it quantifies. We demonstrate this quantifier to validate the zip code in Fig. 14.20 at line 33. Including a comma after the number enclosed in braces matches at least *n* occurrences of the quantified expression. The set of braces containing two numbers (`{n,m}`) matches between *n* and *m* occurrences of the expression that it qualifies. Quantifiers may be applied to patterns enclosed in parentheses to create more complex regular expressions.

Quantifier	Matches
*	Matches zero or more occurrences of the pattern.
+	Matches one or more occurrences of the pattern.
?	Matches zero or one occurrences of the pattern.
{*n*}	Matches exactly *n* occurrences.
{*n*,}	Matches at least *n* occurrences.
{*n*,*m*}	Matches between *n* and *m* (inclusive) occurrences.

Fig. 14.22 | Quantifiers used in regular expressions.

All of the quantifiers are **greedy**. This means that they'll match as many occurrences as they can as long as the match is still successful. However, if any of these quantifiers is followed by a question mark (?), the quantifier becomes **reluctant** (sometimes called **lazy**). It then will match as few occurrences as possible as long as the match is still successful.

The zip code (line 33 in Fig. 14.20) matches a digit five times. This regular expression uses the digit character class and a quantifier with the digit 5 between braces. The phone number (line 38 in Fig. 14.20) matches three digits (the first one cannot be zero) followed by a dash followed by three more digits (again the first one cannot be zero) followed by four more digits.

`String` method `matches` checks whether an entire `String` conforms to a regular expression. For example, we want to accept `"Smith"` as a last name, but not `"9@Smith#"`. If only a substring matches the regular expression, method `matches` returns `false`.

14.7.1 Replacing Substrings and Splitting Strings

Sometimes it's useful to replace parts of a string or to split a string into pieces. For this purpose, class `String` provides methods **`replaceAll`**, **`replaceFirst`** and **`split`**. These methods are demonstrated in Fig. 14.23.

```java
// Fig. 14.23: RegexSubstitution.java
// String methods replaceFirst, replaceAll and split.
import java.util.Arrays;

public class RegexSubstitution {
   public static void main(String[] args) {
      String firstString = "This sentence ends in 5 stars *****";
      String secondString = "1, 2, 3, 4, 5, 6, 7, 8";

      System.out.printf("Original String 1: %s%n", firstString);

      // replace '*' with '^'
      firstString = firstString.replaceAll("\\*", "^");

      System.out.printf("^ substituted for *: %s%n", firstString);

      // replace 'stars' with 'carets'
      firstString = firstString.replaceAll("stars", "carets");

      System.out.printf(
         "\"carets\" substituted for \"stars\": %s%n", firstString);

      // replace words with 'word'
      System.out.printf("Every word replaced by \"word\": %s%n%n",
         firstString.replaceAll("\\w+", "word"));

      System.out.printf("Original String 2: %s%n", secondString);

```

Fig. 14.23 | `String` methods `replaceFirst`, `replaceAll` and `split`. (Part 1 of 2.)

```
29         // replace first three digits with 'digit'
30         for (int i = 0; i < 3; i++) {
31            secondString = secondString.replaceFirst("\\d", "digit");
32         }
33
34         System.out.printf(
35            "First 3 digits replaced by \"digit\" : %s%n", secondString);
36
37         System.out.print("String split at commas: ");
38         String[] results = secondString.split(",\\s*"); // split on commas
39         System.out.println(Arrays.toString(results));
40      }
41   }
```

```
Original String 1: This sentence ends in 5 stars *****
^ substituted for *: This sentence ends in 5 stars ^^^^^
"carets" substituted for "stars": This sentence ends in 5 carets ^^^^^
Every word replaced by "word": word word word word word word ^^^^^

Original String 2: 1, 2, 3, 4, 5, 6, 7, 8
First 3 digits replaced by "digit" : digit, digit, digit, 4, 5, 6, 7, 8
String split at commas: [digit, digit, digit, 4, 5, 6, 7, 8]
```

Fig. 14.23 | `String` methods `replaceFirst`, `replaceAll` and `split`. (Part 2 of 2.)

Method `replaceAll` replaces text in a `String` with new text (the second argument) wherever the original `String` matches a regular expression (the first argument). Line 13 replaces every instance of `"*"` in `firstString` with `"^"`. The regular expression (`"\\*"`) precedes character `*` with two backslashes. Normally, `*` is a quantifier indicating that a regular expression should match *any number of occurrences* of a preceding pattern. However, in line 13, we want to find all occurrences of the literal character `*`—to do this, we must escape character `*` with character `\`. Escaping a special regular-expression character with `\` instructs the matching engine to find the actual character. Since the expression is stored in a Java `String` and `\` is a special character in Java `String`s, we must include an additional `\`. So the Java `String` `"\\*"` represents the regular-expression pattern `\*` which matches a single `*` character in the search string. In line 18, every match for the regular expression `"stars"` in `firstString` is replaced with `"carets"`. Line 25 uses `replaceAll` to replace all words in the string with `"word"`.

Method `replaceFirst` (line 31) replaces the first occurrence of a pattern match. Java `String`s are immutable; therefore, method `replaceFirst` returns a new `String` in which the appropriate characters have been replaced. This line takes the original `String` and replaces it with the `String` returned by `replaceFirst`. By iterating three times we replace the first three instances of a digit (`\d`) in `secondString` with the text `"digit"`.

Method `split` divides a `String` into several substrings. The original is broken in any location that matches a specified regular expression. Method `split` returns an array of `String`s containing the substrings between matches for the regular expression. In line 38, we use method `split` to tokenize a `String` of comma-separated integers. The argument is the regular expression that locates the delimiter. In this case, we use the regular expression `",\s*"` to separate the substrings wherever a comma occurs—again, the Java `String` `",\\s*"` represents the regular expression `,\s*`. By matching any white-space characters, we eliminate extra spaces from the resulting substrings. The commas and white-space characters are not returned as part of the substrings. Line 39 uses `Arrays` method `toString` to display the contents of array `results` in square brackets and separated by commas.

14.7.2 Classes Pattern and Matcher

In addition to the regular-expression capabilities of class `String`, Java provides other classes in package `java.util.regex` that help developers manipulate regular expressions. Class **`Pattern`** represents a regular expression. Class **`Matcher`** contains both a regular-expression pattern and a `CharSequence` in which to search for the pattern.

`CharSequence` (package `java.lang`) is an *interface* that allows read access to a sequence of characters. The interface requires that the methods `charAt`, `length`, `subSequence` and `toString` be declared. Both `String` and `StringBuilder` implement interface `CharSequence`, so an instance of either of these classes can be used with class `Matcher`.

Common Programming Error 14.2

A regular expression can be tested against an object of any class that implements interface `CharSequence`, but the regular expression must be a `String`. Attempting to create a regular expression as a `StringBuilder` is an error.

If a regular expression will be used only once, `static Pattern` method **`matches`** can be used. This method takes a `String` that specifies the regular expression and a `CharSequence` on which to perform the match. This method returns a `boolean` indicating whether the search object (the second argument) *matches* the regular expression.

If a regular expression will be used more than once (in a loop, for example), it's more efficient to use `static Pattern` method **`compile`** to create a specific `Pattern` object for that regular expression. This method receives a `String` representing the regular expression and returns a new `Pattern` object, which can then be used to call method **`matcher`**. This method receives a `CharSequence` to search and returns a `Matcher` object.

`Matcher` provides method **`matches`**, which performs the same task as `Pattern` method `matches`, but receives no arguments—the search pattern and search object are encapsulated in the `Matcher` object. Class `Matcher` provides other methods, including **`find`**, **`lookingAt`**, **`replaceFirst`** and **`replaceAll`**.

Figure 14.24 presents a simple example that employs regular expressions. This program matches birthdays against a regular expression. The expression matches only birthdays that do not occur in April and that belong to people whose names begin with `"J"`.

```
// Fig. 14.24: RegexMatches.java
// Classes Pattern and Matcher.
import java.util.regex.Matcher;
import java.util.regex.Pattern;

public class RegexMatches {
   public static void main(String[] args) {
      // create regular expression
      Pattern expression =
         Pattern.compile("J.*\\d[0-35-9]-\\d\\d-\\d\\d");
```

Fig. 14.24 | Classes `Pattern` and `Matcher`. (Part 1 of 2.)

```
11
12        String string1 = "Jane's Birthday is 05-12-75\n" +
13           "Dave's Birthday is 11-04-68\n" +
14           "John's Birthday is 04-28-73\n" +
15           "Joe's Birthday is 12-17-77";
16
17        // match regular expression to string and print matches
18        Matcher matcher = expression.matcher(string1);
19
20        while (matcher.find()) {
21           System.out.println(matcher.group());
22        }
23     }
24  }
```

```
Jane's Birthday is 05-12-75
Joe's Birthday is 12-17-77
```

Fig. 14.24 | Classes `Pattern` and `Matcher`. (Part 2 of 2.)

Lines 9–10 create a `Pattern` by invoking its `static` method `compile`. The dot character "`.`" in the regular expression (line 10) matches any single character except a newline. Line 18 creates the `Matcher` object for the compiled regular expression and the matching sequence (`string1`). Lines 20–22 use a `while` loop to *iterate* through the `String`. `Matcher` method `find` (line 20) attempts to match a piece of the search object to the search pattern. Each call to `find` starts at the point where the last call ended, so multiple matches can be found. `Matcher` method `lookingAt` performs the same way, except that it always starts from the beginning of the search object and will always find the *first* match if there is one.

Common Programming Error 14.3

Method `matches` *(from class* `String`*,* `Pattern` *or* `Matcher`*) will return* `true` *only if the entire search object matches the regular expression. Methods* `find` *and* `lookingAt` *(from class* `Matcher`*) will return* `true` *if a portion of the search object matches the regular expression.*

Line 21 uses `Matcher` method **group**, which returns the `String` from the search object that matches the search pattern. The `String` that's returned is the one that was last matched by a call to `find` or `lookingAt`. The output in Fig. 14.24 shows the two matches that were found in `string1`.

8 *Java SE 8*

As you'll see in Section 17.13, you can combine regular-expression processing with Java SE 8 lambdas and streams to implement powerful `String`- and file processing applications.

9 *Java SE 9: New* **`Matcher`** *Methods*

Java SE 9 adds several new `Matcher` method overloads—`appendReplacement`, `appendTail`, `replaceAll`, `results` and `replaceFirst`. Methods `appendReplacement` and `appendTail` simply receive `StringBuilder`s rather than `StringBuffer`s. Methods `replaceAll`, `results` and `replaceFirst` are meant for use with lambdas and streams. We'll show these three methods in Chapter 17.

14.8 Wrap-Up

In this chapter, you learned about more String methods for selecting portions of Strings and manipulating Strings. You learned about the Character class and some of the methods it declares to handle chars. The chapter also discussed the capabilities of the StringBuilder class for creating Strings. The end of the chapter discussed regular expressions, which provide a powerful capability to search and match portions of Strings that fit a particular pattern. In the next chapter, you'll learn about file processing, including how persistent data is stored and retrieved.

Summary

Section 14.2 Fundamentals of Characters and Strings

- A character literal's value (p. 565) is its integer value in Unicode (p. 565). Strings can include letters, digits and special characters such as +, -, *, / and $. A string in Java is an object of class String. String literals (p. 566) are written in a program in double quotes.

Section 14.3 Class String

- String objects are immutable (p. 567)—after they're created, their character contents cannot be changed.
- String method length (p. 567) returns the number of characters in a String.
- String method charAt (p. 567) returns the character at a specific position.
- String method regionMatches (p. 569) compares portions of two strings for equality.
- String method equals tests for equality. The method returns true if the contents of the Strings are equal, false otherwise. Method equals uses a lexicographical comparison (p. 571) for Strings.
- When primitive-type values are compared with ==, the result is true if both values are identical. When references are compared with ==, the result is true if both refer to the same object.
- Java treats all string literals with the same contents as a single String object.
- String method equalsIgnoreCase performs a case-insensitive string comparison.
- String method compareTo uses a lexicographical comparison and returns 0 if the Strings are equal, a negative number if the string that calls compareTo is less than the argument String and a positive number if the string that calls compareTo is greater than than the argument String.
- String methods startsWith and endsWith (p. 572) determine whether a string starts with or ends with the specified characters, respectively.
- String method indexOf locates the first occurrence of a character or a substring in a string. String method lastIndexOf locates the last occurrence of a character or a substring in a string.
- String method substring copies and returns part of an existing string object.
- String method concat (p. 576) concatenates two string objects and returns a new string object.
- String method replace returns a new string object that replaces every occurrence in a String of its first character argument with its second character argument. An overloaded version of this method enables you to replace substrings rather than individual characters.
- String method toUpperCase (p. 578) returns a new string with uppercase letters in the positions where the original string had lowercase letters. String method toLowerCase (p. 578) returns a new string with lowercase letters in the positions where the original string had uppercase letters.

- `String` method `trim` (p. 578) returns a new string object in which all white-space characters (e.g., spaces, newlines and tabs) have been removed from the beginning and end of a string.
- `String` method `toCharArray` (p. 578) returns a `char` array containing a copy of the string's characters.
- `String` class `static` method `valueOf` returns its argument converted to a string.

Section 14.4 Class `StringBuilder`

- Class `StringBuilder` provides constructors that enable `StringBuilders` to be initialized with no characters and an initial capacity of 16 characters, with no characters and an initial capacity specified in the integer argument, or with a copy of the characters of the `String` argument and an initial capacity that's the number of characters in the `String` argument plus 16.
- `StringBuilder` method `length` (p. 581) returns the number of characters currently stored in a `StringBuilder`. `StringBuilder` method `capacity` (p. 581) returns the number of characters that can be stored in a `StringBuilder` without allocating more memory.
- `StringBuilder` method `ensureCapacity` (p. 581) ensures that a `StringBuilder` has at least the specified capacity. Method `setLength` increases or decreases the length of a `StringBuilder`.
- `StringBuilder` method `charAt` (p. 582) returns the character at the specified index. Method `setCharAt` (p. 582) sets the character at the specified position. `StringBuilder` method `getChars` (p. 582) copies characters in the `StringBuilder` into the character array passed as an argument.
- `StringBuilder`'s overloaded `append` methods (p. 583) add primitive-type, character-array, `String`, `Object` or `CharSequence` values to the end of a `StringBuilder`.
- `StringBuilder`'s overloaded `insert` (p. 585) methods insert primitive-type, character-array, `String`, `Object` or `CharSequence` values at any position in a `StringBuilder`.

Section 14.5 Class `Character`

- `Character` method `isDefined` (p. 588) determines whether a character is in the Unicode character set.
- `Character` method `isDigit` (p. 588) determines whether a character is a defined Unicode digit.
- `Character` method `isJavaIdentifierStart` (p. 588) determines whether a character can be used as the first character of a Java identifier. `Character` method `isJavaIdentifierPart` (p. 588) determines whether a character can be used in an identifier.
- `Character` method `isLetter` (p. 588) determines whether a character is a letter. `Character` method `isLetterOrDigit` (p. 588) determines whether a character is a letter or a digit.
- `Character` method `isLowerCase` (p. 588) determines whether a character is a lowercase letter. `Character` method `isUpperCase` (p. 588) determines whether a character is an uppercase letter.
- `Character` method `toUpperCase` (p. 588) converts a character to its uppercase equivalent. `Character` method `toLowerCase` (p. 588) converts a character to its lowercase equivalent.
- `Character` method `digit` (p. 589) converts its character argument into an integer in the number system specified by its integer argument `radix` (p. 589). `Character` method `forDigit` (p. 589) converts its integer argument `digit` into a character in the number system specified by its integer argument `radix`.
- `Character` method `charValue` (p. 590) returns the `char` stored in a `Character` object. `Character` method `toString` returns a `String` representation of a `Character`.

Section 14.6 Tokenizing `Strings`

- Class `String`'s `split` method (p. 591) tokenizes a `String` based on the delimiter specified as an argument and returns an array of `Strings` containing the tokens (p. 591).

Section 14.7 Regular Expressions, Class **Pattern** *and Class* **Matcher**

- Regular expressions (p. 592) are `String`s that describe search patterns for matching characters in other `String`s. They're useful for validating input and ensuring that data is in a particular format.
- `String` method `matches` (p. 592) receives a string that specifies the regular expression and matches the contents of the `String` object on which it's called to the regular expression. The method returns a `boolean` indicating whether the match succeeded.
- A character class is an escape sequence that represents a group of characters. Each character class matches a single character in the string we're attempting to match with the regular expression.
- A word character (`\w`; p. 592) is any letter (uppercase or lowercase), any digit or the underscore character.
- A white-space character (`\s`) is a space, a tab, a carriage return, a newline or a form feed.
- A digit (`\d`) is any numeric character.
- To match a set of characters that does not have a predefined character class (p. 592), use square brackets, `[]`. Ranges can be represented by placing a dash (-) between two characters. If the first character in the brackets is `"^"`, the expression accepts any character other than those indicated.
- When the regular expression operator `"*"` appears in a regular expression, the program attempts to match zero or more occurrences of the subexpression immediately preceding the `"*"`.
- Operator `"+"` attempts to match one or more occurrences of the subexpression preceding it.
- The character `"|"` allows a match of the expression to its left or to its right.
- Parentheses () are used to group parts of the regular expression.
- The asterisk (*) and plus (+) are formally called quantifiers (p. 596).
- A quantifier affects only the subexpression immediately preceding it.
- Quantifier question mark (?) matches zero or one occurrences of the expression that it quantifies.
- A set of braces containing one number (`{`*n*`}`) matches exactly *n* occurrences of the expression it quantifies. Including a comma after the number enclosed in braces matches at least *n* occurrences.
- A set of braces containing two numbers (`{`*n*`,`*m*`}`) matches between *n* and *m* occurrences of the expression that it qualifies.
- Quantifiers are greedy (p. 597)—they'll match as many occurrences as they can as long as the match is successful. If a quantifier is followed by a question mark (?), the quantifier becomes reluctant (p. 597), matching as few occurrences as possible as long as the match is successful.
- `String` method `replaceAll` (p. 597) replaces text in a string with new text (the second argument) wherever the original string matches a regular expression (the first argument).
- Escaping a special regular-expression character with a \ instructs the regular-expression matching engine to find the actual character, as opposed to what it represents in a regular expression.
- `String` method `replaceFirst` (p. 597) replaces the first occurrence of a pattern match and returns a new string in which the appropriate characters have been replaced.
- `String` method `split` divides a string into substrings at any location that matches a specified regular expression and returns an array of the substrings.
- Class `Pattern` (p. 599) represents a regular expression.
- Class `Matcher` (p. 599) contains a regular-expression pattern and a `CharSequence` in which to search.
- `CharSequence` is an interface (p. 599) that allows read access to a sequence of characters. Both `String` and `StringBuilder` implement this interface, so they can be used with class `Matcher`.

- If a regular expression will be used only once, static `Pattern` method `matches` (p. 599) takes a string that specifies the regular expression and a `CharSequence` on which to perform the match. This method returns a `boolean` indicating whether the search object matches the regular expression.
- If a regular expression will be used more than once, it's more efficient to use static `Pattern` method `compile` (p. 599) to create a specific `Pattern` object for that regular expression. This method receives a string representing the pattern and returns a new `Pattern` object.
- `Pattern` method `matcher` (p. 599) receives a `CharSequence` to search and returns a `Matcher` object. `Matcher` method `matches` (p. 599) performs the same task as `Pattern` method `matches` but without arguments.
- `Matcher` method `find` (p. 599) attempts to match a piece of the search object to the search pattern. Each call to this method starts at the point where the last call ended, so multiple matches can be found.
- `Matcher` method `lookingAt` (p. 599) performs the same as `find`, except that it always starts from the beginning of the search object and will always find the first match if there is one.
- `Matcher` method `group` (p. 600) returns the string from the search object that matches the search pattern. The string returned is the one that was last matched by a call to `find` or `lookingAt`.

Self-Review Exercises

14.1 State whether each of the following is *true* or *false*. If *false*, explain why.

a) When `String` objects are compared using `==`, the result is `true` if the `Strings` contain the same values.

b) A `String` can be modified after it's created.

14.2 For each of the following, write a single statement that performs the indicated task:

a) Compare the string in `s1` to the string in `s2` for equality of contents.

b) Append the string `s2` to the string `s1`, using `+=`.

c) Determine the length of the string in `s1`.

Answers to Self-Review Exercises

14.1 Answers for a) and b):

a) False. `String` objects are compared using operator `==` to determine whether they're the same object in memory.

b) False. `String` objects are immutable and cannot be modified after they're created. `StringBuilder` objects can be modified after they're created.

14.2 Answers for a) through c):

a) `s1.equals(s2)`

b) `s1 += s2;`

c) `s1.length()`

Exercises

14.3 *(Comparing `Strings`)* Write an application that uses `String` method `compareTo` to compare two strings input by the user. Output whether the first string is less than, equal to or greater than the second.

14.4 *(Comparing Portions of `Strings`)* Write an application that uses `String` method `regionMatches` to compare two strings input by the user. The application should input the number of characters to be compared and the starting index of the comparison. The application should state whether the compared characters are equal. Ignore the case of the characters when performing the comparison.

14.5 *(Random Sentences)* Write an application that uses random-number generation to create sentences. Use four arrays of strings called `article`, `noun`, `verb` and `preposition`. Create a sentence by selecting a word at random from each array in the following order: `article`, `noun`, `verb`, `preposition`, `article` and `noun`. As each word is picked, concatenate it to the previous words in the sentence. The words should be separated by spaces. When the final sentence is output, it should start with a capital letter and end with a period. The application should generate and display 20 sentences.

The article array should contain the articles `"the"`, `"a"`, `"one"`, `"some"` and `"any"`; the noun array should contain the nouns `"boy"`, `"girl"`, `"dog"`, `"town"` and `"car"`; the verb array should contain the verbs `"drove"`, `"jumped"`, `"ran"`, `"walked"` and `"skipped"`; the preposition array should contain the prepositions `"to"`, `"from"`, `"over"`, `"under"` and `"on"`.

14.6 *(Project: Limericks)* A limerick is a humorous five-line verse in which the first and second lines rhyme with the fifth, and the third line rhymes with the fourth. Using techniques similar to those developed in Exercise 14.5, write a Java application that produces random limericks. Polishing this application to produce good limericks is a challenging problem, but the result will be worth the effort!

14.7 *(Pig Latin)* Write an application that encodes English-language phrases into pig Latin. Pig Latin is a form of coded language. There are many different ways to form pig Latin phrases. For simplicity, use the following algorithm:

To form a pig Latin phrase from an English-language phrase, tokenize the phrase into words with `String` method `split`. To translate each English word into a pig Latin word, place the first letter of the English word at the end of the word and add the letters "ay." Thus, the word "jump" becomes "umpjay," the word "the" becomes "hetay," and the word "computer" becomes "omputercay." Blanks between words remain as blanks. Assume the following: The English phrase consists of words separated by blanks, there are no punctuation marks and all words have two or more letters. Method `printLatinWord` should display each word. Each token is passed to method `printLatinWord` to print the pig Latin word. Enable the user to input the sentence. Then display the converted sentence.

14.8 *(Tokenizing Telephone Numbers)* Write an application that inputs a telephone number as a string in the form `(555) 555-5555`. The application should use `String` method `split` to extract the area code as a token, the first three digits of the phone number as a token and the last four digits of the phone number as a token. The seven digits of the phone number should be concatenated into one string. Both the area code and the phone number should be printed. Remember that you'll have to change delimiter characters during the tokenization process.

14.9 *(Displaying a Sentence with Its Words Reversed)* Write an application that inputs a line of text, tokenizes the line with `String` method `split` and outputs the tokens in reverse order. Use space characters as delimiters.

14.10 *(Displaying `Strings` in Uppercase and Lowercase)* Write an application that inputs a line of text and outputs the text twice—once in all uppercase letters and once in all lowercase letters.

14.11 *(Searching `Strings`)* Write an application that inputs a line of text and a search character and uses `String` method `indexOf` to determine the number of occurrences of the character in the text.

14.12 *(Searching `Strings`)* Write an application based on the application in Exercise 14.11 that inputs a line of text and uses `String` method `indexOf` to determine the total number of occurrences of each letter of the alphabet in the text. Uppercase and lowercase letters should be counted together. Store the totals for each letter in an array, and print the values in tabular format after the totals have been determined.

14.13 *(Tokenizing and Comparing `Strings`)* Write an application that reads a line of text, tokenizes the line using space characters as delimiters and outputs only those words beginning with the letter `"b"`.

14.14 *(Tokenizing and Comparing `Strings`)* Write an application that reads a line of text, tokenizes it using space characters as delimiters and outputs only those words ending with the letters `"ED"`.

14.15 *(Converting `int` Values to Characters)* Write an application that inputs an integer code for a character and displays the corresponding character. Modify this application so that it generates all possible three-digit codes in the range from 000 to 255 and attempts to print the corresponding characters.

14.16 *(Defining Your Own `String` Methods)* Write your own versions of `String` search methods `indexOf` and `lastIndexOf`.

14.17 *(Creating Three-Letter `Strings` from a Five-Letter Word)* Write an application that reads a five-letter word from the user and produces every possible three-letter string that can be derived from the letters of that word. For example, the three-letter words produced from the word "bathe" include "ate," "bat," "bet," "tab," "hat," "the" and "tea."

Special Section: String-Manipulation Exercises

The preceding exercises are keyed to the text and designed to test your understanding of fundamental string-manipulation concepts. This section includes a collection of intermediate and advanced string-manipulation exercises. You should find these problems challenging, yet entertaining. The problems vary considerably in difficulty. Some require an hour or two of application writing and implementation. Others are useful for lab assignments that might require two or three weeks of study and implementation. Some are challenging term projects.

14.18 *(Text Analysis)* String manipulation enables interesting approaches to analyzing the writings of great authors. Much attention has been focused on whether William Shakespeare ever lived. Some scholars believe there's substantial evidence indicating that Christopher Marlowe actually penned the masterpieces attributed to Shakespeare. Researchers have used computers to find similarities in the writings of these two authors. This exercise examines three methods for analyzing texts with a computer.

a) Write an application that reads a line of text from the keyboard and prints a table indicating the number of occurrences of each letter of the alphabet in the text. For example, the phrase

```
To be, or not to be: that is the question:
```

contains one "a," two "b's," no "c's," and so on.

b) Write an application that reads a line of text and prints a table indicating the number of one-letter words, two-letter words, three-letter words, and so on, appearing in the text. For example, Fig. 14.25 shows the counts for the phrase

```
Whether 'tis nobler in the mind to suffer
```

c) Write an application that reads a line of text and prints a table indicating the number of occurrences of each different word in the text. The application should include the words in the table in the same order in which they appear in the text. For example, the lines

```
To be, or not to be: that is the question:
Whether 'tis nobler in the mind to suffer
```

contain the word "to" three times, the word "be" two times, the word "or" once, etc.

Word length	Occurrences
1	0
2	2
3	1
4	2 (including 'tis)
5	0
6	2
7	1

Fig. 14.25 | Word-length counts for the string `"Whether 'tis nobler in the mind to suffer"`.

14.19 *(Printing Dates in Various Formats)* Dates are printed in several common formats. Two of the more common formats are

```
04/25/1955 and April 25, 1955
```

Write an application that reads a date in the first format and prints it in the second format.

14.20 *(Check Protection)* Computers are frequently employed in check-writing systems, such as payroll and accounts payable applications. There are many strange stories about weekly paychecks being printed (by mistake) for amounts in excess of $1 million. Incorrect amounts are printed by computerized check-writing systems because of human error or machine failure. Systems designers build controls into their systems to prevent such erroneous checks from being issued.

Another serious problem is the intentional alteration of a check amount by someone who plans to cash a check fraudulently. To prevent a dollar amount from being altered, some computerized check-writing systems employ a technique called check protection. Checks designed for imprinting by computer contain a fixed number of spaces in which the computer may print an amount. Suppose a paycheck contains eight blank spaces in which the computer is supposed to print the amount of a weekly paycheck. If the amount is large, then all eight of the spaces will be filled. For example,

```
1,230.60 (check amount)
--------
12345678 (position numbers)
```

On the other hand, if the amount is less than $1000, then several of the spaces would ordinarily be left blank. For example,

```
   99.87
--------
12345678
```

contains three blank spaces. If a check is printed with blank spaces, it's easier for someone to alter the amount. To prevent alteration, many check-writing systems insert *leading asterisks* to protect the amount as follows:

```
***99.87
--------
12345678
```

Write an application that inputs a dollar amount to be printed on a check, then prints the amount in check-protected format with leading asterisks if necessary. Assume that nine spaces are available for printing the amount.

14.21 *(Writing the Word Equivalent of a Check Amount)* Continuing the discussion in Exercise 14.20, we reiterate the importance of designing check-writing systems to prevent alteration of check amounts. One common security method requires that the amount be written in numbers and spelled out in words as well. Even if someone is able to alter the numerical amount of the check, it's extremely difficult to change the amount in words. Write an application that inputs a numeric check amount that's less than $1000 and writes the word equivalent of the amount. For example, the amount 112.43 should be written as

```
ONE hundred TWELVE and 43/100
```

14.22 *(Morse Code)* Perhaps the most famous of all coding schemes is the Morse code, developed by Samuel Morse in 1832 for use with the telegraph system. The Morse code assigns a series of dots and dashes to each letter of the alphabet, each digit, and a few special characters (e.g., period, comma, colon, semicolon). In sound-oriented systems, the dot represents a short sound and the dash a long sound. Other representations of dots and dashes are used with light-oriented systems and signal-flag systems. Separation between words is indicated by a space or, simply, the absence of a dot or dash. In a sound-oriented system, a space is indicated by a short time during which no sound is transmitted. The international version of the Morse code appears in Fig. 14.26.

Character	Code	Character	Code	Character	Code
A	.-	N	-.	*Digits*	
B	-...	O	---	1	.----
C	-.-.	P	.--.	2	..---
D	-..	Q	--.-	3	...--
E	.	R	.-.	4	....-
F	..-.	S	...	5	.....
G	--.	T	-	6	-....
H	....	U	..-	7	--...
I	..	V	...-	8	---..
J	.---	W	.--	9	----.
K	-.-	X	-..-	0	-----
L	.-..	Y	-.--		
M	--	Z	--..		

Fig. 14.26 | Letters and digits as expressed in international Morse code.

Write an application that reads an English-language phrase and encodes it into Morse code. Also write an application that reads a phrase in Morse code and converts it into the English-language equivalent. Use one blank between each Morse-coded letter and three blanks between each Morse-coded word.

14.23 *(Metric Conversions)* Write an application that will assist the user with metric conversions. Your application should allow the user to specify the names of the units as strings (i.e., centimeters, liters, grams, and so on, for the metric system and inches, quarts, pounds, and so on, for the English system) and should respond to simple questions, such as

```
"How many inches are in 2 meters?"
"How many liters are in 10 quarts?"
```

Your application should recognize invalid conversions. For example, the question

```
"How many feet are in 5 kilograms?"
```

is not meaningful because `"feet"` is a unit of length, whereas `"kilograms"` is a unit of mass.

Special Section: Challenging String-Manipulation Projects

14.24 *(Project: A Spelling Checker)* Many apps you use daily have built-in spell checkers. In this project, you're asked to develop your own spell-checker utility. We make suggestions to help get you started. You should then consider adding more capabilities. Use a computerized dictionary (if you have access to one) as a source of words.

Why do we type so many words with incorrect spellings? In some cases, it's because we simply do not know the correct spelling, so we make a best guess. In some cases, it's because we transpose two letters (e.g., "defualt" instead of "default"). Sometimes we double-type a letter accidentally (e.g., "hanndy" instead of "handy"). Sometimes we type a nearby key instead of the one we intended (e.g., "biryhday" instead of "birthday"), and so on.

Design and implement a spell-checker application in Java. Your application should maintain an array `wordList` of strings. Enable the user to enter these strings. [*Note:* In Chapter 15, we introduce file processing. With this capability, you can obtain the words for the spell checker from a computerized dictionary stored in a file.]

Your application should ask a user to enter a word. The application should then look up that word in the `wordList` array. If the word is in the array, your application should print `"Word is spelled correctly."` If the word is not in the array, your application should print `"Word is not spelled correctly."` Then your application should try to locate other words in `wordList` that might be the word the user intended to type. For example, you can try all possible single transpositions of adjacent letters to discover that the word "default" is a direct match to a word in `wordList`. Of course, this implies that your application will check all other single transpositions, such as "edfault," "dfeault," "deafult," "defalut" and "defautl." When you find a new word that matches one in `wordList`, print it in a message, such as

```
Did you mean "default"?
```

Implement other tests, such as replacing each double letter with a single letter, and any other tests you can develop to improve the value of your spell checker.

14.25 *(Project: A Crossword-Puzzle Generator)* Most people have worked a crossword puzzle, but few have ever attempted to generate one. Generating a crossword puzzle is suggested here as a string-manipulation project requiring substantial sophistication and effort.

There are many issues the programmer must resolve to get even the simplest crossword-puzzle-generator application working. For example, how do you represent the grid of a crossword puzzle inside the computer? Should you use a series of strings or two-dimensional arrays?

The programmer needs a source of words (i.e., a computerized dictionary) that can be directly referenced by the application. In what form should these words be stored to facilitate the complex manipulations required by the application?

If you're really ambitious, you'll want to generate the clues portion of the puzzle, in which the brief hints for each across word and each down word are printed. Merely printing a version of the blank puzzle itself is not a simple problem.

Making a Difference

14.26 *(Cooking with Healthier Ingredients)* Obesity in America is increasing at an alarming rate. Check the map from the Centers for Disease Control and Prevention (CDC) at `http://www.cdc.gov/obesity/data/adult.html`, which shows obesity trends in the United States over the last 20 years. As obesity increases, so do occurrences of related problems (e.g., heart disease, high blood pressure, high cholesterol, type 2 diabetes). Write a program that helps users choose healthier ingredients when cooking, and helps those allergic to certain foods (e.g., nuts, gluten) find substitutes. The program should read a recipe from the user and suggest healthier replacements for some of the ingredients. For simplicity, your program should assume the recipe has no abbreviations for measures such as teaspoons, cups, and tablespoons, and uses numerical digits for quantities (e.g., 1 egg, 2 cups) rather than spelling them out (one egg, two cups). Some common substitutions are shown in Fig. 14.27. Your program should display a warning such as, "Always consult your physician before making significant changes to your diet."

Ingredient	Substitution
1 cup sour cream	1 cup yogurt
1 cup milk	1/2 cup evaporated milk and 1/2 cup water
1 teaspoon lemon juice	1/2 teaspoon vinegar
1 cup sugar	1/2 cup honey, 1 cup molasses or 1/4 cup agave nectar
1 cup butter	1 cup margarine or yogurt
1 cup flour	1 cup rye or rice flour
1 cup mayonnaise	1 cup cottage cheese or 1/8 cup mayonnaise and 7/8 cup yogurt
1 egg	2 tablespoons cornstarch, arrowroot flour or potato starch or 2 egg whites or 1/2 of a large banana (mashed)
1 cup milk	1 cup soy milk
1/4 cup oil	1/4 cup applesauce
white bread	whole-grain bread

Fig. 14.27 | Ingredient substitutions.

Your program should take into consideration that replacements are not always one-for-one. For example, if a cake recipe calls for three eggs, it might reasonably use six egg whites instead. Conversion data for measurements and substitutes can be obtained at websites such as:

```
http://chinesefood.about.com/od/recipeconversionfaqs/f/usmetricrecipes.htm
http://www.pioneerthinking.com/eggsub.html
http://www.gourmetsleuth.com/conversions.htm
```

Your program should consider the user's health concerns, such as high cholesterol, high blood pressure, weight loss, gluten allergy, and so on. For high cholesterol, the program should suggest substitutes for eggs and dairy products; if the user wishes to lose weight, low-calorie substitutes for ingredients such as sugar should be suggested.

14.27 *(Spam Scanner)* Spam (or junk e-mail) costs U.S. organizations billions of dollars a year in spam-prevention software, equipment, network resources, bandwidth, and lost productivity. Research online some of the most common spam e-mail messages and words, and check your own junk e-mail folder. Create a list of 30 words and phrases commonly found in spam messages. Write an application in which the user enters an e-mail message. Then, scan the message for each of the 30 keywords or phrases. For each occurrence of one of these within the message, add a point to the message's "spam score." Next, rate the likelihood that the message is spam, based on the number of points it received.

14.28 *(SMS Language)* Short Message Service (SMS) is a communications service that allows sending text messages of 160 or fewer characters between mobile phones. With the proliferation of mobile-phone use worldwide, SMS is being used in many developing nations for political purposes (e.g., voicing opinions and opposition), for reporting news about natural disasters, and so on. Since the length of SMS messages is limited, SMS Language—abbreviations of common words and phrases in mobile text messages, e-mails, instant messages, etc.—is often used. For example, "in my opinion" is "imo" in SMS Language. Research SMS Language online. Write a GUI application in which the user can enter a message using SMS Language, then click a button to translate it into English (or your own language). Also provide a mechanism to translate text written in English (or your own language) into SMS Language. One potential problem is that one SMS abbreviation could expand into a variety of phrases. For example, IMO (as used above) could also stand for "International Maritime Organization," "in memory of," etc.

15 Files, Input/Output Streams, NIO and XML Serialization

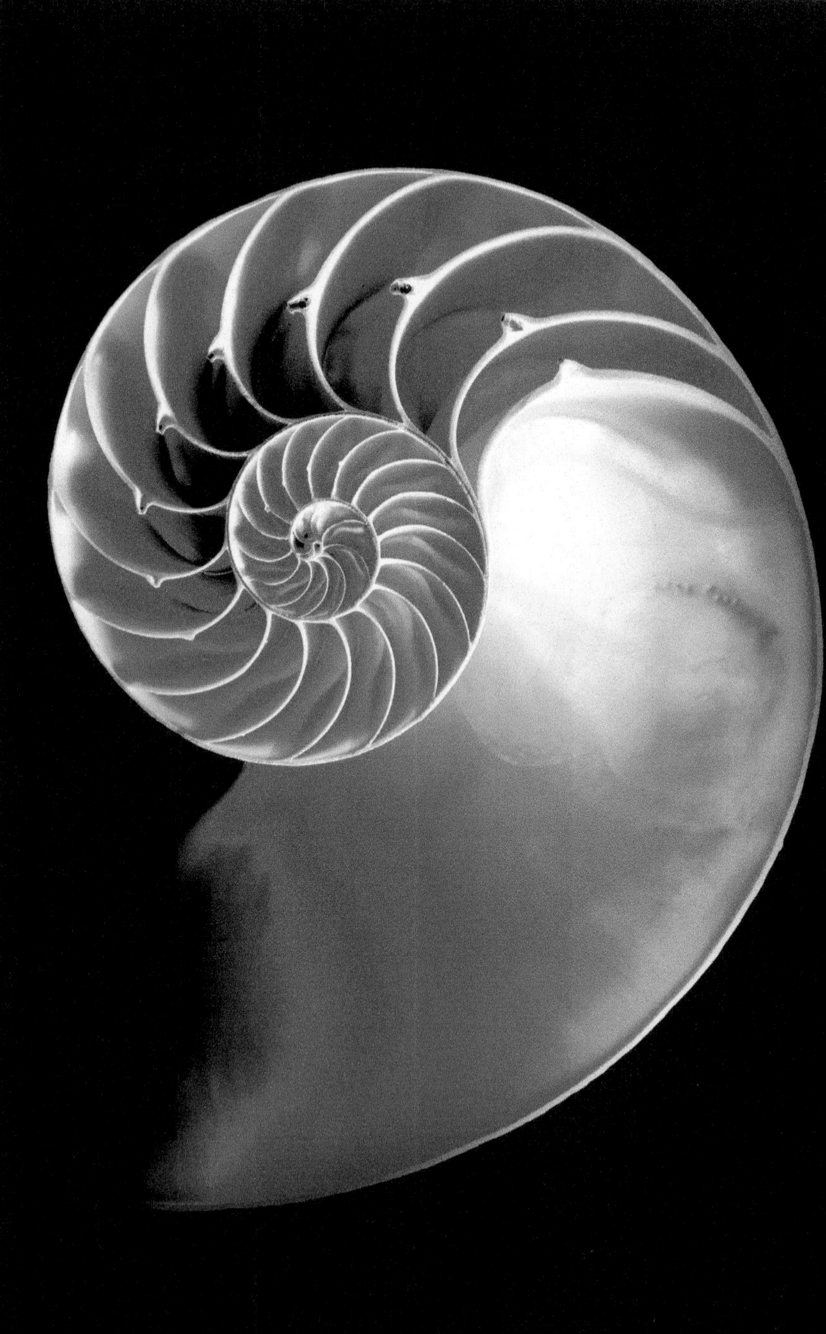

Objectives

In this chapter you'll:

- Create, read, write and update files.
- Retrieve information about files and directories using features of the NIO.2 APIs.
- Learn the differences between text files and binary files.
- Use class `Formatter` to output text to a file.
- Use class `Scanner` to input text from a file.
- Use sequential file processing to develop a real-world credit-inquiry program.
- Write objects to and read objects from a file using XML serialization and the JAXB (Java Architecture for XML Binding) APIs.
- Use a `JFileChooser` dialog to allow users to select files or directories on disk.
- Optionally use `java.io` interfaces and classes to perform byte-based and character-based input and output.

Outline

15.1 Introduction

Data stored in variables and arrays is *temporary*—it's lost when a local variable goes out of scope or when the program terminates. For long-term retention of data, even after the programs that create the data terminate, computers use **files**. You use files every day for tasks such as writing a document or creating a spreadsheet. Computers store files on **secondary storage devices**, including hard disks, flash drives, DVDs and more. Data maintained in files is **persistent data**—it exists beyond the duration of program execution. In this chapter, we explain how Java programs create, update and process files.

We begin by discussing Java's architecture for handling files programmatically. Next we explain that data can be stored in *text files* and *binary files*—and the differences between them. We demonstrate retrieving information about files and directories using classes `Paths` and `Files` and interfaces `Path` and `DirectoryStream` (package `java.nio.file`), then discuss writing to and reading from files. We create and manipulate text files. As you'll learn, however, it's awkward to read data from text files back into object form. Many object-oriented languages (including Java) provide convenient ways to write objects to and read objects from files (known as *serialization* and *deserialization*). To demonstrate this, we recreate some of our sequential programs that used text files, this time by storing objects in and retrieving objects from files. We discuss databases in Chapter 24, Accessing Databases with JDBC, and Chapter 29, Java Persistence API (JPA).

15.2 Files and Streams

Java views each file as a sequential **stream of bytes** (Fig. 15.1).[1] Every operating system provides a mechanism to determine the end of a file, such as an **end-of-file marker** or a count of the total bytes in the file that's recorded in a system-maintained administrative data structure. A Java program processing a stream of bytes simply receives an indication from the operating system when it reaches the end of the stream—the program does *not*

1. Java's NIO APIs also include classes and interfaces that implement so-called channel-based architecture for high-performance I/O. These topics are beyond the scope of this book.

need to know how the underlying platform represents files or streams. In some cases, the end-of-file indication occurs as an exception. In others, the indication is a return value from a method invoked on a stream-processing object.

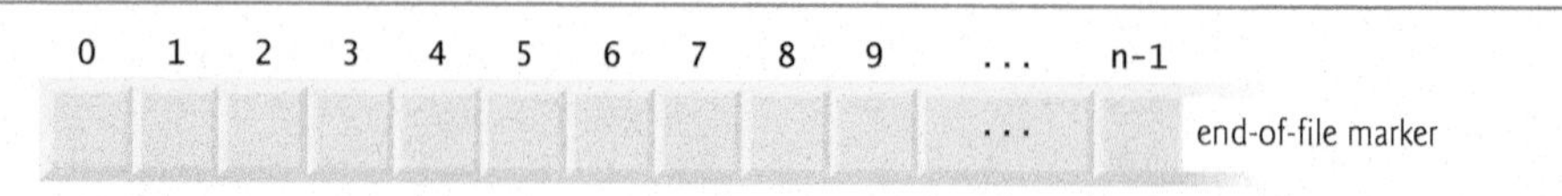

Fig. 15.1 | Java's view of a file of *n* bytes.

Byte-Based and Character-Based Streams

File streams can be used to input and output data as bytes or characters.

- **Byte-based streams** output and input data in its *binary* format—a `char` is two bytes, an `int` is four bytes, a `double` is eight bytes, etc.
- **Character-based streams** output and input data as a *sequence of characters* in which every character is two bytes—the number of bytes for a given value depends on the number of characters in that value. For example, the value `2000000000` requires 20 bytes (10 characters at two bytes per character) but the value `7` requires only two bytes (1 character at two bytes per character).

Files created using byte-based streams are **binary files**, while files created using character-based streams are **text files**. Text files can be read by text editors, while binary files are read by programs that understand the file's specific content and its ordering. A numeric value in a binary file can be used in calculations, whereas the character `5` is simply a character that can be used in a string of text, as in `"Sarah Miller is 15 years old"`.

Standard Input, Standard Output and Standard Error Streams

A Java program **opens** a file by creating an object and associating a stream of bytes or characters with it. The object's constructor interacts with the operating system to *open* the file. Java can also associate streams with different devices. When a Java program begins executing, it creates three stream objects that are associated with devices—`System.in`, `System.out` and `System.err`. The `System.in` (standard input stream) object normally enables a program to input bytes from the keyboard. The `System.out` (standard output stream) object normally enables a program to output character data to the screen. The `System.err` (standard error stream) object normally enables a program to output character-based error messages to the screen. Each stream can be **redirected**. For `System.in`, this capability enables the program to read bytes from a different source. For `System.out` and `System.err`, it enables the output to be sent to a different location, such as a file on disk. Class `System` provides methods **`setIn`**, **`setOut`** and **`setErr`** to redirected the standard input, output and error streams, respectively.

The `java.io` and `java.nio` Packages

Java programs perform stream-based processing with classes and interfaces from package **`java.io`** and the subpackages of **`java.nio`**—Java's New I/O APIs that were first introduced in Java SE 6 and have been enhanced since. There are also other packages throughout the Java APIs containing classes and interfaces based on those in the `java.io` and `java.nio` packages.

Character-based input and output can be performed with classes `Scanner` and **`Formatter`**, as you'll see in Section 15.4. You've used class `Scanner` extensively to input data from the keyboard. `Scanner` also can read data from a file. Class `Formatter` enables formatted data to be output to any text-based stream in a manner similar to method `System.out.printf`. Appendix I presents the details of formatted output with `printf`. All these features can be used to format text files as well. In Chapter 28, we use stream classes to implement networking applications.

Java SE 8 Adds Another Type of Stream 8

Chapter 17, Lambdas and Streams, introduces a new type of stream that's used to process collections of elements (like arrays and `ArrayList`s), rather than the streams of bytes we discuss in this chapter's file-processing examples. In Section 17.13, we use the `Files` method `lines` to create one of these new streams containing the lines of text in a file.

15.3 Using NIO Classes and Interfaces to Get File and Directory Information

Interfaces `Path` and `DirectoryStream` and classes `Paths` and `Files` (all from package `java.nio.file`) are useful for retrieving information about files and directories on disk:

- **`Path`** interface—Objects of classes that implement `Path` represent the location of a file or directory. `Path` objects do not open files or provide any file-processing capabilities. Class **`File`** (package `java.io`) also is used commonly for this purpose.
- **`Paths`** class—Provides `static` methods used to get a `Path` object representing a file or directory location.
- **`Files`** class—Provides `static` methods for common file and directory manipulations, such as copying files; creating and deleting files and directories; getting information about files and directories; reading the contents of files; getting objects that allow you to manipulate the contents of files and directories; and more.
- **`DirectoryStream`** interface—Objects of classes that implement this interface enable a program to iterate through the contents of a directory.

*Creating **`Path`** Objects*

You'll use class `static` method **`get`** of class `Paths` to convert a `String` representing a file's or directory's location into a `Path` object. You can then use the methods of interface `Path` and class `Files` to determine information about the specified file or directory. We discuss several such methods momentarily. For complete lists of their methods, visit:

```
http://docs.oracle.com/javase/8/docs/api/java/nio/file/Path.html
http://docs.oracle.com/javase/8/docs/api/java/nio/file/Files.html
```

Absolute vs. Relative Paths

A file or directory's path specifies its location on disk. The path includes some or all of the directories leading to the file or directory. An **absolute path** contains *all* directories, starting with the **root directory**, that lead to a specific file or directory. Every file or directory on a particular disk drive has the *same* root directory in its path. A **relative path** is "relative" to another directory—for example, a path relative to the directory in which the application began executing.

Getting **Path** *Objects from URIs*

An overloaded version of `Files` `static` method `get` uses a `URI` object to locate the file or directory. A **Uniform Resource Identifier (URI)** is a more general form of the **Uniform Resource Locators (URLs)** that are used to locate websites. For example, the URL `http://www.deitel.com/` is the URL for the Deitel & Associates website. URIs for locating files vary across operating systems. On Windows platforms, the URI

```
file://C:/data.txt
```

identifies the file `data.txt` stored in the root directory of the C: drive. On UNIX/Linux platforms, the URI

```
file:/home/student/data.txt
```

identifies the file `data.txt` stored in the `home` directory of the user `student`.

Example: Getting File and Directory Information

Figure 15.2 prompts the user to enter a file or directory name, then uses classes `Paths`, `Path`, `Files` and `DirectoryStream` to output information about that file or directory.

```java
// Fig. 15.2: FileAndDirectoryInfo.java
// File class used to obtain file and directory information.
import java.io.IOException;
import java.nio.file.DirectoryStream;
import java.nio.file.Files;
import java.nio.file.Path;
import java.nio.file.Paths;
import java.util.Scanner;

public class FileAndDirectoryInfo {
   public static void main(String[] args) throws IOException {
      Scanner input = new Scanner(System.in);

      System.out.println("Enter file or directory name:");

      // create Path object based on user input
      Path path = Paths.get(input.nextLine());

      if (Files.exists(path)) { // if path exists, output info about it
         // display file (or directory) information
         System.out.printf("%n%s exists%n", path.getFileName());
         System.out.printf("%s a directory%n",
            Files.isDirectory(path) ? "Is" : "Is not");
         System.out.printf("%s an absolute path%n",
            path.isAbsolute() ? "Is" : "Is not");
         System.out.printf("Last modified: %s%n",
            Files.getLastModifiedTime(path));
         System.out.printf("Size: %s%n", Files.size(path));
         System.out.printf("Path: %s%n", path);
         System.out.printf("Absolute path: %s%n", path.toAbsolutePath());

```

Fig. 15.2 | `File` class used to obtain file and directory information. (Part 1 of 2.)

```
32          if (Files.isDirectory(path)) { // output directory listing
33             System.out.printf("%nDirectory contents:%n");
34
35             // object for iterating through a directory's contents
36             DirectoryStream<Path> directoryStream =
37                Files.newDirectoryStream(path);
38
39             for (Path p : directoryStream) {
40                System.out.println(p);
41             }
42          }
43       }
44       else { // not file or directory, output error message
45          System.out.printf("%s does not exist%n", path);
46       }
47    } // end main
48 } // end class FileAndDirectoryInfo
```

```
Enter file or directory name:
c:\examples\ch15

ch15 exists
Is a directory
Is an absolute path
Last modified: 2013-11-08T19:50:00.838256Z
Size: 4096
Path: c:\examples\ch15
Absolute path: c:\examples\ch15

Directory contents:
C:\examples\ch15\fig15_02
C:\examples\ch15\fig15_12_13
C:\examples\ch15\SerializationApps
C:\examples\ch15\TextFileApps
```

```
Enter file or directory name:
C:\examples\ch15\fig15_02\FileAndDirectoryInfo.java

FileAndDirectoryInfo.java exists
Is not a directory
Is an absolute path
Last modified: 2013-11-08T19:59:01.848255Z
Size: 2952
Path: C:\examples\ch15\fig15_02\FileAndDirectoryInfo.java
Absolute path: C:\examples\ch15\fig15_02\FileAndDirectoryInfo.java
```

Fig. 15.2 | `File` class used to obtain file and directory information. (Part 2 of 2.)

The program begins by prompting the user for a file or directory (line 14). Line 17 inputs the filename or directory name and passes it to `Paths` `static` method `get`, which converts the `String` to a `Path`. Line 19 invokes `Files` `static` method **`exists`**, which receives a `Path` and determines whether it exists (either as a file or as a directory) on disk.

If the name does not exist, control proceeds to line 45, which displays a message containing the Path's String representation followed by "does not exist." Otherwise, lines 21–42 execute:

- Path method **getFileName** (line 21) gets the String name of the file or directory without any location information.
- Files static method **isDirectory** (line 23) receives a Path and returns a boolean indicating whether that Path represents a directory on disk.
- Path method **isAbsolute** (line 25) returns a boolean indicating whether that Path represents an absolute path to a file or directory.
- Files static method **getLastModifiedTime** (line 27) receives a Path and returns a FileTime (package java.nio.file.attribute) indicating when the file was last modified. The program outputs the FileTime's default String representation.
- Files static method **size** (line 28) receives a Path and returns a long representing the number of bytes in the file or directory. For directories, the value returned is platform specific.
- Path method **toString** (called implicitly at line 29) returns a String representing the Path.
- Path method **toAbsolutePath** (line 30) converts the Path on which it's called to an absolute path.

If the Path represents a directory (line 32), lines 36–37 use Files static method **newDirectoryStream** to get a DirectoryStream<Path> containing Path objects for the directory's contents. Lines 39–41 display the String representation of each Path in the DirectoryStream<Path>. Note that DirectoryStream is a generic type like ArrayList (Section 7.16).

The first output of this program demonstrates a Path for the folder containing this chapter's examples. The second output demonstrates a Path for this example's source-code file. In both cases, we specified an absolute path.

Error-Prevention Tip 15.1

Once you've confirmed that a Path exists, it's still possible that the methods demonstrated in Fig. 15.2 will throw IOExceptions. For example, the file or directory represented by the Path could be deleted from the system after the call to Files method exists and before the other statements in lines 21–42 execute. Industrial strength file- and directory-processing programs require extensive exception handling to deal with such possibilities.

Separator Characters

A **separator character** is used to separate directories and files in a path. On a Windows computer, the *separator character* is a backslash (\). On a Linux or macOS system, it's a forward slash (/). Java processes both characters identically in a pathname. For example, if we were to use the path

```
c:\Program Files\Java\jdk1.6.0_11\demo/jfc
```

which employs each separator character, Java would still process the path properly.

Good Programming Practice 15.1

When building `String`s that represent path information, use `File.separator` to obtain the local computer's proper separator character rather than explicitly using / or \. This constant is a `String` consisting of one character—the proper separator for the system.

Common Programming Error 15.1

Using \ as a directory separator rather than \\ in a string literal is a logic error. A single \ indicates that the \ followed by the next character represents an escape sequence. Use \\ to insert a \ in a string literal.

15.4 Sequential Text Files

Next, we create and manipulate *sequential files* in which records are stored in order by the record-key field. We begin with *text files*, enabling the reader to quickly create and edit human-readable files. We discuss creating, writing data to, reading data from and updating sequential text files. We also include a credit-inquiry program that retrieves data from a file. The programs in Sections 15.4.1–15.4.3 are all in the chapter's `TextFileApps` directory so that they can manipulate the same text file, which is also stored in that directory.

15.4.1 Creating a Sequential Text File

Java imposes no structure on a file—notions such as records do not exist as part of the Java language. Therefore, you must structure files to meet the requirements of your applications. In the example that follows, we see how to impose a *keyed* record structure on a file.

The program in this section creates a simple sequential file that might be used in an accounts receivable system to keep track of the amounts owed to a company by its credit clients. For each client, the program obtains from the user an account number and the client's name and balance (i.e., the amount the client owes the company for goods and services received). Each client's data constitutes a "record" for that client. This application uses the account number as the *record key*—the file's records will be created and maintained in account-number order. The program assumes that the user enters the records in account-number order. In a comprehensive accounts receivable system (based on sequential files), a *sorting* capability would be provided so that the user could enter the records in *any* order. The records would then be sorted and written to the file.

Class `CreateTextFile`

Class `CreateTextFile` (Fig. 15.3) uses a `Formatter` to output formatted `Strings`, using the same formatting capabilities as method `System.out.printf`. A `Formatter` object can output to various locations, such as to a command window or to a file, as we do in this example. The `Formatter` object is instantiated in the `try`-with-resources statement (line 13; introduced in Section 11.12)—recall that `try`-with-resources will close its resource(s) when the `try` block terminates successfully or due to an exception. The constructor we use here takes one argument—a `String` containing the name of the file, including its path. If a path is not specified, as is the case here, the JVM assumes that the file is in the directory from which the program was executed. For text files, we use the `.txt` file extension. If the file does *not* exist, it will be *created*. If an *existing* file is opened, its contents are **truncated**—all the data in the file is *discarded*. If no exception occurs, the file is open for writing and the resulting Formatter object can be used to write data to the file.

```
// Fig. 15.3: CreateTextFile.java
// Writing data to a sequential text file with class Formatter.
import java.io.FileNotFoundException;
import java.lang.SecurityException;
import java.util.Formatter;
import java.util.FormatterClosedException;
import java.util.NoSuchElementException;
import java.util.Scanner;

public class CreateTextFile {
   public static void main(String[] args) {
      // open clients.txt, output data to the file then close clients.txt
      try (Formatter output = new Formatter("clients.txt")) {
         Scanner input = new Scanner(System.in);
         System.out.printf("%s%n%s%n? ",
            "Enter account number, first name, last name and balance.",
            "Enter end-of-file indicator to end input.");

         while (input.hasNext()) { // loop until end-of-file indicator
            try {
               // output new record to file; assumes valid input
               output.format("%d %s %s %.2f%n", input.nextInt(),
                  input.next(), input.next(), input.nextDouble());
            }
            catch (NoSuchElementException elementException) {
               System.err.println("Invalid input. Please try again.");
               input.nextLine(); // discard input so user can try again
            }

            System.out.print("? ");
         }
      }
      catch (SecurityException | FileNotFoundException |
         FormatterClosedException e) {
         e.printStackTrace();
      }
   }
}
```

```
Enter account number, first name, last name and balance.
Enter end-of-file indicator to end input.
? 100 Bob Blue 24.98
? 200 Steve Green -345.67
? 300 Pam White 0.00
? 400 Sam Red -42.16
? 500 Sue Yellow 224.62
? ^Z
```

Fig. 15.3 | Writing data to a sequential text file with class Formatter.

Lines 33–36 are a multi-`catch` which handles several exceptions:

- the **`SecurityException`** that occurs if the user does not have permission to write data to the file opened in line 13
- the **`FileNotFoundException`** that occurs if the file does not exist and a new file cannot be created, or if there's an error *opening* the file in line 13, and
- the **`FormatterClosedException`** that occurs if the `Formatter` object is closed when you attempt to use it in lines 22–23 to write into a file.

For these exceptions, we display a stack trace, then the program terminates.

Writing Data to the File

Lines 15–17 prompt the user to enter the various fields for each record or the end-of-file key sequence when data entry is complete. Figure 15.4 lists the key combinations for entering end-of-file for various computer systems' command windows—some IDEs do not support these for console-based input (so you might have to execute the programs from command windows). Line 19 uses `Scanner` method `hasNext` to determine whether the end-of-file key combination has been entered. The loop executes until `hasNext` encounters end-of-file.

Operating system	Key combination
macOS and Linux	*<Enter> <Ctrl> d*
Windows	*<Ctrl> z*

Fig. 15.4 | End-of-file key combinations.

Lines 22–23 use a `Scanner` to read data from the user, then output the data as a record using the `Formatter`. Each `Scanner` input method throws a **`NoSuchElementException`** (handled in lines 25–28) if the data is in the wrong format (e.g., a `String` when an `int` is expected) or if there's no more data to input.

If no exception occurs, the record's information is output using method **`format`**, which can perform identical formatting to `System.out.printf`. Method `format` writes a formatted `String` to the `Formatter` object's output destination—the file `clients.txt`. The format string `"%d %s %s %.2f%n"` indicates that the current record will be stored as an integer (the account number) followed by a `String` (the first name), another `String` (the last name) and a floating-point value (the balance). Each piece of information is separated from the next by a space, and the double value (the balance) is output with two digits to the right of the decimal point (as indicated by the `.2` in `%.2f`). The data in the text file can be viewed with a text editor or retrieved later by a program designed to read the file (Section 15.4.2). [*Note:* You can also output data to a text file using class **`java.io.PrintWriter`**, which provides `format` and `printf` methods for outputting formatted data.]

When the user enters the end-of-file key combination, the try-with-resources statement closes the `Formatter` and the underlying output file by calling `Formatter` method **`close`**. If a program does not explicitly call method `close`, the operating system normally will close the file when program execution terminates—this is an example of operating-system "housekeeping." However, you should always explicitly close a file when it's no longer needed.

Sample Output

The sample data for this application is shown in Fig. 15.5. In the sample output, the user enters information for five accounts, then enters end-of-file to signal that data entry is complete. The sample output does not show how the data records actually appear in the file. In the next section, to verify that the file was created successfully, we present a program that reads the file and prints its contents. Because this is a text file, you can also verify the information simply by opening the file in a text editor.

Sample data			
100	Bob	Blue	24.98
200	Steve	Green	-345.67
300	Pam	White	0.00
400	Sam	Red	-42.16
500	Sue	Yellow	224.62

Fig. 15.5 | Sample data for the program in Fig. 15.3.

15.4.2 Reading Data from a Sequential Text File

Data is stored in files so that it may be retrieved for processing when needed. Section 15.4.1 demonstrated how to create a file for sequential access. This section shows how to read data sequentially from a text file. We demonstrate how class `Scanner` can be used to input data from a file rather than the keyboard. The application (Fig. 15.6) reads records from the file `"clients.txt"` created by the application of Section 15.4.1 and displays the record's contents. Line 14 creates the `Scanner` that will be used to retrieve input from the file.

```
1  // Fig. 15.6: ReadTextFile.java
2  // This program reads a text file and displays each record.
3  import java.io.IOException;
4  import java.lang.IllegalStateException;
5  import java.nio.file.Files;
6  import java.nio.file.Path;
7  import java.nio.file.Paths;
8  import java.util.NoSuchElementException;
9  import java.util.Scanner;
10
11 public class ReadTextFile {
12    public static void main(String[] args) {
13       // open clients.txt, read its contents and close the file
14       try(Scanner input = new Scanner(Paths.get("clients.txt"))) {
15          System.out.printf("%-10s%-12s%-12s%10s%n", "Account",
16             "First Name", "Last Name", "Balance");
17
```

Fig. 15.6 | Sequential file reading using a `Scanner`. (Part 1 of 2.)

```
18          // read record from file
19          while (input.hasNext()) { // while there is more to read
20             // display record contents
21             System.out.printf("%-10d%-12s%-12s%10.2f%n", input.nextInt(),
22                input.next(), input.next(), input.nextDouble());
23          }
24       }
25       catch (IOException | NoSuchElementException |
26          IllegalStateException e) {
27          e.printStackTrace();
28       }
29    }
30 }
```

```
Account   First Name  Last Name      Balance
100       Bob         Blue             24.98
200       Steve       Green          -345.67
300       Pam         White             0.00
400       Sam         Red             -42.16
500       Sue         Yellow          224.62
```

Fig. 15.6 | Sequential file reading using a `Scanner`. (Part 2 of 2.)

The `try`-with-resources statement opens the file for reading by instantiating a `Scanner` object (line 14). We pass a `Path` object to the constructor, which specifies that the `Scanner` object will read from the file `"clients.txt"` located in the directory from which the application executes. If the file cannot be found, an `IOException` occurs. The exception is handled in lines 25–28.

Lines 15–16 display headers for the columns in the application's output. Lines 19–23 read and display the file's content until the *end-of-file marker* is reached—in which case, method `hasNext` will return `false` at line 19. Lines 21–22 use `Scanner` methods `nextInt`, `next` and `nextDouble` to input an `int` (the account number), two `Strings` (the first and last names) and a `double` value (the balance). Each record is one line of data in the file. If the information in the file is not properly formed (e.g., there's a last name where there should be a balance), a `NoSuchElementException` occurs when the record is input. If the `Scanner` was closed before the data was input, an **`IllegalStateException`** occurs. These exceptions are handled in lines 25–28. Note in the format string in line 21 that the account number, first name and last name are left aligned, while the balance is right aligned and output with two digits of precision. Each iteration of the loop inputs one line of text from the text file, which represents one record. When the loop terminates and line 24 is reached, the `try`-with-resources statement implicitly calls the `Scanner`'s **`close`** method to close `Scanner` and the file.

15.4.3 Case Study: A Credit-Inquiry Program

To retrieve data sequentially from a file, programs start from the beginning of the file and read *all* the data consecutively until the desired information is found. It might be necessary to process the file sequentially several times (from the beginning of the file) during the execution of a program. Class `Scanner` does *not* allow repositioning to the beginning of the file. If it's necessary to read the file again, the program must *close* the file and *reopen* it.

The program in Figs. 15.7–15.8 allows a credit manager to obtain lists of customers with *zero balances* (i.e., customers who do not owe any money), customers with *credit balances* (i.e., customers to whom the company owes money) and customers with *debit balances* (i.e., customers who owe the company money for goods and services received). A credit balance is a *negative* amount, a debit balance a *positive* amount.

`MenuOption` enum

We begin by creating an `enum` type (Fig. 15.7) to define the different menu options the credit manager will have—this is required if you need to provide specific values for the `enum` constants. The options and their values are listed in lines 5–8.

```
1  // Fig. 15.7: MenuOption.java
2  // enum type for the credit-inquiry program's options.
3  public enum MenuOption {
4     // declare contents of enum type
5     ZERO_BALANCE(1),
6     CREDIT_BALANCE(2),
7     DEBIT_BALANCE(3),
8     END(4);
9
10    private final int value; // current menu option
11
12    // constructor
13    private MenuOption(int value) {this.value = value;}
14 }
```

Fig. 15.7 | `enum` type for the credit-inquiry program's menu options.

`CreditInquiry` Class

Figure 15.8 contains the functionality for the credit-inquiry program. The program displays a text menu and allows the credit manager to enter one of three options to obtain credit information:

- Option 1 (`ZERO_BALANCE`) displays accounts with zero balances.
- Option 2 (`CREDIT_BALANCE`) displays accounts with credit (negative) balances.
- Option 3 (`DEBIT_BALANCE`) displays accounts with debit (positive) balances.
- Option 4 (`END`) terminates program execution.

```
// Fig. 15.8: CreditInquiry.java
// This program reads a file sequentially and displays the
// contents based on the type of account the user requests
// (credit balance, debit balance or zero balance).
import java.io.IOException;
import java.lang.IllegalStateException;
import java.nio.file.Paths;
import java.util.NoSuchElementException;
import java.util.Scanner;
```

Fig. 15.8 | Credit-inquiry program. (Part 1 of 4.)

```

public class CreditInquiry {
   private final static MenuOption[] choices = MenuOption.values();

   public static void main(String[] args) {
      Scanner input = new Scanner(System.in);

      // get user's request (e.g., zero, credit or debit balance)
      MenuOption accountType = getRequest(input);

      while (accountType != MenuOption.END) {
         switch (accountType) {
            case ZERO_BALANCE:
               System.out.printf("%nAccounts with zero balances:%n");
               break;
            case CREDIT_BALANCE:
               System.out.printf("%nAccounts with credit balances:%n");
               break;
            case DEBIT_BALANCE:
               System.out.printf("%nAccounts with debit balances:%n");
               break;
         }

         readRecords(accountType);
         accountType = getRequest(input); // get user's request
      }
   }

   // obtain request from user
   private static MenuOption getRequest(Scanner input) {
      int request = 4;

      // display request options
      System.out.printf("%nEnter request%n%s%n%s%n%s%n%s%n",
         " 1 - List accounts with zero balances",
         " 2 - List accounts with credit balances",
         " 3 - List accounts with debit balances",
         " 4 - Terminate program");

      try {
         do { // input user request
            System.out.printf("%n? ");
            request = input.nextInt();
         } while ((request < 1) || (request > 4));
      }
      catch (NoSuchElementException noSuchElementException) {
         System.err.println("Invalid input. Terminating.");
      }

      return choices[request - 1]; // return enum value for option
   }

```

Fig. 15.8 | Credit-inquiry program. (Part 2 of 4.)

```
   // read records from file and display only records of appropriate type
   private static void readRecords(MenuOption accountType) {
      // open file and process contents
      try (Scanner input = new Scanner(Paths.get("clients.txt"))) {
         while (input.hasNext()) { // more data to read
            int accountNumber = input.nextInt();
            String firstName = input.next();
            String lastName = input.next();
            double balance = input.nextDouble();

            // if proper account type, display record
            if (shouldDisplay(accountType, balance)) {
               System.out.printf("%-10d%-12s%-12s%10.2f%n", accountNumber,
                  firstName, lastName, balance);
            }
            else {
               input.nextLine(); // discard the rest of the current record
            }
         }
      }
      catch (NoSuchElementException | IllegalStateException |
         IOException e) {
         System.err.println("Error processing file. Terminating.");
         System.exit(1);
      }
   }

   // use record type to determine if record should be displayed
   private static boolean shouldDisplay(
      MenuOption option, double balance) {
      if ((option == MenuOption.CREDIT_BALANCE) && (balance < 0)) {
         return true;
      }
      else if ((option == MenuOption.DEBIT_BALANCE) && (balance > 0)) {
         return true;
      }
      else if ((option == MenuOption.ZERO_BALANCE) && (balance == 0)) {
         return true;
      }

      return false;
   }
}
```

```
Enter request
 1 - List accounts with zero balances
 2 - List accounts with credit balances
 3 - List accounts with debit balances
 4 - Terminate program

? 1
```

Fig. 15.8 | Credit-inquiry program. (Part 3 of 4.)

```
Accounts with zero balances:
300         Pam          White               0.00

Enter request
 1 - List accounts with zero balances
 2 - List accounts with credit balances
 3 - List accounts with debit balances
 4 - Terminate program

? 2

Accounts with credit balances:
200         Steve        Green            -345.67
400         Sam          Red               -42.16

Enter request
 1 - List accounts with zero balances
 2 - List accounts with credit balances
 3 - List accounts with debit balances
 4 - Terminate program

? 3

Accounts with debit balances:
100         Bob          Blue               24.98
500         Sue          Yellow            224.62

Enter request
 1 - List accounts with zero balances
 2 - List accounts with credit balances
 3 - List accounts with debit balances
 4 - Terminate program

? 4
```

Fig. 15.8 | Credit-inquiry program. (Part 4 of 4.)

The record information is collected by reading through the file and determining if each record satisfies the criteria for the selected account type. Line 18 in `main` calls method `getRequest` (lines 39–60) to display the menu options, translates the number typed by the user into a `MenuOption` and stores the result in `MenuOption` variable `accountType`. Lines 20–35 loop until the user specifies that the program should terminate. Lines 21–31 display a header for the current set of records to be output to the screen. Line 33 calls method `readRecords` (lines 63–87), which loops through the file and reads every record.

Method `readRecords` uses a `try`-with-resources statement to create a `Scanner` that opens the file for reading (line 65). The file will be opened for reading with a new `Scanner` object each time `readRecords` is called, so that we can again read from the beginning of the file. Lines 67–70 read a record. Line 73 calls method `shouldDisplay` (lines 90–103) to determine whether the current record satisfies the account type requested. If `shouldDisplay` returns `true`, the program displays the account information. When the *end-of-file marker* is reached, the loop terminates and the `try`-with-resources statement closes the `Scanner` and the file. Once all the records have been read, control returns to `main` and `getRequest` is called again (line 34) to retrieve the user's next menu option.

15.4.4 Updating Sequential Files

The data in many sequential files cannot be modified without the risk of destroying other data in the file. For example, if the name "`White`" needs to be changed to "`Worthington`", the old name cannot simply be overwritten, because the new name requires more space. The record for `White` was written to the file as

```
300 Pam White 0.00
```

If the record is rewritten beginning at the same location in the file using the new name, the record will be

```
300 Pam Worthington 0.00
```

The new record is larger (has more characters) than the original record. "`Worthington`" would overwrite the "`0.00`" in the current record, and the characters beyond the second "`o`" in "`Worthington`" will overwrite the beginning of the next sequential record in the file. The problem here is that fields in a text file—and hence records—can vary in size. For example, 7, 14, –117, 2074 and 27383 are all `int`s stored in the same number of bytes (4) internally, but they're different-sized fields when written to a file as text. Therefore, records in a sequential file are not usually updated in place—instead, the entire file is rewritten. To make the preceding name change, the records before `300 Pam White 0.00` would be copied to a new file, the new record (which can be of a different size than the one it replaces) would be written and the records after `300 Pam White 0.00` would be copied to the new file. Rewriting the entire file is uneconomical to update just one record, but reasonable if a substantial number of records need to be updated.

15.5 XML Serialization

In Section 15.4, we demonstrated how to write the individual fields of a record into a file as text, and how to read those fields from a file. Sometimes we want to write an entire object to or read an entire object from a file or—as you'll see in the online REST Web Services chapter—over a network connection. As we mentioned in Chapter 12, XML (eXtensible Markup Language) is a widely used language for describing data. XML is one format commonly used to represent objects. In our online web services chapter, we'll also use another common format called JSON (JavaScript Object Notation) to transmit objects over the Internet. We chose XML in this section rather than JSON, because the APIs for manipulating objects as XML are built into Java SE, whereas the APIs for manipulating objects as JSON are part of Java EE (Enterprise Edition).

In this section, we'll manipulate objects using **JAXB (Java Architecture for XML Binding)**. As you'll see, the JAXB enables you to perform **XML serialization**—which JAXB refers to as **marshaling**. A **serialized object** is represented by XML that includes the object's data. After a serialized object has been written into a file, it can be read from the file and **deserialized**—that is, the XML that represents the object and its data can be used to recreate the object in memory.

15.5.1 Creating a Sequential File Using XML Serialization

The serialization we show in this section is performed with character-based streams, so the result will be a text file that you can view in standard text editors. We begin by creating and writing serialized objects to a file.

Declaring Class **Account**

We begin by defining class `Account` (Fig. 15.9), which encapsulates the client record information used by the serialization examples. All the classes for this example and the one in Section 15.5.2 are located in the `SerializationApps` directory with the chapter's examples. Class `Account` contains `private` instance variables `account`, `firstName`, `lastName` and `balance` (lines 4–7) and *set* and *get* methods for accessing these instance variables. Though the *set* methods do not validate the data in this example, generally they should.

```
1  // Fig. 15.9: Account.java
2  // Account class for storing records as objects.
3  public class Account {
4     private int accountNumber;
5     private String firstName;
6     private String lastName;
7     private double balance;
8
9     // initializes an Account with default values
10    public Account() {this(0, "", "", 0.0);}
11
12    // initializes an Account with provided values
13    public Account(int accountNumber, String firstName,
14       String lastName, double balance) {
15       this.accountNumber = accountNumber;
16       this.firstName = firstName;
17       this.lastName = lastName;
18       this.balance = balance;
19    }
20
21    // get account number
22    public int getAccountNumber() {return accountNumber;}
23
24    // set account number
25    public void setAccountNumber(int accountNumber)
26       {this.accountNumber = accountNumber;}
27
28    // get first name
29    public String getFirstName() {return firstName;}
30
31    // set first name
32    public void setFirstName(String firstName)
33       {this.firstName = firstName;}
34
35    // get last name
36    public String getLastName() {return lastName;}
37
38    // set last name
39    public void setLastName(String lastName) {this.lastName = lastName;}
40
41    // get balance
42    public double getBalance() {return balance;}
43
```

Fig. 15.9 | Account class for storing records as objects. (Part 1 of 2.)

```
44      // set balance
45      public void setBalance(double balance) {this.balance = balance;}
46   }
```

Fig. 15.9 | Account class for storing records as objects. (Part 2 of 2.)

Plain Old Java Objects

JAXB works with **POJOs (plain old Java objects)**—no special superclasses or interfaces are required for XML-serialization support. By default, JAXB serializes only an object's `public` instance variables and `public` *read–write* properties. Recall from Section 13.4.1 that a read–write property is defined by creating *get* and *set* methods with specific naming conventions. In class `Account`, methods `getAccountNumber` and `setAccountNumber` (lines 22–26) define a read–write property named `accountNumber`. Similarly, the *get* and *set* methods in lines 29–45 define the read–write properties `firstName`, `lastName` and `balance`. The class must also provide a public default or no-argument constructor to recreate the objects when they're read from the file.

Declaring Class **Accounts**

As you'll see in Fig. 15.11, this example stores `Account` objects in a `List<Account>`, then serializes the entire `List` into a file with one operation. To serialize a `List`, it must be defined as an instance variable of a class. For that reason, we encapsulate the `List<Account>` in class `Accounts` (Fig. 15.10).

```
1   // Fig. 15.10: Accounts.java
2   // Maintains a List<Account>
3   import java.util.ArrayList;
4   import java.util.List;
5   import javax.xml.bind.annotation.XmlElement;
6
7   public class Accounts {
8      // @XmlElement specifies XML element name for each object in the List
9      @XmlElement(name="account")
10     private List<Account> accounts = new ArrayList<>(); // stores Accounts
11
12     // returns the List<Accounts>
13     public List<Account> getAccounts() {return accounts;}
14  }
```

Fig. 15.10 | Account class for serializable objects.

Lines 9–10 declare and initialize the `List<Account>` instance variable `accounts`. JAXB enables you to customize many aspects of XML serialization, such as serializing a private instance variable or a read-only property. The annotation **`@XMLElement`** (line 9; package **`javax.xml.bind.annotation`**) indicates that the `private` instance variable should be serialized. We'll discuss the annotation's `name` argument shortly. The annotation is required because the instance variable is not `public` and there's no corresponding `public` read–write property.

Writing XML Serialized Objects to a File

The program of Fig. 15.11 serializes an `Accounts` object to a text file. The program is similar to the one in Section 15.4, so we focus only on the new features. Line 9 imports the **`JAXB` class** from package `javax.xml.bind`. This package contains many related classes that implement the XML serializations we perform, but the `JAXB` class contains easy-to-use `static` methods that perform the most common operations.

```
1  // Fig. 15.11: CreateSequentialFile.java
2  // Writing objects to a file with JAXB and BufferedWriter.
3  import java.io.BufferedWriter;
4  import java.io.IOException;
5  import java.nio.file.Files;
6  import java.nio.file.Paths;
7  import java.util.NoSuchElementException;
8  import java.util.Scanner;
9  import javax.xml.bind.JAXB;
10
11 public class CreateSequentialFile {
12    public static void main(String[] args) {
13       // open clients.xml, write objects to it then close file
14       try(BufferedWriter output =
15          Files.newBufferedWriter(Paths.get("clients.xml"))) {
16
17          Scanner input = new Scanner(System.in);
18
19          // stores the Accounts before XML serialization
20          Accounts accounts = new Accounts();
21
22          System.out.printf("%s%n%s%n? ",
23             "Enter account number, first name, last name and balance.",
24             "Enter end-of-file indicator to end input.");
25
26          while (input.hasNext()) { // loop until end-of-file indicator
27             try {
28                // create new record
29                Account record = new Account(input.nextInt(),
30                   input.next(), input.next(), input.nextDouble());
31
32                // add to AccountList
33                accounts.getAccounts().add(record);
34             }
35             catch (NoSuchElementException elementException) {
36                System.err.println("Invalid input. Please try again.");
37                input.nextLine(); // discard input so user can try again
38             }
39
40             System.out.print("? ");
41          }
42
43          // write AccountList's XML to output
44          JAXB.marshal(accounts, output);
45       }
```

Fig. 15.11 | Writing objects to a file with `JAXB` and `BufferedWriter`. (Part 1 of 2.)

```
46          catch (IOException ioException) {
47             System.err.println("Error opening file. Terminating.");
48          }
49       }
50    }
```

```
Enter account number, first name, last name and balance.
Enter end-of-file indicator to end input.
? 100 Bob Blue 24.98
? 200 Steve Green -345.67
? 300 Pam White 0.00
? 400 Sam Red -42.16
? 500 Sue Yellow 224.62
? ^Z
```

Fig. 15.11 | Writing objects to a file with `JAXB` and `BufferedWriter`. (Part 2 of 2.)

To open the file, lines 14–15 call `Files` `static` method **`newBufferedWriter`**, which receives a `Path` specifying the file to open for writing (`"clients.xml"`) and—if the file exists—returns a **`BufferedWriter`** that class `JAXB` will use to write text to the file. Existing files that are opened for output in this manner are *truncated.* The standard filename extension for XML files is `.xml`. Lines 14–15 throw an **`IOException`** if a problem occurs while opening the file—such as, when the program does not have permission to access the file or when a read-only file is opened for writing. If so, the program displays an error message (lines 46–48), then terminates. Otherwise, variable `output` can be used to write to the file.

Line 20 creates the `Accounts` object that contains the `List<Account>`. Lines 26–41 input each record, create an `Account` object (lines 29–30) and add to the `List` (line 33).

When the user enters the end-of-file indicator to terminate input, line 44 uses class `JAXB`'s `static` method **`marshal`** to serialize as XML the `Accounts` object containing the `List<Account>`. The first argument is the object to serialize. The second argument to this particular overload of method `marshal` is a `Writer` (package `java.io`) that's used to output the XML—`BufferedWriter` is a subclass of `Writer`. The `BufferedWriter` obtained in lines 14–15 outputs the XML to a file.

Note that only one statement is required to write the *entire* `Accounts` object and all of the objects in its `List<Account>`. In the sample execution for the program in Fig. 15.11, we entered information for five accounts—the same information shown in Fig. 15.5.

The XML Output

Figure 15.12 shows the contents of the file `clients.xml`. Though you do not need to know XML to work with this example, note that the XML is human readable. When JAXB serializes an object of a class, it uses the class's name with a lowercase first letter as the corresponding XML element name, so the `accounts` element (lines 2–33) represents the `Accounts` object.

Recall that line 9 in class `Accounts` (Fig. 15.10) preceded the `List<Account>` instance variable with the annotation

```
@XmlElement(name="account")
```

In addition to enabling JAXB to serialize the instance variable, this annotation specifies the XML element name (`"account"`) used to represent each of the `List`'s `Account` objects in the serialized output. For example, lines 3–8 in Fig. 15.12 represent the `Account` for `Bob Blue`. If we did not specify the annotation's `name` argument, the instance variable's name (`accounts`) would have been used as the XML element name. Many other aspects of JAXB XML serialization are customizable. For more details, see

```
https://docs.oracle.com/javase/tutorial/jaxb/intro/
```

```
1  <?xml version="1.0" encoding="UTF-8" standalone="yes"?>
2  <accounts>
3      <account>
4          <accountNumber>100</accountNumber>
5          <balance>24.98</balance>
6          <firstName>Bob</firstName>
7          <lastName>Blue</lastName>
8      </account>
9      <account>
10         <accountNumber>200</accountNumber>
11         <balance>-345.67</balance>
12         <firstName>Steve</firstName>
13         <lastName>Green</lastName>
14     </account>
15     <account>
16         <accountNumber>300</accountNumber>
17         <balance>0.0</balance>
18         <firstName>Pam</firstName>
19         <lastName>White</lastName>
20     </account>
21     <account>
22         <accountNumber>400</accountNumber>
23         <balance>-42.16</balance>
24         <firstName>Sam</firstName>
25         <lastName>Red</lastName>
26     </account>
27     <account>
28         <accountNumber>500</accountNumber>
29         <balance>224.62</balance>
30         <firstName>Sue</firstName>
31         <lastName>Yellow</lastName>
32     </account>
33 </accounts>
```

Fig. 15.12 | Contents of `clients.xml`.

Each of class `Account`'s property has a corresponding XML element with the same name as the property. For example, lines 4–7 are the XML elements for `Bob Blue`'s `accountNumber`, `balance`, `firstName` and `lastName`—JAXB placed the XML elements in alphabetical order, though this is not required or guaranteed. Within each of these elements is the corresponding property's value—`100` for the `accountNumber`, `24.98` for the balance, `Bob` for the `firstName` and `Blue` for the `lastName`. Lines 9–32 represent the other four `Account` objects that we input into the program in the sample execution.

15.5.2 Reading and Deserializing Data from a Sequential File

The preceding section showed how to create a file containing XML serialized objects. In this section, we discuss how to *read serialized data* from a file. Figure 15.13 reads objects from the file created by the program in Section 15.5.1, then displays the contents. The program opens the file for input by calling `Files` `static` method **`newBufferedReader`**, which receives a `Path` specifying the file to open and, if the file exists and no exceptions occur, returns a **`BufferedReader`** for reading from the file.

```java
// Fig. 15.13: ReadSequentialFile.java
// Reading a file of XML serialized objects with JAXB and a
// BufferedReader and displaying each object.
import java.io.BufferedReader;
import java.io.IOException;
import java.nio.file.Files;
import java.nio.file.Paths;
import javax.xml.bind.JAXB;

public class ReadSequentialFile {
   public static void main(String[] args) {
      // try to open file for deserialization
      try(BufferedReader input =
         Files.newBufferedReader(Paths.get("clients.xml"))) {
         // unmarshal the file's contents
         Accounts accounts = JAXB.unmarshal(input, Accounts.class);

         // display contents
         System.out.printf("%-10s%-12s%-12s%10s%n", "Account",
            "First Name", "Last Name", "Balance");

         for (Account account : accounts.getAccounts()) {
            System.out.printf("%-10d%-12s%-12s%10.2f%n",
               account.getAccountNumber(), account.getFirstName(),
               account.getLastName(), account.getBalance());
         }
      }
      catch (IOException ioException) {
         System.err.println("Error opening file.");
      }
   }
}
```

```
Account   First Name  Last Name      Balance
100       Bob         Blue             24.98
200       Steve       Green          -345.67
300       Pam         White             0.00
400       Sam         Red             -42.16
500       Sue         Yellow          224.62

No more records
```

Fig. 15.13 | Reading a file of XML serialized objects with `JAXB` and a `BufferedReader` and displaying each object.

Line 16 uses JAXB static method **unmarshal** to read the contents of clients.xml and convert the XML into an Accounts object. The overload of unmarshal used here reads XML from a Reader (package java.io) and creates an object of the type specified as the second argument—BufferedReader is a subclass of Reader. The BufferedReader obtained in lines 13–14 reads text from a file. Method unmarshal's second argument is a Class<T> object (package java.lang) representing the type of the object to create from the XML—the notation Accounts.class is a Java compiler shorthand for

```
new Class<Accounts>
```

Once again, note that one statement reads the entire file and recreates the Accounts object. If no exceptions occur, lines 19–26 display the contents of the Accounts object.

15.6 FileChooser and DirectoryChooser Dialogs

JavaFX classes **FileChooser** and **DirectoryChooser** (package javafx.stage) display dialogs that enable the user to select a file or directory, respectively. To demonstrate these dialogs, we enhance the example in Section 15.3. The example (Figs. 15.14–15.15) contains a JavaFX graphical user interface, but still displays the same data as the earlier example.

Creating the JavaFX GUI

The GUI (Fig. 15.15(a)) consists of a 600-by-400 BorderPane with the **fx:id** borderPane:

- In the BorderPane's top, we placed a **ToolBar** layout (from the Scene Builder **Library**'s **Containers** section), which arranges its controls horizontally (by default) or vertically. Typically, you place ToolBars at your GUI's edges, such as in a BorderPane's top, right, bottom or left areas.
- In the BorderPane's center, we placed a **TextArea** control with the **fx:id** textArea. We set the control's **Text** property to "Select file or directory" and enabled its **Wrap Text** property to ensure that long lines of text wrap to the next line. If there are more lines of text to display than vertical lines in the TextArea, the control will show a vertical scrollbar. (When **Wrap Text** is not enabled, the TextArea also shows a horizontal scrollbar if the text is too wide to display.)

By default, the ToolBar you drag onto your layout has one Button. You can drag other controls onto the ToolBar and, if necessary, remove the default Button. We added a second Button. For the first Button, we set:

- the **Text** property to "Select File",
- the **fx:id** property to selectFileButton and
- the **On Action** event handler to selectFileButtonPressed.

For the second Button, we set:

- the **Text** property to "Select Directory",
- the **fx:id** property to selectDirectoryButton and
- the **On Action** event handler to selectDirectoryButtonPressed.

Finally, we specified FileChooserTestController as the FXML's controller.

Class That Launches the App

Class `FileChooserTest` (Fig. 15.14) launches the JavaFX application, using the same techniques you learned in Chapters 12–13.

```
// Fig. 15.14: FileChooserTest.java
// App to test classes FileChooser and DirectoryChooser.
import javafx.application.Application;
import javafx.fxml.FXMLLoader;
import javafx.scene.Parent;
import javafx.scene.Scene;
import javafx.stage.Stage;

public class FileChooserTest extends Application {
   @Override
   public void start(Stage stage) throws Exception {
      Parent root =
         FXMLLoader.load(getClass().getResource("FileChooserTest.fxml"));

      Scene scene = new Scene(root);
      stage.setTitle("File Chooser Test"); // displayed in title bar
      stage.setScene(scene);
      stage.show();
   }

   public static void main(String[] args) {
      launch(args);
   }
}
```

Fig. 15.14 | Demonstrating `JFileChooser`.

Controller Class

Class `FileChooserTestController` (Fig. 15.15) responds to the `Buttons`' events. Both event handlers call method `analyzePath` (defined in lines 70–110) to determine whether a `Path` is a file or directory, display information about the `Path` and, if it's a directory, list its contents.

```
1  // Fig. 15.15: FileChooserTestController.java
2  // Displays information about a selected file or folder.
3  import java.io.File;
4  import java.io.IOException;
5  import java.nio.file.DirectoryStream;
6  import java.nio.file.Files;
7  import java.nio.file.Path;
8  import java.nio.file.Paths;
9  import javafx.event.ActionEvent;
10 import javafx.fxml.FXML;
11 import javafx.scene.control.Button;
12 import javafx.scene.control.TextArea;
```

Fig. 15.15 | Displays information about a selected file or folder. (Part 1 of 5.)

```
import javafx.scene.layout.BorderPane;
import javafx.stage.DirectoryChooser;
import javafx.stage.FileChooser;

public class FileChooserTestController {
   @FXML private BorderPane borderPane;
   @FXML private Button selectFileButton;
   @FXML private Button selectDirectoryButton;
   @FXML private TextArea textArea;

   // handles selectFileButton's events
   @FXML
   private void selectFileButtonPressed(ActionEvent e) {
      // configure dialog allowing selection of a file
      FileChooser fileChooser = new FileChooser();
      fileChooser.setTitle("Select File");

      // display files in folder from which the app was launched
      fileChooser.setInitialDirectory(new File("."));

      // display the FileChooser
      File file = fileChooser.showOpenDialog(
         borderPane.getScene().getWindow());

      // process selected Path or display a message
      if (file != null) {
         analyzePath(file.toPath());
      }
      else {
         textArea.setText("Select file or directory");
      }
   }

   // handles selectDirectoryButton's events
   @FXML
   private void selectDirectoryButtonPressed(ActionEvent e) {
      // configure dialog allowing selection of a directory
      DirectoryChooser directoryChooser = new DirectoryChooser();
      directoryChooser.setTitle("Select Directory");

      // display folder from which the app was launched
      directoryChooser.setInitialDirectory(new File("."));

      // display the FileChooser
      File file = directoryChooser.showDialog(
         borderPane.getScene().getWindow());

      // process selected Path or display a message
      if (file != null) {
         analyzePath(file.toPath());
      }
```

Fig. 15.15 | Displays information about a selected file or folder. (Part 2 of 5.)

```
      else {
         textArea.setText("Select file or directory");
      }
   }

   // display information about file or directory user specifies
   public void analyzePath(Path path) {
      try {
         // if the file or directory exists, display its info
         if (path != null && Files.exists(path)) {
            // gather file (or directory) information
            StringBuilder builder = new StringBuilder();
            builder.append(String.format("%s:%n", path.getFileName()));
            builder.append(String.format("%s a directory%n",
               Files.isDirectory(path) ? "Is" : "Is not"));
            builder.append(String.format("%s an absolute path%n",
               path.isAbsolute() ? "Is" : "Is not"));
            builder.append(String.format("Last modified: %s%n",
               Files.getLastModifiedTime(path)));
            builder.append(String.format("Size: %s%n", Files.size(path)));
            builder.append(String.format("Path: %s%n", path));
            builder.append(String.format("Absolute path: %s%n",
               path.toAbsolutePath()));

            if (Files.isDirectory(path)) { // output directory listing
               builder.append(String.format("%nDirectory contents:%n"));

               // object for iterating through a directory's contents
               DirectoryStream<Path> directoryStream =
                  Files.newDirectoryStream(path);

               for (Path p : directoryStream) {
                  builder.append(String.format("%s%n", p));
               }
            }

            // display file or directory info
            textArea.setText(builder.toString());
         }
         else { // Path does not exist
            textArea.setText("Path does not exist");
         }
      }
      catch (IOException ioException) {
         textArea.setText(ioException.toString());
      }
   }
}
```

Fig. 15.15 | Displays information about a selected file or folder. (Part 3 of 5.)

a) Initial app window.

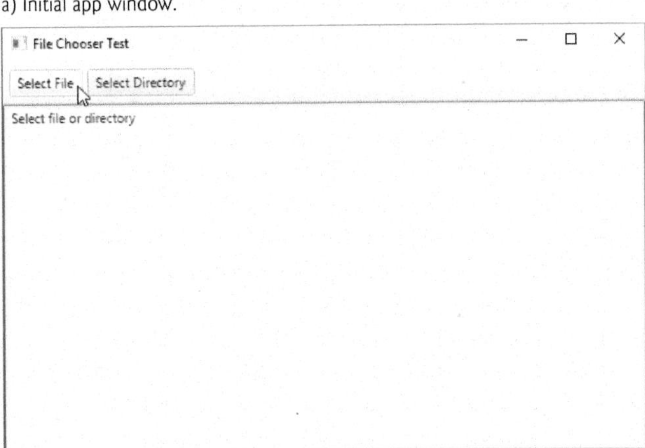

b) Selecting `FileChooserTest.java` from the `FileChooser` dialog displayed when the user clicked the **Select File** `Button`.

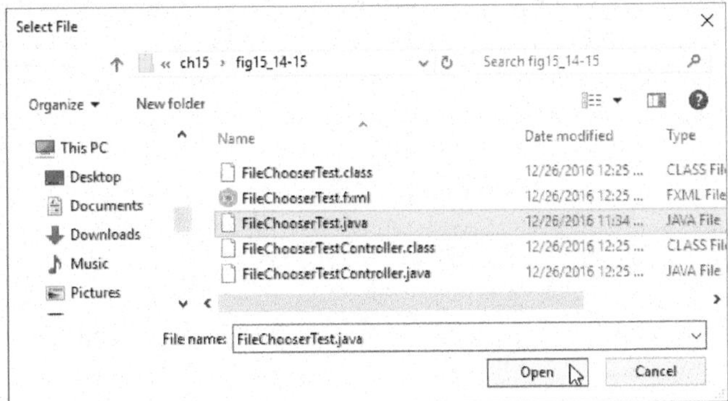

c) Displaying information about the file `FileChooserTest.java`.

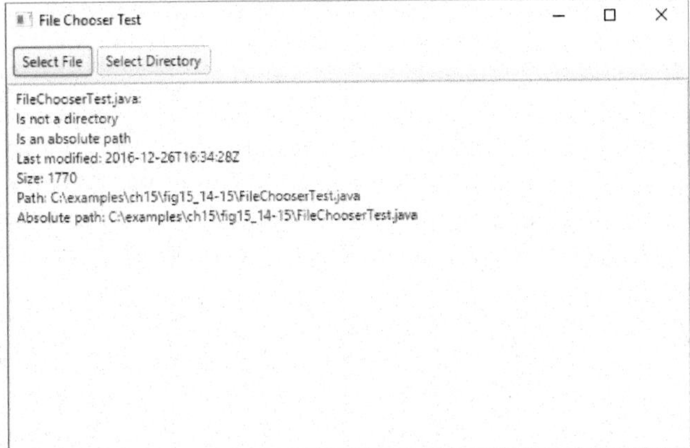

Fig. 15.15 | Displays information about a selected file or folder. (Part 4 of 5.)

d) Selecting `fig15_14-15` from the `DirectoryChooser` dialog displayed when the user clicked the **Select Directory** `Button`.

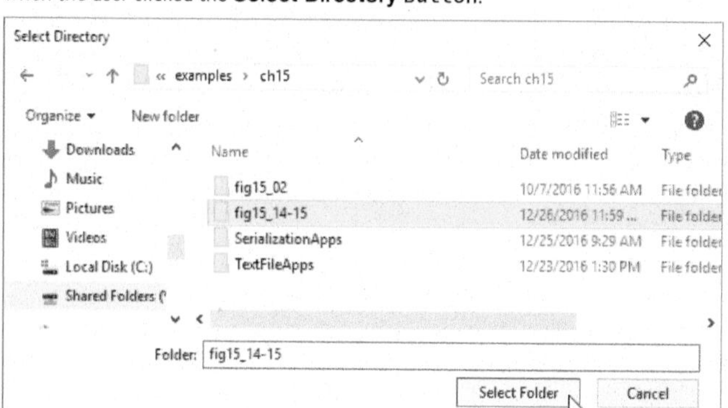

e) Displaying information about the directory `fig15_14-15`.

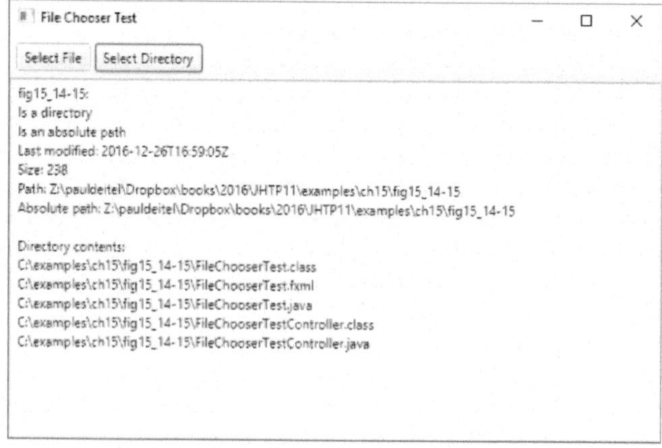

Fig. 15.15 | Displays information about a selected file or folder. (Part 5 of 5.)

Method `selectFileButtonPressed`

When the user presses the **Select File** button, method `selectFileButtonPressed` (lines 24–44) creates, configures and displays a `FileChooser`. Line 28 sets the text displayed in the `FileChooser`'s title bar. Line 31 specifies the initial directory that should be opened when the `FileChooser` is displayed. Method `setInitialDirectory` receives a `File` object representing the directory's location—`"."` represents the current folder from which the app was launched.

Lines 34–35 display the `FileChooser` by calling its **`showOpenDialog`** method to display a dialog with an **Open** button for opening a file. There's also a **`showSaveDialog`** method that displays a dialog with a **Save** button for saving a file. This method receives as its argument a reference to the app's `Window`. A non-`null` argument makes the `FileChooser` a modal dialog that prevents the user from interacting with the rest of the app until the dialog is dismissed—when the user selects a file or clicks **Cancel**. To obtain the app's `Window`, we use the `borderPane`'s `getScene` method to get a reference to its parent Scene, then use the Scene's getWindow method to get a reference to the Window containing the Scene.

Method showOpenDialog returns a File representing the selected file's location, or null if the user clicks the **Cancel** button. If the File is not null, line 39 calls analyzePath to display the selected file's information—File method **toPath** returns a Path object representing the location. Otherwise, line 42 displays a message in the TextArea telling the user to select a file or directory. The screen captures in Fig. 15.15(b) and (c) show the FileChooser dialog with the FileChooserTest.java file selected and, after the user presses the **Open** button, the file's information displayed.

Method selectDirectoryButtonPressed

When the user presses the **Select Directory** button, method selectDirectoryButtonPressed (lines 47–67) creates, configures and displays a DirectoryChooser. The method performs the same tasks as method selectFileButtonPressed. The key difference is line 57, which calls DirectoryChooser method **showDialog** to display the dialog—there are not separate open and save dialogs for selecting folders. Method showDialog returns a File representing the location of the selected directory, or null if the user clicks **Cancel**. If the File is not null, line 62 calls analyzePath to display information about the selected directory. Otherwise, line 65 displays a message in the TextArea telling the user to select a file or directory. The screen captures in Fig. 15.15(d) and (e) show the FileChooser dialog with the fig15_14-15 directory selected and, after the user presses the **Open** button, the directory's information displayed.

15.7 (Optional) Additional java.io Classes

This section overviews additional interfaces and classes (from package java.io).

15.7.1 Interfaces and Classes for Byte-Based Input and Output

InputStream and OutputStream are abstract classes that declare methods for performing byte-based input and output, respectively.

Pipe Streams

Pipes are synchronized communication channels between threads. We discuss threads in Chapter 23. Java provides **PipedOutputStream** (a subclass of OutputStream) and **PipedInputStream** (a subclass of InputStream) to establish pipes between two threads in a program. One thread sends data to another by writing to a PipedOutputStream. The target thread reads information from the pipe via a PipedInputStream.

Filter Streams

A **FilterInputStream** filters an InputStream, and a FilterOutputStream filters an OutputStream. **Filtering** means simply that the filter stream provides additional functionality, such as aggregating bytes into meaningful primitive-type units. FilterInputStream and FilterOutputStream are typically used as superclasses, so some of their filtering capabilities are provided by their subclasses.

A **PrintStream** (a subclass of FilterOutputStream) performs text output to the specified stream. Actually, we've been using PrintStream output throughout the text to this point—System.out and System.err are PrintStream objects.

Data Streams

Reading data as raw bytes is fast, but crude. Usually, programs read data as aggregates of bytes that form `int`s, `float`s, `double`s and so on. Java programs can use several classes to input and output data in aggregate form.

Interface `DataInput` describes methods for reading primitive types from an input stream. Classes **`DataInputStream`** and `RandomAccessFile` each implement this interface to read sets of bytes and view them as primitive-type values. Interface `DataInput` includes methods such as `readBoolean`, `readByte`, `readChar`, `readDouble`, `readFloat`, `readFully` (for `byte` arrays), `readInt`, `readLong`, `readShort`, `readUnsignedByte`, `readUnsignedShort`, `readUTF` (for reading Unicode characters encoded by Java—we discuss UTF encoding in Appendix H) and `skipBytes`.

Interface `DataOutput` describes a set of methods for writing primitive types to an output stream. Classes **`DataOutputStream`** (a subclass of `FilterOutputStream`) and `RandomAccessFile` each implement this interface to write primitive-type values as bytes. Interface `DataOutput` includes overloaded versions of method `write` (for a `byte` or for a `byte` array) and methods `writeBoolean`, `writeByte`, `writeBytes`, `writeChar`, `writeChars` (for Unicode `String`s), `writeDouble`, `writeFloat`, `writeInt`, `writeLong`, `writeShort` and `writeUTF` (to output text modified for Unicode).

Buffered Streams

Buffering is an I/O-performance-enhancement technique. With a **`BufferedOutputStream`** (a subclass of class `FilterOutputStream`), each output statement does *not* necessarily result in an actual physical transfer of data to the output device (which is a slow operation compared to processor and main memory speeds). Rather, each output operation is directed to a region in memory called a **buffer** that's large enough to hold the data of many output operations. Then, actual transfer to the output device is performed in one large **physical output operation** each time the buffer fills. The output operations directed to the output buffer in memory are often called **logical output operations.** With a `BufferedOutputStream`, a partially filled buffer can be forced out to the device at any time by invoking the stream object's **`flush`** method.

Using buffering can greatly increase the performance of an application. Typical I/O operations are extremely slow compared with the speed of accessing data in computer memory. Buffering reduces the number of I/O operations by first combining smaller outputs together in memory. The number of actual physical I/O operations is small compared with the number of I/O requests issued by the program. Thus, the program that's using buffering is more efficient.

Performance Tip 15.1

Buffered I/O can yield significant performance improvements over unbuffered I/O.

With a **`BufferedInputStream`** (a subclass of class `FilterInputStream`), many "logical" chunks of data from a file are read as one large **physical input operation** into a memory buffer. As a program requests each new chunk of data, it's taken from the buffer. (This procedure is sometimes referred to as a **logical input operation.**) When the buffer is empty, the next actual physical input operation from the input device is performed to read in the next group of "logical" chunks of data. Thus, the number of actual physical input operations is small compared with the number of read requests issued by the program.

Memory-Based **byte** *Array Steams*

Java stream I/O includes capabilities for inputting from byte arrays in memory and outputting to byte arrays in memory. A ByteArrayInputStream (a subclass of InputStream) reads from a byte array in memory. A ByteArrayOutputStream (a subclass of OutputStream) outputs to a byte array in memory. One use of byte-array I/O is *data validation.* A program can input an entire line at a time from the input stream into a byte array. Then a validation routine can scrutinize the contents of the byte array and correct the data if necessary. Finally, the program can proceed to input from the byte array, "knowing" that the input data is in the proper format. Outputting to a byte array is a nice way to take advantage of the powerful output-formatting capabilities of Java streams. For example, data can be stored in a byte array, using the same formatting that will be displayed at a later time, and the byte array can then be output to a file to preserve the formatting.

Sequencing Input from Multiple Streams

A SequenceInputStream (a subclass of InputStream) logically concatenates several InputStreams—the program sees the group as one continuous InputStream. When the program reaches the end of one input stream, that stream closes, and the next stream in the sequence opens.

15.7.2 Interfaces and Classes for Character-Based Input and Output

In addition to the byte-based streams, Java provides the **Reader** and **Writer** abstract classes, which are character-based streams like those you used for text-file processing in Section 15.4. Most of the byte-based streams have corresponding character-based concrete Reader or Writer classes.

Character-Based Buffering **Readers** *and* **Writers**

Classes BufferedReader (a subclass of abstract class Reader) and BufferedWriter (a subclass of abstract class Writer) enable buffering for character-based streams. Remember that character-based streams use Unicode characters—such streams can process data in any language that the Unicode character set represents.

Memory-Based **char** *Array* **Readers** *and* **Writers**

Classes **CharArrayReader** and **CharArrayWriter** read and write, respectively, a stream of characters to a char array. A **LineNumberReader** (a subclass of BufferedReader) is a buffered character stream that keeps track of the number of lines read—newlines, returns and carriage-return–line-feed combinations increment the line count. Keeping track of line numbers can be useful if the program needs to inform the reader of an error on a specific line.

Character-Based File, Pipe and String **Readers** *and* **Writers**

An InputStream can be converted to a Reader via class **InputStreamReader**. Similarly, an OutputStream can be converted to a Writer via class **OutputStreamWriter**. Class FileReader (a subclass of InputStreamReader) and class FileWriter (a subclass of OutputStreamWriter) read characters from and write characters to a file, respectively. Class

PipedReader and class PipedWriter implement piped-character streams for transferring data between threads. Class StringReader and StringWriter read characters from and write characters to Strings, respectively. A PrintWriter writes characters to a stream.

15.8 Wrap-Up

In this chapter, you learned how to manipulate persistent data. We compared byte-based and character-based streams, and introduced several classes from packages java.io and java.nio.file. You used classes Files and Paths and interfaces Path and DirectoryStream to retrieve information about files and directories. You used sequential file processing to manipulate records that are stored in order by the record-key field. You used XML serialization to store and retrieve entire objects. The chapter concluded with a small example of using a JFileChooser dialog to allow users to easily select files from a GUI. The next chapter discusses Java's classes for manipulating collections of data—such as class ArrayList, which we introduced in Section 7.16.

Summary

Section 15.1 Introduction

- Computers use files for long-term retention of large amounts of persistent data (p. 613), even after the programs that created the data terminate.
- Computers store files on secondary storage devices (p. 613), such as solid-state drives.

Section 15.2 Files and Streams

- Java views each file as a sequential stream of bytes (p. 613).
- Every operating system provides a mechanism to determine the end of a file, such as an end-of-file marker (p. 613) or a count of the total bytes in the file.
- Byte-based streams (p. 614) represent data in binary format.
- Character-based streams (p. 614) represent data as sequences of characters.
- Files created using byte-based streams are binary files (p. 614). Files created using character-based streams are text files (p. 614). Text files can be read by text editors, whereas binary files are read by a program that converts the data to a human-readable format.
- Java also can associate streams with different devices. Three stream objects are associated with devices when a Java program begins executing—System.in, System.out and System.err.

Section 15.3 Using NIO Classes and Interfaces to Get File and Directory Information

- A Path (p. 615) represents the location of a file or directory. Path objects do not open files or provide any file-processing capabilities.
- Class Paths (p. 615) is used to get a Path object representing a file or directory location.
- Class Files (p. 615) provides static methods for common file and directory manipulations, including methods for copying files; creating and deleting files and directories; getting information about files and directories; reading the contents of files; getting objects that allow you to manipulate the contents of files and directories; and more.
- A DirectoryStream (p. 615) enables a program to iterate through the contents of a directory.

- The `static` method `get` (p. 615) of class `Paths` converts a `String` representing a file's or directory's location into a `Path` object.
- Character-based input and output can be performed with classes `Scanner` and `Formatter`.
- Class `Formatter` (p. 615) enables formatted data to be output to the screen or to a file in a manner similar to `System.out.printf`.
- An absolute path (p. 615) contains all the directories, starting with the root directory (p. 615), that lead to a specific file or directory. Every file or directory on a disk drive has the same root directory in its path.
- A relative path (p. 615) starts from the directory in which the application began executing.
- `Files` `static` method `exists` (p. 617) receives a `Path` and determines whether it exists (either as a file or as a directory) on disk.
- `Path` method `getFileName` (p. 618) gets the `String` name of a file or directory without any location information.
- `Files` `static` method `isDirectory` (p. 618) receives a `Path` and returns a `boolean` indicating whether that `Path` represents a directory on disk.
- `Path` method `isAbsolute` (p. 618) returns a `boolean` indicating whether a `Path` represents an absolute path to a file or directory.
- `Files` `static` method `getLastModifiedTime` (p. 618) receives a `Path` and returns a `FileTime` (package `java.nio.file.attribute`) indicating when the file was last modified.
- `Files` `static` method `size` (p. 618) receives a `Path` and returns a `long` representing the number of bytes in the file or directory. For directories, the value returned is platform specific.
- `Path` method `toString` (p. 618) returns a `String` representation of the `Path`.
- `Path` method `toAbsolutePath` (p. 618) converts the `Path` on which it's called to an absolute path.
- `Files` `static` method `newDirectoryStream` (p. 618) returns a `DirectoryStream<Path>` containing `Path` objects for a directory's contents.
- A separator character (p. 618) is used to separate directories and files in the path.

Section 15.4 Sequential Text Files
- Java imposes no structure on a file. You must structure files to meet your application's needs.
- To retrieve data sequentially from a file, programs normally start from the beginning of the file and read all the data consecutively until the desired information is found.
- Data in many sequential files cannot be modified without the risk of destroying other data in the file. Records in a sequential file are usually updated by rewriting the entire file.

Section 15.5 XML Serialization
- JAXB (Java Architecture for XML Binding) enables you to perform XML serialization, which JAXB refers to as marshaling.
- An XML serialized object is represented as XML that includes the object's data.
- After a serialized object has been written into a file, it can be read from the file and deserialized.

Section 15.5.1 Creating a Sequential File Using XML Serialization
- JAXB works with POJOs (plain old Java objects).
- By default, JAXB serializes an object's `public` instance variables and `public` read–write properties. The class must also provide a public default or no-argument constructor to recreate the objects when they're read from the file.

- To serialize a `List`, it must be defined as an instance variable of a class.
- JAXB enables you to customize many aspects of XML serialization.
- The annotation `@XMLElement` (package `javax.xml.bind.annotation`) indicates that an instance variable should be serialized and optionally specifies the XML element's name.
- Class `JAXB` (package `javax.xml.bind`) performs XML serialization.
- `Files` `static` method `newBufferedWriter` receives a `Path` specifying a file to open for writing and, if the file exists, returns a `BufferedWriter` that can be used to write text to the file. Existing files that are opened for output in this manner are truncated.
- The standard filename extension for XML files is `.xml`.
- `JAXB` `static` method `marshal` serializes an object to XML format. The arguments are the object to serialize and a `Writer` (package `java.io`) that's used to output the XML.
- Class `BufferedWriter` extends `Writer`.
- When JAXB serializes an object of a class, it uses the class's name with a lowercase first letter as the corresponding XML element name.
- Each property's XML element has the same name as the property.

Section 15.5.2 Reading and Deserializing Data from a Sequential File

- `Files` `static` method `newBufferedReader` receives a `Path` specifying a file to open and, if the file exists, returns a `BufferedReader` that can be used to read text from the file.
- `JAXB` `static` method `unmarshal` reads the contents of a file and converts the XML into an object of the type specified by the method's second argument. The second argument is a `Class<T>` object (package `java.lang`) representing the type of the object to create.
- The notation *ClassName*`.class` is shorthand notation for `new Class<`*ClassName*`>`.

Section 15.6 `FileChooser` and `DirectoryChooser` Dialogs

- JavaFX classes `FileChooser` and `DirectoryChooser` (package `javafx.stage`) display dialogs that enable the user to easily select a file or directory, respectively.
- A `ToolBar` layout (located in the Scene Builder **Library**'s **Containers** section) arranges its controls horizontally (by default) or vertically.
- A `TextArea` control displays multiple lines of text. Its **Wrap Text** property ensures that long lines of text wrap to the next line.
- If there's too much text to display, the `TextArea` will show a vertical scrollbar. When **Wrap Text** is not set, the `TextArea` also can show a horizontal scrollbar.
- By default, the `ToolBar` you drag onto your layout has one `Button`. You can drag additional controls onto the `ToolBar` and, if necessary, remove the default `Button`.
- `FileChooser` method `setInitialDirectory` receives a `File` object representing the folder that should initially be displayed in the dialog.
- `FileChooser` method `showOpenDialog` displays an open dialog—there is also a `showSaveDialog` method that displays a dialog for saving a file. This method receives as its argument a reference to the app's `Window`. Supplying a non-`null` argument makes the `FileChooser` a modal dialog. It prevents the user from interacting with the rest of the app until the dialog is dismissed.
- Method `showOpenDialog` returns a `File` representing the location of the selected file, or `null` if the user clicks the **Cancel** button.
- `File` method `toPath` returns a `Path` object representing a location.
- `DirectoryChooser` method `showDialog` displays the dialog. This method returns a `File` representing the location of the selected directory, or `null` if the user clicks the **Cancel** button.

Section 15.7 (Optional) Additional `java.io` Classes

- `InputStream` and `OutputStream` are `abstract` classes for performing byte-based I/O.
- Pipes (p. 641) are synchronized communication channels between threads. One thread sends data via a `PipedOutputStream` (p. 641). The target thread reads information from the pipe via a `PipedInputStream` (p. 641).
- A filter stream (p. 641) provides additional functionality, such as aggregating data bytes into meaningful primitive-type units. `FilterInputStream` (p. 641) and `FilterOutputStream` are typically extended, so some of their filtering capabilities are provided by their concrete subclasses.
- A `PrintStream` (p. 641) performs text output. `System.out` and `System.err` are `PrintStreams`.
- Interface `DataInput` describes methods for reading primitive types from an input stream. Classes `DataInputStream` (p. 642) and `RandomAccessFile` each implement this interface.
- Interface `DataOutput` describes methods for writing primitive types to an output stream. Classes `DataOutputStream` (p. 642) and `RandomAccessFile` each implement this interface.
- Buffering is an I/O-performance-enhancement technique. Buffering reduces the number of I/O operations by combining smaller outputs together in memory. The number of physical I/O operations is much smaller than the number of I/O requests issued by the program.
- With a `BufferedOutputStream` (p. 642) each output operation is directed to a buffer (p. 642) large enough to hold the data of many output operations. Transfer to the output device is performed in one large physical output operation (p. 642) when the buffer fills. A partially filled buffer can be forced out to the device at any time by invoking the stream object's `flush` method (p. 642).
- With a `BufferedInputStream` (p. 642), many "logical" chunks of data from a file are read as one large physical input operation (p. 642) into a memory buffer. As a program requests data, it's taken from the buffer. When the buffer is empty, the next actual physical input operation is performed.
- A `ByteArrayInputStream` reads from a `byte` array in memory. A `ByteArrayOutputStream` outputs to a `byte` array in memory.
- A `SequenceInputStream` concatenates several `InputStreams`. When the program reaches the end of an input stream, that stream closes, and the next stream in the sequence opens.
- The `Reader` (p. 643) and `Writer` (p. 643) `abstract` classes are Unicode character-based streams. Most byte-based streams have corresponding character-based concrete `Reader` or `Writer` classes.
- Classes `BufferedReader` and `BufferedWriter` buffer character-based streams.
- Classes `CharArrayReader` (p. 643) and `CharArrayWriter` (p. 643) manipulate `char` arrays.
- A `LineNumberReader` (p. 643) is a buffered character stream that tracks the number of lines read.
- Classes `FileReader` (p. 643) and `FileWriter` (p. 643) perform character-based file I/O.
- Class `PipedReader` (p. 644) and class `PipedWriter` (p. 644) implement piped-character streams for transferring data between threads.
- Class `StringReader` (p. 644) and `StringWriter` (p. 644) read characters from and write characters to `Strings`, respectively. A `PrintWriter` writes characters to a stream.

Self-Review Exercises

15.1 Determine whether each of the following statements is *true* or *false*. If *false*, explain why.

a) You must explicitly create the stream objects `System.in`, `System.out` and `System.err`.
b) When reading data from a file using class `Scanner`, if you wish to read data in the file multiple times, the file must be closed and reopened to read from the beginning of the file.
c) `Files` `static` method `exists` receives a `Path` and determines whether it exists (either as a file or as a directory) on disk.

d) XML files are not human readable in a text editor.
e) An absolute path contains all the directories, starting with the root directory, that lead to a specific file or directory.
f) Class `Formatter` contains method `printf`, which enables formatted data to be output to the screen or to a file.

15.2 Complete the following tasks, assuming that each applies to the same program:
a) Write a statement that opens file `"oldmast.txt"` for input—use `Scanner` variable `inOldMaster`.
b) Write a statement that opens file `"trans.txt"` for input—use `Scanner` variable `inTransaction`.
c) Write a statement that opens file `"newmast.txt"` for output (and creation)—use `Formatter` variable `outNewMaster`.
d) Write the statements needed to read a record from the file `"oldmast.txt"`. Use the data to create an object of class `Account`—use `Scanner` variable `inOldMaster`. Assume that class `Account` is the same as the `Account` class in Fig. 15.9.
e) Write the statements needed to read a record from the file `"trans.txt"`. The record is an object of class `TransactionRecord`—use `Scanner` variable `inTransaction`. Assume that class `TransactionRecord` contains method `setAccount` (which takes an `int`) to set the account number and method `setAmount` (which takes a `double`) to set the amount of the transaction.
f) Write a statement that outputs a record to the file `"newmast.txt"`. The record is an object of type `Account`—use `Formatter` variable `outNewMaster`.

15.3 Write a statement that performs each of the following tasks:
a) Output an `Accounts` object named `accounts` using XML serialization and a `BufferedWriter` named `writer`.
a) Input an XML serialized object into an `Accounts` object named `accounts` using a `BufferedReader` named `reader`.

Answers to Self-Review Exercises

15.1 a) False. These three streams are created for you when a Java application begins executing. b) True. c) True. d) False. XML files are both computer and machine readable. e) True. f) False. Class `Formatter` contains method `format`, which enables formatted data to be output to the screen or to a file.

15.2 Answers for a) through f):

a)
```
Scanner oldmastInput = new Scanner(Paths.get("oldmast.txt"));
```
b)
```
Scanner inTransaction = new Scanner(Paths.get("trans.txt"));
```
c)
```
Formatter outNewMaster = new Formatter("newmast.txt");
```
d)
```
Account account = new Account();
account.setAccount(inOldMaster.nextInt());
account.setFirstName(inOldMaster.next());
account.setLastName(inOldMaster.next());
account.setBalance(inOldMaster.nextDouble());
```
e)
```
TransactionRecord transaction = new Transaction();
transaction.setAccount(inTransaction.nextInt());
transaction.setAmount(inTransaction.nextDouble());
```
f)
```
outNewMaster.format("%d %s %s %.2f%n",
   account.getAccount(), account.getFirstName(),
   account.getLastName(), account.getBalance());
```

15.3 Answers for a) and b):

a) `JAXB.marshal(accounts, writer);`

b) `Accounts account = JAXB.unmarshal(reader, Accounts.class);`

Exercises

15.4 *(File Matching)* Self-Review Exercise 15.2 asked you to write a series of single statements. Actually, these statements form the core of an important type of file-processing program—namely, a file-matching program. In commercial data processing, it's common to have several files in each application system. In an accounts receivable system, for example, there's generally a master file containing detailed information about each customer, such as the customer's name, address, telephone number, outstanding balance, credit limit, discount terms, contract arrangements and possibly a condensed history of recent purchases and cash payments.

As transactions occur (i.e., sales are made and payments arrive in the mail), information about them is entered into a file. At the end of each business period (a month for some companies, a week for others, and a day in some cases), the file of transactions (called `"trans.txt"`) is applied to the master file (called `"oldmast.txt"`) to update each account's purchase and payment record. During an update, the master file is rewritten as the file `"newmast.txt"`, which is then used at the end of the next business period to begin the updating process again.

File-matching programs must deal with certain problems that do not arise in single-file programs. For example, a match does not always occur. If a customer on the master file has not made any purchases or cash payments in the current business period, no record for this customer will appear on the transaction file. Similarly, a customer who did make some purchases or cash payments could have just moved to this community, and if so, the company may not have had a chance to create a master record for this customer.

Write a complete file-matching accounts receivable program. Use the account number on each file as the record key for matching purposes. Assume that each file is a sequential text file with records stored in increasing account-number order.

a) Define class `TransactionRecord`. Objects of this class contain an account number and amount for the transaction. Provide methods to modify and retrieve these values.

b) Modify class `Account` in Fig. 15.9 to include method `combine`, which takes a `TransactionRecord` object and combines the balance of the `Account` object and the amount value of the `TransactionRecord` object.

c) Write a program to create data for testing the program. Use the sample account data in Figs. 15.16 and 15.17. Run the program to create the files `trans.txt` and `oldmast.txt` to be used by your file-matching program.

Master file account number	Name	Balance
100	Alan Jones	348.17
300	Mary Smith	27.19
500	Sam Sharp	0.00
700	Suzy Green	-14.22

Fig. 15.16 | Sample data for master file.

d) Create class `FileMatch` to perform the file-matching functionality. The class should contain methods that read `oldmast.txt` and `trans.txt`. When a match occurs (i.e., records with the same account number appear in both the master file and the transaction

Transaction file account number	Transaction amount
100	27.14
300	62.11
400	100.56
900	82.17

Fig. 15.17 | Sample data for transaction file.

file), add the dollar amount in the transaction record to the current balance in the master record, and write the `"newmast.txt"` record. (Assume that purchases are indicated by positive amounts in the transaction file and payments by negative amounts.) When there's a master record for a particular account, but no corresponding transaction record, merely write the master record to `"newmast.txt"`. When there's a transaction record, but no corresponding master record, print to a log file the message `"Unmatched transaction record for account number..."` (fill in the account number from the transaction record). The log file should be a text file named `"log.txt"`.

15.5 *(File Matching with Multiple Transactions)* It's possible (and actually common) to have several transaction records with the same record key. This situation occurs, for example, when a customer makes several purchases and cash payments during a business period. Rewrite your accounts receivable file-matching program from Exercise 15.4 to provide for the possibility of handling several transaction records with the same record key. Modify the test data of `CreateData.java` to include the additional transaction records in Fig. 15.18.

Account number	Dollar amount
300	83.89
700	80.78
700	1.53

Fig. 15.18 | Additional transaction records.

15.6 *(File Matching with XML Serialization)* Recreate your solution for Exercise 15.5 using XML serialization. You may want to create applications to read the data stored in the `.xml` files—the code in Section 15.5.2 can be modified for this purpose.

15.7 *(Telephone-Number Word Generator)* Standard telephone keypads contain the digits zero through nine. The numbers two through nine each have three letters associated with them (Fig. 15.19). Many people find it difficult to memorize phone numbers, so they use the correspondence between digits and letters to develop seven-letter words that correspond to their phone numbers. For example, a person whose telephone number is 686-2377 might use the correspondence indicated in Fig. 15.19 to develop the seven-letter word "NUMBERS." Every seven-letter word corresponds to exactly one seven-digit telephone number. A restaurant wishing to increase its takeout business could surely do so with the number 825-3688 (i.e., "TAKEOUT").

Every seven-letter phone number corresponds to many different seven-letter words, but most of these words represent unrecognizable juxtapositions of letters. It's possible, however, that the owner of a barbershop would be pleased to know that the shop's telephone number, 424-7288, corresponds to "HAIRCUT." A veterinarian with the phone number 738-2273 would be pleased to

Digit	Letters	Digit	Letters	Digit	Letters
2	A B C	5	J K L	8	T U V
3	D E F	6	M N O	9	W X Y
4	G H I	7	P R S		

Fig. 15.19 | Telephone keypad digits and letters.

know that the number corresponds to the letters "PETCARE." An automotive dealership would be pleased to know that the dealership number, 639-2277, corresponds to "NEWCARS."

Write a program that, given a seven-digit number, uses a `Formatter` object to write to a file every possible seven-letter word combination corresponding to that number. There are 2,187 (3^7) such combinations. Avoid phone numbers with the digits 0 and 1.

15.8 *(Student Poll)* Figure 7.8 contains an array of survey responses that's hard coded into the program. Suppose we wish to process survey results that are stored in a file. This exercise requires two separate programs. First, create an application that prompts the user for survey responses and outputs each response to a file. Use a `Formatter` to create a file called `numbers.txt`. Each integer should be written using method `format`. Then modify the program in Fig. 7.8 to read the survey responses from `numbers.txt`. The responses should be read from the file by using a `Scanner`. Use method `nextInt` to input one integer at a time from the file. The program should continue to read responses until it reaches the end of the file. The results should be output to the text file `"output.txt"`.

Making a Difference

15.9 *(Phishing Scanner)* Phishing is a form of identity theft in which, in an e-mail, a sender posing as a trustworthy source attempts to acquire private information, such as your user names, passwords, credit-card numbers and social security number. Phishing e-mails claiming to be from popular banks, credit-card companies, auction sites, social networks and online payment services may look quite legitimate. These fraudulent messages often provide links to spoofed (fake) websites where you're asked to enter sensitive information.

Search online for phishing scams. Also check out the Anti-Phishing Working Group

`http://www.antiphishing.org`

and the FBI's Cyber Investigations website

`http://www.fbi.gov/about-us/investigate/cyber/cyber`

where you'll find information about the latest scams and how to protect yourself.

Create a list of 30 words, phrases and company names commonly found in phishing messages. Assign a point value to each based on your estimate of its likelihood to be in a phishing message (e.g., one point if it's somewhat likely, two points if moderately likely, or three points if highly likely). Write an application that scans a file of text for these terms and phrases. For each occurrence of a keyword or phrase within the text file, add the assigned point value to the total points for that word or phrase. For each keyword or phrase found, output one line with the word or phrase, the number of occurrences and the point total. Then show the point total for the entire message. Does your program assign a high point total to some actual phishing e-mails you've received? Does it assign a high point total to some legitimate e-mails you've received?

16 Generic Collections

Objectives

In this chapter you'll:

- Learn what collections are.
- Use class `Arrays` for array manipulations.
- Learn the type-wrapper classes that enable programs to process primitive data values as objects.
- Understand the boxing and unboxing that occurs automatically between objects of the type-wrapper classes and their corresponding primitive types.
- Use prebuilt generic data structures from the collections framework.
- Use various algorithms of the `Collections` class to process collections.
- Use iterators to "walk through" a collection.
- Learn about synchronization and modifiability wrappers.
- Learn about Java SE 9's new factory methods for creating small immutable `List`s, `Set`s and `Map`s.

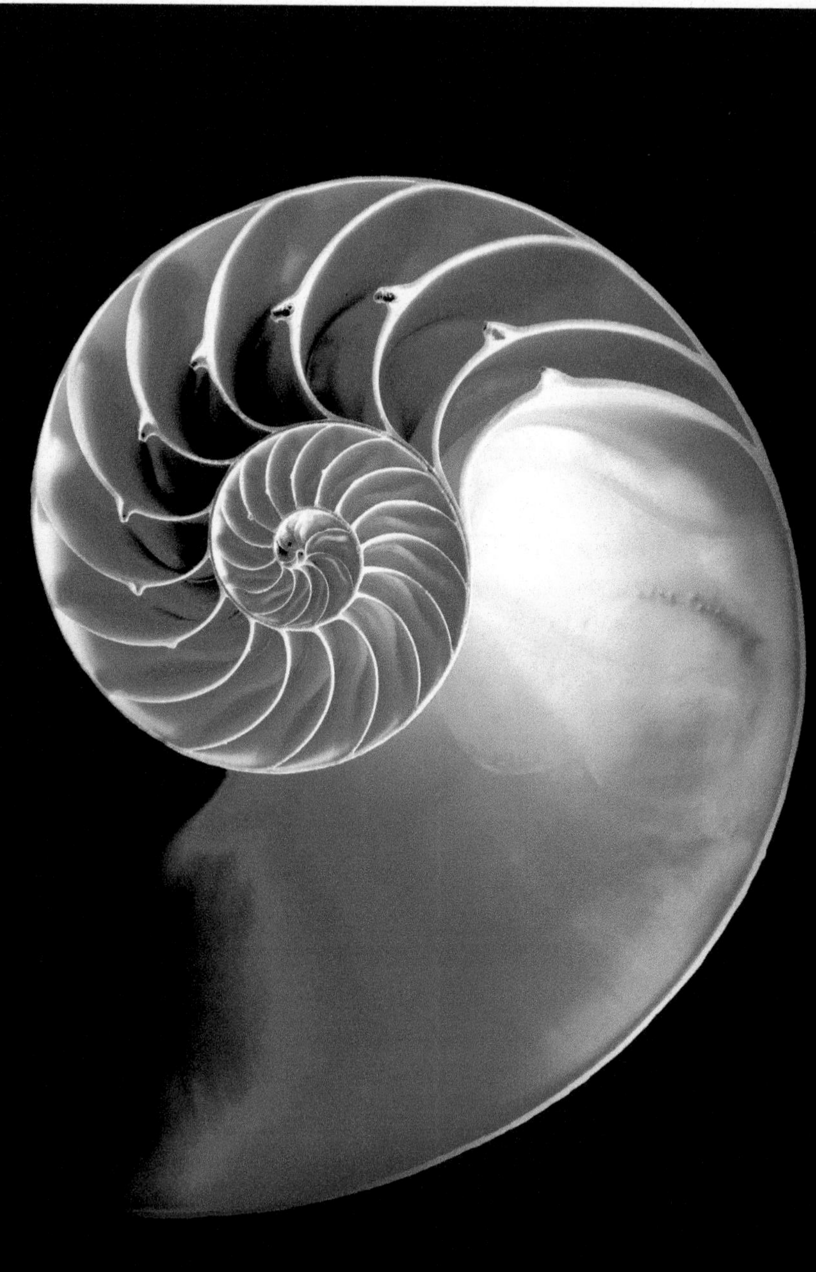

Outline

16.1 Introduction

In Section 7.16, we introduced the generic `ArrayList` collection—a dynamically resizable array-like data structure that stores references to objects of a type that you specify when you create the `ArrayList`. In this chapter, we continue our discussion of the Java **collections framework**, which contains many other *prebuilt* generic data-structures.

Some examples of collections are your favorite songs stored on your smartphone or media player, your contacts list, the cards you hold in a card game, the members of your favorite sports team and the courses you take at school.

We discuss the collections-framework interfaces that declare the capabilities of each collection type, various classes that implement these interfaces, methods that process collection objects, and **iterators** that "walk through" collections.

Java SE 8

After reading Chapter 17, Lambdas and Streams, you'll be able to reimplement many of Chapter 16's examples in a more concise and elegant manner, and in a way that makes them easier to parallelize to improve performance on today's multi-core systems. In Chapter 23, Concurrency, you'll learn how to improve performance on multi-core systems using Java's *concurrent collections* and *parallel stream* operations. 8

Java SE 9

Section 16.14 introduces Java SE 9's new *convenience factory methods*, which help you create small immutable collections that cannot be modified once they're created. 9

16.2 Collections Overview

A **collection** is a data structure—actually, an object—that can hold references to other objects. Usually, collections contain references to objects of any type that has the *is-a* relationship with the collection's element type. The collections-framework interfaces declare the operations to be performed generically on various types of collections. Figure 16.1 lists some of the collections-framework interfaces. Several implementations of these interfaces are provided within the framework. You may also provide your own implementations.

Interface	Description
`Collection`	The root interface in the collections hierarchy from which interfaces `Set`, `Queue` and `List` are derived.
`Set`	A collection that does *not* contain duplicates.
`List`	An ordered collection that *can* contain duplicate elements.
`Map`	A collection that associates keys to values and *cannot* contain duplicate keys. `Map` does not derive from `Collection`.
`Queue`	Typically a *first-in, first-out* collection that models a *waiting line*; other orders can be specified.

Fig. 16.1 | Some collections-framework interfaces.

`Object`-Based Collections

The collections-framework classes and interfaces are members of package `java.util`. In early Java versions, the collections framework classes stored and manipulated *only* `Object` references, enabling you to store *any* object in a collection, because all classes directly or indirectly derive from class `Object`. Programs normally need to process *specific* types of objects. As a result, the `Object` references obtained from a collection needed to be *downcast* to an appropriate type to allow the program to process the objects correctly. As we discussed in Chapter 10, downcasting generally should be avoided.

Generic Collections

To eliminate this problem, the collections framework was enhanced with the *generics* capabilities that we introduced with generic `ArrayList`s in Chapter 7 and that we discuss in more detail in Chapter 20, Generic Classes and Methods: A Deeper Look. Generics enable you to specify the *exact type* that will be stored in a collection and give you the benefits of *compile-time type checking*—the compiler issues error messages if you use inappropriate types in your collections. Once you specify the type stored in a generic collection, any reference you retrieve from the collection will have that type. This eliminates the need for explicit type casts that can throw `ClassCastException`s if the referenced object is *not* of the appropriate type. In addition, the generic collections are *backward compatible* with Java code that was written before generics were introduced.

Good Programming Practice 16.1

Avoid reinventing the wheel—rather than building your own data structures, use the interfaces and collections from the Java collections framework, which have been carefully tested and tuned to meet most application requirements.

Choosing a Collection

The documentation for each collection discusses its memory requirements and its methods' performance characteristics for operations such as adding and removing elements, searching for elements, sorting elements and more. Before choosing a collection, review the online documentation for the collection category you're considering (`Set`, `List`, `Map`, `Queue`, etc.), then choose the implementation that best meets your application's needs. Chapter 19, Searching, Sorting and Big O, discusses a means for describing how hard an algorithm works to perform its task—based on the number of data items to be processed. After reading Chapter 19, you'll better understand each collection's performance characteristics as described in the online documentation.

16.3 Type-Wrapper Classes

Each primitive type (listed in Appendix D) has a corresponding **type-wrapper class** (in package `java.lang`). These classes are called **`Boolean`**, **`Byte`**, **`Character`**, **`Double`**, **`Float`**, **`Integer`**, **`Long`** and **`Short`**. These enable you to manipulate primitive-type values as objects. This is important, because the data structures that we reuse or develop in Chapters 16–21 manipulate and share *objects*—they cannot manipulate variables of primitive types. However, they can manipulate objects of the type-wrapper classes, because every class ultimately derives from `Object`.

Each of the numeric type-wrapper classes—`Byte`, `Short`, `Integer`, `Long`, `Float` and `Double`—extends class `Number`. Also, the type-wrapper classes are `final` classes, so you cannot extend them. Primitive types do not have methods, so the methods related to a primitive type are located in the corresponding type-wrapper class (e.g., method `parseInt`, which converts a `String` to an `int` value, is located in class `Integer`).

16.4 Autoboxing and Auto-Unboxing

Java provides boxing and unboxing conversions that automatically convert between primitive-type values and type-wrapper objects. A **boxing conversion** converts a value of a primitive type to an object of the corresponding type-wrapper class. An **unboxing conversion** converts an object of a type-wrapper class to a value of the corresponding primitive type. These conversions—called **autoboxing** and **auto-unboxing**—are performed automatically. Consider the following statements:

```
Integer[] integerArray = new Integer[5]; // create integerArray
integerArray[0] = 10; // assign Integer 10 to integerArray[0]
int value = integerArray[0]; // get int value of Integer
```

In this case, autoboxing occurs when assigning an `int` value (`10`) to `integerArray[0]`, because `integerArray` stores references to `Integer` objects, not `int` values. Auto-unboxing occurs when assigning `integerArray[0]` to `int` variable `value`, because variable `value` stores an `int` value, not a reference to an `Integer` object. Boxing conversions also occur in conditions, which can evaluate to primitive `boolean` values or `Boolean` objects. Many of the examples in Chapters 16–21 use these conversions to store primitive values in and retrieve them from data structures.

16.5 Interface `Collection` and Class `Collections`

Interface `Collection` contains **bulk operations** (i.e., operations performed on an *entire* collection) for operations such as *adding*, *clearing* and *comparing* objects (or elements) in a collection. A `Collection` can also be converted to an array. In addition, interface `Collec-`

tion provides a method that returns an **Iterator** object, which allows a program to walk through the collection and remove elements from it during the iteration. We discuss class Iterator in Section 16.6.1. Other methods of interface Collection enable a program to determine a collection's *size* and whether a collection is *empty*.

Software Engineering Observation 16.1

Collection is used commonly as a parameter type in methods to allow polymorphic processing of all objects that implement interface Collection.

Software Engineering Observation 16.2

Most collection implementations provide a constructor that takes a Collection argument, thereby allowing a new collection to be constructed containing the elements of the specified collection.

Class **Collections** provides static convenience methods that *search*, *sort* and perform other operations on collections. Section 16.7 discusses Collections methods in detail. We also cover Collections' **wrapper methods** that enable you to treat a collection as a *synchronized collection* (Section 16.11) or an *unmodifiable collection* (Section 16.12). Synchronized collections are for use with multithreading (discussed in Chapter 23), which enables programs to perform operations *in parallel*. When two or more threads of a program *share* a collection, problems might occur. As an analogy, consider a traffic intersection. If all cars were allowed to access the intersection at the same time, collisions might occur. For this reason, traffic lights are provided to control access to the intersection. Similarly, we can *synchronize* access to a collection to ensure that only *one* thread manipulates the collection at a time. The synchronization wrapper methods of class Collections return synchronized versions of collections that can be shared among threads in a program. Chapter 23 also discusses some classes from the java.util.concurrent package, which provides more robust collections for use in multithreaded applications. Unmodifiable collections are useful when clients of a class need to *view* a collection's elements, but they should *not* be allowed to *modify* the collection by adding and removing elements.

16.6 Lists

A List (sometimes called a **sequence**) is a Collection of elements in sequence that can contain duplicate elements. Like array indices, List indices are zero based (i.e., the first element's index is zero). In addition to the methods inherited from Collection, List provides methods for manipulating elements via their indices, manipulating a specified range of elements, searching for elements and obtaining a **ListIterator** to access the elements.

Interface List is implemented by several classes, including **ArrayList** and **LinkedList**. Autoboxing occurs when you add primitive-type values to objects of these classes, because they store only references to objects. Class ArrayList is a resizable-array implementations of List. Inserting an element between existing elements of an ArrayList is an *inefficient* operation—all elements after the new one must be moved out of the way, which could be an expensive operation in a collection with a large number of elements. A LinkedList enables *efficient* insertion (or removal) of elements in the middle of a collection, but is much less efficient than an ArrayList for jumping to a specific element in the collection. We discuss the architecture of linked lists in Chapter 21.

The following two subsections demonstrate the `List` and `Collection` capabilities. Section 16.6.1 removes elements from an `ArrayList` with an `Iterator`. Section 16.6.2 uses `ListIterator` and several `List`- and `LinkedList`-specific methods.

16.6.1 ArrayList and Iterator

Figure 16.2 uses an `ArrayList` (introduced in Section 7.16) to demonstrate several capabilities of interface `Collection`. The program places two `Color` arrays in `ArrayList`s and uses an `Iterator` to remove elements in the second `ArrayList` collection from the first.

```
// Fig. 16.2: CollectionTest.java
// Collection interface demonstrated via an ArrayList object.
import java.util.List;
import java.util.ArrayList;
import java.util.Collection;
import java.util.Iterator;

public class CollectionTest {
   public static void main(String[] args) {
      // add elements in colors array to list
      String[] colors = {"MAGENTA", "RED", "WHITE", "BLUE", "CYAN"};
      List<String> list = new ArrayList<String>();

      for (String color : colors) {
         list.add(color); // adds color to end of list
      }

      // add elements in removeColors array to removeList
      String[] removeColors = {"RED", "WHITE", "BLUE"};
      List<String> removeList = new ArrayList<String>();

      for (String color : removeColors) {
         removeList.add(color);
      }

      // output list contents
      System.out.println("ArrayList: ");

      for (int count = 0; count < list.size(); count++) {
         System.out.printf("%s ", list.get(count));
      }

      // remove from list the colors contained in removeList
      removeColors(list, removeList);

      // output list contents
      System.out.printf("%n%nArrayList after calling removeColors:%n");

      for (String color : list) {
         System.out.printf("%s ", color);
      }
   }
```

Fig. 16.2 | `Collection` interface demonstrated via an `ArrayList` object. (Part 1 of 2.)

```
43
44    // remove colors specified in collection2 from collection1
45    private static void removeColors(Collection<String> collection1,
46       Collection<String> collection2) {
47       // get iterator
48       Iterator<String> iterator = collection1.iterator();
49
50       // loop while collection has items
51       while (iterator.hasNext()) {
52          if (collection2.contains(iterator.next())) {
53             iterator.remove(); // remove current element
54          }
55       }
56    }
57 }
```

```
ArrayList:
MAGENTA RED WHITE BLUE CYAN

ArrayList after calling removeColors:
MAGENTA CYAN
```

Fig. 16.2 | `Collection` interface demonstrated via an `ArrayList` object. (Part 2 of 2.)

Lines 11 and 19 declare and initialize `String` arrays `colors` and `removeColors`. Lines 12 and 20 create `ArrayList<String>` objects and assign their references to `List<String>` variables `list` and `removeList`, respectively. Recall that `ArrayList` is a *generic* class, so we can specify a *type argument* (`String` in this case) to indicate the type of the elements in each list. Because you specify the type to store in a collection at compile time, generic collections provide compile-time *type safety* that allows the compiler to catch attempts to use invalid types. For example, you cannot store `Employee`s in a collection of `String`s.

Lines 14–16 populate `list` with `String`s stored in array `colors`, and lines 22–24 populate `removeList` with `String`s stored in array `removeColors` using **`List` method `add`**, which adds elements to the end of the `List`. Lines 29–31 output each element of `list`. Line 29 calls **`List` method `size`** to get the number of elements in the `ArrayList`. Line 30 uses **`List` method `get`** to retrieve individual element values. Lines 29–31 also could have used the enhanced `for` statement.

Line 34 calls method `removeColors` (lines 45–56), passing `list` and `removeList` as arguments. Method `removeColors` deletes the `String`s in `removeList` from the `String`s in `list`. Lines 39–41 print `list`'s elements after `removeColors` completes its task.

Method `removeColors` declares two `Collection<String>` parameters (lines 45–46)—any two `Collection`s containing `String`s can be passed as arguments. The method accesses the elements of the first `Collection` (`collection1`) via an `Iterator`. Line 48 calls **`Collection` method `iterator`** to get an `Iterator` for the `Collection`. Interfaces `Collection` and `Iterator` are generic types. The loop-continuation condition (line 51) calls **`Iterator` method `hasNext`** to determine whether there are more elements to iterate through. Method `hasNext` returns `true` if another element exists and `false` otherwise.

The `if` condition in line 52 calls **`Iterator` method `next`** to obtain a reference to the next element, then uses method **`contains`** of the second `Collection` (`collection2`) to determine whether `collection2` contains the element returned by `next`. If so, line 53 calls **`Iterator` method `remove`** to remove the element from the `Collection collection1`.

Common Programming Error 16.1

If a collection is modified by one of its methods after an iterator is created for that collection, the iterator immediately becomes invalid—any operation performed with the iterator fails immediately and throws a `ConcurrentModificationException`. For this reason, iterators are said to be "fail fast." Fail-fast iterators help ensure that a modifiable collection is not manipulated by two or more threads at the same time, which could corrupt the collection. In Chapter 23, Concurrency, you'll learn about concurrent collections (package `java.util.concurrent`) that can be safely manipulated by multiple concurrent threads.

Software Engineering Observation 16.3

We refer to the `ArrayList`s in this example via `List` variables. This makes our code more flexible and easier to modify—if we later determine that `LinkedList`s would be more appropriate, only the lines where we created the `ArrayList` objects (lines 12 and 20) need to be modified. In general, when you create a collection object, refer to that object with a variable of the corresponding collection interface type. Similarly, implementing method `removeColors` to receive `Collection` references enables the method to be used with any collection that implements the interface `Collection`.

Type Inference with the <> Notation

Lines 12 and 20 specify the type stored in the `ArrayList` (that is, `String`) on the left and right sides of the initialization statements. You also can use *type inferencing* with `<>`—known as the **diamond notation**—in statements that declare and create generic type variables and objects. For example, line 12 can be written as:

```
List<String> list = new ArrayList<>();
```

In this case, Java uses the type in angle brackets on the left of the declaration (that is, `String`) as the type stored in the `ArrayList` created on the right side of the declaration. We'll use this syntax for the remaining examples in this chapter.

16.6.2 `LinkedList`

Figure 16.3 demonstrates various operations on `LinkedList`s. The program creates two `LinkedList`s of `String`s. The elements of one `List` are added to the other. Then all the `String`s are converted to uppercase, and a range of elements is deleted.

```
// Fig. 16.3: ListTest.java
// Lists, LinkedLists and ListIterators.
import java.util.List;
import java.util.LinkedList;
import java.util.ListIterator;

public class ListTest {
   public static void main(String[] args) {
```

Fig. 16.3 | `List`s, `LinkedList`s and `ListIterator`s. (Part 1 of 3.)

```
      // add colors elements to list1
      String[] colors =
         {"black", "yellow", "green", "blue", "violet", "silver"};
      List<String> list1 = new LinkedList<>();

      for (String color : colors) {
         list1.add(color);
      }

      // add colors2 elements to list2
      String[] colors2 =
         {"gold", "white", "brown", "blue", "gray", "silver"};
      List<String> list2 = new LinkedList<>();

      for (String color : colors2) {
         list2.add(color);
      }

      list1.addAll(list2); // concatenate lists
      list2 = null; // release resources
      printList(list1); // print list1 elements

      convertToUppercaseStrings(list1); // convert to uppercase string
      printList(list1); // print list1 elements

      System.out.printf("%nDeleting elements 4 to 6...");
      removeItems(list1, 4, 7); // remove items 4-6 from list
      printList(list1); // print list1 elements
      printReversedList(list1); // print list in reverse order
   }

   // output List contents
   private static void printList(List<String> list) {
      System.out.printf("%nlist:%n");

      for (String color : list) {
         System.out.printf("%s ", color);
      }

      System.out.println();
   }

   // locate String objects and convert to uppercase
   private static void convertToUppercaseStrings(List<String> list) {
      ListIterator<String> iterator = list.listIterator();

      while (iterator.hasNext()) {
         String color = iterator.next(); // get item
         iterator.set(color.toUpperCase()); // convert to upper case
      }
   }

```

Fig. 16.3 | Lists, LinkedLists and ListIterators. (Part 2 of 3.)

```
61    // obtain sublist and use clear method to delete sublist items
62    private static void removeItems(List<String> list,
63       int start, int end) {
64       list.subList(start, end).clear(); // remove items
65    }
66
67    // print reversed list
68    private static void printReversedList(List<String> list) {
69       ListIterator<String> iterator = list.listIterator(list.size());
70
71       System.out.printf("%nReversed List:%n");
72
73       // print list in reverse order
74       while (iterator.hasPrevious()) {
75          System.out.printf("%s ", iterator.previous());
76       }
77    }
78 }
```

```
list:
black yellow green blue violet silver gold white brown blue gray silver

list:
BLACK YELLOW GREEN BLUE VIOLET SILVER GOLD WHITE BROWN BLUE GRAY SILVER

Deleting elements 4 to 6...
list:
BLACK YELLOW GREEN BLUE WHITE BROWN BLUE GRAY SILVER

Reversed List:
SILVER GRAY BLUE BROWN WHITE BLUE GREEN YELLOW BLACK
```

Fig. 16.3 | Lists, LinkedLists and ListIterators. (Part 3 of 3.)

Lines 12 and 21 create LinkedLists list1 and list2 of type String. LinkedList is a generic class that has one type parameter, for which we specify the type argument String in this example. Lines 14–16 and 23–25 call List method add to *append* elements from arrays colors and colors2 to the *ends* of list1 and list2, respectively.

Line 27 calls **List method addAll** to *append all elements* of list2 to the end of list1. Line 28 sets list2 to null, because list2 is no longer needed. Line 29 calls method printList (lines 41–49) to output list1's contents. Line 31 calls method convertToUppercaseStrings (lines 52–59) to convert each String element to uppercase, then line 32 calls printList again to display the modified Strings. Line 35 calls method removeItems (lines 62–65) to remove the range of elements starting at index 4 up to, but not including, index 7 of the list. Line 37 calls method printReversedList (lines 68–77) to print the list in reverse order.

Method convertToUppercaseStrings

Method convertToUppercaseStrings (lines 52–59) changes lowercase String elements in its List argument to uppercase Strings. Line 53 calls **List method listIterator** to get the List's **bidirectional iterator** (i.e., one that can traverse a List *backward* or *for-*

ward). ListIterator is also a generic class. In this example, the ListIterator references String objects, because method listIterator is called on a List of Strings. Line 55 calls method hasNext to determine whether the List *contains another element*. Line 56 gets the next String in the List. Line 57 calls **String method toUpperCase** to get an uppercase version of the String and calls **ListIterator method set** to replace the current String to which iterator refers with the String returned by method toUpperCase. Like method toUpperCase, **String method toLowerCase** returns a lowercase version of the String.

Method removeItems

Method removeItems (lines 62–65) *removes a range of items* from the list. Line 64 calls **List method subList** to obtain a portion of the List (called a **sublist**). This is called a **range-view method**, which enables the program to view a portion of the list. The sublist is simply a view into the List on which subList is called. Method subList takes as arguments the beginning and ending index for the sublist. The ending index is *not* part of the range of the sublist. In this example, line 35 passes 4 for the beginning index and 7 for the ending index to subList. The sublist returned is the set of elements with indices 4 through 6. Next, the program calls **List method clear** on the sublist to remove the elements of the sublist from the List. Any changes made to a sublist are also made to the original List.

Method printReversedList

Method printReversedList (lines 68–77) prints the list backward. Line 69 calls List method listIterator with the starting position as an argument (in our case, the last element in the list) to get a *bidirectional iterator* for the list. **List method size** returns the number of items in the List. The while condition (line 74) calls **ListIterator's hasPrevious method** to determine whether there are more elements while traversing the list *backward*. Line 75 calls **ListIterator's previous method** to get the previous element from the list and outputs it to the standard output stream.

Views into Collections and Arrays *Method* asList

Class Arrays provides static method **asList** to *view* an array (sometimes called the **backing array**) as a **List** collection. A List view allows you to manipulate the array as if it were a list. This is useful for adding the elements in an array to a collection and for sorting array elements. The next example demonstrates how to create a LinkedList with a List view of an array, because we cannot pass the array to a LinkedList constructor. Sorting array elements with a List view is demonstrated in Fig. 16.7. Any modifications made through the List view change the array, and any modifications made to the array change the List view. The only operation permitted on the view returned by asList is *set*, which changes the value of the view and the backing array. Any other attempts to change the view (such as adding or removing elements) result in an **UnsupportedOperationException**.

Viewing Arrays as Lists *and Converting* Lists *to Arrays*

Figure 16.4 uses Arrays method asList to view an array as a List and uses **List method toArray** to get an array from a LinkedList collection. The program calls method asList to create a List view of an array, which is used to initialize a LinkedList object, then adds a series of Strings to the LinkedList and calls method toArray to obtain an array containing references to the Strings.

```
1  // Fig. 16.4: UsingToArray.java
2  // Viewing arrays as Lists and converting Lists to arrays.
3  import java.util.LinkedList;
4  import java.util.Arrays;
5
6  public class UsingToArray {
7     public static void main(String[] args) {
8        String[] colors = {"black", "blue", "yellow"};
9        LinkedList<String> links = new LinkedList<>(Arrays.asList(colors));
10
11       links.addLast("red"); // add as last item
12       links.add("pink"); // add to the end
13       links.add(3, "green"); // add at 3rd index
14       links.addFirst("cyan"); // add as first item
15
16       // get LinkedList elements as an array
17       colors = links.toArray(new String[links.size()]);
18
19       System.out.println("colors: ");
20
21       for (String color : colors) {
22          System.out.println(color);
23       }
24    }
25 }
```

```
colors:
cyan
black
blue
yellow
green
red
pink
```

Fig. 16.4 | Viewing arrays as `Lists` and converting `Lists` to arrays.

Line 9 constructs a `LinkedList` of `Strings` containing the elements of array `colors`. `Arrays` method `asList` returns a `List` view of the array, then uses that to initialize the `LinkedList` with its constructor that receives a `Collection` as an argument (a `List` *is a* `Collection`). Line 11 calls **`LinkedList` method `addLast`** to add `"red"` to the end of `links`. Lines 12–13 call **`LinkedList` method `add`** to add `"pink"` as the last element and `"green"` as the element at index `3` (i.e., the fourth element). Method `addLast` works identically to the single-argument `add` method. Line 14 calls **`LinkedList` method `addFirst`** to add `"cyan"` as the new first item in the `LinkedList`. The `add` operations are permitted because they operate on the `LinkedList` object, not the view returned by `asList`. [*Note:* When `"cyan"` is added as the first element, `"green"` becomes the fifth element in the `LinkedList`.]

Line 17 calls interface `List`'s `toArray` method to get a `String` array from `links`. The array is a copy of the list's elements—modifying the array's contents does *not* modify the list. The array passed to method `toArray` is of the type that you'd like method `toArray` to return. If the number of elements in that array is greater than or equal to the number of elements in the `LinkedList`, `toArray` copies the list's elements into its array argument and returns that array. If the LinkedList has more elements than the number of elements in the array passed to toArray, toArray *allocates a new array* of the same type it receives as an argument, *copies* the list's elements into the new array and returns the new array.

Common Programming Error 16.2

Passing an array that contains data as toArray's argument can cause logic errors. If the array's number of elements is smaller than the number of elements in the list on which toArray is called, a new array is allocated to store the list's elements—without preserving the array argument's elements. *If the array's number of elements is greater than the number of elements in the list, the array's elements (starting at index zero) are overwritten with the list's elements. The first element of the remainder of the array is set to null to indicate the end of the list.*

16.7 Collections Methods

Class Collections provides several high-performance algorithms for manipulating collection elements. The algorithms (Fig. 16.5) are implemented as static methods. The methods sort, binarySearch, reverse, shuffle, fill and copy operate on Lists. Methods min, max, addAll, frequency and disjoint operate on Collections.

Software Engineering Observation 16.4

The collections framework methods are polymorphic. That is, each can operate on objects that implement specific interfaces, regardless of the underlying implementations.

Method	Description
sort	Sorts the elements of a List.
binarySearch	Locates an object in a List, using the efficient binary search algorithm which we introduced in Section 7.15 and discuss in detail in Section 19.4.
reverse	Reverses the elements of a List.
shuffle	Randomly orders a List's elements.
fill	Sets every List element to refer to a specified object.
copy	Copies references from one List into another.
min	Returns the smallest element in a Collection.
max	Returns the largest element in a Collection.
addAll	Appends all elements in an array to a Collection.
frequency	Calculates how many collection elements are equal to the specified element.
disjoint	Determines whether two collections have no elements in common.

Fig. 16.5 | Some Collections methods.

16.7.1 Method sort

Method **sort** sorts the elements of a List. The elements' type must implement interface **Comparable**. The order is determined by the natural order of the elements' type as implemented by a compareTo method. For example, the natural order for numeric values is ascending order, and the natural order for Strings is based on their lexicographical ordering (Section 14.3). Method compareTo is declared in interface Comparable and is sometimes called the **natural comparison method**. The sort call may specify as a second argument a **Comparator** object that determines an alternative ordering of the elements.

Sorting in Ascending Order

Figure 16.6 uses Collections method sort to order the elements of a List in *ascending* order (line 15). Line 12 creates list as a List of Strings. Lines 13 and 16 each use an *implicit* call to the list's toString method to output the list contents in the format shown in the output.

```
1  // Fig. 16.6: Sort1.java
2  // Collections method sort.
3  import java.util.List;
4  import java.util.Arrays;
5  import java.util.Collections;
6
7  public class Sort1 {
8     public static void main(String[] args) {
9        String[] suits = {"Hearts", "Diamonds", "Clubs", "Spades"};
10
11       // Create and display a list containing the suits array elements
12       List<String> list = Arrays.asList(suits);
13       System.out.printf("Unsorted array elements: %s%n", list);
14
15       Collections.sort(list); // sort ArrayList
16       System.out.printf("Sorted array elements: %s%n", list);
17    }
18 }
```

```
Unsorted array elements: [Hearts, Diamonds, Clubs, Spades]
Sorted array elements: [Clubs, Diamonds, Hearts, Spades]
```

Fig. 16.6 | Collections method sort.

Sorting in Descending Order

Figure 16.7 sorts the same list of strings used in Fig. 16.6 in *descending* order. The example introduces the Comparator interface, which is used for sorting a Collection's elements in a different order. Line 16 calls Collections's method sort to order the List in descending order. The **static Collections method reverseOrder** returns a Comparator object that orders the collection's elements in reverse order. Because the collection being sorted is a List<String>, reverseOrder returns a Comparator<String>.

```
1  // Fig. 16.7: Sort2.java
2  // Using a Comparator object with method sort.
3  import java.util.List;
```

Fig. 16.7 | Collections method sort with a Comparator object. (Part 1 of 2.)

```java
import java.util.Arrays;
import java.util.Collections;

public class Sort2 {
   public static void main(String[] args) {
      String[] suits = {"Hearts", "Diamonds", "Clubs", "Spades"};

      // Create and display a list containing the suits array elements
      List<String> list = Arrays.asList(suits); // create List
      System.out.printf("Unsorted array elements: %s%n", list);

      // sort in descending order using a comparator
      Collections.sort(list, Collections.reverseOrder());
      System.out.printf("Sorted list elements: %s%n", list);
   }
}
```

```
Unsorted array elements: [Hearts, Diamonds, Clubs, Spades]
Sorted list elements: [Spades, Hearts, Diamonds, Clubs]
```

Fig. 16.7 | `Collections` method `sort` with a `Comparator` object. (Part 2 of 2.)

Sorting with a `Comparator`

Figure 16.8 creates a custom `Comparator` class, named `TimeComparator`, that implements interface `Comparator` to compare two `Time2` objects. Class `Time2`, declared in Fig. 8.5, represents times with hours, minutes and seconds.

```java
// Fig. 16.8: TimeComparator.java
// Custom Comparator class that compares two Time2 objects.
import java.util.Comparator;

public class TimeComparator implements Comparator<Time2> {
   @Override
   public int compare(Time2 time1, Time2 time2) {
      int hourDifference = time1.getHour() - time2.getHour();

      if (hourDifference != 0) { // test the hour first
         return hourDifference;
      }

      int minuteDifference = time1.getMinute() - time2.getMinute();

      if (minuteDifference != 0) { // then test the minute
         return minuteDifference;
      }

      int secondDifference = time1.getSecond() - time2.getSecond();
      return secondDifference;
   }
}
```

Fig. 16.8 | Custom `Comparator` class that compares two `Time2` objects.

Class `TimeComparator` implements interface `Comparator`, a generic type that takes one type argument (in this case `Time2`). A class that implements `Comparator` must declare a `compare` method that receives two arguments and returns a *negative* integer if the first argument is *less than* the second, 0 if the arguments are *equal* or a *positive* integer if the first argument is *greater than* the second. Method `compare` (lines 6–22) performs comparisons between `Time2` objects. Line 8 calculates the difference between the hours of the two `Time2` objects. If the hours are different (line 10), then we return this value. If this value is *positive*, then the first hour is greater than the second and the first time is greater than the second. If this value is *negative*, then the first hour is less than the second and the first time is less than the second. If this value is zero, the hours are the same and we must test the minutes (and maybe the seconds) to determine which time is greater.

Figure 16.9 sorts a list using the custom `Comparator` class `TimeComparator`. Line 9 creates an `ArrayList` of `Time2` objects. Recall that both `ArrayList` and `List` are generic types and accept a type argument that specifies the element type of the collection. Lines 11–15 create five `Time2` objects and add them to this list. Line 21 calls method `sort`, passing it an object of our `TimeComparator` class (Fig. 16.8).

```
1  // Fig. 16.9: Sort3.java
2  // Collections method sort with a custom Comparator object.
3  import java.util.List;
4  import java.util.ArrayList;
5  import java.util.Collections;
6
7  public class Sort3 {
8     public static void main(String[] args) {
9        List<Time2> list = new ArrayList<>(); // create List
10
11       list.add(new Time2(6, 24, 34));
12       list.add(new Time2(18, 14, 58));
13       list.add(new Time2(6, 5, 34));
14       list.add(new Time2(12, 14, 58));
15       list.add(new Time2(6, 24, 22));
16
17       // output List elements
18       System.out.printf("Unsorted array elements:%n%s%n", list);
19
20       // sort in order using a comparator
21       Collections.sort(list, new TimeComparator());
22
23       // output List elements
24       System.out.printf("Sorted list elements:%n%s%n", list);
25    }
26 }
```

```
Unsorted array elements:
[6:24:34 AM, 6:14:58 PM, 6:05:34 AM, 12:14:58 PM, 6:24:22 AM]
Sorted list elements:
[6:05:34 AM, 6:24:22 AM, 6:24:34 AM, 12:14:58 PM, 6:14:58 PM]
```

Fig. 16.9 | `Collections` method `sort` with a custom `Comparator` object.

16.7.2 Method shuffle

Method **shuffle** randomly orders a List's elements. Chapter 7 presented a card shuffling and dealing simulation that shuffled a deck of cards with a loop. Figure 16.10 uses method shuffle to shuffle a deck of Card objects that might be used in a card-game simulator.

Class Card (lines 8–32) represents a card in a deck of cards. Each Card has a face and a suit. Lines 9–11 declare two enum types—Face and Suit—which represent the face and the suit of the card, respectively. Method toString (lines 29–31) returns a String containing the face and suit of the Card separated by the string " of ". When an enum constant is converted to a String, the constant's identifier is used as the String representation. Normally we would use all uppercase letters for enum constants. In this example, we chose to use capital letters for only the first letter of each enum constant because we want the card to be displayed with initial capital letters for the face and the suit (e.g., "Ace of Spades").

```
1  // Fig. 16.10: DeckOfCards.java
2  // Card shuffling and dealing with Collections method shuffle.
3  import java.util.List;
4  import java.util.Arrays;
5  import java.util.Collections;
6
7  // class to represent a Card in a deck of cards
8  class Card {
9     public enum Face {Ace, Deuce, Three, Four, Five, Six,
10       Seven, Eight, Nine, Ten, Jack, Queen, King }
11    public enum Suit {Clubs, Diamonds, Hearts, Spades}
12
13    private final Face face;
14    private final Suit suit;
15
16    // constructor
17    public Card(Face face, Suit suit) {
18        this.face = face;
19        this.suit = suit;
20    }
21
22    // return face of the card
23    public Face getFace() {return face;}
24
25    // return suit of Card
26    public Suit getSuit() {return suit;}
27
28    // return String representation of Card
29    public String toString() {
30       return String.format("%s of %s", face, suit);
31    }
32 }
33
34 // class DeckOfCards declaration
35 public class DeckOfCards {
36    private List<Card> list; // declare List that will store Cards
```

Fig. 16.10 | Card shuffling and dealing with Collections method shuffle. (Part 1 of 2.)

```
37
38      // set up deck of Cards and shuffle
39      public DeckOfCards() {
40         Card[] deck = new Card[52];
41         int count = 0; // number of cards
42
43         // populate deck with Card objects
44         for (Card.Suit suit : Card.Suit.values()) {
45            for (Card.Face face : Card.Face.values()) {
46               deck[count] = new Card(face, suit);
47               ++count;
48            }
49         }
50
51         list = Arrays.asList(deck); // get List
52         Collections.shuffle(list);  // shuffle deck
53      }
54
55      // output deck
56      public void printCards() {
57         // display 52 cards in four columns
58         for (int i = 0; i < list.size(); i++) {
59            System.out.printf("%-19s%s", list.get(i),
60               ((i + 1) % 4 == 0) ? System.lineSeparator() : "");
61         }
62      }
63
64      public static void main(String[] args) {
65         DeckOfCards cards = new DeckOfCards();
66         cards.printCards();
67      }
68   }
```

```
Deuce of Clubs     Six of Spades      Nine of Diamonds   Ten of Hearts
Three of Diamonds  Five of Clubs      Deuce of Diamonds  Seven of Clubs
Three of Spades    Six of Diamonds    King of Clubs      Jack of Hearts
Ten of Spades      King of Diamonds   Eight of Spades    Six of Hearts
Nine of Clubs      Ten of Diamonds    Eight of Diamonds  Eight of Hearts
Ten of Clubs       Five of Hearts     Ace of Clubs       Deuce of Hearts
Queen of Diamonds  Ace of Diamonds    Four of Clubs      Nine of Hearts
Ace of Spades      Deuce of Spades    Ace of Hearts      Jack of Diamonds
Seven of Diamonds  Three of Hearts    Four of Spades     Four of Diamonds
Seven of Spades    King of Hearts     Seven of Hearts    Five of Diamonds
Eight of Clubs     Three of Clubs     Queen of Clubs     Queen of Spades
Six of Clubs       Nine of Spades     Four of Hearts     Jack of Clubs
Five of Spades     King of Spades     Jack of Spades     Queen of Hearts
```

Fig. 16.10 | Card shuffling and dealing with `Collections` method `shuffle`. (Part 2 of 2.)

Lines 44–49 populate the `deck` array with cards that have unique face and suit combinations. Both `Face` and `Suit` are `public static enum` types of class `Card`. To use these `enum` types outside of class `Card`, you must qualify each `enum`'s type name with the name of the class in which it resides (i.e., `Card`) and a dot (`.`) separator. Hence, lines 44 and 45 use `Card.Suit` and `Card.Face` to declare the control variables of the `for` statements. Recall that method values of an enum type returns an array that contains all the constants of the enum type. Lines 44–49 use enhanced for statements to construct 52 new Cards.

The shuffling occurs in line 52, which calls static Collections method shuffle to shuffle the Cards. Method shuffle requires a List argument, so we must obtain a List view of the array before we can shuffle it. Line 51 invokes static method asList of class Arrays to get a List view of the deck array.

Method printCards (lines 56–62) displays the deck of cards in four columns. In each iteration of the loop, lines 59–60 output a card left-justified in a 19-character field followed by either a newline or an empty string based on the number of cards output so far. If the number of cards is divisible by 4, a newline is output; otherwise, the empty string is output. Note that line 60 uses System method **lineSeparator** to get the platform-independent newline character to output after every four cards.

16.7.3 Methods reverse, fill, copy, max and min

Class Collections provides methods for *reversing*, *filling* and *copying* Lists. **Collections method reverse** reverses the order of the elements in a List, and **method fill** *overwrites* elements in a List with a specified value. The fill operation is useful for reinitializing a List. **Method copy** takes two arguments—a destination List and a source List. Each element in the source List is copied to the destination List. The destination List must be at least as long as the source List; otherwise, an IndexOutOfBoundsException occurs. If the destination List is longer, the elements not overwritten are unchanged.

Each method we've seen so far operates on Lists. Methods **min** and **max** each operate on any Collection. Method min returns the smallest element in a Collection, and method max returns the largest element in a Collection. Both of these methods can be called with a Comparator object as a second argument to perform *custom comparisons* of objects, such as the TimeComparator in Fig. 16.9. Figure 16.11 demonstrates methods reverse, fill, copy, max and min.

```
// Fig. 16.11: Algorithms1.java
// Collections methods reverse, fill, copy, max and min.
import java.util.List;
import java.util.Arrays;
import java.util.Collections;

public class Algorithms1 {
   public static void main(String[] args) {
      // create and display a List<Character>
      Character[] letters = {'P', 'C', 'M'};
      List<Character> list = Arrays.asList(letters); // get List
      System.out.println("list contains: ");
      output(list);

      // reverse and display the List<Character>
      Collections.reverse(list); // reverse order the elements
      System.out.printf("%nAfter calling reverse, list contains:%n");
      output(list);

```

Fig. 16.11 | Collections methods reverse, fill, copy, max and min. (Part 1 of 2.)

```
20        // create copyList from an array of 3 Characters
21        Character[] lettersCopy = new Character[3];
22        List<Character> copyList = Arrays.asList(lettersCopy);
23
24        // copy the contents of list into copyList
25        Collections.copy(copyList, list);
26        System.out.printf("%nAfter copying, copyList contains:%n");
27        output(copyList);
28
29        // fill list with Rs
30        Collections.fill(list, 'R');
31        System.out.printf("%nAfter calling fill, list contains:%n");
32        output(list);
33     }
34
35     // output List information
36     private static void output(List<Character> listRef) {
37        System.out.print("The list is: ");
38
39        for (Character element : listRef) {
40           System.out.printf("%s ", element);
41        }
42
43        System.out.printf("%nMax: %s", Collections.max(listRef));
44        System.out.printf("  Min: %s%n", Collections.min(listRef));
45     }
46  }
```

```
list contains:
The list is: P C M
Max: P  Min: C

After calling reverse, list contains:
The list is: M C P
Max: P  Min: C

After copying, copyList contains:
The list is: M C P
Max: P  Min: C

After calling fill, list contains:
The list is: R R R
Max: R  Min: R
```

Fig. 16.11 | Collections methods reverse, fill, copy, max and min. (Part 2 of 2.)

Line 11 creates List<Character> variable list and initializes it with a List view of the Character array letters. Lines 12–13 output the current contents of the List. Line 16 calls Collections method reverse to reverse the order of list. Method reverse takes one List argument. Since list is a List view of the array letters, the array's elements are now in reverse order. The reversed contents are output in lines 17–18. Line 25 uses Collections method copy to copy list's elements into copyList. Changes to copyList do not change letters, because copyList is a separate List that's not a List view of the array letters. Method copy requires two List arguments—the destination List and the source List. Line 30 calls Collections method fill to place the character 'R' in each list element. Because list is a List view of the array letters, this operation changes each element in letters to 'R'. Method fill requires a List for the first argument and an object of the List's element type for the second argument—in this case, the object is the *boxed* Character version of 'R'. Lines 43–44 in method output call Collections methods max and min to find the largest and the smallest element of a Collection, respectively. Recall that interface List extends interface Collection, so a List *is a* Collection.

16.7.4 Method binarySearch

The high-speed binary search algorithm—which we discuss in detail in Section 19.4—is built into the Java collections framework as a static **Collections method binarySearch**. This method locates an object in a List (e.g., a LinkedList or an ArrayList). If the object is found, its index is returned. If the object is not found, binarySearch returns a negative value. Method binarySearch determines this negative value by first calculating the insertion point and making its sign negative. Then, binarySearch subtracts 1 from the insertion point to obtain the return value, which guarantees that method binarySearch returns positive numbers (>= 0) if and only if the object is found. If multiple elements in the list match the search key, there's no guarantee which one will be located first. Figure 16.12 uses method binarySearch to search for a series of strings in an ArrayList.

```java
// Fig. 16.12: BinarySearchTest.java
// Collections method binarySearch.
import java.util.List;
import java.util.Arrays;
import java.util.Collections;
import java.util.ArrayList;

public class BinarySearchTest {
   public static void main(String[] args) {
      // create an ArrayList<String> from the contents of colors array
      String[] colors = {"red", "white", "blue", "black", "yellow",
         "purple", "tan", "pink"};
      List<String> list = new ArrayList<>(Arrays.asList(colors));

      Collections.sort(list); // sort the ArrayList
      System.out.printf("Sorted ArrayList: %s%n", list);

      // search list for various values
      printSearchResults(list, "black");
      printSearchResults(list, "red");
      printSearchResults(list, "pink");
      printSearchResults(list, "aqua"); // below lowest
      printSearchResults(list, "gray"); // does not exist
      printSearchResults(list, "teal"); // does not exist
   }

```

Fig. 16.12 | Collections method binarySearch. (Part 1 of 2.)

```
27      // perform search and display result
28      private static void printSearchResults(
29         List<String> list, String key) {
30
31         System.out.printf("%nSearching for: %s%n", key);
32         int result = Collections.binarySearch(list, key);
33
34         if (result >= 0) {
35            System.out.printf("Found at index %d%n", result);
36         }
37         else {
38            System.out.printf("Not Found (%d)%n",result);
39         }
40      }
41   }
```

```
Sorted ArrayList: [black, blue, pink, purple, red, tan, white, yellow]

Searching for: black
Found at index 0

Searching for: red
Found at index 4

Searching for: pink
Found at index 2

Searching for: aqua
Not Found (-1)

Searching for: gray
Not Found (-3)

Searching for: teal
Not Found (-7)
```

Fig. 16.12 | `Collections` method `binarySearch`. (Part 2 of 2.)

Line 13 initializes `list` with an `ArrayList` containing a copy of the elements in array `colors`. `Collections` method `binarySearch` expects its `List` argument's elements to be sorted in *ascending* order, so line 15 uses `Collections` method `sort` to sort the list. If the `List` argument's elements are *not* sorted, `binarySearch`'s result is *undefined*. Line 16 outputs the sorted list. Lines 19–24 call method `printSearchResults` (lines 28–41) to perform searches and output the results. Line 32 calls `Collections` method `binarySearch` to search `list` for the specified `key`. Method `binarySearch` takes a `List` as the first argument and the search key as the second argument. Lines 34–39 output the results of the search. An overloaded version of `binarySearch` takes a `Comparator` object as its third argument, which specifies how `binarySearch` should compare the search key to the `List`'s elements.

16.7.5 Methods `addAll`, `frequency` and `disjoint`

Class `Collections` also provides the methods `addAll`, `frequency` and `disjoint`. **`Collections` method `addAll`** takes two arguments—a `Collection` into which to *insert* the new element(s) and an array (or variable-length argument list) that provides elements to be inserted. **`Collections` method `frequency`** takes two arguments—a `Collection` to be searched and an `Object` to be searched for in the collection. Method `frequency` returns the number of times that the second argument appears in the collection. **`Collections` method `disjoint`** takes two `Collection`s and returns `true` if they have *no elements in common*. Figure 16.13 demonstrates the use of methods `addAll`, `frequency` and `disjoint`.

```java
// Fig. 16.13: Algorithms2.java
// Collections methods addAll, frequency and disjoint.
import java.util.ArrayList;
import java.util.List;
import java.util.Arrays;
import java.util.Collections;

public class Algorithms2 {
   public static void main(String[] args) {
      // initialize list1 and list2
      String[] colors = {"red", "white", "yellow", "blue"};
      List<String> list1 = Arrays.asList(colors);
      ArrayList<String> list2 = new ArrayList<>();

      list2.add("black"); // add "black" to the end of list2
      list2.add("red"); // add "red" to the end of list2
      list2.add("green"); // add "green" to the end of list2

      System.out.print("Before addAll, list2 contains: ");

      // display elements in list2
      for (String s : list2) {
         System.out.printf("%s ", s);
      }

      Collections.addAll(list2, colors); // add colors Strings to list2

      System.out.printf("%nAfter addAll, list2 contains: ");

      // display elements in list2
      for (String s : list2) {
         System.out.printf("%s ", s);
      }

      // get frequency of "red"
      int frequency = Collections.frequency(list2, "red");
      System.out.printf("%nFrequency of red in list2: %d%n", frequency);

      // check whether list1 and list2 have elements in common
      boolean disjoint = Collections.disjoint(list1, list2);

      System.out.printf("list1 and list2 %s elements in common%n",
         (disjoint ? "do not have" : "have"));
   }
}
```

Fig. 16.13 | `Collections` methods `addAll`, `frequency` and `disjoint`. (Part 1 of 2.)

```
Before addAll, list2 contains: black red green
After addAll, list2 contains: black red green red white yellow blue
Frequency of red in list2: 2
list1 and list2 have elements in common
```

Fig. 16.13 | `Collections` methods `addAll`, `frequency` and `disjoint`. (Part 2 of 2.)

Line 12 initializes `list1` with elements in array `colors`, and lines 15–17 add `Strings` `"black"`, `"red"` and `"green"` to `list2`. Line 26 invokes method `addAll` to add elements in array `colors` to `list2`. Line 36 gets the frequency of `String` `"red"` in `list2` using method `frequency`. Line 40 invokes method `disjoint` to test whether `Collections` `list1` and `list2` have elements in common, which they do in this example.

16.8 Class PriorityQueue and Interface Queue

Recall that a queue is a collection that represents a waiting line—typically, *insertions* are made at the back of a queue and *deletions* are made from the front. In Section 21.6, we'll discuss and implement a queue data structure. In Chapter 23, Concurrency, we'll use concurrent queues. In this section, we investigate Java's **`Queue`** interface and **`PriorityQueue`** class from package `java.util`. Interface `Queue` extends interface `Collection` and provides additional operations for *inserting*, *removing* and *inspecting* elements in a queue. `PriorityQueue`, which implements the `Queue` interface, orders elements by their natural ordering as specified by `Comparable` elements' `compareTo` method or by a `Comparator` object that's supplied to the constructor.

Class `PriorityQueue` provides functionality that enables *insertions in sorted order* into the underlying data structure and *deletions* from the *front* of the underlying data structure. When adding elements to a `PriorityQueue`, the elements are inserted in priority order such that the *highest-priority element* (i.e., the largest value) will be the first element removed from the `PriorityQueue`.

The common `PriorityQueue` operations are **`offer`** to *insert* an element at the appropriate location based on priority order, **`poll`** to *remove* the highest-priority element of the priority queue (i.e., the head of the queue), **`peek`** to get a reference to the highest-priority element of the priority queue (without removing that element), **`clear`** to *remove all elements* in the priority queue and **`size`** to get the number of elements in the priority queue.

Figure 16.14 demonstrates class `PriorityQueue`. Line 8 creates a `PriorityQueue` that stores `Doubles` with an *initial capacity* of `11` elements and orders the elements according to the object's natural ordering (the defaults for a `PriorityQueue`). `PriorityQueue` is a generic class. Line 8 instantiates a `PriorityQueue` with a type argument `Double`. Class `PriorityQueue` provides several additional constructors. One of these takes an `int` and a `Comparator` object to create a `PriorityQueue` with the *initial capacity* specified by the `int` and the *ordering* by the `Comparator`. Lines 11–13 use method `offer` to add elements to the priority queue. Method `offer` throws a `NullPointerException` if the program attempts to add a `null` object to the queue. The loop in lines 18–21 uses method `size` to determine whether the priority queue is *empty* (line 18). While there are more elements, line 19 uses `PriorityQueue` method `peek` to retrieve the *highest-priority element* in the queue for output (*without* actually removing it from the queue). Line 20 removes the highest-priority element in the queue with method `poll`, which returns the removed element.

```
// Fig. 16.14: PriorityQueueTest.java
// PriorityQueue test program.
import java.util.PriorityQueue;

public class PriorityQueueTest {
   public static void main(String[] args) {
      // queue of capacity 11
      PriorityQueue<Double> queue = new PriorityQueue<>();

      // insert elements to queue
      queue.offer(3.2);
      queue.offer(9.8);
      queue.offer(5.4);

      System.out.print("Polling from queue: ");

      // display elements in queue
      while (queue.size() > 0) {
         System.out.printf("%.1f ", queue.peek()); // view top element
         queue.poll(); // remove top element
      }
   }
}
```

```
Polling from queue: 3.2 5.4 9.8
```

Fig. 16.14 | `PriorityQueue` test program.

16.9 Sets

A `Set` is a collection of unique elements (i.e., no duplicates). The collections framework contains several `Set` implementations, including **`HashSet`** and **`TreeSet`**. `HashSet` stores its elements (unordered) in a *hash table*, and `TreeSet` stores its elements (ordered) in a *tree*. Hash tables are presented in Section 16.10. Trees are discussed in Section 21.7. Figure 16.15 uses a `HashSet` to *remove duplicate strings* from a `List`. Recall that both `List` and `Collection` are generic types, so line 14 creates a `List` that contains `String` objects, and line 18 passes the collection to method `printNonDuplicates` (lines 22–33), which takes a `Collection` argument. Line 24 constructs a `HashSet<String>` from the `Collection<String>` argument. By definition, `Set`s do *not* contain duplicates, so when the `HashSet` is constructed, it *removes any duplicates* in the `Collection`. Lines 28–30 output elements in the `Set`.

```
1  // Fig. 16.15: SetTest.java
2  // HashSet used to remove duplicate values from array of strings.
3  import java.util.List;
4  import java.util.Arrays;
5  import java.util.HashSet;
6  import java.util.Set;
7  import java.util.Collection;
```

Fig. 16.15 | `HashSet` used to remove duplicate values from an array of strings. (Part 1 of 2.)

```

public class SetTest {
   public static void main(String[] args) {
      // create and display a List<String>
      String[] colors = {"red", "white", "blue", "green", "gray",
         "orange", "tan", "white", "cyan", "peach", "gray", "orange"};
      List<String> list = Arrays.asList(colors);
      System.out.printf("List: %s%n", list);

      // eliminate duplicates then print the unique values
      printNonDuplicates(list);
   }

   // create a Set from a Collection to eliminate duplicates
   private static void printNonDuplicates(Collection<String> values) {
      // create a HashSet
      Set<String> set = new HashSet<>(values);

      System.out.printf("%nNonduplicates are: ");

      for (String value : set) {
         System.out.printf("%s ", value);
      }

      System.out.println();
   }
}
```

```
List: [red, white, blue, green, gray, orange, tan, white, cyan, peach, gray,
orange]

Nonduplicates are: tan green peach cyan red orange gray white blue
```

Fig. 16.15 | `HashSet` used to remove duplicate values from an array of strings. (Part 2 of 2.)

Sorted Sets

The collections framework also includes the **`SortedSet` interface** (which extends `Set`) for sets that maintain their elements in *sorted* order—either the *elements' natural order* (e.g., numbers are in *ascending* order) or an order specified by a `Comparator`. Class `TreeSet` implements `SortedSet`. The program in Fig. 16.16 places `Strings` into a `TreeSet`. The `Strings` are sorted as they're added to the `TreeSet`. This example also demonstrates *range-view* methods, which enable a program to view a portion of a collection.

```
// Fig. 16.16: SortedSetTest.java
// Using SortedSets and TreeSets.
import java.util.Arrays;
import java.util.SortedSet;
import java.util.TreeSet;

```

Fig. 16.16 | Using `SortedSets` and `TreeSets`. (Part 1 of 2.)

```
 7  public class SortedSetTest {
 8     public static void main(String[] args) {
 9        // create TreeSet from array colors
10        String[] colors = {"yellow", "green", "black", "tan", "grey",
11           "white", "orange", "red", "green"};
12        SortedSet<String> tree = new TreeSet<>(Arrays.asList(colors));
13
14        System.out.print("sorted set: ");
15        printSet(tree);
16
17        // get headSet based on "orange"
18        System.out.print("headSet (\"orange\"):  ");
19        printSet(tree.headSet("orange"));
20
21        // get tailSet based upon "orange"
22        System.out.print("tailSet (\"orange\"):  ");
23        printSet(tree.tailSet("orange"));
24
25        // get first and last elements
26        System.out.printf("first: %s%n", tree.first());
27        System.out.printf("last : %s%n", tree.last());
28     }
29
30     // output SortedSet using enhanced for statement
31     private static void printSet(SortedSet<String> set) {
32        for (String s : set) {
33           System.out.printf("%s ", s);
34        }
35
36        System.out.println();
37     }
38  }
```

```
sorted set: black green grey orange red tan white yellow
headSet ("orange"):  black green grey
tailSet ("orange"):  orange red tan white yellow
first: black
last : yellow
```

Fig. 16.16 | Using SortedSets and TreeSets. (Part 2 of 2.)

Line 12 creates a TreeSet<String> that contains the elements of array colors, then assigns the new TreeSet<String> to SortedSet<String> variable tree. Line 15 outputs the initial set of strings using method printSet (lines 31–37), which we discuss momentarily. Line 19 calls **TreeSet method headSet** to get a subset of the TreeSet in which every element is less than "orange". The view returned from headSet is then output with printSet. If any changes are made to the subset, they'll *also* be made to the original TreeSet, because the subset returned by headSet is a view of the TreeSet.

Line 23 calls **TreeSet method tailSet** to get a subset in which each element is greater than or equal to "orange", then outputs the result. Any changes made through the tailSet view are made to the original TreeSet. Lines 26–27 call **SortedSet methods first** and **last** to get the smallest and largest elements of the set, respectively.

Method `printSet` (lines 31–37) accepts a `SortedSet` as an argument and prints it. Lines 32–34 print each element of the `SortedSet` using the enhanced `for` statement.

16.10 Maps

`Maps` associate *keys* to *values*. The keys in a `Map` must be *unique*, but the associated values need not be. If a `Map` contains both unique keys and unique values, it's said to implement a **one-to-one mapping**. If only the keys are unique, the `Map` is said to implement a **many-to-one mapping**—many keys can map to one value.

`Maps` differ from `Sets` in that `Maps` contain keys and values, whereas `Sets` contain only values. Two classes that implement interface `Map` are **`HashMap`** and **`TreeMap`**. `HashMaps` store elements in hash tables, and `TreeMaps` store elements in trees. This section discusses hash tables and provides an example that uses a `HashMap` to store key–value pairs. **Interface `SortedMap`** extends `Map` and maintains its keys in *sorted* order—either the elements' *natural* order or an order specified by a `Comparator`. Class `TreeMap` implements `SortedMap`.

`Map` *Implementation with Hash Tables*

When a program creates objects, it may need to store and retrieve them efficiently. Storing and retrieving information with arrays is efficient if some aspect of your data directly matches a numerical key value and if the *keys are unique* and tightly packed. If you have 100 employees with nine-digit social security numbers and you want to store and retrieve employee data by using the social security number as a key, the task will require an array with over 800 million elements, because nine-digit Social Security numbers must begin with 001–899 (excluding 666) as per the Social Security Administration's website

```
http://www.socialsecurity.gov/employer/randomization.html
```

This is impractical for virtually all applications that use social security numbers as keys. A program having so large an array could achieve high performance for both storing and retrieving employee records by simply using the social security number as the array index.

Numerous applications have this problem—namely, that either the keys are of the wrong type (e.g., not positive integers that correspond to array subscripts) or they're of the right type, but *sparsely* spread over a *huge range*. What is needed is a high-speed scheme for converting keys such as social security numbers, inventory part numbers and the like into unique array indices. Then, when an application needs to store something, the scheme can convert the application's key rapidly into an index, and the record can be stored at that slot in the array. Retrieval is accomplished the same way: Once the application has a key for which it wants to retrieve a data record, the application simply applies the conversion to the key—this produces the array index where the data is stored and retrieved.

The scheme we describe here is the basis of a technique called **hashing**. Why the name? When we convert a key into an array index, we literally scramble the bits, forming a kind of "mishmashed," or hashed, number. The number actually has no real significance beyond its usefulness in storing and retrieving a particular data record.

A glitch in the scheme is called a **collision**—this occurs when two different keys "hash into" the same cell (or element) in the array. We cannot store two values in the same space, so we need to find an alternative home for all values beyond the first that hash to a particular array index. There are many schemes for doing this. One is to "hash again" (i.e., to apply another hashing transformation to the key to provide the next candidate cell in the array). The hashing process is designed to *distribute* the values throughout the table, so the assumption is that an available cell will be found with just a few hashes.

Another scheme uses one hash to locate the first candidate cell. If that cell is occupied, successive cells are searched in order until an available cell is found. Retrieval works the same way: The key is hashed once to determine the initial location and check whether it contains the desired data. If it does, the search is finished. If it does not, successive cells are searched linearly until the desired data is found.

The most popular solution to hash-table collisions is to have each cell of the table be a hash "bucket," typically a linked list of all the key–value pairs that hash to that cell. This is the solution that Java's `HashMap` class (from package `java.util`) uses. `HashMap` implements the `Map` interface.

A hash table's **load factor** affects the performance of hashing schemes. The load factor is the ratio of the number of occupied cells in the hash table to the total number of cells in the hash table. The closer this ratio gets to 1.0, the greater the chance of collisions.

Performance Tip 16.1

The load factor in a hash table is a classic example of a memory-space/execution-time trade-off: By increasing the load factor, we get better memory utilization, but the program runs slower, due to increased hashing collisions. By decreasing the load factor, we get better program speed, because of reduced hashing collisions, but we get poorer memory utilization, because a larger portion of the hash table remains empty.

Computer-science students study hashing schemes in courses called "Data Structures" and "Algorithms." Class `HashMap` enables you to use hashing without having to implement hash-table mechanisms—a classic example of reuse. This concept is profoundly important in our study of object-oriented programming. As discussed in earlier chapters, classes encapsulate and hide complexity (i.e., implementation details) and offer user-friendly interfaces. Properly crafting classes to exhibit such behavior is one of the most valued skills in the field of object-oriented programming. Figure 16.17 uses a `HashMap` to count the number of occurrences of each word in a string.

Line 12 creates an empty `HashMap` with a *default initial capacity* (16 elements) and a default load factor (0.75)—these defaults are built into the implementation of `HashMap`. When the number of occupied slots in the `HashMap` becomes greater than the capacity times the load factor, the capacity is doubled automatically. `HashMap` is a generic class that takes two type arguments—the type of key (i.e., `String`) and the type of value (i.e., `Integer`). Recall that the type arguments passed to a generic class must be reference types, hence the second type argument is `Integer`, not `int`.

```
1 // Fig. 16.17: WordTypeCount.java
2 // Program counts the number of occurrences of each word in a String.
3 import java.util.Map;
4 import java.util.HashMap;
5 import java.util.Set;
6 import java.util.TreeSet;
7 import java.util.Scanner;
```

Fig. 16.17 | Program counts the number of occurrences of each word in a `String`. (Part 1 of 3.)

```java

public class WordTypeCount {
   public static void main(String[] args) {
      // create HashMap to store String keys and Integer values
      Map<String, Integer> myMap = new HashMap<>();

      createMap(myMap); // create map based on user input
      displayMap(myMap); // display map content
   }

   // create map from user input
   private static void createMap(Map<String, Integer> map) {
      Scanner scanner = new Scanner(System.in); // create scanner
      System.out.println("Enter a string:"); // prompt for user input
      String input = scanner.nextLine();

      // tokenize the input
      String[] tokens = input.split(" ");

      // processing input text
      for (String token : tokens) {
         String word = token.toLowerCase(); // get lowercase word

         // if the map contains the word
         if (map.containsKey(word)) { // is word in map?
            int count = map.get(word); // get current count
            map.put(word, count + 1); // increment count
         }
         else {
            map.put(word, 1); // add new word with a count of 1 to map
         }
      }
   }

   // display map content
   private static void displayMap(Map<String, Integer> map) {
      Set<String> keys = map.keySet(); // get keys

      // sort keys
      TreeSet<String> sortedKeys = new TreeSet<>(keys);

      System.out.printf("%nMap contains:%nKey\t\tValue%n");

      // generate output for each key in map
      for (String key : sortedKeys) {
         System.out.printf("%-10s%10s%n", key, map.get(key));
      }

      System.out.printf(
         "%nsize: %d%nisEmpty: %b%n", map.size(), map.isEmpty());
   }
}
```

Fig. 16.17 | Program counts the number of occurrences of each word in a `String`. (Part 2 of 3.)

```
Enter a string:
this is a sample sentence with several words this is another sample
sentence with several different words

Map contains:
Key             Value
a                   1
another             1
different           1
is                  2
sample              2
sentence            2
several             2
this                2
with                2
words               2

size: 10
isEmpty: false
```

Fig. 16.17 | Program counts the number of occurrences of each word in a `String`. (Part 3 of 3.)

Line 14 calls method `createMap` (lines 19–40), which uses a `Map` to store the number of occurrences of each word in the sentence. Line 22 obtains the user input, and line 25 tokenizes it. For each token, lines 28–39 convert the token to lowercase letters (line 29), then call **`Map` method `containsKey`** (line 32) to determine whether the word is in the map (and thus has occurred previously in the string). If the `Map` does *not* contain the word, line 37 uses **`Map` method `put`** to create a new entry, with the word as the key and an `Integer` object containing `1` as the value. Autoboxing occurs when the program passes integer `1` to method `put`, because the map stores the number of occurrences as an `Integer`. If the word does exist in the map, line 33 uses **`Map` method `get`** to obtain the key's associated value (the count) in the map. Line 34 increments that value and uses `put` to replace the key's associated value. Method `put` returns the key's prior associated value, or `null` if the key was not in the map.

Error-Prevention Tip 16.1

Always use immutable keys with a `Map`. The key determines where the corresponding value is placed. If the key has changed since the insert operation, when you subsequently attempt to retrieve that value, it might not be found. In this chapter's examples, we use `String`s as keys and `String`s are immutable.

Method `displayMap` (lines 43–58) displays all the entries in the map. It uses **`HashMap` method `keySet`** (line 44) to get a set of the keys. The keys have type `String` in the map, so method `keySet` returns a generic type `Set` with type parameter specified to be `String`. Line 47 creates a `TreeSet` of the keys, in which the keys are sorted. Lines 52–54 access each key and its value in the map. Line 53 displays each key and its value using format specifier `%-10s` to *left align* each key and format specifier `%10s` to *right align* each value. The keys are displayed in *ascending* order. Line 57 calls **`Map` method `size`** to get the number of key–value pairs in the `Map`, and calls **`Map` method `isEmpty`**, which returns a `boolean` indicating whether the `Map` is empty.

16.11 Synchronized Collections

In Chapter 23, we discuss *multithreading*. The collections in the collections framework are *unsynchronized* by default, so they can operate efficiently when multithreading is not required. Because they're unsynchronized, however, concurrent access to a `Collection` by multiple threads could cause indeterminate results or fatal errors—as we demonstrate in Chapter 23. To prevent potential threading problems, **synchronization wrappers** are provided for collections that might be accessed by multiple threads. A **wrapper** object receives method calls, adds thread synchronization (to prevent concurrent access to the collection) and *delegates* the calls to the wrapped collection object. The `Collections` class provides `static` methods for wrapping collections as synchronized versions. Method headers for some synchronization wrappers are listed in Fig. 16.18. Details on these methods are available at `http://docs.oracle.com/javase/8/docs/api/java/util/Collections.html`. Each method takes a collection and returns its *synchronized view*. For example, the following code creates a synchronized `List` (`list2`) that stores `String` objects:

```
List<String> list1 = new ArrayList<>();
List<String> list2 = Collections.synchronizedList(list1);
```

More robust collections for concurrent access are provided in the `java.util.concurrent` package, which we introduce in Chapter 23.

`public static` method headers
`<T> Collection<T> synchronizedCollection(Collection<T> c)`
`<T> List<T> synchronizedList(List<T> aList)`
`<T> Set<T> synchronizedSet(Set<T> s)`
`<T> SortedSet<T> synchronizedSortedSet(SortedSet<T> s)`
`<K, V> Map<K, V> synchronizedMap(Map<K, V> m)`
`<K, V> SortedMap<K, V> synchronizedSortedMap(SortedMap<K, V> m)`

Fig. 16.18 | Some synchronization wrapper methods.

16.12 Unmodifiable Collections

The `Collections` class provides a set of `static` methods that create **unmodifiable wrappers** for collections. Unmodifiable wrappers throw `UnsupportedOperationExceptions` if attempts are made to modify the collection. In an unmodifiable collection, the references stored in the collection are not modifiable, but the objects they refer *are modifiable* unless they belong to an immutable class like `String`. Headers for some of these methods are listed in Fig. 16.19. Details about these methods are available at `http://docs.oracle.com/javase/8/docs/api/java/util/Collections.html`. All these methods take a generic type and return an unmodifiable view of the generic type. For example, the following code creates an unmodifiable `List` (`list2`) that stores `String` objects:

```
List<String> list1 = new ArrayList<>();
List<String> list2 = Collections.unmodifiableList(list1);
```

Software Engineering Observation 16.5

You can use an unmodifiable wrapper to create a collection that offers read-only access to others, while allowing read–write access to yourself. You do this simply by giving others a reference to the unmodifiable wrapper while retaining for yourself a reference to the original collection.

public static method headers

```
<T> Collection<T> unmodifiableCollection(Collection<T> c)
<T> List<T> unmodifiableList(List<T> aList)
<T> Set<T> unmodifiableSet(Set<T> s)
<T> SortedSet<T> unmodifiableSortedSet(SortedSet<T> s)
<K, V> Map<K, V> unmodifiableMap(Map<K, V> m)
<K, V> SortedMap<K, V> unmodifiableSortedMap(SortedMap<K, V> m)
```

Fig. 16.19 | Some unmodifiable wrapper methods.

16.13 Abstract Implementations

The collections framework provides various abstract implementations of `Collection` interfaces from which you can quickly "flesh out" complete customized implementations. These abstract implementations include a thin `Collection` implementation called an **`AbstractCollection`**, a `List` implementation that allows *array-like access* to its elements called an **`AbstractList`**, a `Map` implementation called an **`AbstractMap`**, a `List` implementation that allows *sequential access* (from beginning to end) to its elements called an **`AbstractSequentialList`**, a `Set` implementation called an **`AbstractSet`** and a `Queue` implementation called **`AbstractQueue`**. You can learn more about these classes at `http://docs.oracle.com/javase/8/docs/api/java/util/package-summary.html`. To write a *custom* implementation, you can extend the abstract implementation that best meets your needs, implement each of the class's `abstract` methods and override the class's concrete methods as necessary.

9

16.14 Java SE 9: Convenience Factory Methods for Immutable Collections[1]

Java SE 9 adds new `static` *convenience factory methods* to interfaces `List`, `Set` and `Map` that enable you to create small *immutable* collections—they cannot be modified once they are created (JEP 269). We introduced factory methods in Section 10.12—the word *factory* indicates that these methods create objects. They're *convenient* because you simply pass the elements as arguments to a convenience factory method, which creates the collection and adds the elements to the collection for you.

1. If any changes occur to the new Java SE 9 content in this section, we'll post updates on the book's website at `http://www.deitel.com/books/jhtp11`. This example requires JDK 9 to execute.

The collections returned by the unmodifiable wrappers we discussed in Section 16.12 create *immutable views* of *mutable collections*—the reference to the original mutable collection can still be used to modify the collection. The convenience factory methods instead return custom collection objects that are truly immutable and optimized to store small collections. In Chapters 17 and 23, we explain how using lambdas and streams with immutable entities can help you create "parallelizable" code that will run more efficiently on today's multi-core architectures. Figure 16.20 demonstrates these convenience factory methods for a `List`, a `Set` and two `Map`s.

Common Programming Error 16.3

Calling any method that attempts to modify a collection returned by the `List`, `Set` or `Map` convenience factory methods results in an `UnsupportedOperationException`.

Software Engineering Observation 16.6

In Java, collection elements are always references to objects. The objects referenced by an immutable collection may still be mutable.

```java
// Fig. 16.20: FactoryMethods.java
// Java SE 9 collection factory methods.
import java.util.List;
import java.util.Map;
import java.util.Set;

public class FactoryMethods {
   public static void main(String[] args) {
      // create a List
      List<String> colorList = List.of("red", "orange", "yellow",
         "green", "blue", "indigo", "violet");
      System.out.printf("colorList: %s%n%n", colorList);

      // create a Set
      Set<String> colorSet = Set.of("red", "orange", "yellow",
         "green", "blue", "indigo", "violet");
      System.out.printf("colorSet: %s%n%n", colorSet);

      // create a Map using method "of"
      Map<String, Integer> dayMap = Map.of("Monday", 1, "Tuesday", 2,
         "Wednesday", 3, "Thursday", 4, "Friday", 5, "Saturday", 6,
         "Sunday", 7);
      System.out.printf("dayMap: %s%n%n", dayMap);

      // create a Map using method "ofEntries" for more than 10 pairs
      Map<String, Integer> daysPerMonthMap = Map.ofEntries(
         Map.entry("January", 31),
         Map.entry("February", 28),
         Map.entry("March", 31),
         Map.entry("April", 30),
         Map.entry("May", 31),
         Map.entry("June", 30),
```

Fig. 16.20 | Java SE 9 collection factory methods. (Part 1 of 2.)

```
33             Map.entry("July", 31),
34             Map.entry("August", 31),
35             Map.entry("September", 30),
36             Map.entry("October", 31),
37             Map.entry("November", 30),
38             Map.entry("December", 31)
39          );
40          System.out.printf("monthMap: %s%n", daysPerMonthMap);
41       }
42    }
```

```
colorList: [red, orange, yellow, green, blue, indigo, violet]

colorSet: [yellow, green, red, blue, violet, indigo, orange]

dayMap: {Tuesday=2, Wednesday=3, Friday=5, Thursday=4, Saturday=6, Monday=1,
Sunday=7}

monthMap: {April=30, February=28, September=30, July=31, October=31,
November=30, December=31, March=31, January=31, June=30, May=31, August=31}
```

```
colorList: [red, orange, yellow, green, blue, indigo, violet]

colorSet: [violet, yellow, orange, green, blue, red, indigo]

dayMap: {Saturday=6, Tuesday=2, Wednesday=3, Sunday=7, Monday=1, Thursday=4,
Friday=5}

monthMap: {February=28, August=31, July=31, November=30, April=30, May=31,
December=31, September=30, January=31, March=31, June=30, October=31}
```

Fig. 16.20 | Java SE 9 collection factory methods. (Part 2 of 2.)

`List` *Interface's Convenience Factory Method* `of`

Lines 10–11 use the `List` convenience factory method `of` to create an immutable `List<String>`. Method `of` has overloads for `List`s of zero to 10 elements and an additional overload that can receive any number of elements. Line 12 displays the `String` representation of the `List`'s contents—recall that this automatically iterates through the `List`'s elements to create the `String`. Also, the returned `List`'s elements are guaranteed to be in the *same* order as method `of`'s arguments.

Performance Tip 16.2

The collections returned by the convenience factory methods are optimized for up to 10 elements (for `Lists` *and* `Sets`*) or key–value pairs (for* `Maps`*).*

Software Engineering Observation 16.7

Method `of` *is overloaded for zero to 10 elements because research showed that these handle the vast majority of cases in which immutable collections are needed.*

Performance Tip 16.3

Method `of`*'s overloads for zero to 10 elements eliminate the extra overhead of processing variable-length argument lists. This improves the performance of applications that create small immutable collections.*

Common Programming Error 16.4

The collections returned by the convenience factory methods are not allowed to contain `null` *values—these methods throw a* `NullPointerException` *if any argument is* `null`*.*

`Set` *Interface's Convenience Factory Method* `of`

Lines 15–16 use the `Set` convenience factory method **`of`** to create an immutable `Set<String>`. As with `List`'s method `of`, `Set`'s method `of` has overloads for `Set`s of zero to 10 elements and an additional overload that can receive any number of elements. Line 17 displays the `String` representation of the `Set`'s contents. Note that we showed two sample outputs of this program and that the order of the `Set`'s elements is *different* in each output. According to the `Set` interface's documentation, the iteration order is *unspecified* for `Set`s returned by the convenience factory methods—as the outputs show, that order can change between executions.

Common Programming Error 16.5

`Set`*'s method* `of` *throws an* `IllegalArgumentException` *if any of its arguments are duplicates.*

`Map` *Interface's Convenience Factory Method* `of`

Lines 20–22 use `Map`'s convenience factory method **`of`** to create an immutable `Map<String, Integer>`. As with `List` and `Set`, `Map`'s method `of` has overloads for `Map`s of zero to 10 key–value pairs. Each pair of arguments (for example, `"Monday"` and `1` in line 20) represents one key–value pair. For `Map`s with more than 10 key–value pairs, interface `Map` provides the method `ofEntries` (which we discuss momentarily). Line 23 displays the `String` representation of the `Map`'s contents. According to the `Map` interface's documentation, the iteration order is *unspecified* for the keys in `Map`s returned by the convenience factory methods—as the outputs show, that order can change between program executions.

Common Programming Error 16.6

`Map`*'s methods* `of` *and* `ofEntries` *each throw an* `IllegalArgumentException` *if any of the keys are duplicates.*

`Map` *Interface's Convenience Factory Method* `ofEntries`

Lines 26–39 use the `Map` convenience factory method **`ofEntries`** to create an immutable `Map<String, Integer>`. Each of this method's variable number of arguments is the result of a call to `Map`'s `static` method **`entry`**, which creates and returns a **`Map.Entry`** object representing one key–value pair. Line 40 displays the `String` representation of the `Map`'s contents. The outputs confirm once again that the iteration order of a `Map`'s keys can change between program executions.

16.15 Wrap-Up

This chapter introduced the Java collections framework. You learned the collection hierarchy and how to use the collections-framework interfaces to program with collections polymorphically. You used classes `ArrayList` and `LinkedList`, which both implement the `List` interface. We presented Java's built-in interface and class for manipulating queues. You used several predefined methods for manipulating collections. You learned how to use the `Set` interface and class `HashSet` to manipulate an unordered collection of unique values. We continued our presentation of sets with the `SortedSet` interface and class `TreeSet` for manipulating a sorted collection of unique values. You then learned about Java's interfaces and classes for manipulating key–value pairs—`Map`, `SortedMap`, `HashMap` and `TreeMap`. We discussed the `Collections` class's `static` methods for obtaining unmodifiable and synchronized views of collections. Finally, we introduced Java SE 9's new convenience factory methods for creating immutable `List`s, `Set`s and `Map`s. For additional information, visit `http://docs.oracle.com/javase/8/docs/technotes/guides/collections`.

In Chapter 17, Lambdas and Streams, you'll use Java SE 8's functional programming capabilities to simplify collection operations. In Chapter 23, Concurrency, you'll learn how to improve performance on multi-core systems using Java's concurrent collections and parallel-stream operations.

Summary

Section 16.1 Introduction

- The Java collections framework provides prebuilt data structures and methods to manipulate them.

Section 16.2 Collections Overview

- A collection is an object that can hold references to other objects.
- The classes and interfaces of the collections framework are in package `java.util`.
- Interfaces `Set` and `List` extend `Collection` (p. 654), which contains operations for adding, clearing and comparing objects in a collection.

Section 16.3 Type-Wrapper Classes

- Type-wrapper classes (e.g., `Integer`, `Double`, `Boolean`) enable programmers to manipulate primitive-type values as objects (p. 655). Objects of these classes can be used in collections.

Section 16.4 Autoboxing and Auto-Unboxing

- Boxing (p. 655) converts a primitive value to an object of the corresponding type-wrapper class. Unboxing (p. 655) converts a type-wrapper object to the corresponding primitive value.
- Java performs boxing conversions and unboxing conversions automatically.

Section 16.5 Interface `Collection` and Class `Collections`

- `Collection` method `iterator` (p. 658) obtains a collection's `Iterator` (p. 656).
- Class `Collections` (p. 656) provides `static` methods for manipulating collections.

Section 16.6 Lists

- Interface `List` is implemented by classes `ArrayList` and `LinkedList`. `ArrayList` (p. 656) is a resizable-array implementation. `LinkedList` (p. 656) is a linkedlist implementation of a `List`.

- Java supports type inferencing with the <> notation in statements that declare and create generic type variables and objects.
- Iterator method hasNext (p. 658) determines whether a Collection contains another element. Method next returns a reference to the next object in the Collection and advances the Iterator.
- A List (p. 662) is an Collection of elements in sequence that can contain duplicate elements.
- Method subList (p. 662) returns a view into a List. Changes made to this view are also made to the List.
- Method clear (p. 662) removes elements from a List.
- Method toArray (p. 662) returns the contents of a collection as an array.

Section 16.7 **Collections** *Methods*

- Algorithms sort (p. 664), binarySearch, reverse (p. 670), shuffle (p. 668), fill (p. 670), copy operate on Lists. Algorithms min and max (p. 670) operate on Collections.
- Algorithm addAll appends all the elements in an array to a collection (p. 673), frequency (p. 674) calculates how many elements in the collection are equal to the specified element, and disjoint (p. 674) determines whether two collections have elements in common.
- Algorithms min and max find the smallest and largest items in a collection.
- The Comparator interface (p. 665) provides a means of sorting a Collection's elements in an order other than their natural order.
- Collections method reverseOrder (p. 665) returns a Comparator object that can be used with sort to sort a collection's elements in reverse order.
- Algorithm shuffle (p. 668) randomly orders the elements of a List.
- Algorithm binarySearch (p. 672) locates a key in a sorted List.

Section 16.8 Class **PriorityQueue** *and Interface* **Queue**

- Interface Queue (p. 675) extends interface Collection and provides additional operations for inserting, removing and inspecting elements in a queue.
- PriorityQueue (p. 675) implements interface Queue and orders elements by their natural ordering or by a Comparator object that's supplied to the constructor.
- PriorityQueue method offer (p. 675) inserts an element at the appropriate location based on priority order. Method poll (p. 675) removes the highest-priority element of the priority queue. Method peek (peek) gets a reference to the highest-priority element of the priority queue. Method clear (p. 675) removes all elements in the priority queue. Method size (p. 675) gets the number of elements in the priority queue.

Section 16.9 Sets

- A Set (p. 676) is an unordered Collection that contains no duplicate elements. HashSet (p. 676) stores its elements in a hash table. TreeSet (p. 676) stores its elements in a tree.
- Interface SortedSet (p. 677) extends Set and represents a set that maintains its elements in sorted order. Class TreeSet implements SortedSet.
- TreeSet method headSet (p. 678) gets a TreeSet view containing elements that are less than a specified element. Method tailSet (p. 678) gets a TreeSet view containing elements that are greater than or equal to a specified element. Any changes made to these views are made to the original TreeSet.

Section 16.10 Maps

- Maps (p. 679) store key–value pairs and cannot contain duplicate keys. HashMaps (p. 679) store elements in a hash table, and TreeMaps (p. 679) store elements in a tree.
- HashMap takes two type arguments—the type of key and the type of value.
- HashMap method put (p. 682) adds a key–value pair to a HashMap. Method get (p. 682) locates the value associated with the specified key. Method isEmpty (p. 682) determines if the map is empty.
- HashMap method keySet (p. 682) returns a set of the keys. Map method size (p. 682) returns the number of key–value pairs in the Map.
- Interface SortedMap (p. 679) extends Map and represents a map that maintains its keys in sorted order. Class TreeMap implements SortedMap.

Section 16.11 Synchronized Collections

- Collections from the collections framework are unsynchronized. Synchronization wrappers (p. 683) are provided for collections that can be accessed by multiple threads simultaneously.

Section 16.12 Unmodifiable Collections

- Unmodifiable collection wrappers (p. 683) throw UnsupportedOperationExceptions (p. 662) if attempts are made to modify the collection.

Section 16.13 Abstract Implementations

- The collections framework provides various abstract implementations of collection interfaces from which you can quickly flesh out complete customized implementations.

Section 16.14 Java SE 9: Convenience Factory Methods for Immutable Collections

- Java SE 9 adds new static convenience factory methods to interfaces List, Set and Map that enable you to create small immutable collections—they cannot be modified once they are created.
- The convenience factory methods return custom collection objects that are truly immutable and optimized to store small collections.
- List convenience factory method of creates an immutable List.
- List method of has overloads for Lists of zero to 10 elements and an additional overload that can receive any number of elements. The returned List's elements are guaranteed to be in the same order as method of's arguments.
- Set convenience factory method of creates an immutable Set.
- Set method of has overloads for Sets of zero to 10 elements and an additional overload that can receive any number of elements.
- The iteration order is unspecified for Sets returned by the convenience factory methods.
- Map convenience factory method of creates an immutable Map.
- Map method of has overloads for Maps of zero to 10 key–value pairs. Each pair of arguments represents one key–value pair.
- The iteration order is unspecified for the keys in Maps returned by the convenience factory methods.
- For Maps with more than 10 key–value pairs, Map convenience factory method ofEntries creates an immutable Map. Each argument to this method is the result of a call to Map's static method entry, which creates and returns a Map.Entry object representing one key–value pair.

Self-Review Exercises

16.1 Fill in the blanks in each of the following statements:

a) A(n) ________ is used to iterate through a collection and can remove elements from the collection during the iteration.
b) An element in a `List` can be accessed by using the element's ________.
c) Assuming that `myArray` contains references to `Double` objects, ________ occurs when the statement "`myArray[0] = 1.25;`" executes.
d) Class ________ provides the capabilities of array-like data structures that can resize themselves dynamically.
e) You can use a(n) ________ to create a collection that offers only read-only access to others while allowing read–write access to yourself.
f) Assuming that `myArray` contains references to `Double` objects, ________ occurs when the statement "`double number = myArray[0];`" executes.
g) `Collections` algorithm ________ determines if two collections have elements in common.

16.2 Determine whether each statement is *true* or *false*. If *false*, explain why.

a) Values of primitive types may be stored directly in a collection.
b) A `Set` can contain duplicate values.
c) A `Map` can contain duplicate keys.
d) A `LinkedList` can contain duplicate values.
e) `Collections` is an `interface`.
f) `Iterators` can remove elements.
g) With hashing, as the load factor increases, the chance of collisions decreases.
h) A `PriorityQueue` permits `null` elements.

Answers to Self-Review Exercises

16.1 a) `Iterator`. b) index. c) autoboxing. d) `ArrayList`. e) unmodifiable wrapper. f) auto-unboxing. g) `disjoint`.

16.2 Answers for a) through h):

a) False. Autoboxing occurs when adding a primitive type to a collection, which means the primitive type is converted to its corresponding type-wrapper class.
b) False. A `Set` cannot contain duplicate values.
c) False. A `Map` cannot contain duplicate keys.
d) True.
e) False. `Collections` is a `class`; `Collection` is an `interface`.
f) True.
g) False. As the load factor increases, fewer slots are available relative to the total number of slots, so the chance of a collision increases.
h) False. Attempting to insert a `null` element causes a `NullPointerException`.

Exercises

16.3 Define each of the following terms:

a) `Collection`
b) `Collections`
c) `Comparator`
d) `List`
e) load factor
f) collision

g) space/time trade-off in hashing
h) `HashMap`

16.4 Explain why inserting additional elements into an `ArrayList` object whose current size is less than its capacity is a relatively fast operation and why inserting additional elements into an `ArrayList` object whose current size is at its capacity is a relatively slow operation.

16.5 Briefly answer the following questions:
a) What is the primary difference between a `Set` and a `Map`?
b) What happens when you add a primitive type (e.g., `double`) value to a collection?
c) Can you print all the elements in a collection without using an `Iterator`? If yes, how?

16.6 Explain briefly the operation of each of the following `Iterator`-related methods:
a) `iterator`
b) `hasNext`
c) `next`

16.7 Explain briefly the operation of each of the following methods of class `HashMap`:
a) `put`
b) `get`
c) `isEmpty`
d) `containsKey`
e) `keySet`

16.8 Determine whether each of the following statements is *true* or *false*. If *false*, explain why.
a) Elements in a `Collection` must be sorted in ascending order before a `binarySearch` may be performed.
b) Method `first` gets the first element in a `TreeSet`.
c) A `List` created with `Arrays` method `asList` is resizable.

16.9 Rewrite lines 10–25 in Fig. 16.3 to be more concise by using the `asList` method and the `LinkedList` constructor that takes a `Collection` argument.

16.10 *(Duplicate Elimination)* Write a program that reads in a series of first names and eliminates duplicates by storing them in a `Set`. Allow the user to search for a first name.

16.11 *(Counting Letters)* Modify the program of Fig. 16.17 to count the number of occurrences of each letter rather than of each word. For example, the string `"HELLO THERE"` contains two `H`s, three `E`s, two `L`s, one `O`, one `T` and one `R`. Display the results.

16.12 *(Color Chooser)* Use a `HashMap` to create a reusable class for choosing one of the 13 predefined colors in class `Color`. The names of the colors should be used as keys, and the predefined `Color` objects should be used as values. Use your new class in an application that allows the user to select a color and draw a shape in that color.

16.13 *(Counting Duplicate Words)* Write a program that determines and prints the number of duplicate words in a sentence. Treat uppercase and lowercase letters the same. Ignore punctuation.

16.14 *(Inserting Elements in a `LinkedList` in Sorted Order)* Write a program that inserts 25 random integers from 0 to 100 in order into a `LinkedList` object. The program should sort the elements, then calculate the sum of the elements and the floating-point average of the elements.

16.15 *(Copying and Reversing `LinkedList`s)* Write a program that creates a `LinkedList` object of 10 characters, then creates a second `LinkedList` object containing a copy of the first list, but in reverse order.

16.16 *(Prime Numbers and Prime Factors)* Write a program that takes a whole number input from a user and determines whether it's prime. If the number is not prime, display its unique prime factors. Remember that a prime number's factors are only 1 and the prime number itself. Every number that's not prime has a unique prime factorization. For example, consider the number 54. The prime factors of 54 are 2, 3, 3 and 3. When the values are multiplied together, the result is 54. For the number 54, the prime factors output should be 2 and 3. Use `Set`s as part of your solution.

16.17 *(Sorting Words with a `TreeSet`)* Write a program that uses a `String` method `split` to tokenize a line of text input by the user and places each token in a `TreeSet`. Print the elements of the `TreeSet`. [*Note:* This should cause the elements to be printed in ascending sorted order.]

16.18 *(Changing a `PriorityQueue`'s Sort Order)* The output of Fig. 16.14 shows that `PriorityQueue` orders `Double` elements in ascending order. Rewrite Fig. 16.14 so that it orders `Double` elements in descending order (i.e., `9.8` should be the highest-priority element rather than `3.2`).

17 Lambdas and Streams

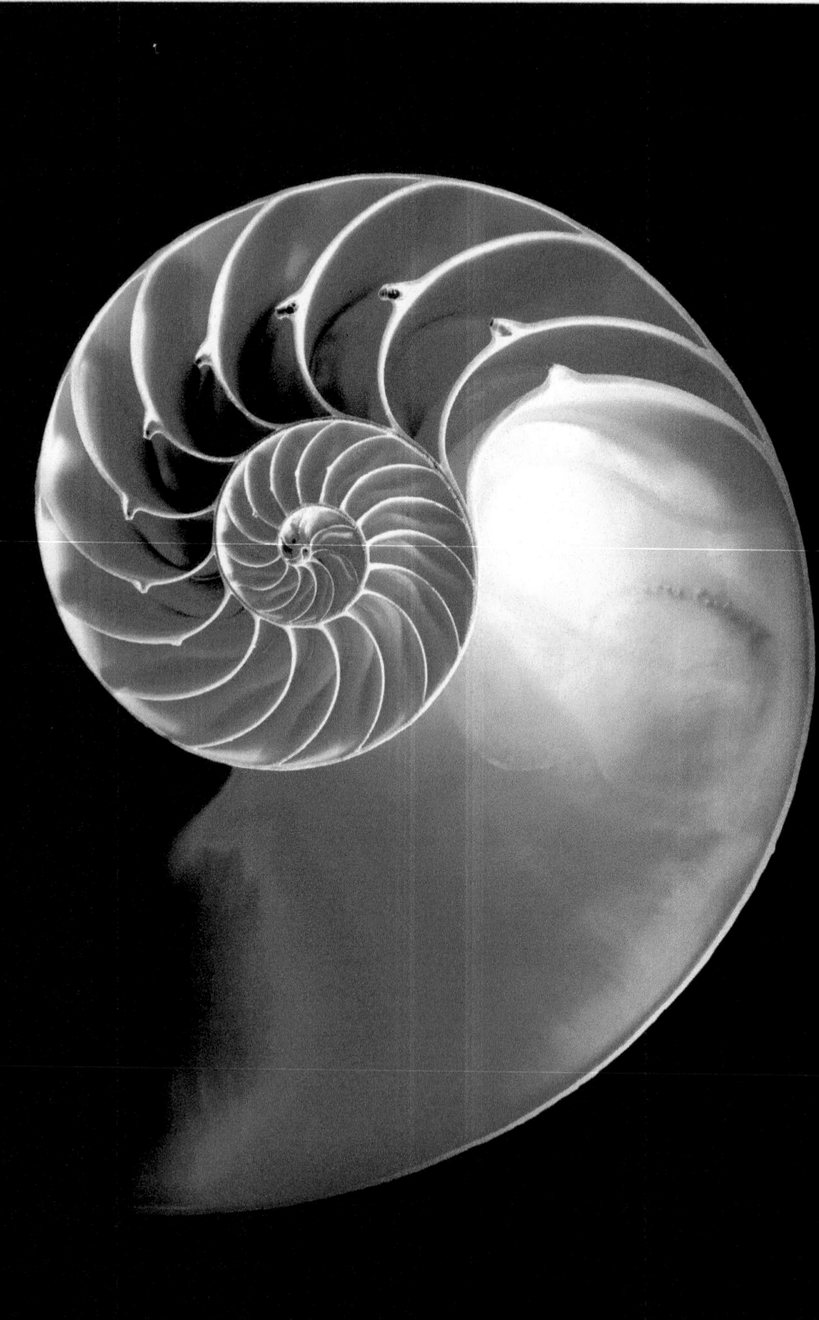

Objectives

In this chapter you'll:

- Learn various functional-programming techniques and how they complement object-oriented programming.
- Use lambdas and streams to simplify tasks that process sequences of elements.
- Learn what streams are and how stream pipelines are formed from stream sources, intermediate operations and terminal operations.
- Create streams representing ranges of `int` values and random `int` values.
- Implement functional interfaces with lambdas.
- Perform on `IntStream`s intermediate operations `filter`, `map`, `mapToObj` and `sorted`, and terminal operations `forEach`, `count`, `min`, `max`, `sum`, `average` and `reduce`.
- Perform on `Stream`s intermediate operations `distinct`, `filter`, `map`, `mapToDouble` and `sorted`, and terminal operations `collect`, `forEach`, `findFirst` and `reduce`.
- Process infinite streams.
- Implement event handlers with lambdas.

Outline

17.1 Introduction[1]

The way you think about Java programming is about to change profoundly. Prior to Java SE 8, Java supported three programming paradigms—*procedural programming*, *object-ori-*

1. We were privileged to have Brian Goetz, Oracle's Java Language Architect and Specification Lead for Java SE 8's Project Lambda, and co-author of *Java Concurrency in Practice*, do a detailed review of *Java How to Program, 10/e*. He thoroughly scrutinized the version of this chapter that appeared in that edition and provided many additional suggestions that are reflected in this new edition, *Java How to Program, 11/e*. Any remaining faults in the book are our own.

8 *ented programming* and *generic programming*. Java SE 8 added *lambdas* and *streams*[2]—key technologies of *functional programming*.

In this chapter, we'll use lambdas and streams to write certain kinds of programs faster, simpler, more concisely and with fewer bugs than with previous techniques. In Chapter 23, Concurrency, you'll see that such programs can be easier to *parallelize* (i.e., perform multiple operations simultaneously) so that you can take advantage of multi-core architectures to enhance performance—a key goal of lambdas and streams.

Software Engineering Observation 17.1

You'll see in Chapter 23, Concurrency that it's hard to create parallel tasks that operate correctly if those tasks modify a program's state (that is, its variables' values). So the techniques that you'll learn in this chapter focus on immutability—not modifying the data source being processed or any other program state.

This chapter presents many examples of lambdas and streams (Fig. 17.1), beginning with several showing better ways to implement tasks you programmed in Chapter 5. The first several examples are presented in a manner that allows them to be covered in the context of earlier chapters. For this reason, some terminology is discussed later in this chapter. Figure 17.2 shows additional lambdas and streams coverage in later chapters.

Section	May be covered after
Sections 17.2–17.4 introduce basic lambda and streams capabilities that process ranges of integers and eliminate the need for counter-controlled repetition.	Chapter 5, Control Statements: Part 2; Logical Operators
Section 17.6 introduces method references and uses them with lambdas and streams to process ranges of integers	Chapter 6, Methods: A Deeper Look
Section 17.7 presents lambda and streams capabilities that process one-dimensional arrays.	Chapter 7, Arrays and `ArrayLists`
Sections 17.8–17.9 discuss key functional interfaces and additional lambda concepts, and tie these into the chapter's earlier examples. Section 10.10 introduced Java SE 8's enhanced interface features (`default` methods, `static` methods and the concept of functional interfaces) that support functional-programming techniques in Java.	Chapter 10, Object-Oriented Programming: Polymorphism and Interfaces
Section 17.16 shows how to use a lambda to implement a JavaFX event-listener functional interface.	Chapter 12, JavaFX Graphical User Interfaces: Part 1,
Section 17.11 shows how to use lambdas and streams to process collections of `String` objects.	Chapter 14, Strings, Characters and Regular Expressions

Fig. 17.1 | This chapter's lambdas and streams discussions and examples. (Part 1 of 2.)

2. The streams we discuss in this chapter are not the same as the input/output streams we discuss in Chapter 15, Files, Input/Output Streams, NIO and XML Serialization, in which a program reads a stream of bytes from or writes a stream of bytes to a file. Section 17.13 uses lambdas and streams to manipulate the contents of a file.

Section	May be covered after
Section 17.13 shows how to use lambdas and streams to process lines of text from a file—the example in this section also uses some regular expression capabilities from Chapter 14.	Chapter 15, Files, Input/Output Streams, NIO and XML Serialization

Fig. 17.1 | This chapter's lambdas and streams discussions and examples. (Part 2 of 2.)

Coverage	Chapter
Uses lambdas to implement Swing event-listener functional interfaces.	Chapter 35, Swing GUI Components: Part 2
Shows that functional programs are easier to parallelize so that they can take advantage of multi-core architectures to enhance performance. Demonstrates parallel stream processing. Shows that `Arrays` method `parallelSort` can improve performance on multi-core vs. single-core architectures when sorting large arrays.	Chapter 23, Concurrency
Uses lambdas to implement Swing event-listener functional interfaces.	Chapter 26, Swing GUI Components: Part 1
Uses streams to process database query results.	Chapter 29, Java Persistence API (JPA)

Fig. 17.2 | Later lambdas and streams coverage.

17.2 Streams and Reduction

[This section demonstrates how streams can be used to simplify programming tasks that you learned in Chapter 5, Control Statements: Part 2; Logical Operators.]

In counter-controlled iteration, you typically determine *what* you want to accomplish then specify precisely *how* to accomplish it using a `for` loop. In this section, we'll investigate that approach, then show you a better way to accomplish the same tasks.

17.2.1 Summing the Integers from 1 through 10 with a for Loop

Let's assume that *what* you want to accomplish is to sum the integers from 1 through 10. In Chapter 5, you saw that you can do this with a counter-controlled loop:

```
int total = 0;

for (int number = 1; number <= 10; number++) {
   total += number;
}
```

This loop specifies precisely *how* to perform the task—with a `for` statement that processes each value of control variable `number` from 1 through 10, adding `number`'s current value to `total` once per loop iteration and incrementing number after each addition operation. This is known as **external iteration**, because *you* specify all the iteration details.

17.2.2 External Iteration with for Is Error Prone

Let's consider potential problems with the preceding code. As implemented, the loop requires two variables (`total` and `number`) that the code *mutates* (that is, modifies) during each loop iteration. Every time you write code that modifies a variable, it's possible to introduce an error into your code. There are several opportunities for error in the preceding code. For example, you could:

- initialize the variable `total` incorrectly
- initialize the `for` loop's control variable `number` incorrectly
- use the wrong loop-continuation condition
- increment control variable `number` incorrectly or
- incorrectly add each value of `number` to the `total`.

In addition, as the tasks you perform get more complicated, understanding *how* the code works gets in the way of understanding *what* it does. This makes the code harder to read, debug and modify, and more likely to contain errors.

17.2.3 Summing with a Stream and Reduction

Now let's take a different approach, specifying *what* to do rather than *how* to do it. In Fig. 17.3, we specify only *what* we want to accomplish—that is, sum the integers from 1 through 10—then simply let Java's **`IntStream`** class (package **`java.util.stream`**) deal with *how* to do it. The key to this program is the following expression in lines 9–10

```
IntStream.rangeClosed(1, 10)
         .sum()
```

which can be read as, "for the stream of `int` values in the range 1 through 10, calculate the sum" or more simply "sum the numbers from 1 through 10." In this code, notice that there is neither a counter-control variable nor a variable to store the total—this is because `IntStream` conveniently defines `rangeClosed` and `sum`.

```
1  // Fig. 17.3: StreamReduce.java
2  // Sum the integers from 1 through 10 with IntStream.
3  import java.util.stream.IntStream;
4
5  public class StreamReduce {
6     public static void main(String[] args) {
7        // sum the integers from 1 through 10
8        System.out.printf("Sum of 1 through 10 is: %d%n",
9           IntStream.rangeClosed(1, 10)
10                   .sum());
11    }
12 }
```

```
Sum of 1 through 10 is: 55
```

Fig. 17.3 | Sum the integers from 1 through 10 with `IntStream`.

Streams and Stream Pipelines

The chained method calls in lines 9–10 create a **stream pipeline.** A **stream** is a sequence of elements on which you perform tasks, and the stream pipeline moves the stream's elements through a sequence of tasks (or *processing steps*).

Good Programming Practice 17.1

When using chained method calls, align the dots (.) vertically for readability as we did in lines 9–10 of Fig. 17.3.

Specifying the Data Source

A stream pipeline typically begins with a method call that creates the stream—this is known as the *data source.* Line 9 specifies the data source with the method call

```
IntStream.rangeClosed(1, 10)
```

which creates an `IntStream` representing an ordered range of `int` values.

Here, we use the `static` method **`rangeClosed`** to create an `IntStream` containing the ordered sequence of `int` elements `1`, `2`, `3`, `4`, `5`, `6`, `7`, `8`, `9` and `10`. The method is named `rangeClosed`, because it produces a *closed range* of values—that is, a range of elements that includes *both* of the method's arguments (`1` and `10`). `IntStream` also provides method **`range`**, which produces a *half-open range* of values from its first argument up to, but not including, its second argument—for example,

```
IntStream.range(1, 10)
```

produces an `IntStream` containing the ordered sequence of `int` elements `1`, `2`, `3`, `4`, `5`, `6`, `7`, `8` and `9`, but *not* 10.

Calculating the Sum of the `IntStream`'s Elements

Next, line 10 completes the stream pipeline with the processing step

```
.sum()
```

This invokes the `IntStream`'s **`sum`** instance method, which returns the sum of all the `int`s in the stream—in this case, the sum of the integers from 1 through 10.

The processing step performed by method `sum` is known as a **reduction**—it reduces the stream of values to a *single* value (the sum). This is one of several predefined `IntStream` reductions—Section 17.7 presents the predefined reductions `count`, `min`, `max`, `average` and `summaryStatistics`, as well as the `reduce` method for defining your own reductions.

Processing the Stream Pipeline

A **terminal operation** initiates a stream pipeline's processing and produces a result. `IntStream` method `sum` is a terminal operation that produces the sum of the stream's elements. Similarly, the reductions `count`, `min`, `max`, `average`, `summaryStatistics` and `reduce` are all terminal operations. You'll see other terminal operations throughout this chapter. Section 17.3.3 discusses terminal operations in more detail.

17.2.4 Internal Iteration

The key to the preceding example is that it specifies *what* we want the task to accomplish—calculating the sum of the integers from 1 through 10—rather than *how* to accomplish it.

This is an example of **declarative programming** (specifying *what*) vs. **imperative programming** (specifying *how*). We broke the goal into two simple tasks—producing the numbers in a closed range (1–10) and calculating their sum. Internally, the `IntStream` (that is, the data source itself) already knows how to perform each of these tasks. We did *not* need to specify *how* to iterate through the elements or declare and use *any* mutable variables. This is known as **internal iteration**, because `IntStream` handles all the iteration details—a key aspect of **functional programming**. Unlike external iteration with the `for` statement, the primary potential for error in line 9 of Fig. 17.3 is specifying the incorrect starting and/or ending values as arguments. Once you're used to it, stream pipeline code also can be easier to read.

Software Engineering Observation 17.2

Functional-programming techniques enable you to write higher-level code, because many of the details are implemented for you by the Java streams library. Your code becomes more concise, which improves productivity and can help you rapidly prototype programs.

Software Engineering Observation 17.3

Functional-programming techniques eliminate large classes of errors, such as off-by-one errors (because iteration details are hidden from you by the libraries) and incorrectly modifying variables (because you focus on immutability and thus do not modify data). This makes it easier to write correct programs.

17.3 Mapping and Lambdas

[This section demonstrates how streams can be used to simplify programming tasks that you learned in Chapter 5, Control Statements: Part 2; Logical Operators.]

The preceding example specified a stream pipeline containing only a data source and a terminal operation that produced a result. Most stream pipelines also contain **intermediate operations** that specify tasks to perform on a stream's elements before a terminal operation produces a result.

In this example, we introduce a common intermediate operation called **mapping**, which transforms a stream's elements to new values. The result is a stream with the same number of elements containing the transformation's results. Sometimes the mapped elements are of different types from the original stream's elements.

To demonstrate mapping, let's revisit the program of Fig. 5.5 in which we calculated the sum of the even integers from 2 through 20 using external iteration, as follows:

```
int total = 0;

for (int number = 2; number <= 20; number += 2) {
   total += number;
}
```

Figure 17.4 reimplements this task using streams and internal iteration.

```
1  // Fig. 17.4: StreamMapReduce.java
2  // Sum the even integers from 2 through 20 with IntStream.
3  import java.util.stream.IntStream;
4
5  public class StreamMapReduce {
6     public static void main(String[] args) {
7        // sum the even integers from 2 through 20
8        System.out.printf("Sum of the even ints from 2 through 20 is: %d%n",
9           IntStream.rangeClosed(1, 10)                 // 1...10
10                   .map((int x) -> {return x * 2;}) // multiply by 2
11                   .sum());                         // sum
12    }
13 }
```

```
Sum of the even ints from 2 through 20 is: 110
```

Fig. 17.4 | Sum the even integers from 2 through 20 with `IntStream`.

The stream pipeline in lines 9–11 performs three chained method calls:

- Line 9 creates the data source—an `IntStream` containing the elements `1`, `2`, `3`, `4`, `5`, `6`, `7`, `8`, `9` and `10`.
- Line 10, which we'll discuss in detail momentarily, performs a processing step that maps each element (`x`) in the stream to that element multiplied by 2. The result is a stream of the even integers `2`, `4`, `6`, `8`, `10`, `12`, `14`, `16`, `18` and `20`.
- Line 11 reduces the stream's elements to a single value—the `sum` of the elements. This is the terminal operation that initiates the pipeline's processing, then `sum`s the stream's elements.

The new feature here is the mapping operation in line 10, which in this case multiplies each stream element by 2. `IntStream` method **`map`** receives as its argument (line 10)

```
(int x) -> {return x * 2;}
```

which you'll see in the next section is an alternate notation for "a *method* that receives an `int` parameter `x` and returns that value multiplied by `2`." For each element in the stream, `map` calls this method, passing to it the current stream element. The method's return value becomes part of the new stream that `map` returns.

17.3.1 Lambda Expressions

As you'll see throughout this chapter, many intermediate and terminal stream operations receive methods as arguments. Method `map`'s argument in line 10

```
(int x) -> {return x * 2;}
```

is called a **lambda expression** (or simply a **lambda**), which represents an *anonymous method*—that is, a *method without a name.* Though a lambda expression's syntax does not look like the methods you've seen previously, the left side does look like a method parameter list and the right side does look like a method body. We explain the syntax details shortly.

Lambda expressions enable you to create methods that can be treated as data. You can:

- pass lambdas as arguments to other methods (like `map`, or even other lambdas)
- assign lambda expressions to variables for later use and
- return lambda expressions from methods.

You'll see that these are powerful capabilities.

Software Engineering Observation 17.4

Lambdas and streams enable you to combine many benefits of functional-programming techniques with the benefits of object-oriented programming.

17.3.2 Lambda Syntax

A lambda consists of a *parameter list* followed by the **arrow token** (`->`) and a body, as in:

```
(parameterList) -> {statements}
```

The lambda in line 10

```
(int x) -> {return x * 2;}
```

receives an `int`, multiplies its value by `2` and returns the result. In this case, the body is a *statement block* that may contain statements enclosed in curly braces. The compiler *infers* from the lambda that it returns an `int`, because the parameter `x` is an `int` and the literal `2` is an `int`—multiplying an `int` by an `int` yields an `int` result. As in a method declaration, lambdas specify parameters in a comma-separated list. The preceding lambda is similar to the method

```
int multiplyBy2(int x) {
   return x * 2;
}
```

but the lambda does not have a name and the compiler infers its return type. There are several variations of the lambda syntax.

Eliminating a Lambda's Parameter Type(s)

A lambda's parameter type(s) usually may be omitted, as in:

```
(x) -> {return x * 2;}
```

in which case, the compiler infers the parameter and return types by the lambda's context—we'll say more about this later. If for any reason the compiler cannot infer the parameter or return types (e.g., if there are multiple type possibilities), it generates an error.

Simplifying the Lambda's Body

If the body contains only one expression, the `return` keyword, curly braces and semicolon may be omitted, as in:

```
(x) -> x * 2
```

In this case, the lambda *implicitly* returns the expression's value.

Simplifying the Lambda's Parameter List

If the parameter list contains only one parameter, the parentheses may be omitted, as in:

```
x -> x * 2
```

Lambdas with Empty Parameter Lists
To define a lambda with an empty parameter list, use empty parentheses to the left of the arrow token (->), as in:

```
() -> System.out.println("Welcome to lambdas!")
```

Method References
In addition, to the preceding lambda-syntax variations, there are specialized shorthand forms of lambdas that are known as *method references*, which we introduce in Section 17.6.

17.3.3 Intermediate and Terminal Operations

In the stream pipeline shown in lines 9–11, `map` is an intermediate operation and `sum` is a terminal operation. Method `map` is one of many intermediate operations that specify tasks to perform on a stream's elements.

Lazy and Eager Operations
Intermediate operations use **lazy evaluation**—each intermediate operation results in a new stream object, but does not perform any operations on the stream's elements until a terminal operation is called to produce a result. This allows library developers to optimize stream-processing performance. For example, if you have 1,000,000 `Person` objects and you're looking for the *first* one with the last name `"Jones"`, rather than processing all 1,000,000 elements, stream processing can terminate as soon as the first matching `Person` object is found.

Performance Tip 17.1
Lazy evaluation helps improve performance by ensuring that operations are performed only if necessary.

Terminal operations are **eager**—they perform the requested operation when they're called. We say more about lazy and eager operations as we encounter them throughout the chapter. You'll see how lazy operations can improve performance in Section 17.5, which discusses how a stream pipeline's intermediate operations are applied to each stream element. Figures 17.5 and 17.6 show some common intermediate and terminal operations, respectively.

Common intermediate stream operations	
`filter`	Returns a stream containing only the elements that satisfy a condition (known as a *predicate*). The new stream often has fewer elements than the original stream.
`distinct`	Returns a stream containing only the unique elements—duplicates are eliminated.
`limit`	Returns a stream with the specified number of elements from the beginning of the original stream.

Fig. 17.5 | Common intermediate stream operations. (Part 1 of 2.)

Common intermediate stream operations	
`map`	Returns a stream in which each of the original stream's elements is mapped to a new value (possibly of a different type)—for example, mapping numeric values to the squares of the numeric values or mapping numeric grades to letter grades (A, B C, D or F). The new stream has the same number of elements as the original stream.
`sorted`	Returns a stream in which the elements are in sorted order. The new stream has the same number of elements as the original stream. We'll show how to specify both ascending and descending order.

Fig. 17.5 | Common intermediate stream operations. (Part 2 of 2.)

Common terminal stream operations	
`forEach`	Performs processing on every element in a stream (for example, display each element).
Reduction operations—*Take all values in the stream and return a single value*	
`average`	Returns the *average* of the elements in a numeric stream.
`count`	Returns the *number of elements* in the stream.
`max`	Returns the *maximum* value in a stream.
`min`	Returns the *minimum* value in a stream.
`reduce`	Reduces the elements of a collection to a *single value* using an associative accumulation function (for example, a lambda that adds two elements and returns the sum).

Fig. 17.6 | Common terminal stream operations.

17.4 Filtering

[This section demonstrates how streams can be used to simplify programming tasks that you learned in Chapter 5, Control Statements: Part 2; Logical Operators.]

Another common intermediate stream operation is *filtering* elements to select those that match a condition—known as a *predicate*. For example, the following code selects the even integers in the range 1–10, multiplies each by 3 and sums the results:

```
int total = 0;

for (int x = 1; x <= 10; x++) {
   if (x % 2 == 0) { // if x is even
      total += x * 3;
   }
}
```

Figure 17.7 reimplements this loop using streams.

```
1  // Fig. 17.7: StreamFilterMapReduce.java
2  // Triple the even ints from 2 through 10 then sum them with IntStream.
3  import java.util.stream.IntStream;
4
5  public class StreamFilterMapReduce {
6     public static void main(String[] args) {
7        // sum the triples of the even integers from 2 through 10
8        System.out.printf(
9           "Sum of the triples of the even ints from 2 through 10 is: %d%n",
10          IntStream.rangeClosed(1, 10)
11                   .filter(x -> x % 2 == 0)
12                   .map(x -> x * 3)
13                   .sum());
14    }
15 }
```

```
Sum of the triples of the even ints from 2 through 10 is: 90
```

Fig. 17.7 | Triple the even `int`s from 2 through 10 then sum them with `IntStream`.

The stream pipeline in lines 10–13 performs four chained method calls:

- Line 10 creates the data source—an `IntStream` for the closed range 1 through 10.
- Line 11, which we'll discuss in detail momentarily, filters the stream's elements by selecting only the elements that are divisible by 2 (that is, the even integers), producing a stream of the even integers from 2, 4, 6, 8 and 10.
- Line 12 maps each element (x) in the stream to that element times 3, producing a stream of the even integers from 6, 12, 18, 24 and 30.
- Line 13 reduces the stream to the sum of its elements (90).

The new feature here is the filtering operation in line 11. `IntStream` method **`filter`** receives as its argument a method that takes one parameter and returns a `boolean` result. If the result is `true` for a given element, that element is included in the resulting stream.

The lambda in line 11:

```
x -> x % 2 == 0
```

determines whether its `int` argument is divisible by `2` (that is, the remainder after dividing by `2` is `0`) and, if so, returns `true`; otherwise, the lambda returns `false`. For each element in the stream, `filter` calls the method that it receives as an argument, passing to the method the current stream element. If the method's return value is `true`, the corresponding element becomes part of the intermediate stream that `filter` returns.

Line 11 creates an intermediate stream representing only the elements that are divisible by `2`. Next, line 12 uses `map` to create an intermediate stream representing the even integers (2, 4, 6, 8 and 10) that are multiplied by 3 (6, 12, 18, 24 and 30). Line 13 initiates the stream processing with a call to the *terminal* operation `sum`. At this point, the combined processing steps are applied to each element, then `sum` returns the total of the elements that remain in the stream. We discuss this further in the next section.

Error-Prevention Tip 17.1

The order of the operations in a stream pipeline matters. For example, `filter`*ing the even numbers from 1–10 yields 2, 4, 6, 8, 10, then* `map`*ping them to twice their values yields 4, 8, 12, 16 and 20. On the other hand,* `map`*ping the numbers from 1–10 to twice their values yields 2, 4, 6, 8, 10, 12, 14, 16, 18 and 20, then* `filter`*ing the even numbers gives all of those values, because they're all even before the* `filter` *operation is performed.*

The stream pipeline shown in this example could have been implemented by using only `map` and `sum`. Exercise 17.18 asks you to eliminate the `filter` operation.

17.5 How Elements Move Through Stream Pipelines

Section 17.3 mentioned that each intermediate operation results in a new stream. Each new stream is simply an object representing the processing steps that have been specified to that point in the pipeline. Chaining intermediate-operation method calls adds to the set of processing steps to perform on each stream element. The last stream object in the stream pipeline contains all the processing steps to perform on each stream element.

When you initiate a stream pipeline with a terminal operation, the intermediate operations' processing steps are applied for a given stream element *before* they are applied to the next stream element. So the stream pipeline in Fig. 17.7 operates as follows:

For each element
  If the element is an even integer
    Multiply the element by 3 and add the result to the total

To prove this, consider a modified version of Fig. 17.7's stream pipeline in which each lambda displays the intermediate operation's name and the current stream element's value:

```
IntStream.rangeClosed(1, 10)
         .filter(
            x -> {
               System.out.printf("%nfilter: %d%n", x);
               return x % 2 == 0;
            })
         .map(
            x -> {
               System.out.println("map: " + x);
               return x * 3;
            })
         .sum()
```

The modified pipeline's output below (we added the comments) clearly shows that each even integer's `map` step is applied *before* the next stream element's `filter` step:

```
filter: 1 // odd so no map step is performed for this element

filter: 2 // even so a map step is performed next
map: 2

filter: 3 // odd so no map step is performed for this element

filter: 4 // even so a map step is performed next
map: 4
```

```
filter: 5 // odd so no map step is performed for this element

filter: 6 // even so a map step is performed next
map: 6

filter: 7 // odd so no map step is performed for this element

filter: 8 // even so a map step is performed next
map: 8

filter: 9 // odd so no map step is performed for this element

filter: 10 // even so a map step is performed next
map: 10
```

For the odd elements, the `map` step was *not* performed. When a `filter` step returns `false`, the element's remaining processing steps are *ignored* because that element is not included in the results. (This version of Fig. 17.7 is located in a subfolder with that example.)

17.6 Method References

[This section demonstrates how streams can be used to simplify programming tasks that you learned in Chapter 6, Methods: A Deeper Look.]

For a lambda that simply calls another method, you can replace the lambda with that method's name—known as a **method reference**. The compiler converts a method reference into an appropriate lambda expression.

Like Fig. 6.6, Fig. 17.8 uses `SecureRandom` to obtain random numbers in the range 1–6. The program uses streams to create the random values and method references to help display the results. We walk through the code in Sections 17.6.1–17.6.4.

```java
// Fig. 17.8: RandomIntegers.java
// Shifted and scaled random integers.
import java.security.SecureRandom;
import java.util.stream.Collectors;

public class RandomIntegers {
   public static void main(String[] args) {
      SecureRandom randomNumbers = new SecureRandom();

      // display 10 random integers on separate lines
      System.out.println("Random numbers on separate lines:");
      randomNumbers.ints(10, 1, 7)
                   .forEach(System.out::println);

      // display 10 random integers on the same line
      String numbers =
         randomNumbers.ints(10, 1, 7)
                      .mapToObj(String::valueOf)
                      .collect(Collectors.joining(" "));
```

Fig. 17.8 | Shifted and scaled random integers. (Part 1 of 2.)

```
20          System.out.printf("%nRandom numbers on one line: %s%n", numbers);
21
22      }
23   }
```

```
Random numbers on separate lines:
4
3
4
5
1
5
5
3
6
5

Random numbers on one line: 4 6 2 5 6 4 3 2 4 1
```

Fig. 17.8 | Shifted and scaled random integers. (Part 2 of 2.)

17.6.1 Creating an `IntStream` of Random Values

Class `SecureRandom`'s **`ints`** method returns an `IntStream` of random numbers. In the stream pipeline of lines 12–13

```
randomNumbers.ints(10, 1, 7)
```

creates an `IntStream` data source with the specified number of random `int` values (`10`) in the range starting with the first argument (`1`) up to, but not including, the second argument (`7`). So, line 12 produces an `IntStream` of `10` random integers in the range 1–6.

17.6.2 Performing a Task on Each Stream Element with `forEach` and a Method Reference

Next, line 13 of the stream pipeline uses `IntStream` method **`forEach`** (a terminal operation) to perform a task on each stream element. Method `forEach` receives as its argument a method that takes one parameter and performs a task using the parameter's value.

The argument to `forEach`

```
System.out::println
```

in this case is a method reference—a shorthand notation for a lambda that calls the specified method. A method reference of the form

objectName`::`*instanceMethodName*

is a **bound instance method reference**—"bound" means the *specific* object to the left of the `::` (`System.out`) *must* be used to call the instance method to the right of the `::` (`println`).

The compiler converts `System.out::println` into a one-parameter lambda like

```
x -> System.out.println(x)
```

that passes the lambda's argument—the current stream element (represented by x)—to the System.out object's println instance method, which implicitly outputs the String representation of the argument. The stream pipeline of lines 12–13 is equivalent to the following for loop:

```
for (int i = 1; i <= 10; i++) {
   System.out.println(1 + randomNumbers.nextInt(6));
}
```

17.6.3 Mapping Integers to String Objects with mapToObj

The stream pipeline in lines 16–19

```
String numbers =
   randomNumbers.ints(10, 1, 7)
                .mapToObj(String::valueOf)
                .collect(Collectors.joining(" "));
```

creates a String containing 10 random integers in the range 1–6 separated by spaces. The pipeline performs three chained method calls:

- Line 17 creates the data source—an IntStream of 10 random integers from 1–6.
- Line 18 maps each int to its String representation, resulting in an intermediate stream of Strings. The IntStream method map that we've used previously returns another IntStream. To map to Strings, we use instead the IntStream method **mapToObj**, which enables you to map from ints to a stream of reference-type elements. Like map, mapToObject expects a one-parameter method that returns a result. In this example, mapToObj's argument is a **static method reference** of the form *ClassName*::*staticMethodName*. The compiler converts String::valueOf (which returns its argument's String representation) into a one-parameter lambda that calls valueOf, passing the current stream element as an argument, as in

```
x -> String.valueOf(x)
```

- Line 19, which we discuss in more detail in Section 17.6.4, uses the Stream terminal operation **collect** to concatenate all the Strings, separating each from the next with a space. Method collect is a form of reduction because it returns one object—in this case, a String.

Line 20 then displays the resulting String.

17.6.4 Concatenating Strings with collect

Consider line 19 of Fig. 17.8. The Stream terminal operation collect uses a *collector* to gather the stream's elements into a single object—often a collection. This is similar to a reduction, but collect returns an object containing the stream's elements, whereas reduce returns a single value of the stream's element type. In this example, we use a predefined collector returned by the static **Collectors** method **joining**. This collector creates a concatenated String representation of the stream's elements, appending each element to the String separated from the previous element by the joining method's argument (in this case, a space). Method collect then returns the resulting String. We discuss other collectors throughout this chapter.

17.7 IntStream Operations

[This section demonstrates how lambdas and streams can be used to simplify programming tasks like those you learned in Chapter 7, Arrays and **ArrayLists**.*]*

Figure 17.9 demonstrates additional `IntStream` operations on streams created from arrays. The `IntStream` techniques shown in this and the prior examples also apply to **`LongStream`s** and **`DoubleStream`s** for `long` and `double` values, respectively. We walk through the code in Sections 17.7.1–17.7.4.

```
// Fig. 17.9: IntStreamOperations.java
// Demonstrating IntStream operations.
import java.util.Arrays;
import java.util.stream.Collectors;
import java.util.stream.IntStream;

public class IntStreamOperations {
   public static void main(String[] args) {
      int[] values = {3, 10, 6, 1, 4, 8, 2, 5, 9, 7};

      // display original values
      System.out.print("Original values: ");
      System.out.println(
         IntStream.of(values)
                  .mapToObj(String::valueOf)
                  .collect(Collectors.joining(" ")));

      // count, min, max, sum and average of the values
      System.out.printf("%nCount: %d%n", IntStream.of(values).count());
      System.out.printf("Min: %d%n",
         IntStream.of(values).min().getAsInt());
      System.out.printf("Max: %d%n",
         IntStream.of(values).max().getAsInt());
      System.out.printf("Sum: %d%n", IntStream.of(values).sum());
      System.out.printf("Average: %.2f%n",
         IntStream.of(values).average().getAsDouble());

      // sum of values with reduce method
      System.out.printf("%nSum via reduce method: %d%n",
         IntStream.of(values)
                  .reduce(0, (x, y) -> x + y));

      // product of values with reduce method
      System.out.printf("Product via reduce method: %d%n",
         IntStream.of(values)
                  .reduce((x, y) -> x * y).getAsInt());

      // sum of squares of values with map and sum methods
      System.out.printf("Sum of squares via map and sum: %d%n%n",
         IntStream.of(values)
                  .map(x -> x * x)
                  .sum());
```

Fig. 17.9 | Demonstrating `IntStream` operations. (Part 1 of 2.)

```
43
44        // displaying the elements in sorted order
45        System.out.printf("Values displayed in sorted order: %s%n",
46           IntStream.of(values)
47                    .sorted()
48                    .mapToObj(String::valueOf)
49                    .collect(Collectors.joining(" ")));
50     }
51  }
```

```
Original values: 3 10 6 1 4 8 2 5 9 7

Count: 10
Min: 1
Max: 10
Sum: 55
Average: 5.50

Sum via reduce method: 55
Product via reduce method: 3628800
Sum of squares via map and sum: 385

Values displayed in sorted order: 1 2 3 4 5 6 7 8 9 10
```

Fig. 17.9 | Demonstrating `IntStream` operations. (Part 2 of 2.)

17.7.1 Creating an IntStream and Displaying Its Values

`IntStream` `static` method **`of`** (line 14) receives an `int` array argument and returns an `IntStream` for processing the array's values. The stream pipeline in lines 14–16

```
IntStream.of(values)
         .mapToObj(String::valueOf)
         .collect(Collectors.joining(" ")));
```

displays the stream's elements. First, line 14 creates an `IntStream` for the `values` array, then lines 15–16 use the `mapToObj` and `collect` methods as shown Fig. 17.8 to obtain a `String` representation of the stream's elements separated by spaces. We use this technique several times in this example and subsequent examples to display stream elements.

This example repeatedly creates an `IntStream` from the array `values` using:

```
IntStream.of(values)
```

You might think that we could simply store the stream and reuse it. However, once a stream pipeline is processed with a terminal operation, *the stream cannot be reused*, because it does not maintain a copy of the original data source.

17.7.2 Terminal Operations count, min, max, sum and average

Class `IntStream` provides various terminal operations for common stream reductions on streams of `int` values:

- **`count`** (line 19) returns the number of elements in the stream.
- **`min`** (line 21) returns an **`OptionalInt`** (package `java.util`) possibly containing the smallest `int` in the stream. For any stream, it's possible that there are *no ele-*

ments in the stream. Returning OptionalInt enables method min to return the minimum value if the stream contains *at least one element.* In this example, we know the stream has 10 elements, so we call class OptionalInt's **getAsInt** method to obtain the minimum value. If there were no *elements*, the OptionalInt would not contain an int and getAsInt would throw a NoSuchElementException. To prevent this, you can instead call method **orElse**, which returns the OptionalInt's value if there is one, or the value you pass to orElse, otherwise.

- max (line 23) returns an OptionalInt possibly containing the largest int in the stream. Again, we call the OptionalInt's getAsInt method to get the largest value, because we know this stream contains elements.
- sum (line 24) returns the sum of all the ints in the stream.
- **average** (line 26) returns an **OptionalDouble** (package java.util) possibly containing the average of the ints in the stream as a value of type double. In this example, we know the stream has elements, so we call class OptionalDouble's **getAsDouble** method to obtain the average. If there were no *elements*, the OptionalDouble would not contain the average and getAsDouble would throw a NoSuchElementException. As with OptionalInt, to prevent this exception, you can instead call method **orElse**, which returns the OptionalDouble's value if there is one, or the value you pass to orElse, otherwise.

Class IntStream also provides method **summaryStatistics** that performs the count, min, max, sum and average operations *in one pass* of an IntStream's elements and returns the results as an **IntSummaryStatistics** object (package java.util). This provides a significant performance boost over reprocessing an IntStream repeatedly for each individual operation. This object has methods for obtaining each result and a toString method that summarizes all the results. For example, the statement:

```
System.out.println(IntStream.of(values).summaryStatistics());
```

produces:

```
IntSummaryStatistics{count=10, sum=55, min=1, average=5.500000,
max=10}
```

for the array values in Fig. 17.9.

17.7.3 Terminal Operation reduce

So far, we've presented various predefined IntStream reductions. You can define your own reductions via an IntStream's **reduce** method—in fact, each terminal operation discussed in Section 17.7.2 is a specialized implementation of reduce. The stream pipeline in lines 30–31

```
IntStream.of(values)
         .reduce(0, (x, y) -> x + y)
```

shows how to total an IntStream's values using reduce, rather than sum.

The first argument to reduce (0) is the operation's **identity value**—a value that, when combined with any stream element (using the lambda in the reduce's second argument), produces the element's original value. For example, when summing the elements, the identity value is 0, because any int value added to 0 results in the original int value. Similarly, when getting the product of the elements the identity value is 1, because any `int` value multiplied by 1 results in the original `int` value.

Method `reduce`'s second argument is a method that receives two `int` values (representing the left and right operands of a binary operator), performs a calculation with the values and returns the result. The lambda

```
(x, y) -> x + y
```

adds the values. A lambda with two or more parameters *must* enclose them in parentheses.

Error-Prevention Tip 17.2

The operation specified by a `reduce`'s argument must be associative—that is, the order in which `reduce` applies the operation to the stream's elements must not matter. This is important, because `reduce` is allowed to apply its operation to the stream elements in any order. A non-associative operation could yield different results based on the processing order. For example, subtraction is not an associative operation—the expression 7 – (5 – 3) yields 5 whereas the expression (7 – 5) – 3 yields –1. Associative `reduce` operations are critical for parallel streams (Chapter 23) that split operations across multiple cores for better performance. Exercise 23.19 explores this issue further.

Based on the stream's elements

```
3 10 6 1 4 8 2 5 9 7
```

the reduction's evaluation proceeds as follows:

```
0 + 3 --> 3
3 + 10 --> 13
13 + 6 --> 19
19 + 1 --> 20
20 + 4 --> 24
24 + 8 --> 32
32 + 2 --> 34
34 + 5 --> 39
39 + 9 --> 48
48 + 7 --> 55
```

Notice that the first calculation uses the identity value (0) as the left operand and each subsequent calculation uses the result of the prior calculation as the left operand. The reduction process continues producing a running total of the `IntStream`'s values until they've all been used, at which point the final sum is returned.

Calculating the Product of the Values with Method `reduce`

The stream pipeline in lines 35–36

```
IntStream.of(values)
        .reduce((x, y) -> x * y).getAsInt()
```

uses the one-argument version of method `reduce`, which returns an `OptionalInt` that, if the stream has elements, contains the product of the `IntStream`'s values; otherwise, the `OptionalInt` does not contain a result.

Based on the stream's elements

```
3 10 6 1 4 8 2 5 9 7
```

the reduction's evaluation proceeds as follows:

```
3 * 10 --> 30
30 * 6 --> 180
180 * 1 --> 180
180 * 4 --> 720
720 * 8 --> 5,760
5,760 * 2 --> 11,520
11,520 * 5 --> 57,600
57,600 * 9 --> 518,400
518,400 * 7 --> 3,628,800
```

This process continues producing a running product of the `IntStream`'s values until they've all been used, at which point the final product is returned.

We could have used the two-parameter `reduce` method, as in:

```
IntStream.of(values)
         .reduce(1, (x, y) -> x * y)
```

However, if the stream were empty, this version of `reduce` would return the identity value (`1`), which would not be the expected result for an empty stream.

Summing the Squares of the Values

Now consider summing the squares of the stream's elements. When implementing your stream pipelines, it's helpful to break down the processing steps into easy-to-understand tasks. Summing the squares of the stream's elements requires two distinct tasks:

- squaring the value of each stream element
- summing the resulting values.

Rather than defining this with a `reduce` method call, the stream pipeline in lines 40–42

```
IntStream.of(values)
         .map(x -> x * x)
         .sum());
```

uses the `map` and `sum` methods to compose the sum-of-squares operation. First `map` produces a new `IntStream` containing the original element's squares, then `sum` totals the resulting stream's elements.

17.7.4 Sorting `IntStream` Values

In Section 7.15, you learned how to sort arrays with the `sort static` method of class `Arrays`. You also may sort the elements of a stream. The stream pipeline in lines 46–49

```
IntStream.of(values)
         .sorted()
         .mapToObj(String::valueOf)
         .collect(Collectors.joining(" ")));
```

sorts the stream's elements and displays each value followed by a space. `IntStream` intermediate operation **`sorted`** orders the elements of the stream into *ascending* order by default. Like `filter`, `sorted` is a *lazy* operation that's performed only when a terminal operation initiates the stream pipeline's processing.

17.8 Functional Interfaces

[This section requires the interface concepts introduced in Sections 10.9–10.10.]

Section 10.10 introduced Java SE 8's enhanced interface features—`default` methods and `static` methods—and discussed the concept of a *functional interface*—an interface that contains exactly one `abstract` method (and may also contain `default` and `static` methods). Such interfaces are also known as *single abstract method* (SAM) interfaces. Functional interfaces are used extensively in functional-style Java programming. Functional programmers work with so-called *pure functions* that have *referential transparency*—that is, they:

- depend only on their parameters
- have no side-effects and
- do not maintain any state.

In Java, pure functions are methods that implement functional interfaces—typically defined as lambdas, like those you've seen so far in this chapter's examples. State changes occur by passing data from method to method. No data is shared.

Software Engineering Observation 17.5

Pure functions are safer because they do not modify a program's state (variables). This also makes them less error prone and thus easier to test, modify and debug.

Functional Interfaces in Package `java.util.function`

Package `java.util.function` contains several functional interfaces. Figure 17.10 shows the six basic generic functional interfaces, several of which you've already used in this chapter's examples. Throughout the table, `T` and `R` are generic type names that represent the type of the object on which the functional interface operates and the return type of a method, respectively. Many other functional interfaces in package `java.util.function` are specialized versions of those in Fig. 17.10. Most are for use with `int`, `long` and `double` primitive values. There are also generic customizations of `Consumer`, `Function` and `Predicate` for binary operations—that is, methods that take two arguments. For each `IntStream` method we've shown that receives a lambda, the method's parameter is actually an `int`-specialized version of one of these interfaces.

Interface	Description
`BinaryOperator<T>`	Represents a method that takes two parameters of the same type and returns a value of that type. Performs a task using the parameters (such as a calculation) and returns the result. The lambdas you passed to `IntStream` method `reduce` (Section 17.7) implemented `IntBinaryOperator`—an `int` specific version of `BinaryOperator`.
`Consumer<T>`	Represents a one-parameter method that returns `void`. Performs a task using its parameter, such as outputting the object, invoking a method of the object, etc. The lambda you passed to `IntStream` method `forEach` (Section 17.6) implemented interface `IntConsumer`—an `int`-specialized version of `Consumer`. Later sections present several more examples of `Consumers`.

Fig. 17.10 | The six basic generic functional interfaces in package `java.util.function`.

Interface	Description
`Function<T,R>`	Represents a one-parameter method that performs a task on the parameter and returns a result—possibly of a different type than the parameter. The lambda you passed to `IntStream` method `mapToObj` (Section 17.6) implemented interface `IntFunction`—an `int`-specialized version of `Function`. Later sections present several more examples of `Functions`.
`Predicate<T>`	Represents a one-parameter method that returns a `boolean` result. Determines whether the parameter satisfies a condition. The lambda you passed to `IntStream` method `filter` (Section 17.4) implemented interface `IntPredicate`—an `int`-specialized version of `Predicate`. Later sections present several more examples of `Predicates`.
`Supplier<T>`	Represents a no-parameter method that returns a result. Often used to create a collection object in which a stream operation's results are placed. You'll see several examples of `Suppliers` starting in Section 17.13.
`UnaryOperator<T>`	Represents a one-parameter method that returns a result of the same type as its parameter. The lambdas you passed in Section 17.3 to `IntStream` method `map` implemented `IntUnaryOperator`—an `int`-specialized version of `UnaryOperator`. Later sections present several more examples of `UnaryOperators`.

Fig. 17.10 | The six basic generic functional interfaces in package `java.util.function`.

17.9 Lambdas: A Deeper Look

Type Inference and a Lambda's Target Type

Lambda expressions can be used anywhere functional interfaces are expected. The Java compiler can usually *infer* the types of a lambda's parameters and the type returned by a lambda from the context in which the lambda is used. This is determined by the lambda's **target type**—the functional-interface type that's expected where the lambda appears in the code. For example, in the call to `IntStream` method `map` from stream pipeline in Fig. 17.4

```
IntStream.rangeClosed(1, 10)
         .map((int x) -> {return x * 2;})
         .sum()
```

the target type is `IntUnaryOperator`, which represents a method that takes one `int` parameter and returns an `int` result. In this case, the lambda parameter's type is explicitly declared to be `int` and the compiler *infers* the lambda's return type as int, because that's what an `IntUnaryOperator` requires.

The compiler also can *infer* a lambda parameter's type. For example, in the call to `IntStream` method `filter` from stream pipeline in Fig. 17.7

```
IntStream.rangeClosed(1, 10)
         .filter(x -> x % 2 == 0)
         .map(x -> x * 3)
         .sum()
```

the target type is `IntPredicate`, which represents a method that takes one `int` parameter and returns a `boolean` result. In this case, the compiler *infers* the lambda parameter `x`'s type as `int`, because that's what an `IntPredicate` requires. We generally let the compiler *infer* the lambda parameter's type in our examples.

Scope and Lambdas

Unlike methods, lambdas do not have their own scope. So, for example, you cannot shadow an enclosing method's local variables with lambda parameters that have the same names. A compilaton error occurs in this case, because the method's local variables and the lambda parameters are in the *same* scope.

Capturing Lambdas and `final` Local Variables

A lambda that refers to a local variable from the enclosing method (known as the lambda's *lexical scope*) is a **capturing lambda**. For such a lambda, the compiler captures the local variable's value and stores it with the lambda to ensure that the lambda can use the value when the lambda *eventually* executes. This is important, because you can pass a lambda to another method that executes the lambda *after* its lexical scope *no longer exists.*

Any local variable that a lambda references in its lexical scope must be `final`. Such a variable either can be explicitly declared `final` or it can be *effectively* `final` (Java SE 8). For an effectively `final` variable, the compiler *infers* that the local variable could have been declared `final`, because its enclosing method never modifies the variable after it's declared and initialized.

17.10 Stream<Integer> Manipulations

[This section requires the interface concepts introduced in Sections 10.9–10.10.]

So far, we've processed `IntStreams`. A **`Stream`** performs tasks on reference-type objects. `IntStream` is simply an `int`-optimized `Stream` that provides methods for common `int` operations. Figure 17.11 performs *filtering* and *sorting* on a `Stream<Integer>`, using techniques similar to those in prior examples, and shows how to place a stream pipeline's results into a new collection for subsequent processing. We'll work with `Streams` of other reference types in subsequent examples.

```
// Fig. 17.11: ArraysAndStreams.java
// Demonstrating lambdas and streams with an array of Integers.
import java.util.Arrays;
import java.util.List;
import java.util.stream.Collectors;

public class ArraysAndStreams {
   public static void main(String[] args) {
      Integer[] values = {2, 9, 5, 0, 3, 7, 1, 4, 8, 6};

      // display original values
      System.out.printf("Original values: %s%n", Arrays.asList(values));

```

Fig. 17.11 | Demonstrating lambdas and streams with an array of `Integers`. (Part 1 of 2.)

```
14          // sort values in ascending order with streams
15          System.out.printf("Sorted values: %s%n",
16             Arrays.stream(values)
17                   .sorted()
18                   .collect(Collectors.toList()));
19
20          // values greater than 4
21          List<Integer> greaterThan4 =
22             Arrays.stream(values)
23                   .filter(value -> value > 4)
24                   .collect(Collectors.toList());
25          System.out.printf("Values greater than 4: %s%n", greaterThan4);
26
27          // filter values greater than 4 then sort the results
28          System.out.printf("Sorted values greater than 4: %s%n",
29             Arrays.stream(values)
30                   .filter(value -> value > 4)
31                   .sorted()
32                   .collect(Collectors.toList()));
33
34          // greaterThan4 List sorted with streams
35          System.out.printf(
36             "Values greater than 4 (ascending with streams): %s%n",
37             greaterThan4.stream()
38                   .sorted()
39                   .collect(Collectors.toList()));
40       }
41    }
```

```
Original values: [2, 9, 5, 0, 3, 7, 1, 4, 8, 6]
Sorted values: [0, 1, 2, 3, 4, 5, 6, 7, 8, 9]
Values greater than 4: [9, 5, 7, 8, 6]
Sorted values greater than 4: [5, 6, 7, 8, 9]
Values greater than 4 (ascending with streams): [5, 6, 7, 8, 9]
```

Fig. 17.11 | Demonstrating lambdas and streams with an array of `Integers`. (Part 2 of 2.)

Throughout this example, we use the `Integer` array `values` (line 9) that's initialized with `int` values—the compiler *boxes* each `int` into an `Integer` object. Line 12 displays the contents of `values` before we perform any stream processing. `Arrays` method **`asList`** creates a `List<Integer>` view of the `values` array. The generic interface `List` (discussed in more detail in Chapter 16) is implemented by collections like `ArrayList` (Chapter 7). Line 12 displays the `List<Integer>`'s default `String` representation, which consists of square brackets (`[` and `]`) containing a comma-separated list of elements—we use this `String` representation throughout the example. We walk through the remainder of the code in Sections 17.10.1–17.10.5.

17.10.1 Creating a Stream<Integer>

Class `Arrays` **`stream`** method can be used to create a `Stream` from an array of objects—for example, line 16 produces a `Stream<Integer>`, because `stream`'s argument is an array of `Integers`. Interface **`Stream`** (package `java.util.stream`) is a generic interface for performing stream operations on any *reference* type. The types of objects that are processed are determined by the Stream's source.

Class Arrays also provides overloaded versions of method stream for creating IntStreams, LongStreams and DoubleStreams from int, long and double arrays or from ranges of elements in the arrays.

17.10.2 Sorting a Stream and Collecting the Results

The stream pipeline in lines 16–18

```
Arrays.stream(values)
      .sorted()
      .collect(Collectors.toList())
```

uses stream techniques to sort the values array and collect the results in a List<Integer>. First, line 16 creates a Stream<Integer> from values. Next, line 17 calls Stream method sorted to sort the elements—this results in an intermediate Stream<Integer> with the values in *ascending* order. (Section 17.11.3 discusses how to sort in descending order.)

Creating a New Collection Containing a Stream Pipeline's Results

When processing streams, you often create *new* collections containing the results so that you can perform operations on them later. To do so, you can use Stream's terminal operation **collect** (Fig. 17.11, line 18). As the stream pipeline is processed, method collect performs a **mutable reduction operation** that creates a List, Map or Set and modifies it by placing the stream pipeline's results into the collection. You may also use the mutable reduction operation **toArray** to place the results in a new array of the Stream's element type.

The version of method collect in line 18 receives as its argument an object that implements interface **Collector** (package java.util.stream), which specifies how to perform the mutable reduction. Class Collectors (package java.util.stream) provides static methods that return predefined Collector implementations. Collectors method **toList** (line 18) returns a Collector that places the Stream<Integer>'s elements into a List<Integer> collection. In lines 15–18, the resulting List<Integer> is displayed with an *implicit* call to its toString method.

A mutable reduction optionally performs a final data transformation. For example, in Fig. 17.8, we called IntStream method collect with the object returned by Collectors method joining. Behind the scenes, this Collector used a **StringJoiner** (package java.util) to concatenate the stream elements' String representations, then called the StringJoiner's toString method to transform the result into a String. We show additional Collectors in Section 17.12. For more predefined Collectors, visit:

```
https://docs.oracle.com/javase/8/docs/api/java/util/stream/
   Collectors.html
```

17.10.3 Filtering a Stream and Storing the Results for Later Use

The stream pipline in lines 21–24 of Fig. 17.11

```
List<Integer> greaterThan4 =
   Arrays.stream(values)
         .filter(value -> value > 4)
         .collect(Collectors.toList());
```

creates a `Stream<Integer>`, `filter`s the stream to locate all the values greater than 4 and `collect`s the results into a `List<Integer>`. `Stream` method `filter`'s lambda argument implements the functional interface `Predicate` (package `java.util.function`), which represents a one-parameter method that returns a `boolean` indicating whether the parameter value satisfies the predicate.

We assign the stream pipeline's resulting `List<Integer>` to variable `greaterThan4`, which is used in line 25 to display the values greater than 4 and used again in lines 37–39 to perform additional operations on only the values greater than 4.

17.10.4 Filtering and Sorting a `Stream` and Collecting the Results

The stream pipeline in lines 29–32

```
Arrays.stream(values)
      .filter(value -> value > 4)
      .sorted()
      .collect(Collectors.toList())
```

displays the values greater than 4 in sorted order. First, line 29 creates a `Stream<Integer>`. Then line 30 `filter`s the elements to locate all the values greater than 4. Next, line 31 indicates that we'd like the results `sorted`. Finally, line 32 `collect`s the results into a `List<Integer>`, which is then displayed as a `String`.

Performance Tip 17.2

Call `filter` before `sorted` so that the stream pipeline sorts only the elements that will be in the stream pipeline's result.

17.10.5 Sorting Previously Collected Results

The stream pipeline in lines 37–39

```
greaterThan4.stream()
            .sorted()
            .collect(Collectors.toList()));
```

uses the `greaterThan4` collection created in lines 21–24 to show additional processing on the results of a prior stream pipeline. `List` method **`stream`** creates the stream. Then we sort the elements and `collect` the results into a new `List<Integer>` and display its `String` representation.

17.11 `Stream<String>` Manipulations

[This section demonstrates how lambdas and streams can be used to simplify programming tasks that you learned in Chapter 14, Strings, Characters and Regular Expressions.]

So far, we've manipulated only streams of `int` values and `Integer` objects. Figure 17.12 performs similar stream operations on a `Stream<String>`. In addition, we demonstrate *case-insensitive sorting* and sorting in *descending* order. Throughout this example, we use the `String` array `strings` (lines 9–10) that's initialized with color names—some with an initial uppercase letter. Line 13 displays the contents of `strings` *before* we perform any stream processing. We walk through the rest of the code in Sections 17.11.1–17.11.3.

```
1  // Fig. 17.12: ArraysAndStreams2.java
2  // Demonstrating lambdas and streams with an array of Strings.
3  import java.util.Arrays;
4  import java.util.Comparator;
5  import java.util.stream.Collectors;
6
7  public class ArraysAndStreams2 {
8     public static void main(String[] args) {
9        String[] strings =
10          {"Red", "orange", "Yellow", "green", "Blue", "indigo", "Violet"};
11
12       // display original strings
13       System.out.printf("Original strings: %s%n", Arrays.asList(strings));
14
15       // strings in uppercase
16       System.out.printf("strings in uppercase: %s%n",
17          Arrays.stream(strings)
18                .map(String::toUpperCase)
19                .collect(Collectors.toList()));
20
21       // strings less than "n" (case insensitive) sorted ascending
22       System.out.printf("strings less than n sorted ascending: %s%n",
23          Arrays.stream(strings)
24                .filter(s -> s.compareToIgnoreCase("n") < 0)
25                .sorted(String.CASE_INSENSITIVE_ORDER)
26                .collect(Collectors.toList()));
27
28       // strings less than "n" (case insensitive) sorted descending
29       System.out.printf("strings less than n sorted descending: %s%n",
30          Arrays.stream(strings)
31                .filter(s -> s.compareToIgnoreCase("n") < 0)
32                .sorted(String.CASE_INSENSITIVE_ORDER.reversed())
33                .collect(Collectors.toList()));
34    }
35 }
```

```
Original strings: [Red, orange, Yellow, green, Blue, indigo, Violet]
strings in uppercase: [RED, ORANGE, YELLOW, GREEN, BLUE, INDIGO, VIOLET]
strings less than n sorted ascending: [Blue, green, indigo]
strings less than n sorted descending: [indigo, green, Blue]
```

Fig. 17.12 | Demonstrating lambdas and streams with an array of Strings.

17.11.1 Mapping Strings to Uppercase

The stream pipeline in lines 17–19

```
Arrays.stream(strings)
      .map(String::toUpperCase)
      .collect(Collectors.toList()));
```

displays the Strings in uppercase letters. To do so, line 17 creates a Stream<String> from the array strings, then line 18 maps each String to its uppercase version by calling String instance method toUpperCase on each stream element.

Stream method map receives an object that implements the Function functional interface, representing a one-parameter method that performs a task with its parameter then returns the result. In this case, we pass to map an **unbound instance method reference** of the form *ClassName*::*instanceMethodName* (String::toUpperCase). "Unbound" means that the method reference does not indicate the specific object on which the method will be called—the compiler converts this to a one-parameter lambda that invokes the instance method on the lambda's parameter, which must have type *ClassName*. In this case, the compiler converts String::toUpperCase into a lambda like

```
s -> s.toUpperCase()
```

which returns the uppercase version of the lambda's argument. Line 19 collects the results into a List<String> that we output as a String.

17.11.2 Filtering Strings Then Sorting Them in Case-Insensitive Ascending Order

The stream pipeline in lines 23–26

```
Arrays.stream(strings)
      .filter(s -> s.compareToIgnoreCase("n") < 0)
      .sorted(String.CASE_INSENSITIVE_ORDER)
      .collect(Collectors.toList())
```

filters and sort the Strings. Line 23 creates a Stream<String> from the array strings, then line 24 calls Stream method filter to locate all the Strings that are less than "n", using a *case-insensitive* comparison in the Predicate lambda. Line 25 sorts the results and line 26 collects them into a List<String> that we output as a String.

In this case, line 25 invokes the version of Stream method sorted that receives a Comparator as an argument. A Comparator defines a compare method that returns a negative value if the first value being compared is less than the second, 0 if they're equal and a positive value if the first value is greater than the second. By default, method sorted uses the *natural order* for the type—for Strings, the natural order is case sensitive, which means that "Z" is less than "a". Passing the predefined Comparator String.CASE_INSENSITIVE_ORDER performs a *case-insensitive* sort.

17.11.3 Filtering Strings Then Sorting Them in Case-Insensitive Descending Order

The stream pipeline in lines 30–33

```
Arrays.stream(strings)
      .filter(s -> s.compareToIgnoreCase("n") < 0)
      .sorted(String.CASE_INSENSITIVE_ORDER.reversed())
      .collect(Collectors.toList()));
```

performs the same tasks as lines 23–26, but sorts the Strings in *descending* order. Functional interface Comparator contains default method **reversed**, which reverses an existing Comparator's ordering. When you apply reversed to String.CASE_INSENSITIVE_ORDER, sorted performs a case-insensitive sort and places the Strings in *descending* order

17.12 Stream<Employee> Manipulations

[This section demonstrates how lambdas and streams can be used to simplify programming tasks that you learned in Chapter 16, Generic Collections.]

The previous examples in this chapter performed stream manipulations on primitive types (like `int`) and Java class library types (like `Integer` and `String`). Of course, you also may perform operations on collections of programmer-defined types.

The example in Figs. 17.13–17.21 demonstrates various lambda and stream capabilities using a `Stream<Employee>`. Class `Employee` (Fig. 17.13) represents an employee with a first name, last name, salary and department and provides methods for getting these values. In addition, the class provides a `getName` method (lines 39–41) that returns the combined first and last name as a `String`, and a `toString` method (lines 44–48) that returns a formatted `String` containing the employee's first name, last name, salary and department. We walk through the rest of the code in Sections 17.12.1–17.12.7

```
1  // Fig. 17.13: Employee.java
2  // Employee class.
3  public class Employee {
4     private String firstName;
5     private String lastName;
6     private double salary;
7     private String department;
8
9     // constructor
10    public Employee(String firstName, String lastName,
11       double salary, String department) {
12       this.firstName = firstName;
13       this.lastName = lastName;
14       this.salary = salary;
15       this.department = department;
16    }
17
18    // get firstName
19    public String getFirstName() {
20       return firstName;
21    }
22
23    // get lastName
24    public String getLastName() {
25       return lastName;
26    }
27
28    // get salary
29    public double getSalary() {
30       return salary;
31    }
32
```

Fig. 17.13 | Employee class for use in Figs. 17.14–17.21. (Part 1 of 2.)

```java
    // get department
    public String getDepartment() {
       return department;
    }

    // return Employee's first and last name combined
    public String getName() {
       return String.format("%s %s", getFirstName(), getLastName());
    }

    // return a String containing the Employee's information
    @Override
    public String toString() {
       return String.format("%-8s %-8s %8.2f   %s",
          getFirstName(), getLastName(), getSalary(), getDepartment());
    }
 }
```

Fig. 17.13 | `Employee` class for use in Figs. 17.14–17.21. (Part 2 of 2.)

17.12.1 Creating and Displaying a `List<Employee>`

Class `ProcessingEmployees` (Figs. 17.14–17.21) is split into several figures so we can keep the discussions of the example's lambda and streams operations close to the corresponding code. Each figure also contains the portion of the program's output that correspond to code shown in that figure.

Figure 17.14 creates an array of `Employees` (lines 15–22) and gets its `List` view (line 25). Line 29 creates a `Stream<Employee>`, then uses `Stream` method `forEach` to display each `Employee`'s `String` representation. `Stream` method `forEach` expects as its argument an object that implements the `Consumer` functional interface, which represents an action to perform on each element of the stream—the corresponding method receives one argument and returns `void`. The bound instance method reference `System.out::println` is converted by the compiler into a one-parameter lambda that passes the lambda's argument—an `Employee`—to the `System.out` object's `println` instance method, which implicitly calls class `Employee`'s `toString` method to get the `String` representation. Figure 17.14's output shows the results of displaying each `Employee`'s `String` representation (line 29)—in this case, `Stream` method `forEach` passes each `Employee` to the `System.out` object's `println` method, which calls the `Employee`'s `toString` method.

```java
1  // Fig. 17.14: ProcessingEmployees.java
2  // Processing streams of Employee objects.
3  import java.util.Arrays;
4  import java.util.Comparator;
5  import java.util.List;
6  import java.util.Map;
7  import java.util.TreeMap;
8  import java.util.function.Function;
9  import java.util.function.Predicate;
```

Fig. 17.14 | Processing streams of `Employee` objects. (Part 1 of 2.)

```
10 import java.util.stream.Collectors;
11
12 public class ProcessingEmployees {
13    public static void main(String[] args) {
14       // initialize array of Employees
15       Employee[] employees = {
16          new Employee("Jason", "Red", 5000, "IT"),
17          new Employee("Ashley", "Green", 7600, "IT"),
18          new Employee("Matthew", "Indigo", 3587.5, "Sales"),
19          new Employee("James", "Indigo", 4700.77, "Marketing"),
20          new Employee("Luke", "Indigo", 6200, "IT"),
21          new Employee("Jason", "Blue", 3200, "Sales"),
22          new Employee("Wendy", "Brown", 4236.4, "Marketing")};
23
24       // get List view of the Employees
25       List<Employee> list = Arrays.asList(employees);
26
27       // display all Employees
28       System.out.println("Complete Employee list:");
29       list.stream().forEach(System.out::println);
30
```

```
Complete Employee list:
Jason     Red       5000.00   IT
Ashley    Green     7600.00   IT
Matthew   Indigo    3587.50   Sales
James     Indigo    4700.77   Marketing
Luke      Indigo    6200.00   IT
Jason     Blue      3200.00   Sales
Wendy     Brown     4236.40   Marketing
```

Fig. 17.14 | Processing streams of `Employee` objects. (Part 2 of 2.)

Java SE 9: Creating an Immutable `List<Employee>` with `List` Method `of` 9

In Fig. 17.14, we first created an array of `Employees` (lines 15–22), then obtained a `List` view of the array (line 25). Recall from Chapter 16 that in Java SE 9, you can populate an immutable `List` directly via `List` `static` method `of`, as in:

```
List<Employee> list = List.of(
   new Employee("Jason", "Red", 5000, "IT"),
   new Employee("Ashley", "Green", 7600, "IT"),
   new Employee("Matthew", "Indigo", 3587.5, "Sales"),
   new Employee("James", "Indigo", 4700.77, "Marketing"),
   new Employee("Luke", "Indigo", 6200, "IT"),
   new Employee("Jason", "Blue", 3200, "Sales"),
   new Employee("Wendy", "Brown", 4236.4, "Marketing"));
```

17.12.2 Filtering `Employees` with Salaries in a Specified Range

So far, we've used lambdas only by passing them directly as arguments to stream methods. Figure 17.15 demonstrates storing a lambda in a variable for later use. Lines 32–33 declare a variable of the functional interface type `Predicate<Employee>` and initialize it with a one-parameter lambda that returns a `boolean` (as required by `Predicate`). The lambda returns true if an `Employee`'s salary is in the range 4000 to 6000. We use the stored lambda in lines 40 and 47 to filter `Employees`.

```
31        // Predicate that returns true for salaries in the range $4000-$6000
32        Predicate<Employee> fourToSixThousand =
33           e -> (e.getSalary() >= 4000 && e.getSalary() <= 6000);
34
35        // Display Employees with salaries in the range $4000-$6000
36        // sorted into ascending order by salary
37        System.out.printf(
38           "%nEmployees earning $4000-$6000 per month sorted by salary:%n");
39        list.stream()
40            .filter(fourToSixThousand)
41            .sorted(Comparator.comparing(Employee::getSalary))
42            .forEach(System.out::println);
43
44        // Display first Employee with salary in the range $4000-$6000
45        System.out.printf("%nFirst employee who earns $4000-$6000:%n%s%n",
46           list.stream()
47               .filter(fourToSixThousand)
48               .findFirst()
49               .get());
50
```

```
Employees earning $4000-$6000 per month sorted by salary:
Wendy     Brown      4236.40   Marketing
James     Indigo     4700.77   Marketing
Jason     Red        5000.00   IT

First employee who earns $4000-$6000:
Jason     Red        5000.00   IT
```

Fig. 17.15 | Filtering `Employees` with salaries in the range $4000–$6000.

The stream pipeline in lines 39–42 performs the following tasks:

- Line 39 creates a `Stream<Employee>`.
- Line 40 filters the stream using the `Predicate` named `fourToSixThousand`.
- Line 41 sorts *by salary* the `Employees` that remain in the stream. To create a salary `Comparator`, we use the `Comparator` interface's `static` method `comparing`, which receives a `Function` that performs a task on its argument and returns the result. The unbound instance method reference `Employee::getSalary` is converted by the compiler into a one-parameter lambda that calls `getSalary` on its `Employee` argument. The `Comparator` returned by method `comparing` calls its `Function` argument on each of two `Employee` objects, then returns a negative value if the first `Employee`'s salary is less than the second, 0 if they're equal and a positive value if the first `Employee`'s salary is greater than the second. `Stream` method `sorted` uses these values to order the `Employees`.
- Finally, line 42 performs the terminal `forEach` operation that processes the stream pipeline and outputs the `Employees` sorted by salary.

Short-Circuit Stream Pipeline Processing

In Section 5.9, you studied short-circuit evaluation with the logical AND (&&) and logical OR (||) operators. One of the nice performance features of lazy evaluation is the ability to perform *short-circuit evaluation*—that is, to stop processing the stream pipeline as soon as the desired result is available. Line 48 of Fig. 17.15 demonstrates `Stream` method **`findFirst`**—a *short-circuiting terminal operation* that processes the stream pipeline and terminates processing as soon as the *first* object from the stream's intermediate operation(s) is found. Based on the original list of `Employees`, the stream pipeline in lines 46–49

```
list.stream()
    .filter(fourToSixThousand)
    .findFirst()
    .get()
```

which filters `Employees` with salaries in the range $4000–$6000—proceeds as follows:

- The `Predicate fourToSixThousand` is applied to the first `Employee` (Jason Red). His salary ($5000.00) is in the range $4000–$6000, so the `Predicate` returns `true` and processing of the stream terminates *immediately*, having processed only one of the eight objects in the stream.
- Method `findFirst` then returns an `Optional` (in this case, an `Optional<Employee>`) containing the object that was found, if any. The call to `Optional` method `get` (line 49) returns the matching `Employee` object in this example. Even if the stream contained millions of `Employee` objects, the `filter` operation would be performed only until a match was found.

We knew from this example's `Employees` that this pipeline would find at least one `Employee` with a salary in the range 4000–6000. So, we called `Optional` method `get` without first checking whether the `Optional` contained a result. If `findFirst` yields an empty `Optional`, this would cause a `NoSuchElementException`.

Error-Prevention Tip 17.3

For a stream operation that returns an `Optional<T>`, store the result in a variable of that type, then use the object's `isPresent` method to confirm that there is a result, before calling the `Optional`'s `get` method. This prevents `NoSuchElementException`s.

Method `findFirst` is one of several search-related terminal operations. Figure 17.16 shows several similar `Stream` methods.

Search-related terminal stream operations	
`findAny`	Similar to `findFirst`, but finds and returns *any* stream element based on the prior intermediate operations. Immediately terminates processing of the stream pipeline once such an element is found. Typically, `findFirst` is used with sequential streams and `findAny` is used with parallel streams (Section 23.13).
`anyMatch`	Determines whether *any* stream elements match a specified condition. Returns `true` if at least one stream element matches and `false` otherwise. Immediately terminates processing of the stream pipeline if an element matches.

Fig. 17.16 | Search-related terminal stream operations. (Part 1 of 2.)

Search-related terminal stream operations	
`allMatch`	Determines whether *all* of the elements in the stream match a specified condition. Returns `true` if so and `false` otherwise. Immediately terminates processing of the stream pipeline if any element does not match.

Fig. 17.16 | Search-related terminal stream operations. (Part 2 of 2.)

17.12.3 Sorting Employees By Multiple Fields

Figure 17.17 shows how to use streams to sort objects by *multiple* fields. In this example, we sort `Employees` by last name, then, for `Employees` with the same last name, we also sort them by first name. To do so, we begin by creating two `Functions` that each receive an `Employee` and return a `String`:

- `byFirstName` (line 52) is assigned a method reference for `Employee` instance method `getFirstName`
- `byLastName` (line 53) is assigned a method reference for `Employee` instance method `getLastName`

Next, we use these `Functions` to create a `Comparator` (`lastThenFirst`; lines 56–57) that first compares two `Employees` by last name, then compares them by first name. We use `Comparator` method `comparing` to create a `Comparator` that calls `Function` `byLastName` on an `Employee` to get its last name. On the resulting `Comparator`, we call `Comparator` method **`thenComparing`** to create a *composed* `Comparator` that first compares `Employees` by last name and, *if the last names are equal*, then compares them by first name. Lines 62–64 use this new `lastThenFirst` `Comparator` to sort the `Employees` in *ascending* order, then display the results. We reuse the `Comparator` in lines 69–71, but call its `reversed` method to indicate that the `Employees` should be sorted in *descending* order by last name, then first name. Lines 52–57 may be expressed more concisely as:

```
Comparator<Employee> lastThenFirst =
   Comparator.comparing(Employee::getLastName)
          .thenComparing(Employee::getFirstName);
```

```
51       // Functions for getting first and last names from an Employee
52       Function<Employee, String> byFirstName = Employee::getFirstName;
53       Function<Employee, String> byLastName = Employee::getLastName;
54
55       // Comparator for comparing Employees by first name then last name
56       Comparator<Employee> lastThenFirst =
57          Comparator.comparing(byLastName).thenComparing(byFirstName);
58
59       // sort employees by last name, then first name
60       System.out.printf(
61          "%nEmployees in ascending order by last name then first:%n");
62       list.stream()
63           .sorted(lastThenFirst)
64           .forEach(System.out::println);
```

Fig. 17.17 | Sorting `Employees` by last name then first name. (Part 1 of 2.)

```

      // sort employees in descending order by last name, then first name
      System.out.printf(
         "%nEmployees in descending order by last name then first:%n");
      list.stream()
          .sorted(lastThenFirst.reversed())
          .forEach(System.out::println);

```

```
Employees in ascending order by last name then first:
Jason    Blue      3200.00  Sales
Wendy    Brown     4236.40  Marketing
Ashley   Green     7600.00  IT
James    Indigo    4700.77  Marketing
Luke     Indigo    6200.00  IT
Matthew  Indigo    3587.50  Sales
Jason    Red       5000.00  IT

Employees in descending order by last name then first:
Jason    Red       5000.00  IT
Matthew  Indigo    3587.50  Sales
Luke     Indigo    6200.00  IT
James    Indigo    4700.77  Marketing
Ashley   Green     7600.00  IT
Wendy    Brown     4236.40  Marketing
Jason    Blue      3200.00  Sales
```

Fig. 17.17 | Sorting `Employees` by last name then first name. (Part 2 of 2.)

Aside: Composing Lambda Expressions

Many functional interfaces in the package `java.util.function` package provide `default` methods that enable you to compose functionality. For example, consider the interface `IntPredicate`, which contains three `default` methods:

- **and**—performs a *logical AND* with *short-circuit evaluation* between the `IntPredicate` on which it's called and the `IntPredicate` it receives as an argument.
- **negate**—*reverses* the `boolean` value of the `IntPredicate` on which it's called.
- **or**—performs a *logical OR* with *short-circuit evaluation* between the `IntPredicate` on which it's called and the `IntPredicate` it receives as an argument.

You can use these methods and `IntPredicate` objects to compose more complex conditions. For example, consider the following two `IntPredicates` that are each initialized with lambdas:

```
IntPredicate even = value -> value % 2 == 0;
IntPredicate greaterThan5 = value -> value > 5;
```

To locate all the even integers greater than 5 in an `IntStream`, you could pass to `IntStream` method `filter` the following composed `IntPredicate`:

```
even.and(greaterThan5)
```

Like `IntPredicate`, functional interface `Predicate` represents a method that returns a `boolean` indicating whether its argument satisfies a condition. `Predicate` also contains methods **and** and **or** for combining predicates, and **negate** for reversing a predicate's boolean value.

17.12.4 Mapping Employees to Unique-Last-Name Strings

You previously used map operations to perform calculations on int values, to convert ints to Strings and to convert Strings to uppercase letters. Figure 17.18 maps objects of one type (Employee) to objects of a different type (String). The stream pipeline in lines 75–79 performs the following tasks:

- Line 75 creates a Stream<Employee>.
- Line 76 maps the Employees to their last names using the unbound instance-method reference Employee::getName as method map's Function argument. The result is a Stream<String> containing only the Employees' last names.
- Line 77 calls Stream method **distinct** on the Stream<String> to eliminate any duplicate Strings—the resulting stream contains only unique last names.
- Line 78 sorts the unique last names.
- Finally, line 79 performs a terminal forEach operation that processes the stream pipeline and outputs the unique last names in sorted order.

Lines 84–87 sort the Employees by last name then, first name, then map the Employees to Strings with Employee instance method getName (line 86) and display the sorted names in a terminal forEach operation.

```
73        // display unique employee last names sorted
74        System.out.printf("%nUnique employee last names:%n");
75        list.stream()
76            .map(Employee::getLastName)
77            .distinct()
78            .sorted()
79            .forEach(System.out::println);
80
81        // display only first and last names
82        System.out.printf(
83           "%nEmployee names in order by last name then first name:%n");
84        list.stream()
85            .sorted(lastThenFirst)
86            .map(Employee::getName)
87            .forEach(System.out::println);
88
```

```
Unique employee last names:
Blue
Brown
Green
Indigo
Red
```

Fig. 17.18 | Mapping Employee objects to last names and whole names. (Part 1 of 2.)

```
Employee names in order by last name then first name:
Jason Blue
Wendy Brown
Ashley Green
James Indigo
Luke Indigo
Matthew Indigo
Jason Red
```

Fig. 17.18 | Mapping `Employee` objects to last names and whole names. (Part 2 of 2.)

17.12.5 Grouping Employees By Department

Previously, we've used the terminal stream operation `collect` to concatenate stream elements into a `String` representation and to place stream elements into `List` collections. Figure 17.19 uses `Stream` method `collect` (line 93) to group `Employees` by department.

```
89          // group Employees by department
90          System.out.printf("%nEmployees by department:%n");
91          Map<String, List<Employee>> groupedByDepartment =
92             list.stream()
93                 .collect(Collectors.groupingBy(Employee::getDepartment));
94          groupedByDepartment.forEach(
95             (department, employeesInDepartment) -> {
96                System.out.printf("%n%s%n", department);
97                employeesInDepartment.forEach(
98                   employee -> System.out.printf("   %s%n", employee));
99             }
100         );
101
```

```
Employees by department:

Sales
   Matthew  Indigo    3587.50   Sales
   Jason    Blue      3200.00   Sales

IT
   Jason    Red       5000.00   IT
   Ashley   Green     7600.00   IT
   Luke     Indigo    6200.00   IT

Marketing
   James    Indigo    4700.77   Marketing
   Wendy    Brown     4236.40   Marketing
```

Fig. 17.19 | Grouping `Employees` by department.

Recall that `collect`'s argument is a `Collector` that specifies how to summarize the data into a useful form. In this case, we use the `Collector` returned by `Collectors static` method **`groupingBy`**, which receives a `Function` that classifies the objects in the stream.

The values returned by this `Function` are used as the keys in a `Map` collection. The corresponding values, by default, are `List`s containing the stream elements in a given category.

When method `collect` is used with this `Collector`, the result is a `Map<String, List<Employee>>` in which each `String` key is a department and each `List<Employee>` contains the `Employee`s in that department. We assign this `Map` to variable `groupedByDepartment`, which we use in lines 94–100 to display the `Employee`s grouped by department. `Map` method **`forEach`** performs an operation on each of the `Map`'s key–value pairs—in this case, the keys are departments and the values are collections of the `Employee`s in a given department. The argument to this method is an object that implements functional interface **`BiConsumer`**, which represents a two-parameter method that does not return a result. For a `Map`, the first parameter represents the key and the second represents the corresponding value.

17.12.6 Counting the Number of `Employees` in Each Department

Figure 17.20 once again demonstrates `Stream` method `collect` and `Collectors` `static` method `groupingBy`, but in this case we count the number of `Employee`s in each department. The technique shown here enables us to combine grouping and reduction into a single operation.

```
102        // count number of Employees in each department
103        System.out.printf("%nCount of Employees by department:%n");
104        Map<String, Long> employeeCountByDepartment =
105           list.stream()
106               .collect(Collectors.groupingBy(Employee::getDepartment,
107                  Collectors.counting()));
108        employeeCountByDepartment.forEach(
109           (department, count) -> System.out.printf(
110              "%s has %d employee(s)%n", department, count));
111
```

```
Count of Employees by department:
Sales has 2 employee(s)
IT has 3 employee(s)
Marketing has 2 employee(s)
```

Fig. 17.20 | Counting the number of `Employees` in each department.

The stream pipeline in lines 104–107 produces a `Map<String, Long>` in which each `String` key is a department name and the corresponding `Long` value is the number of `Employee`s in that department. In this case, we use a version of `Collectors` `static` method `groupingBy` that receives two arguments:

- the first is a `Function` that classifies the objects in the stream and
- the second is another `Collector` (known as the **downstream `Collector`**) that's used to collect the objects classified by the `Function`.

We use a call to `Collectors` `static` method `counting` as the second argument. This resulting `Collector` reduces the elements in a given classification to a count of those elements, rather than collecting them into a List. Lines 108–110 then output the key–value pairs from the resulting Map<String, Long>.

17.12.7 Summing and Averaging Employee Salaries

Previously, we showed that streams of primitive-type elements can be mapped to streams of objects with method mapToObj (found in classes IntStream, LongStream and DoubleStream). Similarly, a Stream of objects may be mapped to an IntStream, LongStream or DoubleStream. Figure 17.21 demonstrates Stream method **mapToDouble** (lines 116, 123 and 129), which maps objects to double values and returns a DoubleStream. In this case, we map Employee objects to their salaries so that we can calculate the *sum* and *average*.

Method mapToDouble receives an object that implements the functional interface **ToDoubleFunction** (package java.util.function), which represents a one-parameter method that returns a double value. Lines 116, 123 and 129 each pass to mapToDouble the unbound instance-method reference Employee::getSalary, which returns the current Employee's salary as a double. The compiler converts this method reference into a one-parameter lambda that calls getSalary on its Employee argument.

```
112         // sum of Employee salaries with DoubleStream sum method
113         System.out.printf(
114            "%nSum of Employees' salaries (via sum method): %.2f%n",
115            list.stream()
116                .mapToDouble(Employee::getSalary)
117                .sum());
118
119         // calculate sum of Employee salaries with Stream reduce method
120         System.out.printf(
121            "Sum of Employees' salaries (via reduce method): %.2f%n",
122            list.stream()
123                .mapToDouble(Employee::getSalary)
124                .reduce(0, (value1, value2) -> value1 + value2));
125
126         // average of Employee salaries with DoubleStream average method
127         System.out.printf("Average of Employees' salaries: %.2f%n",
128            list.stream()
129                .mapToDouble(Employee::getSalary)
130                .average()
131                .getAsDouble());
132      }
133   }
```

```
Sum of Employees' salaries (via sum method): 34524.67
Sum of Employees' salaries (via reduce method): 34525.67
Average of Employees' salaries: 4932.10
```

Fig. 17.21 | Summing and averaging Employee salaries.

Lines 115–117 create a Stream<Employee>, map it to a DoubleStream, then invoke DoubleStream method sum to total the Employees' salaries. Lines 122–124 also sum the

Employees' salaries, but do so using DoubleStream method reduce rather than sum—note that the lambda in line 124 could be replaced with the static method reference

```
Double::sum
```

Class Double's sum method receives two doubles and returns their sum.

Finally, lines 128–131 calculate the average of the Employees' salaries using DoubleStream method average, which returns an OptionalDouble in case the DoubleStream does not contain any elements. Here, we know the stream has elements, so we simply call OptionalDouble method getAsDouble to get the result.

17.13 Creating a Stream<String> from a File

Figure 17.22 uses lambdas and streams to summarize the number of occurrences of each word in a file, then display a summary of the words in alphabetical order grouped by starting letter. This is commonly called a concordance:

```
http://en.wikipedia.org/wiki/Concordance_(publishing)
```

Concordances are often used to analyze published works. For example, concordances of William Shakespeare's and Christopher Marlowe's works (among others) have been used to question whether they are the same person. Figure 17.23 shows the program's output. Line 14 of Fig. 17.22 creates a regular expression Pattern that we'll use to split lines of text into their individual words. The Pattern \s+ represents one or more consecutive white-space characters—recall that because \ indicates an escape sequence in a String, we must specify each \ in a regular expression as \\. As written, this program assumes that the file it reads contains no punctuation, but you could use regular-expression techniques from Section 14.7 to remove punctuation.

```
1  // Fig. 17.22: StreamOfLines.java
2  // Counting word occurrences in a text file.
3  import java.io.IOException;
4  import java.nio.file.Files;
5  import java.nio.file.Paths;
6  import java.util.Map;
7  import java.util.TreeMap;
8  import java.util.regex.Pattern;
9  import java.util.stream.Collectors;
10
11 public class StreamOfLines {
12    public static void main(String[] args) throws IOException {
13       // Regex that matches one or more consecutive whitespace characters
14       Pattern pattern = Pattern.compile("\\s+");
15
16       // count occurrences of each word in a Stream<String> sorted by word
17       Map<String, Long> wordCounts =
18          Files.lines(Paths.get("Chapter2Paragraph.txt"))
19               .flatMap(line -> pattern.splitAsStream(line))
20               .collect(Collectors.groupingBy(String::toLowerCase,
21                  TreeMap::new, Collectors.counting()));
```

Fig. 17.22 | Counting word occurrences in a text file. (Part 1 of 2.)

```

      // display the words grouped by starting letter
      wordCounts.entrySet()
         .stream()
         .collect(
            Collectors.groupingBy(entry -> entry.getKey().charAt(0),
               TreeMap::new, Collectors.toList()))
         .forEach((letter, wordList) -> {
            System.out.printf("%n%C%n", letter);
            wordList.stream().forEach(word -> System.out.printf(
               "%13s: %d%n", word.getKey(), word.getValue()));
         });
   }
}
```

Fig. 17.22 | Counting word occurrences in a text file. (Part 2 of 2.)

```
A
            a: 2
          and: 3
  application: 2
   arithmetic: 1

B
        begin: 1

C
  calculates: 1
 calculations: 1
      chapter: 1
     chapters: 1
  commandline: 1
     compares: 1
   comparison: 1
      compile: 1
     computer: 1
D
    decisions: 1
 demonstrates: 1
      display: 1
     displays: 2

E
      example: 1
     examples: 1

F
          for: 1
         from: 1

H
          how: 2

I
       inputs: 1
     instruct: 1
   introduces: 1

J
         java: 1
          jdk: 1

L
         last: 1
        later: 1
        learn: 1

M
         make: 1
     messages: 2

N
      numbers: 2

O
      obtains: 1
           of: 1
           on: 1
       output: 1

P
      perform: 1
      present: 1
      program: 1
  programming: 1
     programs: 2

R
       result: 1
      results: 2
          run: 1

S
         save: 1
       screen: 1
         show: 1
          sum: 1

T
         that: 3
          the: 7
        their: 2
         then: 2
         this: 2
           to: 4
        tools: 1
          two: 2

U
          use: 2
         user: 1

W
           we: 2
         with: 1

Y
       you'll: 2
```

Fig. 17.23 | Output of Fig. 17.22 arranged in three columns.

Summarizing the Occurrences of Each Word in the File

The stream pipeline in lines 17–21

```
Map<String, Long> wordCounts =
   Files.lines(Paths.get("Chapter2Paragraph.txt"))
        .flatMap(line -> pattern.splitAsStream(line))
        .collect(Collectors.groupingBy(String::toLowerCase,
           TreeMap::new, Collectors.counting()));
```

summarizes the contents of the text file "`Chapter2Paragraph.txt`" (which is located in the folder with the example) into a `Map<String, Long>` in which each `String` key is a word in the file and the corresponding `Long` value is the number of occurrences of that word. The pipeline performs the following tasks:

8
- Line 18 calls `Files` method **`lines`** (added in Java SE 8) which returns a `Stream<String>` that reads lines of text from a file and returns each line as a `String`. Class `Files` (package `java.nio.file`) is one of many classes throughout the Java APIs which provide methods that return `Streams`.
- Line 19 uses `Stream` method **`flatMap`** to break each line of text into its separate words. Method `flatMap` receives a `Function` that maps an object into a stream of elements. In this case, the object is a `String` containing words and the result is a `Stream<String>` for the individual words. The lambda in line 19 passes the `String` representing a line of text to `Pattern` method **`splitAsStream`** (added in
8 Java SE 8), which uses the regular expression specified in the `Pattern` (line 14) to tokenize the `String` into its individual words. The result of line 19 is a `Stream<String>` for the individual words in all the lines of text. (This lambda could be replaced with the method reference `pattern::splitAsStream`.)
- Lines 20–21 use `Stream` method `collect` to count the frequency of each word and place the words and their counts into a `TreeMap<String, Long>`—a `TreeMap` because maintains its keys in sorted order. Here, we use a version of `Collectors` method `groupingBy` that receives three arguments—a classifier, a `Map` factory and a downstream `Collector`. The classifier is a `Function` that returns objects for use as keys in the resulting `Map`—the method reference `String::toLowerCase` converts each word to lowercase. The `Map` factory is an object that implements interface `Supplier` and returns a new `Map` collection—here we use the **constructor reference** `TreeMap::new`, which returns a `TreeMap` that maintains its keys in sorted order. The compiler converts a constructor reference into a parameterless lambda that returns a new `TreeMap`. `Collectors.counting()` is the downstream `Collector` that determines the number of occurrences of each key in the stream. The `TreeMap`'s key type is determined by the classifier `Function`'s return type (`String`), and the `TreeMap`'s value type is determined by the downstream collector—`Collectors.counting()` returns a `Long`.

Displaying the Summary Grouped by Starting Letter

Next, the stream pipeline in lines 24–33 groups the key–value pairs in the `Map wordCounts` by the keys' first letter:

```
wordCounts.entrySet()
          .stream()
          .collect(
             Collectors.groupingBy(entry -> entry.getKey().charAt(0),
               TreeMap::new, Collectors.toList()))
          .forEach((letter, wordList) -> {
             System.out.printf("%n%C%n", letter);
             wordList.stream().forEach(word -> System.out.printf(
                "%13s: %d%n", word.getKey(), word.getValue()));
          });
```

This produces a new `Map` in which each key is a `Character` and the corresponding value is a `List` of the key–value pairs in `wordCounts` in which the key starts with the `Character`. The statement performs the following tasks:

- First we need to get a `Stream` for processing the key–value pairs in `wordCounts`. Interface `Map` does not contain any methods that return `Stream`s. So, line 24 calls `Map` method `entrySet` on `wordCounts` to get a `Set` of **`Map.Entry`** objects that each contain one key–value pair from `wordCounts`. This produces an object of type `Set<Map.Entry<String, Long>>`.
- Line 25 calls `Set` method `stream` to get a `Stream<Map.Entry<String, Long>>`.
- Lines 26–28 call `Stream` method `collect` with three arguments—a classifier, a `Map` factory and a downstream `Collector`. The classifier `Function` in this case gets the key from the `Map.Entry` then uses `String` method `charAt` to get the key's first character—this becomes a `Character` key in the resulting `Map`. Once again, we use the constructor reference `TreeMap::new` as the `Map` factory to create a `TreeMap` that maintains its keys in sorted order. The downstream `Collector` (`Collectors.toList()`) places the `Map.Entry` objects into a `List` collection. The result of `collect` is a `Map<Character, List<Map.Entry<String, Long>>>`.
- Finally, to display the summary of the words and their counts by letter (i.e., the concordance), lines 29–33 pass a lambda to `Map` method `forEach`. The lambda (a `BiConsumer`) receives two parameters—`letter` and `wordList` represent the `Character` key and the `List` value, respectively, for each key–value pair in the `Map` produced by the preceding `collect` operation. The body of this lambda has two statements, so it *must* be enclosed in curly braces. The statement in line 30 displays the `Character` key on its own line. The statement in lines 31–32 gets a `Stream<Map.Entry<String, Long>>` from the `wordList`, then calls `Stream` method `forEach` to display the key and value from each `Map.Entry` object.

17.14 Streams of Random Values

Figure 6.7 summarized 60,000,000 rolls of a six-sided die using *external iteration* (a `for` loop) and a `switch` statement that determined which counter to increment. We then displayed the results using separate statements that performed external iteration. In Fig. 7.7, we reimplemented Fig. 6.7, replacing the entire `switch` statement with a single statement that incremented counters in an array—that version of rolling the die still used external iteration to produce and summarize 60,000,000 random rolls and to display the final results. Both prior versions of this example used mutable variables to control the external iteration and to summarize the results. Figure 17.24 reimplements those programs with a *single statement* that does it all, using lambdas, streams, internal iteration and *no mutable variables* to roll the die 60,000,000 times, calculate the frequencies and display the results.

Performance Tip 17.3

The techniques that `SecureRandom` *uses to produce secure random numbers are significantly slower than those used by* `Random` *(package* `java.util`*). For this reason, Fig. 17.24 may appear to freeze when you run it—on our computers, it took over one minute to complete. To save time, you can speed this example's execution by using class* `Random`*. However, industrial-strength applications should use secure random numbers. Exercise 17.25 asks you to time Fig. 17.24's stream pipeline, then Exercise 23.18 asks you time the pipeline using parallel streams to see if the performance improvems on a multicore system.*

```java
// Fig. 17.24: RandomIntStream.java
// Rolling a die 60,000,000 times with streams
import java.security.SecureRandom;
import java.util.function.Function;
import java.util.stream.Collectors;

public class RandomIntStream {
   public static void main(String[] args) {
      SecureRandom random = new SecureRandom();

      // roll a die 60,000,000 times and summarize the results
      System.out.printf("%-6s%s%n", "Face", "Frequency");
      random.ints(60_000_000, 1, 7)
            .boxed()
            .collect(Collectors.groupingBy(Function.identity(),
               Collectors.counting()))
            .forEach((face, frequency) ->
               System.out.printf("%-6d%d%n", face, frequency));
   }
}
```

```
Face  Frequency
1     9992993
2     10000363
3     10002272
4     10003810
5     10000321
6     10000241
```

Fig. 17.24 | Rolling a die 60,000,000 times with streams.

Class `SecureRandom` has overloaded methods `ints`, **`longs`** and **`doubles`**, which it inherits from class `Random` (package `java.util`). These methods return an `IntStream`, a `LongStream` or a `DoubleStream`, respectively, that represent streams of random numbers. Each method has four overloads. We describe the `ints` overloads here—methods `longs` and `doubles` perform the same tasks for streams of `long` and `double` values, respectively:

- `ints()`—creates an `IntStream` for an *infinite stream* (Section 17.15) of random `int` values.

- `ints(long)`—creates an `IntStream` with the specified number of random `ints`.
- `ints(int, int)`—creates an `IntStream` for an *infinite stream* of random `int` values in the half-open range starting with the first argument and up to, but not including, the second argument.
- `ints(long, int, int)`—creates an `IntStream` with the specified number of random `int` values in the range starting with the first argument and up to, but not including, the second argument.

Line 13 uses the last overloaded version of `ints` (which we introduced in Section 17.6) to create an `IntStream` of 60,000,000 random integer values in the range 1–6.

Converting an `IntStream` *to a* `Stream<Integer>`

We summarize the roll frequencies in this example by collecting them into a `Map<Integer, Long>` in which each `Integer` key is a side of the die and each `Long` value is the frequency of that side. Unfortunately, Java does not allow primitive values in collections, so to summarize the results in a `Map`, we must first convert the `IntStream` to a `Stream<Integer>`. We do this by calling `IntStream` method **`boxed`**.

Summarizing the Die Frequencies

Lines 15–16 call `Stream` method `collect` to summarize the results into a `Map<Integer, Long>`. The first argument to `Collectors` method `groupingBy` (line 15) calls `static` method **`identity`** from interface `Function`, which creates a `Function` that simply returns its argument. This allows the actual random values to be used as the `Map`'s keys. The second argument to method `groupingBy` counts the number of occurrences of each key.

Displaying the Results

Lines 17–18 call the resulting `Map`'s `forEach` method to display the summary of the results. This method receives an object that implements the `BiConsumer` functional interface as an argument. Recall that for `Map`s, the first parameter represents the key and the second represents the corresponding value. The lambda in lines 17–18 uses parameter `face` as the key and `frequency` as the value, and displays the face and frequency.

17.15 Infinite Streams

A data structure, such as an array or a collection, always represents a finite number of elements—all the elements are stored in memory, and memory is finite. Of course, any stream created from a finite data structure will have a finite number of elements, as has been the case in this chapter's prior examples.

Lazy evaluation makes it possible to work with **infinite streams** that represent an unknown, potentially infinite, number of elements. For example, you could define a method `nextPrime` that produces the next prime number in sequence every time you call it. You could then use this to define an infinite stream that *conceptually* represents all prime numbers. However, because streams are lazy until you perform a terminal operation, you can use intermediate operations to restrict the total number of elements that are actually calculated when a terminal operation is performed. Consider the following pseudocode stream pipeline:

Create an infinite stream representing all prime numbers
If the prime number is less than 10,000
Display the prime number

Even though we begin with an infinite stream, only the finite set of primes less than 10,000 would be displayed.

You create infinite streams with the stream-interfaces methods `iterate` and `generate`. For the purpose of this discussion, we'll use the `IntStream` version of these methods.

`IntStream` *Method* `iterate`

Consider the following infinite stream pipeline:

```
IntStream.iterate(1, x -> x + 1)
         .forEach(System.out::println);
```

`IntStream` method **`iterate`** generates an ordered sequence of values starting with the seed value (`1`) in its first argument. Each subsequent element is produced by applying to the preceding value in the sequence the `IntUnaryOperator` specified as `iterate`'s second argument. The preceding pipeline generates the infinite sequence 1, 2, 3, 4, 5, …, but this pipeline has a problem. We did not specify how many elements to produce, so this is the equivalent of an infinite loop.

Limiting an Infinite Stream's Number of Elements

One way to limit the total number of elements that an infinite stream produces is the short-circuiting terminal operation **`limit`**, which specifies the maximum number of elements to process from a stream. In the case of an infinite stream, `limit` terminates the infinite generation of elements. So, the following stream pipeline

```
IntStream.iterate(1, x -> x + 1)
         .limit(10)
         .forEach(System.out::println);
```

begins with an infinite stream, but limits the total number of elements produced to `10`, so it displays the numbers from 1 through 10. Similarly, the pipeline

```
IntStream.iterate(1, x -> x + 1)
         .map(x -> x * x)
         .limit(10)
         .sum()
```

starts with an infinite stream, but sums only the squares of the integers from 1 through 10.

Error-Prevention Tip 17.4

Ensure that stream pipelines using methods that produce infinite streams `limit` *the number of elements to produce.*

`IntStream` *Method* `generate`

You also may create unordered infinite streams using method **`generate`**, which receives an `IntSupplier` representing a method that takes no arguments and returns an `int`. For example, if you have a `SecureRandom` object named `random`, the following stream pipeline generates and displays 10 random integers:

```
IntStream.generate(() -> random.nextInt())
         .limit(10)
         .forEach(System.out::println);
```

This is equivalent to using `SecureRandom`'s no-argument `ints` method (Section 17.14):

```
SecureRandom.ints()
         .limit(10)
         .forEach(System.out::println);
```

17.16 Lambda Event Handlers

In Section 12.5.5, you learned how to implement an event handler using an anonymous inner class. Event-listener interfaces with one `abstract` method—like `ChangeListener`—are functional interfaces. For such interfaces, you can implement event handlers with lambdas. For example, the following `Slider` event handler from Fig. 12.23:

```
tipPercentageSlider.valueProperty().addListener(
   new ChangeListener<Number>() {
      @Override
      public void changed(ObservableValue<? extends Number> ov,
         Number oldValue, Number newValue) {
         tipPercentage =
            BigDecimal.valueOf(newValue.intValue() / 100.0);
         tipPercentageLabel.setText(percent.format(tipPercentage));
      }
   }
);
```

can be implemented more concisely with a lambda as

```
tipPercentageSlider.valueProperty().addListener(
   (ov, oldValue, newValue) -> {
      tipPercentage =
         BigDecimal.valueOf(newValue.intValue() / 100.0);
      tipPercentageLabel.setText(percent.format(tipPercentage));
   });
```

For a simple event handler, a lambda significantly reduces the amount of code you need to write.

17.17 Additional Notes on Java SE 8 Interfaces

Java SE 8 Interfaces Allow Inheritance of Method Implementations 8

Functional interfaces *must* contain only one `abstract` method, but may also contain `default` methods and `static` methods that are fully implemented in the interface declarations. For example, the `Function` interface—which is used extensively in functional programming—has methods `apply` (`abstract`), `compose` (`default`), `andThen` (`default`) and `identity` (`static`).

When a class implements an interface with `default` methods and does *not* override them, the class inherits the `default` methods' implementations. An interface's designer can now evolve an interface by adding new `default` and `static` methods without breaking existing code that implements the interface. For example, interface `Comparator`

(Section 16.7.1) now contains many default and static methods, but older classes that implement this interface will still compile and operate properly in Java SE 8.

Recall that one class can implement many interfaces. If a class implements two or more unrelated interfaces that provide a default method with the same signature, the implementing class *must* override that method; otherwise, a compilation error occurs.

8 *Java SE 8:* **@FunctionalInterface** *Annotation*

You can create your own functional interfaces by ensuring that each contains only one abstract method and zero or more default and/or static methods. Though not required, you can declare that an interface is a functional interface by preceding it with the **@FunctionalInterface annotation**. The compiler will then ensure that the interface contains only one abstract method; otherwise, it will generate a compilation error.

17.18 Wrap-Up

In this chapter, you worked with lambdas, streams and functional interfaces. We presented many examples, often showing simpler ways to implement tasks that you programmed in earlier chapters.

You learned how to process elements in an IntStream—a stream of int values. You created an IntStream representing a closed range of ints, then used intermediate and terminal stream operations to create and process a stream pipeline that produced a result. We used lambdas to create anonymous methods that implemented functional interfaces and passed these lambdas to methods in stream pipelines to specify the processing steps for the streams' elements. We also created IntStreams from existing arrays of int values.

We discussed how a stream's intermediate processing steps are applied to each element before moving onto the next. We showed how to use a forEach terminal operation to perform an operation on each stream element. We used reduction operations to count the number of stream elements, determine the minimum and maximum values, and sum and average the values. You also used method reduce to create your own reduction operations.

You used intermediate operations to filter elements that matched a predicate and map elements to new values—in each case, these operations produced intermediate streams on which you could perform additional processing. You also learned how to sort elements in ascending and descending order and how to sort objects by multiple fields.

We demonstrated how to store a stream pipeline's results in a collection by using various predefined Collector implementations provided by class Collectors. You also learned how to use a Collector to group elements into categories.

You learned that various classes can create stream data sources. For example, you used Files method lines to get a Stream<String> that read lines of text from a file and used SecureRandom method ints to get an IntStream of random values. You also learned how to convert an IntStream into a Stream<Integer> (via method boxed) so that you could use Stream method collect to summarize the frequencies of the Integer values and store the results in a Map.

We introduced infinite streams and showed how to limit the number of elements they generate. You saw how to implement an event-handling functional interface using a lambda. Finally, we presented some additional information about Java SE 8 interfaces and streams. In the next chapter, we discuss recursive programming in which methods call themselves either directly or indirectly.

Summary

Section 17.1 Introduction

- Java SE 8 added lambdas and streams—key technologies of functional programming.
- Lambdas and streams enable you to write certain kinds of programs faster, simpler, more concisely and with fewer bugs than with previous techniques.

Section 17.2 Streams and Reduction

- In counter-controlled iteration, you typically determine *what* you want to accomplish, then specify precisely *how* to accomplish it using a `for` loop.

Section 17.2.1 Summing the Integers from 1 through 10 with a `for` Loop

- With external iteration *you* specify all the iteration details.

Section 17.2.2 External Iteration with `for` Is Error Prone

- External iteration mutates variables during each loop iteration.
- Every time you write code that modifies a variable, it's possible to introduce an error.

Section 17.2.3 Summing with a Stream and Reduction

- Class `IntStream` (package `java.util.stream`) conveniently defines methods that enable you to avoid counter-controlled iteration.
- A stream is a sequence of elements on which you perform tasks.
- A stream pipeline moves the stream's elements through a sequence of tasks (or processing steps).
- A stream pipeline typically begins with a method call that creates the stream—this is known as the data source.
- `IntStream` `static` method `rangeClosed` creates an `IntStream` containing a closed range of values—that is, a range of elements that includes both of the method's arguments.
- `IntStream` method `range` produces a half-open range of values from its first argument up to, but not including, its second argument.
- `IntStream`'s `sum` instance method returns the sum of all the `int`s in the stream.
- Method `sum` performs a reduction—it reduces the stream of values to a single value. Other predefined reductions include `count`, `min`, `max`, `average` and `summaryStatistics`, as well as the `reduce` method for defining your own reductions.
- A terminal operation initiates a stream pipeline's processing and produces a result.
- `IntStream` method `sum` is a terminal operation that produces the sum of the stream's elements.

Section 17.2.4 Internal Iteration

- Internally, the `IntStream` already knows how to iterate through its elements without you having to declare and use any mutable variables. This is known as internal iteration, because `IntStream` handles all the iteration details—a key aspect of functional programming.
- Once you're used to it, stream pipeline code also can be easier to read.

Section 17.3 Mapping and Lambdas

- Most stream pipelines contain intermediate operations that specify tasks to perform on a stream's elements before a terminal operation produces a result.
- A mapping intermediate operation transforms a stream's elements to new values. The result is a stream with the same number of elements containing the transformation's results. Sometimes the mapped elements are of different types from the original stream's elements.

- `IntStream` method `map` receives as its argument an object representing a method with one parameter that returns a result.
- For each element in the stream, `map` calls the method it receives as an argument, passing to the method the current stream element. The method's return value becomes part of the new stream that `map` returns.

Section 17.3.1 Lambda Expressions

- Many intermediate and terminal stream operations receive methods as arguments, typically implemented as lambda expressions.
- A lambda expression represents an anonymous method—that is, a method without a name.
- Lambda expressions (or lambdas for short) enable you to create methods that can be treated as data. You can pass lambda expressions as arguments to other methods, assign lambda expressions to variables for later use and return lambda expressions from methods.

Section 17.3.2 Lambda Syntax

- A lambda consists of a *parameter list* followed by the arrow token (`->`) and a body, as in:

```
(parameterList) -> {statements}
```

- The body is a statement block that may contain one or more statements enclosed in curly braces.
- The compiler infers the return type from the lambda's context.
- As in a method declaration, lambdas specify multiple parameters in a comma-separated list.
- A lambda's parameter type(s) usually may be omitted, in which case the compiler infers the parameter and return types by the lambda's context.
- If the body contains only one expression, the `return` keyword, curly braces and semicolon may be omitted from the body. In this case, the lambda implicitly returns the expression's value.
- If the parameter list contains only one parameter, the parentheses may be omitted.
- To define a lambda with an empty parameter list, use empty parentheses to the left of the arrow token (`->`).

Section 17.3.3 Intermediate and Terminal Operations

- Intermediate operations are lazy—each intermediate operation results in a new stream object, but does not perform any operations on the stream's elements until a terminal operation is called to produce a result. This allows library developers to optimize stream-processing performance.
- Terminal operations are eager—they perform the requested operation when they're called.

Section 17.4 Filtering

- Another common intermediate stream operation is filtering elements to select those that match a condition—known as a predicate.
- `IntStream` method `filter` receives as its argument a method that takes one parameter and returns a `boolean` result. If the result is `true` for a given element, that element is included in the resulting stream.
- When a terminal operation is performed, the combined processing steps specified by intermediate operations are applied to each element.

Section 17.5 How Elements Move Through Stream Pipelines

- Each new stream is an object representing all the processing steps that have been specified to that point in the pipeline.

- Chaining intermediate operations adds to the set of processing steps to perform on each stream element.
- The last stream object in the stream pipeline contains all the processing steps to perform on each stream element.
- When you initiate a stream pipeline with a terminal operation, all of the processing steps specified by the pipeline's intermediate operations are applied for a given stream element *before* they are applied to the next stream element.

Section 17.6 Method References
- Anywhere a lambda can be used, you can use an existing method's name via a method reference—the compiler converts each method reference into an appropriate lambda expression.
- You use method references when a lambda would simply call the corresponding method.

Section 17.6.1 Creating an `IntStream` of Random Values
- Class `SecureRandom`'s `ints` method returns an `IntStream` of random numbers.

Section 17.6.2 Performing a Task on Each Stream Element with `forEach` and a Method Reference
- `IntStream` method `forEach` (a terminal operation) performs a task on each stream element.
- Method `forEach` receives as its argument a method that takes one parameter and performs a task using the parameter's value.
- A method reference is a shorthand notation for a lambda that calls the specified method.
- A method reference of the form *objectName*`::`*instanceMethodName* is a bound instance-method reference, indicating that the specific object to the left of the `::` must be used to call the instance method to the right of the `::`. The compiler converts the method reference into a one-parameter lambda in which the lambda's body calls the method on the specified object, passing the current stream element as an argument.

Section 17.6.3 Mapping Integers to String Objects with `mapToObj`
- `IntStream` method `map` returns another `IntStream`.
- `IntStream` method `mapToObj` maps from `int`s to a stream of reference-type elements.
- A `static` method reference has the form *ClassName*`::`*staticMethodName*, which the compiler converts into a one-parameter lambda that calls the static method on the specified class, passing the current stream element as an argument.
- The `Stream` terminal operation `collect` can be used concatenate `String` stream elements. Method `collect` is a form of reduction because it returns one object.

Section 17.6.4 Concatenating Strings with `collect`
- The `Stream` terminal operation `collect` receives as its argument a collector object that specifies how to gather the stream's elements into a single object.
- The predefined collector returned by the `Collectors` `static` method `joining` creates a concatenated `String` representation of the stream's elements, separating each element from the next by the `joining` method's argument. Method `collect` then returns the resulting `String`.

Section 17.7 `IntStream` Operations
- `LongStream`s and `DoubleStream`s process streams of `long` and `double` values, respectively.

Section 17.7.1 Creating an **`IntStream`** *and Displaying Its Values*

- `IntStream` `static` method `of` receives an `int` array argument and returns an `IntStream` for processing the array's values.
- Once a stream pipeline is processed with a terminal operation, the stream cannot be reused, because it does not maintain a copy of the original data source.

Section 17.7.2 Terminal Operations **`count`**, **`min`**, **`max`**, **`sum`** *and* **`average`**

- `IntStream` method `count` returns the number of elements in the stream.
- `IntStream` method `min` returns an `OptionalInt` (package `java.util`) possibly containing the smallest `int` in the stream.
- For any stream, it's possible that there are no elements in the stream. Returning `OptionalInt` enables method `min` to return the minimum value if the stream contains at least one element.
- `OptionalInt`'s `getAsInt` method obtains the value, if there is one; otherwise, it throws a `NoSuchElementException`.
- `IntStream` method `max` returns an `OptionalInt` possibly containing the largest `int` in the stream.
- `IntStream` method `average` returns an `OptionalDouble` (package `java.util`) possibly containing the average of the `int`s in the stream as a value of type `double`. `OptionalDouble`'s `getAsDouble` method obtains the value, if there is one; otherwise, it throws a `NoSuchElementException`.
- `IntStream` method `summaryStatistics` performs the `count`, `min`, `max`, `sum` and `average` operations *in one pass* of an `IntStream`'s elements and returns the results as an `IntSummaryStatistics` object (package `java.util`).

Section 17.7.3 Terminal Operation **`reduce`**

- You can define your own reductions via an `IntStream`'s `reduce` method.
- The first argument to `reduce` is the operation's identity value—a value that, when combined with any stream element (using the lambda in the `reduce`'s second argument), produces the element's original value.
- Method `reduce`'s second argument is a method that receives two `int` values (the left and right operands of a binary operator), performs a calculation with the values and returns the result.
- The one-argument `reduce` method returns an `OptionalInt` that, if the stream has elements, contains the result. Rather than beginning the reduction with an identity value and the stream's first element, the one-argument `reduce` method begins with the stream's first two elements.
- When implementing your stream pipelines, it's helpful to break down the processing steps into easy-to-understand tasks.

Section 17.7.4 Sorting **`IntStream`** *Values*

- `IntStream` intermediate operation `sorted` orders the elements of the stream into ascending order by default.

Section 17.8 Functional Interfaces

- A functional interface contains exactly one `abstract` method. Such interfaces are also known as single abstract method (SAM) interfaces.
- Functional programmers work with so-called pure functions that depend only on their parameters—they have no side-effects and do not maintain any state.
- Pure functions are implementations of functional interfaces—typically defined as lambdas.
- Package `java.util.function` contains several functional interfaces.

Section 17.9 Lambdas: A Deeper Look

- Lambda expressions can be used anywhere functional interfaces are expected.
- The Java compiler can usually infer the types of a lambda's parameters and the type returned by a lambda from the context in which the lambda is used. This is determined by the lambda's target type—the functional-interface type that's expected where the lambda appears in the code.
- Unlike methods, lambdas do not have their own scope.
- A lambda that refers to a local variable from the enclosing method (known as the lambda's lexical scope) is a capturing lambda. The compiler captures the local variable's value and stores it with the lambda to ensure that the lambda can use the value when the lambda eventually executes.
- Any local variable that a lambda references in its lexical scope must be `final` or effectively `final`.
- If the compiler infers that a local variable could have been declared `final`, because its enclosing method never modifies the variable after it's declared and initialized, then the variable is effectively `final`.

Section 17.10 `Stream<Integer>` Manipulations

- `Stream`s can perform tasks on objects of reference types.
- `Arrays` method `asList` creates a `List` view of an array.

Section 17.10.1 Creating a `Stream<Integer>`

- `Arrays` method `stream` can be used to create a `Stream` from an array of objects.
- Interface `Stream` (package `java.util.stream`) is a generic interface for performing stream operations on any reference type.
- Class `Arrays` also provides overloaded versions of method `stream` for creating `IntStream`s, `LongStream`s and `DoubleStream`s from `int`, `long` and `double` arrays or from ranges of elements in the arrays.

Section 17.10.2 Sorting a `Stream` and Collecting the Results

- When processing streams, you often create new collections containing the results so that you can perform operations on them at a later time. To create a collection, you can use `Stream`'s terminal operation `collect`.
- Method `collect` performs a mutable reduction operation that creates a `List`, `Map` or `Set` and modifies it by placing the results of the stream pipeline into the collection.
- The mutable reduction `toArray` places the results in a new array of a `Stream`'s element type.
- A `Collector` (package `java.util.stream`) specifies how to perform a mutable reduction.
- Class `Collectors` (package `java.util.stream`) provides `static` methods that return predefined `Collector` implementations.
- `Collectors` method `toList` returns a `Collector` that places a `Stream`'s elements in a `List`.

Section 17.10.3 Filtering a `Stream` and Storing the Results for Later Use

- `Stream` method `filter`'s lambda argument implements the functional interface `Predicate` (package `java.util.function`), which represents a one-parameter method that returns a `boolean` indicating whether the parameter value satisfies the predicate.

Section 17.10.5 Sorting Previously Collected Results

- `List` method `stream` creates a `Stream` from the collection.

Section 17.11.1 Mapping `String`*s to Uppercase*

- `Stream` method `map` receives as an argument an object that implements the functional interface `Function`. This interface represents a one-parameter method that performs a task with its parameter then returns the result.
- An unbound instance-method reference has the form *ClassName*`::`*instanceMethodName*. The compiler converts this to a one-parameter lambda that invokes the instance method on the lambda's parameter, which must have type *ClassName*.

Section 17.11.2 Filtering `String`*s Then Sorting Them in Case-Insensitive Ascending Order*

- An overload of `Stream` method `sorted` receives a `Comparator`, which defines a `compare` method that returns a negative value if the first value being compared is less than the second, 0 if they're equal and a positive value if the first value is greater than the second.
- By default, method `sorted` uses the natural order for the type. Passing the predefined `Comparator` `String.CASE_INSENSITIVE_ORDER` performs a case-insensitive sort.

Section 17.11.3 Filtering `String`*s Then Sorting Them in Case-Insensitive Descending Order*

- Functional interface `Comparator` contains `default` method `reversed`, which reverses an existing `Comparator`'s ordering.

Section 17.12.1 Creating and Displaying a `List<Employee>`

- `Stream` method `forEach` expects as its argument an object that implements the `Consumer` functional interface, which represents an action to perform on each element of the stream—the corresponding method receives one argument and returns `void`.

Section 17.12.2 Filtering `Employee`*s with Salaries in a Specified Range*

- You can store a lambda in a variable for later use.
- The `Comparator` interface's `static` method `comparing` receives a `Function` that performs a task on its argument and returns the result. The `Comparator` returned by method `comparing` calls its `Function` argument on each of two stream elements, then returns a negative value if the first is less than the second, 0 if they're equal and a positive value if the first is greater than the second.
- One of the nice performance features of lazy evaluation is the ability to perform short-circuit evaluation to stop processing the stream pipeline as soon as the desired result is available.
- `Stream` method `findFirst`—a short-circuiting terminal operation—processes the stream pipeline and terminates processing as soon as the first object from the stream's intermediate operation(s) is found.
- Method `findFirst` then returns an `Optional` containing the object that was found, if any. `Optional` method `get` returns the matching object; otherwise, it throws a `NoSuchElementException`.

Section 17.12.3 Sorting `Employee`*s By Multiple Fields*

- `Comparator`s may be composed via `default` method `thenComparing`.
- Many functional interfaces in the package `java.util.function` package provide `default` methods that enable you to compose functionality.
- Interface `IntPredicate`'s `default` method `and` performs a logical AND with short-circuit evaluation between the `IntPredicate` on which it's called and the one it receives as an argument.
- Interface `IntPredicate`'s `default` method `negate` reverses the `boolean` value of the `IntPredicate` on which it's called.

- Interface `IntPredicate`'s `default` method `or` performs a logical OR with short-circuit evaluation between the `IntPredicate` on which it's called and the one it receives as an argument.
- Interface `Predicate` represents a method that returns a `boolean` indicating whether its object argument satisfies a condition. `Predicate` also contains methods `and` and `or` for combining predicates, and `negate` for reversing a predicate's `boolean` value.

Section 17.12.4 Mapping `Employees` to Unique Last Name `Strings`

- `Stream` method `distinct` eliminates any duplicates in the stream.

Section 17.12.5 Grouping `Employees` By Department

- The `Collector` returned by `Collectors` `static` method `groupingBy` receives a `Function` that classifies the objects in the stream. The values returned by this `Function` are used as the keys in a `Map` collection. The corresponding values, by default, are `Lists` containing the stream elements in a given category.
- `Map` method `forEach` performs an operation on each of the `Map`'s key–value pairs. The argument to this method is an object that implements functional interface `BiConsumer`, which represents a two-parameter method that does not return a result. For a `Map`, the first parameter represents the key and the second represents the corresponding value.

Section 17.12.6 Counting the Number of `Employees` in Each Department

- `Collectors` `static` method `groupingBy` with two arguments receives a `Function` that classifies the objects in the stream and another `Collector` (known as the downstream `Collector`) that's used to collect the objects classified by the `Function`.
- `Collectors` `static` method `counting` reduces the elements in a given classification to a count of those elements, rather than collecting them into a `List`.

Section 17.12.7 Summing and Averaging `Employee` Salaries

- `Stream` method `mapToDouble` maps objects to `double` values and returns a `DoubleStream`.
- Method `mapToDouble` receives a `ToDoubleFunction` (package `java.util.function`), which represents a one-parameter method that returns a `double` value.
- `DoubleStream` method `average` returns an `OptionalDouble` in case the `DoubleStream` does not contain any elements.

Section 17.13 Creating a `Stream<String>` from a File

- `Files` method `lines` creates a `Stream<String>` for reading the lines of text from a file.
- `Stream` method `flatMap` receives a `Function` that maps an object into a stream—e.g., a line of text into words.
- `Pattern` method `splitAsStream` uses a regular expression to tokenize a `String`.
- `Collectors` method `groupingBy` with three arguments receives a classifier, a `Map` factory and a downstream `Collector`. The classifier `Function` returns objects which are used as keys in the resulting `Map`. The `Map` factory is an object that implements interface `Supplier` and returns a new `Map` collection. The downstream `Collector` determines how to collect each group's elements.
- `Map` method `entrySet` returns a `Set` of `Map.Entry` objects containing the `Map`'s key–value pairs.
- `Set` method `stream` returns a stream for processing the `Set`'s elements.

Section 17.14 Streams of Random Values

- Class `SecureRandom`'s methods `ints`, `longs` and `doubles` (inherited from class `Random`) return `IntStream`, `LongStream` and `DoubleStream`, respectively, for streams of random numbers.

- Method `ints` with no arguments creates an `IntStream` for an infinite stream of random `int` values. An infinite stream is a stream with an unknown number of elements—you use a short-circuiting terminal operation to complete processing on an infinite stream.
- Method `ints` with a `long` argument creates an `IntStream` with the specified number of random `int` values.
- Method `ints` with two `int` arguments creates an `IntStream` for an infinite stream of random `int` values in the range starting with the first argument and up to, but not including, the second.
- Method `ints` with a `long` and two `int` arguments creates an `IntStream` with the specified number of random `int` values in the range from the first argument and up to, but not including, the second.
- To convert an `IntStream` to a `Stream<Integer>` call `IntStream` method `boxed`.
- `Function static` method `identity` creates a `Function` that simply returns its argument.

Section 17.15 Infinite Streams

- Java's stream interfaces also support data sources that represent an unknown, potentially infinite, number of elements. These are known as infinite streams
- `IntStream` method `iterate` generates an ordered sequence of values starting with a seed value in its first argument. Each subsequent element is produced by applying to the preceding value in the sequence the `IntUnaryOperator` specified as `iterate`'s second argument.
- You can limit the total number of elements that an infinite stream produces by calling `limit`, which specifies the maximum number of elements to process from a stream.
- You also may create unordered infinite streams using method `generate` which receives an `IntSupplier`. This interface represents a method that takes no arguments and returns an `int`.

Section 17.16 Lambda Event Handlers

- Some event-listener interfaces are functional interfaces. For such interfaces, you can implement event handlers with lambdas. For a simple event handler, a lambda significantly reduces the amount of code you need to write.

Section 17.17 Additional Notes on Java SE 8 Interfaces

- Functional interfaces must contain only one `abstract` method, but may also contain `default` methods and `static` methods that are fully implemented in the interface declarations.
- When a class implements an interface with `default` methods and does not override them, the class inherits the `default`' implementations. An interface's designer can evolve an interface by adding new `default` and `static` methods without breaking existing code that implements the interface.
- If one class inherits the same `default` method from two interfaces, the class must override that method; otherwise, the compiler will generate a compilation error.
- You can create your own functional interfaces by ensuring that each contains only one `abstract` method and zero or more `default` and/or `static` methods.
- You can declare that an interface is a functional interface by preceding it with the `@FunctionalInterface` annotation. The compiler will then ensure that the interface contains only one `abstract` method; otherwise, it'll generate a compilation error.

Self-Review Exercises

17.1 Fill in the blanks in each of the following statements:

a) Lambda expressions implement ________.

b) With ________ iteration the library determines how to access all the elements in a collection to perform a task.

c) Functional programs are easier to ________ (i.e., perform multiple operations simultaneously) so that your programs can take advantage of multi-core architectures to enhance performance.
d) An implementation of the functional interface ________ takes two `T` arguments, performs an operation on them (such as a calculation) and returns a value of type `T`.
e) An implementation of the functional interface ________ takes a `T` argument and returns a `boolean`, and tests whether the `T` argument satisfies a condition.
f) A(n) ________ represents an anonymous method—a shorthand notation for implementing a functional interface.
g) Intermediate stream operations are ________—they aren't performed until a terminal operation is invoked.
h) The terminal stream operation ________ performs processing on every element in a stream.
i) ________ lambdas use local variables from the enclosing lexical scope.
j) A performance feature of lazy evaluation is the ability to perform ________ evaluation—that is, to stop processing the stream pipeline as soon as the desired result is available.
k) For `Map`s, a `BiConsumer`'s first parameter represents the ________ and its second represents the corresponding ________.

17.2 State whether each of the following is *true* or *false*. If *false*, explain why.
a) Lambda expressions can be used anywhere functional interfaces are expected.
b) Terminal operations are lazy—they perform the requested operation when they are called.
c) Method `reduce`'s first argument is formally called an identity value—a value that, when combined with a stream element using the `IntBinaryOperator`, produces the stream element's original value. For example, when summing the elements, the identity value is 1, and when getting the product of the elements, the identity value is 0.
d) `Stream` method `findFirst` is a short-circuiting terminal operation that processes the stream pipeline but terminates processing as soon as an object is found.
e) `Stream` method `flatMap` receives a `Function` that maps a stream into an object. For example, the object could be a `String` containing words and the result could be another intermediate `Stream<String>` for the individual words.
f) When a class implements an interface with `default` methods and overrides them, the class inherits the `default` methods' implementations. An interface's designer can now evolve an interface by adding new `default` and `static` methods without breaking existing code that implements the interface.

17.3 Write a lambda or method reference for each of the following tasks:
a) Write a lambda that can that can be passed to a method with an `IntConsumer` parameter. The lambda should display its argument followed by a space.
b) Write a method reference that can be used in place of the following lambda:

```
(String s) -> {return s.toUpperCase();}
```

c) Write a no-argument lambda that implicitly returns the `String` `"Welcome to lambdas!"`.
d) Write a method reference for `Math` method `sqrt`.
e) Create a one-parameter lambda that returns the cube of its argument.

Answers to Self-Review Exercises

17.1 a) functional interfaces. b) internal. c) parallelize. d) `BinaryOperator<T>`. e) `Predicate<T>`. f) lambda expression. g) lazy. h) `forEach`. i) Capturing. j) short-circuit. k) key, value.

17.2 a) True. b) False. Terminal operations are *eager*—they perform the requested operation when they are called. c) False. When summing the elements, the identity value is 0, and when getting the product of the elements, the identity value is 1. d) True. e) False. `Stream` method `flatMap` receives a `Function` that maps an object into a stream. f) False. Should say: "...does not override them, ..." instead of "overrides them."

17.3 Answers for a) through e):

a) `value -> System.out.printf("%d ", value)`
b) `String::toUpperCase`
c) `() -> "Welcome to lambdas!"`
d) `Math::sqrt`
e) `value -> value * value * value`

Exercises

17.4 Fill in the blanks in each of the following statements:

a) Stream ________ are formed from stream sources, intermediate operations and terminal operations.
b) The following code uses the technique of ________ iteration:

```
int sum = 0;

for (int counter = 0; counter < values.length; counter++) {
   sum += values[counter];
}
```

c) Functional programming capabilities focus on ________—not modifying the data source being processed or any other program state.
d) An implementation of the functional interface ________ takes a `T` argument and returns `void`, and performs a task with its `T` argument, such as outputting the object, invoking a method of the object, etc.
e) An implementation of the functional interface ________ takes no arguments and produces a value of type `T`—this is often used to create a collection object in which a stream operation's results are placed.
f) Streams are objects that implement interface `Stream` and enable you to perform functional programming tasks on ________ of elements.
g) The intermediate stream operation ________ results in a stream containing only the elements that satisfy a condition.
h) ________ place the results of processing a stream pipeline into a collection such as a `List`, `Set` or `Map`.
i) Calls to `filter` and other intermediate streams are lazy—they aren't evaluated until an eager ________ operation is performed.
j) `Pattern` method ________ uses a regular expression to tokenize a `String` and create a stream.
k) Functional interfaces *must* contain only one ________ method, but may also contain ________ and `static` methods that are fully implemented in the interface declarations.

17.5 State whether each of the following is *true* or *false*. If *false*, explain why.

a) An intermediate operation specifies tasks to perform on the stream's elements; this is efficient because it avoids creating a new stream.
b) Reduction operations take all values in the stream and turn them into a new stream.
c) If you need an ordered sequence of `int` values, you can create an `IntStream` containing such values with `IntStream` methods `range` and `rangeClosed`. Both methods take two

int arguments representing the range of values. Method rangeClosed produces a sequence of values from its first argument up to, but not including, its second argument. Method range produces a sequence of values including both of its arguments.

d) Class Files (package java.nio.file) is one of many classes throughout the Java APIs that have been enhanced to support Streams.
e) Interface Map does not contain any methods that return Streams.
f) The Function interface has methods apply (abstract), compose (abstract), andThen (default) and identity (static).
g) If one class inherits the same default method from two interfaces, the class *must* override that method; otherwise, the compiler does not know which method to use, so it generates a compilation error.

17.6 Write a lambda or method reference for each of the following tasks:

a) Write a lambda expression that receives two double parameters a and b and returns their product. Use the lambda form that explicitly lists the type of each parameter.
b) Rewrite the lambda expression in Part (a) using the lambda form that does not list the type of each parameter.
c) Rewrite the lambda expression in Part (b) using the lambda form that implicitly returns the value of the lambda's body expression.
d) Write a no-argument lambda that implicitly returns the string "Welcome to lambdas!".
e) Write a constructor reference for class ArrayList.
f) Reimplement the following statement using a lambda as the event handler:

```
slider.valueProperty().addListener(
   new ChangeListener<Number>() {
      @Override
      public void changed(ObservableValue<? extends Number> ov,
         Number oldValue, Number newValue) {
         System.out.printf("The slider's new value is %s%n", newValue);
      }
   }
);
```

17.7 What's wrong with the following stream pipeline?

```
list.stream()
    .filter(value -> value % 2 != 0)
    .sum()
```

17.8 Assuming that list is a List<Integer>, explain in detail the stream pipeline:

```
list.stream()
    .filter(value -> value % 2 != 0)
    .reduce(0, Integer::sum)
```

17.9 Assuming that random is a SecureRandom object, explain in detail the stream pipeline:

```
random.ints(1000000, 1, 3)
      .boxed()
      .collect(Collectors.groupingBy(Function.identity(),
         Collectors.counting()))
      .forEach((side, frequency) ->
         System.out.printf("%-6d%d%n", side, frequency));
```

17.10 *(Summarizing the Characters in a File)* Modify the program of Fig. 17.22 to summarize the number of occurrences of every character in the file.

17.11 *(Summarizing the File Types in a Directory)* Section 15.3 demonstrated how to get information about files and directories on disk. In addition, you used a `DirectoryStream` to display the contents of a directory. Interface `DirectoryStream` now contains `default` method `entries`, which returns a `Stream`. Use the techniques from Section 15.3, `DirectoryStream` method `entries`, lambdas and streams to summarize the types of files in a specified directory.

17.12 *(Manipulating a `Stream<Invoice>`)* Use the class `Invoice` provided in the `exercises` folder with this chapter's examples to create an array of `Invoice` objects. Use the sample data shown in Fig. 17.25. Class `Invoice` includes four instance variables—a `partNumber` (type `String`), a `partDescription` (type `String`), a `quantity` of the item being purchased (type `int`) and a `pricePerItem` (type `double`) and corresponding *get* methods. Perform the following queries on the array of `Invoice` objects and display the results:

a) Use streams to sort the `Invoice` objects by `partDescription`, then display the results.
b) Use streams to sort the `Invoice` objects by `pricePerItem`, then display the results.
c) Use streams to map each `Invoice` to its `partDescription` and `quantity`, sort the results by `quantity`, then display the results.
d) Use streams to map each `Invoice` to its `partDescription` and the value of the `Invoice` (i.e., `quantity * pricePerItem`). Order the results by `Invoice` value.
e) Modify Part (d) to select the `Invoice` values in the range $200 to $500.
f) Find any one `Invoice` in which the `partDescription` contains the word `"saw"`.

Part number	Part description	Quantity	Price
83	Electric sander	7	57.98
24	Power saw	18	99.99
7	Sledge hammer	11	21.50
77	Hammer	76	11.99
39	Lawn mower	3	79.50
68	Screwdriver	106	6.99
56	Jig saw	21	11.00
3	Wrench	34	7.50

Fig. 17.25 | Sample data for Exercise 17.12.

17.13 *(Duplicate Word Removal)* Write a program that inputs a sentence from the user (assume no punctuation), then determines and displays the unique words in alphabetical order. Treat uppercase and lowercase letters the same.

17.14 *(Sorting Letters and Removing Duplicates)* Write a program that inserts 30 random letters into a `List<Character>`. Perform the following operations and display your results:

a) Sort the `List` in ascending order.
b) Sort the `List` in descending order.
c) Display the `List` in ascending order with duplicates removed.

17.15 *(Stream Performance)* Answer the following questions with regard to the stream pipeline in Fig. 17.7:

a) How many times does the `filter` operation call its lambda argument?
b) How many times does the `map` operation call its lambda argument?
c) If you reverse the `filter` and `map` operations in the stream pipeline, how many times does the `map` operation call its lambda argument?

17.16 *(`IntStream` Filtering and Sorting)* Use `SecureRandom` method `ints` to generate a stream of 50 random numbers in the range 1 to 999, then filter the resulting stream elements to select only the odd numbers and display the results in sorted order.

17.17 *(Calculating `Employee` Average Salaries by Department)* Modify the `Stream<Employee>` example in Section 17.12 so that it uses stream capabilities to display the average `Employee` salary by department.

17.18 *(Summing the Triples of the Even Integers from 2 through 10)* The example of Fig. 17.7 summed the triples of the even integers from 2 through 10. We used `filter` and `map` in the stream pipeline to demonstrate both in one stream pipeline. Reimplement Fig. 17.7's stream pipeline using only `map` (similar to Fig. 17.4).

17.19 *(Calculating the Class Average with an `IntStream`)* Figures 4.8 and 4.10 demonstrated calculating a class average with counter-controlled repetition and sentinel-controlled repetition, respectively. Create a program that reads integer grades and stores them in an `ArrayList`, then use stream processing to perform the average calculation.

17.20 *(Mapping Integer Grades to Letter Grades)* Create a program that reads integer grades and stores them in an `ArrayList`, then use stream processing to display each grade's letter equivalent (A, B, C, D or F).

17.21 *(Calculating the Average of the Elements in a Two-Dimensional Array)* Figure 7.19 defined a two-dimensional array of grades with 10 rows and three columns, representing 10 students' grades on three exams. Use a stream pipeline to calculate the average of all the grades. For this exercise, use `Stream` method `of` to create a stream from the two-dimensional array and `Stream` method `flatMapToInt` to map each row into a stream of `int` values.

17.22 *(Calculating the Average of the Elements in a Two-Dimensional Array)* Figure 7.19 defined a two-dimensional array of grades with 10 rows and three columns, representing 10 students' grades on three exams. Use streams to calculate the students' individual averages.

17.23 *(Finding the First Person with a Specified Last Name)* Create a collection of `Person` objects in which each `Person` has a `firstName` and a `lastName`. Use streams to locate the first `Person` object containing the last name `Jones`. Ensure that several `Person` objects in your collection have that last name.

17.24 *(Infinite Streams of Prime Integers)* Use an infinite stream of integers to display the first *n* prime numbers, where *n* is input by the user.

17.25 *(Timing 60,000,000 Die Rolls)* In Fig. 17.24, we implemented a stream pipeline that rolled a die 60,000,000 times using values produced by `SecureRandom` method `ints`. Package `java.time` contains types `Instant` and `Duration` that you can use to capture the time before and after evaluating the stream pipeline, then calculate the difference between the `Instant`s to determine the total time. Use `Instant`'s `static` method `now` to get the current time. To determine the difference between two `Instant`s, use class `Duration`'s `static` method `between`, which returns a `Duration` object containing the time difference. `Duration` provides methods like `toMillis` to return a duration in milliseconds. Use these timing techniques to time the original stream pipeline's operation, then do so again using class `Random` from package `java.util`, rather than `SecureRandom`.

18 Recursion

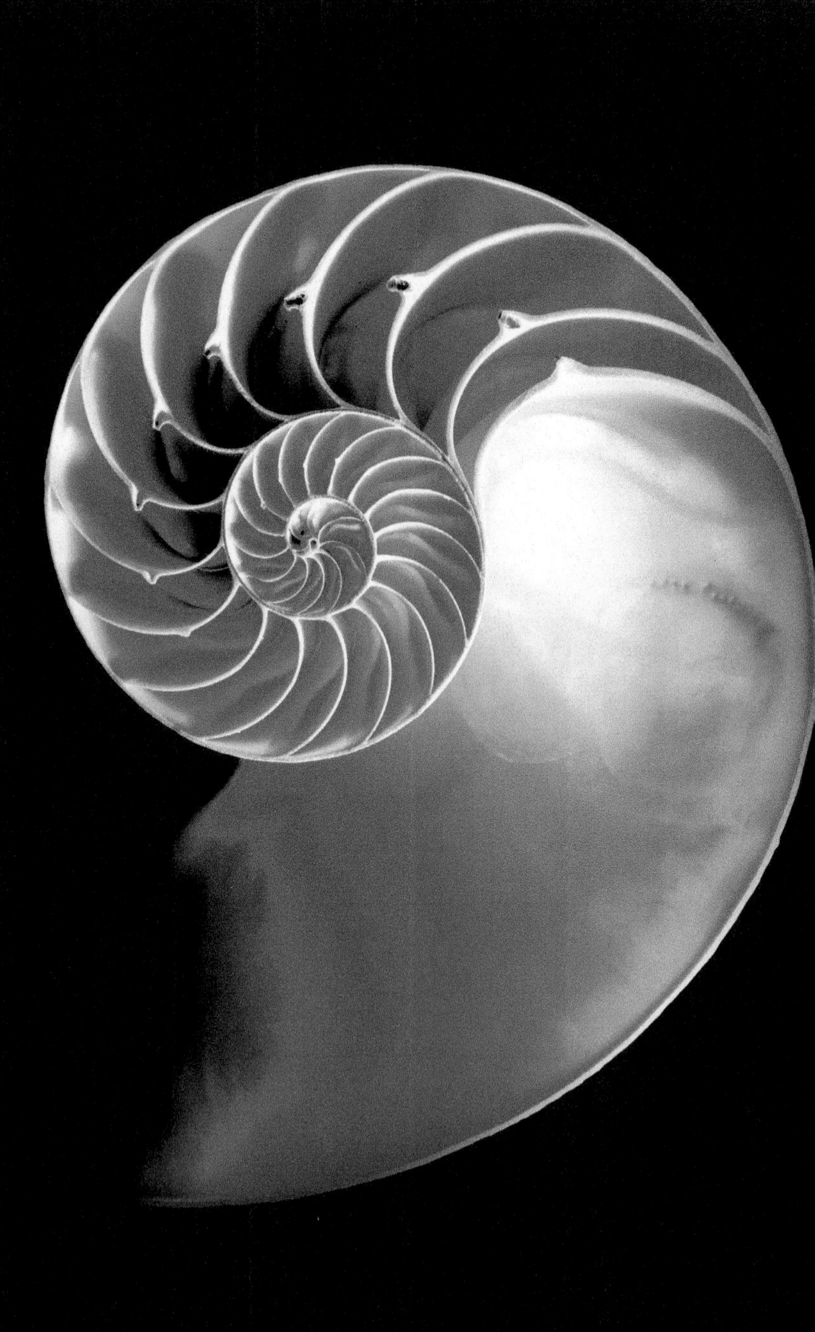

Objectives

In this chapter you'll:

- Learn the concept of recursion.
- Write and use recursive methods.
- Determine the base case and recursion step in a recursive algorithm.
- Learn how recursive method calls are handled by the system.
- Learn the differences between recursion and iteration, and when to use each.
- Learn what fractals are and how to draw them using recursion and JavaFX's `Canvas` and `GraphicsContext` classes.
- Learn what recursive backtracking is and why it's an effective problem-solving technique.

Outline

18.1 Introduction

The programs we've discussed so far are generally structured as methods that call one another in a hierarchical manner. For some problems, it's useful to have a method *call itself*—this is known as a **recursive method.** Such a method can call itself either *directly* or *indirectly through another method.* Recursion is an important topic discussed at length in upper-level computer-science courses. Here, we consider recursion conceptually, then present several examples of recursive methods. Figure 18.1 summarizes the book's recursion examples and exercises.

Chapter	Recursion examples and exercises in this book
18	Factorial Method (Figs. 18.3 and 18.4) Fibonacci Method (Fig. 18.5) Towers of Hanoi (Fig. 18.11) Fractals (Fig. 18.20) What Does This Code Do? (Exercise 18.7, Exercise 18.12 and Exercise 18.13) Find the Error in the Following Code (Exercise 18.8) Raising an Integer to an Integer Power (Exercise 18.9) Visualizing Recursion (Exercise 18.10) Greatest Common Divisor (Exercise 18.11) Determine Whether a String Is a Palindrome (Exercise 18.14) Eight Queens (Exercise 18.15) Print an Array (Exercise 18.16) Print an Array Backward (Exercise 18.17) Minimum Value in an Array (Exercise 18.18) Star Fractal (Exercise 18.19) Maze Traversal Using Recursive Backtracking (Exercise 18.20) Generating Mazes Randomly (Exercise 18.21) Mazes of Any Size (Exercise 18.22) Time to Calculate a Fibonacci Number (Exercise 18.23) Koch Curve (Exercise 18.24) Koch Snowflake (Exercise 18.25) Recursive File and Directory Manipulation (Exercise 18.26)

Fig. 18.1 | Summary of the recursion examples and exercises in this text. (Part 1 of 2.)

Chapter	Recursion examples and exercises in this book
19	Merge Sort (Fig. 19.6) Linear Search (Exercise 19.8) Binary Search (Exercise 19.9) Quicksort (Exercise 19.10)
21	Binary-Tree Insert (Fig. 21.15) Preorder Traversal of a Binary Tree (Fig. 21.15) Inorder Traversal of a Binary Tree (Fig. 21.15) Postorder Traversal of a Binary Tree (Fig. 21.15) Print a Linked List Backward (Exercise 21.20) Search a Linked List (Exercise 21.21)

Fig. 18.1 | Summary of the recursion examples and exercises in this text. (Part 2 of 2.)

18.2 Recursion Concepts

Recursive problem-solving approaches have a number of elements in common. When a recursive method is called to solve a problem, it actually is capable of solving only the *simplest case(s)*, or **base case**(s). If the method is called with a *base case*, it returns a result. If the method is called with a more complex problem, it divides the problem into two conceptual pieces—a piece that the method knows how to do and a piece that it does not know how to do. To make recursion feasible, the latter piece must resemble the original problem, but be a slightly simpler or smaller version of it. Because this new problem resembles the original problem, the method calls a fresh *copy* of itself to work on the smaller problem—this is referred to as a **recursive call** and is also called the **recursion step**. The recursion step normally includes a `return` statement, because its result will be combined with the portion of the problem the method knew how to solve to form a result that will be passed back to the original caller. This concept of separating the problem into two smaller portions is a form of the *divide-and-conquer* approach introduced in Chapter 6.

The recursion step executes while the original method call is still active (i.e., it has not finished executing). It can result in many more recursive calls as the method divides each new subproblem into two conceptual pieces. For the recursion to eventually terminate, each time the method calls itself with a simpler version of the original problem, the sequence of smaller and smaller problems must *converge on a base case*. When the method recognizes the base case, it returns a result to the previous copy of the method. A sequence of returns ensues until the original method call returns the final result to the caller. We'll illustrate this process with a concrete example in Section 18.3.

A recursive method may call another method, which may in turn make a call back to the recursive method. This is known as an **indirect recursive call** or **indirect recursion**. For example, method `A` calls method `B`, which makes a call back to method `A`. This is still recursion, because the second call to method `A` is made while the first call to method `A` is active—that is, the first call to method `A` has not yet finished executing (because it's waiting on method `B` to return a result to it) and has not returned to method `A`'s original caller.

Recursive Directory Structures

To better understand the concept of recursion, let's look at an example that's quite familiar to computer users—the recursive definition of a file-system directory on a computer. A computer normally stores related files in a directory. A directory can be empty, can contain files and/or can contain other directories (usually referred to as subdirectories). Each of these subdirectories, in turn, may also contain both files and directories. If we want to list each file in a directory (including all the files in the directory's subdirectories), we need to create a method that first lists the initial directory's files, then makes recursive calls to list the files in each of that directory's subdirectories. The base case occurs when a directory is reached that does not contain any subdirectories. At this point, all the files in the original directory have been listed and no further recursion is necessary. Exercise 18.26 asks you to write a program that recursively walks a directory structure.

18.3 Example Using Recursion: Factorials

Let's write a recursive program to perform a popular mathematical calculation. Consider the *factorial* of a positive integer *n*, written *n*! (pronounced "*n* factorial"), which is the product

$$n \cdot (n-1) \cdot (n-2) \cdot \ldots \cdot 1$$

with 1! equal to 1 and 0! defined to be 1. For example, 5! is the product $5 \cdot 4 \cdot 3 \cdot 2 \cdot 1$, which is equal to 120.

The factorial of integer `number` (where `number` ≥ 0) can be calculated *iteratively* (non-recursively) using a `for` statement as follows:

```
factorial = 1;
for (int counter = number; counter >= 1; counter--) {
   factorial *= counter;
}
```

A recursive declaration of the factorial calculation for integers greater than 1 is arrived at by observing the following relationship:

$$n! = n \cdot (n-1)!$$

For example, 5! is clearly equal to $5 \cdot 4!$, as shown by the following equations:

$$5! = 5 \cdot 4 \cdot 3 \cdot 2 \cdot 1$$
$$5! = 5 \cdot (4 \cdot 3 \cdot 2 \cdot 1)$$
$$5! = 5 \cdot (4!)$$

The evaluation of 5! would proceed as shown in Fig. 18.2. Figure 18.2(a) shows how the succession of recursive calls proceeds until 1! (the base case) is evaluated to be 1, which terminates the recursion. Figure 18.2(b) shows the values returned from each recursive call to its caller until the final value is calculated and returned.

Figure 18.3 uses recursion to calculate and print the factorials of the integers 0 through 21. The recursive method `factorial` (lines 6–13) first tests to determine whether a *terminating condition* (line 7) is `true`. If `number` is less than or equal to `1` (the base case), `factorial` returns `1`, no further recursion is necessary and the method returns. (A precondition of calling method `factorial` in this example is that its argument must be nonnegative.) If `number` is greater than `1`, line 11 expresses the problem as the product of `number`

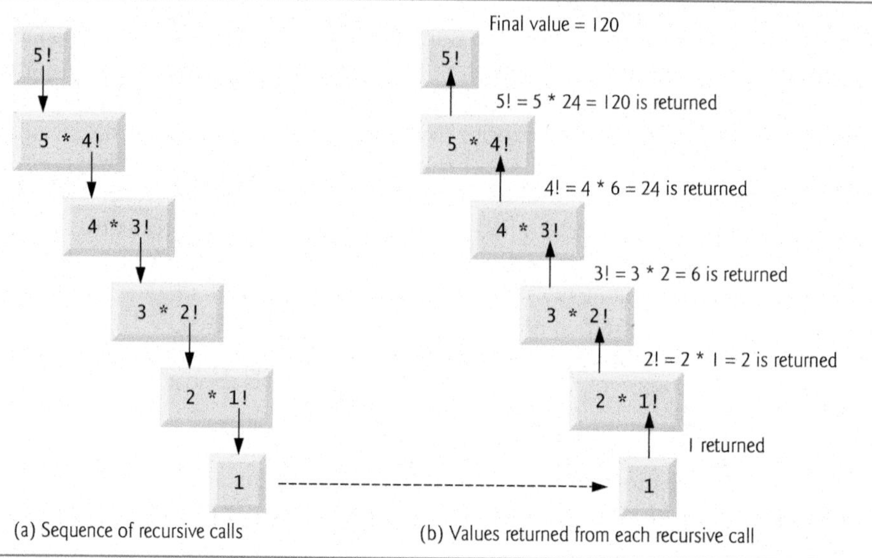

Fig. 18.2 | Recursive evaluation of 5!.

and a recursive call to `factorial` evaluating the factorial of `number - 1`, which is a slightly smaller problem than the original calculation, `factorial(number)`.

Common Programming Error 18.1

Either omitting the base case or writing the recursion step incorrectly so that it does not converge on the base case can cause a logic error known as ***infinite recursion****, where recursive calls are continuously made until memory is exhausted or the method-call stack overflows. This error is analogous to the problem of an infinite loop in an iterative (nonrecursive) solution.*

```
// Fig. 18.3: FactorialCalculator.java
// Recursive factorial method.

public class FactorialCalculator {
   // recursive method factorial (assumes its parameter is >= 0)
   public static long factorial(long number) {
      if (number <= 1) { // test for base case
         return 1; // base cases: 0! = 1 and 1! = 1
      }
      else { // recursion step
         return number * factorial(number - 1);
      }
   }

   public static void main(String[] args) {
      // calculate the factorials of 0 through 21
      for (int counter = 0; counter <= 21; counter++) {
```

Fig. 18.3 | Recursive factorial method. (Part 1 of 2.)

```
18            System.out.printf("%d! = %d%n", counter, factorial(counter));
19         }
20      }
21   }
```

```
0! = 1
1! = 1
2! = 2
3! = 6
4! = 24
5! = 120
...
12! = 479001600 —— 12! causes overflow for int variables
...
20! = 2432902008176640000
21! = -4249290049419214848 —— 21! causes overflow for long variables
```

Fig. 18.3 | Recursive factorial method. (Part 2 of 2.)

Method `main` (lines 15–20) displays the factorials of 0–21.[1] The call to the `factorial` method occurs in line 18. Method `factorial` receives a parameter of type `long` and returns a result of type `long`. The program's output shows that factorial values become large quickly. We use type `long` (which can represent relatively large integers) so the program can calculate factorials greater than 12!. Unfortunately, the `factorial` method produces large values so quickly that we exceed the largest `long` value when we attempt to calculate 21!, as you can see in the last line of the program's output.

Due to the limitations of integral types, `float` or `double` variables may ultimately be needed to calculate factorials of larger numbers. This points to a weakness in some programming languages—namely, that they aren't easily *extended with new types* to handle unique application requirements. As we saw in Chapter 9, Java is an *extensible* language that allows us to create arbitrarily large integers if we wish. In fact, package `java.math` provides classes **`BigInteger`** and `BigDecimal` explicitly for arbitrary precision calculations that cannot be performed with primitive types. You can learn more about these classes at

```
http://docs.oracle.com/javase/8/docs/api/java/math/BigInteger.html
http://docs.oracle.com/javase/8/docs/api/java/math/BigDecimal.html
```

Calculating Factorials with Lambdas and Streams

If you've read Chapter 17, consider doing Exercise 18.28, which asks you to calculate factorials using lambdas and streams, rather than recursion. 8

18.4 Reimplementing Class `FactorialCalculator` Using `BigInteger`

Figure 18.4 reimplements class `FactorialCalculator` using `BigInteger` variables. To demonstrate larger values than what `long` variables can store, we calculate the factorials of the numbers 0–50. Line 3 imports class `BigInteger` from package `java.math`. The new

1. The `for` loops in the `main` methods of this chapter's examples could be implemented with lambdas and streams by using `IntStream` and its `rangeClosed` and `forEach` methods (see Exercise 18.27). 8

factorial method (lines 7–15) receives a BigInteger as an argument and returns a BigInteger.

```
1  // Fig. 18.4: FactorialCalculator.java
2  // Recursive factorial method.
3  import java.math.BigInteger;
4
5  public class FactorialCalculator {
6     // recursive method factorial (assumes its parameter is >= 0)
7     public static BigInteger factorial(BigInteger number) {
8        if (number.compareTo(BigInteger.ONE) <= 0) { // test base case
9           return BigInteger.ONE; // base cases: 0! = 1 and 1! = 1
10       }
11       else { // recursion step
12          return number.multiply(
13             factorial(number.subtract(BigInteger.ONE)));
14       }
15    }
16
17    public static void main(String[] args) {
18       // calculate the factorials of 0 through 50
19       for (int counter = 0; counter <= 50; counter++) {
20          System.out.printf("%d! = %d%n", counter,
21             factorial(BigInteger.valueOf(counter)));
22       }
23    }
24 }
```

```
0! = 1
1! = 1
2! = 2
3! = 6
...
21! = 51090942171709440000 —— 21! and larger values no longer cause overflow
22! = 1124000727777607680000
...
47! = 258623241511168180642964355153611979969197632389120000000000
48! = 12413915592536072670862289047373375038521486354677760000000000
49! = 608281864034267560872252163321295376887552831379210240000000000
50! = 30414093201713378043612608166064768844377641568960512000000000000
```

Fig. 18.4 | Factorial calculations with a recursive method.

Since BigInteger is *not* a primitive type, we can't use the arithmetic, relational and equality operators with BigIntegers; instead, we must use BigInteger methods to perform these tasks. Line 8 tests for the base case using BigInteger method **compareTo**. This method compares the BigInteger number that calls the method to the method's BigInteger argument. The method returns -1 if the BigInteger that calls the method is less than the argument, 0 if they're equal or 1 if the BigInteger that calls the method is greater than the argument. Line 8 compares the BigInteger number with the BigInteger constant **ONE**, which represents the integer value 1. If compareTo returns -1 or 0, then number is less than or equal to 1 (the base case) and the method returns the constant

`BigInteger.ONE`. Otherwise, lines 12–13 perform the recursion step using `BigInteger` methods **`multiply`** and **`subtract`** to implement the calculations required to multiply `number` by the factorial of `number - 1`. The program's output shows that `BigInteger` handles the large values produced by the factorial calculation.

Calculating Factorials with Lambdas and Streams

If you've read Chapter 17, consider doing Exercise 18.28, which asks you to calculate fac- 8
torials using lambdas and streams, rather than recursion.

18.5 Example Using Recursion: Fibonacci Series

The **Fibonacci series,**

0, 1, 1, 2, 3, 5, 8, 13, 21, ...

begins with 0 and 1 and has the property that each subsequent Fibonacci number is the sum of the previous two. This series occurs in nature and describes a form of spiral. The ratio of successive Fibonacci numbers converges on a constant value of 1.618..., a number that has been called the **golden ratio** or the **golden mean.** Humans tend to find the golden mean aesthetically pleasing. Architects often design windows, rooms and buildings whose length and width are in the ratio of the golden mean. Postcards are often designed with a golden-mean length-to-width ratio.

The Fibonacci series may be defined recursively as follows:

$$\text{fibonacci}(0) = 0$$
$$\text{fibonacci}(1) = 1$$
$$\text{fibonacci}(n) = \text{fibonacci}(n-1) + \text{fibonacci}(n-2)$$

There are *two base cases* for the Fibonacci calculation: `fibonacci(0)` is defined to be 0, and `fibonacci(1)` to be 1. Figure 18.5 calculates the *i*th Fibonacci number recursively, using method `fibonacci` (lines 9–18). Method `main` (lines 20–26) tests `fibonacci`, displaying the Fibonacci values of 0–40. The variable `counter` created in the `for` header (line 22) indicates which Fibonacci number to calculate for each iteration of the loop. Fibonacci numbers tend to become large quickly (though not as quickly as factorials). Therefore, we use type `BigInteger` as the parameter type and the return type of method `fibonacci`.

```
 1  // Fig. 18.5: FibonacciCalculator.java
 2  // Recursive fibonacci method.
 3  import java.math.BigInteger;
 4
 5  public class FibonacciCalculator {
 6     private static BigInteger TWO = BigInteger.valueOf(2);
 7
 8     // recursive declaration of method fibonacci
 9     public static BigInteger fibonacci(BigInteger number) {
10        if (number.equals(BigInteger.ZERO) ||
11              number.equals(BigInteger.ONE)) { // base cases
12           return number;
13        }
```

Fig. 18.5 | Recursive fibonacci method. (Part 1 of 2.)

```
14          else { // recursion step
15             return fibonacci(number.subtract(BigInteger.ONE)).add(
16                fibonacci(number.subtract(TWO)));
17          }
18       }
19
20       public static void main(String[] args) {
21          // displays the fibonacci values from 0-40
22          for (int counter = 0; counter <= 40; counter++) {
23             System.out.printf("Fibonacci of %d is: %d%n", counter,
24               fibonacci(BigInteger.valueOf(counter)));
25          }
26       }
27    }
```

```
Fibonacci of 0 is: 0
Fibonacci of 1 is: 1
Fibonacci of 2 is: 1
Fibonacci of 3 is: 2
Fibonacci of 4 is: 3
Fibonacci of 5 is: 5
Fibonacci of 6 is: 8
Fibonacci of 7 is: 13
Fibonacci of 8 is: 21
Fibonacci of 9 is: 34
Fibonacci of 10 is: 55
...
Fibonacci of 37 is: 24157817
Fibonacci of 38 is: 39088169
Fibonacci of 39 is: 63245986
Fibonacci of 40 is: 102334155
```

Fig. 18.5 | Recursive fibonacci method. (Part 2 of 2.)

The call to method `fibonacci` (line 24) from `main` is *not* a recursive call, but all subsequent calls to `fibonacci` performed from lines 15–16 *are* recursive, because at that point the calls are initiated by method `fibonacci` itself. Each time `fibonacci` is called, it immediately tests for the *base cases*—`number` equal to 0 or `number` equal to 1 (lines 10–11). We use `BigInteger` constants **`ZERO`** and `ONE` to represent the values 0 and 1, respectively. If the condition in lines 10–11 is `true`, `fibonacci` simply returns `number`, because `fibonacci(0)` is 0 and `fibonacci(1)` is 1. Interestingly, if `number` is greater than 1, the recursion step generates *two* recursive calls (lines 15–16), each for a slightly smaller problem than the original call to `fibonacci`. Lines 15–16 use `BigInteger` methods **`add`** and `subtract` to help implement the recursive step. We also use a constant of type `BigInteger` named `TWO` that we defined at line 6.

Analyzing the Calls to Method `Fibonacci`

Figure 18.6 shows how method `fibonacci` evaluates `fibonacci(3)`. At the bottom of the figure we're left with the values 1, 0 and 1—the results of evaluating the *base cases*. The first two return values (from left to right), 1 and 0, are returned as the values for the calls `fibonacci(1)` and `fibonacci(0)`. The sum 1 plus 0 is returned as the value of `fibonac-`

ci(2). This is added to the result (1) of the call to fibonacci(1), producing the value 2. This final value is then returned as the value of fibonacci(3).

Figure 18.6 raises some interesting issues about *the order in which Java compilers evaluate the operands of operators*. This order is different from that in which operators are applied to their operands—namely, the order dictated by the rules of operator precedence. From Figure 18.6, it appears that while fibonacci(3) is being evaluated, two recursive calls will be made—fibonacci(2) and fibonacci(1). But in what order will they be made? *The Java language specifies that the order of evaluation of the operands is from left to right.* Thus, the call fibonacci(2) is made first and the call fibonacci(1) second.

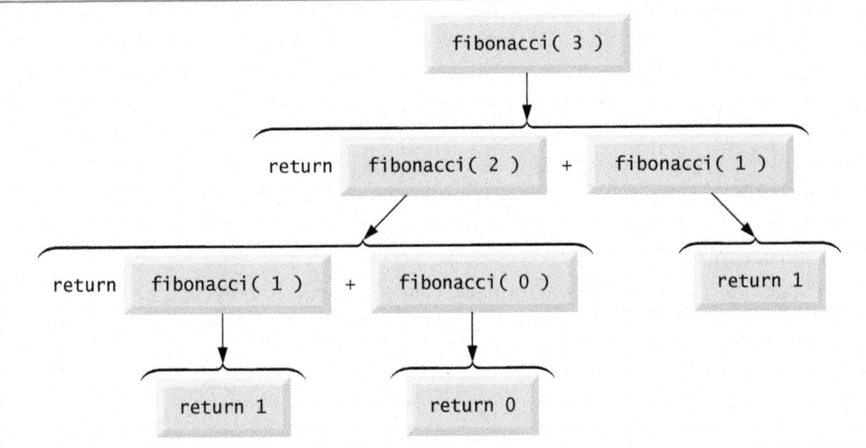

Fig. 18.6 | Set of recursive calls for fibonacci(3).

Complexity Issues

A word of caution is in order about recursive programs like the one we use here to generate Fibonacci numbers. Each invocation of the fibonacci method that does not match one of the *base cases* (0 or 1) results in *two more recursive calls* to the fibonacci method. Hence, this set of recursive calls rapidly gets out of hand. Calculating the Fibonacci value of 20 with the program in Fig. 18.5 requires 21,891 calls to the fibonacci method; calculating the Fibonacci value of 30 requires 2,692,537 calls! As you try to calculate larger Fibonacci values, you'll notice that each consecutive Fibonacci number you use the application to calculate results in a substantial increase in calculation time and in the number of calls to the fibonacci method. For example, the Fibonacci value of 31 requires 4,356,617 calls, and the Fibonacci value of 32 requires 7,049,155 calls! As you can see, the number of calls to fibonacci increases quickly—1,664,080 additional calls between Fibonacci values of 30 and 31 and 2,692,538 additional calls between Fibonacci values of 31 and 32! The difference in the number of calls made between Fibonacci values of 31 and 32 is more than 1.5 times the difference in the number of calls for Fibonacci values between 30 and 31. Problems of this nature can humble even the world's most powerful computers.

[*Note:* In the field of complexity theory, computer scientists study how hard algorithms work to complete their tasks. Complexity issues are discussed in detail in the upper-level computer science curriculum course generally called "Algorithms." We introduce various complexity issues in Chapter 19, Searching, Sorting and Big O.]

In this chapter's exercises, you'll enhance the Fibonacci program of Fig. 18.5 so that it calculates the approximate amount of time required to perform the calculation. For this purpose, you'll call `static System` method `currentTimeMillis`, which takes no arguments and returns the computer's current time in milliseconds since January 1, 1970.

Performance Tip 18.1

Avoid Fibonacci-style recursive programs, because they result in an exponential "explosion" of method calls.

8 *Calculating Fibonacci Numbers with Lambdas and Streams*

If you've read Chapter 17, consider doing Exercise 18.29, which asks you to calculate Fibonacci numbers using lambdas and streams, rather than recursion.

18.6 Recursion and the Method-Call Stack

In Chapter 6, the *stack* data structure was introduced in the context of understanding how Java performs method calls. We discussed both the *method-call stack* and *stack frames*. In this section, we'll use these concepts to demonstrate how the program-execution stack handles *recursive* method calls.

Let's begin by returning to the Fibonacci example—specifically, calling method `fibonacci` with the value `3`, as in Fig. 18.6. To show the *order* in which the method calls' stack frames are placed on the stack, we've lettered the method calls in Fig. 18.7.

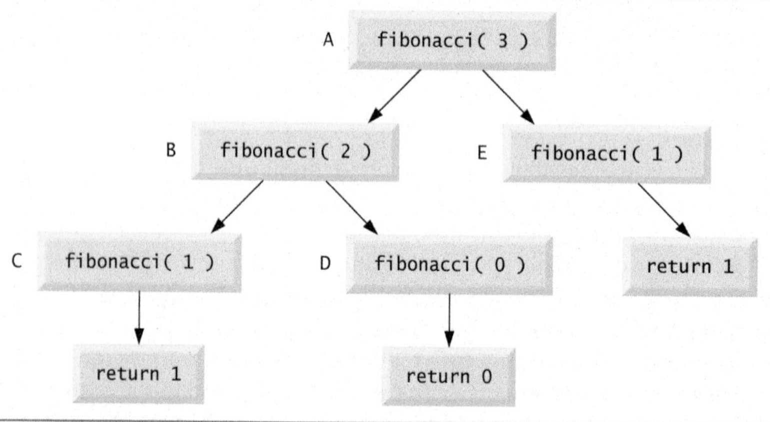

Fig. 18.7 | Method calls made within the call `fibonacci(3)`.

When the first method call (`A`) is made, a *stack frame* containing the value of the local variable `number` (`3`, in this case) is *pushed* onto the *program-execution stack*. This stack, including the stack frame for method call `A`, is illustrated in part (a) of Fig. 18.8. [*Note:* We use a simplified stack here. An actual program-execution stack and its stack frames would be more complex than in Fig. 18.8, containing such information as where the method call is to *return* to when it has completed execution.]

Within method call `A`, method calls `B` and `E` are made. The original method call has not yet completed, so its stack frame remains on the stack. The first method call to be

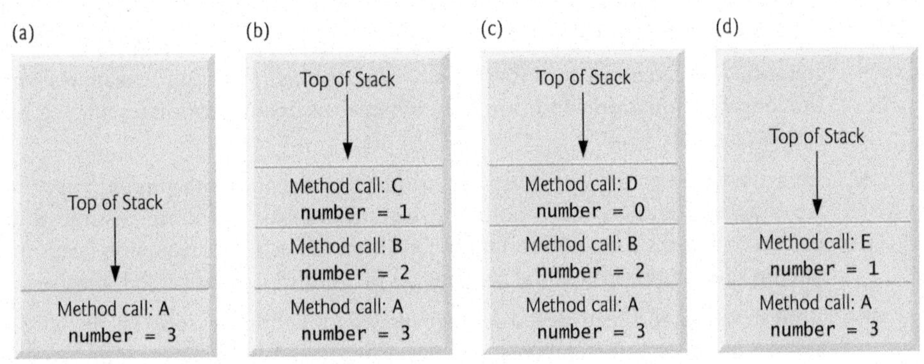

Fig. 18.8 | Method calls on the program-execution stack.

made from within `A` is method call `B`, so the stack frame for method call `B` is pushed onto the stack on top of the one for method call `A`. Method call `B` must execute and complete before method call `E` is made.

Within method call `B`, method calls `C` and `D` will be made. Method call `C` is made first, and its stack frame is pushed onto the stack [part (b) of Fig. 18.8]. Method call `B` has not yet finished, and its stack frame is still on the method-call stack. When method call `C` executes, it makes no further method calls, but simply returns the value `1`. When this method returns, its stack frame is popped off the top of the stack. The method call at the top of the stack is now `B`, which continues to execute by performing method call `D`. The stack frame for method call `D` is pushed onto the stack [part (c) of Fig. 18.8]. Method call `D` completes without making any more method calls and returns the value `0`. The stack frame for this method call is then popped off the stack.

Now, both method calls made from within method call `B` have returned. Method call `B` continues to execute, returning the value `1`. Method call `B` completes, and its stack frame is popped off the stack. At this point, the stack frame for method call `A` is at the top of the stack and the method continues its execution. This method makes method call `E`, whose stack frame is now pushed onto the stack [part (d) of Fig. 18.8]. Method call `E` completes and returns the value `1`. The stack frame for this method call is popped off the stack, and once again method call `A` continues to execute.

At this point, method call `A` will not make any other method calls and can finish its execution, returning the value `2` to `A`'s caller (`fibonacci(3) = 2`). `A`'s stack frame is popped off the stack. The executing method is always the one whose stack frame is at the top of the stack, and the stack frame for that method contains the values of its local variables.

18.7 Recursion vs. Iteration

We've studied methods `factorial` and `fibonacci`, which can easily be implemented either recursively or iteratively. In this section, we compare the two approaches and discuss why you might choose one approach over the other in a particular situation.

Both iteration and recursion are *based on a control statement*: Iteration uses an iteration statement (e.g., `for`, `while` or `do...while`), whereas recursion uses a selection statement (e.g., `if`, `if...else` or `switch`):

- Both iteration and recursion involve *iteration*: Iteration explicitly uses an iteration statement, whereas recursion achieves iteration through repeated method calls.
- Iteration and recursion each involve a *termination test*: Iteration terminates when the loop-continuation condition fails, whereas recursion terminates when a base case is reached.
- Iteration with counter-controlled iteration and recursion both *gradually approach termination*: Iteration keeps modifying a counter until the counter assumes a value that makes the loop-continuation condition fail, whereas recursion keeps producing smaller versions of the original problem until the base case is reached.
- Both iteration and recursion *can occur infinitely*: An infinite loop occurs with iteration if the loop-continuation test never becomes false, whereas infinite recursion occurs if the recursion step does not reduce the problem each time in a manner that converges on the base case, or if the base case is not tested.

To illustrate the differences between iteration and recursion, let's examine an iterative solution to the factorial problem (Fig. 18.9, lines 10–12). Here we use an iteration statement, rather than a selection statement (Fig. 18.3, lines 7–12). Both solutions use a termination test. In the recursive solution (Fig. 18.3), line 7 tests for the *base case*. In Fig. 18.9's iterative solution, line 10 tests the loop-continuation condition—if the test fails, the loop terminates. Finally, instead of producing smaller versions of the original problem, the iterative solution uses a counter that is modified until the loop-continuation condition becomes `false`.

```
1  // Fig. 18.9: FactorialCalculator.java
2  // Iterative factorial method.
3
4  public class FactorialCalculator {
5     // iterative declaration of method factorial
6     public long factorial(long number) {
7        long result = 1;
8
9        // iteratively calculate factorial
10       for (long i = number; i >= 1; i--) {
11          result *= i;
12       }
13
14       return result;
15    }
16
17    public static void main(String[] args) {
18       // calculate the factorials of 0 through 10
19       for (int counter = 0; counter <= 10; counter++) {
20          System.out.printf("%d! = %d%n", counter, factorial(counter));
21       }
22    }
23 }
```

Fig. 18.9 | Iterative factorial method. (Part 1 of 2.)

```
0! = 1
1! = 1
2! = 2
3! = 6
4! = 24
5! = 120
6! = 720
7! = 5040
8! = 40320
9! = 362880
10! = 3628800
```

Fig. 18.9 | Iterative factorial method. (Part 2 of 2.)

Recursion has many *negatives*. It repeatedly invokes the mechanism, and consequently the *overhead, of method calls*. This iteration can be *expensive* in terms of both processor time and memory space. Each recursive call causes another *copy* of the method (actually, only the method's variables, stored in the stack frame) to be created—this set of copies *can consume considerable memory space*. Since iteration occurs within a method, repeated method calls and extra memory assignment are avoided.

Software Engineering Observation 18.1

Any problem that can be solved recursively can be solved iteratively and vice versa. A recursive approach is preferred over an iterative approach when the recursive approach more naturally mirrors the problem and results in a program that's easier to understand and debug. A recursive approach can often be implemented with fewer lines of code. Another reason to choose a recursive approach is that an iterative one might not be apparent.

Performance Tip 18.2

When performance is crucial, you might want to try various iterative and recursive approaches to see which achieve your goal.

Common Programming Error 18.2

Accidentally having a nonrecursive method call itself either directly or indirectly through another method can cause infinite recursion.

18.8 Towers of Hanoi

Earlier in this chapter we studied methods that can be easily implemented both recursively and iteratively. Now, we present a problem whose recursive solution demonstrates the elegance of recursion, and whose iterative solution may not be as apparent.

The **Towers of Hanoi** is one of the classic problems every budding computer scientist must grapple with. Legend has it that in a temple in the Far East, priests are attempting to move a stack of golden disks from one diamond peg to another (Fig. 18.10). The initial stack has 64 disks threaded onto one peg and arranged from bottom to top by decreasing size. The priests are attempting to move the stack from one peg to another under the constraints that exactly one disk is moved at a time and at no time may a larger disk be placed above a smaller disk. Three pegs are provided, one being used for temporarily holding disks. Supposedly, the world will end when the priests complete their task, so there's little incentive for us to facilitate their efforts.

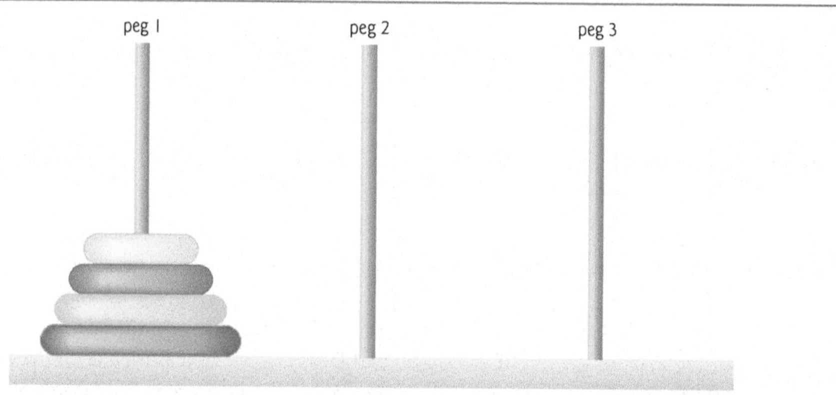

Fig. 18.10 | Towers of Hanoi for the case with four disks.

Let's assume that the priests are attempting to move the disks from peg 1 to peg 3. We wish to develop an algorithm that prints the precise sequence of peg-to-peg disk transfers.

If we try to find an iterative solution, we'll likely find ourselves hopelessly "knotted up" in managing the disks. Instead, attacking this problem recursively quickly yields a solution. Moving n disks can be viewed in terms of moving only $n - 1$ disks (hence the recursion) as follows:

1. Move $n - 1$ disks from peg 1 to peg 2, using peg 3 as a temporary holding area.
2. Move the last disk (the largest) from peg 1 to peg 3.
3. Move $n - 1$ disks from peg 2 to peg 3, using peg 1 as a temporary holding area.

The process ends when the last task involves moving $n = 1$ disk (i.e., the base case). This task is accomplished by moving the disk, without using a temporary holding area.

In Fig. 18.11, method `solveTowers` (lines 5–22) solves the Towers of Hanoi, given the total number of disks (in this case `3`), the starting peg, the ending peg, and the temporary holding peg as parameters.

```
1  // Fig. 18.11: TowersOfHanoi.java
2  // Towers of Hanoi solution with a recursive method.
3  public class TowersOfHanoi {
4     // recursively move disks between towers
5     public static void solveTowers(int disks, int sourcePeg,
6        int destinationPeg, int tempPeg) {
7        // base case -- only one disk to move
8        if (disks == 1) {
9           System.out.printf("%n%d --> %d", sourcePeg, destinationPeg);
10          return;
11       }
```

Fig. 18.11 | Towers of Hanoi solution with a recursive method. (Part 1 of 2.)

```
12
13          // recursion step -- move (disk - 1) disks from sourcePeg
14          // to tempPeg using destinationPeg
15          solveTowers(disks - 1, sourcePeg, tempPeg, destinationPeg);
16
17          // move last disk from sourcePeg to destinationPeg
18          System.out.printf("%n%d --> %d", sourcePeg, destinationPeg);
19
20          // move (disks - 1) disks from tempPeg to destinationPeg
21          solveTowers(disks - 1, tempPeg, destinationPeg, sourcePeg);
22       }
23
24       public static void main(String[] args) {
25          int startPeg = 1; // value 1 used to indicate startPeg in output
26          int endPeg = 3; // value 3 used to indicate endPeg in output
27          int tempPeg = 2; // value 2 used to indicate tempPeg in output
28          int totalDisks = 3; // number of disks
29
30          // initial nonrecursive call: move all disks.
31          solveTowers(totalDisks, startPeg, endPeg, tempPeg);
32       }
33    }
```

```
1 --> 3
1 --> 2
3 --> 2
1 --> 3
2 --> 1
2 --> 3
1 --> 3
```

Fig. 18.11 | Towers of Hanoi solution with a recursive method. (Part 2 of 2.)

The base case (lines 8–11) occurs when only one disk needs to be moved from the starting peg to the ending peg. The recursion step (lines 15–21) moves `disks - 1` disks (line 15) from the first peg (`sourcePeg`) to the temporary holding peg (`tempPeg`). When all but one of the disks have been moved to the temporary peg, line 18 moves the largest disk from the start peg to the destination peg. Line 21 finishes the rest of the moves by calling the method `solveTowers` to recursively move `disks - 1` disks from the temporary peg (`tempPeg`) to the destination peg (`destinationPeg`), this time using the first peg (`sourcePeg`) as the temporary peg. Line 31 in `main` calls the recursive `solveTowers` method, which outputs the steps to the command prompt.

18.9 Fractals

A **fractal** is a geometric figure that can be generated from a pattern repeated recursively (Fig. 18.12). The figure is modified by recursively applying the pattern to each segment of the original figure. Although such figures had been studied before the 20th century, it was the mathematician Benoit Mandelbrot who in the 1970s introduced the term "fractal," along with the specifics of how a fractal is created and the practical applications of fractals. Mandelbrot's fractal geometry provides mathematical models for many complex forms found in nature, such as mountains, clouds and coastlines. Fractals have many uses in mathematics and science. They can be used to better understand systems or patterns that appear in nature (e.g., ecosystems), in the human body (e.g., in the folds of the brain), or in the universe (e.g., galaxy clusters). Not all fractals resemble objects in nature. Drawing fractals has become a popular art form. Fractals have a **self-similar property**—when subdivided into parts, each resembles a reduced-size copy of the whole. Many fractals yield an exact copy of the original when a portion of the fractal is magnified—such a fractal is said to be **strictly self-similar**.

18.9.1 Koch Curve Fractal

As an example, let's look at the strictly self-similar **Koch Curve** fractal (Fig. 18.12). It's formed by removing the middle third of each line in the drawing and replacing it with two lines that form a point, such that if the middle third of the original line remained, an equilateral triangle would be formed. Formulas for creating fractals often involve removing all or part of the previous fractal image. This pattern has already been determined for this fractal—we focus here on how to use those formulas in a recursive solution.

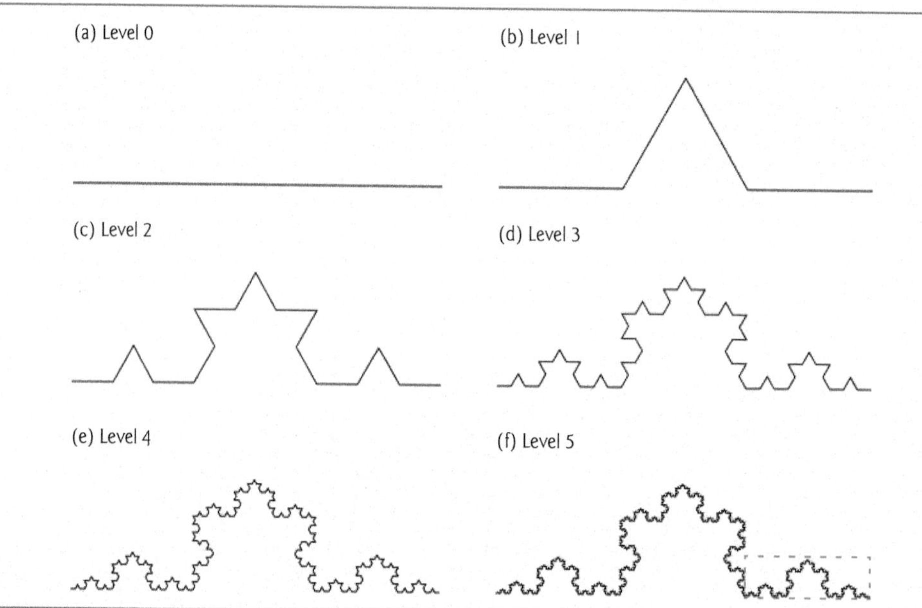

Fig. 18.12 | Koch Curve fractal.

We start with a straight line (Fig. 18.12(a)) and apply the pattern, creating a triangle from the middle third (Fig. 18.12(b)). We then apply the pattern again to each straight line, resulting in Fig. 18.12(c). Each time the pattern is applied, we say that the fractal is at a new **level**, or **depth** (sometimes the term **order** is also used). Fractals can be displayed at many levels—for example, a fractal at level 3 has had three iterations of the pattern applied (Fig. 18.12(d)). After only a few iterations, this fractal begins to look like a portion of a snowflake (Fig. 18.12(e and f)). Since this is a strictly self-similar fractal, each portion of it contains an exact copy of the fractal. In Fig. 18.12(f), for example, we've highlighted a portion of the fractal with a dashed box. If the image in this box were increased in size, it would look exactly like the entire fractal of part (f). Exercise 18.24 asks you to use the drawing techniques you'll learn in this section to implement the Koch Curve.

A similar fractal, the **Koch Snowflake**, is similar to the Koch Curve but begins with a triangle rather than a line. The same pattern is applied to each side of the triangle, resulting in an image that looks like an enclosed snowflake. Exercise 18.25 asks you to research the Koch Snowflake, then create an app that draws it.

18.9.2 (Optional) Case Study: Lo Feather Fractal

We now demonstrate using recursion to draw fractals by writing a program to create a strictly self-similar fractal. We call this the "Lo feather fractal," named for Sin Han Lo, a Deitel & Associates colleague who created it. The fractal will eventually resemble one-half of a feather (see the outputs in Fig. 18.20). The base case, or fractal level of 0, begins as a line between two points, `A` and `B` (Fig. 18.13). To create the next higher level, we find the midpoint (`C`) of the line. To calculate the location of point `C`, use the following formula:

```
xC = (xA + xB) / 2;
yC = (yA + yB) / 2;
```

[*Note:* The `x` and `y` to the left of each letter refer to the *x*-coordinate and *y*-coordinate of that point, respectively. For example, `xA` refers to the *x*-coordinate of point `A`, while `yC` refers to the *y*-coordinate of point `C`. In our diagrams we denote the point by its letter, followed by two numbers representing the *x*- and *y*-coordinates.]

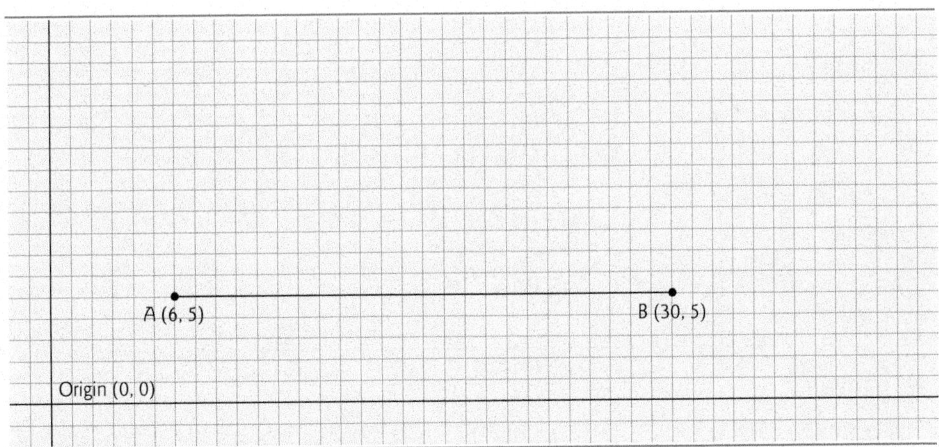

Fig. 18.13 | "Lo feather fractal" at level 0.

To create this fractal, we also must find a point `D` that lies left of segment `AC` and creates an isosceles right triangle `ADC`. To calculate point `D`'s location, use the formulas:

```
xD = xA + (xC - xA) / 2 - (yC - yA) / 2;
yD = yA + (yC - yA) / 2 + (xC - xA) / 2;
```

We now move from level 0 to level 1 as follows: First, add points `C` and `D` (as in Fig. 18.14). Then, remove the original line and add segments `DA`, `DC` and `DB`. The remaining lines will curve at an angle, causing our fractal to look like a feather.

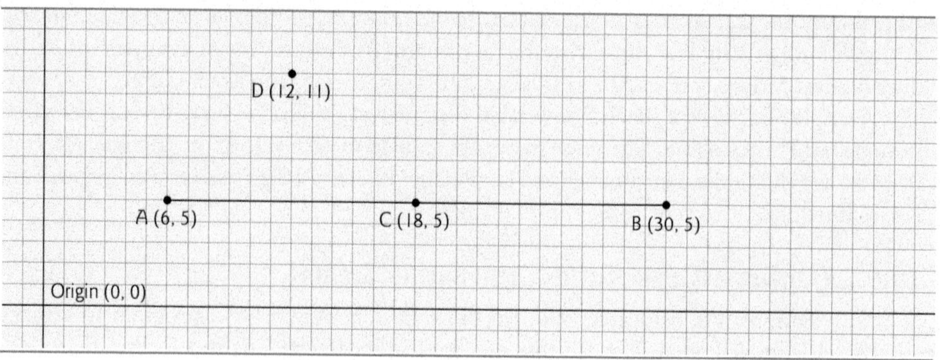

Fig. 18.14 | Determining points C and D for level 1 of the "Lo feather fractal."

For the next level of the fractal, this algorithm is repeated on each of the three lines in level 1. For each line, the formulas above are applied, where the former point `D` is now considered to be point `A`, while the other end of each line is considered to be point `B`. Figure 18.15 contains the line from level 0 (now a dashed line) and the three added lines from level 1. We've changed point `D` to be point `A`, and the original points `A`, `C` and `B` to `B1`, `B2` and `B3`, respectively. The preceding formulas have been used to find the new points `C` and `D` on each line. These points are also numbered 1–3 to keep track of which point is associated with each line. The points `C1` and `D1`, for example, represent points `C` and `D` associated with the line formed from points `A` to `B1`.

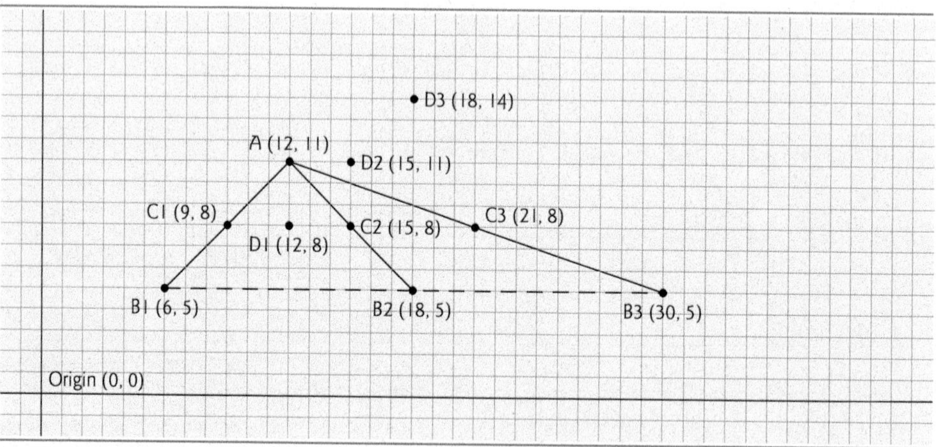

Fig. 18.15 | "Lo feather fractal" at level 1, with C and D points determined for level 2. [*Note:* The fractal at level 0 is included as a dashed line as a reminder of where the line was located in relation to the current fractal.]

To achieve level 2, the three lines in Fig. 18.15 are removed and replaced with new lines from the `C` and `D` points just added. Figure 18.16 shows the new lines (the lines from level 2 are shown as dashed lines for your convenience).

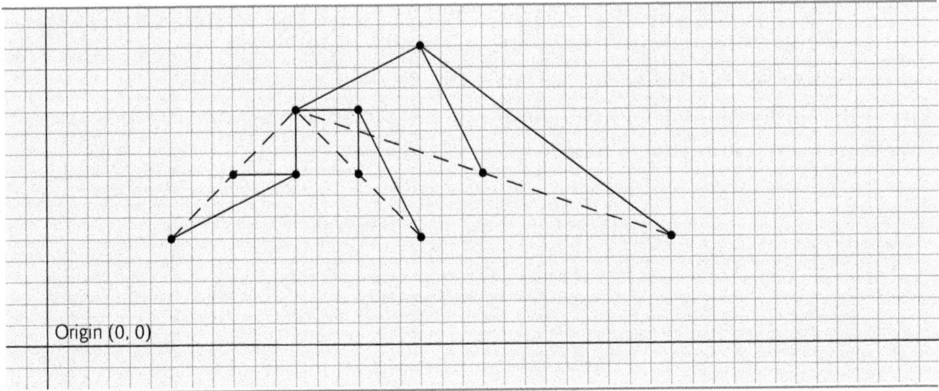

Fig. 18.16 | "Lo feather fractal" at level 2, with dashed lines from level 1 provided.

Figure 18.17 shows level 2 without the dashed lines from level 1. Once this process has been repeated several times, the fractal will begin to look like one-half of a feather, as shown in the output of Fig. 18.20.

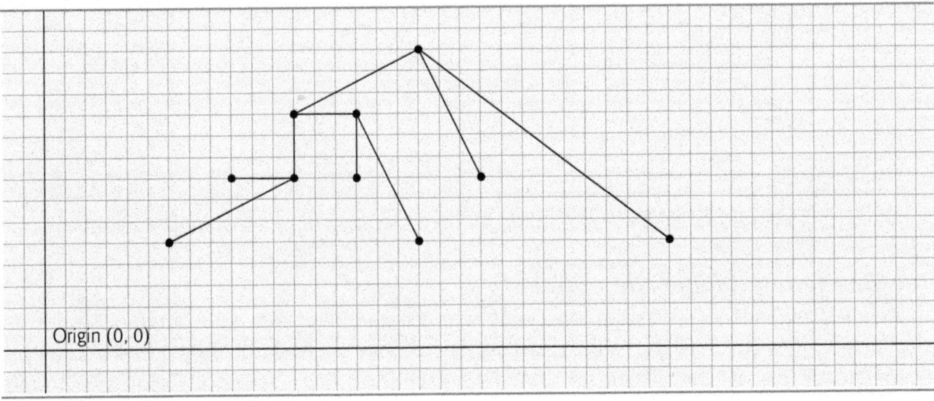

Fig. 18.17 | "Lo feather fractal" at level 2.

18.9.3 (Optional) Fractal App GUI

In this section and the next, we build a JavaFX **Fractal** app that displays the Lo Fractal—we do not show the example's `Application` subclass, because it performs the same tasks we demonstrated in Chapters 12–13 to load and display the app's FXML.

Figure 18.18 shows the GUI with the **fx:id** values for the controls we access programmatically. Like the **Painter** app in Section 13.3, this app uses a `BorderPane` layout with a with a white background color:

- In the top area, we placed a `ToolBar` (located in the Scene Builder **Library**'s **Containers** section). A `ToolBar` layout arranges its controls horizontally (by default) or vertically. Typically, you place `ToolBar`s at your GUI's edges, such as in a `BorderPane`'s top, left, bottom or right areas.
- In the center, we placed a 400-by-480 pixel `Canvas` (from the Scene Builder **Library**'s **Miscellaneous** section). **Canvas** is a `Node` subclass in which you can draw

graphics using a **GraphicsContext** (both in the package javafx.scene.canvas). We show you how to draw a line in a specific color in this example and discuss classes Canvas and GraphicsContext in detail in Section 22.10.

To size the BorderPane layout to its contents, we reset its **Pref Width** and **Pref Height** property values (as you learned in Chapter 13) to USE_COMPUTED_SIZE.

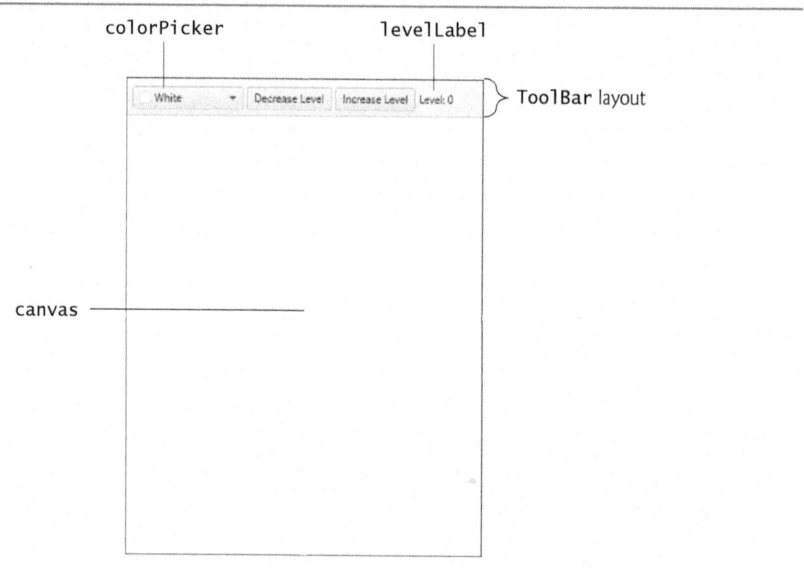

Fig. 18.18 | **Fractal** GUI labeled with **fx:id**s for the programmatically manipulated controls.

ToolBar and Its Additional Controls

By default, the ToolBar you drag onto your layout has one Button. You can drag additional controls onto the ToolBar and, if necessary, remove the default Button. We added a ColorPicker control (with **fx:id** colorPicker), another Button and a Label (with **fx:id** levelLabel). For the two Buttons and the Label, we set their text as shown in Fig. 18.18.

ColorPicker

A **ColorPicker** provides a predefined color-selecting GUI that, by default, enables the user to choose colors by color swatches (small squares of sample colors). Initially, the selected color is **White**. We'll programmatically set this to **Blue** in the app's controller. Figure 18.19 shows the ColorPicker's default GUI and the **Custom Colors** GUI that appears when you click the ColorPicker's **Custom Color...** link. The **Custom Colors** GUI enables you to select any custom color.

Event Handlers

When the user selects a color in the default GUI or customizes a color and presses **Save** in the **Custom Colors** GUI, an ActionEvent occurs. In Scene Builder, for the ColorPicker's **On Action** event handler, we specified colorSelected. In addition, for the **Decrease Level** and **Increase Level** Button's **On Action** events handlers, we specified decreaseLevelButtonPressed and increaseLevelButtonPressed, respectively.

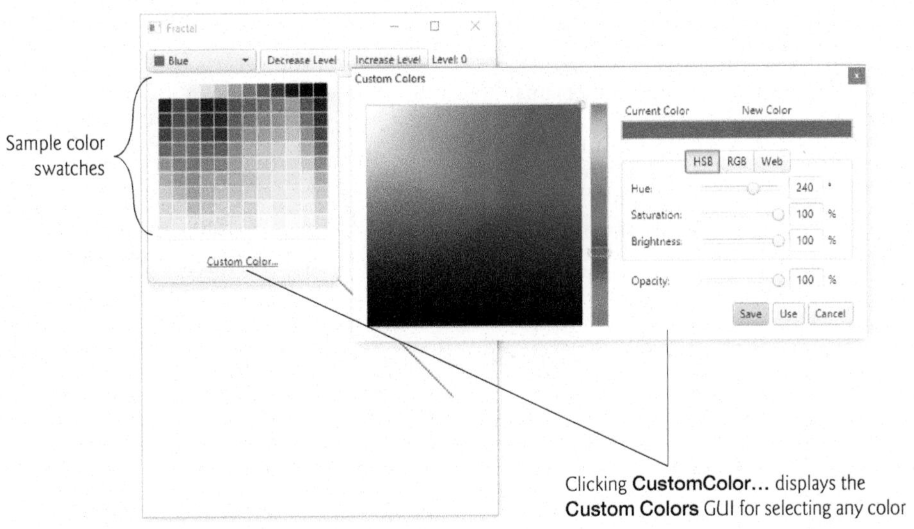

Fig. 18.19 | `ColorPicker`'s predefined GUI.

18.9.4 (Optional) `FractalController` Class

Figure 18.20 presents class `FractalController`, which defines the app's event handlers and the methods for drawing the Lo Fractal recursively. The outputs show the development of the fractal from levels 0–5, then for levels 8 and 11. If we focus on one of the arms of this fractal, it will be identical to the whole image. This property defines the fractal to be strictly self-similar.

```
// Fig. 18.20: FractalController.java
// Drawing the "Lo feather fractal" using recursion.
import javafx.event.ActionEvent;
import javafx.fxml.FXML;
import javafx.scene.canvas.Canvas;
import javafx.scene.canvas.GraphicsContext;
import javafx.scene.control.ColorPicker;
import javafx.scene.control.Label;
import javafx.scene.paint.Color;
import javafx.scene.shape.Line;

public class FractalController {
   // constants
   private static final int MIN_LEVEL = 0;
   private static final int MAX_LEVEL = 15;

   // instance variables that refer to GUI components
   @FXML private Canvas canvas;
   @FXML private ColorPicker colorPicker;
   @FXML private Label levelLabel;

```

Fig. 18.20 | Drawing the "Lo feather fractal" using recursion. (Part 1 of 4.)

```
   // other instance variables
   private Color currentColor = Color.BLUE;
   private int level = MIN_LEVEL; // initial fractal level
   private GraphicsContext gc; // used to draw on Canvas

   // initialize the controller
   public void initialize() {
      levelLabel.setText("Level: " + level);
      colorPicker.setValue(currentColor); // start with purple
      gc = canvas.getGraphicsContext2D(); // get the GraphicsContext
      drawFractal();
   }

   // sets currentColor when user chooses a new Color
   @FXML
   void colorSelected(ActionEvent event) {
      currentColor = colorPicker.getValue(); // get new Color
      drawFractal();
   }

   // decrease level and redraw fractal
   @FXML
   void decreaseLevelButtonPressed(ActionEvent event) {
      if (level > MIN_LEVEL) {
         --level;
         levelLabel.setText("Level: " + level);
         drawFractal();
      }
   }

   // increase level and redraw fractal
   @FXML
   void increaseLevelButtonPressed(ActionEvent event) {
      if (level < MAX_LEVEL) {
         ++level;
         levelLabel.setText("Level: " + level);
         drawFractal();
      }
   }

   // clear Canvas, set drawing color and draw the fractal
   private void drawFractal() {
      gc.clearRect(0, 0, canvas.getWidth(), canvas.getHeight());
      gc.setStroke(currentColor);
      drawFractal(level, 40, 40, 350, 350);
   }

   // draw fractal recursively
   public void drawFractal(int level, int xA, int yA, int xB, int yB) {
      // base case: draw a line connecting two given points
      if (level == 0) {
         gc.strokeLine(xA, yA, xB, yB);
      }
```

Fig. 18.20 | Drawing the "Lo feather fractal" using recursion. (Part 2 of 4.)

```
      else { // recursion step: determine new points, draw next level
         // calculate midpoint between (xA, yA) and (xB, yB)
         int xC = (xA + xB) / 2;
         int yC = (yA + yB) / 2;

         // calculate the fourth point (xD, yD) which forms an
         // isosceles right triangle between (xA, yA) and (xC, yC)
         // where the right angle is at (xD, yD)
         int xD = xA + (xC - xA) / 2 - (yC - yA) / 2;
         int yD = yA + (yC - yA) / 2 + (xC - xA) / 2;

         // recursively draw the Fractal
         drawFractal(level - 1, xD, yD, xA, yA);
         drawFractal(level - 1, xD, yD, xC, yC);
         drawFractal(level - 1, xD, yD, xB, yB);
      }
   }
}
```

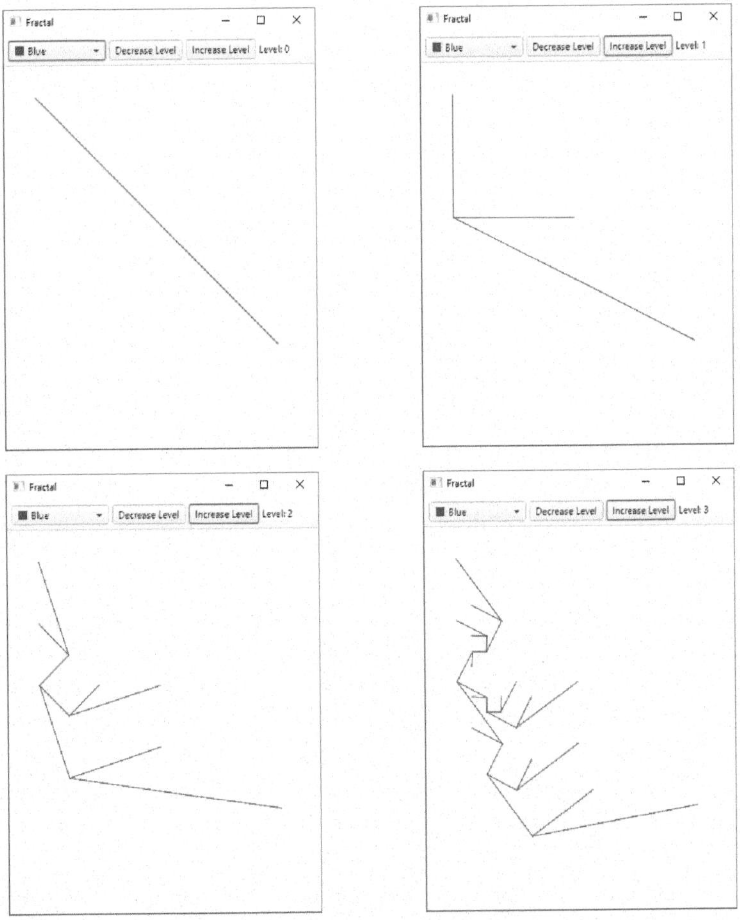

Fig. 18.20 | Drawing the "Lo feather fractal" using recursion. (Part 3 of 4.)

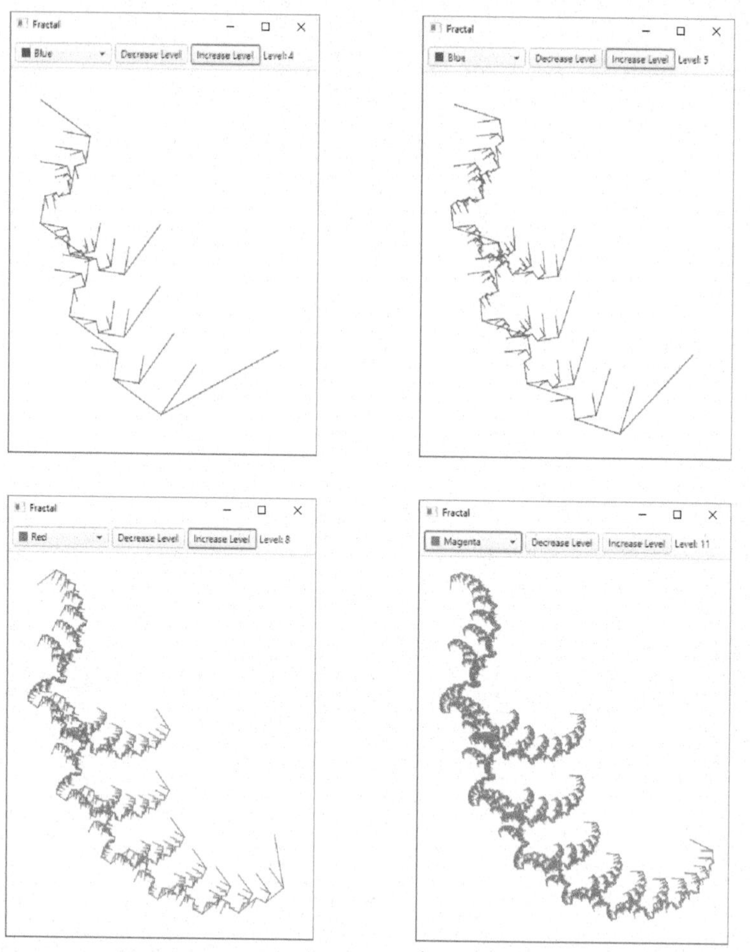

Fig. 18.20 | Drawing the "Lo feather fractal" using recursion. (Part 4 of 4.)

`FractalController` *Fields*

Lines 14–25 declare the class's fields:

- The constants `MIN_LEVEL` and `MAX_LEVEL` (lines 14–15) specify the range of Lo Fractal levels this app can draw. Once you get to level 15, the changes in the fractal (at this size) become difficult to see, so we set 15 as the maximum level. Around level 13 and higher, the fractal rendering becomes *slower* due to the details to be drawn.
- Lines 18–20 declare the `@FXML` instance variables that will reference the GUI's controls that we programmatically manipulate. Recall that these are initialized by the `FXMLLoader`.
- Line 23 declares the `Color` variable `currentColor` and initialize it to the constant `Color.BLUE`. Class **`Color`** (package `javafx.scene.paint`) contains various constants for common colors and provides methods for creating custom colors.

- Line 24 declares the `int` variable `level`, which maintains the current fractal level.
- Line 25 declares the `GraphicsContext` variable `gc`, which will be used to draw on the app's `Canvas`.

`initialize` *Method*

When the app's controller is created and initialized, method initialize (lines 28–33):

- Sets the `levelLabel`'s initial text to indicate level 0.
- Sets the initial value of the `colorPicker` to `currentColor` (`Color.BLUE`).
- Gets the `canvas`'s `GraphicsContext` that will be used to draw lines in the currently selected color.
- Calls `drawFractal` (lines 63–67) to draw level 0 of the fractal.

`colorSelected` *Event Handler*

When the user choses a new color, the `colorPicker`'s `colorSelected` event handler (lines 36–40) uses `ColorPicker` method **`getValue`** to get the currently selected color, then calls `drawFractal` (lines 63–67) to redraw the fractal in the new color and current `level`.

`decreaseLevelButtonPressed` *and* `increaseLevelButtonPressed` *Event Handlers*

When the user presses the **Decrease Level** or **Increase Level** `Buttons`, the corresponding event handler (lines 43–50 or 53–60) executes. These event handlers decrease or increase the level, set the `levelLabel`'s text accordingly and call `drawFractal` (lines 63–67) to redraw the fractal for the new `level` and `currentColor`. Attempting to decrease the `level` below `MIN_LEVEL` or above `MAX_LEVEL` does nothing in this app.

`drawFractal` *Method with No Arguments*

Each time method `drawFractal` is called, it uses `GraphicsContext` method **`clearRect`** to clear any prior drawing. This method clears a rectangular area by setting the contents of the specified area to the `Canvas`'s background color. The method's four arguments are the *x*- and *y*-coordinates of the rectangle's upper-left corner and the width and height of the rectangle. In this case, we clear the entire `Canvas`—methods **`getWidth`** and **`getHeight`** return the `Canvas`'s width and height, respectively.

Next, line 65 calls `GraphicsContext` method **`setStroke`** to set the drawing color to the `currentColor`. Then line 66 makes the first call to the overloaded *recursive* method `drawFractal` (lines 70–91) to draw the fractal.

`drawFractal` *Method with Five Arguments*

Lines 70–91 define the recursive method that creates the fractal. This method takes five parameters: the level of the Lo Fractal to draw and four integers that specify the *x*- and *y*-coordinates of two points. The base case for this method (line 72) occurs when `level` equals `0`, at which time line 73 uses `GraphicsContext` method **`strokeLine`** to draw a line between the two points the current call to `drawFractal` received as arguments.

In the recursive step (lines 75–90), lines 77–84 calculate

- (`xC`, `yC`)—the midpoint between (`xA`, `yA`) and (`xB`, `yB`), and
- (`xD`, `yD`)—the point that creates a right isosceles triangle with (`xA`, `yA`) and (`xC`, `yC`).

Then, lines 87–89 make three recursive calls on three different sets of points.

Since no lines will be drawn until the base case is reached, the distance between two points decreases on each recursive call. As the level of recursion increases, the fractal becomes smoother and more detailed. The shape of this fractal stabilizes as the level approaches 12—that is, the shape of the fractal remains approximately the same and the additional details become hard to perceive. Fractals will stabilize at different levels based on their shape and size.

18.10 Recursive Backtracking

Our recursive methods all have a similar architecture—if the base case is reached, return a result; if not, make one or more recursive calls. This section explores a more complex recursive technique that finds a path through a maze, returning true if there's a possible solution. The solution involves moving through the maze one step at a time, where moves can be made by going down, right, up or left (diagonal moves are not permitted). From the current location in the maze (starting with the entry point), the following steps are taken: For each possible direction, the move is made in that direction and a recursive call is made to solve the remainder of the maze from the new location. When a dead end is reached (i.e., we cannot take any more steps forward without hitting a wall), we *back up* to the previous location and try to go in a different direction. If no other direction can be taken, we back up again. This process continues until we find a point in the maze where a move *can* be made in another direction. Once such a location is found, we move in the new direction and continue with another recursive call to solve the rest of the maze.

To back up to the previous location in the maze, our recursive method simply returns false, moving up the method-call chain to the previous recursive call (which references the previous location in the maze). Using recursion to return to an earlier decision point is known as **recursive backtracking**. If one set of recursive calls does not result in a solution to the problem, the program *backs up* to the previous decision point and makes a different decision, often resulting in another set of recursive calls. In this example, the previous decision point is the previous location in the maze, and the decision to be made is the direction that the next move should take. One direction has led to a *dead end*, so the search continues with a *different* direction. The recursive backtracking solution to the maze problem uses recursion to return only *partway* up the method-call chain, then try a different direction. If the backtracking reaches the entry location of the maze and the paths in all directions have been attempted, the maze does not have a solution.

The exercises ask you to implement recursive backtracking solutions to the maze problem (Exercises 18.20–18.22) and the Eight Queens problem (Exercise 18.15), which attempts to find a way to place eight queens on an empty chessboard so that no queen is "attacking" any other (i.e., no two queens are in the same row, in the same column or along the same diagonal).

18.11 Wrap-Up

In this chapter, you learned how to create recursive methods—i.e., methods that call themselves. You learned that recursive methods typically divide a problem into two conceptual pieces—a piece that the method knows how to do (the base case) and a piece that the method does not know how to do (the recursion step). The recursion step is a slightly smaller version of the original problem and is performed by a recursive method call. You saw some popular recursion examples, including calculating factorials and producing values in the Fibonacci series. You then learned how recursion works "under the hood," including the order in which recursive method calls are pushed on or popped off the program-execution stack. Next, you compared recursive and iterative approaches. You learned how to use recursion to solve more complex problems—the Towers of Hanoi and displaying fractals. The chapter concluded with an introduction to recursive backtracking, a technique for solving problems that involves backing up through recursive calls to try different possible solutions. In the next chapter, you'll learn numerous techniques for sorting lists of data and searching for an item in a list of data, and you'll explore the circumstances under which each searching and sorting technique should be used.

Summary

Section 18.1 Introduction

- A recursive method (p. 757) calls itself directly or indirectly through another method.

Section 18.2 Recursion Concepts

- When a recursive method is called (p. 758) to solve a problem, it can solve only the simplest case(s), or base case(s). If called with a base case (p. 758), the method returns a result.
- If a recursive method is called with a more complex problem than a base case, it typically divides the problem into two conceptual pieces—a piece that the method knows how to do and a piece that it does not know how to do.
- To make recursion feasible, the piece that the method does not know how to do must resemble the original problem, but be a slightly simpler or smaller version of it. Because this new problem resembles the original problem, the method calls a fresh copy of itself to work on the smaller problem—this is called the recursion step (p. 758).
- For recursion to eventually terminate, each time a method calls itself with a simpler version of the original problem, the sequence of smaller and smaller problems must converge on a base case. When, the method recognizes the base case, it returns a result to the previous copy of the method.
- A recursive call may be a call to another method, which in turn makes a call back to the original method. Such a process still results in a recursive call to the original method. This is known as an indirect recursive call or indirect recursion (p. 758).

Section 18.3 Example Using Recursion: Factorials

- Either omitting the base case or writing the recursion step incorrectly so that it does not converge on the base case can cause infinite recursion (p. 760), eventually exhausting memory. This error is analogous to the problem of an infinite loop in an iterative (nonrecursive) solution.

Section 18.5 Example Using Recursion: Fibonacci Series

- The Fibonacci series (p. 763) begins with 0 and 1 and has the property that each subsequent Fibonacci number is the sum of the preceding two.
- The ratio of successive Fibonacci numbers converges on a constant value of 1.618..., a number that has been called the golden ratio or the golden mean (p. 763).
- Some recursive solutions, such as Fibonacci, result in an "explosion" of method calls.

Section 18.6 Recursion and the Method-Call Stack

- The executing method is always the one whose stack frame is at the top of the stack, and the stack frame for that method contains the values of its local variables.

Section 18.7 Recursion vs. Iteration

- Both iteration and recursion are based on a control statement: Iteration uses an iteration statement, recursion a selection statement.
- Both iteration and recursion involve iteration: Iteration explicitly uses an iteration statement, whereas recursion achieves iteration through repeated method calls.
- Iteration and recursion each involve a termination test: Iteration terminates when the loop-continuation condition fails, recursion when a base case is recognized.
- Iteration with counter-controlled iteration and recursion each gradually approach termination: Iteration keeps modifying a counter until the counter assumes a value that makes the loop-continuation condition fail, whereas recursion keeps producing simpler versions of the original problem until the base case is reached.
- Both iteration and recursion can occur infinitely: An infinite loop occurs with iteration if the loop-continuation test never becomes false, whereas infinite recursion occurs if the recursion step does not reduce the problem each time in a manner that converges on the base case.
- Recursion repeatedly invokes the mechanism, and consequently the overhead, of method calls.
- Any problem that can be solved recursively can also be solved iteratively.
- A recursive approach is normally preferred over an iterative approach when it more naturally mirrors the problem and results in a program that is easier to understand and debug.
- A recursive approach can often be implemented with few lines of code, but a corresponding iterative approach might take a large amount of code. Another reason to choose a recursive solution is that an iterative solution might not be apparent.

Section 18.9 Fractals

- A fractal (p. 771) is a geometric figure that is generated from a pattern repeated recursively an infinite number of times.
- Fractals have a self-similar property (p. 772)—subparts are reduced-size copies of the whole.
- A `ToolBar` layout arranges its controls horizontally (by default) or vertically. Typically, you place `ToolBar`s at your GUI's edges.
- `Canvas` is a subclass of `Node` in which you can draw graphics using an object of class `GraphicsContext`. Both classes are in the package `javafx.scene.canvas`.
- By default, the `ToolBar` you drag onto your layout has one `Button`. You can drag additional controls onto the `ToolBar` and, if necessary, remove the default `Button`.
- A `ColorPicker` provides a predefined color-selecting GUI that, by default, enables the user to choose colors by color swatches (small squares of sample colors), but also provides a **Custom Colors** GUI for selecting any custom color.
- When the user selects a color in the default GUI or customizes a color and presses **Save** in the **Custom Colors** GUI an `ActionEvent` occurs.
- Class `Color` (package `javafx.scene.paint`) contains various constants for common colors and provides methods for creating custom colors.
- `ColorPicker` method `getValue` returns the currently selected color.
- `GraphicsContext` method `clearRect` clears a rectangular area of a `Canvas`.
- `Canvas` methods `getWidth` and `getHeight` return the `Canvas`'s width and height, respectively.

- `GraphicsContext` method `setStroke` sets the drawing color.
- `GraphicsContext` method `strokeLine` draws a line between two points.

Section 18.10 Recursive Backtracking

- In recursive backtracking (p. 782), if one set of recursive calls does not result in a solution to the problem, the program backs up to the previous decision point and makes a different decision, often resulting in another set of recursive calls.

Self-Review Exercises

18.1 State whether each of the following is *true* or *false*. If *false*, explain why.

a) A method that calls itself indirectly is not an example of recursion.
b) Recursion can be efficient in computation because of reduced memory-space usage.
c) When a recursive method is called to solve a problem, it actually is capable of solving only the simplest case(s), or base case(s).
d) To make recursion feasible, the recursion step in a recursive solution must resemble the original problem, but be a slightly larger version of it.

18.2 A ________ is needed to terminate recursion.

a) recursion step
b) `break` statement
c) `void` return type
d) base case

18.3 The first call to invoke a recursive method is ________.

a) not recursive
b) recursive
c) the recursion step
d) none of the above

18.4 Each time a fractal's pattern is applied, the fractal is said to be at a new ________.

a) width
b) height
c) level
d) volume

18.5 Iteration and recursion each involve a(n) ________.

a) iteration statement
b) termination test
c) counter variable
d) none of the above

18.6 Fill in the blanks in each of the following statements:

a) The ratio of successive Fibonacci numbers converges on a constant value of 1.618..., a number that has been called the ________ or the ________.
b) Iteration normally uses an iteration statement, whereas recursion normally uses a(n) ________ statement.
c) Fractals have a(n) ________ property—when subdivided into parts, each is a reduced-size copy of the whole.

Answers to Self-Review Exercises

18.1 a) False. A method that calls itself in this manner is an example of indirect recursion. b) False. Recursion can be inefficient in computation because of multiple method calls and excessive memory-space usage. c) True. d) False. To make recursion feasible, the recursion step in a recursive solution must resemble the original problem, but be a slightly *smaller* version of it.

18.2 d.

18.3 a.

18.4 c.

18.5 b.

18.6 a) golden ratio, golden mean. b) selection. c) self-similar.

Exercises

18.7 What does the following code do?

```
public int mystery(int a, int b) {
   if (b == 1) {
      return a;
   }
   else {
      return a + mystery(a, b - 1);
   }
}
```

18.8 Find the error(s) in the following recursive method, and explain how to correct it (them). This method should find the sum of the values from 0 to `n`.

```
public int sum(int n) {
   if (n == 0) {
      return 0;
   }
   else {
      return n + sum(n);
   }
}
```

18.9 ***(Recursive*** **`power`** ***Method)*** Write a recursive method `power(base, exponent)` that, when called, returns

$$base^{\ exponent}$$

For example, `power(3,4)` = 3 * 3 * 3 * 3. Assume that `exponent` is an integer greater than or equal to 1. *Hint:* The recursion step should use the relationship

$$base^{\ exponent} = base \cdot base^{\ exponent - 1}$$

and the terminating condition occurs when `exponent` is equal to `1`, because

$$base^{1} = base$$

Incorporate this method into a program that enables the user to enter the `base` and `exponent`.

18.10 ***(Visualizing Recursion)*** It's interesting to watch recursion "in action." Modify the factorial method in Fig. 18.3 to print its local variable and recursive-call parameter. For each recursive call, display the outputs on a separate line and add a level of indentation. Do your utmost to make the outputs clear, interesting and meaningful. Your goal here is to design and implement an output format that makes it easier to understand recursion. You may want to add such display capabilities to other recursion examples and exercises throughout the text.

18.11 *(Greatest Common Divisor)* The greatest common divisor of integers `x` and `y` is the largest integer that evenly divides into both `x` and `y`. Write a recursive method `gcd` that returns the greatest common divisor of `x` and `y`. The `gcd` of `x` and `y` is defined recursively as follows: If `y` is equal to `0`, then `gcd(x, y)` is `x`; otherwise, `gcd(x, y)` is `gcd(y, x % y)`, where `%` is the remainder operator. Use this method to replace the one you wrote in the application of Exercise 6.27.

18.12 What does the following program do?

```java
// Exercise 18.12: MysteryClass.java
public class MysteryClass {
   public static int mystery(int[] array2, int size) {
      if (size == 1) {
         return array2[0];
      }
      else {
         return array2[size - 1] + mystery(array2, size - 1);
      }
   }

   public static void main(String[] args) {
      int[] array = {1, 2, 3, 4, 5, 6, 7, 8, 9, 10};

      int result = mystery(array, array.length);
      System.out.printf("Result is: %d%n", result);
   }
}
```

18.13 What does the following program do?

```java
// Exercise 18.13: SomeClass.java
public class SomeClass {
   public static String someMethod(int[] array2, int x)
      if (x < array2.length) {
         return String.format(
            "%s%d ", someMethod(array2, x + 1), array2[x]);
      }
      else {
         return "";
      }
   }

   public static void main(String[] args) {
      int[] array = {1, 2, 3, 4, 5, 6, 7, 8, 9, 10};
      String results = someMethod(array, 0);
      System.out.println(results);
   }
}
```

18.14 *(Palindromes)* A palindrome is a string that is spelled the same way forward and backward. Some examples of palindromes are "radar," "able was i ere i saw elba" and (if spaces are ignored) "a man a plan a canal panama." Write a recursive method `testPalindrome` that returns `boolean` value `true` if the string stored in an array is a palindrome and `false` otherwise. The method should ignore spaces and punctuation in the string. [*Hint:* `String` method `toCharArray` gets a `char` array containing the `String`'s characters.]

18.15 *(Eight Queens)* A puzzler for chess buffs is the Eight Queens problem, which asks: Is it possible to place eight queens on an empty chessboard so that no queen is "attacking" any other (i.e., no two queens are in the same row, in the same column or along the same diagonal)? For example, if a queen is placed in the upper-left corner of the board, no other queens could be placed in any of the marked squares shown in Fig. 18.21. Solve the problem recursively. [*Hint:* Your solution should begin with the first column and look for a location in that column where a queen can be placed—initially, place the queen in the first row. The solution should then recursively search the remaining columns. In the first few columns, there will be several locations where a queen may be placed. Take the first available location. If a column is reached with no possible location for a queen, the program should return to the previous column, and move the queen in that column to a new row. This continuous backing up and trying new alternatives is an example of recursive backtracking.]

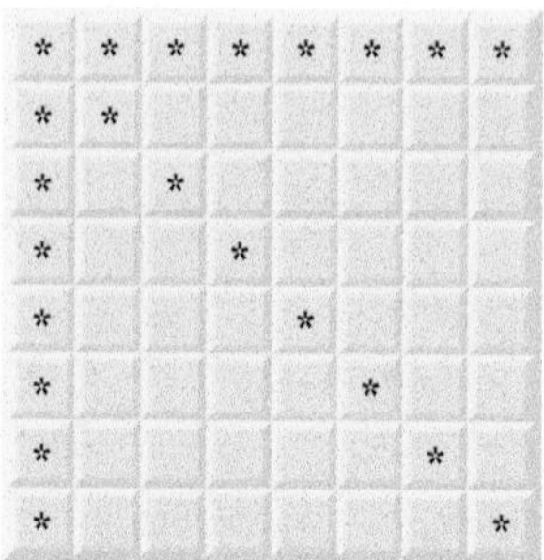

Fig. 18.21 | Squares eliminated by placing a queen in the upper-left corner of a chessboard.

18.16 *(Print an Array)* Write a recursive method `printArray` that displays all the elements in an array of integers, separated by spaces.

18.17 *(Print an Array Backward)* Write a recursive method `stringReverse` that takes a character array containing a string as an argument and prints the string backward.

18.18 *(Find the Minimum Value in an Array)* Write a recursive method `recursiveMinimum` that determines the smallest element in an array of integers. The method should return when it receives an array of one element.

18.19 *(Fractals)* Repeat the fractal pattern in Section 18.9 to form a star with several colors. Begin with five lines (see Fig. 18.22) instead of one, where each line is a different arm of the star. Apply the "Lo feather fractal" pattern to each arm of the star.

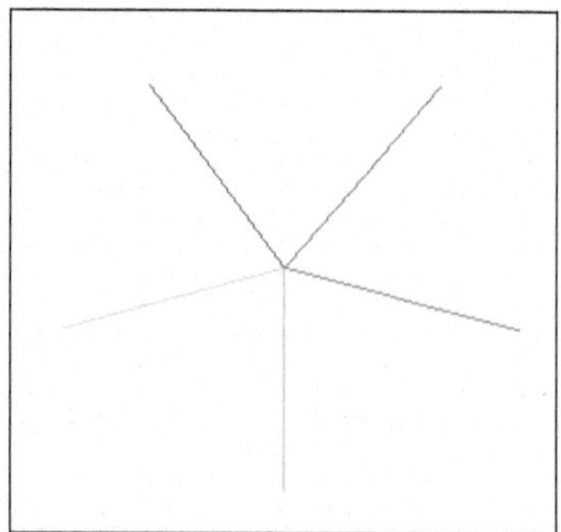

Fig. 18.22 | Sample outputs for Exercise 18.19.

18.20 *(Maze Traversal Using Recursive Backtracking)* The grid of #s and dots (.) in Fig. 18.23 is a two-dimensional array representation of a maze. The #s represent the walls of the maze, and the dots represent locations in the possible paths through the maze. A move can be made only to a location in the array that contains a dot.

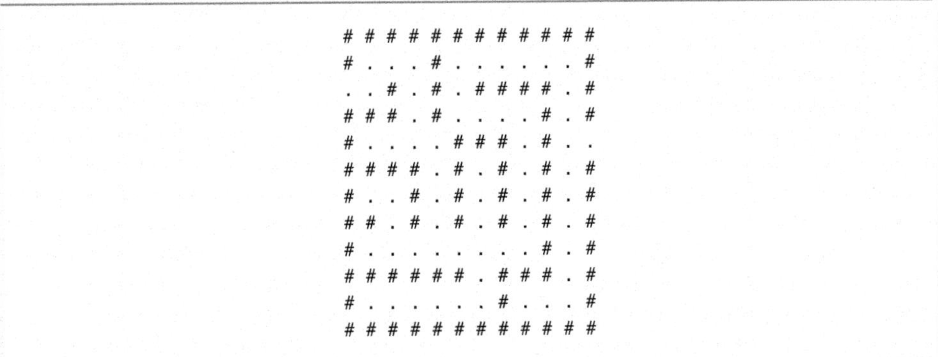

```
# # # # # # # # # # # #
# . . . # . . . . . . #
. . # . # . # # # # . #
# # # . # . . . . # . #
# . . . . # # # . # . .
# # # # . # . # . # . #
# . . # . # . # . # . #
# # . # . # . # . # . #
# . . . . . . . . # . #
# # # # # # . # # # . #
# . . . . . . # . . . #
# # # # # # # # # # # #
```

Fig. 18.23 | Two-dimensional array representation of a maze.

Write a recursive method (`mazeTraversal`) to walk through mazes like the one in Fig. 18.23. The method should receive as arguments a 12-by-12 character array representing the maze and the current location in the maze (the first time this method is called, the current location should be the entry point of the maze). As `mazeTraversal` attempts to locate the exit, it should place the character `x` in each square in the path. There's a simple algorithm for walking through a maze that guarantees finding the exit (assuming there's an exit). If there's no exit, you'll arrive at the starting location again. The algorithm is as follows: From the current location in the maze, try to move one space in any of the possible directions (down, right, up or left). If it's possible to move in at least one direction, call `mazeTraversal` recursively, passing the new spot on the maze as the current spot. If it's not possible to go in any direction, "back up" to a previous location in the maze and try a new direction for that location (this is an example of recursive backtracking). Program the method to display the maze after each move so the user can watch as the maze is solved. The final output of the maze should display only the path needed to solve the maze—if going in a particular direction results in a dead end, the x's going in that direction should not be displayed. [*Hint:* To display only the final path, it may be helpful to mark off spots that result in a dead end with another character (such as `'0'`).]

18.21 *(Generating Mazes Randomly)* Write a method `mazeGenerator` that takes as an argument a two-dimensional 12-by-12 character array and randomly produces a maze. The method should also provide the starting and ending locations of the maze. Test your method `mazeTraversal` from Exercise 18.20, using several randomly generated mazes.

18.22 *(Mazes of Any Size)* Generalize methods `mazeTraversal` and `mazeGenerator` of Exercise 18.20 and Exercise 18.21 to process mazes of any width and height.

18.23 *(Time to Calculate Fibonacci Numbers)* Enhance the Fibonacci program of Fig. 18.5 so that it calculates the approximate amount of time required to perform the calculation and the number of calls made to the recursive method. For this purpose, call `static System` method `currentTimeMillis`, which takes no arguments and returns the computer's current time in milliseconds. Call this method twice—once before and once after the call to `fibonacci`. Save each value and calculate the difference in the times to determine how many milliseconds were required to perform the calculation. Then, add a variable to the `FibonacciCalculator` class, and use this variable to determine the number of calls made to method `fibonacci`. Display your results.

18.24 *(Project: Koch Curve)* Using the techniques you learned in Section 18.9, implement an application that draws the Koch Curve.

18.25 *(Project: Koch Snowflake)* Research the Koch Snowflake online then, using the techniques you learned in Section 18.9, implement an application that draws the Koch Snowflake.

8

Lambdas and Streams Exercises

18.26 *(Project: Recursive File and Directory Manipulation)* Using the `String`-processing capabilities of Chapter 14, the file and directory capabilities of Section 15.3 and a `Map` Section 16.10, create an application that *recursively* walks a directory structure supplied by the user and reports the number of files of each file type (such as `.java`, `.txt`, `.class`, `.docx`, etc.) that exist in the specified directory path. Display the filename extensions in sorted order. Next, investigate method `walk` of class the `Files`. This method returns a stream that walks a directory and its subdirectories and returns the contents to you as a stream. Then, reimplement the first part of this exercise, using lambdas and streams, rather than recursion.

18.27 *(Project: Converting `for` Loops to Lambdas and Streams)* Each of the counter-controlled `for` loops we used in this chapter's examples can be implemented using `IntStream`'s `rangeClosed` method to produce a range of values, then using `IntStream`'s `forEach` method to specify a lambda to execute for each value. The lambda argument to `forEach` could, for example, call method `factorial` (Figs. 18.3–18.4) or method `fibonacci` (Fig. 18.5) and display the result.

18.28 *(Project: Calculating Factorials with Lambdas and Streams)* Reimplement the `factorial` methods of Figs. 18.3–18.4 to calculate factorials using lambdas and streams, rather than recursion.

18.29 *(Project: Calculating Fibonacci Numbers with Lambdas and Streams)* Reimplement the `fibonacci` method of Fig. 18.5 to calculate Fibonacci numbers using lambdas and streams, rather than recursion.

19

Searching, Sorting and Big O

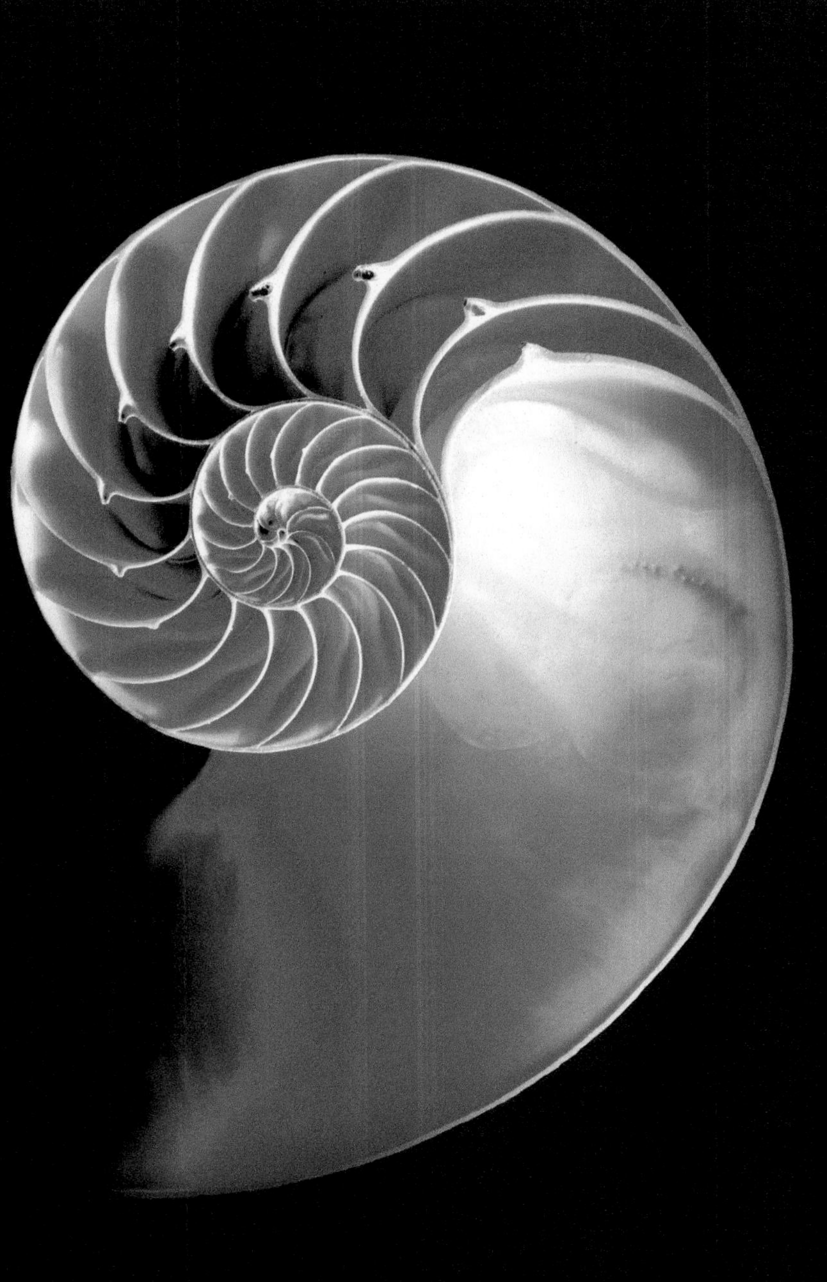

Objectives

In this chapter you'll:

- Search for a given value in an array using linear search and binary search.
- Sort arrays using the iterative selection and insertion sort algorithms.
- Sort arrays using the recursive merge sort algorithm.
- Determine the efficiency of searching and sorting algorithms.
- Be introduced to Big O notation for comparing the efficiency of algorithms.

Outline

19.1 Introduction

Searching data involves determining whether a value (referred to as the **search key**) is present in the data and, if so, finding its location. Two popular search algorithms are the simple linear search and the faster but more complex binary search. **Sorting** places data in ascending or descending order, based on one or more **sort keys**. A list of names could be sorted alphabetically, bank accounts could be sorted by account number, employee payroll records could be sorted by social security number, and so on. This chapter introduces two simple sorting algorithms, the selection sort and the insertion sort, along with the more efficient but more complex merge sort. Figure 19.1 summarizes the searching and sorting algorithms discussed in the examples and exercises of this book.

Software Engineering Observation 19.1

In apps that require searching and sorting, use the predefined capabilities of the Java Collections API (Chapter 16). The techniques in this chapter are provided to introduce students to the concepts behind searching and sorting algorithms—upper-level computer-science courses typically discuss such algorithms in detail.

Chapter	Algorithm	Location
Searching Algorithms:		
16	`binarySearch` method of class `Collections`	Fig. 16.12
19	Linear search	Section 19.2
	Binary search	Section 19.4
	Recursive linear search	Exercise 19.8
	Recursive binary search	Exercise 19.9
21	Linear search of a `List`	Exercise 21.21
	Binary tree search	Exercise 21.23

Fig. 19.1 | Searching and sorting algorithms covered in this text. (Part 1 of 2.)

Chapter	Algorithm	Location
Sorting Algorithms:		
16	`sort` method of class `Collections`	Figs. 16.6–16.9
	`SortedSet` collection	Fig. 16.16
19	Selection sort	Section 19.6
	Insertion sort	Section 19.7
	Recursive merge sort	Section 19.8
	Bubble sort	Exercises 19.5 and 19.6
	Bucket sort	Exercise 19.7
	Recursive quicksort	Exercise 19.10
21	Binary tree sort	Section 21.7

Fig. 19.1 | Searching and sorting algorithms covered in this text. (Part 2 of 2.)

A Note About Counter-Controlled `for` Loops in the Examples

Throughout this chapter, we use many counter-controlled `for` loops to demonstrate the mechanics of searching and sorting with various algorithms. Many of these loops now can be implemented using Java SE 8's streams capabilities (Chapter 17). 8

19.2 Linear Search

Looking up a phone number, finding a website via a search engine and checking the definition of a word in a dictionary all involve searching large amounts of data. This section and Section 19.4 discuss two common search algorithms—one that's easy to program yet relatively inefficient (linear search) and one that's relatively efficient but more complex to program (binary search).

Linear Search Algorithm

The **linear search algorithm** searches each element in an array sequentially. If the search key does not match an element in the array, the algorithm tests each element, and when the end of the array is reached, informs the user that the search key is not present. If the search key is in the array, the algorithm tests each element until it finds one that matches the search key and returns the index of that element.

As an example, consider an array containing the following values

```
34   56   2   10   77   51   93   30   5   52
```

and a program that's searching for 51. Using the linear search algorithm, the program first checks whether 34 matches the search key. It does not, so the algorithm checks whether 56 matches the search key. The program continues moving through the array sequentially, testing 2, then 10, then 77. When the program tests 51, which matches the search key, the program returns the index 5, which is the location of 51 in the array. If, after checking every array element, the program determines that the search key does not match any element in the array, it returns a sentinel value (e.g., `-1`).

Linear Search Implementation

Class `LinearSearchTest` (Fig. 19.2) contains `static` method `linearSearch` for performing searches of an `int` array and `main` for testing `linearSearch`.

```
// Fig. 19.2: LinearSearchTest.java
// Sequentially searching an array for an item.
import java.security.SecureRandom;
import java.util.Arrays;
import java.util.Scanner;

public class LinearSearchTest {
   // perform a linear search on the data
   public static int linearSearch(int data[], int searchKey) {
      // loop through array sequentially
      for (int index = 0; index < data.length; index++) {
         if (data[index] == searchKey) {
            return index; // return index of integer
         }
      }

      return -1; // integer was not found
   }

   public static void main(String[] args) {
      Scanner input = new Scanner(System.in);
      SecureRandom generator = new SecureRandom();

      int[] data = new int[10]; // create array

      for (int i = 0; i < data.length; i++) { // populate array
         data[i] = 10 + generator.nextInt(90);
      }

      System.out.printf("%s%n%n", Arrays.toString(data)); // display array

      // get input from user
      System.out.print("Please enter an integer value (-1 to quit): ");
      int searchInt = input.nextInt();

      // repeatedly input an integer; -1 terminates the program
      while (searchInt != -1) {
         int position = linearSearch(data, searchInt); // perform search

         if (position == -1) { // not found
            System.out.printf("%d was not found%n%n", searchInt);
         }
         else { // found
            System.out.printf("%d was found in position %d%n%n",
               searchInt, position);
         }

```

Fig. 19.2 | Sequentially searching an array for an item. (Part 1 of 2.)

```
48            // get input from user
49            System.out.print("Please enter an integer value (-1 to quit): ");
50            searchInt = input.nextInt();
51         }
52      }
53   }
```

```
[59, 97, 34, 90, 79, 56, 24, 51, 30, 69]

Please enter an integer value (-1 to quit): 79
79 was found in position 4

Please enter an integer value (-1 to quit): 61
61 was not found

Please enter an integer value (-1 to quit): 51
51 was found in position 7

Please enter an integer value (-1 to quit): -1
```

Fig. 19.2 | Sequentially searching an array for an item. (Part 2 of 2.)

Method `linearSearch`

Method `linearSearch` (lines 9–18) performs the linear search. The method receives as parameters the array to search (`data`) and the `searchKey`. Lines 11–15 loop through the elements in the array `data`. Line 12 compares each with `searchKey`. If the values are equal, line 13 returns the *index* of the element. If there are *duplicate* values in the array, linear search returns the index of the *first* element in the array that matches the search key. If the loop ends without finding the value, line 17 returns `-1`.

Method `main`

Method `main` allows the user to search an array. Lines 24–28 create an array of `10` `int`s and populate it with random `int`s from `10`–`99`. Then, line 30 displays the array's contents using `Arrays` `static` method `toString`, which returns a `String` representation of the array with the elements in square brackets (`[` and `]`) and separated by commas.

Lines 33–34 prompt the user for and store the search key. Line 38 calls method `linearSearch` to determine whether `searchInt` is in the array `data`. If it's not, `linearSearch` returns `-1` and the program notifies the user (line 41). If `searchInt` is in the array, `linearSearch` returns the position of the element, which the program outputs in lines 44–45. Lines 49–50 get the next search key from the user.

Generating Arrays of Random Values with Java SE 8 Streams 8

Recall from Section 17.14 that you can use `SecureRandom` method `ints` to generate streams of random values. In Fig. 19.2, lines 24–28 can be replaced by

```
int[] data = generator.ints(10, 10, 91).toArray();
```

The first argument to `ints` (`10`) is the number of elements in the stream. The second and third arguments indicate that the random values `ints` produces will be in the range `10` up to, but not including, `91` (that is, `10`–`90`). On the resulting `IntStream`, we call `toArray` to get an `int` array containing the `10` random values. In this chapter's subsequent examples, we'll use this streams-based technique, rather than `for` statements to populate the arrays. We'll still use `for` statements to enable us to create visual outputs showing how the searching and sorting algorithms work.

19.3 Big O Notation

Searching algorithms all accomplish the *same* goal—finding an element (or elements) matching a given search key, if such an element does, in fact, exist. There are, however, a number of things that differentiate search algorithms from one another. *The major difference is the amount of effort they require to complete the search.* One way to describe this effort is with **Big O notation**, which indicates how hard an algorithm may have to work to solve a problem. For searching and sorting algorithms, this depends particularly on how many data elements there are. In this chapter, we use Big O to describe the worst-case run times for various searching and sorting algorithms.

19.3.1 $O(1)$ Algorithms

Suppose an algorithm is designed to test whether the first element of an array is equal to the second. If the array has 10 elements, this algorithm requires one comparison. If the array has 1000 elements, it still requires one comparison. In fact, the algorithm is completely independent of the number of elements in the array. This algorithm is said to have a **constant run time**, which is represented in Big O notation as $O(1)$ and pronounced as "order one." An algorithm that's $O(1)$ does not necessarily require only one comparison. $O(1)$ just means that the number of comparisons is *constant*—it does not grow as the size of the array increases. An algorithm that tests whether the first element of an array is equal to any of the next three elements is still $O(1)$ even though it requires three comparisons.

19.3.2 $O(n)$ Algorithms

An algorithm that tests whether the first array element is equal to *any* of the other array elements will require at most $n - 1$ comparisons, where n is the number of array elements. If the array has 10 elements, this algorithm requires up to nine comparisons. If the array has 1000 elements, it requires up to 999 comparisons. As n grows larger, the n part of the expression $n - 1$ "dominates," and subtracting one becomes inconsequential. Big O is designed to highlight these dominant terms and ignore terms that become unimportant as n grows. For this reason, an algorithm that requires a total of $n - 1$ comparisons (such as the one we described earlier) is said to be $O(n)$. An $O(n)$ algorithm is referred to as having a **linear run time.** $O(n)$ is often pronounced "on the order of n" or simply "order n."

19.3.3 $O(n^2)$ Algorithms

Now suppose you have an algorithm that tests whether *any* element of an array is duplicated elsewhere in the array. The first element must be compared with every other element in the array. The second element must be compared with every other element except the first (it was already compared to the first). The third element must be compared with every other element except the first two. In the end, this algorithm will end up making $(n - 1) + (n - 2) + \ldots + 2 + 1$ or $n^2/2 - n/2$ comparisons. As n increases, the n^2 term dominates and the n term becomes inconsequential. Again, Big O notation highlights the n^2 term, leaving $n/2$. But, as we'll soon see, constant factors are omitted in Big O notation.

Big O is concerned with how an algorithm's run time grows in relation to the number of items processed. Suppose an algorithm requires n^2 comparisons. With four elements, the algorithm requires 16 comparisons; with eight elements, 64 comparisons. With this algorithm, *doubling* the number of elements *quadruples* the number of comparisons. Consider a similar algorithm requiring $n^2/2$ comparisons. With four elements, the algorithm requires eight comparisons; with eight elements, 32 comparisons. Again, *doubling* the number of elements *quadruples* the number of comparisons. Both of these algorithms grow as the square of n, so Big O ignores the constant, and both algorithms are considered to be $O(n^2)$, which is referred to as **quadratic run time** and pronounced "on the order of n-squared" or more simply "order n-squared."

When n is small, $O(n^2)$ algorithms (on today's computers) will not noticeably affect performance, but as n grows, you'll start to notice performance degradation. An $O(n^2)$ algorithm running on a million-element array would require a trillion "operations" (where each could execute several machine instructions). We tested one of this chapter's $O(n^2)$ algorithms on a current desktop computer and it ran for seven minutes. A billion-element array (not unusual in today's big data applications) would require a quintillion operations, which on that same desktop computer would take approximately 13.3 years to complete! $O(n^2)$ algorithms, unfortunately, are easy to write, as you'll see in this chapter. You'll also see algorithms with more favorable Big O measures. These efficient algorithms often take a bit more cleverness and work to create, but their superior performance can be well worth the extra effort, especially as n gets large and as algorithms are integrated into larger programs.

19.3.4 Big O of the Linear Search

The linear search algorithm runs in $O(n)$ time. The worst case in this algorithm is that every element must be checked to determine whether the search item exists in the array. If the size of the array is *doubled*, the number of comparisons that the algorithm must perform is also *doubled*. Linear search can provide outstanding performance if the element matching the search key happens to be at or near the front of the array. But we seek algorithms that perform well, on average, across *all* searches, including those where the element matching the search key is near the end of the array.

Linear search is easy to program, but it can be slow compared to other search algorithms. If a program needs to perform many searches on large arrays, it's better to implement a more efficient algorithm, such as the binary search, which we present next.

Performance Tip 19.1

Sometimes the simplest algorithms perform poorly. Their virtue often is that they're easy to program, test and debug. Sometimes more complex algorithms are required to realize maximum performance.

19.4 Binary Search

The **binary search algorithm** is more efficient than linear search, but it requires that the array be sorted. The first iteration of this algorithm tests the *middle* element in the array. If this matches the search key, the algorithm ends. Assuming the array is sorted in *ascending* order, then if the search key is *less than* the middle element, it cannot match any element in the second half of the array and the algorithm continues with only the first half of the array (i.e., the first element up to, but not including, the middle element). If the search key is *greater than* the middle element, it cannot match any element in the first half of the array and the algorithm continues with only the second half (i.e., the element *after* the middle element through the last element). Each iteration tests the middle value of the remaining portion of the array. If the search key does not match the element, the algorithm eliminates half of the remaining elements. The algorithm ends by either finding an element that matches the search key or reducing the subarray to zero size.

Example
As an example consider the sorted 15-element array

```
2  3  5  10  27  30  34  51  56  65  77  81  82  93  99
```

and a search key of 65. A program implementing the binary search algorithm would first check whether 51 is the search key (because 51 is the *middle* element of the array). The search key (65) is larger than 51, so 51 is ignored along with the first half of the array (all elements smaller than 51), leaving

```
56  65  77  81  82  93  99
```

Next, the algorithm checks whether 81 (the middle element of the remainder of the array) matches the search key. The search key (65) is smaller than 81, so 81 is discarded along with the elements larger than 81. After just two tests, the algorithm has narrowed the number of values to check to only three (56, 65 and 77). It then checks 65 (which indeed matches the search key) and returns the index of the array element containing 65. This algorithm required just three comparisons to determine whether the search key matched an element of the array. Using a linear search algorithm would have required 10 comparisons. [*Note:* In this example, we've chosen to use an array with 15 elements so that there will always be an obvious middle element in the array. With an even number of elements, the middle of the array lies between two elements. We implement the algorithm to choose the higher of those two elements.]

19.4.1 Binary Search Implementation

Class `BinarySearchTest` (Fig. 19.3) contains:

- `static` method `binarySearch` to search an `int` array for a specified key,
- `static` method `remainingElements` to display the remaining elements in the array being searched, and
- `main` to test method `binarySearch`.

The `main` method (lines 60–89) is nearly identical to `main` in Fig. 19.2. In this program,
8 line 65 creates a 15-element stream (Java SE 8) of random values, sorts the values into ascending order, then converts the stream's elements to an array of `int`s. Recall that the binary search algorithm will work only on a *sorted* array. The first line of output from this program shows the sorted array of `int`s. When the user instructs the program to search for `18`, the program first tests the middle element, which is `57` (as indicated by `*`) in our sample execution. The search key is less than `57`, so the program eliminates the second half of the array and tests the middle element from the first half. The search key is smaller than `36`, so the program eliminates the second half of the array, leaving only three elements. Finally, the program checks `18` (which matches the search key) and returns the index `1`.

```java
// Fig. 19.3: BinarySearchTest.java
// Use binary search to locate an item in an array.
import java.security.SecureRandom;
import java.util.Arrays;
import java.util.Scanner;

public class BinarySearchTest {
   // perform a binary search on the data
   public static int binarySearch(int[] data, int key) {
      int low = 0; // low end of the search area
      int high = data.length - 1; // high end of the search area
      int middle = (low + high + 1) / 2; // middle element
      int location = -1; // return value; -1 if not found

      do { // loop to search for element
         // print remaining elements of array
         System.out.print(remainingElements(data, low, high));

         // output spaces for alignment
         for (int i = 0; i < middle; i++) {
            System.out.print("   ");
         }
         System.out.println(" * "); // indicate current middle

         // if the element is found at the middle
         if (key == data[middle]) {
            location = middle; // location is the current middle
         }
         else if (key < data[middle]) { // middle element is too high
            high = middle - 1; // eliminate the higher half
         }
         else { // middle element is too low
            low = middle + 1; // eliminate the lower half
         }

         middle = (low + high + 1) / 2; // recalculate the middle
      } while ((low <= high) && (location == -1));

      return location; // return location of search key
   }

   // method to output certain values in array
   private static String remainingElements(
      int[] data, int low, int high) {
      StringBuilder temporary = new StringBuilder();

      // append spaces for alignment
      for (int i = 0; i < low; i++) {
         temporary.append("   ");
      }

```

Fig. 19.3 | Use binary search to locate an item in an array (the * in the output marks the middle element). (Part 1 of 3.)

```
      // append elements left in array
      for (int i = low; i <= high; i++) {
         temporary.append(data[i] + " ");
      }

      return String.format("%s%n", temporary);
   }

   public static void main(String[] args) {
      Scanner input = new Scanner(System.in);
      SecureRandom generator = new SecureRandom();

      // create array of 15 random integers in sorted order
      int[] data = generator.ints(15, 10, 91).sorted().toArray();
      System.out.printf("%s%n%n", Arrays.toString(data)); // display array

      // get input from user
      System.out.print("Please enter an integer value (-1 to quit): ");
      int searchInt = input.nextInt();

      // repeatedly input an integer; -1 terminates the program
      while (searchInt != -1) {
         // perform search
         int location = binarySearch(data, searchInt);

         if (location == -1) { // not found
            System.out.printf("%d was not found%n%n", searchInt);
         }
         else { // found
            System.out.printf("%d was found in position %d%n%n",
               searchInt, location);
         }

         // get input from user
         System.out.print("Please enter an integer value (-1 to quit): ");
         searchInt = input.nextInt();
      }
   }
}
```

```
[13, 18, 29, 36, 42, 47, 56, 57, 63, 68, 80, 81, 82, 88, 88]

Please enter an integer value (-1 to quit): 18
13 18 29 36 42 47 56 57 63 68 80 81 82 88 88
                     *
13 18 29 36 42 47 56
         *
13 18 29
   *
18 was found in position 1
```

Fig. 19.3 | Use binary search to locate an item in an array (the * in the output marks the middle element). (Part 2 of 3.)

```
Please enter an integer value (-1 to quit): 82
13 18 29 36 42 47 56 57 63 68 80 81 82 88 88
                      *
                        63 68 80 81 82 88 88
                                 *
                                    82 88 88
                                       *
                                    82
                                    *

82 was found in position 12

Please enter an integer value (-1 to quit): 69
13 18 29 36 42 47 56 57 63 68 80 81 82 88 88
                      *
                        63 68 80 81 82 88 88
                                 *
                        63 68 80
                           *
                              80
                              *
69 was not found

Please enter an integer value (-1 to quit): -1
```

Fig. 19.3 | Use binary search to locate an item in an array (the * in the output marks the middle element). (Part 3 of 3.)

Lines 9–40 declare method `binarySearch`, which receives as parameters the array to search (`data`) and the search key (`key`). Lines 10–12 calculate the `low` end index, `high` end index and `middle` index of the portion of the array that the program is currently searching. At the beginning of the method, the `low` end is `0`, the `high` end is the length of the array minus `1` and the `middle` is the average of these two values. Line 13 initializes the `location` of the element to `-1`—the value that will be returned if the `key` is not found. Lines 15–37 loop until `low` is greater than `high` (this occurs when the `key` is not found) or `location` does not equal `-1` (indicating that the `key` was found). Line 26 tests whether the value in the `middle` element is equal to the `key`. If so, line 27 assigns `middle` to `location`, the loop terminates and `location` is returned to the caller. Each iteration of the loop tests a single value (line 26) and *eliminates half of the remaining values in the array* (lines 29–31 or 32–34) if the value is not the `key`.

19.4.2 Efficiency of the Binary Search

In the worst-case scenario, searching a *sorted* array of 1023 elements takes *only 10 comparisons* when using a binary search. Repeatedly dividing 1023 by 2 (because after each comparison we can eliminate half the array) and rounding down (because we also remove the middle element) yields the values 511, 255, 127, 63, 31, 15, 7, 3, 1 and 0. The number 1023 ($2^{10} - 1$) is divided by 2 only 10 times to get the value 0, which indicates that there are no more elements to test. Dividing by 2 is equivalent to one comparison in the binary search algorithm. Thus, an array of 1,048,575 ($2^{20} - 1$) elements takes a *maximum of 20 comparisons* to find the key, and an array of over one billion elements takes a *maximum of 30 comparisons* to find the key. This is a tremendous improvement in performance over the linear search. For a one-billion-element array, this is a difference between an average of 500 million comparisons for the linear search and a maximum of only 30 comparisons for the binary search! The maximum number of comparisons needed for the binary search of any sorted array is the exponent of the first power of 2 greater than the number of elements in the array, which is represented as $\log_2 n$. All logarithms grow at roughly the same rate, so in big O notation the base can be omitted. This results in a big O of $O(\log n)$ for a binary search, which is also known as **logarithmic run time** and pronounced as "order log n."

19.5 Sorting Algorithms

Sorting data (i.e., placing the data into some particular order, such as ascending or descending) is one of the most important computing applications. A bank sorts all transactions by account number so that it can prepare individual bank statements at the end of each month. Telephone companies sort their lists of accounts by last name and, further, by first name to make it easy to find phone numbers. Virtually every organization must sort some data, and often massive amounts of it. Sorting data is an intriguing, computer-intensive problem that has attracted intense research efforts.

An important item to understand about sorting is that the end result—the sorted array—will be the *same* no matter which algorithm you use to sort the array. The choice of algorithm affects only the run time and memory use of the program. The rest of this chapter introduces three common sorting algorithms. The first two—*selection sort* and *insertion sort*—are easy to program but *inefficient*. The last algorithm—*merge sort*—is much *faster* than selection sort and insertion sort but *harder to program*. We focus on sorting arrays of primitive-type data, namely `int`s. It's possible to sort arrays of class objects as well, as we demonstrated in Section 16.7.1 by using the built-in sorting capabilities of the Collections API.

19.6 Selection Sort

Selection sort is a simple, but inefficient, sorting algorithm. If you're sorting in increasing order, its first iteration selects the *smallest* element in the array and swaps it with the first element. The second iteration selects the *second-smallest* item (which is the smallest item of the remaining elements) and swaps it with the second element. The algorithm continues until the last iteration selects the *second-largest* element and swaps it with the second-to-last index, leaving the largest element in the last index. After the ith iteration, the smallest i items of the array will be sorted into increasing order in the first i elements of the array.

As an example, consider the array

```
34  56  4  10  77  51  93  30  5  52
```

A program that implements selection sort first determines the smallest element (4) of this array, which is contained in index 2. The program swaps 4 with 34, resulting in

```
4  56  34  10  77  51  93  30  5  52
```

The program then determines the smallest value of the remaining elements (all elements except 4), which is 5, contained in index 8. The program swaps 5 with 56, resulting in

```
4  5  34  10  77  51  93  30  56  52
```

On the third iteration, the program determines the next smallest value (10) and swaps it with 34.

```
4   5   10   34   77   51   93   30   56   52
```

The process continues until the array is fully sorted.

```
4   5   10   30   34   51   52   56   77   93
```

After the first iteration, the smallest element is in the first position. After the second iteration, the two smallest elements are in order in the first two positions. After the third iteration, the three smallest elements are in order in the first three positions.

19.6.1 Selection Sort Implementation

Class `SelectionSortTest` (Fig. 19.4) contains:

- `static` method `selectionSort` to sort an `int` array using the selection sort algorithm,
- `static` method `swap` to swap the values of two array elements,
- `static` method `printPass` to display the array contents after each pass, and
- `main` to test method `selectionSort`.

In method `main`, line 61 uses Java SE 8 streams to create an array of `int`s named `data` and populate it with random `int`s in the range 10–99. Line 64 calls method `selectionSort` to sort the array's elements into ascending order.

```
1   // Fig. 19.4: SelectionSortTest.java
2   // Sorting an array with selection sort.
3   import java.security.SecureRandom;
4   import java.util.Arrays;
5
6   public class SelectionSortTest {
7      // sort array using selection sort
8      public static void selectionSort(int[] data) {
9         // loop over data.length - 1 elements
10        for (int i = 0; i < data.length - 1; i++) {
11           int smallest = i; // first index of remaining array
12
13           // loop to find index of smallest element
14           for (int index = i + 1; index < data.length; index++) {
15              if (data[index] < data[smallest]) {
16                 smallest = index;
17              }
18           }
19
20           swap(data, i, smallest); // swap smallest element into position
21           printPass(data, i + 1, smallest); // output pass of algorithm
22        }
23     }
24
```

Fig. 19.4 | Sorting an array with selection sort. (Part 1 of 3.)

```
   // helper method to swap values in two elements
   private static void swap(int[] data, int first, int second) {
      int temporary = data[first]; // store first in temporary
      data[first] = data[second]; // replace first with second
      data[second] = temporary; // put temporary in second
   }

   // print a pass of the algorithm
   private static void printPass(int[] data, int pass, int index) {
      System.out.printf("after pass %2d: ", pass);

      // output elements till selected item
      for (int i = 0; i < index; i++) {
         System.out.printf("%d  ", data[i]);
      }

      System.out.printf("%d* ", data[index]); // indicate swap

      // finish outputting array
      for (int i = index + 1; i < data.length; i++) {
         System.out.printf("%d  ", data[i]);
      }

      System.out.printf("%n               "); // for alignment

      // indicate amount of array that's sorted
      for (int j = 0; j < pass; j++) {
         System.out.print("--  ");
      }
      System.out.println();
   }

   public static void main(String[] args) {
      SecureRandom generator = new SecureRandom();

      // create unordered array of 10 random ints
      int[] data = generator.ints(10, 10, 91).toArray();

      System.out.printf("Unsorted array: %s%n%n", Arrays.toString(data));
      selectionSort(data); // sort array
      System.out.printf("%nSorted array: %s%n", Arrays.toString(data));
   }
}
```

```
Unsorted array: [40, 60, 59, 46, 98, 82, 23, 51, 31, 36]

after pass  1: 23  60  59  46  98  82  40* 51  31  36
               --
after pass  2: 23  31  59  46  98  82  40  51  60* 36
               --  --
after pass  3: 23  31  36  46  98  82  40  51  60  59*
               --  --  --
```

Fig. 19.4 | Sorting an array with selection sort. (Part 2 of 3.)

```
after pass  4: 23  31  36  40  98  82  46* 51  60  59
               --  --  --  --
after pass  5: 23  31  36  40  46  82  98* 51  60  59
               --  --  --  --  --
after pass  6: 23  31  36  40  46  51  98  82* 60  59
               --  --  --  --  --  --
after pass  7: 23  31  36  40  46  51  59  82  60  98*
               --  --  --  --  --  --  --
after pass  8: 23  31  36  40  46  51  59  60  82* 98
               --  --  --  --  --  --  --  --
after pass  9: 23  31  36  40  46  51  59  60  82* 98
               --  --  --  --  --  --  --  --  --

Sorted array: [23, 31, 36, 40, 46, 51, 59, 60, 82, 98]
```

Fig. 19.4 | Sorting an array with selection sort. (Part 3 of 3.)

Methods `selectionSort` *and* `swap`

Lines 8–23 declare the `selectionSort` method. Lines 10–22 loop `data.length - 1` times. Line 11 declares and initializes (to the current index `i`) the variable `smallest`, which stores the index of the smallest element in the remaining array. Lines 14–18 loop over the remaining elements in the array. For each of these elements, line 15 compares its value to the value of the smallest element. If the current element is smaller than the smallest element, line 16 assigns the current element's index to `smallest`. When this loop finishes, `smallest` will contain the index of the smallest element in the remaining array. Line 20 calls method `swap` (lines 26–30) to place the smallest remaining element in the next ordered spot in the array.

Methods `printPass`

Method `printPass` uses dashes (lines 51–53) to indicate the array's sorted portion after each pass. An asterisk is placed next to the position of the element that was swapped with the smallest element on that pass. On each pass, the element next to the asterisk (specified at line 41) and the element above the rightmost set of dashes were swapped.

19.6.2 Efficiency of the Selection Sort

The selection sort algorithm runs in $O(n^2)$ time. Method `selectionSort` uses nested `for` loops. The outer one (lines 10–22) iterates over the first $n - 1$ elements in the array, swapping the smallest remaining item into its sorted position. The inner loop (lines 14–18) iterates over each item in the remaining array, searching for the smallest element. This loop executes $n - 1$ times during the first iteration of the outer loop, $n - 2$ times during the second iteration, then $n - 3$, …, 3, 2, 1. This inner loop will iterate a total of $n(n - 1)/2$ or $(n^2 - n)/2$. In Big O notation, smaller terms drop out and constants are ignored, leaving a Big O of $O(n^2)$.

19.7 Insertion Sort

Insertion sort is another *simple, but inefficient,* sorting algorithm. The first iteration of this algorithm takes the *second element* in the array and, if it's *less than* the *first element, swaps* *it with the first element.* The second iteration looks at the third element and inserts it into the correct position with respect to the first two, so all three elements are in order. At the *i*th iteration of this algorithm, the first *i* elements in the original array will be sorted.

Consider as an example the following array, which is identical to the one used in the discussion of selection sort.

```
34   56   4   10   77   51   93   30   5   52
```

A program that implements the insertion sort algorithm will first look at the first two elements of the array, 34 and 56. These are already in order, so the program continues. (If they were out of order, the program would swap them.)

In the next iteration, the program looks at the third value, 4. This value is less than 56, so the program stores 4 in a temporary variable and moves 56 one element to the right. The program then checks and determines that 4 is less than 34, so it moves 34 one element to the right. The program has now reached the beginning of the array, so it places 4 in the zeroth element. The array now is

```
4   34   56   10   77   51   93   30   5   52
```

In the next iteration, the program stores 10 in a temporary variable. Then it compares 10 to 56 and moves 56 one element to the right because it's larger than 10. The program then compares 10 to 34, moving 34 right one element. When the program compares 10 to 4, it observes that 10 is larger than 4 and places 10 in element 1. The array now is

```
4   10   34   56   77   51   93   30   5   52
```

Using this algorithm, at the *i*th iteration, the first *i* elements of the original array are sorted, but they may not be in their final locations—smaller values may be located later in the array.

19.7.1 Insertion Sort Implementation

Class `InsertionSortTest` (Fig. 19.5) contains:

- `static` method `insertionSort` to sort `int`s using the insertion sort algorithm,
- `static` method `printPass` to display the array contents after each pass, and
- `main` to test method `insertionSort`.

Method `main` (lines 51–60) is identical to `main` in Fig. 19.4 except that line 58 calls method `insertionSort` to sort the array's elements into ascending order.

```
1  // Fig. 19.5: InsertionSortTest.java
2  // Sorting an array with insertion sort.
3  import java.security.SecureRandom;
4  import java.util.Arrays;
5
6  public class InsertionSortTest {
7     // sort array using insertion sort
8     public static void insertionSort(int[] data) {
```

Fig. 19.5 | Sorting an array with insertion sort. (Part 1 of 3.)

```
      // loop over data.length - 1 elements
      for (int next = 1; next < data.length; next++) {
         int insert = data[next]; // value to insert
         int moveItem = next; // location to place element

         // search for place to put current element
         while (moveItem > 0 && data[moveItem - 1] > insert) {
            // shift element right one slot
            data[moveItem] = data[moveItem - 1];
            moveItem--;
         }

         data[moveItem] = insert; // place inserted element
         printPass(data, next, moveItem); // output pass of algorithm
      }
   }

   // print a pass of the algorithm
   public static void printPass(int[] data, int pass, int index) {
      System.out.printf("after pass %2d: ", pass);

      // output elements till swapped item
      for (int i = 0; i < index; i++) {
         System.out.printf("%d  ", data[i]);
      }

      System.out.printf("%d* ", data[index]); // indicate swap

      // finish outputting array
      for (int i = index + 1; i < data.length; i++) {
         System.out.printf("%d  ", data[i]);
      }

      System.out.printf("%n               "); // for alignment

      // indicate amount of array that's sorted
      for (int i = 0; i <= pass; i++) {
         System.out.print("--  ");
      }
      System.out.println();
   }

   public static void main(String[] args) {
      SecureRandom generator = new SecureRandom();

      // create unordered array of 10 random ints
      int[] data = generator.ints(10, 10, 91).toArray();

      System.out.printf("Unsorted array: %s%n%n", Arrays.toString(data));
      insertionSort(data); // sort array
      System.out.printf("%nSorted array: %s%n", Arrays.toString(data));
   }
}
```

Fig. 19.5 | Sorting an array with insertion sort. (Part 2 of 3.)

```
Unsorted array: [34, 96, 12, 87, 40, 80, 16, 50, 30, 45]

after pass  1: 34   96*  12   87   40   80   16   50   30   45
               --   --
after pass  2: 12*  34   96   87   40   80   16   50   30   45
               --   --   --
after pass  3: 12   34   87*  96   40   80   16   50   30   45
               --   --   --   --
after pass  4: 12   34   40*  87   96   80   16   50   30   45
               --   --   --   --   --
after pass  5: 12   34   40   80*  87   96   16   50   30   45
               --   --   --   --   --   --
after pass  6: 12   16*  34   40   80   87   96   50   30   45
               --   --   --   --   --   --   --
after pass  7: 12   16   34   40   50*  80   87   96   30   45
               --   --   --   --   --   --   --   --
after pass  8: 12   16   30*  34   40   50   80   87   96   45
               --   --   --   --   --   --   --   --   --
after pass  9: 12   16   30   34   40   45*  50   80   87   96
               --   --   --   --   --   --   --   --   --   --

Sorted array: [12, 16, 30, 34, 40, 45, 50, 80, 87, 96]
```

Fig. 19.5 | Sorting an array with insertion sort. (Part 3 of 3.)

Method `insertionSort`

Lines 8–24 declare the `insertionSort` method. Lines 10–23 loop over `data.length - 1` items in the array. In each iteration, line 11 declares and initializes variable `insert`, which holds the value of the element that will be inserted into the sorted portion of the array. Line 12 declares and initializes the variable `moveItem`, which keeps track of where to insert the element. Lines 15–19 loop to locate the correct position where the element should be inserted. The loop will terminate either when the program reaches the front of the array or when it reaches an element that's less than the value to be inserted. Line 17 moves an element to the right in the array, and line 18 decrements the position at which to insert the next element. After the loop ends, line 21 inserts the element into place.

Method `printPass`

The output of method `printPass` (lines 27–49) uses dashes to indicate the portion of the array that's sorted after each pass. An asterisk is placed next to the element that was inserted into place on that pass.

19.7.2 Efficiency of the Insertion Sort

The insertion sort algorithm also runs in $O(n^2)$ time. Like selection sort, the implementation of insertion sort (lines 8–24) contains two loops. The `for` loop (lines 10–23) iterates `data.length - 1` times, inserting an element into the appropriate position in the elements sorted so far. For the purposes of this application, `data.length - 1` is equivalent to $n - 1$ (as `data.length` is the size of the array). The `while` loop (lines 15–19) iterates over the preceding elements in the array. In the worst case, this `while` loop will require $n - 1$ comparisons. Each individual loop runs in $O(n)$ time. In Big O notation, nested loops mean that you must *multiply* the number of comparisons. For each iteration of an outer loop, there will be a certain number of iterations of the inner loop. In this algorithm, for each $O(n)$ iterations of the outer loop, there will be $O(n)$ iterations of the inner loop. Multiplying these values results in a Big O of $O(n^2)$.

19.8 Merge Sort

Merge sort is an *efficient* sorting algorithm but is conceptually *more complex* than selection sort and insertion sort. The merge sort algorithm sorts an array by *splitting* it into two equal-sized subarrays, *sorting* each subarray, then *merging* them into one larger array. With an odd number of elements, the algorithm creates the two subarrays such that one has one more element than the other.

The implementation of merge sort in this example is recursive. The base case is an array with one element, which is, of course, sorted, so the merge sort immediately returns in this case. The recursion step splits the array into two approximately equal pieces, recursively sorts them, then merges the two sorted arrays into one larger, sorted array.

Suppose the algorithm has already merged smaller arrays to create sorted arrays A:

```
4  10  34  56  77
```

and B:

```
5  30  51  52  93
```

Merge sort combines these two arrays into one larger, sorted array. The smallest element in A is 4 (located in the zeroth index of A). The smallest element in B is 5 (located in the zeroth index of B). In order to determine the smallest element in the larger array, the algorithm compares 4 and 5. The value from A is smaller, so 4 becomes the first element in the merged array. The algorithm continues by comparing 10 (the second element in A) to 5 (the first element in B). The value from B is smaller, so 5 becomes the second element in the larger array. The algorithm continues by comparing 10 to 30, with 10 becoming the third element in the array, and so on.

19.8.1 Merge Sort Implementation

Figure 19.6 declares the `MergeSortTest` class, which contains:

- `static` method `mergeSort` to initiate the sorting of an `int` array using the merge sort algorithm,
- `static` method `sortArray` to perform the recursive merge sort algorithm—this is called by method `mergeSort`,
- `static` method `merge` to merge two sorted subarrays into a single sorted subarray,
- `static` method `subarrayString` to get a subarray's `String` representation for output purposes, and
- `main` to test method `mergeSort`.

Method `main` (lines 104–113) is identical to `main` in Figs. 19.4–19.5 except that line 111 calls method `mergeSort` to sort the array elements into ascending order. The output from this program displays the splits and merges performed by merge sort, showing the progress of the sort at each step of the algorithm. It's well worth your time to step through these outputs to fully understand this elegant sorting algorithm.

```
// Fig. 19.6: MergeSortTest.java
// Sorting an array with merge sort.
import java.security.SecureRandom;
import java.util.Arrays;

public class MergeSortTest {
   // calls recursive sortArray method to begin merge sorting
   public static void mergeSort(int[] data) {
      sortArray(data, 0, data.length - 1); // sort entire array
   }

   // splits array, sorts subarrays and merges subarrays into sorted array
   private static void sortArray(int[] data, int low, int high) {
      // test base case; size of array equals 1
      if ((high - low) >= 1) { // if not base case
         int middle1 = (low + high) / 2; // calculate middle of array
         int middle2 = middle1 + 1; // calculate next element over

         // output split step
         System.out.printf("split:    %s%n",
            subarrayString(data, low, high));
         System.out.printf("          %s%n",
            subarrayString(data, low, middle1));
         System.out.printf("          %s%n%n",
            subarrayString(data, middle2, high));

         // split array in half; sort each half (recursive calls)
         sortArray(data, low, middle1); // first half of array
         sortArray(data, middle2, high); // second half of array

         // merge two sorted arrays after split calls return
         merge (data, low, middle1, middle2, high);
      }
   }

   // merge two sorted subarrays into one sorted subarray
   private static void merge(int[] data, int left, int middle1,
      int middle2, int right) {

      int leftIndex = left; // index into left subarray
      int rightIndex = middle2; // index into right subarray
      int combinedIndex = left; // index into temporary working array
      int[] combined = new int[data.length]; // working array

      // output two subarrays before merging
      System.out.printf("merge:    %s%n",
         subarrayString(data, left, middle1));
      System.out.printf("          %s%n",
         subarrayString(data, middle2, right));
```

Fig. 19.6 | Sorting an array with merge sort. (Part 1 of 4.)

```java

      // merge arrays until reaching end of either
      while (leftIndex <= middle1 && rightIndex <= right) {
         // place smaller of two current elements into result
         // and move to next space in arrays
         if (data[leftIndex] <= data[rightIndex]) {
            combined[combinedIndex++] = data[leftIndex++];
         }
         else {
            combined[combinedIndex++] = data[rightIndex++];
         }
      }

      // if left array is empty
      if (leftIndex == middle2) {
         // copy in rest of right array
         while (rightIndex <= right) {
            combined[combinedIndex++] = data[rightIndex++];
         }
      }
      else { // right array is empty
         // copy in rest of left array
         while (leftIndex <= middle1) {
            combined[combinedIndex++] = data[leftIndex++];
         }
      }

      // copy values back into original array
      for (int i = left; i <= right; i++) {
         data[i] = combined[i];
      }

      // output merged array
      System.out.printf("          %s%n%n",
         subarrayString(data, left, right));
   }

   // method to output certain values in array
   private static String subarrayString(int[] data, int low, int high) {
      StringBuilder temporary = new StringBuilder();

      // output spaces for alignment
      for (int i = 0; i < low; i++) {
         temporary.append("   ");
      }

      // output elements left in array
      for (int i = low; i <= high; i++) {
         temporary.append(" " + data[i]);
      }

      return temporary.toString();
   }
```

Fig. 19.6 | Sorting an array with merge sort. (Part 2 of 4.)

```
    public static void main(String[] args) {
       SecureRandom generator = new SecureRandom();

       // create unordered array of 10 random ints
       int[] data = generator.ints(10, 10, 91).toArray();

       System.out.printf("Unsorted array: %s%n%n", Arrays.toString(data));
       mergeSort(data); // sort array
       System.out.printf("Sorted array: %s%n", Arrays.toString(data));
    }
 }
```

```
Unsorted array:
[75, 56, 85, 90, 49, 26, 12, 48, 40, 47]

split:    75 56 85 90 49 26 12 48 40 47
          75 56 85 90 49
                         26 12 48 40 47

split:    75 56 85 90 49
          75 56 85
                   90 49

split:    75 56 85
          75 56
                85

split:    75 56
          75
             56

merge:    75
             56
          56 75

merge:    56 75
                85
          56 75 85

split:             90 49
                   90
                      49

merge:             90
                      49
                   49 90

merge:    56 75 85
                   49 90
          49 56 75 85 90

split:                   26 12 48 40 47
                         26 12 48
                                  40 47
```

Fig. 19.6 | Sorting an array with merge sort. (Part 3 of 4.)

```
split:                  26 12 48
                        26 12
                              48

split:                  26 12
                        26
                           12

merge:                  26
                           12
                        12 26

merge:                  12 26
                              48
                        12 26 48

split:                           40 47
                                 40
                                    47

merge:                           40
                                    47
                                 40 47

merge:                  12 26 48
                                 40 47
                        12 26 40 47 48

merge:     49 56 75 85 90
                        12 26 40 47 48
           12 26 40 47 48 49 56 75 85 90

Sorted array: [12, 26, 40, 47, 48, 49, 56, 75, 85, 90]
```

Fig. 19.6 | Sorting an array with merge sort. (Part 4 of 4.)

Method `mergeSort`

Lines 8–10 of Fig. 19.6 declare the `mergeSort` method. Line 9 calls method `sortArray` with `0` and `data.length - 1` as the arguments—corresponding to the beginning and ending indices, respectively, of the array to be sorted. These values tell method `sortArray` to operate on the entire array.

Recursive Method `sortArray`

Method `sortArray` (lines 13–34) performs the recursive merge sort algorithm. Line 15 tests the base case. If the size of the array is `1`, the array is already sorted, so the method returns immediately. If the size of the array is greater than `1`, the method splits the array in two, recursively calls method `sortArray` to sort the two subarrays, then merges them. Line 28 recursively calls method `sortArray` on the first half of the array, and line 29 recursively calls method `sortArray` on the second half. When these two method calls return, each half of the array has been sorted. Line 32 calls method `merge` (lines 37–85) on the two halves of the array to combine the two sorted arrays into one larger sorted array.

Method **merge**

Lines 37–85 declare method `merge`. Lines 52–61 in `merge` loop until the end of either subarray is reached. Line 55 tests which element at the beginning of the arrays is smaller. If the element in the left array is smaller, line 56 places it in position in the combined array. If the element in the right array is smaller, line 59 places it in position in the combined array. When the `while` loop completes, one entire subarray has been placed in the combined array, but the other subarray still contains data. Line 64 tests whether the left array has reached the end. If so, lines 66–68 fill the combined array with the elements of the right array. If the left array has not reached the end, then the right array must have reached the end, and lines 72–74 fill the combined array with the elements of the left array. Finally, lines 78–80 copy the combined array into the original array.

19.8.2 Efficiency of the Merge Sort

Merge sort is *far more efficient* than insertion or selection sort. Consider the first (nonrecursive) call to `sortArray`. This results in two recursive calls to `sortArray` with subarrays each approximately half the original array's size, and a single call to `merge`, which requires, at worst, $n - 1$ comparisons to fill the original array, which is $O(n)$. (Recall that each array element can be chosen by comparing one element from each subarray.) The two calls to `sortArray` result in four more recursive `sortArray` calls, each with a subarray approximately a quarter of the original array's size, along with two calls to `merge` that each require, at worst, $n/2 - 1$ comparisons, for a total number of comparisons of $O(n)$. This process continues, each `sortArray` call generating two additional `sortArray` calls and a `merge` call, until the algorithm has *split* the array into one-element subarrays. At each level, $O(n)$ comparisons are required to *merge* the subarrays. Each level splits the arrays in half, so doubling the array size requires one more level. Quadrupling the array size requires two more levels. This pattern is logarithmic and results in $\log_2 n$ levels. This results in a total efficiency of $O(n \log n)$.

19.9 Big O Summary for This Chapter's Searching and Sorting Algorithms

Figure 19.7 summarizes the searching and sorting algorithms covered in this chapter with the Big O for each. Figure 19.8 lists the Big O values we've covered in this chapter along with a number of values for n to highlight the differences in the growth rates.

Algorithm	Location	Big O
Searching Algorithms:		
Linear search	Section 19.2	$O(n)$
Binary search	Section 19.4	$O(\log n)$
Recursive linear search	Exercise 19.8	$O(n)$
Recursive binary search	Exercise 19.9	$O(\log n)$

Fig. 19.7 | Searching and sorting algorithms with Big O values. (Part 1 of 2.)

Algorithm	Location	Big O
Sorting Algorithms:		
Selection sort	Section 19.6	$O(n^2)$
Insertion sort	Section 19.7	$O(n^2)$
Merge sort	Section 19.8	$O(n \log n)$
Bubble sort	Exercises 19.5 and 19.6	$O(n^2)$

Fig. 19.7 | Searching and sorting algorithms with Big O values. (Part 2 of 2.)

$n =$	$O(\log n)$	$O(n)$	$O(n \log n)$	$O(n^2)$
1	0	1	0	1
2	1	2	2	4
3	1	3	3	9
4	1	4	4	16
5	1	5	5	25
10	1	10	10	100
100	2	100	200	10,000
1000	3	1000	3000	10^6
1,000,000	6	1,000,000	6,000,000	10^{12}
1,000,000,000	9	1,000,000,000	9,000,000,000	10^{18}

Fig. 19.8 | Number of comparisons for common Big O notations.

19.10 Massive Parallelism and Parallel Algorithms

Today's multi-core desktop computers typically have two, four or eight cores. We're headed towards a world of massive parallelism where instead of two, four or eight, we could be talking about thousands and eventually millions or more processors.

The ultimate search would be to employ massive parallelism to check every cell simultaneously, in which case, you could determine whether a particular value is in an array in one "cycle" of the hardware.

In Chapter 23, Concurrency, we'll talk more about how parallel algorithms and multi-core hardware can improve the performance of searching and sorting algorithms.

19.11 Wrap-Up

This chapter introduced searching and sorting. We discussed two searching algorithms—linear search and binary search—and three sorting algorithms—selection sort, insertion sort and merge sort. We introduced Big O notation, which helps you analyze the efficiency of an algorithm. The next two chapters continue our discussion of dynamic data structures that can grow or shrink at execution time. Chapter 20 demonstrates how to use Java's generics capabilities to implement generic methods and classes. Chapter 21 discusses the details of implementing generic data structures. Each of the algorithms in this chapter is "single threaded"—in Chapter 23, Concurrency, we'll discuss multithreading and how it can help you program for better performance on today's multi-core systems.

Summary

Section 19.1 Introduction

- Searching (p. 792) involves determining if a search key is in the data and, if so, finding its location.
- Sorting (p. 792) involves arranging data into order.

Section 19.2 Linear Search

- The linear search algorithm (p. 793) searches each element in the array sequentially until it finds the correct element, or until it reaches the end of the array without finding the element.

Section 19.3 Big O Notation

- A major difference among searching algorithms is the amount of effort they require.
- Big O notation (p. 796) describes an algorithm's efficiency in terms of the work required to solve a problem. For searching and sorting algorithms typically it depends on the number of elements in the data.
- An algorithm that's $O(1)$ does not necessarily require only one comparison (p. 796). It just means that the number of comparisons does not grow as the size of the array increases.
- An $O(n)$ algorithm is referred to as having a linear run time (p. 796).
- Big O highlights dominant factors and ignores terms that become unimportant with high n values.
- Big O notation is concerned with the growth rate of algorithm run times, so constants are ignored.
- The linear search algorithm runs in $O(n)$ time.
- The worst case in linear search is that every element must be checked to determine whether the search key (p. 797) exists, which occurs if the search key is the last array element or is not present.

Section 19.4 Binary Search

- Binary search (p. 797) is more efficient than linear search, but it requires that the array be sorted.
- The first iteration of binary search tests the middle element in the array. If this is the search key, the algorithm returns its location. If the search key is less than the middle element, the search continues with the first half of the array. If the search key is greater than the middle element, the search continues with the second half of the array. Each iteration tests the middle value of the remaining array and, if the element is not found, eliminates half of the remaining elements.
- Binary search is a more efficient searching algorithm than linear search because each comparison eliminates from consideration half of the elements in the array.
- Binary search runs in $O(\log n)$ time because each step removes half of the remaining elements; this is also known as logarithmic run time (p. 802).
- If the array size is doubled, binary search requires only one extra comparison.

Section 19.6 Selection Sort

- Selection sort (p. 802) is a simple, but inefficient, sorting algorithm.
- The sort begins by selecting the smallest item and swaps it with the first element. The second iteration selects the second-smallest item (which is the smallest remaining item) and swaps it with the second element. The sort continues until the last iteration selects the second-largest element and swaps it with the second-to-last element, leaving the largest element in the last index. At the ith iteration of selection sort, the smallest i items of the whole array are sorted into the first i indices.
- The selection sort algorithm runs in $O(n^2)$ time.

Section 19.7 Insertion Sort

- The first iteration of insertion sort (p. 805) takes the second element in the array and, if it's less than the first element, swaps it with the first element. The second iteration looks at the third element and inserts it in the correct position with respect to the first two elements. After the ith iteration of insertion sort, the first i elements in the original array are sorted.
- The insertion sort algorithm runs in $O(n^2)$ time (p. 809).

Section 19.8 Merge Sort

- Merge sort (p. 809) is a sorting algorithm that's faster, but more complex to implement, than selection sort and insertion sort. The merge sort algorithm sorts an array by splitting it into two equal-sized subarrays, sorting each subarray recursively and merging the subarrays into one larger array.
- Merge sort's base case is an array with one element. A one-element array is already sorted, so merge sort immediately returns when it's called with a one-element array. The merge part of merge sort takes two sorted arrays and combines them into one larger sorted array.
- Merge sort performs the merge by looking at the first element in each array, which is also the smallest element in the array. Merge sort takes the smallest of these and places it in the first element of the larger array. If there are still elements in the subarray, merge sort looks at the second of these (which is now the smallest element remaining) and compares it to the first element in the other subarray. Merge sort continues this process until the larger array is filled.
- In the worst case, the first call to merge sort has to make $O(n)$ comparisons to fill the n slots in the final array.
- The merging portion of the merge sort algorithm is performed on two subarrays, each of approximately size $n/2$. Merging each of these subarrays requires $n/2 - 1$ comparisons for each subarray, or $O(n)$ comparisons total. This pattern continues as each level works on twice as many arrays, but each is half the size of the previous array.
- Similar to binary search, splitting the arrays in half results in $\log n$ levels for a total efficiency of $O(n \log n)$ (p. 814).

Self-Review Exercises

19.1 Fill in the blanks in each of the following statements:

a) A selection sort application would take approximately ________ times as long to run on a 128-element array as on a 32-element array.

b) The efficiency of merge sort is ________.

19.2 What key aspect of both the binary search and the merge sort accounts for the logarithmic portion of their respective Big Os?

19.3 In what sense is the insertion sort superior to the merge sort? In what sense is the merge sort superior to the insertion sort?

19.4 In the text, we say that after the merge sort splits the array into two subarrays, it then sorts these two subarrays and merges them. Why might someone be puzzled by our statement that "it then sorts these two subarrays"?

Answers to Self-Review Exercises

19.1 a) 16, because an $O(n^2)$ algorithm takes 16 times as long to sort four times as much information. b) $O(n \log n)$.

19.2 Both of these algorithms incorporate "halving"—somehow reducing something by half. The binary search eliminates from consideration one-half of the array after each comparison. The merge sort splits the array in half each time it's called.

19.3 The insertion sort is easier to understand and to program than the merge sort. The merge sort is far more efficient [$O(n \log n)$] than the insertion sort [$O(n^2)$].

19.4 In a sense, it does not really sort these two subarrays. It simply keeps splitting the original array in half until it provides a one-element subarray, which is, of course, sorted. It then builds up the original two subarrays by merging these one-element arrays to form larger subarrays, which are then merged, and so on.

Exercises

19.5 *(Bubble Sort)* Implement bubble sort—another simple yet inefficient sorting technique. It's called bubble sort or sinking sort because smaller values gradually "bubble" their way to the top of the array (i.e., towards the first element) like air bubbles rising in water, while the larger values sink to the bottom (end) of the array. The technique uses nested loops to make several passes through the array. Each pass compares successive pairs of elements. If a pair is in increasing order (or the values are equal), the bubble sort leaves the values as they are. If a pair is in decreasing order, the bubble sort swaps their values in the array. The first pass compares the first two elements of the array and swaps their values if necessary. It then compares the second and third elements in the array. The end of this pass compares the last two elements in the array and swaps them if necessary. After one pass, the largest element will be in the last index. After two passes, the largest two elements will be in the last two indices. Explain why bubble sort is an $O(n^2)$ algorithm.

19.6 *(Enhanced Bubble Sort)* Make the following simple modifications to improve the performance of the bubble sort you developed in Exercise 19.5:

a) After the first pass, the largest number is guaranteed to be in the highest-numbered array element; after the second pass, the two highest numbers are "in place"; and so on. Instead of making nine comparisons on every pass for a ten-element array, modify the bubble sort to make eight comparisons on the second pass, seven on the third pass, and so on.
b) The data in the array may already be in proper or near-proper order, so why make nine passes if fewer will suffice? Modify the sort to check at the end of each pass whether any swaps have been made. If there were none, the data must already be sorted, so the program should terminate. If swaps have been made, at least one more pass is needed.

19.7 *(Bucket Sort)* A bucket sort begins with a one-dimensional array of positive integers to be sorted and a two-dimensional array of integers with rows indexed from 0 to 9 and columns indexed from 0 to $n - 1$, where n is the number of values to be sorted. Each row of the two-dimensional array is referred to as a *bucket*. Write a class named `BucketSort` containing a method called `sort` that operates as follows:

a) Place each value of the one-dimensional array into a row of the bucket array, based on the value's "ones" (rightmost) digit. For example, 97 is placed in row 7, 3 is placed in row 3 and 100 is placed in row 0. This procedure is called a *distribution pass*.

b) Loop through the bucket array row by row, and copy the values back to the original array. This procedure is called a *gathering pass*. The new order of the preceding values in the one-dimensional array is 100, 3 and 97.
c) Repeat this process for each subsequent digit position (tens, hundreds, thousands, etc.). On the second (tens digit) pass, 100 is placed in row 0, 3 is placed in row 0 (because 3 has no tens digit) and 97 is placed in row 9. After the gathering pass, the order of the values in the one-dimensional array is 100, 3 and 97. On the third (hundreds digit) pass, 100 is placed in row 1, 3 is placed in row 0 and 97 is placed in row 0 (after the 3). After this last gathering pass, the original array is in sorted order.

The two-dimensional array of buckets is 10 times the length of the integer array being sorted. This sorting technique provides better performance than a bubble sort, but requires much more memory—the bubble sort requires space for only one additional element of data. This comparison is an example of the space/time trade-off: The bucket sort uses more memory than the bubble sort, but performs better. This version of the bucket sort requires copying all the data back to the original array on each pass. Another possibility is to create a second two-dimensional bucket array and repeatedly swap the data between the two bucket arrays.

19.8 *(Recursive Linear Search)* Modify Fig. 19.2 to use recursive method `recursiveLinearSearch` to perform a linear search of the array. The method should receive the search key and starting index as arguments. If the search key is found, return its index in the array; otherwise, return `-1`. Each call to the recursive method should check one index in the array.

19.9 *(Recursive Binary Search)* Modify Fig. 19.3 to use recursive method `recursiveBinarySearch` to perform a binary search of the array. The method should receive the search key, starting index and ending index as arguments. If the search key is found, return its index in the array. If the search key is not found, return `-1`.

19.10 *(Quicksort)* The recursive sorting technique called quicksort uses the following basic algorithm for a one-dimensional array of values:

a) *Partitioning Step*: Take the first element of the unsorted array and determine its final location in the sorted array (i.e., all values to the left of the element in the array are less than the element, and all values to the right of the element in the array are greater than the element—we show how to do this below). We now have one element in its proper location and two unsorted subarrays.
b) *Recursive Step*: Perform *Step 1* on each unsorted subarray. Each time *Step 1* is performed on a subarray, another element is placed in its final location of the sorted array, and two unsorted subarrays are created. When a subarray consists of one element, that element is in its final location (because a one-element array is already sorted).

The basic algorithm seems simple enough, but how do we determine the final position of the first element of each subarray? As an example, consider the following set of values (the element in bold is the partitioning element—it will be placed in its final location in the sorted array):

37 2 6 4 89 8 10 12 68 45

Starting from the rightmost element of the array, compare each element with **37** until an element less than **37** is found; then swap **37** and that element. The first element less than **37** is 12, so **37** and 12 are swapped. The new array is

12 2 6 4 89 8 10 **37** 68 45

Element 12 is in italics to indicate that it was just swapped with **37**.

Starting from the left of the array, but beginning with the element after 12, compare each element with 37 until an element greater than 37 is found—then swap 37 and that element. The first element greater than 37 is 89, so 37 and 89 are swapped. The new array is

12 2 6 4 37 8 10 *89* 68 45

Starting flrom the right, but beginning with the element before 89, compare each element with 37 until an element less than 37 is found—then swap 37 and that element. The first element less than 37 is 10, so 37 and 10 are swapped. The new array is

12 2 6 4 *10* 8 37 89 68 45

Starting from the left, but beginning with the element after 10, compare each element with 37 until an element greater than 37 is found—then swap 37 and that element. There are no more elements greater than 37, so when we compare 37 with itself, we know that 37 has been placed in its final location in the sorted array. Every value to the left of 37 is smaller than it, and every value to the right of 37 is larger than it.

Once the partition has been applied on the previous array, there are two unsorted subarrays. The subarray with values less than 37 contains 12, 2, 6, 4, 10 and 8. The subarray with values greater than 37 contains 89, 68 and 45. The sort continues recursively, with both subarrays being partitioned in the same manner as the original array.

Based on the preceding discussion, write recursive method `quickSortHelper` to sort a one-dimensional integer array. The method should receive as arguments a starting index and an ending index on the original array being sorted.

Making a Difference

19.11 *(Visualization of Sorting Algorithms)* In earlier chapters, we showed how computers can help improve the learning process. In this chapter, you studied a variety of sorting algorithms. Each has the same goal—to produce a sorted array—but each algorithm operates differently. It's helpful to use graphics, animation and sound to make each algorithm "come alive." Search the popular video sites online for "sorting algorithm visualization" and write a description of how you'd go about implementing your own. In Chapter 22, JavaFX Graphics and Multimedia, and Chapter 23, Concurrency, you'll learn the techniques that will enable you to implement your own multimedia sorting application.

Generic Classes and Methods: A Deeper Look

20

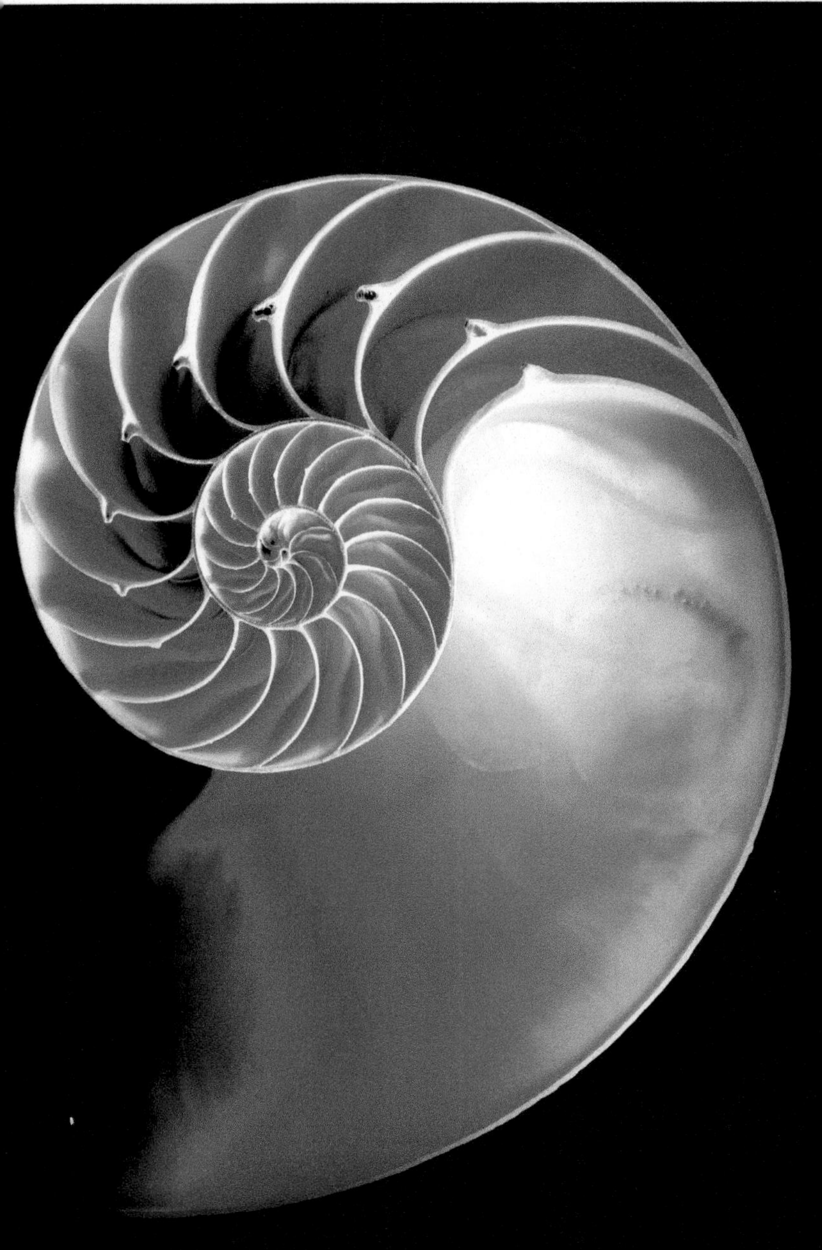

Objectives

In this chapter you'll:

- Create generic methods that perform identical tasks on arguments of different types.
- Create a generic `Stack` class that can be used to store objects of any class or interface type.
- Learn about compile-time translation of generic methods and classes.
- Learn how to overload generic methods with non-generic or generic methods.
- Use wildcards when precise type information about a parameter is not required in the method body.

Outline

20.1 Introduction

You've used existing generic methods and classes in Chapters 7 and 16. In this chapter, you'll learn how to write your own.

It would be nice if we could write a single `sort` method to sort the elements in an `Integer` array, a `String` array or an array of any type that supports ordering (i.e., its elements can be compared). It would also be nice if we could write a single `Stack` class that could be used as a `Stack` of integers, a `Stack` of floating-point numbers, a `Stack` of `Strings` or a `Stack` of any other type. It would be even nicer if we could detect type mismatches at *compile time*—known as **compile-time type safety**. For example, if a `Stack` should store only integers, an attempt to push a `String` onto that `Stack` should issue a *compilation* error. This chapter discusses **generics**—specifically **generic methods** and **generic classes**—which provide the means to create the type-safe general models mentioned above.

20.2 Motivation for Generic Methods

Overloaded methods are often used to perform *similar* operations on *different* types of data. To motivate generic methods, let's begin with an example (Fig. 20.1) containing overloaded `printArray` methods (lines 20–27, 30–37 and 40–47) that print the `String` representations of the elements of an `Integer` array, a `Double` array and a `Character` array, respectively. We could have used arrays of primitive types `int`, `double` and `char`. We're using arrays of the type-wrapper classes to set up our generic method example, because *only reference types can be used to specify generic types in generic methods and classes.*

```
1  // Fig. 20.1: OverloadedMethods.java
2  // Printing array elements using overloaded methods.
3
4  public class OverloadedMethods {
5     public static void main(String[] args) {
6        // create arrays of Integer, Double and Character
7        Integer[] integerArray = {1, 2, 3, 4, 5, 6};
8        Double[] doubleArray = {1.1, 2.2, 3.3, 4.4, 5.5, 6.6, 7.7};
9        Character[] characterArray = {'H', 'E', 'L', 'L', 'O'};
10
```

Fig. 20.1 | Printing array elements using overloaded methods. (Part 1 of 2.)

```
11        System.out.printf("Array integerArray contains: ");
12        printArray(integerArray); // pass an Integer array
13        System.out.printf("Array doubleArray contains: ");
14        printArray(doubleArray); // pass a Double array
15        System.out.printf("Array characterArray contains: ");
16        printArray(characterArray); // pass a Character array
17     }
18
19     // method printArray to print Integer array
20     public static void printArray(Integer[] inputArray) {
21        // display array elements
22        for (Integer element : inputArray) {
23           System.out.printf("%s ", element);
24        }
25
26        System.out.println();
27     }
28
29     // method printArray to print Double array
30     public static void printArray(Double[] inputArray) {
31        // display array elements
32        for (Double element : inputArray) {
33           System.out.printf("%s ", element);
34        }
35
36        System.out.println();
37     }
38
39     // method printArray to print Character array
40     public static void printArray(Character[] inputArray) {
41        // display array elements
42        for (Character element : inputArray) {
43           System.out.printf("%s ", element);
44        }
45
46        System.out.println();
47     }
48  }
```

```
Array integerArray contains: 1 2 3 4 5 6
Array doubleArray contains: 1.1 2.2 3.3 4.4 5.5 6.6 7.7
Array characterArray contains: H E L L O
```

Fig. 20.1 | Printing array elements using overloaded methods. (Part 2 of 2.)

The program begins by declaring and initializing three arrays—six-element `Integer` array `integerArray` (line 7), seven-element `Double` array `doubleArray` (line 8) and five-element `Character` array `characterArray` (line 9). Then lines 11–16 display the contents of each array.

When the compiler encounters a method call, it attempts to locate a method declaration with the same name and with parameters that match the argument types in the call. In this example, each `printArray` call matches one of the `printArray` method declarations. For example, line 12 calls `printArray` with `integerArray` as its argument. The compiler determines the argument's type (i.e., `Integer[]`) and attempts to locate a `printArray` method that specifies an `Integer[]` parameter (lines 20–27), then sets up a call to that method. Similarly, when the compiler encounters the call at line 14, it determines the argument's type (i.e., `Double[]`), then attempts to locate a `printArray` method that specifies a `Double[]` parameter (lines 30–37), then sets up a call to that method. Finally, when the compiler encounters the call at line 16, it determines the argument's type (i.e., `Character[]`), then attempts to locate a `printArray` method that specifies a `Character[]` parameter (lines 40–47), then sets up a call to that method.

Common Features in the Overloaded `printArray` *Methods*

Study each `printArray` method. The array element type appears in each method's header (lines 20, 30 and 40) and `for`-statement header (lines 22, 32 and 42). If we were to replace the element types in each method with a generic name—`T` by convention—then all three methods would look like the one in Fig. 20.2. It appears that if we can replace the array element type in each of the three methods with a *single generic type*, then we should be able to declare *one* `printArray` method that can display the `String` representations of the elements of *any* array that contains objects. The method in Fig. 20.2 is similar to the generic `printArray` method declaration you'll see in Section 20.3. The one shown here *will not compile*—we use this simply to show that the three `printArray` methods of Fig. 20.1 are identical except for the types they process.

```
public static void printArray(T[] inputArray) {
   // display array elements
   for (T element : inputArray)  {
      System.out.printf("%s ", element);
   }

   System.out.println();
}
```

Fig. 20.2 | `printArray` method in which actual type names are replaced with a generic type name (in this case `T`).

20.3 Generic Methods: Implementation and Compile-Time Translation

If the operations performed by several overloaded methods are *identical* for each argument type, the overloaded methods can be more conveniently coded using a generic method. You can write a single generic method declaration that can be called with arguments of different types. Based on the types of the arguments passed to the generic method, the compiler handles each method call appropriately. At *compilation time*, the compiler ensures the *type safety* of your code, preventing many runtime errors.

Figure 20.3 reimplements Fig. 20.1 using a generic `printArray` method (lines 20–27 of Fig. 20.3). The `printArray` calls in lines 12, 14 and 16 are identical to those of Fig. 20.1, and the outputs of the two applications are identical. This demonstrates the expressive power of generics.

```
1  // Fig. 20.3: GenericMethodTest.java
2  // Printing array elements using generic method printArray.
3
4  public class GenericMethodTest {
5     public static void main(String[] args) {
6        // create arrays of Integer, Double and Character
7        Integer[] integerArray = {1, 2, 3, 4, 5};
8        Double[] doubleArray = {1.1, 2.2, 3.3, 4.4, 5.5, 6.6, 7.7};
9        Character[] characterArray = {'H', 'E', 'L', 'L', 'O'};
10
11       System.out.printf("Array integerArray contains: ");
12       printArray(integerArray); // pass an Integer array
13       System.out.printf("Array doubleArray contains: ");
14       printArray(doubleArray); // pass a Double array
15       System.out.printf("Array characterArray contains: ");
16       printArray(characterArray); // pass a Character array
17    }
18
19    // generic method printArray
20    public static <T> void printArray(T[] inputArray) {
21       // display array elements
22       for (T element : inputArray) {
23          System.out.printf("%s ", element);
24       }
25
26       System.out.println();
27    }
28 }
```

```
Array integerArray contains: 1 2 3 4 5
Array doubleArray contains: 1.1 2.2 3.3 4.4 5.5 6.6 7.7
Array characterArray contains: H E L L O
```

Fig. 20.3 | Printing array elements using generic method `printArray`.

Type Parameter Section of a Generic Method

All generic method declarations have a **type-parameter section** (line 20; `<T>` in this example) delimited by **angle brackets** that precedes the method's return type. Each type-parameter section contains one or more **type parameters**, separated by commas. A type parameter, also known as a **type variable**, is an identifier that specifies a generic type name. The type parameters can be used to declare the return type, parameters and local variables in a generic method declaration, and they act as placeholders for the types of the arguments passed to the generic method, which are known as **actual type arguments**. A generic method's body is declared like that of any other method. *Type parameters can represent only reference types*—not primitive types (like `int`, `double` and `char`). Also, the type-parameter names throughout the method declaration must match those declared in the type-parameter section. For example, line 22 declares `element` as type `T`, which matches the type parameter (`T`) declared in line 20. A type parameter can be declared only once in the type-parameter section but can appear more than once in the method's parameter list. For example, the type-parameter name `T` appears twice in the following method's parameter list:

```
public static <T> T maximum(T value1, T value2)
```

Type-parameter names need not be unique among different generic methods. In method `printArray`, `T` appears in the same two locations where the overloaded `printArray` methods of Fig. 20.1 specified `Integer`, `Double` or `Character` as the array element type. The remainder of `printArray` is identical to the versions presented in Fig. 20.1.

Good Programming Practice 20.1

The letters `T` (for "type"), `E` (for "element"), `K` (for "key") and `V` (for "value") are commonly used as type parameters. For other common ones, see `http://docs.oracle.com/javase/tutorial/java/generics/types.html`.

Testing the Generic `printArray` Method

As in Fig. 20.1, the program in Fig. 20.3 begins by declaring and initializing six-element `Integer` array `integerArray` (line 7), seven-element `Double` array `doubleArray` (line 8) and five-element `Character` array `characterArray` (line 9). Then each array is output by calling `printArray` (lines 12, 14 and 16)—once with argument `integerArray`, once with argument `doubleArray` and once with argument `characterArray`.

When the compiler encounters line 12, it first determines argument `integerArray`'s type (i.e., `Integer[]`) and attempts to locate a method named `printArray` that specifies a single `Integer[]` parameter. There's no such method in this example. Next, the compiler determines whether there's a generic method named `printArray` that specifies a single array parameter and uses a type parameter to represent the array element type. The compiler determines that `printArray` (lines 20–27) is a match and sets up a call to the method. The same process is repeated for the calls to method `printArray` at lines 14 and 16.

Common Programming Error 20.1

If the compiler cannot match a method call to a nongeneric or a generic method declaration, a compilation error occurs.

Common Programming Error 20.2

If the compiler doesn't find a method declaration that matches a method call exactly, but does find two or more methods that can satisfy the method call, a compilation error occurs. For the complete details of resolving calls to overloaded and generic methods, see `http://docs.oracle.com/javase/specs/jls/se8/html/jls-15.html#jls-15.12`.

In addition to setting up the method calls, the compiler also determines whether the operations in the method body can be applied to elements of the type stored in the array argument. The only operation performed on the array elements in this example is to output their `String` representation. Line 23 performs an *implicit `toString` call* on every `element`. *To work with generics, every element of the array must be an object of a class or interface type.* Since all objects have a `toString` method, the compiler is satisfied that line 23 performs a *valid* operation for any object in `printArray`'s array argument. The `toString` methods of classes `Integer`, `Double` and `Character` return the `String` representations of the underlying `int`, `double` or `char` value, respectively.

Erasure at Compilation Time

When the compiler translates generic method `printArray` into Java bytecodes, it removes the type-parameter section and *replaces the type parameters with actual types*. This process is known as **erasure**. By default all generic types are replaced with type `Object`. So the compiled version of method `printArray` appears as shown in Fig. 20.4—there's only *one* copy of this code, which is used for all `printArray` calls in the example. This is quite different from similar mechanisms in other programming languages, such as C++'s templates, in which a *separate copy of the source code* is generated and compiled for *every* type passed as an argument to the method. As you'll see in Section 20.4, the translation and compilation of generics is a bit more involved than what we've discussed in this section.

By declaring `printArray` as a generic method in Fig. 20.3, we eliminated the need for the overloaded methods of Fig. 20.1 and created a reusable method that can output the `String` representations of the elements in any array that contains objects. However, this particular example could have simply declared the `printArray` method as shown in Fig. 20.4, using an `Object` array as the parameter. This would have yielded the same results, because any `Object` can be output as a `String`. In a generic method, the benefits become more apparent when you place restrictions on the type parameters, as we demonstrate in the next section.

```
public static void printArray(Object[] inputArray) {
   // display array elements
   for (Object element : inputArray) {
      System.out.printf("%s ", element);
   }

   System.out.println();
}
```

Fig. 20.4 | Generic method `printArray` after the compiler performs erasure.

20.4 Additional Compile-Time Translation Issues: Methods That Use a Type Parameter as the Return Type

Let's consider a generic method in which type parameters are used in the return type and in the parameter list (Fig. 20.5). The application uses a generic method `maximum` to determine and return the largest of its three arguments of the same type. Unfortunately, *the relational operator > cannot be used with reference types*. However, it's possible to compare two objects of the same class if that class implements the generic **interface `Comparable<T>`** (from package `java.lang`). All the type-wrapper classes for primitive types implement this interface. **Generic interfaces** enable you to specify, with a single interface declaration, a set of related types. `Comparable<T>` objects have a **`compareTo` method**. For example, two `Integer` objects, `integer1` and `integer2`, can be compared with the expression:

```
integer1.compareTo(integer2)
```

When you declare a class that implements `Comparable<T>`, you must define method `compareTo` such that it compares the contents of two objects of that class and returns the comparison results. Method `compareTo` *must* return

- `0` if the objects are equal,
- a negative integer if `object1` is less than `object2` or
- a positive integer if `object1` is greater than `object2`.

For example, class Integer's compareTo method compares the int values stored in two Integer objects. A benefit of implementing interface Comparable<T> is that Comparable<T> objects can be used with the sorting and searching methods of class Collections (package java.util). We discussed those methods in Chapter 16. In this example, we'll use method compareTo in method maximum to help determine the largest value.

```
1  // Fig. 20.5: MaximumTest.java
2  // Generic method maximum returns the largest of three objects.
3
4  public class MaximumTest {
5     public static void main(String[] args) {
6        System.out.printf("Maximum of %d, %d and %d is %d%n", 3, 4, 5,
7           maximum(3, 4, 5));
8        System.out.printf("Maximum of %.1f, %.1f and %.1f is %.1f%n",
9           6.6, 8.8, 7.7, maximum(6.6, 8.8, 7.7));
10       System.out.printf("Maximum of %s, %s and %s is %s%n", "pear",
11          "apple", "orange", maximum("pear", "apple", "orange"));
12    }
13
14    // determines the largest of three Comparable objects
15    public static <T extends Comparable<T>> T maximum(T x, T y, T z) {
16       T max = x; // assume x is initially the largest
17
18       if (y.compareTo(max) > 0) {
19          max = y; // y is the largest so far
20       }
21
22       if (z.compareTo(max) > 0) {
23          max = z; // z is the largest
24       }
25
26       return max; // returns the largest object
27    }
28 }
```

```
Maximum of 3, 4 and 5 is 5
Maximum of 6.6, 8.8 and 7.7 is 8.8
Maximum of pear, apple and orange is pear
```

Fig. 20.5 | Generic method maximum with an upper bound on its type parameter.

Generic Method **maximum** *and Specifying a Type Parameter's Upper Bound*

Generic method maximum (lines 15–27) uses type parameter T as its return type (line 15), as the type of method parameters x, y and z (line 15), and as the type of local variable max (line 16). The type-parameter section specifies that T extends Comparable<T>—only objects of classes that implement interface Comparable<T> can be used with this method. Comparable<T> is known as the type parameter's **upper bound**. By default, Object is the upper bound, meaning that an object of any type can be used. Type-parameter declarations that bound the parameter always use keyword extends regardless of whether the type parameter extends a class or implements an interface. The upper bound may be a comma-separated list that contains zero or one class and zero or more interfaces.

Method `maximum`'s type parameter is more restrictive than the one specified for `printArray` in Fig. 20.3, which was able to output arrays containing any type of object. The `Comparable<T>` restriction is important, because not all objects can be compared. However, `Comparable<T>` objects are guaranteed to have a `compareTo` method.

Method `maximum` uses the same algorithm that we used in Section 6.4 to determine the largest of its three arguments. The method assumes that its first argument (`x`) is the largest and assigns it to local variable `max` (line 16 of Fig. 20.5). Next, the `if` statement at lines 18–20 determines whether `y` is greater than `max`. The condition invokes `y`'s `compareTo` method with the expression `y.compareTo(max)`, which returns a negative integer, `0` or a positive integer, to determine `y`'s relationship to `max`. If the return value of the `compareTo` is greater than `0`, then `y` is greater and is assigned to variable `max`. Similarly, the `if` statement at lines 22–24 determines whether `z` is greater than `max` and, if so, assigns `z` to `max`. Then line 26 returns `max` to the caller.

Calling Method `maximum`

In `main`, line 7 calls `maximum` with the integers `3`, `4` and `5`. When the compiler encounters this call, it first looks for a `maximum` method that takes three arguments of type `int`. There's no such method, so the compiler looks for a generic method that can be used and finds generic method `maximum`. However, recall that the arguments to a generic method must be of a *reference type*. So the compiler autoboxes the three `int` values as `Integer` objects and specifies that the three `Integer` objects will be passed to `maximum`. Class `Integer` (package `java.lang`) implements the `Comparable<Integer>` interface such that method `compareTo` compares the `int` values in two `Integer` objects. Therefore, `Integer`s are valid arguments to method `maximum`. When the `Integer` representing the maximum is returned, we attempt to output it with the `%d` format specifier, which outputs an `int` primitive-type value. So `maximum`'s return value is output as an `int` value.

A similar process occurs for the three `double` arguments passed to `maximum` in line 9. Each `double` is autoboxed as a `Double` object and passed to `maximum`. Again, this is allowed because class `Double` (package `java.lang`) implements the `Comparable<Double>` interface. The `Double` returned by `maximum` is output with the format specifier `%.1f`, which outputs a `double` primitive-type value. So `maximum`'s return value is auto-unboxed and output as a `double`. The call to `maximum` in line 11 receives three `String`s, which are also `Comparable<String>` objects. We intentionally placed the largest value in a different position in each method call (lines 7, 9 and 11) to show that the generic method always finds the maximum value, regardless of its position in the argument list.

Erasure and the Upper Bound of a Type Parameter

When the compiler translates method `maximum` into bytecodes, it uses erasure to replace the type parameters with actual types. In Fig. 20.3, all generic types were replaced with type `Object`. Actually, all type parameters are replaced with the ***upper bound*** of the type parameter, which is specified in the type-parameter section. Figure 20.6 simulates the erasure of method maximum's types by showing the method's source code after the type-parameter section is removed and type parameter `T` is replaced with the upper bound, `Comparable`, throughout the method declaration. The erasure of `Comparable<T>` is simply `Comparable`.

```
public static Comparable maximum(Comparable x, Comparable y,
   Comparable z) {

   Comparable max = x; // assume x is initially the largest

   if (y.compareTo(max) > 0) {
      max = y; // y is the largest so far
   }

   if (z.compareTo(max) > 0) {
      max = z; // z is the largest
   }

   return max; // returns the largest object
}
```

Fig. 20.6 | Generic method `maximum` after erasure is performed by the compiler.

After erasure, method `maximum` specifies that it returns type `Comparable`. However, the calling method does not expect to receive a `Comparable`. It expects to receive an object of the same type that was passed to `maximum` as an argument—`Integer`, `Double` or `String` in this example. When the compiler replaces the type-parameter information with the upper-bound type in the method declaration, it also inserts *explicit cast operations* in front of each method call to ensure that the returned value is of the type expected by the caller. Thus, the call to `maximum` in line 7 (Fig. 20.5) is preceded by an `Integer` cast, as in

```
(Integer) maximum(3, 4, 5)
```

the call to `maximum` in line 9 is preceded by a `Double` cast, as in

```
(Double) maximum(6.6, 8.8, 7.7)
```

and the call to `maximum` in line 11 is preceded by a `String` cast, as in

```
(String) maximum("pear", "apple", "orange")
```

In each case, the type of the cast for the return value is *inferred* from the types of the method arguments in the particular method call, because, according to the method declaration, the return type and the argument types match. Without generics, you'd be responsible for implementing the cast operation.

20.5 Overloading Generic Methods

A generic method may be overloaded like any other method. A class can provide two or more generic methods that specify the same method name but different method parameters. For example, generic method `printArray` of Fig. 20.3 could be overloaded with another `printArray` generic method with the additional parameters `lowSubscript` and `highSubscript` to specify the portion of the array to output (see Exercise 20.5).

A generic method can also be overloaded by nongeneric methods. When the compiler encounters a method call, it searches for the method declaration that best matches the method name and the argument types specified in the call—an error occurs if two or more overloaded methods both could be considered best matches. For example, generic method printArray of Fig. 20.3 could be overloaded with a version that's specific to Strings, which outputs the Strings in neat, tabular format (see Exercise 20.6).

20.6 Generic Classes

A data structure, such as a stack, can be understood *independently* of the element type it manipulates. Generic classes provide a means for describing the concept of a stack (or any other class) in a *type-independent* manner. We can then instantiate *type-specific* objects of the generic class. Generics provide a nice opportunity for software reusability.

Once you have a generic class, you can use a simple, concise notation to indicate the type(s) that should be used in place of the class's type parameter(s). At compilation time, the compiler ensures the *type safety* of your code and uses the *erasure* techniques described in Sections 20.3–20.4 to enable your client code to interact with the generic class.

One generic Stack class, for example, could be the basis for creating many logical Stack classes (e.g., "Stack of Double," "Stack of Integer," "Stack of Character," "Stack of Employee"). These classes are known as **parameterized classes** or **parameterized types** because they accept one or more type parameters. Recall that type parameters represent only *reference types*, which means the Stack generic class cannot be instantiated with primitive types. However, we can instantiate a Stack that stores objects of Java's type-wrapper classes and allow Java to use *autoboxing* to convert the primitive values into objects. Recall that autoboxing occurs when a value of a primitive type (e.g., int) is pushed onto a Stack that contains wrapper-class objects (e.g., Integer). *Auto-unboxing* occurs when an object of the wrapper class is popped off the Stack and assigned to a primitive-type variable.

Implementing a Generic Stack *Class*

Figure 20.7 declares a generic Stack class for demonstration purposes—the java.util package already contains a generic Stack class. A generic class declaration looks like a non-generic one, but the class name is followed by *a type-parameter section* (line 6). In this case, type parameter E represents the *element* type the Stack will manipulate. As with generic methods, the type-parameter section of a generic class can have one or more type parameters separated by commas. (You'll create a generic class with two type parameters in Exercise 20.8.) Type parameter E is used throughout the Stack class declaration to represent the element type. This example implements a Stack as an ArrayList.

```
1  // Fig. 20.7: Stack.java
2  // Stack generic class declaration.
3  import java.util.ArrayList;
4  import java.util.NoSuchElementException;
5
6  public class Stack<E> {
7     private final ArrayList<E> elements; // ArrayList stores stack elements
8
9     // no-argument constructor creates a stack of the default size
10    public Stack() {
11       this(10); // default stack size
12    }
```

Fig. 20.7 | Stack generic class declaration. (Part 1 of 2.)

```
13
14     // constructor creates a stack of the specified number of elements
15     public Stack(int capacity) {
16        int initCapacity = capacity > 0 ? capacity : 10; // validate
17        elements = new ArrayList<E>(initCapacity); // create ArrayList
18     }
19
20     // push element onto stack
21     public void push(E pushValue) {
22        elements.add(pushValue); // place pushValue on Stack
23     }
24
25     // return the top element if not empty; else throw exception
26     public E pop() {
27        if (elements.isEmpty()) { // if stack is empty
28           throw new NoSuchElementException("Stack is empty, cannot pop");
29        }
30
31        // remove and return top element of Stack
32        return elements.remove(elements.size() - 1);
33     }
34  }
```

Fig. 20.7 | Stack generic class declaration. (Part 2 of 2.)

Class Stack declares variable elements as an ArrayList<E> (line 7). This ArrayList will store the Stack's elements. As you know, an ArrayList can grow dynamically, so objects of our Stack class can also grow dynamically. The Stack class's no-argument constructor (lines 10–12) invokes the one-argument constructor (lines 15–18) to create a Stack in which the underlying ArrayList has a capacity of 10 elements. The one-argument constructor can also be called directly to create a Stack with a specified initial capacity. Line 16 validates the constructor's argument. Line 17 creates the ArrayList of the specified capacity (or 10 if the capacity was invalid).

Method push (lines 21–23) uses ArrayList method add to append the pushed item to the end of the ArrayList elements. The last element in the ArrayList represents the stack's *top*.

Method pop (lines 26–33) first determines whether an attempt is being made to pop an element from an empty Stack. If so, line 28 throws a NoSuchElementException (package java.util). Otherwise, line 32 returns the Stack's top element by removing the underlying ArrayList's last element.

As with generic methods, when a generic class is compiled, the compiler performs *erasure* on the class's type parameters and replaces them with their upper bounds. For class Stack (Fig. 20.7), no upper bound is specified, so the default upper bound, Object, is used. The scope of a generic class's type parameter is the entire class. However, type parameters *cannot* be used in a class's static variable declarations.

Testing the Generic Stack *Class*

Now, let's consider the application (Fig. 20.8) that uses the Stack generic class (Fig. 20.7). Lines 11–12 in Fig. 20.8 create and initialize variables of type Stack<Double> (pronounced "Stack of Double") and Stack<Integer> (pronounced "Stack of Integer"). The types Double and Integer are known as the Stack's **type arguments**. The compiler uses them to replace the type parameters so that it can perform type checking and insert cast operations as necessary. We'll discuss the cast operations in more detail shortly. Lines 11–12 instantiate doubleStack with a capacity of 5 and integerStack with a capacity of 10 (the default). Lines 15–16 and 19–20 call methods testPushDouble (lines 24–33), testPopDouble (lines 36–52), testPushInteger (lines 55–64) and testPopInteger (lines 67–83), respectively, to demonstrate the two Stacks in this example.

```
1  // Fig. 20.8: StackTest.java
2  // Stack generic class test program.
3  import java.util.NoSuchElementException;
4
5  public class StackTest {
6     public static void main(String[] args) {
7        double[] doubleElements = {1.1, 2.2, 3.3, 4.4, 5.5};
8        int[] integerElements = {1, 2, 3, 4, 5, 6, 7, 8, 9, 10};
9
10       // Create a Stack<Double> and a Stack<Integer>
11       Stack<Double> doubleStack = new Stack<>(5);
12       Stack<Integer> integerStack = new Stack<>();
13
14       // push elements of doubleElements onto doubleStack
15       testPushDouble(doubleStack, doubleElements);
16       testPopDouble(doubleStack); // pop from doubleStack
17
18       // push elements of integerElements onto integerStack
19       testPushInteger(integerStack, integerElements);
20       testPopInteger(integerStack); // pop from integerStack
21    }
22
23    // test push method with double stack
24    private static void testPushDouble(
25       Stack<Double> stack, double[] values) {
26       System.out.printf("%nPushing elements onto doubleStack%n");
27
28       // push elements to Stack
29       for (double value : values) {
30          System.out.printf("%.1f ", value);
31          stack.push(value); // push onto doubleStack
32       }
33    }
34
35    // test pop method with double stack
36    private static void testPopDouble(Stack<Double> stack) {
37       // pop elements from stack
38       try {
39          System.out.printf("%nPopping elements from doubleStack%n");
40          double popValue; // store element removed from stack
41
```

Fig. 20.8 | Stack generic class test program. (Part 1 of 3.)

```
         // remove all elements from Stack
         while (true) {
            popValue = stack.pop(); // pop from doubleStack
            System.out.printf("%.1f ", popValue);
         }
      }
      catch(NoSuchElementException noSuchElementException) {
         System.err.println();
         noSuchElementException.printStackTrace();
      }
   }

   // test push method with integer stack
   private static void testPushInteger(
      Stack<Integer> stack, int[] values) {
      System.out.printf("%nPushing elements onto integerStack%n");

      // push elements to Stack
      for (int value : values) {
         System.out.printf("%d ", value);
         stack.push(value); // push onto integerStack
      }
   }

   // test pop method with integer stack
   private static void testPopInteger(Stack<Integer> stack) {
      // pop elements from stack
      try {
         System.out.printf("%nPopping elements from integerStack%n");
         int popValue; // store element removed from stack

         // remove all elements from Stack
         while (true) {
            popValue = stack.pop(); // pop from intStack
            System.out.printf("%d ", popValue);
         }
      }
      catch(NoSuchElementException noSuchElementException) {
         System.err.println();
         noSuchElementException.printStackTrace();
      }
   }
}
```

```
Pushing elements onto doubleStack
1.1 2.2 3.3 4.4 5.5
Popping elements from doubleStack
5.5 4.4 3.3 2.2 1.1
java.util.NoSuchElementException: Stack is empty, cannot pop
        at Stack.pop(Stack.java:28)
        at StackTest.testPopDouble(StackTest.java:44)
        at StackTest.main(StackTest.java:16)
```

Fig. 20.8 | Stack generic class test program. (Part 2 of 3.)

```
Pushing elements onto integerStack
1 2 3 4 5 6 7 8 9 10
Popping elements from integerStack
10 9 8 7 6 5 4 3 2 1
java.util.NoSuchElementException: Stack is empty, cannot pop
        at Stack.pop(Stack.java:28)
        at StackTest.testPopInteger(StackTest.java:75)
        at StackTest.main(StackTest.java:20)
```

Fig. 20.8 | Stack generic class test program. (Part 3 of 3.)

Methods `testPushDouble` *and* `testPopDouble`

Method `testPushDouble` (lines 24–33) invokes method `push` (line 31) to place the `double` values 1.1, 2.2, 3.3, 4.4 and 5.5 from array `doubleElements` onto `doubleStack`. *Autoboxing* occurs in line 31 when the program tries to push a primitive `double` value onto the `doubleStack`, which stores only references to `Double` objects.

Method `testPopDouble` (lines 36–52) invokes `Stack` method `pop` (line 44) in an infinite loop (lines 43–46) to remove all the values from the stack. The output shows that the values indeed pop off in last-in, first-out order (the defining characteristic of stacks). When the loop attempts to `pop` a sixth value, the `doubleStack` is empty, so `pop` throws a `NoSuchElementException`, which causes the program to proceed to the `catch` block (lines 48–51). The stack trace indicates the exception that occurred and shows that method `pop` generated the exception at line 28 of the file `Stack.java` (Fig. 20.7). The trace also shows that `pop` was called by `StackTest` method `testPopDouble` at line 44 (Fig. 20.8) of `StackTest.java` and that method `testPopDouble` was called from method `main` at line 16 of `StackTest.java`. This information enables you to determine the methods that were on the method-call stack at the time the exception occurred. Because the program catches the exception, the exception is considered to have been handled and the program can continue executing.

Auto-unboxing occurs in line 44 when the program assigns the `Double` object popped from the stack to a `double` primitive variable. Recall from Section 20.4 that the compiler inserts casts to ensure that the proper types are returned from generic methods. After erasure, `Stack` method `pop` returns type `Object`, but the client code in `testPopDouble` expects to receive a `double` when method `pop` returns. So the compiler inserts a `Double` cast, as in

```
popValue = (Double) stack.pop();
```

The value assigned to `popValue` will be *unboxed* from the `Double` object returned by `pop`.

Methods `testPushInteger` *and* `testPopInteger`

Method `testPushInteger` (lines 55–64) invokes `Stack` method `push` to place values onto `integerStack` until it's full. Method `testPopInteger` (lines 67–83) invokes `Stack` method `pop` to remove values from `integerStack`. Once again, the values are popped in last-in, first-out order. During *erasure*, the compiler recognizes that the client code in method `testPopInteger` expects to receive an `int` when method `pop` returns. So the compiler inserts an `Integer` cast, as in

```
popValue = (Integer) stack.pop();
```

The value assigned to `popValue` will be unboxed from the `Integer` object returned by `pop`.

Creating Generic Methods to Test Class `Stack<E>`

The code in methods `testPushDouble` and `testPushInteger` is *almost identical* for pushing values onto a `Stack<Double>` or a `Stack<Integer>`, respectively, and the code in methods `testPopDouble` and `testPopInteger` is almost identical for popping values from a `Stack<Double>` or a `Stack<Integer>`, respectively. This presents another opportunity to use generic methods. Figure 20.9 declares generic method `testPush` (lines 24–33) to perform the same tasks as `testPushDouble` and `testPushInteger` in Fig. 20.8—that is, `push` values onto a `Stack<E>`. Similarly, generic method `testPop` (Fig. 20.9, lines 36–52) performs the same tasks as `testPopDouble` and `testPopInteger` in Fig. 20.8—that is, `pop` values off a `Stack<E>`. The output of Fig. 20.9 precisely matches that of Fig. 20.8.

```
1  // Fig. 20.9: StackTest2.java
2  // Passing generic Stack objects to generic methods.
3  import java.util.NoSuchElementException;
4
5  public class StackTest2 {
6     public static void main(String[] args) {
7        Double[] doubleElements = {1.1, 2.2, 3.3, 4.4, 5.5};
8        Integer[] integerElements = {1, 2, 3, 4, 5, 6, 7, 8, 9, 10};
9
10       // Create a Stack<Double> and a Stack<Integer>
11       Stack<Double> doubleStack = new Stack<>(5);
12       Stack<Integer> integerStack = new Stack<>();
13
14       // push elements of doubleElements onto doubleStack
15       testPush("doubleStack", doubleStack, doubleElements);
16       testPop("doubleStack", doubleStack); // pop from doubleStack
17
18       // push elements of integerElements onto integerStack
19       testPush("integerStack", integerStack, integerElements);
20       testPop("integerStack", integerStack); // pop from integerStack
21    }
22
23    // generic method testPush pushes elements onto a Stack
24    public static <E> void testPush(String name , Stack<E> stack,
25       E[] elements) {
26       System.out.printf("%nPushing elements onto %s%n", name);
27
28       // push elements onto Stack
29       for (E element : elements) {
30          System.out.printf("%s ", element);
31          stack.push(element); // push element onto stack
32       }
33    }
34
35    // generic method testPop pops elements from a Stack
36    public static <E> void testPop(String name, Stack<E> stack) {
37       // pop elements from stack
38       try {
39          System.out.printf("%nPopping elements from %s%n", name);
40          E popValue; // store element removed from stack
```

Fig. 20.9 | Passing generic `Stack` objects to generic methods. (Part 1 of 2.)

```
41
42            // remove all elements from Stack
43            while (true) {
44               popValue = stack.pop();
45               System.out.printf("%s ", popValue);
46            }
47         }
48         catch(NoSuchElementException noSuchElementException) {
49            System.out.println();
50            noSuchElementException.printStackTrace();
51         }
52      }
53   }
```

```
Pushing elements onto doubleStack
1.1 2.2 3.3 4.4 5.5
Popping elements from doubleStack
5.5 4.4 3.3 2.2 1.1
java.util.NoSuchElementException: Stack is empty, cannot pop
        at Stack.pop(Stack.java:28)
        at StackTest2.testPop(StackTest2.java:44)
        at StackTest2.main(StackTest2.java:16)

Pushing elements onto integerStack
1 2 3 4 5 6 7 8 9 10
Popping elements from integerStack
10 9 8 7 6 5 4 3 2 1
java.util.NoSuchElementException: Stack is empty, cannot pop
        at Stack.pop(Stack.java:28)
        at StackTest2.testPop(StackTest2.java:44)
        at StackTest2.main(StackTest2.java:20)
```

Fig. 20.9 | Passing generic `Stack` objects to generic methods. (Part 2 of 2.)

Lines 11–12 create the `Stack<Double>` and `Stack<Integer>` objects, respectively. Lines 15–16 and 19–20 invoke generic methods `testPush` and `testPop` to test the `Stack` objects. Type parameters can represent only reference types, so to be able to pass arrays `doubleElements` and `integerElements` to generic method `testPush`, the arrays declared in lines 7–8 must be declared with the wrapper types `Double` and `Integer`. When these arrays are initialized with primitive values, the compiler *autoboxes* each primitive value.

Generic method `testPush` (lines 24–33) uses type parameter `E` (specified at line 24) to represent the data type stored in the `Stack<E>`. The generic method takes three arguments—a `String` that represents the name of the `Stack<E>` object for output purposes, a reference to an object of type `Stack<E>` and an array of type `E`—the type of elements that will be pushed onto `Stack<E>`. The compiler enforces *consistency* between the type of the `Stack` and the elements that will be pushed onto the `Stack` when `push` is invoked, which is the real value of the generic method call. Generic method `testPop` (lines 36–52) takes two arguments—a `String` that represents the name of the `Stack<E>` object for output purposes and a reference to an object of type `Stack<E>`.

20.7 Wildcards in Methods That Accept Type Parameters

In this section, we introduce a powerful generics concept known as **wildcards**. Let's consider an example that motivates wildcards (Fig. 20.10). Suppose that you'd like to implement a generic method sum that totals the numbers in a collection, such as a List. You'd begin by inserting the numbers in the collection. Because generic classes can be used only with class or interface types, the numbers would be *autoboxed* as objects of the type-wrapper classes. For example, any int value would be *autoboxed* as an Integer object, and any double value would be *autoboxed* as a Double object. We'd like to be able to total all the numbers in the List regardless of their type. For this reason, we'll declare the List with the type argument Number, which is the superclass of both Integer and Double. In addition, method sum will receive a parameter of type List<Number> and total its elements.

```java
// Fig. 20.10: TotalNumbers.java
// Totaling the numbers in a List<Number>.
import java.util.ArrayList;
import java.util.List;

public class TotalNumbers {
   public static void main(String[] args) {
      // create, initialize and output List of Numbers containing
      // both Integers and Doubles, then display total of the elements
      Number[] numbers = {1, 2.4, 3, 4.1}; // Integers and Doubles
      List<Number> numberList = new ArrayList<>();

      for (Number element : numbers) {
         numberList.add(element); // place each number in numberList
      }

      System.out.printf("numberList contains: %s%n", numberList);
      System.out.printf("Total of the elements in numberList: %.1f%n",
         sum(numberList));
   }

   // calculate total of List elements
   public static double sum(List<Number> list) {
      double total = 0; // initialize total

      // calculate sum
      for (Number element : list) {
         total += element.doubleValue();
      }

      return total;
   }
}
```

```
numberList contains: [1, 2.4, 3, 4.1]
Total of the elements in numberList: 10.5
```

Fig. 20.10 | Totaling the numbers in a List<Number>.

Line 10 declares and initializes an array of Numbers. Because the initializers are primitive values, Java *autoboxes* each primitive value as an object of its corresponding wrapper type. The int values 1 and 3 are *autoboxed* as Integer objects, and the double values 2.4 and 4.1 are *autoboxed* as Double objects. Line 11 creates an ArrayList object that stores Numbers and assigns it to List variable numberList.

Lines 13–15 traverse array numbers and place each element in numberList. Line 17 outputs the List's contents by implicitly invoking the List's toString method. Lines 18–19 display the sum of the elements that is returned by the call to method sum.

Method sum (lines 23–32) receives a List of Numbers and calculates the total of its Numbers. The method uses double values to perform the calculations and returns the result as a double. Lines 27–29 total the List's elements. The for statement assigns each Number to variable element, then uses **Number method doubleValue** to obtain the Number's underlying primitive value as a double. The result is added to total. When the loop terminates, line 31 returns the total.

Implementing Method sum *with a Wildcard Type Argument in Its Parameter*

Recall that the purpose of method sum in Fig. 20.10 was to total any type of Numbers stored in a List. We created a List of Numbers that contained both Integer and Double objects. The output of Fig. 20.10 demonstrates that method sum worked properly. Given that method sum can total the elements of a List of Numbers, you might expect that the method would also work for Lists that contain elements of only one numeric type, such as List<Integer>. So we modified class TotalNumbers to create a List of Integers and pass it to method sum. When we compile the program, the compiler issues the following error message:

```
TotalNumbersErrors.java:19: error: incompatible types:
List<Integer> cannot be converted to List<Number>
```

Although Number is the superclass of Integer, the compiler doesn't consider the type List<Number> to be a supertype of List<Integer>. If it were, then every operation we could perform on a List<Number> would also work on a List<Integer>. Consider the fact that you can add a Double object to a List<Number> because a Double *is a* Number, but you cannot add a Double object to a List<Integer> because a Double *is not an* Integer. Thus, the subtype relationship does not hold.

How do we create a more flexible version of method sum that can total the elements of any List containing elements of any subclass of Number? This is where **wildcard type arguments** are important. Wildcards enable you to specify method parameters, return values, variables or fields, and so on, that act as supertypes or subtypes of parameterized types. In Fig. 20.11, method sum's parameter is declared in line 52 with the type:

```
List<? extends Number>
```

A wildcard type argument is denoted by a question mark (?), which represents an "unknown type." In this case, the wildcard extends class Number, which means that the wildcard has an upper bound of Number. Thus, the unknown-type argument must be either Number or a subclass of Number. With the wildcard type argument, method sum can receive an argument a List containing any type of Number, such as a List<Integer> (line 20), List<Double> (line 34) or List<Number> (line 48).

```
// Fig. 20.11: WildcardTest.java
// Wildcard test program.
import java.util.ArrayList;
import java.util.List;

public class WildcardTest {
   public static void main(String[] args) {
      // create, initialize and output List of Integers, then
      // display total of the elements
      Integer[] integers = {1, 2, 3, 4, 5};
      List<Integer> integerList = new ArrayList<>();

      // insert elements in integerList
      for (Integer element : integers) {
         integerList.add(element);
      }

      System.out.printf("integerList contains: %s%n", integerList);
      System.out.printf("Total of the elements in integerList: %.0f%n%n",
         sum(integerList));

      // create, initialize and output List of Doubles, then
      // display total of the elements
      Double[] doubles = {1.1, 3.3, 5.5};
      List<Double> doubleList = new ArrayList<>();

      // insert elements in doubleList
      for (Double element : doubles) {
         doubleList.add(element);
      }

      System.out.printf("doubleList contains: %s%n", doubleList);
      System.out.printf("Total of the elements in doubleList: %.1f%n%n",
         sum(doubleList));

      // create, initialize and output List of Numbers containing
      // both Integers and Doubles, then display total of the elements
      Number[] numbers = {1, 2.4, 3, 4.1}; // Integers and Doubles
      List<Number> numberList = new ArrayList<>();

      // insert elements in numberList
      for (Number element : numbers) {
         numberList.add(element);
      }

      System.out.printf("numberList contains: %s%n", numberList);
      System.out.printf("Total of the elements in numberList: %.1f%n",
         sum(numberList));
   }

```

Fig. 20.11 | Wildcard test program. (Part 1 of 2.)

```
51    // total the elements; using a wildcard in the List parameter
52    public static double sum(List<? extends Number> list) {
53       double total = 0; // initialize total
54
55       // calculate sum
56       for (Number element : list) {
57          total += element.doubleValue();
58       }
59
60       return total;
61    }
62 }
```

```
integerList contains: [1, 2, 3, 4, 5]
Total of the elements in integerList: 15

doubleList contains: [1.1, 3.3, 5.5]
Total of the elements in doubleList: 9.9

numberList contains: [1, 2.4, 3, 4.1]
Total of the elements in numberList: 10.5
```

Fig. 20.11 | Wildcard test program. (Part 2 of 2.)

Lines 10–20 create and initialize a `List<Integer>`, output its elements and total them by calling method `sum` (line 20). Lines 24–34 and 38–48 perform the same operations for a `List<Double>` and a `List<Number>` that contains `Integer`s and `Double`s.

In method `sum` (lines 52–61), although the `List` argument's element types are not directly known by the method, they're known to be at least of type `Number`, because the wildcard was specified with the upper bound `Number`. For this reason line 57 is allowed, because all `Number` objects have a `doubleValue` method.

Wildcard Restrictions

Because the wildcard (?) in the method's header (line 52) does not specify a type-parameter name, you cannot use it as a type name throughout the method's body (i.e., you cannot replace `Number` with `?` in line 56). You could, however, declare method `sum` as follows:

```
public static <T extends Number> double sum(List<T> list)
```

which allows the method to receive a `List` that contains elements of any `Number` subclass. You could then use the type parameter `T` throughout the method body.

If the wildcard is specified without an upper bound, then only the methods of type `Object` can be invoked on values of the wildcard type. Also, methods that use wildcards in their parameter's type arguments cannot be used to add elements to a collection referenced by the parameter.

Common Programming Error 20.3

Using a wildcard in a method's type-parameter section or using a wildcard as an explicit type of a variable in the method body is a syntax error.

20.8 Wrap-Up

This chapter introduced generics. You saw how to declare generic methods and classes with type parameters specified in type-parameter sections. We showed how to specify the upper bound for a type parameter and how the Java compiler uses erasure and casts to support multiple types with generic methods and classes. You also saw how to use wildcards in a generic method or a generic class.

In Chapter 21, you'll learn how to implement your own custom dynamic data structures that can grow or shrink at execution time. In particular, you'll implement these data structures using the generics capabilities you learned in this chapter.

Summary

Section 20.1 Introduction

- Generic methods enable you to specify, with one method declaration, a set of related methods.
- Generic classes and interfaces enable you to specify sets of related types.

Section 20.2 Motivation for Generic Methods

- Overloaded methods are often used to perform similar operations on different types of data.
- When the compiler encounters a method call, it attempts to locate a method declaration with a name and parameters that are compatible with the argument types in the method call.

Section 20.3 Generic Methods: Implementation and Compile-Time Translation

- If the operations performed by several overloaded methods are identical for each argument type, they can be more compactly and conveniently coded using a generic method. A single generic method declaration can be called with arguments of different data types. Based on the types of the arguments passed to a generic method, the compiler handles each method call appropriately.
- All generic method declarations have a type-parameter section (p. 825) delimited by angle brackets (< and >) that precedes the method's return type (p. 825).
- A type-parameter section contains one or more type parameters separated by commas.
- A type parameter (p. 825) is an identifier that specifies a generic type name. Type parameters can be used as the return type, parameter types and local variable types in a generic method declaration, and they act as placeholders for the types of the arguments passed to the generic method, which are known as actual type arguments (p. 825). Type parameters can represent only reference types.
- Type-parameter names used throughout a method declaration must match those declared in the type-parameter section. A type-parameter name can be declared only once in the type-parameter section but can appear more than once in the method's parameter list.
- When the compiler encounters a method call, it determines the argument types and attempts to locate a method with the same name and parameters that match the argument types. If there's no such method, the compiler searches for methods with the same name and compatible parameters and for matching generic methods.
- Objects of a class that implements interface `Comparable` can be compared with the interface's `compareTo` method (p. 827), which returns `0` if the objects are equal, a negative integer if the first object is less than the second, or a positive integer if the first object is greater than the second.
- All the type-wrapper classes for primitive types implement `Comparable`.
- `Comparable` objects can be used with the sorting and searching methods of class `Collections`.

- When a generic method is compiled, the compiler performs erasure to remove the type-parameter section and replace the type parameters with actual types. By default each type parameter is replaced with its upper bound, which is `Object` unless specified otherwise.

Section 20.4 Additional Compile-Time Translation Issues: Methods That Use a Type Parameter as the Return Type

- When erasure is performed on a method that returns a type variable, explicit casts are inserted in front of each method call to ensure that the returned value has the type expected by the caller.

Section 20.5 Overloading Generic Methods

- A generic method may be overloaded with other generic methods or with nongeneric methods.

Section 20.6 Generic Classes

- Generic classes provide a means for describing a class in a type-independent manner. We can then instantiate type-specific objects of the generic class.
- A generic class declaration looks like a nongeneric class declaration, except that the class name is followed by a type-parameter section. The type-parameter section of a generic class can have one or more type parameters separated by commas.
- When a generic class is compiled, the compiler performs erasure on the class's type parameters and replaces them with their upper bounds.
- Type parameters cannot be used in a class's `static` declarations.
- When instantiating an object of a generic class, the types specified in angle brackets after the class name are known as type arguments (p. 833). The compiler uses them to replace the type parameters so that it can perform type checking and insert cast operations as necessary.

Section 20.7 Wildcards in Methods That Accept Type Parameters

- Class `Number` is the superclass of both `Integer` and `Double`.
- `Number` method `doubleValue` (p. 839) obtains the `Number`'s underlying value as a `double`.
- Wildcard type arguments enable you to specify method parameters, return values, variables, and so on, that act as supertypes of parameterized types. A wildcard type argument is denoted by `?` (p. 839), which represents an "unknown type." A wildcard can also have an upper bound.
- Because a wildcard (`?`) is not a type-parameter name, you cannot use it as a type name throughout a method's body.
- If a wildcard is specified without an upper bound, then only the methods of type `Object` can be invoked on values of the wildcard type.
- Methods that use wildcards as type arguments (p. 839) cannot be used to add elements to a collection referenced by the parameter.

Self-Review Exercises

20.1 State whether each of the following is *true* or *false*. If *false*, explain why.

a) A generic method cannot have the same method name as a nongeneric method.
b) All generic method declarations have a type-parameter section that immediately precedes the method name.
c) A generic method can be overloaded by another generic method with the same method name but different method parameters.
d) A type parameter can be declared only once in the type-parameter section but can appear more than once in the method's parameter list.

e) Type-parameter names among different generic methods must be unique.
f) The scope of a generic class's type parameter is the entire class except its `static` members.

20.2 Fill in the blanks in each of the following:
a) ________ and ________ enable you to specify, with a single method declaration, a set of related methods, or with a single class declaration, a set of related types, respectively.
b) A type-parameter section is delimited by ________.
c) A generic method's ________ can be used to specify the method's argument types, to specify the method's return type and to declare variables within the method.
d) In a generic class declaration, the class name is followed by a(n) ________.
e) The syntax ________ specifies that the upper bound of a wildcard is type `T`.

Answers to Self-Review Exercises

20.1 a) False. Generic and nongeneric methods can have the same method name. A generic method can overload another generic method with the same method name but different method parameters. A generic method also can be overloaded by providing nongeneric methods with the same method name and number of arguments. b) False. All generic method declarations that use named type parameters (as opposed to wildcards) have a type-parameter section that immediately precedes the method's return type. c) True. d) True. e) False. Type-parameter names among different generic methods need not be unique. f) True.

20.2 a) Generic methods, generic classes. b) angle brackets (`<` and `>`). c) type parameters. d) type-parameter section. e) `? extends T`.

Exercises

20.3 *(Explain Notation)* Explain the use of the following notation in a Java program:

```
public class Array<T> { }
```

20.4 *(Generic Method* **`selectionSort`***)* Write a generic method `selectionSort` based on the sort program of Fig. 19.4. Write a test program that inputs, sorts and outputs an `Integer` array and a `Float` array. [*Hint:* Use `<T extends Comparable<T>>` in the type-parameter section for method `selectionSort`, so that you can use method `compareTo` to compare the objects of the type that `T` represents.]

20.5 *(Overloaded Generic Method* **`printArray`***)* Overload generic method `printArray` of Fig. 20.3 so that it takes two additional integer arguments, `lowSubscript` and `highSubscript`. A call to this method prints only the designated portion of the array. Validate `lowSubscript` and `highSubscript`. If either is out of range, the overloaded `printArray` method should throw an `InvalidSubscriptException`; otherwise, `printArray` should return the number of elements printed. Then modify `main` to exercise both versions of `printArray` on arrays `integerArray`, `doubleArray` and `characterArray`. Test all capabilities of both versions of `printArray`.

20.6 *(Overloading a Generic Method with a Nongeneric Method))* Overload generic method `printArray` of Fig. 20.3 with a nongeneric version that specifically prints an array of `String`s in neat, tabular format, as shown in the sample output that follows:

```
Array stringArray contains:
one      two      three    four
five     six      seven    eight
```

20.7 *(Generic **isEqualTo** Method)* Write a simple generic version of method `isEqualTo` that compares its two arguments with the `equals` method and returns `true` if they're equal and `false` otherwise. Use this generic method in a program that calls `isEqualTo` with a variety of built-in types, such as `Object` or `Integer`. When you run this program, are the objects passed to `isEqualTo` compared based on their contents or their references?

20.8 *(Generic Class **Pair**)* Write a generic class `Pair` which has two type parameters—`F` and `S`—each representing the type of the first and second element of the pair, respectively. Add *get* and *set* methods for the first and second elements of the pair. [*Hint:* The class header should be `public class Pair<F, S>`.]

20.9 *(Overloading Generic Methods)* How can generic methods be overloaded?

20.10 *(Overload Resolution)* The compiler performs a matching process to determine which method to call when a method is invoked. Under what circumstances does an attempt to make a match result in a compile-time error?

20.11 *(What Does this Statement Do?)* Explain why a Java program might use the statement

```
List<Employee> workerList = new ArrayList<>();
```

21 Custom Generic Data Structures

Objectives

In this chapter you'll:

- Form linked data structures using references, self-referential classes, recursion and generics.
- Create and manipulate dynamic data structures, such as linked lists, queues, stacks and binary trees.
- Learn various important applications of linked data structures.
- Create reusable data structures with composition.
- Organize classes in packages to promote reuse.

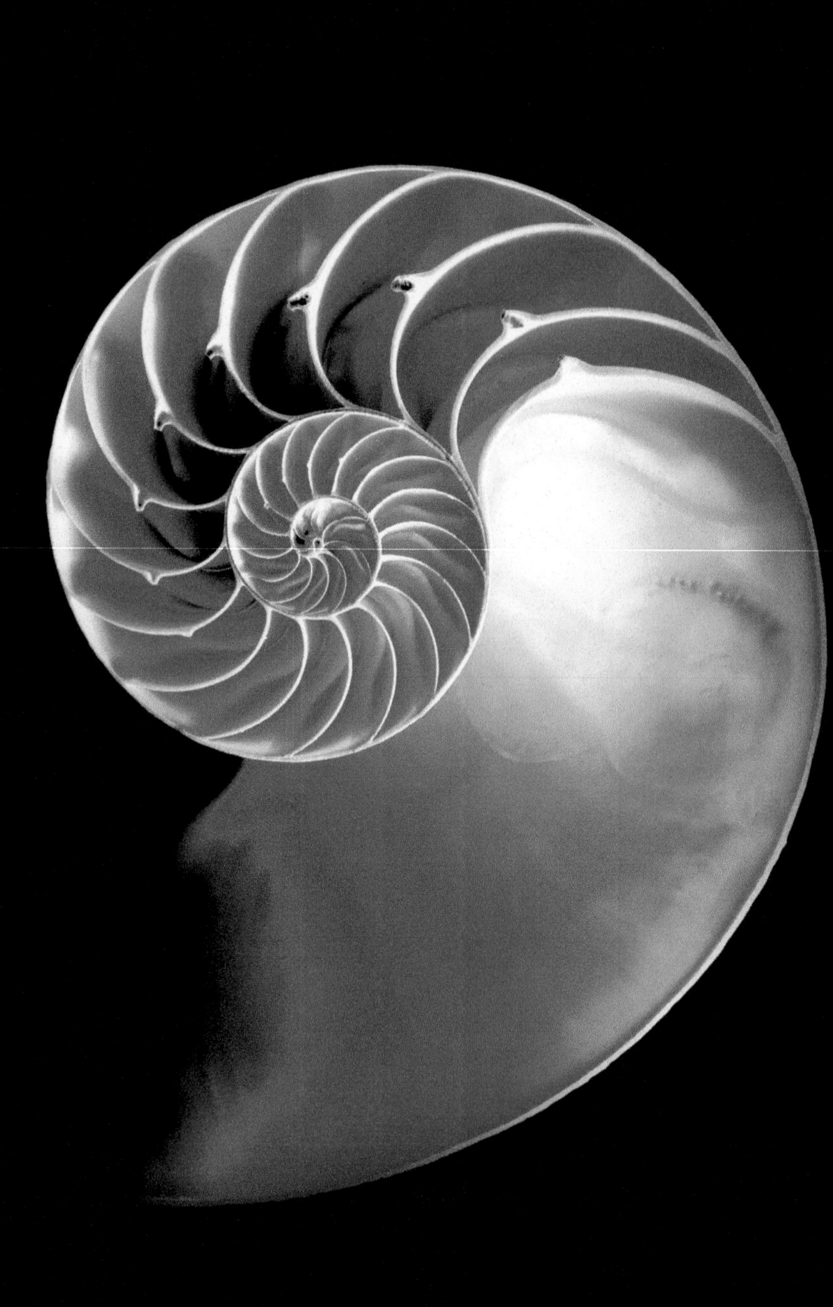

Outline

21.1 Introduction

This chapter shows how to build **dynamic data structures** that grow and shrink at execution time. **Linked lists** are collections of data items "linked up in a chain"—insertions and deletions can be made *anywhere* in a linked list. **Stacks** are important in compilers and operating systems; insertions and deletions are made only at one end of a stack—its **top**. **Queues** represent waiting lines; insertions are made at the back (also referred to as the **tail**) of a queue and deletions are made from the front (also referred to as the **head**). **Binary trees** facilitate high-speed searching and sorting of data, eliminating duplicate data items efficiently, representing file-system directories, compiling expressions into machine language and many other interesting applications.

We discuss each of these major data-structure types and implement programs that create and manipulate them. We use classes and composition to create them for reusability and maintainability. We also explain how to organize classes into your own packages to promote reuse. We include this chapter for computer-science and computer-engineering students who need to know how to build linked data structures.

Software Engineering Observation 21.1

The vast majority of software developers should use the predefined generic collection classes that we discussed in Chapter 16, rather than developing customized linked data structures.

"Building Your Own Compiler" Project

If you feel ambitious, you might want to attempt the major project described in the Building Your Own Compiler special exercise section. You've been using a Java compiler to translate your Java programs to bytecodes so that you could execute these programs. In this project, you'll build your own compiler. It will read statements written in a simple, yet powerful high-level language similar to early versions of the popular language BASIC and translate these statements into Simpletron Machine Language (SML) instructions—SML is the language you learned in the Chapter 7 special section, Building Your Own Computer. Your Simpletron Simulator program will then execute the SML program produced by your compiler! Implementing this project by using an object-oriented approach will give you an opportunity to exercise most of what you've learned in this book. The special section carefully walks you through the specifications of the high-level language and describes the algorithms you'll need to convert each high-level language statement into machine-language instructions. If you enjoy being challenged, you might attempt the enhancements to both the compiler and the Simpletron Simulator suggested in the exercises.

21.2 Self-Referential Classes

A **self-referential class** contains an instance variable that refers to another object of the same class type. For example, the generic `Node` class declaration

```
class Node<E> {
   private E data;
   private Node<E> nextNode; // reference to next linked node
   public Node(E data) { /* constructor body */ }
   public void setData(E data) { /* method body */ }
   public E getData() { /* method body */ }
   public void setNext(Node<E> next) { /* method body */ }
   public Node<E> getNext() { /* method body */ }
}
```

has two `private` instance variables—`data` (of the generic type `E`) and `Node<E>` variable `nextNode`. Variable `nextNode` references a `Node<E>` object, an object of the same class being declared here—hence the term "self-referential class." Field `nextNode` is a **link**—it "links" an object of type `Node<E>` to another object of the same type. Type `Node<E>` also has five methods: a constructor that receives a value to initialize `data`, a `setData` method to set the value of `data`, a `getData` method to return the value of `data`, a `setNext` method to set the value of `nextNode` and a `getNext` method to return a reference to the next node.

Programs can link self-referential objects together to form such useful data structures as lists, queues, stacks and trees. Figure 21.1 illustrates two self-referential objects linked together to form a list—`15` and `10` are the `data` values in `Node<Integer>` objects. A backslash (\)—representing a `null` reference—is placed in the link member of the second self-referential object to indicate that the link does *not* refer to another object. The backslash is illustrative; it does not correspond to the backslash character in Java. By convention, in code we use `null` to indicate the end of a data structure.

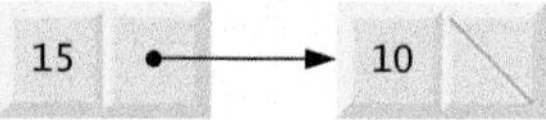

Fig. 21.1 | Self-referential-class objects linked together.

21.3 Dynamic Memory Allocation

Creating and maintaining dynamic data structures requires **dynamic memory allocation**—allowing a program to obtain more memory space at execution time to hold new nodes and to release space no longer needed. Remember that Java does not require you to explicitly release dynamically allocated memory. Rather, Java performs automatic *garbage collection* of objects that are no longer referenced in a program.

The limit for dynamic memory allocation can be as large as the amount of available physical memory in the computer or the amount of available disk space in a virtual-memory system. Often the limits are much smaller, because the computer's available memory must be shared among many applications.

The declaration and class-instance-creation expression

```
// 10 is nodeToAdd's data
Node<Integer> nodeToAdd = new Node<Integer>(10);
```

allocates a `Node<Integer>` object and returns a reference to it, which is assigned to `nodeToAdd`. If *insufficient memory* is available, the preceding expression throws an `OutOfMemoryError`. The sections that follow discuss lists, stacks, queues and trees—all of which use dynamic memory allocation and self-referential classes to create dynamic data structures.

21.4 Linked Lists

A linked list is a linear collection (i.e., a sequence) of self-referential-class objects, called **nodes**, connected by reference *links*—hence, the term "linked" list. Typically, a program accesses a linked list via a reference to its first node. The program accesses each subsequent node via the link reference stored in the previous node. By convention, the link reference in the last node of the list is set to `null` to indicate "end of list." Data is stored in and removed from linked lists dynamically—the program creates and deletes nodes as necessary. Stacks and queues are also linear data structures and, as we'll see, are constrained versions of linked lists. Trees are *nonlinear* data structures.

Lists of data can be stored in conventional Java arrays, but linked lists provide several advantages. A linked list is appropriate when the number of data elements to be represented in the data structure is *unpredictable*. Linked lists are dynamic, so the length of a list can increase or decrease as necessary, whereas the size of a conventional Java array cannot be altered—it's fixed when the program creates the array. [Of course, `ArrayList`s *can* grow and shrink.] Conventional arrays can become full. Linked lists become full only when the system has *insufficient memory* to satisfy dynamic storage allocation requests. Package `java.util` contains class `LinkedList` (discussed in Chapter 16) for implementing and manipulating linked lists that grow and shrink during program execution.

Performance Tip 21.1

After locating the insertion point, insertion into a linked list is fast—only two references have to be modified. All existing node objects remain at their current locations in memory.

Linked lists can be maintained in sorted order simply by inserting each new element at the proper point in the list. (It does, of course, take time to *locate* the proper insertion point.) *Existing list elements do not need to be moved.*

Performance Tip 21.2

Insertion and deletion in a sorted array can be time consuming—all the elements following the inserted or deleted element must be shifted appropriately.

21.4.1 Singly Linked Lists

Linked list nodes normally are *not stored contiguously* in memory. Rather, they're logically contiguous. Figure 21.2 illustrates a linked list with several nodes. This diagram presents a **singly linked list**—each node contains one reference to the next node in the list. Often, linked lists are implemented as *doubly linked lists*—each node contains a reference to the next node in the list *and* a reference to the preceding one.

Performance Tip 21.3

The elements of an array are contiguous in memory. This allows immediate access to any array element, because its address can be calculated directly as its offset from the beginning of the array. Linked lists do not afford such immediate access—an element can be accessed only by traversing the list from the front (or the back in a doubly linked list).

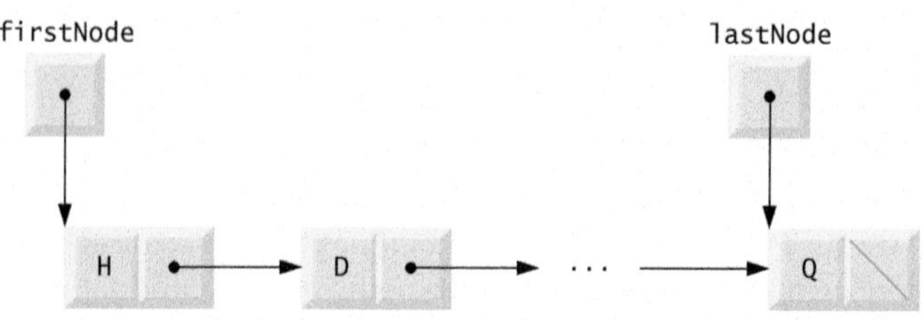

Fig. 21.2 | Linked-list graphical representation.

21.4.2 Implementing a Generic `List` Class

The program of Figs. 21.3–21.4 uses an object of our generic `List` class to manipulate a list of miscellaneous objects. The program consists of three classes—`ListNode` (Fig. 21.3, lines 8–28), `List` (Fig. 21.3, lines 31–132) and `ListTest` (Fig. 21.4). Encapsulated in each `List` object is a linked list of `ListNode` objects.

[*Note:* The `List` and `ListNode` classes are placed in the package `com.deitel.datastructures`, so that they can be reused throughout this chapter. In Section 21.4.10, we discuss the `package` statement (line 3 of Fig. 21.3) and show how to compile and run programs that use classes in your own packages.]

```
1  // Fig. 21.3: List.java
2  // ListNode and List class declarations.
3  package com.deitel.datastructures;
4
5  import java.util.NoSuchElementException;
6
7  // class to represent one node in a list
8  class ListNode<E> {
9     // package access members; List can access these directly
10    E data; // data for this node
11    ListNode<E> nextNode; // reference to the next node in the list
12
13    // constructor creates a ListNode that refers to object
14    ListNode(E object) {this(object, null);}
15
```

Fig. 21.3 | `ListNode` and `List` class declarations. (Part 1 of 4.)

```
   // constructor creates ListNode that refers to the specified
   // object and to the next ListNode
   ListNode(E object, ListNode<E> node) {
      data = object;
      nextNode = node;
   }

   // return reference to data in node
   E getData() {return data;}

   // return reference to next node in list
   ListNode<E> getNext() {return nextNode;}
}

// class List definition
public class List<E> {
   private ListNode<E> firstNode;
   private ListNode<E> lastNode;
   private String name; // string like "list" used in printing

   // constructor creates empty List with "list" as the name
   public List() {this("list");}

   // constructor creates an empty List with a name
   public List(String listName) {
      name = listName;
      firstNode = lastNode = null;
   }

   // insert item at front of List
   public void insertAtFront(E insertItem) {
      if (isEmpty()) { // firstNode and lastNode refer to same object
         firstNode = lastNode = new ListNode<E>(insertItem);
      }
      else { // firstNode refers to new node
         firstNode = new ListNode<E>(insertItem, firstNode);
      }
   }

   // insert item at end of List
   public void insertAtBack(E insertItem) {
      if (isEmpty()) { // firstNode and lastNode refer to same object
         firstNode = lastNode = new ListNode<E>(insertItem);
      }
      else { // lastNode's nextNode refers to new node
         lastNode = lastNode.nextNode = new ListNode<E>(insertItem);
      }
   }

   // remove first node from List
   public E removeFromFront() throws NoSuchElementException {
      if (isEmpty()) { // throw exception if List is empty
```

Fig. 21.3 | `ListNode` and `List` class declarations. (Part 2 of 4.)

```
         throw new NoSuchElementException(name + " is empty");
      }

      E removedItem = firstNode.data; // retrieve data being removed

      // update references firstNode and lastNode
      if (firstNode == lastNode) {
         firstNode = lastNode = null;
      }
      else {
         firstNode = firstNode.nextNode;
      }

      return removedItem; // return removed node data
   }

   // remove last node from List
   public E removeFromBack() throws NoSuchElementException {
      if (isEmpty()) { // throw exception if List is empty
         throw new NoSuchElementException(name + " is empty");
      }

      E removedItem = lastNode.data; // retrieve data being removed

      // update references firstNode and lastNode
      if (firstNode == lastNode) {
         firstNode = lastNode = null;
      }
      else { // locate new last node
         ListNode<E> current = firstNode;

         // loop while current node does not refer to lastNode
         while (current.nextNode != lastNode) {
            current = current.nextNode;
         }

         lastNode = current; // current is new lastNode
         current.nextNode = null;
      }

      return removedItem; // return removed node data
   }

   // determine whether list is empty; returns true if so
   public boolean isEmpty() {return firstNode == null;}

   // output list contents
   public void print() {
      if (isEmpty()) {
         System.out.printf("Empty %s%n", name);
         return;
      }

```

Fig. 21.3 | `ListNode` and `List` class declarations. (Part 3 of 4.)

```
121         System.out.printf("The %s is: ", name);
122         ListNode<E> current = firstNode;
123
124         // while not at end of list, output current node's data
125         while (current != null) {
126            System.out.printf("%s ", current.data);
127            current = current.nextNode;
128         }
129
130         System.out.println();
131      }
132   }
```

Fig. 21.3 | `ListNode` and `List` class declarations. (Part 4 of 4.)

21.4.3 Generic Classes ListNode and List

Generic class `ListNode` (Fig. 21.3, lines 8–28) declares package-access fields `data` and `nextNode`. The `data` field is a reference of type `E`, so its type will be determined when the client code creates the corresponding `List` object. Variable `nextNode` stores a reference to the next `ListNode` object in the linked list (or `null` if the node is the last one in the list).

Lines 32–33 of class `List` (lines 31–132) declare references to the first and last `ListNode`s in a `List` (`firstNode` and `lastNode`, respectively). The constructors (lines 37 and 40–43) initialize both references to `null`. The most important methods of class `List` are `insertAtFront` (lines 46–53), `insertAtBack` (lines 56–63), `removeFromFront` (lines 66–82) and `removeFromBack` (lines 85–109). Method `isEmpty` (line 112) is a *predicate method* that determines whether the list is empty (i.e., the reference to the first node of the list is `null`). Predicate methods typically test a condition and do not modify the object on which they're called. If the list is empty, method `isEmpty` returns `true`; otherwise, it returns `false`. Method `print` (lines 115–131) displays the list's contents. We discuss class `List`'s methods in more detail after we discuss class `ListTest`.

21.4.4 Class ListTest

Method `main` of class `ListTest` (Fig. 21.4) creates a `List<Integer>` object (line 8), then inserts objects at the beginning of the list using method `insertAtFront`, inserts objects at the end of the list using method `insertAtBack`, deletes objects from the front of the list using method `removeFromFront` and deletes objects from the end of the list using method `removeFromBack`. After each insert and remove operation, `ListTest` calls `List` method `print` to display the current list contents. If an attempt is made to remove an item from an empty list, a `NoSuchElementException` is thrown, so the method calls to `removeFromFront` and `removeFromBack` are placed in a `try` block that's followed by an appropriate exception handler. Notice in lines 11, 13, 15 and 17 that the application passes literal primitive `int` values to methods `insertAtFront` and `insertAtBack`. Each of these methods was declared with a parameter of the generic type `E` (Fig. 21.3, lines 46 and 56). Since this example manipulates a `List<Integer>`, the type `E` represents the type-wrapper class `Integer`. In this case, the JVM *autoboxes* each literal value in an `Integer` object, and that object is actually inserted into the list.

```java
// Fig. 21.4: ListTest.java
// ListTest class to demonstrate List capabilities.
import com.deitel.datastructures.List;
import java.util.NoSuchElementException;

public class ListTest {
   public static void main(String[] args) {
      List<Integer> list = new List<>();

      // insert integers in list
      list.insertAtFront(-1);
      list.print();
      list.insertAtFront(0);
      list.print();
      list.insertAtBack(1);
      list.print();
      list.insertAtBack(5);
      list.print();

      // remove objects from list; print after each removal
      try {
         int removedItem = list.removeFromFront();
         System.out.printf("%n%d removed%n", removedItem);
         list.print();

         removedItem = list.removeFromFront();
         System.out.printf("%n%d removed%n", removedItem);
         list.print();

         removedItem = list.removeFromBack();
         System.out.printf("%n%d removed%n", removedItem);
         list.print();

         removedItem = list.removeFromBack();
         System.out.printf("%n%d removed%n", removedItem);
         list.print();
      }
      catch (NoSuchElementException noSuchElementException) {
         noSuchElementException.printStackTrace();
      }
   }
}
```

```
The list is: -1
The list is: 0 -1
The list is: 0 -1 1
The list is: 0 -1 1 5

0 removed
The list is: -1 1 5

-1 removed
The list is: 1 5
```

Fig. 21.4 | ListTest class to demonstrate List capabilities. (Part 1 of 2.)

```
5 removed
The list is: 1

1 removed
Empty list
```

Fig. 21.4 | `ListTest` class to demonstrate `List` capabilities. (Part 2 of 2.)

21.4.5 List Method insertAtFront

Now we discuss each method of class `List` (Fig. 21.3) in detail and provide diagrams showing the reference manipulations performed by methods `insertAtFront`, `insertAtBack`, `removeFromFront` and `removeFromBack`. Method `insertAtFront` (lines 46–53 of Fig. 21.3) places a new node at the front of the list. The steps are:

1. Call `isEmpty` to determine whether the list is empty (line 47).
2. If the list is empty, assign to `firstNode` and `lastNode` the new `ListNode` that was initialized with `insertItem` (line 48). (Recall that assignment operators evaluate right to left.) The `ListNode` constructor at line 14 calls the `ListNode` constructor at lines 18–21 to set instance variable `data` to refer to the `insertItem` and to set reference `nextNode` to `null`, because this is the first and last node in the list.
3. If the list is not empty, the new node is "linked" into the list by setting `firstNode` to a new `ListNode` object and initializing that object with `insertItem` and `firstNode` (line 51). When the `ListNode` constructor (lines 18–21) executes, it sets instance variable `data` to refer to the `insertItem` passed as an argument and performs the insertion by setting the `nextNode` reference of the new node to the `ListNode` passed as an argument, which previously was the first node.

In Fig. 21.5, part (a) shows a list and a new node during the `insertAtFront` operation and before the program links the new node into the list. The dotted arrows in part (b) illustrate *Step 3* of the `insertAtFront` operation that enables the node containing `12` to become the new first node in the list.

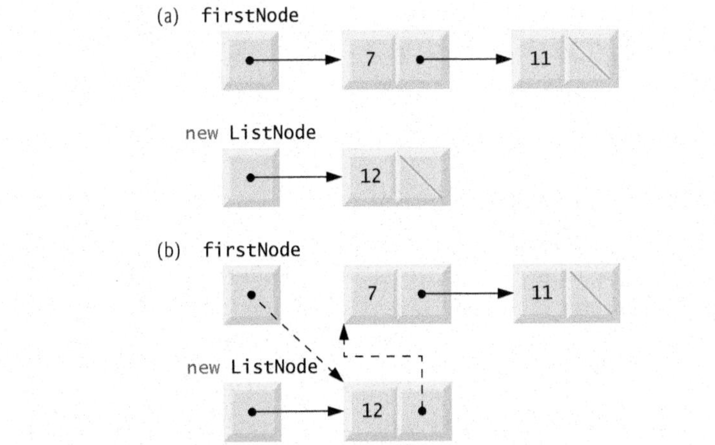

Fig. 21.5 | Graphical representation of operation `insertAtFront`.

21.4.6 List Method insertAtBack

Method `insertAtBack` (lines 56–63 of Fig. 21.3) places a new node at the back of the list. The steps are:

1. Call `isEmpty` to determine whether the list is empty (line 57).
2. If the list is empty, assign to `firstNode` and `lastNode` the new `ListNode` that was initialized with `insertItem` (line 58). The `ListNode` constructor at line 14 calls the constructor at lines 18–21 to set instance variable `data` to refer to the `insertItem` passed as an argument and to set reference `nextNode` to `null`.
3. If the list is not empty, line 61 links the new node into the list by assigning to `lastNode` and `lastNode.nextNode` the reference to the new `ListNode` that was initialized with `insertItem`. `ListNode`'s constructor (line 14) sets instance variable `data` to refer to the `insertItem` passed as an argument and sets reference `nextNode` to `null`, because this is the last node in the list.

In Fig. 21.6, part (a) shows a list and a new node during the `insertAtBack` operation and before linking the new node into the list. The dotted arrows in part (b) illustrate *Step 3* of method `insertAtBack`, which adds the new node to the end of a list that's not empty.

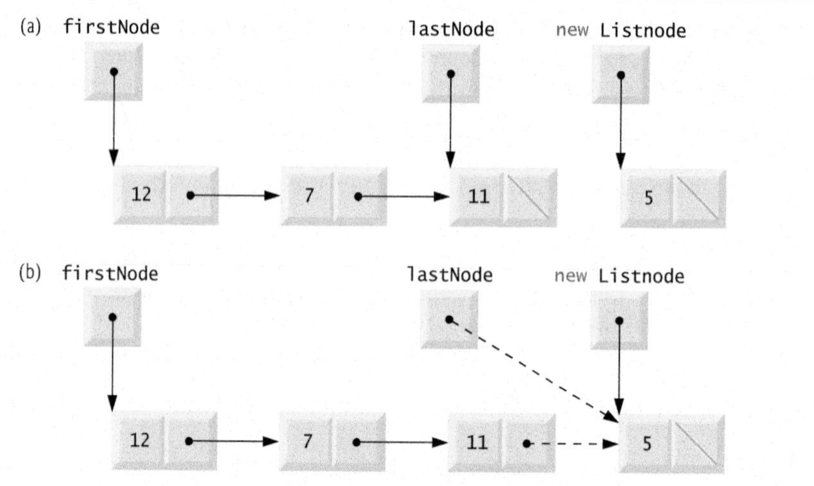

Fig. 21.6 | Graphical representation of operation `insertAtBack`.

21.4.7 List Method removeFromFront

Method `removeFromFront` (lines 66–82 of Fig. 21.3) removes the first node of the list and returns a reference to the removed data. If the list is empty when the program calls this method, the method throws an `NoSuchElementException` (lines 67–69). Otherwise, the method returns a reference to the removed data. The steps are:

1. Assign `firstNode.data` (the data being removed) to `removedItem` (line 71).
2. If `firstNode` and `lastNode` refer to the same object (line 74), the list has only one element at this time. So, the method sets `firstNode` and `lastNode` to `null` (line 75) to remove the node from the list (leaving the list empty).

3. If the list has more than one node, then the method leaves reference `lastNode` as is and assigns the value of `firstNode.nextNode` to `firstNode` (line 78). Thus, `firstNode` references the node that was previously the second node in the list.
4. Return the `removedItem` reference (line 81).

In Fig. 21.7, part (a) illustrates the list before the removal operation. The dashed lines and arrows in part (b) show the reference manipulations.

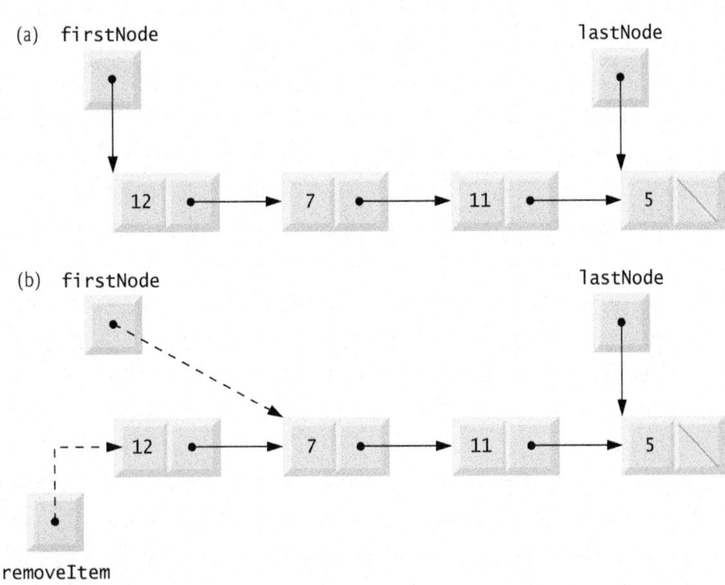

Fig. 21.7 | Graphical representation of operation `removeFromFront`.

21.4.8 List Method removeFromBack

Method `removeFromBack` (lines 85–109 of Fig. 21.3) removes the last node of a list and returns a reference to the removed data. The method throws a `NoSuchElementException` (lines 86–88) if the list is empty when the program calls this method. The steps are:

1. Assign `lastNode.data` (the data being removed) to `removedItem` (line 90).
2. If the `firstNode` and `lastNode` refer to the same object (line 93), the list has only one element at this time. So, line 94 sets `firstNode` and `lastNode` to `null` to remove that node from the list (leaving the list empty).
3. If the list has more than one node, create the `ListNode` reference `current` and assign it `firstNode` (line 97).
4. Now "walk the list" with `current` until it references the node before the last node. The `while` loop (lines 100–102) assigns `current.nextNode` to `current` as long as `current.nextNode` (the next node in the list) is not `lastNode`.
5. After locating the second-to-last node, assign `current` to `lastNode` (line 104) to update which node is last in the list.

6. Set the `current.nextNode` to `null` (line 105) to remove the last node from the list and terminate the list at the current node.
7. Return the `removedItem` reference (line 108).

In Fig. 21.8, part (a) illustrates the list before the removal operation. The dashed lines and arrows in part (b) show the reference manipulations. [We limited the `List` insertion and removal operations to the front and the back of the list. In Exercise 21.26, you'll enhance the `List` class to enable insertions and deletions *anywhere* in the `List`.]

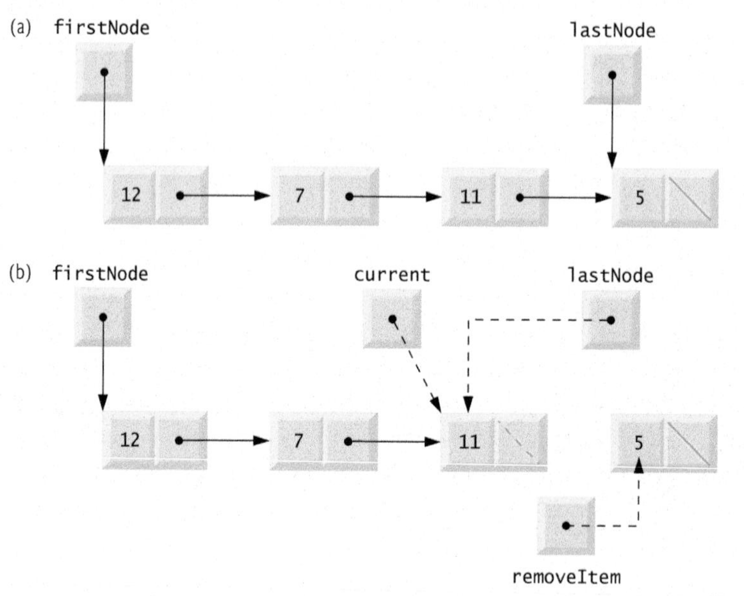

Fig. 21.8 | Graphical representation of operation `removeFromBack`.

21.4.9 `List` Method `print`

Method `print` (lines 115–131 of Fig. 21.3) first determines whether the list is empty (lines 116–119) and, if so, displays a message and returns control to the calling method. Otherwise, `print` outputs the list's data. Line 122 creates `ListNode current` and initializes it with `firstNode`. While `current` is not `null`, there are more items in the list. Therefore, line 126 outputs a string representation of `current.data`. Line 127 moves to the next node in the list by assigning the value of reference `current.nextNode` to `current`. This printing algorithm is identical for linked lists, stacks and queues.

21.4.10 Creating Your Own Packages

As you know, the Java API types (classes, interfaces and `enum`s) are organized in *packages* that group related types. Packages facilitate software reuse by enabling programs to `import` existing classes, rather than *copying* them into the folders of each program that uses them. Programmers use packages to organize program components, especially in large programs. For example, you might have one package containing the types that make up your program's graphical user interface, another for the types that manage your application's data and another for the types that communicate with servers over a network. In addition, packages help you specify unique names for every type you declare, which (as we'll discuss) helps prevent class-name conflicts. This section introduces how to create and use your own packages. Much of what we discuss here is handled for you by IDEs such as NetBeans, Eclipse and IntelliJ IDEA. We focus on creating and using packages with the JDK's command-line tools.

Steps for Declaring a Reusable Class

Before a class can be imported into multiple programs, it must be placed in a package to make it reusable. The steps for creating a reusable class are:

1. Declare one or more `public` types (classes, interfaces and `enum`s). Only `public` types can be reused outside the package in which they're declared.
2. Choose a unique package name and add a **package declaration** to the source-code file for each reusable type that should be part of the package.
3. Compile the types so that they're placed in the appropriate package directory.
4. Import the reusable types into a program and use them.

We'll now discuss each of these steps in more detail.

Step 1: Creating `public` *Types for Reuse*

For *Step 1*, you declare the types that will be placed in the package, including both the reusable types and any supporting types. In Fig. 21.3, class `List` is `public`, so it's reusable outside its package. Class `ListNode`, however, is not `public`, so it can be used *only* by class `List` and any other types declared in the *same* package. If a source-code file contains more than one type, all types in the file are placed in the same package when the file is compiled.

Step 2: Adding the `package` *Statements*

For *Step 2*, you provide a `package` declaration containing the package's name. All source-code files containing types that should be part of the same package must contain the *same* `package` declaration. Figure 21.3 contains:

```
package com.deitel.datastructures;
```

indicating that all the types declared in this file—`ListNode` and `List` in Fig. 21.3—are part of the `com.deitel.datastructures` package.

Each Java source-code file may contain only *one* `package` declaration, and it must *precede* all other declarations and statements. If no `package` statement is provided in a Java source-code file, the types declared in that file are placed in the so-called *default package* and are accessible only to other classes in the default package that are located in the *same directory*. All prior programs in this book have used this default package.

Package Naming Conventions

A package name's parts are separated by dots (`.`), and there typically are two or more parts. To ensure *unique* package names, you typically begin the name with your institution's or company's Internet domain name in reverse order—e.g., our domain name is `deitel.com`, so we begin our package names with `com.deitel`. For the domain name *yourcollege*`.edu`, you'd begin the package name with `edu.`*yourcollege*.

After the reversed domain name, you can specify additional parts in a package name. If you're part of a university with many schools or company with many divisions, you might use the school or division name as the next part of the package name. Similarly, if the types are for a specific project, you might include the project name as part of the package name. We chose `datastructures` as the next part in our package name to indicate that classes `ListNode` and `List` are from this data-structures chapter.

Fully Qualified Names

The `package` name is part of the **fully qualified type name**, so the name of class `List` is actually `com.deitel.datastructures.List`. You can use this fully qualified name in your programs, or you can `import` the class and use its **simple name** (the class name by itself—`List`) in the program. If another package also contains a `List` class, the fully qualified class names can be used to distinguish between the classes in the program and prevent a **name conflict** (also called a **name collision**).

Step 3: Compiling Packaged Types

Step 3 is to compile the class so that it's stored in the appropriate package. When a Java file containing a `package` declaration is compiled, the resulting class file is placed in a directory specified by the declaration. Classes in the package `com.deitel.datastructures` are placed in the directory

```
com
   deitel
      datastructures
```

The names in the `package` declaration specify the exact location of the package's classes.

The `javac` command-line option **`-d`** causes the compiler to create the directories based on the `package` declaration. The option also specifies where the top-level directory in the package name should be placed on your system—you may specify a relative or complete path to this location. For example, the command

```
javac -d . List.java
```

specifies that the first directory in our package name (`com`) should be placed in the current directory. The period (`.`) after `-d` in the preceding command represents the *current directory* on the Windows, UNIX, Linux and macOS operating systems (and several others as well). Similarly, the command

```
javac -d .. List.java
```

specifies that the first directory in our package name (`com`) should be placed in the *parent* directory—we did this for all the reusable classes in this chapter. Once you compile with the `-d` option, the package's `datastructures` directory contains the files `ListNode.class` and `List.class`.

Step 4: Importing Types from Your Package

Once types are compiled into a package, they can be imported (*Step 4*). Class `ListTest` (Fig. 21.4) is in the *default package* because its `.java` file does not contain a `package` declaration. Class `ListTest` is in a *different* package from `List`, so you must either `import` class `List` so that class `ListTest` can use it (line 3 of Fig. 21.4) or you must *fully qualify* the name `List` everywhere it's used throughout class `ListTest`. For example, line 8 of Fig. 21.4 could have been written as:

```
com.deitel.datastructures.List<Integer> list =
   new com.deitel.datastructures.List<>();
```

Single-Type-Import vs. Type-Import-On-Demand Declarations

Lines 3–4 of Fig. 21.4 are **single-type-import declarations**—they each specify *one* class to import. When a source-code file uses *multiple* classes from a package, you can import those classes with a a **type-import-on-demand declaration** of the form

```
import packagename.*;
```

which uses an asterisk (*) at its end to inform the compiler that *all* `public` classes from the *packagename* package can be used without fully qualifying their names in the file containing the `import`. Only those classes that are *used* are loaded at execution time. The preceding `import` allows you to use the simple name of any type from the *packagename* package. Throughout this book, we provide single-type-import declarations as a form of documentation to show you specifically which types are used in each program.

Common Programming Error 21.1

Using the `import` declaration `import java.*;` causes a compilation error. You must specify the full package name from which you want to import classes.

Error-Prevention Tip 21.1

Using single-type-import declarations helps avoid naming conflicts by importing only the types you actually use in your code.

Specifying the Classpath When Compiling a Program

When compiling `ListTest`, `javac` must locate the `.class` files for class `List` to ensure that class `ListTest` uses it correctly. The compiler uses a special object called a **class loader** to locate the classes it needs. The class loader begins by searching the standard Java classes that are bundled with the JDK. Then it searches for **optional packages**. Java provides an **extension mechanism** that enables new (optional) packages to be added to Java for development and execution purposes. If the class is not found in the standard Java classes or in the extension classes, the class loader searches the **classpath**—a list of directories or **archive files** containing reusable types. Each directory or archive file is separated from the next by a **directory separator**—a semicolon (;) on Windows or a colon (:) on UNIX/Linux/macOS. Archive files are individual files that contain directories of other files, typically in a compressed format. For example, the standard classes used by your programs are contained in the archive file `rt.jar`, which is installed with the JDK. Archive files normally end with the `.jar` or `.zip` filename extensions.

By default, the classpath consists only of the current directory. However, the classpath can be modified by

1. providing the **`-classpath`** *listOfDirectories* option to the `javac` compiler or
2. setting the **CLASSPATH environment variable** (a special variable that you define and the operating system maintains so that programs can search for classes in the specified locations).

If you compile `ListTest.java` without specifying the `-classpath` option, as in

```
javac ListTest.java
```

the class loader assumes that the additional package(s) used by the `ListTest` program are in the *current directory*. As we mentioned, we placed our package in the *parent* directory so that it could be used by other programs in this chapter. To compile `ListTest.java`, use the command

```
javac -classpath .;.. ListTest.java
```

on Windows or the command

```
javac -classpath .:.. ListTest.java
```

on UNIX/Linux/macOS. The `.` in the classpath enables the class loader to locate `ListTest` in the current directory. The `..` enables the class loader to locate the contents of package `com.deitel.datastructures` in the parent directory. The `-classpath` option may also be abbreviated as **`-cp`**.

Common Programming Error 21.2

Specifying an explicit classpath eliminates the current directory from the classpath. This prevents classes in the current directory (including packages in the current directory) from loading properly. If classes must be loaded from the current directory, include a dot (.) in the classpath to specify the current directory.

Software Engineering Observation 21.2

In general, it's a better practice to use the `-classpath` option of the compiler, rather than the `CLASSPATH` environment variable, to specify the classpath for a program. This enables each program to have its own classpath.

Error-Prevention Tip 21.2

Specifying the classpath with the `CLASSPATH` environment variable can cause subtle and difficult-to-locate errors in programs that use different versions of the same package.

Specifying the Classpath When Executing a Program

When you execute a program, the JVM must be able to locate the `.class` files for the program's classes. Like the compiler, the `java` command uses a *class loader* that searches the standard classes and extension classes first, then searches the classpath (the current directory by default). The classpath can be specified explicitly by using the same techniques discussed for the compiler. As with the compiler, it's better to specify an individual program's classpath via command-line JVM options. You can specify the classpath in the `java` command via the **`-classpath`** or **`-cp`** command-line options, followed by a list of directories or archive files. Again, if classes must be loaded from the current directory, be sure to include a dot (.) in the classpath to specify the current directory. To execute the `ListTest` program, use the following command:

```
java -classpath .;.. ListTest
```

(Again, use : rather than ; on UNIX/Linux/macOS.) *You'll need to use similar `javac` and `java` commands for each of this chapter's remaining examples.* For more about the classpath, visit `docs.oracle.com/javase/8/docs/technotes/tools/index.html#general`.

21.5 Stacks

A stack is a constrained list—*new nodes can be added to and removed from a stack only at the top*. For this reason, a stack is referred to as a **last-in, first-out** (**LIFO**) data structure. The link member in the bottom node is set to null to indicate the bottom of the stack. A stack is not required to be implemented as a linked list—it can also be implemented using an array or an ArrayList, for example.

Stack Operations

The primary methods for manipulating a stack are **push** and **pop**, which add a new node to the top of the stack and remove a node from the top of the stack, respectively. Method pop also returns the data from the popped node.

Stack Applications

Stacks have many interesting applications. For example, when a program calls a method, the called method must know how to return to its caller, so the return address of the calling method is pushed onto the program-execution stack (discussed in Section 6.6). If a series of method calls occurs, the successive return addresses are pushed onto the stack in last-in, first-out order so that each method can return to its caller. Stacks support recursive method calls in the *same* manner as they do conventional nonrecursive method calls.

The program-execution stack also contains the memory for local variables on each invocation of a method during a program's execution. When the method returns to its caller, the memory for that method's local variables is popped off the stack, and those variables are no longer known to the program. If the local variable is a reference and the object to which it referred has no other variables referring to it, the object can be garbage collected.

Compilers use stacks to evaluate arithmetic expressions and generate machine-language code to process them. The exercises in this chapter explore several applications of stacks, including using them to develop a complete working compiler.

Stack<E> Class That Contains a List<E>

We take advantage of the close relationship between lists and stacks to implement a stack class by reusing the List<E> class (Fig. 21.3). We use *composition* by including a reference to a List object as a private instance variable. This chapter's list, stack and queue data structures are implemented to store references to objects of any type to encourage further reusability. Class Stack<E> (Fig. 21.9) is declared in package com.deitel.datastructures (line 3) for reuse. Stack<E>'s source-code file does not import List<E>, because the classes are in the same package. Use the following command to compile class Stack:

```
javac -d .. -cp .. Stack.java
```

```
1  // Fig. 21.9: Stack.java
2  // Stack uses a composed List object.
3  package com.deitel.datastructures;
4
5  import java.util.NoSuchElementException;
6
7  public class Stack<E> {
```

Fig. 21.9 | Stack uses a composed List object. (Part 1 of 2.)

```
8       private List<E> stackList;
9
10      // constructor
11      public Stack() {stackList = new List<E>("stack");}
12
13      // add object to stack
14      public void push(E object) {stackList.insertAtFront(object);}
15
16      // remove object from stack
17      public E pop() throws NoSuchElementException {
18         return stackList.removeFromFront();
19      }
20
21      // determine if stack is empty
22      public boolean isEmpty() {return stackList.isEmpty();}
23
24      // output stack contents
25      public void print() {stackList.print();}
26   }
```

Fig. 21.9 | Stack uses a composed List object. (Part 2 of 2.)

Stack<E> Methods

Class Stack<E> has four methods—push, pop, isEmpty and print—which are essentially List<E>'s insertAtFront, removeFromFront, isEmpty and print methods. List<E>'s other methods (such as insertAtBack and removeFromBack) should not be accessible to Stack<E> client code—composing a private List<E> (line 8) to implement our Stack<E>'s capabilities, rather than inheritance, enables us to hide the remaining List<E> methods.

We implement each Stack<E> method as a call to a List<E> method. This is called **delegation**—each Stack<E> method delegates its work to the appropriate List<E> method. In particular, Stack<E> delegates calls to List<E> methods insertAtFront (line 14), removeFromFront (line 18), isEmpty (line 22) and print (line 25).

Testing Class Stack<E>

Class StackTest (Fig. 21.10) creates a Stack<Integer> object called stack (line 8). The program pushes ints onto the stack (lines 11, 13, 15 and 17). *Autoboxing* converts each argument to an Integer. Lines 21–33 pop the objects from the stack. If pop is invoked on an empty stack, the method throws a NoSuchElementException. In this case, the program displays the exception's stack trace, which shows the methods on the program-execution stack at the time the exception occurred. The program outputs the contents of the stack after each pop operation. Use the following commands to compile and run class StackTest:

```
javac -cp .;.. StackTest.java
java -cp .;.. StackTest
```

```
1   // Fig. 21.10: StackTest.java
2   // Stack manipulation program.
3   import com.deitel.datastructures.Stack;
```

Fig. 21.10 | Stack manipulation program. (Part 1 of 2.)

```
import java.util.NoSuchElementException;

public class StackTest {
   public static void main(String[] args) {
      Stack<Integer> stack = new Stack<>();

      // use push method
      stack.push(-1);
      stack.print();
      stack.push(0);
      stack.print();
      stack.push(1);
      stack.print();
      stack.push(5);
      stack.print();

      // remove items from stack
      boolean continueLoop = true;

      while (continueLoop) {
         try {
            int removedItem = stack.pop(); // remove top element
            System.out.printf("%n%d popped%n", removedItem);
            stack.print();
         }
         catch (NoSuchElementException noSuchElementException) {
            continueLoop = false;
            noSuchElementException.printStackTrace();
         }
      }
   }
}
```

```
The stack is: -1
The stack is: 0 -1
The stack is: 1  0 -1
The stack is: 5  1  0 -1

5 popped
The stack is: 1 0 -1

1 popped
The stack is: 0 -1

0 popped
The stack is: -1

-1 popped
Empty stack
java.util.NoSuchElementException: stack is empty
        at com.deitel.datastructures.List.removeFromFront(List.java:68)
        at com.deitel.datastructures.Stack.pop(Stack.java:18)
        at StackTest.main(StackTest.java:25)
```

Fig. 21.10 | Stack manipulation program. (Part 2 of 2.)

21.6 Queues

Another commonly used data structure is the queue. A queue is similar to a checkout line in a supermarket—the cashier services the person at the *beginning* of the line *first*. Other customers enter the line only at the end and wait for service.

Queue Operations

Queue nodes are removed only from the head (or front) of the queue and are inserted only at the tail (or end). For this reason, a queue is a **first-in, first-out** (**FIFO**) data structure. The insert and remove operations are known as **enqueue** and **dequeue**.

Queue Applications

Queues have many uses in computer systems. Each core in a computer CPU can service only one application at a time. Each application requiring processor time can be placed in a queue. The application at the front of the queue is the next to receive service. Each application gradually advances to the front as the applications before it receive service.

Queues are also used to support **print spooling**. For example, a single printer might be shared by all users of a network. Many users can send print jobs to the printer, even when the printer is already busy. These print jobs can be placed in a queue until the printer becomes available. A program called a **spooler** manages the queue to ensure that, as each print job completes, the next one is sent to the printer.

Information packets also *wait* in queues in computer networks. Each time a packet arrives at a network node, it must be routed to the next node along the path to the packet's final destination. The routing node routes one packet at a time, so additional packets are enqueued until the router can route them.

A file server in a computer network handles file-access requests from many clients throughout the network. Servers have a limited capacity to service requests from clients. When that capacity is exceeded, client requests *wait* in queues.

Queue<E> *Class That Contains a* **List<E>**

Figure 21.11 creates a Queue<E> class that contains a List<E> (Fig. 21.3) object and provides methods enqueue, dequeue, isEmpty and print. Class List<E> contains some methods (e.g., insertAtFront and removeFromBack) that shouldn't be accessible through Queue<E>'s public interface. Using composition enables us to hide class List<E>'s other public methods from Queue<E>'s client code. Each Queue<E> method delegates to a List<E> method—enqueue calls List<E> method insertAtBack (Fig. 21.11, line 14), dequeue calls List<E> method removeFromFront (line 18), isEmpty calls List<E> method isEmpty (line 22) and print calls List<E> method print (line 25). For reuse, class Queue<E> is declared in package com.deitel.datastructures. Again, we do not import List<E> because it's in the same package.

```
1  // Fig. 21.11: Queue.java
2  // Queue uses class List.
3  package com.deitel.datastructures;
4
5  import java.util.NoSuchElementException;
```

Fig. 21.11 | Queue uses class List. (Part 1 of 2.)

```java

public class Queue<E> {
   private List<E> queueList;

   // constructor
   public Queue() {queueList = new List<E>("queue");}

   // add object to queue
   public void enqueue(E object) {queueList.insertAtBack(object);}

   // remove object from queue
   public E dequeue() throws NoSuchElementException {
      return queueList.removeFromFront();
   }

   // determine if queue is empty
   public boolean isEmpty() {return queueList.isEmpty();}

   // output queue contents
   public void print() {queueList.print();}
}
```

Fig. 21.11 | Queue uses class `List`. (Part 2 of 2.)

Testing Class **Queue<E>**

Class `QueueTest`'s (Fig. 21.12) `main` method creates and initializes `Queue<E>` variable `queue` (line 8). Lines 11, 13, 15 and 17 enqueue four integers, taking advantage of *autoboxing* to insert `Integer` objects into the queue. Lines 21–33 dequeue the objects in first-in, first-out order. When the queue is empty, method `dequeue` throws a `NoSuchElementException` and the program displays the exception's stack trace.

```java
1  // Fig. 21.12: QueueTest.java
2  // Class QueueTest.
3  import com.deitel.datastructures.Queue;
4  import java.util.NoSuchElementException;
5
6  public class QueueTest {
7     public static void main(String[] args) {
8        Queue<Integer> queue = new Queue<>();
9
10       // use enqueue method
11       queue.enqueue(-1);
12       queue.print();
13       queue.enqueue(0);
14       queue.print();
15       queue.enqueue(1);
16       queue.print();
17       queue.enqueue(5);
18       queue.print();
19
```

Fig. 21.12 | Class `QueueTest`. (Part 1 of 2.)

```
      // remove objects from queue
      boolean continueLoop = true;

      while (continueLoop) {
         try {
            int removedItem = queue.dequeue(); // remove head element
            System.out.printf("%n%d dequeued%n", removedItem);
            queue.print();
         }
         catch (NoSuchElementException noSuchElementException) {
            continueLoop = false;
            noSuchElementException.printStackTrace();
         }
      }
   }
}
```

```
The queue is: -1
The queue is: -1 0
The queue is: -1 0 1
The queue is: -1 0 1 5

-1 dequeued
The queue is: 0 1 5

0 dequeued
The queue is: 1 5

1 dequeued
The queue is: 5

5 dequeued
Empty queue
java.util.NoSuchElementException: queue is empty
        at com.deitel.datastructures.List.removeFromFront(List.java:68)
        at com.deitel.datastructures.Queue.dequeue(Queue.java:18)
        at QueueTest.main(QueueTest.java:25)
```

Fig. 21.12 | Class QueueTest. (Part 2 of 2.)

21.7 Trees

Lists, stacks and queues are **linear data structures** (i.e., **sequences**). A tree is a nonlinear, two-dimensional data structure with special properties. Tree nodes contain two or more links. This section discusses binary trees (Fig. 21.13) whose nodes each contain two links (one or both of which may be null). The **root node** is the first node in a tree. Each link in the root node refers to a **child**. The **left child** is the first node in the **left subtree** (also known as the root node of the left subtree), and the **right child** is the first node in the **right subtree** (also known as the root node of the right subtree). The children of a specific node are called **siblings**. A node with no children is a **leaf node**. Computer scientists normally draw trees from the root node down—the opposite of the way most trees grow in nature.

In our example, we create a special binary tree called a **binary search tree**. Such a tree (with no duplicate node values) has the characteristic that the values in any left subtree are less than the value in that subtree's parent node, and the values in any right subtree are

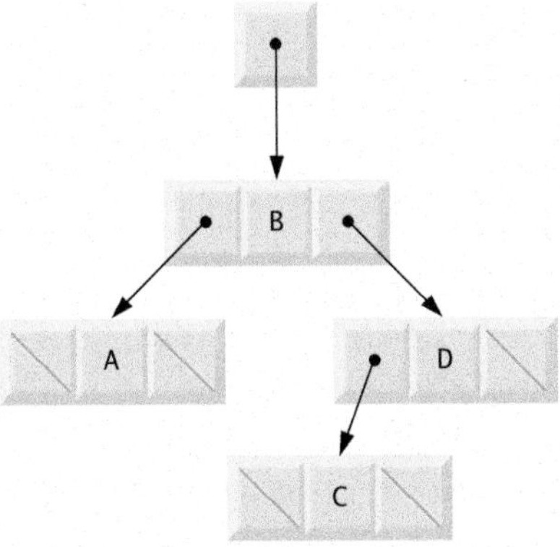

Fig. 21.13 | Binary tree graphical representation.

greater than the value in that subtree's parent node. Figure 21.14 illustrates a binary search tree with 12 integer values. The shape of the binary search tree that corresponds to a set of data can vary, depending on the order in which the values are inserted into the tree.

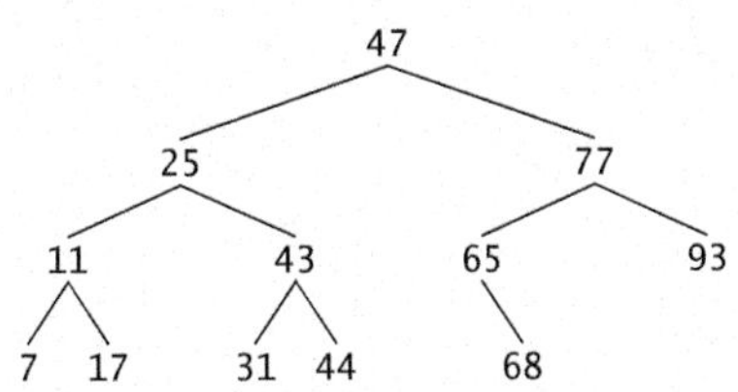

Fig. 21.14 | Binary search tree containing 12 values.

Figures 21.15–21.16 create a generic binary-search-tree class and use it to manipulate a tree of integers. The application in Fig. 21.16 *traverses* the tree (i.e., walks through its nodes) using recursive **inorder, preorder** and **postorder traversals** (trees are almost always processed recursively). The program generates 10 random numbers and inserts each into the tree. Class `Tree<E>` is declared in package `com.deitel.datastructures` for reuse.

```
// Fig. 21.15: Tree.java
// TreeNode and Tree class declarations for a binary search tree.
package com.deitel.datastructures;

// class TreeNode definition
class TreeNode<E extends Comparable<E>> {
   // package access members
   TreeNode<E> leftNode;
   E data; // node value
   TreeNode<E> rightNode;
```

Fig. 21.15 | `TreeNode` and `Tree` class declarations for a binary search tree. (Part 1 of 3.)

```

   // constructor initializes data and makes this a leaf node
   public TreeNode(E nodeData) {
      data = nodeData;
      leftNode = rightNode = null; // node has no children
   }

   // locate insertion point and insert new node; ignore duplicate values
   public void insert(E insertValue) {
      // insert in left subtree
      if (insertValue.compareTo(data) < 0) {
         // insert new TreeNode
         if (leftNode == null) {
            leftNode = new TreeNode<E>(insertValue);
         }
         else { // continue traversing left subtree recursively
            leftNode.insert(insertValue);
         }
      }
      // insert in right subtree
      else if (insertValue.compareTo(data) > 0) {
         // insert new TreeNode
         if (rightNode == null) {
            rightNode = new TreeNode<E>(insertValue);
         }
         else { // continue traversing right subtree recursively
            rightNode.insert(insertValue);
         }
      }
   }
}

// class Tree definition
public class Tree<E extends Comparable<E>> {
   private TreeNode<E> root;

   // constructor initializes an empty Tree of integers
   public Tree() {root = null;}

   // insert a new node in the binary search tree
   public void insertNode(E insertValue) {
      if (root == null) {
         root = new TreeNode<E>(insertValue); // create root node
      }
      else {
         root.insert(insertValue); // call the insert method
      }
   }

   // begin preorder traversal
   public void preorderTraversal() {preorderHelper(root);}

```

Fig. 21.15 | TreeNode and Tree class declarations for a binary search tree. (Part 2 of 3.)

```
    // recursive method to perform preorder traversal
    private void preorderHelper(TreeNode<E> node) {
       if (node == null) {
          return;
       }

       System.out.printf("%s ", node.data); // output node data
       preorderHelper(node.leftNode); // traverse left subtree
       preorderHelper(node.rightNode); // traverse right subtree
    }

    // begin inorder traversal
    public void inorderTraversal() {inorderHelper(root);}

    // recursive method to perform inorder traversal
    private void inorderHelper(TreeNode<E> node) {
       if (node == null) {
          return;
       }

       inorderHelper(node.leftNode); // traverse left subtree
       System.out.printf("%s ", node.data); // output node data
       inorderHelper(node.rightNode); // traverse right subtree
    }

    // begin postorder traversal
    public void postorderTraversal() {postorderHelper(root);}

    // recursive method to perform postorder traversal
    private void postorderHelper(TreeNode<E> node) {
       if (node == null) {
          return;
       }

       postorderHelper(node.leftNode); // traverse left subtree
       postorderHelper(node.rightNode); // traverse right subtree
       System.out.printf("%s ", node.data); // output node data
    }
}
```

Fig. 21.15 | TreeNode and Tree class declarations for a binary search tree. (Part 3 of 3.)

```
// Fig. 21.16: TreeTest.java
// Binary tree test program.
import java.security.SecureRandom;
import com.deitel.datastructures.Tree;

public class TreeTest {
   public static void main(String[] args) {
      Tree<Integer> tree = new Tree<Integer>();
      SecureRandom randomNumber = new SecureRandom();
```

Fig. 21.16 | Binary tree test program. (Part 1 of 2.)

```
10
11         System.out.println("Inserting the following values: ");
12
13         // insert 10 random integers from 0-99 in tree
14         for (int i = 1; i <= 10; i++) {
15            int value = randomNumber.nextInt(100);
16            System.out.printf("%d ", value);
17            tree.insertNode(value);
18         }
19
20         System.out.printf("%n%nPreorder traversal%n");
21         tree.preorderTraversal();
22
23         System.out.printf("%n%nInorder traversal%n");
24         tree.inorderTraversal();
25
26         System.out.printf("%n%nPostorder traversal%n");
27         tree.postorderTraversal();
28         System.out.println();
29      }
30   }
```

```
Inserting the following values:
49 64 14 34 85 64 46 14 37 55

Preorder traversal
49 14 34 46 37 64 55 85

Inorder traversal
14 34 37 46 49 55 64 85

Postorder traversal
37 46 34 14 55 85 64 49
```

Fig. 21.16 | Binary tree test program. (Part 2 of 2.)

Let's walk through the binary tree program. Method `main` of class `TreeTest` (Fig. 21.16) begins by instantiating an empty `Tree<E>` object and assigning its reference to variable `tree` (line 8). Lines 14–18 randomly generate 10 integers, each of which is inserted into the binary tree by calling method `insertNode` (line 17). The program then performs preorder, inorder and postorder traversals (these will be explained shortly) of `tree` (lines 21, 24 and 27, respectively).

Overview of Class `Tree<E>`

Class `Tree<E>` (Fig. 21.15, lines 44–101) requires its type argument to implement interface `Comparable`, so that each value inserted in the tree can be *compared* with the existing values to find the insertion point. The class's `private` `root` (line 45) instance variable is a `TreeNode<E>` reference to the tree's root node. `Tree<E>`'s constructor (line 48) initializes `root` to `null` to indicate that the tree is *empty*. The class contains method `insertNode` (lines 51–58) to insert a new node in the tree and methods `preorderTraversal` (line 61), `inorderTraversal` (line 75) and `postorderTraversal` (line 89) to initiate tree traversals. Each of these methods calls a recursive `private` utility method to perform the traversal operations on the tree's internal representation.

Tree *Method* insertNode

Class `Tree<E>`'s method `insertNode` (lines 51–58) first determines whether the tree is empty. If so, line 53 creates a new `TreeNode`, initializes it with the value being inserted in the tree and assigns the new node to reference `root`. If the tree is not empty, line 61 calls `TreeNode` method `insert` (lines 19–40), which recursively determines the new node's location in the tree, then inserts the node at that location. A node can be inserted only as a leaf node in a binary search tree.

TreeNode *Method* insert

`TreeNode<E>` method `insert` compares the value to insert with the `data` value in the current node. If the insert value is less than the current node's data (line 21), the program determines whether the left subtree is empty (line 23). If so, line 24 allocates a new `TreeNode`, initializes it with the value being inserted and assigns the new node to reference `leftNode`. Otherwise, line 27 recursively calls `insert` for the left subtree to insert the value into the left subtree. If the insert value is greater than the current node's data (line 31), the program determines whether the right subtree is empty (line 33). If so, line 34 allocates a new `TreeNode`, initializes it with the value being inserted and assigns the new node to reference `rightNode`. Otherwise, line 37 recursively calls `insert` for the right subtree to insert the value in the right subtree.

The binary search tree facilitates **duplicate elimination**. While building a tree, the insertion operation recognizes attempts to insert a duplicate value, because a duplicate follows the same "go left" or "go right" decisions on each comparison as the original value did. Thus, the insertion operation eventually compares the duplicate with a node containing the same value. At this point, the insertion operation can decide to *discard* the duplicate value (as we do in this example). In our `Tree<E>` implementation, if the `insertValue` is already in the tree, it's simply ignored. Note that the two duplicate values in the 15 randomly generated values were ignored.

Tree<E> *Methods* preorderTraversal. inorderTraversal *and* postorderTraversal

Methods `preorderTraversal`, `inorderTraversal` and `postorderTraversal` call `Tree` helper methods `preorderHelper` (lines 64–72), `inorderHelper` (lines 78–86) and `postorderHelper` (lines 92–100), respectively, to traverse the tree and print the node values.

Reference `root` is an *implementation detail* that a programmer should not be able to access. By providing these helper methods, class `Tree<E>` enables client code to initiate a traversal without having to pass the `root` node to the method. Methods `preorderTraversal`, `inorderTraversal` and `postorderTraversal` pass the private `root` reference to the appropriate helper method to initiate a traversal. The base case for each helper method determines whether the reference it receives is `null` and, if so, returns immediately.

Let's begin with our inorder traversal of the binary search tree, which prints the node values in *ascending order*. The process of creating a binary search tree actually sorts the data; thus, it's called the **binary tree sort**. Method `inorderHelper` (lines 78–86) defines the steps for an inorder traversal:

1. Traverse the left subtree with a call to `inorderHelper` (line 83).
2. Process the value in the node (line 84).
3. Traverse the right subtree with a call to `inorderHelper` (line 85).

The inorder traversal does not process the value in a node until the values in that node's left subtree are processed. The inorder traversal of the tree in Fig. 21.17 is

```
6 13 17 27 33 42 48
```

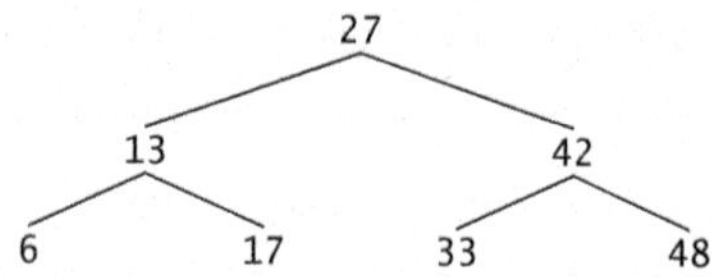

Fig. 21.17 | Binary search tree with seven values.

Method `preorderHelper` (Fig. 21.15, lines 64–72) defines a preorder traversal's steps:

1. Process the value in the node (line 69).
2. Traverse the left subtree with a call to `preorderHelper` (line 70).
3. Traverse the right subtree with a call to `preorderHelper` (line 71).

The preorder traversal processes the value in each node as the node is visited. After processing the value in a particular node, it processes the values in the left subtree, then processes the values in the right subtree. The preorder traversal of the tree in Fig. 21.17 is

```
27 13 6 17 42 33 48
```

Method `postorderHelper` (Fig. 21.15, lines 92–100) defines a postorder traversal's steps:

1. Traverse the left subtree with a call to `postorderHelper` (line 97).
2. Traverse the right subtree with a call to `postorderHelper` (line 98).
3. Process the value in the node (line 99).

The postorder traversal processes the value in each node after the values of all that node's children are processed. The `postorderTraversal` of the tree in Fig. 21.17 is

```
6 17 13 33 48 42 27
```

Binary Tree Search Performance

Searching a binary tree for a value that matches a key value is fast, especially for **tightly packed** (or **balanced**) **trees.** In a tightly packed tree, each level contains about twice as many elements as the previous level. Figure 21.17 is a tightly packed binary tree. A tightly packed binary search tree with n elements has $\log_2 n$ levels. Thus, at most $\log_2 n$ comparisons are required either to find a match or to determine that no match exists. Searching a (tightly packed) 1000-element binary search tree requires at most 10 comparisons, because $2^{10} > 1000$. Searching a (tightly packed) 1,000,000-element binary search tree requires at most 20 comparisons, because $2^{20} > 1{,}000{,}000$.

Other Tree Algorithms

The chapter exercises present algorithms for several other binary tree operations, such as deleting an item from a binary tree, printing a binary tree in a two-dimensional tree format and performing a **level-order traversal of a binary tree**. The level-order traversal visits the nodes of the tree row by row, starting at the root-node level. On each level of the tree, a level-order traversal visits the nodes from left to right. Other binary tree exercises include allowing a binary search tree to contain duplicate values, inserting string values in a binary tree and determining how many levels are contained in a binary tree.

21.8 Wrap-Up

This chapter completes our presentation of data structures. We began in Chapter 16 with an introduction to the built-in collections of the Java Collections Framework and continued in Chapter 20 by showing you how to implement generic methods and collections. In this chapter, you learned to build generic dynamic data structures that grow and shrink at execution time. You learned that linked lists are collections of data items that are "linked up in a chain." You also saw that an application can perform insertions and deletions at the beginning and end of a linked list. You learned that the stack and queue data structures are constrained versions of lists. For stacks, you saw that insertions and deletions are made only at the top. For queues that represent waiting lines, you saw that insertions are made at the tail and deletions are made from the head. You also learned the binary tree data structure. You saw a binary search tree that facilitated high-speed searching and sorting of data and eliminating duplicate data items efficiently. Throughout the chapter, you learned how to create and package these data structures for reusability and maintainability.

In the next chapter, we'll demonstrate additional JavaFX features, including graphics, multimedia and customizing a GUI's look-and-feel with JavaFX's CSS (Cascading Style Sheets) capabilities.

Summary

Section 21.1 Introduction

- Dynamic data structures (p. 847) can grow and shrink at execution time.
- Linked lists (p. 847) are collections of data items "linked up in a chain"—insertions and deletions can be made anywhere in a linked list.
- Stacks (p. 847) are important in compilers and operating systems—insertions and deletions are made only at the top (p. 847) of a stack.
- In a queue, insertions are made at the tail (p. 847) and deletions are made from the head (p. 847).
- Binary trees (p. 847) facilitate high-speed searching and sorting, eliminating duplicate data items efficiently, representing file-system directories and compiling expressions into machine language.

Section 21.2 Self-Referential Classes

- A self-referential class (p. 848) contains a reference that refers to another object of the same class type. Self-referential objects can be linked together to form dynamic data structures.

Section 21.3 Dynamic Memory Allocation

- The limit for dynamic memory allocation (p. 848) can be as large as the available physical memory in the computer or the available disk space in a virtual-memory system. Often the limits are much smaller, because the computer's available memory must be shared among many applications.
- If no memory is available, an `OutOfMemoryError` is thrown.

Section 21.4 Linked Lists

- A linked list is accessed via a reference to the first node of the list. Each subsequent node is accessed via the link-reference member stored in the previous node.
- By convention, the link reference in the last node of a list is set to `null` to mark the end of the list.
- A node can contain data of any type, including objects of other classes.
- A linked list is appropriate when the number of data elements to be stored is unpredictable. Linked lists are dynamic, so the length of a list can increase or decrease as necessary.
- The size of a "conventional" Java array cannot be altered—it's fixed at creation time.
- List nodes normally are not stored in contiguous memory. Rather, they're logically contiguous.
- Packages help manage program components and facilitate software reuse.
- Packages provide a convention for unique type names that helps prevent naming conflicts (p. 859).
- Before a type can be imported into multiple programs, it must be placed in a package. There can be only one `package` declaration (p. 859) in each Java source-code file, and it must precede all other declarations and statements in the file.
- Every package name should start with your Internet domain name in reverse order. After the domain name is reversed, you can choose any other names you want for your package.
- When compiling types in a package, the `javac` command-line option `-d` (p. 860) specifies where to store the package and causes the compiler to create the package's directories if they do not exist.
- The `package` name is part of the fully qualified type name (p. 860).
- A single-type-import declaration (p. 861) specifies one class to import. A type-import-on-demand declaration (p. 861) imports only the classes that the program uses from a particular package.
- The compiler uses a class loader (p. 861) to locate the classes it needs in the classpath. The classpath consists of a list of directories or archive files, each separated by a directory separator (p. 861).
- The classpath for the compiler and JVM can be specified by providing the `-classpath` or `-cp` option (p. 862) to the `javac` or `java` command, or by setting the `CLASSPATH` environment variable. If classes must be loaded from the current directory, include a dot (`.`) in the classpath.

Section 21.5 Stacks

- A stack is a last-in, first-out (LIFO) data structure (p. 863). The primary methods used to manipulate a stack are `push` (p. 863) and `pop` (p. 863), which add a new node to the stack's top and remove a node from the top, respectively. Method `pop` returns the removed node's data.
- When a method call is made, the called method must know how to return to its caller, so the return address is pushed onto the program-execution stack. If a series of method calls occurs, the successive return values are pushed onto the stack in last-in, first-out order.
- The program-execution stack also contains the memory for the method's local variables on each method invocation. When the method returns to its caller, the space for that method's local variables is popped off the stack, and those variables are no longer available to the program.
- Stacks are used by compilers to evaluate arithmetic expressions and generate machine-language code to process the expressions.
- The technique of implementing each stack method as a call to a `List` method is called delegation—the stack method invoked delegates (p. 864) the call to the appropriate `List` method.

Section 21.6 Queues

- A queue is similar to a checkout line in a supermarket—the first person in line is serviced first, and other customers enter the line only at the end and wait to be serviced.
- Queue nodes are removed only from the head of the queue and are inserted only at the tail. For this reason, a queue is referred to as a first-in, first-out FIFO data structure.
- The insert and remove operations for a queue are known as `enqueue` (p. 866) and `dequeue` (p. 866).
- Queues have many uses in computer systems. Each core can service only one application at a time. Entries for the other applications are placed in a queue. The entry at the front of the queue is the next to receive service. Each entry gradually advances to the front of the queue as applications receive service.

Section 21.7 Trees

- A tree is a nonlinear, two-dimensional data structure. Tree nodes contain two or more links.
- A binary tree (p. 868) is a tree whose nodes all contain two links. The root node (p. 868) is the first node in a tree.
- Each link in the root node refers to a child (p. 868). The left child (p. 868) is the first node in the left subtree (p. 868), and the right child (p. 868) is the first node in the right subtree (p. 868).
- The children of a node are called siblings (p. 868). A node with no children is a leaf node (p. 868).
- In a binary search tree (p. 868) with no duplicate values, the values in any left subtree are less than the value in the subtree's parent node, and the values in any right subtree are greater than the value in the subtree's parent node. A node can be inserted only as a leaf node in a binary search tree.
- An inorder traversal (p. 869) of a binary search tree processes the node values in ascending order.
- In a preorder traversal (p. 869), the value in each node is processed as the node is visited. Then the values in the left subtree are processed, then the values in the right subtree.
- In a postorder traversal (p. 869), the value in each node is processed after the values of its children.
- The binary search tree facilitates duplicate elimination (p. 873). As the tree is created, attempts to insert a duplicate value are recognized, because a duplicate follows the same "go left" or "go right" decisions on each comparison as the original value did. Thus, the duplicate eventually is compared with a node containing the same value. The duplicate value can be discarded at this point.
- In a tightly packed tree (p. 874), each level contains about twice as many elements as the previous one. So a tightly packed binary search tree with n elements has $\log_2 n$ levels, and thus at most $\log_2 n$ comparisons would have to be made either to find a match or to determine that no match exists. Searching a (tightly packed) 1000-element binary search tree requires at most 10 comparisons, because $2^{10} > 1000$. Searching a (tightly packed) 1,000,000-element binary search tree requires at most 20 comparisons, because $2^{20} > 1{,}000{,}000$.

Self-Review Exercises

21.1 Fill in the blanks in each of the following statements:

a) A self-________ class is used to form dynamic data structures that can grow and shrink at execution time.

b) A(n) ________ is a constrained version of a linked list in which nodes can be inserted and deleted only from the start of the list.

c) A method that does not alter a linked list, but simply looks at it to determine whether it's empty, is referred to as a(n) ________ method.
d) A queue is referred to as a(n) ________ data structure because the first nodes inserted are the first ones removed.
e) The reference to the next node in a linked list is referred to as a(n) ________.
f) Automatically reclaiming dynamically allocated memory in Java is called ________.
g) A(n) ________ is a constrained version of a linked list in which nodes can be inserted only at the end of the list and deleted only from the start of the list.
h) A(n) ________ is a nonlinear, two-dimensional data structure that contains nodes with two or more links.
i) A stack is referred to as a(n) ________ data structure because the last node inserted is the first node removed.
j) The nodes of a(n) ________ tree contain two link members.
k) The first node of a tree is the ________ node.
l) Each link in a tree node refers to a(n) ________ or ________ of that node.
m) A tree node that has no children is called a(n) ________ node.
n) The three traversal algorithms we mentioned in the text for binary search trees are ________, ________ and ________.
o) When compiling types in a package, the `javac` command-line option ________ specifies where to store the package and causes the compiler to create the package's directories if they do not exist.
p) The compiler uses a(n) ________ to locate the classes it needs in the classpath.
q) The classpath for the compiler and JVM can be specified with the ________ option to the `javac` or `java` command, or by setting the ________ environment variable.
r) There can be only one ________ in a Java source-code file, and it must precede all other declarations and statements in the file.

21.2 What are the differences between a linked list and a stack?

21.3 What are the differences between a stack and a queue?

21.4 Comment on how each of the following entities or concepts contributes to the reusability of data structures:
a) Classes
b) Composition

21.5 Provide the inorder, preorder and postorder traversals of the binary search tree of Fig. 21.18.

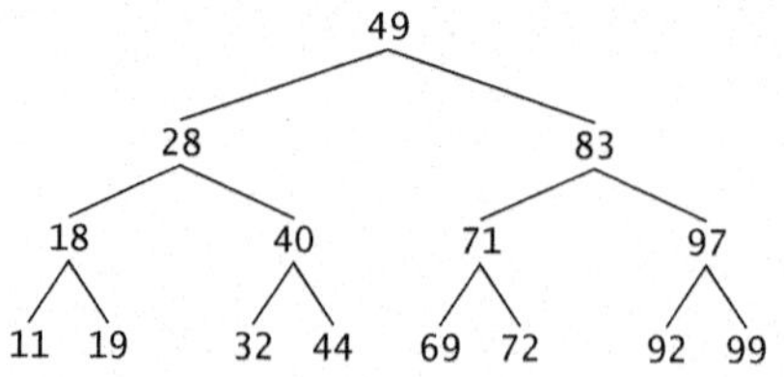

49
28 83
18 40 71 97
11 19 32 44 69 72 92 99

Fig. 21.18 | Binary search tree with 15 nodes.

Answers to Self-Review Exercises

21.1 a) referential. b) stack. c) predicate. d) first-in, first-out (FIFO). e) link. f) garbage collection. g) queue. h) tree. i) last-in, first-out (LIFO). j) binary. k) root. l) child or subtree. m) leaf.

n) inorder, preorder, postorder. o) `-d`. p) class loader. q) `-classpath` or `-cp`, `CLASSPATH`. r) `package` declaration.

21.2 It's possible to insert a node anywhere and remove a node from anywhere in a linked list. Nodes in a stack may be inserted only at the top of the stack and removed only from the top.

21.3 A queue is a FIFO data structure—nodes may be inserted at the tail and deleted from the head. A stack is a LIFO data structure that has a single reference to the stack's top, where both insertion and deletion of nodes are performed.

21.4 Answers for a) and b):

a) Classes allow us to create as many data structure objects as we wish.
b) Composition enables a class to reuse code by storing a reference to an instance of another class in a field. Public methods of the instance can be called by methods in the class that contains the reference.

21.5 The inorder traversal is

```
11 18 19 28 32 40 44 49 69 71 72 83 92 97 99
```

The preorder traversal is

```
49 28 18 11 19 40 32 44 83 71 69 72 97 92 99
```

The postorder traversal is

```
11 19 18 32 44 40 28 69 72 71 92 99 97 83 49
```

Exercises

21.6 *(Concatenating Lists)* Write a program that concatenates two linked-list objects of characters. Class `ListConcatenate` should include a `static` method `concatenate` that takes references to both list objects as arguments and concatenates the second list to the first list.

21.7 *(Inserting into an Ordered List)* Write a program that inserts 25 random integers from 0 to 100 in order into a linked-list object. For this exercise, you'll need to modify the `List<E>` class (Fig. 21.3) to maintain an ordered list. Name the new version of the class `SortedList`.

21.8 *(Merging Ordered Lists)* Modify the `SortedList` class from Exercise 21.7 to include a `merge` method that can merge the `SortedList` it receives as an argument with the `SortedList` that calls the method. Write an application to test method `merge`.

21.9 *(Copying a List Backward)* Write a `static` method `reverseCopy` that receives a `List<E>` as an argument and returns a copy of that `List<E>` with its elements reversed. Test this method in an application.

21.10 *(Printing a Sentence in Reverse Using a Stack)* Write a program that inputs a line of text and uses a stack to display the words of the line in reverse order.

21.11 *(Palindrome Tester)* Write a program that uses a stack to determine whether a string is a palindrome (i.e., the string is spelled identically backward and forward). The program should ignore spaces and punctuation.

21.12 *(Infix-to-Postfix Converter)* Stacks are used by compilers to help in the process of evaluating expressions and generating machine-language code. In this and the next exercise, we investigate how compilers evaluate arithmetic expressions consisting only of constants, operators and parentheses.

Humans generally write expressions like `3 + 4` and `7 / 9` in which the operator (`+` or `/` here) is written between its operands—this is called *infix notation*. Computers "prefer" *postfix notation*, in which the operator is written to the right of its two operands. The preceding infix expressions would appear in postfix notation as `3 4 +` and `7 9 /`, respectively.

To evaluate a complex infix expression, a compiler would first convert the expression to postfix notation and evaluate the postfix version. Each of these algorithms requires only a single left-to-right pass of the expression. Each algorithm uses a stack object in support of its operation, but each uses the stack for a different purpose.

In this exercise, you'll write a Java version of the infix-to-postfix conversion algorithm. In the next exercise, you'll write a Java version of the postfix expression evaluation algorithm. In a later exercise, you'll discover that code you write in this exercise can help you implement a complete working compiler.

Write class `InfixToPostfixConverter` to convert an ordinary infix arithmetic expression (assume a valid expression is entered) with single-digit integers such as

```
(6 + 2) * 5 - 8 / 4
```

to a postfix expression. The postfix version (no parentheses are needed) of the this infix expression is

```
6 2 + 5 * 8 4 / -
```

The program should read the expression into `StringBuffer infix` and use the stack class implemented in this chapter to help create the postfix expression in `StringBuffer postfix`. The algorithm for creating a postfix expression is shown in Fig. 21.19.

Push a left parenthesis `'('` *onto the stack.*
Append a right parenthesis `')'` *to the end of* `infix`*.*

While the stack is not empty, read `infix` *from left to right and do the following:*
    If the current character in `infix` *is a digit, append it to* `postfix`*.*

    If the current character in `infix` *is a left parenthesis, push it onto the stack.*

    If the current character in `infix` *is an operator:*
        Pop operators (if there are any) at the top of the stack while they have equal or higher precedence than the current operator, and append the popped operators to `postfix`*.*
        Push the current character in `infix` *onto the stack.*

    If the current character in `infix` *is a right parenthesis:*
        Pop operators from the top of the stack and append them to `postfix` *until a left parenthesis is at the top of the stack.*
        Pop (and discard) the left parenthesis from the stack.

Fig. 21.19 | Algorithm for creating a postfix expression.

The following arithmetic operations are allowed in an expression:

- `+` addition
- `-` subtraction
- `*` multiplication
- `/` division
- `^` exponentiation
- `%` remainder

The stack should be maintained with stack nodes, each containing data and a reference to the next stack node. Some methods you may want to provide are as follows:

a) Method `convertToPostfix`, which converts the infix expression to postfix notation.
b) Method `isOperator`, which determines whether `c` is an operator.
c) Method `precedence`, which determines whether the precedence of `operator1` (from the infix expression) is less than, equal to or greater than that of `operator2` (from the stack). The method returns `true` if `operator1` has lower precedence than `operator2`. Otherwise, `false` is returned.
d) Method `peek` (this should be added to the stack class), which returns the top value of the stack without popping the stack.

21.13 ***(Postfix Evaluator)*** Write class `PostfixEvaluator` that evaluates a postfix expression such as

```
6 2 + 5 * 8 4 / -
```

The program should read a postfix expression consisting of digits and operators into a `StringBuffer`. The program should read the expression and evaluate it (assume it's valid). The algorithm to evaluate a postfix expression is showing in Fig. 21.20.

```
1  Append a right parenthesis ')' to the end of the postfix expression. When the right-parenthesis
2  character is encountered, no further processing is necessary.
3
4  Until the right parenthesis is encountered, read the expression from left to right.
5     If the current character is a digit, do the following:
6        Push its integer value onto the stack (the integer value of a digit character is its
7        value in the Unicode character set minus the value of '0' in Unicode).
8
9     Otherwise, if the current character is an operator:
10       Pop the two top elements of the stack into variables x and y.
11       Calculate y operator x.
12       Push the result of the calculation onto the stack.
13
14 When the right parenthesis is encountered in the expression, pop the top value of the stack. This is the
15 result of the postfix expression.
```

Fig. 21.20 | Algorithm for evaluating a postfix expression.

[*Note:* In lines 4–12 above (based on the sample expression at the beginning of this exercise), if the operator is `'/'`, the top of the stack is `4` and the next element in the stack is `40`, then pop `4` into `x`, pop `40` into `y`, evaluate `40 / 4` and push the result, `10`, back on the stack. This note also applies to other operators.] The arithmetic operations allowed in an expression are: `+` (addition), `-` (subtraction), `*` (multiplication), `/` (division), `^` (exponentiation) and `%` (remainder).

The stack should be maintained using the modified stack class from Exercise 21.12. You may want to provide the following methods:

a) Method `evaluatePostfixExpression`, which evaluates the postfix expression.
b) Method `calculate`, which evaluates the expression `op1 operator op2`.

21.14 ***(Postfix Evaluator Modification)*** Modify the postfix evaluator program of Exercise 21.13 so that it can process integer operands larger than 9.

21.15 ***(Supermarket Simulation)*** Write a program that simulates a checkout line at a supermarket. The line is a queue object. Customers (i.e., customer objects) arrive at random integer intervals of from 1 to 4 minutes. Also, each customer is serviced at random integer intervals of from 1 to 4 minutes. Obviously, the rates need to be balanced. If the average arrival rate is larger than the average service rate, the queue will grow infinitely. Even with "balanced" rates, randomness can still cause long lines. Run the supermarket simulation for a 12-hour day (720 minutes), using the algorithm in Fig. 21.21. Then answer each of the following:

a) What is the maximum number of customers in the queue at any time?
b) What is the longest wait any one customer experiences?
c) What happens if the arrival interval is changed from 1 to 4 minutes to 1 to 3 minutes?

```
Choose a random integer between 1 and 4 to determine the minute at which the first customer arrives.

At the first customer's arrival time, do the following:
    Determine customer's service time (random integer from 1 to 4).
    Begin servicing the customer.
    Schedule arrival time of next customer (random integer 1 to 4 added to the current time).

For each simulated minute of the day, consider the following:
    If the next customer arrives, proceed as follows:
        Say so.
        Enqueue the customer.
        Schedule the arrival time of the next customer.

    If service was completed for the last customer, do the following:
        Say so.
        Dequeue next customer to be serviced.
        Determine customer's service completion time (random integer from 1 to 4 added to the
            current time).
```

Fig. 21.21 | Algorithm for the supermarket simulation.

21.16 ***(Allowing Duplicates in a Binary Tree)*** Modify Figs. 21.15 and 21.16 to allow the binary tree to contain duplicates.

21.17 ***(Processing a Binary Search Tree of `Strings`)*** Write a program based on the program of Figs. 21.15 and 21.16 that inputs a line of text, tokenizes it into separate words, inserts the words in a binary search tree and prints the inorder, preorder and postorder traversals of the tree.

21.18 ***(Duplicate Elimination)*** In this chapter, we saw that duplicate elimination is straightforward when creating a binary search tree. Describe how you'd perform duplicate elimination when using only a one-dimensional array. Compare the performance of array-based duplicate elimination with the performance of binary-search-tree-based duplicate elimination.

21.19 ***(Depth of a Binary Tree)*** Modify Figs. 21.15 and 21.16 so the `Tree` class provides a method `getDepth` that determines how many levels are in the tree. Test the method in an application that inserts 20 random integers into a `Tree`.

21.20 ***(Recursively Print a List Backward)*** Modify the `List<E>` class of Fig. 21.3 to include method `printListBackward` that recursively outputs the items in a linked-list object in reverse order. Write a test program that creates a list of integers and prints the list in reverse order.

21.21 ***(Recursively Search a List)*** Modify the `List<E>` class of Fig. 21.3 to include method `search` that recursively searches a linked-list object for a specified value. The method should return a reference to the value if it's found; otherwise, it should return `null`. Use your method in a test program that creates a list of integers. The program should prompt the user for a value to locate in the list.

21.22 *(Binary Tree Delete)* In this exercise, we discuss deleting items from binary search trees. The deletion algorithm is not as straightforward as the insertion algorithm. Three cases are encountered when deleting an item—the item is contained in a leaf node (i.e., it has no children), or in a node that has one child or in a node that has two children.

If the item to be deleted is contained in a leaf node, the node is deleted and the reference in the parent node is set to null.

If the item to be deleted is contained in a node with one child, the reference in the parent node is set to reference the child node and the node containing the data item is deleted. This causes the child node to take the place of the deleted node in the tree.

The last case is the most difficult. When a node with two children is deleted, another node in the tree must take its place. However, the reference in the parent node cannot simply be assigned to reference one of the children of the node to be deleted. In most cases, the resulting binary search tree would not embody the following characteristic of binary search trees (with no duplicate values): *The values in any left subtree are less than the value in the parent node, and the values in any right subtree are greater than the value in the parent node.*

Which node is used as a *replacement node* to maintain this characteristic? It's either the node containing the largest value in the tree less than the value in the node being deleted, or the node containing the smallest value in the tree greater than the value in the node being deleted. Let's consider the node with the smaller value. In a binary search tree, the largest value less than a parent's value is located in the left subtree of the parent node and is guaranteed to be contained in the rightmost node of the subtree. This node is located by walking down the left subtree to the right until the reference to the right child of the current node is null. We're now referencing the replacement node, which is either a leaf node or a node with one child to its left. If the replacement node is a leaf node, the steps to perform the deletion are as follows:

a) Store the reference to the node to be deleted in a temporary reference variable.
b) Set the reference in the parent of the node being deleted to reference the replacement node.
c) Set the reference in the parent of the replacement node to `null`.
d) Set the reference to the right subtree in the replacement node to reference the right subtree of the node to be deleted.
e) Set the reference to the left subtree in the replacement node to reference the left subtree of the node to be deleted.

The deletion steps for a replacement node with a left child are similar to those for a replacement node with no children, but the algorithm also must move the child into the replacement node's position in the tree. If the replacement node is a node with a left child, the steps to perform the deletion are as follows:

a) Store the reference to the node to be deleted in a temporary reference variable.
b) Set the reference in the parent of the node being deleted to refer to the replacement node.
c) Set the reference in the parent of the replacement node to reference the left child of the replacement node.
d) Set the reference to the right subtree in the replacement node to reference the right subtree of the node to be deleted.
e) Set the reference to the left subtree in the replacement node to reference the left subtree of the node to be deleted.

Write method `deleteNode`, which takes as its argument the value to delete. Method `deleteNode` should locate in the tree the node containing the value to delete and use the algorithms discussed here to delete the node. If the value is not found in the tree, the method should display a message saying so. Modify the program of Figs. 21.15 and 21.16 to use this method. After deleting an item, call the methods `inorderTraversal`, `preorderTraversal` and `postorderTraversal` to confirm that the delete operation was performed correctly.

21.23 *(Binary Tree Search)* Modify class `Tree` of Fig. 21.15 to include method `contains`, which attempts to locate a specified value in a binary-search-tree object. The method should take as an argument a search key to locate. If the node containing the search key is found, the method should return a reference to that node's data; otherwise, it should return `null`.

21.24 *(Level-Order Binary Tree Traversal)* The program of Figs. 21.15 and 21.16 illustrated three recursive methods of traversing a binary tree—inorder, preorder and postorder traversals. This exercise presents the *level-order traversal* of a binary tree, in which the node values are printed level by level, starting at the root-node level. The nodes on each level are printed from left to right. The level-order traversal is not a recursive algorithm. It uses a queue object to control the output of the nodes. The algorithm is shown in Fig. 21.22. Write method `levelOrder` to perform a level-order traversal of a binary tree object. Modify the program of Figs. 21.15 and 21.16 to use this method. [*Note:* You'll also need to use the queue-processing methods of Fig. 21.11 in this program.]

```
Insert the root node in the queue.

While there are nodes left in the queue, do the following:
    Get the next node in the queue.
    Print the node's value.

    If the reference to the left child of the node is not null:
        Insert the left child node in the queue.

    If the reference to the right child of the node is not null:
        Insert the right child node in the queue.
```

Fig. 21.22 | Algorithm for a level-order binary tree traversal.

21.25 *(Printing Trees)* Modify class `Tree` of Fig. 21.15 to include a recursive `outputTree` method to display a binary tree object. The method should output the tree row by row, with the top of the tree at the left of the screen and the bottom of the tree toward the right. Each row is output vertically. For example, the binary tree illustrated in Fig. 21.18 is output as shown in Fig. 21.23.

The rightmost leaf node appears at the output's top in the rightmost column and the root node appears at the output's left. Each column starts five spaces to the right of the preceding column. Method `outputTree` should receive an argument `totalSpaces` representing the number of spaces preceding the value to be output. (This variable should start at zero so that the root node is output at the left of the screen.) The method uses a modified inorder traversal to output the tree—it starts at the rightmost node in the tree and works back to the left. The algorithm is in Fig. 21.24.

21.26 *(Insert/Delete Anywhere in a Linked List)* Our linked-list class allowed insertions and deletions at only the front and the back of the linked list. These capabilities were convenient for us when we used composition to produce a stack class and a queue class with minimal code simply by reusing the list class. Linked lists are normally more general than those we provided. Modify the linked-list class we developed in this chapter to handle insertions and deletions *anywhere* in the list. Create diagrams comparable to Figs. 21.5 (`insertAtFront`), 21.6 (`insertAtBack`), 21.7 (`removeFromFront`) and 21.8 (`removeFromBack`) that show how to insert a new node in the middle of a linked list and how to remove an existing node from the middle of a linked list.

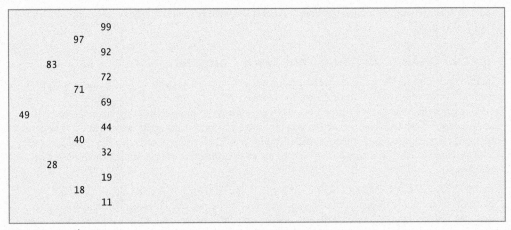

Fig. 21.23 | Sample output of recursive method `outputTree`.

```
While the reference to the current node is not null, perform the following:
    Recursively call outputTree with the right subtree of the current node and totalSpaces + 5.
    Use a for statement to count from 1 to totalSpaces and output spaces.
    Output the value in the current node.
    Set the reference to the current node to refer to the left subtree of the current node.
    Increment totalSpaces by 5.
```

Fig. 21.24 | Algorithm for printing a binary tree.

21.27 ***(Lists and Queues without Tail References)*** Our linked-list implementation (Fig. 21.3) used both a `firstNode` and a `lastNode`. The `lastNode` was useful for the `insertAtBack` and `removeFromBack` methods of the `List` class. The `insertAtBack` method corresponds to the `enqueue` method of the `Queue` class. Rewrite the `List` class so that it does not use a `lastNode`. Thus, any operations on the tail of a list must begin searching the list from the front. Does this affect our implementation of the `Queue` class (Fig. 21.11)?

21.28 ***(Performance of Binary Tree Sorting and Searching)*** One problem with the binary tree sort is that the order in which the data is inserted affects the shape of the tree—for the same collection of data, different orderings can yield binary trees of dramatically different shapes. The performance of the binary tree sorting and searching algorithms is sensitive to the shape of the binary tree. What shape would a binary tree have if its data were inserted in increasing order? in decreasing order? What shape should the tree have to achieve maximal searching performance?

21.29 ***(Indexed Lists)*** As presented in the text, linked lists must be searched sequentially. For large lists, this can result in poor performance. A common technique for improving list-searching performance is to create and maintain an index to the list. An index is a set of references to key places in the list. For example, an application that searches a large list of names could improve performance by creating an index with 26 entries—one for each letter of the alphabet. A search operation for a last name beginning with 'Y' would then first search the index to determine where the 'Y' entries began, then "jump into" the list at that point and search linearly until the desired name was found. This would be much faster than searching the linked list from the beginning. Use the `List` class of Fig. 21.3 as the basis of an `IndexedList` class. Write a program that demonstrates the operation of indexed lists. Be sure to include methods `insertInIndexedList`, `searchIndexedList` and `deleteFromIndexedList`.

Special Section: Building Your Own Compiler

In Exercises 7.36–7.38, we introduced Simpletron Machine Language (SML), and you implemented a Simpletron computer simulator to execute SML programs. In Exercises 21.30–21.34, we build a compiler that converts programs written in a high-level programming language to SML. This section "ties" together the entire programming process. You'll write programs in this new high-level language, compile them on the compiler you build and run them on the simulator you built in Exercise 7.37. You should make every effort to implement your compiler in an object-oriented manner.

21.30 *(The Simple Language)* Before we begin building the compiler, we discuss a simple, yet powerful high-level language similar to early versions of the popular language BASIC. We call the language *Simple*. Every Simple *statement* consists of a *line number* and a Simple *instruction*. Line numbers must appear in ascending order. Each instruction begins with one of the following Simple *commands*: `rem`, `input`, `let`, `print`, `goto`, `if/goto` or `end` (see Fig. 21.25). All commands except `end` can be used repeatedly. Simple evaluates only integer expressions using the `+`, `-`, `*` and `/` operators. These operators have the same precedence as in Java. Parentheses can be used to change the order of evaluation of an expression.

Command	Example statement	Description
`rem`	`50 rem this is a remark`	Any text following the command `rem` is for documentation purposes only and is ignored by the compiler.
`input`	`30 input x`	Display a question mark to prompt the user to enter an integer. Read that integer from the keyboard and store the integer in `x`.
`let`	`80 let u = 4 * (j - 56)`	Assign `u` the value of `4 * (j - 56)`. Note that an arbitrarily complex expression can appear to the right of the equal sign.
`print`	`10 print w`	Display the value of `w`.
`goto`	`70 goto 45`	Transfer program control to line `45`.
`if/goto`	`35 if i == z goto 80`	Compare `i` and `z` for equality and transfer program control to line `80` if the condition is true; otherwise, continue execution with the next statement.
`end`	`99 end`	Terminate program execution.

Fig. 21.25 | Simple commands.

Our Simple compiler recognizes only lowercase letters. All characters in a Simple file should be lowercase. (Uppercase letters result in a syntax error unless they appear in a `rem` statement, in which case they are ignored.) A *variable name* is a single letter. Simple does not allow descriptive variable names, so variables should be explained in remarks to indicate their use in a program. Simple uses only integer variables. Simple does not have variable declarations—merely mentioning a variable name in a program causes the variable to be declared and initialized to zero. The syntax of Simple does not allow string manipulation (reading a string, writing a string, comparing strings, and so on). If a string is encountered in a Simple program (after a command other than `rem`), the compiler generates a syntax error. The first version of our compiler assumes that Simple programs are entered correctly. Exercise 21.33 asks the reader to modify the compiler to perform syntax error checking.

Simple uses the conditional if/goto and unconditional goto statements to alter the flow of control during program execution. If the condition in the if/goto statement is true, control is transferred to a specific line of the program. The following relational and equality operators are valid in an if/goto statement: <, >, <=, >=, == or !=. The precedence of these operators is the same as in Java.

Let's now consider several programs that demonstrate Simple's features. The first program (Fig. 21.26) reads two integers from the keyboard, stores the values in variables a and b and computes and prints their sum (stored in variable c).

```
10 rem   determine and print the sum of two integers
15 rem
20 rem   input the two integers
30 input a
40 input b
45 rem
50 rem   add integers and store result in c
60 let c = a + b
65 rem
70 rem   print the result
80 print c
90 rem   terminate program execution
99 end
```

Fig. 21.26 | Simple program that determines the sum of two integers.

The program of Fig. 21.27 determines and prints the larger of two integers. The integers are input from the keyboard and stored in s and t. The if/goto statement tests the condition s >= t. If the condition is true, control is transferred to line 90 and s is output; otherwise, t is output and control is transferred to the end statement in line 99, where the program terminates.

```
10 rem   determine and print the larger of two integers
20 input s
30 input t
32 rem
35 rem   test if s >= t
40 if s >= t goto 90
45 rem
50 rem   t is greater than s, so print t
60 print t
70 goto 99
75 rem
80 rem   s is greater than or equal to t, so print s
90 print s
99 end
```

Fig. 21.27 | Simple program that finds the larger of two integers.

Simple does not provide a repetition statement (such as Java's for, while or do...while). However, Simple can simulate each of Java's repetition statements by using the if/goto and goto statements. Figure 21.28 uses a sentinel-controlled loop to calculate the squares of several integers. Each integer is input from the keyboard and stored in variable j. If the value entered is the sentinel value

-9999, control is transferred to line 99, where the program terminates. Otherwise, k is assigned the square of j, k is output to the screen and control is passed to line 20, where the next integer is input.

```
10 rem   calculate the squares of several integers
20 input j
23 rem
25 rem   test for sentinel value
30 if j == -9999 goto 99
33 rem
35 rem   calculate square of j and assign result to k
40 let k = j * j
50 print k
53 rem
55 rem   loop to get next j
60 goto 20
99 end
```

Fig. 21.28 | Calculate the squares of several integers.

Using the sample programs of Figs. 21.26–21.28 as your guide, write a Simple program to accomplish each of the following:

a) Input three integers, determine their average and print the result.
b) Use a sentinel-controlled loop to input 10 integers and compute and print their sum.
c) Use a counter-controlled loop to input 7 integers, some positive and some negative, and compute and print their average.
d) Input a series of integers and determine and print the largest. The first integer input indicates how many numbers should be processed.
e) Input 10 integers and print the smallest.
f) Calculate and print the sum of the even integers from 2 to 30.
g) Calculate and print the product of the odd integers from 1 to 9.

21.31 *(Building a Compiler. Prerequisites: Complete Exercises 7.36, 7.37, 21.12, 21.13 and 21.30)* Now that the Simple language has been presented (Exercise 21.30), we discuss how to build a Simple compiler. First, we consider the process by which a Simple program is converted to SML and executed by the Simpletron simulator (see Fig. 21.29). A file containing a Simple program is read by the compiler and converted to SML code. The SML code is output to a file on disk, in which SML instructions appear one per line. The SML file is then loaded into the Simpletron simulator, and the results are sent to a file on disk and to the screen. Note that the Simpletron program developed in Exercise 7.37 took its input from the keyboard. It must be modified to read from a file so it can run the programs produced by our compiler.

The Simple compiler performs two *passes* of the Simple program to convert it to SML. The first pass constructs a *symbol table* (object) in which every *line number* (object), *variable name* (object) and *constant* (object) of the Simple program is stored with its type and corresponding location in the final SML code (the symbol table is discussed in detail below). The first pass also produces the corresponding SML instruction object(s) for each of the Simple statements. If the Simple program contains statements that transfer control to a line later in the program, the first pass results in an SML program containing some "unfinished" instructions. The second pass of the compiler locates and completes the unfinished instructions and outputs the SML program to a file.

First Pass

The compiler begins by reading one statement of the Simple program into memory. The line must be separated into its individual *tokens* (i.e., "pieces" of a statement) for processing and compilation.

(The StreamTokenizer class from the java.io package can be used.) Recall that every statement begins with a line number followed by a command. As the compiler breaks a statement into tokens, if the token is a line number, a variable or a constant, it's placed in the symbol table. A line number is placed in the symbol table only if it's the first token in a statement. The symbolTable object is an array of TableEntry objects representing each symbol in the program. There is no restriction on the number of symbols that can appear in the program. Therefore, the symbolTable for a particular program could be large. Make it a 100-element array for now. You can increase or decrease its size once the program is working.

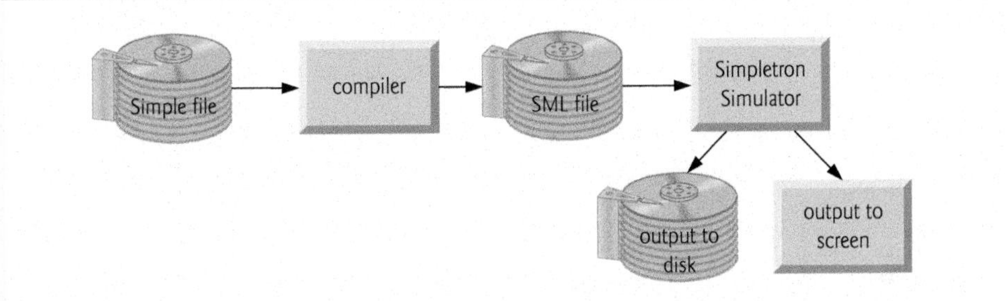

Fig. 21.29 | Writing, compiling and executing a Simple language program.

Each TableEntry object contains three fields. Field symbol is an integer containing the Unicode representation of a variable (remember that variable names are single characters), a line number or a constant. Field type is one of the following characters indicating the symbol's type: 'C' for constant, 'L' for line number or 'V' for variable. Field location contains the Simpletron memory location (00 to 99) to which the symbol refers. Simpletron memory is an array of 100 integers in which SML instructions and data are stored. For a line number, the location is the element in the Simpletron memory array at which the SML instructions for the Simple statement begin. For a variable or constant, the location is the element in the Simpletron memory array in which the variable or constant is stored. Variables and constants are allocated from the end of Simpletron's memory backward. The first variable or constant is stored at location 99, the next at location 98, an so on.

The symbol table plays an integral part in converting Simple programs to SML. We learned in Chapter 7 that an SML instruction is a four-digit integer comprised of two parts—the *operation code* and the *operand*. The operation code is determined by commands in Simple. For example, the simple command input corresponds to SML operation code 10 (read), and the Simple command print corresponds to SML operation code 11 (write). The operand is a memory location containing the data on which the operation code performs its task (e.g., operation code 10 reads a value from the keyboard and stores it in the memory location specified by the operand). The compiler searches symbolTable to determine the Simpletron memory location for each symbol, so the corresponding location can be used to complete the SML instructions.

The compilation of each Simple statement is based on its command. For example, after the line number in a rem statement is inserted in the symbol table, the remainder of the statement is ignored by the compiler, because a remark is for documentation purposes only. The input, print, goto and end statements correspond to the SML *read, write, branch* (to a specific location) and *halt* instructions. Statements containing these Simple commands are converted directly to SML. [*Note:* A goto statement may contain an unresolved reference if the specified line number refers to a statement further into the Simple program file; this is sometimes called a forward reference.]

When a goto statement is compiled with an unresolved reference, the SML instruction must be *flagged* to indicate that the second pass of the compiler must complete the instruction. The flags are stored in a 100-element array flags of type int in which each element is initialized to -1. If the memory location to which a line number in the Simple program refers is not yet known (i.e., it's not in the symbol table), the line number is stored in array `flags` in the element with the same index as the incomplete instruction. The operand of the incomplete instruction is set to `00` temporarily. For example, an unconditional branch instruction (making a forward reference) is left as `+4000` until the second pass of the compiler. The second pass will be described shortly.

Compilation of `if/goto` and `let` statements is more complicated than for other statements—they are the only statements that produce more than one SML instruction. For an `if/goto` statement, the compiler produces code to test the condition and to branch to another line if necessary. The result of the branch could be an unresolved reference. Each of the relational and equality operators can be simulated by using SML's *branch zero* and *branch negative* instructions (or possibly a combination of both).

For a `let` statement, the compiler produces code to evaluate an arbitrarily complex arithmetic expression consisting of integer variables and/or constants. Expressions should separate each operand and operator with spaces. Exercises 21.12 and 21.13 presented the infix-to-postfix conversion algorithm and the postfix evaluation algorithm used by compilers to evaluate expressions. Before proceeding with your compiler, you should complete each of these exercises. When a compiler encounters an expression, it converts the expression from infix notation to postfix notation, then evaluates the postfix expression.

How is it that the compiler produces the machine language to evaluate an expression containing variables? The postfix evaluation algorithm contains a "hook" where the compiler can generate SML instructions rather than actually evaluating the expression. To enable this "hook" in the compiler, the postfix evaluation algorithm must be modified to search the symbol table for each symbol it encounters (and possibly insert it), determine the symbol's corresponding memory location and *push the memory location (instead of the symbol) onto the stack.* When an operator is encountered in the postfix expression, the two memory locations at the top of the stack are popped, and machine language for effecting the operation is produced by using the memory locations as operands. The result of each subexpression is stored in a temporary location in memory and pushed back onto the stack so the evaluation of the postfix expression can continue. When postfix evaluation is complete, the memory location containing the result is the only location left on the stack. This is popped, and SML instructions are generated to assign the result to the variable at the left of the `let` statement.

Second Pass

The second pass of the compiler performs two tasks: Resolve any unresolved references and output the SML code to a file. Resolution of references occurs as follows:

a) Search the `flags` array for an unresolved reference (i.e., an element with a value other than `-1`).
b) Locate the object in array `symbolTable` containing the symbol stored in the `flags` array (be sure that the type of the symbol is `'L'` for line number).
c) Insert the memory location from field `location` into the instruction with the unresolved reference (remember that an instruction containing an unresolved reference has operand `00`).
d) Repeat *Steps (a), (b)* and *(c)* until the end of the `flags` array is reached.

After the resolution process is complete, the entire array containing the SML code is output to a disk file with one SML instruction per line. This file can be read by the Simpletron for execution (after the simulator is modified to read its input from a file). Compiling your first Simple program into an SML file and executing that file should give you a real sense of personal accomplishment.

A Complete Example

The following example illustrates the complete conversion of a Simple program to SML as it will be performed by the Simple compiler. Consider a Simple program that inputs an integer and sums the values from 1 to that integer. The program and the SML instructions produced by the first pass of the Simple compiler are illustrated in Fig. 21.30. The symbol table constructed by the first pass is shown in Fig. 21.31.

Simple program	SML location and instruction	Description
`5 rem sum 1 to x`	*none*	rem ignored
`10 input x`	00 +1099	read x into location 99
`15 rem check y == x`	*none*	rem ignored
`20 if y == x goto 60`	01 +2098	load y (98) into accumulator
	02 +3199	sub x (99) from accumulator
	03 +4200	branch zero to unresolved location
`25 rem   increment y`	*none*	rem ignored
`30 let y = y + 1`	04 +2098	load y into accumulator
	05 +3097	add 1 (97) to accumulator
	06 +2196	store in temporary location 96
	07 +2096	load from temporary location 96
	08 +2198	store accumulator in y
`35 rem   add y to total`	*none*	rem ignored
`40 let t = t + y`	09 +2095	load t (95) into accumulator
	10 +3098	add y to accumulator
	11 +2194	store in temporary location 94
	12 +2094	load from temporary location 94
	13 +2195	store accumulator in t
`45 rem   loop y`	*none*	rem ignored
`50 goto 20`	14 +4001	branch to location 01
`55 rem   output result`	*none*	rem ignored
`60 print t`	15 +1195	output t to screen
`99 end`	16 +4300	terminate execution

Fig. 21.30 | SML instructions produced after the compiler's first pass.

Symbol	Type	Location
5	L	00
10	L	00
'x'	V	99
15	L	01

Fig. 21.31 | Symbol table for program of Fig. 21.30. (Part 1 of 2.)

Symbol	Type	Location
20	L	01
'y'	V	98
25	L	04
30	L	04
1	C	97
35	L	09
40	L	09
't'	V	95
45	L	14
50	L	14
55	L	15
60	L	15
99	L	16

Fig. 21.31 | Symbol table for program of Fig. 21.30. (Part 2 of 2.)

Most Simple statements convert directly to single SML instructions. The exceptions are remarks, the `if/goto` statement in line `20` and the `let` statements. Remarks do not translate into machine language. However, the line number for a remark is placed in the symbol table in case the line number is referenced in a `goto` statement or an `if/goto` statement. Line `20` of the program specifies that, if the condition `y == x` is true, program control is transferred to line `60`. Since line `60` appears later in the program, the first pass of the compiler has not as yet placed `60` in the symbol table. (Statement line numbers are placed in the symbol table only when they appear as the first token in a statement.) Therefore, it's not possible at this time to determine the operand of the SML *branch zero* instruction at location `03` in the array of SML instructions. The compiler places `60` in location `03` of the `flags` array to indicate that the second pass completes this instruction.

We must keep track of the next instruction location in the SML array because there is not a one-to-one correspondence between Simple statements and SML instructions. For example, the `if/goto` statement of line `20` compiles into three SML instructions. Each time an instruction is produced, we must increment the *instruction counter* to the next location in the SML array. Note that the size of Simpletron's memory could present a problem for Simple programs with many statements, variables and constants. It's conceivable that the compiler will run out of memory. To test for this case, your program should contain a *data counter* to keep track of the location at which the next variable or constant will be stored in the SML array. If the value of the instruction counter is larger than the value of the data counter, the SML array is full. In this case, the compilation process should terminate, and the compiler should print an error message indicating that it ran out of memory during compilation. This serves to emphasize that, although the programmer is freed from the burdens of managing memory by the compiler, the compiler itself must carefully determine the placement of instructions and data in memory and must check for such errors as memory being exhausted during the compilation process.

A Step-by-Step View of the Compilation Process

Let's now walk through the compilation process for the Simple program in Fig. 21.30. The compiler reads the first line of the program

```
5 rem sum 1 to x
```

into memory. The first token in the statement (the line number) is determined using a `StringTokenizer` (see Chapter 14). The token returned by the `StringTokenizer` is converted to an integer by using `static` method `Integer.parseInt()`, so the line-number symbol `5` can be located in the symbol table. If the symbol is not found, it's inserted in the symbol table.

We are at the beginning of the program and this is the first line, and no symbols are in the table yet. Therefore, `5` is inserted into the symbol table as type `L` (line number) and assigned the first location in the SML array (`00`). Although this line is a remark, a space in the symbol table is still allocated for the line number (in case it's referenced by a `goto` or an `if/goto`). No SML instruction is generated for a `rem` statement, so the instruction counter is not incremented.

The statement

```
10 input x
```

is tokenized next. The line number `10` is placed in the symbol table as type `L` and assigned the first location in the SML array (`00` because a remark began the program, so the instruction counter is currently `00`). The command `input` indicates that the next token is a variable (only a variable can appear in an `input` statement). `input` corresponds directly to an SML operation code; therefore, the compiler simply has to determine the location of `x` in the SML array. Symbol `x` is not found in the symbol table, so it's inserted into the symbol table as the Unicode representation of `x`, given type `V` and assigned location `99` in the SML array (data storage begins at `99` and is allocated backward). SML code can now be generated for this statement. Operation code `10` (the SML read operation code) is multiplied by 100, and the location of `x` (as determined in the symbol table) is added to complete the instruction. The instruction is then stored in the SML array at location `00`. The instruction counter is incremented by one, because a single SML instruction was produced.

The statement

```
15 rem   check y == x
```

is tokenized next. The symbol table is searched for line number `15` (which is not found). The line number is inserted as type `L` and assigned the next location in the array, `01`. (Remember that `rem` statements do not produce code, so the instruction counter is not incremented.)

The statement

```
20 if y == x goto 60
```

is tokenized next. Line number `20` is inserted in the symbol table and given type `L` at the next location in the SML array `01`. The command `if` indicates that a condition is to be evaluated. The variable `y` is not found in the symbol table, so it's inserted and given the type `V` and the SML location `98`. Next, SML instructions are generated to evaluate the condition. There is no direct equivalent in SML for the `if/goto`; it must be simulated by performing a calculation using `x` and `y` and branching according to the result. If `y` is equal to `x`, the result of subtracting `x` from `y` is zero, so the *branch zero* instruction can be used with the result of the calculation to simulate the `if/goto` statement. The first step requires that `y` be loaded (from SML location `98`) into the accumulator. This produces the instruction `01 +2098`. Next, `x` is subtracted from the accumulator. This produces the instruction `02 +3199`. The value in the accumulator may be zero, positive or negative. The operator is `==`, so we want to *branch zero.* First, the symbol table is searched for the branch location (`60` in this case), which is not found. So, `60` is placed in the `flags` array at location `03`, and the instruction `03 +4200` is generated. (We cannot add the branch location because we've not yet assigned a location to line `60` in the SML array.) The instruction counter is incremented to `04`.

The compiler proceeds to the statement

```
25 rem   increment y
```

The line number `25` is inserted in the symbol table as type `L` and assigned SML location `04`. The instruction counter is not incremented.

When the statement

```
30 let y = y + 1
```

is tokenized, the line number 30 is inserted in the symbol table as type L and assigned SML location 04. Command let indicates that the line is an assignment statement. First, all the symbols on the line are inserted in the symbol table (if they are not already there). The integer 1 is added to the symbol table as type C and assigned SML location 97. Next, the right side of the assignment is converted from infix to postfix notation. Then the postfix expression (y 1 +) is evaluated. Symbol y is located in the symbol table, and its corresponding memory location is pushed onto the stack. Symbol 1 is also located in the symbol table, and its corresponding memory location is pushed onto the stack. When the operator + is encountered, the postfix evaluator pops the stack into the right operand of the operator and pops the stack again into the left operand of the operator, then produces the SML instructions

04 +2098 *(load y)*
05 +3097 *(add 1)*

The result of the expression is stored in a temporary location in memory (96) with the instruction

06 +2196 *(store temporary)*

and the temporary location is pushed onto the stack. Now that the expression has been evaluated, the result must be stored in y (i.e., the variable on the left side of =). So, the temporary location is loaded into the accumulator and the accumulator is stored in y with the instructions

07 +2096 *(load temporary)*
08 +2198 *(store y)*

The reader should immediately notice that SML instructions appear to be redundant. We'll discuss this issue shortly.

When the statement

```
35 rem  add y to total
```

is tokenized, line number 35 is inserted in the symbol table as type L and assigned location 09.

The statement

```
40 let t = t + y
```

is similar to line 30. The variable t is inserted in the symbol table as type V and assigned SML location 95. The instructions follow the same logic and format as line 30, and the instructions 09 +2095, 10 +3098, 11 +2194, 12 +2094 and 13 +2195 are generated. Note that the result of t + y is assigned to temporary location 94 before being assigned to t (95). Once again, the reader should note that the instructions in memory locations 11 and 12 appear to be redundant. Again, we'll discuss this shortly.

The statement

```
45 rem  loop y
```

is a remark, so line 45 is added to the symbol table as type L and assigned SML location 14.

The statement

```
50 goto 20
```

transfers control to line 20. Line number 50 is inserted in the symbol table as type L and assigned SML location 14. The equivalent of goto in SML is the *unconditional branch* (40) instruction that transfers control to a specific SML location. The compiler searches the symbol table for line 20 and finds that it corresponds to SML location 01. The operation code (40) is multiplied by 100, and location 01 is added to it to produce the instruction 14 +4001.

The statement

```
55 rem   output result
```

is a remark, so line 55 is inserted in the symbol table as type L and assigned SML location 15.

The statement

```
60 print t
```

is an output statement. Line number 60 is inserted in the symbol table as type L and assigned SML location 15. The equivalent of print in SML is operation code 11 (*write*). The location of t is determined from the symbol table and added to the result of the operation code multiplied by 100.

The statement

```
99 end
```

is the final line of the program. Line number 99 is stored in the symbol table as type L and assigned SML location 16. The end command produces the SML instruction +4300 (43 is *halt* in SML), which is written as the final instruction in the SML memory array.

This completes the first pass of the compiler. We now consider the second pass. The flags array is searched for values other than -1. Location 03 contains 60, so the compiler knows that instruction 03 is incomplete. The compiler completes the instruction by searching the symbol table for 60, determining its location and adding the location to the incomplete instruction. In this case, the search determines that line 60 corresponds to SML location 15, so the completed instruction 03 +4215 is produced, replacing 03 +4200. The Simple program has now been compiled successfully.

To build the compiler, you'll have to perform each of the following tasks:

a) Modify the Simpletron simulator program you wrote in Exercise 7.37 to take its input from a file specified by the user (see Chapter 15). The simulator should output its results to a disk file in the same format as the screen output. Convert the simulator to be an object-oriented program. In particular, make each part of the hardware an object. Arrange the instruction types into a class hierarchy using inheritance. Then execute the program polymorphically simply by telling each instruction to execute itself with an executeInstruction message.

b) Modify the infix-to-postfix evaluation algorithm of Exercise 21.12 to process multidigit integer operands and single-letter variable-name operands. [*Hint:* Class StringTokenizer can be used to locate each constant and variable in an expression, and constants can be converted from strings to integers by using Integer class method parseInt.] [*Note:* The data representation of the postfix expression must be altered to support variable names and integer constants.]

c) Modify the postfix evaluation algorithm to process multidigit integer operands and variable-name operands. Also, the algorithm should now implement the "hook" discussed earlier so that SML instructions are produced rather than directly evaluating the expression. [*Hint:* Class StringTokenizer can be used to locate each constant and variable in an expression, and constants can be converted from strings to integers by using Integer class method parseInt.] [*Note:* The data representation of the postfix expression must be altered to support variable names and integer constants.]

d) Build the compiler. Incorporate parts b) and c) for evaluating expressions in let statements. Your program should contain a method that performs the first pass of the compiler and a method that performs the second pass of the compiler. Both methods can call other methods to accomplish their tasks. Make your compiler as object oriented as possible.

21.32 ***(Optimizing the Simple Compiler)*** When a program is compiled and converted into SML, a set of instructions is generated. Certain combinations of instructions often repeat themselves, usually in triplets called *productions*. A production normally consists of three instructions, such as *load*, *add* and *store*. For example, Fig. 21.32 illustrates five of the SML instructions that were produced in the compilation of the program in Fig. 21.30. The first three instructions are the production that adds 1 to y. Note that instructions 06 and 07 store the accumulator value in temporary location 96, then load the value back into the accumulator so instruction 08 can store the value in location 98. Often a production is followed by a load instruction for the same location that was just stored. This code can be *optimized* by eliminating the store instruction and the subsequent load instruction that operate on the same memory location, thus enabling the Simpletron to execute the program faster. Figure 21.33 illustrates the optimized SML for the program of Fig. 21.30. Note that there are four fewer instructions in the optimized code—a memory-space savings of 25%.

```
04    +2098  (load)
05    +3097  (add)
06    +2196  (store)
07    +2096  (load)
08    +2198  (store)
```

Fig. 21.32 | Unoptimized code from the program of Fig. 21.30.

Simple program	SML location and instruction	Description
`5 rem sum 1 to x`	*none*	rem ignored
`10 input x`	00 +1099	read x into location 99
`15 rem   check y == x`	*none*	rem ignored
`20 if y == x goto 60`	01 +2098	load y (98) into accumulator
	02 +3199	sub x (99) from accumulator
	03 +4211	branch to location 11 if zero
`25 rem   increment y`	*none*	rem ignored
`30 let y = y + 1`	04 +2098	load y into accumulator
	05 +3097	add 1 (97) to accumulator
	06 +2198	store accumulator in y (98)
`35 rem   add y to total`	*none*	rem ignored
`40 let t = t + y`	07 +2096	load t from location (96)
	08 +3098	add y (98) accumulator
	09 +2196	store accumulator in t (96)
`45 rem   loop y`	*none*	rem ignored
`50 goto 20`	10 +4001	branch to location 01
`55 rem   output result`	*none*	rem ignored
`60 print t`	11 +1196	output t (96) to screen
`99 end`	12 +4300	terminate execution

Fig. 21.33 | Optimized code for the program of Fig. 21.30.

21.33 *(Modifications to the Simple Compiler)* Perform the following modifications to the Simple compiler. Some of these modifications might also require modifications to the Simpletron simulator program written in Exercise 7.37.

a) Allow the remainder operator (`%`) to be used in `let` statements. Simpletron Machine Language must be modified to include a remainder instruction.
b) Allow exponentiation in a `let` statement using `^` as the exponentiation operator. Simpletron Machine Language must be modified to include an exponentiation instruction.
c) Allow the compiler to recognize uppercase and lowercase letters in Simple statements (e.g., `'A'` is equivalent to `'a'`). No modifications to the Simpletron simulator are required.
d) Allow `input` statements to read values for multiple variables such as `input x, y`. No modifications to the Simpletron simulator are required to perform this enhancement to the Simple compiler.
e) Allow the compiler to output multiple values from a single `print` statement, such as `print a, b, c`. No modifications to the Simpletron simulator are required to perform this enhancement.
f) Add syntax-checking capabilities to the compiler so error messages are output when syntax errors are encountered in a Simple program. No modifications to the Simpletron simulator are required.
g) Allow arrays of integers. No modifications to the Simpletron simulator are required to perform this enhancement.
h) Allow subroutines specified by the Simple commands `gosub` and `return`. Command `gosub` passes program control to a subroutine and command `return` passes control back to the statement after the `gosub`. This is similar to a method call in Java. The same subroutine can be called from many `gosub` commands distributed throughout a program. No modifications to the Simpletron simulator are required.
i) Allow repetition statements of the form

```
for x = 2 to 10 step 2
    Simple statements
next
```

This `for` statement loops from `2` to `10` with an increment of `2`. The `next` line marks the end of the body of the `for` line. No modifications to the Simpletron simulator are required.
j) Allow repetition statements of the form

```
for x = 2 to 10
    Simple statements
next
```

This `for` statement loops from `2` to `10` with a default increment of `1`. No modifications to the Simpletron simulator are required.
k) Allow the compiler to process string input and output. This requires the Simpletron simulator to be modified to process and store string values. [*Hint:* Each Simpletron word (i.e., memory location) can be divided into two groups, each holding a two-digit integer. Each two-digit integer represents the Unicode decimal equivalent of a character. Add a machine-language instruction that will print a string beginning at a certain Simpletron memory location. The first half of the Simpletron word at that location is a count of the number of characters in the string (i.e., the length of the string). Each succeeding half-word contains one Unicode character expressed as two decimal digits. The machine-language instruction checks the length and prints the string by translating each two-digit number into its equivalent character.]

l) Allow the compiler to process floating-point values in addition to integers. The Simpletron Simulator must also be modified to process floating-point values.

21.34 *(A Simple Interpreter)* An interpreter is a program that reads a high-level-language program statement, determines the operation to be performed by the statement and executes the operation immediately. The high-level-language program is not converted into machine language first. Interpreters execute more slowly than compilers do, because each statement encountered in the program being interpreted must first be deciphered at execution time. If statements are contained in a loop, they're deciphered each time they are encountered in the loop. Early versions of the BASIC programming language were implemented as interpreters.

Write an interpreter for the Simple language discussed in Exercise 21.30. The program should use the infix-to-postfix converter developed in Exercise 21.12 and the postfix evaluator developed in Exercise 21.13 to evaluate expressions in a `let` statement. The same restrictions placed on the Simple language in Exercise 21.30 should be adhered to in this program. Test the interpreter with the Simple programs written in Exercise 21.30. Compare the results of running these programs in the interpreter with the results of compiling the Simple programs and running them in the Simpletron simulator built in Exercise 7.37.

This page intentionally left blank.

22 JavaFX Graphics and Multimedia

Objectives

In this chapter you'll:

- Use JavaFX graphics and multimedia capabilities to make your apps "come alive" with graphics, animations, audio and video.
- Use external Cascading Style Sheets to customize the look of `Node`s while maintaining their functionality.
- Customize fonts attributes such as font family, size and style.
- Display two-dimensional shape nodes of types `Line`, `Rectangle`, `Circle`, `Ellipse`, `Arc`, `Path`, `Polyline` and `Polygon`.
- Customize the stroke and fill of shapes with solid colors, images and gradients.
- Use `Transform`s to reposition and reorient nodes.
- Display and control video playback with `Media`, `MediaPlayer` and `MediaView`.
- Animate `Node` properties with `Transition` and `Timeline` animations.
- Use an `AnimationTimer` to create frame-by-frame animations.
- Draw graphics on a `Canvas` node.
- Display 3D shapes.

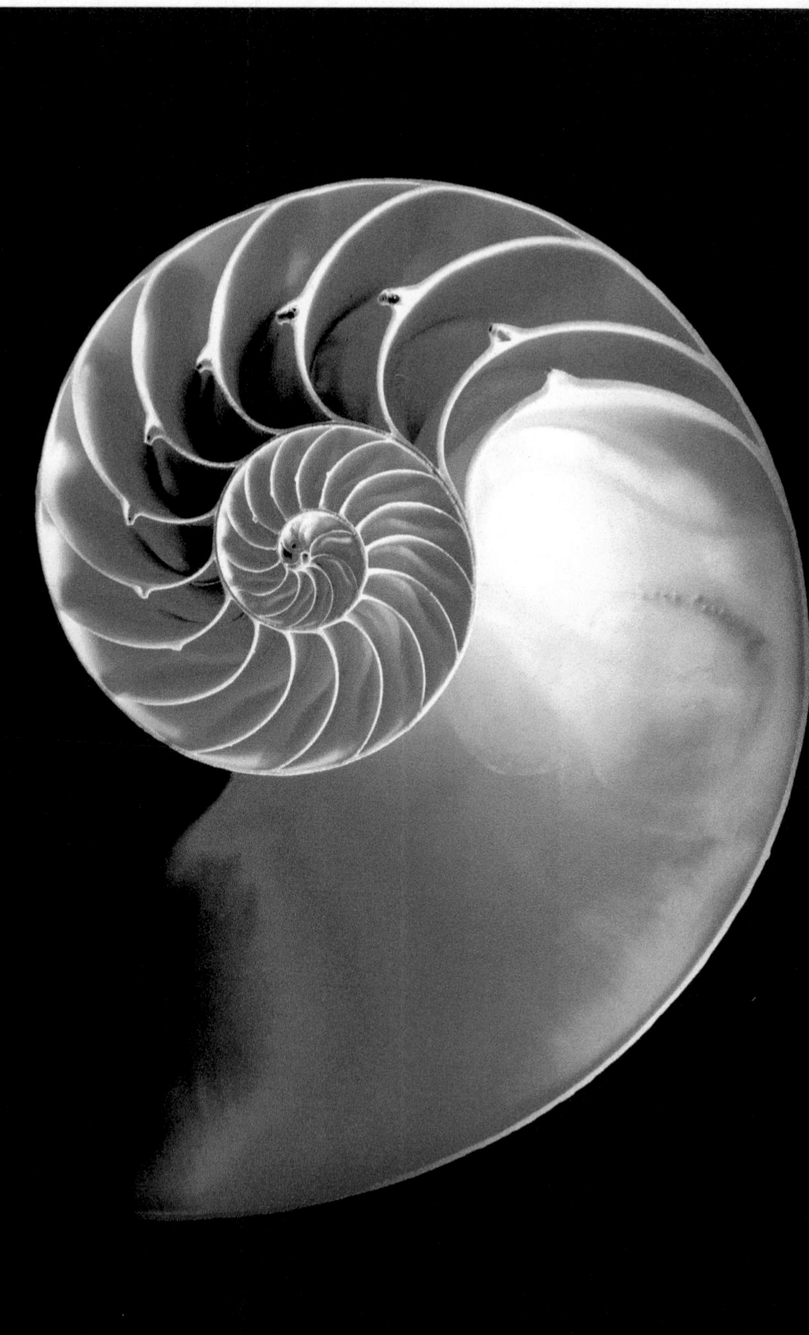

Outline

22.1 Introduction

In this chapter, we continue our discussion of JavaFX from Chapters 12 and 13. Here, we present various JavaFX graphics and multimedia capabilities. You'll:

- Use external Cascading Style Sheets (CSS) to customize the appearance of JavaFX nodes.
- Customize fonts and font attributes used to display text.
- Display two-dimensional shapes, including lines, rectangles, circles, ellipses, arcs, polylines, polygons and custom paths.
- Apply transforms to `Node`s, such as rotating a `Node` around a particular point, scaling, translating (moving) and more.
- Display video and control its playback (e.g., play, pause, stop, and skip to specific time).
- Animate JavaFX `Node`s with `Transition` and `Timeline` animations that change `Node` property values over time. As you'll see, the built-in `Transition` animations change specific JavaFX `Node` properties (such as a `Node`'s stroke and fill colors), but `Timeline` animations can be used to change *any* modifiable `Node` property.
- Create frame-by-frame animations with an `AnimationTimer`.
- Draw two-dimensional graphics on a `Canvas` `Node`.
- Display three-dimensional shapes, including boxes, cylinders and spheres.

Throughout this chapter, we do not show each example's `Application` subclass, because it performs the same tasks we demonstrated in Chapters 12 and 13. Also, some examples do not have controller classes because they simply display JavaFX controls or graphics to demonstrate CSS capabilities.

Project Exercises
At the end of this chapter, we provide dozens of project exercises that you'll find challenging and hopefully entertaining. These will reinforce techniques you've learned and encourage you to investigate additional JavaFX graphics and multimedia capabilities in Oracle's online JavaFX documentation. The **Block Breaker**, **SpotOn**, **Horse Race**, **Cannon** and other exercises will give you experience with game-programming fundamentals.

22.2 Controlling Fonts with Cascading Style Sheets (CSS)

In Chapters 12–13, you built JavaFX GUIs using Scene Builder. You specified a particular JavaFX object's appearance by selecting the object in Scene Builder, then setting its property values in the **Properties** inspector. With this approach, if you want to change the GUI's appearance, you must edit each object. If you have a large GUI in which you want to make the same changes to multiple objects, this can be time consuming and error prone.

In this chapter, we format JavaFX objects using a technology called **Cascading Style Sheets** (CSS) that's typically used to style the elements in web pages. CSS allows you to specify *presentation* (e.g., fonts, spacing, sizes, colors, positioning) separately from the GUI's *structure* and *content* (layout containers, shapes, text, GUI components, etc.). If a JavaFX GUI's presentation is determined entirely by CSS rules, you can simply swap in a new style sheet to change the GUI's appearance.

In this section, you'll use CSS to specify the font properties of several `Label`s and the spacing and padding properties for the `VBox` layout that contains the `Label`s. You'll place **CSS rules** that specify the font properties, spacing and padding in a separate file that ends with the **`.css` filename extension**, then reference that file from the FXML. As you'll see,

- before referencing the CSS file from the FXML, Scene Builder displays the GUI without styling, and
- after referencing the CSS file from the FXML, Scene Builder renders the GUI with the CSS rules applied to the appropriate objects.

For a complete reference that shows

- all the JavaFX CSS properties,
- the JavaFX `Node` types to which the attributes can be applied, and
- the allowed values for each attribute

visit:

```
https://docs.oracle.com/javase/8/javafx/api/javafx/scene/doc-files/
   cssref.html
```

22.2.1 CSS That Styles the GUI

Figure 22.1 presents this app's CSS rules that specify the `VBox`'s and each `Label`'s style. This file is located in the same folder as the rest of the example's files.

***.vbox* CSS Rule—Style Class Selectors**
Lines 4–7 define the `.vbox` CSS rule that will be applied to this app's `VBox` object (lines 8–18 of Fig. 22.2). Each CSS rule begins with a **CSS selector** which specifies the JavaFX objects that will be styled according to the rule. In the `.vbox` CSS rule, `.vbox` is a **style**

```
1  /* Fig. 22.1: FontsCSS.css */
2  /* CSS rules that style the VBox and Labels */
3
4  .vbox {
5     -fx-spacing: 10;
6     -fx-padding: 10;
7  }
8
9  #label1 {
10    -fx-font: bold 14pt Arial;
11 }
12
13 #label2 {
14    -fx-font: 16pt "Times New Roman";
15 }
16
17 #label3 {
18    -fx-font: bold italic 16pt "Courier New";
19 }
20
21 #label4 {
22    -fx-font-size: 14pt;
23    -fx-underline: true;
24 }
25
26 #label5 {
27    -fx-font-size: 14pt;
28 }
29
30 #label5 .text {
31    -fx-strikethrough: true;
32 }
```

Fig. 22.1 | CSS rules that style the `VBox` and `Labels`.

class selector. The CSS properties in this rule are applied to any JavaFX object that has a `styleClass` property with the value `"vbox"`. In CSS, a style class selector begins with a dot (`.`) and is followed by its **class name** (not to be confused with a Java class). By convention, selector names typically have all lowercase letters, and multi-word names separate each word from the next with a dash (`-`).

Each CSS rule's body is delimited by a set of required braces (`{}`) containing the CSS properties that are applied to objects matching the CSS selector. Each JavaFX CSS property name begins with `-fx-`[1] followed by the name of the corresponding JavaFX object's property in all lowercase letters. So, **`-fx-spacing`** in line 5 of Fig. 22.1 defines the value for a JavaFX object's `spacing` property, and **`-fx-padding`** in line 6 defines the value for a JavaFX object's `padding` property. The value of each property is specified to the right of the required colon (`:`). In this case, we set `-fx-spacing` to `10` to place 10 pixels of vertical

1. According to the JavaFX CSS Reference Guide at `https://docs.oracle.com/javase/8/javafx/api/javafx/scene/doc-files/cssref.html`, JavaFX CSS property names are designed to be processed in style sheets that may also contain HTML CSS. For this reason, JavaFX's CSS property names are prefixed with "`-fx-`" to ensure that they have distinct names from their HTML CSS counterparts.

space between objects in the `VBox`, and `-fx-padding` to `10` to separate the `VBox`'s contents from the `VBox`'s edges by 10 pixels at the top, right, bottom and left edges. You also can specify the `-fx-padding` with four values separated by spaces. For example,

```
-fx-padding: 10 5 10 5
```

specifies 10 pixels for the top padding, 5 for the right, 10 for the bottom and 5 for the left. We show how to apply the `.vbox` CSS rule to the `VBox` object in Section 22.2.2.

#label1 CSS Rule—ID Selectors

Lines 9–11 define the `#label1` CSS rule. Selectors that begin with `#` are known as **ID selectors**—they are applied to objects with the specified ID. In this case, the `#label1` selector matches the object with the `fx:id label1`—that is, the `Label` object in line 12 of Fig. 22.2. The `#label1` CSS rule specifies the CSS property

```
-fx-font: bold 14pt Arial;
```

This rule sets an object's `font` property. The object to which this rule applies displays its text in a bold, 14-point, Arial font. The `-fx-font` property can specify all aspects of a font, including its style, weight, size and font family—the size and font family are required. There are also properties for setting each font component: `-fx-font-style`, `-fx-font-weight`, `-fx-font-size` and `-fx-font-family`. These are applied to a JavaFX object's similarly named properties. For more information on specifying CSS font attributes, see

```
https://docs.oracle.com/javase/8/javafx/api/javafx/scene/doc-files/
   cssref.html#typefont
```

For a complete list of CSS selector types and how you can combine them, see

```
https://www.w3.org/TR/css3-selectors/
```

#label2 CSS Rule

Lines 13–15 define the `#label2` CSS rule that will be applied to the `Label` with the `fx:id label2`. The CSS property

```
-fx-font: 16pt "Times New Roman";
```

specifies only the required font size (`16pt`) and font family (`"Times New Roman"`) components—font family names with multiple words must be enclosed in double quotes.

#label3 CSS Rule

Lines 17–19 define the `#label3` CSS rule that will be applied to the `Label` with the `fx:id label3`. The CSS property

```
-fx-font: bold italic 16pt "Courier New";
```

specifies all the font components—weight (`bold`), style (`italic`), size (`16pt`) and font family (`"Courier New"`).

#label4 CSS Rule

Lines 21–24 define the `#label4` CSS rule that will be applied to the `Label` with the `fx:id label4`. The CSS property

```
-fx-font-size: 14pt;
```

specifies the font size `14pt`—all other aspects of this `Label`'s font are inherited from the `Label`'s parent container. The CSS property

```
-fx-underline: true;
```

indicates that the text in the `Label` should be *underlined*—the default value for this property is `false`.

`#label5` CSS Rule

Lines 26–28 define the `#label5` CSS rule that will be applied to the `Label` with the `fx:id` `label5`. The CSS property

```
-fx-font-size: 14pt;
```

specifies the font size `14pt`.

`#label5 .text` CSS Rule

Lines 30–32 define the `#label5 .text` CSS rule that will be applied to the `Text` object within the `Label` that has the `fx:id` value `"label5"`. The selector in this case is a combination of an ID selector and a style class selector. Each `Label` contains a `Text` object with the CSS class `.text`. When applying this CSS rule, JavaFX first locates the object with the ID `label5`, then within that object looks for a nested object that specifies the class `text`.

The CSS property

```
-fx-strikethrough: true;
```

indicates that the text in the `Label` should be displayed with a line through it—the default value for this property is `false`.

22.2.2 FXML That Defines the GUI—Introduction to XML Markup[2]

Figure 22.2 shows the contents of `FontCSS.fxml`—the `FontCSS` app's FXML GUI, which consists of a `VBox` layout element (lines 8–18) containing five `Label` elements (lines 12–16). When you first drag five `Label`s onto the `VBox` and configure their text (Fig. 22.2(a)), all the `Label`s initially have the same appearance in Scene Builder. Also, initially there's no spacing between and around the `Label`s in the `VBox`.

```
1  <?xml version="1.0" encoding="UTF-8"?>
2  <!-- Fig. 22.2: FontCSS.fxml -->
3  <!-- FontCSS GUI that is styled via external CSS -->
4
5  <?import javafx.scene.control.Label?>
6  <?import javafx.scene.layout.VBox?>
7
```

Fig. 22.2 | `FontCSS` GUI that is styled via external CSS. (Part 1 of 2.)

2. In many of this chapter's examples, after creating a GUI in Scene Builder, we used a text editor to format the FXML, remove unnecessary properties that were inserted by Scene Builder and properties that we specified via CSS rules. For this reason, when you build these examples from scratch, your FXML may differ from what's shown in this chapter. You also can set a property to its default value in Scene Builder to remove it from the FXML.

```
8   <VBox styleClass="vbox" stylesheets="@FontCSS.css"
9      xmlns="http://javafx.com/javafx/8.0.60"
10     xmlns:fx="http://javafx.com/fxml/1">
11     <children>
12        <Label fx:id="label1" text="Arial 14pt bold" />
13        <Label fx:id="label2" text="Times New Roman 16pt plain" />
14        <Label fx:id="label3" text="Courier New 16pt bold and italic" />
15        <Label fx:id="label4" text="Default font 14pt with underline" />
16        <Label fx:id="label5" text="Default font 14pt with strikethrough" />
17     </children>
18  </VBox>
```

a) GUI as it appears in Scene Builder *before* referencing the completed CSS file

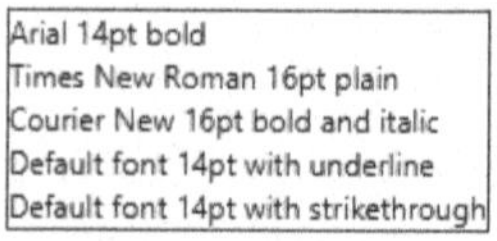

Arial 14pt bold
Times New Roman 16pt plain
Courier New 16pt bold and italic
Default font 14pt with underline
Default font 14pt with strikethrough

b) GUI as it appears in Scene Builder *after* referencing the `FontCSS.css` file containing the rules that style the **VBox** and the **`Label`s**

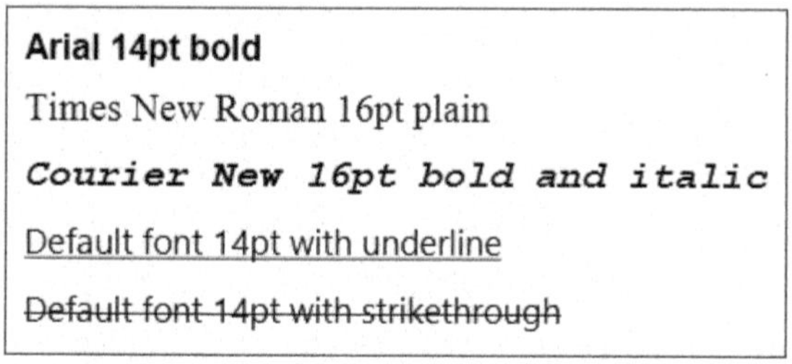

Arial 14pt bold
Times New Roman 16pt plain
Courier New 16pt bold and italic
Default font 14pt with underline
~~Default font 14pt with strikethrough~~

c) GUI as it appears in the *running* application

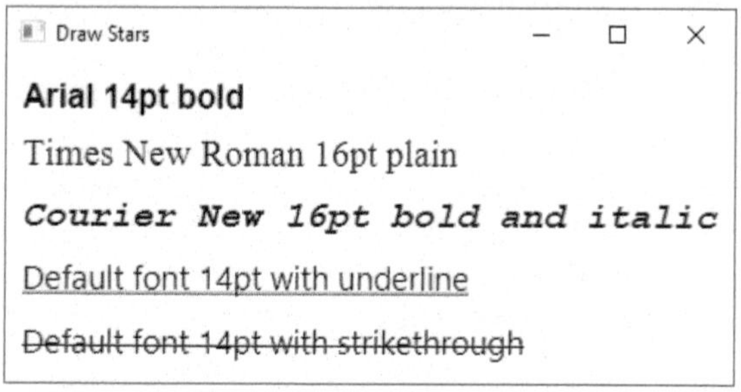

Draw Stars
Arial 14pt bold
Times New Roman 16pt plain
Courier New 16pt bold and italic
Default font 14pt with underline
~~Default font 14pt with strikethrough~~

Fig. 22.2 | `FontCSS` GUI that is styled via external CSS. (Part 2 of 2.)

XML Declaration

Each FXML document begins with an **XML declaration** (line 1), which must be the first line in the file and indicates that the document contains XML markup. For FXML documents, line 1 must appear as shown in Fig. 22.2. The XML declaration's **`version` attribute** specifies the XML syntax version (`1.0`) used in the document. The **`encoding` attribute** specifies the format of the document's character—XML documents typically contain Unicode characters in `UTF-8` format (`https://en.wikipedia.org/wiki/UTF-8`).

Attributes

Each XML attribute has the format

```
name="value"
```

The *name* and *value* are separated by = and the *value* placed in quotation marks (""). Multiple *name=value* pairs are separated by whitespace.

Comments

Lines 2–3 are XML comments, which begin with `<!--` and end with `-->`, and can be placed almost anywhere in an XML document. XML comments can span to multiple lines.

FXML **`import`** *Declarations*

Lines 5–6 are FXML **`import` declarations** that specify the fully qualified names of the JavaFX types used in the document. Such declarations are delimited by `<?import` and `?>`.

Elements

XML documents contain **elements** that specify the document's structure. Most elements are delimited by a **start tag** and an **end tag**:

- A start tag consists of **angle brackets** (< and >) containing the element's name followed by zero or more attributes. For example, the `VBox` element's start tag (lines 8–10) contains four attributes.
- An end tag consists of the element name preceded by a **forward slash** (/) in angle brackets—for example, `</VBox>` in line 18.

An element's start and end tags enclose the element's contents. In this case, lines 11–17 declare other elements that describe the `VBox`'s contents. Every XML document must have exactly one **root element** that contains all the other elements. In Fig. 22.2, `VBox` is the root.

A layout element always contains a **`children`** element (lines 11–17) containing the child `Nodes` that are arranged by that layout. For a `VBox`, the `children` element contains the child `Nodes` in the order they're displayed on the screen from top to bottom. The elements in lines 12–16 represent the `VBox`'s five `Labels`. These are **empty elements** that use the shorthand start-tag-only notation:

```
<ElementName attributes />
```

in which the empty element's start tag ends with `/>` rather than `>`. The empty element:

```
<Label fx:id="label1" text="Arial 14pt bold" />
```

is equivalent to

```
<Label fx:id="label1" text="Arial 14pt bold">
</Label>
```

which does not have content between the start and end tags. Empty elements often have attributes (such as `fx:id` and `text` for each `Label` element).

XML Namespaces

In lines 9–10, the `VBox` attributes

```
xmlns="http://javafx.com/javafx/8.0.60"
xmlns:fx="http://javafx.com/fxml/1"
```

specify the XML namespaces used in FXML markup. An XML **namespace** specifies a collection of element and attribute names that you can use in the document. The attribute

```
xmlns="http://javafx.com/javafx/8.0.60"
```

specifies the default namespace. FXML `import` declarations (like those in lines 5–6) add names to this namespace for use in the document. The attribute

```
xmlns:fx="http://javafx.com/fxml/1"
```

specifies JavaFX's `fx` namespace. Elements and attributes from this namespace (such as the `fx:id` attribute) are used internally by the `FXMLLoader` class. For example, for each FXML element that specifies an `fx:id`, the `FXMLLoader` initializes a corresponding variable in the controller class. The `fx:` in `fx:id` is a **namespace prefix** that specifies the namespace (`fx`) that defines the attribute (`id`). Every element or attribute name in Fig. 22.2 that does not begin with `fx:` is part of the default namespace.

22.2.3 Referencing the CSS File from FXML

For the `Labels` to appear with the fonts shown in Fig. 22.2(b), we must reference the `FontCSS.css` file from the FXML. This enables Scene Builder to apply the CSS rules to the GUI. To reference the CSS file:

1. Select the `VBox` in the Scene Builder.
2. In the **Properties** inspector, click the **+** button under the **Stylesheets** heading.
3. In the dialog that appears, select the `FontCSS.css` file and click **Open**.

This adds the `stylesheets` attribute (line 8)

```
stylesheets="@FontCSS.css"
```

to the `VBox`'s opening tag (lines 8–10). The `@` symbol—called the local resolution operator in FXML—indicates that the file `FontCSS.css` is located relative to the FXML file on disk. No path information is specified here, so the CSS file and the FXML file must be in the same folder.

22.2.4 Specifying the VBox's Style Class

The preceding steps apply the font styles to the `Labels`, based on their ID selectors, but do not apply the spacing and padding to the `VBox`. Recall that for the `VBox` we defined a CSS rule using a *style class selector* with the name `.vbox`. To apply the CSS rule to the `VBox`:

1. Select the `VBox` in the Scene Builder.
2. In the **Properties** inspector, under the **Style Class** heading, specify the value `vbox` *without* the dot, then press *Enter* to complete the setting.

This adds the `styleClass` attribute

```
styleClass="vbox"
```

to the `VBox`'s opening tag (line 8). At this point the GUI appears as in Fig. 22.2(b). You can now run the app to see the output in Fig. 22.2(c).

22.2.5 Programmatically Loading CSS

In the `FontCSS` app, the FXML referenced the CSS style sheet directly (line 8). It's also possible to load CSS files dynamically and add them to a `Scene`'s collection of style sheets. You might do this, for example, in an app that enables users to choose their preferred look-and-feel, such as a light background with dark text vs. a dark background with light text.

To load a stylesheet dynamically, add the following statement to the `Application` subclass's `start` method:

```
scene.getStylesheets().add(
   getClass().getResource("FontCSS.css").toExternalForm());
```

In the preceding statement:

- Inherited `Object` method `getClass` obtains a `Class` object representing the app's `Application` subclass.
- `Class` method `getResource` returns a `URL` representing the location of the file `FontCSS.css`. Method `getResource` looks for the file in the same location from which the `Application` subclass was loaded.
- `URL` method `toExternalForm` returns the `URL`'s `String` representation. This is passed to the `add` method of the `Scene`'s collection of style sheets—this adds the style sheet to the scene.

22.3 Displaying Two-Dimensional Shapes

JavaFX has two ways to draw shapes:

- You can define **`Shape`** and **`Shape3D`** (package **`javafx.scene.shape`**) subclass objects, add them to a container in the JavaFX stage and manipulate them like other JavaFX `Node`s.
- You can add a **`Canvas`** object (package **`javafx.scene.canvas`**) to a container in the JavaFX stage, then draw on it using various `GraphicsContext` methods.

The `BasicShapes` example presented in this section shows you how to display two-dimensional `Shape`s of types **`Line`**, **`Rectangle`**, **`Circle`**, **`Ellipse`** and **`Arc`**. Like other `Node` types, you can drag shapes from the Scene Builder **Library**'s **Shapes** category onto the design area, then configure them via the **Inspector**'s **Properties**, **Layout** and **Code** sections—of course, you also may create objects of any JavaFX `Node` type programmatically.

22.3.1 Defining Two-Dimensional Shapes with FXML

Figure 22.3 shows the completed FXML for the `BasicShapes` app, which references the `BasicShapes.css` file (line 13) that we present in Section 22.3.2. For this app we dragged two `Line`s, a `Rectangle`, a `Circle`, an `Ellipse` and an `Arc` onto a `Pane` layout and configured their dimensions and positions in Scene Builder.

```
1 <?xml version="1.0" encoding="UTF-8"?>
2 <!-- Fig. 22.3: BasicShapes.fxml -->
3 <!-- Defining Shape objects and styling via CSS -->
4
5 <?import javafx.scene.layout.Pane?>
6 <?import javafx.scene.shape.Arc?>
7 <?import javafx.scene.shape.Circle?>
8 <?import javafx.scene.shape.Ellipse?>
```

Fig. 22.3 | Defining `Shape` objects and styling via CSS. (Part 1 of 2.)

```
9  <?import javafx.scene.shape.Line?>
10 <?import javafx.scene.shape.Rectangle?>
11
12 <Pane id="Pane" prefHeight="110.0" prefWidth="630.0"
13    stylesheets="@BasicShapes.css" xmlns="http://javafx.com/javafx/8.0.60"
14    xmlns:fx="http://javafx.com/fxml/1">
15    <children>
16       <Line fx:id="line1" endX="100.0" endY="100.0"
17          startX="10.0" startY="10.0" />
18       <Line fx:id="line2" endX="10.0" endY="100.0"
19          startX="100.0" startY="10.0" />
20       <Rectangle fx:id="rectangle" height="90.0" layoutX="120.0"
21          layoutY="10.0" width="90.0" />
22       <Circle fx:id="circle" centerX="270.0" centerY="55.0"
23          radius="45.0" />
24       <Ellipse fx:id="ellipse" centerX="430.0" centerY="55.0"
25          radiusX="100.0" radiusY="45.0" />
26       <Arc fx:id="arc" centerX="590.0" centerY="55.0" length="270.0"
27          radiusX="45.0" radiusY="45.0" startAngle="45.0" type="ROUND" />
28    </children>
29 </Pane>
```

a) GUI in Scene Builder with CSS applied—Ellipse's image fill does not show.

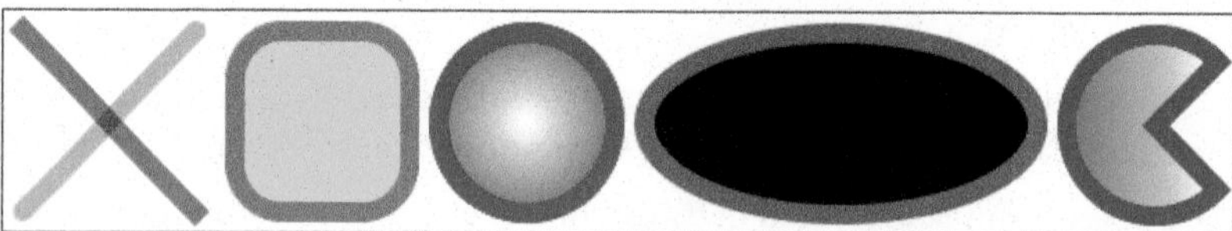

b) GUI in running app—Ellipse's image fill displays correctly.

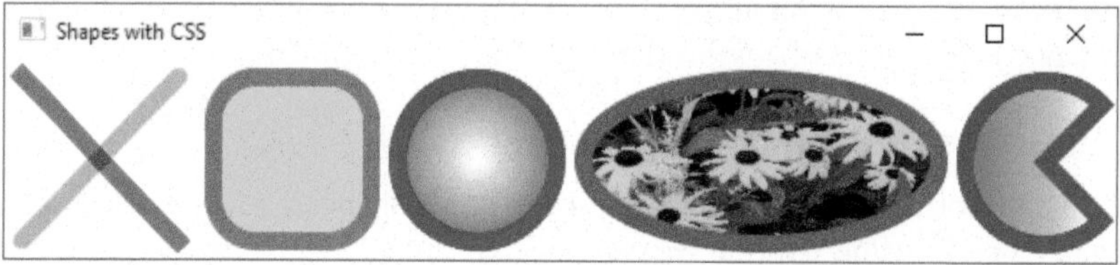

Fig. 22.3 | Defining Shape objects and styling via CSS. (Part 2 of 2.)

For each property you can set in Scene Builder, there is a corresponding attribute in FXML. For example, the `Pane` object's **Pref Height** property in Scene Builder corresponds to the `prefHeight` attribute (line 12) in FXML. When you build this GUI in Scene Builder, use the FXML attribute values shown in Fig. 22.3. Note that as you drag each shape onto your design, Scene Builder automatically configures certain properties, such as the **Fill** and **Stroke** colors for the `Rectangle`, `Circle`, `Ellipse` and `Arc`. For each such property that does not have a corresponding attribute shown in Fig. 22.3, you can remove the attribute either by setting the property to its default value in Scene Builder or by manually editing the FXML.

Lines 6–10 import the shape classes used in the FXML. We also specified `fx:id` values (lines 16 and 18) for the two `Line`s—we use these values in CSS rules with ID selectors to define separate styles for each `Line`. We removed the shapes' `fill`, `stroke` and `strokeType` properties that Scene Builder autogenerated. The default `fill` for a shape is black. The default stroke is a one-pixel black line. The default `strokeType` is centered—based on the stroke's thickness, half the thickness appears inside the shape's bounds and half outside. You also may display a shape's stroke completely inside or outside the shape's bounds. We specify the strokes and fills with the styles in Section 22.3.2.

`Line` *Objects*

Lines 16–17 and 18–19 define two `Line`s. Each connects two endpoints specified by the properties **`startX`**, **`startY`**, **`endX`** and **`endY`**. The *x*- and *y*-coordinates are measured from the top-left corner of the `Pane`, with *x*-coordinates increasing left to right and *y*-coordinates increasing top to bottom. If you specify a `Line`'s **`layoutX`** and **`layoutY`** properties, then the `startX`, `startY`, `endX` and `endY` properties are measured from that point.

`Rectangle` *Object*

Lines 20–21 define a `Rectangle` object. A `Rectangle` is displayed based on its `layoutX`, `layoutY`, **`width`** and **`height`** properties:

- A `Rectangle`'s upper-left corner is positioned at the coordinates specified by the `layoutX` and `layoutY` properties, which are inherited from class `Node`.
- A `Rectangle`'s dimensions are specified by the `width` and `height` properties—in this case they have the same value, so the `Rectangle` defines a square.

`Circle` *Object*

Lines 22–23 define a `Circle` object with its center at the point specified by the **`centerX`** and **`centerY`** properties. The **`radius`** property determines the `Circle`'s size (two times the `radius`) around its center point.

`Ellipse` *Object*

Lines 24–25 define an `Ellipse` object. Like a `Circle`, an `Ellipse`'s center is specified by the **`centerX`** and **`centerY`** properties. You also specify **`radiusX`** and **`radiusY`** properties that help determine the `Ellipse`'s width (left and right of the center point) and height (above and below the center point).

`Arc` *Object*

Lines 26–27 define an `Arc` object. Like an `Ellipse`, an `Arc`'s center is specified by the **`centerX`** and **`centerY`** properties, and the **`radiusX`** and **`radiusY`** properties determine the `Arc`'s width and height. For an `Arc`, you also specify:

- **`length`**—The arc's length in degrees (0–360). Positive values sweep counterclockwise.
- **`startAngle`**—The angle in degrees at which the arc should begin.
- **`type`**—How the arc should be closed. `ROUND` indicates that the starting and ending points of the arc should be connected to the center point by straight lines. You also may choose `OPEN`, which does not connect the start and end points, or `CHORD`, which connects the start and end points with a straight line.

22.3.2 CSS That Styles the Two-Dimensional Shapes

Figure 22.4 shows the CSS for the `BasicShapes` app. In this CSS file, we define two CSS rules with ID selectors (`#line1` and `#line2`) to style the app's two `Line` objects. The remaining rules use **type selectors**, which apply to all objects of a given type. You specify a type selector by using the JavaFX class name.

```
1  /* Fig. 22.4: BasicShapes.css */
2  /* CSS that styles various two-dimensional shapes */
3
4  Line, Rectangle, Circle, Ellipse, Arc {
5      -fx-stroke-width: 10;
6  }
7
8  #line1 {
9      -fx-stroke: red;
10 }
11
12 #line2 {
13     -fx-stroke: rgba(0%, 50%, 0%, 0.5);
14     -fx-stroke-line-cap: round;
15 }
16
17 Rectangle {
18    -fx-stroke: red;
19    -fx-arc-width: 50;
20    -fx-arc-height: 50;
21    -fx-fill: yellow;
22 }
23
24 Circle {
25    -fx-stroke: blue;
26    -fx-fill: radial-gradient(center 50% 50%, radius 60%, white, red);
27 }
28
29 Ellipse {
30    -fx-stroke: green;
31    -fx-fill: image-pattern("yellowflowers.png");
32 }
33
34 Arc {
35    -fx-stroke: purple;
36    -fx-fill: linear-gradient(to right, cyan, white);
37 }
```

Fig. 22.4 | CSS that styles various two-dimensional shapes.

Specifying Common Attributes for Various Objects

The CSS rule in lines 4–6 defines the **`-fx-stroke-width`** CSS property for all the shapes in the app—this property specifies the thickness of the `Line`s and the border thickness of all the other shapes. To apply this rule to multiple shapes we use CSS type selectors in a comma-separated list. So, line 4 indicates that the rule in lines 4–6 should be applied to all objects of types `Line`, `Rectangle`, `Circle`, `Ellipse` and `Arc` in the GUI.

Styling the **Lines**

The CSS rule in lines 8–10 sets the **-fx-stroke** to the solid color red. This rule applies to the Line with the fx:id "line1". This rule is in addition to the rule at lines 4–6, which sets the stroke width for all Lines (and all the other shapes). When JavaFX renders an object, it combines all the CSS rules that apply to the object to determine its appearance. This rule applies to the Line with the fx:id "line1". Colors may be specified as

- named colors (such as "red", "green" and "blue"),
- colors defined by their red, green, blue and alpha (transparency) components,
- colors defined by their hue, saturation, brightness and alpha components,

and more. For details on all the ways to specify color in CSS, see

```
https://docs.oracle.com/javase/8/javafx/api/javafx/scene/doc-files/
   cssref.html#typecolor
```

The CSS rule in lines 12–15 applies to the Line with the fx:id "line2". For this rule, we specified the -fx-stroke property's color using the CSS function **rgba**, which defines a color based on its red, green, blue and alpha (transparency) components. Here we used the version of rgba that receives percentages from 0% to 100% specifying the amount of red, green and blue in the color, and a value from 0.0 (transparent) to 1.0 (opaque) for the alpha component. Line 13 produces a semitransparent green line. You can see the interaction between the two Lines' colors at the intersection point in Fig. 22.3's output windows. The **-fx-stroke-line-cap** CSS property (line 14) indicates that the ends of the Line should be *rounded*—the rounding effect becomes more noticeable with thicker strokes.

Styling the **Rectangle**

For Rectangles, Circles, Ellipses and Arcs you can specify both the -fx-stroke for the shapes' borders and the **-fx-fill**, which specifies the color or pattern that appears inside the shape. The rule in lines 17–22 uses a CSS type selector to indicate that all Rectangles should have red borders (line 18) and yellow fill (line 21). Lines 19–20 define the Rectangle's **-fx-arc-width** and **-fx-arc-height** properties, which specify the width and height of an ellipse that's divided in half horizontally and vertically, then used to round the Rectangle's corners. Because these properties have the same value (50) in this app, the four corners are each one quarter of a circle with a diameter of 50.

Styling the **Circle**

The CSS rule at lines 24–27 applies to all Circle objects. Line 25 sets the Circle's stroke to blue. Line 26 sets the Circle's fill with a **gradient**—colors that transition gradually from one color to the next. You can transition between as many colors as you like and specify the points at which to change colors, called **color stops**. You can use gradients for any property that specifies a color. In this case, we use the CSS function **radial-gradient** in which the color changes gradually from a center point outward. The fill

```
-fx-fill: radial-gradient(center 50% 50%, radius 60%, white, red);
```

indicates that the gradient should begin from a center point at 50% 50%—the middle of the shape horizontally and the middle of the shape vertically. The radius specifies the distance from the center at which an even mixture of the two colors appears. This radial gradient begins with the color `white` in the center and ends with `red` at the outer edge of the `Circle`'s fill. We'll discuss a linear gradient momentarily.

Styling the `Ellipse`

The CSS rule at lines 29–32 applies to all `Ellipse` objects. Line 30 specifies that an `Ellipse` should have a `green` stroke. Line 31 specifies that the `Ellipse`'s fill should be the image in the file `yellowflowers.png`, which is located in this app's folder. This image is provided in the `images` folder with the chapter's examples—if you're building this app from scratch, copy the video into the app's folder on your system. To specify an image as fill, you use the CSS function **`image-pattern`**. [*Note:* At the time of this writing, Scene Builder does not display a shape's fill correctly if it's specified with a CSS `image-pattern`. You must run the example to see the fill, as shown in Fig. 22.3(b).]

Styling the `Arc`

The CSS rule at lines 34–37 applies to all `Arc` objects. Line 35 specifies that an `Arc` should have a `purple` stroke. In this case, line 36

```
-fx-fill: linear-gradient(to right, cyan, white);
```

specifies that the `Arc` should be filled with a **linear gradient**—such gradients gradually transition from one color to the next horizontally, vertically or diagonally. You can transition between as many colors as you like and specify the points at which to change colors. To create a linear gradient, you use the CSS function **`linear-gradient`**. In this case, `to right` indicates that the gradient should start from the shape's left edge and transition through colors to the shape's right edge. We specified only two colors here—`cyan` at the left edge of the gradient and `white` at the right edge—but two or more colors can be specified in the comma-separated list. For more information on all the options for configuring radial gradients, linear gradients and image patterns, see

```
https://docs.oracle.com/javase/8/javafx/api/javafx/scene/doc-files/
   cssref.html#typepaint
```

22.4 `Polylines`, `Polygons` and `Paths`

There are several kinds of JavaFX shapes that enable you to create custom shapes:

- **`Polyline`**—draws a series of connected lines defined by a set of points.
- **`Polygon`**—draws a series of connected lines defined by a set of points and connects the last point to the first point.
- **`Path`**—draws a series of connected **`PathElements`** by moving to a given point, then drawing lines, arcs and curves.

In the `PolyShapes` app, you select which shape you want to display by selecting one of the `RadioButtons` in the left column. You specify a shape's points by clicking throughout the `AnchoredPane` in which the shapes are displayed.

For this example, we do not show the `PolyShapes` subclass of `Application` (located in the example's `PolyShapes.java` file), because it loads the FXML and displays the GUI, as demonstrated in Chapters 12 and 13.

22.4.1 GUI and CSS

This app's GUI (Fig. 22.5) is similar to that of the `Painter` app in Section 13.3. For that reason, we show only the key GUI elements' `fx:id` property values, rather than the complete FXML—each `fx:id` property value ends with the GUI element's type. In this GUI:

- The three `RadioButton`s are part of a `ToggleGroup` with the `fx:id` `"toggleGroup"`. The **Polyline** `RadioButton` should be **Selected** by default. We also set each `RadioButton`'s **On Action** event handler to `shapeRadioButtonSelected`.
- We dragged a `Polyline`, a `Polygon` and a `Path` from the Scene Builder **Library**'s **Shapes** section onto the `Pane` that displays the shapes, and we set their `fx:id`s to `polyline`, `polygon` and `path`, respectively. We set each shape's `visible` property to `false` by selecting the shape in Scene Builder, then unchecking the **Visible** checkbox in the **Properties** inspector. We display only the shape with the selected `RadioButton` at runtime.
- We set the `Pane`'s **On Mouse Clicked** event handler to `drawingAreaMouseClicked`.
- We set the **Clear** `Button`'s **On Action** event handler to `clearButtonPressed`.
- We set the controller class to `PolyShapesController`.
- Finally, we edited the FXML to remove the `Path` object's `<elements>` and the `Polyline` and `Polygon` objects' `<points>`, as we'll set these programmatically in response to the user's mouse-click events.

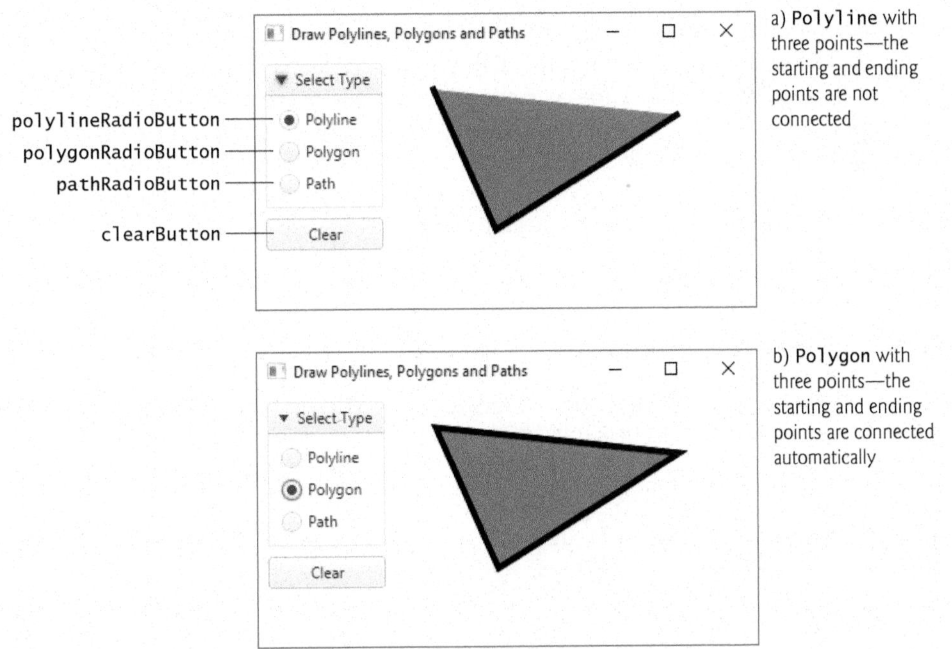

Fig. 22.5 | `Polylines`, `Polygons` and `Paths`. (Part 1 of 2.)

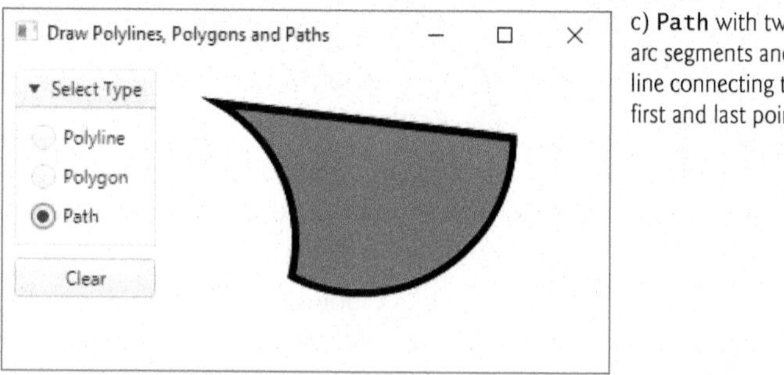

c) Path with two arc segments and a line connecting the first and last points

Fig. 22.5 | Polylines, Polygons and Paths. (Part 2 of 2.)

The PolyShapes.css file defines the properties -fx-stroke, -fx-stroke-width and -fx-fill that are applied to all three shapes in this example. As you can see in Fig. 22.5, the stroke is a thick black line (5 pixels wide) and the fill is red.

```
Polyline, Polygon, Path {
    -fx-stroke: black;
    -fx-stroke-width: 5;
    -fx-fill: red;
}
```

22.4.2 PolyShapesController Class

Figure 22.6 shows this app's PolyShapesController class, which responds to the user's interactions. The enum ShapeType (line 17) defines three constants that we use to determine which shape to display. Lines 20–26 declare the variables that correspond to the GUI components and shapes with fx:ids in the FXML. The shapeType variable (line 29) stores whichever shape type is currently selected in the GUI's RadioButtons—by default, the Polyline will be displayed. As you'll soon see, the sweepFlag variable is used to determine whether an arc in a Path is drawn with a negative or positive sweep angle.

```
1  // Fig. 22.6: PolyShapesController.java
2  // Drawing Polylines, Polygons and Paths.
3  import javafx.event.ActionEvent;
4  import javafx.fxml.FXML;
5  import javafx.scene.control.RadioButton;
6  import javafx.scene.control.ToggleGroup;
7  import javafx.scene.input.MouseEvent;
8  import javafx.scene.shape.ArcTo;
9  import javafx.scene.shape.ClosePath;
10 import javafx.scene.shape.MoveTo;
11 import javafx.scene.shape.Path;
12 import javafx.scene.shape.Polygon;
13 import javafx.scene.shape.Polyline;
14
```

Fig. 22.6 | Drawing Polylines, Polygons and Paths. (Part 1 of 3.)

```
public class PolyShapesController {
   // enum representing shape types
   private enum ShapeType {POLYLINE, POLYGON, PATH};

   // instance variables that refer to GUI components
   @FXML private RadioButton polylineRadioButton;
   @FXML private RadioButton polygonRadioButton;
   @FXML private RadioButton pathRadioButton;
   @FXML private ToggleGroup toggleGroup;
   @FXML private Polyline polyline;
   @FXML private Polygon polygon;
   @FXML private Path path;

   // instance variables for managing state
   private ShapeType shapeType = ShapeType.POLYLINE;
   private boolean sweepFlag = true; // used with arcs in a Path

   // set user data for the RadioButtons and display polyline object
   public void initialize() {
      // user data on a control can be any Object
      polylineRadioButton.setUserData(ShapeType.POLYLINE);
      polygonRadioButton.setUserData(ShapeType.POLYGON);
      pathRadioButton.setUserData(ShapeType.PATH);

      displayShape(); // sets polyline's visibility to true when app loads
   }

   // handles drawingArea's onMouseClicked event
   @FXML
   private void drawingAreaMouseClicked(MouseEvent e) {
      polyline.getPoints().addAll(e.getX(), e.getY());
      polygon.getPoints().addAll(e.getX(), e.getY());

      // if path is empty, move to first click position and close path
      if (path.getElements().isEmpty()) {
         path.getElements().add(new MoveTo(e.getX(), e.getY()));
         path.getElements().add(new ClosePath());
      }
      else { // insert a new path segment before the ClosePath element
         // create an arc segment and insert it in the path
         ArcTo arcTo = new ArcTo();
         arcTo.setX(e.getX());
         arcTo.setY(e.getY());
         arcTo.setRadiusX(100.0);
         arcTo.setRadiusY(100.0);
         arcTo.setSweepFlag(sweepFlag);
         sweepFlag = !sweepFlag;
         path.getElements().add(path.getElements().size() - 1, arcTo);
      }
   }

```

Fig. 22.6 | Drawing Polylines, Polygons and Paths. (Part 2 of 3.)

```
66       // handles color RadioButton's ActionEvents
67       @FXML
68       private void shapeRadioButtonSelected(ActionEvent e) {
69          // user data for each color RadioButton is a ShapeType constant
70          shapeType =
71             (ShapeType) toggleGroup.getSelectedToggle().getUserData();
72          displayShape(); // display the currently selected shape
73       }
74
75       // displays currently selected shape
76       private void displayShape() {
77          polyline.setVisible(shapeType == ShapeType.POLYLINE);
78          polygon.setVisible(shapeType == ShapeType.POLYGON);
79          path.setVisible(shapeType == ShapeType.PATH);
80       }
81
82       // resets each shape
83       @FXML
84       private void clearButtonPressed(ActionEvent event) {
85          polyline.getPoints().clear();
86          polygon.getPoints().clear();
87          path.getElements().clear();
88       }
89    }
```

Fig. 22.6 | Drawing `Polylines`, `Polygons` and `Paths`. (Part 3 of 3.)

Method `initialize`

Recall from Section 13.3.1 that you can associate any `Object` with each JavaFX control via its `setUserData` method. For the shape `RadioButtons` in this app, we store the specific `ShapeType` that the `RadioButton` represents (lines 35–37). We use these values when handling the `RadioButton` events to set the `shapeType` instance variable. Line 39 then calls method `displayShape` to display the currently selected shape (the `Polyline` by default). Initially, the shape is not visible because it does not yet have any points.

Method `drawingAreaMouseClicked`

When the user clicks the app's `Pane`, method `drawingAreaMouseClicked` (lines 43–64) modifies all three shapes to incorporate the new point at which the user clicked. `Polylines` and `Polygons` store their points as a collection of `Double` values in which the first two values represent the first point's location, the next two values represent the second point's location, etc. Line 45 gets the `polyline` object's collection of points, then adds the new click point to the collection by calling its `addAll` method and passing the `MouseEvent`'s *x*- and *y*-coordinate values. This adds the new point's information to the end of the collection. Line 46 performs the same task for the `polygon` object.

Lines 49–63 manipulate the `path` object. A `Path` is represented by a collection of **`PathElements`**. The subclasses of `PathElement` used in this example are:

- **`MoveTo`**—Moves to a specific position without drawing anything.

- `ArcTo`—Draws an arc from the previous `PathElement`'s endpoint to the specified location. We'll discuss this in more detail momentarily.
- `ClosePath`—Closes the path by drawing a straight line from the end point of the last `PathElement` to the start point of the first `PathElement`.

Other `PathElements` not covered here include `LineTo`, `HLineTo`, `VLineTo`, `CubicCurveTo` and `QuadCurveTo`.

When the user clicks the `Pane`, line 49 checks whether the `Path` contains elements. If not, line 50 moves the starting point of the `path` to the mouse-click location by adding a `MoveTo` element to the path's `PathElements` collection. Then line 51 adds a new `ClosePath` element to complete the path. For each subsequent mouse-click event, lines 55–60 create an `ArcTo` element and line 62 inserts it before the `ClosePath` element by calling the `PathElements` collection's `add` method that receives an index as its first argument.

Lines 56–57 set the `ArcTo` element's end point to the `MouseEvent`'s coordinates. The arc is drawn as a piece of an ellipse for which you specify the horizontal radius and vertical radius (lines 58–59). Line 60 sets the `ArcTo`'s `sweepFlag`, which determines whether the arc sweeps in the positive angle direction (`true`; counter clockwise) or the negative angle direction (`false`; clockwise). By default an `ArcTo` element is drawn as the shortest arc between the last `PathElement`'s end point and the point specified by the `ArcTo` element. To sweep the arc the long way around the ellipse, set the `ArcTo`'s `largeArcFlag` to `true`. For each mouse click, line 61 reverses the value of our controller class's `sweepFlag` instance variable so that the `ArcTo` elements toggle between positive and negative angles for variety.

Method `shapeRadioButtonSelected`

When the user clicks a shape `RadioButton`, lines 70–71 set the controller's `shapeType` instance variable, then line 72 calls method `displayShape` to display the selected shape. Try creating a `Polyline` of several points, then changing to the `Polygon` and `Path` to see how the points are used in each shape.

Method `displayShape`

Lines 77–79 simply set the visibility of the three shapes, based on the current `shapeType`. The currently selected shape's visibility is set to `true` to display the shape, and the other shapes' visibility is set to `false` to hide those shapes.

Method `clearButtonPressed`

When the user clicks the **Clear** `Button`, lines 85–86 clear the `polyline`'s and `polygon`'s collections of points, and line 87 clears the `path`'s collection of `PathElements`. The user can then begin drawing a new shape by clicking the `Pane`.

22.5 Transforms

A **transform** can be applied to any UI element to *reposition* or *reorient* the element. The built-in JavaFX transforms are subclasses of **`Transform`**. Some of these subclasses include:

- **`Translate`**—*moves* an object to a new location.
- **`Rotate`**—*rotates* an object around a point and by a specified rotation angle.
- **`Scale`**—*scales* an object's size by the specified amounts.

The next example draws stars using the Polygon control and uses Rotate transforms to create a circle of randomly colored stars. The FXML for this app consists of an empty 300-by-300 Pane layout with the fx:id "pane". We also set the controller class to DrawStarsController. Figure 22.7 shows the app's controller and a sample output.

Method initialize (lines 14–37) defines the stars, applies the transforms and attaches the stars to the app's pane. Lines 16–18 define the points of a star as an array of type Double—the collection of points stored in a Polygon is implemented with a generic collection, so you must use type Double rather than double (recall that primitive types cannot be used in Java generics). Each pair of values in the array represents the *x*- and *y*-coordinates of one point in the Polygon. We defined ten points in the array.

```
1  // Fig. 22.7: DrawStarsController.java
2  // Create a circle of stars using Polygons and Rotate transforms
3  import java.security.SecureRandom;
4  import javafx.fxml.FXML;
5  import javafx.scene.layout.Pane;
6  import javafx.scene.paint.Color;
7  import javafx.scene.shape.Polygon;
8  import javafx.scene.transform.Transform;
9
10 public class DrawStarsController {
11    @FXML private Pane pane;
12    private static final SecureRandom random = new SecureRandom();
13
14    public void initialize() {
15       // points that define a five-pointed star shape
16       Double[] points = {205.0,150.0, 217.0,186.0, 259.0,186.0,
17          223.0,204.0, 233.0,246.0, 205.0,222.0, 177.0,246.0, 187.0,204.0,
18          151.0,186.0, 193.0,186.0};
19
20       // create 18 stars
21       for (int count = 0; count < 18; ++count) {
22          // create a new Polygon and copy existing points into it
23          Polygon newStar = new Polygon();
24          newStar.getPoints().addAll(points);
25
26          // create random Color and set as newStar's fill
27          newStar.setStroke(Color.GREY);
28          newStar.setFill(Color.rgb(random.nextInt(255),
29             random.nextInt(255), random.nextInt(255),
30             random.nextDouble()));
31
32          // apply a rotation to the shape
33          newStar.getTransforms().add(
34             Transform.rotate(count * 20, 150, 150));
35          pane.getChildren().add(newStar);
36       }
37    }
38 }
```

Fig. 22.7 | Create a circle of stars using Polygons and Rotate transforms. (Part 1 of 2.)

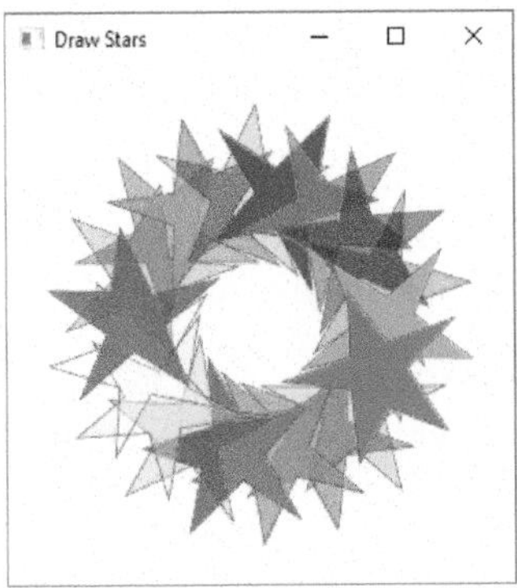

Fig. 22.7 | Create a circle of stars using `Polygons` and `Rotate` transforms. (Part 2 of 2.)

During each iteration of the loop, lines 23–34 create a `Polygon` using the points in the `points` array and apply a different `Rotate` transform. This results in the circle of `Polygons` in the screen capture. To generate the random colors for each star, we use a `SecureRandom` object to create three random values from 0–255 for the red, green and blue components of the color, and one random value from 0.0–1.0 for the color's alpha transparency value. We pass those values to class `Color`'s `static` `rgb` method to create a `Color`.

To apply a rotation to the new `Polygon`, we add a `Rotate` transform to the `Polygon`'s collection of `Transforms` (lines 33–34). To create the `Rotate` transform object, we invoke class `Transform`'s `static` method **`rotate`** (line 34), which returns a `Rotate` object. The method's first argument is the rotation angle. Each iteration of the loop assigns a new rotation-angle value by using the control variable multiplied by 20 as the `rotate` method's first argument. The method's next two arguments are the *x*- and *y*-coordinates of the point of rotation around which the `Polygon` rotates. The center of the circle of stars is the point *(150, 150)*, because we rotated all 18 stars around that point. Adding each `Polygon` as a new child element of the `pane` object allows the `Polygon` to be rendered on screen.

22.6 Playing Video with Media, MediaPlayer and MediaViewer

Many of today's most popular apps are multimedia intensive. JavaFX provides audio and video multimedia capabilities via the classes of package **`javafx.scene.media`**:

- For simple audio playback you can use class **`AudioClip`**.
- For audio playback with more playback controls and for video playback you can use classes **`Media`**, **`MediaPlayer`** and **`MediaView`**.

In this section, you'll build a basic video player. We'll explain classes `Media`, `MediaPlayer` and `MediaView` as we encounter them in the project's controller class (Section 22.6.2). The video used in this example is from NASA's multimedia library[3] and was downloaded from

```
http://www.nasa.gov/centers/kennedy/multimedia/HD-index.html
```

3. For NASA's terms of use, visit `http://www.nasa.gov/multimedia/guidelines/`.

The video file sts117.mp4 is provided in the video folder with this chapter's examples. When building the app from scratch, copy the video onto the app's folder.

Media Formats

For video, JavaFX supports MPEG-4 (also called MP4) and Flash Video formats. We downloaded a Windows WMV version of the video file used in this example, then converted it to MP4 via a free online video converter.[4]

ControlsFX Library's **ExceptionDialog**

ExceptionDialog is one of many additional JavaFX controls available through the open-source project ControlsFX at

```
http://controlsfx.org
```

We use an ExceptionDialog in this app to display a message to the user if an error occurs during media playback.

You can download the latest version of ControlsFX from the preceding web page, then extract the contents of the ZIP file. Place the extracted ControlsFX JAR file (named controlsfx-8.40.12.jar at the time of this writing) in your project's folder—a JAR file is a compressed archive like a ZIP file, but contains Java class files and their corresponding resources. We included a copy of the JAR file with the final example.

Compiling and Running the App with ControlsFX

To compile this app, you must specify the JAR file as part of the app's classpath. To do so, use the javac command's -classpath option, as in:

```
javac -classpath .;controlsfx-8.40.12.jar *.java
```

Similary, to run the app, use the java command's -cp option, as in

```
java -cp .;controlsfx-8.40.12.jar VideoPlayer
```

In the preceding commands, Linux and macOS users should use a colon (:) rather than a semicolon(;). The classpath in each command specifies the current folder containing the app's files—this is represented by the dot (.)—and the name of the JAR file containing the ControlsFX classes (including ExceptionDialog).

22.6.1 VideoPlayer GUI

Figure 22.8 shows the completed VideoPlayer.fxml file and two sample screen captures of the final running VideoPlayer app. The GUI's layout is a BorderPane consisting of

- a MediaView (located in the Scene Builder **Library**'s **Controls** section) with the fx:id mediaView and
- a ToolBar (located in the Scene Builder **Library**'s **Containers** section) containing one Button with the fx:id playPauseButton and the text "Play". The controller method playPauseButtonPressed responds when the Button is pressed.

We placed the MediaView in the BorderPane's center region (lines 25–27) so that it occupies all available space in the BorderPane, and we placed the ToolBar in the BorderPane's

4. There are many free online and downloadable video-format conversion tools. We used the one at https://convertio.co/video-converter/.

bottom region (lines 15–24). By default, Scene Builder adds one `Button` to the `ToolBar` when you drag the `ToolBar` onto your layout. You can then add other controls to the `ToolBar` as necessary. We set the controller class to `VideoPlayerController`.

```
1  <?xml version="1.0" encoding="UTF-8"?>
2  <!-- Fig. 22.8: VideoPlayer.fxml -->
3  <!-- VideoPlayer GUI with a MediaView and a Button -->
4
5  <?import javafx.scene.control.Button?>
6  <?import javafx.scene.control.ToolBar?>
7  <?import javafx.scene.layout.BorderPane?>
8  <?import javafx.scene.media.MediaView?>
9
10 <BorderPane prefHeight="400.0" prefWidth="600.0"
11    style="-fx-background-color: black;"
12    xmlns="http://javafx.com/javafx/8.0.60"
13    xmlns:fx="http://javafx.com/fxml/1"
14    fx:controller="VideoPlayerController">
15    <bottom>
16       <ToolBar prefHeight="40.0" prefWidth="200.0"
17          BorderPane.alignment="CENTER">
18          <items>
19             <Button fx:id="playPauseButton"
20                onAction="#playPauseButtonPressed" prefHeight="25.0"
21                prefWidth="60.0" text="Play" />
22          </items>
23       </ToolBar>
24    </bottom>
25    <center>
26       <MediaView fx:id="mediaView" BorderPane.alignment="CENTER" />
27    </center>
28 </BorderPane>
```

Fig. 22.8 | `VideoPlayer` GUI with a `MediaView` and a `Button`. Video courtesy of NASA—see `http://www.nasa.gov/multimedia/guidelines/` for usage guidelines. (Part 1 of 2.)

Fig. 22.8 | `VideoPlayer` GUI with a `MediaView` and a `Button`. Video courtesy of NASA—see `http://www.nasa.gov/multimedia/guidelines/` for usage guidelines. (Part 2 of 2.)

22.6.2 `VideoPlayerController` Class

Figure 22.9 shows the completed `VideoPlayerController` class, which configures video playback and responds to state changes from the `MediaPlayer` and the events when the user presses the `playPauseButton`. The controller uses classes `Media`, `MediaPlayer` and `MediaView` as follows:

- A `Media` object specifies the location of the media to play and provides access to various information about the media, such as its duration, dimensions and more.
- A `MediaPlayer` object loads a `Media` object and controls playback. In addition, a `MediaPlayer` transitions through its various states (*ready*, *playing*, *paused*, etc.) during media loading and playback. As you'll see, you can provide `Runnable`s that execute in response to these state transitions.
- A `MediaView` object displays the `Media` being played by a given `MediaPlayer` object.

```
// Fig. 22.9: VideoPlayerController.java
// Using Media, MediaPlayer and MediaView to play a video.
import java.net.URL;
import javafx.beans.binding.Bindings;
import javafx.beans.property.DoubleProperty;
import javafx.event.ActionEvent;
import javafx.fxml.FXML;
import javafx.scene.control.Button;
import javafx.scene.media.Media;
import javafx.scene.media.MediaPlayer;
```

Fig. 22.9 | Using `Media`, `MediaPlayer` and `MediaView` to play a video. (Part 1 of 3.)

```
import javafx.scene.media.MediaView;
import javafx.util.Duration;
import org.controlsfx.dialog.ExceptionDialog;

public class VideoPlayerController {
   @FXML private MediaView mediaView;
   @FXML private Button playPauseButton;
   private MediaPlayer mediaPlayer;
   private boolean playing = false;

   public void initialize() {
      // get URL of the video file
      URL url = VideoPlayerController.class.getResource("sts117.mp4");

      // create a Media object for the specified URL
      Media media = new Media(url.toExternalForm());

      // create a MediaPlayer to control Media playback
      mediaPlayer = new MediaPlayer(media);

      // specify which MediaPlayer to display in the MediaView
      mediaView.setMediaPlayer(mediaPlayer);

      // set handler to be called when the video completes playing
      mediaPlayer.setOnEndOfMedia(
         new Runnable() {
            public void run() {
               playing = false;
               playPauseButton.setText("Play");
               mediaPlayer.seek(Duration.ZERO);
               mediaPlayer.pause();
            }
         }
      );

      // set handler that displays an ExceptionDialog if an error occurs
      mediaPlayer.setOnError(
         new Runnable() {
            public void run() {
               ExceptionDialog dialog =
                  new ExceptionDialog(mediaPlayer.getError());
               dialog.showAndWait();
            }
         }
      );

      // set handler that resizes window to video size once ready to play
      mediaPlayer.setOnReady(
         new Runnable() {
            public void run() {
               DoubleProperty width = mediaView.fitWidthProperty();
               DoubleProperty height = mediaView.fitHeightProperty();
```

Fig. 22.9 | Using Media, MediaPlayer and MediaView to play a video. (Part 2 of 3.)

```
63                width.bind(Bindings.selectDouble(
64                   mediaView.sceneProperty(), "width"));
65                height.bind(Bindings.selectDouble(
66                   mediaView.sceneProperty(), "height"));
67             }
68          }
69       );
70    }
71
72    // toggle media playback and the text on the playPauseButton
73    @FXML
74    private void playPauseButtonPressed(ActionEvent e) {
75       playing = !playing;
76
77       if (playing) {
78          playPauseButton.setText("Pause");
79          mediaPlayer.play();
80       }
81       else {
82          playPauseButton.setText("Play");
83          mediaPlayer.pause();
84       }
85    }
86 }
```

Fig. 22.9 | Using `Media`, `MediaPlayer` and `MediaView` to play a video. (Part 3 of 3.)

Instance Variables

Lines 16–19 declare the controller's instance variables. When the app loads, the `mediaView` variable (line 16) is assigned a reference to the `MediaView` object declared in the app's FXML. The `mediaPlayer` variable (line 18) is configured in method `initialize` to load the video specified by a `Media` object and used by method `playPauseButtonPressed` (lines 73–85) to play and pause the video.

Creating a `Media` Object Representing the Video to Play

Method `initialize` configures media playback and registers event handlers for `MediaPlayer` events. Line 23 gets a `URL` representing the location of the `sts117.mp4` video file. The notation

```
VideoPlayerController.class
```

creates a `Class` object representing the `VideoPlayerController` class. This is equivalent to calling inherited method `getClass()`. Next line 26 creates a `Media` object representing the video. The argument to the `Media` constructor is a `String` representing the video's location, which we obtain with `URL` method `toExternalForm`. The URL `String` can represent a local file on your computer or can be a location on the web. The `Media` constructor throws various exceptions, including `MediaExceptions` if the media cannot be found or is not of a supported media format.

Creating a `MediaPlayer` Object to Load the Video and Control Playback

To load the video and prepare it for playback, you must associate it with a `MediaPlayer` object (line 29). Playing multiple videos requires a separate `MediaPlayer` for each `Media` object. However, a given Media object can be associated with multiple MediaPlayers. The MediaPlayer constructor throws a NullPointerException if the Media is null or a MediaException if a problem occurs during construction of the MediaPlayer object.

Attaching the **MediaPlayer** *Object to the* **MediaView** *to Display the Video*

A MediaPlayer does not provide a view in which to display video. For this purpose, you must associate a MediaPlayer with a MediaView. When the MediaView already exists—such as when it's created in FXML—you call the MediaView's **setMediaPlayer** method (line 32) to perform this task. When creating a MediaView object programmatically, you can pass the MediaPlayer to the MediaView's constructor. A MediaView is like any other Node in the scene graph, so you can apply CSS styles, transforms and animations (Sections 22.7–22.9) to it as well.

Configuring Event Handlers for **MediaPlayer** *Events*

A MediaPlayer transitions through various states. Some common states include *ready*, *playing* and *paused*. For these and other states, you can execute a task as the MediaPlayer enters the corresponding state. In addition, you can specify tasks that execute when the end of media playback is reached or when an error occurs during playback. To perform a task for a given state, you specify an object that implements the **Runnable** interface (package java.lang). This interface contains a no-parameter run method that returns void.

For example, lines 35–44 call the MediaPlayer's **setOnEndOfMedia** method, passing an object of an anonymous inner class that implements interface Runnable to execute when video playback completes. Line 38 sets the boolean instance variable playing to false and line 39 changes the text on the playPauseButton to "Play" to indicate that the user can click the Button to play the video again. Line 40 calls MediaPlayer method **seek** to move to the beginning of the video and line 41 pauses the video.

Lines 47–55 call the MediaPlayer's **setOnError** method to specify a task to perform if the MediaPlayer enters the *error* state, indicating that an error occurred during playback. In this case, we display an ExceptionDialog containing the MediaPlayer's error message. Calling the ExceptionDialog's showAndWait method indicates that the app must wait for the user to dismiss the dialog before continuing.

Binding the **MediaViewer's** *Size to the Scene's Size*

Lines 58–69 call the MediaPlayer's **setOnReady** method to specify a task to perform if the MediaPlayer enters the *ready* state. We use property bindings to bind the MediaView's width and height properties to the scene's width and height properties so that the MediaView resizes with app's window. A Node's sceneProperty returns a ReadOnlyObjectProperty<Scene> that you can use to access to the Scene in which the Node is displayed. The ReadOnlyObjectProperty<Scene> represents an object that has many properties. To bind to a specific properties of that object, you can use the methods of class **Bindings** (package javafx.beans.binding) to select the corresponding properties. The Scene's width and height are each DoubleProperty objects. Bindings method **selectDouble** gets a reference to a DoubleProperty. The method's first argument is the object that contains the property and the second argument is the name of the property to which you'd like to bind.

Method `playPauseButtonPressed`

The event handler `playPauseButtonPressed` (lines 73–85) toggles video playback. When `playing` is `true`, line 78 sets the `playPauseButton`'s text to `"Pause"` and line 79 calls the `MediaPlayer`'s **`play`** method; otherwise, line 82 sets the `playPauseButton`'s text to `"Play"` and line 83 calls the `MediaPlayer`'s **`pause`** method.

8

Using Java SE 8 Lambdas to Implement the **`Runnable`***s*

Each of the anonymous inner classes in this controller's `initialize` method can be implemented more concisely using lambdas as shown in Section 17.16.

22.7 Transition Animations

Animations in JavaFX apps transition a `Node`'s property values from one value to another in a specified amount of time. Most properties of a `Node` can be animated. This section focuses on several of JavaFX's predefined **`Transition`** animations from the **`javafx.animations`** package. By default, the subclasses that define `Transition` animations change the values of specific `Node` properties. For example, a `FadeTransition` changes the value of a `Node`'s `opacity` property (which specifies whether the `Node` is opaque or transparent) over time, whereas a `PathTransition` changes a `Node`'s location by moving it along a `Path` over time. Though we show sample screen captures for all the animation examples, the best way to experience each is to run the examples yourself.

22.7.1 `TransitionAnimations.fxml`

Figure 22.10 shows this app's GUI and screen captures of the running application. When you click the `startButton` (lines 17–19), its `startButtonPressed` event handler in the app's controller creates a sequence of `Transition` animations for the `Rectangle` (lines 15–16) and plays them. The `Rectangle` is styled with the following CSS from the file `TransitionAnimations.css`:

```
Rectangle {
    -fx-stroke-width: 10;
    -fx-stroke: red;
    -fx-arc-width: 50;
    -fx-arc-height: 50;
    -fx-fill: yellow;
}
```

which produces a rounded rectangle with a 10-pixel red border and yellow fill.

```
1  <?xml version="1.0" encoding="UTF-8"?>
2  <!-- Fig. 22.10: TransitionAnimations.fxml -->
3  <!-- FXML for a Rectangle and Button -->
4
5  <?import javafx.scene.control.Button?>
6  <?import javafx.scene.layout.Pane?>
7  <?import javafx.scene.shape.Rectangle?>
8
```

Fig. 22.10 | FXML for a `Rectangle` and `Button`. (Part 1 of 3.)

```
<Pane id="Pane" prefHeight="200.0" prefWidth="180.0"
   stylesheets="@TransitionAnimations.css"
   xmlns="http://javafx.com/javafx/8.0.60"
   xmlns:fx="http://javafx.com/fxml/1"
   fx:controller="TransitionAnimationsController">
   <children>
      <Rectangle fx:id="rectangle" height="90.0" layoutX="45.0"
         layoutY="45.0" width="90.0" />
      <Button fx:id="startButton" layoutX="38.0" layoutY="161.0"
         mnemonicParsing="false"
         onAction="#startButtonPressed" text="Start Animations" />
   </children>
</Pane>
```

a) Initial **Rectangle**

b) **Rectangle** undergoing parallel fill and stroke transitions

c) **Rectangle** undergoing a fade transition

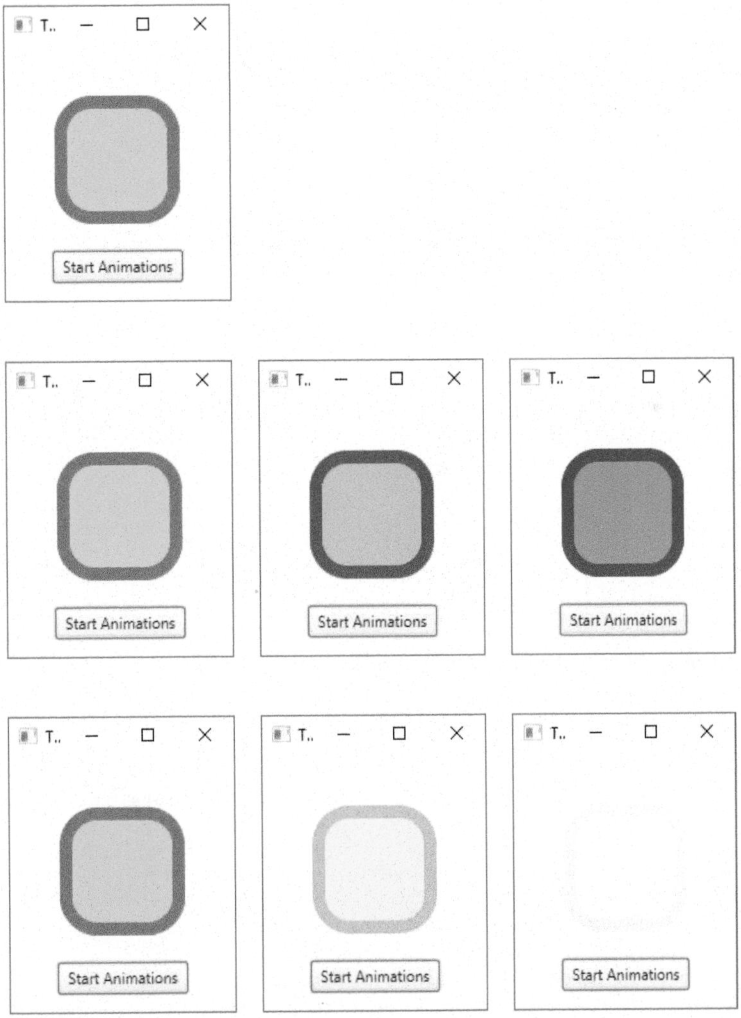

Fig. 22.10 | FXML for a **Rectangle** and **Button**. (Part 2 of 3.)

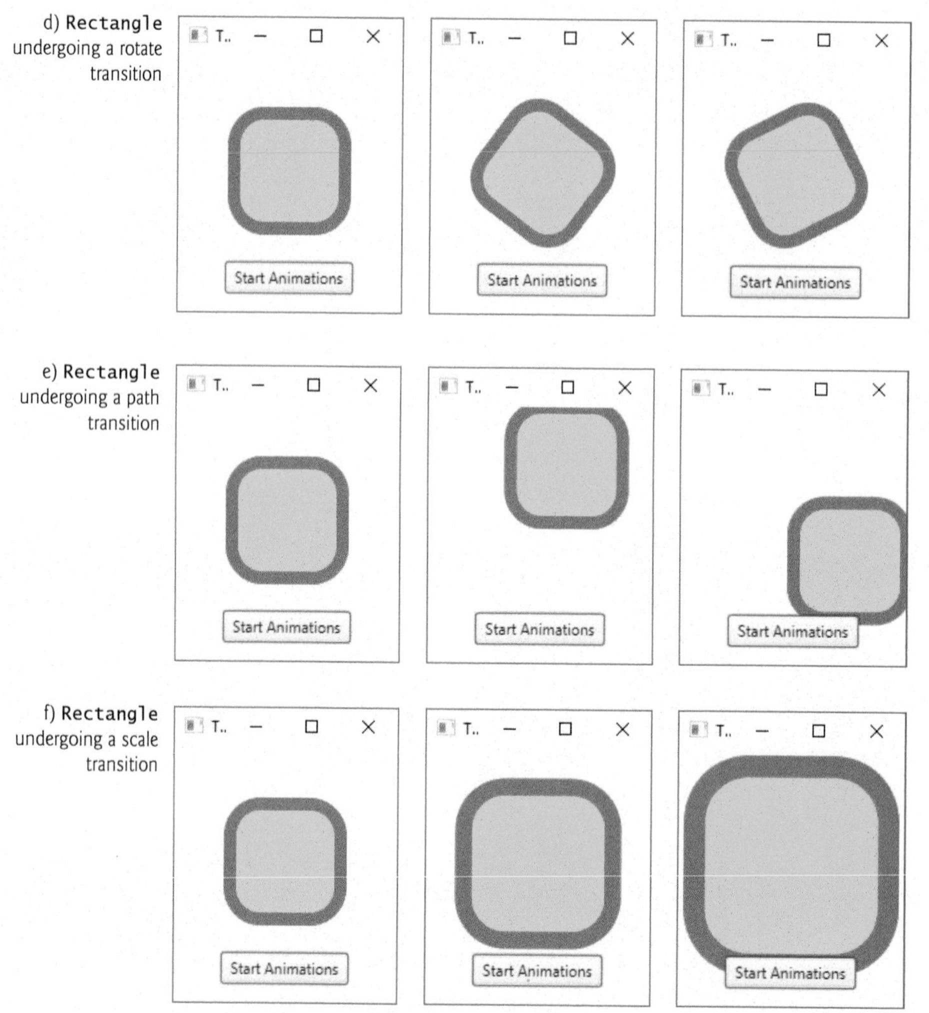

Fig. 22.10 | FXML for a `Rectangle` and `Button`. (Part 3 of 3.)

22.7.2 `TransitionAnimationsController` Class

Figure 22.11 shows this app's controller class, which defines the `startButton`'s event handler (lines 25–87). This event handler defines several animations that are played in sequence.

```
1  // Fig. 22.11: TransitionAnimationsController.java
2  // Applying Transition animations to a Rectangle.
3  import javafx.animation.FadeTransition;
4  import javafx.animation.FillTransition;
5  import javafx.animation.Interpolator;
6  import javafx.animation.ParallelTransition;
```

Fig. 22.11 | Applying `Transition` animations to a `Rectangle`. (Part 1 of 3.)

```
import javafx.animation.PathTransition;
import javafx.animation.RotateTransition;
import javafx.animation.ScaleTransition;
import javafx.animation.SequentialTransition;
import javafx.animation.StrokeTransition;
import javafx.event.ActionEvent;
import javafx.fxml.FXML;
import javafx.scene.paint.Color;
import javafx.scene.shape.LineTo;
import javafx.scene.shape.MoveTo;
import javafx.scene.shape.Path;
import javafx.scene.shape.Rectangle;
import javafx.util.Duration;

public class TransitionAnimationsController {
   @FXML private Rectangle rectangle;

   // configure and start transition animations
   @FXML
   private void startButtonPressed(ActionEvent event) {
      // transition that changes a shape's fill
      FillTransition fillTransition =
         new FillTransition(Duration.seconds(1));
      fillTransition.setToValue(Color.CYAN);
      fillTransition.setCycleCount(2);

      // each even cycle plays transition in reverse to restore original
      fillTransition.setAutoReverse(true);

      // transition that changes a shape's stroke over time
      StrokeTransition strokeTransition =
         new StrokeTransition(Duration.seconds(1));
      strokeTransition.setToValue(Color.BLUE);
      strokeTransition.setCycleCount(2);
      strokeTransition.setAutoReverse(true);

      // parallelizes multiple transitions
      ParallelTransition parallelTransition =
         new ParallelTransition(fillTransition, strokeTransition);

      // transition that changes a node's opacity over time
      FadeTransition fadeTransition =
         new FadeTransition(Duration.seconds(1));
      fadeTransition.setFromValue(1.0); // opaque
      fadeTransition.setToValue(0.0); // transparent
      fadeTransition.setCycleCount(2);
      fadeTransition.setAutoReverse(true);

      // transition that rotates a node
      RotateTransition rotateTransition =
         new RotateTransition(Duration.seconds(1));
      rotateTransition.setByAngle(360.0);
```

Fig. 22.11 | Applying `Transition` animations to a `Rectangle`. (Part 2 of 3.)

```
59          rotateTransition.setCycleCount(2);
60          rotateTransition.setInterpolator(Interpolator.EASE_BOTH);
61          rotateTransition.setAutoReverse(true);
62
63          // transition that moves a node along a Path
64          Path path = new Path(new MoveTo(45, 45), new LineTo(45, 0),
65             new LineTo(90, 0), new LineTo(90, 90), new LineTo(0, 90));
66          PathTransition translateTransition =
67             new PathTransition(Duration.seconds(2), path);
68          translateTransition.setCycleCount(2);
69          translateTransition.setInterpolator(Interpolator.EASE_IN);
70          translateTransition.setAutoReverse(true);
71
72          // transition that scales a shape to make it larger or smaller
73          ScaleTransition scaleTransition =
74             new ScaleTransition(Duration.seconds(1));
75          scaleTransition.setByX(0.75);
76          scaleTransition.setByY(0.75);
77          scaleTransition.setCycleCount(2);
78          scaleTransition.setInterpolator(Interpolator.EASE_OUT);
79          scaleTransition.setAutoReverse(true);
80
81          // transition that applies a sequence of transitions to a node
82          SequentialTransition sequentialTransition =
83             new SequentialTransition (rectangle, parallelTransition,
84                fadeTransition, rotateTransition, translateTransition,
85                scaleTransition);
86          sequentialTransition.play(); // play the transition
87       }
88    }
```

Fig. 22.11 | Applying `Transition` animations to a `Rectangle`. (Part 3 of 3.)

`FillTransition`

Lines 28–34 configure a one-second **`FillTransition`** that changes a shape's fill color. Line 30 specifies the color (`CYAN`) to which the fill will transition. Line 31 sets the animations cycle count to 2—this specifies the number of iterations of the transition to perform over the specified duration. Line 34 specifies that the animation should automatically play itself in reverse once the initial transition is complete. For this animation, during the first cycle the fill color changes from the original fill color to `CYAN`, and during the second cycle the animation transitions back to the original fill color.

`StrokeTransition`

Lines 37–41 configure a one-second **`StrokeTransition`** that changes a shape's stroke color. Line 39 specifies the color (`BLUE`) to which the stroke will transition. Line 40 sets the animations cycle count to 2, and line 41 specifies that the animation should automatically play itself in reverse once the initial transition is complete. For this animation, during the first cycle the stroke color changes from the original stroke color to `BLUE`, and during the second cycle the animation transitions back to the original stroke color.

ParallelTransition

Lines 44–45 configure a **ParallelTransition** that performs multiple transitions at the same time (that is, in parallel). The ParallelTransition constructor receives a variable number of Transitions as a comma-separated list. In this case, the FillTransition and StrokeTransition will be performed in parallel on the app's Rectangle.

FadeTransition

Lines 48–53 configure a one-second **FadeTransition** that changes a Node's opacity. Line 50 specifies the initial opacity—1.0 is fully opaque. Line 51 specifies the final opacity—0.0 is fully transparent. Once again, we set the cycle count to 2 and specified that the animation should auto-reverse itself.

RotateTransition

Lines 56–61 configure a one-second **RotateTransition** that rotates a Node. You can rotate a Node by a specified number of degrees (line 58) or you can use other RotateTransition methods to specify a start angle and end angle. Each Transition animation uses an **Interpolator** to calculate new property values throughout the animation's duration. The default is a **LINEAR** Interpolator which evenly divides the property value changes over the animation's duration. For the RotateTransition, line 60 uses the Interpolator **EASE_BOTH**, which changes the rotation slowly at first (known as "easing in"), speeds up the rotation in the middle of the animation, then slows the rotation again to complete the animation (known as "easing out"). For a list of all the predefined Interpolators, see

```
https://docs.oracle.com/javase/8/javafx/api/javafx/animation/
    Interpolator.html
```

PathTransition

Lines 64–70 configure a two-second **PathTransition** that changes a shape's position by moving it along a Path. Lines 64–65 create the Path, which is specified as the second argument to the PathTransition constructor. A **LineTo** object draws a straight line from the previous PathElement's endpoint to the specified location. Line 69 specifies that this animation should use the Interpolator **EASE_IN**, which changes the position slowly at first, before performing the animation at full speed.

ScaleTransition

Lines 73–79 configure a one-second **ScaleTransition** that changes a Node's size. Line 75 specifies that the object will be scaled 75% larger along the *x*-axis (i.e., horizontally), and line 76 specifies that the object will be scaled 75% larger along the *y*-axis (i.e., vertically). Line 78 specifies that this animation should use the Interpolator **EASE_OUT**, which begins scaling the shape at full speed, then slows down as the animation completes.

SequentialTransition

Lines 82–86 configure a **SequentialTransition** that performs a sequence of transitions—as each completes, the next one in the sequence begins executing. The SequentialTransition constructor receives the Node to which the sequence of animations will be applied, followed by a comma-separated list of Transitions to perform. In fact, every transition animation class has a constructor that enables you to specify a Node. For this example, we did not specify Nodes when creating the other transitions, because they're all applied by the SequentialTransition to the Rectangle. Every Transition has a **play** method (line 86) that begins the animation. Calling `play` on the `SequentialTransition` automatically calls `play` on each animation in the sequence.

22.8 Timeline Animations

In this section, we continue our animation discussion with a **Timeline** animation that bounces a `Circle` object around the app's `Pane` over time. A `Timeline` animation can change any `Node` property that's modifiable. You specify how to change property values with one or more **KeyFrame** objects that the `Timeline` animation performs in sequence. For this app, we'll specify a single `KeyFrame` that modifies a `Circle`'s location, then we'll play that `KeyFrame` indefinitely. Figure 22.12 shows the app's FXML, which defines a `Circle` object with a five-pixel black border and the fill color `DODGERBLUE`.

```
<?xml version="1.0" encoding="UTF-8"?>
<!-- Fig. 22.12: TimelineAnimation.fxml -->
<!-- FXML for a Circle that will be animated by the controller -->

<?import javafx.scene.layout.Pane?>
<?import javafx.scene.shape.Circle?>

<Pane id="Pane" fx:id="pane" prefHeight="400.0"
   prefWidth="600.0" xmlns:fx="http://javafx.com/fxml/1"
   xmlns="http://javafx.com/javafx/8.0.60"
   fx:controller="TimelineAnimationController">
   <children>
      <Circle fx:id="c" fill="DODGERBLUE" layoutX="142.0" layoutY="143.0"
         radius="40.0" stroke="BLACK" strokeType="INSIDE"
         strokeWidth="5.0" />
   </children>
</Pane>
```

Fig. 22.12 | FXML for a `Circle` that will be animated by the controller.

The application's controller (Fig. 22.13) configures then plays the `Timeline` animation in the `initialize` method. Lines 22–45 define the animation, line 48 specifies that the animation should cycle indefinitely (until the program terminates or the animation's `stop` method is called) and line 49 plays the animation.

```
1  // Fig. 22.13: TimelineAnimationController.java
2  // Bounce a circle around a window using a Timeline animation
3  import java.security.SecureRandom;
4  import javafx.animation.KeyFrame;
5  import javafx.animation.Timeline;
6  import javafx.event.ActionEvent;
7  import javafx.event.EventHandler;
8  import javafx.fxml.FXML;
9  import javafx.geometry.Bounds;
10 import javafx.scene.layout.Pane;
```

Fig. 22.13 | Bounce a circle around a window using a `Timeline` animation. (Part 1 of 3.)

```
import javafx.scene.shape.Circle;
import javafx.util.Duration;

public class TimelineAnimationController {
   @FXML Circle c;
   @FXML Pane pane;

   public void initialize() {
      SecureRandom random = new SecureRandom();

      // define a timeline animation
      Timeline timelineAnimation = new Timeline(
         new KeyFrame(Duration.millis(10),
            new EventHandler<ActionEvent>() {
               int dx = 1 + random.nextInt(5);
               int dy = 1 + random.nextInt(5);

               // move the circle by the dx and dy amounts
               @Override
               public void handle(final ActionEvent e) {
                  c.setLayoutX(c.getLayoutX() + dx);
                  c.setLayoutY(c.getLayoutY() + dy);
                  Bounds bounds = pane.getBoundsInLocal();

                  if (hitRightOrLeftEdge(bounds)) {
                     dx *= -1;
                  }

                  if (hitTopOrBottom(bounds)) {
                     dy *= -1;
                  }
               }
            }
         )
      );

      // indicate that the timeline animation should run indefinitely
      timelineAnimation.setCycleCount(Timeline.INDEFINITE);
      timelineAnimation.play();
   }

   // determines whether the circle hit the left or right of the window
   private boolean hitRightOrLeftEdge(Bounds bounds) {
      return (c.getLayoutX() <= (bounds.getMinX() + c.getRadius())) ||
         (c.getLayoutX() >= (bounds.getMaxX() - c.getRadius()));
   }

   // determines whether the circle hit the top or bottom of the window
   private boolean hitTopOrBottom(Bounds bounds) {
      return (c.getLayoutY() <= (bounds.getMinY() + c.getRadius())) ||
         (c.getLayoutY() >= (bounds.getMaxY() - c.getRadius()));
   }
}
```

Fig. 22.13 | Bounce a circle around a window using a `Timeline` animation. (Part 2 of 3.)

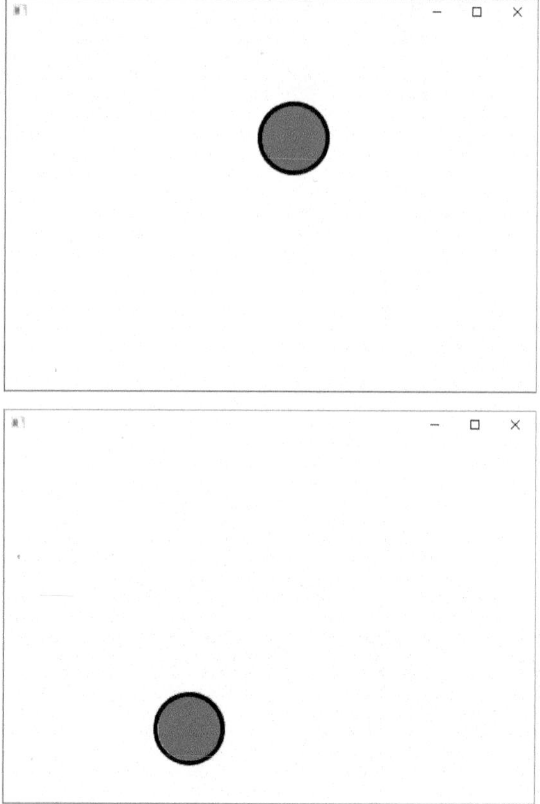

Fig. 22.13 | Bounce a circle around a window using a `Timeline` animation. (Part 3 of 3.)

Creating the `Timeline`

The `Timeline` constructor used in lines 22–45 can receive a comma-separated list of `KeyFrame`s as arguments—in this case, we pass a single `KeyFrame`. Each `KeyFrame` issues an `ActionEvent` at a particular time in the animation. The app can respond to the event by changing a `Node`'s property values. The `KeyFrame` constructor used here specifies that, after 10 milliseconds, the `ActionEvent` will occur. Because we set the `Timeline`'s cycle count to `Timeline.INDEFINITE`, the `Timeline` will perform this `KeyFrame` every 10 milliseconds. Lines 24–43 define the `EventHandler` for the `KeyFrame`'s `ActionEvent`.

`KeyFrame`*'s* `EventHandler`

In the `KeyFrame`'s `EventHandler` we define instance variables `dx` and `dy` (lines 25–26) and initialize them with randomly chosen values that will be used to change the `Circle`'s *x*- and *y*-coordinates each time the `KeyFrame` plays. The `EventHandler`'s `handle` method (lines 29–42) adds these values to the `Circle`'s *x*- and *y*-coordinates (lines 31–32). Next, lines 35–41 perform bounds checking to determine whether the `Circle` has collided with any of the `Pane`'s edges. If the `Circle` hits the left or right edge, line 36 multiplies the value of `dx` by `-1` to reverse the `Circle`'s horizontal direction. If the `Circle` hits the top or bottom edge, line 40 multiplies the value of `dx` by `-1` to reverse the `Circle`'s horizontal direction.

22.9 Frame-by-Frame Animation with AnimationTimer

A third way to implement JavaFX animations is via an **AnimationTimer** (package javafx.animation), which enables you to define frame-by-frame animations. You specify how your objects should move in a given frame, then JavaFX aggregates all of the drawing operations and displays the frame. This can be used with objects in the scene graph or to draw shapes in a Canvas. JavaFX calls the **handle** method of every AnimationTimer before it draws an animation frame.

For smooth animation, JavaFX tries to display animation frames at 60 frames per second. This frame rate varies based on the animation's complexity, the processor speed and how busy the processor is at a given time. For this reason, method handle receives a time stamp in nanoseconds (billionths of a second) that you can use to determine the elapsed time since the last animation frame, then you can scale the movements of your objects accordingly. This enables you to define animations that operate at the same overall speed, regardless of the frame rate on a given device.

Figure 22.14 reimplements the animation in Fig. 22.13 using an AnimationTimer. The FXML is identical (other than the filename and controller class name). Much of the code is identical to Fig. 22.13—we've highlighted the key changes, which we discuss below.

```java
// Fig. 22.14: BallAnimationTimerController.java
// Bounce a circle around a window using an AnimationTimer subclass.
import java.security.SecureRandom;
import javafx.animation.AnimationTimer;
import javafx.fxml.FXML;
import javafx.geometry.Bounds;
import javafx.scene.layout.Pane;
import javafx.scene.shape.Circle;
import javafx.util.Duration;

public class BallAnimationTimerController {
   @FXML private Circle c;
   @FXML private Pane pane;

   public void initialize() {
      SecureRandom random = new SecureRandom();

      // define a timeline animation
      AnimationTimer timer = new AnimationTimer() {
         int dx = 1 + random.nextInt(5);
         int dy = 1 + random.nextInt(5);
         int velocity = 60; // used to scale distance changes
         long previousTime = System.nanoTime(); // time since app launch

         // specify how to move Circle for current animation frame
         @Override
         public void handle(long now) {
            double elapsedTime = (now - previousTime) / 1000000000.0;
            previousTime = now;
            double scale = elapsedTime * velocity;
```

Fig. 22.14 | Bounce a circle around a window using an AnimationTimer subclass. (Part 1 of 2.)

```
31
32                Bounds bounds = pane.getBoundsInLocal();
33                c.setLayoutX(c.getLayoutX() + dx * scale);
34                c.setLayoutY(c.getLayoutY() + dy * scale);
35
36                if (hitRightOrLeftEdge(bounds)) {
37                   dx *= -1;
38                }
39
40                if (hitTopOrBottom(bounds)) {
41                   dy *= -1;
42                }
43             }
44          };
45
46          timer.start();
47       }
48
49       // determines whether the circle hit left/right of the window
50       private boolean hitRightOrLeftEdge(Bounds bounds) {
51          return (c.getLayoutX() <= (bounds.getMinX() + c.getRadius())) ||
52             (c.getLayoutX() >= (bounds.getMaxX() - c.getRadius()));
53       }
54
55       // determines whether the circle hit top/bottom of the window
56       private boolean hitTopOrBottom(Bounds bounds) {
57          return (c.getLayoutY() <= (bounds.getMinY() + c.getRadius())) ||
58             (c.getLayoutY() >= (bounds.getMaxY() - c.getRadius()));
59       }
60    }
```

Fig. 22.14 | Bounce a circle around a window using an `AnimationTimer` subclass. (Part 2 of 2.)

Extending `abstract` *Class* `AnimationTimer`

Class `AnimationTimer` is an `abstract` class, so you must create a subclass. In this example, lines 19–44 create an anonymous inner class that extends `AnimationTimer`. Lines 20–23 define the anonymous inner class's instance variables:

- As in Fig. 22.13, `dx` and `dy` incrementally change the `Circle`'s position and are chosen randomly so the `Circle` moves at different speeds during each execution.
- Variable `velocity` is used as a multiplier to determine the actual distance moved in each animation frame—we discuss this again momentarily.
- Variable `previousTime` represents the time stamp (in nanoseconds) of the previous animation frame—this will be used to determine the elapsed time between frames. We initialized `previousTime` to `System.nanoTime()`, which returns the number of nanoseconds since the JVM launched the app. Each call to `handle` also receives as its argument the number of nanoseconds since the JVM launched the app.

Overriding Method `handle`

Lines 26–43 override `AnimationTimer` method `handle`, which specifies what to do during each animation frame:

- Line 28 calculates the `elapsedTime` in *seconds* since the last animation frame. If method `handle` truly is called 60 times per second, the elapsed time between frames will be approximately 0.0167 seconds—that is, 1/60 of a second.
- Line 29 stores the time stamp in `previousTime` for use in the *next* animation frame.
- When we change the `Circle`'s `layoutX` and `layoutY` (lines 33–34), we multiply `dx` and `dy` by the `scale` (line 30). In Fig. 22.13, the `Circle`'s speed was determined by moving between one and five pixels along the *x*- and *y*-axes every 10 milliseconds—the larger the values, the faster the `Circle` moved. If we scale `dx` or `dy` by just `elapsedTime`, we'd move the `Circle` only small fractions of `dx` and `dy` during each frame—approximately 0.0167 seconds (1/60 of a second) to 0.083 seconds (5/60 of a second), based on their randomly chosen values. For this reason, we multiply the `elapsedTime` by the `velocity` (60) to scale the movement in each frame. This results in values that are approximately one to five pixels, as in Fig. 22.13.

22.10 Drawing on a Canvas

So far, you've displayed and manipulated JavaFX two-dimensional shape objects that reside in the scene graph. In this section, we demonstrate similar drawing capabilities using the `javafx.scene.canvas` package, which contains two classes:

- Class **`Canvas`** is a subclass of `Node` in which you can draw graphics.
- Class **`GraphicsContext`** performs the drawing operations on a `Canvas`.

As you'll see, a `GraphicsContext` object enables you to specify the same drawing characteristics that you've previously used on `Shape` objects. However, with a `GraphicsContext`, you must set these characteristics and draw the shapes programmatically. To demonstrate various `Canvas` capabilities, Fig. 22.15 re-implements Section 22.3's `BasicShapes` example. Here, you'll see various JavaFX classes and `enum`s (from packages `javafx.scene.image`, `javafx.scene.paint` and `javafx.scene.shape`) that JavaFX's CSS capabilities use behind the scenes to style `Shape`s.

Performance Tip 22.1

A `Canvas` typically is preferred for performance-oriented graphics, such as those in games with moving elements.

```
// Fig. 22.15: CanvasShapesController.java
// Drawing on a Canvas.
import javafx.fxml.FXML;
import javafx.scene.canvas.Canvas;
import javafx.scene.canvas.GraphicsContext;
import javafx.scene.image.Image;
import javafx.scene.paint.Color;
import javafx.scene.paint.CycleMethod;
import javafx.scene.paint.ImagePattern;
```

Fig. 22.15 | Drawing on a `Canvas`. (Part 1 of 3.)

```
import javafx.scene.paint.LinearGradient;
import javafx.scene.paint.RadialGradient;
import javafx.scene.paint.Stop;
import javafx.scene.shape.ArcType;
import javafx.scene.shape.StrokeLineCap;

public class CanvasShapesController {
   // instance variables that refer to GUI components
   @FXML private Canvas drawingCanvas;

   // draw on the Canvas
   public void initialize() {
      GraphicsContext gc = drawingCanvas.getGraphicsContext2D();
      gc.setLineWidth(10); // set all stroke widths

      // draw red line
      gc.setStroke(Color.RED);
      gc.strokeLine(10, 10, 100, 100);

      // draw green line
      gc.setGlobalAlpha(0.5); // half transparent
      gc.setLineCap(StrokeLineCap.ROUND);
      gc.setStroke(Color.GREEN);
      gc.strokeLine(100, 10, 10, 100);

      gc.setGlobalAlpha(1.0); // reset alpha transparency

      // draw rounded rect with red border and yellow fill
      gc.setStroke(Color.RED);
      gc.setFill(Color.YELLOW);
      gc.fillRoundRect(120, 10, 90, 90, 50, 50);
      gc.strokeRoundRect(120, 10, 90, 90, 50, 50);

      // draw circle with blue border and red/white radial gradient fill
      gc.setStroke(Color.BLUE);
      Stop[] stopsRadial =
         {new Stop(0, Color.RED), new Stop(1, Color.WHITE)};
      RadialGradient radialGradient = new RadialGradient(0, 0, 0.5, 0.5,
         0.6, true, CycleMethod.NO_CYCLE, stopsRadial);
      gc.setFill(radialGradient);
      gc.fillOval(230, 10, 90, 90);
      gc.strokeOval(230, 10, 90, 90);

      // draw ellipse with green border and image fill
      gc.setStroke(Color.GREEN);
      gc.setFill(new ImagePattern(new Image("yellowflowers.png")));
      gc.fillOval(340, 10, 200, 90);
      gc.strokeOval(340, 10, 200, 90);

      // draw arc with purple border and cyan/white linear gradient fill
      gc.setStroke(Color.PURPLE);
      Stop[] stopsLinear =
         {new Stop(0, Color.CYAN), new Stop(1, Color.WHITE)};
```

Fig. 22.15 | Drawing on a Canvas. (Part 2 of 3.)

```
63         LinearGradient linearGradient = new LinearGradient(0, 0, 1, 0,
64            true, CycleMethod.NO_CYCLE, stopsLinear);
65         gc.setFill(linearGradient);
66         gc.fillArc(560, 10, 90, 90, 45, 270, ArcType.ROUND);
67         gc.strokeArc(560, 10, 90, 90, 45, 270, ArcType.ROUND);
68      }
69   }
```

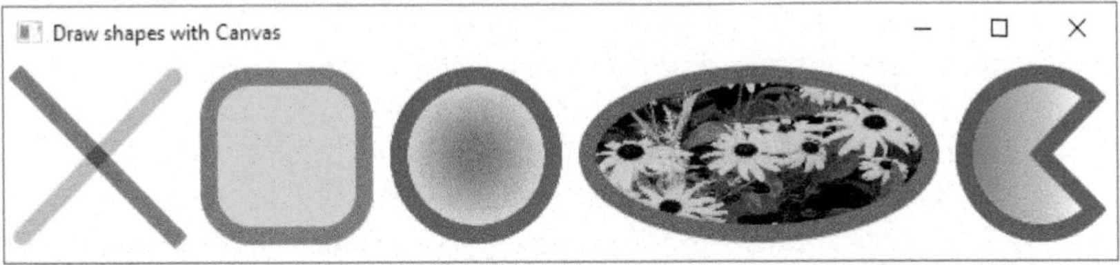

Fig. 22.15 | Drawing on a Canvas. (Part 3 of 3.)

Obtaining the **GraphicsContext**

To draw on a `Canvas`, you first obtain its `GraphicsContext` by calling `Canvas` method **`getGraphicsContext2D`** (line 22).

Setting the Line Width for All the Shapes

When you set a `GraphicsContext`'s drawing characteristics, they're applied (as appropriate) to all subsequent shapes you draw. For example, line 23 calls **`setLineWidth`** to specify the `GraphicsContext`'s line thickness (`10`). All subsequent `GraphicsContext` method calls that draw lines or shape borders will use this setting. This is similar to the `-fx-stroke-width` CSS attribute we specified for all shapes in Fig. 22.4.

Drawing Lines

Lines 26–33 draw the red and green lines:

- `GraphicsContext`'s **`setStroke`** method (lines 26 and 32) specifies the **`Paint`** object (package `javafx.scene.paint`) used to draw the line. The `Paint` can be any of the subclasses **`Color`**, **`ImagePattern`**, **`LinearGradient`** or **`RadialGradient`** (all from package `javafx.scene.paint`). We demonstrate each of these in this example—`Color` for the lines and `Color`, `ImagePattern`, `LinearGradient` or `RadialGradient` as the fills for other shapes.
- `GraphicsContext`'s **`strokeLine`** method (lines 27 and 33) draws a line using the current `Paint` object that's set as the stroke. The four arguments are the *x*-*y* coordinates of the start and end points, respectively.
- `GraphicsContext`'s **`setLineCap`** method (line 31) sets line cap, like the CSS property `-fx-stroke-line-cap` in Fig. 22.4. The argument to this method must be constant from the `enum` **`StrokeLineCap`** (package `javafx.scene.shape`). Here we round the line ends.
- `GraphicsContext`'s **`setGlobalAlpha`** method (line 30) sets the alpha transparency of all subsequent shapes you draw. For the green line we used `0.5`, which is 50% transparent. After drawing the green line, we reset this to the default `1.0` (line 35), so that subsequent shapes are fully opaque.

Drawing a Rounded Rectangle

Lines 38–41 draw a rounded rectangle with a red border:

- Line 38 sets the border color to `Color.RED`.
- `GraphicsContext`'s **`setFill`** method (lines 39, 49, 55 and 65) specifies the `Paint` object that fills a shape. Here we fill the rectangle with `Color.YELLOW`.
- `GraphicsContext`'s **`fillRoundRect`** method draws a *filled* rectangle with rounded corners using the current `Paint` object set as the fill. The method's first four arguments represent the rectangle's upper-left *x*-coordinate, upper-left *y*-coordinate, width and height, respectively. The last two arguments represent the arc width and arc height that are used to round the corners. These work identically to the CSS properties `-fx-arc-width` and `-fx-arc-height` properties in Fig. 22.4. `GraphicsContext` also provides a **`fillRect`** method that draws a rectangle without rounded corners.
- `GraphicsContext`'s **`strokeRoundRect`** method has the same arguments as `fillRoundRect`, but draws a hollow rectangle with rounded corners. `GraphicsContext` also provides a **`strokeRect`** method that draws a rectangle without rounded corners.

Drawing a Circle with a `RadialGradient` *Fill*

Lines 44–51 draw a circle with a blue border and a red-white, radial-gradient fill. Line 44 sets the border color to `Color.BLUE`. Lines 45–48 configure the `RadialGradient`—these lines perform the same tasks as the CSS function `radial-gradient` in Fig. 22.4.

First, lines 45–46 create an array of **`Stop`** objects (package `javafx.scene.paint`) representing the color stops. Each `Stop` has an offset from 0.0 to 1.0 representing the offset (as a percentage) from the gradient's start point and a `Color`. Here the `Stop`s indicate that the radial gradient will transition from red at the gradient's start point to white at its end point.

The `RadialGradient` constructor (lines 47–48) receives as arguments:

- the focus angle, which specifies the direction of the radial gradient's focal point from the gradient's center,
- the distance of the focal point as a percentage (0.0–1.0),
- the center point's *x* and *y* location as percentages (0.0–1.0) of the width and height for the shape being filled,
- a `boolean` indicating whether the gradient should scale to fill its shape,
- a constant from the **`CycleMethod`** enum (package `javafx.scene.paint`) indicating how the color stops are applied, and
- an array of `Stop` objects—this can also be a comma-separated list of `Stop`s or a `List<Stop>` object.

This creates a red-white radial gradient that starts with solid red at the center of the shape and—at 60% of the radial gradient's radius—transitions to white. Line 49 sets the fill to the new `radialGradient`, then lines 50–51 call `GraphicsContext`'s **`fillOval`** and **`strokeOval`** methods to draw a filled oval and hollow oval, respectively. Each method receives as arguments the upper-left *x*-coordinate, upper-left *y*-coordinate, width and height of the rectangular area (that is, the bounding box) in which the oval should be drawn. Because the width and height are the same, these calls draw circles.

Drawing an Oval with an **`ImagePattern`** *Fill*

Lines 54–57 draw an oval with a green border and containing an image:

- Line 54 sets the border color to `Color.GREEN`.
- Line 55 sets the fill to an `ImagePattern`—a subclass of `Paint` that loads an `Image`, either from the local system or from a URL specified as a `String`. `ImagePattern` is the class used by the CSS function `image-pattern` in Fig. 22.4.
- Lines 56–57 draw a filled oval and a hollow oval, respectively.

Drawing an Arc with a **`LinearGradient`** *Fill*

Lines 60–67 draw an arc with a purple border and filled with a cyan-white linear gradient:

- Line 60 sets the border color to `Color.PURPLE`.
- Lines 61–64 configure the `LinearGradient`, which is the class used by CSS function `linear-gradient` in Fig. 22.4. The constructor's first four arguments are the endpoint coordinates that represent the direction and angle of the gradient—if the *x*-coordinates are the same, the gradient is vertical; if the *y*-coordinates are the same, the gradient is horizontal and all other linear gradients follow a diagonal line. When these values are specified in the range 0.0 to 1.0 and the constructor's fifth argument is `true`, the gradient is scaled to fill the shape. The next argument is the `CycleMethod`. The last argument is an array of `Stop` objects—again, this can be a comma-separated list of `Stop`s or a `List<Stop>` object.

Lines 66–67 call `GraphicsContext`'s **`fillArc`** and **`strokeArc`** methods to draw a filled arc and hollow arc, respectively. Each method receives as arguments

- the upper-left *x*-coordinate, upper-left *y*-coordinate, width and height of the rectangular area (that is, the bounding box) in which the oval should be drawn,
- the start angle and sweep of the arc in degrees, and
- a constant from the **`ArcType`** `enum` (package `javafx.scene.shape`)

Additional **`GraphicsContext`** *Features*

There are many additional `GraphicsContext` features, which you can explore at

```
https://docs.oracle.com/javase/8/javafx/api/javafx/scene/canvas/
    GraphicsContext.html
```

Some of the capabilities that we did not discuss here include:

- Drawing and filling text—similar to the font features in Section 22.2.
- Drawing and filling polylines, polygons and paths—similar to the corresponding `Shape` subclasses in Section 22.4.
- Applying effects and transforms—similar to the transforms in Section 22.5.
- Drawing images.
- Manipulating the individual pixels of a drawing in a `Canvas` via a `PixelWriter`.
- Saving and restoring graphics characteristics via the save and `restore` methods.

22.11 Three-Dimensional Shapes

Throughout this chapter, we've demonstrated many two-dimensional graphics capabilities. In Java SE 8, JavaFX added several three-dimensional shapes and corresponding capabilities. The three-dimensional shapes are subclasses of **`Shape3D`** from the package `javafx.scene.shape`. In this section, you'll use Scene Builder to create a **`Box`**, a **`Cylinder`** and a **`Sphere`** and specify several of their properties. Then, in the app's controller, you'll create so-called *materials* that apply color and images to the 3D shapes.

FXML for the `Box`*,* `Cylinder` *and* `Sphere`

Figure 22.16 shows the completed FXML that we created with Scene Builder:

- Lines 16–21 define the `Box` object.
- Lines 22–27 define the `Cylinder` object.
- Lines 28–29 define the `Sphere` object.

We dragged objects of each of these `Shape3D` subclasses from the Scene Builder **Library**'s **Shapes** section onto the design area and gave them the **fx:id** values `box`, `cylinder` and `sphere`, respectively. We also set the controller to `ThreeDimensionalShapesController`.[5]

```
1  <?xml version="1.0" encoding="UTF-8"?>
2  <!-- ThreeDimensionalShapes.fxml -->
3  <!-- FXML that displays a Box, Cylinder and Sphere -->
4
5  <?import javafx.geometry.Point3D?>
6  <?import javafx.scene.layout.Pane?>
7  <?import javafx.scene.shape.Box?>
8  <?import javafx.scene.shape.Cylinder?>
9  <?import javafx.scene.shape.Sphere?>
10
11 <Pane prefHeight="200.0" prefWidth="510.0"
12    xmlns="http://javafx.com/javafx/8.0.60"
13    xmlns:fx="http://javafx.com/fxml/1"
14    fx:controller="ThreeDimensionalShapesController">
15    <children>
16       <Box fx:id="box" depth="100.0" height="100.0" layoutX="100.0"
17          layoutY="100.0" rotate="30.0" width="100.0">
18          <rotationAxis>
19             <Point3D x="1.0" y="1.0" z="1.0" />
20          </rotationAxis>
21       </Box>
22       <Cylinder fx:id="cylinder" height="100.0" layoutX="265.0"
23          layoutY="100.0" radius="50.0" rotate="-45.0">
24          <rotationAxis>
25             <Point3D x="1.0" y="1.0" z="1.0" />
```

Fig. 22.16 | FXML that displays a `Box`, `Cylinder` and `Sphere`. (Part 1 of 2.)

5. At the time of this writing, when you drag three-dimensional shapes onto the Scene Builder design area, their dimensions are set to small values by default—a `Box`'s **Width**, **Height** and **Depth** are set to 2, a `Cylinder`'s **Height** and **Radius** are set to 2 and `0.77`, and a `Sphere`'s **Radius** is set to `0.77`. You may need to select them in the **Hierarchy** pane to set their properties.

```
            </rotationAxis>
        </Cylinder>
        <Sphere fx:id="sphere" layoutX="430.0" layoutY="100.0"
            radius="60.0" />
    </children>
</Pane>
```

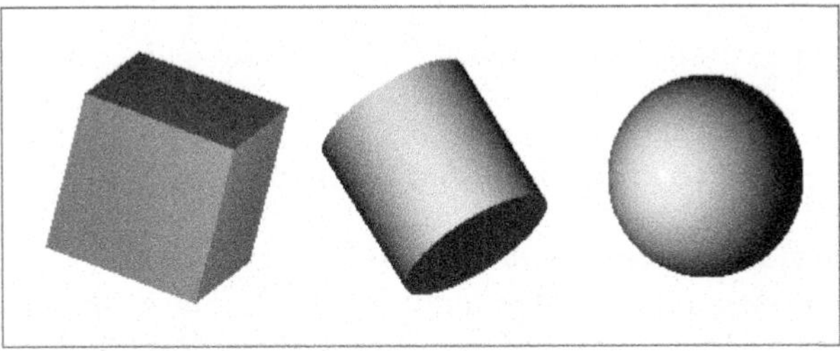

Fig. 22.16 | FXML that displays a `Box`, `Cylinder` and `Sphere`. (Part 2 of 2.)

As you can see in the screen capture of Figure 22.16, all three shapes initially are gray. The shading you see in Scene Builder comes from the scene's default lighting. Though we do not use them in this example, package `javafx.scene`'s `AmbientLight` and `PointLight` classes can be used to add your own lighting effects. You can also use camera objects to view the scene from different angles and distances. These are located in the Scene Builder **Library**'s **3D** section. For more information on lighting and cameras, see

```
https://docs.oracle.com/javase/8/javafx/graphics-tutorial/javafx-
    3d-graphics.htm
```

We ask you to investigate these capabilities and use them in Exercise 22.11.

`Box` *Properties*

Configure the `Box`'s properties in Scene Builder as follows:

- Set **Width, Height** and **Depth** to `100`, making a cube. The depth is measured along the *z*-axis which runs perpendicular to your screen—when you move objects along the *z*-axis they get bigger as they're brought toward you and smaller as they're moved away from you.
- Set **Layout X** and **Layout Y** to `100` to specify the location of the cube.
- Set **Rotate** to `30` to specify the rotation angle in degrees. Positive values rotate counter-clockwise.
- For **Rotation Axis**, set the **X**, **Y** and **Z** values to `1` to indicate that the **Rotate** angle should be used to rotate the cube 30 degrees around *each* axis.

To see how the **Rotate** angle and **Rotation Axis** values affect the `Box`'s rotation, try setting two of the three **Rotation Axis** values to `0`, then changing the **Rotate** angle.

`Cylinder` *Properties*

Configure the `Cylinder`'s properties in Scene Builder as follows:

- Set **Height** to `100.0` and **Radius** to `50`.

- Set **Layout X** and **Layout Y** to `265` and `100`, respectively.
- Set **Rotate** to `-45` to specify the rotation angle in degrees. Negative values rotate clockwise.
- For **Rotation Axis**, set the **X**, **Y** and **Z** values to `1` to indicate that the **Rotate** angle should be applied to all three axes.

`Sphere` *Properties*

Configure the `Sphere`'s properties in Scene Builder as follows:

- Set **Radius** to `60`.
- Set **Layout X** and **Layout Y** to `430` and `100`, respectively.

`ThreeDimensionalShapesController` *Class*

Figure 22.17 shows this app's controller and final output. The colors and images you see on the final shapes are created by applying so-called materials to the shapes. JavaFX class **`PhongMaterial`** (package `javafx.scene.paint`) is used to define materials. The name "Phong" is a 3D graphics term—*phong shading* is technique for applying color and shading to 3D surfaces. For more details on this technique, visit

```
https://en.wikipedia.org/wiki/Phong_shading
```

```java
// Fig. 22.17: ThreeDimensionalShapesController.java
// Setting the material displayed on 3D shapes.
import javafx.fxml.FXML;
import javafx.scene.paint.Color;
import javafx.scene.paint.PhongMaterial;
import javafx.scene.image.Image;
import javafx.scene.shape.Box;
import javafx.scene.shape.Cylinder;
import javafx.scene.shape.Sphere;

public class ThreeDimensionalShapesController {
   // instance variables that refer to 3D shapes
   @FXML private Box box;
   @FXML private Cylinder cylinder;
   @FXML private Sphere sphere;

   // set the material for each 3D shape
   public void initialize() {
      // define material for the Box object
      PhongMaterial boxMaterial = new PhongMaterial();
      boxMaterial.setDiffuseColor(Color.CYAN);
      box.setMaterial(boxMaterial);

      // define material for the Cylinder object
      PhongMaterial cylinderMaterial = new PhongMaterial();
      cylinderMaterial.setDiffuseMap(new Image("yellowflowers.png"));
      cylinder.setMaterial(cylinderMaterial);

```

Fig. 22.17 | Setting the material displayed on 3D shapes. (Part 1 of 2.)

```
29         // define material for the Sphere object
30         PhongMaterial sphereMaterial = new PhongMaterial();
31         sphereMaterial.setDiffuseColor(Color.RED);
32         sphereMaterial.setSpecularColor(Color.WHITE);
33         sphereMaterial.setSpecularPower(32);
34         sphere.setMaterial(sphereMaterial);
35      }
36   }
```

Fig. 22.17 | Setting the material displayed on 3D shapes. (Part 2 of 2.)

`PhongMaterial` *for the* `Box`

Lines 20–22 configure and set the `Box` object's `PhongMaterial`. Method **`setDiffuseColor`** sets the color that's applied to the `Box`'s surfaces (that is, sides). The scene's lighting effects determine the shades of the color applied to each visible surface. These shades change, based on the angle from which the light shines on the objects.

`PhongMaterial` *for the* `Cylinder`

Lines 25–27 configure and set the `Cylinder` object's `PhongMaterial`. Method **`setDiffuseMap`** sets the `Image` that's applied to the `Cylinder`'s surfaces. Again, the scene's lighting affects how the image is shaded on the surfaces. In the output, notice that the image is darker at the left and right edges (where less light reaches) and barely visible on the bottom (where almost no light reaches).

`PhongMaterial` *for the* `Sphere`

Lines 30–34 configure and set the `Sphere` object's `PhongMaterial`. We set the diffuse color to red. Method **`setSpecularColor`** sets the color of a bright spot that makes a 3D shape appear shiny. Method **`setSpecularPower`** determines the intensity of that spot. Try experimenting with different specular powers to see changes in the bright spot's intensity.

22.12 Wrap-Up

In this chapter, we completed our discussion of JavaFX that began in Chapters 12 and 13. Here, we presented various JavaFX graphics and multimedia capabilities.

We used external Cascading Style Sheets (CSS) to customize the appearance of JavaFX `Node`s, including `Label`s and objects of various `Shape` subclasses. We displayed two-dimensional shapes, including lines, rectangles, circles, ellipses, arcs, polylines, polygons and custom paths.

We showed how to apply a transform to a `Node`, rotating 18 `Polygon` objects around a specific point to create a circle of star shapes. We created a simple video player using class `Media` to specify the video's location, class `MediaPlayer` to load the video and control its playback and class `MediaView` to display the video.

We animated `Nodes` with `Transition` and `Timeline` animations that change `Node` properties to new values over time. We used built-in `Transition` animations to change specific JavaFX `Node` properties (such as a `Node`'s stroke and fill colors, opacity, angle of rotation and scale). We used `Timeline` animations with `KeyFrames` to bounce a `Circle` around a window, and showed that such animations can be used to change any modifiable `Node` property. We also showed how to create frame-by-frame animations with `AnimationTimer`.

Next, we presented various capabilities for drawing on a `Canvas Node` using a `GraphicsContext` object. You saw that `GraphicsContext` supports many of the same drawing characteristics and shapes that you can implement with `Shape Nodes`. Finally, we showed the three-dimensional shapes `Box`, `Cylinder` and `Sphere`, and demonstrated how to use materials to apply color and images to them. For more information on JavaFX, visit the FX Experience blog at

```
http://fxexperience.com/
```

Summary

Section 22.2 Controlling Fonts with Cascading Style Sheets (CSS)

- JavaFX objects can be formatted using Cascading Style Sheets (CSS).
- CSS allows you to specify presentation (e.g., fonts, spacing, sizes, colors, positioning) separately from the GUI's structure and content (layout containers, shapes, text, GUI components, etc.).

Section 22.2.1 CSS That Styles the GUI

- Each CSS rule begins with a CSS selector which specifies the JavaFX objects that will be styled according to the rule.
- A rule with a style class selector applies to any object that has a `styleClass` property with the class name. In CSS, a style class selector begins with a dot (`.`) and is followed by its class name.
- Each CSS rule's body is delimited by a set of required braces (`{}`) containing the CSS properties that are applied to objects matching the CSS selector.
- Each JavaFX CSS property name begins with `-fx-` followed by the name of the corresponding JavaFX object's property in all lowercase letters.
- The `-fx-spacing` property specifies vertical space between objects.
- The `-fx-padding` property separates an object from its container's edges.
- Selectors that begin with # are known as ID selectors—they are applied to objects with the specified ID.
- The `-fx-font` property can specify all aspects of a font, including its style, weight, size and font family—the size and font family are required.
- Font properties also may be specified with `-fx-font-style`, `-fx-font-weight`, `-fx-font-size` and `-fx-font-family`. These are applied to a JavaFX object's similarly named properties.

Section 22.2.2 FXML That Defines the GUI—Introduction to XML Markup

- Each FXML document begins with an XML declaration, which must be the first line in the file and indicates that the document contains XML markup.
- Each XML attribute has a *name* and *value* separated by `=`, and the *value* is placed in quotation marks (`""`). Multiple *name*=*value* pairs are separated by whitespace.
- XML comments begin with `<!--` and end with `-->` and can span multiple lines.
- An FXML `import` declaration specifies the fully qualified name of a JavaFX type used in the document. Such declarations are delimited by `<?import` and `?>`.
- XML documents contain elements that specify the document's structure. Most elements are delimited by a start tag and an end tag.
- A start tag consists of angle brackets (`<` and `>`) containing the element's name followed by zero or more attributes.
- An end tag consists of the element name preceded by a forward slash (`/`) in angle brackets.
- Every XML document must have exactly one root element that contains all the other elements.
- An FXML layout element's `children` element contains the child `Nodes` arranged by that layout.
- Empty elements use the shorthand start-tag-only notation in which the empty element's start tag ends with `/>`, rather than `>`.
- An XML namespace specifies a collection of element and attribute names that you can use in the document.

Section 22.2.3 Referencing the CSS File from FXML

- If you reference a CSS file from FXML, Scene Builder can apply the CSS rules to the GUI.
- The `@` symbol—called the local resolution operator in FXML—indicates that a file is located relative to the FXML file on disk.

Section 22.2.4 Specifying the `VBox`'s Style Class

- To apply a CSS class to an object in Scene Builder, set the object's **Style Class** to the CSS class name without the dot (`.`).

Section 22.2.5 Programmatically Loading CSS

- It's possible to load CSS files dynamically and add them to a `Scene`'s collection of style sheets, which you can access via the `getStyleSheets` method.

Section 22.3 Displaying Two-Dimensional Shapes

- You can add objects of subclasses of `Shape` and `Shape3D` (package `javafx.scene.shape`) to a container in the JavaFX stage.
- You can add a `Canvas` object (package `javafx.scene.canvas`) to a container in the JavaFX stage, then draw on it using various `Canvas` methods.
- Like other `Node` types, you can drag shapes from the Scene Builder **Library**'s **Shapes** category onto the design area, then configure them via the **Properties**, **Layout** and **Code Inspectors**. You also may create objects of any JavaFX `Node` type programmatically.

Section 22.3.1 Defining Two-Dimensional Shapes with FXML

- For each property you can set in Scene Builder, there is a corresponding attribute in FXML.
- As you drag each shape onto your design, Scene Builder automatically configures certain properties, such as the **Fill** and **Stroke** colors for `Rectangles`, `Circles`, `Ellipses` and `Arcs`.

- You can remove an attribute either by setting the property to its default value in Scene Builder or by manually editing the FXML.
- The default `fill` for a shape is black.
- The default stroke is a one-pixel black line.
- The default `strokeType` is centered, based on the stroke's thickness—half the thickness appears inside the shape's bounds and half outside. You also may display a shape's stroke completely inside or outside the shape's bounds.
- A `Line` connects two endpoints specified by the properties `startX`, `startY`, `endX` and `endY`.
- The *x*- and *y*-coordinate values are measured by default from the top-left corner of the layout, with *x*-coordinates increasing left to right and *y*-coordinates increasing top to bottom.
- If you specify a `Line`'s `layoutX` and `layoutY` properties, then the `startX`, `startY`, `endX` and `endY` properties are measured from that point.
- A `Rectangle` is displayed based on its `layoutX`, `layoutY`, `width` and `height` properties. The upper-left corner is positioned at the coordinates specified by the `layoutX` and `layoutY` properties.
- A `Circle` object is centered at the point specified by the `centerX` and `centerY` properties. The `radius` property determines the `Circle`'s size around its center point.
- An `Ellipse`'s center is specified by the `centerX` and `centerY` properties. Its `radiusX` and `radiusY` properties determine the `Ellipse`'s width and height.
- An `Arcs`'s center is specified by the `centerX` and `centerY` properties, and the properties `radiusX` and `radiusY` determine the `Arc`'s width and height. You must also specify the `Arc`'s `length`, `startAngle` and `type`.

Section 22.3.2 CSS That Styles the Two-Dimensional Shapes

- You specify a CSS type selector by using the JavaFX class name.
- When JavaFX renders an object, it combines all the CSS rules that apply to the object to determine its appearance.
- Colors may be specified as named colors (such as `"red"`, `"green"` and `"blue"`), RGBA colors, colors defined by their hue, saturation, brightness and alpha components and more.
- CSS function `rgba` defines a color based on its red, green, blue and alpha components.
- The `-fx-stroke-line-cap` CSS property indicates how lines should be terminated.
- The `-fx-fill` CSS property specifies the color or pattern that appears inside a shape.
- A `Rectangle`'s `-fx-arc-width` and `-fx-arc-height` properties specify the width and height of an ellipse that's divided in half horizontally and vertically, then used to round the `Rectangle`'s corners.
- A gradient defines colors that transition gradually from one color to the next.
- CSS function `radial-gradient` produces color changes gradually from a center point outward.
- To specify an image as fill, you use the CSS function `image-pattern`.
- A linear gradient gradually transitions between colors horizontally, vertically or diagonally.

Section 22.4 `Polylines`, `Polygons` and `Paths`

- A `Polyline` draws a series of connected lines defined by a set of points.
- A `Polygon` draws a series of connected lines defined by a set of points and connects the last point to the first point.
- A `Path` draws a series of connected `PathElements` by moving to a given point, then drawing lines, arcs and curves.

Section 22.4.2 `PolyshapesController` *Class*

- A `Path` is represented by a collection of `PathElements`.
- The `MoveTo` subclass of `PathElement` moves to a specific position without drawing anything.
- The `ArcTo` subclass of `PathElement` draws an arc from the previous `PathElement`'s endpoint to the specified location.
- The `ClosePath` subclass of `PathElement` closes the path by drawing a straight line from the end point of the last `PathElement` to the start point of the first `PathElement`.
- An `ArcTo`'s `sweepFlag` determines whether the arc sweeps in the positive angle direction (`true`; counter clockwise) or the negative angle direction (`false`; clockwise).
- By default an `ArcTo` element is drawn as the shortest arc between the last `PathElement`'s end point and the point specified by the `ArcTo` element. To sweep the arc the long way around the ellipse, set the `ArcTo`'s `largeArcFlag` to `true`.

Section 22.5 Transforms

- A transform can be applied to any UI element to reposition or reorient the graphic.
- A `Translate` transform moves an object to a new location.
- A `Rotate` transform rotates an object around a point and by a specified rotation angle.
- A `Scale` transform scales an object's size by the specified amounts.
- To create a `Rotate` transform, invoke class `Transform`'s `static` method `rotate`, which returns a `Rotate` object. The method's first argument is the rotation angle. The method's next two arguments are the *x*- and *y*-coordinates of the point of rotation around which the `Shape` rotates.

Section 22.6 Playing Video with `Media`*,* `MediaPlayer` *and* `MediaViewer`

- JavaFX's audio and video capabilities are located in package `javafx.scene.media`.
- For simple audio playback you can use class `AudioClip`. For audio playback with more playback controls and for video playback you can use classes `Media`, `MediaPlayer` and `MediaView`.
- For video, JavaFX supports MPEG-4 (also called MP4) and Flash Video formats.

Section 22.6.1 VideoPlayer GUI

- `MediaView` is located in the Scene Builder **Library**'s **Controls** section.
- `ToolBar` is located in the Scene Builder **Library**'s **Containers** section. By default, Scene Builder adds one `Button` to a `ToolBar` when you drag the `ToolBar` onto your layout.

Section 22.6.2 `VideoPlayerController` *Class*

- A `Media` object specifies the location of the media to play and provides access to various information about the media, such as its duration, dimensions and more.
- A `MediaPlayer` object loads a `Media` object and controls playback. In addition, a `MediaPlayer` transitions through its various states during media loading and playback. You can provide `Runnables` that execute in response to state transitions.
- A `MediaView` object displays the `Media` being played by a given `MediaPlayer` object.
- To load a video and prepare it for playback, you must associate it with a `MediaPlayer` object.
- Playing multiple videos requires a separate `MediaPlayer` for each `Media` object. However, a given `Media` object can be associated with multiple `MediaPlayers`.
- A `MediaPlayer` does not provide a view in which to display video. For this purpose, you must associate a `MediaPlayer` with a `MediaView`. When a `MediaView` already exists—such as when it's created in FXML—you call the `MediaView`'s `setMediaPlayer` method to perform this task.

- When creating a MediaView object programmatically, you can pass a MediaPlayer to the MediaView's constructor.
- A MediaView is like any other Node in the scene graph, so you can apply CSS styles, transforms and animations to it.
- Some common MediaPlayer states include *ready*, *playing* and *paused*.
- To perform a task for a given state, you specify an object that implements the Runnable interface (package java.lang). This interface contains a no-parameter run method that returns void.
- MediaPlayer's setOnEndOfMedia method receives a Runnable object that should execute when video playback completes.
- MediaPlayer method seek moves to a specified time in the media clip.
- MediaPlayer's setOnError method receives a Runnable object that should execute if the MediaPlayer enters the *error* state, indicating that an error occurred during playback.
- MediaPlayer's setOnReady method receives a Runnable object that should execute if the MediaPlayer enters the *ready* state.
- A Node's sceneProperty returns a ReadOnlyObjectProperty<Scene> that you can use to access to the Scene in which the Node is displayed.
- To bind to a specific properties of an object, you can use the methods of class Bindings (package javafx.beans.binding) to select the corresponding properties.
- Bindings method selectDouble gets a reference to a DoubleProperty.

Section 22.7 **Transition** *Animations*
- Transition animations change a Node's property values from one value to another in a specified amount of time. Most properties of a Node can be animated.
- By default, the subclasses that define Transition animations (package javafx.animations) change the values of specific Node properties.

Section 22.7.2 **TransitionAnimationsController** *Class*
- A FillTransition changes a shape's fill color.
- A StrokeTransition changes a shape's stroke color.
- A ParallelTransition performs multiple transitions at the same time (that is, in parallel).
- A FadeTransition changes a Node's opacity.
- A RotateTransition rotates a Node.
- Each Transition animation uses an Interpolator to calculate new property values throughout the animation's duration.
- The Interpolator EASE_BOTH begins the animation slowly at first (known as "easing in"), speeds up the in the middle, then slows again to complete the animation (known as "easing out").
- A PathTransition changes a shape's position by moving it along a Path.
- The LineTo subclass of PathElement draws a straight line from the previous PathElement's endpoint to the specified location.
- The Interpolator EASE_IN begins an animation slowly at first, then continues at full speed.
- A ScaleTransition changes a Node's size.
- The Interpolator EASE_OUT begins an animation at full speed, then slows down as the animation completes.

- A SequentialTransition performs a sequence of transitions—as each completes, the next one in the sequence begins executing.
- Every Transition has a play method that begins the animation.

Section 22.8 **Timeline** *Animations*

- A Timeline animation can change any Node property that's modifiable. You specify how to change property values with one or more KeyFrame objects that the Timeline animation performs in sequence.
- Each KeyFrame issues an ActionEvent at a particular time in the animation. The app can respond to the event by changing a Node's property values.
- Setting an animation's cycle count to Timeline.INDEFINITE performs an animation until its stop method is called or the program terminates.

Section 22.9 Frame-By-Frame Animation with **AnimationTimer**

- An AnimationTimer (package javafx.animation) enables you to define frame-by-frame animations. You specify how your objects should move in a given frame, then JavaFX aggregates all of the drawing operations and displays the frame.
- JavaFX calls the handle method of every AnimationTimer before it draws an animation frame.
- For smooth animation, JavaFX tries to display animation frames at 60 frames per second.
- Method handle receives a time stamp in nanoseconds (billionths of a second) that you can use to determine the elapsed time since the last animation frame, then you can scale the movements of your objects accordingly. This enables you to define animations that operate at the same overall speed, regardless of the frame rate on a given device.
- Class AnimationTimer is an abstract class, so you must create a subclass to use it.

Section 22.10 Drawing on a **Canvas**

- Package javafx.scene.canvas contains two classes: Canvas is a subclass of Node in which you can draw graphics, and GraphicsContext performs the drawing operations on a Canvas.
- To draw on a Canvas, you must first obtain its GraphicsContext by calling Canvas method getGraphicsContext2D.
- When you set a GraphicsContext's drawing characteristics, they're applied (as appropriate) to all subsequent shapes you draw. For example, if you call setLineWidth to specify the GraphicsContext's line thickness, all subsequent GraphicsContext method calls that draw lines or shape borders will use this setting.
- GraphicsContext's setStroke method specifies the Paint object (package javafx.scene.paint) used to draw the line. The Paint can be any of the subclasses Color, ImagePattern, LinearGradient or RadialGradient.
- GraphicsContext's strokeLine method draws a line using the current Paint object that's set as the stroke. The four arguments are the *x-y* coordinates of the start and end points, respectively.
- GraphicsContext's setLineCap method sets line cap.
- GraphicsContext's setGlobalAlpha method sets the alpha transparency of all subsequent shapes you draw.
- GraphicsContext's setFill method specifies the Paint object used to fill a shape.
- GraphicsContext's strokeRoundRect method draws a hollow rectangle with rounded corners.
- GraphicsContext's fillRoundRect method has the same arguments as strokeRoundRect, but uses the current Paint object set as the fill to draw a filled rectangle with rounded corners.

- GraphicsContext's strokeRect method draws a hollow rectangle without rounded corners.
- GraphicsContext's fillRect method draws a filled rectangle without rounded corners.
- A RadialGradient specifies a gradient that radiates outward from a focal point.
- Stop objects represent color stops in a gradient.
- GraphicsContext's fillOval and strokeOval methods draw a filled and hollow oval, respectively.
- ImagePattern is a subclass of Paint that loads an Image, either from the local system or from a URL specified as a String.
- A LinearGradient specifies a gradient that transitions between colors along a straight line.
- GraphicsContext's fillArc and strokeArc methods draw filled and hollow arcs, respectively.

Section 22.11 Three-Dimensional Shapes

- The three-dimensional shapes are subclasses of Shape3D from the package javafx.scene.shape. These include Box, Cylinder and Sphere.
- The shading you see for three-dimensional shapes in Scene Builder comes from the scene's default lighting. Package javafx.scene's AmbientLight and PointLight classes can be used to add your own lighting effects.
- You can use camera objects to view a scene from different angles and distances.
- An object's depth is measured along the *z*-axis, which runs perpendicular to your screen—when you move objects along the *z*-axis they get bigger as they're brought toward you and smaller as they're moved away from you.
- Colors and images on three-dimensional shapes are created by applying materials to the shapes.
- JavaFX class PhongMaterial is used to define materials.
- The name "Phong" is a 3D graphics term—phong shading is a technique for applying color and shading to 3D surfaces.
- PhongMaterial method setDiffuseColor sets the color that's applied to a three-dimensional shape's surface(s). The scene's lighting effects determine the shades of the color that are applied to each visible surface.
- PhongMaterial method setDiffuseMap sets the Image that's applied to a three-dimensional shape's surface(s).
- PhongMaterial method setSpecularColor sets the color of a bright spot that makes a 3D shape appear shiny. PhongMaterial method setSpecularPower determines the intensity of that spot.

Self-Review Exercises

22.1 Fill in the blanks in each of the following statements:

a) Selectors that begin with ________ are known as ID selectors—they are applied to objects with the specified ID.
b) XML comments begin with ________ and end with --> and can span multiple lines.
c) The *x*- and *y*-coordinate values are measured by default from the ________ corner of the layout, with *x*-coordinates increasing left to right and *y*-coordinates increasing top to bottom.
d) The ________ CSS property indicates how lines should be terminated.
e) A(n) ________ defines colors that transition gradually from one color to the next.
f) A(n) ________ can be applied to any UI element to reposition or reorient the graphic.
g) To perform a task for a given state of a MediaPlayer, you specify an object that implements interface ________ (package java.lang).
h) A FadeTransition changes a Node's ________.

i) Each Transition animation uses a(n) ________ to calculate new property values throughout the animation's duration.
j) Package javafx.scene.canvas contains two classes: Canvas is a subclass of Node in which you can draw graphics and ________ performs the drawing operations on a Canvas.
k) ________ objects represent color stops in a gradient.
l) Colors and images you see on three-dimensional shapes are created by applying ________ to the shapes.
m) JavaFX class ________ is used to define materials.

22.2 State whether each of the following is *true* or *false*. If *false*, explain why.
a) Each CSS rule begins with a CSS collector which specifies the JavaFX objects that will be styled according to the rule.
b) An XML start tag consists of square brackets ([and]) containing the element's name followed by zero or more attributes.
c) It's possible to load CSS files dynamically and add them to a Scene's collection of style sheets, which you can access via the getStyleSheets method.
d) For each property you set in Scene Builder, there is a corresponding attribute in FXML.
e) You specify a CSS type selector by using the JavaFX class name.
f) A Polyline draws a series of connected lines defined by a set of points and connects the last point to the first point.
g) PathElement subclass MoveTo moves to a specific position without drawing anything.
h) For video, JavaFX supports MPEG-4 (also called MP4) and Flash Video formats.
i) Playing multiple videos requires a separate MediaPlayer for each Media object.
j) Transition animations change a Node's property values from one value to another in a specified amount of time. Only one property of a Node can be animated.
k) Setting an animation's cycle count to Timeline.INFINITE performs an animation until its stop method is called or the program terminates.
l) For smooth animation, JavaFX tries to display animation frames at 30 frames per second.
m) You cannot define animations that operate at the same overall speed, regardless of the frame rate on a given device.
n) Class AnimationTimer is a concrete class.
o) If you call setLineWidth to specify the GraphicsContext's line thickness, all subsequent GraphicsContext method calls that draw lines or shape borders will use this setting.
p) A three-dimensional object's depth is measured along the *z*-axis which runs parallel to your screen.
q) PhongMaterial method setSpecularColor sets the color of a bright spot that makes a 3D shape appear shiny. PhongMaterial method setSpecularPower determines the intensity of that spot.

Answers to Self-Review Exercises

22.1 a) #. b) <!--. c) top-left. d) -fx-stroke-line-cap. e) gradient. f) transform. g) Runnable. h) opacity. i) Interpolator. j) GraphicsContext. k) Stop. l) materials. m) PhongMaterial.

22.2 a) False. Each CSS rule begins with a CSS selector which specifies the JavaFX objects that will be styled according to the rule. b) False. A start tag consists of angle brackets (< and >) containing the element's name followed by zero or more attributes. c) True. d) True. e) True. f) False. A Polygon draws a series of connected lines defined by a set of points and connects the last point to the first point. g) True. h) True. i) True. j) False. Most properties of a Node can be animated. k) False. Setting an animation's cycle count to Timeline.INDEFINITE performs an animation until its stop method is called or the program terminates. l) False. For smooth animation, JavaFX tries to display animation frames at 60 frames per second. m) False. Method `handle` receives a time stamp in nanoseconds (billionths of a second) that you can use to determine the elapsed time since the last animation frame, so you can define animations that operate at the same overall speed, regardless of the frame rate on a given device. n) False. Class `AnimationTimer` is an `abstract` class, so you must create a subclass to use it. o) True. p) A three-dimensional object's depth is measured along the *z*-axis, which runs perpendicular to your screen. q) True.

Exercises

22.3 *(Enhanced* ***`DrawStars`*** *app)* Modify the `DrawStars` example in Section 22.5 so that all the stars have `Rotate` transition animations that execute indefinitely—that is, set each animation's cycle count to `Animation.INDEFINITE`.

22.4 *(****`PolyLine`*** *app)* Create an app in which, as the user moves the mouse cursor around the window, a `Circle` and `Polyline` follow the cursor. The app should appear as shown in Fig. 22.18. There should always be a `Circle` centered at the current mouse-cursor location, and that location should also be the first point in the `Polyline`. As you respond to each mouse-move event, use the mouse cursor's location as the `Circle`'s new center and insert that location at the *beginning* of the `Polyline`'s points collection. The `Polyline`'s length should not increase forever—once the `Polyline` reaches 50 points, remove the last point each time you insert a new first point.

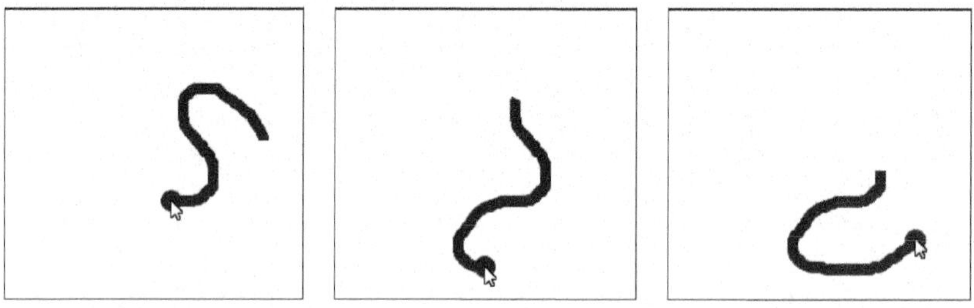

Fig. 22.18 | `Circle` and `Polyline` follow the mouse cursor inside the window.

22.5 *(****`UsingGradients`*** *app)* Create a `UsingGradients` app that displays a `Rectangle` and enables the user to fill it with a radial or a linear gradient. The app should enable users to modify either gradient by specifying the RGBA values for the starting and ending gradient colors. Use `RadioButtons` to allow the user to select the gradient type. [*Hint:* You'll need to programmatically create and apply the gradients in this example.]

Project Exercises

[*Note to Instructors:* **No solutions are provided for these projects.]**

22.6 *(Creating Static Art with a* ***`Canvas`*** *Node)* Create an art app similar to the **Painter** app in Section 13.3 that allows you to draw shapes by clicking and dragging the mouse in a `Canvas`. Include options for:

a) selecting the shape to draw—line, rectangle or oval.
b) changing the line color and line thickness.
c) specifying the fill color for rectangles and ovals.

Provide red, green and blue sliders that allow you to select the RGBA color for the line or fill. Include a color swatch below the three sliders so that as you move each slider, the color swatch shows you the current drawing color. Also include options that allow you to turn the cursor into an eraser and to clear the entire drawing.

22.7 *(Creating Static Art with* **Shapes** *in the Scene Graph)* Create an art app similar to the **Painter** app in Section 13.3 that allows you to draw shapes by clicking and dragging the mouse in a `Pane` and adding an appropriate `Shape` object to the scene graph. Include options for:

a) selecting the Shape subclass to draw—`Line`, `Rectangle`, `Circle` or `Ellipse`.
b) changing the stroke color and thickness.
c) specifying the fill color for `Rectangles`, `Circles` or `Ellipses`.

Provide red, green and blue sliders that allow you to select the RGBA color for the line or fill. Include a color swatch below the three sliders so that as you move each slider, the color swatch shows you the current drawing color. Also include options that allow you to undo the last shape and to clear the entire drawing. Enable the user to select an existing shape and move it or delete it.

22.8 *(Random 2D Dynamic Art with* **Canvas** *and* **AnimationTimer***)* Write an app that continuously draws shapes of your choosing on a `Canvas`. Use random positions, sizes, locations, line widths, fills and alpha transparencies. The shapes should randomly move around the `Canvas` in different directions and at different speeds.

22.9 *(Random 2D Dynamic Art with* **Shapes***, the Scene Graph and* **AnimationTimers***)* Write an app that continuously displays `Shape` subclass objects on a `Pane` with random sizes, locations, stroke widths, fills and alpha transparencies. The `Shapes` should randomly move around the `Canvas` in different directions and at different speeds. You'll need to programmatically create and manipulate the `Shapes`, then configure their settings similarly to how you specified a `GraphicsContext`'s settings in Section 22.10. Each `Shape` you create should have its own `AnimationTimer`.

22.10 *(Random 3D Animated Art with the Scene Graph and* **AnimationTimers***)* Using the techniques you learned in Section 22.11, create an app that continuously displays `Boxes`, `Cylinders` and `Spheres` on a `Pane` with random sizes, locations and diffuse colors. For each three-dimensional shape, create an `AnimationTimer` that moves and rotates the shape around. For bounds-testing purposes assume the depth of the *z*-axis is 400 pixels. As the shape moves along the *z*-axis it should shrink when moving away from the user and grow when moving towards the user.

22.11 *(Experimenting with 3D Lighting and Camera Effects Capabilities)* JavaFX supports lighting and camera effects. The classes for these are `AmbientLight`, `PointLight`, `ParallelCamera` and `PerspectiveCamera` (package `javafx.scene`). Investigate each of these classes, then modify Exercise 22.10 to incorporate these capabilities. Provide a GUI that enables the user to control where the lights and cameras are located in the scene and which are active at a given time.

22.12 *(***Hangman Game** *App Using* **Shapes** *and the Scene Graph)* Recreate the classic word game Hangman. At the start of the game, display a dashed line with one dash representing each letter in the word to be guessed. As a hint to the user, provide either a category for the word (e.g., sport or landmark) or the word's definition. Ask the user to enter a letter. If the letter is in the word, display it in the location of the corresponding dash. Otherwise, draw part of the hangman stick figure. The game ends when the user completes the word or the entire hangman stick figure is drawn to the screen.

22.13 *(***Block Breaker** *Game Using* **Shapes** *and the Scene Graph)* Use the bouncing-ball animation techniques you learned in Section 22.8 to create a **Block Breaker** game with

a) a bouncing ball (a `Circle`),
b) several rows and columns of blocks (`Rectangles`) in red, yellow, blue or green (randomly selected for each block), and
c) a paddle (another `Rectangle`) at the bottom of the app.

When the app begins executing, the ball is sitting on top of the paddle, which is located at the bottom-center of the window. The user clicks the mouse to set the ball in motion toward the blocks—that is, its `dy` value is initially negative. When the ball hits a block, that block should be removed from the screen and the ball should bounce back towards the blocker—that is, its `dy` value becomes positive, similar to bouncing off the top of the `Pane` in Section 22.8's app. If the ball hits the left or right side of the `Pane` it should bounce in the opposite direction, as in Section 22.8's app. To move the ball toward the blocks again, the user must move the paddle (by moving the mouse left or right in the window) so the ball will bounce off the paddle to change directions. The `dx` value should change only when the ball hits the `Pane`'s left or right side. For this version of the app, set the `dx` and `dy` values to `2`. You can test for collisions between the ball and the blocks or paddle by using the `Shape` class's `static intersect` method.

The user should begin with three lives—if the ball misses the paddle and falls off the bottom of the screen, the user should lose a life. The game ends when the user either clears all the blocks or loses all three lives. Award points for each block that's destroyed with more points for blocks in the higher rows.

22.14 *(Enhanced **Block Breaker** Game)* Modify the **Block Breaker** game in Exercise 22.13 as follows:

a) When the ball hits the paddle, change its `dx` value and direction based on the intersection point. For example, assume the paddle has three "zones." If the ball hits the left zone, `dx` should be set to `-5` so the ball moves to the left by 5 pixels each time its location changes. If the ball hits the right zone, `dx` should be set to `5` so the ball moves to the right by 5 pixels each time its location changes. If the ball hits the center zone, it should keep moving in the same *x* direction by 2 pixels each time its location changes.
b) Add multiple levels. In each level, the ball's speed should increase by 10% and the size of the paddle should decrease by 5%.
c) Provide a continuous mode in which as the user clears a row, the existing blocks move down a row and a new row of blocks is added at the top.

22.15 *(**Word Search** App with the Scene Graph)* Create a grid of letters that fills the screen. Hidden in the grid should be at least ten words. The words may be horizontal, vertical or diagonal, and, in each case, forward, backward, up or down. Allow the user to highlight the words by dragging the mouse across the letters on the screen or clicking each letter of the word. Include a timer. The less time it takes the user to complete the game (that is, to highlight all the letters of all the legitimate words), the higher the score.

22.16 *(Animated **Fractal** App with `Canvas`)* Using the animation techniques you learned in this chapter, modify the fractal app of Section 18.9 to animate the Lo fractal. Provide options that allow the user to specify the number of levels, then animate the fractal from level 1 to the user-specified level. Draw the lines in random colors.

22.17 *(**Kaleidescope** App with `Canvas`)* Create an app that simulates a kaleidoscope. Allow the user to click a `Button` to clear the screen and draw another kaleidoscope image.

22.18 *(**Game of Snake** App with `Canvas`)* Research the Game of Snake online and develop an app that allows a user to play the game.

22.19 *(**Digital Clock** App with the Scene Graph and `Timeline` Animation)* Create an app that displays a digital clock on the screen in a `Label`. Include alarm-clock functionality. Use a `Timeline` animation that executes once per second.

22.20 *(**Analog Clock** App with `Canvas` and an `Animation Timer`)* Create an app that displays an analog clock with hour, minute and second hands that move appropriately as the time changes. Use an `AnimationTimer` and scale the movement of the second hand based on the elapsed time between animation frames.

22.21 *(Animated **Towers of Hanoi** App with `Shapes`, the Scene Graph and `PathTransitions`)* Section 18.8 presented the recursive Towers of Hanoi. Write a animated solution to the Towers of Hanoi that shows the disks moving between pegs. Allow the user to enter the number of disks.

22.22 *(Text Shadow on a* `Shape` *in the Scene Graph)* Display a `Label` containing the phrase `"JavaFX"` and apply a drop shadow to the text. Investigate the JavaFX CSS function `dropshadow` at `https://docs.oracle.com/javase/8/javafx/api/javafx/scene/doc-files/cssref.html`, then use a dropshadow as the value of the CSS property `-fx-effect`, which can be applied to any `Node`.

22.23 *(Linear and Radial Gradients for* `Shapes` *in the Scene Graph)* Create shapes with a variety of linear and radial gradients. Investigate the JavaFX CSS gradient capabilities at `https://docs.oracle.com/javase/8/javafx/api/javafx/scene/doc-files/cssref.html`.

22.24 *(Shadows for a* `Rectangle` *in the Scene Graph)* Create an app that displays a rectangle with a shadow and allows the user to control the shadow using `Sliders`. Investigate class `DropShadow` (package `javafx.scene.effect`). Use `Node` method `setEffect` to apply the `DropShadow`.

22.25 *(Concentric Circles on a* `Canvas`*)* Write an app that draws eight concentric circles in a `Canvas`. For each new circle, increase the radius value by 5 pixels. Choose the circles' colors, randomly.

22.26 *(*`ImageView` *Manipulation in the Scene Graph)* Write an app that converts a color image in an `ImageView` to `SepiaTone` (package `javafx.scene.effect`).

22.27 *(Randomly Erasing an Image on a* `Canvas`*)* Suppose an image is displayed on a `Canvas`. One way to erase the image is simply to set every pixel to the same color immediately, but the visual effect is dull. Write an app that displays an image, then erases it by using random-number generation to select individual pixels to erase. After most of the image is erased, erase all the remaining pixels at once. You might try several variants of this problem. For example, you might display lines, circles or shapes randomly to erase regions of the screen. Investigate interface `PixelWriter` (package `javafx.scene.image`), which can be used to manipulate pixels in a `Canvas`. Use `GraphicsContext`'s `getPixelWriter` method to obtain the `PixelWriter`.

22.28 *(Scrolling Marquee Sign on a* `Canvas`*)* Create an app that scrolls dotted characters from right to left (or from left to right if that's appropriate for your language) across a marquee-like display sign. As an option, display the text in a continuous loop, so that after the text disappears at one end, it reappears at the other.

22.29 *(Scrolling-Image Marquee on a* `Canvas`*)* Create an app that scrolls a series of images across a marquee screen on a `Canvas`.

22.30 *(One-Armed Bandit on a* `Canvas`*)* Develop a multimedia simulation of a "one-armed bandit." Have three spinning wheels. Place symbols and images of various fruits on each wheel. Use random-number generation to simulate the spinning of each wheel and the stopping of each wheel on a symbol. Play sounds for each of the wheels spinning, a sound when each wheel stops moving and a loud ringing sound when all three wheels stop on the same fruit.

22.31 *(Game of Pool on a* `Canvas`*)* Create a multimedia-based simulation of the game of pool. Each player takes turns using the mouse to position a pool cue and hit it against the ball at the appropriate angle to try to make other balls fall into the pockets. Your app should keep score.

22.32 *(15 Puzzle Using* `Labels` *in the Scene Graph)* Create an app that enables the user to play the game of 15. The game has a 4-by-4 board with a total of 16 slots. One slot is empty; the others are occupied by 15 square tiles numbered 1 through 15. The user can move any tile next to the currently empty slot into that slot by clicking that tile. Your app should create the board with the tiles in random order. The goal is to arrange the tiles into sequential order, row by row—that is, 1–4 in the first row, 5–8 in the second row, 9–12 in the third row and 13–15 in the fourth row.

22.33 *(Eyesight Tester with* `Canvas`*)* You've probably had your eyesight tested. In these exams, you're asked to cover one eye, then read out loud the letters from an eyesight chart called a Snellen chart. The letters are arranged in 11 rows and include only the letters C, D, E, F, L, N, O, P, T, Z. The first row has one letter in a very large font. As you move down, the number of letters in each row increases by one and the font size of the letters decreases, ending with a row of 11 letters in a very small font. Your ability to read the letters accurately measures your visual acuity. Create an eyesight-testing chart similar to the Snellen chart (`http://en.wikipedia.org/wiki/Snellen_chart`) used by medical professionals. The chart is meant to be read from 20 feet away, so scale the fonts accordingly, given that you're sitting close to your screen.

22.34 *(**SpotOn** Game App Using **Shapes** in the Scene Graph)* The **SpotOn** game tests a user's reflexes by requiring the user to click moving spots before they disappear (Fig. 22.19). All of the required images and sounds for this exercise are located in the `exerciseResources` folder with this chapter's examples, though you also can use free images and sounds from many websites or create your own.

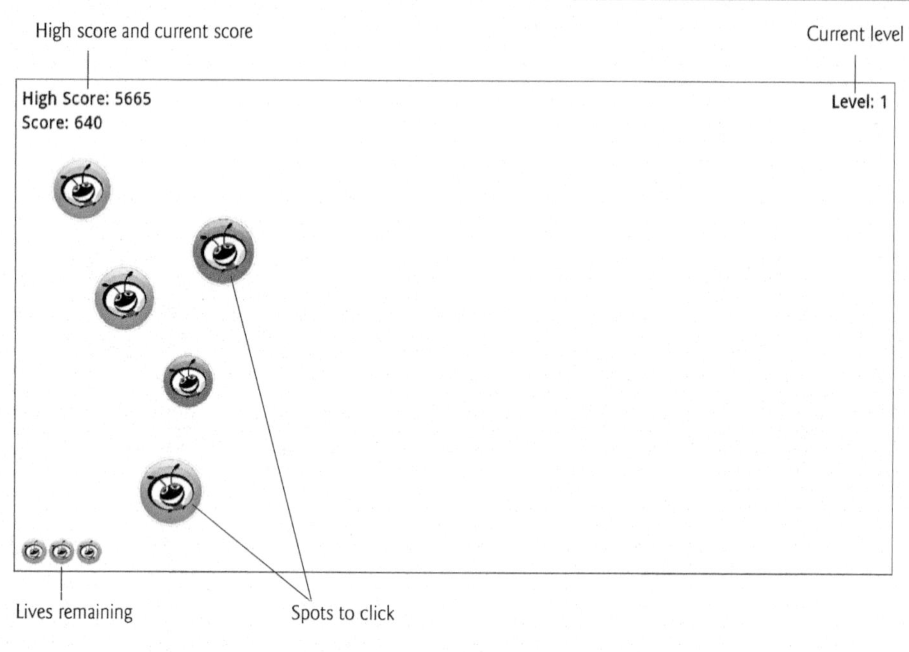

Fig. 22.19 | **SpotOn** game app.

In this game, the spots shrink as they move, making them harder to click. The game begins on level one, and the user reaches each higher level by clicking 10 spots. The higher the level, the faster the spots move—making the game increasingly challenging. When the user clicks a spot, the app plays a "hit" sound (`hit.mp3`) and the spot disappears. Points are awarded for each clicked spot—10 times the current level. Accuracy is important—any click that isn't on a spot plays a "miss" sound (`miss.mp3`) and decreases the score by 15 times the current level.

The user begins the game with *three* additional lives, which are displayed in the bottom-left corner of the app. If a spot disappears before the user clicks it, the app plays a "flushing" sound (`disappear.mp3`) sound and the user loses a life. The user gains a life for reaching each new level, up to a maximum of *seven* lives. When no lives remain and a spot's animation ends before the spot is clicked, the game ends and displays an `Alert` dialog (package `javafx.scene.control`).

Create the **SpotOn** game app. Define a `Spot` subclass of `Circle` that encapsulates a spot's data and functionality. For each `Spot`:

a) Fill its circle with one of the spot images (`red_spot.png` or `green_spot.png`)—specify the fill as you did for the `Ellipse` in Fig. 22.3.
b) Provide a random start point and a random end point and ensure that the `Spot` is completely within the `Pane`'s bounds.
c) Provide an event handler that responds to a mouse click within the `Spots` bounds, which you can set via the inherited `Node` method `setOnMouseClicked`.
d) To make each `Spot` move, use a `ParallelTransition` (Section 22.7) consisting of a `ScaleTransition` that reduces the size of a spot from its original size to 25% of its original size, and a `PathTransition` that moves the spot from its start point to its end point. Register an event handler that executes when the `ParallelTransition` runs to completion—in this case, the user should lose a life because the spot was not clicked.

A `TimelineAnimation` (Section 22.8) should create the five initial spots—one every half-second. After that, each subsequent spot should be created when the user successfully clicks a spot or when a spot completes its animation and has not been clicked. To check for clicks that miss a spot, register a mouse-click handler for the app's `Pane`.

22.35 *(Horse Race Game App)* Amusement parks have many variations of the horse race in which your horse moves in response to your rolling balls into a hole, hitting a target with a water gun, etc. Modify the **SpotOn** game in Exercise 22.34 to move an `ImageView` containing a horse image across the screen. The horse should move only when the user successfully clicks a spot. If the user clicks the screen but misses a spot, the horse should move backward. Use a `PathAnimation` to move the horse in response to each successful click. You can also play a `RotateAnimation` in parallel to rock the horse back and forth as it moves. Locate online a public domain, downloadable audio clip of the William Tell Overture (such as the one at `https://archive.org/details/WilliamTellOverture_414`) and play it in the background during the race.

22.36 *(Cannon Game App with `Canvas` and `AnimationTimer`)* [*Note:* This game requires some two-dimensional analytic geometry and some basic trigonometry to determine the angle of the cannon.] The **Cannon** game app challenges you to destroy nine targets before a ten-second time limit expires (Fig. 22.20). All of the required sounds for this exercise are located in the `exerciseResources` folder with this chapter's examples, though you also can use free sounds from many websites or create your own.

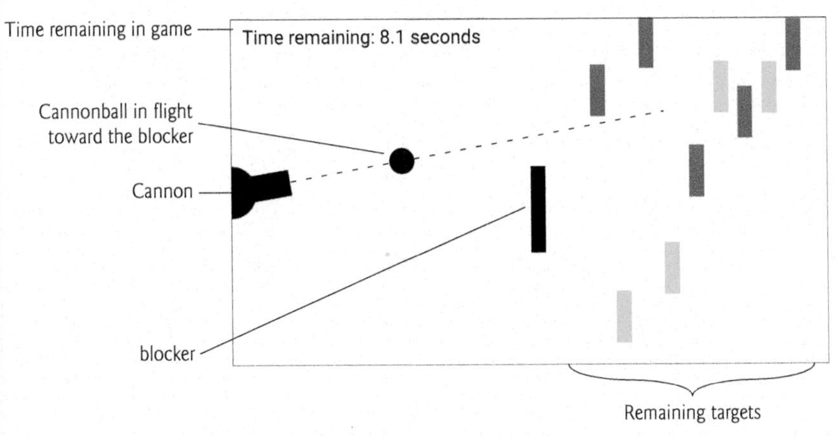

Fig. 22.20 | Completed **Cannon Game** app.

The game consists of a *cannon*, a *cannonball*, nine *targets* and a *blocker* that defends the targets—the blocker cannot be destroyed. The blocker and each target move *vertically* at different speeds, reversing direction when they hit the `Canvas`'s top or bottom. You aim and fire the cannon by clicking the mouse—the cannon's barrel then rotates to aim at the click point and fires the cannonball in a straight line in that direction.

You win by destroying all nine targets before time expires—if the timer reaches zero, you lose. When you destroy a target, the time remaining increases by a three-second time bonus. When you hit the blocker, the time remaining decreases by a three-second time penalty. When the game ends, the app displays an `Alert` dialog (package `javafx.scene.control`) indicating whether you won or lost, and showing the number of shots fired and the elapsed time.

When you fire the cannon, the game plays a *firing sound* (`cannon_fire.wav`) and a cannonball begins moving from the cannon's barrel toward the blocker and targets. When a cannonball hits a target, a *glass-breaking sound* (`target_hit.wav`) plays and that target disappears. When the cannonball hits the blocker, a *hit sound* (`blocker_hit.wav`) plays and the cannonball bounces back toward the cannon.

Use a `Canvas` to implement the game's graphics. This app should perform its animations manually by updating the game elements using `AnimationTimers` as shown in Section 22.9. Consider defining classes that represent the various game elements—each class can define its own `AnimationTimer` to specify how to move a game element of that type.

For simplicity, perform collision detection, based on the cannonball's bounding box—that is, the square area in which the cannonball is drawn—rather than the cannoball's circular area. If the cannonball's bounding box intersects with the blocker's or a target's bounds, then a collision occurred. In the next exercise, you'll reimplement the **Cannon** game with `Shapes` in the scene graph. As you'll see, class `Shape` provides capabilities for more precise collision detection, based on actual shapes, rather than the imprecise rectangular bounding you'll use in this exercise.

[*Note:* Many of today's games are implemented with game-development frameworks that provide more sophisticated "pixel-perfect" collision-detection capabilities. Some frameworks include physics engines that can simulate real-world attributes like mass, gravity, friction, speed, acceleration and more. There are various free and fee-based frameworks available for developing from the simplest 2D games to the most complex 3D console-style games (such as games for Sony's PlayStation® and Microsoft's Xbox®).]

22.37 *(Cannon Game App with* **`Shapes`** *and* **`TransitionAnimations`***)* Reimplement Exercise 22.36 using `Circles` and `Rectangles` to represent the game elements and `TransitionAnimations` to move them. Class `Shape` provides `static` method `intersect` that can be used for collision detection, based on the actual shapes (that is, a `Circle` for the cannonball and `Rectangles` for the blocker and targets), rather than the imprecise, simplified, bounding-box approach used in Exercise 22.36.

22.38 *(Cannon Game Enhancements)* Add the following **Cannon** game enhancements and others of your choosing:

a) Add an "explosion animation" each time the cannonball hits one of the targets. Match the animation with the "explosion sound" that plays when a target is hit.
b) Play a sound when the blocker hits the top or the bottom of the screen.
c) Play a sound when the target hits the top ot the bottom of the screen.
d) Add a trail to the cannonball; erase it when the cannonball hits the target.

23 Concurrency

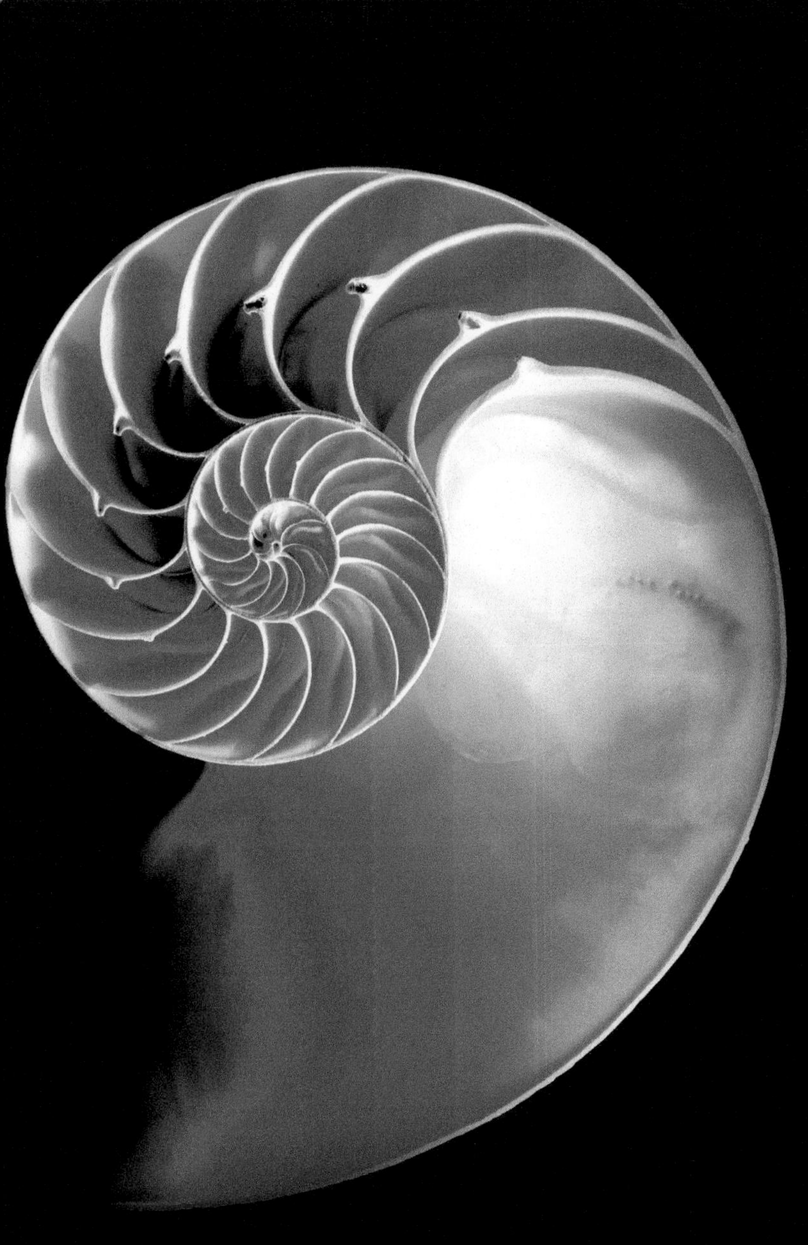

Objectives

In this chapter you'll:

- Understand concurrency, parallelism and multithreading.
- Learn the thread life cycle.
- Use `ExecutorService` to launch concurrent threads that execute `Runnable`s.
- Use `synchronized` methods to coordinate access to shared mutable data.
- Understand producer/consumer relationships.
- Use JavaFX's concurrency APIs to update GUIs in a thread-safe manner.
- Compare the performance of `Arrays` methods `sort` and `parallelSort` on a multi-core system.
- Use parallel streams for better performance on multi-core systems.
- Use `CompletableFuture`s to execute long calculations asynchronously and get the results in the future.

Outline

23.1 Introduction

[*Note: Sections marked "Advanced" are intended for readers who wish a deeper treatment of concurrency and may be skipped by readers preferring only basic coverage.*] It would be nice if we could focus our attention on performing only one task at a time and doing it well. That's usually difficult to do in a complex world in which there's so much going on at once. This chapter presents Java's capabilities for creating and managing multiple tasks. As we'll demonstrate, this can greatly improve program performance and responsiveness.

When we say that two tasks are operating **concurrently**, we mean that they're both *making progress* at once. Until the early 2000s, most computers had only a single processor. Operating systems on such computers execute tasks concurrently by rapidly switching between them, doing a small portion of each before moving on to the next, so that all tasks keep progressing. For example, it's common for personal computers to compile a program, send a file to a printer, receive electronic mail messages over a network and more, concurrently. Since its inception, Java has supported concurrency.

When we say that two tasks are operating **in parallel**, we mean that they're executing *simultaneously*. In this sense, parallelism is a subset of concurrency. The human body performs a great variety of operations in parallel. Respiration, blood circulation, digestion, thinking and walking, for example, can occur in parallel, as can all the senses—sight, hearing, touch, smell and taste. It's believed that this parallelism is possible because the human brain is thought to contain billions of "processors." Today's multi-core computers have multiple processors that can perform tasks in parallel.

Java Concurrency

Java makes concurrency available to you through the language and APIs. Java programs can have multiple **threads of execution**, each with its own method-call stack and program counter, allowing it to execute concurrently with other threads while sharing with them application-wide resources such as memory and file handles. This capability is called **multithreading**.

Performance Tip 23.1

A problem with single-threaded applications that can lead to poor responsiveness is that lengthy activities must complete before *others can begin. In a multithreaded application, threads can be distributed across multiple cores (if available) so that multiple tasks execute in parallel and the application can operate more efficiently. Multithreading can also increase performance on single-processor systems—when one thread cannot proceed (because, for example, it's waiting for the result of an I/O operation), another can use the processor.*

Concurrent Programming Uses

We'll discuss many applications of **concurrent programming**. For example, when streaming an audio or video over the Internet, the user may not want to wait until the entire audio or video downloads before starting the playback. To solve this problem, multiple threads can be used—one to download the audio or video (later in the chapter we'll refer to this as a *producer*), and another to play it (later in the chapter we'll refer to this as a *consumer*). These activities proceed concurrently. To avoid choppy playback, the threads are **synchronized** (that is, their actions are coordinated) so that the player thread doesn't begin until there's a sufficient amount of the audio or video in memory to keep the player thread busy. Producer and consumer threads *share memory*—we'll show how to coordinate these threads to ensure correct execution. The Java Virtual Machine (JVM) creates threads to run programs and threads to perform housekeeping tasks such as garbage collection.

Concurrent Programming Is Difficult

Writing multithreaded programs can be tricky. Although the human mind can perform functions concurrently, people find it difficult to jump between parallel trains of thought. To see why multithreaded programs can be difficult to write and understand, try the following experiment: Open three books to page 1, and try reading the books concurrently. Read a few words from the first book, then a few from the second, then a few from the third, then loop back and read the next few words from the first book, and so on. After this experiment, you'll appreciate many of the challenges of multithreading—switching between the books, reading briefly, remembering your place in each book, moving the book you're reading closer so that you can see it and pushing the books you're not reading aside—and, amid all this chaos, trying to comprehend the content of the books!

Use the Prebuilt Classes of the Concurrency APIs Whenever Possible

Programming concurrent applications is difficult and error prone. If you must use synchronization in a program, follow these guidelines:

1. *The vast majority of programmers should use existing collection classes and interfaces from the concurrency APIs that manage synchronization for you—such as the* `Array-`

`BlockingQueue` *class (an implementation of interface* `BlockingQueue`*) we discuss in Section 23.6.* Two other concurrency API classes that you'll use frequently are `LinkedBlockingQueue` and `ConcurrentHashMap` (each summarized in Fig. 23.22). The concurrency API classes are written by experts, have been thoroughly tested and debugged, operate efficiently and help you avoid common traps and pitfalls. Section 23.10 overviews Java's prebuilt concurrent collections.

2. For advanced programmers who want to control synchronization, use the `synchronized` keyword and `Object` methods `wait`, `notify` and `notifyAll`, which we discuss in the optional Section 23.7.
3. Only the most advanced programmers should use `Lock`s and `Condition`s, which we introduce in the optional Section 23.9, and classes like `LinkedTransferQueue`—an implementation of interface `TransferQueue`—which we summarize in Fig. 23.22.

You might want to read our discussions of the more advanced features mentioned in items 2 and 3, even though you most likely will not use them. We explain these because:

- They provide a solid basis for understanding how concurrent applications synchronize access to shared memory.
- By showing you the complexity involved in using these low-level features, we hope to impress upon you the message: *Use the simpler prebuilt concurrency capabilities whenever possible.*

23.2 Thread States and Life Cycle

At any time, a thread is said to be in one of several **thread states**—illustrated in the UML state diagram in Fig. 23.1. Several of the terms in the diagram are defined in later sections. We include this discussion to help you understand what's going on "under the hood" in a Java multithreaded environment. Java hides most of this detail from you, greatly simplifying the task of developing multithreaded applications.

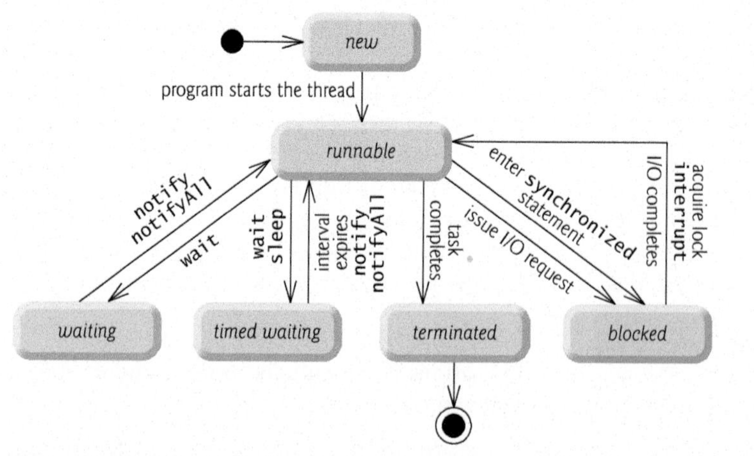

Fig. 23.1 | Thread life-cycle UML state diagram.

23.2.1 *New* and *Runnable* States

A new thread begins its life cycle in the ***new*** state. It remains in this state until the program starts the thread, which places it in the ***runnable*** state. A thread in the *runnable* state is considered to be executing its task.

23.2.2 *Waiting* State

Sometimes a *runnable* thread transitions to the ***waiting*** state while it waits for another thread to perform a task. A *waiting* thread transitions back to the *runnable* state only when another thread notifies it to continue executing.

23.2.3 *Timed Waiting* State

A *runnable* thread can enter the ***timed waiting*** state for a specified interval of time. It transitions back to the *runnable* state when that time interval expires or when the event it's waiting for occurs. *Timed waiting* threads and *waiting* threads cannot use a processor, even if one is available. A *runnable* thread can transition to the *timed waiting* state if it provides an optional wait interval when it's waiting for another thread to perform a task. Such a thread returns to the *runnable* state when it's notified by another thread or when the timed interval expires—whichever comes first. Another way to place a thread in the *timed waiting* state is to put a *runnable* thread to sleep—a **sleeping thread** remains in the *timed waiting* state for a designated period of time (called a **sleep interval**), after which it returns to the *runnable* state. Threads sleep when they momentarily do not have work to perform. For example, a word processor may contain a thread that periodically backs up (i.e., writes a copy of) the current document to disk for recovery purposes. If the thread did not sleep between successive backups, it would require a loop in which it continually tested whether it should write a copy of the document to disk. This loop would consume processor time without performing productive work, thus reducing system performance. In this case, it's more efficient for the thread to specify a sleep interval (equal to the period between successive backups) and enter the *timed waiting* state. This thread is returned to the *runnable* state when its sleep interval expires, at which point it writes a copy of the document to disk and reenters the *timed waiting* state.

23.2.4 *Blocked* State

A *runnable* thread transitions to the ***blocked*** state when it attempts to perform a task that cannot be completed immediately and it must temporarily wait until that task completes. For example, when a thread issues an input/output request, the operating system blocks the thread from executing until that I/O request completes—at that point, the *blocked* thread transitions to the *runnable* state, so it can resume execution. A *blocked* thread cannot use a processor, even if one is available.

23.2.5 *Terminated* State

A *runnable* thread enters the ***terminated*** state (sometimes called the ***dead*** state) when it successfully completes its task or otherwise terminates (perhaps due to an error). In the UML state diagram of Fig. 23.1, the *terminated* state is followed by the UML final state (the bull's-eye symbol) to indicate the end of the state transitions.

23.2.6 Operating-System View of the *Runnable* State

At the operating system level, Java's *runnable* state typically encompasses *two separate* states (Fig. 23.2). The operating system hides these states from the JVM, which sees only the *runnable* state. When a thread first transitions to the *runnable* state from the *new* state, it's in the ***ready*** state. A *ready* thread enters the ***running*** state (i.e., begins executing) when the operating system assigns it to a processor—also known as **dispatching the thread.** In most operating systems, each thread is given a small amount of processor time—called a **quantum** or **timeslice**—with which to perform its task. Deciding how large the quantum should be is a key topic in operating systems courses. When its quantum expires, the thread returns to the *ready* state, and the operating system assigns another thread to the processor. Transitions between the *ready* and *running* states are handled solely by the operating system. The JVM does not "see" the transitions—it simply views the thread as being *runnable* and leaves it up to the operating system to transition the thread between *ready* and *running.* The process that an operating system uses to determine which thread to dispatch is called **thread scheduling** and is dependent on thread priorities.

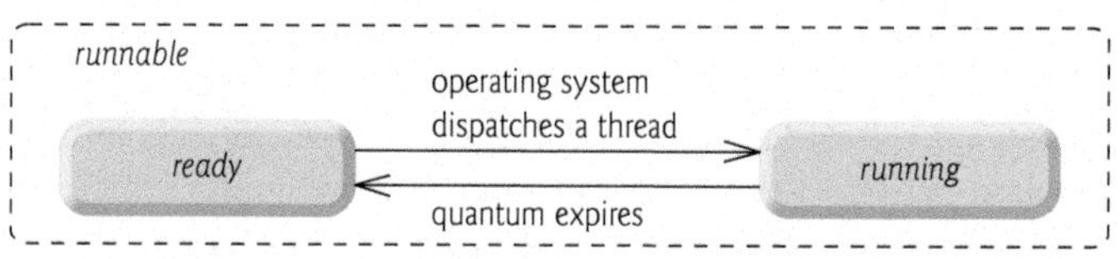

Fig. 23.2 | Operating system's internal view of Java's *runnable* state.

23.2.7 Thread Priorities and Thread Scheduling

Every Java thread has a **thread priority** that helps determine the order in which threads are scheduled. Each new thread inherits the priority of the thread that created it. Informally, higher-priority threads are more important to a program and should be allocated processor time before lower-priority threads. *Nevertheless, thread priorities cannot guarantee the order in which threads execute.*

It's recommended that you do not explicitly create and use `Threads` *to implement concurrency, but rather use the* `Executor` *interface (described in Section 23.3).* The `Thread` class does contain some useful `static` methods, which you *will* use later in the chapter.

Most operating systems support timeslicing, which enables threads of equal priority to share a processor. Without timeslicing, each thread in a set of equal-priority threads runs to completion (unless it leaves the *runnable* state and enters the *waiting* or *timed waiting* state, or gets interrupted by a higher-priority thread) before other threads of equal priority get a chance to execute. With timeslicing, even if a thread has *not* finished executing when its quantum expires, the processor is taken away from the thread and given to the next thread of equal priority, if one is available.

An *operating system's* **thread scheduler** determines which thread runs next. One simple thread-scheduler implementation keeps the highest-priority thread *running* at all times and, if there's more than one highest-priority thread, ensures that all such threads execute for a quantum each in **round-robin** fashion. This process continues until all threads run to completion.

Software Engineering Observation 23.1

Java provides higher-level concurrency utilities to hide much of this complexity and make multithreaded programming less error prone. Thread priorities are used behind the scenes to interact with the operating system, but most programmers who use Java multithreading will not be concerned with setting and adjusting thread priorities.

Portability Tip 23.1

Thread scheduling is platform dependent—the behavior of a multithreaded program could vary across different Java implementations.

23.2.8 Indefinite Postponement and Deadlock

When a higher-priority thread enters the *ready* state, the operating system generally preempts the *running* thread (an operation known as **preemptive scheduling**). Depending on the operating system, a steady influx of higher-priority threads could postpone—possibly indefinitely—the execution of lower-priority threads. Such **indefinite postponement** is sometimes referred to more colorfully as **starvation**. Operating systems employ a technique called *aging* to prevent starvation—as a thread waits in the *ready* state, the operating system gradually increases the thread's priority to ensure that the thread will eventually run.

Another problem related to indefinite postponement is called **deadlock**. This occurs when a waiting thread (let's call this thread1) cannot proceed because it's waiting (either directly or indirectly) for another thread (let's call this thread2) to proceed, while simultaneously thread2 cannot proceed because it's waiting (either directly or indirectly) for thread1 to proceed. The two threads are waiting for each other, so the actions that would enable each thread to continue execution can never occur.

23.3 Creating and Executing Threads with the Executor Framework

This section demonstrates how to perform concurrent tasks in an application by using `Executor`s and `Runnable` objects.

Creating Concurrent Tasks with the `Runnable` *Interface*

You implement the **`Runnable`** interface (of package `java.lang`) to specify a task that can execute concurrently with other tasks. The `Runnable` interface declares the single method **`run`**, which contains the code that defines the task that a `Runnable` object should perform.

Executing `Runnable` *Objects with an* `Executor`

To allow a `Runnable` to perform its task, you must execute it. An **`Executor`** object executes `Runnable`s. It does this by creating and managing a group of threads called a **thread pool**. When an `Executor` begins executing a `Runnable`, the `Executor` calls the `Runnable` object's `run` method.

The `Executor` interface declares a single method named **`execute`** which accepts a `Runnable` as an argument. The `Executor` assigns every `Runnable` passed to its `execute` method to one of the available threads in the thread pool. If there are no available threads, the `Executor` creates a new thread or waits for a thread to become available and assigns that thread the `Runnable` that was passed to method `execute`.

Using an Executor has many advantages over creating threads yourself. Executors can *reuse existing threads* to eliminate the overhead of creating a new thread for each task and can improve performance by *optimizing the number of threads* to ensure that the processor stays busy, without creating so many threads that the application runs out of resources.

Software Engineering Observation 23.2

Though it's possible to create threads explicitly, it's recommended that you use the Executor *interface to manage the execution of* Runnable *objects.*

Using Class Executors *to Obtain an* ExecutorService

The **ExecutorService interface** (of package java.util.concurrent) *extends* Executor and declares various methods for managing the life cycle of an Executor. You obtain an ExecutorService object by calling one of the static methods declared in class **Executors** (of package java.util.concurrent). We use interface ExecutorService and a method of class Executors in our example (Fig. 23.4), which executes three tasks.

Implementing the Runnable *Interface*

Class PrintTask (Fig. 23.3) implements Runnable (line 5), *so that multiple* PrintTask*s can execute concurrently*. Variable sleepTime (line 7) stores a random integer value from 0 to 5 seconds created in the PrintTask constructor (line 15). Each thread running a PrintTask sleeps for the amount of time specified by sleepTime, then outputs its task's name and a message indicating that it's done sleeping.

```
1  // Fig. 23.3: PrintTask.java
2  // PrintTask class sleeps for a random time from 0 to 5 seconds
3  import java.security.SecureRandom;
4
5  public class PrintTask implements Runnable {
6     private static final SecureRandom generator = new SecureRandom();
7     private final int sleepTime; // random sleep time for thread
8     private final String taskName;
9
10    // constructor
11    public PrintTask(String taskName) {
12       this.taskName = taskName;
13
14       // pick random sleep time between 0 and 5 seconds
15       sleepTime = generator.nextInt(5000); // milliseconds
16    }
17
18    // method run contains the code that a thread will execute
19    @Override
20    public void run() {
21       try { // put thread to sleep for sleepTime amount of time
22          System.out.printf("%s going to sleep for %d milliseconds.%n",
23             taskName, sleepTime);
24          Thread.sleep(sleepTime); // put thread to sleep
25       }
```

Fig. 23.3 | PrintTask class sleeps for a random time from 0 to 5 seconds. (Part 1 of 2.)

```
26          catch (InterruptedException exception) {
27             exception.printStackTrace();
28             Thread.currentThread().interrupt(); // re-interrupt the thread
29          }
30
31          // print task name
32          System.out.printf("%s done sleeping%n", taskName);
33       }
34    }
```

Fig. 23.3 | `PrintTask` class sleeps for a random time from 0 to 5 seconds. (Part 2 of 2.)

A `PrintTask` executes when a thread calls the `PrintTask`'s `run` method. Lines 22–23 display a message indicating the currently executing task's name and that the task is going to sleep for `sleepTime` milliseconds. Line 24 invokes `static` `Thread` method **`sleep`** to place the thread in the *timed waiting* state for the specified amount of time. At this point, the thread loses the processor, and the system allows another thread to execute. When the thread awakens, it reenters the *runnable* state. When the `PrintTask` is assigned to a processor again, line 32 outputs a message indicating that the task is done sleeping, then method `run` terminates. The `catch` at lines 26–29 is required because method `sleep` might throw a *checked* **`InterruptedException`** if a sleeping thread's **`interrupt`** method is called.

Let the Thread Handle `InterruptedException`*s*

It's considered good practice to let the executing thread handle `InterruptedException`s. Normally, you'd do this by declaring that method `run` throws the exception, rather than catching the exception. However, recall from Chapter 11 that when you override a method, the `throws` clause may contain only the same or a subset of the exception types declared in the original method's `throws` clause. `Runnable` method `run` does not have a `throws` clause, so we cannot provide one in line 20. To ensure that the executing thread receives the `InterruptedException`, line 28 first obtains a reference to the currently executing `Thread` by calling `static` method **`currentThread`**, then uses that `Thread`'s `interrupt` method to deliver the `InterruptedException` to the current thread.[1]

Using the `ExecutorService` *to Manage Threads That Execute* `PrintTask`*s*

Figure 23.4 uses an `ExecutorService` object to manage threads that execute `PrintTask`s (as defined in Fig. 23.3). Lines 9–11 in Fig. 23.4 create and name three `PrintTask`s to execute. Line 16 uses `Executors` method **`newCachedThreadPool`** to obtain an `ExecutorService` that creates new threads if no existing threads are available to reuse. These threads are used by the `ExecutorService` to execute the `Runnable`s.

```
1   // Fig. 23.4: TaskExecutor.java
2   // Using an ExecutorService to execute Runnables.
3   import java.util.concurrent.Executors;
```

Fig. 23.4 | Using an `ExecutorService` to execute `Runnable`s. (Part 1 of 2.)

1. For detailed information on handling thread interruptions, see Chapter 7 of *Java Concurrency in Practice* by Brian Goetz, et al., Addison-Wesley Professional, 2006.

```
4   import java.util.concurrent.ExecutorService;
5
6   public class TaskExecutor {
7      public static void main(String[] args) {
8         // create and name each runnable
9         PrintTask task1 = new PrintTask("task1");
10        PrintTask task2 = new PrintTask("task2");
11        PrintTask task3 = new PrintTask("task3");
12
13        System.out.println("Starting Executor");
14
15        // create ExecutorService to manage threads
16        ExecutorService executorService = Executors.newCachedThreadPool();
17
18        // start the three PrintTasks
19        executorService.execute(task1); // start task1
20        executorService.execute(task2); // start task2
21        executorService.execute(task3); // start task3
22
23        // shut down ExecutorService--it decides when to shut down threads
24        executorService.shutdown();
25
26        System.out.printf("Tasks started, main ends.%n%n");
27     }
28  }
```

```
Starting Executor
Tasks started, main ends

task1 going to sleep for 4806 milliseconds
task2 going to sleep for 2513 milliseconds
task3 going to sleep for 1132 milliseconds
task3 done sleeping
task2 done sleeping
task1 done sleeping
```

```
Starting Executor
task1 going to sleep for 3161 milliseconds.
task3 going to sleep for 532 milliseconds.
task2 going to sleep for 3440 milliseconds.
Tasks started, main ends.

task3 done sleeping
task1 done sleeping
task2 done sleeping
```

Fig. 23.4 | Using an ExecutorService to execute Runnables. (Part 2 of 2.)

Lines 19–21 each invoke the ExecutorService's execute method, which executes its Runnable argument (in this case a PrintTask) at some time in the future. The specified task may execute in one of the threads in the ExecutorService's thread pool, in a new thread created to execute it, or in the thread that called the execute method—the ExecutorService manages these details. Method execute returns immediately from each invocation—the program does *not* wait for each PrintTask to finish. Line 24 calls ExecutorService method **shutdown**, which prevents the ExecutorService from accepting new tasks, but *continues executing tasks that have already been submitted.* Once all of the previously submitted tasks have completed, the ExecutorService terminates. Line 26 outputs a message indicating that the tasks were started and the main thread is finishing its execution.

Main Thread

The code in main executes in the **main thread**, which is created by the JVM. The code in the run method of PrintTask (lines 19–33 of Fig. 23.3) executes whenever the Executor starts each PrintTask—again, sometime after they're passed to the ExecutorService's execute method (Fig. 23.4, lines 19–21). When main terminates, the program itself continues running until the submitted tasks complete.

Sample Outputs

The sample outputs show each task's name and sleep time as the thread goes to sleep. The thread with the shortest sleep time *in most cases* awakens first, indicates that it's done sleeping and terminates. In Section 23.8, we discuss multithreading issues that could prevent the thread with the shortest sleep time from awakening first. In the first output, the main thread terminates *before* any of the PrintTasks output their names and sleep times. This shows that the main thread runs to completion before any of the PrintTasks gets a chance to run. In the second output, all of the PrintTasks output their names and sleep times *before* the main thread terminates. This shows that the PrintTasks started executing before the main thread terminated. Also, notice in the second example output, task3 goes to sleep before task2, even though we passed task2 to the ExecutorService's execute method before task3. This illustrates the fact that *we cannot predict the order in which the tasks will start executing, even if we know the order in which they were created and started.*

Waiting for Previously Scheduled Tasks to Terminate

After scheduling tasks to execute, you'll typically want to *wait for the tasks to complete*—for example, so that you can use the tasks' results. After calling method shutdown, you can call ExecutorService method awaitTermination to wait for scheduled tasks to complete. We demonstrate this in Fig. 23.7. We purposely did not call awaitTermination in Fig. 23.4 to demonstrate that a program can continue executing after the main thread terminates.

23.4 Thread Synchronization

When multiple threads share an object and it's *modified* by one or more of them, indeterminate results may occur (as we'll see in the examples) unless access to the shared object is managed properly. If one thread is in the process of updating a shared object and another thread also tries to update it, it's uncertain which thread's update takes effect. Similarly, if one thread is in the process of updating a shared object and another thread tries to read it, it's uncertain whether the reading thread will see the old value or the new one. In such cases, the program's behavior cannot be trusted—sometimes the program will produce the correct results, and sometimes it won't, and there won't be any indication that the shared object was manipulated incorrectly.

The problem can be solved by giving only one thread at a time *exclusive access* to code that accesses the shared object. During that time, other threads desiring to access the object are kept waiting. When the thread with exclusive access finishes accessing the object, one of the waiting threads is allowed to proceed. This process, called **thread synchronization**, coordinates access to shared data by multiple concurrent threads. By synchronizing threads in this manner, you can ensure that each thread accessing a shared object *excludes* all other threads from doing so simultaneously—this is called **mutual exclusion**.

23.4.1 Immutable Data

Actually, thread synchronization is necessary *only* for shared **mutable data**, i.e., data that may *change* during its lifetime. With shared **immutable data** that will *not* change, it's not possible for a thread to see old or incorrect values as a result of another thread's manipulation of that data.

When you share *immutable data* across threads, declare the corresponding data fields `final` to indicate that the variables's values will *not* change after they're initialized. This prevents accidental modification of the shared data, which could compromise thread safety. *Labeling object references as* `final` *indicates that the reference will not change, but it does not guarantee that the referenced object is immutable—this depends entirely on the object's properties.* But, it's still good practice to mark references that will not change as `final`.

Software Engineering Observation 23.3

Always declare data fields that you do not expect to change as `final`*. Primitive variables that are declared as* `final` *can safely be shared across threads. An object reference that's declared as* `final` *ensures that the object it refers to will be fully constructed and initialized before it's used by the program, and prevents the reference from pointing to another object.*

23.4.2 Monitors

A common way to perform synchronization is to use Java's built-in **monitors**. Every object has a monitor and a **monitor lock** (or **intrinsic lock**). The monitor ensures that its object's monitor lock is held by a maximum of only one thread at any time. Monitors and monitor locks can thus be used to enforce mutual exclusion. If an operation requires the executing thread to *hold a lock* while the operation is performed, a thread must *acquire the lock* before proceeding with the operation. Other threads attempting to perform an operation that requires the same lock will be *blocked* until the first thread *releases the lock*, at which point the *blocked* threads may attempt to acquire the lock and proceed with the operation.

To specify that a thread must hold a monitor lock to execute a block of code, the code should be placed in a **`synchronized` statement**. Such code is said to be **guarded** by the monitor lock; a thread must **acquire the lock** to execute the guarded statements. The monitor allows only one thread at a time to execute statements within `synchronized` statements that lock on the same object, as only one thread at a time can hold the monitor lock. The `synchronized` statements are declared using the **`synchronized` keyword**:

```
synchronized (object) {
   statements
}
```

where *object* is the object whose monitor lock will be acquired; *object* is normally `this` if it's the object in which the `synchronized` statement appears. If several `synchronized` statements in different threads are trying to execute on an object at the same time, only one of them may be active on the object—all the other threads attempting to enter a `synchronized` statement on the same object are placed in the *blocked* state.

When a `synchronized` statement finishes executing, the object's monitor lock is released and one of the *blocked* threads attempting to enter a `synchronized` statement can be allowed to acquire the lock to proceed. Java also allows **`synchronized` methods**. Before executing, a `synchronized` instance method must acquire the lock on the object that's used to call the method. Similarly, a `static synchronized` method must acquire the lock on a `Class` object that represents the class in which the method is declared. A `Class` object is the execution-time representation of a class that the JVM has loaded into memory.

Software Engineering Observation 23.4

Using a `synchronized` *block to enforce mutual exclusion is an example of the design pattern known as the Java Monitor Pattern (see Section 4.2.1 of* Java Concurrency in Practice *by Brian Goetz, et al., Addison-Wesley Professional, 2006).*

23.4.3 Unsynchronized Mutable Data Sharing

First, we illustrate the dangers of sharing an object across threads *without* proper synchronization. In this example (Figs. 23.5–23.7), two `Runnable`s maintain references to a single integer array. Each `Runnable` writes three values to the array, then terminates. This may seem harmless, but we'll see that it can result in errors if the array is manipulated without synchronization.

Class `SimpleArray`

We'll *share* a `SimpleArray` object (Fig. 23.5) across multiple threads. `SimpleArray` will enable those threads to place `int` values into `array` (declared at line 8). Line 9 initializes variable `writeIndex`, which determines the array element that should be written to next. The constructor (line 12) creates an integer array of the desired size.

```
1  // Fig. 23.5: SimpleArray.java
2  // Class that manages an integer array to be shared by multiple threads.
3  import java.security.SecureRandom;
4  import java.util.Arrays;
5
6  public class SimpleArray { // CAUTION: NOT THREAD SAFE!
7     private static final SecureRandom generator = new SecureRandom();
8     private final int[] array; // the shared integer array
9     private int writeIndex = 0; // shared index of next element to write
10
11    // construct a SimpleArray of a given size
12    public SimpleArray(int size) {array = new int[size];}
13
```

Fig. 23.5 | Class that manages an integer array to be shared by multiple threads. (*Caution:* The example of Figs. 23.5–23.7 is *not* thread safe.) (Part 1 of 2.)

```
14      // add a value to the shared array
15      public void add(int value) {
16         int position = writeIndex; // store the write index
17
18         try {
19            // put thread to sleep for 0-499 milliseconds
20            Thread.sleep(generator.nextInt(500));
21         }
22         catch (InterruptedException ex) {
23            Thread.currentThread().interrupt(); // re-interrupt the thread
24         }
25
26         // put value in the appropriate element
27         array[position] = value;
28         System.out.printf("%s wrote %2d to element %d.%n",
29            Thread.currentThread().getName(), value, position);
30
31         ++writeIndex; // increment index of element to be written next
32         System.out.printf("Next write index: %d%n", writeIndex);
33      }
34
35      // used for outputting the contents of the shared integer array
36      @Override
37      public String toString() {
38         return Arrays.toString(array);
39      }
40   }
```

Fig. 23.5 | Class that manages an integer array to be shared by multiple threads. (*Caution:* The example of Figs. 23.5–23.7 is *not* thread safe.) (Part 2 of 2.)

Method add (lines 15–33) places a new value into the array. Line 16 stores the current writeIndex value. Line 20 puts the thread that invokes add to sleep for a random interval from 0 to 499 milliseconds. We do this for demonstration purposes to make the problems associated with *unsynchronized access to shared mutable data* more obvious. After the thread is done sleeping, line 27 inserts the value passed to add into the array at the element specified by position. Lines 28–29 display the executing thread's name, the value that was added and the value's index in the array. In line 29, the expression

```
Thread.currentThread().getName()
```

first obtains a reference to the currently executing Thread, then uses its getName method to obtain its name. Line 31 increments writeIndex so that the next call to add will insert a value in the array's next element. Lines 36–39 override method toString to create a String representation of the array's contents.

Class ArrayWriter

Class ArrayWriter (Fig. 23.6) implements the interface Runnable to define a task for inserting values in a SimpleArray object. The constructor (lines 9–12) receives an int representing the first value this task will insert in a SimpleArray object and a reference to the SimpleArray object to manipulate. Line 17 invokes SimpleArray method add. The task completes after lines 16–18 add three consecutive integers beginning with startValue.

```java
// Fig. 23.6: ArrayWriter.java
// Adds integers to an array shared with other Runnables
import java.lang.Runnable;

public class ArrayWriter implements Runnable {
   private final SimpleArray sharedSimpleArray;
   private final int startValue;

   public ArrayWriter(int value, SimpleArray array) {
      startValue = value;
      sharedSimpleArray = array;
   }

   @Override
   public void run() {
      for (int i = startValue; i < startValue + 3; i++) {
         sharedSimpleArray.add(i); // add an element to the shared array
      }
   }
}
```

Fig. 23.6 | Adds integers to an array shared with other `Runnables`. (*Caution:* The example of Figs. 23.5–23.7 is *not* thread safe.)

Class `SharedArrayTest`

Class `SharedArrayTest` (Fig. 23.7) executes two `ArrayWriter` tasks that add values to a single `SimpleArray` object. Line 10 constructs a six-element `SimpleArray` object. Lines 13–14 create two new `ArrayWriter` tasks, one that places the values `1` through `3` in the `SimpleArray` object, and one that places the values `11` through `13`. Lines 17–19 create an `ExecutorService` and execute the two `ArrayWriters`. Line 21 invokes the `ExecutorService`'s `shutDown` method to prevent it from accepting additional tasks and to enable the application to terminate when the currently executing tasks complete execution.

```java
1  // Fig. 23.7: SharedArrayTest.java
2  // Executing two Runnables to add elements to a shared SimpleArray.
3  import java.util.concurrent.Executors;
4  import java.util.concurrent.ExecutorService;
5  import java.util.concurrent.TimeUnit;
6
7  public class SharedArrayTest {
8     public static void main(String[] arg) {
9        // construct the shared object
10       SimpleArray sharedSimpleArray = new SimpleArray(6);
11
12       // create two tasks to write to the shared SimpleArray
13       ArrayWriter writer1 = new ArrayWriter(1, sharedSimpleArray);
14       ArrayWriter writer2 = new ArrayWriter(11, sharedSimpleArray);
```

Fig. 23.7 | Executing two `Runnables` to add elements to a shared array—the italicized text is our commentary, which is not part of the program's output. (*Caution:* The example of Figs. 23.5–23.7 is *not* thread safe.) (Part 1 of 2.)

```
15
16         // execute the tasks with an ExecutorService
17         ExecutorService executorService = Executors.newCachedThreadPool();
18         executorService.execute(writer1);
19         executorService.execute(writer2);
20
21         executorService.shutdown();
22
23         try {
24            // wait 1 minute for both writers to finish executing
25            boolean tasksEnded =
26               executorService.awaitTermination(1, TimeUnit.MINUTES);
27
28            if (tasksEnded) {
29               System.out.printf("%nContents of SimpleArray:%n");
30               System.out.println(sharedSimpleArray); // print contents
31            }
32            else {
33               System.out.println(
34                  "Timed out while waiting for tasks to finish.");
35            }
36         }
37         catch (InterruptedException ex) {
38            ex.printStackTrace();
39         }
40      }
41   }
```

```
pool-1-thread-1 wrote  1 to element 0.  — pool-1-thread-1 wrote 1 to element 0
Next write index: 1
pool-1-thread-1 wrote  2 to element 1.
Next write index: 2
pool-1-thread-1 wrote  3 to element 2.
Next write index: 3
pool-1-thread-2 wrote 11 to element 0.  — pool-1-thread-2 overwrote element 0's value
Next write index: 4
pool-1-thread-2 wrote 12 to element 4.
Next write index: 5
pool-1-thread-2 wrote 13 to element 5.
Next write index: 6

Contents of SimpleArray:
[11, 2, 3, 0, 12, 13]
```

Fig. 23.7 | Executing two `Runnable`s to add elements to a shared array—the italicized text is our commentary, which is not part of the program's output. (*Caution:* The example of Figs. 23.5–23.7 is *not* thread safe.) (Part 2 of 2.)

`ExecutorService` *Method* `awaitTermination`

Recall that `ExecutorService` method `shutdown` returns immediately. Thus any code that appears *after* the call to `ExecutorService` method `shutdown` in line 21 *will continue executing as long as the* `main` *thread is still assigned to a processor*. We'd like to output the `Sim-`

`SimpleArray` object to show you the results *after* the threads complete their tasks. So, we need the program to wait for the threads to complete before `main` outputs the `SimpleArray` object's contents. Interface `ExecutorService` provides the **`awaitTermination`** method for this purpose. This method returns control to its caller either when all tasks executing in the `ExecutorService` complete or when the specified timeout elapses. If all tasks are completed before `awaitTermination` times out, this method returns `true`; otherwise it returns `false`. The two arguments to `awaitTermination` represent a timeout value and a unit of measure specified with a constant from class `TimeUnit` (in this case, `TimeUnit.MINUTES`).

Method `awaitTermination` throws an `InterruptedException` if the calling thread is interrupted while waiting for other threads to terminate. Because we catch this exception in the application's `main` method, there's no need to re-interrupt the `main` thread, as this program will terminate as soon as `main` terminates.

In this example, if *both* tasks complete before `awaitTermination` times out, line 30 displays the `SimpleArray` object's contents. Otherwise, lines 33–34 display a message indicating that the tasks did not finish executing before `awaitTermination` timed out.

Sample Program Output

Figure 23.7's output shows the problems (highlighted in the output) that can be caused by *failure to synchronize access to shared mutable data.* The value `1` was written to element `0`, then *overwritten* later by the value `11`. Also, when `writeIndex` was incremented to 3, *nothing was written to that element*, as indicated by the 0 in that element of the array.

Recall that we call `Thread` method `sleep` between operations on the shared mutable data to emphasize the *unpredictability of thread scheduling* and to increase the likelihood of producing erroneous output. Even if these operations were allowed to proceed at their normal pace, you could still see errors in the program's output. However, modern processors can handle `SimpleArray` method `add`'s operations so quickly that you might not see the errors caused by the two threads executing this method concurrently, even if you tested the program dozens of times.

One of the challenges of multithreaded programming is spotting the errors—they may occur so infrequently and unpredictably that a broken program does not produce incorrect results during testing, creating the illusion that the program is correct. This is all the more reason to use predefined collections that handle the synchronization for you.

23.4.4 Synchronized Mutable Data Sharing—Making Operations Atomic

Figure 23.7's output errors can be attributed to the fact that the shared `SimpleArray` is not **thread safe**—it's susceptible to errors if it's *accessed concurrently by multiple threads.* The problem lies in method `add`, which stores the `writeIndex` value, places a new value in that element, then increments `writeIndex`. This would not present a problem in a single-threaded program. However, if one thread obtains the `writeIndex` value, there's no guarantee that another thread will not come along and increment `writeIndex` *before* the first thread has had a chance to place a value in the array. If this happens, the first thread will be writing to the array based on a **stale value** of `writeIndex`—that is, a value that's no longer valid. Another possibility is that one thread might obtain the `writeIndex` value *after* another thread adds an element to the array but *before* `writeIndex` is incremented. In this case, too, the first thread would use an invalid `writeIndex` value.

SimpleArray is *not thread safe because it allows any number of threads to read and modify shared mutable data concurrently*, which can cause errors. To make SimpleArray thread safe, we must ensure that no two threads can access its shared mutable data at the same time. While one thread is in the process of storing writeIndex, adding a value to the array, and incrementing writeIndex, *no other thread* may read or change the value of writeIndex or modify the contents of the array at any point during these three operations. In other words, we want these three operations—storing writeIndex, writing to the array, incrementing writeIndex—to be an **atomic operation**, which cannot be divided into smaller suboperations. (As you'll see in later examples, read operations on shared mutable data should also be atomic.) We can simulate atomicity by ensuring that only one thread carries out the three operations at a time. Any other threads that need to perform the operation must *wait* until the first thread has finished the add operation in its entirety.

Atomicity can be achieved using the synchronized keyword. By placing our three suboperations in a synchronized statement or synchronized method, we allow only one thread at a time to acquire the lock and perform the operations. When that thread has completed all of the operations in the synchronized block and releases the lock, another thread may acquire the lock and begin executing the operations. This ensures that a thread executing the operations will see the actual values of the shared mutable data and that *these values will not change unexpectedly in the middle of the operations as a result of another thread's modifying them.*

Software Engineering Observation 23.5

Place all accesses to mutable data that may be shared by multiple threads inside synchronized *statements or* synchronized *methods that synchronize on the same lock. When performing multiple operations on shared mutable data, hold the lock for the entirety of the operation to ensure that the operation is effectively atomic.*

Class SimpleArray with Synchronization

Figure 23.8 displays class SimpleArray with the proper synchronization. Notice that it's identical to the SimpleArray class of Fig. 23.5, except that add is now a synchronized method (line 18 of Fig. 23.8). So, only one thread at a time can execute this method. We reuse classes ArrayWriter (Fig. 23.6) and SharedArrayTest (Fig. 23.7) from the previous example, so we do not show them again here.

```
1   // Fig. 23.8: SimpleArray.java
2   // Class that manages an integer array to be shared by multiple
3   // threads with synchronization.
4   import java.security.SecureRandom;
5   import java.util.Arrays;
6
7   public class SimpleArray {
8      private static final SecureRandom generator = new SecureRandom();
9      private final int[] array; // the shared integer array
10     private int writeIndex = 0; // index of next element to be written
11
```

Fig. 23.8 | Class that manages an integer array to be shared by multiple threads with synchronization. (Part 1 of 2.)

```
12      // construct a SimpleArray of a given size
13      public SimpleArray(int size) {
14         array = new int[size];
15      }
16
17      // add a value to the shared array
18      public synchronized void add(int value) {
19         int position = writeIndex; // store the write index
20
21         try {
22            // in real applications, you shouldn't sleep while holding a lock
23            Thread.sleep(generator.nextInt(500)); // for demo only
24         }
25         catch (InterruptedException ex) {
26            Thread.currentThread().interrupt();
27         }
28
29         // put value in the appropriate element
30         array[position] = value;
31         System.out.printf("%s wrote %2d to element %d.%n",
32            Thread.currentThread().getName(), value, position);
33
34         ++writeIndex; // increment index of element to be written next
35         System.out.printf("Next write index: %d%n", writeIndex);
36      }
37
38      // used for outputting the contents of the shared integer array
39      @Override
40      public synchronized String toString() {
41         return Arrays.toString(array);
42      }
43   }
```

```
pool-1-thread-1 wrote  1 to element 0.
Next write index: 1
pool-1-thread-2 wrote 11 to element 1.
Next write index: 2
pool-1-thread-2 wrote 12 to element 2.
Next write index: 3
pool-1-thread-2 wrote 13 to element 3.
Next write index: 4
pool-1-thread-1 wrote  2 to element 4.
Next write index: 5
pool-1-thread-1 wrote  3 to element 5.
Next write index: 6

Contents of SimpleArray:
[1, 11, 12, 13, 2, 3]
```

Fig. 23.8 | Class that manages an integer array to be shared by multiple threads with synchronization. (Part 2 of 2.)

Line 18 declares method add as `synchronized`, making all of the operations in this method behave as a single, atomic operation. Line 19 performs the first suboperation—

storing the value of `writeIndex`. Line 30 performs the second suboperation, writing a value to the element at the index `position`. Line 34 performs the third suboperation, incrementing `writeIndex`. When the method finishes executing at line 36, the executing thread implicitly *releases* the `SimpleArray` object's lock, making it possible for another thread to begin executing the `add` method.

In the `synchronized` `add` method, we print messages to the console indicating the progress of threads as they execute this method, in addition to performing the actual operations required to insert a value in the array. We do this so that the messages will be printed in the correct order, allowing us to see whether the method is properly synchronized by comparing these outputs with those of the previous, unsynchronized example. We continue to output messages from `synchronized` blocks in later examples for *demonstration purposes only*; typically, however, I/O *should not* be performed in `synchronized` blocks, because it's important to minimize the amount of time that an object is "locked." [*Note:* **Line 23 in this example calls `Thread` method `sleep` (for demo purposes only) to emphasize the unpredictability of thread scheduling. You should never call `sleep` while holding a lock in a real application.**]

Performance Tip 23.2

Keep the duration of `synchronized` statements as short as possible while maintaining the needed synchronization. This minimizes the wait time for blocked threads. Avoid performing I/O, lengthy calculations and operations that do not require synchronization while holding a lock.

23.5 Producer/Consumer Relationship without Synchronization

In a **producer/consumer relationship**, the **producer** portion of an application generates data and *stores it in a shared object*, and the **consumer** portion of the application *reads data from the shared object*. The producer/consumer relationship separates the task of identifying work to be done from the tasks involved in actually carrying out the work.

Examples of Producer/Consumer Relationship

One example of a common producer/consumer relationship is **print spooling**. Although a printer might not be available when you want to print from an application (i.e., the producer), you can still "complete" the print task, as the data is temporarily placed on disk until the printer becomes available. Similarly, when the printer (i.e., a consumer) is available, it doesn't have to wait until a current user wants to print. The spooled print jobs can be printed as soon as the printer becomes available. Another example of the producer/consumer relationship is an application that copies data onto DVDs by placing data in a fixed-size buffer, which is emptied as the DVD drive "burns" the data onto the DVD.

Synchronization and State Dependence

In a multithreaded producer/consumer relationship, a **producer thread** generates data and places it in a shared object called a **buffer**. A **consumer thread** reads data from the buffer. This relationship requires *synchronization* to ensure that values are produced and consumed properly. All operations on *mutable* data that's shared by multiple threads (e.g., the data in the buffer) must be guarded with a lock to prevent corruption, as discussed in

Section 23.4. Operations on the buffer data shared by a producer and consumer thread are also **state dependent**—the operations should proceed only if the buffer is in the correct state. If the buffer is in a *not-full state*, the producer may produce; if the buffer is in a *not-empty state*, the consumer may consume. All operations that access the buffer must use synchronization to ensure that data is written to the buffer or read from the buffer only if the buffer is in the proper state. If the producer attempting to put the next data into the buffer determines that it's full, the producer thread must *wait* until there's space to write a new value. If a consumer thread finds the buffer empty or finds that the previous data has already been read, the consumer must also *wait* for new data to become available. Other examples of state dependence are that you can't drive your car if its gas tank is empty and you can't put more gas into the tank if it's already full.

Logic Errors from Lack of Synchronization

Consider how logic errors can arise if we do not synchronize access among multiple threads manipulating shared mutable data. Our next example (Figs. 23.9–23.13) implements a producer/consumer relationship *without the proper synchronization.* A producer thread writes the numbers 1 through 10 into a shared buffer—a single memory location shared between two threads (a single `int` variable called `buffer` in line 5 of Fig. 23.12 in this example). The consumer thread reads this data from the shared buffer and displays the data. The program's output shows the values that the producer writes (produces) into the shared buffer and the values that the consumer reads (consumes) from the shared buffer.

Each value the producer thread writes to the shared buffer must be consumed *exactly once* by the consumer thread. However, the threads in this example are not synchronized. Therefore, *data can be lost or garbled if the producer places new data into the shared buffer before the consumer reads the previous data.* Also, data can be incorrectly *duplicated* if the consumer consumes data again before the producer produces the next value. To show these possibilities, the consumer thread in the following example keeps a total of all the values it reads. The producer thread produces values from 1 through 10. If the consumer reads each value produced once and only once, the total will be 55. However, if you execute this program several times, you'll see that the total is not always 55 (as shown in the outputs in Fig. 23.13). To emphasize the point, the producer and consumer threads in the example each sleep for random intervals of up to three seconds between performing their tasks. Thus, we do not know when the producer thread will attempt to write a new value, or when the consumer thread will attempt to read a value.

Interface `Buffer`

The program consists of interface `Buffer` (Fig. 23.9) and classes `Producer` (Fig. 23.10), `Consumer` (Fig. 23.11), `UnsynchronizedBuffer` (Fig. 23.12) and `SharedBufferTest` (Fig. 23.13). Interface `Buffer` (Fig. 23.9) declares methods `blockingPut` (line 5) and `blockingGet` (line 8) that a `Buffer` (such as `UnsynchronizedBuffer`) must implement to enable the `Producer` thread to place a value in the `Buffer` and the `Consumer` thread to retrieve a value from the `Buffer`, respectively. In subsequent examples, methods `blockingPut` and `blockingGet` will call methods that throw `InterruptedException`s—typically this indicates that a method temporarily could be blocked from performing a task. We declare each method with a `throws` clause here so that we don't have to modify this interface for the later examples.

```java
// Fig. 23.9: Buffer.java
// Buffer interface specifies methods called by Producer and Consumer.
public interface Buffer {
   // place int value into Buffer
   public void blockingPut(int value) throws InterruptedException;

   // return int value from Buffer
   public int blockingGet() throws InterruptedException;
}
```

Fig. 23.9 | Buffer interface specifies methods called by `Producer` and `Consumer`. (*Caution:* The example of Figs. 23.9–23.13 is *not* thread safe.)

Class Producer

Class `Producer` (Fig. 23.10) implements the `Runnable` interface, allowing it to be executed as a task in a separate thread. The constructor (lines 10–12) initializes the `Buffer` reference `sharedLocation` with an object created in `main` (line 13 of Fig. 23.13) and passed to the constructor. As we'll see, this is an `UnsynchronizedBuffer` object that implements interface `Buffer` *without synchronizing access to the shared object.*

```java
1  // Fig. 23.10: Producer.java
2  // Producer with a run method that inserts the values 1 to 10 in buffer.
3  import java.security.SecureRandom;
4
5  public class Producer implements Runnable {
6     private static final SecureRandom generator = new SecureRandom();
7     private final Buffer sharedLocation; // reference to shared object
8
9     // constructor
10    public Producer(Buffer sharedLocation) {
11       this.sharedLocation = sharedLocation;
12    }
13
14    // store values from 1 to 10 in sharedLocation
15    @Override
16    public void run() {
17       int sum = 0;
18
19       for (int count = 1; count <= 10; count++) {
20          try { // sleep 0 to 3 seconds, then place value in Buffer
21             Thread.sleep(generator.nextInt(3000)); // random sleep
22             sharedLocation.blockingPut(count); // set value in buffer
23             sum += count; // increment sum of values
24             System.out.printf("\t%2d%n", sum);
25          }
26          catch (InterruptedException exception) {
27             Thread.currentThread().interrupt();
28          }
29       }
```

Fig. 23.10 | `Producer` with a `run` method that inserts the values 1 to 10 in buffer. (*Caution:* The example of Figs. 23.9–23.13 is *not* thread safe.) (Part 1 of 2.)

```
30
31         System.out.printf(
32            "Producer done producing%nTerminating Producer%n");
33      }
34   }
```

Fig. 23.10 | `Producer` with a `run` method that inserts the values 1 to 10 in buffer. (*Caution:* The example of Figs. 23.9–23.13 is *not* thread safe.) (Part 2 of 2.)

The `Producer` thread in this program executes the tasks specified in the method `run` (Fig. 23.10, lines 15–33). Each iteration of its loop invokes `Thread` method `sleep` (line 21) to place the `Producer` thread into the *timed waiting* state for a random time interval between 0 and 3 seconds. When the thread awakens, line 22 passes the value of control variable `count` to the `Buffer` object's `blockingPut` method to set the shared buffer's value. Lines 23–24 keep a total of all the values produced so far and output that value. When the loop completes, lines 31–32 display a message indicating that the `Producer` has finished producing data and is terminating. Next, method `run` terminates, which indicates that the `Producer` completed its task. Any method called from a `Runnable`'s `run` method (e.g., `Buffer` method `blockingPut`) executes as part of that task's thread of execution. This fact becomes important in Sections 23.6–23.8 when we add synchronization to the producer/consumer relationship.

Class `Consumer`

Class `Consumer` (Fig. 23.11) also implements interface `Runnable`, allowing the `Consumer` to execute concurrently with the `Producer`. Lines 10–12 initialize `Buffer` reference `sharedLocation` with an object that implements the `Buffer` interface (created in `main`, Fig. 23.13) and passed to the constructor as the parameter `sharedLocation`. As we'll see, this is the same `UnsynchronizedBuffer` object that's used to initialize the `Producer` object—thus, the two threads share the same object. The `Consumer` thread in this program performs the tasks specified in method `run`. Lines 19–29 in Fig. 23.11 iterate 10 times. Each iteration invokes `Thread` method `sleep` (line 22) to put the `Consumer` thread into the *timed waiting* state for up to 3 seconds. Next, line 23 uses the `Buffer`'s `blockingGet` method to retrieve the value in the shared buffer, then adds the value to variable `sum`. Line 24 displays the total of all the values consumed so far. When the loop completes, lines 31–32 display the sum of the consumed values. Then method `run` terminates, which indicates that the `Consumer` completed its task. Once both threads enter the *terminated* state, the program ends.

```
1  // Fig. 23.11: Consumer.java
2  // Consumer with a run method that loops, reading 10 values from buffer.
3  import java.security.SecureRandom;
4
5  public class Consumer implements Runnable {
6     private static final SecureRandom generator = new SecureRandom();
7     private final Buffer sharedLocation; // reference to shared object
8
```

Fig. 23.11 | `Consumer` with a `run` method that loops, reading 10 values from buffer. (*Caution:* The example of Figs. 23.9–23.13 is *not* thread safe.) (Part 1 of 2.)

```java
    // constructor
    public Consumer(Buffer sharedLocation) {
       this.sharedLocation = sharedLocation;
    }

    // read sharedLocation's value 10 times and sum the values
    @Override
    public void run() {
       int sum = 0;

       for (int count = 1; count <= 10; count++) {
          // sleep 0 to 3 seconds, read value from buffer and add to sum
          try {
             Thread.sleep(generator.nextInt(3000));
             sum += sharedLocation.blockingGet();
             System.out.printf("\t\t\t%2d%n", sum);
          }
          catch (InterruptedException exception) {
             Thread.currentThread().interrupt();
          }
       }

       System.out.printf("%n%s %d%n%s%n",
          "Consumer read values totaling", sum, "Terminating Consumer");
    }
 }
```

Fig. 23.11 | Consumer with a run method that loops, reading 10 values from buffer. (*Caution:* The example of Figs. 23.9–23.13 is *not* thread safe.) (Part 2 of 2.)

We Call Thread *Method* sleep *Only for Demonstration Purposes*

We call method sleep in method run of the Producer and Consumer classes to emphasize the fact that, *in multithreaded applications, it's unpredictable when each thread will perform its task and for how long it will perform the task when it has a processor.* Normally, these thread-scheduling issues are beyond the control of the Java developer. In this program, our thread's tasks are quite simple—the Producer writes the values 1 to 10 to the buffer, and the Consumer reads 10 values from the buffer and adds each value to variable sum. Without the sleep method call, and if the Producer executes first, given today's phenomenally fast processors, the Producer would likely complete its task before the Consumer got a chance to execute. If the Consumer executed first, it would likely consume garbage data ten times, then terminate before the Producer could produce the first real value.

Class UnsynchronizedBuffer *Does Not Synchronize Access to the Buffer*

Class UnsynchronizedBuffer (Fig. 23.12) implements interface Buffer (line 4), but does *not* synchronize access to the buffer's state—we purposely do this to demonstrate the problems that occur when multiple threads access *shared* mutable data *without* synchronization. Line 5 declares instance variable buffer and initializes it to -1. This value is used to demonstrate the case in which the Consumer attempts to consume a value *before* the Producer ever places a value in buffer. Again, methods blockingPut (lines 8–12) and blockingGet (lines 15–19) do *not* synchronize access to the buffer instance variable. Method `blockingPut` simply assigns its argument to `buffer` (line 11), and method `blockingGet` simply returns the value of `buffer` (line 18). As you'll see in Fig. 23.13, `UnsynchronizedBuffer` object is shared between the `Producer` and the `Consumer`.

```
1  // Fig. 23.12: UnsynchronizedBuffer.java
2  // UnsynchronizedBuffer maintains the shared integer that is accessed by
3  // a producer thread and a consumer thread.
4  public class UnsynchronizedBuffer implements Buffer {
5     private int buffer = -1; // shared by producer and consumer threads
6
7     // place value into buffer
8     @Override
9     public void blockingPut(int value) throws InterruptedException {
10       System.out.printf("Producer writes\t%2d", value);
11       buffer = value;
12    }
13
14    // return value from buffer
15    @Override
16    public int blockingGet() throws InterruptedException {
17       System.out.printf("Consumer reads\t%2d", buffer);
18       return buffer;
19    }
20 }
```

Fig. 23.12 | `UnsynchronizedBuffer` maintains the shared integer that is accessed by a producer thread and a consumer thread. (*Caution:* The example of Fig. 23.9–Fig. 23.13 is *not* thread safe.)

Class `SharedBufferTest`

In class `SharedBufferTest` (Fig. 23.13), line 10 creates an `ExecutorService` to execute the `Producer` and `Consumer` `Runnables`. Line 13 creates an `UnsynchronizedBuffer` and assigns it to `Buffer` variable `sharedLocation`. This object stores the data that the `Producer` and `Consumer` threads will share. Lines 22–23 create and execute the `Producer` and `Consumer`. The `Producer` and `Consumer` constructors are each passed the same `Buffer` object (`sharedLocation`), so each object refers to the same `Buffer`. These lines also implicitly launch the threads and call each `Runnable`'s `run` method. Finally, line 25 calls method `shutdown` so that the application can terminate when the threads executing the `Producer` and `Consumer` complete their tasks and line 26 waits for the scheduled tasks to complete. When `main` terminates, the main thread of execution enters the *terminated* state.

```
1  // Fig. 23.13: SharedBufferTest.java
2  // Application with two threads manipulating an unsynchronized buffer.
3  import java.util.concurrent.ExecutorService;
4  import java.util.concurrent.Executors;
5  import java.util.concurrent.TimeUnit;
6
```

Fig. 23.13 | Application with two threads manipulating an unsynchronized buffer—the italicized text in the output is our commentary, which is not part of the program's output. (*Caution:* The example of Figs. 23.9–23.13 is *not* thread safe.) (Part 1 of 3.)

```
public class SharedBufferTest {
   public static void main(String[] args) throws InterruptedException {
      // create new thread pool
      ExecutorService executorService = Executors.newCachedThreadPool();

      // create UnsynchronizedBuffer to store ints
      Buffer sharedLocation = new UnsynchronizedBuffer();

      System.out.println(
         "Action\t\tValue\tSum of Produced\tSum of Consumed");
      System.out.printf(
         "------\t\t-----\t---------------\t---------------%n%n");

      // execute the Producer and Consumer, giving each
      // access to the sharedLocation
      executorService.execute(new Producer(sharedLocation));
      executorService.execute(new Consumer(sharedLocation));

      executorService.shutdown(); // terminate app when tasks complete
      executorService.awaitTermination(1, TimeUnit.MINUTES);
   }
}
```

```
Action          Value   Sum of Produced Sum of Consumed
------          -----   --------------- ---------------

Producer writes  1       1
Producer writes  2       3                      — 1 lost
Producer writes  3       6                      — 2 lost
Consumer reads   3                      3
Producer writes  4       10
Consumer reads   4                      7
Producer writes  5       15
Producer writes  6       21                     — 5 lost
Producer writes  7       28                     — 6 lost
Consumer reads   7                      14
Consumer reads   7                      21      — 7 read again
Producer writes  8       36
Consumer reads   8                      29
Consumer reads   8                      37      — 8 read again
Producer writes  9       45
Producer writes 10       55                     — 9 lost

Producer done producing
Terminating Producer
Consumer reads  10                      47
Consumer reads  10                      57      — 10 read again
Consumer reads  10                      67      — 10 read again
Consumer reads  10                      77      — 10 read again

Consumer read values totaling 77
Terminating Consumer
```

Fig. 23.13 | Application with two threads manipulating an unsynchronized buffer—the italicized text in the output is our commentary, which is not part of the program's output. (*Caution:* The example of Figs. 23.9–23.13 is *not* thread safe.) (Part 2 of 3.)

```
Action           Value   Sum of Produced Sum of Consumed
------           -----   --------------- ---------------

Consumer reads   -1                           -1 — reads -1 bad data
Producer writes   1         1
Consumer reads    1                            0
Consumer reads    1                            1 — 1 read again
Consumer reads    1                            2 — 1 read again
Consumer reads    1                            3 — 1 read again
Consumer reads    1                            4 — 1 read again
Producer writes   2         3
Consumer reads    2                            6
Producer writes   3         6
Consumer reads    3                            9
Producer writes   4        10
Consumer reads    4                           13
Producer writes   5        15
Producer writes   6        21                    — 5 lost
Consumer reads    6                           19

Consumer read values totaling 19
Terminating Consumer
Producer writes   7        28                    — 7 never read
Producer writes   8        36                    — 8 never read
Producer writes   9        45                    — 9 never read
Producer writes 10         55                    — 9 never read

Producer done producing
Terminating Producer
```

Fig. 23.13 | Application with two threads manipulating an unsynchronized buffer—the italicized text in the output is our commentary, which is not part of the program's output. (*Caution:* The example of Figs. 23.9–23.13 is *not* thread safe.) (Part 3 of 3.)

Recall that the `Producer` should execute first, and every value it produces should be consumed exactly once by the `Consumer`. However, in the first output of Fig. 23.13, notice that the `Producer` writes `1`, `2` and `3` before the `Consumer` reads its first value (`3`). Therefore, the values `1` and `2` are *lost*. Later, `5`, `6` and `9` are *lost*, while `7` and `8` are *read twice* and `10` is read four times. So the first output produces an incorrect total of 77, instead of the correct total of 55. (Lines in the output where the `Producer` or `Consumer` acted out of order are highlighted.) In the second output, the `Consumer` reads the value `-1` *before* the `Producer` ever writes a value. The `Consumer` reads the value `1` *five times* before the `Producer` writes the value `2`. Meanwhile, `5`, `7`, `8`, `9` and `10` are all *lost*—the last four because the `Consumer` terminates *before* the `Producer`. The result is an incorrect consumer total of 19.

Error-Prevention Tip 23.1

Access to a shared object by concurrent threads must be controlled carefully or a program may produce incorrect results.

To solve the problems of *lost* and *duplicated* data, Section 23.6 presents an example in which we use an `ArrayBlockingQueue` (from package `java.util.concurrent`) to synchronize access to the shared object, guaranteeing that each and every value will be processed once and only once.

23.6 Producer/Consumer Relationship: ArrayBlockingQueue

The best way to synchronize producer and consumer threads is to use classes from Java's `java.util.concurrent` package that *encapsulate the synchronization for you*. Java includes the class **`ArrayBlockingQueue`**—a fully implemented, *thread-safe buffer class* that implements interface **`BlockingQueue`**. This interface declares methods **`put`** and **`take`**. Method `put` places an element at the end of the `BlockingQueue`, waiting if the queue is full. Method `take` removes an element from the head of the `BlockingQueue`, waiting if the queue is empty. These methods make class `ArrayBlockingQueue` a good choice for implementing a shared buffer. Because method `put` blocks until there's room in the buffer to write data, and method `take` blocks until there's new data to read, the producer must produce a value first, the consumer correctly consumes only after the producer writes a value and the producer correctly produces the next value (after the first) only after the consumer reads the previous (or first) value. `ArrayBlockingQueue` stores the shared mutable data in an array, the size of which is specified as `ArrayBlockingQueue`'s constructor argument. An `ArrayBlockingQueue` is fixed in size and will not expand to accommodate extra elements.

Class `BlockingBuffer`

Figures 23.14–23.15 demonstrate a `Producer` and a `Consumer` accessing an `ArrayBlockingQueue`. Class `BlockingBuffer` (Fig. 23.14) uses an `ArrayBlockingQueue` object that stores an `Integer` (line 6). Line 9 creates the `ArrayBlockingQueue` and passes `1` to the constructor so that the object holds a single value to mimic the `UnsynchronizedBuffer` example in Fig. 23.12. We discuss *multiple-element buffers* in Section 23.8. Because our `BlockingBuffer` class uses the *thread-safe* `ArrayBlockingQueue` class to manage all of its shared state (the shared buffer in this case), `BlockingBuffer` is itself *thread safe*, even though we have not implemented the synchronization ourselves.

```
1  // Fig. 23.14: BlockingBuffer.java
2  // Creating a synchronized buffer using an ArrayBlockingQueue.
3  import java.util.concurrent.ArrayBlockingQueue;
4
5  public class BlockingBuffer implements Buffer {
6     private final ArrayBlockingQueue<Integer> buffer; // shared buffer
7
8     public BlockingBuffer() {
9        buffer = new ArrayBlockingQueue<Integer>(1);
10    }
11
12    // place value into buffer
13    @Override
14    public void blockingPut(int value) throws InterruptedException {
15       buffer.put(value); // place value in buffer
16       System.out.printf("%s%2d\t%s%d%n", "Producer writes ", value,
17          "Buffer cells occupied: ", buffer.size());
18    }
19
```

Fig. 23.14 | Creating a synchronized buffer using an `ArrayBlockingQueue`. (Part 1 of 2.)

```
20       // return value from buffer
21       @Override
22       public int blockingGet() throws InterruptedException {
23          int readValue = buffer.take(); // remove value from buffer
24          System.out.printf("%s %2d\t%s%d%n", "Consumer reads ",
25             readValue, "Buffer cells occupied: ", buffer.size());
26
27          return readValue;
28       }
29    }
```

Fig. 23.14 | Creating a synchronized buffer using an ArrayBlockingQueue. (Part 2 of 2.)

`BlockingBuffer` implements interface `Buffer` (Fig. 23.9) and uses classes `Producer` (Fig. 23.10 modified to remove line 24) and `Consumer` (Fig. 23.11 modified to remove line 24) from the example in Section 23.5. This approach demonstrates encapsulated synchronization—*the threads accessing the shared object are unaware that their buffer accesses are now synchronized.* The synchronization is handled entirely in the `blockingPut` and `blockingGet` methods of `BlockingBuffer` by calling the synchronized `ArrayBlockingQueue` methods `put` and `take`, respectively. Thus, the `Producer` and `Consumer` `Runnables` are properly synchronized simply by calling the shared object's `blockingPut` and `blockingGet` methods.

Line 15 in method `blockingPut` (Fig. 23.14) calls the `ArrayBlockingQueue` object's `put` method. This method call blocks if necessary until there's room in the `buffer` to place the `value`. Method `blockingGet` calls the `ArrayBlockingQueue` object's `take` method (line 23). This method call *blocks* if necessary until there's an element in the `buffer` to remove. Lines 16–17 and 24–25 use the `ArrayBlockingQueue` object's **`size`** method to display the total number of elements currently in the `ArrayBlockingQueue`.

Class `BlockingBufferTest`

Class `BlockingBufferTest` (Fig. 23.15) contains the `main` method that launches the application. Line 11 creates an `ExecutorService`, and line 14 creates a `BlockingBuffer` object and assigns its reference to the `Buffer` variable `sharedLocation`. Lines 16–17 execute the `Producer` and `Consumer` `Runnables`. Line 19 calls method `shutdown` to end the application when the threads finish executing the `Producer` and `Consumer` tasks, and line 20 waits for the scheduled tasks to complete.

```
1  // Fig. 23.15: BlockingBufferTest.java
2  // Two threads manipulating a blocking buffer that properly
3  // implements the producer/consumer relationship.
4  import java.util.concurrent.ExecutorService;
5  import java.util.concurrent.Executors;
6  import java.util.concurrent.TimeUnit;
7
8  public class BlockingBufferTest {
9     public static void main(String[] args) throws InterruptedException {
```

Fig. 23.15 | Two threads manipulating a blocking buffer that properly implements the producer/consumer relationship. (Part 1 of 2.)

```
        // create new thread pool
        ExecutorService executorService = Executors.newCachedThreadPool();

        // create BlockingBuffer to store ints
        Buffer sharedLocation = new BlockingBuffer();

        executorService.execute(new Producer(sharedLocation));
        executorService.execute(new Consumer(sharedLocation));

        executorService.shutdown();
        executorService.awaitTermination(1, TimeUnit.MINUTES);
    }
}
```

```
Producer writes  1      Buffer cells occupied: 1
Consumer reads   1      Buffer cells occupied: 0
Producer writes  2      Buffer cells occupied: 1
Consumer reads   2      Buffer cells occupied: 0
Producer writes  3      Buffer cells occupied: 1
Consumer reads   3      Buffer cells occupied: 0
Producer writes  4      Buffer cells occupied: 1
Consumer reads   4      Buffer cells occupied: 0
Producer writes  5      Buffer cells occupied: 1
Consumer reads   5      Buffer cells occupied: 0
Producer writes  6      Buffer cells occupied: 1
Consumer reads   6      Buffer cells occupied: 0
Producer writes  7      Buffer cells occupied: 1
Consumer reads   7      Buffer cells occupied: 0
Producer writes  8      Buffer cells occupied: 1
Consumer reads   8      Buffer cells occupied: 0
Producer writes  9      Buffer cells occupied: 1
Consumer reads   9      Buffer cells occupied: 0
Producer writes 10      Buffer cells occupied: 1

Producer done producing
Terminating Producer
Consumer reads  10      Buffer cells occupied: 0

Consumer read values totaling 55
Terminating Consumer
```

Fig. 23.15 | Two threads manipulating a blocking buffer that properly implements the producer/consumer relationship. (Part 2 of 2.)

While methods `put` and `take` of `ArrayBlockingQueue` are properly synchronized, `BlockingBuffer` methods `blockingPut` and `blockingGet` (Fig. 23.14) are not declared to be synchronized. Thus, the statements performed in method `blockingPut`—the `put` operation (Fig. 23.14, line 15) and the output (lines 16–17)—are *not atomic*; nor are the statements in method `blockingGet`—the `take` operation (line 23) and the output (lines 24–25). So there's no guarantee that each output will occur immediately after the corresponding `put` or `take` operation, and the outputs may appear out of order. Even if they do, the `ArrayBlockingQueue` object is properly synchronizing access to the data, as evidenced by the fact that the sum of values read by the consumer is always correct.

23.7 (Advanced) Producer/Consumer Relationship with synchronized, wait, notify and notifyAll

[*Note:* This section is intended for *advanced* programmers who want to control synchronization.[2]] The previous example showed how multiple threads can share a single-element buffer in a thread-safe manner by using the `ArrayBlockingQueue` class that encapsulates the synchronization necessary to protect the shared mutable data. For educational purposes, we now explain how you can implement a shared buffer yourself using the `synchronized` keyword and methods of class `Object`. *Using an* `ArrayBlockingQueue` *generally results in more-maintainable, better-performing code.*

After identifying the shared mutable data and the *synchronization policy* (i.e., associating the data with a lock that guards it), the next step in synchronizing access to the buffer is to implement methods `blockingGet` and `blockingPut` as `synchronized` methods. This requires that a thread obtain the *monitor lock* on the `Buffer` object before attempting to access the buffer data, but it does not automatically ensure that threads proceed with an operation only if the buffer is in the proper state. We need a way to allow our threads to *wait*, depending on whether certain conditions are true. In the case of placing a new item in the buffer, the condition that allows the operation to proceed is that the *buffer is not full.* In the case of fetching an item from the buffer, the condition that allows the operation to proceed is that the *buffer is not empty*. If the condition in question is true, the operation may proceed; if it's false, the thread must *wait* until it becomes true. When a thread is waiting on a condition, it's removed from contention for the processor and placed into the *waiting* state and the lock it holds is released.

Methods `wait`*,* `notify` *and* `notifyAll`

`Object` methods `wait`, `notify` and `notifyAll` can be used with conditions to make threads *wait* when they cannot perform their tasks. If a thread obtains the *monitor lock* on an object, then determines that it cannot continue with its task on that object until some condition is satisfied, the thread can call `Object` method **`wait`** on the `synchronized` object; this *releases the monitor lock* on the object, and the thread waits in the *waiting* state while the other threads try to enter the object's `synchronized` statement(s) or method(s). When a thread executing a `synchronized` statement (or method) completes or satisfies the condition on which another thread may be waiting, it can call `Object` method **`notify`** on the `synchronized` object to allow a waiting thread to transition to the *runnable* state again. At this point, the thread that was transitioned from the *waiting* state to the *runnable* state can attempt to *reacquire the monitor lock* on the object. Even if the thread is able to reacquire the monitor lock, it still might not be able to perform its task at this time—in which case the thread will reenter the *waiting* state and implicitly *release the monitor lock.* If a thread calls **`notifyAll`** on the `synchronized` object, then *all* the threads waiting for the monitor lock become eligible to *reacquire the lock* (that is, they all transition to the *runnable* state).

Remember that only *one* thread at a time can obtain the monitor lock on the object—other threads that attempt to acquire the same monitor lock will be *blocked* until the mon-

2. For detailed information on `wait`, `notify` and `notifyAll`, see Chapter 14 of *Java Concurrency in Practice* by Brian Goetz, et al., Addison-Wesley Professional, 2006.

itor lock becomes available again (i.e., until no other thread is executing in a `synchronized` statement on that object).

Common Programming Error 23.1

It's an error if a thread issues a `wait`, a `notify` or a `notifyAll` on an object without having acquired a lock for it. This causes an `IllegalMonitorStateException`.

Error-Prevention Tip 23.2

It's a good practice to use `notifyAll` to notify waiting *threads to become* runnable. *Doing so avoids the possibility that your program would forget about waiting threads, which would otherwise starve.*

Figures 23.16 and 23.17 demonstrate a `Producer` and a `Consumer` accessing a shared buffer with synchronization. In this case, the `Producer` always produces a value *first*, the `Consumer` correctly consumes only *after* the `Producer` produces a value and the `Producer` correctly produces the next value only after the `Consumer` consumes the previous (or first) value. We reuse interface `Buffer` and classes `Producer` and `Consumer` from the example in Section 23.5, except that line 24 is removed from class `Producer` and class `Consumer`.

Class `SynchronizedBuffer`

The synchronization is handled in class `SynchronizedBuffer`'s `blockingPut` and `blockingGet` methods (Fig. 23.16). Thus, the `Producer`'s and `Consumer`'s `run` methods simply call the shared object's `synchronized` `blockingPut` and `blockingGet` methods. Again, we output messages from the `synchronized` methods for demonstration purposes only—I/O *should not* be performed in `synchronized` blocks, because it's important to minimize the amount of time that an object is "locked."

```
// Fig. 23.16: SynchronizedBuffer.java
// Synchronizing access to shared mutable data using Object
// methods wait and notifyAll.
public class SynchronizedBuffer implements Buffer {
   private int buffer = -1; // shared by producer and consumer threads
   private boolean occupied = false;

   // place value into buffer
   @Override
   public synchronized void blockingPut(int value)
      throws InterruptedException {
      // while there are no empty locations, place thread in waiting state
      while (occupied) {
         // output thread information and buffer information, then wait
         System.out.println("Producer tries to write."); // for demo only
         displayState("Buffer full. Producer waits."); // for demo only
         wait();
      }

      buffer = value; // set new buffer value
```

Fig. 23.16 | Synchronizing access to shared mutable data using `Object` methods `wait` and `notifyAll`. (Part 1 of 2.)

```
21
22          // indicate producer cannot store another value
23          // until consumer retrieves current buffer value
24          occupied = true;
25
26          displayState("Producer writes " + buffer); // for demo only
27
28          notifyAll(); // tell waiting thread(s) to enter runnable state
29       } // end method blockingPut; releases lock on SynchronizedBuffer
30
31       // return value from buffer
32       @Override
33       public synchronized int blockingGet() throws InterruptedException {
34          // while no data to read, place thread in waiting state
35          while (!occupied) {
36             // output thread information and buffer information, then wait
37             System.out.println("Consumer tries to read."); // for demo only
38             displayState("Buffer empty. Consumer waits."); // for demo only
39             wait();
40          }
41
42          // indicate that producer can store another value
43          // because consumer just retrieved buffer value
44          occupied = false;
45
46          displayState("Consumer reads " + buffer); // for demo only
47
48          notifyAll(); // tell waiting thread(s) to enter runnable state
49
50          return buffer;
51       } // end method blockingGet; releases lock on SynchronizedBuffer
52
53       // display current operation and buffer state; for demo only
54       private synchronized void displayState(String operation) {
55          System.out.printf("%-40s%d\t\t%b%n%n", operation, buffer, occupied);
56       }
57    }
```

Fig. 23.16 | Synchronizing access to shared mutable data using `Object` methods `wait` and `notifyAll`. (Part 2 of 2.)

Fields and Methods of Class `SynchronizedBuffer`

Class `SynchronizedBuffer` contains fields `buffer` (line 5) and `occupied` (line 6)—you must synchronize access to *both* fields to ensure that class `SynchronizedBuffer` is thread safe. Methods `blockingPut` (lines 9–29) and `blockingGet` (lines 32–51) are declared as `synchronized`—only *one* thread can call either of these methods at a time on a particular `SynchronizedBuffer` object. Field `occupied` is used to determine whether it's the `Producer`'s or the `Consumer`'s turn to perform a task. This field is used in conditional expressions in both the `blockingPut` and `blockingGet` methods. If `occupied` is `false`, then `buffer` is empty, so the `Consumer` cannot read the value of `buffer`, but the `Producer` can place a value into `buffer`. If `occupied` is `true`, the `Consumer` can read a value from `buffer`, but the `Producer` cannot place a value into `buffer`.

Method `blockingPut` *and the* **Producer** *Thread*

When the `Producer` thread's `run` method invokes `synchronized` method `blockingPut`, the thread attempts to acquire the `SynchronizedBuffer` object's monitor lock. If the monitor lock is available, the `Producer` thread *implicitly* acquires the lock. Then the loop at lines 13–18 first determines whether `occupied` is `true`. If so, `buffer` is *full* and we want to wait until the buffer is empty, so line 15 outputs a message indicating that the `Producer` thread is trying to write a value, and line 16 invokes method `displayState` (lines 54–56) to output another message indicating that `buffer` is *full* and that the `Producer` thread is *waiting* until there's space. Line 17 invokes method `wait` (inherited from `Object` by `SynchronizedBuffer`) to place the thread that called method `blockingPut` (i.e., the `Producer` thread) in the *waiting* state for the `SynchronizedBuffer` object. The call to `wait` causes the calling thread to *implicitly* release the lock on the `SynchronizedBuffer` object. This is important because the thread cannot currently perform its task and because other threads (in this case, the `Consumer`) should be allowed to access the object to allow the condition (`occupied`) to change. Now another thread can attempt to acquire the `SynchronizedBuffer` object's lock and invoke the object's `blockingPut` or `blockingGet` method.

The `Producer` thread remains in the *waiting* state until another thread *notifies* the `Producer` that it may proceed—at which point the `Producer` returns to the *runnable* state and attempts to implicitly reacquire the lock on the `SynchronizedBuffer` object. If the lock is available, the `Producer` thread reacquires it, and method `blockingPut` continues executing with the next statement after the `wait` call. Because `wait` is called in a loop, the loop-continuation condition is tested again to determine whether the thread can proceed. If not, then `wait` is invoked again—otherwise, method `blockingPut` continues with the next statement after the loop.

Line 20 in method `blockingPut` assigns the `value` to the `buffer`. Line 24 sets `occupied` to `true` to indicate that the `buffer` now contains a value (i.e., a consumer can read the value, but a `Producer` cannot yet put another value there). Line 26 invokes method `displayState` to output a message indicating that the `Producer` is writing a new value into the `buffer`. Line 28 invokes method `notifyAll` (inherited from `Object`). If any threads are *waiting* on the `SynchronizedBuffer` object's monitor lock, those threads enter the *runnable* state and can now attempt to *reacquire the lock*. Method `notifyAll` returns immediately, and method `blockingPut` then returns to the caller (i.e., the `Producer`'s `run` method). When method `blockingPut` returns, it *implicitly releases the monitor lock* on the `SynchronizedBuffer` object.

Method `blockingGet` *and the* **Consumer** *Thread*

Methods `blockingGet` and `blockingPut` are implemented similarly. When the `Consumer` thread's `run` method invokes `synchronized` method `blockingGet`, the thread attempts to *acquire the monitor lock* on the `SynchronizedBuffer` object. If the lock is available, the `Consumer` thread acquires it. Then the `while` loop at lines 35–40 determines whether `occupied` is `false`. If so, the buffer is empty, so line 37 outputs a message indicating that the `Consumer` thread is trying to read a value, and line 38 invokes method `displayState` to output a message indicating that the buffer is *empty* and that the `Consumer` thread is *waiting*. Line 39 invokes method `wait` to place the thread that called method `blockingGet` (i.e., the `Consumer`) in the *waiting* state for the `SynchronizedBuffer` object. Again, the call to `wait` causes the calling thread to *implicitly release the lock* on the `SynchronizedBuffer` object, so another thread can attempt to acquire the `SynchronizedBuffer` object's lock and invoke the object's blockingPut or blockingGet method. If the lock on the SynchronizedBuffer is not available (e.g., if the Producer has not yet returned from method blockingPut), the Consumer is *blocked* until the lock becomes available.

The Consumer thread remains in the *waiting* state until it's *notified* by another thread that it may proceed—at which point the Consumer thread returns to the *runnable* state and attempts to *implicitly reacquire the lock* on the SynchronizedBuffer object. If the lock is available, the Consumer reacquires it, and method blockingGet continues executing with the next statement after wait. Because wait is called in a loop, the loop-continuation condition is tested again to determine whether the thread can proceed with its execution. If not, wait is invoked again—otherwise, method blockingGet continues with the next statement after the loop. Line 44 sets occupied to false to indicate that buffer is now empty (i.e., a Consumer cannot read the value, but a Producer can place another value in buffer), line 46 calls method displayState to indicate that the consumer is reading and line 48 invokes method notifyAll. If any threads are in the *waiting* state for the lock on this SynchronizedBuffer object, they enter the *runnable* state and can now attempt to *reacquire the lock*. Method notifyAll returns immediately, then method blockingGet returns the value of buffer to its caller. When method blockingGet returns (line 50), the lock on the SynchronizedBuffer object is *implicitly released.*

Error-Prevention Tip 23.3

Always invoke method wait *in a loop that tests the condition the task is waiting on. It's possible that a thread will reenter the runnable state (via a timed wait or another thread calling* notifyAll*) before the condition is satisfied. Testing the condition again ensures that the thread will not erroneously execute if it was notified early.*

Method displayState *Is Also* synchronized

Notice that method displayState is a synchronized method. This is important because it, too, reads the SynchronizedBuffer's shared mutable data. Though only one thread at a time may acquire a given object's lock, one thread may acquire the same object's lock *multiple* times—this is known as a **reentrant lock** and enables one synchronized method to invoke another on the same object.

Testing Class SynchronizedBuffer

Class SharedBufferTest2 (Fig. 23.17) is similar to class SharedBufferTest (Fig. 23.13). Line 10 creates an ExecutorService to run the Producer and Consumer tasks. Line 13 creates a SynchronizedBuffer object and assigns its reference to Buffer variable sharedLocation. This object stores the data that will be shared between the Producer and Consumer. Lines 15–16 display the column heads for the output. Lines 19–20 execute a Producer and a Consumer. Finally, line 22 calls method shutdown to end the application when the Producer and Consumer complete their tasks, and line 23 waits for the scheduled tasks to complete. When method main ends, the main thread of execution terminates.

```
1  // Fig. 23.17: SharedBufferTest2.java
2  // Two threads correctly manipulating a synchronized buffer.
3  import java.util.concurrent.ExecutorService;
```

Fig. 23.17 | Two threads correctly manipulating a synchronized buffer. (Part 1 of 3.)

```java
import java.util.concurrent.Executors;
import java.util.concurrent.TimeUnit;

public class SharedBufferTest2 {
   public static void main(String[] args) throws InterruptedException {
      // create a newCachedThreadPool
      ExecutorService executorService = Executors.newCachedThreadPool();

      // create SynchronizedBuffer to store ints
      Buffer sharedLocation = new SynchronizedBuffer();

      System.out.printf("%-40s%s\t\t%s%n%-40s%s%n%n", "Operation",
         "Buffer", "Occupied", "---------", "------\t\t--------");

      // execute the Producer and Consumer tasks
      executorService.execute(new Producer(sharedLocation));
      executorService.execute(new Consumer(sharedLocation));

      executorService.shutdown();
      executorService.awaitTermination(1, TimeUnit.MINUTES);
   }
}
```

```
Operation                               Buffer          Occupied
---------                               ------          --------

Consumer tries to read.
Buffer empty. Consumer waits.           -1              false

Producer writes 1                       1               true

Consumer reads 1                        1               false

Consumer tries to read.
Buffer empty. Consumer waits.           1               false

Producer writes 2                       2               true

Consumer reads 2                        2               false

Producer writes 3                       3               true

Consumer reads 3                        3               false

Producer writes 4                       4               true

Producer tries to write.
Buffer full. Producer waits.            4               true

Consumer reads 4                        4               false

Producer writes 5                       5               true

Consumer reads 5                        5               false

Producer writes 6                       6               true
```

Fig. 23.17 | Two threads correctly manipulating a synchronized buffer. (Part 2 of 3.)

```
Producer tries to write.
Buffer full. Producer waits.          6          true

Consumer reads 6                      6          false

Producer writes 7                     7          true

Producer tries to write.
Buffer full. Producer waits.          7          true

Consumer reads 7                      7          false

Producer writes 8                     8          true

Consumer reads 8                      8          false

Consumer tries to read.
Buffer empty. Consumer waits.         8          false

Producer writes 9                     9          true

Consumer reads 9                      9          false

Consumer tries to read.
Buffer empty. Consumer waits.         9          false

Producer writes 10                    10         true

Consumer reads 10                     10         false


Producer done producing
Terminating Producer

Consumer read values totaling 55
Terminating Consumer
```

Fig. 23.17 | Two threads correctly manipulating a synchronized buffer. (Part 3 of 3.)

Study the outputs in Fig. 23.17. Observe that *every integer produced is consumed exactly once—no values are lost, and no values are consumed more than once.* The synchronization ensures that the `Producer` produces a value only when the buffer is *empty* and the `Consumer` consumes only when the buffer is *full*. The `Producer` always goes first, the `Consumer` *waits* if the `Producer` has not produced since the `Consumer` last consumed, and the `Producer` waits if the `Consumer` has not yet consumed the value that the `Producer` most recently produced. Execute this program several times to confirm that every integer produced is consumed exactly *once*. In the sample output, note the highlighted lines indicating when the `Producer` and `Consumer` must *wait* to perform their respective tasks.

23.8 (Advanced) Producer/Consumer Relationship: Bounded Buffers

The program in Section 23.7 uses thread synchronization to guarantee that two threads manipulate data in a shared buffer correctly. However, the application may not perform optimally. If the two threads operate at different speeds, one of them will spend more (or most) of its time waiting. For example, in the program in Section 23.7 we shared a single integer variable between the two threads. If the `Producer` thread produces values *faster* than the `Consumer` can consume them, then the `Producer` thread *waits* for the `Consumer`, because there are no other locations in the buffer in which to place the next value. Similarly, if the `Consumer` consumes values *faster* than the `Producer` produces them, the `Consumer` *waits* until the `Producer` places the next value in the shared buffer. Even when we have threads that operate at the *same* relative speeds, those threads may occasionally become "out of sync" over a period of time, causing one of them to *wait* for the other.

Performance Tip 23.3

We cannot make assumptions about the relative speeds of concurrent threads—*interactions that occur with the operating system, the network, the user and other components can cause the threads to operate at different and ever-changing speeds. When this happens, threads wait. When threads wait excessively, programs become less efficient, interactive programs become less responsive and applications suffer longer delays.*

Bounded Buffers

To minimize the amount of waiting time for threads that share resources and operate at the same average speeds, we can implement a **bounded buffer** that provides a fixed number of buffer cells into which the `Producer` can place values, and from which the `Consumer` can retrieve those values. (In fact, the `ArrayBlockingQueue` class in Section 23.6 is a bounded buffer.) If the `Producer` temporarily produces values faster than the `Consumer` can consume them, the `Producer` can write additional values into the extra buffer cells, if any are available. This capability enables the `Producer` to perform its task even though the `Consumer` is not ready to retrieve the current value being produced. Similarly, if the `Consumer` temporarily consumes faster than the `Producer` produces new values, the `Consumer` can read additional values (if there are any) from the buffer. This enables the `Consumer` to keep busy even though the `Producer` is not ready to produce additional values. An example of the producer/consumer relationship that uses a bounded buffer is video streaming, which we discussed in Section 23.1.

Even a *bounded buffer* is inappropriate if the `Producer` and the `Consumer` operate consistently at different speeds. If the `Consumer` always executes faster than the `Producer`, then a buffer containing one location is enough. If the `Producer` always executes faster, only a buffer with an "infinite" number of locations would be able to absorb the extra production. However, if the `Producer` and `Consumer` execute at about the same average speed, a bounded buffer helps to smooth the effects of any occasional speeding up or slowing down in either thread's execution.

The key to using a *bounded buffer* with a `Producer` and `Consumer` that operate at about the same speed is to provide the buffer with enough locations to handle the anticipated "extra" production. If, over a period of time, we determine that the `Producer` often produces as many as three more values than the `Consumer` can consume, we can provide a buffer of at least three cells to handle the extra production. Making the buffer too small would cause threads to wait longer.

[*Note:* As we mention in Fig. 23.22, `ArrayBlockingQueue` can work with multiple producers and multiple consumers. For example, a factory that produces its product very fast will need to have many more delivery trucks (i.e., consumers) to remove those products quickly from the warehousing area (i.e., the bounded buffer) so that the factory can continue to produce products at full capacity.]

Performance Tip 23.4

Even when using a bounded buffer, *it's possible that a producer thread could fill the buffer, which would force the producer to wait until a consumer consumed a value to free an element in the buffer. Similarly, if the buffer is empty at any given time, a consumer thread must wait until the producer produces another value. The key to using a bounded buffer is to optimize the buffer size to minimize the amount of thread wait time, while not wasting space.*

Bounded Buffers Using `ArrayBlockingQueue`

The simplest way to implement a bounded buffer is to use an `ArrayBlockingQueue` for the buffer so that *all of the synchronization details are handled for you*. This can be done by modifying the example from Section 23.6 to pass the desired size for the bounded buffer into the `ArrayBlockingQueue` constructor. Rather than repeat our previous `ArrayBlockingQueue` example with a different size, we instead present an example that illustrates how you can build a bounded buffer yourself. Again, using an `ArrayBlockingQueue` will result in more-maintainable and better-performing code. In Exercise 23.13, we ask you to reimplement this section's example, using the Java Concurrency API techniques presented in Section 23.9.

Implementing Your Own Bounded Buffer as a Circular Buffer

The program in Figs. 23.18 and 23.19 demonstrates a `Producer` and a `Consumer` accessing a *bounded buffer with synchronization*. Again, we reuse interface `Buffer` and classes `Producer` and `Consumer` from the example in Section 23.5, except that line 24 is removed from class `Producer` and class `Consumer`. We implement the bounded buffer (Fig. 23.18) as a **circular buffer** that uses a shared array of three elements. A circular buffer writes into and reads from the array elements in order, beginning at the first cell and moving toward the last. When a `Producer` or `Consumer` reaches the last element, it returns to the first and begins writing or reading, respectively, from there. In this version of the producer/consumer relationship, the `Consumer` consumes a value only when the array is not empty and the `Producer` produces a value only when the array is not full. Once again, the output statements used in this class's `synchronized` methods are for *demonstration purposes only*.

```
// Fig. 23.18: CircularBuffer.java
// Synchronizing access to a shared three-element bounded buffer.
public class CircularBuffer implements Buffer {
   private final int[] buffer = {-1, -1, -1}; // shared buffer

   private int occupiedCells = 0; // count number of buffers used
   private int writeIndex = 0; // index of next element to write to
   private int readIndex = 0; // index of next element to read

   // place value into buffer
   @Override
   public synchronized void blockingPut(int value)
      throws InterruptedException {
```

Fig. 23.18 | Synchronizing access to a shared three-element bounded buffer. (Part 1 of 3.)

```

      // wait until buffer has space available, then write value;
      // while no empty locations, place thread in blocked state
      while (occupiedCells == buffer.length) {
         System.out.printf("Buffer is full. Producer waits.%n");
         wait(); // wait until a buffer cell is free
      }

      buffer[writeIndex] = value; // set new buffer value

      // update circular write index
      writeIndex = (writeIndex + 1) % buffer.length;

      ++occupiedCells; // one more buffer cell is full
      displayState("Producer writes " + value);
      notifyAll(); // notify threads waiting to read from buffer
   }

   // return value from buffer
   @Override
   public synchronized int blockingGet() throws InterruptedException {
      // wait until buffer has data, then read value;
      // while no data to read, place thread in waiting state
      while (occupiedCells == 0) {
         System.out.printf("Buffer is empty. Consumer waits.%n");
         wait(); // wait until a buffer cell is filled
      }

      int readValue = buffer[readIndex]; // read value from buffer

      // update circular read index
      readIndex = (readIndex + 1) % buffer.length;

      --occupiedCells; // one fewer buffer cells are occupied
      displayState("Consumer reads " + readValue);
      notifyAll(); // notify threads waiting to write to buffer

      return readValue;
   }

   // display current operation and buffer state
   public synchronized void displayState(String operation) {
      // output operation and number of occupied buffer cells
      System.out.printf("%s%s%d)%n%s", operation,
         " (buffer cells occupied: ", occupiedCells, "buffer cells:  ");

      for (int value : buffer) {
         System.out.printf(" %2d  ", value); // output values in buffer
      }

      System.out.printf("%n               ");

```

Fig. 23.18 | Synchronizing access to a shared three-element bounded buffer. (Part 2 of 3.)

```
66         for (int i = 0; i < buffer.length; i++) {
67            System.out.print("---- ");
68         }
69
70         System.out.printf("%n               ");
71
72         for (int i = 0; i < buffer.length; i++) {
73            if (i == writeIndex && i == readIndex) {
74               System.out.print(" WR"); // both write and read index
75            }
76            else if (i == writeIndex) {
77               System.out.print(" W   "); // just write index
78            }
79            else if (i == readIndex) {
80               System.out.print("  R  "); // just read index
81            }
82            else {
83               System.out.print("     "); // neither index
84            }
85         }
86
87         System.out.printf("%n%n");
88      }
89   }
```

Fig. 23.18 | Synchronizing access to a shared three-element bounded buffer. (Part 3 of 3.)

Line 4 initializes array `buffer` as a three-element `int` array that represents the circular buffer. Variable `occupiedCells` (line 6) counts the number of elements in `buffer` that contain data to be read. When `occupiedCells` is `0`, the circular buffer is *empty* and the `Consumer` must *wait*—when `occupiedCells` is `3` (the size of the circular buffer), the circular buffer is *full* and the `Producer` must *wait*. Variable `writeIndex` (line 7) indicates the next location in which a value can be placed by a `Producer`. Variable `readIndex` (line 8) indicates the position from which the next value can be read by a `Consumer`. `CircularBuffer`'s instance variables are *all* part of the class's shared mutable data, thus access to all of these variables must be synchronized to ensure that a `CircularBuffer` is thread safe.

`CircularBuffer` Method `blockingPut`

`CircularBuffer` method `blockingPut` (lines 11–30) performs the same tasks as in Fig. 23.16, with a few modifications. The loop at lines 17–20 of Figs. 23.18 determines whether the `Producer` must *wait* (i.e., all buffer cells are *full*). If so, line 18 indicates that the `Producer` is *waiting* to perform its task. Then line 19 invokes method `wait`, causing the `Producer` thread to *release* the `CircularBuffer`'s *lock* and *wait* until there's space for a new value to be written into the buffer. When execution continues at line 22 after the `while` loop, the value written by the `Producer` is placed in the circular buffer at location `writeIndex`. Then line 25 updates `writeIndex` for the next call to `CircularBuffer` method `blockingPut`. This line is the key to the buffer's *circularity*. When `writeIndex` is incremented *past the end of the buffer*, the line sets it to `0`. Line 27 increments `occupiedCells`, because there's now one more value in the buffer that the `Consumer` can read. Next, line 28 invokes method `displayState` (lines 55–88) to update the output with the value produced, the number of occupied buffer cells, the contents of the buffer cells and the current `writeIndex` and `readIndex`. Line 29 invokes method `notifyAll` to transition *waiting* threads to the *runnable* state, so that a waiting `Consumer` thread (if there is one) can now try again to read a value from the buffer.

`CircularBuffer` Method `blockingGet`

`CircularBuffer` method `blockingGet` (lines 33–52) also performs the same tasks as it did in Fig. 23.16, with a few minor modifications. The loop at lines 37–40 (Fig. 23.18) determines whether the `Consumer` must wait (i.e., all buffer cells are *empty*). If the `Consumer` must *wait*, line 38 updates the output to indicate that the `Consumer` is *waiting* to perform its task. Then line 39 invokes method `wait`, causing the current thread to *release the lock* on the `CircularBuffer` and *wait* until data is available to read. When execution eventually continues at line 42 after a `notifyAll` call from the `Producer`, `readValue` is assigned the value at location `readIndex` in the circular buffer. Then line 45 updates `readIndex` for the next call to `CircularBuffer` method `blockingGet`. This line and line 25 implement the *circularity* of the buffer. Line 47 decrements `occupiedCells`, because there's now one more position in the buffer in which the `Producer` thread can place a value. Line 48 invokes method `displayState` to update the output with the consumed value, the number of occupied buffer cells, the contents of the buffer cells and the current `writeIndex` and `readIndex`. Line 49 invokes method `notifyAll` to allow any `Producer` threads *waiting to write* into the `CircularBuffer` object to attempt to write again. Then line 51 returns the consumed value to the caller.

`CircularBuffer` Method `displayState`

Method `displayState` (lines 55–88) outputs the application's state. Lines 60–62 output the values of the buffer cells, using a `"%2d"` format specifier to print the contents of each buffer with a leading space if it's a single digit. Lines 72–85 output the current `writeIndex` and `readIndex` with the letters `W` and `R`, respectively. Once again, `displayState` is a synchronized method because it accesses class `CircularBuffer`'s shared mutable data.

Testing Class `CircularBuffer`

Class `CircularBufferTest` (Fig. 23.19) contains the `main` method that launches the application. Line 10 creates the `ExecutorService`, and line 13 creates a `CircularBuffer` object and assigns its reference to `CircularBuffer` variable `sharedLocation`. Line 16 invokes the `CircularBuffer`'s `displayState` method to show the initial state of the buffer. Lines 19–20 execute the `Producer` and `Consumer` tasks. Line 22 calls method `shutdown` to end the application when the threads complete the `Producer` and `Consumer` tasks, and line 23 waits for the tasks to complete.

```
1  // Fig. 23.19: CircularBufferTest.java
2  // Producer and Consumer threads correctly manipulating a circular buffer.
3  import java.util.concurrent.ExecutorService;
4  import java.util.concurrent.Executors;
5  import java.util.concurrent.TimeUnit;
6
7  public class CircularBufferTest {
```

Fig. 23.19 | `Producer` and `Consumer` threads correctly manipulating a circular buffer. (Part 1 of 4.)

```
   public static void main(String[] args) throws InterruptedException {
      // create new thread pool
      ExecutorService executorService = Executors.newCachedThreadPool();

      // create CircularBuffer to store ints
      CircularBuffer sharedLocation = new CircularBuffer();

      // display the initial state of the CircularBuffer
      sharedLocation.displayState("Initial State");

      // execute the Producer and Consumer tasks
      executorService.execute(new Producer(sharedLocation));
      executorService.execute(new Consumer(sharedLocation));

      executorService.shutdown();
      executorService.awaitTermination(1, TimeUnit.MINUTES);
   }
}
```

```
Initial State (buffer cells occupied: 0)
buffer cells:   -1   -1   -1
               ---- ---- ----
                WR

Producer writes 1 (buffer cells occupied: 1)
buffer cells:    1   -1   -1
               ---- ---- ----
                 R    W

Consumer reads 1 (buffer cells occupied: 0)
buffer cells:    1   -1   -1
               ---- ---- ----
                     WR

Buffer is empty. Consumer waits.
Producer writes 2 (buffer cells occupied: 1)
buffer cells:    1    2   -1
               ---- ---- ----
                      R    W

Consumer reads 2 (buffer cells occupied: 0)
buffer cells:    1    2   -1
               ---- ---- ----
                          WR

Producer writes 3 (buffer cells occupied: 1)
buffer cells:    1    2    3
               ---- ---- ----
                W          R

Consumer reads 3 (buffer cells occupied: 0)
buffer cells:    1    2    3
               ---- ---- ----
                WR
```

Fig. 23.19 | Producer and Consumer threads correctly manipulating a circular buffer. (Part 2 of 4.)

```
Producer writes 4 (buffer cells occupied: 1)
buffer cells:    4    2    3
               ---- ---- ----
                 R    W

Producer writes 5 (buffer cells occupied: 2)
buffer cells:    4    5    3
               ---- ---- ----
                 R         W

Consumer reads 4 (buffer cells occupied: 1)
buffer cells:    4    5    3
               ---- ---- ----
                      R    W

Producer writes 6 (buffer cells occupied: 2)
buffer cells:    4    5    6
               ---- ---- ----
                W     R

Producer writes 7 (buffer cells occupied: 3)
buffer cells:    7    5    6
               ---- ---- ----
                     WR

Consumer reads 5 (buffer cells occupied: 2)
buffer cells:    7    5    6
               ---- ---- ----
                     W    R

Producer writes 8 (buffer cells occupied: 3)
buffer cells:    7    8    6
               ---- ---- ----
                          WR

Consumer reads 6 (buffer cells occupied: 2)
buffer cells:    7    8    6
               ---- ---- ----
                 R         W

Consumer reads 7 (buffer cells occupied: 1)
buffer cells:    7    8    6
               ---- ---- ----
                      R    W

Producer writes 9 (buffer cells occupied: 2)
buffer cells:    7    8    9
               ---- ---- ----
                W     R

Consumer reads 8 (buffer cells occupied: 1)
buffer cells:    7    8    9
               ---- ---- ----
                W          R
```

Fig. 23.19 | Producer and Consumer threads correctly manipulating a circular buffer. (Part 3 of 4.)

```
Consumer reads 9 (buffer cells occupied: 0)
buffer cells:    7    8    9
               ---- ---- ----
                WR

Producer writes 10 (buffer cells occupied: 1)
buffer cells:   10    8    9
               ---- ---- ----
                 R    W


Producer done producing
Terminating Producer
Consumer reads 10 (buffer cells occupied: 0)
buffer cells:   10    8    9
               ---- ---- ----
                     WR


Consumer read values totaling: 55
Terminating Consumer
```

Fig. 23.19 | Producer and Consumer threads correctly manipulating a circular buffer. (Part 4 of 4.)

Each time the Producer writes a value or the Consumer reads a value, the program outputs a message indicating the action performed (a read or a write), the contents of buffer, and the location of writeIndex and readIndex. In the output of Fig. 23.19, the Producer first writes the value 1. The buffer then contains the value 1 in the first cell and the value -1 (the default value that we use for output purposes) in the other two cells. The write index is updated to the second cell, while the read index stays at the first cell. Next, the Consumer reads 1. The buffer contains the same values, but the read index has been updated to the second cell. The Consumer then tries to read again, but the buffer is empty and the Consumer is forced to wait. Only once in this execution of the program was it necessary for either thread to wait.

23.9 (Advanced) Producer/Consumer Relationship: The Lock and Condition Interfaces

Though the synchronized keyword provides for most basic thread-synchronization needs, Java provides other tools to assist in developing concurrent programs. In this section, we discuss the Lock and Condition interfaces. These interfaces give you more precise control over thread synchronization, but are more complicated to use. *Only the most advanced programmers should use these interfaces.*

Interface **Lock** *and Class* **ReentrantLock**

Any object can contain a reference to an object that implements the **Lock** interface (of package java.util.concurrent.locks). A thread calls the Lock's **lock** method (analogous to entering a synchronized block) to acquire the lock. Once a Lock has been obtained by one thread, the Lock object will not allow another thread to obtain the Lock until the first thread releases the Lock (by calling the Lock's **unlock** method—analogous to exiting a `synchronized` block). If several threads are trying to call method `lock` on the same `Lock` object at the same time, only one of these threads can obtain the lock—all the others are placed in the *waiting* state for that lock. When a thread calls method `unlock`, the lock on the object is released and a waiting thread attempting to lock the object proceeds.

Error-Prevention Tip 23.4

Place calls to `Lock` *method* `unlock` *in a* `finally` *block. If an exception is thrown,* `unlock` *must still be called or deadlock could occur.*

Class **`ReentrantLock`** (of package `java.util.concurrent.locks`) is a basic implementation of the `Lock` interface. The constructor for a `ReentrantLock` takes a `boolean` argument that specifies whether the lock has a **fairness policy**. If the argument is `true`, the `ReentrantLock`'s fairness policy is "the longest-waiting thread will acquire the lock when it's available." Such a fairness policy guarantees that *indefinite postponement* (also called *starvation*) cannot occur. If the fairness policy argument is set to `false`, there's no guarantee as to which waiting thread will acquire the lock when it's available.

Software Engineering Observation 23.6

Using a `ReentrantLock` *with a fairness policy avoids indefinite postponement.*

Performance Tip 23.5

In most cases, a non-fair lock is preferable, because using a fair lock can decrease program performance.

Condition Objects and Interface `Condition`

If a thread that owns a `Lock` determines that it cannot continue with its task until some condition is satisfied, the thread can wait on a **condition object**. Using `Lock` objects allows you to explicitly declare the condition objects on which a thread may need to wait. For example, in the producer/consumer relationship, producers can wait on *one* object and consumers can wait on *another*. This is not possible when using the `synchronized` keywords and an object's built-in monitor lock.

Condition objects are associated with a specific `Lock` and are created by calling a `Lock`'s **`newCondition`** method, which returns an object that implements the **`Condition`** interface (package `java.util.concurrent.locks`). To wait on a `Condition`, the thread can call its **`await`** method (analogous to `Object` method `wait`). This immediately releases the associated `Lock` and places the thread in the *waiting* state for that `Condition`. Other threads can then try to obtain the `Lock`.

When a *runnable* thread completes a task and determines that the *waiting* thread can now continue, the *runnable* thread can call `Condition` method **`signal`** (analogous to `Object` method `notify`) to allow a thread in that `Condition`'s *waiting* state to return to the *runnable* state. At this point, the thread that transitioned from the *waiting* state to the *runnable* state can attempt to reacquire the `Lock`. Even if it's able to *reacquire* the `Lock`, the thread still might not be able to perform its task at this time—in which case the thread can call the `Condition`'s `await` method to *release* the `Lock` and reenter the *waiting* state.

If multiple threads are in a `Condition`'s *waiting* state when `signal` is called, the default implementation of `Condition` signals the longest-waiting thread to transition to the *runnable* state. If a thread calls Condition method **signalAll** (analogous to Object method notifyAll), then all the threads waiting for that condition transition to the *runnable* state and become eligible to reacquire the Lock. Only one of those threads can obtain the Lock on the object—the others will wait until the Lock becomes available again. If the Lock has a *fairness policy*, the longest-waiting thread acquires the Lock. When a thread is finished with a shared object, it must call method unlock to release the Lock.

Error-Prevention Tip 23.5

When multiple threads manipulate a shared object using locks, ensure that if one thread calls method await *to enter the* waiting *state for a condition object, a separate thread eventually will call* Condition *method* signal *to transition the thread waiting on the condition object back to the* runnable *state. If multiple threads may be waiting on the condition object, a separate thread can call* Condition *method* signalAll *as a safeguard to ensure that all the waiting threads have another opportunity to perform their tasks. If this is not done, starvation might occur.*

Common Programming Error 23.2

An IllegalMonitorStateException *occurs if a thread issues an* await, *a* signal, *or a* signalAll *on a* Condition *object that was created from a* ReentrantLock *without having acquired the lock for that* Condition *object.*

Lock *and* Condition *vs. the* synchronized *Keyword*

In some applications, using Lock and Condition objects may be preferable to using the synchronized keyword. Locks allow you to *interrupt* waiting threads or to specify a *timeout* for waiting to acquire a lock, which is not possible using the synchronized keyword. Also, a Lock is *not* constrained to be acquired and released in the *same* block of code, which is the case with the synchronized keyword. Condition objects allow you to specify multiple conditions on which threads may *wait*. Thus, it's possible to indicate to waiting threads that a specific condition object is now true by calling signal or signalAll on that Condition object. With synchronized, there's no way to explicitly state the condition on which threads are waiting, and thus there's no way to notify threads waiting on one condition that they may proceed without also signaling threads waiting on any other conditions. There are other possible advantages to using Lock and Condition objects, but generally it's best to use the synchronized keyword unless your application requires advanced synchronization capabilities.

Software Engineering Observation 23.7

Think of Lock *and* Condition *as an advanced version of* synchronized. Lock *and* Condition *support timed waits, interruptible waits and multiple* Condition *queues per* Lock*—if you do not need one of these features, you do not need* Lock *and* Condition.

Error-Prevention Tip 23.6

Using interfaces Lock *and* Condition *is error prone—*unlock *is not guaranteed to be called, whereas the monitor in a* synchronized *statement will always be released when the statement completes execution. Of course, you can guarantee that* unlock *will be called if it's placed in a* finally *block, as we do in Fig. 23.20.*

Using `Lock`*s and* `Condition`*s to Implement Synchronization*

We now implement the producer/consumer relationship using `Lock` and `Condition` objects to coordinate access to a shared single-element buffer (Figs. 23.20 and 23.21). In this case, each produced value is correctly consumed exactly once. Again, we reuse interface `Buffer` and classes `Producer` and `Consumer` from the example in Section 23.5, except that line 24 is removed from class `Producer` and class `Consumer`.

Class `SynchronizedBuffer`

Class `SynchronizedBuffer` (Fig. 23.20) contains five fields. Line 10 initializes `Lock` instance variable `accessLock` with a new `ReentrantLock`. We did not specify a *fairness policy* in this example, because at any time only a single `Producer` or `Consumer` will be waiting to acquire the `Lock`. Lines 13–14 create two `Condition`s using `Lock` method `newCondition`:

- `Condition canWrite` contains a queue for a `Producer` thread waiting while the buffer is *full* (i.e., there's data in the buffer that the `Consumer` has not read yet). If the buffer is *full*, the `Producer` calls method `await` on this `Condition`. When the `Consumer` reads data from a *full* buffer, it calls method `signal` on this `Condition`.
- `Condition canRead` contains a queue for a `Consumer` thread waiting while the buffer is *empty* (i.e., there's no data in the buffer for the `Consumer` to read). If the buffer is *empty*, the `Consumer` calls method `await` on this `Condition`. When the `Producer` writes to the *empty* buffer, it calls method `signal` on this `Condition`.

The `int` variable `buffer` (line 16) holds the shared mutable data. The `boolean` variable `occupied` (line 17) keeps track of whether the buffer currently holds data (that the `Consumer` should read).

```
1  // Fig. 23.20: SynchronizedBuffer.java
2  // Synchronizing access to a shared integer using the Lock and Condition
3  // interfaces
4  import java.util.concurrent.locks.Lock;
5  import java.util.concurrent.locks.ReentrantLock;
6  import java.util.concurrent.locks.Condition;
7
8  public class SynchronizedBuffer implements Buffer {
9     // Lock to control synchronization with this buffer
10    private final Lock accessLock = new ReentrantLock();
11
12    // conditions to control reading and writing
13    private final Condition canWrite = accessLock.newCondition();
14    private final Condition canRead = accessLock.newCondition();
15
16    private int buffer = -1; // shared by producer and consumer threads
17    private boolean occupied = false; // whether buffer is occupied
18
19    // place int value into buffer
20    @Override
21    public void blockingPut(int value) throws InterruptedException {
22       accessLock.lock(); // lock this object
```

Fig. 23.20 | Synchronizing access to a shared integer using the `Lock` and `Condition` interfaces. (Part 1 of 3.)

```java

      // output thread information and buffer information, then wait
      try {
         // while buffer is not empty, place thread in waiting state
         while (occupied) {
            System.out.println("Producer tries to write.");
            displayState("Buffer full. Producer waits.");
            canWrite.await(); // wait until buffer is empty
         }

         buffer = value; // set new buffer value

         // indicate producer cannot store another value
         // until consumer retrieves current buffer value
         occupied = true;

         displayState("Producer writes " + buffer);

         // signal any threads waiting to read from buffer
         canRead.signalAll();
      }
      finally {
         accessLock.unlock(); // unlock this object
      }
   }

   // return value from buffer
   @Override
   public int blockingGet() throws InterruptedException {
      int readValue = 0; // initialize value read from buffer
      accessLock.lock(); // lock this object

      // output thread information and buffer information, then wait
      try {
         // if there is no data to read, place thread in waiting state
         while (!occupied) {
            System.out.println("Consumer tries to read.");
            displayState("Buffer empty. Consumer waits.");
            canRead.await(); // wait until buffer is full
         }

         // indicate that producer can store another value
         // because consumer just retrieved buffer value
         occupied = false;

         readValue = buffer; // retrieve value from buffer
         displayState("Consumer reads " + readValue);

         // signal any threads waiting for buffer to be empty
         canWrite.signalAll();
      }
```

Fig. 23.20 | Synchronizing access to a shared integer using the Lock and Condition interfaces. (Part 2 of 3.)

```
74          finally {
75             accessLock.unlock(); // unlock this object
76          }
77
78          return readValue;
79       }
80
81       // display current operation and buffer state
82       private void displayState(String operation) {
83          try {
84             accessLock.lock(); // lock this object
85             System.out.printf("%-40s%d\t\t%b%n%n", operation, buffer,
86                occupied);
87          }
88          finally {
89             accessLock.unlock(); // unlock this object
90          }
91       }
92    }
```

Fig. 23.20 | Synchronizing access to a shared integer using the `Lock` and `Condition` interfaces. (Part 3 of 3.)

Method `blockingPut` calls method `lock` on the `SynchronizedBuffer`'s `accessLock` (line 22). If the lock is *available* (i.e., no other thread has acquired it), this thread now owns the lock and the thread continues. If the lock is *unavailable* (i.e., it's held by another thread), method `lock` waits until the lock is released. After the lock is acquired, lines 25–43 execute. Line 27 determines whether `buffer` is full. If it is, lines 28–29 display a message indicating that the thread will *wait*. Line 30 calls `Condition` method `await` on the `canWrite` condition object, which temporarily releases the `SynchronizedBuffer`'s `Lock` and *waits* for a signal from the `Consumer` that `buffer` is available for writing. When `buffer` is available, the method proceeds, writing to `buffer` (line 33), setting `occupied` to `true` (line 37) and displaying a message indicating that the producer wrote a value (line 39). Line 42 calls `Condition` method `signal` on the condition object `canRead` to notify the waiting `Consumer` (if there is one) that the buffer has new data. Line 45 calls method `unlock` from a `finally` block to *release* the lock and allow the `Consumer` to proceed.

Line 53 of method `blockingGet` calls method `lock` to *acquire* the `Lock`. This method *waits* until the `Lock` is *available*. Once the `Lock` is *acquired*, line 58 determines whether the buffer is *empty*. If so, line 61 calls method `await` on condition object `canRead`. Recall that method `signal` is called on variable `canRead` in the `blockingPut` method (line 42). When the `Condition` object is *signaled*, the `blockingGet` method continues. Lines 66–69 set `occupied` to `false`, store the value of `buffer` in `readValue` and output the `readValue`. Then line 72 *signals* the condition object `canWrite`. This awakens the `Producer` if it's indeed *waiting* for the buffer to be *emptied*. Line 75 calls method `unlock` from a `finally` block to *release* the lock, and line 78 returns `readValue` to the caller.

Common Programming Error 23.3

Forgetting to `signal` a waiting thread is a logic error. The thread will remain in the waiting *state, preventing it from proceeding. This can lead to indefinite postponement or deadlock.*

Class **SharedBufferTest2**

Class SharedBufferTest2 (Fig. 23.21) is identical to that of Fig. 23.17. Study the outputs in Fig. 23.21. *Observe that every integer produced is consumed exactly once—no values are lost, and no values are consumed more than once.* The Lock and Condition objects ensure that the Producer and Consumer cannot perform their tasks unless it's their turn. The Producer *must* go first, the Consumer *must wait* if the Producer has not produced since the Consumer last consumed and the Producer *must wait* if the Consumer has not yet consumed the value that the Producer most recently produced. Execute this program several times to confirm that every integer produced is consumed exactly once. In the sample output, note the highlighted lines indicating when the Producer and Consumer must *wait* to perform their respective tasks.

```
// Fig. 23.21: SharedBufferTest2.java
// Two threads manipulating a synchronized buffer.
import java.util.concurrent.ExecutorService;
import java.util.concurrent.Executors;
import java.util.concurrent.TimeUnit;

public class SharedBufferTest2 {
   public static void main(String[] args) throws InterruptedException {
      // create new thread pool
      ExecutorService executorService = Executors.newCachedThreadPool();

      // create SynchronizedBuffer to store ints
      Buffer sharedLocation = new SynchronizedBuffer();

      System.out.printf("%-40s%s\t\t%s%n%-40s%s%n%n", "Operation",
         "Buffer", "Occupied", "---------", "------\t\t--------");

      // execute the Producer and Consumer tasks
      executorService.execute(new Producer(sharedLocation));
      executorService.execute(new Consumer(sharedLocation));

      executorService.shutdown();
      executorService.awaitTermination(1, TimeUnit.MINUTES);
   }
}
```

```
Operation                               Buffer          Occupied
---------                               ------          --------

Producer writes 1                       1               true

Producer tries to write.
Buffer full. Producer waits.            1               true

Consumer reads 1                        1               false

Producer writes 2                       2               true

Producer tries to write.
Buffer full. Producer waits.            2               true
```

Fig. 23.21 | Two threads manipulating a synchronized buffer. (Part 1 of 2.)

```
Consumer reads 2                      2                false
Producer writes 3                     3                true
Consumer reads 3                      3                false
Producer writes 4                     4                true
Consumer reads 4                      4                false
Consumer tries to read.
Buffer empty. Consumer waits.         4                false
Producer writes 5                     5                true
Consumer reads 5                      5                false
Consumer tries to read.
Buffer empty. Consumer waits.         5                false
Producer writes 6                     6                true
Consumer reads 6                      6                false
Producer writes 7                     7                true
Consumer reads 7                      7                false
Producer writes 8                     8                true
Consumer reads 8                      8                false
Producer writes 9                     9                true
Consumer reads 9                      9                false
Producer writes 10                    10               true

Producer done producing
Terminating Producer
Consumer reads 10                     10               false

Consumer read values totaling 55
Terminating Consumer
```

Fig. 23.21 | Two threads manipulating a synchronized buffer. (Part 2 of 2.)

23.10 Concurrent Collections

In Chapter 16, we introduced various collections from the Java Collections API. We also mentioned that you can obtain *synchronized* versions of those collections to allow only one thread at a time to access a collection that might be shared among several threads. The collections from the `java.util.concurrent` package are specifically designed and optimized for sharing collections among multiple threads.

Figure 23.22 lists the many concurrent collections in package `java.util.concurrent`. The entries for `ConcurrentHashMap` and `LinkedBlockingQueue` are shown in **bold**
8 because these are by far the most frequently used concurrent collections. Like the collections introduced in Chapter 16, the concurrent collections were enhanced in Java SE 8 to

support lambdas. However, rather than providing methods to support streams, the concurrent collections provide their own implementations of various stream-like operations—e.g., `ConcurrentHashMap` has methods `forEach`, `reduce` and `search`—that are designed and optimized for concurrent collections that are shared among threads. For more information on the concurrent collections, visit

```
http://docs.oracle.com/javase/8/docs/api/java/util/concurrent/
   package-summary.html
```

Collection	Description
`ArrayBlockingQueue`	A fixed-size queue that supports the producer/consumer relationship—possibly with many producers and consumers.
`ConcurrentHashMap`	**A hash-based map (similar to the `HashMap` introduced in Chapter 16) that allows an arbitrary number of reader threads and a limited number of writer threads. This and the `LinkedBlockingQueue` are by far the most frequently used concurrent collections.**
`ConcurrentLinkedDeque`	A concurrent linked-list implementation of a double-ended queue.
`ConcurrentLinkedQueue`	A concurrent linked-list implementation of a queue that can grow dynamically.
`ConcurrentSkipListMap`	A concurrent map that is sorted by its keys.
`ConcurrentSkipListSet`	A sorted concurrent set.
`CopyOnWriteArrayList`	A thread-safe `ArrayList`. Each operation that modifies the collection first creates a new copy of the contents. Used when the collection is traversed much more frequently than the collection's contents are modified.
`CopyOnWriteArraySet`	A set that's implemented using `CopyOnWriteArrayList`.
`DelayQueue`	A variable-size queue containing `Delayed` objects. An object can be removed only after its delay has expired.
`LinkedBlockingDeque`	A double-ended blocking queue implemented as a linked list that can optionally be fixed in size.
`LinkedBlockingQueue`	**A blocking queue implemented as a linked list that can optionally be fixed in size. This and the `ConcurrentHashMap` are by far the most frequently used concurrent collections.**
`LinkedTransferQueue`	A linked-list implementation of interface `TransferQueue`. Each producer has the option of waiting for a consumer to take an element being inserted (via method `transfer`) or simply placing the element into the queue (via method `put`). Also provides overloaded method `tryTransfer` to immediately transfer an element to a waiting consumer or to do so within a specified timeout period. If the transfer cannot be completed, the element is not placed in the queue. Typically used in applications that pass messages between threads.
`PriorityBlockingQueue`	A variable-length priority-based blocking queue (like a `PriorityQueue`).
`SynchronousQueue`	[For experts.] A blocking queue implementation that does not have an internal capacity. Each insert operation by one thread must wait for a remove operation from another thread and vice versa.

Fig. 23.22 | Concurrent collections summary (package `java.util.concurrent`).

23.11 Multithreading in JavaFX

JavaFX applications present a unique set of challenges for multithreaded programming. All JavaFX applications have a single thread, called the **JavaFX application thread**, to handle interactions with the application's controls. Typical interactions include *rendering controls* or *processing user actions* such as mouse clicks. All tasks that require interaction with an application's GUI are placed in an *event queue* and are executed sequentially by the JavaFX application thread.

JavaFX's scene graph is not thread safe—its nodes cannot be manipulated by multiple threads without the risk of incorrect results that might corrupt the scene graph. Unlike the other examples presented in this chapter, thread safety in JavaFX applications is achieved not by synchronizing thread actions, but by *ensuring that programs manipulate the scene graph from only the JavaFX application thread.* This technique is called **thread confinement.** Allowing just one thread to access non-thread-safe objects eliminates the possibility of corruption due to multiple threads accessing these objects concurrently.

It's acceptable to perform brief tasks on the JavaFX application thread in sequence with GUI component manipulations—like calculating tips and totals in Chapter 12's **Tip Calculator** app. If an application must perform a lengthy task in response to a user interaction, the JavaFX application thread cannot render controls or respond to events while the thread is tied up in that task. This causes the GUI to become unresponsive. It's preferable to handle long-running tasks in separate threads, freeing the JavaFX application thread to continue managing other GUI interactions. Of course, you must update the GUI with the computation's results from the JavaFX application thread, rather than from the worker thread that performed the computation.[3]

`Platform` *Method* `runLater`

JavaFX provides multiple mechanisms for updating the GUI from other threads. One is to call the `static` method **`runLater`** of class **`Platform`** (package `javafx.application`). This method receives a `Runnable` and schedules it on the JavaFX application thread for execution at some point in the future. Such `Runnable`s should perform only small updates, so the GUI remains responsive.

Class `Task` *and Interface* `Worker`

Long-running or compute-intensive tasks should be performed on separate worker threads, not the JavaFX application thread. Package **`javafx.concurrent`** provides interface `Worker` and classes `Task` and `ScheduledService` for this purpose:

- A **`Worker`** is a task that should execute using one or more separate threads.
- Class **`Task`** is a `Worker` implementation that enables you to perform a task (such as a long-running computation) in a worker thread and update the GUI from the JavaFX application thread based on the task's results. `Task` implements several interfaces, including `Runnable`, so a `Task` object can be scheduled to execute in a

3. Like JavaFX, Swing uses a single thread for handling interactions and displaying the GUI. Swing's similar capabilities to the JavaFX concurrency features discussed in this section are located in package `javax.swing`. Class `SwingUtilities` method `invokeLater` schedules a `Runnable` for later execution in the so-called event-dispatch thread. Class `SwingWorker` performs a long-running task in a worker thread and can display results in the GUI from the event-dispatch thread.

separate thread. Class `Task` also provides methods that are guaranteed to update its properties in the JavaFX application thread—as you'll see, this enables programs to bind a `Task`'s properties to GUI controls for automatic updating. Once a `Task` completes, it cannot be restarted—performing the `Task` again requires a new `Task` object. We'll demonstrate `Task`s in the next two examples.

- Class **`ScheduledService`** is a `Worker` implementation that creates and manages a `Task`. Unlike a `Task`, a `ScheduledService` can be reset and restarted. It also can be configured to automatically restart both after successful completion and if it fails due to an exception.

23.11.1 Performing Computations in a Worker Thread: Fibonacci Numbers

In the next example, the user enters a number *n* and the program gets the *n*th Fibonacci number, which we calculate using the recursive algorithm discussed in Section 18.5. Since the algorithm is time consuming for large values, we use a `Task` object to perform the recursive calculation in a worker thread. The GUI also provides a separate set of components that displays the next Fibonacci number in the sequence with each click of a `Button`. This set of components performs its short computation directly in the event dispatch thread. The program is capable of producing up to the 92nd Fibonacci number—subsequent values are outside the range that can be represented by a `long`. Recall that you can use class `BigInteger` to represent arbitrarily large integer values.

Creating a Task

Class `FibonacciTask` (Fig. 23.23) extends `Task<Long>` (line 5) to perform the recursive Fibonacci calculation in a *worker thread.* The instance variable `n` (line 6) represents the Fibonacci number to calculate. Overridden `Task` method **`call`** (lines 14–20) computes the *n*th Fibonacci number and returns the result. The `Task`'s type parameter `Long` (line 5) determines `call`'s return type (line 15). Inherited `Task` method **`updateMessage`** (called in lines 16 and 18) updates the `Task`'s `message` property in the *JavaFX application thread.* As you'll see in Fig. 23.25, this enables us to bind JavaFX controls to `FibonacciTask`'s `message` property to display messages while the task is executing.

```
1  // Fig. 23.23: FibonacciTask.java
2  // Task subclass for calculating Fibonacci numbers in the background
3  import javafx.concurrent.Task;
4
5  public class FibonacciTask extends Task<Long> {
6     private final int n; // Fibonacci number to calculate
7
8     // constructor
9     public FibonacciTask(int n) {
10       this.n = n;
11    }
12
```

Fig. 23.23 | Task subclass for calculating Fibonacci numbers in the background. (Part 1 of 2.)

```
13       // long-running code to be run in a worker thread
14       @Override
15       protected Long call() {
16          updateMessage("Calculating...");
17          long result = fibonacci(n);
18          updateMessage("Done calculating.");
19          return result;
20       }
21
22       // recursive method fibonacci; calculates nth Fibonacci number
23       public long fibonacci(long number) {
24          if (number == 0 || number == 1) {
25             return number;
26          }
27          else {
28             return fibonacci(number - 1) + fibonacci(number - 2);
29          }
30       }
31    }
```

Fig. 23.23 | `Task` subclass for calculating Fibonacci numbers in the background. (Part 2 of 2.)

When the worker thread enters the *running* state, `FibonacciTask`'s `call` method begins executing. First, line 16 calls the inherited `updateMessage` method to update the `FibonacciTask`'s `message` property, indicating that the task is calculating. Next, line 17 invokes recursive method `fibonacci` (lines 23–30) with instance variable `n`'s value as the argument. When `fibonacci` returns, line 18 updates `FibonacciTask`'s `message` property again to indicate that the calculation completed, then line 19 returns the result to the JavaFX application thread.

`FibonacciNumbers` GUI

Figure 23.24 shows the app's GUI (defined in `FibonacciNumbers.fxml`) labeled with its **fx:ids**. Here we point out only the key elements and the event-handling methods you'll see in class `FibonacciNumbersController` (Fig. 23.25). For the complete layout details, open `FibonacciNumbers.fxml` in Scene Builder. The GUI's primary layout is a `VBox` containing two `TitledPane`s. The controller class defines two event handlers:

- `goButtonPressed` is called when the **Go** `Button` is pressed—this launches the worker thread to calculate a Fibonacci number recursively.
- `nextNumberButtonPressed` is called when the **Next Number** `Button` is pressed—this calculates the next Fibonacci number in the sequence. Initially the app displays the Fibonacci of 0 (which is 0).

We do not show the JavaFX `Application` subclass (located in `FibonacciNumbers.java`), because it performs the same tasks you've seen previously to load the app's FXML GUI and initialize the controller.

Class `FibonacciNumbersController`

Class `FibonacciNumbersController` (Fig. 23.25) displays a window containing two sets of controls:

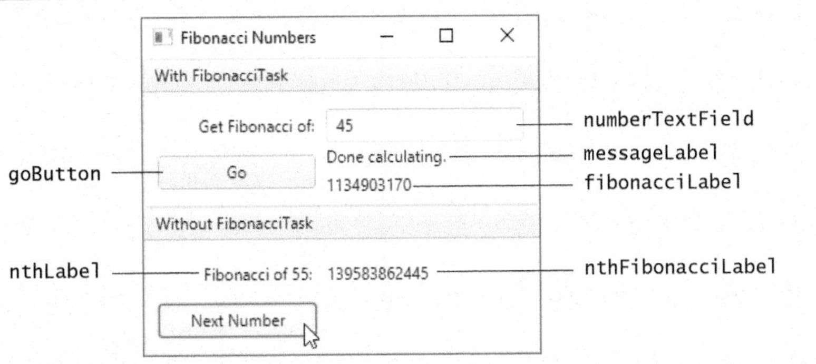

Fig. 23.24 | `FibonacciNumbers` GUI with its **fx:id**s.

- The **With FibonacciTask** `TitledPane` provides controls that enable the user to enter a Fibonacci number to calculate and launch a `FibonacciTask` in a worker thread. `Label`s in this `TitledPane` display the `FibonacciTask`'s message property value as it's updated and the final result of the `FibonacciTask` once it's available.
- The **Without FibonacciTask** `TitledPane` provides the **Next Number** `Button` that enables the user to calculate the next Fibonacci number in sequence. `Label`s in this `TitledPane` display which Fibonacci number is being calculated (that is, `"Fibonacci of` *n*`"`) and the corresponding Fibonacci value.

Instance variables `n1` and `n2` (lines 20–21) contain the previous two Fibonacci numbers in the sequence and are initialized to `0` and `1`, respectively. Instance variable `number` (initialized to `1` in line 22) keeps track of which Fibonacci value will be calculated and displayed next when the user clicks the **Next Number** `Button`—so the first time this `Button` is clicked, the Fibonacci of 1 is displayed.

```
1  // Fig. 23.25: FibonacciNumbersController.java
2  // Using a Task to perform a long calculation
3  // outside the JavaFX application thread.
4  import java.util.concurrent.Executors;
5  import java.util.concurrent.ExecutorService;
6  import javafx.event.ActionEvent;
7  import javafx.fxml.FXML;
8  import javafx.scene.control.Button;
9  import javafx.scene.control.Label;
10 import javafx.scene.control.TextField;
11
12 public class FibonacciNumbersController {
13    @FXML private TextField numberTextField;
14    @FXML private Button goButton;
15    @FXML private Label messageLabel;
16    @FXML private Label fibonacciLabel;
17    @FXML private Label nthLabel;
18    @FXML private Label nthFibonacciLabel;
```

Fig. 23.25 | Using a `Task` to perform a long calculation outside the JavaFX application thread. (Part 1 of 3.)

```

   private long n1 = 0; // initialize with Fibonacci of 0
   private long n2 = 1; // initialize with Fibonacci of 1
   private int number = 1; // current Fibonacci number to display

   // starts FibonacciTask to calculate in background
   @FXML
   void goButtonPressed(ActionEvent event) {
      // get Fibonacci number to calculate
      try {
         int input = Integer.parseInt(numberTextField.getText());

         // create, configure and launch FibonacciTask
         FibonacciTask task = new FibonacciTask(input);

         // display task's messages in messageLabel
         messageLabel.textProperty().bind(task.messageProperty());

         // clear fibonacciLabel when task starts
         task.setOnRunning((succeededEvent) -> {
            goButton.setDisable(true);
            fibonacciLabel.setText("");
         });

         // set fibonacciLabel when task completes successfully
         task.setOnSucceeded((succeededEvent) -> {
            fibonacciLabel.setText(task.getValue().toString());
            goButton.setDisable(false);
         });

         // create ExecutorService to manage threads
         ExecutorService executorService =
            Executors.newFixedThreadPool(1); // pool of one thread
         executorService.execute(task); // start the task
         executorService.shutdown();
      }
      catch (NumberFormatException e) {
         numberTextField.setText("Enter an integer");
         numberTextField.selectAll();
         numberTextField.requestFocus();
      }
   }

   // calculates next Fibonacci value
   @FXML
   void nextNumberButtonPressed(ActionEvent event) {
      // display the next Fibonacci number
      nthLabel.setText("Fibonacci of " + number + ": ");
      nthFibonacciLabel.setText(String.valueOf(n2));
      long temp = n1 + n2;
      n1 = n2;
```

Fig. 23.25 | Using a Task to perform a long calculation outside the JavaFX application thread. (Part 2 of 3.)

```
70          n2 = temp;
71          ++number;
72       }
73    }
```

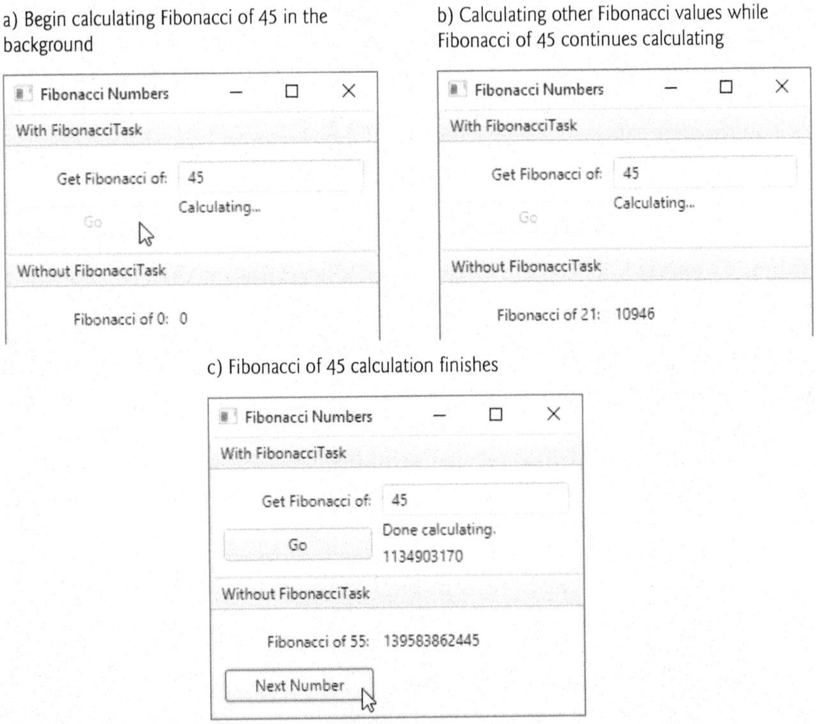

a) Begin calculating Fibonacci of 45 in the background

b) Calculating other Fibonacci values while Fibonacci of 45 continues calculating

c) Fibonacci of 45 calculation finishes

Fig. 23.25 | Using a `Task` to perform a long calculation outside the JavaFX application thread. (Part 3 of 3.)

Method `goButtonPressed`

When the user clicks the **Go** `Button`, method `goButtonPressed` (lines 25–60) executes. Line 29 gets the value entered in the `numberTextField` and attempts to parse it as an integer. If this fails, lines 56–58 prompt the user to enter an integer, select the text in the `numberTextField` and give the `numberTextField` the focus, so the user can immediately enter a new value in the `numberTextField`.

Line 32 creates a new `FibonacciTask` object, passing the constructor the user-entered value. Line 35 binds the `messageLabel`'s `text` property (a `StringProperty`) to the `FibonacciTask`'s `message` property (a `ReadOnlyStringProperty`)—when `FibonacciTask` updates this property, the `messageLabel` displays the new value.

All `Worker`s transition through various states. Class `Task`—an implementation of `Worker`—enables you to register listeners for several of these states:

- Lines 38–41 use `Task` method **`setOnRunning`** to register a listener (implemented as a lambda) that's invoked when the `Task` enters the *running* state—that is, when the `Task` has been assigned a processor and begins executing its `call` method. In this case, we disable the goButton so the user cannot launch another FibonacciTask until the current one completes, then we clear the fibonacciLabel (so an old result is not displayed when a new FibonacciTask begins).

- Lines 44–47 use Task method **setOnSucceeded** to register a listener (implemented as a lambda) that's invoked when the Task enters the *succeeded* state—that is, when the Task successfully runs to completion. In this case, we call the Task's **getValue** method (from interface Worker) to obtain the result, which we convert to a String, then display in the fibonacciLabel. Then we enable the goButton so the user can start a new FibonacciTask.

You also can register listeners for a Task's *canceled, failed* and *scheduled* states.

Finally, lines 50–53 use an ExecutorService to launch the FibonacciTask (line 52), which schedules it for execution in a separate worker thread. Method execute does not wait for the FibonacciTask to finish executing. It returns immediately, allowing the GUI to continue processing other events while the computation is performed.

Method nextNumberButtonPressed

If the user clicks the **Next Number** Button, method nextNumberButtonPressed (lines 63–72) executes. Lines 66–67 update the nthLabel to show which Fibonacci number is being displayed, then update nthFibonacciLabel to display n2's value. Next, lines 68–71 add the previous two Fibonacci numbers stored in n1 and n2 to determine the next number in the sequence (which will be displayed on the next call to nextNumberButtonPressed), update n1 and n2 to their new values and increment number.

The code for these calculations is in method nextNumberButtonPressed, so they're performed on the *JavaFX application thread.* Handling such short computations in this thread does not cause the GUI to become unresponsive, as with the recursive algorithm for calculating the Fibonacci of a large number. Because the longer Fibonacci computation is performed in a separate worker thread, it's possible to click the **Next Number** Button to get the next Fibonacci number while the recursive computation is still in progress.

23.11.2 Processing Intermediate Results: Sieve of Eratosthenes

Class Task provides additional methods and properties that enable you to update a GUI with a Task's intermediate results as the Task continues executing in a Worker thread. The next example uses the following Task methods and properties:

- Method **updateProgress** updates a Task's **progress** property, which represents the percentage completion.
- Method **updateValue** updates a Task's **value** property, which holds each intermediate value.

Like updateMessage, updateProgress and updateValue are guaranteed to update the corresponding properties in the JavaFX application thread.

A Task *to Find Prime Numbers*

Figure 23.26 presents class PrimeCalculatorTask, which extends Task<Integer> to compute the first *n* prime numbers in a *worker thread.* As you'll see in the FindPrimesController (Fig. 23.28), we'll bind this Task's progress property to a ProgressBar control so the app can provide a visual indication of the portion of the Task that has been completed.

The controller also registers a listener for the `value` property's changes—we'll store each prime value in an `ObservableList` that's bound to a `ListView`.

```
// Fig. 23.26: PrimeCalculatorTask.java
// Calculates the first n primes, publishing them as they are found.
import java.util.Arrays;
import javafx.concurrent.Task;

public class PrimeCalculatorTask extends Task<Integer> {
   private final boolean[] primes; // boolean array for finding primes

   // constructor
   public PrimeCalculatorTask(int max) {
      primes = new boolean[max];
      Arrays.fill(primes, true); // initialize all primes elements to true
   }

   // long-running code to be run in a worker thread
   @Override
   protected Integer call() {
      int count = 0; // the number of primes found

      // starting at index 2 (the first prime number), cycle through and
      // set to false elements with indices that are multiples of i
      for (int i = 2; i < primes.length; i++) {
         if (isCancelled()) { // if calculation has been canceled
            updateMessage("Cancelled");
            return 0;
         }
         else {
            try {
               Thread.sleep(10); // slow the thread
            }
            catch (InterruptedException ex) {
               updateMessage("Interrupted");
               return 0;
            }

            updateProgress(i + 1, primes.length);

            if (primes[i]) { // i is prime
               ++count;
               updateMessage(String.format("Found %d primes", count));
               updateValue(i); // intermediate result

               // eliminate multiples of i
               for (int j = i + i; j < primes.length; j += i) {
                  primes[j] = false; // i is not prime
               }
            }
         }
      }
```

Fig. 23.26 | Calculates the first *n* primes, publishing them as they are found. (Part 1 of 2.)

```
50
51            return 0;
52        }
53    }
```

Fig. 23.26 | Calculates the first *n* primes, publishing them as they are found. (Part 2 of 2.)

Constructor

The constructor (lines 10–13) receives an integer indicating the upper limit of the prime numbers to locate, creates the `boolean` array `primes` and initializes its elements to `true`.

Sieve of Eratosthenes

`PrimeCalculatorTask` uses the `primes` array and the **Sieve of Eratosthenes** algorithm (described in Exercise 7.27) to find all primes less than `max`. The Sieve of Eratosthenes takes a list of integers and, beginning with the first prime number, filters out all multiples of that prime. It then moves to the next prime, which will be the next number that's not yet filtered out, and eliminates all of its multiples. It continues until the end of the list is reached and all nonprimes have been filtered out. Algorithmically, we begin with element `2` of the `boolean` array and set the cells corresponding to all values that are multiples of 2 to `false` to indicate that they're divisible by 2 and thus not prime. We then move to the next array element, check whether it's `true`, and if so set all of its multiples to `false` to indicate that they're divisible by the current index. When the whole array has been traversed in this way, all indices that contain `true` are prime, as they have no divisors.

Overridden `Task` *Method* `call`

In method `call` (lines 16–52), the control variable `i` for the loop (lines 22–49) represents the current index for implementing the Sieve of Eratosthenes. Line 23 calls the inherited `Task` method **`isCancelled`** to determine whether the user has clicked the **Cancel** button. If so, line 24 updates the `Task`'s `message` property, then line 25 returns `0` to terminate the `Task` immediately.

If the calculation isn't canceled, line 29 puts the currently executing thread to sleep for 10 milliseconds. We discuss the reason for this shortly. Line 36 calls `Task`'s `updateProgress` method to update the `progress` property in the JavaFX application thread. The percentage completion is determined by dividing the method's first argument by its second argument.

Next, line 38 tests whether the current `primes` element is `true` (and thus prime). If so, line 39 increments the `count` of prime numbers found so far and line 40 updates the `Task`'s `message` property with a `String` containing the `count`. Then, line 41 passes the index `i` to method `updateValue`, which updates `Task`'s `value` property in the JavaFX application thread—as you'll see in the controller, we process this *intermediate result* and display it the GUI. When the entire array has been traversed, line 51 returns `0`, which we ignore in the controller, because it is not a prime number.

Because the computation progresses quickly, publishing values often, updates can pile up on the JavaFX application thread, causing it to ignore some updates. This is why for demonstration purposes we put the worker thread to *sleep* for 10 milliseconds during each iteration of the loop. The calculation is slowed just enough to allow the JavaFX application thread to keep up with the updates and enable the GUI to remain responsive.

`FindPrimes` GUI

Figure 23.27 shows the app's GUI (defined in `FindPrimes.fxml`) labeled with its **fx:ids**. Here we point out only the key elements and the event-handling methods you'll see in class `FindPrimesController` (Fig. 23.28). For the complete layout details, open `FindPrimes.fxml` in Scene Builder. The GUI's primary layout is a `BorderPane` containing two `ToolBar`s in the top and bottom areas. The controller class defines two event handlers:

- `getPrimesButtonPressed` is called when the **Get Primes** `Button` is pressed—this launches the worker thread to find prime numbers less than the value input by the user.
- `cancelButtonPressed` is called when the **Cancel** `Button` is pressed—this terminates the worker thread.

We do not show the JavaFX `Application` subclass (located in `FindPrimes.java`), because it performs the same tasks you've seen previously to load the app's FXML GUI and initialize the controller.

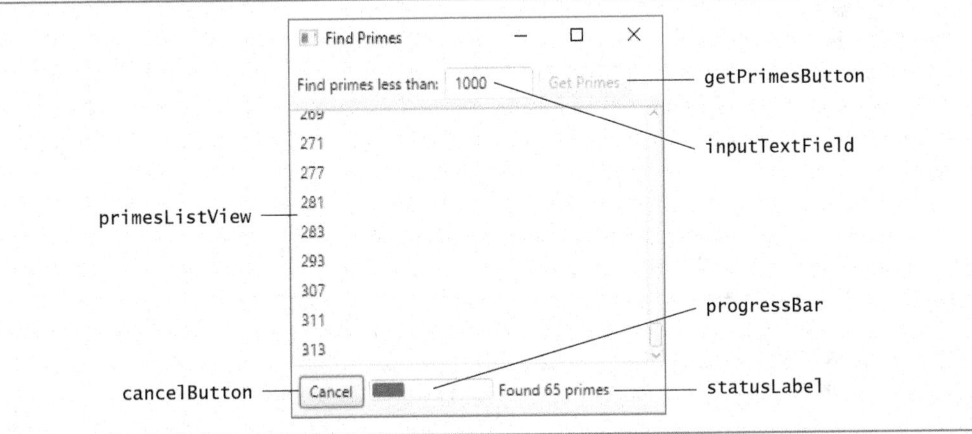

Fig. 23.27 | `FindPrimes` GUI with its **fx:ids**.

Class `FindPrimesController`

Class `FindPrimesController` (Fig. 23.28) creates an `ObservableList<Integer>` (lines 24–25) and binds it to the app's `primesListView` (line 30). The controller also provides the event handlers for the **Get Primes** and **Cancel** `Button`s.

```
1  // Fig. 23.28: FindPrimesController.java
2  // Displaying prime numbers as they're calculated; updating a ProgressBar
3  import java.util.concurrent.Executors;
4  import java.util.concurrent.ExecutorService;
5  import javafx.collections.FXCollections;
6  import javafx.collections.ObservableList;
7  import javafx.event.ActionEvent;
```

Fig. 23.28 | Displaying prime numbers as they're calculated and updating a `ProgressBar`. (Part 1 of 4.)

```
import javafx.fxml.FXML;
import javafx.scene.control.Button;
import javafx.scene.control.Label;
import javafx.scene.control.ListView;
import javafx.scene.control.ProgressBar;
import javafx.scene.control.TextField;

public class FindPrimesController {
   @FXML private TextField inputTextField;
   @FXML private Button getPrimesButton;
   @FXML private ListView<Integer> primesListView;
   @FXML private Button cancelButton;
   @FXML private ProgressBar progressBar;
   @FXML private Label statusLabel;

   // stores the list of primes received from PrimeCalculatorTask
   private ObservableList<Integer> primes =
      FXCollections.observableArrayList();
   private PrimeCalculatorTask task; // finds prime numbers

   // binds primesListView's items to the ObservableList primes
   public void initialize() {
      primesListView.setItems(primes);
   }

   // start calculating primes in the background
   @FXML
   void getPrimesButtonPressed(ActionEvent event) {
      primes.clear();

      // get Fibonacci number to calculate
      try {
         int input = Integer.parseInt(inputTextField.getText());
         task = new PrimeCalculatorTask(input); // create task

         // display task's messages in statusLabel
         statusLabel.textProperty().bind(task.messageProperty());

         // update progressBar based on task's progressProperty
         progressBar.progressProperty().bind(task.progressProperty());

         // store intermediate results in the ObservableList primes
         task.valueProperty().addListener(
            (observable, oldValue, newValue) -> {
               if (newValue != 0) { // task returns 0 when it terminates
                  primes.add(newValue);
                  primesListView.scrollTo(
                     primesListView.getItems().size());
               }
            });

```

Fig. 23.28 | Displaying prime numbers as they're calculated and updating a `ProgressBar`. (Part 2 of 4.)

```
         // when task begins,
         // disable getPrimesButton and enable cancelButton
         task.setOnRunning((succeededEvent) -> {
            getPrimesButton.setDisable(true);
            cancelButton.setDisable(false);
         });

         // when task completes successfully,
         // enable getPrimesButton and disable cancelButton
         task.setOnSucceeded((succeededEvent) -> {
            getPrimesButton.setDisable(false);
            cancelButton.setDisable(true);
         });

         // create ExecutorService to manage threads
         ExecutorService executorService =
            Executors.newFixedThreadPool(1);
         executorService.execute(task); // start the task
         executorService.shutdown();
      }
      catch (NumberFormatException e) {
         inputTextField.setText("Enter an integer");
         inputTextField.selectAll();
         inputTextField.requestFocus();
      }
   }

   // cancel task when user presses Cancel Button
   @FXML
   void cancelButtonPressed(ActionEvent event) {
      if (task != null) {
         task.cancel(); // terminate the task
         getPrimesButton.setDisable(false);
         cancelButton.setDisable(true);
      }
   }
}
```

Find Primes

Find primes less than: 1000 Get Primes

Cancel

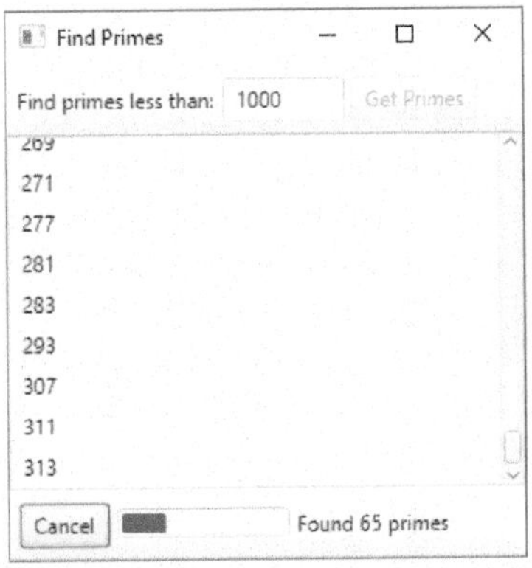

Find Primes

Find primes less than: 1000 Get Primes

269
271
277
281
283
293
307
311
313

Cancel Found 65 primes

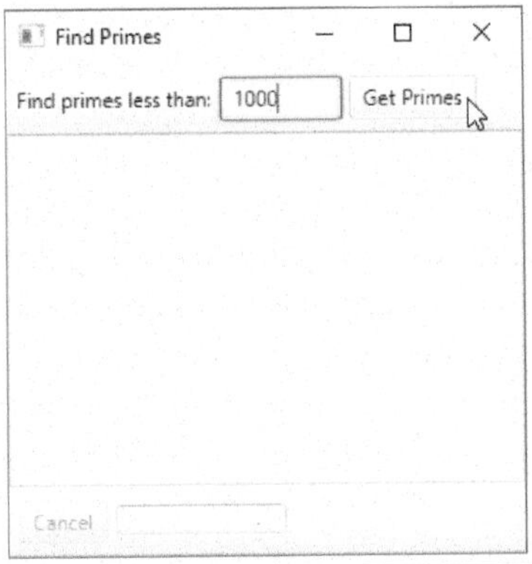

Fig. 23.28 | Displaying prime numbers as they're calculated and updating a `ProgressBar`. (Part 3 of 4.)

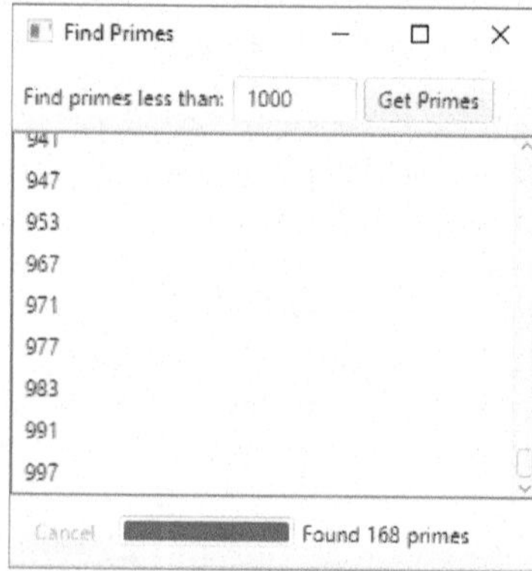

Fig. 23.28 | Displaying prime numbers as they're calculated and updating a `ProgressBar`. (Part 4 of 4.)

Method `getPrimesButtonPressed`

When the user presses the **Get Primes** `Button`, method `getPrimesButtonPressed` creates a `PrimeCalculatorTask` (line 41), then configures various property bindings and event listeners:

- Line 44 binds the `statusLabel`'s `text` property to the task's `message` property to update the `statusLabel` automatically as new primes are found.
- Line 47 binds the `progressBar`'s `progress` property to the task's `progress` property to update the `progressBar` automatically with the percentage completion.
- Lines 50–57 register a `ChangeListener` (using a lambda) that gets invoked each time the task's `value` property changes. If the `newValue` of the property is not `0` (indicating that the task terminated), line 53 adds the `newValue` to the `ObservableList<Integer>` named `primes`—recall that this is bound to the `primesListView`, which displays the list's elements. Next, lines 54–55 scroll the `ListView` to its last element so the user can see the new values being displayed.
- Lines 61–71 register listeners for the task's *running* and *succeeded* state changes. We use these to enable and disable the app's `Buttons` based on the task's state.
- Lines 74–77 launch the task in a separate thread.

Method `cancelButtonPressed`

When the user presses the **Cancel** `Button`, method `cancelButtonPressed` calls the `PrimeCalculatorTask`'s inherited **`cancel`** method (line 90) to terminate the task, then enables the `getPrimesButton` and disables the `cancelButton`.

8 23.12 `sort`/`parallelSort` Timings with the Java SE 8 Date/Time API

In Section 7.15, we used class `Arrays`'s `static` method `sort` to sort an array and we introduced `static` method `parallelSort` for sorting large arrays more efficiently on multi-core systems. Figure 23.29 uses both methods to sort 100,000,000 element arrays of random int values so that we can demonstrate parallelSort's performance improvement of over sort on a multi-core system (we ran this example on a quad-core system).[4]

```
// Fig. 23.29: SortComparison.java
// Comparing performance of Arrays methods sort and parallelSort.
import java.time.Duration;
import java.time.Instant;
import java.text.NumberFormat;
import java.util.Arrays;
import java.util.Random;

public class SortComparison {
   public static void main(String[] args) {
      Random random = new Random();

      // create array of random ints, then copy it
      int[] array1 = random.ints(100_000_000).toArray();
      int[] array2 = array1.clone();

      // time the sorting of array1 with Arrays method sort
      System.out.println("Starting sort");
      Instant sortStart = Instant.now();
      Arrays.sort(array1);
      Instant sortEnd = Instant.now();

      // display timing results
      long sortTime = Duration.between(sortStart, sortEnd).toMillis();
      System.out.printf("Total time in milliseconds: %d%n%n", sortTime);

      // time the sorting of array2 with Arrays method parallelSort
      System.out.println("Starting parallelSort");
      Instant parallelSortStart = Instant.now();
      Arrays.parallelSort(array2);
      Instant parallelSortEnd = Instant.now();

      // display timing results
      long parallelSortTime =
         Duration.between(parallelSortStart, parallelSortEnd).toMillis();
      System.out.printf("Total time in milliseconds: %d%n%n",
         parallelSortTime);

      // display time difference as a percentage
      String percentage = NumberFormat.getPercentInstance().format(
         (double) (sortTime - parallelSortTime) / parallelSortTime);
      System.out.printf("sort took %s more time than parallelSort%n",
         percentage);
   }
}
```

Fig. 23.29 | Comparing performance of Arrays methods sort and parallelSort. (Part 1 of 2.)

4. To create the 100,000,000 element array in this example, we used Random rather than SecureRandom, because Random executes significantly faster.

```
Starting sort
Total time in milliseconds: 8883

Starting parallelSort
Total time in milliseconds: 2143

sort took 315% more time than parallelSort
```

Fig. 23.29 | Comparing performance of `Arrays` methods `sort` and `parallelSort`. (Part 2 of 2.)

Creating the Arrays

Line 14 uses `Random` method `ints` to create an `IntStream` of 100,000,000 random `int` values, then calls `IntStream` method `toArray` to place the values into an array. Line 15 calls method `clone` to make a copy of `array1` so that the calls to both `sort` and `parallelSort` work with the same set of values.

Timing `Arrays` *Method* `sort` *with Date/Time API Classes* `Instant` *and* `Duration`

Lines 19 and 21 each call class `Instant`'s `static` method **`now`** to get the current time before and after the call to `sort`. To determine the difference between two `Instant`s, line 24 uses class `Duration`'s `static` method **`between`**, which returns a `Duration` object containing the time difference. Next, we call `Duration` method **`toMillis`** to get the difference in milliseconds.

Timing `Arrays` *Method* `parallelSort` *with Date/Time API Classes* `Instant` *and* `Duration`

Lines 29–31 time the call to `Arrays` method `parallelSort`. Then, lines 34–35 calculate the difference between the `Instant`s.

Displaying the Percentage Difference Between the Sorting Times

Lines 40–41 use a `NumberFormat` (package `java.text`) to format the ratio of the sort times as a percentage. `NumberFormat` `static` method **`getPercentInstance`** returns a `NumberFormat` that's used to format a number as a percentage. `NumberFormat` method `format` performs the formatting. As you can see in the sample output, the `sort` method took over *300% more time* than `parallelSort` to sort the 100,000,000 random `int` values.[5]

Other Parallel Array Operations

In addition to method `parallelSort`, class `Arrays` now contains methods `parallelSetAll` and `parallelPrefix`, which perform the following tasks:

- **`parallelSetAll`**—Fills an array with values produced by a generator function that receives an `int` and returns a value of type `int`, `long`, `double` or the array's element type. Depending on which overload of method `parallelSetAll` is used, the generator function is an implementation of `IntUnaryOperator` (for `int` arrays), `IntToLongFunction` (for `long` arrays), `IntToDoubleFunction` (for `double` arrays) or `IntFunction<T>` (for arrays of any non-primitive type).

5. Depending on your computer's setup, number of cores, whether your operating system is running in a virtual machine, etc., you could see significantly different performance.

- **`parallelPrefix`**—Applies a `BinaryOperator` to the current and previous array elements and stores the result in the current element. For example, consider:

```
int[] values = {1, 2, 3, 4, 5};
Arrays.parallelPrefix(values, (x, y) -> x + y);
```

This call to `parallelPrefix` uses a `BinaryOperator` that *adds* two values. After the call completes, the array contains 1, 3, 6, 10 and 15. Similarly, the following call to `parallelPrefix`, uses a `BinaryOperator` that *multiplies* two values. After the call completes, the array contains 1, 2, 6, 24 and 120:

```
int[] values = {1, 2, 3, 4, 5};
Arrays.parallelPrefix(values, (x, y) -> x * y);
```

23.13 Java SE 8: Sequential vs. Parallel Streams 8

In Chapter 17, you learned about Java SE 8 lambdas and streams. We mentioned that streams are easy to *parallelize,* enabling programs to benefit from enhanced performance on multi-core systems. Using the timing capabilities introduced in Section 23.12, Fig. 23.30 demonstrates both *sequential* and *parallel* stream operations on a 50,000,000-element array of random `long` values (created at line 15) to compare the performance.

```
1  // Fig. 23.30: StreamStatisticsComparison.java
2  // Comparing performance of sequential and parallel stream operations.
3  import java.time.Duration;
4  import java.time.Instant;
5  import java.util.Arrays;
6  import java.util.LongSummaryStatistics;
7  import java.util.stream.LongStream;
8  import java.util.Random;
9
10 public class StreamStatisticsComparison {
11    public static void main(String[] args) {
12       Random random = new Random();
13
14       // create array of random long values
15       long[] values = random.longs(50_000_000, 1, 1001).toArray();
16
17       // perform calculations separately
18       Instant separateStart = Instant.now();
19       long count = Arrays.stream(values).count();
20       long sum = Arrays.stream(values).sum();
21       long min = Arrays.stream(values).min().getAsLong();
22       long max = Arrays.stream(values).max().getAsLong();
23       double average = Arrays.stream(values).average().getAsDouble();
24       Instant separateEnd = Instant.now();
25
26       // display results
27       System.out.println("Calculations performed separately");
28       System.out.printf("    count: %,d%n", count);
```

Fig. 23.30 | Comparing performance of sequential and parallel stream operations. (Part 1 of 3.)

```
      System.out.printf("     sum: %,d%n", sum);
      System.out.printf("     min: %,d%n", min);
      System.out.printf("     max: %,d%n", max);
      System.out.printf(" average: %f%n", average);
      System.out.printf("Total time in milliseconds: %d%n%n",
         Duration.between(separateStart, separateEnd).toMillis());

      // time summaryStatistics operation with sequential stream
      LongStream stream1 = Arrays.stream(values);
      System.out.println("Calculating statistics on sequential stream");
      Instant sequentialStart = Instant.now();
      LongSummaryStatistics results1 = stream1.summaryStatistics();
      Instant sequentialEnd = Instant.now();

      // display results
      displayStatistics(results1);
      System.out.printf("Total time in milliseconds: %d%n%n",
         Duration.between(sequentialStart, sequentialEnd).toMillis());

      // time sum operation with parallel stream
      LongStream stream2 = Arrays.stream(values).parallel();
      System.out.println("Calculating statistics on parallel stream");
      Instant parallelStart = Instant.now();
      LongSummaryStatistics results2 = stream2.summaryStatistics();
      Instant parallelEnd = Instant.now();

      // display results
      displayStatistics(results1);
      System.out.printf("Total time in milliseconds: %d%n%n",
         Duration.between(parallelStart, parallelEnd).toMillis());
   }

   // display's LongSummaryStatistics values
   private static void displayStatistics(LongSummaryStatistics stats) {
      System.out.println("Statistics");
      System.out.printf("   count: %,d%n", stats.getCount());
      System.out.printf("     sum: %,d%n", stats.getSum());
      System.out.printf("     min: %,d%n", stats.getMin());
      System.out.printf("     max: %,d%n", stats.getMax());
      System.out.printf(" average: %f%n", stats.getAverage());
   }
}
```

```
Calculations performed separately
    count: 50,000,000
      sum: 25,025,212,218
      min: 1
      max: 1,000
  average: 500.504244
Total time in milliseconds: 710
```

Fig. 23.30 | Comparing performance of sequential and parallel stream operations. (Part 2 of 3.)

```
Calculating statistics on sequential stream
Statistics
    count: 50,000,000
      sum: 25,025,212,218
      min: 1
      max: 1,000
  average: 500.504244
Total time in milliseconds: 305

Calculating statistics on parallel stream
Statistics
    count: 50,000,000
      sum: 25,025,212,218
      min: 1
      max: 1,000
  average: 500.504244
Total time in milliseconds: 143
```

Fig. 23.30 | Comparing performance of sequential and parallel stream operations. (Part 3 of 3.)

Performing Stream Operations with Separate Passes of a Sequential Stream

Section 17.7 demonstrated various numerical operations on `IntStreams`. Lines 18–24 of Fig. 23.30 perform and time the `count`, `sum`, `min`, `max` and `average` stream operations each performed individually on a `LongStream` returned by `Arrays` method `stream`. Lines 27–34 then display the results and the total time required to perform all five operations.

Performing Stream Operations with a Single Pass of a Sequential Stream

Lines 37–46 demonstrate the performance improvement you get by using `LongStream` method `summaryStatistics` to determine the count, sum, minimum value, maximum value and average in one pass of a *sequential* `LongStream`—all streams are sequential by default. This operation took approximately 43% of the time required to perform the five operations separately.

Performing Stream Operations with a Single Pass of a Parallel Stream

Lines 49–50 demonstrate the performance improvement you get by using `LongStream` method `summaryStatistics` on a *parallel* `LongStream`. To obtain a parallel stream that can take advantage of multi-core processors, simply invoke method `parallel` on an existing stream. As you can see from the sample output, performing the operations on a parallel stream decreased the total time required even further—taking approximately 47% of the calculation time for the sequential `LongStream` and just 20% of the time required to perform the five operations separately.

23.14 (Advanced) Interfaces Callable and Future

Interface `Runnable` provides only the most basic functionality for multithreaded programming. In fact, this interface has limitations. Suppose a `Runnable` is performing a long calculation and the application wants to retrieve the result of that calculation. The `run` method cannot return a value, so *shared mutable data* would be required to pass the value back to the calling thread. As you now know, this would require thread synchronization.

The **`Callable`** interface (of package `java.util.concurrent`) fixes this limitation. The interface declares a single method named **`call`** which returns a value representing the result of the `Callable`'s task—such as the result of a long-running calculation.

An application that creates a `Callable` likely wants to run it concurrently with other `Runnable`s and `Callable`s. `ExecutorService` method **`submit`** executes its `Callable` argument and returns an object of type **`Future`** (of package `java.util.concurrent`), which represents the `Callable`'s future result. The `Future` interface **`get`** method *blocks* the calling thread, and waits for the `Callable` to complete and return its result. The interface also provides methods that enable you to cancel a `Callable`'s execution, determine whether the `Callable` was canceled and determine whether the `Callable` completed its task.

Executing Aysnchronous Tasks with `CompletableFuture`

8 Java SE 8 introduced class **`CompletableFuture`** (package `java.util.concurrent`), which implements the `Future` interface and enables you to *asynchronously* execute `Runnable`s that perform tasks or `Supplier`s that return values. Interface **`Supplier`**, like interface `Callable`, is a functional interface with a single method (in this case, `get`) that receives no arguments and returns a result. Class `CompletableFuture` provides many additional capabilities for advanced programmers, such as creating `CompletableFuture`s without executing them immediately, composing one or more `CompletableFuture`s so that you can wait for any or all of them to complete, executing code after a `CompletableFuture` completes and more.

Figure 23.31 performs two long-running calculations sequentially, then performs them again asynchronously using `CompletableFuture`s to demonstrate the performance improvement from asynchronous execution on a multi-core system. For demonstration purposes, our long-running calculation is performed by a recursive `fibonacci` method (lines 69–76; similar to the one presented in Section 18.5). For larger Fibonacci values, the recursive implementation can require *significant* computation time—in practice, it's much faster to calculate Fibonacci values using a loop.

```
1  // Fig. 23.31: FibonacciDemo.java
2  // Fibonacci calculations performed synchronously and asynchronously
3  import java.time.Duration;
4  import java.text.NumberFormat;
5  import java.time.Instant;
6  import java.util.concurrent.CompletableFuture;
7  import java.util.concurrent.ExecutionException;
8
9  // class that stores two Instants in time
10 class TimeData {
11    public Instant start;
12    public Instant end;
13
14    // return total time in seconds
15    public double timeInSeconds() {
16       return Duration.between(start, end).toMillis() / 1000.0;
17    }
18 }
19
```

Fig. 23.31 | Fibonacci calculations performed synchronously and asynchronously. (Part 1 of 3.)

```java
public class FibonacciDemo {
   public static void main(String[] args)
      throws InterruptedException, ExecutionException {

      // perform synchronous fibonacci(45) and fibonacci(44) calculations
      System.out.println("Synchronous Long Running Calculations");
      TimeData synchronousResult1 = startFibonacci(45);
      TimeData synchronousResult2 = startFibonacci(44);
      double synchronousTime =
         calculateTime(synchronousResult1, synchronousResult2);
      System.out.printf(
         "  Total calculation time = %.3f seconds%n", synchronousTime);

      // perform asynchronous fibonacci(45) and fibonacci(44) calculations
      System.out.printf("%nAsynchronous Long Running Calculations%n");
      CompletableFuture<TimeData> futureResult1 =
         CompletableFuture.supplyAsync(() -> startFibonacci(45));
      CompletableFuture<TimeData> futureResult2 =
         CompletableFuture.supplyAsync(() -> startFibonacci(44));

      // wait for results from the asynchronous operations
      TimeData asynchronousResult1 = futureResult1.get();
      TimeData asynchronousResult2 = futureResult2.get();
      double asynchronousTime =
         calculateTime(asynchronousResult1, asynchronousResult2);
      System.out.printf(
         "  Total calculation time = %.3f seconds%n", asynchronousTime);

      // display time difference as a percentage
      String percentage = NumberFormat.getPercentInstance().format(
         (synchronousTime - asynchronousTime) / asynchronousTime);
      System.out.printf("%nSynchronous calculations took %s" +
         " more time than the asynchronous ones%n", percentage);
   }

   // executes function fibonacci asynchronously
   private static TimeData startFibonacci(int n) {
      // create a TimeData object to store times
      TimeData timeData = new TimeData();

      System.out.printf("  Calculating fibonacci(%d)%n", n);
      timeData.start = Instant.now();
      long fibonacciValue = fibonacci(n);
      timeData.end = Instant.now();
      displayResult(n, fibonacciValue, timeData);
      return timeData;
   }

   // recursive method fibonacci; calculates nth Fibonacci number
   private static long fibonacci(long n) {
      if (n == 0 || n == 1) {
         return n;
      }
```

Fig. 23.31 | Fibonacci calculations performed synchronously and asynchronously. (Part 2 of 3.)

```
      else {
         return fibonacci(n - 1) + fibonacci(n - 2);
      }
   }

   // display fibonacci calculation result and total calculation time
   private static void displayResult(
      int n, long value, TimeData timeData) {

      System.out.printf("  fibonacci(%d) = %d%n", n, value);
      System.out.printf(
         "  Calculation time for fibonacci(%d) = %.3f seconds%n",
         n, timeData.timeInSeconds());
   }

   // display fibonacci calculation result and total calculation time
   private static double calculateTime(
      TimeData result1, TimeData result2) {

      TimeData bothThreads = new TimeData();

      // determine earlier start time
      bothThreads.start = result1.start.compareTo(result2.start) < 0 ?
         result1.start : result2.start;

      // determine later end time
      bothThreads.end = result1.end.compareTo(result2.end) > 0 ?
         result1.end : result2.end;

      return bothThreads.timeInSeconds();
   }
}
```

```
Synchronous Long Running Calculations
  Calculating fibonacci(45)
  fibonacci(45) = 1134903170
  Calculation time for fibonacci(45) = 4.395 seconds
  Calculating fibonacci(44)
  fibonacci(44) = 701408733
  Calculation time for fibonacci(44) = 2.722 seconds
  Total calculation time = 7.122 seconds

Asynchronous Long Running Calculations
  Calculating fibonacci(45)
  Calculating fibonacci(44)
  fibonacci(44) = 701408733
  Calculation time for fibonacci(44) = 2.707 seconds
  fibonacci(45) = 1134903170
  Calculation time for fibonacci(45) = 4.403 seconds
  Total calculation time = 4.403 seconds

Synchronous calculations took 62% more time than the asynchronous ones
```

Fig. 23.31 | Fibonacci calculations performed synchronously and asynchronously. (Part 3 of 3.)

Class `TimeData`

Class `TimeData` (lines 10–18) stores two `Instant`s representing the start and end time of a task, and provides method `timeInSeconds` to calculate the total time between them. We use `TimeData` objects throughout this example to calculate the time required to perform Fibonacci calculations.

Method `startFibonacci` *for Performing and Timing Fibonacci Calculations*

Method `startFibonacci` (lines 56–66) is called several times in `main` (lines 26, 27, 36 and 38) to initiate Fibonacci calculations and to calculate the time each calculation requires. The method receives the Fibonacci number to calculate and performs the following tasks:

- Line 58 creates a `TimeData` object to store the calculation's start and end times.
- Line 60 displays the Fibonacci number to be calculated.
- Line 61 stores the current time before method `fibonacci` is called.
- Line 62 calls method `fibonacci` to perform the calculation.
- Line 63 stores the current time after the call to `fibonacci` completes.
- Line 64 displays the result and the total time required for the calculation.
- Line 65 returns the `TimeData` object for use in method `main`.

Performing Fibonacci Calculations Synchronously

Method `main` first demonstrates synchronous Fibonacci calculations. Line 26 calls `startFibonacci(45)` to initiate the `fibonacci(45)` calculation and store the `TimeData` object containing the calculation's start and end times. When this call completes, line 27 calls `startFibonacci(44)` to initiate the `fibonacci(44)` calculation and store its `TimeData`. Next, lines 28–29 pass both `TimeData` objects to method `calculateTime` (lines 89–103), which returns the total calculation time in seconds. Lines 30–31 display the total calculation time for the synchronous Fibonacci calculations.

Performing Fibonacci Calculations Asynchronously

Lines 35–38 in `main` launch the asynchronous Fibonacci calculations in separate threads. `CompletableFuture` `static` method **`supplyAsync`** executes an asynchronous task that returns a value. The method receives as its argument an object that implements interface `Supplier`—in this case, we use lambdas with empty parameter lists to invoke `startFibonacci(45)` (line 36) and `startFibonacci(44)` (line 38). The compiler infers that `supplyAsync` returns a `CompletableFuture<TimeData>` because method `startFibonacci` returns type `TimeData`. Class `CompletableFuture` also provides `static` method **`runAsync`** to execute an asynchronous task that does not return a result—this method receives a `Runnable`.

Getting the Asynchronous Calculations' Results

Class `CompletableFuture` implements interface `Future`, so we can obtain the asynchronous tasks' results by calling `Future` method `get` (lines 41–42). These are *blocking* calls—they cause the `main` thread to *wait* until the asynchronous tasks complete and return their results. In our case, the results are `TimeData` objects. Once both tasks return, lines 43–44 pass both `TimeData` objects to method `calculateTime` (lines 89–103) to get the total calculation time in seconds. Then, lines 45–46 display the total calculation time for the asynchronous Fibonacci calculations. Finally, lines 49–52 calculate and display the percentage difference in execution time for the synchronous and asynchronous calculations.

Program Outputs
On our quad-core computer, the synchronous calculations took a total of 7.122 seconds. Though the individual asynchronous calculations took approximately the same amount of time as the corresponding synchronous calculations, the total time for the asynchronous calculations was only 4.403 seconds, because the two calculations were actually performed *in parallel*. As you can see in the output, the synchronous calculations took 62% more time to complete, so asynchronous execution provided a significant performance improvement.

23.15 (Advanced) Fork/Join Framework

Java's concurrency APIs include the Fork/Join framework, which helps programmers parallelize algorithms. The framework is beyond the scope of this book. Experts tell us that most Java programmers will nevertheless benefit by the Fork/Join framework's use "behind the scenes" in the Java API and other third-party libraries. For example, the parallel capabilities of Java SE 8 streams are implemented using this framework.

The Fork/Join framework is particularly well suited to divide-and-conquer-style algorithms, such as the recursive merge sort that we implemented in Section 19.8. Recall that the recursive merge-sort algorithm sorts an array by *splitting* it into two equal-sized subarrays, *sorting* each subarray, then *merging* them into one larger array. Each subarray is sorted by performing the same algorithm on the subarray. For algorithms like merge sort, the Fork/Join framework can be used to create concurrent tasks so that they can be distributed across multiple processors and be truly performed in parallel—the details of assigning the tasks to different processors are handled for you by the framework. Exercises 23.20–23.21 ask you to further investigate the Fork/Join Framework and use it to reimplement the recursive merge sort and quicksort algorithms. Exercise 23.22 asks why you might not want to take the time and effort to reimplement the binary search algorithm with Fork/Join. To learn more about Fork/Join, see the following Oracle tutorial and other online tutorials:

```
https://docs.oracle.com/javase/tutorial/essential/concurrency/
   forkjoin.html
```

23.16 Wrap-Up

In this chapter, we presented Java's concurrency capabilities for enhancing application performance on multi-core systems. You learned the differences between concurrent and parallel execution. We discussed that Java makes concurrency available to you through multithreading. You also learned that the JVM itself creates threads to run a program, and that it also can create threads to perform housekeeping tasks such as garbage collection.

We discussed the life cycle of a thread and the states that a thread may occupy during its lifetime. Next, we presented the interface `Runnable`, which is used to specify a task that can execute concurrently with other tasks. This interface's `run` method is invoked by the thread executing the task. Then we showed how to use the `Executor` interface to manage the execution of `Runnable` objects via thread pools, which can reuse existing threads to eliminate the overhead of creating a new thread for each task and can improve performance by optimizing the number of threads to ensure that the processor stays busy.

You learned that when multiple threads share an object and one or more of them modify that object, indeterminate results may occur unless access to the shared object is managed properly. We showed you how to solve this problem via thread synchronization, which coordinates access to shared mutable data by multiple concurrent threads. You learned several techniques for performing synchronization—first with the built-in class `ArrayBlockingQueue` (which handles *all* the synchronization details for you), then with Java's built-in monitors and the `synchronized` keyword, and finally with interfaces `Lock` and `Condition`.

We discussed the fact that JavaFX GUIs are not thread safe, so all interactions with and modifications to the GUI must be performed in the JavaFX application thread. We also discussed the problems associated with performing long-running calculations in that thread. Then we showed how you can use class `Task` to perform long-running calculations in worker threads. You learned how to use a `Task`'s properties to display the results of a `Task` in a GUI when the calculation completed and how to display intermediate results while the calculation was still in process.

We revisited the `Arrays` class's `sort` and `parallelSort` methods to demonstrate the benefit of using a parallel sorting algorithm on a multi-core processor. We used the Java SE 8 Date/Time API's `Instant` and `Duration` classes to time the sort operations.

You learned that Java SE 8 streams are easy to parallelize, enabling programs to benefit from enhanced performance on multi-core systems, and that to obtain a parallel stream, you simply invoke method `parallel` on an existing stream.

We discussed the `Callable` and `Future` interfaces, which enable you to execute tasks that return results and to obtain those results, respectively. We then presented an example of performing long-running tasks synchronously and asynchronously using Java SE 8's `CompletableFuture` class. In the next chapter, we introduce database-application development with Java's JDBC API.

Summary

Section 23.1 Introduction

- Two tasks that are operating concurrently are both making progress at once.
- Two tasks that are operating in parallel are executing simultaneously. In this sense, parallelism is a subset of concurrency. Today's multi-core computers have multiple processors that can perform tasks in parallel.
- Java makes concurrency available to you through the language and APIs.
- Java programs can have multiple threads of execution, where each thread has its own method-call stack and program counter, allowing it to execute concurrently with other threads. This capability is called multithreading.
- In a multithreaded application, threads can be distributed across multiple processors (if available) so that multiple tasks execute in parallel and the application can operate more efficiently.
- The JVM creates threads to run a program and for housekeeping tasks such as garbage collection.
- Multithreading can also increase performance on single-processor systems—when one thread cannot proceed (because, for example, it's waiting for the result of an I/O operation), another can use the processor.
- The vast majority of programmers should use existing collection classes and interfaces from the concurrency APIs that manage synchronization for you.

Section 23.2 Thread States and Life Cycle

- A new thread begins its life cycle in the *new* state (p. 967). When the program starts the thread, it's placed in the *runnable* state. A thread in the *runnable* state is considered to be executing its task.
- A *runnable* thread transitions to the *waiting* state (p. 967) to wait for another thread to perform a task. A *waiting* thread transitions to *runnable* when another thread notifies it to continue executing.
- A *runnable* thread can enter the *timed waiting* state (p. 967) for a specified interval of time, transitioning back to *runnable* when that time interval expires or when the event it's waiting for occurs.
- A *runnable* thread can transition to the *timed waiting* state if it provides an optional wait interval when it's waiting for another thread to perform a task. Such a thread will return to the *runnable* state when it's notified by another thread or when the timed interval expires.
- A sleeping thread (p. 967) remains in the *timed waiting* state for a designated period of time, after which it returns to the *runnable* state.
- A *runnable* thread transitions to the *blocked* state (p. 967) when it attempts to perform a task that cannot be completed immediately and the thread must temporarily wait until that task completes. At that point, the *blocked* thread transitions to the *runnable* state, so it can resume execution.
- A *runnable* thread enters the *terminated* state (p. 967) when it successfully completes its task or otherwise terminates (perhaps due to an error).
- At the operating-system level, the *runnable* state (p. 968) encompasses two separate states. When a thread first transitions to the *runnable* state from the *new* state, it's in the *ready* state (p. 968). A *ready* thread enters the *running* state (p. 968) when the operating system dispatches it.
- Most operating systems allot a quantum (p. 968) in which a thread performs its task. When this expires, the thread returns to the *ready* state and another thread is assigned to the processor.
- Thread scheduling determines which thread to dispatch based on thread priorities.
- The job of an operating system's thread scheduler (p. 968) is to determine which thread runs next.
- When a higher-priority thread enters the *ready* state, the operating system generally preempts the currently *running* thread (an operation known as preemptive scheduling; p. 969).
- Depending on the operating system, higher-priority threads could postpone—possibly indefinitely (p. 969)—the execution of lower-priority threads.

Section 23.3 Creating and Executing Threads with the **Executor** *Framework*

- A `Runnable` (p. 969) object represents a task that can execute concurrently with other tasks.
- Interface `Runnable` declares method `run` (p. 969) in which you place the code that defines the task to perform. The thread executing a `Runnable` calls method `run` to perform the task.
- A program will not terminate until its last thread completes execution.
- You cannot predict the order in which threads will be scheduled, even if you know the order in which they were created and started.
- Use the `Executor` interface (p. 969) to manage the execution of `Runnable` objects. An `Executor` object typically creates and manages a group of threads—called a thread pool (p. 969). `Executors` (p. 970) can reuse existing threads and can improve performance by optimizing the number of threads to ensure that the processor stays busy.
- `Executor` method `execute` (p. 969) receives a `Runnable` and assigns it to an available thread in a thread pool. If there are none, the `Executor` creates a new thread or waits for one to become available.
- Interface `ExecutorService` (of package `java.util.concurrent`; p. 970) extends interface `Executor` and declares other methods for managing the life cycle of an `Executor`. An object that implements the `ExecutorService` interface can be created using `static` methods declared in class `Executors` (of package `java.util.concurrent`).

- `Executors` method `newCachedThreadPool` (p. 971) returns an `ExecutorService` that creates new threads if no existing threads are available to reuse.
- `ExecutorService` method `execute` executes its `Runnable` sometime in the future. The method returns immediately from each invocation—the program does not wait for each task to finish.
- `ExecutorService` method `shutdown` (p. 973) notifies the `ExecutorService` to stop accepting new tasks, but continues executing existing tasks and terminates when those tasks complete execution.

Section 23.4 Thread Synchronization

- Thread synchronization (p. 974) coordinates access to shared mutable data by multiple concurrent threads.
- By synchronizing threads, you can ensure that each thread accessing a shared object excludes all other threads from doing so simultaneously—this is called mutual exclusion (p. 974).
- A common way to perform synchronization is to use Java's built-in monitors. Every object has a monitor and a monitor lock (p. 974). The monitor ensures that its object's monitor lock is held by a maximum of only one thread at any time, and thus can be used to enforce mutual exclusion.
- If an operation requires the executing thread to hold a lock while the operation is performed, a thread must acquire the lock (p. 974) before it can proceed with the operation. Any other threads attempting to perform an operation that requires the same lock will be *blocked* until the first thread releases the lock, at which point the *blocked* threads may attempt to acquire the lock.
- To specify that a thread must hold a monitor lock to execute a block of code, the code should be placed in a `synchronized` statement (p. 974). Such code is said to be guarded by the monitor lock.
- The `synchronized` statements are declared using the `synchronized` keyword:

```
synchronized (object) {
   statements
}
```

  where *object* is the object whose monitor lock will be acquired; *object* is normally `this` if it's the object in which the `synchronized` statement appears.
- Java also allows `synchronized` methods (p. 975). Before executing, a `synchronized` instance method must acquire the lock on the object that's used to call the method. Similary, a `static synchronized` method must acquire the lock on a `Class` object that represents the class in which the method is declared. A `Class` object is the execution-time representation of a class that the JVM has loaded into memory
- `ExecutorService` method `awaitTermination` (p. 979) forces a program to wait for threads to terminate. It returns control to its caller either when all tasks executing in the `ExecutorService` complete or when the specified timeout elapses. If all tasks complete before the timeout elapses, the method returns `true`; otherwise, it returns `false`.
- You can simulate atomicity (p. 980) by ensuring that only one thread performs a set of operations at a time. Atomicity can be achieved with `synchronized` statements or `synchronized` methods.
- When you share immutable data across threads, you should declare the corresponding data fields `final` to indicate that the variables' values will not change after they're initialized.

Section 23.5 Producer/Consumer Relationship without Synchronization

- In a multithreaded producer/consumer relationship (p. 982), a producer thread generates data and places it in a shared object called a buffer. A consumer thread reads data from the buffer.
- Operations on a buffer data shared by a producer and a consumer should proceed only if the buffer is in the correct state. If the buffer is not full, the producer may produce; if the buffer is not empty, the consumer may consume. If the buffer is full when the producer attempts to write into

it, the producer must wait until there's space. If the buffer is empty or the previous value was already read, the consumer must wait for new data to become available.

Section 23.6 Producer/Consumer Relationship: **`ArrayBlockingQueue`**

- `ArrayBlockingQueue` (p. 990) is a fully implemented buffer class from package `java.util.concurrent` that implements the `BlockingQueue` interface.
- An `ArrayBlockingQueue` can implement a shared buffer in a producer/consumer relationship. Method `put` (p. 990) places an element at the end of the `BlockingQueue`, waiting if the queue is full. Method `take` (p. 990) removes an element from the head of the `BlockingQueue`, waiting if the queue is empty.
- `ArrayBlockingQueue` stores shared mutable data in an array that's sized with an argument passed to the constructor. Once created, an `ArrayBlockingQueue` is fixed in size.

Section 23.7 (Advanced) Producer/Consumer Relationship with **`synchronized`**, **`wait`**, **`notify`** *and* **`notifyAll`**

- You can implement a shared buffer yourself using the `synchronized` keyword and `Object` methods `wait`, `notify` and `notifyAll` (p. 993).
- A thread can call `Object` method `wait` to release an object's monitor lock, and wait in the *waiting* state while the other threads try to enter the object's `synchronized` statement(s) or method(s).
- When a thread executing a `synchronized` statement (or method) completes or satisfies the condition on which another thread may be waiting, it can call `Object` method `notify` (p. 993) to allow a waiting thread to transition to the *runnable* state. At this point, the thread that was transitioned can attempt to reacquire the monitor lock on the object.
- If a thread calls `notifyAll` (p. 993), then all the threads waiting for the monitor lock become eligible to reacquire the lock (that is, they all transition to the *runnable* state).

Section 23.8 (Advanced) Producer/Consumer Relationship: Bounded Buffers

- You cannot make assumptions about the relative speeds of concurrent threads.
- A bounded buffer (p. 1000) can be used to minimize the amount of waiting time for threads that share resources and operate at the same average speeds. If the producer temporarily produces values faster than the consumer can consume them, the producer can write additional values into the extra buffer space (if any are available). If the consumer consumes faster than the producer produces new values, the consumer can read additional values (if there are any) from the buffer.
- The key to using a bounded buffer with a producer and consumer that operate at about the same speed is to provide the buffer with enough locations to handle the anticipated "extra" production.
- The simplest way to implement a bounded buffer is to use an `ArrayBlockingQueue` for the buffer so that all of the synchronization details are handled for you.

Section 23.9 (Advanced) Producer/Consumer Relationship: The **`Lock`** *and* **`Condition`** *Interfaces*

- The `Lock` and `Condition` interfaces (p. 1007) give programmers more precise control over thread synchronization, but are more complicated to use.
- Any object can contain a reference to an object that implements the `Lock` interface (of package `java.util.concurrent.locks`). A thread calls a `Lock`'s `lock` method (p. 1007) to acquire the lock. Once a `Lock` has been obtained by one thread, the `Lock` will not allow another thread to obtain it until the first thread releases it (by calling the `Lock`'s `unlock` method; p. 1007).

- If several threads are trying to call method `lock` on the same `Lock` object at the same time, only one thread can obtain the lock—the others are placed in the *waiting* state. When a thread calls `unlock`, the object's lock is released and a waiting thread attempting to lock the object proceeds.
- Class `ReentrantLock` (p. 1008) is a basic implementation of the `Lock` interface.
- The `ReentrantLock` constructor takes a `boolean` that specifies whether the lock has a fairness policy (p. 1008). If `true`, the `ReentrantLock`'s fairness policy is "the longest-waiting thread will acquire the lock when it's available"—this prevents indefinite postponement. If the argument is set to `false`, there's no guarantee as to which waiting thread will acquire the lock when it's available.
- If a thread that owns a `Lock` determines that it cannot continue with its task until some condition is satisfied, the thread can wait on a condition object (p. 1008). Using `Lock` objects allows you to explicitly declare the condition objects on which a thread may need to wait.
- `Condition` (p. 1008) objects are associated with a specific `Lock` and are created by calling `Lock` method `newCondition`, which returns a `Condition` object. To wait on a `Condition`, the thread can call the `Condition`'s `await` method. This immediately releases the associated `Lock` and places the thread in the *waiting* state for that `Condition`. Other threads can then try to obtain the `Lock`.
- When a *runnable* thread completes a task and determines that a *waiting* thread can now continue, the *runnable* thread can call `Condition` method `signal` to allow a thread in that `Condition`'s *waiting* state to return to the *runnable* state. At this point, the thread that transitioned from the *waiting* state to the *runnable* state can attempt to reacquire the `Lock`.
- If multiple threads are in a `Condition`'s *waiting* state when `signal` is called, the default implementation of `Condition` signals the longest-waiting thread to transition to the *runnable* state.
- If a thread calls `Condition` method `signalAll`, then all the threads waiting for that condition transition to the *runnable* state and become eligible to reacquire the `Lock`.
- When a thread is finished with a shared object, it must call method `unlock` to release the `Lock`.
- `Lock`s allow you to interrupt waiting threads or to specify a timeout for waiting to acquire a lock—not possible with `synchronized`. Also, a `Lock` object is not constrained to be acquired and released in the same block of code, which is the case with the `synchronized` keyword.
- `Condition` objects allow you to specify multiple conditions on which threads may wait. Thus, it's possible to indicate to waiting threads that a specific condition object is now true by calling that `Condition` object's `signal` or `signallAll` methods (p. 1008). With `synchronized`, there's no way to explicitly state the condition on which threads are waiting.

Section 23.10 Concurrent Collections

- The collections from the `java.util.concurrent` package are specifically designed and optimized for sharing collections among multiple threads.
- The concurrent collections provide their own implementations of various stream-like operations—e.g., `ConcurrentHashMap` has methods `forEach`, `reduce` and `search`—that are designed and optimized for concurrent collections that are shared among threads.

Section 23.11 Multithreading in JavaFX

- All JavaFX applications have a single thread, called the JavaFX application thread, to handle interactions with the application's controls. All tasks that require interaction with an application's GUI are placed in an event queue and are executed sequentially by the JavaFX application thread.
- Thread safety in JavaFX applications is achieved not by synchronizing thread actions, but by ensuring that the scene graph is accessed from only the JavaFX application thread. This technique is called thread confinement.
- You should handle long-running computations in separate threads.

- The `static` method `runLater` of class `Platform` (package `javafx.application`) receives a `Runnable` and schedules it on the JavaFX application thread for execution at some point in the future. Such `Runnable`s should be used to perform small updates, so the GUI remains responsive.
- Package `javafx.concurrent` provides interface `Worker` and classes `Task` and `ScheduledService` for implementing long-running tasks outside the JavaFX application thread.
- A `Worker` is a task that should execute using one or more separate threads.
- Class `Task` is a `Worker` implementation that enables you to perform a task in a worker thread and update the GUI from the JavaFX application thread based on the task's results.
- `Task` implements several interfaces, including `Runnable`, so a `Task` object can be scheduled to execute in a separate thread.
- Class `Task` provides methods that are guaranteed to update its properties in the JavaFX application thread.
- Once a `Task` completes, it cannot be restarted.
- Class `ScheduledService` is a `Worker` implementation that creates and manages a `Task`. Unlike a `Task`, a `ScheduledService` can be reset and restarted. It also can be configured to automatically restart both after successful completion and if it fails due to an exception.

Section 23.11.1 Performing Computations in a Worker Thread: Fibonacci Numbers

- `Task` method `call` performs a `Task`'s work and returns the result. The `Task`'s type parameter indicates `call`'s return type.
- Inherited `Task` method `updateMessage` updates a `Task`'s `message` property in the JavaFX application thread.
- You can bind JavaFX controls to a `Task`'s properties to display their values.
- All `Workers` transition through various states. Class `Task`—an implementation of `Worker`—enables you to register listeners for several of these states.
- `Task` method `setOnRunning` registers a listener that's invoked when a `Task` enters the *running* state—that is, when the `Task`'s `call` method begins executing in a worker thread.
- `Task` method `setOnSucceeded` registers a listener that's invoked when the `Task` enters the *succeeded* state—that is, when the `Task` successfully runs to completion.
- `Task`'s `getValue` method (from interface `Worker`) obtains a `Task`'s result.
- You also can register listeners for a `Task`'s *canceled, failed* and *scheduled* states.

Section 23.11.2 Processing Intermediate Results: Sieve of Eratosthenes

- Class `Task` provides additional methods and properties that enable you to update a GUI with a `Task`'s intermediate results as the `Task` continues executing in a `Worker` thread.
- Method `updateProgress` updates a `Task`'s `progress` property, which represents the percentage completion.
- Method `updateValue` updates a `Task`'s `value` property, which holds each intermediate value.
- Like `updateMessage`, `updateProgress` and `updateValue` are guaranteed to update the corresponding properties in the JavaFX application thread.
- `Task` method `isCancelled` returns true if the `Task` has been canceled.
- `Task`'s inherited `cancel` method terminates the task.

Section 23.12 `sort`/`parallelSort` Timings with the Java SE 8 Date/Time API

- Class `Instant`'s `static` method `now` gets the current time.

- To determine the difference between two `Instant`s, use class `Duration`'s `static` method `between`, which returns a `Duration` object containing the time difference.
- `Duration` method `toMillis` returns the `Duration` as a `long` value milliseconds.
- `NumberFormat` `static` method `getPercentInstance` returns a `NumberFormat` that's used to format a number as a percentage.
- `NumberFormat` method `format` returns a `String` representation of its argument in the specified numeric format.
- `Arrays` `static` method `parallelSetAll` fills an array with values produced by a generator function that receives an `int` and returns a value of type `int`, `long`, `double` or the array's element type. Depending on which overload of method `parallelSetAll` is used, the generator function is an object of a class that implements `IntToDoubleFunction` (for double arrays), `IntUnaryOperator` (for int arrays), `IntToLongFunction` (for long arrays) or `IntFunction<T>` (for arrays of any non-primitive type).
- `Arrays` `static` method `parallelPrefix` applies a `BinaryOperator` to the current and previous array elements and stores the result in the current element.

Section 23.13 Java SE 8: Sequential vs. Parallel Streams

- Streams are easy to parallelize, enabling programs to benefit from enhanced performance on multi-core systems.
- To obtain a parallel stream, simply invoke method `parallel` on an existing stream.

Section 23.14 (Advanced) Interfaces `Callable` *and* `Future`

- The `Callable` (p. 1034) interface (of package `java.util.concurrent`) declares a single method named `call` that allows a task to return a value.
- `ExecutorService` method `submit` (p. 1034) executes a `Callable` passed in as its argument. Method `submit` returns an object of type `Future` (of package `java.util.concurrent`) that represents the future result of the executing `Callable`.
- Interface `Future` (p. 1034) declares method `get` to return the result of the `Callable`. The interface also provides methods that enable you to cancel a `Callable`'s execution, determine whether the `Callable` was cancelled and determine whether the `Callable` completed its task.
- Java SE 8 introduces a new `CompletableFuture` class (package `java.util.concurrent`; p. 1034), which implements the `Future` interface and enables you to asynchronously execute `Runnable`s that perform tasks or `Supplier`s that return values.
- Interface `Supplier` (p. 1034), like interface `Callable`, is a functional interface with a single method (in this case, `get`) that receives no arguments and returns a result.
- `CompletableFuture` `static` method `supplyAsync` (p. 1033) asynchronously executes a `Supplier` task that returns a value.
- `CompletableFuture` `static` method `runAsync` (p. 1034) asynchronously executes a `Runnable` task that does not return a result.
- `CompletableFuture` method `get` is a blocking method—it causes the calling thread to wait until the asynchronous task completes and returns its results.

Section 23.15 (Advanced) Fork/Join Framework

- Java's concurrency APIs include the Fork/join framework, which helps programmers parallelize algorithms. The Fork/join framework is particularly well suited to divide-and-conquer-style algorithms, like the merge sort.

Self-Review Exercises

23.1 Fill in the blanks in each of the following statements:

a) A thread enters the *terminated* state when ________.

b) To pause for a designated number of milliseconds and resume execution, a thread should call method ________ of class ________.

c) A *runnable* thread can enter the ________ state for a specified interval of time.

d) At the operating-system level, the *runnable* state actually encompasses two separate states, ________ and ________.

e) `Runnable`s are executed using a class that implements the ________ interface.

f) `ExecutorService` method ________ prevents the `ExecutorService` from accepting new tasks, but continues executing tasks that have already been submitted.

g) In a(n) ________ relationship, the ________ generates data and stores it in a shared object, and the ________ reads data from the shared object.

h) Only one thread at a time can execute a(n) ________ statement or block.

23.2 *(Advanced Optional Sections)* Fill in the blanks in each of the following statements:

a) Method ________ of class `Condition` moves a single thread in an object's *waiting* state to the *runnable* state.

b) Method ________ of class `Condition` moves every thread in an object's *waiting* state to the *runnable* state.

c) A thread can call method ________ on a `Condition` object to release the associated `Lock` and place that thread in the ________ state.

d) Class ________ implements the `BlockingQueue` interface using an array.

e) Class `Instant`'s `static` method ________ gets the current time.

f) `Duration` method ________ returns the `Duration` as a `long` value milliseconds.

g) `NumberFormat` `static` method ________ returns a `NumberFormat` that's used to format a number as a percentage.

h) `NumberFormat` method ________ returns a `String` representation of its argument in the specified numeric format.

i) `Arrays` `static` method ________ fills an array with values produced by a generator function.

j) `Arrays` `static` method ________ applies a `BinaryOperator` to the current and previous array elements and stores the result in the current element.

k) To obtain a parallel stream, simply invoke method ________ on an existing stream.

l) Among its many features a `CompletableFuture` enables you to asynchronously execute ________ that perform tasks or ________ that return values.

23.3 State whether each of the following is *true* or *false*. If *false*, explain why.

a) A thread is not *runnable* if it has terminated.

b) Some operating systems use timeslicing with threads. Therefore, they can enable threads to preempt threads of the same priority.

c) When the thread's quantum expires, the thread returns to the *running* state as the operating system assigns it to a processor.

d) On a single-processor system without timeslicing, each thread in a set of equal-priority threads (with no other threads present) runs to completion before other threads of equal priority get a chance to execute.

23.4 *(Advanced Optional Sections)* State whether each of the following is *true* or *false*. If *false*, explain why.

a) To determine the difference between two `Instant`s, use class `Duration`'s `static` method `difference`, which returns a `Duration` object containing the time difference.

b) Streams are easy to parallelize, enabling programs to benefit from enhanced performance on multi-core systems.
c) Interface `Supplier`, like interface `Callable`, is a functional interface with a single method that receives no arguments and returns a result.
d) `CompletableFuture` `static` method `runAsync` asynchronously executes a `Supplier` task that returns a value.
e) `CompletableFuture` `static` method `supplyAsync` asynchronously executes a `Runnable` task that does not return a result.

Exercises

23.1 a) it complete its task (or terminates due to an error). b) `sleep`, `Thread`. c) *timed waiting*. d) *ready*, *running*. e) `Executor`. f) `shutdown`. g) producer/consumer, producer, consumer. h) `synchronized`.

23.2 a) `signal`. b) `signalAll`. c) `await`, *waiting*. d) `ArrayBlockingQueue`. e) `now`. f) `toMillis`. g) `getPercentInstance`. h) `format`. i) `parallelSetAll`. j) `parallelPrefix`. k) `parallel`. l) `Runnables`, `Suppliers`.

23.3 a) True. b) False. Timeslicing allows a thread to execute until its timeslice (or quantum) expires. Then other threads of equal priority can execute. c) False. When a thread's quantum expires, the thread returns to the *ready* state and the operating system assigns to the processor another thread. d) True.

23.4 a) False. The `Duration` method for calculating the difference between two `Instants` is named `between`. b) True. c) True. d) False. The method that asynchronously executes a `Supplier` is `supplyAsync`. e) False. The method that asynchronously executes a `Runnable` is `runAsync`.

Exercises

23.5 *(True or False)* State whether each of the following is *true* or *false*. If *false*, explain why.
a) Method `sleep` does not consume processor time while a thread sleeps.
b) JavaFX components are thread safe.
c) *(Advanced)* Declaring a method `synchronized` guarantees that deadlock cannot occur.
d) *(Advanced)* Once a `ReentrantLock` has been obtained by a thread, the `ReentrantLock` object will not allow another thread to obtain the lock until the first thread releases it.

23.6 *(Multithreading Terms)* Define each of the following terms.
a) thread
b) multithreading
c) *runnable* state
d) *timed waiting* state
e) preemptive scheduling
f) `Runnable` interface
g) producer/consumer relationship
h) quantum

23.7 *(Advanced: Multithreading Terms)* Discuss each of the following terms in the context of Java's threading mechanisms:
a) `synchronized`
b) `wait`
c) `notify`
d) `notifyAll`
e) `Lock`
f) `Condition`

23.8 *(Blocked State)* List the reasons for entering the *blocked* state. For each of these, describe how the program will normally leave the *blocked* state and enter the *runnable* state.

23.9 *(Deadlock and Indefinite Postponement)* Two problems that can occur in systems that allow threads to wait are deadlock, in which one or more threads will wait forever for an event that cannot occur, and indefinite postponement, in which one or more threads will be delayed for some unpredictably long time. Give an example of how each of these problems can occur in multithreaded Java programs.

23.10 *(Bouncing Ball)* Write a program that uses the JavaFX threading techniques introduced in this chapter to bounce a blue ball inside a `Pane`. The ball should begin moving in a random direction from the point where the user clicks the mouse. When the ball hits the edge of the `Pane`, it should bounce off the edge and continue in the opposite direction.

23.11 *(Bouncing Balls)* Modify the program in Exercise 23.10 to add a new ball each time the user clicks the mouse. Provide for a minimum of 20 balls. Randomly choose the color for each new ball.

23.12 *(Bouncing Balls with Shadows)* Modify the program in Exercise 23.11 to add shadows. As a ball moves, draw a solid black oval at the bottom of the `Pane`. You may consider adding a 3-D effect by increasing or decreasing the size of each ball when it hits the edge of the `Pane`.

23.13 *(Advanced: Circular Buffer with `Lock`s and `Condition`s)* Reimplement the example in Section 23.8 using the `Lock` and `Condition` concepts presented in Section 23.9.

23.14 *(Bounded Buffer: A Real-World Example)* Describe how a highway off-ramp onto a local road is a good example of a producer/consumer relationship with a bounded buffer. In particular, discuss how the designers might choose the size of the off-ramp.

Parallel Streams

For Exercises 23.15–23.17, you may need to create larger data sets to see a significant performance difference.

23.15 *(Summarizing the Words in a File)* Reimplement Fig. 17.22 using parallel streams. Use the Date/Time API timing techniques you learned in Section 23.12 to compare the time required for the sequential and parallel versions of the program.

23.16 *(Summarizing the Characters in a File)* Reimplement Exercise 17.10 using parallel streams. Use the Date/Time API timing techniques you learned in Section 23.12 to compare the time required for the sequential and parallel versions of the program.

23.17 *(Summarizing the File Types in a Directory)* Reimplement Exercise 17.11 using parallel streams. Use the Date/Time API timing techniques you learned in Section 23.12 to compare the time required for the sequential and parallel versions of the program.

23.18 *(Parallelizing and Timing 60,000,000 Die Rolls)* In Fig. 17.24, we implemented a stream pipeline that rolled a die 60,000,000 times using values produced by `SecureRandom` method `ints`. Use the same timing techniques you used in Exercise 17.25 to time the original stream pipeline's operation, then perform and time the operation using a parallel stream. Any improvement?

23.19 *(Calculating the Sum of the Squares)* Section 17.7.3 used `map` and `sum` to calculate the sum of the squares of an `IntStream`'s values. Reimplement stream pipeline in Fig. 17.9 to replace `map` and `sum` with the following `reduce`, which receives a lambda that does *not* represent an associative operation:

```
.reduce((x, y) -> x + y * y)
```

Error-Prevention Tip 17.2 cautioned you that `reduce`'s argument *must* be an associative operation. Execute the reimplemented stream pipeline using a parallel stream. Does it produce the correct sum of the squares of the `IntStream`'s values?

Parallel Sorting and Searching Projects

For the following project exercises, research the Fork/Join Framework's capabilities for parallelizing recursive algorithms, then use the Fork/Join Framework to implement the specified algorithms.

23.20 *(Project: Recursive Merge Sort with Fork/Join)* Section 19.8 demonstrated the recursive merge sort algorithm. Reimplement the program of Fig. 19.6 using the Fork/Join Framework.

23.21 *(Project: Recursive Quicksort with Fork/Join)* In Exercise 19.10, you implemented the recursive quicksort algorithm. Reimplement the quicksort using the Fork/Join Framework.

23.22 *(Project: Recursive Binary Search with Fork/Join)* In Exercises 23.20–23.21, you reimplemented recursive sorting algorithms using the Fork/Join Framework. Why might you *not* want to invest the effort into applying this technique to a recursive binary search algorithm?

24 Accessing Databases with JDBC

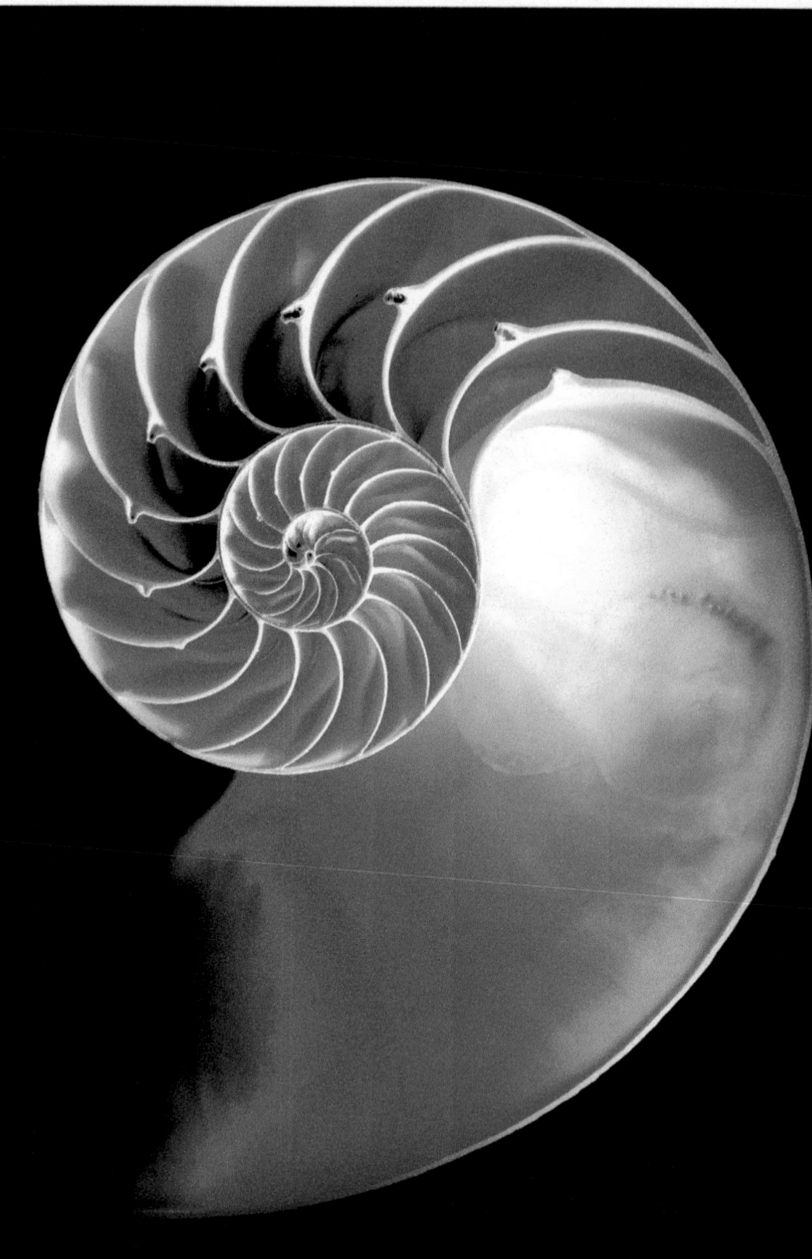

Objectives

In this chapter you'll:

- Learn relational database concepts.
- Use Structured Query Language (SQL) to retrieve data from and manipulate data in a database.
- Use the JDBC™ API's classes and interfaces to manipulate databases.
- Use JDBC's automatic JDBC driver discovery.
- Embed a Swing GUI control into a JavaFX scene graph via a `SwingNode`.
- Use Swing's `JTable` and a `TableModel` to populate a `JTable` with a `ResultSet`'s data.
- Sort and filter a `JTable`'s contents.
- Use the `RowSet` interface from package `javax.sql` to simplify connecting to and interacting with databases.
- Create precompiled SQL statements with parameters via `PreparedStatement`s.
- Learn how transaction processing makes database applications more robust.

Outline

24.1 Introduction

A **database** is an organized collection of data. There are many different strategies for organizing data to facilitate easy access and manipulation. A **database management system** (**DBMS**) provides mechanisms for storing, organizing, retrieving and modifying data for many users. Database management systems allow for the access and storage of data without concern for the internal representation of data.

Structured Query Language

Today's most popular database systems are *relational databases* (Section 24.2). A language called **SQL**—pronounced "sequel," or as its individual letters—is the international standard language used almost universally with relational databases to perform **queries** (i.e., to request information that satisfies given criteria) and to manipulate data. [*Note:* As you learn about SQL, you'll see some authors writing "a SQL statement" (which assumes the pronunciation "sequel") and others writing "an SQL statement" (which assumes that the individual letters are pronounced). In this book we pronounce SQL as "sequel."]

Popular Relational Database Management Systems

Some popular proprietary **relational database management systems** (**RDBMSs**) are Microsoft SQL Server, Oracle, Sybase and IBM DB2, PostgreSQL, MariaDB and MySQL are popular *open-source* DBMSs that can be downloaded and used *freely* by anyone. JDK 8 comes with a pure-Java RDBMS called Java DB—the Oracle-branded version of Apache Derby™.

JDBC

Java programs interact with databases using the **Java Database Connectivity** (JDBC™) API. A **JDBC driver** enables Java applications to connect to a database in a particular DBMS and allows you to manipulate that database using the JDBC API.

Software Engineering Observation 24.1

The JDBC API is portable—the same code can manipulate databases in various RDBMSs.

Most popular database management systems provide JDBC drivers. In this chapter, we introduce JDBC and use it to manipulate Java DB databases. The techniques we demonstrate here can be used to manipulate other databases that have JDBC drivers. If not, third-party vendors provide JDBC drivers for many DBMSs.

Java Persistence API (JPA)

In online Chapter 29, we introduce Java Persistence API (JPA). In that chapter, you'll learn how to autogenerate Java classes that represent the tables in a database and the relationships between them—known as object-relational mapping—then use objects of those classes to interact with a database. As you'll see, storing data in and retrieving data from a database will be handled for you—many of the JDBC techniques you learn in this chapter typically are hidden from you by JPA.

9 *JDK 9 Note*

As of JDK 9, Oracle no longer bundles Java DB with the JDK. If you're using JDK 9 with this chapter, follow the download and installation instructions for Apache Derby at

```
http://db.apache.org/derby/papers/DerbyTut/
   install_software.html#derby
```

before proceeding with this chapter's examples.

24.2 Relational Databases

A **relational database** is a logical representation of data that allows the data to be accessed without consideration of its physical structure. A relational database stores data in **tables**. Figure 24.1 illustrates a sample table that might be used in a personnel system. The table name is `Employee`, and its primary purpose is to store the attributes of employees. Tables are composed of **rows**, each describing a single entity—in Fig. 24.1, an employee. Rows are composed of **columns** in which values are stored. This table consists of six rows. The `Number` column of each row is the table's **primary key**—a column (or group of columns) with a value that is *unique* for each row. This guarantees that each row can be identified by its primary key. Good examples of primary-key columns are a social security number, an employee ID number and a part number in an inventory system, as values in each of these columns are guaranteed to be unique. The rows in Fig. 24.1 are displayed in order by primary key. In this case, the rows are listed in ascending order by primary key, but they could be listed in descending order or in no particular order at all.

Each column represents a different data attribute. Rows are unique (by primary key) within a table, but particular column values may be duplicated between rows. For example, three different rows in the `Employee` table's `Department` column contain number 413.

	Number	Name	Department	Salary	Location
	23603	Jones	413	1100	New Jersey
	24568	Kerwin	413	2000	New Jersey
Row	34589	Larson	642	1800	Los Angeles
	35761	Myers	611	1400	Orlando
	47132	Neumann	413	9000	New Jersey
	78321	Stephens	611	8500	Orlando
	Primary key		Column		

Fig. 24.1 | `Employee` table sample data.

Selecting Data Subsets
Different users of a database are often interested in different data and different relationships among the data. Most users require only subsets of the rows and columns. Queries specify which subsets of the data to select from a table. You use SQL to define queries. For example, you might select data from the `Employee` table to create a result that shows where each department is located, presenting the data sorted in increasing order by department number. This result is shown in Fig. 24.2. SQL is discussed in Section 24.4.

Department	Location
413	New Jersey
611	Orlando
642	Los Angeles

Fig. 24.2 | Distinct `Department` and `Location` data from the `Employees` table.

24.3 A books Database

We introduce relational databases in the context of this chapter's `books` database, which you'll use in several examples. Before we discuss SQL, we discuss the *tables* of the `books` database. We use this database to introduce various database concepts, including how to use SQL to obtain information from the database and to manipulate the data. We provide a script to create the database. You can find the script in the examples directory for this chapter. Section 24.5 explains how to use this script.

***Authors** Table*
The database consists of three tables: `Authors`, `AuthorISBN` and `Titles`. The `Authors` table (described in Fig. 24.3) consists of three columns that maintain each author's unique ID number, first name and last name. Figure 24.4 contains sample data from the `Authors` table.

Column	Description
AuthorID	Author's ID number in the database. In the books database, this integer column is defined as autoincremented—for each row inserted in this table, the AuthorID value is increased by 1 automatically to ensure that each row has a unique AuthorID. This column represents the table's primary key. Autoincremented columns are so-called identity columns. The SQL script we provide for this database uses the SQL **IDENTITY** keyword to mark the AuthorID column as an identity column. For more information on using the IDENTITY keyword and creating databases, see the Java DB Developer's Guide at http://docs.oracle.com/javadb/10.10.1.2/devguide/derbydev.pdf.
FirstName	Author's first name (a string).
LastName	Author's last name (a string).

Fig. 24.3 | Authors table from the books database.

AuthorID	FirstName	LastName
1	Paul	Deitel
2	Harvey	Deitel
3	Abbey	Deitel
4	Dan	Quirk
5	Michael	Morgano

Fig. 24.4 | Sample data from the Authors table.

Titles Table

The Titles table described in Fig. 24.5 consists of four columns that maintain information about each book in the database, including its ISBN, title, edition number and copyright year. Figure 24.6 contains the data from the Titles table.

Column	Description
ISBN	ISBN of the book (a string). The table's primary key. ISBN is an abbreviation for "International Standard Book Number"—a numbering scheme that publishers use to give every book a unique identification number.
Title	Title of the book (a string).
EditionNumber	Edition number of the book (an integer).
Copyright	Copyright year of the book (a string).

Fig. 24.5 | Titles table from the books database.

ISBN	Title	EditionNumber	Copyright
0132151006	Internet & World Wide Web How to Program	5	2012
0133807800	Java How to Program	10	2015
0132575655	Java How to Program, Late Objects Version	10	2015
013299044X	C How to Program	7	2013
0132990601	Simply Visual Basic 2010	4	2013
0133406954	Visual Basic 2012 How to Program	6	2014
0133379337	Visual C# 2012 How to Program	5	2014
0136151574	Visual C++ 2008 How to Program	2	2008
0133378713	C++ How to Program	9	2014
0133570924	Android How to Program	2	2015
0133570924	Android for Programmers: An App-Driven Approach, Volume 1	2	2014
0132121360	Android for Programmers: An App-Driven Approach	1	2012

Fig. 24.6 | Sample data from the `Titles` table of the `books` database .

`AuthorISBN` *Table*

The `AuthorISBN` table (described in Fig. 24.7) consists of two columns that maintain ISBNs for each book and their corresponding authors' ID numbers. This table associates authors with their books. The `AuthorID` column is a **foreign key**—a column in this table that matches the primary-key column in another table (that is, `AuthorID` in the `Authors` table). The `ISBN` column is also a foreign key—it matches the primary-key column (that is, `ISBN`) in the `Titles` table. A database might consist of many tables. A goal when designing a database is to *minimize* the amount of *duplicated* data among the database's tables. Foreign keys, which are specified when a database table is created in the database, link the data in *multiple* tables. Together the `AuthorID` and `ISBN` columns in this table form a *composite primary key*. Every row in this table *uniquely* matches *one* author to *one* book's ISBN. Figure 24.8 contains the data from the `AuthorISBN` table of the `books` database. [*Note:* To save space, we split the table into two columns, each containing the `AuthorID` and `ISBN` columns.]

Column	Description
`AuthorID`	The author's ID number, a foreign key to the `Authors` table.
`ISBN`	The ISBN for a book, a foreign key to the `Titles` table.

Fig. 24.7 | `AuthorISBN` table from the `books` database.

Every foreign-key value must appear as another table's primary-key value so the DBMS can ensure that the foreign key value is valid—this is known as the **Rule of Referential Integrity**. For example, the DBMS ensures that the `AuthorID` value for a particular

AuthorID	ISBN	AuthorID	ISBN
1	0132151006	2	0133379337
2	0132151006	1	0136151574
3	0132151006	2	0136151574
1	0133807800	4	0136151574
2	0133807800	1	0133378713
1	0132575655	2	0133378713
2	0132575655	1	0133764036
1	013299044X	2	0133764036
2	013299044X	3	0133764036
1	0132990601	1	0133570924
2	0132990601	2	0133570924
3	0132990601	3	0133570924
1	0133406954	1	0132121360
2	0133406954	2	0132121360
3	0133406954	3	0132121360
1	0133379337	5	0132121360

Fig. 24.8 | Sample data from the `AuthorISBN` table of `books`.

row of the `AuthorISBN` table is valid by checking that there is a row in the `Authors` table with that `AuthorID` as the primary key.

Foreign keys also allow *related* data in *multiple* tables to be *selected* from those tables—this is known as **joining** the data. There is a **one-to-many relationship** between a primary key and a corresponding foreign key (for example, one author can write many books and one book can be written by many authors). This means that a foreign key can appear *many* times in its own table but only *once* (as the primary key) in another table. For example, the `ISBN 0132151006` can appear in several rows of `AuthorISBN` (because this book has several authors) but only once in `Titles`, where `ISBN` is the primary key.

Entity-Relationship (ER) Diagram

There's a one-to-many relationship between a primary key and a corresponding foreign key (e.g., one author can write many books). A foreign key can appear many times in its own table, but only once (as the primary key) in another table. Figure 24.9 is an **entity-relationship (ER) diagram** for the `books` database. This diagram shows the *database tables* and the *relationships* among them. The first compartment in each box contains the table's name, and the remaining compartments contain the table's columns. The names in italic are primary keys. *A table's primary key uniquely identifies each row in the table.* Every row must have a primary-key value, and that value must be unique in the table. This is known as the **Rule of Entity Integrity**. Again, for the `AuthorISBN` table, the primary key is the combination of both columns—this is known as a composite primary key.

The lines connecting the tables represent the *relationships* among the tables. Consider the line between the `Authors` and `AuthorISBN` tables. On the `Authors` end, there's a `1`, and

Fig. 24.9 | Table relationships in the books database.

on the AuthorISBN end, an infinity symbol (∞). This indicates a *one-to-many relationship*—for *each* author in the Authors table, there can be an *arbitrary number* of ISBNs for books written by that author in the AuthorISBN table (that is, an author can write *any* number of books). The relationship line links the AuthorID column in the Authors table (where AuthorID is the primary key) to the AuthorID column in the AuthorISBN table (where AuthorID is a foreign key)—the line between the tables links the primary key to the matching foreign key.

The line between the Titles and AuthorISBN tables illustrates a *one-to-many relationship*—one book can be written by many authors. Note that the line between the tables links the primary key ISBN in table Titles to the corresponding foreign key in table AuthorISBN. The relationships in Fig. 24.9 illustrate that the sole purpose of the AuthorISBN table is to provide a **many-to-many relationship** between the Authors and Titles tables—an author can write *many* books, and a book can have *many* authors.

24.4 SQL

We now discuss SQL in the context of our books database. You'll be able to use the SQL discussed here in the examples later in the chapter. The next several subsections demonstrate SQL queries and statements using the SQL keywords in Fig. 24.10. Other SQL keywords are beyond this text's scope.

SQL keyword	Description
SELECT	Retrieves data from one or more tables.
FROM	Tables involved in the query. Required in every SELECT.
WHERE	Criteria for selection that determine the rows to be retrieved, deleted or updated. Optional in a SQL statement.
GROUP BY	Criteria for grouping rows. Optional in a SELECT query.
ORDER BY	Criteria for ordering rows. Optional in a SELECT query.
INNER JOIN	Merge rows from multiple tables.
INSERT	Insert rows into a specified table.
UPDATE	Update rows in a specified table.
DELETE	Delete rows from a specified table.

Fig. 24.10 | SQL query keywords.

24.4.1 Basic SELECT Query

Let's consider several SQL queries that extract information from database `books`. A SQL query "selects" rows and columns from one or more tables in a database. Such selections are performed by queries with the **SELECT** keyword. The basic form of a `SELECT` query is

```
SELECT * FROM tableName
```

in which the **asterisk** (*) *wildcard character* indicates that all columns from the *tableName* table should be retrieved. For example, to retrieve all the data in the `Authors` table, use

```
SELECT * FROM Authors
```

Most programs do not require all the data in a table. To retrieve only specific columns, replace the * with a comma-separated list of column names. For example, to retrieve only the columns `AuthorID` and `LastName` for all rows in the `Authors` table, use the query

```
SELECT AuthorID, LastName FROM Authors
```

This query returns the data listed in Fig. 24.11.

AuthorID	LastName	AuthorID	LastName
1	Deitel	4	Quirk
2	Deitel	5	Morgano
3	Deitel		

Fig. 24.11 | Sample `AuthorID` and `LastName` data from the `Authors` table.

Software Engineering Observation 24.2

In general, you process results by knowing in advance the column order—for example, selecting `AuthorID` and `LastName` from `Authors` ensures that the columns will appear in the result in that exact order. Selecting columns by name avoids returning unneeded columns and protects against changes in the actual database column order. Programs can then process result columns by specifying the column number in the result (starting from number 1 for the first column).

Common Programming Error 24.1

If you assume that the columns are always returned in the same order from a query that uses the asterisk (*), the program may process the results incorrectly. If the column order in the table(s) changes or if additional columns are added at a later time, the order of the columns in the result will change accordingly.

24.4.2 WHERE Clause

In most cases, it's necessary to locate rows in a database that satisfy certain **selection criteria**. Only rows that satisfy the selection criteria (formally called **predicates**) are selected. SQL uses the optional **WHERE clause** in a query to specify the selection criteria for the query. The basic form of a query with selection criteria is

```
SELECT columnName1, columnName2, … FROM tableName WHERE criteria
```

For example, to select the `Title`, `EditionNumber` and `Copyright` columns from table `Titles` for which the `Copyright` date is greater than `2013`, use the query

```
SELECT Title, EditionNumber, Copyright
   FROM Titles
   WHERE Copyright > '2013'
```

Strings in SQL are delimited by single (`'`) rather than double (`"`) quotes. Figure 24.12 shows the result of the preceding query.

Title	EditionNumber	Copyright
Java How to Program	10	2015
Java How to Program, Late Objects Version	10	2015
Visual Basic 2012 How to Program	6	2014
Visual C# 2012 How to Program	5	2014
C++ How to Program	9	2014
Android How to Program	2	2015
Android for Programmers: An App-Driven Approach, Volume 1	2	2014

Fig. 24.12 | Sampling of titles with copyrights after 2013 from table `Titles`.

Pattern Matching: Zero or More Characters

The `WHERE` clause criteria can contain the operators `<`, `>`, `<=`, `>=`, `=`, `<>` (not equal) and `LIKE`. Operator **`LIKE`** is used for **pattern matching** with wildcard characters **percent** (**`%`**) and **underscore** (**`_`**). Pattern matching allows SQL to search for strings that match a given pattern.

A pattern that contains a percent character (`%`) searches for strings that have zero or more characters at the percent character's position in the pattern. For example, the next query locates the rows of all the authors whose last name starts with the letter `D`:

```
SELECT AuthorID, FirstName, LastName
   FROM Authors
   WHERE LastName LIKE 'D%'
```

This query selects the two rows shown in Fig. 24.13—three of the five authors have a last name starting with the letter `D` (followed by zero or more characters). The `%` symbol in the `WHERE` clause's `LIKE` pattern indicates that any number of characters can appear after the letter `D` in the `LastName`. The pattern string is surrounded by single-quote characters.

AuthorID	FirstName	LastName
1	Paul	Deitel
2	Harvey	Deitel
3	Abbey	Deitel

Fig. 24.13 | Authors whose last name starts with `D` from the `Authors` table.

Portability Tip 24.1

See the documentation for your database system to determine whether SQL is case sensitive on your system and to determine the syntax for SQL keywords, such as the `LIKE` operator.

Pattern Matching: Any Character

An underscore (_) in the pattern string indicates a single wildcard character at that position in the pattern. For example, the following query locates the rows of all the authors whose last names start with any character (specified by _), followed by the letter o, followed by any number of additional characters (specified by %):

```
SELECT AuthorID, FirstName, LastName
   FROM Authors
   WHERE LastName LIKE '_o%'
```

The preceding query produces the row shown in Fig. 24.14, because only one author in our database has a last name that contains the letter o as its second letter.

AuthorID	FirstName	LastName
5	Michael	Morgano

Fig. 24.14 | The only author from the `Authors` table whose last name contains o as the second letter.

24.4.3 ORDER BY Clause

The rows in the result of a query can be sorted into ascending or descending order by using the optional **ORDER BY clause**. The basic form of a query with an `ORDER BY` clause is

```
SELECT columnName1, columnName2, ... FROM tableName ORDER BY column ASC
SELECT columnName1, columnName2, ... FROM tableName ORDER BY column DESC
```

where `ASC` specifies ascending order (lowest to highest), `DESC` specifies descending order (highest to lowest) and *column* specifies the column on which the sort is based. For example, to obtain the list of authors in ascending order by last name (Fig. 24.15), use the query

```
SELECT AuthorID, FirstName, LastName
   FROM Authors
   ORDER BY LastName ASC
```

AuthorID	FirstName	LastName
1	Paul	Deitel
2	Harvey	Deitel
3	Abbey	Deitel
5	Michael	Morgano
4	Dan	Quirk

Fig. 24.15 | Sample data from table `Authors` in ascending order by `LastName`.

Sorting in Descending Order

The default sorting order is ascending, so ASC is optional. To obtain the same list of authors in descending order by last name (Fig. 24.16), use the query

```
SELECT AuthorID, FirstName, LastName
   FROM Authors
   ORDER BY LastName DESC
```

AuthorID	FirstName	LastName
4	Dan	Quirk
5	Michael	Morgano
1	Paul	Deitel
2	Harvey	Deitel
3	Abbey	Deitel

Fig. 24.16 | Sample data from table Authors in descending order by LastName.

Sorting By Multiple Columns

Multiple columns can be used for sorting with an ORDER BY clause of the form

```
ORDER BY column1 sortingOrder, column2 sortingOrder, ...
```

where *sortingOrder* is either ASC or DESC. The *sortingOrder* does not have to be identical for each column. The query

```
SELECT AuthorID, FirstName, LastName
   FROM Authors
   ORDER BY LastName, FirstName
```

sorts all the rows in ascending order by last name, then by first name. If any rows have the same last-name value, they're returned sorted by first name (Fig. 24.17).

AuthorID	FirstName	LastName
3	Abbey	Deitel
2	Harvey	Deitel
1	Paul	Deitel
5	Michael	Morgano
4	Dan	Quirk

Fig. 24.17 | Sample data from Authors in ascending order by LastName and FirstName.

Combining the WHERE and ORDER BY Clauses

The WHERE and ORDER BY clauses can be combined in one query, as in

```
SELECT ISBN, Title, EditionNumber, Copyright
   FROM Titles
   WHERE Title LIKE '%How to Program'
   ORDER BY Title ASC
```

which returns the `ISBN`, `Title`, `EditionNumber` and `Copyright` of each book in the `Titles` table that has a `Title` ending with `"How to Program"` and sorts them in ascending order by `Title`. The query results are shown in Fig. 24.18.

ISBN	Title	EditionNumber	Copyright
0133764036	Android How to Program	2	2015
013299044X	C How to Program	7	2013
0133378713	C++ How to Program	9	2014
0132151006	Internet & World Wide Web How to Program	5	2012
0133807800	Java How to Program	10	2015
0133406954	Visual Basic 2012 How to Program	6	2014
0133379337	Visual C# 2012 How to Program	5	2014
0136151574	Visual C++ 2008 How to Program	2	2008

Fig. 24.18 | Sampling of books from table `Titles` whose titles end with `How to Program` in ascending order by `Title`.

24.4.4 Merging Data from Multiple Tables: INNER JOIN

Database designers often split related data into separate tables to ensure that a database does not store data redundantly. For example, in the `books` database, the `AuthorISB` table stores the relationship data between authors and their corresponding titles. If we did not separate this information into individual tables, we'd need to include author information with each entry in the `Titles` table. This would result in the database's storing *duplicate* author information for authors who wrote multiple books. Often, it's necessary to merge data from multiple tables into a single result. Referred to as joining the tables, this is specified by an **`INNER JOIN`** operator, which merges rows from two tables by matching values in columns that are common to the tables. The basic form of an `INNER JOIN` is:

```
SELECT columnName1, columnName2, ...
FROM table1
INNER JOIN table2
   ON table1.columnName = table2.columnName
```

The **`ON` clause** of the `INNER JOIN` specifies the columns from each table that are compared to determine which rows are merged—one is a primary key and the other is a foreign key in the tables being joined. For example, the following query produces a list of authors accompanied by the ISBNs for books written by each author:

```
SELECT FirstName, LastName, ISBN
FROM Authors
INNER JOIN AuthorISBN
   ON Authors.AuthorID = AuthorISBN.AuthorID
ORDER BY LastName, FirstName
```

The query merges the `FirstName` and `LastName` columns from table `Authors` with the `ISBN` column from table `AuthorISBN`, sorting the results in ascending order by `LastName` and FirstName. Note the use of the syntax *tableName*.*columnName* in the ON clause. This syntax, called a **qualified name**, specifies the columns from each table that should be compared to join the tables. The "*tableName*." syntax is required if the columns have the same name in both tables. The same syntax can be used in any SQL statement to distinguish columns in different tables that have the same name. In some systems, table names qualified with the database name can be used to perform cross-database queries. As always, the query can contain an ORDER BY clause. Figure 24.19 shows the results of the preceding query, ordered by LastName and FirstName.

Common Programming Error 24.2

Failure to qualify names for columns that have the same name in two or more tables is an error. In such cases, the statement must precede those column names with their table names and a dot (e.g., Authors.AuthorID*).*

FirstName	LastName	ISBN	FirstName	LastName	ISBN
Abbey	Deitel	0132121360	Harvey	Deitel	013299044X
Abbey	Deitel	0133570924	Harvey	Deitel	0132575655
Abbey	Deitel	0133764036	Paul	Deitel	0133406954
Abbey	Deitel	0133406954	Paul	Deitel	0132990601
Abbey	Deitel	0132990601	Paul	Deitel	0132121360
Abbey	Deitel	0132151006	Paul	Deitel	0133570924
Harvey	Deitel	0132121360	Paul	Deitel	0133764036
Harvey	Deitel	0133570924	Paul	Deitel	0133378713
Harvey	Deitel	0133807800	Paul	Deitel	0136151574
Harvey	Deitel	0132151006	Paul	Deitel	0133379337
Harvey	Deitel	0133764036	Paul	Deitel	013299044X
Harvey	Deitel	0133378713	Paul	Deitel	0132575655
Harvey	Deitel	0136151574	Paul	Deitel	0133807800
Harvey	Deitel	0133379337	Paul	Deitel	0132151006
Harvey	Deitel	0133406954	Michael	Morgano	0132121360
Harvey	Deitel	0132990601	Dan	Quirk	0136151574

Fig. 24.19 | Sampling of authors and ISBNs for the books they have written in ascending order by LastName and FirstName.

24.4.5 INSERT Statement

The **INSERT** statement inserts a row into a table. The basic form of this statement is

```
INSERT INTO tableName (columnName1, columnName2, ..., columnNameN)
   VALUES (value1, value2, ..., valueN)
```

where *tableName* is the table in which to insert the row. The *tableName* is followed by a comma-separated list of column names in parentheses (this list is not required if the INSERT operation specifies a value for every column of the table in the correct order). The list of column names is followed by the SQL keyword **VALUES** and a comma-separated list of values in parentheses. The values specified here must match the columns specified after the table name in both order and type (e.g., if *columnName1* is supposed to be the `FirstName` column, then *value1* should be a string in single quotes representing the first name). Always explicitly list the columns when inserting rows. If the table's column order changes or a new column is added, using only `VALUES` may cause an error. The `INSERT` statement

```
INSERT INTO Authors (FirstName, LastName)
   VALUES ('Sue', 'Red')
```

inserts a row into the `Authors` table. The statement indicates that values are provided for the `FirstName` and `LastName` columns. The corresponding values are `'Sue'` and `'Smith'`. We do not specify an `AuthorID` in this example because `AuthorID` is an autoincremented column in the `Authors` table. For every row added to this table, the DBMS assigns a unique `AuthorID` value that is the next value in the autoincremented sequence (i.e., 1, 2, 3 and so on). In this case, Sue Red would be assigned `AuthorID` number 6. Figure 24.20 shows the `Authors` table after the `INSERT` operation. [*Note:* Not every database management system supports autoincremented columns. Check the documentation for your DBMS for alternatives to autoincremented columns.]

Common Programming Error 24.3

SQL delimits strings with single quotes ('). A string containing a single quote (e.g., O'Malley) must have two single quotes in the position where the single quote appears (e.g., `'O''Malley'`*). The first acts as an escape character for the second. Not escaping single-quote characters in a string that's part of a SQL statement is a SQL syntax error.*

Common Programming Error 24.4

It's normally an error to specify a value for an autoincrement column.

AuthorID	FirstName	LastName
1	Paul	Deitel
2	Harvey	Deitel
3	Abbey	Deitel
4	Dan	Quirk
5	Michael	Morgano
6	Sue	Red

Fig. 24.20 | Sample data from table `Authors` after an `INSERT` operation.

24.4.6 UPDATE Statement

An **UPDATE** statement modifies data in a table. Its basic form is

```
UPDATE tableName
   SET columnName1 = value1, columnName2 = value2, …, columnNameN = valueN
   WHERE criteria
```

where *tableName* is the table to update. The *tableName* is followed by keyword **SET** and a comma-separated list of *columnName* = *value* pairs. The optional WHERE clause provides criteria that determine which rows to update. Though not required, the WHERE clause is typically used, unless a change is to be made to every row. The UPDATE statement

```
UPDATE Authors
   SET LastName = 'Black'
   WHERE LastName = 'Red' AND FirstName = 'Sue'
```

updates a row in the Authors table. The statement indicates that LastName will be assigned the value Black for the row where LastName is Red and FirstName is Sue. [*Note:* If there are multiple matching rows, this statement will modify *all* such rows to have the last name "Black."] If we know the AuthorID in advance of the UPDATE operation (possibly because we searched for it previously), the WHERE clause can be simplified as follows:

```
WHERE AuthorID = 6
```

Figure 24.21 shows the Authors table after the UPDATE operation has taken place.

AuthorID	FirstName	LastName
1	Paul	Deitel
2	Harvey	Deitel
3	Abbey	Deitel
4	Dan	Quirk
5	Michael	Morgano
6	Sue	Black

Fig. 24.21 | Sample data from table Authors after an UPDATE operation.

24.4.7 DELETE Statement

A SQL **DELETE** statement removes rows from a table. Its basic form is

```
DELETE FROM tableName WHERE criteria
```

where *tableName* is the table from which to delete. The optional WHERE clause specifies the criteria used to determine which rows to delete. If this clause is omitted, all the table's rows are deleted. The DELETE statement

```
DELETE FROM Authors
   WHERE LastName = 'Black' AND FirstName = 'Sue'
```

deletes the row for Sue Black in the Authors table. If we know the AuthorID in advance of the DELETE operation, the WHERE clause can be simplified as follows:

```
WHERE AuthorID = 6
```

Figure 24.22 shows the Authors table after the DELETE operation has taken place.

AuthorID	FirstName	LastName
1	Paul	Deitel
2	Harvey	Deitel
3	Abbey	Deitel
4	Dan	Quirk
5	Michael	Morgano

Fig. 24.22 | Sample data from table `Authors` after a `DELETE` operation.

24.5 Setting Up a Java DB Database[1]

This chapter's examples use the pure Java database **Java DB**, which is installed with Oracle's JDK on Windows, macOS and Linux. Before you can execute this chapter's applications, you must set up in Java DB the `books` database that's used in Sections 24.6–24.8 and the `addressbook` database that's used in Section 24.9.

For this chapter, you'll be using the embedded version of Java DB. This means that the database you manipulate in each example must be located in that example's folder. This chapter's examples are located in two subfolders of the `ch24` examples folder—`books_examples` and `addressbook_example`. Java DB may also act as a server that can receive database requests over a network, but that is beyond this chapter's scope.

JDK Installation Folders

The Java DB software is located in the `db` subdirectory of your JDK's installation directory. The directories listed below are for Oracle's JDK 8 update 112:

- 32-bit JDK on Windows: `C:\Program Files (x86)\Java\jdk1.8.0_112`
- 64-bit JDK on Windows: `C:\Program Files\Java\jdk1.8.0_112`
- macOS:
  `/Library/Java/JavaVirtualMachines/jdk1.8.0_112.jdk/Contents/Home`
- Ubuntu Linux: `/usr/lib/jvm/java-8-oracle`

For Linux, the install location depends on the installer you use and possibly the version of Linux that you use. We used Ubuntu Linux for testing purposes.

Depending on your platform, the JDK installation folder's name might differ if you're using a different JDK version. In the following instructions, you should update the JDK installation folder's name based on the JDK version you're using.

Java DB Configuration

Java DB comes with several files that enable you to configure and run it. Before executing these files from a command window, you must set the environment variable `JAVA_HOME` to refer to the JDK's exact installation directory listed above (or the location where you in-

1. If you're using JDK 9 with this chapter, see the note in Section 24.1 about downloading and installing Apache Derby. You'll also need to update the instructions in Section 24.5, based on Apache Derby's installation folder on your computer.

stalled the JDK if it differs from those listed above). See the Before You Begin section of this book for information on setting environment variables.

24.5.1 Creating the Chapter's Databases on Windows

After setting the `JAVA_HOME` environment variable, perform the following steps:

1. Run Notepad as an administrator. To do this on Windows 7, select **Start > All Programs > Accessories**, right click Notepad and select **Run as administrator**. On Windows 10, search for Notepad, right click it in the search results and select **Advanced** in the app bar, then select **Run as administrator**.
2. From Notepad, open the batch file `setEmbeddedCP.bat` that is located in the JDK installation folder's `db\bin` folder.
3. Locate the line

```
@rem set DERBY_INSTALL=
```

and change it to

```
@set DERBY_INSTALL=%JAVA_HOME%\db
```

Save your changes and close this file.

4. Open a Command Prompt window and change to the JDK installation folder's `db\bin` folder. Then, type `setEmbeddedCP.bat` and press *Enter* to set the environment variables required by Java DB.
5. Use the `cd` command to change to this chapter's examples folder, then to the subfolder `books_examples`. This folder contains a SQL script `books.sql` that builds the `books` database.
6. Execute the following command (with the quote marks) to start the Java DB command-line tool—the double quotes are necessary because the path that the environment variable `%JAVA_HOME%` represents contains a space.

```
"%JAVA_HOME%\db\bin\ij"
```

7. At the `ij>` prompt type the following command and press *Enter* to create the `books` database in the current directory and to create the user `deitel` with the password `deitel` for accessing the database:

```
connect 'jdbc:derby:books;create=true;user=deitel;
    password=deitel';
```

8. To create the database table and insert sample data in it, we've provided the file `books.sql` in this example's directory. To execute this SQL script, type

```
run 'books.sql';
```

Once you create the database, you can execute the SQL statements presented in Section 24.4 to confirm their execution. Each command you enter at the `ij>` prompt must be terminated with a semicolon (;).

9. Change directories to the `addressbook_example` subfolder of the `ch24` examples folder, which contains the SQL script `addressbook.sql` that builds the `addressbook` database. Repeat *Steps 6–9*. In each step, replace `books` with `addressbook`.

10. To terminate the Java DB command-line tool, type

```
exit;
```

You're now ready to execute this chapter's examples.

24.5.2 Creating the Chapter's Databases on macOS

After setting the `JAVA_HOME` environment variable, perform the following steps:

1. Open a Terminal, then type:

   ```
   DERBY_HOME=/Library/Java/JavaVirtualMachines/jdk1.8.0_112/
       Contents/Home/db
   ```

   and press *Enter*. Then type

   ```
   export DERBY_HOME
   ```

   and press *Enter*. This specifies where Java DB is located on your Mac.
2. In the Terminal window, change directories to the JDK installation folder's `db/bin` folder. Then, type `./setEmbeddedCP` and press *Enter* to set the environment variables required by Java DB.
3. In the Terminal window, use the `cd` command to change to the `books_examples` directory. This directory contains a SQL script `books.sql` that builds the `books` database.
4. Execute the following command to start the command-line tool for interacting with Java DB:

   ```
   $JAVA_HOME/db/bin/ij
   ```

5. Perform *Steps 7–9* of Section 24.5.1 to create the `books` database.

You're now ready to execute this chapter's examples.

24.5.3 Creating the Chapter's Databases on Linux

After setting the `JAVA_HOME` environment variable, perform the following steps:

1. Open a shell window.
2. Perform the steps in Section 24.5.2, but in *Step 1*, set `DERBY_HOME` to

   `DERBY_HOME=`*YourLinuxJDKInstallationFolder*`/db`

   On our Ubuntu Linux system, this was:

   ```
   DERBY_HOME=/usr/lib/jvm/java-7-oracle/db
   ```

You're now ready to execute this chapter's examples.

24.6 Connecting to and Querying a Database

The example of Fig. 24.23 performs a simple query on the `books` database that retrieves the entire `Authors` table and displays the data. The program illustrates connecting to the database, querying the database and processing the result. The discussion that follows presents the key JDBC aspects of the program.

```
// Fig. 24.23: DisplayAuthors.java
// Displaying the contents of the Authors table.
import java.sql.Connection;
import java.sql.Statement;
import java.sql.DriverManager;
import java.sql.ResultSet;
import java.sql.ResultSetMetaData;
import java.sql.SQLException;

public class DisplayAuthors {
   public static void main(String args[]) {
      final String DATABASE_URL = "jdbc:derby:books";
      final String SELECT_QUERY =
         "SELECT authorID, firstName, lastName FROM authors";

      // use try-with-resources to connect to and query the database
      try (
         Connection connection = DriverManager.getConnection(
            DATABASE_URL, "deitel", "deitel");
         Statement statement = connection.createStatement();
         ResultSet resultSet = statement.executeQuery(SELECT_QUERY)) {

         // get ResultSet's meta data
         ResultSetMetaData metaData = resultSet.getMetaData();
         int numberOfColumns = metaData.getColumnCount();

         System.out.printf("Authors Table of Books Database:%n%n");

         // display the names of the columns in the ResultSet
         for (int i = 1; i <= numberOfColumns; i++) {
            System.out.printf("%-8s\t", metaData.getColumnName(i));
         }
         System.out.println();

         // display query results
         while (resultSet.next()) {
            for (int i = 1; i <= numberOfColumns; i++) {
               System.out.printf("%-8s\t", resultSet.getObject(i));
            }
            System.out.println();
         }
      }
      catch (SQLException sqlException) {
         sqlException.printStackTrace();
      }
   }
}
```

Fig. 24.23 | Displaying the contents of the Authors table. (Part 1 of 2.)

```
Authors Table of Books Database:

AUTHORID            FIRSTNAME           LASTNAME
1                   Paul                Deitel
2                   Harvey              Deitel
3                   Abbey               Deitel
4                   Dan                 Quirk
5                   Michael             Morgano
```

Fig. 24.23 | Displaying the contents of the Authors table. (Part 2 of 2.)

Lines 3–8 import the JDBC interfaces and classes from package `java.sql` used in this program. Method `main` connects to the `books` database, queries the database, displays the query result and closes the database connection. Line 12 declares a `String` constant for the database URL. This identifies the name of the database to connect to, as well as information about the protocol used by the JDBC driver (discussed shortly). Lines 13–14 declare a `String` constant representing the SQL query that will select the `authorID`, `firstName` and `lastName` columns from the database's `authors` table.

24.6.1 Automatic Driver Discovery

JDBC supports **automatic driver discovery**—it loads the database driver into memory for you. To ensure that the program can locate the driver class, you must include the class's location in the program's classpath when you execute the program. You did this for Java DB in Section 24.5 when you executed the `setEmbeddedCP.bat` or `setEmbeddedCP` file on your system—that step configured a `CLASSPATH` environment variable in the command window for your platform. After doing so, you can run this application simply using the command

```
java DisplayAuthors
```

24.6.2 Connecting to the Database

The JDBC interfaces we use in this example extend the `AutoCloseable` interface, so you can use objects that implement these interfaces with the `try`-with-resources statement (lines 17–45). Lines 18–21 create this example's `AutoCloseable` objects, which are closed when the `try` block terminates (line 42) or if an exception occurs during the `try` block's execution. Each object created in the parentheses following keyword `try` must be separated from the next by a semicolon (;).

Lines 18–19 create a **`Connection`** object that manages the connection between the Java program and the database. `Connection` objects enable programs to create SQL statements that manipulate databases. The program initializes `connection` with the result of a call to the **`DriverManager`** class's `static` method **`getConnection`**. The method's arguments are:

- a `String` that specifies the database URL,
- a `String` that specifies the username, and
- a `String` that specifies the password.

This method attempts to connect to the database specified by its URL argument—if it cannot, it throws a **`SQLException`** (package `java.sql`). The username and password for the `books` database were set in Section 24.5 when you created the database. If you used a different username and password there, you'll need to replace the username (second argument) and password (third argument) passed to method `getConnection` in lines 18–19.

The URL locates the database. In this chapter's examples, the database is on the local computer, but it could reside on a network. The URL `jdbc:derby:books` specifies:

- the protocol for communication (`jdbc`),
- the **subprotocol** for communication (`derby`), and
- the database name (`books`).

The subprotocol `derby` indicates that the program uses a Java DB/Apache Derby-specific subprotocol to connect to the database—recall that Java DB is simply the Oracle branded version of Apache Derby. Figure 24.24 lists the JDBC driver names and database URL formats of several popular RDBMSs.

Software Engineering Observation 24.3

Most database management systems require the user to log in before accessing the database contents. `DriverManager` *method* `getConnection` *is overloaded with versions that enable the program to supply the username and password to gain access.*

RDBMS	Database URL format
MySQL	`jdbc:mysql://`*hostname*`:`*portNumber*`/`*databaseName*
ORACLE	`jdbc:oracle:thin:@`*hostname*`:`*portNumber*`:`*databaseName*
DB2	`jdbc:db2:`*hostname*`:`*portNumber*`/`*databaseName*
PostgreSQL	`jdbc:postgresql://`*hostname*`:`*portNumber*`/`*databaseName*
Java DB/Apache Derby	`jdbc:derby:`*dataBaseName* (embedded; used in this chapter) `jdbc:derby://`*hostname*`:`*portNumber*`/`*databaseName* (network)
Microsoft SQL Server	`jdbc:sqlserver://`*hostname*`:`*portNumber*`;databaseName=`*dataBaseName*
Sybase	`jdbc:sybase:Tds:`*hostname*`:`*portNumber*`/`*databaseName*

Fig. 24.24 | Popular JDBC database URL formats.

24.6.3 Creating a `Statement` for Executing Queries

Line 20 of Fig. 24.23 invokes `Connection` method **`createStatement`** to obtain an object that implements interface `Statement` (package `java.sql`). You use a **`Statement`** object to submit SQL statements to the database.

24.6.4 Executing a Query

Line 21 uses the `Statement` object's **`executeQuery`** method to submit a query that selects all the author information from the `Authors` table. This method returns an object that implements interface **`ResultSet`** and contains the query results.

24.6.5 Processing a Query's ResultSet

Lines 24–41 process the ResultSet. Line 24 obtains the ResultSet's **ResultSetMetaData** object (package java.sql). The **metadata** describes the ResultSet's contents. Programs can use metadata programmatically to obtain information about the ResultSet's column names and types. Line 25 uses ResultSetMetaData method **getColumnCount** to retrieve the number of columns in the ResultSet. Lines 30–32 display the column names.

Software Engineering Observation 24.4

Metadata enables programs to process ResultSet contents dynamically when detailed information about the ResultSet is not known in advance.

Lines 36–41 display the data in each ResultSet row. First, the program positions the ResultSet cursor (which points to the row being processed) to the first row. Method **next** (line 36) returns boolean value true if it's able to position to the next row; otherwise, the method returns false to indicate that the end of the ResultSet has been reached.

Common Programming Error 24.5

Initially, a ResultSet cursor is positioned before the first row. A SQLException occurs if you attempt to access a ResultSet's contents before positioning the ResultSet cursor to the first row with method next.

If the ResultSet has rows, lines 37–39 extract and display the contents of each column in the current row. Each column can be extracted as a specific Java type—ResultSetMetaData method **getColumnType** returns a constant integer from class **Types** (package java.sql) indicating a given column's type. Programs can use these values in a switch statement to invoke ResultSet methods that return the column values as appropriate Java types. For example, if the a column's type is Types.INTEGER, ResultSet method **getInt** gets the column value as an int. For simplicity, this example treats each value as an Object. We retrieve each column value with ResultSet method **getObject** (line 38), then display the Object's String representation. ResultSet *get* methods typically receive as an argument either a column number (as an int) or a column name (as a String) indicating which column's value to obtain. Unlike array indices, ResultSet *column numbers start at 1.*

Common Programming Error 24.6

Specifying column index 0 when obtaining values from a ResultSet causes a SQLException—the first column index in a ResultSet is always 1.

Performance Tip 24.1

If a query specifies the exact columns to select from the database, the ResultSet contains the columns in the specified order. For this scenario, using the column number to obtain the column's value is more efficient than using the column name. The column number provides direct access to the specified column. Using the column name requires a search of the column names to locate the appropriate column.

Error-Prevention Tip 24.1

Using column names to obtain values from a ResultSet produces code that is less error prone than obtaining values by column number—you don't need to remember the column order. Also, if the column order changes, your code does not have to change.

When the end of the try block is reached (line 42), the close method is called on the ResultSet, Statement and Connection objects that were obtained at the beginning of the try-with-resources statement.

Common Programming Error 24.7

A SQLException occurs if you attempt to manipulate a ResultSet after closing the Statement that created it. The ResultSet is discarded when the Statement is closed.

Software Engineering Observation 24.5

Each Statement object can open only one ResultSet object at a time. When a Statement returns a new ResultSet, the Statement closes the prior ResultSet. To use multiple ResultSets in parallel, separate Statement objects must return the ResultSets.

24.7 Querying the books Database

Next, we present a DisplayQueryResults app that allows you to enter a SQL query and see its results. The GUI uses a combination of JavaFX and Swing controls. We display the query results in a Swing **JTable** (package javax.swing), which can be populated dynamically from a ResultSet via a **TableModel** (package javax.swing.table). A TableModel provides methods that a JTable can call to access a ResultSet's data. Though JavaFX's TableView control provides data-binding capabilities (like those in Chapter 13), the combination of JTable and TableModel is more powerful for displaying ResultSet data.

24.7.1 ResultSetTableModel Class

Class ResultSetTableModel (Fig. 24.25) is a TableModel that performs the connection to the database and maintains the ResultSet. The class extends class **AbstractTableModel** (package javax.swing.table), which implements interface TableModel. ResultSetTableModel overrides TableModel methods **getColumnClass**, **getColumnCount**, **getColumnName**, **getRowCount** and **getValueAt**, based on the current ResultSet. The default implementations of TableModel methods isCellEditable and setValueAt (provided by AbstractTableModel) are not overridden, because this example does not support editing the JTable cells. The default implementations of TableModel methods **addTableModelListener** and **removeTableModelListener** (provided by AbstractTableModel) are not overridden, because the AbstractTableModel implementations of these methods properly add and remove listeners for the events that occur when a TableModel changes.

```
// Fig. 24.25: ResultSetTableModel.java
// A TableModel that supplies ResultSet data to a JTable.
import java.sql.Connection;
import java.sql.Statement;
import java.sql.DriverManager;
import java.sql.ResultSet;
import java.sql.ResultSetMetaData;
import java.sql.SQLException;
import javax.swing.table.AbstractTableModel;

```

Fig. 24.25 | A TableModel that supplies ResultSet data to a JTable. (Part 1 of 5.)

```
// ResultSet rows and columns are counted from 1 and JTable
// rows and columns are counted from 0. When processing
// ResultSet rows or columns for use in a JTable, it is
// necessary to add 1 to the row or column number to manipulate
// the appropriate ResultSet column (i.e., JTable column 0 is
// ResultSet column 1 and JTable row 0 is ResultSet row 1).
public class ResultSetTableModel extends AbstractTableModel {
   private final Connection connection;
   private final Statement statement;
   private ResultSet resultSet;
   private ResultSetMetaData metaData;
   private int numberOfRows;

   // keep track of database connection status
   private boolean connectedToDatabase = false;

   // constructor initializes resultSet and obtains its metadata object;
   // determines number of rows
   public ResultSetTableModel(String url, String username,
      String password, String query) throws SQLException {
      // connect to database
      connection = DriverManager.getConnection(url, username, password);

      // create Statement to query database
      statement = connection.createStatement(
         ResultSet.TYPE_SCROLL_INSENSITIVE, ResultSet.CONCUR_READ_ONLY);

      // update database connection status
      connectedToDatabase = true;

      // set query and execute it
      setQuery(query);
   }

   // get class that represents column type
   public Class getColumnClass(int column) throws IllegalStateException {
      // ensure database connection is available
      if (!connectedToDatabase) {
         throw new IllegalStateException("Not Connected to Database");
      }

      // determine Java class of column
      try {
         String className = metaData.getColumnClassName(column + 1);

         // return Class object that represents className
         return Class.forName(className);
      }
      catch (Exception exception) {
         exception.printStackTrace();
      }

```

Fig. 24.25 | A `TableModel` that supplies `ResultSet` data to a `JTable`. (Part 2 of 5.)

```
         return Object.class; // if problems occur above, assume type Object
      }

      // get number of columns in ResultSet
      public int getColumnCount() throws IllegalStateException {
         // ensure database connection is available
         if (!connectedToDatabase) {
            throw new IllegalStateException("Not Connected to Database");
         }

         // determine number of columns
         try {
            return metaData.getColumnCount();
         }
         catch (SQLException sqlException) {
            sqlException.printStackTrace();
         }

         return 0; // if problems occur above, return 0 for number of columns
      }

      // get name of a particular column in ResultSet
      public String getColumnName(int column) throws IllegalStateException {
         // ensure database connection is available
         if (!connectedToDatabase) {
            throw new IllegalStateException("Not Connected to Database");
         }

         // determine column name
         try {
            return metaData.getColumnName(column + 1);
         }
         catch (SQLException sqlException) {
            sqlException.printStackTrace();
         }

         return ""; // if problems, return empty string for column name
      }

      // return number of rows in ResultSet
      public int getRowCount() throws IllegalStateException {
         // ensure database connection is available
         if (!connectedToDatabase) {
            throw new IllegalStateException("Not Connected to Database");
         }

         return numberOfRows;
      }

      // obtain value in particular row and column
      public Object getValueAt(int row, int column)
         throws IllegalStateException {
```

Fig. 24.25 | A TableModel that supplies ResultSet data to a JTable. (Part 3 of 5.)

```

      // ensure database connection is available
      if (!connectedToDatabase) {
         throw new IllegalStateException("Not Connected to Database");
      }

      // obtain a value at specified ResultSet row and column
      try {
         resultSet.absolute(row + 1);
         return resultSet.getObject(column + 1);
      }
      catch (SQLException sqlException) {
         sqlException.printStackTrace();
      }

      return ""; // if problems, return empty string object
   }

   // set new database query string
   public void setQuery(String query)
      throws SQLException, IllegalStateException {

      // ensure database connection is available
      if (!connectedToDatabase) {
         throw new IllegalStateException("Not Connected to Database");
      }

      // specify query and execute it
      resultSet = statement.executeQuery(query);

      // obtain metadata for ResultSet
      metaData = resultSet.getMetaData();

      // determine number of rows in ResultSet
      resultSet.last(); // move to last row
      numberOfRows = resultSet.getRow(); // get row number


      fireTableStructureChanged(); // notify JTable that model has changed
   }

   // close Statement and Connection
   public void disconnectFromDatabase() {
      if (connectedToDatabase) {
         // close Statement and Connection
         try {
            resultSet.close();
            statement.close();
            connection.close();
         }
         catch (SQLException sqlException) {
            sqlException.printStackTrace();
         }
```

Fig. 24.25 | A `TableModel` that supplies `ResultSet` data to a `JTable`. (Part 4 of 5.)

```
168          finally { // update database connection status
169             connectedToDatabase = false;
170          }
171       }
172    }
173 }
```

Fig. 24.25 | A TableModel that supplies ResultSet data to a JTable. (Part 5 of 5.)

ResultSetTableModel Constructor

The ResultSetTableModel constructor (lines 29–43) accepts four String arguments—the URL of the database, the username, the password and the default query to perform. The constructor throws any exceptions that occur back to the application that created the ResultSetTableModel object, so that the application can determine how to handle the exception (e.g., report an error and terminate the application). Line 32 establishes a connection to the database. Lines 35–36 invoke Connection method createStatement to create a Statement object. This example uses a version of createStatement that takes two arguments—the result set type and the result set concurrency. The **result set type** (Fig. 24.26) specifies whether the ResultSet's cursor is able to scroll in both directions or forward only and whether the ResultSet is sensitive to changes made to the underlying data.

Portability Tip 24.2

Some JDBC drivers do not support scrollable ResultSets. In such cases, the driver typically returns a ResultSet in which the cursor can move only forward. For more information, see your database driver documentation.

Common Programming Error 24.8

Attempting to move the cursor backward through a ResultSet when the database driver does not support backward scrolling causes a SQLFeatureNotSupportedException.

ResultSet constant	Description
TYPE_FORWARD_ONLY	Specifies that a ResultSet's cursor can move only in the forward direction (i.e., from the first to the last row in the ResultSet).
TYPE_SCROLL_INSENSITIVE	Specifies that a ResultSet's cursor can scroll in either direction and that the changes made to the underlying data during ResultSet processing are not reflected in the ResultSet unless the program queries the database again.
TYPE_SCROLL_SENSITIVE	Specifies that a ResultSet's cursor can scroll in either direction and that the changes made to the underlying data during ResultSet processing are reflected immediately in the ResultSet.

Fig. 24.26 | ResultSet constants for specifying ResultSet type.

ResultSets that are sensitive to changes reflect those changes immediately after they're made with methods of interface ResultSet. If a ResultSet is insensitive to changes, the query that produced the ResultSet must be executed again to reflect any changes made. The **result set concurrency** (Fig. 24.27) specifies whether the ResultSet can be updated with ResultSet's update methods. This example uses a ResultSet that is scrollable, insensitive to changes and read-only. Line 42 (Fig. 24.25) invokes method setQuery (lines 134–154) to perform the default query.

ResultSet static concurrency constant	Description
CONCUR_READ_ONLY	Specifies that a ResultSet can't be updated—changes to the ResultSet contents cannot be reflected in the database with ResultSet's update methods.
CONCUR_UPDATABLE	Specifies that a ResultSet can be updated (i.e., changes to its contents can be reflected in the database with ResultSet's update methods).

Fig. 24.27 | ResultSet constants for specifying result properties.

Portability Tip 24.3

Some JDBC drivers do not support updatable ResultSets. In such cases, the driver typically returns a read-only ResultSet. For more information, see your database driver documentation.

Common Programming Error 24.9

Attempting to update a ResultSet when the database driver does not support updatable ResultSets causes SQLFeatureNotSupportedExceptions.

ResultSetTableModel Method getColumnClass

Method getColumnClass (lines 46–64) returns a Class object that represents the superclass of all objects in a particular column. The JTable uses this information to configure the default cell renderer and cell editor for that column in the JTable. Line 54 uses ResultSetMetaData method **getColumnClassName** to obtain the fully qualified class name for the specified column. Line 57 loads the class and returns the corresponding Class object. If an exception occurs, the catch in lines 59–61 prints a stack trace and line 63 returns Object.class—the Class instance that represents class Object—as the default type. [*Note:* Line 54 uses the argument column + 1. Like arrays, JTable row and column numbers are counted from 0. However, ResultSet row and column numbers are counted from 1. Thus, when processing ResultSet rows or columns for use in a JTable, it's necessary to add 1 to the row or column number to manipulate the appropriate ResultSet row or column.]

ResultSetTableModel Method getColumnCount

Method getColumnCount (lines 67–82) returns the number of columns in the model's underlying ResultSet. Line 75 uses ResultSetMetaData method **getColumnCount** to obtain the number of columns in the ResultSet. If an exception occurs, the catch in lines 77–79 prints a stack trace and line 81 returns 0 as the default number of columns.

ResultSetTableModel *Method* getColumnName

Method getColumnName (lines 85–100) returns the name of the column in the model's underlying ResultSet. Line 93 uses ResultSetMetaData method **getColumnName** to obtain the column name from the ResultSet. If an exception occurs, the catch in lines 95–97 prints a stack trace and line 99 returns the empty string as the default column name.

ResultSetTableModel *Method* getRowCount

Method getRowCount (lines 103–110) returns the number of rows in the model's underlying ResultSet. When method setQuery (lines 134–154) performs a query, it stores the number of rows in variable numberOfRows.

ResultSetTableModel *Method* getValueAt

Method getValueAt (lines 113–131) returns the Object in a particular row and column of the model's underlying ResultSet. Line 123 uses ResultSet method **absolute** to position the ResultSet cursor to a specific row. Line 124 uses ResultSet method getObject to obtain the Object in a specific column of the current row. If an exception occurs, the catch in lines 126–128 prints a stack trace and line 130 returns an empty string as the default value.

ResultSetTableModel *Method* setQuery

Method setQuery (lines 134–154) executes the query it receives as an argument to obtain a new ResultSet (line 143). Line 146 gets the ResultSetMetaData for the new ResultSet. Line 149 uses ResultSet method **last** to position the ResultSet cursor at the last row in the ResultSet. [*Note:* This can be slow if the table contains many rows.] Line 150 uses ResultSet method **getRow** to obtain the row number for the current row in the ResultSet. Line 153 invokes method **fireTableStructureChanged** (inherited from class AbstractTableModel) to notify any JTable using this ResultSetTableModel object as its model that the structure of the model has changed. This causes the JTable to repopulate its rows and columns with the new ResultSet data. Method setQuery throws any exceptions that occur in its body back to the application that invoked setQuery.

ResultSetTableModel *Method* disconnectFromDatabase

Method disconnectFromDatabase (lines 157–172) implements an appropriate termination method for class ResultSetTableModel. A class designer should provide a public method that clients of the class must invoke explicitly to free resources that an object has used. In this case, method disconnectFromDatabase closes the ResultSet, Statement and Connection (lines 161–163). Clients of the ResultSetTableModel class should always invoke this method when ResultSetTableModel is no longer needed. Before the method releases resources, line 158 verifies whether the app is currently connected to the database. If not, the method returns. Method disconnectFromDatabase sets connectedToDatabase to false (line 169) to ensure that clients do not use an instance of ResultSetTableModel after that instance has already been terminated. The other methods in class ResultSetTableModel each throw an IllegalStateException if connectedToDatabase is false.

24.7.2 DisplayQueryResults App's GUI

Figure 24.28 shows the app's GUI (defined in `DisplayQueryResults.fxml`) labeled with its **fx:ids**. You've built many FXML GUIs in prior chapters, so we point out only the key elements and the event-handler methods implemented in class `DisplayQueryResultsController` (Fig. 24.29). For the complete layout details, open the file `DisplayQueryResults.fxml` in Scene Builder or view the FXML in a text editor. The GUI's primary layout is a `BorderPane` with the **fx:id** `borderPane`—we use this in the controller class to dynamically add a `SwingNode` containing the `JTable` to the `BorderPane`'s center (Section 24.7.3). The `BorderPane`'s top and bottom areas contain `GridPane`s with the app's other controls. The controller class defines two event-handling methods:

- `submitQueryButtonPressed` is called when the **Submit Query** `Button` is clicked.
- `applyFilterButtonPressed` is called when the the **Apply Filter** `Button` is clicked.

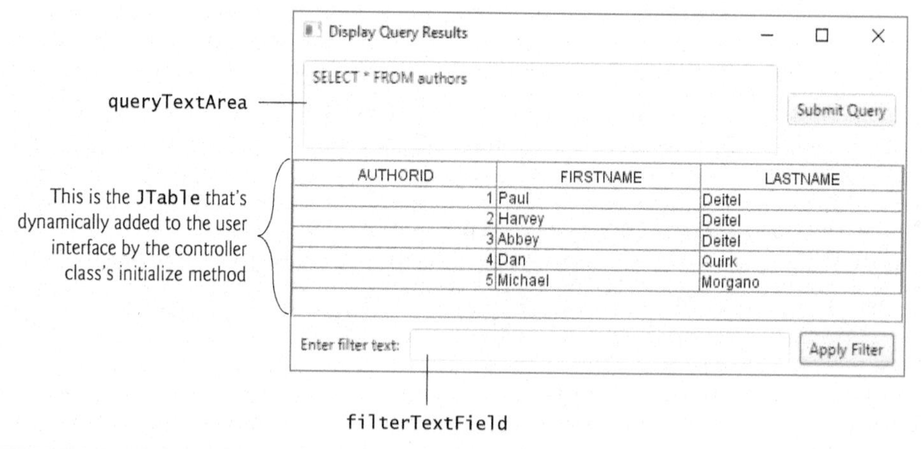

Fig. 24.28 | `DisplayQueryResults` app's GUI.

24.7.3 DisplayQueryResultsController Class

Class `DisplayQueryResultsController` (Fig. 24.29) completes the GUI, interacts with the `ResultSetTableModel` via a `JTable` object and responds to the GUI's events. We do not show the JavaFX `Application` subclass here (located in `DisplayQueryResults.java`), because it performs the same tasks you've seen previously to load the app's FXML GUI and initialize the controller.

```java
// Fig. 24.29: DisplayQueryResultsController.java
// Controller for the DisplayQueryResults app
import java.sql.SQLException;
import java.util.regex.PatternSyntaxException;

import javafx.embed.swing.SwingNode;
import javafx.event.ActionEvent;
```

Fig. 24.29 | Controller for the `DisplayQueryResults` app. (Part 1 of 4.)

```
import javafx.fxml.FXML;
import javafx.scene.control.Alert;
import javafx.scene.control.Alert.AlertType;
import javafx.scene.control.TextArea;
import javafx.scene.control.TextField;
import javafx.scene.layout.BorderPane;

import javax.swing.JScrollPane;
import javax.swing.JTable;
import javax.swing.RowFilter;
import javax.swing.table.TableModel;
import javax.swing.table.TableRowSorter;

public class DisplayQueryResultsController {
   @FXML private BorderPane borderPane;
   @FXML private TextArea queryTextArea;
   @FXML private TextField filterTextField;

   // database URL, username and password
   private static final String DATABASE_URL = "jdbc:derby:books";
   private static final String USERNAME = "deitel";
   private static final String PASSWORD = "deitel";

   // default query retrieves all data from Authors table
   private static final String DEFAULT_QUERY = "SELECT * FROM authors";

   // used for configuring JTable to display and sort data
   private ResultSetTableModel tableModel;
   private TableRowSorter<TableModel> sorter;

   public void initialize() {
      queryTextArea.setText(DEFAULT_QUERY);

      // create ResultSetTableModel and display database table
      try {
         // create TableModel for results of DEFAULT_QUERY
         tableModel = new ResultSetTableModel(DATABASE_URL,
            USERNAME, PASSWORD, DEFAULT_QUERY);

         // create JTable based on the tableModel
         JTable resultTable = new JTable(tableModel);

         // set up row sorting for JTable
         sorter = new TableRowSorter<TableModel>(tableModel);
         resultTable.setRowSorter(sorter);

         // configure SwingNode to display JTable, then add to borderPane
         SwingNode swingNode = new SwingNode();
         swingNode.setContent(new JScrollPane(resultTable));
         borderPane.setCenter(swingNode);
      }
      catch (SQLException sqlException) {
```

Fig. 24.29 | Controller for the DisplayQueryResults app. (Part 2 of 4.)

```
            displayAlert(AlertType.ERROR, "Database Error",
               sqlException.getMessage());
            tableModel.disconnectFromDatabase(); // close connection
            System.exit(1); // terminate application
         }
      }

      // query the database and display results in JTable
      @FXML
      void submitQueryButtonPressed(ActionEvent event) {
         // perform a new query
         try {
            tableModel.setQuery(queryTextArea.getText());
         }
         catch (SQLException sqlException) {
            displayAlert(AlertType.ERROR, "Database Error",
               sqlException.getMessage());

            // try to recover from invalid user query
            // by executing default query
            try {
               tableModel.setQuery(DEFAULT_QUERY);
               queryTextArea.setText(DEFAULT_QUERY);
            }
            catch (SQLException sqlException2) {
               displayAlert(AlertType.ERROR, "Database Error",
                  sqlException2.getMessage());
               tableModel.disconnectFromDatabase(); // close connection
               System.exit(1); // terminate application
            }
         }
      }

      // apply specified filter to results
      @FXML
      void applyFilterButtonPressed(ActionEvent event) {
         String text = filterTextField.getText();

         if (text.length() == 0) {
            sorter.setRowFilter(null);
         }
         else {
            try {
               sorter.setRowFilter(RowFilter.regexFilter(text));
            }
            catch (PatternSyntaxException pse) {
               displayAlert(AlertType.ERROR, "Regex Error",
                  "Bad regex pattern");
            }
         }
      }

      // display an Alert dialog
```

Fig. 24.29 | Controller for the `DisplayQueryResults` app. (Part 3 of 4.)

```
    private void displayAlert(
       AlertType type, String title, String message) {
       Alert alert = new Alert(type);
       alert.setTitle(title);
       alert.setContentText(message);
       alert.showAndWait();
    }
}
```

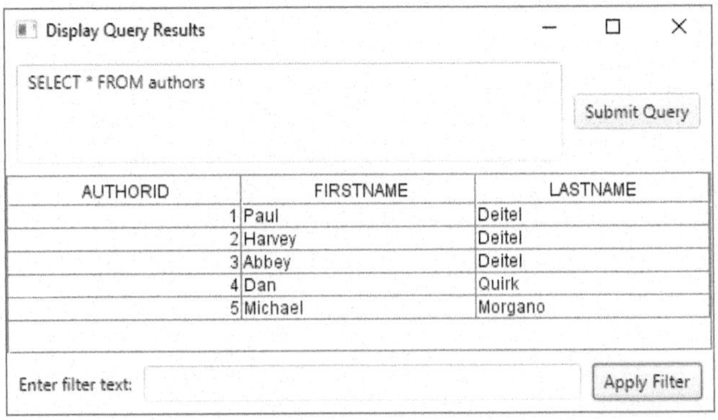

Display Query Results

SELECT * FROM authors

Submit Query

AUTHORID	FIRSTNAME	LASTNAME
1	Paul	Deitel
2	Harvey	Deitel
3	Abbey	Deitel
4	Dan	Quirk
5	Michael	Morgano

Enter filter text: Apply Filter

a) Displaying all authors from the **Authors** table.

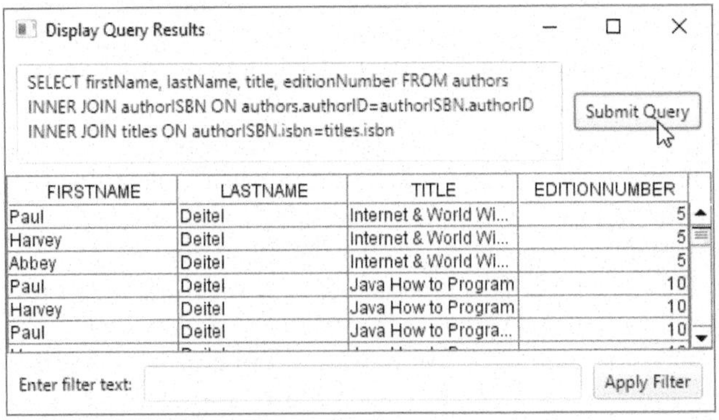

Display Query Results

SELECT firstName, lastName, title, editionNumber FROM authors
INNER JOIN authorISBN ON authors.authorID=authorISBN.authorID
INNER JOIN titles ON authorISBN.isbn=titles.isbn

Submit Query

FIRSTNAME	LASTNAME	TITLE	EDITIONNUMBER
Paul	Deitel	Internet & World Wi...	5
Harvey	Deitel	Internet & World Wi...	5
Abbey	Deitel	Internet & World Wi...	5
Paul	Deitel	Java How to Program	10
Harvey	Deitel	Java How to Program	10
Paul	Deitel	Java How to Progra...	10

Enter filter text: Apply Filter

b) Displaying the authors' first and last names joined with the titles and edition numbers of the books they've authored.

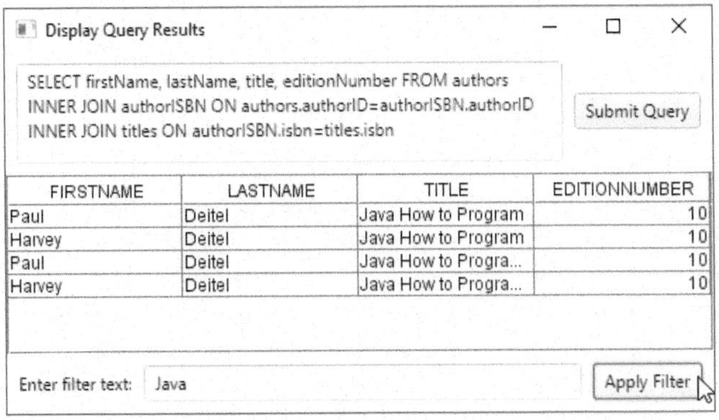

Display Query Results

SELECT firstName, lastName, title, editionNumber FROM authors
INNER JOIN authorISBN ON authors.authorID=authorISBN.authorID
INNER JOIN titles ON authorISBN.isbn=titles.isbn

Submit Query

FIRSTNAME	LASTNAME	TITLE	EDITIONNUMBER
Paul	Deitel	Java How to Program	10
Harvey	Deitel	Java How to Program	10
Paul	Deitel	Java How to Progra...	10
Harvey	Deitel	Java How to Progra...	10

Enter filter text: Java Apply Filter

c) Filtering the results of the previous query to show only the books with Java in the title.

Fig. 24.29 | Controller for the `DisplayQueryResults` app. (Part 4 of 4.)

`static` *Fields*

Lines 27–29 and 32 declare the URL, username, password and default query that are passed to the `ResultSetTableModel` constructor to make the initial connection to the database and perform the default query.

Method `initialize`

When the `FXMLLoader` calls the controller's `initialize` method, lines 44–45 create a `ResultSetTableModel` object, assign it to instance variable `tableModel` (declared at line 35) and complete the GUI. Line 48 creates the `JTable` object that will display the `ResultSetTableModel`'s `ResultSet`. Here we use the `JTable` constructor that receives a `TableModel` object. This constructor registers the `JTable` as a listener for `TableModelEvents` generated by the `ResultSetTableModel`. When such events occur—for example, when you enter a new query and press **Submit Query**—the `JTable` automatically updates itself, based on the `ResultSetTableModel`'s current `ResultSet`. If an exception occurs when the `ResultSetTableModel` attempts to perform the default query, lines 59–64 catch the exception, display an `Alert` dialog (by calling method `displayAlert` in lines 113–119), close the connection and terminate the app.

`JTable`s allow users to sort rows by the data in a specific column. Line 51 creates a **`TableRowSorter`** (from package **`javax.swing.table`**) and assigns it to instance variable `sorter` (declared at line 36). The `TableRowSorter` uses our `ResultSetTableModel` to sort rows in the `JTable`. When the user clicks a particular `JTable` column's title, the `TableRowSorter` interacts with the underlying `TableModel` to reorder the rows based on that column's data. Line 52 uses `JTable` method **`setRowSorter`** to specify the `TableRowSorter` for `resultTable`.

8 Lines 55–57 create and configure a **`SwingNode`**. This Java SE 8 class enables you to embed Swing GUI controls in JavaFX GUIs. The argument to `SwingNode` method **`setContent`** is a `JComponent`—the superclass of all Swing GUI controls. In this case, we pass a new **`JScrollPane`** object—a subclass of `JComponent`—that we initialize with the `JTable`. A `JScrollPane` provides scrollbars for Swing GUI components that have more content to display than can fit in their area on the screen. For a `JTable`, depending on its number of rows and columns, the `JScrollPane` automatically provides vertical and horizontal scrollbars as necessary. Line 57 attaches the `SwingNode` to the `BoderPane`'s center area.

Software Engineering Observation 24.6

Class `SwingNode` enables you to reuse existing Swing GUIs or specific Swing controls by embedding them in new JavaFX apps.

Method `submitQueryButtonPressed`

When the user clicks the **Submit Query** `Button`, method `submitQueryButtonPressed` (lines 68–91) invokes `ResultSetTableModel` method `setQuery` (line 72) to execute the new query. If the user's query fails (for example, because of a syntax error in the user's input), lines 81–82 execute the default query. If the default query also fails, there could be a more serious error, so line 87 ensures that the database connection is closed and line 88 terminates the program. The screen captures in Fig. 24.29 show the results of two queries. Figure 24.29(a) shows the default query that retrieves all the data from table `Authors` of database `books`. Figure 24.29(b) shows a query that selects each author's first name and last name from the `Authors` table and combines that information with the titles and edition numbers of all that author's books from the `Titles` table. Try entering your own queries in the text area and clicking the **Submit Query** button to execute the query.

Method `applyFilterButtonPressed`

`JTable`s can show subsets of the data from the underlying `TableModel`—this is known as filtering the data. When the user enters text in the `filterTextField` and presses the **Apply Filter** `Button`, method `applyFilterButtonPressed` (lines 94–110) executes. Line 96 obtains the filter text. If the user did not specify filter text, line 99 uses `JTable` method **`setRowFilter`** to remove any prior filter by setting the filter to `null`. Otherwise, line 103 uses `setRowFilter` to specify a **`RowFilter`** (from package `javax.swing`) based on the user's input. Class `RowFilter` provides several methods for creating filters. The `static` method **`regexFilter`** receives a `String` containing a regular expression pattern as its argument and an optional set of indices that specify which columns to filter. If no indices are specified, then all the columns are searched. In this example, the regular expression pattern is the text the user typed. Once the filter is set, the data displayed in the `JTable` is updated based on the filtered `TableModel`. Figure 24.29(c) shows the results of the query in Fig. 24.29(b) filtered to show only records that contain the word `"Java"`.

Method `displayAlert`

When an exception occurs, the app calls method `displayAlert` (lines 113–119) to create and display an **`Alert`** dialog (package `javafx.scene.control`) containing a message. Line 115 creates the dialog, passing its `AlertType` to the constructor. The `AlertType.ERROR` constant displays an error-message dialog with a red icon containing an **X** to indicate an error. Line 116 sets the title that appears in the dialog's title bar. Line 117 sets the message that appears inside the dialog. Finally, line 118 calls `Alert` method `showAndWait`, which makes this a modal dialog. The user must close the dialog before interacting with the rest of the app.

24.8 RowSet Interface

In the preceding examples, you learned how to query a database by explicitly establishing a `Connection` to the database, preparing a `Statement` for querying the database and executing the query. In this section, we demonstrate the **`RowSet` interface**, which configures the database connection and prepares query statements automatically. The interface `RowSet` provides several *set* methods that allow you to specify the properties needed to establish a connection (such as the database URL, username and password of the database) and create a `Statement` (such as a query). `RowSet` also provides several *get* methods that return these properties.

Connected and Disconnected `RowSet`*s*

There are two types of `RowSet` objects—connected and disconnected. A **connected `RowSet`** object connects to the database once and remains connected while the object is in use. A **disconnected `RowSet`** object connects to the database, executes a query to retrieve the data from the database and then closes the connection. A program may change the data in a disconnected `RowSet` while it's disconnected. Modified data then can be updated in the database after a disconnected `RowSet` reestablishes the connection with the database.

Package **`javax.sql.rowset`** contains two subinterfaces of `RowSet`—`JdbcRowSet` and `CachedRowSet`. **`JdbcRowSet`**, a connected `RowSet`, acts as a wrapper around a `ResultSet` object and allows you to scroll through and update the rows in the `ResultSet`. Recall that by default, a `ResultSet` object is nonscrollable and read only—you must explicitly set the result-set type constant to `TYPE_SCROLL_INSENSITIVE` and set the result-set concurrency constant to `CONCUR_UPDATABLE` to make a `ResultSet` object scrollable and updatable. A `JdbcRowSet` object is scrollable and updatable by default. **`CachedRowSet`**, a disconnected `RowSet`, caches the data of a `ResultSet` in memory and disconnects from the database. Like `JdbcRowSet`, a `CachedRowSet` object is scrollable and updatable by default. A `CachedRowSet` object is also *serializable*, so it can be passed between Java applications through a network, such as the Internet. However, `CachedRowSet` has a limitation—the amount of data that can be stored in memory is limited. Package `javax.sql.rowset` contains three other subinterfaces of `RowSet`.

Portability Tip 24.4

A `RowSet` can provide scrolling capability for drivers that do not support scrollable `ResultSets`.

Using a RowSet

Figure 24.30 reimplements the example of Fig. 24.23 using a `RowSet`. Rather than establish the connection and create a `Statement` explicitly, Fig. 24.30 uses a `JdbcRowSet` object to create a `Connection` and a `Statement` automatically.

```
// Fig. 24.30: JdbcRowSetTest.java
// Displaying the contents of the Authors table using JdbcRowSet.
import java.sql.ResultSetMetaData;
import java.sql.SQLException;
import javax.sql.rowset.JdbcRowSet;
import javax.sql.rowset.RowSetProvider;

public class JdbcRowSetTest {
   // JDBC driver name and database URL
   private static final String DATABASE_URL = "jdbc:derby:books";
   private static final String USERNAME = "deitel";
   private static final String PASSWORD = "deitel";

   public static void main(String args[]) {
      // connect to database books and query database
      try (JdbcRowSet rowSet =
         RowSetProvider.newFactory().createJdbcRowSet()) {

         // specify JdbcRowSet properties
         rowSet.setUrl(DATABASE_URL);
         rowSet.setUsername(USERNAME);
         rowSet.setPassword(PASSWORD);
         rowSet.setCommand("SELECT * FROM Authors"); // set query
         rowSet.execute(); // execute query

         // process query results
         ResultSetMetaData metaData = rowSet.getMetaData();
         int numberOfColumns = metaData.getColumnCount();
```

Fig. 24.30 | Displaying the contents of the `Authors` table using `JdbcRowSet`. (Part 1 of 2.)

```
29            System.out.printf("Authors Table of Books Database:%n%n");
30
31            // display rowset header
32            for (int i = 1; i <= numberOfColumns; i++) {
33               System.out.printf("%-8s\t", metaData.getColumnName(i));
34            }
35            System.out.println();
36
37            // display each row
38            while (rowSet.next()) {
39               for (int i = 1; i <= numberOfColumns; i++) {
40                  System.out.printf("%-8s\t", rowSet.getObject(i));
41               }
42               System.out.println();
43            }
44         }
45         catch (SQLException sqlException) {
46            sqlException.printStackTrace();
47            System.exit(1);
48         }
49      }
50   }
```

```
Authors Table of Books Database:

AUTHORID        FIRSTNAME       LASTNAME
1               Paul            Deitel
2               Harvey          Deitel
3               Abbey           Deitel
4               Dan             Quirk
5               Michael         Morgano
```

Fig. 24.30 | Displaying the contents of the `Authors` table using `JdbcRowSet`. (Part 2 of 2.)

Class **`RowSetProvider`** (package `javax.sql.rowset`) provides `static` method **`newFactory`** which returns an object that implements the **`RowSetFactory`** interface (package `javax.sql.rowset`). This object can be used to create various types of `RowSets`. Lines 16–17 in the `try`-with-resources statement use `RowSetFactory` method **`createJdbcRowSet`** to obtain a `JdbcRowSet` object.

Lines 20–22 set the `RowSet` properties that the `DriverManager` uses to establish a database connection. Line 20 invokes `JdbcRowSet` method **`setUrl`** to specify the database URL. Line 21 invokes `JdbcRowSet` method **`setUsername`** to specify the username. Line 22 invokes `JdbcRowSet` method **`setPassword`** to specify the password. Line 23 invokes `JdbcRowSet` method **`setCommand`** to specify the SQL query that will populate the `RowSet`. Line 24 invokes `JdbcRowSet` method **`execute`** to execute the SQL query. Method `execute` performs four actions—it establishes a `Connection` to the database, prepares the query `Statement`, executes the query and stores the `ResultSet` returned by the query. The `Connection`, `Statement` and `ResultSet` are encapsulated in the `JdbcRowSet` object.

The remaining code is almost identical to Fig. 24.23, except that line 27 (Fig. 24.30) obtains a `ResultSetMetaData` object from the `JdbcRowSet`, line 38 uses the `JdbcRowSet`'s next method to get the next row of the result and line 40 uses the JdbcRowSet's getObject method to obtain a column's value. When the end of the try block is reached, the try-with-resources statement invokes JdbcRowSet method **close** to close the RowSet's encapsulated ResultSet, Statement and Connection. In a CachedRowSet, invoking close also releases the resources held by that RowSet. The application's output is identical to Fig. 24.23.

24.9 PreparedStatements

A **PreparedStatement** enables you to create compiled SQL statements that execute more efficiently than Statements. PreparedStatements also can specify parameters, making them more flexible than Statements—you can execute the same query repeatedly with different parameter values. For example, in the books database, you might want to locate all book titles for an author with a specific last and first name, and you might want to execute that query for several authors. With a PreparedStatement, that query is defined as:

```
PreparedStatement authorBooks = connection.prepareStatement(
   "SELECT LastName, FirstName, Title " +
   "FROM Authors INNER JOIN AuthorISBN " +
      "ON Authors.AuthorID=AuthorISBN.AuthorID " +
   "INNER JOIN Titles " +
      "ON AuthorISBN.ISBN=Titles.ISBN " +
   "WHERE LastName = ? AND FirstName = ?");
```

The two question marks (?) in the preceding SQL statement's last line are placeholders for values that will be passed to the database as part of the query. Before executing a PreparedStatement, the program must specify the values by using the PreparedStatement interface's *set* methods.

For the preceding query, both parameters are strings that can be set with PreparedStatement method **setString** as follows:

```
authorBooks.setString(1, "Deitel");
authorBooks.setString(2, "Paul");
```

Method setString's first argument represents the parameter number being set, and the second argument is that parameter's value. Parameter numbers are *counted from 1*, starting with the first question mark (?). When the program executes the preceding PreparedStatement with the parameter values set above, the SQL passed to the database is

```
SELECT LastName, FirstName, Title
FROM Authors INNER JOIN AuthorISBN
   ON Authors.AuthorID=AuthorISBN.AuthorID
INNER JOIN Titles
   ON AuthorISBN.ISBN=Titles.ISBN
WHERE LastName = 'Deitel' AND FirstName = 'Paul'
```

Method setString automatically escapes String parameter values as necessary. For example, if the last name is O'Brien, the statement

```
authorBooks.setString(1, "O'Brien");
```

escapes the ' character in O'Brien by replacing it with two single-quote characters, so that the ' appears correctly in the database.

Performance Tip 24.2

`PreparedStatement`s are more efficient than `Statement`s when executing SQL statements multiple times and with different parameter values.

Error-Prevention Tip 24.2

Use `PreparedStatement`s with parameters for queries that receive `String` values as arguments to ensure that the `String`s are quoted properly in the SQL statement.

Error-Prevention Tip 24.3

`PreparedStatement`s help prevent SQL injection attacks, which typically occur in SQL statements that include user input improperly. To avoid this security issue, use `PreparedStatement`s in which user input can be supplied only via parameters—indicated with ? when creating a `PreparedStatement`. Once you've created such a `PreparedStatement`, you can use its set methods to specify the user input as arguments for those parameters.

Interface `PreparedStatement` provides *set* methods for each supported SQL type. It's important to use the *set* method that's appropriate for the parameter's SQL type in the database—`SQLException`s occur when a program attempts to convert a parameter value to an incorrect type.

24.9.1 AddressBook App That Uses PreparedStatements

We now present an `AddressBook` JavaFX app that enables you to browse existing entries, add new entries and search for entries with a last name that begins with the specified characters. Our `addressbook` Java DB database (created in Section 24.5) contains an `Addresses` table with the columns `AddressID`, `FirstName`, `LastName`, `Email` and `PhoneNumber`. The column `AddressID` is an auto-incremented identity column in the `Addresses` table.

24.9.2 Class Person

Our `AddressBook` loads data into `Person` objects (Fig. 24.31). Each represents one entry in the `addressbook` database. The class contains instance variables for the address ID, first name, last name, email address and phone number, as well as *set* and *get* methods for manipulating these fields and a `toString` method that returns the `Person`'s name in the format

```
last name, first name
```

Though we do not use the address ID in this example, we included it in class `Person` for use in Exercises 24.7–24.8.

```java
// Fig. 24.31: Person.java
// Person class that represents an entry in an address book.
public class Person {
   private int addressID;
   private String firstName;
   private String lastName;
   private String email;
   private String phoneNumber;
```

Fig. 24.31 | `Person` class that represents an entry in an address book. (Part 1 of 2.)

```java

   // constructor
   public Person() {}

   // constructor
   public Person(int addressID, String firstName, String lastName,
      String email, String phoneNumber) {
      setAddressID(addressID);
      setFirstName(firstName);
      setLastName(lastName);
      setEmail(email);
      setPhoneNumber(phoneNumber);
   }

   // sets the addressID
   public void setAddressID(int addressID) {this.addressID = addressID;}

   // returns the addressID
   public int getAddressID() {return addressID;}

   // sets the firstName
   public void setFirstName(String firstName) {
      this.firstName = firstName;
   }

   // returns the first name
   public String getFirstName() {return firstName;}

   // sets the lastName
   public void setLastName(String lastName) {this.lastName = lastName;}

   // returns the last name
   public String getLastName() {return lastName;}

   // sets the email address
   public void setEmail(String email) {this.email = email;}

   // returns the email address
   public String getEmail() {return email;}

   // sets the phone number
   public void setPhoneNumber(String phoneNumber) {
      this.phoneNumber = phoneNumber;
   }

   // returns the phone number
   public String getPhoneNumber() {return phoneNumber;}

   // returns the string representation of the Person's name
   @Override
   public String toString()
      {return getLastName() + ", " + getFirstName();}
}
```

Fig. 24.31 | Person class that represents an entry in an address book. (Part 2 of 2.)

24.9.3 Class PersonQueries

Class `PersonQueries` (Fig. 24.32) manages the **Address Book** application's database connection and creates the `PreparedStatements` for interacting with the database. Lines 17–19 declare three `PreparedStatement` variables. The constructor (lines 22–47) connects to the database at lines 24–25.

```
1  // Fig. 24.32: PersonQueries.java
2  // PreparedStatements used by the Address Book application.
3  import java.sql.Connection;
4  import java.sql.DriverManager;
5  import java.sql.PreparedStatement;
6  import java.sql.ResultSet;
7  import java.sql.SQLException;
8  import java.util.List;
9  import java.util.ArrayList;
10 
11 public class PersonQueries {
12    private static final String URL = "jdbc:derby:AddressBook";
13    private static final String USERNAME = "deitel";
14    private static final String PASSWORD = "deitel";
15 
16    private Connection connection; // manages connection
17    private PreparedStatement selectAllPeople;
18    private PreparedStatement selectPeopleByLastName;
19    private PreparedStatement insertNewPerson;
20 
21    // constructor
22    public PersonQueries() {
23       try {
24          connection =
25             DriverManager.getConnection(URL, USERNAME, PASSWORD);
26 
27          // create query that selects all entries in the AddressBook
28          selectAllPeople = connection.prepareStatement(
29             "SELECT * FROM Addresses ORDER BY LastName, FirstName");
30 
31          // create query that selects entries with last names
32          // that begin with the specified characters
33          selectPeopleByLastName = connection.prepareStatement(
34             "SELECT * FROM Addresses WHERE LastName LIKE ? " +
35             "ORDER BY LastName, FirstName");
36 
37          // create insert that adds a new entry into the database
38          insertNewPerson = connection.prepareStatement(
39             "INSERT INTO Addresses " +
40             "(FirstName, LastName, Email, PhoneNumber) " +
41             "VALUES (?, ?, ?, ?)");
42       }
43       catch (SQLException sqlException) {
44          sqlException.printStackTrace();
```

Fig. 24.32 | `PreparedStatements` used by the **Address Book** application. (Part 1 of 3.)

```
         System.exit(1);
      }
   }

   // select all of the addresses in the database
   public List<Person> getAllPeople() {
      // executeQuery returns ResultSet containing matching entries
      try (ResultSet resultSet = selectAllPeople.executeQuery()) {
         List<Person> results = new ArrayList<Person>();

         while (resultSet.next()) {
            results.add(new Person(
               resultSet.getInt("AddressID"),
               resultSet.getString("FirstName"),
               resultSet.getString("LastName"),
               resultSet.getString("Email"),
               resultSet.getString("PhoneNumber")));
         }

         return results;
      }
      catch (SQLException sqlException) {
         sqlException.printStackTrace();
      }

      return null;
   }

   // select person by last name
   public List<Person> getPeopleByLastName(String lastName) {
      try {
         selectPeopleByLastName.setString(1, lastName); // set last name
      }
      catch (SQLException sqlException) {
         sqlException.printStackTrace();
         return null;
      }

      // executeQuery returns ResultSet containing matching entries
      try (ResultSet resultSet = selectPeopleByLastName.executeQuery()) {
         List<Person> results = new ArrayList<Person>();

         while (resultSet.next()) {
            results.add(new Person(
               resultSet.getInt("addressID"),
               resultSet.getString("FirstName"),
               resultSet.getString("LastName"),
               resultSet.getString("Email"),
               resultSet.getString("PhoneNumber")));
         }

         return results;
      }
```

Fig. 24.32 | PreparedStatements used by the **Address Book** application. (Part 2 of 3.)

```
98         catch (SQLException sqlException) {
99            sqlException.printStackTrace();
100           return null;
101        }
102     }
103
104     // add an entry
105     public int addPerson(String firstName, String lastName,
106        String email, String phoneNumber) {
107
108        // insert the new entry; returns # of rows updated
109        try {
110           // set parameters
111           insertNewPerson.setString(1, firstName);
112           insertNewPerson.setString(2, lastName);
113           insertNewPerson.setString(3, email);
114           insertNewPerson.setString(4, phoneNumber);
115
116           return insertNewPerson.executeUpdate();
117        }
118        catch (SQLException sqlException) {
119           sqlException.printStackTrace();
120           return 0;
121        }
122     }
123
124     // close the database connection
125     public void close() {
126        try {
127           connection.close();
128        }
129        catch (SQLException sqlException) {
130           sqlException.printStackTrace();
131        }
132     }
133  }
```

Fig. 24.32 | `PreparedStatements` used by the **Address Book** application. (Part 3 of 3.)

Creating `PreparedStatement`*s*

Lines 28–29 invoke `Connection` method **`prepareStatement`** to create the `PreparedStatement` `selectAllPeople` that selects all the rows in the `Addresses` table and sorts them by last name, then by first name. Lines 33–35 create the `PreparedStatement` `selectPeopleByLastName` with a parameter. This statement uses the SQL `LIKE` operator to search the `Addresses` table by last name. The `?` character specifies the last-name parameter—as you'll see, the text we set as this parameter's value will end with `%`, so that the database will return entries for last names that start with the characters entered by the user. Lines 38–41 create the `PreparedStatement` `insertNewPerson` with four parameters that represent the first name, last name, email address and phone number for a new entry. Again, notice the `?` characters used to represent these parameters.

`PersonQueries` *Method* `getAllPeople`

Method `getAllPeople` (lines 50–71) executes `PreparedStatement selectAllPeople` (line 52) by calling method **`executeQuery`**, which returns a `ResultSet` containing the rows that match the query (in this case, all the rows in the `Addresses` table). Lines 55–62 place the query results in an `ArrayList<Person>`, which is returned to the caller at line 64.

`PersonQueries` *Method* `getPeopleByLastName`

Method `getPeopleByLastName` (lines 74–102) uses `PreparedStatement` method `setString` to set the parameter of `selectPeopleByLastName` (line 76). Then, line 84 executes the query and lines 87–94 place the query results in an `ArrayList<Person>`. Line 96 returns the `ArrayList` to the caller.

`PersonQueries` *Methods* `addPerson` *and* `Close`

Method `addPerson` (lines 105–122) uses `PreparedStatement` method `setString` (lines 111–114) to set the parameters for the `insertNewPerson PreparedStatement`. Line 116 uses `PreparedStatement` method **`executeUpdate`** to update the database by inserting the new record. This method returns an integer indicating the number of rows that were updated (or inserted) in the database. Method `close` (lines 125–132) simply closes the database connection.

24.9.4 AddressBook GUI

Figure 24.33 shows the app's GUI (defined in `AddressBook.fxml`) labeled with its **fx:ids**. Here we point out only the key elements and their event-handler methods, which you'll see in class `AddressBookController` (Fig. 24.34). For the complete layout details, open `AddressBook.fxml` in Scene Builder. The GUI's primary layout is a `BorderPane`. The controller class defines three event-handling methods:

- `addEntryButtonPressed` is called when the **Add Entry** `Button` is pressed.
- `findButtonPressed` is called when the **Find** `Button` is pressed.
- `browseAllButtonPressed` is called when the **Browse All** `Button` is pressed.

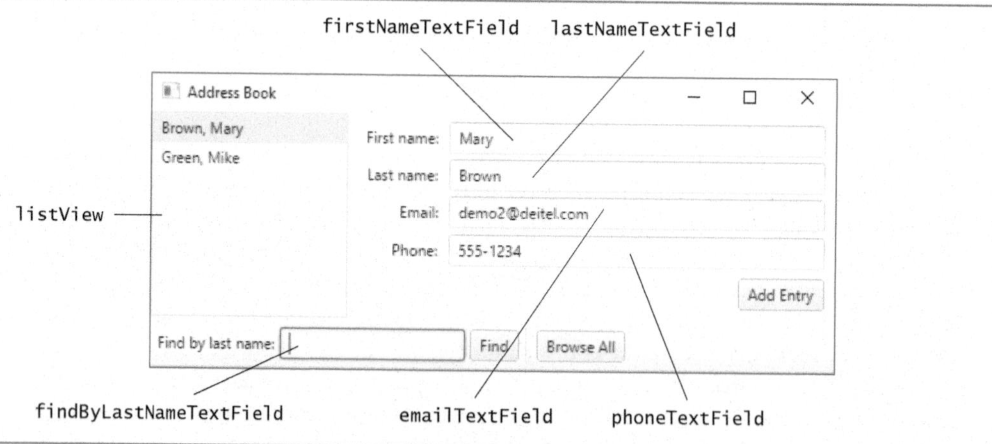

Fig. 24.33 | `AddressBook` GUI with its **fx:ids**.

24.9.5 Class AddressBookController

The AddressBookController (Fig. 24.34) class uses a PersonQueries object to interact with the database. We do not show the JavaFX Application subclass here (located in AddressBook.java), because it performs the same tasks you've seen previously to load the app's FXML GUI and initialize the controller.

```
// Fig. 24.34: AddressBookController.java
// Controller for the AddressBook app
import java.util.List;
import javafx.application.Platform;
import javafx.collections.FXCollections;
import javafx.collections.ObservableList;
import javafx.event.ActionEvent;
import javafx.fxml.FXML;
import javafx.scene.control.Alert;
import javafx.scene.control.Alert.AlertType;
import javafx.scene.control.ListView;
import javafx.scene.control.TextField;

public class AddressBookController {
   @FXML private ListView<Person> listView; // displays contact names
   @FXML private TextField firstNameTextField;
   @FXML private TextField lastNameTextField;
   @FXML private TextField emailTextField;
   @FXML private TextField phoneTextField;
   @FXML private TextField findByLastNameTextField;

   // interacts with the database
   private final PersonQueries personQueries = new PersonQueries();

   // stores list of Person objects that results from a database query
   private final ObservableList<Person> contactList =
      FXCollections.observableArrayList();

   // populate listView and set up listener for selection events
   public void initialize() {
      listView.setItems(contactList); // bind to contactsList
      getAllEntries(); // populates contactList, which updates listView

      // when ListView selection changes, display selected person's data
      listView.getSelectionModel().selectedItemProperty().addListener(
         (observableValue, oldValue, newValue) -> {
            displayContact(newValue);
         }
      );
   }

   // get all the entries from the database to populate contactList
   private void getAllEntries() {
      contactList.setAll(personQueries.getAllPeople());
```

Fig. 24.34 | Controller for the AddressBook app. (Part 1 of 4.)

```
         selectFirstEntry();
      }

      // select first item in listView
      private void selectFirstEntry() {
         listView.getSelectionModel().selectFirst();
      }

      // display contact information
      private void displayContact(Person person) {
         if (person != null) {
            firstNameTextField.setText(person.getFirstName());
            lastNameTextField.setText(person.getLastName());
            emailTextField.setText(person.getEmail());
            phoneTextField.setText(person.getPhoneNumber());
         }
         else {
            firstNameTextField.clear();
            lastNameTextField.clear();
            emailTextField.clear();
            phoneTextField.clear();
         }
      }

      // add a new entry
      @FXML
      void addEntryButtonPressed(ActionEvent event) {
         int result = personQueries.addPerson(
            firstNameTextField.getText(), lastNameTextField.getText(),
            emailTextField.getText(), phoneTextField.getText());

         if (result == 1) {
            displayAlert(AlertType.INFORMATION, "Entry Added",
               "New entry successfully added.");
         }
         else {
            displayAlert(AlertType.ERROR, "Entry Not Added",
               "Unable to add entry.");
         }

         getAllEntries();
      }

      // find entries with the specified last name
      @FXML
      void findButtonPressed(ActionEvent event) {
         List<Person> people = personQueries.getPeopleByLastName(
            findByLastNameTextField.getText() + "%");

         if (people.size() > 0) { // display all entries
            contactList.setAll(people);
            selectFirstEntry();
         }
```

Fig. 24.34 | Controller for the AddressBook app. (Part 2 of 4.)

```
      else {
         displayAlert(AlertType.INFORMATION, "Lastname Not Found",
            "There are no entries with the specified last name.");
      }
   }

   // browse all the entries
   @FXML
   void browseAllButtonPressed(ActionEvent event) {
      getAllEntries();
   }

   // display an Alert dialog
   private void displayAlert(
      AlertType type, String title, String message) {
      Alert alert = new Alert(type);
      alert.setTitle(title);
      alert.setContentText(message);
      alert.showAndWait();
   }
}
```

a) Initial **Address Book** screen showing entries.

b) Viewing the entry for **Green, Mike**.

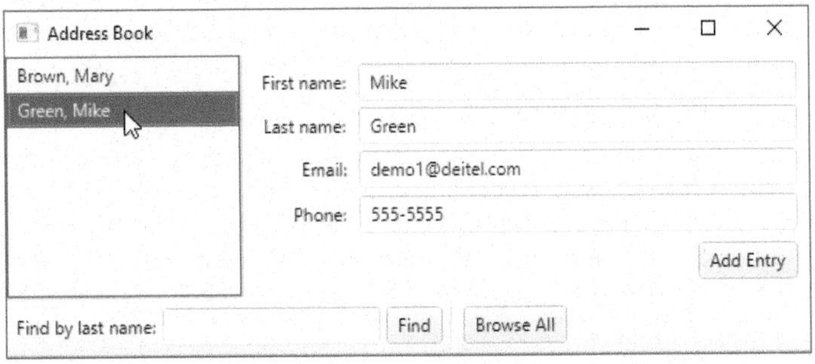

Fig. 24.34 | Controller for the `AddressBook` app. (Part 3 of 4.)

c) Adding a new entry for **Sue Green**.

d) Searching for last names that start with **Gr**.

e) Returning to the complete list by clicking **Browse All**.

Fig. 24.34 | Controller for the AddressBook app. (Part 4 of 4.)

Instance Variables

Line 23 creates the PersonQueries object. We use the same techniques to populate the ListView that we used in Section 13.5, so lines 26–27 create an ObservableList<Person> named contactList to store the Person objects returned by the PersonQueries object.

Method initialize

When the FXMLLoader initializes the controller, method initialize (lines 30–40) performs the following tasks:

- Line 31 binds the `contactList` to the `ListView`, so that each time this `ObservableList<Person>` changes, the `ListView` will update its list of items.
- Line 32 calls method `getAllEntries` (declared in lines 43–46) to get all the entries from the database and place them in the `contactList`.
- Lines 35–39 register a `ChangeListener` that displays the selected contact when the user selects a new item in the `ListView`. In this case, we used a lambda expression to create the event handler (Fig. 13.15 showed a similar `ChangeListener` defined as an anonymous inner class).

Methods `getAllEntries` *and* `selectFirstEntry`

When the app first executes, when the user clicks the **Browse All** `Button` and when the user adds a new entry to the database, method `getEntries` (lines 43–46) calls `PersonQueries` method `getAllPeople` (line 44) to obtain all the entries. The resulting `List<Person>` is passed to `ObservableList` method `setAll` to replace the `contactList`'s contents. At this point, the `ListView` updates its list of items based on the new contents of `contactList`.

Next line 45 selects the first item in the `ListView` by calling method `selectFirstEntry` (lines 49–51). Line 50 selects the `ListView`'s first item to display that contact's data.

Method `displayContact`

When an item is selected in the `ListView`, the `ChangeListener` registered in method `initialize` calls `displayContact` (lines 54–67) to display the selected `Person`'s data. If the argument is `null`, the method clears the `TextField`'s contents.

Method `addEntryButtonPressed`

To add a new entry into the database, you can enter the first name, last name, email and phone number (the `AddressID` will *autoincrement*) in the `TextFields` that display contact information, then press the **Add Entry** `Button`. Method `addEntryButtonPressed` (lines 70–86) calls `PersonQueries` method `addPerson` (lines 72–74) to add the new entry to the database. Line 85 calls `getAllEntries` to obtain the updated database contents and display them in the `ListView`.

Method `findButtonPressed`

When the user presses the **Find** `Button`, method `findButtonPressed` (lines 89–102) is called. Lines 91–92 call `PersonQueries` method `getPeopleByLastName` to search the database. Note that line 92 appends a `%` to the text input by the user. This enables the corresponding SQL query, which contains a `LIKE` operator, to locate last names that begin with the characters the user typed in the `findByLastNameTextField`. If there are several such entries, they're all displayed in the `ListView` when the `contactList` is updated (line 95) and the first one is selected (line 96).

Method `browseAllButtonPressed`

When the user presses the **Browse All** `Button`, method `browseAllButtonPressed` (lines 105–108) simply calls method `getAllEntries` to get all the database entries and display them in the `ListView`.

24.10 Stored Procedures

Many database-management systems can store individual or sets of SQL statements in a database, so that programs accessing that database can invoke them. Such named collections of SQL statements are called **stored procedures**. JDBC enables programs to invoke stored procedures using objects that implement the interface **`CallableStatement`**. `CallableStatement`s can receive arguments specified with the methods inherited from interface `PreparedStatement`. In addition, `CallableStatement`s can specify **output parameters** in which a stored procedure can place return values. Interface `CallableStatement` includes methods to specify which parameters in a stored procedure are output parameters. The interface also includes methods to obtain the values of output parameters returned from a stored procedure.

Portability Tip 24.5

Although the syntax for creating stored procedures differs across database management systems, the interface `CallableStatement` provides a uniform interface for specifying input and output parameters for stored procedures and for invoking stored procedures.

Portability Tip 24.6

According to the Java API documentation for interface `CallableStatement`, for maximum portability between database systems, programs should process the update counts (which indicate how many rows were updated) or `ResultSet`s returned from a `CallableStatement` before obtaining the values of any output parameters.

24.11 Transaction Processing

Many database applications require guarantees that a series of database insertions, updates and deletions executes properly before the application continues processing the next database operation. For example, when you transfer money electronically between bank accounts, several factors determine if the transaction is successful. You begin by specifying the source account and the amount you wish to transfer from that account to a destination account. Next, you specify the destination account. The bank checks the source account to determine whether its funds are sufficient to complete the transfer. If so, the bank withdraws the specified amount and, if all goes well, deposits it into the destination account to complete the transfer. What happens if the transfer fails after the bank withdraws the money from the source account? In a proper banking system, the bank redeposits the money in the source account. How would you feel if the money was subtracted from your source account and the bank *did not* deposit the money in the destination account?

Transaction processing enables a program that interacts with a database to *treat a database operation (or set of operations) as a single operation*. Such an operation also is known as an **atomic operation** or a **transaction**. At the end of a transaction, a decision can be made either to **commit the transaction** or **roll back the transaction**. Committing the transaction finalizes the database operation(s); all insertions, updates and deletions performed as part of the transaction cannot be reversed without performing a new database operation. Rolling back the transaction leaves the database in its state prior to the database operation. This is useful when a portion of a transaction fails to complete properly. In our bank-account-transfer discussion, the transaction would be rolled back if the deposit could not be made into the destination account.

Java provides transaction processing via methods of interface `Connection`. Method **`setAutoCommit`** specifies whether each SQL statement commits after it completes (a `true` argument) or whether several SQL statements should be grouped as a transaction (a `false` argument). If the argument to `setAutoCommit` is `false`, the program must follow the last SQL statement in the transaction with a call to `Connection` method **`commit`** (to commit the changes to the database) or `Connection` method **`rollback`** (to return the database to its state prior to the transaction). Interface `Connection` also provides method **`getAutoCommit`** to determine the autocommit state for the `Connection`.

24.12 Wrap-Up

In this chapter, you learned basic database concepts, how to query and manipulate data in a database using SQL and how to use JDBC to allow Java applications to interact with Java DB databases. You learned about the SQL commands `SELECT`, `INSERT`, `UPDATE` and `DELETE`, as well as clauses such as `WHERE`, `ORDER BY` and `INNER JOIN`.

You created and configured databases in Java DB by using predefined SQL scripts. You learned the steps for obtaining a `Connection` to the database, creating a `Statement` to interact with the database's data, executing the statement and processing the results. You incorporated a Swing `JTable` component into a JavaFX GUI via a `SwingNode` and used a `TableModel` to bind `ResultSet` data to the `JTable`.

Next, you used a `RowSet` to simplify the process of connecting to a database and creating statements. You used `PreparedStatements` to create precompiled SQL statements. We also provided overviews of `CallableStatements` and transaction processing. In the next chapter, you'll learn about JShell—Java 9's REPL (read-evaluate-print loop) that enables you to quickly explore, discover and experiment with Java language and API features.

Summary

Section 24.1 Introduction

- A database (p. 1051) is an integrated collection of data. A database management system (DBMS; p. 1051) provides mechanisms for storing, organizing, retrieving and modifying data.
- Today's most popular database management systems are relational database (p. 1051) systems.
- SQL (p. 1051) is the international standard language used to query (p. 1051) and manipulate relational data.
- Java programs interact with databases using the Java Database Connectivity (JDBC™) API—software that facilitates communications between a database management system and a program.
- A JDBC driver (p. 1052) enables Java applications to connect to a database in a particular DBMS and allows you to retrieve and manipulate database data.

Section 24.2 Relational Databases

- A relational database (p. 1052) stores data in tables (p. 1052). Tables are composed of rows (p. 1052), and rows are composed of columns in which values are stored.
- A table's primary key (p. 1052) has a unique value in each row.
- Each column (p. 1052) of a table represents a different attribute.

Section 24.3 A **books** *Database*

- The primary key can be composed of more than one column.
- An identity column is the SQL standard way to represent an autoincremented (p. 1054) column. The SQL `IDENTITY` keyword (p. 1054) marks a column as an identity column.
- A foreign key is a column in a table that must match the primary-key column in another table. This is known as the Rule of Referential Integrity (p. 1055).
- A one-to-many relationship (p. 1056) between tables indicates that a row in one table can have many related rows in a separate table.
- Every row must have a primary-key value, and that value must be unique in the table. This is known as the Rule of Entity Integrity (p. 1056).
- Foreign keys enable information from multiple tables to be joined together. There's a one-to-many relationship between a primary key and its corresponding foreign key.

Section 24.4.1 Basic **SELECT** *Query*

- The basic form of a query (p. 1058) is

  `SELECT * FROM` *tableName*

  where the asterisk (`*`; p. 1058) indicates that all columns from *tableName* should be selected, and *tableName* specifies the table in the database from which rows will be retrieved.
- To retrieve specific columns, replace the `*` with a comma-separated list of column names.

Section 24.4.2 **WHERE** *Clause*

- The optional `WHERE` clause (p. 1058) in a query specifies the selection criteria for the query. The basic form of a query with selection criteria (p. 1058) is

  `SELECT` *columnName1*, *columnName2*, … `FROM` *tableName* `WHERE` *criteria*

- The `WHERE` clause can contain operators `<`, `>`, `<=`, `>=`, `=`, `<>` and `LIKE`. `LIKE` (p. 1059) is used for string pattern matching (p. 1059) with wildcard characters percent (`%`) and underscore (`_`).
- A percent character (`%`; p. 1059) in a pattern indicates that a string matching the pattern can have zero or more characters at the percent character's location in the pattern.
- An underscore (`_`; p. 1059) in the pattern string indicates a single character at that position in the pattern.

Section 24.4.3 **ORDER BY** *Clause*

- A query's result can be sorted with the `ORDER BY` clause (p. 1060). The simplest form of an `ORDER BY` clause is

  `SELECT` *columnName1*, *columnName2*, … `FROM` *tableName* `ORDER BY` *column* `ASC`
  `SELECT` *columnName1*, *columnName2*, … `FROM` *tableName* `ORDER BY` *column* `DESC`

  where `ASC` specifies ascending order, `DESC` specifies descending order and *column* specifies the column on which the sort is based. The default sorting order is ascending, so `ASC` is optional.
- Multiple columns can be used for ordering purposes with an `ORDER BY` clause of the form

  `ORDER BY` *column1 sortingOrder*, *column2 sortingOrder*, …

- The `WHERE` and `ORDER BY` clauses can be combined in one query. If used, `ORDER BY` must be the last clause in the query.

Section 24.4.4 Merging Data from Multiple Tables: INNER JOIN

- An INNER JOIN (p. 1062) merges rows from two tables by matching values in columns that are common to the tables. The basic form for the INNER JOIN operator is:

```
SELECT columnName1, columnName2, ...
FROM table1
INNER JOIN table2
   ON table1.columnName = table2.columnName
```

  The ON clause (p. 1062) specifies the columns from each table that are compared to determine which rows are joined. If a SQL statement uses columns with the same name from multiple tables, the column names must be fully qualified (p. 1063) by prefixing them with their table names and a dot (.).

Section 24.4.5 INSERT *Statement*

- An INSERT statement (p. 1063) inserts a new row into a table. The basic form of this statement is

```
INSERT INTO tableName (columnName1, columnName2, ..., columnNameN)
   VALUES (value1, value2, ..., valueN)
```

  where *tableName* is the table in which to insert the row. The *tableName* is followed by a comma-separated list of column names in parentheses. The list of column names is followed by the SQL keyword VALUES (p. 1064) and a comma-separated list of values in parentheses.

- SQL uses single quotes (') to delimit strings. To specify a string containing a single quote in SQL, escape the single quote with another single quote (i.e., '').

Section 24.4.6 UPDATE *Statement*

- An UPDATE statement (p. 1064) modifies data in a table. The basic form of an UPDATE statement is

```
UPDATE tableName
   SET columnName1 = value1, columnName2 = value2, ..., columnNameN = valueN
   WHERE criteria
```

  where *tableName* is the table to update. Keyword SET (p. 1065) is followed by a comma-separated list of *columnName* = *value* pairs. The optional WHERE clause determines which rows to update.

Section 24.4.7 DELETE *Statement*

- A DELETE statement (p. 1065) removes rows from a table. The simplest DELETE statement form is

```
DELETE FROM tableName WHERE criteria
```

  where *tableName* is the table from which to delete a row (or rows). The optional WHERE *criteria* determines which rows to delete. If this clause is omitted, all the table's rows are deleted.

Section 24.5 Setting Up a Java DB Database

- Oracle's pure Java database Java DB (p. 1066) is installed with the JDK on Windows, macOS and Linux.
- Java DB has both an embedded version and a network version.
- The Java DB software is located in the db subdirectory of your JDK's installation directory.
- Java DB comes with several files that enable you to configure and run it. Before executing these files from a command window, you must set the environment variable JAVA_HOME to refer to the JDK's exact installation directory.

- You use the `setEmbeddedCP.bat` or `setEmbeddedCP` file (depending on your OS platform) to configure the `CLASSPATH` for working with Java DB embedded databases.
- The Java DB `ij` tool allows you to interact with Java DB from the command line. You can use it to create databases, run SQL scripts and perform SQL queries. Each command you enter at the `ij>` prompt must be terminated with a semicolon (`;`).

Section 24.6 Connecting to and Querying a Database

- Package `java.sql` contains classes and interfaces for accessing relational databases in Java.
- A `Connection` object (p. 1070) manages the connection between a Java program and a database. `Connection` objects enable programs to create SQL statements that access data.
- `DriverManager` (p. 1070) method `getConnection` (p. 1070) attempts to connect to a database at a URL that specifies the protocol for communication, the subprotocol (p. 1071) for communication and the database name.
- `Connection` method `createStatement` (p. 1071) creates a `Statement` object (p. 1071), which can be used to submit SQL statements to the database.
- `Statement` method `executeQuery` (p. 1071) executes a query and returns a `ResultSet` object (p. 1071). `ResultSet` methods enable a program to manipulate query results.
- A `ResultSetMetaData` object (p. 1072) describes a `ResultSet`'s contents. Programs can use metadata programmatically to obtain information about the `ResultSet` column names and types.
- `ResultSetMetaData` method `getColumnCount` (p. 1072) retrieves the number of `ResultSet` columns.
- `ResultSet` method `next` (p. 1072) positions the `ResultSet` cursor to the next row and returns `true` if the row exists; otherwise, it returns `false`. This method must be called to begin processing a `ResultSet` because the cursor is initially positioned before the first row.
- It's possible to extract each `ResultSet` column as a specific Java type. `ResultSetMetaData` method `getColumnType` (p. 1072) returns a `Types` (p. 1072) constant (package `java.sql`) indicating the column's type.
- `ResultSet` *get* methods typically receive as an argument either a column number (as an `int`) or a column name (as a `String`) indicating which column's value to obtain.
- `ResultSet` row and column numbers start at 1.
- Each `Statement` object can open only one `ResultSet` at a time. When a `Statement` returns a new `ResultSet`, the `Statement` closes the prior `ResultSet`.

Section 24.7 Querying the **`books`** *Database*

- `TableModel` (p. 1073) method `getColumnClass` (p. 1073) returns a `Class` object that represents the superclass of all objects in a particular column. A `JTable` (p. 1073) uses this information to set up the default cell renderer and cell editor for that column in a `JTable`.
- `Connection` method `createStatement` has an overloaded version that receives the result type and concurrency. The result type specifies whether the `ResultSet`'s cursor is able to scroll in both directions or forward only and whether the `ResultSet` is sensitive to changes. The result concurrency (p. 1078) specifies whether the `ResultSet` can be updated.
- Some JDBC drivers (p. 1078) do not support scrollable or updatable `ResultSet`s.
- `ResultSetMetaData` method `getColumnClassName` (p. 1078) obtains a column's fully qualified class name.
- `TableModel` method `getColumnCount` (p. 1078) returns the number of columns in the `ResultSet`.
- `TableModel` method `getColumnName` (p. 1078) returns a column name in the `ResultSet`.

- `ResultSetMetaData` method `getColumnName` (p. 1079) obtains a `ResultSet` column's name.
- `TableModel` method `getRowCount` (p. 1078) returns the number of rows in the model.
- `TableModel` method `getValueAt` (p. 1078) returns the `Object` at a particular row and column of the model's underlying `ResultSet`.
- `ResultSet` method `absolute` (p. 1079) positions the `ResultSet` cursor at a specific row.
- `AbstractTableModel` method `fireTableStructureChanged` (p. 1079) notifies a `JTable` that its model has changed and the `JTable` needs updating.
- A `TableRowSorter` (from package `javax.swing.table`) provides row-sorting capabilities for a `JTable`.
- A `SwingNode` enables you to embed Swing GUI controls in JavaFX GUIs.
- The argument to `SwingNode` method `setContent` is a `JComponent`—the superclass of all Swing GUI controls.
- A `JScrollPane` provides scrollbars for Swing GUI components that have more content to display than can fit in their area on the screen.
- `JTables` can show subsets of the data from the underlying `TableModel`—this is known as filtering the data.
- `JTable` method `setRowFilter` specifies a `RowFilter` (from package `javax.swing`), which provides several methods for creating filters. The `static` method `regexFilter` receives a `String` containing a regular expression pattern as its argument and an optional set of indices that specify which columns to filter. If no indices are specified, then all the columns are searched.

Section 24.8 **`RowSet`** *Interface*

- Interface `RowSet` (p. 1085) configures a database connection and executes a query automatically.
- A connected `RowSet` (p. 1085) remains connected to the database while the object is in use. A disconnected `RowSet` (p. 1085) connects, executes a query, then closes the connection.
- `JdbcRowSet` (p. 1085) (a connected `RowSet`) wraps a `ResultSet` object and allows you to scroll and update its rows. Unlike a `ResultSet` object, a `JdbcRowSet` is scrollable and updatable by default.
- `CachedRowSet` (p. 1086), a disconnected `RowSet`, caches a `ResultSet`'s data in memory. A `CachedRowSet` is scrollable and updatable. A `CachedRowSet` is also serializable.
- Class `RowSetProvider` (package `javax.sql.rowset`; p. 1087) provides `static` method `newFactory` which returns an object that implements interface `RowSetFactory` (package `javax.sql.rowset`) that can be used to create various types of `RowSets`.
- `RowSetFactory` (p. 1087) method `createJdbcRowSet` returns a `JdbcRowSet` object.
- `JdbcRowSet` method `setUrl` specifies the database URL.
- `JdbcRowSet` method `setUsername` specifies the username.
- `JdbcRowSet` method `setPassword` specifies the password.
- `JdbcRowSet` method `setCommand` specifies the SQL query that will be used to populate a `RowSet`.
- `JdbcRowSet` method `execute` executes the SQL query. Method `execute` establishes a `Connection` to the database, prepares the query `Statement`, executes the query and stores the `ResultSet` returned by query. The `Connection`, `Statement` and `ResultSet` are encapsulated in the `JdbcRowSet` object.

Section 24.9 **`PreparedStatements`**

- `PreparedStatements` (p. 1088) are compiled, so they execute more efficiently than `Statements`.
- `PreparedStatements` can have parameters, so the same query can execute with different arguments.

- A parameter is specified with a question mark (?) in the SQL statement. Before executing a PreparedStatement, you must use PreparedStatement's *set* methods to specify the arguments.
- PreparedStatement method setString's (p. 1088) first argument represents the parameter number being set, and the second argument is that parameter's value.
- Parameter numbers are counted from 1, starting with the first question mark (?).
- Method setString automatically escapes String parameter values as necessary.
- Interface PreparedStatement provides set methods for each supported SQL type.

Section 24.10 Stored Procedures

- JDBC enables programs to invoke stored procedures (p. 1100) using CallableStatement (p. 1100) objects.
- CallableStatement can specify input parameters. CallableStatement can specify output parameters (p. 1100) in which a stored procedure can place return values.

Section 24.11 Transaction Processing

- Transaction processing (p. 1100) enables a program that interacts with a database to treat a database operation (or set of operations) as a single operation—known as an atomic operation (p. 1100) or a transaction (p. 1100).
- At the end of a transaction, a decision can be made to either commit or roll back the transaction.
- Committing a transaction (p. 1100) finalizes the database operation(s)—inserts, updates and deletes cannot be reversed without performing a new database operation.
- Rolling back a transaction (p. 1100) leaves the database in its state prior to the database operation.
- Java provides transaction processing via methods of interface Connection.
- Method setAutoCommit (p. 1101) specifies whether each SQL statement commits after it completes (a true argument) or whether several SQL statements should be grouped as a transaction.
- When autocommit is disabled, the program must follow the last SQL statement in the transaction with a call to Connection method commit (to commit the changes to the database; p. 1101) or Connection method rollback (to return the database to its state prior to the transaction; p. 1101).
- Method getAutoCommit (p. 1101) determines the autocommit state for the Connection.

Self-Review Exercise

24.1 Fill in the blanks in each of the following statements:

a) The international standard database language is ________.
b) A table in a database consists of ________ and ________.
c) Statement objects return SQL query results as ________ objects.
d) The ________ uniquely identifies each row in a table.
e) SQL keyword ________ is followed by the selection criteria that specify the rows to select in a query.
f) SQL keywords ________ specify the order in which rows are sorted in a query.
g) Merging rows from multiple database tables is called ________ the tables.
h) A(n) ________ is an organized collection of data.
i) A(n) ________ is a set of columns whose values match the primary-key values of another table.
j) ________ method ________ is used to obtain a Connection to a database.
k) Interface ________ helps manage the connection between a Java program and a database.

l) A(n) ________ object is used to submit a query to a database.
m) Unlike a `ResultSet` object, ________ and ________ objects are scrollable and updatable by default.
n) ________, a disconnected `RowSet`, caches the data of a `ResultSet` in memory.

Answers to Self-Review Exercise

24.1 a) SQL. b) rows, columns. c) `ResultSet`. d) primary key. e) `WHERE`. f) `ORDER BY`. g) joining. h) database. i) foreign key. j) `DriverManager`, `getConnection`. k) `Connection`. l) `Statement`. m) `JdbcRowSet`, `CachedRowSet`. n) `CachedRowSet`.

Exercises

24.2 *(Query Application for the* **books** *Database)* Using the techniques shown in this chapter, define a complete query application for the `books` database. Provide the following predefined queries:

a) Select all authors from the `Authors` table.
b) Select a specific author and list all books for that author. Include each book's title, year and ISBN. Order the information alphabetically by the author's last name, then by first name.
c) Select a specific title and list all authors for that title. Order the authors alphabetically by last name then by first name.
d) Provide any other queries you feel are appropriate.

Display a `ComboBox` with appropriate names for each predefined query. Also allow users to supply their own queries. A `ComboBox` is similar to a `ListView`, but displays its items in a drop-down list.

24.3 *(Data-Manipulation Application for the* **books** *Database)* Define a data-manipulation application for the `books` database. The user should be able to edit existing data and add new data to the database (obeying referential and entity integrity constraints). Allow the user to edit the database in the following ways:

a) Add a new author.
b) Edit the existing information for an author.
c) Add a new title for an author. (Remember that the book must have an entry in the `AuthorISBN` table.).
d) Add a new entry in the `AuthorISBN` table to link authors with titles.

24.4 *(Employee Database)* In Section 10.5, we introduced an employee-payroll hierarchy to calculate each employee's payroll. In this exercise, we provide a database of employees that corresponds to the employee-payroll hierarchy. (A SQL script to create the `Employees` database is provided with the examples for this chapter.) Write an application that allows the user to:

a) Add employees to the `Employee` table.
b) Add payroll information to the appropriate table for each new employee. For example, for a salaried employee add the payroll information to the `SalariedEmployees` table.

Figure 24.35 is the entity-relationship diagram for the `employees` database.

24.5 *(Employee Database Query Application)* Modify Exercise 24.4 to provide a `ComboBox` and a `TextArea` to allow the user to perform a query that is either selected from the `ComboBox` or input into the `TextArea`. Sample predefined queries should include:

a) Select all employees working in department SALES.
b) Select hourly employees working over 30 hours.
c) Select all commission employees in descending order of the commission rate.

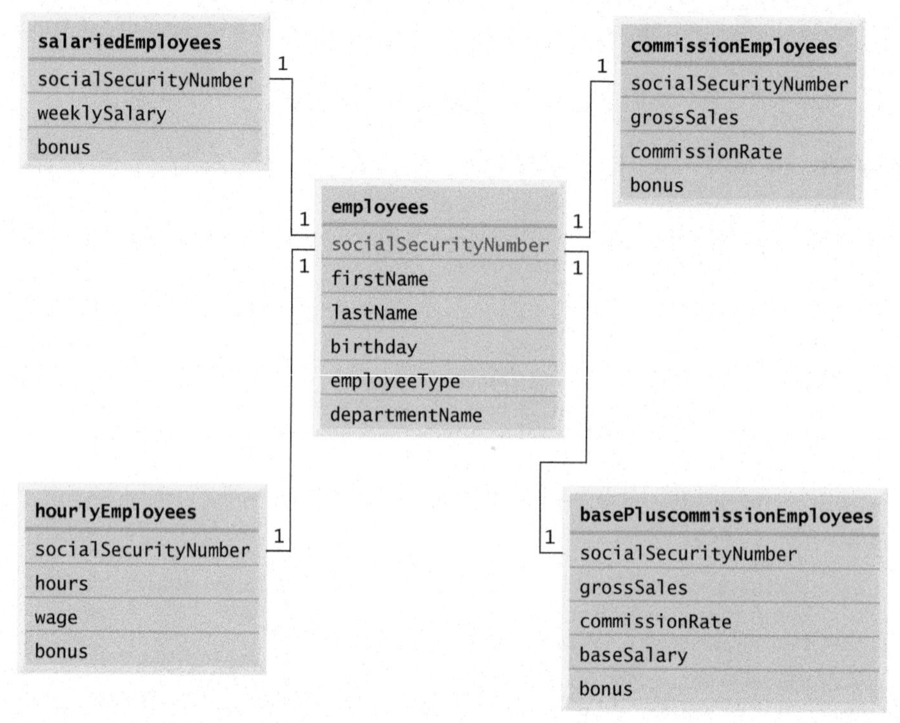

Fig. 24.35 | Table relationships in the `employees` database.

24.6 *(Employee Database Data-Manipulation Application)* Modify Exercise 24.5 to perform the following tasks:

a) Increase base salary by 10% for all base-plus-commission employees.
b) If the employee's birthday is in the current month, add a $100 bonus.
c) For all commission employees with gross sales over $10,000, add a $100 bonus.

24.7 *(Address-Book Modification: Update an Existing Entry)* Modify the program in Section 24.9 to include a method named `updatePerson` in class `PersonQueries`. The method should update an existing entry in the database. Provide an **Update** `Button`. When the user presses this `Button`, an event handler in the controller class should call `PersonQueries` method `updatePerson` to update the currently displayed contact with the data in the `TextFields`.

24.8 *(Address-Book Modification: Delete an Existing Entry)* Modify the program of Exercise 24.7 to include a method named `deletePerson` in class `PersonQueries`. The method should delete an existing entry in the database. Provide a **Delete** `Button`. When the user presses this `Button`, an event handler in the controller class should call `PersonQueries` method `deletePerson` to remove the currently selected contact, then update the `ListView` with the current set of entries in the database and select the first entry.

24.9 *(Optional Project: ATM Case Study with a Database)* Modify the optional ATM Case Study (located with this book's online chapters—see the inside front cover of the book) to use an actual database to store the account information. We provide a SQL script with the chapter's examples to create the `BankDatabase`, which has a single table consisting of four columns—`AccountNumber` (an `int`), `PIN` (an `int`), `AvailableBalance` (a `double`) and `TotalBalance` (a `double`).

Introduction to JShell: Java 9's REPL for Interactive Java

25

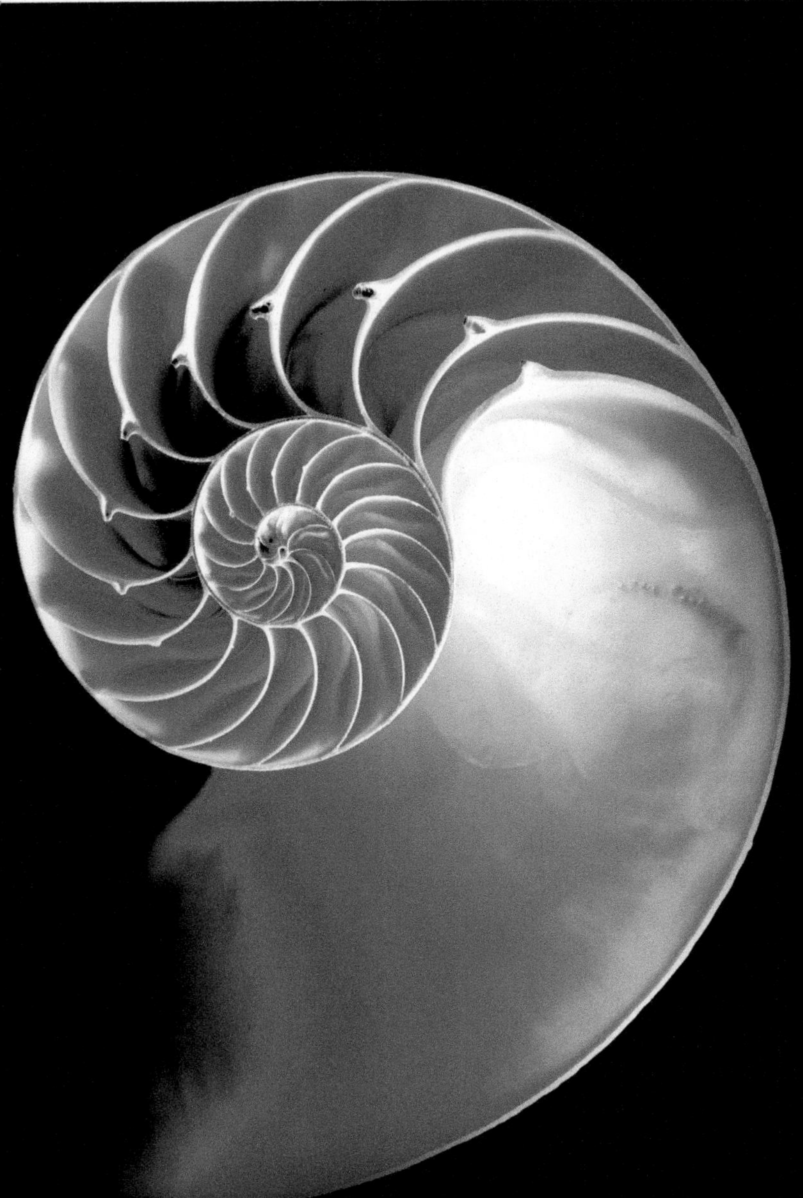

Objectives

In this chapter you'll:

- See how using JShell can enhance the learning and software development processes by enabling you to explore, discover and experiment with Java language and API features.
- Start a JShell session.
- Execute code snippets.
- Declare variables explicitly.
- Evaluate expressions.
- Edit existing code snippets.
- Declare and use a class.
- Save snippets to a file.
- Open a file of JShell snippets and evaluate them.
- Auto-complete code and JShell commands.
- Display method parameters and overloads.
- Discover and explore with the Java API documentation in JShell.
- Declare and use methods.
- Forward reference a method that has not yet been declared.
- See how JShell wraps exceptions.
- Import custom packages for use in a JShell session.
- Control JShell's feedback level.

Outline

25.1 Introduction

As educators, it's a joy to write this chapter on what may be the most important pedagogic improvement in Java since its inception more than two decades ago. The Java community—by far the largest programming language community in the world—has grown to more than 10 million developers. But along the way, not much has been done to improve
9 the learning process for novice programmers. That changes dramatically in Java 9 with the introduction of **JShell**—Java's **REPL (read-evaluate-print loop)**.[1]

---

1. We'd like to thank Robert Field at Oracle—the head of the JShell/REPL effort. We interacted with Mr. Field extensively as we developed Chapter 25. He answered our many questions. We reported JShell bugs and made suggestions for improvement.

Instructors have indicated a preference in introductory programming courses for languages with REPLs—and now Java has a rich REPL implementation. And with the new JShell APIs, third parties will build JShell and related interactive-development tools into the major IDEs like Eclipse, IntelliJ, NetBeans and others. Java 9 and JShell are evolving rapidly, so we've placed all our Java 9 content online—we'll keep it up-to-date as Java 9 evolves.

What is JShell?

What's the magic? It's simple. JShell provides a fast and friendly environment that enables you to quickly explore, discover and experiment with Java language features and its extensive libraries. REPLs like the one in JShell have been around for decades. In the 1960s, one of the earliest REPLs made convenient interactive development possible in the LISP programming language. Students of that era, like one of your authors, Harvey Deitel, found it fast and fun to use.

JShell replaces the tedious cycle of editing, compiling and executing with its read-evaluate-print loop. Rather than complete programs, you write **JShell commands** and Java code snippets. When you enter a snippet, JShell *immediately* **reads** it, **evaluates** it and **prints** the results that help you see the effects of your code. Then it **loops** to perform this process again for the next snippet. As you work through Chapter 25's scores of examples and exercises, you'll see how JShell and its instant feedback keep your attention, enhance your performance and speed the learning and software development processes.

Code Comes Alive

As you know, we emphasize the value of the live-code teaching approach in our books, focusing on *complete*, working programs. JShell brings this right down to the individual snippet level. Your code literally comes alive as you enter each line. Of course, you'll still make occasional errors as you enter your snippets. JShell reports compilation errors to you on a snippet-by-snippet basis. You can use this capability, for example, to test the items in our Common Programming Error tips and see the errors as they occur.

Kinds of Snippets

Snippets can be expressions, individual statements, multi-line statements and larger entities, like methods and classes. JShell supports all but a few Java features, but there are some differences designed to facilitate JShell's explore–discover–experiment capabilities. In JShell, methods do not need to be in classes, expressions and statements do not need to be in methods, and you do not need a `main` method (other differences are in Section 25.14). Eliminating this infrastructure saves you considerable time, especially compared to the lengthy repeated edit, compile and execute cycles of complete programs. And because JShell automatically displays the results of evaluating your expressions and statements, you do not need as many print statements as we use throughout this book's traditional Java code examples.

Discovery with Auto-Completion

We include a detailed treatment of **auto-completion**—a key discovery feature that speeds the coding process. After you type a portion of a name (class, method, variable, etc.) and press the *Tab* key, JShell completes the name for you or provides a list of all possible names that begin with what you've typed so far. You can then easily display method parameters and even the documentation that describes those methods.

Rapid Prototyping

Professional developers will commonly use JShell for rapid prototyping but not for full-out software development. Once you develop and test a small chunk of code, you can then paste it in to your larger project.

How This Chapter Is Organized

Chapter 25 is optional. For those who want to use JShell, the chapter has been designed as a series of units, paced to certain earlier chapters of the print book. Each unit begins with a statement like: "This section may be read after Chapter 2." So you'd begin by reading through Chapter 2, then read the corresponding section of this chapter—and similarly for subsequent chapters.

The Chapter 2 JShell Exercises

As you work your way through this chapter, execute each snippet and command in JShell to confirm that the features work as advertised. Sections 25.3–25.4 are designed to be read after Chapter 2. Once you read these sections, we recommend that you do Chapter 25's dozens of self-review exercises. JShell encourages you to "learn by doing," so the exercises have you write and test code snippets that exercise many of Chapter 2's Java features.

The self-review exercises are small and to the point, and the answers are provided to help you quickly get comfortable with JShell's capabilities. When you're done you'll have a great sense of what JShell is all about. Please tell us what you think of this new Java tool. Thanks!

Instead of rambling on about the advantages of JShell, we're going to let JShell itself convince you. If you have any questions as you work through the following examples and exercises, just write to us at `deitel@deitel.com` and we'll always respond promptly.

9

25.2 Installing JDK 9

Java 9 and its JShell are early access technologies that are still under development. This introduction to JShell is based on JDK 9 build 152. To use JShell, you must first install JDK 9, which is available in early access form at

```
https://jdk9.java.net/download/
```

The Before You Begin section that follows the Preface discusses the JDK version numbering schemes, then shows how to manage multiple JDK installations on your particular platform.

25.3 Introduction to JShell

[*Note:* This section may be read after studying Chapter 2, Introduction to Java Applications; Input/Output and Operators.]

In Chapter 2, to create a Java application, you:

1. created a class containing a `main` method.
2. declared in `main` the statements that will execute when you run the program.
3. compiled the program and fixed any compilation errors that occurred. This step had to be repeated until the program compiled without errors.
4. ran the program to see the results.

By automatically compiling and executing code as you complete each expression or statement, JShell eliminates the overhead of

- creating a class containing the code you wish to test,
- compiling the class and
- executing the class.

Instead, you can focus on interactively discovering and experimenting with Java's language and API features. If you enter code that does not compile, JShell immediately reports the errors. You can then use JShell's editing features to quickly fix and re-execute the code.

25.3.1 Starting a JShell Session

To start a JShell session in:

- Microsoft Windows, open a **Command Prompt** then type `jshell` and press *Enter*.
- macOS (formerly OS X), open a **Terminal** window then type the following command and press *Enter*.

```
$JAVA_HOME/bin/jshell
```

- Linux, open a shell window then type `jshell` and press *Enter*.

The preceding commands execute a new JShell session and display the following message and the **`jshell>` prompt**:

```
|  Welcome to JShell -- Version 9-ea
|  For an introduction type: /help intro

jshell>
```

In the first line above, "`Version 9-ea`" indicates that you're using the ea (that is, early access) version of JDK 9. JShell precedes informational messages with vertical bars (|). You are now ready to enter Java code or JShell commands. 9

25.3.2 Executing Statements

[*Note:* As you work through this chapter, type the same code and JShell commands that we show at each `jshell>` prompt to ensure that what you see on your screen will match what we show in the sample outputs.]

JShell has two input types:

- Java code (which the JShell documentation refers to as **snippets**) and
- JShell commands.

In this section and Section 25.3.3, we begin with Java code snippets. Subsequent sections introduce JShell commands.

You can type any expression or statement at the `jshell>` prompt then press *Enter* to execute the code and see its results immediately. Consider the program of Fig. 2.1, which we show again in Fig. 25.1. To demonstrate how `System.out.println` works, this program required many lines of code and comments, which you had to write, compile and execute. Even without the comments, five code lines were still required (lines 4 and 6–9).

```
1 // Fig. 25.1: Welcome1.java
2 // Text-printing program.
3
4 public class Welcome1 {
5    // main method begins execution of Java application
6    public static void main(String[] args) {
7       System.out.println("Welcome to Java Programming!");
8    } // end method main
9 } // end class Welcome1
```

```
Welcome to Java Programming!
```

Fig. 25.1 | Text-printing program.

In JShell, you can execute the statement in line 7 without creating all the infrastructure of class `Welcome1` and its `main` method:

```
jshell> System.out.println("Welcome to Java Programming!")
Welcome to Java Programming!

jshell>
```

In this case, JShell displays the snippet's command-line output below the initial `jshell>` prompt and the statement you entered. Per our convention, we show user inputs in bold.

Notice that we did not enter the preceding statement's semicolon (`;`). JShell adds *only* terminating semicolons.[2] You need to add a semicolon if the end of the statement is not the end of the line—for example, if the statement is inside braces (`{` and `}`). Also, if there is more than one statement on a line then you need a semicolon between statements, but not after the last statement.

The blank line before the second `jshell>` prompt is the result of the newline displayed by method `println` and the newline that JShell always displays before each `jshell>` prompt. Using `print` rather than `println` eliminates the blank line:

```
jshell> System.out.print("Welcome to Java Programming!")
Welcome to Java Programming!
jshell>
```

JShell keeps track of everything you type, which can be useful for re-executing prior statements and modifying statements to update the tasks they perform.

25.3.3 Declaring Variables Explicitly

Almost anything you can declare in a typical Java source-code file also can be declared in JShell (Section 25.14 discusses some of the features you cannot use). For example, you can explicitly declare a variable as follows:

```
jshell> int number1
number1 ==> 0

jshell>
```

2. Not requiring semicolons is one example of how JShell reinterprets standard Java for convenient interactive use. We discuss several of these throughout the chapter and summarize them in Section 25.14.

When you enter a variable declaration, JShell displays the variable's name (in this case, `number1`) followed by `==>` (which means, "has the value") and the variable's initial value (`0`). If you do not specify an initial value explicitly, the variable is initialized to its type's default value—in this case, `0` for an `int` variable.

A variable can be initialized in its declaration—let's redeclare `number1`:

```
jshell> int number1 = 30
number1 ==> 30

jshell>
```

JShell displays

```
number1 ==> 30
```

to indicate that `number1` now has the value `30`. When you declare a new variable with the *same name* as another variable in the current JShell session, JShell replaces the first declaration with the new one.[3] Because `number1` was declared previously, we could have simply assigned `number1` a value, as in

```
jshell> number1 = 45
number1 ==> 45

jshell>
```

Compilation Errors in JShell

You must declare variables before using them in JShell. The following declaration of `int` variable `sum` attempts to use a variable named `number2` that we have not yet declared, so JShell reports a compilation error, indicating that the compiler was unable to find a variable named `number2`:

```
jshell> int sum = number1 + number2
|  Error:
|  cannot find symbol
|    symbol:   variable number2
|  int sum = number1 + number2;
|                      ^-----^

jshell>
```

The error message uses the notation `^-----^` to highlight the error in the statement. No error is reported for the previously declared variable `number1`. Because this snippet has a compilation error, it's invalid. However, JShell still maintains the snippet as part of the JShell session's history, which includes valid snippets, invalid snippets and commands that you've typed. As you'll soon see, you can recall this invalid snippet and execute it again later. JShell's **`/history`** command displays the current session's history—that is, *everything* you've typed:

3. Redeclaring an existing variable is another example of how JShell reinterprets standard Java for interactive use. This behavior is different from how the Java compiler handles a new declaration of an existing variable—such a "double declaration" generates a compilation error.

```
jshell> /history

System.out.println("Welcome to Java Programming!")
System.out.print("Welcome to Java Programming!")
int number1
int number1 = 45
number1 = 45
int sum = number1 + number2
/history

jshell>
```

Fixing the Error

JShell makes it easy to fix a prior error and re-execute a snippet. Let's fix the preceding error by first declaring `number2` with the value `72`:

```
jshell> int number2 = 72
number2 ==> 72

jshell>
```

Subsequent snippets can now use `number2`—in a moment, you'll re-execute the snippet that declared and initialized `sum` with `number1 + number2`.

Recalling and Re-executing a Previous Snippet

Now that both `number1` and `number2` are declared, we can declare the `int` variable `sum`. You can use the up and down arrow keys to navigate backward and forward through the snippets and JShell commands you've entered previously. Rather than retyping `sum`'s declaration, you can press the up arrow key three times to recall the declaration that failed previously. JShell recalls your prior inputs in reverse order—the last line of text you typed is recalled first. So, the first time you press the up arrow key, the following appears at the `jshell>` prompt:

```
jshell> int number2 = 72
```

The second time you press the up arrow key, the `/history` command appears:

```
jshell> /history
```

The third time you press the up arrow key, `sum`'s prior declaration appears:

```
jshell> int sum = number1 + number2
```

Now you can press *Enter* to re-execute the snippet that declares and initializes `sum`:

```
jshell> int sum = number1 + number2
sum ==> 117

jshell>
```

JShell adds the values of `number1` (`45`) and `number2` (`72`), stores the result in the new `sum` variable, then shows `sum`'s value (`117`).

25.3.4 Listing and Executing Prior Snippets

You can view a list of all previous valid Java code snippets with JShell's **`/list`** command—JShell displays the snippets in the order you entered them:

```
jshell> /list

   1 : System.out.println("Welcome to Java Programming!")
   2 : System.out.print("Welcome to Java Programming!")
   4 : int number1 = 30;
   5 : number1 = 45
   6 : int number2 = 72;
   7 : int sum = number1 + number2;

jshell>
```

Each valid snippet is identified by a sequential **snippet ID**. The snippet with ID 3 is *missing* above, because we replaced that original snippet

```
int number1
```

with the one that has the ID 4 in the preceding `/list`. Note that `/list` may not display everything that `/history` does. As you recall, if you omit a terminating semicolon, JShell inserts it for you behind the scenes. When you say `/list`, *only* the declarations (snippets 4, 6 and 7) actually show the semicolons that JShell inserted.

Snippet 1 above is just an expression. If we type it with a terminating semicolon, it's an **expression statement.**

Executing Snippets By ID Number

You can execute any prior snippet by typing */id*, where *id* is the snippet's ID. For example, when you enter /1:

```
jshell> /1
System.out.println("Welcome to Java Programming!")
Welcome to Java Programming!

jshell>
```

JShell displays the first snippet we entered, executes it and shows the result.[4] You can re-execute the last snippet you typed (whether it was valid or invalid) with `/!`:

```
jshell> /!
System.out.println("Welcome to Java Programming!")
Welcome to Java Programming!

jshell>
```

JShell assigns an ID to every valid snippet you execute, so even though

```
System.out.println("Welcome to Java Programming!")
```

already exists in this session as snippet `1`, JShell creates a new snippet with the next ID in sequence (in this case, `8` and `9` for the last two snippets). Executing the `/list` command shows that snippets `1`, `8` and `9` are identical:

4. At the time of this writing, you cannot use the */id* command to execute a *range* of previous snippets; however, the JShell command `/reload` can re-execute *all* existing snippets (Section 25.12.3).

```
jshell> /list

   1 : System.out.println("Welcome to Java Programming!")
   2 : System.out.print("Welcome to Java Programming!")
   4 : int number1 = 30;
   5 : number1 = 45
   6 : int number2 = 72;
   7 : int sum = number1 + number2;
   8 : System.out.println("Welcome to Java Programming!")
   9 : System.out.println("Welcome to Java Programming!")

jshell>
```

25.3.5 Evaluating Expressions and Declaring Variables Implicitly

When you enter an expression in JShell, it evaluates the expression, implicitly creates a variable and assigns the expression's value to the variable. **Implicit variables** are named $#, where # is the new snippet's ID.[5] For example:

```
jshell> 11 + 5
$10 ==> 16

jshell>
```

evaluates the expression `11 + 5` and assigns the resulting value (`16`) to the implicitly declared variable `$10`, because there were nine prior valid snippets (even though one was deleted because we redeclared the variable `number1`). JShell *infers* that the type of `$10` is `int`, because the expression `11 + 5` adds two `int` values, producing an `int`. Expressions may also include one or more method calls. The list of snippets is now:

```
jshell> /list

   1 : System.out.println("Welcome to Java Programming!")
   2 : System.out.print("Welcome to Java Programming!")
   4 : int number1 = 30;
   5 : number1 = 45
   6 : int number2 = 72;
   7 : int sum = number1 + number2;
   8 : System.out.println("Welcome to Java Programming!")
   9 : System.out.println("Welcome to Java Programming!")
  10 : 11 + 5

jshell>
```

Note that the implicitly declared variable `$10` appears in the list simply as `10` without the `$`.

25.3.6 Using Implicitly Declared Variables

Like any other declared variable, you can use an implicitly declared variable in an expression. For example, the following assigns to the *existing* variable `sum` the result of adding `number1` (`45`) and `$10` (`16`):

5. Implicitly declared variables are another example of how JShell reinterprets standard Java for interactive use. In regular Java programs you must explicitly declare *every* variable.

```
jshell> sum = number1 + $10
sum ==> 61

jshell>
```

The list of snippets is now:

```
jshell> /list

   1 : System.out.println("Welcome to Java Programming!")
   2 : System.out.print("Welcome to Java Programming!")
   4 : int number1 = 30;
   5 : number1 = 45
   6 : int number2 = 72;
   7 : int sum = number1 + number2;
   8 : System.out.println("Welcome to Java Programming!")
   9 : System.out.println("Welcome to Java Programming!")
  10 : 11 + 5
  11 : sum = number1 + $10

jshell>
```

25.3.7 Viewing a Variable's Value

You can view a variable's value at any time simply by typing its name and pressing *Enter*:

```
jshell> sum
sum ==> 61

jshell>
```

JShell treats the variable name as an expression and simply evaluates its value.

25.3.8 Resetting a JShell Session

You can remove all prior code from a JShell session by entering the `/reset` command:

```
jshell> /reset
|  Resetting state.

jshell> /list

jshell>
```

The subsequent `/list` command shows that all prior snippets were removed. Confirmation messages displayed by JShell, such as

```
|  Resetting state.
```

are helpful when you're first becoming familiar with JShell. In Section 25.12.5, we'll show how you can change the JShell *feedback mode*, making it more or less verbose.

25.3.9 Writing Multiline Statements

Next, we write an `if` statement that determines whether `45` is less than `72`. First, let's store 45 and 72 in implicitly declared variables, as in:

```
jshell> 45
$1 ==> 45

jshell> 72
$2 ==> 72

jshell>
```

Next, begin typing the `if` statement:

```
jshell> if ($1 < $2) {
   ...>
```

JShell knows that the `if` statement is incomplete, because we typed the opening left brace, but did not provide a body or a closing right brace. So, JShell displays the **continuation prompt** `...>` at which you can enter more of the control statement. The following completes and evaluates the `if` statement:

```
jshell> if ($1 < $2) {
   ...>     System.out.printf("%d < %d%n", $1, $2);
   ...> }
45 < 72

jshell>
```

In this case, a second continuation prompt appeared because the `if` statement was still missing its terminating right brace (}). Note that the statement-terminating semicolon (;) at the end of the `System.out.printf` statement in the `if`'s body is required. We manually indented the `if`'s body statement—JShell does *not* add spacing or braces for you as IDEs generally do. Also, JShell assigns each multiline code snippet—such as an `if` statement—only one snippet ID. The list of snippets is now:

```
jshell> /list

   1 : 45
   2 : 72
   3 : if ($1 < $2) {
           System.out.printf("%d < %d%n", $1, $2);
       }

jshell>
```

25.3.10 Editing Code Snippets

Sometimes you might want to create a new snippet, based on an existing snippet in the current JShell session. For example, suppose you want to create an `if` statement that determines whether `$1` is *greater than* `$2`. The statement that performs this task

```
if ($1 > $2) {
    System.out.printf("%d > %d%n", $1, $2);
}
```

is nearly identical to the `if` statement in Section 25.3.9, so it would be easier to edit the existing statement rather than typing the new one from scratch. When you edit a snippet, JShell saves the edited version as a new snippet with the next snippet ID in sequence.

Editing a Single-Line Snippet

To edit a single-line snippet, locate it with the up-arrow key, make your changes within the snippet then press *Enter* to evaluate it. See Section 25.13 for some keyboard shortcuts that can help you edit single-line snippets.

Editing a Multiline Snippet

For a larger snippet that's spread over several lines—such as a `if` statement that contains one or more statements—you can edit the entire snippet by using JShell's **`/edit`** command to open the snippet in the **JShell Edit Pad** (Fig. 25.2). The command

```
/edit
```

opens **JShell Edit Pad** and displays *all* valid code snippets you've entered so far. To edit a specific snippet, include the snippet's ID, as in

```
/edit id
```

So, the command:

```
/edit 3
```

displays the `if` statement from Section 25.3.9 in **JShell Edit Pad** (Fig. 25.2)—no snippet IDs are shown in this window. **JShell Edit Pad**'s window is *modal*—that is, while it's open, you cannot enter code snippets or commands at the JShell prompt.

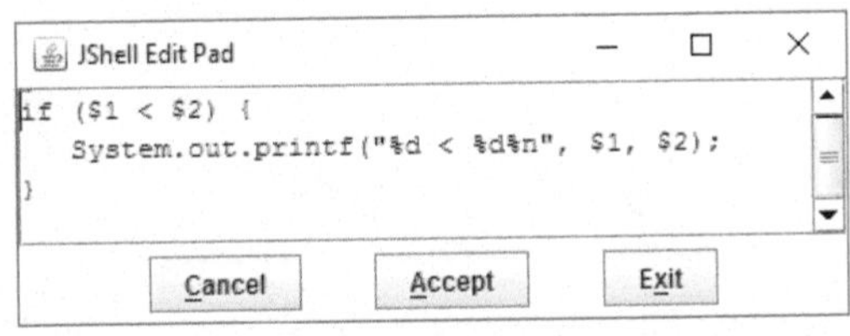

Fig. 25.2 | **JShell Edit Pad** showing the `if` statement from Section 25.3.9.

JShell Edit Pad supports only basic editing capabilities. You can:

- click to insert the cursor at a specific position to begin typing,
- move the cursor via the arrow keys on your keyboard,
- drag the mouse to select text,
- use the *Delete* (*Backspace*) key to delete text,
- cut, copy and paste text using your operating system's keyboard shortcuts, and
- enter text, including new snippets separate from the one(s) you're editing.

In the first and second lines of the `if` statement, select each less than operator (<) and change it to a greater than operator (>), then click **Accept** to create a new `if` statement containing the edited code. When you click **Accept**, JShell also immediately evaluates the new `if` statement and displays its results (if any)—because `$1` (`45`) is *not* greater than `$2` (`72`) the `System.out.printf` statement does not execute,[6] so no additional output is shown in JShell.

If you want to return immediately to the JShell prompt, rather than clicking **Accept**, you could click **Exit** to execute the edited snippet and close **JShell Edit Pad.** Clicking **Cancel** closes **JShell Edit Pad** and discards any changes you made since the last time you clicked **Accept**, or since **JShell Edit Pad** was launched if have not yet clicked **Accept.**

When you change or create multiple snippets then click **Accept** or **Exit**, JShell compares the **JShell Edit Pad** contents with the previously saved snippets. It then executes every modified or new snippet.

Adding a New Snippet Via JShell Edit Pad

To show that **JShell Edit Pad** does, in fact, execute snippets immediately when you click **Accept**, let's change $1's value to 100 by entering the following statement following the `if` statement after the other code in **JShell Edit Pad:**

```
$1 = 100
```

and clicking **Accept** (Fig. 25.3). Each time you modify a variable's value, JShell immediately displays the variable's name and new value:

```
jshell> /edit 3
$1 ==> 100
```

Click **Exit** to close **JShell Edit Pad** and return to the `jshell>` prompt.

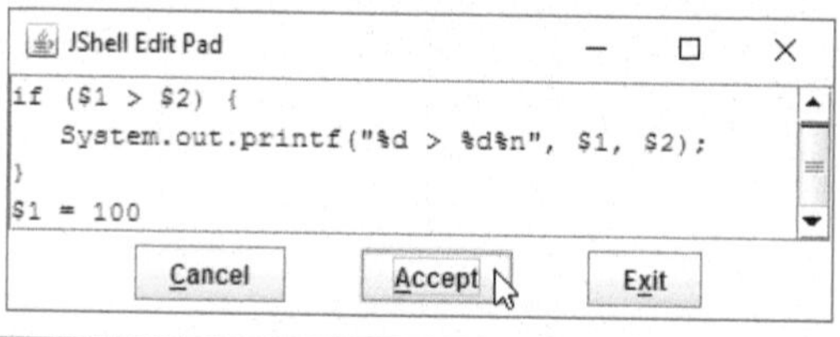

Fig. 25.3 | Entering a new statement following the `if` statement in **JShell Edit Pad**.

The following lists the current snippets—notice that each multiline `if` statement has only one ID:

```
jshell> /list

   1 : 45
   2 : 72
   3 : if ($1 < $2) {
          System.out.printf("%d < %d%n", $1, $2);
       }
   4 : if ($1 > $2) {
          System.out.printf("%d > %d%n", $1, $2);
       }
   5 : $1 = 100

jshell>
```

6. We could have made this an `if...else` statement to show output when the condition is *false*, but this section is meant to be used with Chapter 2 where we introduce only the single-selection `if` statement.

Executing the New `if` *Statement Again*

The following re-executes the new `if` statement (ID 4) with the updated `$1` value:

```
jshell> /4
if ($1 > $2) {
   System.out.printf("%d > %d%n", $1, $2);
}
100 > 72

jshell>
```

The condition `$1 > $2` is now `true`, so the `if` statement's body executes. The list of snippets is now

```
jshell> /list

   1 : 45
   2 : 72
   3 : if ($1 < $2) {
          System.out.printf("%d < %d%n", $1, $2);
       }
   4 : if ($1 > $2) {
          System.out.printf("%d > %d%n", $1, $2);
       }
   5 : $1 = 100
   6 : if ($1 > $2) {
          System.out.printf("%d > %d%n", $1, $2);
       }

jshell>
```

25.3.11 Exiting JShell

To terminate the current JShell session, use the **/exit** command or type the keyboard shortcut *Ctrl* + *d* (or *control* + *d*). This returns you to the command-line prompt in your **Command Prompt** (in Windows), **Terminal** (in macOS) or shell (in Linux—sometimes called **Terminal**, depending on your Linux distribution).

25.4 Command-Line Input in JShell

[*Note:* This section may be read after studying Chapter 2, Introduction to Java Applications; Input/Output and Operators and the preceding sections in this chapter.]

In Chapter 2, we showed command-line input using a `Scanner` object:

```
Scanner input = new Scanner(System.in);

System.out.print("Enter first integer: ");
int number1 = input.nextInt();
```

We created a `Scanner`, prompted the user for input, then used `Scanner` method `nextInt` to read a value. Recall that the program then waited for you to type an integer and press *Enter* before proceeding to the next statement. The on-screen interaction appeared as:

```
Enter first integer: 45
```

This section shows what that interaction looks like in JShell.

*Creating a **Scanner***

Start a new JShell session or /reset the current one, then create a Scanner object:

```
jshell> Scanner input = new Scanner(System.in)
input ==> java.util.Scanner[delimiters=\p{javaWhitespace}+] ...
   \E][infinity string=\Q∞\E]

jshell>
```

You do not need to import Scanner. JShell automatically imports the java.util package and several others—we show the complete list in Section 25.10. When you create an object, JShell displays its text representation. The notation to the right of input ==> is the Scanner's text representation (which you can simply ignore).

Prompting for Input and Reading a Value

Next, prompt the user for input:

```
jshell> System.out.print("Enter first integer: ")
Enter first integer:
jshell>
```

The statement's output is displayed immediately, followed by the next jshell> prompt. Now enter the input statement:

```
jshell> int number1 = input.nextInt()
_
```

At this point, JShell waits for your input. The input cursor is positioned below the jshell> prompt and snippet you just entered—indicated by the underscore (_) above—rather than next to the prompt "Enter first integer:" as it was in Chapter 2. Now type an integer and press *Enter* to assign it to number1—the last snippet's execution is now complete, so the next jshell> prompt appears.:

```
jshell> int number1 = input.nextInt()
45
number1 ==> 45

jshell>
```

Though you can use Scanner for command-line input in JShell, in most cases it's unnecessary. The goal of the preceding interactions was simply to store an integer value in the variable number1. You can accomplish that in JShell with the simple assignment

```
jshell> int number1 = 45
number1 ==> 45

jshell>
```

For this reason, you'll typically use assignments, rather than command-line input in JShell. We introduced Scanner here, because sometimes you'll want to copy code you developed in JShell into a conventional Java program.

25.5 Declaring and Using Classes

[*Note:* This section may be read after studying Chapter 3, Introduction to Classes, Objects, Methods and Strings.]

In Section 25.3, we demonstrated basic JShell capabilities. In this section, we create a class and manipulate an object of that class. We'll use the version of class `Account` presented in Fig. 3.1.

25.5.1 Creating a Class in JShell

Start a new JShell session (or `/reset` the current one), then declare class `Account`—we ignored the comments from Fig. 3.1:

```
jshell> public class Account {
   ...>    private String name;
   ...>
   ...>    public void setName(String name) {
   ...>       this.name = name;
   ...>    }
   ...>
   ...>    public String getName() {
   ...>       return name;
   ...>    }
   ...> }
|  created class Account

jshell>
```

JShell recognizes when you enter the class's closing brace—then displays

```
|  created class Account
```

and issues the next `jshell>` prompt. Note that the semicolons throughout class `Account`'s body are required.

To save time, rather than typing a class's code as shown above, you can load an existing source code file into JShell, as shown in Section 25.5.6. Though you can specify access modifiers like `public` on your classes (and other types), JShell ignores all access modifiers on the top-level types except for `abstract` (discussed in Chapter 10).

Viewing Declared Classes

To view the names of the classes you've declared so far, enter the **/types** command:[7]

```
jshell> /types
|    class Account

jshell>
```

25.5.2 Explicitly Declaring Reference-Type Variables

The following creates the `Account` variable `account`:

```
jshell> Account account
account ==> null

jshell>
```

The default value of a reference-type variable is `null`.

---

7. `/types` actually displays all types you declare, including classes, interfaces and enums.

25.5.3 Creating Objects

You can create new objects. The following creates an `Account` variable named `account` and initializes it with a new object:

```
jshell> account = new Account()
account ==> Account@56ef9176

jshell>
```

The strange notation

```
Account@56ef9176
```

is the default text representation of the new `Account` object. If a class provides a custom text representation, you'll see that instead. We show how to provide a custom text representation for objects of a class in Section 7.6. We discuss the default text representation of objects in Section 9.6. The value after the `@` symbol is the object's *hashcode*. We discuss hashcodes in Section 16.10.

Declaring an Implicit `Account` *Variable Initialized with an* `Account` *Object*

If you create an object with only the expression `new Account()`, JShell assigns the object to an implicit variable of type `Account`, as in:

```
jshell> new Account()
$4 ==> Account@1ed4004b

jshell>
```

Note that this object's hashcode (`1ed4004b`) is different from the prior `Account` object's hashcode (`56ef9176`)—these typically are different, but that's not guaranteed.

Viewing Declared Variables

You can view all the variables you've declared so far with the JShell **`/vars`** command:

```
jshell> /vars
|    Account account = Account@56ef9176
|    Account $4 = Account@1ed4004b

jshell>
```

For each variable, JShell shows the type and variable name followed by an equal sign and the variable's text representation.

25.5.4 Manipulating Objects

Once you have an object, you can call its methods. In fact, you already did this with the `System.out` object by calling its `println`, `print` and `printf` methods in earlier snippets.

The following sets the `account` object's name:

```
jshell> account.setName("Amanda")

jshell>
```

The method `setName` has the return type `void`, so it does not return a value and JShell does not show any additional output.

The following gets the `account` object's name:

```
jshell> account.getName()
$6 ==> "Amanda"

jshell>
```

Method `getName` returns a `String`. When you invoke a method that returns a value, JShell stores the value in an implicitly declared variable. In this case, `$6`'s type is *inferred* to be `String`. Of course, you could have assigned the result of the preceding method call to an explicitly declared variable.

If you invoke a method as part of a larger statement, the return value is used in that statement, rather than stored. For example, the following uses `println` to display the `account` object's name:

```
jshell> System.out.println(account.getName())
Amanda

jshell>
```

25.5.5 Creating a Meaningful Variable Name for an Expression

You can give a meaningful variable name to a value that JShell previously assigned to an implicit variable. For example, with the following snippet recalled

```
jshell> account.getName()
```

on Windows type

Alt + *F1* *v*

on macOS type

Esc + *F1* *v* or *Alt* + *F1* *v*

and on Linux type

Alt + *Enter* *v*

The + notation means that you should you press *both* keys together (e.g. *Alt* and *F1*), then release those keys and press *v*. JShell infers the expression's type and begins a variable declaration for you—`account.getName()` returns a `String`, so JShell inserts `String` and an equal sign (=) before the expression, as in

```
jshell> account.getName()
jshell> String _= account.getName()
```

JShell also positions the cursor (indicated by the _ above) immediately before the = so you can simply type the variable name, as in

```
jshell> String name = account.getName()
name ==> "Amanda"

jshell>
```

When you press *Enter*, JShell evaluates the new snippet and stores the value in the specified variable.

25.5.6 Saving and Opening Code-Snippet Files

You can save all of a session's valid code snippets to a file, which you can then load into a JShell session as needed. To save just the *valid* snippets, use the **/save** command, as in:

```
/save filename
```

By default, the file is created in the folder from which you launched JShell. To store the file in a different location, specify the complete path of the file.

Once you save your snippets, they can be reloaded with the **/open** command:

```
/open filename
```

which executes each snippet in the file.

Using /open to Load Java Source-Code Files

You also can open existing Java source code files using `/open`. For example, let's assume you'd like to experiment with class `Account` from Fig. 3.1 (as you did in Section 25.5.1). Rather than typing its code into JShell, you can save time by loading the class from the source file `Account.java`. In a command window, you'd change to the folder containing `Account.java`, execute JShell, then use the following command to load the class declaration into JShell:

```
/open Account.java
```

To load a file from another folder, you can specify the full pathname of the file to open. In Section 25.10, we'll show how to use existing compiled classes in JShell.

25.6 Discovery with JShell Auto-Completion

[*Note:* This section may be read after studying Chapter 3, Introduction to Classes, Objects, Methods and Strings, and completing Section 25.5.]

JShell can help you write code. When you partially type the name of an existing class, variable or method then press the *Tab* key, JShell does one of the following:

- If no other name matches what you've typed so far, JShell enters the rest of the name for you.
- If there are multiple names that begin with the same letters, JShell displays a list of those names to help you decide what to type next—then you can type the next letter(s) and press *Tab* again to complete the name.
- If no names match what you typed so far, JShell does nothing and your operating system's alert sound plays as feedback.

Auto-completion is normally an IDE feature, but with JShell it's IDE independent.

Let's first list the snippets we've entered since the last `/reset` (from Section 25.5):

```
jshell> /list

   1 : public class Account {
          private String name;
          public void setName(String name) {
             this.name = name;
          }
          public String getName() {
             return name;
          }
       }
   2 : Account account;
   3 : account = new Account()
   4 : new Account()
   5 : account.setName("Amanda")
   6 : account.getName()
   7 : System.out.println(account.getName())
   8 : String name = account.getName();
jshell>
```

25.6.1 Auto-Completing Identifiers

The only variable declared so far that begins with lowercase "a" is `account`, which was declared in snippet 2. Auto-completion is case sensitive, so "a" does not match the class name `Account`. If you type "a" at the `jshell>` prompt:

```
jshell> a
```

then press *Tab*, JShell auto-completes the name:

```
jshell> account
```

If you then enter a dot:

```
jshell> account.
```

then press *Tab*, JShell does not know what method you want to call, so it displays a list of everything—in this case, all the methods—that can appear to the right of the dot:

```
jshell> account.
equals(       getClass()    getName()     hashCode()    notify()
notifyAll()   setName(      toString()    wait(

jshell> account.
```

and follows the list with a new `jshell>` prompt that includes what you've typed so far. The list includes the methods we declared in class `Account` (snippet 1) *and* several methods that all Java classes have (as we discuss in Chapter 9). In the list of method names

- those followed by "`()`" are methods that do not require arguments and
- those followed only by "`(`" are methods that either require at least one argument or that are so-called *overloaded methods*—multiple methods with the same name, but different parameter lists (discussed in Section 6.12).

Let's assume you want to use `Account`'s `setName` method to change the name stored in the `account` object to `"John"`. There's only one method that begins with `"s"`, so you can type `s` then *Tab* to auto-complete `setName`:

```
jshell> account.setName(
```

JShell automatically inserts the method call's opening left parenthesis. Now you can complete the snippet as in:

```
jshell> account.setName("John")

jshell>
```

25.6.2 Auto-Completing JShell Commands

Auto-completion also works for JShell commands. If you type / then press *Tab*, JShell displays the list of JShell commands:

```
jshell> /
/!          /?          /drop       /edit       /env        /exit
/help       /history    /imports    /list       /methods    /open
/reload     /reset      /save       /set        /types      /vars

jshell> /
```

If you then type `h` and press *Tab*, JShell displays only the commands that start with `/h`:

```
jshell> /h
/help       /history

jshell> /h
```

Finally, if you type `"i"` and press *Tab*, JShell auto-completes `/history`. Similarly, if you type `/l` then press *Tab*, JShell auto-completes the command as `/list`, because only that command starts with `/l`.

25.7 Exploring a Class's Members and Viewing Documentation

[*Note:* This section may be read after studying Chapter 6, Methods: A Deeper Look, and the preceding portions of Chapter 25.]

The preceding section introduced basic auto-completion capabilities. When using JShell for experimentation and discovery, you'll often want to learn more about a class before using it. In this section, we'll show you how to:

- view the parameters required by a method so that you can call it correctly
- view the documentation for a method
- view the documentation for a field of a class
- view the documentation for a class, and
- view the list of overloads for a given method.

To demonstrate these features, let's explore class Math. Start a new JShell session or /reset the current one.

25.7.1 Listing Class Math's static Members

As we discussed in Chapter 6, class Math contains only static members—static methods for various mathematical calculations and the static constants PI and E. To view a complete list, type "Math." then press *Tab*:

```
jshell> Math.
E                 IEEEremainder(    PI                abs(
acos(             addExact(         asin(             atan(
atan2(            cbrt(             ceil(             class
copySign(         cos(              cosh(             decrementExact(
exp(              expm1(            floor(            floorDiv(
floorMod(         fma(              getExponent(      hypot(
incrementExact(   log(              log10(            log1p(
max(              min(              multiplyExact(    multiplyFull(
multiplyHigh(     negateExact(      nextAfter(        nextDown(
nextUp(           pow(              random()          rint(
round(            scalb(            signum(           sin(
sinh(             sqrt(             subtractExact(    tan(
tanh(             toDegrees(        toIntExact(       toRadians(
ulp(

jshell> Math.
```

As you know, JShell auto-completion displays a list of everything that can appear to the right of the dot (.). Here we typed a class name and a dot (.), so JShell shows only the class's static members. The names that are not followed by any parentheses (E and PI) are the class's static variables. All the other names are the class's static methods:

- Any method names followed by ()—only random in this case—do not require any arguments.
- Any method names followed by only an opening left parenthesis, (, require at least one argument or are overloaded.

You can easily view the value of the constants PI and E:

```
jshell> Math.PI
$1 ==> 3.141592653589793

jshell> Math.E
$2 ==> 2.718281828459045

jshell>
```

25.7.2 Viewing a Method's Parameters

Let's assume you wish to test Math's pow method (introduced in Section 5.4.2), but you do not know the parameters it requires. You can type

```
Math.p
```

then press *Tab* to auto-complete the name pow:

```
jshell> Math.pow(
```

Since there are no other methods that begin with "pow", JShell also inserts the left parenthesis to indicate the beginning of a method call. Next, you can type *Shift* + *Tab* to view the method's parameters:

```
jshell> Math.pow(
double Math.pow(double a, double b)
<press shift-tab again to see javadoc>

jshell> Math.pow(
```

JShell displays the method's return type, name and complete parameter list followed by the next `jshell>` prompt containing what you've typed so far. As you can see, the method requires two `double` parameters.

25.7.3 Viewing a Method's Documentation

JShell integrates the Java API documentation so you can view documentation conveniently in JShell, rather than requiring you to use a separate web browser. Suppose you'd like to learn more about pow before completing your code snippet. You can press *Shift* + *Tab* again to view the method's Java documentation (known as its javadoc)—we cut out some of the documentation text and replaced it with a vertical ellipsis (...) to save space (try the steps in your own JShell session to see the complete text):

```
jshell> Math.pow(
double Math.pow(double a, double b)
Returns the value of the first argument raised to the power of the
second argument.Special cases:
  * If the second argument is positive or negative zero, then the
    result is 1.0.
.
.
.
<press space for next page, Q to quit>
```

For long documentation, JShell displays part of it, then shows the message

```
<press space for next page, Q to quit>
```

You can press the space key to view the next page of documentation. If you press *Q* (or *q*) or if JShell has already displayed the complete documentation, the next `jshell>` prompt shows the portion of the snippet you've typed so far:

```
jshell> Math.pow(
```

25.7.4 Viewing a `public` Field's Documentation

You can use the *Shift* + *Tab* feature to learn more about a class's `public` fields. For example, if you enter `Math.PI` followed by *Shift* + *Tab*, JShell displays

```
jshell> Math.PI
Math.PI:double
<press shift-tab again to see javadoc>
```

which shows `Math.PI`'s type and indicates that you can use *Shift + Tab* again to view the documentation. Doing so displays:

```
jshell> Math.PI
Math.PI:double
The double value that is closer than any other to pi, the ratio of
the circumference of a circle to its diameter.

jshell> Math.PI
```

and the next `jshell>` prompt shows the portion of the snippet you've typed so far.

25.7.5 Viewing a Class's Documentation

You also can type a class name then *Shift + Tab* to view the class's fully qualified name. For example, typing `Math` then *Shift + Tab* shows:

```
jshell> Math
java.lang.Math
<press shift-tab again to see javadoc>

jshell> Math
```

indicating that class `Math` is in the package `java.lang`. Typing *Shift + Tab* again shows the beginning of the class's documentation:

```
jshell> Math
java.lang.Math
The class Math contains methods for performing basic numeric opera-
tions such as the elementary exponential, logarithm, square root,
and trigonometric functions. Unlike some of the numeric methods of
.
.
.
<press space for next page, Q to quit>
```

In this case, there is more documentation to view, so you can press the space key to view it or *Q* (or *q*) to return to the `jshell>` prompt showing the portion of the snippet you've typed so far:

```
jshell> Math
```

25.7.6 Viewing Method Overloads

Many classes have *overloaded* methods. When you press *Shift + Tab* to view an overloaded method's parameters, JShell displays the complete list of overloads, showing the parameters for every overload. For example, method `Math.abs` has four overloads:

```
jshell> Math.abs(
int Math.abs(int a)
long Math.abs(long a)
float Math.abs(float a)
double Math.abs(double a)
<press shift-tab again to see javadoc>

jshell> Math.abs(
```

When you *Shift* + *Tab* again to view the documentation, JShell shows you the *first* overload's documentation:

```
jshell> Math.abs(
int Math.abs(int a)
Returns the absolute value of an int value.If the argument is not
negative, the argument is returned. If the argument is negative,
the negation of the argument is returned.
.
.
.
<press space for next javadoc, Q to quit>
```

You can then press the space key to view the documentation for the next overload in the list, or you can press *Q* (or *q*) to return to the `jshell>` prompt showing the portion of the snippet you've typed so far.

25.7.7 Exploring Members of a Specific Object

The exploration features shown in Sections 25.7.1–25.7.6 also apply to the members of a specific object. Let's create and explore a `String` object:

```
jshell> String dayName = "Monday"
dayName ==> "Monday"

jshell>
```

To view the methods you can call on the `dayName` object, type "`dayName.`" and press *Tab*:

```
jshell> dayName.
charAt(                chars()                codePointAt(
codePointBefore(       codePointCount(        codePoints()
compareTo(             compareToIgnoreCase(   concat(
contains(              contentEquals(         endsWith(
equals(                equalsIgnoreCase(      getBytes(
getChars(              getClass()             hashCode()
indexOf(               intern()               isEmpty()
lastIndexOf(           length()               matches(
notify()               notifyAll()            offsetByCodePoints(
regionMatches(         replace(               replaceAll(
replaceFirst(          split(                 startsWith(
subSequence(           substring(             toCharArray()
toLowerCase(           toString()             toUpperCase(
trim()                 wait(

jshell> dayName.
```

Exploring toUpperCase

Let's investigate the `toUpperCase` method. Continue by typing "`toU`" and pressing *Tab* to auto-complete its name:

```
jshell> dayName.toUpperCase(
toUpperCase(

jshell> dayName.toUpperCase(
```

Then, type *Shift* + *Tab* to view its parameters:

```
jshell> dayName.toUpperCase(
String String.toUpperCase(Locale locale)
String String.toUpperCase()
<press shift-tab again to see javadoc>

jshell> dayName.toUpperCase(
```

This method has two overloads. You can now use *Shift* + *Tab* to read about each overload, or simply choose the one you wish to use, by specifying the appropriate arguments (if any). In this case, we'll use the no-argument version to create a new `String` containing `MONDAY`, so we simply enter the closing right parenthesis of the method call and press *Enter*:

```
jshell> dayName.toUpperCase()
$2 ==> "MONDAY"

jshell>
```

Exploring `substring`

Let's assume you want to create the new `String` `"DAY"`—a subset of the implicit variable `$2`'s characters. For this purpose class `String` provides the overloaded method `substring`. First type `"$2.subs"` and press *Tab* to auto-complete its the method's name:

```
jshell> $2.substring(
substring(

jshell>
```

Next, use *Shift* + *Tab* to view the method's overloads:

```
jshell> $2.substring(
String String.substring(int beginIndex)
String String.substring(int beginIndex, int endIndex)
<press shift-tab again to see javadoc>

jshell> $2.substring(
```

Next, use *Shift* + *Tab* again to view the first overload's documentation:

```
jshell> $2.substring(
String String.substring(int beginIndex)
Returns a string that is a substring of this string.The substring
begins with the character at the specified index and extends to the
end of this string.
.
.
.
<press space for next javadoc, Q to quit>
```

As you can see from the documentation, this overload of the method enables you to obtain a substring starting from a specific character index (that is, position) and continuing through the end of the `String`. The first character in the `String` is at index `0`. This is the version of the method we wish to use to obtain `"DAY"` from `"MONDAY"`, so we can press *Q* to quit the documentation and return to our code snippet:

```
jshell> $2.substring(
```

Finally, we can complete our call to substring and press *Enter* to view the results:

```
jshell> $2.substring(3)
$3 ==> "DAY"

jshell>
```

25.8 Declaring Methods

[*Note:* This section may be read after studying Chapter 6, Methods: A Deeper Look, and the preceding portions of Chapter 25.]

You can use JShell to prototype methods. For example, let's assume we'd like to write code that displays the cubes of the values from 1 through 10. For the purpose of this discussion, we're going to define two methods:

- Method `displayCubes` will iterate 10 times, calling method `cube` each time.
- Method `cube` will receive one int value and return the cube of that value.

25.8.1 Forward Referencing an Undeclared Method—Declaring Method `displayCubes`

Let's begin with method `displayCubes`. Start a new JShell session or `/reset` the current one, then enter the following method declaration:

```
void displayCubes() {
   for (int i = 1; i <= 10; i++) {
      System.out.println("Cube of " + i + " is " + cube(i));
   }
}
```

When you complete the method declaration, JShell displays:

```
|  created method displayCubes(), however, it cannot be invoked
until method cube(int) is declared

jshell>
```

Again, we *manually* added the indentation. Note that after you type the method body's opening left brace, JShell displays continuation prompts (`...>`) before each subsequent line until you complete the method declaration by entering its closing right brace. Also, although JShell says `"created method displayCubes()"`, it indicates that you cannot call this method until `"cube(int) is declared"`. This is *not* fatal in JShell—it recognizes that `displayCubes` depends on an undeclared method (`cube`)—this is known as **forward referencing** an undeclared method. Once you define `cube`, you can call `displayCubes`.

25.8.2 Declaring a Previously Undeclared Method

Next, let's declare method `cube`, but *purposely make a logic error* by returning the square rather than the cube of its argument:

```
jshell> int cube(int x) {
   ...>     return x * x;
   ...> }
|  created method cube(int)

jshell>
```

At this point, you can use JShell's **/methods** command to see the complete list of methods that are declared in the current JShell session:

```
jshell> /methods
|    displayCubes ()void
|    cube (int)int

jshell>
```

Note that JShell displays each method's return type to the right of the parameter list.

25.8.3 Testing cube and Replacing Its Declaration

Now that method cube is declared, let's test it with the argument 2:

```
jshell> cube(2)
$3 ==> 4

jshell>
```

The method correctly returns the 4 (that is, 2 * 2), based on how the method is implemented. However, our the method's purpose was to calculate the cube of the argument, so the result should have been 8 (2 * 2 * 2). You can edit cube's snippet to correct the problem. Because cube was declared as a multiline snippet, the easiest way to edit the declaration is using **JShell Edit Pad**. You could use /list to determine cube's snippet ID then use /edit followed by the ID to open the snippet. You also edit the method by specifying its name, as in:

```
jshell> /edit cube
```

In the **JShell Edit Pad** window, change cube's body to:

```
    return x * x * x;
```

then press **Exit**. JShell displays:

```
jshell> /edit cube
|  modified method cube(int)

jshell>
```

25.8.4 Testing Updated Method cube and Method displayCubes

Now that method cube is properly declared, let's test it again with the arguments 2 and 10:

```
jshell> cube(2)
$5 ==> 8

jshell> cube(10)
$6 ==> 1000

jshell>
```

The method properly returns the cubes of 2 (that is, 8) and 10 (that is, 1000), and stores the results in the implicit variables $5 and $6.

Now let's test displayCubes. If you type "di" and press *Tab*, JShell auto-completes the name, including the parentheses of the method call, because displayCubes receives no parameters. The following shows the results of the call:

```
jshell> displayCubes()
Cube of 1 is 1
Cube of 2 is 8
Cube of 3 is 27
Cube of 4 is 64
Cube of 5 is 125
Cube of 6 is 216
Cube of 7 is 343
Cube of 8 is 512
Cube of 9 is 729
Cube of 10 is 1000

jshell>
```

25.9 Exceptions

[*Note:* This section may be read after studying Chapter 7 and the preceding sections of Chapter 25.]

In Section 7.5, we introduced Java's exception-handling mechanism, showing how to catch an exception that occurred when we attempted to use an out-of-bounds array index. In JShell, catching exceptions is not required—it automatically catches each exception and displays information about it, then displays the next JShell prompt, so you can continue your session. This is particularly important for *checked exceptions* (Section 11.5) that are required to be caught in regular Java programs—as you know, catching an exception requires wrapping the code in a try...catch statement. By automatically, catching all exceptions, JShell makes it easier for you to *experiment* with methods that throw checked exceptions.

In the following new JShell session, we declare an array of int values, then demonstrate both valid and invalid array-access expressions:

```
jshell> int[] values = {10, 20, 30}
values ==> int[3] { 10, 20, 30 }

jshell> values[1]
$2 ==> 20

jshell> values[10]
|  java.lang.ArrayIndexOutOfBoundsException thrown: 10
|        at (#3:1)

jshell>
```

The snippet values[10] attempts to access an out-of-bounds element—recall that this results in an ArrayIndexOutOfBoundsException. Even though we did not wrap the code in a try...catch, JShell catches the exception and displays the its String representation. This includes the exception's type and an error message (in this case, the invalid index 10), followed by a so-called stack trace indicating where the problem occurred. The notation

```
|        at (#3:1)
```

indicates that the exception occurred at line 1 of the code snippet with the ID 3. Section 6.6 discussed the method-call stack. A stack trace indicates the methods that were on the method-call stack at the time the exception occurred. A typical stack trace contains several "at" lines like the one shown here—one per stack frame. After displaying the stack trace, JShell shows the next jshell> prompt. Chapter 11 discusses stack traces in detail.

25.10 Importing Classes and Adding Packages to the CLASSPATH

[*Note:* This section may be read after studying Chapter 21, Custom Generic Data Structures and the preceding sections of Chapter 25.]

When working in JShell, you can import types from Java 9's packages. In fact, several packages are so commonly used by Java developers that JShell automatically imports them for you. (You can change this with JShell's /set start command—see Section 25.12.)

You can use JShell's **/imports** command to see the current session's list of import declarations. The following listing shows the packages that are auto-imported when you begin a new JShell session:

```
jshell> /imports
|    import java.io.*
|    import java.math.*
|    import java.net.*
|    import java.nio.file.*
|    import java.util.*
|    import java.util.concurrent.*
|    import java.util.function.*
|    import java.util.prefs.*
|    import java.util.regex.*
|    import java.util.stream.*

jshell>
```

The java.lang package's contents are always available in JShell, just as in any Java source-code file.

In addition to the Java API's packages, you can import your own or third-party packages to use their types in JShell. First, you use JShell's **/env -class-path** command to add the packages to JShell's CLASSPATH, which specifies where the additional packages are located. You can then use import declarations to experiment with the packages' contents in JShell.

Using Our Custom Generic List Class

In Chapter 21, we declared a custom generic List data structure and placed it in the package com.deitel.datastructures. Here, we'll add that package to JShell's CLASSPATH, import our List class, then use it in JShell. If you have a current JShell session open, use /exit to terminate it. Then, change directories to the ch21 examples folder and start a new JShell session.

Adding the Location of a Package to the CLASSPATH

The `ch21` folder contains a folder named `com`, which is the first of a nested set of folders that represent the compiled classes in our package `com.deitel.datastructures`. The following uses adds this package to the `CLASSPATH`:

```
jshell> /env -class-path .
|  Setting new options and restoring state.

jshell>
```

The dot (`.`) indicates the current folder from which you launched JShell. You also can specify complete paths to other folders on your system or the paths of JAR (Java archive) files that contain packages of compiled classes.

Importing a Class from the Package

Now, you can import the `List` class for use in JShell. The following shows importing our `List` class and the complete list of imports in the current session:

```
jshell> import com.deitel.datastructures.List

jshell> /imports
|    import java.io.*
|    import java.math.*
|    import java.net.*
|    import java.nio.file.*
|    import java.util.*
|    import java.util.concurrent.*
|    import java.util.function.*
|    import java.util.prefs.*
|    import java.util.regex.*
|    import java.util.stream.*
|    import com.deitel.datastructures.List

jshell>
```

Using the Imported Class

Finally, you can use class `List`. Below we create a `List<String>` and show that JShell's auto-complete capability can display the list of available methods. Then we insert two `String`s into the `List`, displaying its contents after each `insertAtFront` operation:

```
jshell> List<String> list = new List<>()
list ==> com.deitel.datastructures.List@31610302

jshell> list.
equals(          getClass()        hashCode()          insertAtBack(
insertAtFront(   isEmpty()         notify()            notifyAll()
print()          removeFromBack()  removeFromFront()   toString()
wait(

jshell> list.insertAtFront("red")

jshell> list.print()
The list is: red
```

```
jshell> list.insertAtFront("blue")

jshell> list.print()
The list is: blue red

jshell>
```

A Note Regarding `imports`

As you saw at the beginning of this section, JShell imports the entire `java.util` package—which contains the `List` interface (Section 16.6)—in every JShell session. The Java compiler gives precedence to an explicit type `import` for our class `List` like

```
import com.deitel.datastructures.List;
```

vs. an `import`-on-demand like

```
import java.util.*;
```

Had we used the following `import`-on-demand:

```
import com.deitel.datastructures.*;
```

then we would have had to refer to our `List` class by its fully qualified name (that is, `com.deitel.datastructures.List`) to differentiate it from `java.util.List`.

25.11 Using an External Editor

Section 25.3.10 demonstrated **JShell Edit Pad** for editing code snippets. This tool provides only simple editing functionality. Many programmers prefer to use more powerful text editors. Using JShell's **`/set editor`** command, you can specify your preferred text editor. For example, we have a text editor named EditPlus, located on our Windows system at

```
C:\Program Files\EditPlus\editplus.exe
```

The JShell command

```
jshell> /set editor C:\Program Files\EditPlus\editplus.exe
|  Editor set to: C:\Program Files\EditPlus\editplus.exe

jshell>
```

sets `EditPlus` as the snippet editor for the current JShell session. The `/set editor` command's argument is *operating-system specific*. For example, on Ubuntu Linux, you can use the built-in `gedit` text editor with the command

```
/set editor gedit
```

and on macOS,[8] you can use the built-in `TextEdit` application with the command

```
/set editor -wait open -a TextEdit
```

Editing Snippets with a Custom Text Editor

When you're using a custom editor, each time you save snippet edits JShell immediately re-evaluates any snippets that have changed and shows their results (but not the snippets

8. On macOS, the `-wait` option is required so that JShell does not simply open the external editor, then return immediately to the next `jshell>` prompt.

themselves) in the JShell output. The following shows a new JShell session in which we set a custom editor, then performed JShell interactions—we explain momentarily the two lines of output that follow the /edit command:

```
jshell> /set editor C:\Program Files\EditPlus\editplus.exe
|  Editor set to: C:\Program Files\EditPlus\editplus.exe

jshell> int x = 10
x ==> 10

jshell> int y = 10
y ==> 20

jshell> /edit
y ==> 20
10 + 20 = 30
jshell> /list

   1 : int x = 10;
   3 : int y = 20;
   4 : System.out.print(x + " + " + y + " = " + (x + y))

jshell>
```

First we declared the int variables x and y, then we launched the external editor to edit our snippets. Initially, the editor shows the snippets that declare x and y (Fig. 25.4).

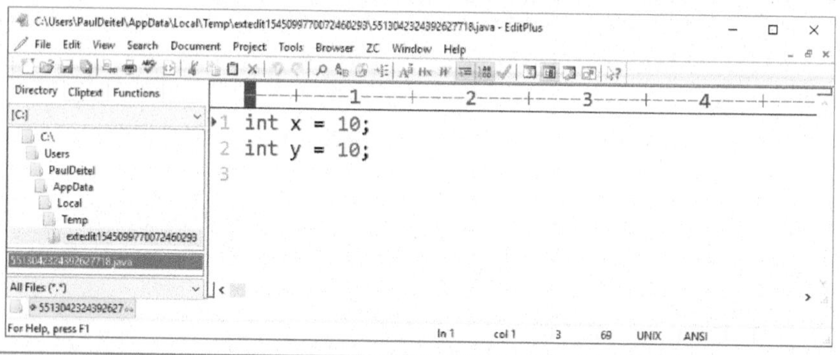

Fig. 25.4 | External editor showing code snippets to edit.

Next, we edited y's declaration, giving it the new value 20, then we added a new snippet to display both values and their sum (Fig. 25.5).

When we saved the edits in our text editor, JShell replaced y's original declaration with the updated one and showed

```
y ==> 20
```

to indicate that y's value changed. Then, JShell executed the new System.out.print snippet and showed its results

```
10 + 20 = 30
```

Finally, when we closed the external editor, JShell displayed the next jshell> prompt.

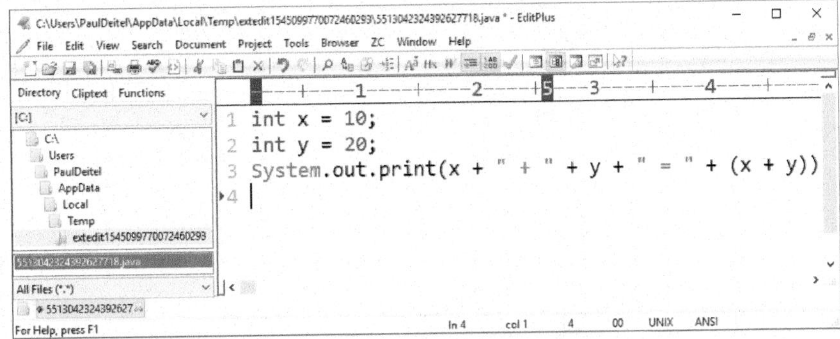

Fig. 25.5 | External editor showing code snippets to edit.

Retaining the Editor Setting

You can retain your editor setting for future JShell sessions as follows:

```
/set editor -retain commandToLaunchYourEditor
```

Restoring the JShell Edit Pad *As the Default Editor*

If you do not retain your custom editor, subsequent JShell sessions will use **JShell Edit Pad**. If you do retain the custom editor, you can restore **JShell Edit Pad** as the default with

```
/set editor -retain -default
```

25.12 Summary of JShell Commands

Figure 25.6 shows the basic JShell commands. Many of these commands have been presented throughout this chapter. Others are discussed in this section.

Command	Description
`/help` or `/?`	Displays JShell's list of commands.
`/help intro`	Displays a brief introduction to JShell.
`/help shortcuts`	Displays a description of several JShell shortcut keys.
`/list`	By default, lists the valid snippets you've entered in the current session. To list all snippets, use `/list -all`.
`/!`	Recalls and re-evaluates the last snippet.
`/`*id*	Recalls and re-evaluates the snippet with the specified *id*.
`/-`*n*	Recalls and re-evaluates a prior snippet—for *n*, `1` is the last snippet, `2` is the second-to-last, etc.
`/edit`	By default, opens a **JShell Edit Pad** window containing the valid snippets you've entered in the current session. See Section 25.11 to learn how to configure an external editor.
`/save`	Saves the current session's valid snippets to a specified file.

Fig. 25.6 | Jshell commands. (Part 1 of 2.)

Command	Description
/open	Opens a specified file of code snippets, loads the snippets into the current session and evaluates the loaded snippets.
/vars	Displays the current session's variables and their corresponding values.
/methods	Displays the signatures of the current session's declared methods.
/types	Displays types declared in the current session.
/imports	Displays the current session's `import` declarations.
/exit	Terminates the current JShell session.
/reset	Resets the current JShell session, deleting all code snippets.
/reload	Reloads a JShell session and executes the valid snippets (Section 25.12.3).
/drop	Deletes a specified snippet from the current session (Section 25.12.4).
/classpath	Adds packages to the classpath used by JShell, so that you can then `import` types from those packages for use in JShell. We discuss creating your own packages in Chapter 21, Custom Generic Data Structures.
/history	Lists everything you've typed in the current JShell session, including all snippets (valid, invalid or overwritten) and JShell commands—the `/list` command shows only snippets, not JShell commands.
/set	Sets various JShell configuration options, such as the editor used in response to the `/edit` command, the text used for the JShell prompts, the imports to specify when a session starts, etc. (Sections 25.12.5–25.12.6).

Fig. 25.6 | Jshell commands. (Part 2 of 2.)

25.12.1 Getting Help in JShell

JShell's help documentation is incorporated directly via the **`/help`** or **`/?`** commands—`/?` is simply a shorthand for `/help`. For a quick introduction to JShell, type:

```
/help intro
```

To display JShell's list of commands, type

```
/help
```

For more information on a given command's options, type

```
/help command
```

For example

```
/help /list
```

displays the `/list` command's more detailed help documentation. Similarly

```
/help /set start
```

displays more detailed help documentation for the `/set` command's `start` option. For a list of the shortcut key combinations in JShell, type

```
/help shortcuts
```

25.12.2 /edit Command: Additional Features

We've discussed using `/edit` to load all valid snippets, a snippet with a specified ID or a method with a specified name into **JShell Edit Pad**. You can specify the identifier for any variable, method or type declaration that you'd like to edit. For example, if the current JShell session contains the declaration of a class named `Account`, the following loads that class into **JShell Edit Pad**:

```
/edit Account
```

25.12.3 /reload Command

At the time of this writing, you cannot use the */id* command to execute a range of previous snippets. However, JShell's **/reload** command can re-execute all valid snippets in the current session. Consider the session from Sections 25.3.9–25.3.10:

```
jshell> /list

   1 : 45
   2 : 72
   3 : if ($1 < $2) {
           System.out.printf("%d < %d%n", $1, $2);
       }
   4 : if ($1 > $2) {
           System.out.printf("%d > %d%n", $1, $2);
       }
   5 : $1 = 100;
   6 : if ($1 > $2) {
           System.out.printf("%d > %d%n", $1, $2);
       }

jshell>
```

The following reloads that session one snippet at a time:

```
jshell> /reload
|  Restarting and restoring state.
-: 45
-: 72
-: if ($1 < $2) {
       System.out.printf("%d < %d%n", $1, $2);
   }
45 < 72
-: if ($1 > $2) {
       System.out.printf("%d > %d%n", $1, $2);
   }
-: $1 = 100
-: if ($1 > $2) {
       System.out.printf("%d > %d%n", $1, $2);
   }
100 > 72

jshell>
```

Each reloaded snippet is preceded by `-:` and in the case of the `if` statements, the output (if any) is shown immediately following each `if` statement. If you prefer not to see the snippets as they reload, you can use the `/reload` command's `-quiet` option:

```
jshell> /reload -quiet
|  Restarting and restoring state.
45 < 72
100 > 72

jshell>
```

In this case, only the results of output statements are displayed. Then, you can view the snippets that were reloaded with the `/list` command.

25.12.4 /drop Command

You can eliminate a snippet from the current session with JShell's **/drop** command followed by a snippet ID or an identifier. The following new JShell session declares a variable `x` and a method `cube`, then drops `x` via its snippet ID and drops `cube` via its identifier:

```
jshell> int x = 10
x ==> 10

jshell> int cube(int y) {return y * y * y;}
|  created method cube(int)

jshell> /list

   1 : int x = 10;
   2 : int cube(int y) {return y * y * y;}

jshell> /drop 1
|  dropped variable x

jshell> /drop cube
|  dropped method cube(int)

jshell> /list

jshell>
```

25.12.5 Feedback Modes

JShell has several feedback modes that determine what gets displayed after each interaction. To change the feedback mode, use JShell's **/set feedback** command:

```
/set feedback mode
```

where *mode* is `concise`, `normal` (the default), `silent` or `verbose`. All of the prior JShell interactions in this chapter used the `normal` mode.

Feedback Mode verbose

Below is a new JShell session in which we used `verbose` mode, which beginning programmers might prefer:

```
jshell> /set feedback verbose
|  Feedback mode: verbose

jshell> int x = 10
x ==> 10
|  created variable x : int

jshell> int cube(int y) {return y * y * y;}
|  created method cube(int)

jshell> cube(x)
$3 ==> 1000
|  created scratch variable $3 : int

jshell> x = 5
x ==> 5
|  assigned to x : int

jshell> cube(x)
$5 ==> 125
|  created scratch variable $5 : int

jshell>
```

Notice the additional feedback indicating that

- variable x was created,
- variable $3 was created on the first call to cube—JShell refers to the implicit variable as a *scratch variable,*
- an int was assigned to the variable x, and
- scratch variable $5 was created on the second call to cube.

Feedback Mode concise

Next, we /reset the session then set the feedback mode to concise and repeat the preceding session:

```
jshell> /set feedback concise
jshell> int x = 10;
jshell> int cube(int y) {return y * y * y;}
jshell> cube(x)
$3 ==> 1000
jshell> x = 5
jshell> cube(x)
$5 ==> 125
jshell>
```

As you can see, the only feedback displayed is the result of each call to cube. If an error occurs, its feedback also will be displayed.

Feedback Mode silent

Next, we /reset the session then set the feedback mode to silent and repeat the preceding session:

```
jshell> /set feedback silent
-> int x = 10;
-> int cube(int y) {return y * y * y;}
-> cube(x)
-> x = 5
-> cube(x)
-> /set feedback normal
|  Feedback mode: normal

jshell>
```

In this case, the `jshell>` prompt becomes `->` and only error feedback will be displayed. You might use this mode if you've copied code from a Java source file and want to paste it into JShell, but do not want to see the feedback for each line.

25.12.6 Other JShell Features Configurable with /set

So far, we've demonstrated the `/set` command's capabilities for setting an external snippet editor and setting feedback modes. The `/set` command provides extensive capabilities for creating custom feedback modes via the commands:

- `/set mode`
- `/set prompt`
- `/set truncation`
- `/set format`

The `/set mode` command creates a user-defined custom feedback mode. Then you can use the other three commands to customize all aspects of JShell's feedback. The details of these commands are beyond the scope of this chapter. For more information, see JShell's help documentation for each of the preceding commands.

Customizing JShell Startup

Section 25.10 showed the set of common packages JShell `imports` at the start of each session. Using JShell's **`/set start`** command

```
/set start filename
```

you can provide a file of Java snippets and JShell commands that will be used in the current session when it restarts due to a `/reset` or `/reload` command. You can also remove all startup snippets with

```
/set start -none
```

or return to the default startup snippets with

```
/set start -default
```

In all three cases, the setting applies only to the current session unless you also include the `-retain` option. For example, the following command indicates that all subsequent JShell sessions should load the specified file of startup snippets and commands:

```
/set start -retain filename
```

You can restore the defaults for future sessions with

```
/set start -retain -default
```

25.13 Keyboard Shortcuts for Snippet Editing

In addition to the commands in Fig. 25.6, JShell supports many keyboard shortcuts for editing code, such as quickly jumping to the beginning or end of a line, or jumping between words in a line. JShell's command-line features are implemented by a library named JLine 2, which provides command-line editing and history capabilites. Figure 25.7 shows a sample of the shortcuts available.

Shortcut	Description
Ctrl + a	Move cursor to beginning of line.
Ctrl + e	Move cursor to end of line.
Alt + b	Move the cursor backwards by one word.
Alt + f	Move the cursor forwards by one word.
Ctrl + r	Perform a search for the last command or snippet containing the characters you type after typing *Ctrl + r*.
Ctrl + t	Reverse the two characters to the left of the cursor.
Ctrl + k	Cut everything from the cursor to the end of the line.
Ctrl + u	Cut everything from the beginning of the line up to, but not including the character at the cursor position.
Ctrl + w	Cut the word before the cursor.
Alt + d	Cut the word after the cursor.

Fig. 25.7 | Some keyboard shortcuts for editing the current snippet at the `jshell>` prompt.

25.14 How JShell Reinterprets Java for Interactive Use

In JShell:

- A `main` method is not required.
- Semicolons are not required on standalone statements.
- Variables do not need to be declared in classes or in methods.
- Methods do not need to be declared inside a class's body.
- Statements do not need to be written inside methods.
- Redeclaring a variable, method or type simply drops the prior declaration and replaces it with the new one, whereas the Java compiler normally would report an error.
- You do not need to catch exceptions, though you can if you need to test exception handling.
- JShell ignores top-level access modifiers (`public`, `private`, `protected`, `static`, `final`)—only `abstract` (Chapter 10) is allowed as a class modifier.
- The `synchronized` keyword (Chapter 23, Concurrency) is ignored.
- `package` statements and Java 9 `module` statements are not allowed. 9

25.15 IDE JShell Support

At the time of this writing, work is just beginning on JShell support in popular IDEs such
8 as NetBeans, IntelliJ IDEA and Eclipse. NetBeans currently has an early access plug-in
that enables you to work with JShell in both Java 8 and Java 9—even though JShell is a
9 Java 9 feature. Some vendors will use JShell's APIs to provide developers with JShell environments that show both the code users type and the results of running that code side-by-side. Some features you might see in IDE JShell support include:

- Source-code syntax coloring for better code readability.
- Automatic source-code indentation and insertion of closing braces (`}`), parentheses (`)`) and brackets (`]`) to save programmers time.
- Debugger integration.
- Project integration, such as being able to automatically use classes in the same project from a JShell session.

25.16 Wrap-Up

9 In this chapter, you used JShell—Java 9's new interactive REPL for exploration, discovery and experimentation. We showed how to start a JShell session and work with various types of code snippets, including statements, variables, expressions, methods and classes—all without having to declare a class containing a `main` method to execute the code.

You saw that you can list the valid snippets in the current session, and recall and execute prior snippets and commands using the up and down arrow keys. You also saw that you can list the current session's variables, methods, types and `imports`. We showed how to clear the current JShell session to remove all existing snippets and how to save snippets to a file then reload them.

We demonstrated JShell's auto-completion capabilities for code and commands, and showed how you can explore a class's members and view documentation directly in JShell. We explored class `Math`, demonstrating how to list its `static` members, how to view a method's parameters and overloads, view a method's documentation and view a `public` field's documentation. We also explored the methods of a `String` object.

You declared methods and forward referenced an undeclared method that you declared later in the session, then saw that you could go back and execute the first method. We also showed that you can replace a method declaration with a new method—in fact, you can replace any declaration of a variable, method or type.

We showed that JShell catches all exceptions and simply displays a stack trace followed by the next `jshell>` prompt, so you can continue the session. You imported an existing compiled class from a package, then used that class in a JShell session.

Next, we summarized and demonstrated various other JShell commands. We showed how to configure a custom snippet editor, view JShell's help documentation, reload a session, drop snippets from a session, configure feedback modes and more. We listed some additional keyboard shortcuts for editing the current snippet at the `jshell>` prompt. Finally, we discussed how JShell reinterprets Java for interactive use and IDE support for JShell.

Self-Review Exercises

We encourage you to use JShell to do Exercises 25.1–25.43 after reading Sections 25.3–25.4. We've included the answers for all these exercises to help you get comfortable with JShell/REPL quickly.

25.1 Confirm that when you use `System.out.println` to display a `String` literal, such as `"Happy Birthday!"`, the quotes (`""`) are not displayed. End your statement with a semicolon.

25.2 Repeat Exercise 25.1, but remove the semicolon at the end of your statement to demonstrate that semicolons in this position are optional in JShell.

25.3 Confirm that JShell does not execute a `//` end-of-line comment.

25.4 Show that an executable statement enclosed in a multiline comment—delimited by `/*` and `*/`—does not execute.

25.5 Show what happens when the following code is entered in JShell:

```
/* incomplete multi-line comment
System.out.println("Welcome to Java Programming!")
/* complete multi-line
comment */
```

25.6 Show that indenting code with spaces does not affect statement execution.

25.7 Declare each of the following variables as type `int` in JShell to determine which are valid and which are invalid?

a) `first`
b) `first number`
c) `first1`
d) `1first`

25.8 Show that braces do not have to occur in matching pairs inside a string literal.

25.9 Show what happens when you type each of the following code snippets into JShell:

a) `System.out.println("seems OK")`
b) `System.out.println("missing something?)`
c) `System.out.println"missing something else?")`

25.10 Demonstrate that after a `System.out.print` the next print results appear on the same line right after the previous one's. [*Hint:* To demonstrate this, reset the current session, enter two `System.out.print` statements, then use the following two commands to save the snippets to a file, then reload and re-execute them:

```
/save mysnippets
/open mysnippets
```

The `/open` command loads the `mysnippets` file's contents then executes them.]

25.11 Demonstrate that after a `System.out.println`, the next text that prints displays its text at the left of the next line. [*Hint:* To demonstrate this, reset the current session, enter a `System.out.println` statement followed by another print statement, then use the following two commands to save the snippets to a file, then reload and re-execute them:

```
/save mysnippets
/open mysnippets
```

The `/open` command loads the `mysnippets` file's contents then executes them.]

25.12 Demonstrate that you can reset a JShell session to remove all prior snippets and start from scratch without having to exit JShell and start a new session.

25.13 Using `System.out.println`, demonstrate that the escape sequence `\n` causes a newline to be issued to the output. Use the string

```
"Welcome\nto\nJShell!"
```

25.14 Demonstrate that the escape sequence \t causes a tab to be issued to the output. Note that your output will depend on how tabs are set on your system. Use the string

```
"before\tafter\nbefore\t\tafter"
```

25.15 Demonstrate what happens when you include a single backslash (\) in a string. Be sure that the character after the backslash does not create a valid escape sequence.

25.16 Display a string containing \\\\ (recall that \\ is an escape sequence for a backslash). How many backslashes are displayed?

25.17 Use the escape sequence \" to display a quoted string.

25.18 What happens when the following code executes in JShell:

```
System.out.println("Happy Birthday!\rSunny")
```

25.19 Consider the following statement

```
System.out.printf("%s%n%s%n", "Welcome to ", "Java Programming!")
```

Make the following intentional errors (separately) to see what happens.

a) Omit the parentheses around the argument list.
b) Omit the commas.
c) Omit one of the `%s%n` sequences.
d) Omit one of the strings (i.e., the second or the third argument).
e) Replace the first `%s` with `%d`.
f) Replace the string `"Welcome to "` with the integer `23`.

25.20 What happens when you enter the `/imports` command in a new JShell session?

25.21 Import class `Scanner` then create a `Scanner` object `input` for reading from `System.in`. What happens when you execute the statement:

```
int number = input.nextInt()
```

and the user enters the string `"hello"`?

25.22 In a new or `/reset` JShell session, repeat Exercise 25.21 without importing class `Scanner` to demonstrate that the package `java.util` is already imported in JShell.

25.23 Demonstrate what happens when you don't precede a `Scanner` input operation with a meaningful prompting message telling the user what to input. Enter the following statements:

```
Scanner input = new Scanner(System.in)
int value = input.nextInt()
```

25.24 Demonstrate that you can't place an `import` statement in a class.

25.25 Demonstrate that identifiers are case sensitive by declaring variables `id` and `ID` of types `String` and `int`, respectively. Also use the `/list` command to show the two snippets representing the separate variables.

25.26 Demonstrate that initialization statements like

```
String month = "April"
int age = 65
```

indeed initialize their variables with the indicated values.

25.27 Demonstrate what happens when you:

a) Add 1 to the largest possible `int` value 2,147,483,647.
b) Subtract 1 from the smallest possible integer –2,147,483,648.

25.28 Demonstrate that large integers like `1234567890` are equivalent to their counterparts with the underscore separators, namely `1_234_567_890`:

a) `1234567890 == 1_234_567_890`
b) Print each of these values and show that you get the same result.
c) Divide each of these values by 2 and show that you get the same result.

25.29 Placing spaces around operators in an arithmetic expression does not affect the value of that expression. In particular, the following expressions are equivalent:

```
17+23
17 + 23
```

Demonstrate this with an `if` statement using the condition

```
(17+23) == (17 + 23)
```

25.30 Demonstrate that the parentheses around the argument `number1 + number2` in the following statement are unnecessary:

```
System.out.printf("Sum is %d%n", (number1 + number2))
```

25.31 Declare the `int` variable `x` and initialize it to `14`, then demonstrate that the subsequent assignment `x = 27` is destructive.

25.32 Demonstrate that printing the value of the following variable is non-destructive:

```
int y = 29
```

25.33 Using the declarations:

```
int b = 7
int m = 9
```

a) Demonstrate that attempting to do algebraic multiplication by placing the variable names next to one another as in `bm` doesn't work in Java.
b) Demonstrate that the Java expression `b * m` indeed multiplies the two operands.

25.34 Use the following expressions to demonstrate that integer division yields an integer result:

a) `8 / 4`
b) `7 / 5`

25.35 Demonstrate what happens when you attempt each of the following integer divisions:

a) `0 / 1`
b) `1 / 0`
c) `0 / 0`

25.36 Demonstrate that the values of the following expressions:

a) `(3 + 4 + 5) / 5`
b) `3 + 4 + 5 / 5`

are different and thus the parentheses in the first expression are required if you want to divide the entire quantity 3 + 4 + 5 by 5.

25.37 Calculate the value of the following expression:

```
5 / 2 * 2 + 4 % 3 + 9 - 3
```

manually being careful to observe the rules of operator precedence. Confirm the result in JShell.

25.38 Test each of the two equality and four relational operators on the two values 7 and 7. For example, `7 == 7`, `7 < 7`, etc.

25.39 Repeat Exercise 25.38 using the values `7` and `9`.

25.40 Repeat Exercise 25.38 using the values `11` and `9`.

25.41 Demonstrate that accidentally placing a semicolon after the right parenthesis of the condition in an if statement can be a logic error.

```
if (3 == 5); {
   System.out.println("3 is equal to 5");
}
```

25.42 Given the following declarations:

```
int x = 1
int y = 2
int z = 3
int a
```

what are the values of a, x, y and z after the following statement executes?

```
a = x = y = z = 10
```

25.43 Manually determine the value of the following expression then use JShell to check your work:

```
(3 * 9 * (3 + (9 * 3 / (3))))
```

Answers to Self-Review Exercises

25.1

```
jshell> System.out.println("Happy Birthday!");
Happy Birthday!

jshell>
```

25.2

```
jshell> System.out.println("Happy Birthday!")
Happy Birthday!

jshell>
```

25.3

```
jshell> // comments are not executable

jshell>
```

25.4

```
jshell> /* opening line of multi-line comment
   ...>    System.out.println("Welcome to Java Programming!")
   ...>    closing line of multi-line comment */

jshell>
```

25.5 There is no compilation error, because the second /* is considered to be part of the first multi-line comment.

```
jshell> /* incomplete multi-line comment
   ...> System.out.println("Welcome to Java Programming!")
   ...> /* complete multi-line
   ...> comment */

jshell>
```

25.6

```
jshell> System.out.println("A")
A

jshell>    System.out.println("A") // indented 3 spaces
A

jshell>       System.out.println("A") // indented 6 spaces
A

jshell>
```

25.7 a) valid. b) invalid (space not allowed). c) valid. d) invalid (can't begin with a digit).

```
jshell> int first
first ==> 0

jshell> int first number
|  Error:
|  ';' expected
|  int first number
|           ^

jshell> int first1
first1 ==> 0

jshell> int 1first
|  Error:
|  '.class' expected
|  int 1first
|     ^
|  Error:
|  not a statement
|  int 1first
|      ^--^
|  Error:
|  unexpected type
|    required: value
|    found:    class
|  int 1first
|  ^--^
|  Error:
|  missing return statement
|  int 1first
|> ^---------^

jshell>
```

25.8

```
jshell> "Unmatched brace { in a string is OK"
$1 ==> "Unmatched brace { in a string is OK"

jshell>
```

25.9

```
jshell> System.out.println("seems OK")
seems OK

jshell> System.out.println("missing something?)
|  Error:
|  unclosed string literal
|  System.out.println("missing something?)
|                     ^

jshell> System.out.println"missing something else?")
|  Error:
|  ';' expected
|  System.out.println"missing something else?")
|                    ^
|  Error:
|  cannot find symbol
|    symbol:   variable println
|  System.out.println"missing something else?")
|  ^----------------^

jshell>
```

25.10

```
jshell> System.out.print("Happy ")
Happy
jshell> System.out.print("Birthday")
Birthday
jshell> /save mysession

jshell> /open mysession
Happy Birthday
jshell>
```

25.11

```
jshell> System.out.println("Happy ")
Happy
jshell> System.out.println("Birthday")
Birthday
jshell> /save mysession

jshell> /open mysession
Happy
Birthday
jshell>
```

25.12

```
jshell> int x = 10
x ==> 10

jshell> int y = 20
y ==> 20
```

(continued...)

```
jshell> x + y
$3 ==> 30

jshell> /reset
|  Resetting state.

jshell> /list

jshell>
```

25.13

```
jshell> System.out.println("Welcome\nto\nJShell!")
Welcome
to
JShell!

jshell>
```

25.14

```
jshell> System.out.println("before\tafter\nbefore\t\tafter")
before  after
before          after

jshell>
```

25.15

```
jshell> System.out.println("Bad escap\e")
|  Error:
|  illegal escape character
|  System.out.println("Bad escap\e")
|                                ^

jshell>
```

25.16 Two.

```
jshell> System.out.println("Displaying backslashes \\\\")
Displaying backslashes \\

jshell>
```

25.17

```
jshell> System.out.println("\"This is a string in quotes\"")
"This is a string in quotes"

jshell>
```

25.18

```
jshell> System.out.println("Happy Birthday!\rSunny")
Sunny Birthday!

jshell>
```

25.19 a)

```
jshell> System.out.printf"%s%n%s%n", "Welcome to ", "Java
Programming!"
|  Error:
|  ';' expected
|  System.out.printf"%s%n%s%n", "Welcome to ", "Java Programming!"
|                   ^
|  Error:
|  cannot find symbol
|    symbol:   variable printf
|  System.out.printf"%s%n%s%n", "Welcome to ", "Java Programming!"
|  ^---------------^

jshell>
```

b)

```
jshell> System.out.printf("%s%n%s%n" "Welcome to " "Java |  Error:
|  ')' expected
|  System.out.printf("%s%n%s%n" "Welcome to " "Java Programming!")
|                              ^

jshell>
```

c)

```
jshell> System.out.printf("%s%n", "Welcome to ", "Java
Programming!")
Welcome to
$6 ==> java.io.PrintStream@6d4b1c02

jshell>
```

d)

```
jshell> System.out.printf("%s%n%s%n", "Welcome to ")
Welcome to
|  java.util.MissingFormatArgumentException thrown: Format
specifier '%s'
|        at Formatter.format (Formatter.java:2524)
|        at PrintStream.format (PrintStream.java:974)
|        at PrintStream.printf (PrintStream.java:870)
|        at (#7:1)

jshell>
```

e)

```
jshell> System.out.printf("%d%n%s%n", "Welcome to ", "Java
Programming!")
|  java.util.IllegalFormatConversionException thrown: d !=
java.lang.String
|        at Formatter$FormatSpecifier.failConversion
(Formatter.java:4275)
|        at Formatter$FormatSpecifier.printInteger
(Formatter.java:2790)
|        at Formatter$FormatSpecifier.print (Formatter.java:2744)
```

(continued...)

```
|        at Formatter.format (Formatter.java:2525)
|        at PrintStream.format (PrintStream.java:974)
|        at PrintStream.printf (PrintStream.java:870)
|        at (#8:1)

jshell>
```

f)

```
jshell> System.out.printf("%s%n%s%n", 23, "Java Programming!")
23
Java Programming!
$9 ==> java.io.PrintStream@6d4b1c02

jshell>
```

25.20

```
jshell> /imports
|    import java.io.*
|    import java.math.*
|    import java.net.*
|    import java.nio.file.*
|    import java.util.*
|    import java.util.concurrent.*
|    import java.util.function.*
|    import java.util.prefs.*
|    import java.util.regex.*
|    import java.util.stream.*

jshell>
```

25.21

```
jshell> import java.util.Scanner

jshell> Scanner input = new Scanner(System.in)
input ==> java.util.Scanner[delimiters=\p{javaWhitespace}+] ...
\E][infinity string=\Q∞\E]

jshell> int number = input.nextInt()
hello
|  java.util.InputMismatchException thrown:
|        at Scanner.throwFor (Scanner.java:860)
|        at Scanner.next (Scanner.java:1497)
|        at Scanner.nextInt (Scanner.java:2161)
|        at Scanner.nextInt (Scanner.java:2115)
|        at (#2:1)

jshell>
```

25.22

```
jshell> Scanner input = new Scanner(System.in)
input ==> java.util.Scanner[delimiters=\p{javaWhitespace}+] ...
\E][infinity string=\Q∞\E]
```

(continued...)

```
jshell> int number = input.nextInt()
hello
|  java.util.InputMismatchException thrown:
|        at Scanner.throwFor (Scanner.java:860)
|        at Scanner.next (Scanner.java:1497)
|        at Scanner.nextInt (Scanner.java:2161)
|        at Scanner.nextInt (Scanner.java:2115)
|        at (#2:1)

jshell>
```

25.23 JShell appears to hang while it waits for the user to type a value and press *Enter*.

```
jshell> Scanner input = new Scanner(System.in)
input ==> java.util.Scanner[delimiters=\p{javaWhitespace}+] ...
\E][infinity string=\Q∞\E]

jshell> int value = input.nextInt()
```

25.24

```
jshell> class Demonstration {
   ...>     import java.util.Scanner;
   ...> }
|  Error:
|  illegal start of type
|     import java.util.Scanner;
|     ^
|  Error:
|  <identifier> expected
|     import java.util.Scanner;
|                             ^

jshell> import java.util.Scanner

jshell> class Demonstration {
   ...> }
|  created class Demonstration

jshell>
```

25.25

```
jshell> /reset
|  Resetting state.

jshell> String id = "Natasha"
id ==> "Natasha"

jshell> int ID = 413
ID ==> 413

jshell> /list
```

(continued...)

```
   1 : String id = "Natasha";
   2 : int ID = 413;

jshell>
```

25.26

```
jshell> String month = "April"
month ==> "April"

jshell> System.out.println(month)
April

jshell> int age = 65
age ==> 65

jshell> System.out.println(age)
65

jshell>
```

25.27

```
jshell> 2147483647 + 1
$9 ==> -2147483648

jshell> -2147483648 - 1
$10 ==> 2147483647

jshell>
```

25.28

```
jshell> 1234567890 == 1_234_567_890
$4 ==> true

jshell> System.out.println(1234567890)
1234567890

jshell> System.out.println(1_234_567_890)
1234567890

jshell> 1234567890 / 2
$5 ==> 617283945

jshell> 1_234_567_890 / 2
$6 ==> 617283945

jshell>
```

25.29

```
jshell> (17+23) == (17 + 23)
$7 ==> true

jshell>
```

25.30

```
jshell> int number1 = 10
number1 ==> 10

jshell> int number2 = 20
number2 ==> 20

jshell> System.out.printf("Sum is %d%n", (number1 + number2))
Sum is 30
$10 ==> java.io.PrintStream@1794d431

jshell> System.out.printf("Sum is %d%n", number1 + number2)
Sum is 30
$11 ==> java.io.PrintStream@1794d431

jshell>
```

25.31

```
jshell> int x = 14
x ==> 14

jshell> x = 27
x ==> 27

jshell>
```

25.32

```
jshell> int y = 29
y ==> 29

jshell> System.out.println(y)
29

jshell> y
y ==> 29
```

25.33

```
jshell> int b = 7
b ==> 7

jshell> int m = 9
m ==> 9

jshell> bm
|  Error:
|  cannot find symbol
|    symbol:   variable bm
|  bm
|  ^^

jshell> b * m
$3 ==> 63

jshell>
```

25.34 a) 2. b) 1.

```
jshell> 8 / 4
$4 ==> 2

jshell> 7 / 5
$5 ==> 1

jshell>
```

25.35

```
jshell> 0 / 1
$6 ==> 0

jshell> 1 / 0
|  java.lang.ArithmeticException thrown: / by zero
|        at (#7:1)

jshell> 0 / 0
|  java.lang.ArithmeticException thrown: / by zero
|        at (#8:1)

jshell>
```

25.36

```
jshell> (3 + 4 + 5) / 5
$9 ==> 2

jshell> 3 + 4 + 5 / 5
$10 ==> 8

jshell>
```

25.37

```
jshell> 5 / 2 * 2 + 4 % 3 + 9 - 3
$11 ==> 11

jshell>
```

25.38

```
jshell> 7 == 7
$12 ==> true

jshell> 7 != 7
$13 ==> false

jshell> 7 < 7
$14 ==> false

jshell> 7 <= 7
$15 ==> true

jshell> 7 > 7
$16 ==> false
```

(continued...)

```
jshell> 7 >= 7
$17 ==> true

jshell>
```

25.39

```
jshell> 7 == 9
$18 ==> false

jshell> 7 != 9
$19 ==> true

jshell> 7 < 9
$20 ==> true

jshell> 7 <= 9
$21 ==> true

jshell> 7 > 9
$22 ==> false

jshell> 7 >= 9
$23 ==> false

jshell>
```

25.40

```
jshell> 11 == 9
$24 ==> false

jshell> 11 != 9
$25 ==> true

jshell> 11 < 9
$26 ==> false

jshell> 11 <= 9
$27 ==> false

jshell> 11 > 9
$28 ==> true

jshell> 11 >= 9
$29 ==> true

jshell>
```

25.41

```
jshell> if (3 == 5); {
   ...>     System.out.println("3 is equal to 5");
   ...> }
3 is equal to 5

jshell>
```

25.42

```
jshell> int x = 1
x ==> 1

jshell> int y = 2
y ==> 2

jshell> int z = 3
z ==> 3

jshell> int a
a ==> 0

jshell> a = x = y = z = 10
a ==> 10

jshell> x
x ==> 10

jshell> y
y ==> 10

jshell> z
z ==> 10

jshell>
```

25.43

```
jshell> (3 * 9 * (3 + (9 * 3 / (3))))
$42 ==> 324

jshell>
```

Chapters on the Web

The following chapters are available at *Java How to Program, 11/e*'s Companion Website (`www.pearsonhighered.com/deitel`) as PDF documents:

- Chapter 26, Swing GUI Components: Part 1
- Chapter 27, Graphics and Java 2D
- Chapter 28, Networking
- Chapter 29, Java Persistence API (JPA)
- Chapter 30, JavaServer™ Faces Web Apps: Part 1
- Chapter 31, JavaServer™ Faces Web Apps: Part 2
- Chapter 32, REST Web Services
- Chapter 33, (Optional) ATM Case Study, Part 1: Object-Oriented Design with the UML
- Chapter 34, (Optional) ATM Case Study, Part 2: Implementing an Object-Oriented Design
- Chapter 35, Swing GUI Components: Part 2
- Chapter 36, Java Module System and Other Java 9 Features

These files can be viewed in Adobe® Reader® (`get.adobe.com/reader`).

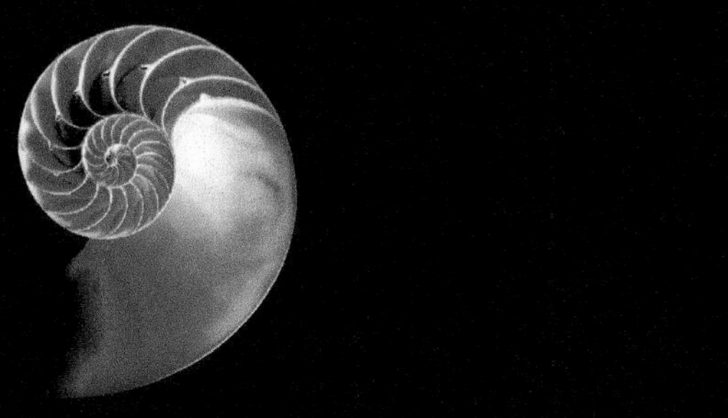

A

Operator Precedence Chart

Operators are shown in decreasing order of precedence from top to bottom (Fig. A.1).

Operator	Description	Associativity
`++` `--`	unary postfix increment unary postfix decrement	right to left

`++`
`--`
`+`
`-`
`!`
`~`
(*type*)
	unary prefix increment
	unary prefix decrement
	unary plus
	unary minus
	unary logical negation
	unary bitwise complement
	unary cast
		right to left

`*`
`/`
`%`
	multiplication
	division
	remainder
		left to right

`+` `-`	addition or string concatenation subtraction	left to right

`<<`
`>>`
`>>>`
	left shift
	signed right shift
	unsigned right shift
		left to right

`<`
`<=`
`>`
`>=`
`instanceof`
	less than
	less than or equal to
	greater than
	greater than or equal to
	type comparison
		left to right

`==` `!=`	is equal to is not equal to	left to right
`&`	bitwise AND boolean logical AND	left to right
`^`	bitwise exclusive OR boolean logical exclusive OR	left to right

Fig. A.1 | Operator precedence chart. (Part 1 of 2.)

Operator	Description	Associativity
|	bitwise inclusive OR boolean logical inclusive OR	left to right
&&	conditional AND	left to right
||	conditional OR	left to right
?:	conditional	right to left
= += -= *= /= %= &= ^= |= <<= >>= >>>=	assignment addition assignment subtraction assignment multiplication assignment division assignment remainder assignment bitwise AND assignment bitwise exclusive OR assignment bitwise inclusive OR assignment bitwise left-shift assignment bitwise signed-right-shift assignment bitwise unsigned-right-shift assignment	right to left

Fig. A.1 | Operator precedence chart. (Part 2 of 2.)

B

ASCII Character Set

<table>
<tr><th></th><th>0</th><th>1</th><th>2</th><th>3</th><th>4</th><th>5</th><th>6</th><th>7</th><th>8</th><th>9</th></tr>
<tr><td>0</td><td>nul</td><td>soh</td><td>stx</td><td>etx</td><td>eot</td><td>enq</td><td>ack</td><td>bel</td><td>bs</td><td>ht</td></tr>
<tr><td>1</td><td>nl</td><td>vt</td><td>ff</td><td>cr</td><td>so</td><td>si</td><td>dle</td><td>dc1</td><td>dc2</td><td>dc3</td></tr>
<tr><td>2</td><td>dc4</td><td>nak</td><td>syn</td><td>etb</td><td>can</td><td>em</td><td>sub</td><td>esc</td><td>fs</td><td>gs</td></tr>
<tr><td>3</td><td>rs</td><td>us</td><td>sp</td><td>!</td><td>"</td><td>#</td><td>$</td><td>%</td><td>&</td><td>'</td></tr>
<tr><td>4</td><td>(</td><td>)</td><td>*</td><td>+</td><td>,</td><td>-</td><td>.</td><td>/</td><td>0</td><td>1</td></tr>
<tr><td>5</td><td>2</td><td>3</td><td>4</td><td>5</td><td>6</td><td>7</td><td>8</td><td>9</td><td>:</td><td>;</td></tr>
<tr><td>6</td><td><</td><td>=</td><td>></td><td>?</td><td>@</td><td>A</td><td>B</td><td>C</td><td>D</td><td>E</td></tr>
<tr><td>7</td><td>F</td><td>G</td><td>H</td><td>I</td><td>J</td><td>K</td><td>L</td><td>M</td><td>N</td><td>O</td></tr>
<tr><td>8</td><td>P</td><td>Q</td><td>R</td><td>S</td><td>T</td><td>U</td><td>V</td><td>W</td><td>X</td><td>Y</td></tr>
<tr><td>9</td><td>Z</td><td>[</td><td>\</td><td>]</td><td>^</td><td>_</td><td>`</td><td>a</td><td>b</td><td>c</td></tr>
<tr><td>10</td><td>d</td><td>e</td><td>f</td><td>g</td><td>h</td><td>i</td><td>j</td><td>k</td><td>l</td><td>m</td></tr>
<tr><td>11</td><td>n</td><td>o</td><td>p</td><td>q</td><td>r</td><td>s</td><td>t</td><td>u</td><td>v</td><td>w</td></tr>
<tr><td>12</td><td>x</td><td>y</td><td>z</td><td>{</td><td>|</td><td>}</td><td>~</td><td>del</td><td></td><td></td></tr>
</table>

Fig. B.1 | ASCII character set.

The digits at the left of the table are the left digits of the decimal equivalents (0–127) of the character codes, and the digits at the top of the table are the right digits of the character codes. For example, the character code for “F” is 70, and the character code for “&” is 38.

Most users of this book are interested in the ASCII character set used to represent English characters on many computers. The ASCII character set is a subset of the Unicode character set used by Java to represent characters from most of the world’s languages. For more information on the Unicode character set, see the online Appendix H.

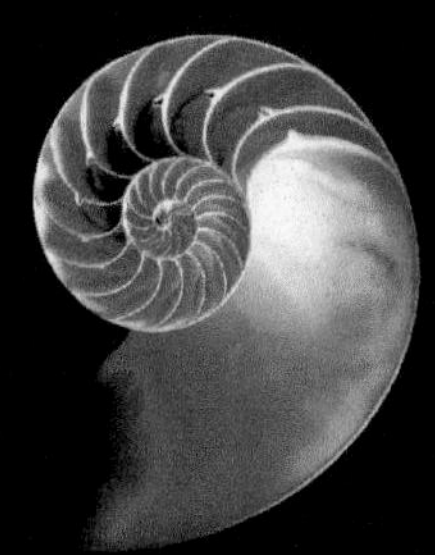

C Keywords and Reserved Words

Java Keywords				
`abstract`	`assert`	`boolean`	`break`	`byte`
`case`	`catch`	`char`	`class`	`continue`
`default`	`do`	`double`	`else`	`enum`
`extends`	`final`	`finally`	`float`	`for`
`if`	`implements`	`import`	`instanceof`	`int`
`interface`	`long`	`native`	`new`	`package`
`private`	`protected`	`public`	`return`	`short`
`static`	`strictfp`	`super`	`switch`	`synchronized`
`this`	`throw`	`throws`	`transient`	`try`
`void`	`volatile`	`while`		
Keywords that are not currently used				
`const`	`goto`			

Fig. C.1 | Java keywords.

Java also contains the reserved words `true` and `false`, which are `boolean` literals, and `null`, which is the literal that represents a reference to nothing. Like keywords, these reserved words cannot be used as identifiers.

D

Primitive Types

Type	Size (bits)	Values	Standard
`boolean`		`true` or `false`	
`char`	16	`'\u0000'` to `'\uFFFF'` (0 to 65535)	(ISO Unicode character set)
`byte`	8	-128 to $+127$ (-2^7 to $2^7 - 1$)	
`short`	16	$-32,768$ to $+32,767$ (-2^{15} to $2^{15} - 1$)	
`int`	32	$-2,147,483,648$ to $+2,147,483,647$ (-2^{31} to $2^{31} - 1$)	
`long`	64	$-9,223,372,036,854,775,808$ to $+9,223,372,036,854,775,807$ (-2^{63} to $2^{63} - 1$)	
`float`	32	*Negative range:* –3.4028234663852886E+38 to –1.40129846432481707e–45 *Positive range:* 1.40129846432481707e–45 to 3.4028234663852886E+38	(IEEE 754 floating point)
`double`	64	*Negative range:* –1.7976931348623157E+308 to –4.94065645841246544e–324 *Positive range:* 4.94065645841246544e–324 to 1.7976931348623157E+308	(IEEE 754 floating point)

Fig. D.1 | Java primitive types.

Notes

- A `boolean`'s representation is specific to each platform's Java Virtual Machine.
- You can use underscores to make numeric literal values more readable. For example, `1_000_000` is equivalent to `1000000`.
- For more information on IEEE 754 visit `http://grouper.ieee.org/groups/754/`. For more information on Unicode, see `http://unicode.org`.

E

Using the Debugger

Objectives

In this appendix you'll:

- Set breakpoints to debug applications.
- Run an application through the debugger with the `run` command.
- Set a breakpoint with the `stop` command.
- Continue execution after a breakpoint is reached with the `cont` command.
- Evaluate expressions with the `print` command.
- Change variable values during program execution with the `set` command.
- Use the `step`, `step up` and `next` commands to control execution.
- See how a field is modified during program execution with the `watch` command.
- Use the `clear` command to list breakpoints or remove a breakpoint.

Outline

E.1 Introduction

In Chapter 2, you learned that there are two types of errors—syntax errors and logic errors—and you learned how to eliminate syntax errors from your code. Logic errors do not prevent the application from compiling successfully, but they do cause an application to produce erroneous results when it runs. The JDK includes software called a **debugger** that allows you to monitor the execution of your applications so you can locate and remove logic errors. The debugger will be one of your most important application development tools. Many IDEs provide their own debuggers similar to the one included in the JDK or provide a graphical user interface to the JDK's debugger.

This appendix demonstrates key features of the JDK's debugger using command-line applications that receive no input from the user. The same debugger features discussed here can be used to debug applications that take user input, but debugging such applications requires a slightly more complex setup. To focus on the debugger features, we've opted to demonstrate the debugger with simple command-line applications involving no user input. For more information on the Java debugger visit `http://docs.oracle.com/javase/8/docs/technotes/tools/windows/jdb.html`.

E.2 Breakpoints and the `run`, `stop`, `cont` and `print` Commands

We begin our study of the debugger by investigating **breakpoints**, which are markers that can be set at any executable line of code. When application execution reaches a breakpoint, execution pauses, allowing you to examine the values of variables to help determine whether logic errors exist. For example, you can examine the value of a variable that stores the result of a calculation to determine whether the calculation was performed correctly. Setting a breakpoint at a line of code that is not executable (such as a comment) causes the debugger to display an error message.

To illustrate the features of the debugger, we use application `AccountTest` (Fig. E.1), which creates and manipulates an object of class `Account` (Fig. 3.8). Execution of `AccountTest` begins in `main`. Line 5 creates an `Account` object with an initial balance of $50.00. Recall that `Account`'s constructor accepts one argument, which specifies the `Account`'s initial `balance`. Lines 8–9 output the initial account balance using `Account` method `getBalance`. Line 11 declares and initializes a local variable `depositAmount`. Lines 13–15 then print `depositAmount` and add it to the `Account`'s `balance` using its `credit` method. Finally, lines 18–19 display the new `balance`. [*Note:* The Appendix E examples directory contains a copy of `Account.java` identical to the one in Fig. 3.8.]

```
// Fig. E.1: AccountTest.java
// Create and manipulate an Account object.
public class AccountTest {
   public static void main(String[] args) {
      Account account = new Account("Jane Green", 50.00);

      // display initial balance of Account object
      System.out.printf("initial account balance: $%.2f%n",
         account.getBalance());

      double depositAmount = 25.0; // deposit amount

      System.out.printf("%nadding %.2f to account balance%n%n",
         depositAmount);
      account.deposit(depositAmount); // add to account balance

      // display new balance
      System.out.printf("new account balance: $%.2f%n",
         account.getBalance());
   }
}
```

```
initial account balance: $50.00

adding 25.00 to account balance

new account balance: $75.00
```

Fig. E.1 | Create and manipulate an `Account` object.

In the following steps, you'll use breakpoints and various debugger commands to examine the value of the variable `depositAmount` declared in `AccountTest` (Fig. E.1).

1. ***Opening a command window and changing directories.*** Open a command window for your platform then change to the `appE` (Appendix E) directory in the book's examples directory.
2. ***Compiling the application for debugging.*** The Java debugger works only with `.class` files that were compiled with the **`-g`** compiler option, which generates information that is used by the debugger to help you debug your applications. Compile the application with the `-g` command-line option by typing `javac -g *.java`. This compiles all of the working directory's `.java` files for debugging.
3. ***Starting the debugger.*** In the command window, type **`jdb`** (Fig. E.2). This command will start the Java debugger and enable you to use its features.

```
C:\examples\appE>javac -g AccountTest.java Account.java

C:\examples\appE>jdb
Initializing jdb ...
>
```

Fig. E.2 | Starting the Java debugger.

4. ***Running an application in the debugger.*** Run the AccountTest application through the debugger by typing **run** AccountTest (Fig. E.3). If you do not set any breakpoints before running your application in the debugger, the application will run just as it would using the java command.

```
C:\examples\appE>jdb
Initializing jdb ...
> run AccountTest
run  AccountTest
Set uncaught java.lang.Throwable
Set deferred uncaught java.lang.Throwable
>
VM Started: initial account balance: $50.00

adding 25.00 to account balance

new account balance: $75.00

The application exited
```

Fig. E.3 | Running the AccountTest application through the debugger.

5. ***Restarting the debugger.*** To make proper use of the debugger, you must set at least one breakpoint before running the application. Restart the debugger by typing jdb.
6. ***Inserting breakpoints in Java.*** You set a breakpoint at a specific line of code in your application. The line numbers used in these steps are from the source code in Fig. E.1. Set a breakpoint at line 8 of Fig. E.1 by typing stop at AccountTest:8 (Fig. E.4). The **stop command** inserts a breakpoint at the line number specified after the command. You can set as many breakpoints as necessary. Set another breakpoint at line 15 of Fig. E.1 by typing stop at AccountTest:15 (Fig. E.4). When the application runs, it suspends execution at any line that contains a breakpoint. The application is said to be in **break mode** when the debugger pauses the application's execution. Breakpoints can be set even after the debugging process has begun. The debugger command stop in, followed by a class name, a period and a method name (e.g., stop in Account.credit) instructs the debugger to set a breakpoint at the first executable statement in the specified method. The debugger pauses execution when program control enters the method.

```
C:\examples\appE>jdb
Initializing jdb ...
> stop at AccountTest:8
Deferring breakpoint AccountTest:8.
It will be set after the class is loaded.
> stop at AccountTest:15
Deferring breakpoint AccountTest:15.
It will be set after the class is loaded.
>
```

Fig. E.4 | Setting breakpoints at lines 8 and 15.

7. ***Running the application and beginning the debugging process.*** Type `run AccountTest` to execute the application and begin the debugging process (Fig. E.5). The debugger prints text indicating that breakpoints were set at lines 8 and 15 of Fig. E.1. It calls each breakpoint a "deferred breakpoint" because each was set before the application began running in the debugger. The application pauses when execution reaches the breakpoint on line 8. At this point, the debugger notifies you that a breakpoint has been reached and it displays the source code at that line (8). That line of code is the next statement that will execute.

```
It will be set after the class is loaded.
>run AccountTest
run  AccountTest
Set uncaught java.lang.Throwable
Set deferred uncaught java.lang.Throwable
>
VM Started: Set deferred breakpoint AccountTest:15
Set deferred breakpoint AccountTest:8

Breakpoint hit: "thread=main", AccountTest.main(), line=8 bci=13
8          System.out.printf("initial account balance: $%.2f%n",

main[1]
```

Fig. E.5 | Restarting the `AccountTest` application.

8. ***Using the* `cont` *command to resume execution.*** Type `cont`. The **`cont` command** causes the application to continue running until the next breakpoint is reached (line 15), at which point the debugger notifies you (Fig. E.6). `AccountTest`'s normal output appears between messages from the debugger.

```
main[1] cont
> initial account balance: $50.00

adding 25.00 to account balance

Breakpoint hit: "thread=main", AccountTest.main(), line=15 bci=60
15          account.deposit(depositAmount); // add to account balance

main[1]
```

Fig. E.6 | Execution reaches the second breakpoint.

9. ***Examining a variable's value.*** Type `print depositAmount` to display the current value stored in the `depositAmount` variable (Fig. E.7). The **`print` command** allows you to peek inside the computer at the value of one of your variables. This command will help you find and eliminate logic errors in your code. The value displayed is `25.0`—the value assigned to `depositAmount` in line 15 of Fig. E.1.

```
main[1] print depositAmount
 depositAmount = 25.0
main[1]
```

Fig. E.7 | Examining the value of variable `depositAmount`.

10. ***Continuing application execution.*** Type `cont` to continue the application's execution. There are no more breakpoints, so the application is no longer in break mode. The application continues executing and eventually terminates (Fig. E.8). The debugger will stop when the application ends.

```
main[1] cont
> new account balance: $75.00

The application exited
```

Fig. E.8 | Continuing application execution and exiting the debugger.

E.3 The print and set Commands

In the preceding section, you learned how to use the debugger's `print` command to examine the value of a variable during program execution. In this section, you'll learn how to use the `print` command to examine the value of more complex expressions. You'll also learn the **set command**, which allows the programmer to assign new values to variables.

For this section, we assume that you've followed *Step 1* and *Step 2* in Section E.2 to open the command window, change to the directory containing the Appendix E examples (e.g., `C:\examples\appE`) and compile the `AccountTest` application (and class `Account`) for debugging.

1. ***Starting debugging.*** In the command window, type `jdb` to start the Java debugger.
2. ***Inserting a breakpoint.*** Set a breakpoint at line 15 in the source code by typing `stop at AccountTest:15`.
3. ***Running the application and reaching a breakpoint.*** Type `run AccountTest` to begin the debugging process (Fig. E.9). This will cause `AccountTest`'s `main` to execute until the breakpoint at line 15 of Fig. E.1 is reached. This suspends application execution and switches the application into break mode. At this point, the program has created an `Account` object and printed the initial balance of the `Account` obtained by calling its `getBalance` method. Line 11 declared and initialized local variable `depositAmount` to `25.0`, and lines 13–14 displayed the `depositAmount`. The statement in line 15 is the next statement that will execute.
4. ***Evaluating arithmetic and boolean expressions.*** Recall from Section E.2 that once the application has entered break mode, you can explore the values of the application's variables using the debugger's `print` command. You can also use the `print` command to evaluate arithmetic and `boolean` expressions. In the command window, type `print depositAmount - 2.0`. The `print` command returns the value `23.0` (Fig. E.10). However, this command does not actually change the value of

```
C:\examples\appE>jdb
Initializing jdb ...
> stop at AccountTest:19
Deferring breakpoint AccountTest:19.
It will be set after the class is loaded.
> run AccountTest
run  AccountTest
Set uncaught java.lang.Throwable
Set deferred uncaught java.lang.Throwable
>
VM Started: Set deferred breakpoint AccountTest:19
initial account balance: $50.00

adding 25.00 to account balance

Breakpoint hit: "thread=main", AccountTest.main(), line=15 bci=60
15          account.deposit(depositAmount); // add to account balance

main[1]
```

Fig. E.9 | Application execution suspended when debugger reaches the breakpoint at line 15.

depositAmount. In the command window, type `print depositAmount == 23.0`. Expressions containing the == symbol are treated as `boolean` expressions. The value returned is `false` (Fig. E.10) because `depositAmount` does not currently contain the value `23.0`—`depositAmount` is still `25.0`.

```
main[1] print depositAmount - 2.0
 depositAmount - 2.0 = 23.0
main[1] print depositAmount == 23.0
 depositAmount == 23.0 = false
main[1]
```

Fig. E.10 | Examining the values of an arithmetic and `boolean` expression.

5. ***Modifying values.*** The debugger allows you to change the values of variables during the application's execution. This can be valuable for experimenting with different values and for locating logic errors in applications. You can use the debugger's `set` command to change the value of a variable. Type `set depositAmount = 75.0`. The debugger changes the value of `depositAmount` and displays its new value (Fig. E.11).

```
main[1] set depositAmount = 75.0
 depositAmount = 75.0 = 75.0
main[1]
```

Fig. E.11 | Modifying values.

6. ***Viewing the application result.*** Type `cont` to continue application execution. Line 19 of `AccountTest` (Fig. E.1) executes, passing `depositAmount` to `Account` method `credit`. Method `main` then displays the new balance. The result is

$125.00 (Fig. E.12). This shows that the preceding step changed the value of depositAmount from its initial value (25.0) to 75.0.

```
main[1] cont
> new account balance: $125.00

The application exited

C:\examples\appE>
```

Fig. E.12 | Output showing new account balance based on altered value of depositAmount.

E.4 Controlling Execution Using the step, step up and next Commands

Sometimes you'll need to execute an application line by line to find and fix errors. Walking through a portion of your application this way can help you verify that a method's code executes correctly. In this section, you'll learn how to use the debugger for this task. The commands you learn in this section allow you to execute a method line by line, execute all the statements of a method at once or execute only the remaining statements of a method (if you've already executed some statements within the method).

Once again, we assume you're working in the directory containing the Appendix E examples and have compiled for debugging with the -g compiler option.

1. ***Starting the debugger.*** Start the debugger by typing jdb.
2. ***Setting a breakpoint.*** Type stop at AccountTest:15 to set a breakpoint at line 15 of Fig. E.1.
3. ***Running the application.*** Run the application by typing run AccountTest. After the application displays its two output messages, the debugger indicates that the breakpoint has been reached and displays the code at line 15. The debugger and application then pause and wait for the next command to be entered.
4. ***Using the step command.*** The **step command** executes the next statement in the application. If the next statement to execute is a method call, control transfers to the called method. The step command enables you to enter a method and study the individual statements of that method. For example, you can use the print and set commands to view and modify the variables within the method. You'll now use the step command to enter the credit method of class Account (Fig. 3.8) by typing step (Fig. E.13). The debugger indicates that the step has been completed and displays the next executable statement—in this case, line 22 of class Account (Fig. 3.8).
5. ***Using the step up command.*** After you've stepped into the credit method, type **step up**. This command executes the remaining statements in the method and returns control to the place where the method was called. The credit method contains only one statement to add the method's parameter amount to instance variable balance. The step up command executes this statement, then pauses before line 18 in AccountTest (Fig. E.1). Thus, the next action to occur will be to

```
main[1] step
>
Step completed: "thread=main", Account.deposit(), line=22 bci=0
22          if (depositAmount > 0.0) { // if the depositAmount is valid

main[1]
```

Fig. E.13 | Stepping into the `credit` method.

print the new account balance (Fig. E.14). In lengthy methods, you may want to look at a few key lines of code, then continue debugging the caller's code. The `step up` command is useful for situations in which you do not want to continue stepping through the entire method line by line.

```
main[1] step up
>
Step completed: "thread=main", AccountTest.main(), line=18 bci=65
18          System.out.printf("new account balance: $%.2f%n",

main[1]
```

Fig. E.14 | Stepping out of a method.

6. ***Using the* `cont` *command to continue execution.*** Enter the `cont` command (Fig. E.15) to display the new balance. At this point the application and the debugger terminate.

```
main[1] cont
> new account balance: $75.00

The application exited

C:\examples\appE>
```

Fig. E.15 | Continuing execution of the `AccountTest` application.

7. ***Restarting the debugger.*** Restart the debugger by typing `jdb`.
8. ***Setting a breakpoint.*** Breakpoints persist only until the end of the debugging session in which they're set—once the debugger exits, all breakpoints are removed. (In Section E.6, you'll learn how to manually clear a breakpoint before the end of the debugging session.) Thus, the breakpoint set for line 15 in *Step 2* no longer exists upon restarting the debugger in *Step 7*. To reset the breakpoint at line 15, once again type `stop at AccountTest:15`.
9. ***Running the application.*** Type `run AccountTest` to run the application. As in *Step 3*, `AccountTest` runs until the breakpoint at line 15 is reached, then the debugger pauses and waits for the next command.

10. *Using the* **next** *command.* Type **next**. This command behaves like the step command, except when the next statement to execute contains a method call. In that case, the called method executes in its entirety and the application advances to the next executable line after the method call (Fig. E.16). Recall from *Step 4* that the step command would enter the called method. In this example, the next command causes Account method credit to execute, then the debugger pauses at line 18 in AccountTest.

```
main[1] next
>
Step completed: "thread=main", AccountTest.main(), line=18 bci=65
18          System.out.printf("new account balance: $%.2f%n",

main[1]
```

Fig. E.16 | Stepping over a method call.

11. *Using the* **exit** *command.* Use the **exit command** to end the debugging session (Fig. E.17). This command causes the AccountTest application to immediately terminate rather than execute the remaining statements in main. When debugging some types of applications (e.g., GUI applications), the application continues to execute even after the debugging session ends.

```
main[1] exit

C:\examples\appE>
```

Fig. E.17 | Exiting the debugger.

E.5 The watch Command

In this section, we present the **watch command**, which tells the debugger to watch a field. When that field is about to change, the debugger will notify you. In this section, you'll learn how to use the watch command to see how the Account object's field balance is modified during the execution of the AccountTest application.

As in the preceding two sections, we assume that you've followed *Step 1* and *Step 2* in Section E.2 to open the command window, change to the correct examples directory and compile classes AccountTest and Account for debugging (i.e., with the -g compiler option).

1. *Starting the debugger.* Start the debugger by typing jdb.
2. *Watching a class's field.* Set a watch on Account's balance field by typing watch Account.balance (Fig. E.18). You can set a watch on any field during execution of the debugger. Whenever the value in a field is about to change, the debugger enters break mode and notifies you that the value will change. Watches can be placed only on fields, not on local variables.
3. *Running the application.* Run the application with the command run AccountTest. The debugger will now notify you that field balance's value will change (Fig. E.19). When the application begins, an instance of Account is cre-

```
C:\examples\appE>jdb
Initializing jdb ...
> watch Account.balance
Deferring watch modification of Account.balance.
It will be set after the class is loaded.
>
```

Fig. E.18 | Setting a watch on `Account`'s `balance` field.

ated with an initial balance of $50.00 and a reference to the `Account` object is assigned to the local variable `account` (line 9, Fig. E.1). Recall from Fig. 3.8 that when the constructor for this object runs, if parameter `initialBalance` is greater than `0.0`, instance variable `balance` is assigned the value of parameter `initialBalance`. The debugger notifies you that the value of `balance` will be set to `50.0`.

```
> run AccountTest
run  AccountTest
Set uncaught java.lang.Throwable
Set deferred uncaught java.lang.Throwable
>
VM Started: Set deferred watch modification of Account.balance

Field (Account.balance) is 0.0, will be 50.0: "thread=main",
Account.<init>(), line=16 bci=17
16             this.balance = balance; // assign it to instance variable balance

main[1]
```

Fig. E.19 | `AccountTest` stops when `account` is created and its `balance` field will be modified.

4. ***Adding money to the account.*** Type `cont` to continue executing the application. The application executes normally before reaching the code on line 15 of Fig. E.1 that calls `Account` method `credit` to raise the `Account` object's `balance` by a specified `amount`. The debugger notifies you that instance variable `balance` will change (Fig. E.20). Although line 15 of class `AccountTest` calls method `deposit`, line 23 (Fig. 3.8) in `Account`'s method `deposit` actually changes the value of `balance`.

```
main[1] cont
> initial account balance: $50.00

adding 25.00 to account balance


Field (Account.balance) is 50.0, will be 75.0: "thread=main",
Account.deposit(), line=23 bci=13
23             balance = balance + depositAmount; // add it to the balance

main[1]
```

Fig. E.20 | Changing the value of `balance` by calling `Account` method `credit`.

5. ***Continuing execution.*** Type cont—the application will finish executing because the application does not attempt any additional changes to balance (Fig. E.21).

```
main[1] cont
> new account balance: $75.00

The application exited

C:\examples\appE>
```

Fig. E.21 | Continuing execution of AccountTest.

6. ***Restarting the debugger and resetting the watch on the variable.*** Type jdb to restart the debugger. Once again, set a watch on the Account instance variable balance by typing the watch Account.balance, then type run AccountTest to run the application.
7. ***Removing the watch on the field.*** Suppose you want to watch a field for only part of a program's execution. You can remove the debugger's watch on variable balance by typing **unwatch** Account.balance (Fig. E.22). Type cont—the application will finish executing without reentering break mode.

```
main[1] unwatch Account.balance
Removed: watch modification of Account.balance
main[1] cont
> initial account balance: $50.00

adding 25.00 to account balance

new account balance: $75.00

The application exited

C:\examples\appE>
```

Fig. E.22 | Removing the watch on variable balance.

E.6 The clear Command

In the preceding section, you learned to use the unwatch command to remove a watch on a field. The debugger also provides the clear command to remove a breakpoint from an application. You'll often need to debug applications containing repetitive actions, such as a loop. You may want to examine the values of variables during several, but possibly not all, of the loop's iterations. If you set a breakpoint in the body of a loop, the debugger will pause before each execution of the line containing a breakpoint. After determining that the loop is working properly, you may want to remove the breakpoint and allow the remaining iterations to proceed normally. In this section, we use the compound interest application in Fig. 5.6 to demonstrate how the debugger behaves when you set a breakpoint in the body of a for statement and how to remove a breakpoint in the middle of a debugging session.

1. ***Opening the command window, changing directories and compiling the application for debugging.*** Open the command window, then change to the directory containing the Appendix E examples. For your convenience, we've provided a copy of the `Interest.java` file in this directory. Compile the application for debugging by typing `javac -g Interest.java`.
2. ***Starting the debugger and setting breakpoints.*** Start the debugger by typing `jdb`. Set breakpoints at lines 10 and 18 of class `Interest` by typing `stop at Interest:10`, then `stop at Interest:18`.
3. ***Running the application.*** Run the application by typing `run Interest`. The application executes until reaching the breakpoint at line 10 (Fig. E.23).

```
It will be set after the class is loaded.
> run Interest
run  Interest
Set uncaught java.lang.Throwable
Set deferred uncaught java.lang.Throwable
>
VM Started: Set deferred breakpoint Interest:18
Set deferred breakpoint Interest:10

Breakpoint hit: "thread=main", Interest.main(), line=10 bci=8
10            System.out.printf("%s%20s%n", "Year", "Amount on deposit");

main[1]
```

Fig. E.23 | Reaching the breakpoint at line 10 in the `Interest` application.

4. ***Continuing execution.*** Type `cont` to continue—line 10 executes, printing the column headings `"Year"` and `"Amount on deposit"`. Line 10 (Fig. 5.6) appears before the `for` statement at lines 13–19 in `Interest` and thus executes only once. Execution continues past line 10 until the breakpoint at line 18 is reached during the first iteration of the `for` statement (Fig. E.24).

```
main[1] cont
> Year   Amount on deposit

Breakpoint hit: "thread=main", Interest.main(), line=18 bci=54
18               System.out.printf("%4d%,20.2f%n", year, amount);

main[1]
```

Fig. E.24 | Reaching the breakpoint at line 18 in the `Interest` application.

5. ***Examining variable values.*** Type `print year` to examine the current value of variable `year` (i.e., the `for`'s control variable). Print the value of variable `amount` too (Fig. E.25).
6. ***Continuing execution.*** Type `cont` to continue execution. Line 18 executes and prints the current values of `year` and `amount`. After the `for` enters its second itera-

```
main[1] print year
 year = 1
main[1] print amount
 amount = 1050.0
main[1]
```

Fig. E.25 | Printing year and amount during the first iteration of Interest's for.

tion, the debugger notifies you that the breakpoint at line 18 has been reached a second time. The debugger pauses each time a line where a breakpoint has been set is about to execute—when the breakpoint appears in a loop, the debugger pauses during each iteration. Print the values of variables `year` and `amount` again to see how the values have changed since the first iteration of the `for` (Fig. E.26).

```
main[1] cont
>    1           1,050.00

Breakpoint hit: "thread=main", Interest.main(), line=18 bci=54
18              System.out.printf("%4d%,20.2f%n", year, amount);

main[1] print amount
 amount = 1102.5
main[1] print year
 year = 2
main[1]
```

Fig. E.26 | Printing year and amount during the second iteration of Interest's for.

7. ***Removing a breakpoint.*** You can display a list of currently set breakpoints by typing **`clear`** (Fig. E.27). Suppose you're satisfied that the `Interest` application's `for` statement is working properly, so you want to remove the breakpoint at line 18 (Fig. 5.6) and allow the remaining iterations of the loop to proceed normally. You can remove the breakpoint at line 18 by typing `clear Interest:18`. Now type `clear` to list the remaining breakpoints in the application. The debugger should indicate that only the breakpoint at line 10 remains (Fig. E.27). This breakpoint has already been reached and thus will no longer affect execution.

```
main[1] clear
Breakpoints set:
        breakpoint Interest:10
        breakpoint Interest:18
main[1] clear Interest:18
Removed: breakpoint Interest:18
main[1] clear
Breakpoints set:
        breakpoint Interest:10
main[1]
```

Fig. E.27 | Removing the breakpoint at line 18.

8. ***Continuing execution after removing a breakpoint.*** Type `cont` to continue execution. Recall that execution last paused before the `printf` statement in line 18 (Fig. 5.6). If the breakpoint at line 18 was removed successfully, continuing the application will produce the correct output for the current and remaining iterations of the `for` statement without the application halting (Fig. E.28).

```
main[1] cont
>    2              1,102.50
   3              1,157.63
   4              1,215.51
   5              1,276.28
   6              1,340.10
   7              1,407.10
   8              1,477.46
   9              1,551.33
  10              1,628.89

The application exited

C:\examples\appE>
```

Fig. E.28 | Application executes without a breakpoint set at line 22.

E.7 Wrap-Up

In this appendix, you learned how to insert and remove breakpoints in the debugger. Breakpoints allow you to pause application execution so you can examine variable values with the debugger's `print` command. This capability will help you locate and fix logic errors in your applications. You saw how to use the `print` command to examine the value of an expression and how to use the `set` command to change the value of a variable. You also learned debugger commands (including the `step`, `step up` and `next` commands) that can be used to determine whether a method is executing correctly. You learned how to use the `watch` command to keep track of a field throughout the life of an application. Finally, you learned how to use the `clear` command to list all the breakpoints set for an application or remove individual breakpoints to continue execution without breakpoints.

Appendices on the Web

The following appendices are available at *Java How to Program, 11/e*'s Companion Website (`www.pearsonhighered.com/deitel`) as PDF documents:

- Appendix F, Using the Java API Documentation
- Appendix G, Creating Documentation with javadoc
- Appendix H, Unicode®
- Appendix I, Formatted Output
- Appendix J, Number Systems
- Appendix K, Bit Manipulation
- Appendix L, Labeled `break` and `continue` Statements
- Appendix M, UML 2: Additional Diagram Types
- Appendix N, Design Patterns

These files can be viewed in Adobe® Reader® (`get.adobe.com/reader`).

Index

[*Note:* Page references for defining occurrences of terms appear in **bold maroon.**]

Symbols

Numerics

A

J

N

O

S

T

U

W

X

Y

Z

ADDITIONAL COMMENTS FROM RECENT EDITIONS REVIEWERS

“Nice breadth of coverage of traditional core Java and programming topics as well as newer areas such as **lambda expressions** and areas becoming more critical such as **concurrent programming**. I like the bank-account class example. Arrays and ArrayLists is a fine chapter. Classes chapters provide a good examination of data-type creation. Nice chapter on exception handling. Very nice coverage of files, streams, serialization, generics and hand-managed, node-based data structures.” —**Evan Golub, University of Maryland**

“A great book for studying the world's most popular programming language. Really good, clear explanation of object-oriented programming fundamentals. Excellent polymorphism chapter. Covers all the essentials of strings. Introduces **JavaFX**, the great new way to develop client applications in Java—I like the use of **Scene Builder** to create the GUI with drag-and-drop design rather than doing it by hand, which shows the way it should be done. Good to see try-with-resources and DirectoryStream. Excellent generic collections chapter. Covers **lambdas and streams** well. Good coverage of **concurrency**.” —**Simon Ritter, Oracle**

“The early introduction of the class concept is clearly presented. A comprehensive overview of control structures and the pitfalls that befall new programmers. I applaud the authors for their topical research and illustrative examples. The arrays exercises are sophisticated and interesting. The clearest explanation of pass-by-value and pass-by-reference that I've encountered. A logical progression of inheritance and the rationale for properly implementing encapsulation in a system involving an inheritance hierarchy. The polymorphism and exception handling discussions are the best I've seen. An excellent strings chapter. I like the recursion discussions of the 'Lo Fractal' and backtracking, which is useful in computer vision applications. A good segue into a data structures course.” —**Ric Heishman, George Mason University**

“Practical top-down, solution approach to teaching programming basics, covering pseudocode, algorithm development and activity diagrams. Of immense value to practitioners and students of the object-oriented approach. Demystifies inheritance and polymorphism, and illustrates their use in getting elegant, simple and maintainable code. The optional OO design case study presents the object-oriented approach in a simple manner, from requirements to Java code.” —**Vinod Varma, Astro Infotech Private Limited**

“Most major concepts are illustrated by complete, annotated programs. Abundant exercises hone your understanding of the material. JDBC is explained well.” —**Shyamal Mitra, University of Texas at Austin**

“Easy-to-read conversational style. Clear code examples propel readers to become proficient in Java.” —**Patty Kraft, San Diego State U.**

“You'll be on your way to becoming a great Java programmer with this book.” —**Peter Pilgrim, Java Champion, Consultant**

“Excellent descriptions of the search and sort algorithms and a gentle introduction to Big O—the examples give the code for the algorithms, and output that creates a picture of how the algorithms work.” —**Diana Franklin, University of California, Santa Barbara**

“Beautiful collections of exercises. Nice illustration of how to use Java to generate impressive graphics.” —**Amr Sabry, Indiana U.**

“The optional OOD ATM case study puts many concepts from previous chapters together in a plan for a large program, showing the object-oriented design process—the discussion of inheritance and polymorphism is especially good.” —**Susan Rodger, Duke University**

“Fantastic textbook and reference. Provides great detail on the latest Java features including **lambdas**. The code examples make it easy to understand the concepts. GUI examples are very good and the exercises are well thought out. Graphics examples are easy to follow; good and challenging exercises.” —**Lance Andersen, Principal Member of the Technical Staff, Oracle**

“Perfect introduction to strings. Best introduction to Java 2D I've seen! The collections framework is well explained. Good introduction to the most essential data structures. A nice introduction to **JavaFX**.” —**Manfred Riem, Java Champion**

“A plethora of well-thought-through exercises. I like the DeckOfCards example, the employee polymorphism example, the clear definitions of regular expressions and the Pig Latin exercise. Good introduction to collections and hashtable performance. Solid **threading** treatment.”
—**Dr. Danny Coward, Oracle**

“The inheritance chapter is excellent; examples are gender neutral which is perfect.”
—**Khallai Taylor, Assistant Professor, Triton College and Adjunct Professor, Lonestar College—Kingwood**

“Good explanation of translating from pseudocode to Java. I like how the book flows. Excellent exception and Java SE 8 interface explanations.”
—**Jorge Vargas, Yumbling, Java Champion**

“The Making a Difference exercises are inspired—they have a contemporary feeling, both in their topics and in the way they encourage the student to gather data from the Internet and bring it back to the question at hand.” —**Vince O'Brien, Pearson Education (our publisher)**

“An admirable job introducing writing simple classes.” —**Marty Allen, University of Wisconsin-La Crosse**